A HISTORY OF THE ISRAELI-PALESTINIAN CONFLICT

INDIANA SERIES IN ARAB
AND ISLAMIC STUDIES

Salih J. Altoma, Iliya Harik, and Mark Tessler, *General editors*

A HISTORY OF THE ISRAELI-PALESTINIAN CONFLICT

Mark Tessler

Indiana University Press

Bloomington and Indianapolis

The paper used in this publication meets the minimum require-
ments of American National Standard for Information Sciences—
Permanence of Paper for Printed Library Materials, ANSI
Z39.48-1984.

⊗™

Manufactured in the United States of America

Library of Congress Cataloging-in-Publication Data

Tessler, Mark A.
    A History of the Israeli-Palestinian conflict / Mark Tessler.
      p. cm. — (Indiana series in Arab and Islamic studies)
    Includes bibliographical references and index.
    ISBN 0-253-35848-5. — ISBN 0-253-20873-4 (pbk.)
      1. Jewish-Arab relations—1917-   2. Israel-Arab conflicts.
I. Title. II. Series.
DS119.7.T443 1994
956—dc20   93-34049

1 2 3 4 5 99 98 97 96 95 94

To Pat, Joelle, Louise, and Sidney

Contents

List of Maps

Preface

THIS BOOK SEEKS not only to provide an objective history of the Israeli-Palestinian conflict but also to encourage an engaged and sympathetic understanding of the parties to this continuing dispute. The aim of this approach may be described as objectivity without detachment.

Many on both sides of the Israeli-Palestinian conflict find it difficult to take the opposing side seriously, not in military or political terms, of course, but as a people with legitimate rights and valid aspirations. On both sides there are those who insist on delegitimizing or even demonizing their adversary, as if the rightness of their cause were justified primarily by the villainy of the opposing party and only secondarily by their own ideals and achievements.

A related concern is the tendency of strongly partisan observers to acquire information selectively. Not only do such people make little effort to distinguish between fact and propaganda, they actively seek out views that confirm opinions already held. Such individuals usually rely on pro-Israeli sources for information about Palestinians or on pro-Palestinian sources for information about Israel, although they loudly complain—and properly so—when their opponents do the same.

The present study rejects these tendencies and offers a different approach. It assumes that both Israeli Jews and Palestinian Arabs have legitimate and inalienable rights. These rights are rooted in the historical experience of each people. Their validity does not depend on the absence of any corresponding rights possessed by the other party to the conflict. Nor can these rights be forfeited; the validity of each people's claims and aspirations transcends the actions of its leaders, who at times may have acted unwisely, or perhaps even unethically.

More generally, this study reflects a conviction that the rights and aspirations of Israelis, Zionists, and Jews, on the one hand, and of Palestinians and Arabs, on the other, cannot be understood properly if seen exclusively, or even primarily, from the perspective of the present-day struggle in Palestine. Although this struggle is the focus of the present volume, it will be approached with a firm belief that Palestinians and Israelis must each be comprehended on their own terms, in the context of their respective histories, and with reference only thereafter to the complaints of their opponents.

Consistent with this approach, the book presupposes that the Israeli-Palestinian conflict is not a struggle between good and evil but rather a confrontation between two peoples who deserve recognition and respect, neither of whom has a monopoly on behavior that is either praiseworthy or condemnable. To some readers, especially those without strong ties to either Palestinians or Israelis, this proposition may seem self-evident. Nevertheless, at least some who approach the subject with powerful partisan attachments will challenge it as fictitious symmetry. In response to this charge, the book advances the view that it is possible to have loyalties and commitments to one of the parties to an intense and protracted conflict and yet to view both that party and its adversary in a manner that abhors prejudice, strives for empathy, eschews mythmaking, and distinguishes as fully as possible between fact and propaganda.

Finally, this study urges readers to pay attention to sources of information and to recognize the importance of diversity in this connection. The chapters that follow provide a wide and varied range of references and suggestions for further reading. The narrative draws upon a large body of research by both Israeli and Palestinian scholars, as well as others. Whenever possible it devotes particular attention to recent works based on original empirical investigations or newly available archival materials.

This approach to the Israeli-Palestinian conflict is advocated not only in the name of objectivity and historical accuracy but with a conviction that there is practical value to what might be called an "approach-approach" perspective. Over the long term, such a perspective offers a basis for hope, leading to the proposition that there are realistic alternatives to conceiving of the struggle between Israelis and Palestinians in zero-sum terms. Both sides will have to make concessions if peace is to be achieved, and neither will find it easy to agree to the necessary compromises. But the political will to accept reasonable formulations, and above all to understand and value the distinction between compromise and capitulation, will be found if each party acknowledges the legitimacy of the other's aspirations, and does so with a recognition that this is established by a fair-minded reading of the historical record.

The dramatic accord between Israel and the PLO, hammered out during months of secret negotiations in Norway and signed at a White House ceremony in September 1993, as this volume goes to press, demonstrates that in the short run, too, the key to fostering movement toward peace lies in acceptance of the rights of both Israelis and Palestinians. The recent agreement leaves many questions unresolved; it is primarily an expression of general principles and defers consideration of the most difficult issues. Thus, while greeted with enthusiasm and hope by a majority of Israelis and Palestinians, it has understandably been viewed with skepticism as well, even by many on both sides who endorse the principles it sets forth. Yet mutual recognition between Israel and the Palestinians is the logical way, indeed the only way, to break the Middle East impasse. The accord is of historic significance, despite the uncertainty that remains and the hard bargaining that lies ahead, precisely because Israelis and Palestinians have taken a step without which there would be almost no possibility of serious and sustained movement toward peace.

Whether or not the Israeli-PLO accord fulfills the hopes it has spawned will depend more than anything else on the parties' willingness to view the principles it espouses as fair and reasonable, and this in turn, as stated, will in large measure depend on how Israelis and Palestinians approach the reading of history. To the extent that each people will take from the historical record an understanding that the other is entitled to recognition and a territorial foundation for the exercise of national rights, and thus is not an undeserving enemy whose struggle over the years has been motivated by pernicious impulses it either will not or cannot contain, to that extent it is likely that most Israelis and Palestinians will see compromise as both a workable and a desirable alternative to continuing conflict.

It is with this conviction, in the belief that there is practical as well as intellectual benefit to be derived from knowledge of the conflict's history, that the present study examines the origins and evolution of the struggle between Israelis and Palestinians. It is in this connection that the book aspires not only to offer an objective and accurate rendering, but also to provide a framework for thinking about the cumulative meaning and eventual resolution of the lingering dispute.

Despite the hopes for the future held out by this perspective, it is neither possible nor desirable to emphasize only the positive, ignoring the forces that have produced turmoil and violence and propelled the Israeli-Palestinian conflict forward. The history to be told in this volume requires attention to difficult and complex issues, often involving a clash of legitimate competing interests. Events that have caused intense pain and anger must be reviewed as well. All of this, together with missed opportunities and the troubling behavior of one party or the other in particular instances, makes up the substance of the Israeli- Palestinian conflict. These realities cannot be avoided or wished away. On the contrary, they must be examined in detail in order to comprehend both the experiences that have brought Palestinians and Israelis to the present historical moment and the obstacles to be overcome in the future if peace is to be achieved.

While early chapters reach back in history to provide a view of Jews and Zionists and of Arabs and Palestinians that is independent of the conflict between them, and also to suggest circumstances in which rival nationalisms might have clashed in Palestine with far less damage and disruption, most of the book is devoted to the events of the last three-quarters of a century, during which a legacy of bitterness, fear, and mistrust has been created. This legacy is the product of violence and tangible loss. Surviving wounds reflect real injuries, including loss of life and physical damage, not merely psychological pressures, symbolic affronts, and insults to dignity and pride.

I have tried to do justice to competing positions when discussing these and other aspects of the conflict. Readers must judge for themselves how responsibility for particular developments should be apportioned among the parties involved. My goal is not to foster specific conclusions about central issues in the conflict but to provide a basis for understanding and evaluating the actions of both Israelis and Palestinians. There will be instances in which readers who identify with one of the parties will believe the position they support has not been presented adequately. Sometimes supporters of both sides may feel ill served. Nevertheless, the volume strives for a nonpartisan point of view; it seeks to present both Palestinian and Israeli analyses and to enable readers to form their own conclusions about the persuasiveness of competing arguments.

This is not to say the narrative regards every argument about every serious question as equally valid. In many instances, it would be a disservice to readers simply to juxtapose competing explanations or interpretations of fact, and in these cases the author's judgment about the quality of evidence or logic will probably be evident. But even in these instances it is hoped that readers will join in the debate, evaluating the judgments of the author as well as the arguments of the protagonists.

Beyond this, however, my aim has been to maintain a stance of considered objectivity. I have tried to represent both sides fairly when fundamental issues are discussed. Similarly, the cumulative effect of the factual information presented should be an understanding and appreciation of both Palestinian and Israeli positions.

As an examination of the past gives way to thoughts about the future, the question of conflict resolution inevitably emerges. However bitter may have been the experiences of Palestinians and Israelis and no matter how one assesses responsibility for creating the conflict, or for failing to resolve it, one must at some point ask whether the future might be different, whether there is not an alternative to continued violence and turmoil. Furthermore, the timing for such an inquiry is fortuitous, since Israel and the PLO have now recognized one another and signed an agreement that holds out the possibility of resolving a dispute which many had come to believe could not be resolved.

In fact, it is not difficult to envision a reasonable solution, one that will simultaneously end Palestinian statelessness and ensure Israeli security. Not all historical injustices can be eliminated, and most will not be forgotten. But the past need not determine the future, just as the history and evolution of the conflict were not preordained. Israelis and Palestinians can break with the past if they have the political will to do so, and any who doubt this need only look to the Israeli-PLO accord for evidence that it is on the parties themselves, and not on history, that the future depends.

The most plausible solution available to Israelis and Palestinians involves partition, meaning that each people would rule over a portion of Palestine, that each would use the territory it controls for the unfettered exercise of its right to self-determination, and that there would be normal and peaceful relations between the two national communities. Partition is not a new idea. It has been proposed by diplomats and commissions of inquiry since the 1930s. Whether or not it should have been accepted when put forward in the past is beside the point when thinking about the future. Partition remains a viable option. Sharing the territory of Palestine would not give either side all that it desires, or believes it deserves, or perhaps actually does deserve in some abstract sense. But it is a solution that recognizes and fulfills the basic requirements of each party, giving both Palestinians and Israelis an indispensable minimum, or more. It offers an alternative to unending struggle and establishes a basis for Israel and Palestine to evolve in ways that will benefit all who live there.

Furthermore, large numbers of Israelis and Palestinians today consider partition an acceptable solution. The principles of territorial compromise and mutual recognition appear to be supported by a majority on both sides of the conflict. To be sure, on both sides there are also hard-liners and rejectionists, those who for ideological reasons oppose territorial compromise and recognition of their longstanding adversary. But such individuals do not predominate in either case, and their ability to prevent progress toward a settlement will be limited if the enemy is not judged to be dangerous and unreasonable. This is why the recent Israeli-PLO accord is so significant. Even if there are disappointments and setbacks as the parties struggle to translate principle into practice, as there almost certainly will be, the agreement confirms that a basis for peace exists. It demonstrates what an accurate reading of history shows to have been the case all along, that there is nothing about the essence of Zionism or of Palestinian nationalism that makes it impossible even to conceive of a solution to the conflict.

The most important obstacles to the achievement of peace are attitudes, perceptions, fears, and symbols, rather than the incompatibility of existential interests. Real interests are in competition with one another, to be sure, but this is not the central problem. Since partition would respect and respond to the fundamental historical aspirations of both Palestinians and Israelis, it follows that the success of present and future peacemaking efforts will depend more than anything else on finding a way to address the psychological and emotional dimensions of the dispute. Majorities on both sides will develop the political will and determination to put the past behind them, to seize or create opportunities for progress toward peace and to refute the arguments of the rejectionists in their own camp, only if they have a view of their adversary that is not distorted by myth and propaganda and that reflects the same empathy and understanding with which they themselves quite rightly ask to be judged.

I return to the need for objectivity without detachment. The key to genuine peace is not to be found in the realm of novel diplomatic formulas or innovative insights about the structure of a solution, although these do remain important, and in some areas, such as the status of Jerusalem, they may well be critical. But the most basic requirement for peace involves the intangibles of tolerance, empathy, trust, and confidence. Only if each party to the conflict is persuaded that the other is not inherently sinister or irrational, but rather has valid claims and has been motivated over the years by legitimate national aspirations, is there likely to be agreement on any formula for compromise and peace, no matter how reasonable that formula might be.

The experiences from which have emerged the perspective that informs this volume reflect a debt to both Israelis and Palestinians, and to many others as well. I was privileged during the 1960s to spend several years of university study in Israel and the Arab world, particularly in Tunisia, and was able during the 1970s and 1980s to make numerous visits for the purpose of research to Israel, the West Bank, Egypt, and North Africa. During the early 1980s, I regularly visited Israel and the occupied territories and wrote about the Israeli-Palestinian conflict under the auspices of the Universities Field Staff International. More recently, I have directed two university affiliation programs supported by grants from the United States Information Agency, one between the University of Wisconsin–Milwaukee and An- Najah National University in Nablus, and the other between UWM and the Hebrew University of Jerusalem. I am indebted to UFSI and to USIA for the support they have provided. I am indebted even more, in a different way, to colleagues at An-Najah and at the Hebrew University, both for their friendship and for their contribution to my continuing education.

I wish to record particular thanks to a number of individuals with whom I have had the great pleasure and privilege to be associated in recent years. This includes Laurie Brand, Iliya Harik, Sharif Kanaana, Baruch Kimmerling, Jacob Landau, Ann Lesch, Moshe Ma'oz, Nadim Rouhana, Emile Sahliyeh, Gabriel Sheffer, Khalil Shikaki, and Jamal Sanad. None, of course, bears any responsibility for the judgments and interpretations contained in this volume. Indeed, each will undoubtedly disagree with some of what I have written. But are all serious and committed scholars from whom I have learned a great deal. I owe an important additional debt to Laurie Brand, Gabriel Sheffer, Emile Sahliyeh, and Baruch Kimmerling for providing valuable comments on drafts of some chapters in this volume.

There are two other individuals whose support has been critical. William F. Halloran, dean of the College of Letters & Science of the University of Wisconsin–Milwaukee, has consistently offered personal encouragement and invaluable assistance, as well as friendship, and I am deeply grateful. I am also deeply grateful to Janet Rabinowitch, senior sponsoring editor at Indiana University Press, not only for her intelligent advice about both editorial and substantive considerations, but above all for her sustained encouragement during the years this volume was in preparation.

I also wish to thank David Long for valuable bibliographic assistance, Jane Lyle for careful copy-editing, and Donna Schenstrom and Paul Beyer for the production of the maps.

Above all, I wish to express my gratitude to my family. My wife, Pat, and my daughter, Joelle, accompanied me on numerous trips to the Middle East, offering companionship, encouragement, and intelligent discussion that greatly enriched these visits. In addition, they graciously accepted my absence when I traveled to the region alone, and during the many hours devoted to research and writing. I am also grateful to my mother, Louise Brown, for her constant encouragement, and for her efforts to instill in me a sense of balance and fairness. I hope she will be justified in the belief that she has been successful.

A Note on Transliteration

Scholarly practice has been followed in most instances in the transliteration of Arabic and Hebrew words, although several exceptions have been made for the benefit of general readers. Diacritical markings are not employed when transliterating Arabic words, unless they are present in quoted passages or in bibliographic citations. Full diacriticals would render the text cumbersome for non-specialists; and partial or modified diacriticals might be awkward as well, without necessarily being of major assistance in pronunciation. The absence of diacritical markings, by contrast, will not prevent specialists from recognizing the original Arabic word. Common English spellings, if they exist, are employed for Arabic names and terms. Thus, for example, the text uses King Hussein rather than King Husayn, Gamal Abdul Nasser rather than Jamal Abd al-Nasir, and sheikh rather than shaykh.

An attempt has been made to unify the spelling of names and terms from Hebrew and Arabic, although it has not been possible to achieve complete consistency. Authors' names and names or other words in titles or quoted passages are reproduced without modification, with the result that some names are spelled in two or more ways; for example, Chaim and Haim, Ya'acov and Yaacov, Muhammad and Mohammad, Daud and Daoud, Abdalla, Abdallah, and Abdullah, and Ain and Ein.

A HISTORY OF THE ISRAELI-PALESTINIAN CONFLICT

PART I

Jews and Arabs before the Conflict
The Congruent Origins of Modern Zionism and Arab Nationalism

THERE ARE SEVERAL reasons to begin a study of the Israeli-Palestinian conflict with a general survey of Jewish and Arab history. One is to dispel the common misconception that the current struggle in Palestine is an extension of an ancient blood feud, fueled by ethnic or religious antagonisms dating back hundreds of years. This view is not only inaccurate, it is also potentially damaging; it promotes distorted judgments about both Jewish and Arab behavior while at the same time diverting attention from considerations that are central to a proper understanding of the conflict in the Middle East.

Present-day issues must be approached with a recognition that neither the Arab-Israeli dispute in general nor the Israeli-Palestinian conflict in particular is based on or driven forward by primordial antagonisms, and that it has in fact been less than a century since Jews and Arabs began to view one another as enemies. A review of Jewish history and Arab history makes this clear, revealing that each unfolded in response to interaction between its own internal dynamics and the wide sweep of world events, and that, in Palestine as well as more broadly, each people occupied but a peripheral place in the evolution of the other until the beginning of the twentieth century. Indeed, as recently as the eve of World War I, the legacy of Jewish-Arab relations was untarnished to the extent that contemporary Zionists and Arab nationalists deemed it worthwhile to explore the possibilities for an alliance between their two movements, with a view toward making common cause in the face of challenges from Europe.

Equally or even more important, not only the Israeli-Palestinian conflict but the parties to this conflict must be understood in a manner informed by history, with a foundation of knowledge that makes it possible to separate fact from propaganda. To arrive at such an understanding and provide this foundation, it is once again necessary to examine Jewish and Arab history during the long centuries before the two peoples confronted one another in Palestine. Neither Jews and Israelis on the one hand nor Arabs and Palestinians on the other can be understood properly if seen primarily, or in the first instance, through the prism of the present-day struggle in the Middle East. Each people must rather be comprehended on its own terms, free from stereotypes and in the context of its own history and culture, and only secondarily, if at all, with reference to the complaints of its adversary. To understand the aspirations and behavior of Jews and Arabs, including the Arabs of Palestine, it is thus essential to examine the historical experiences that have shaped the character of each people and forged its identity and outlook, and to trace this evolution across the centuries and even millennia that preceded the emergence of the Israel-Palestinian conflict. Such an account will lay a foundation for thinking accurately about the parties to the current conflict in Palestine. More positively, it should also foster recognition that, however valid may be the grievances of those with whom each people is presently locked in combat, both Jews and Arabs have ambitions that are legitimate and even praiseworthy.

There is also a remarkable congruence between Jewish and Arab history, and herein resides yet another reason to examine the experience of each people prior to the conflict in Palestine. Indeed, this may be the most important reason of all in the long run. Despite a present-day view that places emphasis on the hostility and conflict between Jews and Arabs, there exists a striking symmetry in the general flow of Jewish and Arab history, and also in the particular way that nationalist movements within each community took shape and entered the arena of contemporary world politics toward the end of the nineteenth century. This symmetry provides a rich resource for dialogue and cooperation should Israelis, Palestinians, and other Arabs one day agree on a formula for resolving the conflict in Palestine and, looking to the future, seek to focus attention on the common elements in their respective national destinies. Should this occur, each people will receive from a knowledge of the other's history not only the insights necessary for accurate judgments about its adversary but also benefits of a more positive nature, including the discovery that Jews and Arabs have much in common, and that each is well suited as a consequence of its own historical experience to appreciate and lend support to the aspirations of the other.

The congruence of Jewish and Arab history prior to the conflict in Palestine is visible in four distinct areas, each of which will be highlighted in the next two chapters. First, Jews and Arabs are both ancient Semitic peoples, with centuries-old bonds of solidarity based on religion, culture, and language. Each constituted a coherent political community long before concepts of modern nationalism were known in Europe, and in each case this community believed in its own Divine origins and sacred mission. The history of the Jews is the history of a people intertwined with that of a religion, and the history of the Muslim religion is equally central to that of the Arabs, such that both Jews and Muslim Arabs established early political communities which they believed to be an expression of God's will. Moreover, again in both cases, this Divine writ was preserved in the form of holy law, the core of which was believed to have been revealed directly by God, and the temporal legitimacy and worldly character of each people's corporate existence was accordingly fashioned in large measure by its acceptance of this body of law as a national constitution. Thus, during their respective classical periods, Jews and Arabs both possessed the elements of peoplehood and transformed themselves into viable political kingdoms, with the members of each polity united by respect for an authoritative legal system and by shared bonds of religion, culture, and civilization.

Second, there is symmetry in the periodization of Jewish and Arab history, both in general and with respect to the emergence of modern nationalism. Each people had once enjoyed an age of high accomplishment, a golden age during which it was able to fulfill its national destiny through action at the center of the Western world's political stage. In each case, however, this classical era was followed by long centuries of decline, by an age of darkness and slumber marked by the loss of political independence and unity and also by a conservative and traditionalist normative ethic. Finally, Jews and Arabs entered a period of renaissance and revitalization in the nineteenth century.

Both peoples characterize this latter period as a time of reawakening, and in each case the timing and the stimuli are highly comparable. Currents of emancipation and nationalism on the part of European states upset the tranquility of traditional communities and led to the emergence of new ideas. Moreover, this parallel history fostered among Jews and Arabs a similar psychological outlook, based on a belief that their ancient identities and destinies remained as relevant as ever, but that the intellectual vigor and political might of other nations could not be denied and, accordingly, that intensified contact with the latter should be an occasion for critical self-examination. With the revered if somewhat idealized memory of a golden age embedded self-consciously in their collective and institutionalized memory, yet recognizing that they were separated from these past glories by many centuries and that they had in the interregnum experienced defeats and indignities and lost the ability to control their own affairs, elements within each community sought to legitimize an accommodation with the modern age and to fashion a strategy of national reconstruction.

A third area of congruence between Jewish and Arab history is to be found in the striking similarity of each people's response to challenges from Europe during the course of the nineteenth century. At the outset this challenge was primarily intellectual, or moral, and the first response of Jews and Arabs was a debate within each community about the relative value of continuity and change. Moreover, as the century wore on and these debates matured, parallel divisions of opinion were in evidence among both peoples. There were radicals, or messianists, whose vision of the future was based on sweeping change and who called for bold new definitions of historic identities and a fundamental transformation of ancient ways of life. Only by embracing the wisdom of the modern age without reservation, they asserted, could their community be truly rejuvenated. There were also orthodox and conservative elements in the ranks of each people. Articulating the viewpoint of the true believer, these individuals rejected calls for modernization and change, insisting that the destiny of their community was in Divine hands and that man must not substitute his own judgment for that of the Creator. These pious traditionalists also asserted that revitalization was a false goal, a pursuit which, however well-intentioned, would in the end rob their community of the very elements that gave it spiritual sustenance and a proud civilization. In between these two positions were Jewish and Arab moderates, men who sought to borrow selectively from European culture and who worked to fashion an authentic synthesis of tradition and modernity. Their goal was to rediscover and preserve the dynamic spirit of their sacred law and venerable culture, and thereafter to use this wisdom to transcend the minutiae of ossified religious practice, which they deemed responsible for stagnation and inner decay, and with it to embrace the opportunities offered by the modern age.

A fourth common element is the manner in which this intellectual ferment and concern with modernization were transformed into nationalism. By the latter years of the nineteenth century, both Jews and Arabs had come to believe that the nations of Europe posed more than an intellectual and cultural challenge. Jews were physically threatened by outbreaks of anti-Semitism in many parts of Europe. Arabs were already under the domination of European colonialism in a number of countries and were confronted by imperialist ideologies based on a foundation of cultural racism. To combat these political and physical challenges, Jews and Arabs both began to articulate platforms possessing nationalist content, calling for political arrangements that would enable each people to organize in its own defense and to manage its own affairs without interference.

Modern political Zionism sought the establishment in Palestine of an autonomous and self-sufficient Jewish colony. This national home would restore the Jewish people to the Biblical Land of Israel, offer Jews a refuge from persecution, and permit construction of a spiritual center where Jewish religious and cultural norms could be put into practice and thereafter evolve. Nationalism in the Arab world, in Palestine as elsewhere, was similarly preoccupied with self-rule and auto-emancipation. Its goal was the construction of political communities run by and for the benefit of the indigenous population. These polities would defend their Arab inhabitants against the challenge of European imperialism, manage the task of improving the material circumstances of Arab life, and provide a framework within which the Arab world could at once defend and revitalize its classical civilization. Although Jews and Arabs would soon clash in Palestine, each people at the outset was irrelevant to the nationalism of the other. Zionists and Arab nationalists were both responding, in very similar ways, to a troubling new aggressiveness on the part of Europe.

These commonalties may one day offer a foundation for reduced hostility between Arabs and Jews, should there eventually be a settlement of the present-day conflict in Palestine, and should the two peoples then seek to understand one another better and to cooperate in charting the future of the Middle East. Indeed, although it is unlikely in the short run, awareness of the congruence of their respective histories might even to some degree lead each people to recognize the legitimacy of the other's aspirations and to approach the conflict between them with greater willingness to seek accommodation and compromise. In the meantime, while attention to the rich and parallel history of Jews and Arabs before there was a conflict in Palestine should not, and will not, divert attention from developments that subsequently placed the two national communities in opposition to one another, this early history remains the logical point of departure for a study of the Israeli-Palestinian conflict. Knowledge of this history is necessary to avoid misconceptions and to put the conflict itself into proper perspective. Even more important, it is essential for a full and proper understanding of the Jewish people, Zionism, and Israel on the one hand, and of the Arabs, the Palestinians, and the nationalism of each on the other. Thus, with these purposes in mind, the next two chapters summarize the history of Jews and Arabs before these two ancient peoples clashed in Palestine and came to regard one another as mortal enemies.

1 | Jewish History and the Emergence of Modern Political Zionism

Early History and Foundations of Nationhood

IT IS INADEQUATE to describe the Jews as a religious group in the modern-day sense of the term. Like Muslims, they are more appropriately regarded as a national community of believers. The Jews' sense of peoplehood is extremely well developed, inextricably bound up with their collective historical experience, with the Land of Israel where they built their ancient kingdoms, and with the sociological and political content of their law.

All of these elements defining the bonds of Jewish peoplehood are made sacred in the eyes of the true believer by the Divine origins attributed to them. The Jewish people considers itself to have been chosen by God, indeed to be *the* people chosen to receive the Holy Testament. Moreover, the role chosen for the Jewish people is not merely to receive the word of God and thereafter to proclaim His existence and transmit His commandments. It is also to found a society and a polity in which men and women will live in a fashion pleasing to the Creator. It is in this sense, too, that believing Jews regard themselves as the chosen people, selected not only to be God's messenger but also, as the orthodox among them say, to be a light unto the nations. Finally, Jewish doctrine asserts that God has granted His chosen people dominion over the Land of Israel, *Eretz Yisrael*, in order that they possess a country in which to construct their commonwealth based on His law. Located in the territory today known as Palestine, and known to the ancients as the Land of Canaan, *Eretz Yisrael* is held to have been promised by God to the patriarch Abraham and his descendants. This promise was reaffirmed and implemented in the form of a solemn covenant between God and the Jews during the time of Moses.

The character of the Jewish people is thus defined both by the temporal aspects of its historical legacy and by a belief that the experience of the Jews is part of a larger Divine plan. The former involve a strong communal identity and the land and the law which in ancient times gave tangible expression to this national spirit, and which continued to shape Jewish thought even after the people of Israel had been driven into exile and dispersed. The latter is the conviction, held not only by devout Jews but also by the true believers of other religions which accept the Hebrew Bible, that the course of Jewish history has been shaped by God's promise of guidance and protection. Therefore, again, the Jews are more than a religious group. They are also a historically legitimated political community possessing many of the attributes associated with nationhood. This duality is well-described by James Parkes, who chooses the term "people" to define the collective consciousness of the Jews. He writes that their history is "that of a people inextricably interwoven with that of a religion. Neither can be told apart from the other. . . . It is best to describe them as a people."[1]

Biblical record and archaeological evidence indicate that the Jews conquered and began to settle the land of Canaan during the thirteenth century before the Christian era (B.C.E.). Moses had given the Israelites political organization and led them out of Egypt, bringing them to the borders of the Promised Land. Then, under Joshua, they initiated a prolonged military campaign in which they gradually took control of the territory and made it their home. Most contemporary scholars believe that it took the Jews many decades to establish hegemony over *Eretz Yisrael*, and that even after it was secured and occupied, Canaanite enclaves remained for some time. Despite accounts in the Book of Joshua which suggest that the land was conquered in a single campaign, planned in advance by Moses and later Joshua, other Biblical testimony is consistent with those archaeological indications suggesting a struggle that lasted as much as a century.[2] In any event, by the twelfth century B.C.E., the period of Judges, the Jews were firmly established in ancient Palestine, and the area of their control included substantial tracts of territory on both sides of the Jordan River. Map 1.1 shows the extent of Israelite control during the century following the conquest. It also indicates the particular region inhabited by each of the original twelve Israelite tribes.

The Israelite political community developed steadily, marked by the growth of national consciousness and the emergence of national institutions and reaching its apogee during the period of monarchical rule under David and Solomon. The establishment of the monarchy, which took shape in the latter half of the eleventh century B.C.E. under Samuel and Saul, modified existing patterns of political organization. Prior to this period, leaders had held temporary mandates and were regarded as thoroughly submissive to the will of God. Now, however, although David and Solomon were both devout and God-fearing leaders, they assumed vastly increased powers and presented themselves as more than simple intermediaries between God and His people. According to one scholar, it is as if Jahweh, the Hebrew God, had "delegated some of his powers to a man. As representative of God to the people, and of the people to God, the king partook of the Divine majesty."[3]

David, who ruled until 960 B.C.E., greatly expanded and strengthened the Israelite kingdom. He had initially established his capital in Hebron, in the region of his own tribe, Judah, but within a few years he captured Jerusalem from the Jebusites and made it the center of his growing empire. Soon the kingdom of the Jews stretched from the Red Sea in the south to what is today the southern part

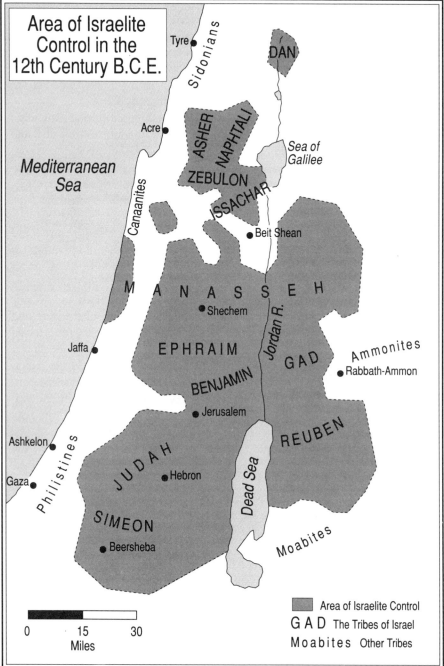

Area of Israelite Control in the 12th Century B.C.E.

of Lebanon, and from the Mediterranean Sea in the east across the Jordan River to Ammon and Moab. In addition, David succeeded in bringing unity to his expanding empire, first gaining allegiance from tribal elders who had formerly resisted the authority of the monarchy and then undermining the power base of these once-independent leaders. Unity and the growth of monarchical power also fostered the emergence of new social groupings, including royal functionaries, government officials, priests, landowners, and merchants.

The kingdom continued to develop and remained united through the reign of Solomon, David's son, who presided over a period of comparative peace and governed the country until 930 B.C.E. Solomon's accomplishments included construction of the royal complex in Jerusalem, consisting of the palace and the Temple; expansion and fortification of many other cities; and creation of an integrated political system for governing the country's twelve administrative districts. He also established an elaborate network of political and commercial relationships with neighboring peoples, making treaties to enhance trade or security and sealing some of them through marriage to women from the ruling families of foreign states. Solomon's reign was marked by pomp and grandeur, and under his leadership Jerusalem became a great city, and Palestine an important country. There were also serious problems, however. Class divisions increased and became more important, with the wealthy benefiting from the growth of the state and its capital, while many common citizens were impoverished by heavy taxes levied to support the state's building program and the luxurious lifestyle of its elite.

The kingdom of the Jews split in two after Solomon's death. In the region of Judea, including Jerusalem and extending southward, the Davidic dynasty continued to hold power. Enjoying comparative stability, it claimed continuity with the past both because it represented the House of David and because the holy Temple of Jerusalem remained within its realm. In the north, however, in the region of Samaria, dissident tribal elements established a rival kingdom, the Kingdom of Israel, which was the larger and more populous of the two competing states, and which soon completely overshadowed the kingdom in Judea. After an initial period of intermittent warfare, commonalities of culture and history led to an alliance between the two Hebrew states, and thereafter the small southern kingdom was gradually transformed into a vassal of the larger one in the north. Israel's capital was at Shechem, the site of present-day Nablus. Among its first kings were Omri and his son, Ahab, who established stable and peaceful relations with neighboring powers and brought prosperity to the country. According to one historian, the dynasty became firmly rooted in the affections of the people, and "Ahab appeared to have regained the glory of the regal days of Solomon."[4]

After several centuries of independence, the Jewish kingdoms in Samaria and Judea were both eventually conquered by powerful neighbors, the former in the last quarter of the eighth century B.C.E. and the latter in the second decade of the sixth century B.C.E. The Kingdom of Israel, which had for some time been distracted and weakened by internal dynastic rivalries, fell to the advancing Assyrian army in 722 B.C.E., after which Samaria was transformed into an Assyrian province and many of its Jewish inhabitants were driven into exile. The kingdom in Judea, called Judah after the tribe of David, did not immediately suffer the same fate; it preserved its independence in the face of the Assyrian challenge by accepting the status of a vassal state. Moreover, it later was able to invade and reoccupy a portion of those provinces in Samaria that had once been part of the Israelite empire and which were now ruled by the Assyrians. Nevertheless, Judah, too, was eventually overrun. During the early years of the sixth century B.C.E. it was besieged by the armies of Babylonia under Nebuchadnezzar. The defenders of Jerusalem were defeated and the city was destroyed in 586 B.C.E. Many Judean Jews were subsequently deported to Babylonia, and for the first time in more than four hundred years the ancient Middle East was without an independent Hebrew state.

The Babylonian conquest of Judah, and with it the destruction of the Temple in Jerusalem, brought to an end the first Jewish Commonwealth in Palestine and closed a critical chapter in the history of the Jewish people. For a time, at least, Palestine ceased to be the political center of Hebrew life. Although a majority of the Jews remained in Palestine following the loss of Israelite independence, the wealthiest and most cultured sectors of Hebrew society were removed to Babylonia, where they appear to have been treated well by local authorities, and where they soon established important centers of Jewish learning and legal scholarship. There was also during this period a flourishing Jewish community in Egypt, the other major empire of the age. This community, which existed prior to the fall of Judah, was also treated well by local officials and was appreciated in particular for its contribution to the commercial and economic life of the country. So far as the Jews remaining in Palestine are concerned, they were primarily peasants, and in the decades immediately following the destruction of Jerusalem they lived a precarious existence marked by poverty and insecurity.

Jewish life nonetheless slowly revived in Palestine, particularly after Cyrus conquered Babylon in 538 B.C.E. and incorporated its provinces into the newly created Persian Empire. Exiled Jews began to return to Palestine in that year, with 42,000 repatriated in an initial wave of immigration, and the Temple in Jerusalem was rebuilt between 520 and 515 B.C.E. Subsequent Persian kings, such as Darius and Artaxerxes I, for the most part supported the reconstruction of Jewish society in Palestine. The Hebrew leader Ezra was granted broad authority by the latter monarch and permitted to establish an administration based on Jewish law that regulated the life of Jews throughout the empire, beyond the borders of Judea and Samaria. Ezra also brought additional Jews back to Jerusalem. Several years later, Nehemiah, originally Artaxerxes' cup-bearer, was made governor of Judea by the Persian king and authorized to rebuild sections of Jerusalem, completing reconstruction of the city's walls in 455 B.C.E.

Palestine became part of the Hellenistic world when Persia fell to Alexander the Great in 332 B.C.E. Despite the importance of this event for the ancient world generally, however, Jewish life was not greatly disturbed by the rise of Alexander's empire. On the one hand, Greek culture did not penetrate deeply into *Eretz Yisrael*, which retained its largely Semitic orientation. On the other, Hellenistic rulers tended to regard the Jews as a distinct national community deserving of autonomy. Judea was granted the status of a semi-independent territory, with Jerusalem its capital and the laws of the Holy Torah its constitution, and Jewish leaders were permitted to exercise authority over all the inhabitants of Judea.

Palestine passed to the Syrian-based Seleucid Empire at the beginning of the second century B.C.E., and within a few years the people of Judea were being oppressed by their new foreign rulers. Antiochus IV plundered the Temple in 169 B.C.E., as his armies passed through Jerusalem while returning from a campaign in Egypt, and the next year he occupied the city and punished its inhabitants. The observance of Jewish law and ritual was outlawed, and the Temple was made over into a shrine for the worship of Zeus. Antiochus also settled non-Jews in Jerusalem in order to further transform the character of Judea's capital.

The Jews rebelled under the leadership of Judah Maccabee, Judah the Hammer, scoring several decisive victories over the Seleucid armies and eventually regaining the independence they had lost more than four centuries earlier. Control over much of Jerusalem was regained in 164 B.C.E., and the Temple was purified and rededicated in that year, an event recalled in the annual celebration of Hanukkah, the Jewish Festival of Lights. Several years later, Judah concluded a treaty with Rome, securing the latter's support for an independent Jewish polity in Judea; and though Judah himself was killed in battle shortly thereafter, guerrilla warfare continued, and in 142 B.C.E. the Seleucid king, Demitrius II, also recognized the independence of Judea. Thus was established the Second Jewish Commonwealth in Palestine.

In 140 B.C.E., an assembly convened in Jerusalem to approve the rule of Judah's sole surviving brother, Simon, thereby resurrecting the Israelite monarchy and establishing a new line of Judean kings, known as the Hasmoneans. Hasmonean leadership was marked by a fusion of political, religious, and military authority, as sanctioned by the Jerusalem assembly. The kingdom also grew stronger under the Hasmoneans, so that, with the growing disintegration of the Seleucid Empire, it was able to recapture Samaria and other parts of *Eretz Yisrael* lying outside Judea. At its zenith, it controlled almost as much territory as had the kingdom of David and Solomon more than eight centuries earlier.

Rome's entry into Palestine opened the concluding chapter in the history of ancient Israel, leading within a few years to the defeat of the Hasmonean state, which at the time had maintained its independence for barely three-quarters of a century. Roman armies under Pompey invaded Jerusalem in 63 B.C.E., capturing the city and, after a three-month siege, taking the area of the Temple Mount as well. The fall of the Israelite capital, made possible in part by internal conflicts that had broken out within the kingdom, also resulted in the loss of thousands of lives. The independence of Judea came to an end with this defeat and the territory thereafter became a province of the Roman Empire.

There was considerable resistance to Roman rule, even though the Jews were granted substantial autonomy by their governors, and the course of Jewish history was fundamentally transformed when this resistance was finally put down. Prior to the reign of Herod (37–4 B.C.E.), Antigonus, the last ruler of the Hasmonean dynasty, succeeded in reestablishing the kingdom of Judea for about three years. Upon Herod's death there was another rebellion, this one unsuccessful. Of much greater consequence was the revolt in Judea from 66 to 70 C.E. Jewish forces overran the Roman garrison in Jerusalem and defeated the army of Rome dispatched from Syria to crush the Israelite uprising, after which they established a government to rule over the whole of Hebrew Palestine.

This brief encounter with renewed independence ended abruptly, however. Nero sent a huge force to put down the revolt. Led by Vespasian and his son, Titus, Roman legions systematically retook the country, finally conquering Jerusalem after a siege that resulted in thousands of Jewish deaths and then destroying the Temple in 70 C.E. Isolated groups in outlying districts for a time continued to resist, although they were soon defeated as well. One band of zealous Jews held out at the desert fortress of Masada, overlooking the Dead Sea, until their stronghold was overrun in 73 C.E. Preferring death to submission, the defenders of Masada took their own lives when they could no longer repel the Romans, an act that is sometimes seen as a symbol both of the Jewish people's fierce desire for independence and of the Jews' readiness to stand against the outside world, whatever the consequences.

The destruction of the Temple in Jerusalem brought an end to all hope of reestablishing the Second Jewish Commonwealth, and thereafter Jewish national life began to disintegrate. Further, the movement of the Jews into a period of exile and dispersion was sealed by the tragic consequences of revolts initiated by Bar Kochba and others in the second century. Although successful at the outset, Roman legions responded to these rebellions with a murderous campaign, in which as many as half a million Jews may have been killed. Many others were deported or forced into slavery. Jews were thereafter forbidden to enter Jerusalem, on pain of death, and the city itself was rebuilt as a pagan center. In addition, discarding the name of Judea, the territory of *Eretz Yisrael* was renamed "Syria Palestina" by the Romans. For the next eight centuries Christianity was the dominant religion in Palestine, after which Islam became the religion of the majority. In the ninth century, too, Aramaic gave way to Arabic as the principal language of the region.

Interwoven with this experience in nationhood and these ties to the land of Palestine is the role of Jewish law in defining the peoplehood of the Jews. The law is sacred; it is given by God and is as tangible a sign of Jewish chosenness as the delivery of ancient Israel into the Promised Land. The law is also comprehensive. It guides the community of believers not only in matters of spirituality and worship but also in the conduct of its daily life and in all aspects of its collective behavior. In other words, orthodox Judaism holds that God gave the Jewish people a national constitution, as well as a land and a sense of communal solidarity, with which to fulfill its Divinely ordained mission.

Jewish law is divided into the Torah and the Talmud. The former contains the five books of the Pentateuch which, according to fundamentalist belief, were delivered to Moses and the Children of Israel at Mount Sinai. According to this interpretation, basic laws were revealed to the whole of the assembled community, and a much larger body of legislation was transmitted to Moses alone, who then caused it to be written down in the form of the Torah's five books. Most Jewish scholars today believe that the Torah was not codified until later, its constituent parts having been written down during different periods by men of varying social and intellectual backgrounds.[5] Although they affirm that the process began with Moses, and also that the prophets who later brought together and codified laws which had been orally transmitted for generations were themselves Divinely guided, many of these scholars nonetheless agree that the Torah probably did not assume its present form until the fifth century B.C.E. Moreover, its inspired authors wrote history and literature, as well as constitutional law. They recounted the fate of Israel in the books of the prophets, and they related songs, proverbs, and tales of inspiration in Writings, or *Ketuvim*. Written later and added to the Torah, Prophets and Writings make up the two remaining canonical divisions of the Hebrew Bible.

The Talmud contains the oral law of the Jews as it was handed down following canonization of the books of the Hebrew Bible. It is composed of two parts, the *Mishnah* and the *Gemara*, the former being the first codification of the Jewish law since the Bible and the latter being commentaries and interpretations of the *Mishnah*. The legal codes presented in the *Mishnah* and discussed in the *Gemara* constitute the *Halakhah*, the body of rabbinical law governing both the spiritual and the civil life of the Jews. The Talmud also contains meditations, folklore, poetry, and philosophical discussions—a kind of post-Biblical literature of the Jews' spiritual and historical experience. This is known as the *Aggadah*.

There is both a Babylonian Talmud and a Jerusalem Talmud. Although the former is much better known and more widely studied, the two documents were written during the same period and are comparable in structure and content. The Babylonian Talmud was compiled and edited by sages at the Academy of Sura in Babylon about 500 C.E. The Jerusalem Talmud was compiled in Tiberias about two hundred years earlier, although the final edition was not completed until the fifth century. According to one scholar, the former is distinguished by the clarity of its definitions and analyses, while the latter is notable for its simplicity and logic.[6] In any event, the Talmud records the experience of the Jews through the

Second Israelite Commonwealth and into the early centuries of their exile and dispersion. Although it was not intended as an authoritative legal code, comparable to the laws of the Holy Bible, it came to be regarded as such. It codified the practices of a political community established to live in conformity with the Divine will and guided by inspired men who integrated spiritual and civil leadership. Thus the *Halakhah* became part of the constitution governing Jewish life, to which Jews strove to conform in the Diaspora following their exodus from Palestine. According to some scholars, *Halakhic* law sometimes even overshadowed the Scriptures which it was created to expound.[7]

Law is central to the peoplehood and political consciousness of the Jews not only because it is considered sacred, constituting a tangible and enduring manifestation of the Jews' Divine destiny, but also because it is comprehensive. The patterns of behavior enjoined upon the faithful are not limited to the obligations of ritual and worship which men and women owe their Creator, or even to the standards of personal morality with which they must struggle to comply in order to find grace in God's eyes and to be granted their reward in the kingdom of life after death. Such patterns of worship and standards of moral conduct are present to be sure, but equally central are codes which govern the more sociological and communal aspects of Jewish life.

The law of the Jews contains countless prescriptions dealing with matters of social, economic, and even political significance. Examples are the requirement that agricultural land lie fallow for one full year after six of cultivation (with the added prescription that it be accorded a second jubilee year after seven such rotations, in the fiftieth year), and the prohibition of lending at interest, no matter how low the rate, to a fellow Jew. The centrality of the temporal preoccupation of Jewish law is illustrated more generally by the following account of *Halakhah*, taken from an anthology prepared by a group of distinguished Jewish scholars. The account also insists upon the humanitarian character of this body of rabbinical law.

> The *Halakhah* teaches the highest esteem for manual work, and contains progressive regulations for the protection of labor which are unrivaled even by the most modern legislation. It is merciful in its penal code, tending toward the abolition of capital punishment, conceiving of legal penalties not as vengeance but as protection for society and treating crime more as a pathological phenomenon than anything else. . . . Restricting private ownership in the interest of public welfare, it calls for a most liberal social order. It considers ethical family life as a prerequisite for a happy society.[8]

Despite its temporal focus, such a body of law cannot be considered secular. It is made sacred by the Divine associations attributed to it. But it is nonetheless a unified system of public law, as well as religious doctrine and a code of personal status, and this in turn makes it a *loi cadre*, indeed a constitution, for the construction of a political community. Thus, coupled with their historical experience in *Eretz Yisrael*, the law of the Torah and the Talmud makes the Jews a people, indeed a nation, rather than a religious group. The concatenation of these communal bonds produces a solidarity that is akin to nationalism, even though it is legitimized by an understanding of Divine as well as natural and historical right. As expressed in the context of the modern-day world by Moses Hess, a mid-nineteenth-century Zionist thinker, this communal solidarity has made the Jews from the beginning of their history a nation in the modern sense—indeed the first such nation.[9]

Classical Zionism and the Middle Centuries

Following destruction of the Second Jewish Commonwealth in Palestine and dispersion of the Jewish people, Jews reaffirmed their chosenness and continued to think of themselves as a political community. Moreover, these notions came together in the form of Zionism, not modern political Zionism but rather classical or traditional religious Zionism, in which Jews expressed their belief that God would in the future bring about an ingathering of the exiles and restore the children of Israel to the Promised Land. This belief reflected not only the Jews' understanding of their historical experience and sociological character but also, and more fundamentally, a faith in the role that God had selected for the Jewish people in His larger plan for the salvation of mankind.

Classical Zionism proclaimed the Jews' continuing and unbreakable tie to Palestine, to the territory they regarded as *Eretz Yisrael*. According to one scholar, "Despite the loss of political independence and the dispersion of the Jewish people, the true home of the Jews remained Jerusalem and the Land of Israel; the idea of eventual return from the four corners of the earth was never abandoned."[10] Moreover, the notions of return and an ingathering of the exiles were visible and salient within the lives of Diaspora Jews. As summarized by one present-day analyst, perhaps with slight hyperbole,

> Most aspects of Jewish life in the Diaspora were intimately linked with Palestine. Jewish rabbinical law favored the settler in the ancient homeland. Religious literature echoed with such sayings as: "It is better to dwell in the deserts of Palestine than in palaces abroad," "Whoever lives in Palestine lives sinless," and "The air of Palestine makes one wise." There was no distinction between the spiritual and the physical Palestine in the minds of most Jews. Although separated from the Holy Land by thousands of miles, to most it seemed closer than the neighboring Christian communities, which were regarded with hostility and fear.[11]

Also central to classical Zionism is the notion of the coming of the Messiah, an event that the faithful believe will bring with it the millennium and be the occasion for the restoration of Jewish national independence in the Holy Land.

There are many passages in the Hebrew Bible, in the Book of Daniel and elsewhere, that foster an expectation of the coming of the Messiah and reflect on the events which will accompany the "end of days." Moreover, there have always been those who believe the secret of this coming is hidden within the text of the Scriptures and who perform calculations aimed at divining the key with which to unlock this mystery. Messianic speculation based on such calculations was not unknown prior to the end of the Second Commonwealth, but it increased substantially in the centuries following the destruction of the Temple, in 70 C.E., as acceptance of the prophecy of the Messiah spread among Jews remaining in Palestine and the growing number in the Diaspora. One scholar accordingly reports that Messianic hopes and beliefs became "an essential part of the Jewish faith and of the Jewish experience of life and history," and that "the heritage of Messianic prophecy was accepted by all—not only in its Biblical form but even more decisively in its subsequent rabbinic development."[12]

Among the reasons given by Jews for their belief that Jesus was not the Messiah is their faith that the Messianic age will bring with it events which have not yet occurred. According to orthodox Jewish thought, there will be a Day of Judgment, on which the dead will be recalled to life and those who have not sinned beyond redemption will be permitted to live forever. This will usher in an era of happiness and perpetual peace. Further, with wickedness banished, the Jews will be delivered from their enemies, and their righteousness and place as the chosen people will be recognized by the nations of the world.[13] Expectations that such an age was near were apparently widespread during the time of Jesus, and some have suggested that Jesus' own teachings may have been largely shaped by the ardor of this contemporary Messianic speculation.[14] In any event, pious Jews continue to await the Messiah and to affirm that His arrival will deliver Israel from its oppressors. With His coming, the Jewish people will be restored to the Promised Land and to its rightful place of leadership among the nations, and at the same time the entire world will be freed from wickedness and sin.

Messianic speculation continued through the ages, there being many false messiahs and many occasions when Jewish mystics proclaimed the Day of Judgment and the arrival of the Messiah to be imminent. Further, the response to these pretensions and proclamations was sometimes intense. For example, during the period of Shabbetai Zebi, a pseudo-messiah from Smyrna who declared himself in 1648 and subsequently traveled to Cairo, Jerusalem, and other destinations in the Eastern Mediterranean, some devout Jews periodically slept with their shoes on and began their meals by eating the meat, in order to be prepared should they be called away without warning by the arrival of the Messiah. Such actions were exceptional, to be sure, characterizing only small bands of the most zealous. Nevertheless, Messianic speculation was a consistent preoccupation among certain elements within the Jewish community from Roman times until well into the modern period.

Much of the activity associated with this phenomenon has been recorded and analyzed in a major treatise by Abba Hillel Silver.[15] Silver also shows the relationship between social and political instability on the one hand and the intensity of Messianic speculation on the other.[16] Accordingly, the anti-Jewish outbursts that ran from the eleventh through the fourteenth centuries often resulted in millenarian enthusiasm, which in turn sometimes expressed itself in sudden migrations to Palestine and also produced the first of European Jewry's pseudo-messiahs. Although Silver's study deals with many ages and dozens of calculators and pseudo-messiahs, the following passage describing the mood in the mid-seventeenth century communicates effectively the fervor that sometimes attended Messianic movements. Silver writes that during this period even many Christians were caught in the grip of a millennial frenzy.

> As the year 1648 approached—the *Anno Mirabile*—the great year heralded by the *Zohar* and many subsequent teachers, the national fever mounted. Fantastic hopes engulfed the whole of Israel, from Safad to London, from Morocco to Poland. The rabbis of Palestine sent an encyclical prayer to be recited at dawn and in the evening in all the lands of the Diaspora, the recitation to be accompanied by lamentation and penance, asking for the restoration of the Kingdom of David and for the remission of the travail-pangs of the Messianic times. Another pastoral letter was dispatched from Palestine to the Diaspora, urging upon all men to forgo strife and to cultivate peace and good will, in preparation for the imminent arrival of the Messiah. Numerous pamphlets on the correct practice of repentance, based on the tradition of Luria, were widely circulated and read. Men prayed and castigated themselves, knowing that the great day was at hand.[17]

Messianic movements and attendant migrations to Palestine were also in evidence during the last half of the seventeenth and the first half of the eighteenth centuries. In 1700, for example, Rabbi Judah Hehassid brought fifteen hundred of his followers to Palestine from Poland and Russia, with the explicit goal of hastening the coming of the Messiah. Messianic pretenders who declared themselves between 1700 and 1740, and who sometimes claimed to be successors of Shabbetai Zebi, included Michael Cardoso from Crete, Mordechai Mokiah from Hungary, Nehemiah Hiyya-Hayyun from the Low Countries, Jacob Querido from Turkey, and Moses Hayyim Luzzatto from Padua, Italy. Still later, in 1777, Rabbi Menachem Mendel brought three hundred disciples from Rumania, Lithuania, and the Ukraine to Safad and Tiberias, and thereafter to Jerusalem.

Although Messianic activity of this sort was episodic, and usually confined to the more pious or even mystic elements of the Jewish community, other manifestations of traditional Zionist conceptions were much more routinized and widespread. Practicing Jews prayed daily for the time when the world would be delivered from evil and the people of Israel would be returned to Jerusalem. They annually lamented the destruction of the Temple on Tisha B'av, one of the most somber days in the Hebrew calendar, and it was also a custom to leave one brick above the door unpainted as a constant reminder of this calamity. Jews further expressed their faith in a return to the Holy Land on many ceremonial occasions. "Next year in Jerusalem," they proclaimed at the annual Passover supper, for example, in remembrance of the exodus from Pharaoh's Egypt and their first journey to the Promised Land.

As expressed by Silver, three factors underlie the Messianic beliefs of the Jewish people: "the loss of national independence and the attendant deprivations, the will to live dominantly and triumphantly as a rehabilitated people in its national home, and the unfaltering faith in divine justice by whose eternal canons the national restoration was infallibly prescribed."[18] These are the dominant and recurring themes of classical Zionism and the elements from which its political significance is derived. They include a lamentation of the Jewish people's exile from Palestine and subsequent dispersion, an affirmation that the Jewish nation's unity of purpose and tie to the Holy Land nonetheless remain and cannot be destroyed, and a profession of the Jews' unshakable faith that a restoration of their kingdom in *Eretz Yisrael* is part of God's plan and will accompany the arrival of Messiah.

As the preceding makes clear, traditional religious Zionism is inextricably bound up with the Jews' definition of themselves as a nation. The Messianic idea expresses and brings together the political, religious, and spiritual destiny of the Jewish people, making the bonds of their peoplehood not only a shared recollection of their Divinely guided history as a nation in Palestine and the sociological content of the law they struggle to observe in their communities scattered throughout the Diaspora, but also a firmly held conviction that they will be gathered together in the future and thus united as they were in the past. Indeed, in the view of one scholar, it is this faith in a common political destiny that explains the enduring existence of the Jews as a distinct people, "bound together by an intense feeling of solidarity, somewhat aloof in its attitude to outsiders, and jealously clinging to the taboos which had been designed for the very purpose of emphasizing and perpetuating its exclusiveness."[19] In other words, "what made the Jews remain Jews was, it seems, their absolute conviction that the Diaspora was but a preliminary expiation of communal sin, a preparation for the coming of the Messiah and the return to a transfigured Holy Land—even though, after the final collapse of the Jewish state, they usually thought of that consummation as belonging to a remote and indefinite future."[20]

While this constellation of beliefs continued to shape Jewish identity and thought into the modern era, Jews for the most part considered themselves passive before God. Indeed, this element of passivity, or patient anticipation, is also central to the definition of classical Zionism. Their sense of community and emotional attachment to *Eretz Yisrael* remained intense, but most Jews nonetheless did not believe it was appropriate to initiate steps toward the reconstruction of their national home in Palestine. On the contrary, such action would indicate a loss of faith and the absence of a willingness to wait for the Creator's plan to unfold in its own Divinely ordained fashion, and this, as a consequence, would rupture the covenant between God and the Jewish people and make illogical and illegitimate any proclamations of Jewish nationhood or any assertion of a continuing tie between Diaspora Jewry and the Land of Israel. The most Jews might do would be to live in a fashion pleasing to the Creator, in the hope that this might hasten the onset of the Messianic age, if in fact the Day of Redemption was not preordained and was thus amenable to modification. In sum, faith, patience, and obedience to God's law, rather than action in the form of physical involvement with the Holy Land, were what the Jews believed to be required of them until the arrival of the Messiah. It is for this reason, notes a prominent Israeli scholar, that the Jews' link to Palestine, for all its emotional and religious ardor, "did not change the praxis of Jewish life in the Diaspora. . . . The belief in the Return to Zion never disappeared, but the historical record shows that on the whole Jews did not relate to the vision of the Return in a more active way than most Christians viewed the Second Coming."[21]

These classical Zionist conceptions provided little motivation for a Jewish return to Palestine. As explained, quite the opposite was in fact the case; it would have been heretical for Jews to arrogate unto themselves the work of God, to believe that they need not await the unfolding of the Divine plan but rather could take into their own hands the fulfillment of a destiny for which they considered themselves chosen by the Creator. Thus, although there was an unbroken Jewish presence in Palestine from the destruction of the Second Commonwealth until the modern era, and while there were also periods of renaissance among the Jews there, during the early years of Ottoman rule in the sixteenth century, for example, the number of Jews residing in the Holy Land after the second century never constituted more than a small proportion either of the country's overall population or of world Jewry. Similarly, although small numbers of Jews traveled to Palestine from the Diaspora throughout the ages, sometimes making visits and sometimes going to settle, most sought only personal spiritual fulfillment and had no thought of contributing to the realization of political or nationalist objectives.

At the dawning of the modern age, in the latter half of the eighteenth century, only 5,000 or so of the estimated 2.5 to 3 million Jews in the world resided in Palestine, a territory which itself had a population of roughly 250,000 to 300,000 at this time. Palestine's population also contained about 25,000 Christians and several thousand Druze, with the rest of its inhabitants being Sunni Muslims. So far as the Jews of the country are concerned, their presence was limited not only in magnitude but also in dispersion, involving concentrations only in Jerusalem and three other cities of special spiritual significance, Hebron, Tiberias, and Safad. Jerusalem contained approximately 50 percent of the total Jewish population of Palestine. Yet as late as 1833 there were only 3,000 Jews in the city. It was not until a decade later that Jews became the largest religious group in Jerusalem, surpassing the Muslims, and they did not become an absolute majority there until the beginning of organized migrations late in the century.[22] Finally, the pious Jews of Palestine in no sense constituted an integrated or self-sufficient political community. Many devoted themselves principally to prayer and study and were dependent upon donations from abroad to support both themselves and their religious institutions.

Outside Palestine, in Europe and the Muslim world, Jews resided in ghettos in the cities and larger towns, and in small villages and hamlets in the rural areas. They were usually limited in the degree to which they could participate in public life outside the ghetto, and they were also often subject to humiliating and degrading restrictions in their relations with non-Jews. According to one satirical account of eighteenth-century Frankfurt, written by a non-Jewish publicist of the day, Jews enjoyed the "loving protection" of authorities: they were forbidden to leave their street on Sundays, so that drunks should not molest them; they were not permitted to marry before the age of twenty-five, so that their offspring should be strong and healthy; on holidays they could leave their homes only at six in the evening, so that the great heat should not cause them any harm; the public gardens and promenades outside the city were closed to them and they had to walk in the fields—to awaken their interest in agriculture; and if a Jew crossed the street and a Christian citizen shouted, "Pay your respects, Jud," the Jew had to remove his hat, no doubt to strengthen the feelings of love and respect between Christian and Jew.[23]

The history of the Jews in Europe, where about 90 percent of world Jewry lived at this time, had for centuries been characterized not only by political inequality and personal humiliation but also, frequently, by physical persecution. Individual Jews might on occasion prosper, or even attain positions of privilege and influence through service to prominent notables and officials. Further, though continuing themes in European Jewish life, intolerance and abuse were much more intense in certain times and places than others. On the whole, however, the Jewish communities of Europe were powerless and dependent and were often the target of anti-Semitic outbursts, many of which were associated with Christian religious fervor. Jews living within the Byzantine Empire were the target of four major campaigns of forced conversion, in 560, 621, 873, and 930, and there were similar campaigns in France in the sixth and seventh centuries, as well as later. Jews were massacred in France and Germany during the Crusades, and there were anti-Jewish riots in England during the Middle Ages. In the late thirteenth century Jews were expelled from England, and they were expelled from France as well in the following century. There were also violent outbursts against the Jews of Germany during this period. On one occasion, for example, nearly two hundred Jews were slaughtered in Frankfurt after the Jewish parents of a converted boy attempted to prevent his baptism. In addition, anti-Jewish riots occurred in Austria in the fifteenth century.

The persecution that Jews had known for half a millennium or more in the Christian states of northern Europe was largely absent in Muslim Spain, which experienced a golden age beginning in the latter half of the eighth century under the enlightened rule of the Umayyad dynasty based in Cordoba. On the contrary, Jewish life was full and prosperous for almost four hundred years, even after the more puritanical Almoravid and Almohad dynasties based in Morocco took control of the area in the eleventh and twelfth centuries respectively. The brilliance of the Jews' own golden age in medieval Spain is symbolized by the myriad accomplishments of Moses Maimonides (1135–1204), who was at once a philosopher, statesman, codifier, and physician. Maimonides produced the *Mishnah-Torah*, a fourteen-volume compilation of all Biblical and rabbinic law. He also wrote *The Guide for the Perplexed*, a philosophical treatise that offered Jews a rational foundation for their faith and was his most important work. On the strength of these and other contributions, Maimonides became the most prominent and influential Jewish figure of the Middle Ages, giving rise to the saying, "From Moses to Moses there was none like Moses."

There were many others who also contributed to the brilliance of Jewish life in Muslim Spain. The succession of distinguished personalities began with Hasdai ibn Shaprut, a tenth-century practicing physician and statesman in the Umayyad court. Among those who followed were Samuel ibn Nagdela, another statesman, Solomon ibn Gabirol and Judah Halevy, the two most outstanding poets of medieval Jewish literature, and Moses Nahmanides and Hasdai Crescas, prominent rabbis and scholars who mounted an intellectual challenge to the philosophical approach to Judaism put forward by Maimonides.

But the fate of Spanish Jews began to change in the thirteenth century, with the defeat of the Muslims by Christian kings who ruled outside of Andalusia. Although the position of Spain's Jewish communities for a time remained secure following the Christian conquest, with Jews at first retaining considerable influence in certain localities, anti-Semitism developed in the fourteenth century and produced growing alarm among Spanish Jews unfamiliar with discrimination and persecution. Jews were massacred in Toledo in 1355, for example, and 1391 was a year of particular tragedy, with mobs attacking the Jewish quarters in Seville, Cordoba, Palma, and elsewhere and killing thousands of defenseless Jews. There were also decrees condemning the Talmud and forbidding Jews to read it, as well as legislation regulating Jewish dress and residence and restricting Jewish enterprise more generally.

Large numbers of Spanish Jews converted to Christianity at this time, further undermining the vitality of their community and contributing to developments that ultimately brought its demise. Jews appear to have had a variety of reasons for abandoning their religion. Many converted in response to anti-Semitism, of course, seeking to avoid persecution and believing it to be the only path open to them. Some of these Jews secretly continued to study the Torah and observe Jewish commandments. Many Jews also converted in response to the appeals of proselytizing Christian clerics, who promised both spiritual and temporal rewards to those who would acknowledge the truth of Christian doctrine and thereby accept salvation. Moreover, at least some of these converts, including some prominent rabbis, appear to have been sincerely convinced that they had been mistaken not to recognize Jesus as the Messiah. Finally, some who abandoned Judaism were simply opportunists, motivated by the hope that as Christians they would have more opportunities for social and personal advancement. But whatever the motivation, these conversions assumed massive proportions after 1391, breaking the spirit of the Spanish Jewish community and sowing the seeds of an even greater tragedy in the years ahead.

While converts from Judaism initially prospered, often attaining wealth and positions of prominence in the government and even the Church, the circumstances of the new Christians changed dramatically in the fifteenth century. Believing that they remained secretly loyal to Judaism, and often motivated as well by resentment of their success, officials of the Christian Church began to charge the converts with heresy and perversion. Now described as *Marranos*, which appears to have meant swine, the converts were harassed and persecuted even more than Jews who had not converted, although the latter continued to suffer as well. The campaign against Marranos reached its peak with the establishment of the Inquisition late in the fifteenth century. Inquisitors spared no effort as they strove to root out "Christian perverts," meaning converts whom they considered disloyal and insincere. Moreover, this drive for purification had a racial as well as a religious connotation, since Inquisitors sometimes described the Jews as a race and demanded a Christianity free from Jewish blood as well as heretical Jewish ideas. In 1481, several converts who had been persuaded to confess their sins were burned alive; and in the years that followed, thousands of cases of alleged deviation were investigated and tried in the courts of the Inquisition, and hundreds of those found guilty were put to death. Other forms of persecution at this time included the passage of laws forbidding converts from holding public office in some areas, attacks on the homes and property of Marranos, and riots in which converts were beaten or worse.

To complete their quest for the purification of Christian Spain, leaders of the Inquisition urged King Ferdinand and Queen Isabella to expel the Jews from the country. With the Marranos broken and Jews now more fearful of conversion than of continuing to practice their religion, this was the obvious next step for those seeking Christian purity, and in 1492 Ferdinand accepted demands pressed by the increasingly influential leaders of the Inquisition and issued an edict to the effect that any Jew remaining in Spain four months thence would be put to death. The Jews were stunned and appealed for reconsideration, offering to pay for the right to remain in the land where their ancestors had lived for the past fifteen centuries. These entreaties were unsuccessful, however, and thereafter hundreds of thousands departed the country, bringing to an end what had been the proudest and most prosperous Jewish community in Europe.[24]

Despite restrictions and episodic violence, Jewish life in the ghettos of Europe also possessed a familiarity and a daily order with which most Jews had become comfortable during the long centuries since the destruction of their last commonwealth in *Eretz Yisrael*. Ruled by their own religious leaders, who rendered judgments based on canons of Hebrew law considered authoritative, they found the routines of life predictable and even satisfying. The communities themselves were for the most part autonomous and inward-looking, upset only during periods of external political turmoil, when pressures from the outside impinged upon them. This pattern was particularly characteristic of the ghettos of Eastern Europe, to which the vast majority of the world's Jews had gravitated in response to the anti-Jewish outbursts in Western Europe during the Crusades and over the course of the thirteenth, fourteenth, and fifteenth centuries. Poland alone is estimated to have had 1.5 million Jews, roughly half the world's total, at the beginning of the nineteenth century.

During the latter years of the premodern era, Jewish life in Eastern Europe, and to a considerable extent elsewhere, thus reflected not only an admixture of the fear and anxiety produced by a long history of anti-Jewish violence and the joyous expectation of eventual redemption derived from a belief in the coming of the Messiah, but also an ahistorical sense that the present represented the natural and inevitable order of things until the onset of the Messianic era. The latter orientation, born of continuity and stability on the one hand and narrowness and parochialism on the other, combining tradition and traditionalism as it were, gave most Jewish communities of this period both an internal strength and a profound conservatism. Moreover, this outlook had become so pervasive and long-standing that it was sometimes regarded as an essential part of the definition of Judaism itself, rather than as the pattern of social organization according to which Jews happened to be living at a particular historical moment. This ethos, which by the end of the eighteenth century had survived for more than a thousand years but was at last on the threshold of a major challenge, is well described by Parkes in *A History of the Jewish People.*

> There was a timelessness about ghetto life, and the gradual acceptance of the idea that the canon of Talmudic interpretation was practically closed led to a similar timelessness about Judaism. There were no new problems seeking interpretation, and the barriers of Jewish life grew closer rather than more distant. The result was that it did not occur to the Jews that there was more than one way to be a Jew, or that there was more than one possibility before the people—at any rate until the Messiah came to change the present dispensation.[25]

First Responses to the Modern Age

The political and ideological climate within which Jews lived began to change in the second half of the eighteenth century, and this in turn produced important changes in Jewish thought and eventually gave rise to modern political Zionism. During this period, and particularly in the wake of the French Revolution, the ideological character of the countries of Western Europe underwent a profound transformation. The medieval association of church and state was abandoned, abruptly in France and more gradually elsewhere, and new concepts of citizenship and political life were introduced. In place of a staid and decaying *ancien régime*, based on royal patrimonialism and institutionalized inequality, France under Napoleon opted for modernization and emancipation.

The French Revolution produced legislation removing many of the restrictions that had long been placed on Jewish life and brought an invitation to Jews to come out of their ghettos and participate in national life on a basis of equality and full partnership. Movement toward granting the Jews full citizenship took place in Germany, too, where in fact the matter had been under discussion prior to the action of the French National Assembly in 1789, and also in Holland and Belgium and then in Scandinavia, Italy, Austria-Hungary, England, and Switzerland. Ottoman Turkey, which ruled over the Muslim countries where most non-European Jews lived, experienced a modernist revolution during this period as well. Citizenship was granted to Turkish Jews in 1839.

One of the most important features of the revolution taking place was that it approached Jews as individuals and not as a political community. As expressed by David Vital, the author of a major study of the origins of modern political Zionism, the Emancipation "took the form, for the most part, of a breaking down of the barriers to the Jew's entry into civil society as an individual, not of the establishment of the Jewish *community* on a basis of equality with other ethnic groups."[26] The formula pronounced before the French National Assembly in 1789 made this clear and explicit: "Aux Juifs comme nation nous ne donnons rien; aux Juifs comme individus nous donnons tout"—nothing for the Jews as a nation, everything for the Jews as individuals.[27] Similarly, in Germany and other countries over which the principles of revolution and emancipation spread during the course of the nineteenth century, there was never any question of recognizing the Jews as a separate nation within the larger polity. What was being offered to the Jews was an opportunity to behave like other citizens—in other words, to divorce Judaism from their political identity and become Jewish Frenchmen, Jewish Germans, and so forth.

The emancipation of European Jewry was protracted and not without setbacks; another of the most salient features of the revolution taking place was its sporadic and irregular character, involving reversals and frequently bringing change to some Jewish communities but not others. In Germany, for example, some of the restrictions that had earlier been lifted were reimposed in 1815 and remained in effect for several more decades. In England, it was not until 1858 that a Jew could be elected to parliament, not until 1870 that Jews could enter university, and not until 1890 that they were granted full citizenship.[28] Nevertheless, the break with the past was striking and deep. As stated once again by Vital, this was "the starting point for the history of *modern* Jewry." Vital describes the changes of the nineteenth century as "a great transformation in the relationship [between Jews and non-Jews] which took place in some parts of Europe, and to a minor extent in the Islamic lands, as a consequence of the Emancipation—the slow and irregular process, often reversed, whereby some, but not all, Jews came to be released from the disabilities under which they had long labored."[29]

The modernist movement among Jews themselves, from which came many of their initial responses to currents of emancipation promising an end to the indignities of Diaspora life, is known as the *haskalah*, or Jewish Enlightenment, a diffuse movement of opinion concerned with Jewish intellectual and cultural development in many fields. The *haskalah*, which had no unifying organization or structure, incorporated different schools of thought and varying points of view about the issues of the day. It was composed of local groups and, as noted by Vital, "the ideas current among, and promoted by, its adherents were rarely formulated with consistency and were often mutually exclusive."[30] There was nevertheless a common ideological foundation that united the disparate elements of the *haskalah*, a foundation that Vital describes as "a compound of dissatisfaction with the condition of their people and a generalized belief in the necessity and the possibility of change through the establishment of a cultural *modus vivendi* between Jewry and the world around it."[31]

The *haskalah* began in Germany in the late eighteenth century, several decades before the introduction of major legislation granting new rights to Jews. Later it flourished in Eastern as well as Western Europe. A son or daughter of the *haskalah* was known as a *maskil*, literally an "enlightened one" (pl. *maskilim*), and a *maskil* was typically highly educated, of middle-class origin, deeply immersed in the broader culture of the European society in which he or she lived, and committed to the principle that both Jew and non-Jew shared a common, universal citizenship. Symbolic of this kind of Jew was the towering figure of Moses Mendelssohn, the leading German Jewish intellectual of the eighteenth century and a man whom many regard as the father of the *haskalah*. Mendelssohn's *Application of Mathematical Proofs to Metaphysics* won the prize of the Berlin Academy of Science in 1763. His *Phaedon; or, The Immortality of the Soul*, a collection of theological and philosophical writings based largely on Plato's *Phaedo*, became a favorite in Enlightenment circles. Although Mendelssohn was of an earlier generation, and thus a pioneer and trailblazer rather than a product of the *haskalah*, the life and work of this "Socrates of Berlin," as he was sometimes known, were brilliant testimony to the fact that a Jew might achieve great prominence in the world of European letters and make major contributions to the general culture.[32]

As indicated, the *haskalah* and the larger movement of ideas of which it was a part were marked by varying responses to the new political climate in which European Jews were beginning to find themselves. First, many urged that new opportunities and improvements in the condition of Jewish life be embraced in the fullest measure, without any hesitation or misplaced nostalgia. By the example of their own conduct and by the content of their writings and statements, they charted for the Jews a future based on the full exercise of their new rights of citizenship and on a narrowing of their behavior and identification as Jews to spheres restricted to spirituality and worship. Oriented toward assimilation and the unrestricted integration of the Jew into European society, they anticipated and welcomed what they saw as a pure revolution: there would be a dramatic reduction of the cultural and behavioral differences between Jews and non-Jews, with all becoming citizens of the world and with each individual, regardless of his or her personal religious beliefs, an equal participant in and contributor to a universal world culture. One major study of Jewish and Zionist thought during this period describes this assimilation-oriented impulse as "messianism." It is not the messianism of traditional Zionism, of course, but it is analogous in that it anticipates and embraces the arrival of a new era, one in which the sorrows of the past will be left behind and Jews will go forward into the bright light of a happy new age. The position of the most dedicated true believers of this new messianism is described by the author of the study, Arthur Hertzberg, in the following terms:

> The assimilationists, those Jews who consciously strove to give up their own identity entirely in order to become undifferentiated individuals in the modern world, were truly messianic. The very completeness and unconditionality of their surrender to the dominant values of the majority were a program for the final solution of the Jewish question: let the Jew become like everybody else, yielding up his claim to chosenness and being relieved of his role as scapegoat. Let society run on its universal and immutable principles, rooted in reason and natural law, which know neither positive nor negative expectations for the Jew. Above all, let him disappear from the center of the stage, his own and the world's, to be one among many equally important small incidents in the history of the world.[33]

This assimilationist, or messianist, orientation, radical and previously unknown in Jewish history, became dominant among middle-class Jews in Western Europe and retained its centrality throughout most of the nineteenth century. It was particularly pronounced among the leading families in major urban centers. Another important study of modern political Zionism illustrates its origins and character with an account of the educated German Jewish women who maintained fashionable salons in Berlin and Vienna. These women were from the most prominent Jewish families of the day. Among their number, for example, were the daughters of Moses Mendelssohn, who himself had close association with many well-known non-Jewish intellectuals, and who in this respect was a generation ahead of his time. Mendelssohn's daughters and other salon women lived in an atmosphere of heady worldliness, which carried assimilation to its logical conclusion and which showed what at least some Jews hoped would be the sweetest fruits of the Emancipation. According to Walter Laqueur, the author of the study, these women entertained statesmen and generals, princes and poets, theologians and philosophers; rare indeed was the influential intellectual who did not, at one time or another, frequent the homes of these women. The German aristocracy found in their salons intelligent conversation, a lively cultural interest, and above all social and intellectual freedom.[34]

Some change-oriented Jews coupled their advocacy of integration into European society with attempts to modernize their own religious and cultural traditions. Among the most important of these efforts was the formation of a movement to reform the study and observance of the Jewish religion. Reform Judaism, which was also influenced by the life and work of Moses Mendelssohn, first made its appearance in Holland and Germany around the beginning of the nineteenth century. One of its goals was the removal of any contradiction between religion and modern life; and among the initiatives undertaken in pursuit of this objective was the creation of societies for the scientific study of Judaism, including investigation of the historical evolution of Jewish rituals and customs. A related development was the promotion of new forms of religious education. Ethical concepts were stressed and, as described in one account, there was a sharp departure from "the old theory that Jewish education was a religious exercise or a spiritual discipline, rather than a means of developing the intellectual and aesthetic potentialities of man."[35]

Another of Reform Judaism's goals was the restructuring of religious activity so as to make it more palatable to educated men and women who identified with general European culture. Changes included the modernization of many ritual observances, prayer in the language of the land, as well as Hebrew, and elimination of certain ceremonial practices deemed to be outmoded. Among the first instances of such reform was a new service introduced during the first decade of the nineteenth century at the synagogue of Israel Jacobson in Westphalia. There were prayers, songs, and sermons in German; an organ and a choir, both unknown in orthodox synagogues, were introduced as well; and, in yet another departure, it was later agreed that men and women should be seated together.[36] Soon this kind of reform service had made its appearance not only in Germany and Holland but also in Austria, Denmark, France, Hungary, and elsewhere. In the eyes of reformers, such changes were not an attack upon religion but rather an attempt to restore its dignity. In their view, the traditional service was mechanical and disorderly, in which prayers were often poorly understood and were accompanied by a steady stream of gossip and banter on the part of assembled worshipers. Such practices appeared quite unseemly to educated men and women and had, they believed, contributed to a decline in the prestige of synagogue life.[37]

Change-oriented Jews placed particular emphasis on education, and advocates of assimilation not only called for the reform of Jewish education but, more generally, insisted on the importance of professional training, and above all declared it to be absolutely critical that Jews undertake the study of general European culture. All of this, they asserted, was necessary for Jews to prosper in the contemporary world. Many also saw language as a critical aspect of Jewish emancipation. The predominance of Yiddish, which was characterized as "mutilated and confused, desolate and arid" by Nephtali Hertz Wessely, one of the early lights of the *haskalah* movement,[38] would have to give way to "correct speech," by which was meant fluency in German or any other national language in a country where Jews lived. In addition, some advocated greater knowledge of Hebrew, with emphasis on the language's grammar and structure rather than its exclusive use for the recitation of religious texts, and in this connection there were also calls for modernization of the ancient language of the Jews.

Although it did not appear until the middle of the nineteenth century, the Alliance Israelite Universelle is another expression of the drive to free Jews from outmoded practices and to foster their cultural integration into European society. An international educational and cultural consortium, established in France in 1860 and dedicated to improving the lot of Jews everywhere, the AIU illustrates particularly well the missionary orientation with which some Jewish messianists approached issues of identity and culture. The AIU's most important work was in the field of education, especially in North Africa, where it eventually associated itself with the cultural policies of French colonialism. In 1862 it opened its first school in Tetouan, Morocco. Although the AIU established schools in many countries, so that its network by 1900 embraced 100 schools and 26,000 pupils, it was in Morocco, Tunisia, and Turkey that the organization concentrated its efforts. Moreover, its own justification of this geographical bias indicates the Alliance's orientation toward a *mission civilisatrice*. AIU leaders judged Jews in Morocco, Turkey, and Tunisia to be in "a deplorable intellectual state" and to have "absolutely no knowledge of modern culture." They were barely able to read and write in Hebrew. AIU spokesmen acknowledged that Jews were more unhappy and persecuted in Russia and other parts of Eastern Europe, but for these latter Jews the "sacred flame of science was never extinguished."[39]

The schools of the AIU offered a self-consciously modern instructional program, which included some study of Hebrew and religion but which was nonetheless explicitly modeled on France's secular educational system. The language of instruction was usually French and, in these cases, courses, books, and tests were for the most part identical to those employed in France. The purpose was to assimilate young Jews into French culture, and to facilitate their successful entry into French society by preparing them to take and pass the standardized national exams given in the metropole. Alliance schools met with resistance from tradition-oriented Jews in some quarters. On the island of Djerba in southern Tunisia, for example, local rabbis succeeded in blocking the establishment of an AIU school in both of the villages where Jews lived. More generally, however, the

AIU steadily expanded the locus of its activities and became, as was its intent, an important agent of assimilation into the mainstream of European culture for hundreds of thousands of traditional Jews in North Africa and elsewhere. The following account, taken from a special 1973 issue of the *Cahiers* of the Alliance, shows how the organization defined its objectives.

> Jews . . . lived like their Arab neighbors, far from the great currents of expansion in industry and science of the Western world, a primitive existence, made more difficult by their special legal status as Jews. . . . Always, since its beginnings more than a century ago, the Alliance sought to instill in the children not only a love of culture and knowledge, but also the respect for the rights of man, and the meaning of the struggle for liberty and for the dignity of the individual. . . . The pure Jewish tradition on the one hand, the Western ideals brought over from France on the other, became the banner under which so many dedicated men and women carried out their task with such devotion.[40]

Some pushed assimilation to its logical conclusion. Marriage to non-Jews occurred with considerable frequency among middle-class Jews in Western Europe, and even conversion to Christianity assumed proportions that more conservative Jews found alarming. The prominent Jewish hostesses of Berlin, for example, including the daughters of Moses Mendelssohn, all became Christian. Moreover, though most educated Jews retained an attachment to the faith of the fathers, or at least to its contemporary expression in the form of Reform Judaism, many of these individuals nonetheless loudly proclaimed the primacy of their identification with the world of their Christian countrymen. They declared their love of the *patrie* and called its capital their new Jerusalem. To a degree, their professions of loyalty were aimed at convincing non-Jews that they were indeed worthy of equality, and some of these expressions were actively encouraged by political authorities. Napoleon had asked, for example, whether the Jew, once emancipated, would be unreservedly loyal to the state, and it is in this context that rabbis and Jewish leaders from France and Italy gathered in Paris in 1812 to affirm their loyalty to the emperor.[41] Nevertheless, though fears of renewed anti-Semitism may have encouraged such declarations, it is also true that many Jews of the Emancipation sincerely and genuinely believed that they were children of a new age, that they were part of a great social movement which was radically reshaping the destiny of all men and women, including the Jews.

Standing against this assimilationist and messianist orientation were those Jews who advocated cultural synthesis or compartmentalization. There were significant intellectual variations both between and within these latter schools of thought, but taken together they stood for cultural accommodation and a definition of Jewish enlightenment in which emphasis was placed on the first as well as the second element in the formula. Hertzberg describes these orientations as "defensive" in character, for they rejected, and sought to defend Judaism against, the pure and complete revolution advocated by assimilationists; they insisted on the transcendental relevance of authentic Jewish values and declared that their mission was to preserve these values, as well as to ameliorate the social and political conditions under which Jews lived. Hertzberg's excellent analysis of this defensive perspective observes that many associated with it viewed the changes taking place around them as constituting a challenge, as well as an opportunity. To a degree, emancipation was even a burden, a *gezerah*, which Hertzberg translates as "a destiny to be accepted with resignation."[42]

Maskilim oriented toward cultural synthesis called for the study of Hebrew, in order that the language be revived and modernized, and also for an integration of the Jews' authentic and esteemed civilization on the one hand and the broader modern and scientific world culture of Europe on the other. The resulting cultural synthesis would provide the normative foundation for a new and progressive Jewish identity, one appropriate to the demands and opportunities of a century committed to emancipation. Through the early years of the nineteenth century, this orientation was prominent among leaders of the German *haskalah*, who, as noted, took their inspiration from the work of Moses Mendelssohn. Their principal goal was the eradication of any contradiction between Judaism and modern life, and they undertook religious and educational reforms designed to remove outmoded norms and patterns of behavior, while at the same time seeking to discover and preserve the transcendent ethical and aesthetic contributions of Jewish civilization. Later in the nineteenth century, this concern with cultural synthesis declined in importance in Western Europe but assumed much greater prominence among Jewish intellectuals in Eastern Europe, who, in a sense, may accordingly be regarded as the truest heirs of the *haskalah*.

Advocates of compartmentalization emphasized the need to maintain a distinction between Jewish and universal values and urged Jews to conform to the one in their private lives and the other in public. "Be a Jew in your home and a man outside" was the admonition of Judah Leib Gordon, a leading figure of the Russian *haskalah* movement.[43] Here, then, the emphasis was less on cultural synthesis than on the dualism of those cultural policies that Jews were enjoined to follow. In many cases, this orientation also encouraged the revival of Hebrew or the reform of various Jewish customs. Thus it was not necessarily an apologist for the traditional practice of Judaism or an uncritical defender of traditional Hebrew-Yiddish culture. In other instances, however, this position was taken by men whose culture and pattern of religious observance differed little from what had been accepted centuries earlier. As described by Raphael Mahler in relation to Germany, these individuals "seized upon German culture without effecting the slightest change in their practice of the Jewish religion, which they identified with the essence of Jewishness."[44] In the same connection, Vital discusses Jews in Eastern Europe whose adoption of Russian was solely instrumental, being little more than "a parallel vehicle of communication and expression."[45]

Religious conversion and intermarriage confirmed the diagnosis of *maskilim* oriented toward cultural synthesis or compartmentalization, those who set themselves apart from traditional and orthodox Judaism but who nonetheless believed that should substantial numbers of Jews abandon their special identity in order to become citizens of the world, the result would be disastrous for the Jewish people. Unrestricted assimilation would ultimately result in the loss of Jewish specificity, in the disappearance of a civilization that was sacred in origin and historically legitimized and in defense of which generations of Jews had endured hardship and persecution. The task that these more moderate *maskilim* set for themselves, both to be defined in their intellectual inquiries and to be lived out in their personal conduct, was thus to bring together authentically Jewish and universal values.

This philosophical orientation is prominently illustrated by Nachman Krochmal's *Guide to the Perplexed of Our Time*, written in Hebrew and published posthumously in 1851. Recalling *The Guide to the Perplexed* of Maimonides, whose great contribution was to unite an analytical appreciation of Judaism with the intellectual vigor of medieval Muslim civilization, Krochmal's work viewed Judaism as an evolving ethos, shaped by historical circumstances rather than immutable and frozen in time, and hence understandable through application of the intellect. In this way, he argued, an interest in Judaism was compatible with a modern spirit, and Jews could identify with the peoplehood or even the nationalism of their own community without either sacrificing rationalism or embracing the mystical faith of the rabbis. Krochmal's emphasis on the Jews as a nation, one among many and shaped by historical forces in the same way as are other nations, makes him an early intellectual contributor to modern political Zionism.[46] Nevertheless, it is his affinity with the preoccupations of the earlier German *haskalah*, his concern to integrate from the analytical perspective of the Hegelian dialectic both the generality of an overarching scientific and material world culture and the specificity of the Jews' own essential contribution to a universal normative order, that gives his work particular interest.

By the third or fourth decade of the nineteenth century, this defensive school of thought was gaining influence among Jewish intellectuals in Eastern Europe, where the Russian *haskalah* continued the tradition of its German precursor while the latter itself gave way to the predominance of more messianist visions of the destiny of European Jewry. Krochmal, for example, lived in Galacia, where Polish was the language of the masses, although German was used by the educated elite. In Russia, which had taken over most of Poland at the end of the eighteenth century and, as a result, now had hegemony over most of Eastern Europe's Jewish communities, the most prominent intellectuals of the *haskalah* included Isaac Bar Levinsohn, both a rabbinical and a modern scholar who was sometimes known as "the Russian Mendelssohn," and whose call for uniting Talmudic and secular studies was put forward in *Learning in Israel* and other books; Judah Leib Gordon, a celebrated poet who wrote in Hebrew and treated themes of Jewish history from Biblical times until his own age; Abraham Mapu, who wrote novels in Hebrew and whose *Love of Zion* became a best-seller; and Peretz Smolenskin, a scholar, author, and editor, who published the monthly journal *Dawn* and who attempted to inspire among his readers a love of the Hebrew language.

Each of these Russian *maskilim* emphasized the importance of balancing continuity and change and of uniting, or at least juxtaposing, both general and particularistic cultural norms. Smolenskin, like Krochmal, saw the Jews as a national community and thus made an intellectual contribution to the eventual emergence of modern political Zionism. Yet he remained a prominent disciple of the *haskalah*, with its European cultural focus and its preoccupation with bringing together universal and Jewish values, and it is in this context that he offered the following rejoinder to those Jews who were prepared to sacrifice their historic identity in return for a place of equality in European society:

> You wish to be like other peoples? So do I. Be, I pray you, be like them. Search and find knowledge, avoid and forsake superstition; above all, be not ashamed of the rock whence you were hewn. Yes, be like the other peoples, proud of your literature, jealous of your self-respect. . . . [47]

Elsewhere, in 1883, Smolenskin offered the following critical account of the German *haskalah*, as it had evolved during the nineteenth century under the influence of men oriented toward assimilation:

> Its aim was not to cultivate knowledge for its own sake but to cast off Judaism and replace it with "enlightenment." The example was set by the exponents and high priests of this doctrine—men without wisdom, who understood neither the past nor the future and did not comprehend the present either. They advanced the strange and preposterous theory that the cause of all our suffering and travail is our rejection of enlightenment; we need only accept and cherish western civilization for the sun of righteousness to dawn upon us. [48]

Yet such admonishments against assimilation were in no sense intended as a defense of the pre-Emancipation status quo or a denial that Jewish life was in need of change. Just as Smolenskin called on the Jews to seek knowledge and forsake superstition, Levinsohn wrote that "art and science are steadily progressing [and] to perfect ourselves in them we must resort to non-Jewish sources." [49] The poet Gordon wrote, "Arise, my people, 'tis time for waking! Lo, the night is o'er, the day is breaking." [50]

While the defensive school of thought within the *haskalah* predominated in Eastern Europe, in contrast to the situation in the West, there were also some Russian Jews whose orientation was toward assimilation. As expressed by Vital, these individuals sought "total merger with, and assimilation into, the Russian people whose pains and quandaries would henceforth become theirs, while their own ancient and specific Jewish agonies were sloughed off in the process." For these Jews, Vital continues, there was "an unspoken alliance with the Russian authorities themselves—for there the *maskilim*'s desire to encourage the acquisition of general, secular culture appeared to meet the authorities' wish to propagate it."[51] An institutional expression of this ideological orientation was the Society for the Diffusion of Enlightenment among the Jews, founded in 1867 by a group of privileged Jews from St. Petersburg. The society's goal was to eradicate Jewish "separatism and fanaticism . . . and aloofness from everything Russian," in order that Jews might become "full-fledged citizens of this country."[52]

At the other end of the ideological spectrum, in what undoubtedly constituted the most important difference between Jewish life in Western and Eastern Europe, the great majority of Jews in the latter region continued to reside in traditional circumstances and were indifferent or even hostile not only to assimilation but to all of the schools of thought encompassed by the *haskalah*. Overwhelmingly located in a region known as the Pale of Settlement, most of which had come under Russian control after the partition of Poland, the Jewish masses lived in urban ghettos or in villages and hamlets that had been stable for centuries, and where currents of emancipation and change on the whole were not intense until late in the nineteenth century. Most residents of these conservative, Yiddish-speaking communities thus knew little beyond the piety and parochialism of traditional Jewish life. Moreover, to the extent that some of these Jews were nonetheless buffeted by the political and ideological transformations sweeping over Europe, one response was a revivalist movement known as *Hasidism*, which was based on mystical interpretations and called for absolute conformity to an ultraorthodox definition of Judaism and Jewish culture.

Contributing to the relative conservatism of Eastern European Jewry were the policies and attitudes that prevailed in Tsarist Russia, which included not only White Russia but also the Ukraine, Lithuania, and, as noted, eastern and central Poland. On the one hand, Russian authorities were slow to grant new rights and opportunities to Jews. For example, it was not until the middle of the nineteenth century, following reform edicts by Alexander II, that Jews were permitted to enter Russian schools and universities. Also, the most important centers of Jewish intellectual life were Odessa and Vilna because the Russian cities of Moscow and St. Petersburg remained closed to Jews for a considerable time. On the other hand, anti-Semitic tendencies within Russian society made popular culture, as well as official policy, a deterrent to the kind of Russification that was required for full immersion in modern society. Jews were the object of antipathy on the part of the peasantry, with whom they dealt as petty merchants and financial agents. They were also strongly disliked in many sectors of the Russian establishment, including the bureaucracy, the military, and the Church. As a result of all of these considerations, it is estimated that only 15 percent of the Jewish children attended Russian-language schools, whereas 85 percent received a traditional religious education. Yiddish remained the mother tongue of 98 percent of the Jews of the Pale.[53]

The religious and cultural changes advocated by the *haskalah* had little attraction for the orthodox masses of the Pale and were vigorously denounced by traditional Jewish leaders, who sometimes reserved their most bitter condemnation not for advocates of assimilation but for *maskilim* whose intellectual posture was more defensive in character. These traditional leaders shared with the defensive school of the *haskalah* a belief that the revolutionary potential of the times posed a threat to Judaism. In their eyes, too, each new conversion or mixed marriage demonstrated a self-evident truth, that destruction of the bonds defining Jewish peoplehood would be the inevitable result of flirtation with false concepts, such as universal citizenship or Reform Judaism. Nevertheless, while in principle the greatest scorn of traditional Jews should thus have been directed at the most assimilated of their coreligionists, they in fact often considered the ideas of the defensive school to be more subversive.

In the view of many orthodox Jews, *maskilim* whose orientation was messianist could at least be identified for the false Jews they were; their option was clear, as were the reasons that it should be rejected by those who cared about Judaism and who saw in the destiny of the Jewish people more than the personal welfare of men and women who happened to be Jewish. On the other hand, *maskilim* who advocated compartmentalization, or especially cultural synthesis, promoted the seductive idea that they were addressing the needs of Judaism, as well as of individual Jews. Such notions were completely erroneous in the judgment of orthodox and traditional Jews. They might be advanced by men who were sincere and of good faith, but the latter's logic was nonetheless flawed. Moreover, once revolutionary changes were introduced and men took unto themselves the right to define the destiny of the chosen people, it was only a matter of time before individuals of lesser sincerity and intelligence would begin to make more selfish choices, after which all attempts to preserve the essence of Judaism would be outrun by events. After all, this had been the legacy of the *haskalah* in Germany, which began by embracing the tradition of Mendelssohn and flowered through the beginning of the nineteenth century, only to produce succeeding generations of Jews who often abandoned the quest for a vibrant Judaism, and who subordinated to their personal desires any thought of preserving that unique essence which sets the Jewish people apart from other nations.

In sum, the first Jewish responses to the modern age ranged across a broad ideological spectrum that included support for change, opposition to change, and a halfway-house orientation favoring a balance of change and continuity. Equally significant, there were intense debates among individuals with differing points of view, creating ideological ferment that was also part of the Jews' response to currents of emancipation and modernization.

Traditional Jews seeking to maintain established patterns of religion and culture were condemned for fatalism, fanaticism, ignorance, and backwardness. Yet their faith and sense of historical continuity enabled them to dismiss such condemnations with little hesitation. In addition, in Eastern Europe, these traditional

Jews had the benefit of numerical strength. *Maskilim* with an assimilationist orientation, who occupied the other end of the ideological spectrum, were accused of arrogance, selfishness, betrayal, superficiality, and mindless imitation. But these Jews, too, had the security that comes with a clear and straightforward historic vision, this one inspired by a belief in the inexorable unfolding of a profound human drama, and by the purity of the revolution of which they believed themselves to be a part. Further, especially in Western Europe, they often derived additional strength from the encouragement of non-Jewish intellectuals and authorities, who praised them for blazing a trail for their coreligionists. Finally, Jews who searched for an alternative to the monolithic poles of continuity and change, who sought an acceptable middle ground and strove for a balance between universalism and authenticity, were called subversive, confused, romantic, and unrealistic. They were also cross-pressured by the less nuanced ideological challenges of orthodox Jews on the one hand and radical assimilationists on the other. Yet they, too, were convinced of the correctness of their position, insisting that the need for balance and synthesis was self-evident and that any other course was sure to be disastrous for the Jews.

The Beginnings of Modern Political Zionism

The intellectual activity of this period attests to the revolutionary character of the circumstances in which Jews found themselves in the nineteenth century. The debate among Jews oriented toward assimilation and those assuming a more defensive posture went forward, with each not only addressing the other but also responding to the criticism directed at it by orthodox rabbis and other traditional Jewish authorities. It was thus an era of dialogue and passionate debate, a liberal age, an age of ideas. As the imagery of *Dawn* or of Judah Leib Gordon's poems suggested, it was also a period of Jewish reawakening. Among the educated, at least, Jews sensed that a long and unhappy age was at last coming to a close, and they emotionally articulated their dreams and fears about the future.

In this intellectual climate there emerged as well some writers who placed emphasis on the national and political aspects of Jewish peoplehood, and who thus became the ideological precursors of modern political Zionism. It is not always possible to associate an individual neatly with a single school of thought, such as messianist, defensive, or, now, Zionist. The ideas of some, moreover, evolved and changed during the course of their intellectual careers. Krochmal and Smolenskin, for example, were sons of the *haskalah* and contributed to the debate surrounding questions of cultural assimilation. Furthermore, Smolenskin wrote, "The land in which we dwell is our country. We once had a land of our own, but it was not the tie that united us. Our Torah is the native land that makes us a people, a nation only in the spiritual sense, but in the normal business of life we are like all other men."[54] Yet Krochmal and Smolenskin are also rightly claimed by modern Zionism. Both emphasized the peoplehood and unity of the Jews. Krochmal analyzed the history of the Jews as a political community and argued that it was through their existence as a nation that they contributed timeless and universal values to the gentile nations of the world. Smolenskin extended this argument. He strongly supported Jewish settlement in Palestine in his later years. Coming eventually to the conclusion that the *haskalah* was for many Jews, even in Eastern Europe, a pretext for abandoning any meaningful Jewish identity, he began to assert that the genius of the Jewish people required for its full development the restoration to the Jews of the land that "once was and still is our own."[55]

Other Jewish intellectuals also articulated Zionist themes during this period. They remained for some time a small minority among the educated and middle-class Jews who addressed themselves to the concerns of a new age. Further, they reaped scorn from more orthodox and traditional Jewish leaders, who condemned their political brand of Zionism as heresy and who insisted upon the Jews' historical understanding that the return to Zion was a destiny to be fulfilled by God and not by man. Nevertheless, there did emerge writers of prominence who, like Krochmal and Smolenskin, proclaimed that the Jews were a nation in the modern sense, who called on the Jewish people to assert their national rights, and who saw the reconstruction of Jewish society in Palestine as the key element in a nationalist program of action. They were not yet thinking about an independent Jewish state in Palestine, and for the most part they saw any return to Palestine in the context of a solution to the temporal problems and needs of the Jewish people, not as a fulfillment of Biblical prophecy. Yet they did insist on the sacred tie of the Jews to the land of *Eretz Yisrael* and on solidarity among Jews based not on a common challenge from the gentile world but rather on the positive attributes of Torah and a God-given national experience. Articulating these themes, they added modern political Zionism to the expanding range of ideological responses that were called up by the revolutionary character of the times.

Major contributors to Zionist thought during this period include Rabbi Yehudah Alkalai, Rabbi Zvi Hirsch Kalischer, Moses Hess, Eliezer Ben Yehudah, Moshe Leib Lilienblum, and Leo Pinsker. Alkalai and Kalischer have been called "pious proto-Zionists."[56] Both remained tied to orthodox Judaism, which they served as rabbis in Serbia and Western Poland respectively, and both were influenced by traditional Jewish conceptions of Messianic redemption. Both also wrote in rabbinical Hebrew. Yet, in addition, each also saw a need for Jewish self-determination that was analogous to the secular nationalisms gaining strength in Europe. Alkalai published an interpretation of Biblical passages in 1845 in which he argued that the Redeemer will not arrive suddenly, and that His coming will be preceded by a number of preparatory steps. Therefore, Jews should begin to return to Palestine and build up the land as part of this preparation. Further, Alkalai placed great emphasis on the revival of spoken Hebrew; breaking with orthodox tradition, which viewed the language as a sacred tongue inappropriate for everyday life, he insisted that a common use of Hebrew was the key to reestablishing unity among the Jews.

Kalischer was rather more explicit in claiming for the Jews the same political rights as the secular nations of Europe, and in urging the Jews to become active in defense of their legitimate national rights. In *Seeking Zion*, first published in 1862, he wrote, "Let us take to heart the examples of the Italians, Poles, and Hungarians, who laid down their lives and possessions in the struggle for national independence, while we, the Children of Israel, who have the most glorious and holiest of lands as our inheritance, are spiritless and silent. We should be ashamed of ourselves."[57]

Moses Hess, an assimilated German Jew who began his intellectual life in the revolutionary socialist movement, and to whom Karl Marx later acknowledged a debt, gradually turned to Zionism as the answer to the problems of the Jews. Hess advocated Jewish assimilation into a universal socialist ethic during his earlier years, but he later came to a different view of the proper relationship between Jewish specificity and universal social and political norms. The course he proposed, based on a fusion of socialism and Jewish nationalism, was set forth in *Rome and Jerusalem*, published in 1862. Hess's vision was the creation of a socialist Jewish commonwealth in Palestine. To Hess, this was a program that would rescue the Jews from assimilation without requiring a rejection of progressive ideas and universal principles. Moreover, not only would it give enlightened Jews a viable alternative to the bourgeois society of Europe, but its emphasis on the rights of the proletariat would appeal to poor Jews in Eastern Europe and the Muslim world, who, Hess believed, might thus be persuaded to migrate to Palestine in substantial numbers. Finally, the commonwealth advocated by Hess would enable the Jews, by their practice and refinement of socialism, to render a service to all progressive peoples, and thereby to fulfill their destiny as a light unto the nations. In this context, too, Hess explicitly advanced the hope that the Arab peoples of Egypt and Syria would achieve independence and base their political communities on a similar fusion of nationalism and socialism.[58] As with many early Zionists, Hess's immediate influence on Jewish thinking was limited. Yet the socialist camp of the modern Zionist movement traces its origins back to Hess, and in retrospect he emerges as one of the most important early advocates of modern political Zionism. His experience also presages the embrace of Zionism by many assimilated Jews a generation later.

Ben Yehudah, Lilienblum, and Pinsker made their contributions to modern political Zionism about two decades later, when the circumstances of European Jewry were once again changing. Ben Yehudah is best known today for his singular contribution to the revival of Hebrew. He not only opposed the rabbis who believed the language should be reserved for matters of religion, he also distinguished himself from those members of the *haskalah* who sought to revive Hebrew but then to limit its use to literature and intellectual life. Ben Yehudah spent decades preparing the first modern dictionary of Hebrew, and his efforts did indeed lay a foundation for Hebrew's eventual development into the language of daily life among Jews in Palestine. Moreover, Ben Yehudah made a direct connection between his efforts to revive Hebrew and a renaissance of the Jewish nation. In a letter to *Dawn*, Smolenskin's review, he declared in 1880, "The Hebrew language can only live if we revive the nation and return it to its fatherland."[59]

Anti-Semitism reappeared in Eastern Europe during this period and had a profound effect upon Jewish political thought. It contributed heavily to the shift toward Zionism of men such as Smolenskin, who, as noted, was a leading figure of the Eastern *haskalah* and who did not embrace Jewish nationalism until later in his life. Lilienblum and Pinsker traveled much the same path, as, eventually, did many others. Jews living under tsarist rule were accorded greater freedom in the 1850s and 1860s; and, residing in Odessa, the most important center of the Russian *haskalah*, both men identified with the liberal tradition of its educated and highly secular Jewish community. Lilienblum flirted with socialism in his early writings. Pinsker had studied medicine at Moscow University and was decorated by the tsar for medical work on behalf of the Russian army during the Crimean War. Thus, when some *yeshivas* (Jewish religious schools) were closed in Russia and other restrictions were placed on Jewish activity in the 1870s, many Jews of the Enlightenment tended to regard these developments as aberrations. Lilienblum, Pinsker, and others were inclined by their experience to view anti-Semitism as a vestige of an earlier era; it was grounded in a lack of education and in religious fanaticism, and thus would slowly fade away as European society continued to evolve. But virulent anti-Jewish pogroms broke out in 1881, bringing disaster to hundreds of thousands of Jews and dashing the illusions of men such as Lilienblum and Pinsker. Even in Odessa, with its progressive tradition and high level of education, there were violent attacks against Jews.

Setting the stage for these pogroms was the assassination of Tsar Alexander II by revolutionary fanatics in 1881. His successor, Alexander III, brought a halt to the gradual reforms that had been taking place in Tsarist Russia and sought to cut the country off from radical ideas, which he attributed to Western European influences. Some reactionary Russian authorities also attributed the social transformations taking place to the nefarious influence of Jews, calling them "the primary bearers of revolutionary infection, the source of all that was vicious in modern capitalism."[60] Such views were encouraged by the new tsar's nationalistic advisors, who believed in the glory of Russia's Slavic civilization, were fanatically loyal to its Orthodox Church, and gave absolute priority to protecting the monarchy and the existing order from both liberal political ideologies and the growing discontent of a peasantry faced with severe economic difficulties. These men loathed the Jews and, since anti-Jewish sentiments were widespread among both the peasantry and much of the elite, they also saw in the Jews an available and convenient actor to cast in the role of villain in their populist railings about the country's problems. One of the most influential of these unofficial advisors to the tsar, Konstantin Pobedonostsev, called the Jews "our great ulcer" and wrote, "They have undermined everything. . . . They are at the root of the revolutionary socialist movement and of regicide. . . . The people as a whole fall into financial slavery to them."[61]

Under the regime of the new tsar, there soon began widespread riots against the Jews, some of which may have been centrally organized, and most of which the government did nothing to prevent.[62] One general declared that he would not endanger the lives of his soldiers to protect the Jews, who, according to the minister of the interior, had brought the pogroms on themselves by their wickedness and unscrupulous economic behavior. Commissions of inquiry were appointed to look into illegal Jewish activities, and some Jews were even placed on trial for conduct said to have aroused the public and produced the rioting.

Meanwhile, anti-Jewish violence raged throughout the remainder of 1881 and into early 1882, and thereafter sporadically during 1883 and 1884. Jewish communities were attacked in Odessa and other cities, especially in the Ukraine, White Russia, and parts of Bessarabia. In the towns and villages of the Pale of Settlement, where the vast majority of Tsarist Russia's approximately five million Jews lived, entire communities were destroyed. By the end of 1881 alone, there had been attacks on 215 Jewish communities. According to one estimate, the number of homeless stood at 20,000, and those who had lost their means of livelihood numbered 100,000.[63] According to a newspaper account of the pogrom in the southern Russian town of Balta in April 1882, "It was a scene of pillage, murder, arson, and rape to make one tremble with horror."[64] Rampaging mobs were often encouraged by local officials, and on some occasions drunken soldiers joined in the destruction and plunder. One Russian official encouraged the reign of terror with a proposed three-part solution to the country's alleged Jewish problem: one-third would be driven out, one-third would be forced to convert, and one-third would be killed.

Although the rioting subsided in 1882, and after 1884 a period of relative calm prevailed for the next two decades, new restrictions continued to be imposed on the Jews of Tsarist Russia. The infamous "May Laws" of 1882 narrowed the territory in which Jews could live and led to the abrupt expulsion of many dwelling elsewhere who could not prove that their residence had been officially authorized. Jews were also barred from owning mortgages and leases, and these measures were applied retroactively so that many Jews were deprived of their homes. Other actions taken in 1882 restricted the ability of Jewish merchants to sell alcohol, allegedly for the purpose of reducing public drunkenness, and curtailed the recruitment of Jews into the Russian navy. Additionally, in

1887, new limits were placed on Jewish entry into universities. The proportion of Jews at any university could not exceed 10 percent in the Pale of Settlement and 5 percent elsewhere, except in Moscow and St. Petersburg, where it was limited to 3 percent.

One consequence of these profound changes in the intellectual climate and physical circumstances within which Russian Jewry found itself was increased interest in modern political Zionism and the course of action it proposed. This was particularly evident, as stated, in the transformed perspective of leading members of the Russian *haskalah*. Men such as Lilienblum and Pinsker could no longer argue that Jews should seek to integrate themselves into the mainstream of European society, taking care at the same time to maintain and defend their Hebrew heritage. Lilienblum wrote in 1883, "Not only can civilization and progress do nothing to eradicate anti-Semitic views, but indirectly they even help them along. . . . Anti-Semitism is the shadow of our new and fine contemporary civilization; it will no more do away with anti-Semitism than the light will destroy the shadow it casts." [65] There was only one viable response for the Jews, he wrote in 1882 in *Let Us Not Confuse the Issues*: "Let us gather our dispersed from Eastern Europe and go up to our land with rejoicing; whoever is on the side of God and His people, let him say, 'I am for Zion.' " [66] Pinsker articulated similar views in his influential booklet *Auto-Emancipation: An Appeal to His People by a Russian Jew*, also published in 1882. Although Palestine was a less central focus of Pinsker's thinking, he embraced Jewish nationalism and pleaded for Jewish self-determination. The Jews should establish a national home, preferably in Palestine, but elsewhere if necessary.

Additionally, beyond shaking the faith of Russian *maskilim* in modernization and progress, the events of this period disturbed and uprooted hundreds of thousands of poorer Jews, Jews who had continued to reside in their traditional communities within the Pale of Settlement and who had previously given little thought to the possibility of redefining their identity or altering their lifestyle. Now, however, radical changes were forced upon most of these Jews. Numerous Jewish villages and hamlets were destroyed and their inhabitants driven into dense urban ghettos where they were no longer able to support themselves. Known as *shtetls*, the small and largely autonomous Jewish communities of the Pale were often rural in character. The quintessential expression of traditional Eastern European Jewish culture, *shtetl* life had survived for almost a thousand years. But the Pale of the *shtetl* began to approach its end after 1881 and, more generally, the Jews of Russia were driven steadily toward pauperism. It is estimated that by the end of the century approximately 40 percent of Russian Jewry was completely dependent on charity. [67]

Migration was an understandable response to the persecution and disorder that began with the pogroms of 1881, and by far the preferred destination for departing Russian Jews was the United States. Between 1881 and the end of the century, about 450,000 Russian Jews reached the United States, in contrast to only 250,000 who had done so between 1800 and 1880. By the end of World War I that number had almost tripled, and it had doubled yet again by 1930. Large numbers of Russian Jews also moved to Central and Western Europe during the last years of the nineteenth century, sometimes going no farther because they lacked the resources to make their way to the United States, and sometimes deciding that the relatively liberal political climate of Austria, Germany, France, and England was sufficiently congenial to make further movement unnecessary. In addition, still other Jews migrated to South America and various dominions within the British colonial empire. All in all, in the largest Jewish migration in history, more than four million Jews departed from Russia during this period, many abandoning the land they had inhabited for more than a millennium.[68]

Some Russian Jews also began to think about migration to Palestine during this period and turned to the ideas being advanced by intellectuals such as Lilienblum and Pinsker. Much of the initial impetus for action came from student groups, whose young members argued passionately not only that the Jews must leave Russia but also that the Jewish people required a national renaissance, and that this could take place only in *Eretz Yisrael*. Known collectively as Hovevei Zion (Lovers of Zion), they formed independent associations in many towns during 1881 and 1882. Also, though coordination remained limited, they came together at a national conference in the city of Kattowitz in Upper Silesia in 1884. A central administrative body was established by the conference and Pinsker was elected president. Lilienblum also became a leader of the Hovevei Zion movement, which had to conduct many of its activities in secret until it was finally granted the status of a legal association by Russian authorities in 1890. Chapters of Hovevei Zion collected money, offered courses in Hebrew and Jewish history, and even provided instruction in self-defense, all of which was viewed as preparation for immigration to Palestine. Lovers of Zion also discussed the nature of the Jewish existence they should seek in Palestine, with some agreeing that a fundamental restructuring of Jewish society was required and that the Jews should once again become an agricultural people, thus returning to the land in a double sense.

One of the first and most active groups to emerge within this framework took the name Bilu, derived from the passage in Isaiah that reads "Bet Ya'acov lechu ve nelcha" (O' House of Jacob, come ye, and let us go). The Bilu group, founded by high-school and university students in Kharkov in 1881, immediately dispatched a small group of settlers to Palestine, some of whom arrived the following year. The efforts of modern Zionism to colonize Palestine are usually dated from the arrival of the *Biluim*; they initiated the first of five identifiable waves of Jewish immigration to Palestine in modern times. A Jew who immigrates to *Eretz Yisrael* is said to make *aliya* (literally an ascent), and the first wave of *aliya* began with the *Biluim* in 1882 and lasted until 1903. The Bilu group itself was tiny. It sent only fifty or sixty settlers to Palestine between 1882 and 1884, and less than twenty of these young Jews remained in the country at the end of the latter year.[69] Nevertheless, the first wave of *aliya*, of which the *Biluim* were the vanguard, approximately doubled the Jewish population of Palestine, raising it to about 50,000 from a pre-1882 total estimated at 24,000.

A manifesto issued by the *Biluim* in 1882 set forth the case for Jewish immigration to the Holy Land and articulated the ideological themes that were coming together to produce and define modern political Zionism: a reawakening of the Jewish people; a rejection of assimilation, as neither desirable nor possible, and a concomitant reaffirmation of Jewish nationhood; the inevitability of anti-Semitism and a need for the Jews to separate themselves physically from the world of Europe; and a continuing God-given link between the Jewish people and *Eretz Yisrael*. The manifesto of the *Biluim* thus declared, in part:

> Sleepest thou, O' our nation? What has thou been doing until 1882? Sleeping and dreaming the false dream of assimilation. . . . Now, thank God, thou art awakened from thy slothful slumber. The pogroms have awakened thee from thy charmed sleep. . . . What do we want. . . . A home in our country. It was given to us by the mercy of God; it is ours as registered in the archives of history.[70]

Theodor Herzl, Ahad Ha'am, and the Evolution of Zionist Thought

Although less violent than in Tsarist Russia, anti-Semitism was also beginning to reappear in Western Europe, where it was eventually to alter the faith of many educated Jews in assimilation and integration. In Germany, economic disorder following the Franco-Prussian war, and especially the financial crisis of 1873, which ruined many German speculators, led to charges that the country was being undermined by corrupt Jewish financiers. In response to the involvement of some Jews in the many scandals that were uncovered, anti-Semitic literature began to appear in the 1870s, and in 1880 a German priest told the Bavarian assembly, "If you wish to assist the starving population . . . make one brief law: Every Jewish peddler is to be shot or hanged."[71] In 1879, leading anti-Semites formed a political party, and associations were also established to encourage the boycott of Jewish merchants. There were expressions of anti-Jewish sentiment in Austria and Hungary as well during this period. In 1895, for example, anti-Semites took control of the municipal council of Vienna and elected one of their number as burgomaster of the city.

Anti-Semitism was rearing its head in France, too, setting in motion a series of events that would soon have a direct and significant impact on the incipient Zionist movement. Various anti-Jewish writings and activities emerged in the 1890s, and to some extent before, such as the publication of *La France Juive* in

1886. In this volume, the author, Edouard Drumont, railed against the financial ruin that Jews were alleged to be bringing to France, as he did in a journal, *La Libre Parole*, which began publication in 1892. Anti-Semitism in France had a populist character during this period. Rather than feeding on religious fervor and anti-Jewish interpretations of Christianity, it was to a considerable degree a response to economic uncertainty and social dislocation, especially among the poorer classes. It was also fueled by the crash of the Panama Canal Investment Company in the mid-1880s, in which thousands of stockholders experienced financial ruin, and in the demise of which several Jews were implicated.

One of those who recorded this rise of anti-Semitic sentiment with forcefulness and concern was a prominent Jewish journalist stationed in Paris, Theodor Herzl. Herzl was a highly assimilated Jew from Vienna, reporting from Paris for the prestigious Viennese newspaper *Neue Freie Presse*. Herzl had had only a limited Jewish education and displayed little interest in matters bearing on the Jews until late in his life. He was not indifferent to Judaism or unaware of the presence of anti-Semitism in his native Austria; in 1883, for example, he resigned from the student fraternity of which he was a member because it had begun to turn toward anti-Semitism. But Herzl's preoccupations during this period of his life nonetheless lay elsewhere. He was typical of the successful and well-educated Jews of Western Europe, oriented toward, and highly integrated into, the society and culture of the Christian majority. Indeed, he was not even aware of the writings of those Jews, such as Hess and Pinsker, who had embraced Jewish nationalism. Herzl himself was not only a well-known journalist but an aspiring playwright as well. Although his plays never received the critical acclaim he desired, his goal was to become an important contributor to German-language literature.

It is this background as an emancipated and assimilated Jew that makes Herzl's subsequent writings on anti-Semitism and his later conversion to Zionism so significant. Just as the intellectual transformation of Smolenskin, Lilienblum, and Pinsker in the face of the pogroms symbolized Zionism's emergence from the fading faith of the Russian *haskalah*, so did Herzl's response to anti-Semitism in France signify the emergence in Western Europe of Jewish intellectuals who had come to the conclusion that their dream of assimilation was impossible.

Herzl began reporting from Paris in 1891, and many of his articles dealt with the growth and increasing acceptability of anti-Jewish rhetoric, including verbal attacks on the Jews by members of the Chamber of Deputies. Herzl himself collected and reprinted many of his dispatches dealing with anti-Jewish themes in a volume published in 1895.[72] In 1894 he published *The New Ghetto*, a play in which his diminishing faith in assimilation is expressed. One of the play's central characters is told that the Jews will never achieve total equality, no matter how educated and emancipated they might become: "When there was a real ghetto, we were not allowed to leave it without permission, on pain of severe punishment. Now the walls and barriers have become invisible. . . . Yet we are still rigidly confined to a moral ghetto."[73]

The critical event in Herzl's conversion to Zionism was the trial and conviction of Captain Alfred Dreyfus, a Jew who had risen to a position of importance in the French army, and who in 1894 was accused of spying for Germany. Dreyfus insisted that he was innocent, but he was nonetheless condemned by court martial and imprisoned on the infamous Devil's Island. Later, when it became evident that there had been irregularities at his trial, he was retried and then, though found guilty again, granted a pardon. Finally, twelve years later, he succeeded in proving his innocence, winning an appeal before the high court and gaining reinstatement into the military.

While many non-Jews believed in Dreyfus's innocence and worked on his behalf, the affair nonetheless had clear and important anti-Jewish overtones. The decision to blame Dreyfus when it was discovered that someone in the military had sold secrets to the Germans was motivated in part by anti-Semitism; and even more important, at least so far as Herzl is concerned, was the anti-Jewish character of widespread popular calls for Dreyfus's conviction. When the captain was stripped of his rank and drummed out of the national military academy, he was met by a screaming mob shouting "à bas les juifs" ("down with the Jews"). Herzl, who had been covering the Dreyfus case for his paper and had written about the effect of the trial on popular attitudes in France, was present on the day that Dreyfus faced the abusive mob outside the Ecole Militaire. The scene he witnessed confirmed his growing belief that anti-Semitism would never disappear and that the Jews would never become truly assimilated.

What Herzl witnessed also led him to conclude that creation of a Jewish state in Palestine was the only viable and permanent solution to the problem of the Jews; and after reaching this conclusion, he immediately sought audiences with wealthy Jews who he hoped would assist in the creation of his proposed state. His first interview, which bore no fruit, was with Baron Maurice von Hirsch, founder of Jewish colonization in Argentina. He then turned to the Rothschilds and, in five days of frantic writing, drafted a sixty-five-page memorandum setting forth his ideas. This was in 1895, and in February 1896 he published *The Jewish State (Der Judenstaat)*, a slender volume that was in fact a revised version of his appeal to the Rothschilds, and which soon became the manifesto of the nascent Zionism movement. The book, which shocked many of Herzl's friends and was radically different from anything he had written previously, was designed for, and achieved, what Vital describes as a "tactical" purpose: "to make the issue public and to draw new allies."[74] *The Jewish State* gained attention among Jews not only in Western Europe but in Eastern Europe as well, where "the local Jewish press, now predominantly favorable, or at least charitably disposed [toward modern political Zionism] was prompt to report the gist of its contents and something of the reactions to it elsewhere."[75]

The Jewish State is uncompromising in its insistence that assimilation is impossible, and that it is futile to wish for the disappearance of anti-Semitism. Anti-Semitism, Herzl writes, "is a misplaced piece of medievalism which civilized nations do not seem able to shake off, try as they will." As for the Jews, "We have sincerely tried everywhere to merge with the national communities in which we live, seeking only to preserve the faith of our fathers. It is not permitted to us. In vain we are loyal patriots, sometimes super loyal; in vain do we make the same sacrifices of life and property as our fellow citizens."[76] Such categorical statements about what Herzl called "the Jewish question" shocked many of his friends. As his newly articulated views and his efforts on their behalf gradually came to the attention of the public, they also disturbed many middle-class Jews who, like Herzl himself in the past, had assumed that integration was both possible and desirable and had fashioned their own lives accordingly. Many continued to embrace this belief, and some charged that Herzl was either an alarmist or an opportunist.

Yet Herzl had not completely lost faith in integration and human progress, and herein lie some of the most interesting and original aspects of his proposal to create a Jewish state. Herzl argued, first, that not only would the creation of a separate Jewish state respond to the needs of the Jews for a refuge from persecution, but it would also be a service to the non-Jewish world, which must surely deplore its odious anti-Semitic impulses. Such passions, however inevitable and unmanageable they might be, were shameful to men and women of an enlightened and progressive age. They were also disturbing of the public order, and they distracted societies from the rational pursuit of their political and social objectives. The non-Jewish world, or at least its leaders, could accordingly be expected to join the Jews in welcoming a solution to the Jewish question, and could even be called upon to assist in bringing about the establishment of a Jewish state in Palestine.

Even more important, the Jewish state, once created, would take its place in the community of nations, and in this collective sense the Jews would indeed become integrated into the modern world order. The Jews were a people, indeed a nation, and their integration was to be on this national basis, not as individuals slipping almost surreptitiously into non-Jewish society. But Herzl's vision of the Jewish state was nonetheless modern; it would be progressive, almost secular, in character, not a Torah-dominated polity fashioned in the image of the Old Testament: "We shall not revert to a lower stage but rise to a higher one. We shall not dwell in mud huts; we shall build new, more beautiful and more modern houses, and possess them in safety."[77]

Herzl's ideas about the character of the Jewish state were thus different from those that had emerged in Eastern Europe, where Pinsker and other Zionists envisioned the creation of a state that would be uniquely and authentically Jewish, one that addressed the spiritual needs of Judaism as well as the temporal needs of the Jews. Herzl's rationalism and modernity led him to see the Jewish polity as a state like any other. It would be progressive not because this was mandated by a God-given mission or rooted in a uniquely Jewish ethical code, but rather because all states should strive for human betterment and because such was the direction of universal evolution. The particulars that Herzl proposed were sometimes, but not always, utopian. For example, he favored a democratic monarchy or an aristocratic republican form of government, believing that most citizens were as yet unprepared for unrestricted democracy. But while the Jews were no more advanced than other nations, neither were they, ultimately, different. They possess the same hopes and failings as others, and their destiny is thus to become a full and equal member of the community of nations, and in this way to play their part in the common quest for a better world.

Herzl devoted his great energy and passion both to international diplomacy on behalf of the Zionist cause and to building up the institutional infrastructure of the nascent Zionist movement. So far as diplomacy is concerned, he traveled extensively and negotiated tirelessly with non-Jewish leaders in the hope of winning international political support. His most important and most persistent efforts were directed at the sultan of Ottoman Turkey, whose authority over Palestine was recognized by the powers of Europe. The sultan was unresponsive, however, largely because of his belief that the Zionists could not be trusted to establish in Palestine a political community that would fully respect the authority of Constantinople.[78] Much of Herzl's subsequent diplomatic travels involved the search for an ally who would be able to exert economic or political pressure for a change in Turkish policy, and for a time it appeared that Kaiser Wilhelm of Germany would provide such assistance. Herzl also sought support for the Zionist cause from other European leaders. For example, he told Russian officials that they could solve the Jewish problem in their country through emigration, if only Russia's neighbor, Turkey, could be persuaded to permit more Jews to settle in Palestine. In addition, he approached Great Britain about possible Jewish settlement in that country's East African colonies. The result of these efforts was meager, but Herzl nonetheless continued his labors, convinced that European and Ottoman leaders would eventually recognize that his proposals served the interests of the non-Jewish world, as well as those of the Jews.

Herzl's accomplishments with respect to institutional development were much more substantial and enduring; he was a catalyst for the establishment of the Zionist Organization, bringing together Jews oriented toward modern Zionism and creating an international structure to support Jewish colonization in Palestine. The landmark event in this process was the First Zionist Congress, which was convened at Herzl's urging in Basel, Switzerland, in 1897 and which was attended by more than two hundred individuals, some representing local Jewish communities and Zionist societies in various countries. The Basel meeting resulted both in the adoption of a formal Programme and in the establishment of an international Zionist Organization, thereby initiating the transformation of modern political Zionism from a diffuse and disorganized ideological tendency into an international movement with a coherent platform and institutional structure. The critical importance of this event is emphasized by most students of Zionism, including Vital, who writes, "Prior to the Congress the spectacle is largely one of disunity, incoherence, painfully slow progress—or none at all— confusion of ideas, dearth of leadership, and, above all, no set policy and no forum in which a set policy can be hammered out and formally adopted. Before the Congress there is, as it were, proto-Zionism." By contrast, after the Basel meeting, "there is Zionism proper."[79]

The Programme adopted at the First Zionist Congress specified that "Zionism aims at the creation of a home for the Jewish people in Palestine to be secured by public law," and it also recorded that this objective would be pursued through the advancement of Jewish settlement in Palestine, through the organizing and unifying of all Jewry, through the strengthening of Jewish national feelings and consciousness, and through efforts to obtain whatever governmental consent was necessary to achieve the aims of Zionism. The congress chose Herzl to lead the movement it had created to carry out this program, his candidacy having been supported, with reservations, by the large delegation from Russia. Herzl also assumed responsibility for the movement's weekly publication, which gave him a critical role in articulating Zionist goals and shaping and mobilizing contemporary Jewish opinion.

A second individual who played an important role at Basel, and thereafter, is Max Nordau, a German-speaking Jew of Hungarian origin who became one of Herzl's closest associates. Like Herzl, Nordau was a prominent journalist, as well as an essayist and a playwright, and he also shared many of the conclusions to which Herzl had come following the Dreyfus affair, including the inevitability of anti-Semitism and the inadequacy of assimilation as a solution to the problem of the Jews. Nordau told the assembled delegates at the First Zionist Congress, in a speech which was a high point of the meeting, that after "a slumber of thirty to sixty years, anti-Semitism broke out once more . . . and his real situation was revealed to the mortified Jew." Further, he stated, "the emancipated Jew is insecure in his relations with his fellow beings. . . . He fears that his character might be recognized as Jewish, and he never has the satisfaction of showing himself as he is in all his thoughts and sentiments. He becomes an inner cripple." Thus, in Nordau's analysis, "Jewish misery has two forms, the material and the moral."[80]

The convening of the First Zionist Congress illustrates the essence of Herzl's contribution to Zionism; it was his effectiveness in advocacy and mobilization, rather than the profundity or imaginativeness of his political thought, that enabled him to play such a critical role in the development of the modern Zionist movement. He did produce one more piece of Zionist literature, *Old-New Land* (*Altneuland*), a projection of Jewish life in Palestine in 1923, which he wrote in 1902. Nevertheless, his main contribution was as an organizer and above all as a publicist, rather than as a theoretician, and in these arenas he labored feverishly until his death in 1904, at the age of forty-four. He used his skill and contacts as a journalist to place Zionism's concerns on the agenda of Jewish and world opinion, and his personal qualities of charm, sincerity, and confidence contributed greatly to his effectiveness in public relations. Thus, while his was not a highly intellectual or a spiritual contribution, Herzl fully deserves his title as the father of modern political Zionism. As explained by a prominent Israeli scholar:

> From the moment Herzl came to his conclusion about the necessity for a national solution to the Jewish problem, he correctly realized that such a momentous and revolutionary task could not be achieved through silent labor at the edge of world politics. Articles in obscure Jewish publications would not mobilize the massive force needed for such a tremendous transformative effort, ideological disputations between a few scores of semiemployed Jewish intellectuals in unheard-of tracts would never get the message across. . . . Herzl was the first to achieve a breakthrough for Zionism in Jewish and world opinion. He turned the quest for a national solution to the plight of the Jewish people from an issue debated at great length and with profound erudition in provincial Hebrew periodicals read by only a handful of Jewish intellectuals in the remote corners of the Russian Pale of Settlement into a subject for world opinion. From a marginal phenomenon of Jewish life he painted the Zionist solution on the canvas of world politics—and it has never left it since.[81]

The institutionalization and unification of the Zionist movement did not end debate among Jews about how to respond to the challenges of the modern age. Modern political Zionism continued to draw criticism from orthodox and traditional quarters, where it was viewed as a usurpation by man of a destiny whose fulfillment could be brought about only by the Deity. For a time it was viewed with suspicion by many highly acculturated Jews, too, including both individual Jews who feared that its growing strength might invite discrimination by calling into question their own political loyalties, and also more organized currents of political opinion within the secularist fold. A prominent example of the latter was the Jewish Socialist Bund, which appeared in the 1890s. The Bund declared its anticipation of a socialist revolution that would end all distinctions based on class and religion and thereby give rise to a social order in which there would no longer be a Jewish question.

In addition to the broader spectrum of Jewish political thought within which modern Zionism was embedded, there was also a significant normative cleavage within Zionist ranks, between two competing centers of ideological gravity that carried forward the debate among *maskilim* of a generation earlier. Herzl, with his emphasis on Jewish normalcy and his conviction that the Jewish state should be like any other polity within the community of nations, represented an evolution of messianist responses to the Emancipation. Nordau was also prominently associated with this view. In the judgment of Herzl, Nordau, and others, the Jews should shed their burden of chosenness and, relieved of the responsibility for making a unique contribution to the betterment of the human condition, they should partake of a new and more universal destiny. True to the vision of radical messianists of the first part of the century, this brand of Zionism accepted the validity of integration and assimilation. It simply added, from its Zionist perspective, that since the Jews were after all a people and not a religious group, this integration should take place on a collective and communal basis. It was the Jewish people, not individual Jews, that should assimilate into a new and secular world order and, as part of a community of progressive and forward-looking nations, participate in the effort to fulfill the potential of an age dedicated to emancipation and enlightenment.

The defensive school of thought of the mid-nineteenth century differentiated itself from these messianist currents, and descendants of this ideological orientation were also prominently represented within the ranks of modern political Zionism. Epitomized by the Russian *haskalah* in the years before the pogroms, the defensive school of thought argued that while Jews should embrace the opportunities and wisdom of the modern age, they should at the same time maintain their special and unique identity. Those within the Zionist movement who carried forward this approach to emancipation and modernity articulated what came to be known as "Cultural" Zionism, in contrast to the "Political" Zionism represented by Herzl and Nordau.

Cultural Zionism insisted that the Jewish state should not seek to be a state like any other but, rather, should wholeheartedly commit to the articulation and projection of its own special character, adapted to, and expressed in terms of, the canons of the modern age. Furthermore, for at least some Cultural Zionists, the justification for this position went beyond the idea that the Jewish people, like any people, should be faithful to its own culture, ethos, and historic identity. Some also believed that the Jewish state should preserve its unique normative heritage in order to carry forward Israel's ethical and spiritual mission to serve humanity, thereby answering once again the call to be a light unto the nations. Thus, the great ideological schism between more radical and more traditional Jews of the Enlightenment, associated for the most part with the differing tendencies that predominated among *maskilim* in Western and Eastern Europe respectively, found its way into the mainstream of modern political Zionism.

The leading figure of Cultural Zionism during this period was Ahad Ha'am, a pseudonym (meaning "one of the people") adopted by a Russian-born Jew whose real name was Asher Ginsberg. Ginsberg was born into a Hasidic family in 1856 and studied at a traditional Talmud-Torah school during his early years. He later settled in Odessa and subsequently embraced the ideas of the *haskalah* and the Lovers of Zion, eventually becoming one of modern Zionism's most prolific writers. He was also a prime contributor to the revival of Hebrew and its transformation into a language of modern prose. Ahad Ha'am charged that while the Zionism of Herzl and Nordau addressed the needs of the Jewish people, temporal and physical needs, it failed to recognize that Zionism must also concern itself with the needs of Judaism, with cultural, ethical, and spiritual needs. Thus, as Ahad Ha'am argued in "The Jewish State and the Jewish Problem," an important essay published in 1897, Herzl's political community might be a state of Jews, but this was not the same thing as a *Jewish* state, which is in fact what he believed to be required.

Ahad Ha'am is a key figure in the intellectual history of modern Zionism precisely because he concerned himself with the normative mission of the Zionist state. Whereas others focused their attention on the immediate and practical problems surrounding the creation of a Jewish homeland, which were of indisputable importance to be sure and which, if not solved, would render all other questions irrelevant, Ahad Ha'am believed it essential to take a longer view. He addressed matters that would remain central to the hopes and aspirations of Zionism even after a Jewish state had been created. One of Ahad Ha'am's concerns was the relationship between the Jewish national home in Palestine and those Jews remaining in the Diaspora, a concern that once again led him to emphasize the spiritual and cultural dimensions of Jewish nationalism. Since many Jews would remain outside of Palestine, the Jewish state would require a national ethic with which Jews everywhere could identify and, equally, that would enhance the ethical and spiritual well-being of Jewish life in the Diaspora. He presented his vision in "The Jewish State and the Jewish Problem," proclaiming that from its historic center "the spirit of Judaism will go forth to the great circumference, to all the communities of the Diaspora, and will breathe new life into them and will preserve their unity."[82]

While insisting upon the centrality of historic Jewish values, Ahad Ha'am nevertheless believed that the essence of these values was not to be found in the narrow religious orthodoxy of the rabbis or in the parochialism of ghetto life prior to the Emancipation. He thus stood in opposition to the traditionalists, as well as to the inheritors of messianism and assimilation. If the latter were misguided, and ultimately un-Jewish, the former were reactionary and, for all their religious knowledge and sincere dedication to Judaism, hopelessly out of touch with the needs of the Jewish state that Zionism sought to establish. The nature of Ahad Ha'am's determination to embrace both modernity and tradition brought criticism from those who identified themselves unambiguously with either of these two normative orientations, leading each to accuse him of being the unwitting ally of the other. But Ahad Ha'am's struggle to find a middle ground, to be a progressive conservative and chart a course between what he considered to be disastrous extremes, makes him tremendously attractive and is in large measure the source of continuing interest in his ideas.

In Ahad Ha'am's view, Zionism would be spurious if it did not lead to a state that was meaningfully and authentically Jewish, and hence different from other states; yet the struggle to balance continuity and change is faced by other peoples, too, as well as by Jews, and "meeting the needs of Judaism" is thus relevant for these peoples' attempts to address the requirements of their own cultural and ethical systems and makes a contribution, thereby, to advancing the general human condition. In other words, although its definition of "normalcy" is very different from that of Herzl, the Cultural Zionism represented by Ahad Ha'am labors to create a society that will accept as legitimate, and then aggressively address, dilemmas and challenges that are widespread and perhaps universal, rather than unique to the Jews. Moreover, if successful in defining the specificity of its Jewishness and in satisfactorily relating its identity to both the past and the present, Zionism, by its wisdom and example, will encourage other peoples struggling to meet the same challenge with respect to their own histories and identities.

Insisting upon authentic Jewish values is not the same as reaching agreement on their definition, however, to say nothing of imposing them on the reality of a Zionist state, and here Ahad Ha'am was in a much more difficult position. He was, of course, assailed by the orthodox rabbis. They saw him as even more dangerous than Herzl, for while the latter spoke in the name of the Jewish people, Ahad Ha'am claimed to be concerned with Judaism itself. Ahad Ha'am's difficulties were further compounded by the limits of his own faith. Though he believed in the unity of the Jewish people and in the sanctity of Jewish ethics, and also in the relevance of Judaism's spiritual destiny to the whole of humanity, he was personally agnostic. Thus, not only was he faced with the need to offer a definition of Judaism that contrasted with that of the rabbis, he also had to reconcile his near-mystical belief in Judaism and his acceptance of the Jews' chosenness with his own agnosticism. This aspect of Ahad Ha'am's life and thought is well described by Hertzberg, who notes that he accepted the "moral genius" of Judaism but regarded its origin as a "secular mystery." He wrote,

> History has not yet satisfactorily explained how it came about that a tiny nation in a corner of Asia produced a unique religious and ethical outlook, which, though it has so profound an influence on the rest of the world, has yet remained foreign to the rest of the world. . . . But every true Jew, be he orthodox or liberal, feels in the depth of his being that there is something in the spirit of our people—though we do not know what it is—which has prevented us from following the rest of the world along the beaten path.[83]

Turning to the construction of a modern and spiritual Jewish culture, based on authentic Jewish values and the enduring moral genius of the Jewish people, Ahad Ha'am ultimately concluded that this was a task for the Zionist state and not a few theoreticians. In the end, his role and that of his disciples was not to fashion a blueprint for such cultural development but rather to inscribe the need to do so indelibly on the Zionist agenda. As expressed by Hertzberg, "The task of creating and clearly defining a modern version of the superior Jewish morality had to be postponed, for only a 'spiritual center' could provide the soil for sure and elemental creativity. Only within its confines would the right choices be made; only there would his values come into their own." [84]

The great significance of Ahad Ha'am and other early Cultural Zionists lies in the fact that realization of their vision has indeed become a central preoccupation of modern Zionism. Among the Jewish community that was beginning to grow up in Palestine, and more recently within present-day Israel and among Jews throughout the world who consider themselves tied to the Jewish state, there is an ongoing concern not only to promote political development and economic well-being, but also to shape the evolution of the Jews' national character and to address the ambiguities and dilemmas of being a Jewish society in the twentieth century. The fulfillment of these latter objectives has often been surrounded by controversy, as Zionists and others with radically differing ideological predispositions contribute to the debate about problems and solutions. But the centrality and critical importance of the task have been widely recognized for some time, and within the ranks of modern political Zionism, the origins of this recognition are to be found in the Cultural Zionism of Ahad Ha'am.

The Zionist Organization and the New Yishuv

During its first years the Zionist movement experienced both significant structural growth and serious divisions and difficulties. Zionist congresses became institutionalized and were convened regularly, at first on an annual basis and then biannually after 1901. In addition, a permanent executive committee was established to guide the day-to-day activities of the Zionist Organization between these meetings. The grass-roots base of the Zionist Organization was also expanding rapidly. The Second Zionist Congress was attended by about 350 delegates, substantially more than a year earlier; and while 117 local Zionist groups had been identified the year before, it was now announced that over 900 such groups were in existence. An additional development at the 1897 Congress was the emergence of a left-wing, socialist-oriented Zionist faction, led by Nachman Syrkin. Further, not only did the socialist left expand in the years that followed, but it was soon joined by an orthodox party, the religious Mizrachi faction of Zionism. There also later emerged a centrist General Zionist faction, whose members did not join the first Zionist political parties and who were known for economic liberalism and the advocacy of private enterprise.

The promotion of Jewish immigration to Palestine and the acquisition of land on which to settle new immigrants were the most important objectives of the newly founded Zionist Organization, and the pursuit of these goals in turn intensified the development of the movement's institutional structure. The Jewish Colonial Trust, established in London in 1899, became the first bank of the Zionist Organization. It was set up as a joint stock company and supported by tens of thousands of Jews who purchased small numbers of shares. The Jewish National Fund (Keren Kayemet) was created in 1901 at the Fifth Congress of the Zionist Organization. Its purpose was to purchase and develop land in Palestine. The JNF was supported by voluntary contributions and also by a small annual tax, the *shekel*, which Zionists levied upon themselves. The property it acquired was held in a common trust, in the name of the entire Jewish people, to be leased at favorable rates to new settlers. The JNF also undertook improvement schemes, such as reforestation and swamp drainage, to develop the land it held.

Financial problems were one of the difficulties facing the new movement. Herzl complained constantly about the lack of funds to support the work of organizing and publicizing Zionist activity, to say nothing of its more fundamental goals. Thus, for example, the Colonial Trust did not succeed in raising the capital called for at the time of its creation. The Rothschild family, though prominent Jewish philanthropists, decided not to participate in the venture. The Zionists also received only limited support from wealthy Jews in Germany and Russia. Much of Herzl's effort was accordingly devoted to fund-raising, a task that he found onerous and which, along with his other ceaseless activities on behalf of the movement, sapped his energies. According to Laqueur, "The Zionist organization was so poor, the income from subscriptions so small, that the executive kept its finances secret for years in order to avoid ridicule."[85]

Another important concern was the political division among Zionist factions. One major cleavage, of course, revolved around the differing ideas of Herzl's Political Zionism and Ahad Ha'am's Cultural Zionism, representing to a considerable degree the dissimilar outlook of Jews in Western Europe and Eastern Europe on the question of Jewish identity. It is somewhat ironic that the Zionist vision of Herzl, a highly assimilated Jew, solicited a stronger response among the poorer and more conservative Jews of Eastern Europe than among Herzl's liberal and middle-class counterparts in the West. Nevertheless, as discussed, Easterners had their own ideas about the content that should be given to Herzl's vision of a Jewish state. Thus, as early as the 1901 congress, there was a demonstration by a group calling itself the Democratic Party and demanding more attention by Zionism to the Jews' historic Hebrew heritage. One of the group's organizers was Chaim Weizmann, a young Russian Jew who was later to inherit the leadership of the movement, and who in 1948 became the first president of Israel. In 1901, however, Weizmann's protest led to a stormy debate on "Zionist culture," which almost split the congress.

A second early division was between the diplomatic and legalistic approach of Herzl and some other Zionist leaders, on the one hand, and those favoring more direct action, on the other. Herzl, true to his view that the Jewish state should be a polity like any other, accepted by the world community of nations, attached great importance to obtaining international support for the creation of a Jewish state. More important than unilateral action in the areas of immigration and settlement, in his view, was the acquisition of an international charter granting the Jews the right to found and develop their homeland in Palestine. It is this belief that led Herzl to his wearying and unsuccessful negotiations with the political leaders of Europe.

Although in part for different reasons, Ahad Ha'am tended to share Herzl's view that Jewish immigration to Palestine should not be undertaken without careful planning and until a suitable legal framework for the construction of the Jewish state could be established. In a series of articles entitled "The Truth from Palestine," written in 1891 and 1893 following visits to Jewish settlements in *Eretz Yisrael*, Ahad Ha'am deplored the ambiguous political status of these communities. They were dependent on the willingness of local officials to tolerate their activities and on the unsteady protection of European consulates. Therefore, although he had no specific plan for a diplomatic initiative and was not a supporter of Political Zionism, Ahad Ha'am, too, like Herzl, considered approval of the Ottoman sultan to be an essential precondition for serious efforts at colonization.[86]

On the other hand, the Democratic Party and other militant opposition elements favored immediate Jewish settlement in *Eretz Yisrael*. Weizmann and his colleagues, who were also sometimes called "Practical Zionists," believed that the success or failure of the Zionist movement would be determined by facts on the ground, not by international charters. Accordingly, it was this group that had pressed for creation of the Jewish National Fund at the Fifth Zionist Congress. In the view of Weizmann, highest priority should be attached to bringing immigrants to Palestine and to cultivating land and creating villages.

Weizmann and his followers not only challenged Herzl on the matter of direct action, they also offered their own utopian vision of the kind of Jewish society that should be constructed in Palestine. In addition to calling for the renaissance of Hebrew culture, Practical Zionists dreamed of creating "a model society founded on social, political and economic equality."[87] According to one scholar, it is no accident that most advocates of this idea were of Russian origin. Tolstoy's theory about regeneration through work, the revolutionary socialism stirring the tsarist empire, and Biblical messianism were the three sources of their inspiration.[88] The ideas of Weizmann and other Practical Zionists steadily gained influence, especially after Herzl died in 1904, worn out and depressed at having failed to secure the international guarantees he so desperately sought.

Herzl's last years were marked by controversy, and particularly significant in this regard were his negotiations with the British about the possibility of creating a Jewish homeland in Uganda and his presentation of this proposal to the Zionist Congress of 1903. The suggestion that Uganda might be suitable for Jewish colonization was first put forward by Joseph Chamberlain, the British colonial secretary, who said that he had thought about Herzl during a recent visit to the interior of British East Africa. Herzl, who at the time had been discussing with the British a scheme for Jewish settlement in Sinai, responded positively to Chamberlain's proposal, in part because of a desire to deepen Zionist-British cooperation and, more generally, to show that his diplomatic efforts were capable of bearing fruit. At the 1903 Zionist Congress, Herzl accordingly recommended that a study commission be dispatched to East Africa to gather information with which to evaluate the Uganda initiative. At the same time, he stressed that Uganda was being proposed not as an alternative to Palestine but, rather, as a place where Jews who were forced to leave their homes might take immediate and temporary refuge. Instead of becoming dispersed throughout the world, these Jews could thus be formed into viable communities, which could later be transferred to Zion.[89]

Despite Herzl's assurances that the plan implied no diminution in Zionism's commitment to a Jewish homeland in Palestine, there was much opposition to the Uganda proposal, even to the idea of sending an investigatory commission. To some, it revealed the inadequacy of Political Zionism; although Herzl insisted that this was not the case, they worried that the plan represented a secularist conception of Zionism and a desire for Jewish normalcy so strong that it mattered little where the Jewish state was located. This view was expressed by Ahad Ha'am, for example, who asserted in an indignant article that there could not have been a more convincing demonstration of the bankruptcy of Political Zionism than Herzl's endorsement of the East Africa plan.[90] Many also saw in the Uganda proposal Herzl's obsession with international legal guarantees, which they described as "diplomatism" and which, as noted, they charged with diverting attention from the much more important work of building up the Jewish presence in Palestine.

The congress approved the Uganda proposal by a vote of 295 to 177, with 100 abstentions. Ironically, perhaps, Herzl's arguments were accepted by the religious faction, Mizrachi, and were opposed most vehemently by Russian delegates, including both socialists and members of Hovevei Zion. But while Herzl's prestige had enabled him to secure passage of the resolution, there was a serious danger that the movement would split. Russian delegates walked out, and when Herzl came to their meeting room to urge their return, he was met with shouts of "Traitor!" After hours of pleading and repeating that he had no thought of abandoning or changing the Zionist program, the dissidents did eventually return, explaining that their exit had been not a partisan protest against Herzl's leadership but an expression of their profound and unshakable conviction that there could be no separation between Zionism and *Eretz Yisrael*. Unity was restored, at least on the surface, but Herzl himself was badly shaken by the experience.

The response to the Uganda scheme removed any ambiguity that might possibly have existed about whether the creation of a Jewish state outside of Palestine would speak to the goals articulated by modern political Zionism. It would not.

The history and religion of the Jewish people demanded that their state be located in the land of their ancestors, in the land to which they were bound by a covenant between themselves and their Creator. Herzl himself explicitly conceded this principle: "that Zionism had to do essentially and necessarily, and perhaps exclusively, with Zion-*Eretz-Yisrael.*"[91] He stated in the debate at the 1903 congress that he had learned a great deal in the course of time, and "I also learned that the solution for us lies only in Palestine."[92]

So far as the commission dispatched to Uganda is concerned, it presented its findings at the 1905 Zionist Congress, by which time Herzl had died, and reported that the territory could accommodate no more than twenty thousand settlers, and that to relocate even this number would be extremely expensive and difficult. But while consideration of the Uganda proposal lasted only two years, with there never being any serious prospect of its implementation, its appearance and demise were significant. If it was a fruitless endeavor from the viewpoint of Practical Zionism, it was nonetheless an important event that helped to clarify the meaning of modern political Zionism.

Beyond this important contribution to the clarification of Zionism's program, the events of the 1903 congress depressed Herzl and added to his weariness and deteriorating health. His diaries of the period convey a foreboding of death, and indeed he did die in July of 1904. But while he was ill and exhausted during the last year of his life, and deeply dispirited that the tangible accomplishments of his efforts appeared so meager, history would render a different verdict about the fruits of his labors. During the eight years following publication of *The Jewish State*, the Zionist idea had moved into the mainstream of contemporary Jewish thought, and a unified structural foundation for Zionist efforts had been put in place. There were hundreds of local groups united in a worldwide Zionist federation, regular annual or biannual conferences, a permanent executive committee, a bank, and the Jewish National Fund. There were also a growing number of Jews in Palestine.

Ideological and tactical differences among Political, Cultural, and Practical Zionism eventually gave way to structured competition among Zionist political parties advocating either secular socialism, capitalist free enterprise, or religious piety. The normative divisions within European Jewry prior to the emergence of modern political Zionism thus found their way into the new movement, which, for all its agreement about the impossibility of assimilation and the need for a Jewish homeland, emerged as an organization marked by structural complexity and ideological pluralism. Such heterogeneity was inevitable in a movement that addressed itself to, and sought support from, all of the Jewish communities scattered throughout the world.

In addition, as Practical Zionists had foreseen, the center of gravity of the evolving Zionist movement gradually shifted away from Europe to the growing Jewish community in Palestine; and similarly, though efforts to obtain international political and legal support for a Jewish homeland remained important, the highest priority was given to immigration, land purchase, and community development in Palestine. The *Yishuv*, as the Jewish community in Palestine was known, increasingly became the focal point of Zionist thought and action. Jewish society in Palestine prior to the beginning of organized Zionist migrations is sometimes described as the old *Yishuv*, in contrast to the new *Yishuv* that Zionism sought to build. As discussed earlier, the inhabitants of the old *Yishuv* were pious and traditional Jews, concentrated in a few cities having special religious significance. The old *Yishuv* was not an integrated and self-sufficient community, nor did it aspire to be; most of its members were poor and many were unable to support themselves. But this situation was changing with the emergence and growth of the new *Yishuv*.

Although construction of the new *Yishuv* is usually dated from the arrival of the Bilu group in 1882, which initiated the First *Aliya*, there had in fact been several modern settlement schemes prior to 1882. In 1839, Sir Moses Montefiore opened negotiations with the Egyptian ruler, Muhammad Ali, discussing the possibility of a loan to Egypt in return for a charter granting the Jews settlement rights in Palestine. Muhammad Ali had come to power in Egypt in 1805 and declared Egypt's autonomy within the Turkish empire. In the years that followed, he had carried out an extensive campaign of modernization and development, for which he badly needed funds, and he had also invaded Palestine and Syria in 1832, driving out the Ottomans and holding the area until 1841. In the wake of renewed Ottoman control, Montefiore's efforts were shelved. In the 1850s, however, he finally succeeded in purchasing land in Palestine for Jewish settlement and for schemes of modernization. Together with the Rothschilds of Paris, he also supported the construction of a modern hospital in Jerusalem and a school that taught modern subjects. Previously, Jews who did not want an orthodox religious education had usually attended the schools of Christian missionaries.

In 1855, at a site outside Jerusalem on the road leading to the coast, Montefiore made the first Jewish land purchase for purposes of agricultural development in the history of modern Palestine. Rumanian Jews from Jerusalem eventually settled there in the 1890s, creating the village of Motza. In 1870, the Alliance Israelite Universelle established an agricultural college, Mikveh Yisrael, near Jaffa on the Mediterranean coast. There was growing recognition that agricultural activity should be a significant part of any program to develop Jewish society in Palestine, and Mikveh Yisrael was founded with the explicit objective of contributing to this effort. Another development prior to 1882 was the establishment of Petah Tikvah, in 1878. Also begun by Rumanian Jews, Petah Tikvah, whose name in Hebrew means "Gate of Hope," was established as an agricultural village on the Plain of Sharon, not far from the site of present-day Tel Aviv. The experiment failed, and the community was abandoned after a time, but a few years later it was refounded by Russian Jews belonging to Hovevei Zion who had come to Palestine as part of the First *Aliya.*

As a result of these developments, about a thousand Jews were making their living from agricultural labor in 1881, having become self-sufficient or, in the words of the U.S. Consul in Jerusalem, having ceased to be "paupers and beggars."[93] Along with other new influences that entered the old *Yishuv* in the 1860s and 1870s, such as the appearance of the first modern Hebrew-language journals—*Halevanon*, which began publication in 1863, and *Havatzellet*, which began in 1870—these developments hinted at the important transformations that were to come. In the judgment of one Zionist scholar, they also readied the old *Yishuv* "to open its gates to new immigrants, ways of life and ideas."[94]

Led by the Hovevei Zion movement, especially in Russia and Rumania, organized migrations began in 1882, with many of the new immigrants at first seeking to establish agricultural communities. The village of Rishon Le-Zion, which means First to Zion, was set up in the summer of 1882 by Russian Jews; and shortly thereafter immigrants from Rumania established themselves in the northern community of Rosh Pina, which had earlier been settled by Jews from Safad and then abandoned. Among the other agriculturally oriented villages that were revived or created during this period were Petah Tikvah, Zichron Ya'acov, Rehovot, and Hadera. Thus, while the vast majority of the Jews who left Eastern Europe in the wake of the pogroms did not immigrate to Palestine, the new *Yishuv* nonetheless experienced significant growth. There were roughly twenty Jewish agricultural settlements in Palestine at the end of the century, and approximately five thousand men and women lived in these communities.[95]

Life in the new *Yishuv* was difficult, however, with agricultural communities in particular experiencing serious problems during the early years of their existence. Most Jewish immigrants were poorly prepared for farming. Nor were they aided by the harsh conditions prevailing where many of their settlements were located. Some for a time lived in caves, and many fell ill, often from malaria. As a result of these conditions, less than 20 percent of the recently arrived immigrants took up residence in new settlements or engaged in self-supporting agricultural activities; and even among this group a substantial number soon abandoned their efforts and sought work in one of the major towns of Palestine, usually doing little to build up the country or to create a unified and modern Jewish society. In addition, many new immigrants gave up on Palestine altogether, returning to Europe or, if possible, making their way to the United States. Some of the new colonies might not have survived at all had it not been for the intervention of European philanthropists, notably Baron Edmond de Rothschild. The baron assisted settlers in Zichron Ya'acov, Rishon Le-Zion, and elsewhere, providing capital and technical advice for the production of wine and other agricultural products. He also purchased much of the production of these colonies.

A related problem from the viewpoint of Zionist ideology is that Jewish agriculturists were often transformed into members of a planter class. Rather than living by the fruits of their own labor, which is what Zionism anticipated and desired, immigrants often became supervisors and overseers of local Arabs, who were hired to do the actual agricultural work. This pattern developed for understandable economic reasons, primarily because Arabs were willing to work for lower wages and fewer benefits than were Jews, and secondarily because they tended to be more experienced and knowledgeable about matters related to farming.[96] Nevertheless, the situation was deplored by many Zionists. For example, this is one of the aspects of life in the new *Yishuv* that so distressed Ahad Ha'am when he visited Palestine in the early 1890s. Many Jews were living more like European *colons* than self-sufficient Zionist pioneers, and in the view of Ahad Ha'am, as well as others, this was a far cry from the "national redemption" to which Zionism was dedicated. In addition, beyond its symbolic significance, this situation had the practical consequence of driving down wages, limiting employment, and generally discouraging Jewish workers from immigrating to Palestine, or remaining there. Concern about these problems sparked an inquiry in 1900 by the General Board of Hebrew Workers in *Eretz Yisrael*, and it led some Zionists in the Diaspora to complain about the "great doubt over the ability of the [Jewish] laborers to survive in *Eretz Yisrael*."[97]

While these features of the First *Aliya* limited its ability to transform radically the character of the *Yishuv*, this wave of Jewish immigration nonetheless made a contribution that was of obvious practical significance and of equal or even greater symbolic value. Lasting until 1903, it increased the population of the *Yishuv* by about 25,000, roughly doubling the number of Jews in Palestine. It also brought the creation of a number of new communities, some of which today are among the most prosperous in Israel. In addition to the agricultural settlements mentioned above, the Jews extended their presence in several cities where they had not previously been numerous, and where their way of life was less traditional than in the historic centers of Jerusalem, Safad, Tiberias, and Hebron. In Jaffa, for example, they built new neighborhoods in 1887 and 1890, bringing the Jewish population of the city to about 3,000. In Haifa, with approximately 1,500 Jews, the first Jewish quarter was founded in 1891. The new *Yishuv* also introduced new norms and values in important areas, often to the displeasure of the leaders of the old *Yishuv*. In 1889, for instance, many farmers defied Jerusalem rabbis who insisted that, in accordance with Jewish law, their land be removed from cultivation during the Jewish sabbatical year (5649). A different kind of departure was the production of the first Hebrew play, written by Moshe Leib Lilienblum and staged in Rehovot in 1890.

In sum, despite numerous mistakes and important limitations, the First *Aliya* is appreciated in retrospect for the start it made in constructing the Zionist state. The new immigrants launched initiatives and laid a foundation. They also braved many hardships, gaining experience that would prove valuable to those who came after them.

Labor Zionism and the Second Aliya

The Second *Aliya* spanned the decade from 1904 through 1913 and brought about 35,000 additional Jews to Palestine. Most new arrivals were from Eastern Europe, especially from Russia, as had been the case with the preceding wave of immigration; and, as was also the case with the First *Aliya*, they represented only a small proportion of the large number of Eastern European Jews who left their homes during this period. Approximately 2.5 million Jews left Russia and other European countries between the onset of the pogroms and the beginning of World War I, of whom only 60,000 or so became permanent residents of Palestine.

The Second *Aliya* was a watershed in the development of the Yishuv and in the translation into reality of Zionism's abstract vision. For one thing, it gave the Jewish community in Palestine, whose population was about 85,000 on the eve of the war, the stability that comes with attainment of a critical mass. It greatly reduced the fragility and sense of isolation that surrounded Jewish life in Palestine, especially for Jews outside the major cities. Even more important, it set in motion a process of serious transformation in the character of the *Yishuv*, beginning its evolution into a modern and integrated polity. Finally, the Second *Aliya* provided the majority of the men and women who were to lead the *Yishuv* on its course toward modern statehood. For a time even after Israel attained independence in 1948, it was led by men and women who arrived in *Eretz Yisrael* as a result of the Second *Aliya*. The pattern of Jewish settlements in Palestine in 1914, at the conclusion of the Second *Aliya* and on the eve of World War I, is shown in Map 1.2.

Two sets of factors shaped the origins and character of the new wave of immigration, one having to do with organization and the other with ideology. With respect to the first consideration, the immigrants of this period benefited greatly from the institutional development that had recently occurred within Zionist ranks. Whereas the Zionist Organization and the Keren Kayemet did not exist when the Lovers of Zion began their migrations to Palestine, those who came with the Second *Aliya* were able to obtain advice and practical assistance from these and other newly created Zionist institutions, which provided support to new immigrants both prior to their departure from Eastern Europe and after their arrival in Palestine. The new immigrants were also able to draw upon the wisdom and hard experience acquired by those who had come before them and initiated construction of the new *Yishuv*. All of this gave the Second *Aliya* much greater organizational coherence than the one it followed, removing at least some of the difficulty and disorder that had attended the first.

With respect to ideology, the new *aliya* was heavily influenced by the principles of revolutionary and utopian socialism being espoused by intellectuals and political activists in Tsarist Russia, and also by the struggle for revolutionary

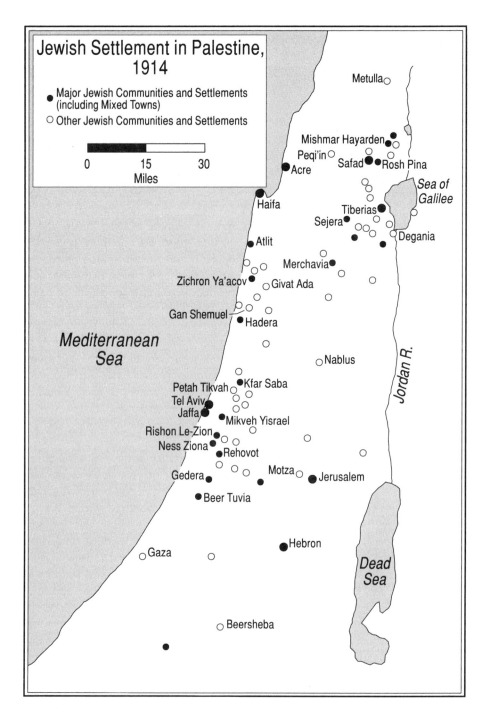

Jewish Settlement in Palestine, 1914

● Major Jewish Communities and Settlements (including Mixed Towns)

○ Other Jewish Communities and Settlements

0   15   30
Miles

Metulla○

Mishmar Hayarden○

Peqi'in○

Safad ●● Rosh Pina

Acre

Sea of Galilee

Haifa

Tiberias

Sejera

Degania

Atlit

Merchavia●

Zichron Ya'acov ●○ Givat Ada

Gan Shemuel

Hadera

Mediterranean Sea

Jordan R.

Nablus

Petah Tikvah

Kfar Saba

Tel Aviv

Jaffa

Mikveh Yisrael

Rishon Le-Zion

Ness Ziona

Rehovot

Gedera

Motza○

Jerusalem

Beer Tuvia

Hebron

○Gaza

Dead Sea

Beersheba

change occurring inside Russia itself. Not all Jews who came to Palestine during this period were ardent socialists, and even many who did embrace socialism could hardly be described as revolutionaries. Nevertheless, a substantial number who joined the Second *Aliya* were not traditional Jews from the parochial communities of the Pale of Settlement but politically conscious Jews who had received a modern education, and the utopian socialist orientation of many of these men and women gave the new wave of immigration its ideological character.

The Second *Aliya* included young people who had supported the revolutionary parties and movements that were formed in Tsarist Russia during the early years of the century, and whose attempts to organize and mobilize the working class had led to the unsuccessful Russian revolution of 1905–1906. Many of these men and women had not originally been oriented toward Zionism but, disappointed that worker uprisings in these years did not produce fundamental change, they now turned to Palestine as a land where they might construct a more egalitarian society.

Still other politically conscious Jews had from the beginning grafted their socialist outlook onto a foundation of Jewish nationalism. Organized into the political parties of Labor Zionism, Poalei Zion (Workers of Zion) and Hapoel Hatzair (The Young Worker), which were formed in the early years of the twentieth century, they argued that the problems of Jewish workers were in substantial measure caused by the contradictions of their life in the Diaspora. These Zionist socialists did sometimes involve themselves in the general struggle of workers inside Russia, and this in turn occasioned debates about whether Zionism would become obsolete should a truly revolutionary society in fact be created in the Diaspora. On the whole, however, even before the failure of the 1905–1906 revolution, Labor Zionists were clear in their advocacy of a Jewish society in Palestine organized along socialist lines, to be based on and sustained by the labor of the Jewish working class.

In addition to the positive attraction of building socialism in Zion, the Second *Aliya* was also in part the product of renewed anti-Semitic violence, which was itself tied up with the ideologies of the period and which for the most part was led by forces seeking to suppress revolutionary change. After nearly twenty years of relative calm, new and even more extensive pogroms took place, beginning in 1903 and reaching the height of their intensity late in 1905. Groups of the extreme right, such as the "Black Hundred," preached a fanatical mixture of nationalism and religious extremism and included violence against Jews in their vigilante attacks on workers' groups and other activists. For example, 45 Jews were killed and many more injured in attacks in Kishinev in April 1903, with similar outbursts following in other cities. The new wave of pogroms became most intense in the fall of 1905, when 810 Jews were killed, and hundreds more wounded, in riots throughout western and southern Russia.[98]

On the ground, in Palestine, the Second *Aliya* was accompanied by a variety of efforts to advance construction of the new *Yishuv*, some of which were more successful than others but all of which, taken together, continued the work of translating Zionism's vision into reality. Among the initiatives tied directly to the Labor Zionist orientation of the Second *Aliya* were the establishment of labor exchanges, workers' kitchens, and a medical insurance program. The latter, Kupat Holim, gradually developed into a comprehensive national sick fund that not only provided health insurance but also maintained an extensive network of clinics.

A particularly important innovation was the creation of new forms of agricultural settlement, the significance of working the land having been vigorously reaffirmed by Labor Zionism. One kind of settlement was the *moshav*, a cooperative agricultural village in which workers own small plots of land but carry out marketing and many aspects of production on a collective basis. A second form of cooperative agriculture appearing at this time was the "national farm," where workers were employed to cultivate land purchased by the Jewish National Fund under the supervision of trained agronomists. A third form, which grew out of the "national farm" scheme, was the *kibbutz*. The first *kibbutz*, Degania, was founded on the southern shores of the Sea of Galilee in 1909.

The early history of Kibbutz Degania sheds light both on the way that new agricultural communities were sometimes formed and on the difficulties that many of them faced in the years before World War I.[99] In 1905, the Jewish Colonization Association had purchased land in Lower Galilee from its Arab owners, and in 1908 the JNF founded a national farm on part of this land. A dispute soon broke out between the farm's managers and its Jewish workers, however, and in 1909 the two sides came to an agreement that was to result in the establishment of Degania. A contract was signed between six workers—five men and one woman—and the Palestine Land Development Company. It provided that while the PLDC would retain ownership of the land, the farm itself would thereafter be run by the workers without interference. It also provided that each of the latter would receive a monthly salary, and that any net profit would be divided equally between the workers and the company. This core group increased in size modestly during the next two years and contained eleven members in 1911, all of whom lived a communal existence and managed the new settlement on a collective basis. The *kibbutz* also hired a number of Jewish workers, who did not belong to the central commune.

The founders of Degania faced hardships in the early years. All of the *kibbutz*'s residents lived in mud huts that had been abandoned by their previous Arab inhabitants, who had been tenant farmers on the land purchased by the JCA and had not been consulted when the tract was sold by its absentee owners. The climate, like the living conditions, was difficult. Two hundred meters below sea level, Degania was exceedingly hot during the long summers, with temperatures above 100 degrees for extended periods. Also, as elsewhere in Palestine, diseases, especially malaria, were common at this time. Finally, Degania was isolated and sometimes dangerous. It was necessary to patrol the fields of the settlement, and sometimes to drive away local Arabs who tried to harvest its crops. There were also occasional skirmishes with Arab bands.

The experience of Degania and other *kibbutzim* made these communal agricultural settlements something of a symbol for the Second *Aliya*. On the one hand, the *kibbutz* represented utopian socialism; its organization was revolutionary and its values emphasized egalitarianism. On the other, it was a tangible expression of the Second *Aliya*'s commitment to Jewish labor and to self-sufficiency. Although various kinds of *kibbutzim* eventually emerged, great emphasis was placed on communalism and egalitarianism, especially in the early years. There was no private property, and decisions not only about production but also about the expenditure of revenues were made on a collective basis. In the name of equality, too, jobs were rotated periodically, such that a person might supervise some aspect of settlement life at one time and then do manual labor in the fields or work in the kitchen at another. Other aspects of this egalitarianism included communal living quarters for children, the abolition of a division of labor based on gender, and communal meals and common services in other areas, such as laundry and home maintenance.

In addition to its emphasis on socialism and equality, Labor Zionism also laid great stress on self-reliance, declaring that Jews should live by the fruits of their own labor and be capable of confronting without assistance whatever difficulties they faced. Consistent with this principle, the *kibbutz* was notable for its autonomy, social cohesion, and ability to provide security. It was a self-contained community, capable of surviving on its own when necessary and of meeting all the needs of its members, and this, too, in addition to its socialist character, made it a symbol for the Second *Aliya* and for Labor Zionism's vision of the new *Yishuv*.

A related dimension of the Second *Aliya*'s drive for self-sufficiency is reflected in what became known as the "conquest of labor," meaning reduction or elimination of the threat that Jewish agricultural workers would be displaced by Arabs, and also, to the extent possible, the transfer to Jews of those jobs in Zionist agricultural communities that were already held by Arab laborers. While local Arabs were usually willing to work long hours for low wages, and were thus attractive employees, Labor Zionism attached great importance to the creation of a Jewish working class and considered it unacceptable that the productivity of the new *Yishuv* should be dependent on the labor of non-Jews. Zionist leaders stated when discussing their conception of a whole and autonomous polity that Jews should be farmers and laborers, as well as merchants and employers. Engaging in a bit of rhetorical hyperbole, some added that in such a political community even the criminals and the prostitutes should be Jewish. Equally important, as noted earlier, the hiring of Jewish workers was essential to provide employment and stimulate immigration, both of which were necessary to promote the development of the *Yishuv*. This combination of symbolic and practical considerations was expressed in the slogan of Hapoel Hatzair, a workers' political party established in 1905: "A necessary condition for the realization of Zionism is the proliferation of Hebrew workers in *Eretz Yisrael* and their entrenchment in all branches of work."[100]

While policies adopted in pursuit of the "conquest of labor" did not bring an end to the widespread use of unskilled Arab labor in Jewish agricultural communities, or even completely eliminate the threat of displacement among unskilled Jewish workers, they did, in the aggregate, contribute to higher wages and greater employment for the Jewish working class. One of these policies was the provision of subsidies for Jewish labor. Sometimes, especially in the early years, employers paid Jews the same wages as Arabs, but the former received additional compensation from public funds. Alternatively, employers agreed to pay Jews higher wages than Arabs, either willingly, as a contribution to the development of the *Yishuv*, or in response to pressure exerted by the increasingly well organized Labor Zionist parties.

Another part of the "conquest of labor," in addition to subsidization, was a general policy of reserving skilled work for Jews whenever possible. Pressure to conform to this policy of monopolization, referenced by the term "entrenchment," was also sometimes exerted by the organized Labor movement. As a result of these policies, as well as other considerations, the wages of Jewish workers rose significantly, both in absolute terms and relative to the pay received by Arab laborers. On the other hand, even with these wage gains, the economic circumstances of many Jewish workers remained precarious.[101]

Also related to the attempt to reduce dependence on Arab labor was a scheme to bring Jews from Yemen to Palestine, in the hope that these "natural" Jewish workers would be oriented toward agriculture and willing to work for the same wages as local Arabs. Zionist officials visited Yemen at the end of 1910, and several thousand Yemenite Jews subsequently responded to the invitation they issued. Upon their arrival in Palestine, they established their own quarters in the vicinity of major villages, and many did indeed go to work on Jewish plantations or in Jewish orchards. But while the presence of the Yemenites added to the demographic mass of the new *Yishuv* and provided a small pool of less expensive Jewish labor, it did not displace a significant number of local Arabs from unskilled work in Jewish agricultural settlements, and it in fact created new problems associated with the marginal social and economic status of many Yemenite Jewish families. According to one Zionist historian, the Yemenites became "a marginal and burdensome social and economic element."[102] In the words of a contemporary account, "Instead of a solution to the old and accursed question of the Hebrew worker, a new problem arose: the question of the Yemenites."[103]

Despite continuing problems and the difficult economic circumstances of some workers, the disorder of the early years gradually diminished during the course of the Second *Aliya* and Jewish agricultural development in Palestine began to assume significant proportions. By 1914 there were forty agricultural villages, with a combined population exceeding 12,000, and regional federations of workers had been established in the Galilee and in Judea. Productivity also increased greatly. More than 100,000 acres were under cultivation by the close of the Second *Aliya*. Citrus fruit and almonds were being grown, in addition to grapes, and unified marketing cooperatives had been established to manage the sale and export of different kinds of produce. Many of the new development schemes attracted investment capital from Jews living in the Diaspora.

Although agriculture was the backbone of the new *Yishuv*, and of the drive for Zionist self-sufficiency, there was also progress in the direction of creating a modern urban population and of establishing an industrial base for the Jewish homeland. The city of Tel Aviv was founded in 1909, established by new immigrants as a garden suburb of Jaffa, and by 1914 its population had grown to about 2,000. The number of Jews in Haifa, another urban center that was comparatively modern in character, had grown to more than 3,000. New industries were also established in both Jaffa and Haifa, including the Stein Iron Works in the former city and the Atid Oil Factory in the latter. Taking its agricultural and urban sectors together, the population of the new *Yishuv* thus grew to more than twice that of the old during the years of the Second *Aliya*; and with its geographic distribution and economic dynamism giving it even greater functional weight, this population of new immigrants succeeded in laying a foundation for the definitive transformation of Jewish society in Palestine.

There were also many important cultural developments during this period, the most significant being the transformation of Hebrew into the lingua franca of the *Yishuv*. The revival of Hebrew was particularly important to Zionists of the Second *Aliya* for two reasons. First, the language would unite immigrants who came from different parts of the Diaspora and brought different linguistic traditions. It would thus contribute in a practical sense to the social integration of the *Yishuv*. Second, the use of Hebrew represented the cultural dimension of Labor Zionism's quest for autonomy and self-sufficiency, it being argued that Jewish society in Palestine should develop on the foundation of its own language and culture, as well as its own labor and economic productivity. Despite fierce opposition from many rabbis, who considered Hebrew a holy tongue that should be reserved for worship and study and should not be profaned by use in the conduct of daily affairs, efforts to transform the ancient language of the Jews into a vehicle of modern communication had been going on for some time. The pioneering work of Eliezer Ben Yehudah, mentioned earlier, began during the First *Aliya*. Ben Yehudah went to Palestine in 1881 and devoted himself to the preparation of a massive dictionary of modern Hebrew, devising terms for countless modern words and concepts that have no direct equivalent in the ancient language. He also waged a determined campaign to persuade others to use the new language. Only during the Second *Aliya*, however, did his efforts and those of others who followed his lead strike a responsive chord among substantial numbers. Now, for the first time, in the new *Yishuv*, Hebrew became the language of daily life among a substantial and growing number of Jews, especially among young people and including common workers as well as persons with higher levels of education.

The use of Hebrew in publishing, education, and other domains increased in this environment and was stimulated further by the establishment in 1904 of a national committee to coordinate efforts to modernize the language. The first Hebrew-language daily newspapers began publication in 1908. One of them, *Hatzevi*, was edited by Ben Yehudah. Most of the periodicals of the Labor Zionist parties were also written in Hebrew at this time. In the field of education, a Hebrew-language teacher-training institute was opened in Jerusalem in 1904; the Herzlia Hebrew Gymnasium, a Hebrew high school that served as a model for modern Jewish secondary schools elsewhere, was opened the next year; and a national network of Hebrew schools, with a combined enrollment of 3,200 pupils, was created in 1912. Still other developments in the cultural life of the *Yishuv*, not all of which pertain to language, include establishment of the Jewish Telegraph Agency in 1904; establishment in the same year of the Habimah Theater, which produced plays by a growing number of authors writing in Hebrew; the founding of the Bezalel School of Art in Jerusalem in 1906; and the beginning of construction in 1912 of a technical university in Haifa. The later institution, the Technion, was the first school of higher learning in the *Yishuv* and eventually grew into a world-renowned center for pure and applied scientific research.

As a result of all these developments, despite the important problems it continued to face, the Jewish *Yishuv* in Palestine was rapidly becoming a viable political community. By the eve of World War I, it had made important strides toward, and perhaps had even attained, a critical demographic mass. It had also made significant progress toward economic viability. Though it was not yet self-sufficient, its economy was characterized by rising levels of productivity and, like its population, was increasingly differentiated. In addition, the *Yishuv* was supported by an increasingly well organized international Zionist movement and possessed social and political institutions that provided basic services and promoted integration in the domestic arena of Palestine. Finally, based in large measure on the revival and modernization of Hebrew, the Jewish population of Palestine was beginning to articulate its own culture and project its own identity. Thus, building on the foundation of previous Jewish immigration to Palestine, the Second *Aliya* brought critical changes, in both kind and degree, in the character of the new *Yishuv*. By the end of 1914, with Europe now plunged into war and repercussions for the Middle East as yet unknown, the Jewish community in Palestine was set firmly, and irrevocably, on a course that gave tangible expression to the ancient national identity of the Jewish people and translated into reality the vision of the Jews' future articulated by modern political Zionism.

2 | Arab History and the Origins of Nationalism in the Arab World

Palestinians, Arabs, and Arabism

THE PALESTINIANS ARE descendants of two ancient peoples, the Canaanites and the Philistines. The former are the earliest known inhabitants of Palestine, which in the Bible is in fact called the Land of Canaan. It is believed that they entered the country around 3000 B.C.E. Canaanite society was not united but rather was composed of autonomous principalities, each ruled by a king who apparently had religious as well as political duties. Jerusalem was one of the cities ruled by the Canaanites, until it fell to the ancient Israelites about 1000 B.C.E. The Philistines, from whom the present name of Palestine is derived, entered the area around 1200 B.C.E. and took up residence in the southern coastal plain. Both the Canaanites and the Philistines were pagans, although some converted to Judaism following the arrival of the Israelites. Many later converted to Christianity, as did a number of Jews, and a majority subsequently embraced Islam, which was introduced by the Arabs in the seventh century.

From the early Middle Ages until the beginning of the twentieth century, the Palestinian people traced its evolution through the collective history of the Arab nation, of which it has now been a part for more than a millennium; and, in turn, the history of the Arab nation during this period cannot be told without reference to the emergence and development of Islam, the religion of most Arabs. At the time of the first Islamic revelations, received by the Prophet Muhammad in Mecca in 610 C.E., Christianity was the principal religion in Palestine, and Aramaic was the most widely used language. The territory had been part of the Roman and later the Byzantine empires, and thus, for many centuries, the principal focus of its political and ideological attention had been directed westward toward the Mediterranean, rather than toward the deserts of Arabia lying to the south and east. The rise of Islam brought important currents of change, however, setting in motion a fundamental transformation of existing political and cultural patterns. Warriors from the Arabian Peninsula carried out raids in Palestine shortly after the death of the Prophet, in 632 C.E., and within a few years the territory had been conquered by the Arabs and incorporated into their rapidly expanding empire.

As elsewhere, many in Palestine embraced the religion of their new rulers.[1]

Islam did not become the religion of the majority in Palestine until the ninth century, and from that period until the present there has remained a sizable Christian minority. At the present time, 10 to 15 percent of the Arabs of Palestinian origin are Christian. But in Palestine, as in other regions conquered by the Arabs, Islam spread rapidly, helped by the ease of conversion, by Muslim acceptance of the Divine revelations of Judaism and Christianity, and by a tolerance which permitted converts to retain many pre-Islamic cultural norms and institutions. The language of the Arabs also gradually spread throughout much of the empire. In Palestine, Arabic became the language of the majority during the ninth century.

The mainstream of Palestinian society thus became assimilated into the dominant normative order of Arab and Islamic civilization, such that most Palestinians today see their Arab identity and their Palestinian identity as inextricably intertwined. These identities operate in tandem to define the substantive content of political consciousness; they are not competing patterns of collective affiliation which Palestinians must seek to compartmentalize, or between which they must choose. While the Jewish minority living in Palestine during the early Islamic centuries did not participate in this assimilative process to the same extent, it is interesting to note that the Jews of Palestine nonetheless welcomed and encouraged the introduction of Arab rule. They believed, correctly, that they would fare better under the hegemony of Muslim Arabs than they had under their former Roman and Byzantine governors. In any event, Palestine was deeply affected by the political and ideological revolution that took place in the Middle East following the introduction of Islam. Most of its inhabitants became Arab during this period, and an understanding of Palestinian history and Palestinian political aspirations accordingly requires attention to experiences that have shaped the Arab world as a whole since the rise of Islam.

The process of acculturation by which the inhabitants of Palestine became Arab is not unique. On the contrary, it is typical of the way in which the religion and language of the Arabian Peninsula spread throughout what is today regarded as the Arab world, creating and giving a normative foundation to what Arabs themselves call *al-watan al-arabi*, the "Arab nation" or the "Arab fatherland." The Arab nation, which is a community of culture and civilization rather than a political entity, at present stretches from Iraq in the east to Morocco in the west, including as distinct geographic regions the Fertile Crescent, the Arabian Gulf, the Nile Valley, and North Africa. The latter is known as the Maghreb, or Arab west. These regions and others were conquered by the Arabs in the seventh century and, as in Palestine, their inhabitants converted to Islam in steadily increasing numbers. Most gradually embraced the language and culture of the Arabs as well, although the extent and rapidity of this assimilative process varied from one location to another.

The North African experience illustrates this process and sheds light on developments in Palestine and elsewhere. Conversion to Islam began shortly after the arrival of the first Arab invaders, less than two decades after the death of the Prophet in 632, whereas the penetration of Arabic and Arab culture was delayed by several centuries. Much of the indigenous Berber population had earlier converted to Judaism and Christianity, and most Berbers embraced Islam readily following the first Arab conquests. Arabic, on the other hand, did not become predominant for at least another four hundred years. In the eastern Maghreb, in the area of present-day Tunisia, interdynastic rivalries sent several hundred thousand Arab warriors into the region in the eleventh century, changing the demographic composition of the population and, for the first time, spreading the language and customs of the Arabs to the countryside and to the poorer sectors of the society. Previously, despite Islamization, these had been the cultural patterns of an alien Arab ruling class. Farther to the west, especially in the more remote mountain regions of Algeria and Morocco, Arabic and Arab culture penetrated more slowly still, with pockets of unassimilated Berbers remaining to this day. Nevertheless, during the first few centuries of the present millennium, the Maghreb became culturally as well as politically a part of the Arab world.

This process of assimilation reveals how Palestinians and others became Arab, and why, despite significant intra-Arab variation in patterns of politics and society, an attachment to Arabism is a central and unifying theme in the identity and political outlook of peoples throughout the Arab world, including the Palestinians. In addition, the substantive content of Arabism is also revealed in this process of assimilation, and this in turn contributes to a proper understanding of the term "Arab." As the Palestinian experience indicates, the essence of Arabism is defined by a set of cultural symbols and patterns of social behavior, and these may be acquired through processes of socialization and acculturation. One becomes Arab by learning and embracing these symbols and behavioral patterns, which thereafter become the basis for both objective and subjective definitions of collective identification.

The Arabs are not a race, since men and women of all races may become Arab by adopting the linguistic, sociological, and cultural attributes that define Arabism. The term "Arab" originally meant someone from the Arabian Peninsula, whence came the people who brought Arabism and Islam, and at this time the term did carry implications of kinship and genealogical descent. It referred to those who not only spoke Arabic but also were members by birth of a tribe of Arabian origin.[2] This early use of the term sometimes referenced as well the Bedouin lifestyle of the original Arab tribes. But definitions based on ethnicity and kinship disappeared as the Arabs forged an expanding empire during the early Islamic centuries, to be replaced by definitions, and self-definitions, that saw Arabism as a civilization and a culture. Further, although use of the term "Arab" to distinguish nomadic from sedentary populations in the Arab world has continued, this usage is colloquial and principally one of popular convenience. It is quite distinct from what Arabs discuss when seeking to define the essence of Arabism or membership in the Arab nation. In these cases, again, they place emphasis on the learned patterns of language, culture, and civilization that they share and with which they choose to identify. As a result, a convenient operational definition of an Arab is one whose mother tongue is Arabic and who believes that the history of the Arabic-speaking peoples is his or her own history.[3]

The preceding makes clear that in order to tell fully and properly the story of the Palestinian people it is necessary to give attention to historical experiences which have shaped the identity of all Arabs, including that of the Palestinians but also of others, and this remains the case even though attributions of nationalism to the Arabs' cultural community are relatively recent. The idea that those who share the bonds of Arabism constitute a natural political community is a twentieth- century phenomenon, the product to a considerable degree of intensified contact with the nationalism and imperialism of Europe. But even without explicit political content, without the assertion that the Arabs are a nation in the present-day sense of the term, there existed for centuries both the common experiences by which Arab peoples from Iraq to Morocco trace their collective history and the tangible attributes of what they all regard as a shared heritage of culture and civilization, with Arabic and Islam as central foci. Therefore, although the Arab world did not conceive of and present itself as a *political* community during the course of its history, and derived its identity as a nation from commonalities of language and civilization rather than a unifying structure of government, its collective history remains the legacy of each of its constituent peoples, among them the Arabs of Palestine, and must accordingly be included in the story of any one of them.

There is also a specifically Palestinian history that requires attention, but the most important and politically salient aspects of this history belong to the twentieth century and are thus part of a later chapter in the story of Palestine's indigenous Arab population. The Palestinians do possess a sense of political community built, in part, on bonds and experiences that make them unique, including centuries of life in their ancestral homeland, their particular response to currents of reform in the nineteenth century, and subsequent confrontations with Zionism and European imperialism. Accordingly, their political identity is defined by membership not only in the Arab nation but in the Palestinian nation as well; they regard themselves as Arabs and embrace without reservation the heritage of the entire Arabic-speaking world, but they also affirm their specificity and place emphasis on factors that set them apart from, as well as tie them to, other Arab peoples. Nevertheless, important as are these latter considerations, they did not come together to create and define a sense of Palestinian peoplehood, or nationalism, until the beginning of the present century. The broader sweep of Arab history is thus an essential component of the Palestinians' own story, central to any attempt to understand their intellectual and political heritage. A general history of the Arabs is in fact the point of departure for an inquiry of this sort. It should precede examination of the relatively recent emergence of Palestinian nationalism and the subsequent evolution, during the twentieth century, of sentiments and institutions giving expression to the national consciousness of the Palestinian people.

There are other important reasons for including a survey of Arab history in a study of the Israeli-Palestinian conflict. One is to foster recognition that the late development of Palestinian nationalism represents a pattern that is common in the Arab world and, as a consequence, that the right to self-determination proclaimed by Palestinians is no less valid than that put forward by the Arab inhabitants of other territorial units. While the more focused and territorially defined national orientation of the Palestinian people is less than a century old, as noted, this is not exceptional within the Arab world, or in many other parts of the Third World for that matter. Indeed, in some Arab countries, among them Libya, Jordan, Saudi Arabia, and Algeria, citizens define themselves today in terms of a political identity that took shape even more recently than that of the Palestinians. Other patterns of territorial identification are older, such as those found in Egypt, Tunisia, Syria, Morocco, and Iraq. Nevertheless, on the whole, the idea that the Arabs of Palestine constitute a distinct people within the larger Arab arena is no more recent, and no more spurious, than the territorially focused identities of the independent states mentioned above.

It may be added that even were this not the case, Palestinians would still possess the right to reside in and rule over their ancestral homeland, managing their own affairs in accordance with the evolving will and consciousness of the majority of their country's citizens. But an examination of Arab history in fact reveals that the Palestinian case is not unique so far as the development of modern nationalism is concerned. Palestinian political consciousness emerged in the context of a general crystallization of separate, territorially focused political identities, which occurred throughout the Arab world during the last part of the nineteenth century and the first part of the twentieth century. It is thus no less indigenous, authentic, and genuine than that of dozens of societies whose claims to self-determination and national independence are today accepted without reservation.

Still another reason for surveying Arab history, equally essential for a proper understanding of the Israeli-Palestinian conflict, is to dispel the widely held misconception that Jews and Muslim Arabs have been fighting in Palestine for hundreds of years, and that the Israeli-Palestinian conflict is consequently an extension of an ancient dispute rooted in primordial religious and ethnic antagonisms. A review of Arab history from pre-Islamic times until the present makes clear that this is not the case. Just as the history of the Jewish people has been shaped by both its own internal dynamics and the wider sweep of world events, and even in Palestine did not include a confrontation with Arabs until a century ago, so the political evolution of the Arabic-speaking world, including its Palestinian component, has been significantly influenced by its interaction with the Jewish people for only one hundred years, perhaps even less. An examination of Arab history, like Jewish history, accordingly provides a substantive foundation for understanding that neither the Arab-Israeli conflict in general nor the Israeli-Palestinian conflict in particular is a millennia-old blood feud. Indeed, as will be discussed in the next chapter, Arab nationalists and Zionists in some instances saw one another as potential allies in the early years of the twentieth century, when each national movement took shape, discovered the other, and sought to defend itself against challenges from Europe that at the time appeared paramount.

Although the Israeli-Palestinian conflict is at its core, there is also a broader conflict between Israel and the independent states of the Arab world, and herein lies yet another reason to examine Arab as well as Palestinian history. The fact that Palestinians are Arabs, and that other Arabs, as well as the Palestinians themselves, recognize and attach significance to this fact, has given the Arab world a compelling interest in the conflict in Palestine. Arab states have joined in the struggle for what they consider the legitimate rights of the Palestinian people, and some have become key actors in the drama. As a result, an account of the collective heritage of the Arab world is important not only because it constitutes an essential component of the Palestinians' political identity, by which the Palestinians continue to be influenced, but also because such an account contributes to fuller comprehension of the motivation and behavior of other major participants in the broader Arab-Israeli conflict.

Finally, of less immediate significance but potentially most important of all in the long run, a survey of Arab history reveals a remarkable congruence with the history of the Jews. The periodization of Arab history and Jewish history is strikingly similar, as are the ways that both modern political Zionism and modern Arab nationalism emerged toward the end of the nineteenth century. This symmetry does not mean that the struggle between Jews and Arabs in Palestine, when it finally crystallized, was any less intense. Ultimately, Zionists and Palestinian Arabs came to regard one another as the most important obstacle to the realization of their respective national aspirations. Nevertheless, this congruence reinforces the important point that the Arab-Jewish conflict is of comparatively recent vintage, that it is not an ancient blood feud, and, further, it suggests a basis for Arab-Jewish dialogue and understanding should there eventually be a resolution of the present-day struggle in Palestine. Recognizing that they have no choice but to live together, Israelis, Palestinians, and other Arabs may one day choose to place emphasis on the common elements in their respective national destinies; and should this occur, an abundant resource will be provided by the striking similarities in the history of each people, during the centuries before there was an Arab-Jewish conflict in Palestine.

Islam and the Periodization of Arab History

The history of the Arabs can be divided into four general periods, each of which is defined, in part, by the circumstances of Islam as well as by the evolving sociological and political order of the Arab world. The history of the Arabs and that of Islam are inextricably intertwined; one cannot be told apart from the other, even though not all Arabs are Muslims and, today, there are hundreds of millions of non-Arab Muslims. As expressed by one Arab scholar, "The Prophet was an Arab, the Quran is written in Arabic, and the Arabs were the 'matter of Islam' [*maddat al-Islam*], the human instrument through which it conquered the world."[4] Also, conversely, Islam is "the creator of the Arab nation, the content of its culture and the object of its collective pride."[5] As a result, "Being a member of the Arab nation is to be conscious of belonging to the Muslim community,"[6] and indeed, until the age of modern nationalism, the religion served as the principal binding force in the Arab world.[7] Such assessments are even to be found in the writings of Christian Arabs and avowed secularists, many of whom see the history and culture of the Muslim community as providing the substantive foundation for their own national identification.[8]

The first of the four periods is that which predates the earliest Islamic revelations. It is known as *jahiliyya*, meaning "ignorance of religious truths," and refers to the circumstances of Arabia prior to the life of the Prophet Muhammad (570–632 C.E.) and the introduction of Islam. Arabs and Muslims regard this as a strife-torn and unenlightened era, even though they also recall its virtues and accomplishments. Among its major characteristics are parochialism, fragmentation, and warfare.

Although not wholly isolated from the Persian and Byzantine cultures which dominated the Middle East during this period, the three centuries preceding the rise of Islam were ones of decline and disorder in the heartland of the Arabs. During the first centuries of the Christian era, the Arabian Peninsula possessed important and flourishing states which, on an intermittent basis, were integrated into the overarching civilizations of the ancient world. These included the Nabatean Kingdom, which controlled trade between the Roman Empire and lands farther to the east, and the Kingdom of Palmyra. These and other states of northern and central Arabia declined rapidly in the fourth century C.E., however, in large measure because of the redirection of trade routes. Trade with the east at this time increasingly became routed either through Egypt and the Red Sea or, alternatively, through the Euphrates Valley and the Persian Gulf. Not long after, the states of southern Arabia, in what is today Yemen, fell into disarray. Thus, at the time of Islam's introduction during the first half of the seventh century, the Arabian Peninsula had long been characterized by disarray, fragmentation, and alienation from the major civilizations of the Middle East.

The bulk of the Arab population at this time was Bedouin and tribal in character, which is also central to the definition that Arabs and Muslims give to the period of *jahiliyya*. In the tribal society of the Arabian Peninsula, the group rather than the individual was the basic social unit, with property held in common and nomadic herding carried out on a communal basis. Tribes possessed low levels of political organization and were fiercely independent, being organized on the basis of real or putative patrilineal descent. Further, intertribal warfare was common, as were raids on settled communities and the occasional caravans that could still be found; and a need for defense against external enemies thus contributed, along with blood ties, to the maintenance of tribal cohesion. Although tinged with ambivalence, the Arab and Muslim view of the Bedouin lifestyle that characterizes the period of *jahiliyya* is ultimately quite negative. The Bedouin are seen as wild and destructive, living an aimless and unproductive existence that is more cruel than noble. From the period of *jahiliyya* until modern times, outsiders, including other Arabs, have for the most part viewed the Bedouin as a threat to established order and an obstacle to the pursuit by civilized society of cultural and material advancement.

Selected aspects of tribal society and culture are judged more favorably. For example, there is a certain, somewhat grudging admiration for the simplicity and purity of desert Arab society, with its independence and egalitarianism, its communal solidarity, and its virtues of honesty, courage, and uncomplaining acceptance of hardship. As one observer notes, Arab philosophers sometimes describe the Bedouin "in terms similar to the eighteenth century European philosophers' 'Natural Man'— simple, pristine, children of God, uncorrupted and untamed by civilization."[9] The early Bedouins' contribution to the language and poetry of the Arabs earns them even more respect, even in the eyes of sophisticated urban Arabs and among many who view the pre-Islamic period as an unenlightened age. Poetry is an art form to which Arab society has long devoted a disproportionate share of its literary creativity, and the origins of this poetic tradition are in the "song language" of pre-Islamic Arabia, described as a language which, "though fed by all dialects and understood everywhere, was still sharply distinguished from daily speech."[10] Moreover, some of the epic poems of the pre-Islamic period continue to be taught and repeated today. Concerning the linguistic and cultural contribution of the early Arabs more generally, classical Arabic, which Islam subsequently made into a language of worldly learning, is derived from the poetic language of early Arabia. Even today, to say that a student of Arabic has studied with the Bedouin is to pay him the highest compliment.

These important cultural contributions notwithstanding, the major attributes of the period of *jahiliyya* are derived from the unincorporated, tribal character of life in the Arabian Peninsula prior to the introduction of Islam. Representing the political world of dissidence and insolence, the Bedouin tribes placed themselves in a posture of opposition to centralized authority and vigorously resisted incorporation into larger political communities. Fierce raiders and warriors who fought with one another and lived according to their own uncomplicated code, the Bedouin also rejected assimilation into the high cultures of the pre-Islamic Middle East and sought to maintain their unique and inward-looking lifestyle. It is this constellation of attributes that gives to the period of *jahiliyya* its dominant characteristics: parochialism, fragmentation, and conflict.

A new era began with the rise of Islam and the construction of a vast Arab and Islamic empire. Although devout Muslims sometimes assert that historical analysis need only distinguish between the period of *jahiliyya* and that of Islam, it is in fact useful to identify three different phases in the evolution of the Arab world following the introduction of Islam. The first of these begins with the life of Muhammad and continues for several centuries, until the demise of the unified political kingdoms established by the Prophet's successors. This period is one of growth, outreach, and expansion, ultimately blossoming into a golden age of intellectual as well as political accomplishment. A subsequent era, beginning in the tenth century or so and spanning the middle centuries of Islam, witnessed the end of the golden age and the onset of a period marked, in relative terms at least, by constriction and decline. This period is sometimes described as the Dark Ages of the Arab world. A final period, which begins in the nineteenth century and continues until the present, is one of reawakening and renaissance. These three eras, as well as that of *jahiliyya*, constitute a convenient and widely accepted periodization of the history of the Arab world.

The intellectual and emotional divide between the age of *jahiliyya* on the one hand and historical periods following the rise of Islam on the other involves more than a contrast between modern society and Bedouin life. It is a moral and symbolic distinction, as well as one that may be viewed through the temporal characteristics of Arab civilization at different points in time. The Bedouins of pre-Islamic Arabia represent man's beginning, noble in some aspects but ultimately primitive and unfulfilled. What comes later, by contrast, represents fulfillment, man's submission to the will of God and his active participation in a community of believers dedicated to living as the Creator intended. As explained by one authority, "The society which did not know Islam was ruled by custom, evolved by men for their own purposes and in ignorance of the commandments of God. . . . The link between human beings in pre-Islamic society was that of a natural relationship, based on blood . . . [whereas] the link between Muslims was a moral link." [11]

Islam is not only a religion in the traditional and relatively narrow Western sense. It is also a culture and a state. This point is consistently stressed by Muslim scholars, one of whom writes, for example, that "Islam, in its precise sense, is a social order, a philosophy of life, a system of economic principles, a rule of government." [12] Concerned with far more than personal piety and individual morality, the Quran is a body of law which establishes, in considerable detail, the social behavior and organization of a political community. Indeed, to the faithful, it is God's word about the kind of polity they should construct and, being both the essential source of guidance on matters of societal organization and the foundation of public as well as personal status law, it is in fact the authoritative constitution of this community, which Muslims call the *umma*.

As with Judaism, the spiritual and temporal are fused in Islam. The social and cultural force of the religion, and the moral authority of its political expression in the *umma*, are seen as a part of the miracle wrought by the message that God transmitted through Muhammad. Accordingly, Islam's golden age of expansion has both a political and a religious dimension, with mutual reinforcement rather than tension between the two. In its political context, the story of this period is that of Muhammad's initial attempts to win converts, his subsequent founding of an Islamic political order in Medina, and ultimately, following his death, Arab conquests leading to the construction of an empire stretching from Spain to India. These earthly accomplishments included not only the exercise and expansion of political power but also intellectual and cultural achievements on a world scale and the crystallization of a rich and vibrant Islamic civilization.

The religious expansion intertwined with these developments involved more than mass conversion to Islam. Most important was the standardization and application of Islamic law, at the center of which was a process of legal interpretation known as *ijtihad*. Indeed the early Islamic centuries are sometimes called the age of *ijtihad*, or the years during which the "gate of *ijtihad*" was open, meaning that not only the text of the law but also its use by Muslims as a practical guide to action had to be rendered authoritative. Thus, even after ambiguities and disagreements about the literal text of the message God had transmitted to Muhammad were resolved, giving rise to the Quran as we know it today, it remained to be determined how generalized injunctions and exhortations should be applied by believers in particular situations.

Moreover, there was a close connection between this process of religio-legal interpretation on the one hand and the political expansion of the Islamic community on the other. Since the growth during this period of the Arab-Islamic state vastly increased the complexity of social life and introduced circumstances not known to Muslims at the time God's Islamic message was transmitted, political development was itself a stimulus to legal development. It regularly introduced new situations, requiring Muslim scholars to seek agreement on how the message of the Holy Book should be interpreted and applied in the face of some new problem or novel circumstance. At the same time, devotion to God's law contributed reciprocally to the community's dynamic outward thrust. Muslims sought to increase the scope and scale of their community, in part, in order to understand their universal doctrine more fully. Mortals may never understand Divine wisdom in its full measure, no matter how devotedly they memorize and recite its expression in the language of men. They may deepen their comprehension, however; and while for individuals this may be done through study and reflection, it is pursued by a community through the process of *ijtihad*. In this way, more of the limitless application of the holy law may become known to man, and the law itself may be more fully and faithfully applied since a body of collective wisdom about its true intent will be accumulated.

The period of Islam and Arab expansion began in 610, when Muhammad received the first of the revelations he was to transmit.[13] This was in Mecca, which at the time was the most important city of the Arabian Peninsula. The oasis community derived much significance from its accepted position as a sanctuary from intertribal warfare. It was also an important center of worship for the pagan cults that prevailed in pre-Islamic Arabia. Muhammad was born in Mecca about 570 C.E. and was thus approximately forty years of age when he delivered the first of the pronouncements that he insisted were the revealed word of God and which, upon authentication, were subsequently collected in the Quran. Quranic verses based on these early revelations are for the most part short and somber. Containing the message of warning and salvation that Muhammad said he had been instructed to convey, they deal principally with such themes as the unity of God, the evils of idol worship, the need to redress injustice, and the approach of a day of moral judgment. The tone and content of these verses differ significantly from those based on revelations transmitted later in Muhammad's life, which are longer and give more direction in matters of personal conduct and societal organization.

Few were receptive to Muhammad's message at the outset. Initial converts included a few family members and friends. Most others were members of the impoverished or slave classes of Mecca. Moreover, though at first the Meccan community and its leaders seemed more indifferent than hostile to Muhammad's teachings, vigorous opposition soon emerged. Some of this was in response to his increasingly intense denunciation of the pantheistic gods that many worshipped, and some was based on his attempts to form and lead an autonomous community within the Meccan state, over which the latter's authority would be limited. Most important, however, was the threat to Meccan prosperity contained in the message Muhammad brought. Not only did Mecca's conservative ruling oligarchy fear the egalitarianism he preached, but widespread acceptance of the monotheism for which he called would reduce the city's importance as a center of pagan worship, on which much of its trade was built. Similarly, submission of the Bedouins to Islam, bringing an end to tribal warfare and the integration of the tribes into a unified political community, would eliminate Mecca's importance as a sanctuary. In view of these challenges to the city's economic base, and to their own control over it, the leaders of Mecca did all within their power to limit Muhammad's influence. Indeed, following repudiation by his clan and the loss of its protection, he was forced to flee from Mecca to nearby Taif in 619; and thereafter, upon his return, he remained in seclusion until he was guaranteed protection by a respected member of his tribe.

A signal event in the formation of the Islamic community was Muhammad's move to the city of Yathrib, later known as Medina, in 622. This is known to Muslims as the *hijra*, the "flight" or "migration," and it is the event from which the Islamic calendar is dated. Located about two hundred miles north of Mecca,

Yathrib was a much less complex community. Its economic foundation was agricultural rather than commercial, and it had neither the extremes of economic stratification nor the sophisticated political organization that characterized Mecca. Further, it was not a center of pagan worship. On the contrary, among its inhabitants were Judaized Arab tribes, making monotheism a familiar part of religious life. Finally, and directly related to the migration of Muhammad and his followers, the town during this period was torn by warfare among rival tribes. Exhausted from conflict and fearful that their community would be completely destroyed, or might fall under the control of its Jewish tribes, Yathrib's pagan leadership invited Muhammad to come to their city with his followers and to serve as arbiter and peacemaker. Some time later Yathrib came to be called Medina, the Arabic word for city, derived from its title of *medinat rasul-Allah*, the city of the Messenger of God.

Medina offered Muhammad an opportunity to move from preaching to practice and to translate into reality the vision revealed to him. This was particularly important, moreover, since Islam's revelations are intended to be the foundation of a worldly community, being more than abstract moral principles and spiritually edifying images. Throughout his life, Muhammad continued to make pronouncements which he claimed were the word of God, and Quranic verses based on the revelations he received at Medina tend to be longer, less poetic, and concerned principally with the conduct of temporal human affairs, in contrast to the affirmations of God's unity, the bold denunciations of injustice, and the somber warnings of judgment that were most common during his years in Mecca.

Medina also offered Muhammad a base from which to expand the Islamic community, and he began by conquering central Arabia's independent Bedouin tribes and forging them into a kind of desert empire. Tribes within Muhammad's community were united and governed by a prohibition of internal warfare. The unconquered pagan tribes, by contrast, were atomized and fiercely independent, and each thus stood alone in the face of overwhelming Muslim strength. Tribes were conquered one by one in this manner, and upon surrender each was integrated into the Islamic community. Conquered tribes were not punished or exploited. Each was merely required to acknowledge the authority of Medina, to renounce warfare against other members of the community and its allies, and, like all Muslims, to pay the *zakkat*, a religious tax.

The submission of the tribes enabled the Muslim community to grow rapidly and expand its power, until great stretches of Arabia were soon within its grip. The power of the Islamic community also attracted the attention of neighboring kingdoms. For example, Cyrus, the Byzantine governor of Egypt, sent gifts to Muhammad and sought good relations with the increasingly powerful Islamic community. With its growing might, the community centered at Medina was soon powerful enough to challenge the cities of Mecca and Taif, and in the important battle of Badr, fought in 624, the Prophet's forces defeated the Meccan armies decisively. The former ultimately triumphed by blockading the city, which in 630 submitted to Muhammad's authority. Muhammad's treatment of Mecca in surrender is significant, too, revealing the Prophet's political acumen and capacity for compromise. Following his victory, Muhammad made the Meccans a partner in the construction of the Islamic community; he devoted great energy to infusing a devotion to Islam among the Meccans and worked to enlist their intellectual sophistication and political capacity in the service of his expanding community.

While Muhammad's political and military skill enabled him to build his empire, he also succeeded in convincing many within the community of the authenticity of the revelations he transmitted. To some, his victory over so formidable an enemy as Mecca appeared to attest to Divine guidance. Many were also impressed by the careful distinction he maintained between his own teachings and advice on the one hand and the pronouncements he proclaimed to be God's word on the other. In many areas, as in the treatment of women, for example, the Prophet expressed his personal conviction that compassion and humane treatment were pleasing in God's sight, even as he transmitted a legal code that formally granted to men certain rights denied to women. In this manner, by announcing edicts which gave legal sanction to behavior that his own teachings sought to discourage, Muhammad's credibility was enhanced.[14]

The achievement of the Quran itself, and most notably its linguistic brilliance, offered the most striking evidence of the Prophet's claims. Muhammad is considered to have been illiterate, yet the language of the Quran is classical Arabic of unsurpassed beauty, a holy tongue said by the faithful to be the language of the angels. This language is in fact regarded as a part of God's gift, and, accordingly, the Quran is said to be incapable of translation. It may be rendered in another language, but the result is not the Quran.[15] Marmaduke Pickthall, who has produced an English version of the holy book, warns that whereas the true Quran is an "inimitable symphony, the very sounds of which move men to tears and ecstasy," his English-speaking readers should expect only a pale imitation.[16] At Mecca, Muhammad appealed to this aspect of his revelations to respond to critics who demanded a miracle. If his recitations were the product of human intelligence, he replied, let others produce just ten verses like them. And since none could, let them accept the Quran as a Divine miracle.[17]

A deep crisis in the community followed Muhammad's unexpected death from a fever in 632. Although his religious role as the Messenger of God could not be carried on by any successor, the political integrity of the Muslim community and the continuity of temporal leadership functions had to be ensured. Muhammad had established no institutionalized structures of leadership or succession, however, and so the community had to devise procedures and criteria for the selection of his successor. The matter was resolved, at least temporarily, with the designation of Abu Bakr, father-in-law of the Prophet and one of the first converts to Islam, who was given the title of *khalifa* (caliph; deputy). Abu Bakr's duties were at the outset ill-defined, being essentially to sustain the political dimension of Muhammad's mission. The office of caliph soon evolved, however, providing the expanding community with a powerful institution of centralized executive and military leadership.

Old and ailing, Abu Bakr died two years later, in 634, and was replaced by Umar, who presided over a dramatic expansion of the Muslim community. During the decade of Umar's rule, until he was killed by a slave of Persian origin in 644, the Islamic state simultaneously eliminated pockets of dissidence in the Arabian Peninsula and established itself in the neighboring territories of Egypt, Palestine, Syria, and Iraq. Egypt, Syria, and Palestine at the time were controlled by Byzantine forces, who had only recently reconquered them in a costly and exhausting war with the Persian Empire. The Persians still controlled Iraq. With both empires seriously weakened by the prolonged warfare between them, the Arabs scored one military victory after another. In 636, in a battle along the Yarmuk River in present-day Jordan, Muslim armies led by Khalid confronted and destroyed Byzantine forces commanded by the emperor, giving the Arabs control of most of Syria and Palestine. In 637, the Arabs decisively defeated a Persian force of superior numbers and took control of Iraq, and victories in 639 and 640 brought most of Egypt into Arab hands as well. Moreover, under Umar's leadership, the Muslim state not only continued its conquests but also introduced an Arab administration in captured provinces. He in fact visited Syria and Palestine in 637 in order to formulate a plan of government and select its leaders. As governor of Syria and Palestine, Umar chose Muawiya, a man from the prominent and powerful Umayyad clan of Mecca.

Uthman was selected to replace Umar, a choice that was somewhat surprising since he was considered to be weak and perhaps even cowardly. His designation as caliph was controversial for another reason as well. Like Muawiya, governor in Damascus, Uthman was from the Umayyad clan of Mecca, which was resented both for its initial opposition to Muhammad and, after Mecca's entry into the Muslim community, for its patrician attitudes and political ambitions. Uthman's weakness and his dependence on his Umayyad clansmen were particularly worrisome, since a strong hand was needed to deal with the problems of the expanding Arab and Islamic empire. For one thing, the central government in Mecca had increasing difficulty asserting its authority over regional governors, some of whom, like Muawiya, had become semi-autonomous. For another, a number of tribes had begun to agitate for greater independence. Finally, some Muslims objected to the materialism that conquests and new wealth had introduced. Uthman was blamed for these challenges and dislocations, being publicly denounced for weakness and nepotism, and in 656 he was murdered by mutinous Arab troops who had come to Medina from their garrison in Egypt to present grievances.

The mutineers established Ali, Muhammad's cousin and son-in-law, as the fourth caliph, and this set the scene for a civil war that changed the course of Arab and Islamic history. Many were willing to accept Ali as caliph in 656. His kin connections to the Prophet made him an appropriate candidate in the judgment of some, and the new caliph was also highly respected for his personal qualities, including piety, loyalty, honesty, and bravery. On the other hand, some opposed his rule, both for personal reasons and because of the way it had come about, violating as it did both the laws of Islam and the customs of the community regarding succession. These opponents included the principal surviving Medinese companions of Muhammad, among them his wife Aisha, known as "Mother of the Faithful." While his critics organized themselves in Mecca, Ali moved the center of his government to Iraq, dividing the empire and leading the caliphate out of Arabia. He defeated Aisha and her associates in battle, but immediately thereafter was challenged by Muawiya from Damascus. Muawiya represented the interests of the Umayyads, who were angered not only by the murder of Uthman but also by Ali's removal of many officials the former caliph had appointed. The two rivals fought a series of battles between 657 and 659, leading first to an arbitrated settlement unfavorable to Ali, and then to additional warfare in which his forces fared poorly. Ali was murdered in 661 by a former supporter dissatisfied with his performance, and thereafter his son acknowledged the authority of the Umayyad governor in Syria. The title of caliph passed to Muawiya, whose authority was soon recognized throughout the empire.

The Age of Expansion

Muawiya established in the House of Umayyad the first of the three successive dynasties that dominated the Arab-Islamic world during the age of its expansion, the others being the Abbasids and the Fatimids. During the next ninety years, from their capital in Damascus, the Umayyads constructed a steadily expanding empire, brought an increasing number of non-Arab Muslims under their control, and laid a foundation for the emergence of a golden age of Islamic civilization. By 669 the Umayyads had built a navy and attacked Cyprus, and the following year they launched the first of a series of attacks on Constantinople. To the east, their armies drove through Persia and into Afghanistan, seizing Kabul in 664. By the early part of the eighth century, they had captured part of India. To the west, they extended earlier gains in North Africa, capturing Carthage in 698 and invading Spain in 711. Following their conquest of the Iberian Peninsula, the Umayyads entered France, where they were finally turned back at Poitiers in 738. About this time they also conquered territory to the north in Georgia and the Caucasus. Thus, Muawiya's ascendance not only marked the end of the Arabian caliphate, it initiated an era during which the Arabs exercised power on a world scale. The empire the Umayyads constructed in only three-quarters of a century was as large and powerful as any the world had seen at that time.

The character of the Umayyad Empire differed markedly from that of the Prophet's community. Although their rule brought increasing numbers of conversions to Islam, the Umayyads were not religious and challenges in the name of Islam gradually emerged. An important related consideration is that, in the fashion of pre-Islamic Mecca, ruling-class solidarity was based primarily on considerations of ethnicity and birth, with the dominant Arab elite forming "not so much a nation as a hereditary social caste which one could only enter by birth." [18] The Umayyad elite lived in luxury and enjoyed many privileges. Many of its members acquired large landholdings, sometimes receiving grants of land from the government, and they often built luxurious estates and devoted vast sums to buildings and furnishings. In the army, Arab soldiers were better paid and received a larger share of booty than non-Arab Muslim warriors. The political organizations of the empire were characteristically Arab at the outset, with a council of sheikhs and institutionalized consultation among tribal leaders. As the empire expanded, however, a permanent government administration came into existence. The institution of the caliphate also eventually became hereditary.

Conquests proceeded much more rapidly than the social and cultural integration of conquered peoples, creating conditions for instability. The new empire included Muslims whose linguistic and cultural heritage was, among others, Persian, Aramaic, Coptic, and Berber. Indeed, the most important Umayyad monuments, the Great Mosque in Damascus and the Dome of the Rock in Jerusalem, testify to the influence of non-Arab cultural forms. Only in Iraq did Arabic assume significant proportions as a language of popular usage during this period. In addition to a large and growing class of non-Arab Muslims, who were known as *mawali*, the number of Christians and Jews under Arab rule increased. Following the tradition of Muhammad, Christians and Jews were known as "People of the Book" and given protected status. Their religious revelations are accepted by Islam, being considered incomplete but nonetheless authentic, and so they enjoyed communal autonomy and religious freedom in return for a higher rate of taxation and deference to Muslim codes in certain areas.

Challenges to Umayyad rule came both from the religious and social discontent of those who opposed the dominant political order and from conflict and intrigues among the Arab tribes themselves. One religious faction that opposed the Umayyads was the Kharijites, who had initially supported Ali but then abandoned him because of his apparent willingness to negotiate with Muawiya. The Kharijites opposed the concept of a centralized state and favored the purity of Muhammad's early community. There was also criticism from men of Islamic learning who disapproved of the imperial style and attendant lack of piety of the Umayyad elite. From these men there developed a class of religious scholars, the *ulama,* whose function was to interpret Muslim law and instruct in its application, and by the eighth century the *ulama* had become outspoken opponents of Umayyad rule.

The most important opposition to Umayyad authority came from the Shia, literally the *Shiatu Ali* or "Partisans of Ali." Although Shiism later evolved into a separate religious tendency within Islam,[19] which is today centered in Iran, it began as an Arab political faction and traces its origins to Ali's earliest supporters. The Shia's strength during the Umayyad period was among the local population of Iraq, where Ali had made his capital upon leaving Arabia, and where the Shia's call for a heredity caliphate in the line of Muhammad found considerable support. The Shia appealed in particular to the discontent of the *mawali,* non-Arab Muslims who for the most part constituted a disadvantaged social class within the Umayyad state. The *mawali* were increasingly resentful of Arab exclusivism and privilege, which they regarded as incompatible with the religious ideals in whose name the caliphate claimed legitimacy.

The most serious crisis began in 743, during a period of disorder following the nineteen-year rule of Hisham. Although there had been conflict and even civil war on previous occasions, the events of this period contributed directly to the fall of the reigning dynasty. The party that led the attack on the Umayyads, and in victory succeeded them, was the Abbasids. In Iraq, Muhammad ibn Ali ibn al-Abbas, descendant of an uncle of the Prophet, declared his opposition to the Umayyads, appealed to the disadvantaged non-Arab Muslim populations of Persia, Iraq, and Syria, and forged an important alliance with both extremist and mainstream Shiite factions. Then, in 747, under the leadership of Abbas's son, Ibrahim, the Abbasids began their assault. Their general was Abu-Muslim, himself a *mawala* from Iraq, and under his command Abbasid forces defeated the Umayyads and brought their control of the empire to an end in 750. Umayyad rule survived only in Spain, where a member of the dynasty headed an independent principality centered in Cordova.

The Abbasids made Iraq the center of the empire they had seized, and during the centuries of their power a rich and synthetic Islamic civilization emerged, with the classical golden age of the Arabs and Muslims in many ways reaching its apogee. Enriched by cultural contributions from Greeks, Persians, and others, Baghdad became the sophisticated city of 1,001 Arabian nights. The first Abbasid caliph, Ibrahim's brother Abu al-Abbas, ruled between 750 and 754. The second, Mansur, another brother, reigned for twenty-one years, until 775. Mansur is regarded as the founder of the Abbasid dynasty. He built Baghdad and established it as his capital in 762.

Among the earliest acts of the Abbasids in power was a repudiation of the Shiite connection that had enabled them to defeat the Umayyads. Despite the retention of certain notions associated with Shiism, such as the hereditary basis of leadership and claims that the caliph ruled by Divine right, the Abbasids defined themselves as orthodox Sunni Muslims. The Shia, bitterly disappointed that the caliphate had not been restored to the line of Ali, retreated to the periphery of the empire and awaited the day when their fortunes might improve.

While the Abbasids' Sunni Islam represented continuity with established custom, the rise of the new dynasty brought changes that in other ways were truly revolutionary. The time of the Umayyads had been a period of conquest and extension, of external expansion. The contribution of the Abbasids, by contrast, was one of cultural, material, and intellectual development, a kind of internal expansion, as it were. Eloquent accounts of the brilliance of this period abound in the literature on Arab and Islamic history. Jacques Berque, for example, compares the classical culture of the Arabs and Muslims with that of the ancient Greeks, calling the Arab "a Greek of the Underworld." Using as a metaphor a Greek statue of the best period, which "is neither detached from nature, which it perfects, nor from man, whom it exalts," he sees in the Islamic attitude toward the world an openness and an instinct for synthesis. It possessed "a quality of wholeness . . . free from original sin, in harmony with itself, and favored by God."[20] Less metaphorical testimony about the civilization to which this attitude gave rise is offered by Gibb, who acknowledges difficulty in trying to summarize in a few words the myriad accomplishments of the Abbasid age. "The ninth and tenth centuries witnessed the climax of Islamic civilization in breadth and creative effort. Industry, commerce, architecture, and the minor arts flourished with immense vitality as Persia, Mesopotamia, Syria, and Egypt brought their contribution to the common stock."[21]

Economic development related to progress in the fields of commerce and industry was especially impressive. The Abbasids profited by their control of trade between Europe and the Far East, which gave them knowledge of both worlds and contributed greatly to the commercial development of their own lands. From ports on the Persian Gulf and the Red Sea, they traveled to East Asia and China, returning with silks, spices, tin, paper, inks, and numerous other products, some of which were for domestic consumption and some of which were re-exported. Domestic processing industries and crafts also contributed significantly to the economic development of the Abbasid empire. A wide variety of goods were produced, some of which were exported. Textiles, clothing, and carpets were probably the most important. Metalworking, too, was highly developed. Indeed, the Arabs improved upon metallurgical procedures acquired from India, becoming famous for the quality of their swords and other steel products and for the art of metal inlay.

Agriculture was also well developed in many parts of the empire. For example, there were extensive irrigation projects in some regions, with Abbasid engineers contributing to these efforts through the development of the water wheel, the water clock, and other technological innovations. Mining, too, was carried out on a significant scale, gold, silver, and copper being the most important minerals. To support all of this economic activity, institutions of banking developed in the ninth century. Large commercial purchases in the bazaar were usually effected by check, rather than in cash, and reports describe a banking system so elaborate that it was possible to draw a check in Baghdad and cash it in Morocco.[22]

Still other developments under the Abbasids included an important evolution of concepts and patterns of government. The Abbasid caliphs asserted that their rule was based on Divine right. They called themselves the deputy of God, rather than the deputy of His messenger, and accordingly transformed their regimes into absolute and full-blown monarchies. Influenced by concepts and styles of Persian origin, the life of the royal court was marked by pomp and ceremony. Access to power was no longer the privilege of men of Arab descent. On the other hand, the Arab traditions of access to rulers and of direct consultation disappeared with the appointment of officials who served as a buffer between the caliph and those who would approach him. A related development was the emergence of a professional bureaucracy, which grew significantly in size, complexity, and organizational coherence. Its members were salaried, and the norms governing their performance and responsibilities became standardized and institutionalized. This administrative network also ceased to be an instrument of Arab exclusivism and dominance. On the contrary, it was an important vehicle of social mobility for many non-Arab Muslims. Finally, later in the Abbasid period, substantial political power passed into the hands of military commanders and regional governors. Although the pomp of court life continued, the exercise of authority became more diffuse and there emerged a differentiation between the institution that presumed to continue the political mission of the Prophet and the real rulers of the Muslim empire.

The greatest achievements of the age were probably intellectual, taking place in virtually all of the arts and sciences, including the master science of law and jurisprudence.[23] In many disciplines the Arabs performed an invaluable service by preserving the scholarly texts of ancient Greece and Rome, which they translated into Arabic and Persian and collected into libraries. Yet they also carried out new studies to advance the state of knowledge. Accomplishments in the field of medicine, for example, include improvements in herbal medicines and syrups, important treatises on surgery, and the development of new diagnostic procedures. Much of this knowledge was brought together in the writings of scholars and physicians, such as Ibn Sina and al-Razi, which were studied in Europe as late as the sixteenth century.

Accomplishments in the field of mathematics were equally or even more important. Contributions included the invention of the zero and advances in algebra, geometry, and trigonometry. Moreover, these gains in mathematical reckoning made possible new developments in other fields, including geography, navigation, astronomy, and optics. The Arabs and Muslims not only mapped dozens of previously uncharted areas, their scholars and scientists determined the length of a terrestrial degree, measured latitude and longitude, developed the magnetic compass and improved the ancient astrolabe, advanced highly accurate theories about the Earth's rotation, built stellar observatories, and prepared astronomical tables that would be employed in Europe for centuries to come. Such a catalogue becomes all the more impressive when contrasted with the isolation and intellectual conservatism of Mecca little more than one hundred years earlier.[24]

Law and jurisprudence are the most fundamental of all the Muslim sciences; the necessity of studying the law, and the ardor with which this obligation is carried out, are probably matched among major religions only by Judaism.[25] The development and study of Islamic law began following the death of the Prophet and concentrated initially on codification, which was largely completed during the Umayyad period. According to tradition, the Quran had to be compiled from "scraps of parchment and leather, tablets of stone, ribs of palm branches, camels' shoulder-blades and ribs, pieces of board and the breasts of men."[26] Written records, moreover, were in Arabic's defective early script, one of whose limitations was the absence of vowels. Thus, early legal scholarship had as its central preoccupations the authentication of records said to contain chapters and verses of the Quran, the pursuit of agreement as to the precise structure of these passages, and, finally, their arrangement into the Quran as we know it today. The Muslim holy book that resulted from this process has 114 chapters, called *suras*, and about 6,000 verses.

Although the Quran, considered the word of God, is both the supreme guide to the behavior of Muslims and the constitution of the *umma*, the community of believers, orthodox Muslims also recognize a second essential component of Islamic law. This is the *Sunna*, which sets down the declarations, customs, and practices of Muhammad and was initially preserved not in written form but through narratives, called *hadiths* (literally tales), which are accounts of the Prophet's sayings and deeds and of the behavior of his community at Medina. In matters where behavior is not clearly prescribed by the Quran, the *Sunna* and *hadiths* are an authoritative guide. Though not the literal word of God, orthodox Muslims consider the *Sunna* holy because it is founded on the life of the Almighty's chosen messenger, and they accordingly accept it as unalterable law, second in authority only to the Quran. The orthodox majority are thus called Sunnis, whereas the minority Shiite wing of Islam incorporates a rejection of the *Sunna* into its denial of the actions of the community following Muhammad's death.

Given both the existence of several hundred thousand *hadiths* which pretended authenticity and the oral foundation on which they all rested, the fashioning of accepted and standardized versions of the *Sunna* preoccupied legal scholars well into the Abbasid period. Each *hadith* had to be evaluated, and this was carried out, in part, by identifying and assessing the veracity of every link in the chain of communication by which a narrative record had been transmitted since the time of the Prophet. The work initially involved constructing biographical dictionaries of the authorities from whose testimony *hadith*s derived and then, after assessing the reliability of each, classifying *hadith*s in terms of their "soundness." Agreement was reached through a process known as *ijma*, literally "consensus," wherein individual judgments and opinions were retained or discarded as a function of their ability to obtain the concurrence of the *ulama*, the community's legal scholars. The *Sunna* thus took the form of collections of those *hadith*s judged to be valid, each of which was preceded by an enumeration of its transmitting authorities, and such a corpus is often referred to simply as "the *Hadith*." By the third Islamic century, corresponding to the ninth century C.E., six collections of *hadith*s had acquired such prominence that they became universally accepted in Sunni Islam, gradually being looked upon as binding and being referred to as "The Six Canonical *Hadith* Works."[27] The works of al-Bukhari and Muslim, who died in 870 and 875 respectively, are considered to be the most "sound" among them. Al-Bukhari, for example, quotes about 7,300 *hadith*s, after having evaluated about 200,000 for possible inclusion and rejecting thousands more without review.

Islamic law, composed of the Quran and the *Sunna*, is known as the *Sharia*, literally the "straight path" in which men should walk to find favor in God's eyes and reach paradise. The Quran and the *Sunna* are the only sources of Muslim law, moreover; legislation introduced by men is without legitimacy in Islamic political theory and, accordingly, there were no legislative institutions either in the Prophet's community or in the empires of succeeding dynasties. But while the *Sharia* is considered complete and immutable, excluding the exercise of all human judgment when its commands and prohibitions are unambiguous, the ability of men and women to comprehend the law's Divine wisdom is limited and guidance is sometimes required in the matter of its application. As a result, early labors devoted to codifying the law were accompanied by a concern on the part of the community for its proper interpretation. This concern, present from the earliest days, intensified as the Muslim community evolved into an empire, and as Muslims were required to pursue the path of God in circumstances not known at the time of the Prophet.

As noted earlier, the process of interpretation is known as *ijtihad*, a term which expresses the religious dimension of the age of Arab and Islamic expansion. Opinions regarding the proper interpretation of the Quran and the *Sunna* in particular circumstances were advanced by individual scholars possessing sufficient intellect and training, and these opinions in turn were evaluated, again, with respect to their ability to generate a consensus among the *ulama*. Jurists and theologians of the eighth and ninth centuries worked out these interpretations in matters of both ritual and doctrine, and early in the tenth century the first collection and unified critical analysis of comments in explanation of the law was published by al-Tabari. Al-Tabari's opus is a vast work of thirty volumes, a landmark in its day which laid a foundation for the more specialized commentaries of later scholars.[28]

Acceptance of the principle of *ijtihad* limited any potential conflict between religious duty on the one hand and social and intellectual development on the other. Indeed, some would argue that the former was an active stimulus to the latter, in that it motivated Muslims to expand the scope and complexity of their society in order that they might come to know more fully the universal truths lying beneath their law's formal text. This position was accepted by the *ulama* during the first centuries of Islam, and it was also given powerful expression by leading Muslim scholars of a later age, such as Ibn Taymiyya and Ibn Khaldoun, who lived in the fourteenth century. *Ijtihad* thus embodies the idea that it is both permissible and necessary to approach the law not in a spirit of slavish devotion and with a suspension of the intellect but rather with an attitude that study is necessary in order that the law's unceasing contribution to human welfare might be grasped. It is this historically legitimized perspective that permits Arabs and Muslims of our own age to assert with accuracy that "Islam exalts reason and freedom, encourages progress and rejects all intermediaries between God and man."[29] This exaltation and encouragement contributed mightily to the growth of Islamic civilization during the age of expansion, and to its numerous accomplishments.

The Age of Decline

Although there is no clear point of demarcation between the period of expansion and the period of decline, and although the brilliance of classical Arab and Islamic civilization continued for a time, destructive changes beginning in the tenth century brought movement toward a new era in the political and intellectual history of the Arab world. First, the lingering Sunni-Shia quarrel about the devolution of the caliphate assumed new vigor and led to the division of the *umma*. Second, and most important according to some, acceptance of the principle of *ijtihad* declined, undermining the liberal spirit of the preceding centuries. Some scholars suggest that the ethic of the new age is summed up by the term *taqlid*, which means "imitation" or "devout conformism" and is usually contrasted with the liberal exercise of reason encouraged by *ijtihad*. The narrowed horizons of the middle Arab centuries are reflected in this conformist mentality, writes one authority: the dreadful *taqlid*, "the enemy of life," crushed the spirit of inquiry and outreach that had previously been dominant.[30] According to another, who compares the Arab world of this period to Europe during the Dark Ages, "scholars devoted themselves to the task of preserving the pale glow of a great civilization with little hope of rekindling its fire or adding to the former blaze, never daring to experiment or tamper for fear of snuffing out what little remained."[31]

In the tenth century, the dominance of the overextended Abbasids was supplanted by that of the Fatimids, Shia who traced their line through the Prophet's daughter, Fatima, and who had departed from the mainstream of Arab life after the Abbasids came to power. The Shiite movement experienced internal divisions during the eighth century, but its principal wing (known also as the Ismailis) took control of Yemen late in the ninth century and then installed itself in Tunisia in 909, the year from which the Fatimid dynasty dates its rule. Claiming to have reestablished the "true caliphate," the Fatimids began to dismember the vast but increasingly decentralized Abbasid empire, taking control of the regional and provincial capitals that had by this time become largely autonomous. The Fatimids captured Egypt and part of western Arabia within a few years, and in 969 they founded the modern city of Cairo and made it their capital. Conquests continued as Palestine and Syria also fell under the control of the Fatimid caliph, whom Shia called "the Imam." Baghdad remained independent and survived as the center of Abbasid rule, but what was preserved of the Abbasid empire was in financial and political disarray by the middle of the century.

The Fatimids did not replace the Abbasids, as the latter had themselves replaced the Umayyads, but the lands of Islam were now divided and fragmented. The tenth century not only saw rival caliphs in Cairo and Baghdad, moreover, in the Fatimid and Abbasid houses respectively, it also witnessed the proclamation of a third caliphate by remnants of the Umayyad dynasty ruling Spain and part of North Africa from their capital in Cordova. Each one of the three principal dynasties of the classical Arab world thus controlled a portion of what had previously been a unified empire. Each also claimed to be the true representative of the political mission of the Prophet, asserting the legitimacy of its own caliph as the proper leader of the *umma*. The result, of course, was that the political unity of the Muslim world came to an end, and the future of the institution which preserved its link to the community governed by the Prophet was placed in doubt.

Though less impressive than under Abbasid rule, intellectual life and material culture were nonetheless rich and varied under the Fatimids. The venerable al-Azhar Mosque University, the oldest university in the world and still the most prestigious center of Islamic higher learning, was founded in Cairo in 972, for example. More generally, the light of Islamic scholarship for a time continued to burn bright, perhaps because, as one historian suggests, the deterioration of a civilization does not occur in a uniform manner and, just as in a diseased human body, it may actually be masked temporarily by an increased stimulation of certain functions.[32] Whereas Abbasid scholarship had been centered in the court of the caliph in Baghdad, dependent largely on the support of a single sovereign, intellectual inquiry was now supported and actively pursued in a number of capitals, including several under Fatimid rule. Fatimid rule was also accompanied by commercial and industrial development, which brought considerable prosperity, especially to Egypt. For example, the Fatimids presided over a flourishing trade with both Europe and India, and their ships and merchants sailed regularly throughout the Mediterranean Sea. Indeed their fleets dominated trade in the eastern Mediterranean, and their principal ports, Alexandria and Tripoli on the Syrian coast, became maritime centers of world importance. In addition to these intellectual and economic accomplishments associated with Fatimid rule, the brilliance of the Islamic golden age for a time continued in the Umayyad capital of Cordova. With a population of half a million, Cordova was in many respects the most sophisticated city of Europe. Its schools remained preeminent in the study of medicine, mathematics, philosophy, poetry, and music, and among its most distinctive creations were its art and architecture, which fused Arab and Byzantine models and added to these its own originality.

During the lengthy reign of Caliph Mustansir, from 1036 to 1094, the Fatimid empire first reached the zenith of its power and then unraveled swiftly during the second half of the eleventh century. Prior to their decline, the Fatimids controlled all of North Africa, Sicily, Egypt, Palestine, Syria, and western Arabia. Their forces even succeeded in capturing Baghdad in the middle of the century, proclaiming the authority of the Fatimid caliph from the Abbasid capital. They were driven out within a year, however, bringing an end to their momentary expansion. Further, in 1049 their governors in Tunisia, the Zirids, declared independence from Cairo and began to name the caliph of Baghdad in official prayers, while an independent Berber kingdom, the Almoravids, established itself in Morocco in 1061 and from Marrakesh ruled an empire stretching from Senegal into Spain. Control of Palestine and Syria fell out of Fatimid hands as well after 1070. Thus, by the end of the century, not only was the Islamic world divided among rival dynasties, but the most powerful of these, the Fatimids, had been largely dismembered.

This political division and fragmentation were accompanied by important normative changes, the most significant, as noted, being a growing inclination among Muslim scholars and theologians to regard the "gate of *ijtihad*" as closed. By the end of the third Islamic century, interpretations of law which were widely shared by the Muslim community's religious leaders had come to be regarded as immutable and Divinely inspired, similar to the original sources from which they were drawn. In the extreme, the consensus of the community, *ijma*, was elevated into a theory of infallibility; as expressed by one scholar, it was agreed, reflexively, that "what the *umma* as a whole accepted and acted on represented a valid consensus of what God intended."[33] Thus, with increasing agreement that continued tolerance of individual interpretation could not be reconciled with respect for the infallible understanding that the *ulama* had fashioned, and with the points of law on which consensus had not yet been reached rapidly diminishing in number and salience, no scholar, however eminent, could any longer qualify as a *mujtahid*, an authoritative interpreter of the law.[34] As a result, inquiry and interpretation were now discouraged rather than approved. Jurists were increasingly bound by the principle of *taqlid*, the call to reject innovation and independent inquiry and instead to "imitate" the doctrines of one's predecessors. To advance any novel interpretation of the text of the law was to be guilty of "innovation," which was tantamount to heresy.[35]

Muslim theology underwent something of a crisis in this environment. By the eleventh century, religious opposition in the form of Islamic mysticism emerged in response to the dry and narrow orthodoxy of the *ulama*. Known as *sufis*, for the ascetic wool (*suf*) garments they frequently wore, Islamic mystics demanded a personal and emotional dimension to their religious experience and claimed to be starved by the detachment of orthodox jurists. The latter, they insisted, saw only the letter of the law and preoccupied themselves with minutiae. Sufism offered a path to religious meaning and fulfillment that was seized by a growing number of men of Islamic learning, the most famous of whom is al-Ghazali, an eleventh-century scholar who remains a towering figure in the literary and theological history of Islam. Although a highly respected professor of religious sciences in Baghdad at the age of thirty-three, this sensitive and intelligent tradition-minded Muslim was unsettled by the conservative world in which he found himself. Searching for meaning not provided by religious orthodoxy, he studied and mastered the natural sciences and philosophies of his day. He deemed them inadequate, too, however, and ultimately found the answer to his search for fulfillment in a "science of the heart" rather than learning of the mind.[36] One of his works, "The Renaissance of Religious Sciences," set out to harmonize theology and mysticism and became, according to one scholar, the most widely quoted Islamic text after the Quran and the classical *hadith* collections.[37]

The changing normative climate not only imposed its rigidity on religious thought and matters of legal interpretation, it undermined as well the intellectual energy and creativity of Islamic civilization more generally. On the one hand, the *ulama* increasingly adopted a posture of hostility toward the secular sciences, which they feared might challenge both the central position of religion and their own privileged status. On the other hand, and more broadly, the new ethos discouraged personal reasoning of any kind and promoted an approach to all learning in which originality and creativity were highly suspect. Knowledge was viewed as a fixed quantity, and even institutions of higher learning were expected to respect and preserve its established boundaries. For all but a few, instruction was restricted to a narrow range of traditional subjects that were learned by rote and recited endlessly, usually without discussion or analytical insight, with the result that philosophy and rationalism were "as good as dead."[38]

The intellectual narrowness of the age was also reflected in an absence of interest in foreign cultures and ideas. In contrast to the classical period, when the Arabs had freely incorporated contributions from other cultures, interest in foreign civilizations was now minimal. Attitudes toward Europe, which was slowly moving out of its own dark age toward an eventual renaissance, were particularly revealing in this respect. Bernard Lewis reports that Europe appeared as "the outer darkness of barbarism from which the sunlit world of Islam had little to fear and less to learn." [39] He quotes an eleventh-century judge to the effect that the people who inhabit the north "lack keenness of understanding and clarity of intelligence, and are overcome by ignorance and foolishness, blindness and stupidity."

Juxtaposed to the Arab world's intellectual stagnation was its loss of political independence. The march of history brought new invaders and conquerors, with the result that political authority passed out of Arab hands. As noted, Umayyad Spain and Fatimid North Africa fell under the control of successive Berber empires during the eleventh and twelfth centuries, first the Almoravids and then the Almohads. In the Arab East, Fatimid and Abbasid remnants also came under attack. The Seljuk Turks, a Sunni Muslim tribe of central Asian origin, captured Baghdad in 1055. Thereafter, they scored victories against the Byzantines and the Fatimids farther to the west, wresting Syria and Palestine from the latter between 1070 and 1080. The Seljuk kingdom came apart within a few years, however, giving rise to a period of disorder that lasted until Egypt and the Fertile Crescent fell under the control of a Kurdish officer named Salah al-Din al-Ayyubi (known in the West as Saladin). Saladin's invasion sealed the fate of the decaying Fatimid empire: its caliph was deposed in 1171 and it was ordered that henceforth the Abbasid caliph in Baghdad be named in the prayers recited in Cairo mosques. Although the Abbasid caliph by now had neither political power nor autonomy, this is an important event that brought to an end the period of multiple pretenders to the caliphate. It also brought the return of Egypt's rulers to the world of Sunni Islam.

Between the thirteenth and fifteenth centuries, the Arab East was ruled by the Mamluks and the Mongols. The Ayyubi state established by Saladin was displaced in the middle of the former century by the Mamluks, at the outset a slave caste of largely Turkish (and sometimes Mongol or Circassian) origin, which was first brought to Egypt to serve as the foundation of a praetorian army. The Mamluk Sultanate ruled Egypt, Palestine, and Syria as an independent state for the next 250 years, bringing a measure of order and stability and permitting Egypt to displace Iraq as the fulcrum of the Arabic-speaking world. On the other hand, the Mamluks were a closed class of alien governors. Turkish or Circassian remained the language of the ruling class, some of whose members could barely speak Arabic.

At about the time the Mamluks were establishing themselves in Egypt and the Fertile Crescent, territories farther to the east were being overrun by the Mongols who, under Hulagu Khan, the grandson of Genghis Khan (1155–1227), captured and sacked Baghdad in 1258. The Mongol armies continued westward to Palestine, where they were stopped by the Mamluks in the battle of Ain Julut in 1260. Although they later embraced Islam in substantial numbers, the Mongol invaders, in contrast to the Seljuks, were not Muslims. They were heathens with no interest in the religion of those they conquered and accordingly, upon taking Baghdad, they killed the reigning caliph and abolished the Abbasid caliphate. The caliphate received a restoration of sorts a few years later, when the Mamluks in Egypt invited a member of the Abbasid family to Cairo and permitted him to reside in the royal court with the title of caliph. Nevertheless, the destruction of this historic institution in 1258 symbolized the darkness and disorder of the age to many Arabs. Even though the *umma* was divided and the caliphate had long since lost any real power, it had continued to symbolize both the sense of community shared by all Muslims and the historic role of the Arabs in carrying forward the Prophet's political mission.

The extensive damage done by the Mongol invasion was physical as well as symbolic. The invaders not only destroyed the proud Abbasid capital, they also massacred many of its inhabitants. A similar fate befell other urban centers, including the Syrian city of Aleppo, for example. An American historian describes the situation following the sack of Baghdad in a manner that conveys much of the general chaos and destruction of the middle centuries of Arab history:

> Further devastation, pestilence, and flood followed the sack. . . . The remnant of the city population shrank within its walls. The peasants tried desperately to avoid contact with all outside their villages. Only the bedouin, who had already withdrawn from the empire, remained virtually untouched. The dreary chronicle of this period would net us little. Men clung to niches as we have imagined some might in the aftermath of nuclear war, desperately trying to survive, not daring to hope to live as they or their fathers had in former times.[40]

In the sixteenth century, the Ottoman Turks took control of most of the Arab world, integrating the Arab provinces into their expanding and increasingly powerful empire and holding these possessions until the dawn of a new era in the political history of the Arabs. The Ottomans toppled the Mamluk state in 1517, adding Egypt, Palestine, and Syria to their domains. They also at this time removed to their capital, Constantinople, the puppet Abbasid caliphate that had been established by the Mamluks, symbolizing the passing of power not only from Arab hands but from the Arab world itself. Later Ottoman sultans asserted that the authority of the caliphate had passed to them, and they sought to employ the connection to legitimize pan-Islamic policies. In any event, the institution remained in Constantinople until 1924, when it was abolished by the founders of the Turkish republic. Shortly after the fall of the Mamluks, the sherif of Mecca surrendered, placing western Arabia under Ottoman sovereignty and giving the

Turks control of the holy cities of Mecca and Medina. A few years later, the Ottomans established themselves in Libya and Algeria in the west and Iraq in the east, and in 1574, after a prolonged struggle with Spain and the indigenous Hafsid dynasty, they also secured control of Tunisia. Finally, in 1639, Iraq, which had broken away, was recaptured from the Persians, bringing almost all the Arab world under Turkish control. Only Morocco, the deserts of Arabia, and Yemen, which gained independence in 1633 after sixty-five years of Ottoman rule, remained outside the empire ruled from Constantinople. Although many provinces eventually gained considerable autonomy, local ruling dynasties evolved from regimes installed by the Ottomans and were justifiably regarded as alien by the Arabic-speaking masses.

The Arab sense of history shaped by this chronology is one of cycles, with a long period of weakness and decline made all the more repugnant by its contrast to the golden age preceding it. Both the brilliance of the former epoch and the darkness of the latter are sometimes exaggerated. The age of expansion knew violence and despotism, as well as political and intellectual sophistication. The period that came after brought continuing advances in selected areas and, under the Ottomans, was characterized by power and accomplishment for Islam if not the Arabs. Nevertheless, the difference in the central tendency of each age is clear and dramatic. However strong might be the tendency in retrospect to embellish its grandeur, that the classical Arab age was one of greatness is beyond dispute. Alternatively, the middle centuries, the era of Arab decline, brought a profound religious, moral, and political crisis. Relegated to the periphery of world history for the first time since the rise of Islam, the Arab world experienced what the nineteenth-century modernist Muhammad Ali called the "Sleep of Ages." By this time, according to one analyst, "the rot of seven centuries had finally eaten its way to the heart and soul of the Arab peoples."[41] Thus, looking back over their history, Arabs often see not only a period of greatness but centuries of separation between that period and their present circumstances.

This Arab psychological and historical perspective has been emphasized by many scholars. As expressed by one leading historian, the Arabs are for the most part uninterested in and unaware of Islamic accomplishments after the Arab downfall. Accordingly, "the Arab sense of bygone splendor is superb. One cannot begin to understand the modern Arab if one lacks a perceptive feeling of this."[42]

The Arab Reawakening and Its Challenges

The historical era in which the Arab world currently finds itself embedded is described by the Arabs themselves as one of renaissance, or *nahda*. This is the fourth and final period in the history of the Arabs, bringing up to the present a story that began during the pre-Islamic era of *jahiliyya* and thereafter traced its evolution first through a golden age of political expansion and intellectual brilliance and then through a darker period marked by fragmentation, constriction, and narrowness. The Arab renaissance began at the end of the eighteenth century and assumed meaningful proportions over the course of the nineteenth century, being driven forward by the introduction, first in Egypt and then elsewhere, of programs of reform and development. During much of this period, the Arab world was responding not only to a growing awareness of its own deficiencies but to political and intellectual challenges emanating from Europe. For this reason, its efforts at reform and development are sometimes characterized as "defensive modernization." Finally, for the most part following World War II, the Arabs regained the independence that had been lost for centuries and, free from external control, undertook to manage the evolution of their self-governing states with a view toward accelerating their cultural renaissance and enhancing their material well-being.

The dawning of the modern era, which in the Arab world may be dated from Napoleon's invasion of Egypt in 1798, took the Arabs largely by surprise. Although there had been commercial connections of reasonable proportions between a number of European countries and Arab ports on the Mediterranean, the Arabs at this time knew little of European society, and relations between the two worlds were limited and superficial. Indeed, with the development of a New World in the Americas and the use of sea routes for trade with the Orient, Europe had for a long time found little reason to direct its interests and energies toward the Arab Middle East. The Ottoman Empire's early victories over Europe also served to insulate the Arab world from European influences. Most Arabs were thus unaware that profound changes had taken place in France, Britain, and elsewhere, and the result was accordingly one of shock and confusion when Napoleon's forces easily defeated the troops sent to repel them and thereby revealed a powerful and sophisticated West to the Egyptians and other Arabs.

The French invasion of Egypt was the first direct military confrontation between Arabs and Europeans since the days of the Crusades and, in the words of Gibb, it "tore aside the veil of apathy which had cut the Arabs off from the new life of Europe and gave the deathblow to medievalism."[43] As expressed by one Arab leader, the Egyptians met Napoleon's forces with little more than a naive belief that "their country belonged to the 'Commander of the Faithful' and was consequently inviolable."[44] Egypt's Turko-Mamluk governors greeted news of the French arrival with disdain, saying, "Let all the Franks come, and we shall crush them beneath our horses' hooves."[45] The Egyptians were thus completely perplexed when Bonaparte's army landed without difficulty and quickly suppressed all efforts at resistance. "The world seemed upside down to the pious Muslims of the day."[46]

Napoleon's occupation of Egypt lasted only three years, but it provided a stimulus for the emergence of a modernist movement determined to end what it regarded as the country's weakness and stagnation, thus making Egypt the center of Arab efforts to bring about a political and cultural renaissance. The founder of this modernist movement was Muhammad Ali, an Ottoman soldier of Macedonian origin who seized control and made himself governor of Egypt in 1805. After clearing the way for reform by removing the ruling class and seizing its extensive landholdings, Muhammad Ali devoted his energies to a broad program of development and change.[47] Not all of Muhammad Ali's innovations were successful, of course. Moreover, corruption was widespread; many state officials were more concerned about themselves than about the welfare of the country. Nevertheless, a new dynamism and sense of purpose were introduced into Egypt, based on a recognition of the weakness of Arab and Islamic society and with efforts at development explicitly guided by the model of modern Europe. Even more important, these efforts succeeded in bringing about a transformation of major proportions. Assessing the accomplishments of Muhammad Ali and his successors less than three-quarters of a century later, in 1876, a British journalist in Alexandria wrote that "Egypt is a marvelous instance of progress. She has advanced as much in seventy years as many other countries have done in five hundred."[48]

Modernization was sought in many fields, including military affairs, government, agriculture, and industry. Recognizing that Europe's power in the first instance manifested itself in superior military ability, Muhammad Ali engaged French advisors and, with their assistance, constructed an army and a navy that were capable of securing Egypt's virtual independence from Turkey. Further, seeking to make Egypt as self-sufficient as possible, he built factories to produce guns, munitions, uniforms, and other necessary goods. Reforms in other areas included the rationalization of government administration. One important development was the creation of a large and well-organized state bureaucracy, staffed by literate civil servants. Another was a restructuring of the system of taxation, with peasants now paying taxes directly to the government rather than through landlords. The modernization of agriculture was yet another of Muhammad Ali's objectives, and accomplishments in this area included the extension and improvement of irrigation and the introduction of new crops, most notably cotton. There was also an important program of land reform; holdings of the former elite were taken over and subdivided among the peasants, who then produced crops directly for the government. Finally, industrial development was reflected in the construction of a modern transportation system, the creation of state-run facilities for the production of textiles and other goods, and a program whereby thousands of workers received government wages for their labor in small workshops or at home.[49]

The most important developments of the period were in the field of education. While Egypt's concern for modern education began as a desire to instruct army officers in the military sciences of Europe, Muhammad Ali soon realized that Europe's strength did not lie principally in its military might or even in its technology; it was the product, above all, of the scientific ideas and organizational concepts upon which these were based. New educational institutions, which incorporated modern subjects and foreign languages into their curricula, were thus established alongside the country's traditional Quranic schools and mosque universities. By 1840 there were approximately fifty primary schools of this sort scattered throughout the country, as well as large preparatory schools in both Cairo and Alexandria. In addition, there were a number of specialized postprimary schools, devoted to such military fields as artillery and cavalry and to practical fields of a nonmilitary nature, including veterinary science, medicine, translation, and civil administration. The students in all of these schools, who soon numbered more than 10,000, were educated entirely at government expense and upon graduation were immediately taken into government service. Europeans, Italians at first and then mostly Frenchmen, were employed as instructors in Muhammad Ali's new schools, although Egyptians were later incorporated into their ranks as well.

Another important dimension of the investment in modern education was the organization of student missions, which were sent to Europe for advanced training in specialized technical fields. The first such mission was sent in 1813. It contained fifteen students who received government scholarships to study military subjects. By the time of Muhammad Ali's death, in 1848, many missions had been sent abroad, principally to France but also to Italy and England. There were also instances of workers who visited European factories to acquire knowledge of modern industrial techniques.[50] Upon returning to Egypt, students were required to translate the texts they had used abroad into Turkish or Arabic. Indeed, it is reported that Muhammad Ali once cut a geography book into three sections, in order that three individuals might participate in its translation and thereby complete the work more quickly. At first, most of the students who received a modern education were either of Turkish origin or Christians from the Levant. The number of Egyptians benefiting from the investment in education increased steadily, however, and there soon emerged a class of indigenous professionals and intellectuals.

Although Egypt was by far the most important center of modernization in the Arab world during the nineteenth century, it was by no means the only country experiencing significant change. There were important local initiatives in several other Arab lands. In addition, an extensive program of reform was undertaken in Turkey, laying a foundation for the diffusion of modernist currents to a number of Arab provinces within the Ottoman Empire. Known collectively as *Tanzimat*, these reforms included sweeping internal political reorganization, the creation of a modern bureaucracy, reorganization of the military, and the establishment of new schools and overseas study missions.

One Arab country where reforms of considerable magnitude were carried out was Tunisia. Although nominally subservient to the authority of the Ottoman sultan, nineteenth-century Tunisia was largely autonomous under the rule of its own monarchical dynasty, the Husaynids. Moreover, despite their Turkish origins, most of the ruling families had intermarried with the local population, and Arabic was by this time the language of the political class.[51] The local monarch was called the *bey*, and it is during the reign of Ahmed Bey, from 1837 to 1855, that extensive efforts at modernization were undertaken. Slavery was abolished, the system of taxation was revised, the military establishment was overhauled and ancillary industries were created, the civil service was restructured, and a state bank was established. In addition, and perhaps most important, there were major innovations in the field of education. Particularly notable was the creation in 1840 of the Bardo Polytechnic School. Designed to train officers for the new Tunisian army, the Bardo school reflected the same concern for education and military modernization that existed in Egypt. With its direction entrusted to Europeans, the school offered mathematics taught by an Italian, military sciences taught by English and French instructors, and the French and Italian languages. The school also provided for the study of Arabic and the Muslim religion.[52]

Another center of change was Syria, where the stimulus for modernization came from two sources. First, there were indigenous Christians who displayed an interest in the new world of Europe, some based on contact with European Catholic missionaries going back to the eighteenth century or earlier. Modern schools were established in many Christian communities, especially in the southwestern coastal region in the area of present-day Lebanon. Moreover, these schools not only taught secular subjects, they also frequently offered instruction in classical Arabic, a language whose use at the time was otherwise largely confined to Muslim religious leaders.

The penetration of Egyptian influences was a second stimulus to change. Muhammad Ali's army invaded Syria in 1831, conquering the country easily and instituting nearly a decade of Egyptian rule. Although the Egyptians were forced out in 1841, after the Turks improved their military fortunes by securing British assistance, Muhammad Ali's governors ruled long enough to introduce important changes and to expand existing modernist currents. The administration of Syria was based on the same principles of centralization and planning that were followed in Egypt. The Egyptians also placed emphasis on religious equality, which enabled the class of educated Christians to expand its activities. Finally, and most important, Egyptian rule helped to "open up" Syria to more direct European influences. As explained by one scholar, "A change in tastes and technology distinguished the Egyptian period, as old ways, old tools and old weapons were quickly judged to be outmoded. . . . The flood gates, once opened by the Egyptians, were never again closed. . . . The Levant began to be tied to the world market on a massive scale and to acquire a taste for the goods and disquieting new ideas of the West."[53]

Often described as "defensive modernization," planned programs of change in Egypt and elsewhere did not seek to remake Arab and Islamic society in the image of Europe but, instead, to borrow from the West only those military and economic principles which were necessary for the Arab world to end its decline and move toward a restoration of its former greatness. Modernists such as Muhammad Ali, Ahmed Bey, and others had no desire to modify the moral or cultural content of Arab and Islamic civilization. Indeed, they continued to believe this civilization superior to that of Europe, and they accordingly sought to preside not over its demise but rather over its renaissance. This civilization, in their view, should once again be a normative order of world significance, and for this reason they were concerned that the borrowing of European ideas be limited to the domains of science, technology, and administration.

Early modernists warned that if the inner content as well as the outer forms of European society were imported, the moral foundations of Arab and Islamic civilization would be undermined, and modernization would thus have failed as a strategy for rejuvenating the Arab world and its culture. The cure, in effect, would have proved more damaging than the disease. Among the dangers about which they expressed concern were diminished piety, a breakdown in the respect for law, increased corruption, the disruption of family life and parental authority, and an end to modesty in the behavior of women. Further, some saw practical as well as moral dangers, predicting that unrestricted cultural borrowing would disturb the natural and God-given order, sap the will and coherence of Arab society, and create such confusion that the Arabs would actually be weaker than before the introduction of modernist programs. It is for this reason, for example, that student missions sent to Europe were kept under strict control and often accompanied by a spiritual guardian. On at least one occasion, Muhammad Ali specifically denied permission to a group of students seeking to make a tour of France in order to learn about French life at first hand.[54] These restrictions were a reflection of the modernists' concern with revitalizing the Arab world's classical civilization, which of course required the preservation of its moral and cultural integrity.

The motivation for defensive modernization lay not only in a desire to restore the power and vitality of the Arab world but, in addition, in an effort to prepare for a political challenge from Europe that was beginning to take shape. As a result of Napoleon's conquest of Egypt, as well their subsequent dealings with France and other European countries, the Arabs recognized that their weakness made them highly vulnerable to foreign domination. Further, their concern intensified as the imperial designs of France, Britain, and several other European states became increasingly clear during the first half of the nineteenth century. It is perhaps ironic that the Arab world sought to discover and import the sources of Europe's strength in part to be able to defend itself against European power. Nevertheless, as with the notion of selective borrowing, this irony illustrates the ambiguous attitude toward Europe that underlay the notion of defensive modernization in the Arab world.

The intention of France and Britain to exercise authority over parts of the Arab world was unmistakable by the 1830s. France invaded Algeria in 1830, conducting military campaigns against those who resisted its occupation and initiating 132 years of colonial rule. The British occupied Aden in 1839, and the authority of the British consul in Syria had come to rival that of the Ottoman governor by the middle of the century. In 1860–1861, a French military invasion of Syria led to the creation of an autonomous Lebanon, which after 1864 was administered by a Christian governor who could be appointed only with the approval of the European powers.

Another important dimension of contemporary European imperialism is the capitulation agreements the Ottoman sultan was forced to accept in Egypt and other parts of the empire. These "capitulations" placed European residents outside the jurisdiction of local courts. Even in crimes against the native population, Europeans possessed complete immunity from the application of local law, a situation which was intolerable to the Arab masses and their leaders.[55] Moreover, when local officials in some cases tried to hold foreign nationals accountable for crimes they had committed, their challenge to the privileged status of Europeans residing in the Arab world, and thereby to the extension of European authority, paved the way for deeper European penetration.

The scope and intensity of efforts associated with defensive modernization were particularly evident in Egypt. Muhammad Ali's successors bore the title of *khedive*, and among the most important of these were his son Said, who governed from 1854 to 1863, and his grandson Ismail, who was *khedive* from 1863 to 1879. Indicative of the kinds of development projects implemented under Said and Ismail was construction of the Cairo-Alexandria railroad, which began in 1851 and was completed in 1857. The level of activity under Ismail was particularly feverish. To develop a modern network of transportation and communications, the Egyptian government constructed more than 900 miles of railroads, 5,000 miles of telegraph, 430 bridges, and the harbor of Alexandria. In addition, it reclaimed over a million acres of land, largely by constructing 8,000 miles of irrigation canals, and built numerous factories and textile mills. The investment in education was equally impressive. For example, the number of government primary schools grew from 185 to 4,685 during Ismail's reign, and overseas educational missions resumed after a hiatus of several years. Yet another accomplishment was the rapid expansion of Egypt's exports, especially during Ismail's early years when the country benefited from a demand for cotton created by the American Civil War. In still other areas, Egypt created a national library and museum, a representative assembly, and a newspaper press.

The most massive project of the period was the construction of the Suez Canal, which restored Egypt to a central position in trade between Europe and the Far East. The canal was the scheme of Ferdinand de Lesseps, a French engineer who, in 1854, secured from Said a concession to build a waterway linking the Mediterranean and the Red Sea. The Egyptian government purchased half the stock in the investment company formed by de Lesseps and also provided nearly 20,000 men to do the digging, in return for which it was to receive 15 percent of the profits from the canal's operation. After delays and financial problems, the canal was completed in 1869, and Ismail celebrated its opening with elaborate ceremonies attended by European heads of state and other foreign dignitaries. Ismail spent lavishly to entertain his guests, using the occasion to show off the fruits of his development efforts and to secure European recognition of his country's virtual independence from Turkey.

Although none could match the accomplishments of Egypt, there were efforts at modernization in several other Arab countries during the second half of the nineteenth century. The case of Tunisia provides a good illustration, particularly during the reign of Khayr al-Din Pasha, premier from 1873 to 1877 under Ahmed Bey's successor. Under Khayr al-Din's leadership, the administration of justice was reorganized, development projects were implemented, taxation procedures were revised, and land reform was carried out. Achievements in the field of education were also impressive. Indeed, in Khayr al-Din's view, these were his government's most important achievements.[56] New primary schools were built and existing ones enlarged, and a modern secondary school, Sadiki College, was established on the model of European lycées.

The Tunisian case also provides another illustration of the logic of defensive modernization. Khayr al-Din's philosophy, set out in a handbook of practical reforms for Muslim states, was similar to that of Muhammad Ali and is summarized as follows by one historian: "Islam is valid, yet Muslims today are weak; Western civilization, although certainly less valid, appears stronger; to right the balance, Muslims must return to their true path, to the fundamentals of their religion, and must at the same time learn the technical skills that have given Western civilization its temporary superiority."[57] This point of view is also clearly reflected in the decree establishing Sadiki College, the most important of Khayr al-Din's contributions to education. The declared purpose of the school was to teach "the Quran, writing and useful knowledge, i.e., juridical sciences, foreign languages, and the rational sciences that might be of use to Muslims, being at the same time not contrary to the faith." In addition, "professors must inculcate in the students a love of the faith by showing them its beauties and excellence. . . . "[58]

Two interrelated dilemmas associated with defensive modernization became increasingly clear as the nineteenth century unfolded. The first dilemma was intellectual and moral in character. Specifically, selective borrowing from Europe was proving much more difficult to operationalize than to define; imported ideas about science, technology, and administration could not be readily separated

from the more general social and cultural norms of the societies where they prevailed, and programs of reform and development were thus bringing the penetration of a much broader range of foreign values than had originally been desired.
The second dilemma was political in nature. Defensive modernization deepened
Europe's interest and involvement in the Arab world, making it less likely that
Europeans would be indifferent to political and economic changes taking place
and, more specifically, sharpening their appetite for imperialist adventures. Thus,
again, the success of modernist efforts produced new obstacles to the very goals
for which they had been pursued, and in the political arena this meant that growing Arab strength and development brought heightened scrutiny from the powerful and potentially expansionist nations of Europe.

The intellectual dilemma associated with defensive modernization had been
recognized for some time, and the dangers it implied had long been articulated
by conservatives and traditionalists who opposed its implementation. These critics insisted that the modernists' conception of progress was flawed, that their
policies would inevitably bring unwanted as well as desired changes, and that the
presence of the former would erode the very religious and cultural values that
modernization was designed to defend, thereby thwarting the Arab and Islamic
renaissance. Modernists countered that the only alternative proposed by conservatives was a rejection of all change, a continuation of the blind adherence to
tradition which had led the Arab and Islamic world into its age of darkness in
the first place. This, of course, was unacceptable. Nevertheless, while traditionalists may not have offered solutions that seemed compelling, the dangers they
identified were real enough, as even some modernists were eventually forced to
acknowledge. For example, a growing number of those educated abroad, or even
in the new schools set up at home, had begun to question the validity of traditional Arab and Islamic civilization. Instead of devoting themselves to technological change in the service of religious and cultural continuity, many in fact advocated more sweeping reforms than their predecessors would ever have dared. This
became increasingly common during the course of the nineteenth century.

The leading intellectual in Egypt during the first half of the nineteenth century was Rifaa Rafi al-Tahtawi, a man whose contribution to Egypt's modernist
movement was enormous and whose own life provided rich material for continuing debates about the benefits and dangers of modernization. Tahtawi received a
traditional education, having studied at the prestigious al-Azhar Mosque University and, after completing his studies, remaining there as a professor. In 1826,
he was selected by Muhammad Ali to lead a large educational mission to France
in order that the students might have spiritual instruction and counsel. Tahtawi
later wrote that at the time he considered Europe to be the "home of the infidel,
the seat of pigheadedness," and he agreed to head the mission only upon the
urging of his mentor at al-Azhar. According to his own account, he then "wept
for leaving behind him the Azhar of the sciences, the home of learning and the

learned."[59] Once in Paris, however, Tahtawi began to question the traditional education he had received and set out to understand the world of Europe as thoroughly as possible. He studied many modern scientific subjects and read works on philosophy, logic, and ancient and modern history. He even read the poetry of Racine and others. The account of his five years in France was published in *al-Takhlis* (The Journey), the first book about Europe in modern Arabic. *Al-Takhlis* was widely read, going through three editions in Arabic and one in Turkish.

After returning to Egypt, Tahtawi founded the School of Languages in 1835 and became director of its Office of Translations. The purpose of the institution was to prepare students for professional schools and to train translators. The Office of Translations, however, was devoted to rendering European works in Arabic and thereby permitting diffusion throughout the Arab world of the ideas they contained. More than two thousand books and pamphlets were translated prior to the school's closing in 1851. Moreover, these translations were not limited to scientific subjects and technical manuals but also included the works of European political philosophers, such as Voltaire and Montesquieu. In addition, the office self-consciously sought to modernize the Arabic language, devising terms for the modern vocabulary of European letters and science and, more generally, working to make the holy language of the Quran a useful medium for writing about contemporary subjects. Tahtawi contributed further to the form and content of modern Arabic literature through his own writings, publishing seventeen books during his lifetime. One of these, *The Path of Egyptian Hearts in the Joys of the Contemporary Arts*, is judged by an Arab scholar to be the single greatest influence on Egyptian thought in the nineteenth century.[60]

Tahtawi's intellectual transformation epitomizes what conservatives saw as the danger of defensive modernization. His writings dealt with virtually all aspects of social life, and the prescriptions he advanced contained many imported ideas. Indeed, he argued that the Arab world needed to borrow broadly rather than selectively and that its well-being required fundamental social and cultural change, as well as technological and scientific adaptation. Tahtawi also criticized al-Azhar for the narrowness of its education, observing that the renowned mosque university had once encouraged the study of secular sciences. Such criticism was of course rejected by the *ulama*, including many of Tahtawi's former teachers. In their view, his insistence that progress and fulfillment required more than adherence to Islamic law was a convincing demonstration that the reformers were dangerous: however sincere these modernists might be, and however restricted the changes they initially advocated, their misguided efforts would have the inevitable consequence of undermining the very normative system to which they claimed allegiance.

Tahtawi offered a different interpretation, however, insisting that he did not seek to undermine Islam but rather to restore its original vigor, and suggesting in this context that it was necessary to revise the prevailing view of *ijtihad*. Instead of seeing the consensus of the *ulama* as immutable and the presentation of alternative interpretations as tantamount to heresy, Tahtawi pointed out that the "door of *ijtihad*" had been open during the golden age of Arab and Islamic expansion, and he called for steps to push it open again. Further, he did not deny that the *ulama* remained responsible for taking the lead in matters of legal interpretation. He simply added that the *ulama* could not fulfill their responsibilities to Islam and to Muslims without a knowledge of the modern world, and that the reform of religious education was accordingly essential. Finally, he argued that Islam recognizes, in certain circumstances, the legitimacy of guidance from a foreign legal code in matters of interpretation.[61] All of this permitted Tahtawi and his supporters to claim that his prescriptions neither neglected nor were hostile to Islamic principles.

These competing analyses reflect the intellectual dilemma embedded in defensive modernization, indicating not only the moral danger it potentially posed but the way in which modernists responded to the charge that their strategy was flawed. Tahtawi's bold views about *ijtihad* were later echoed and expanded by other advocates of change. Seeking to rediscover the religious ethic that had led to Arab and Muslim grandeur in an earlier age, these modernists insisted that their conceptions addressed not only the needs of Muslims but the needs of Islam as well, and that they were indeed contributing to an Arab and Islamic revival. Many also asserted that they understood the true meaning of Islam far better than their conservative critics. In at least some of the areas where conservatives opposed change, such as the behavior of women and other personal status issues, modernists were eventually to argue that it was orthodox legal opinion, rather than their own "new" interpretations, that contradicted the true spirit of Islam. In these and other areas, they maintained, the direction in which the Quran and the Prophet sought to lead was inadequately understood by the *ulama* of their day.

There was also a political dilemma associated with defensive modernization, and this resulted from the imperialist impulse of nineteenth-century Europe. Although designed to make the Arab world strong enough to resist European domination, defensive modernization invited foreign involvement and scrutiny on a scale that in fact increased the likelihood of European intervention. Thus, while the fruits of defensive modernization were impressive, there was a high political cost to be paid for these gains, most notably in Egypt but elsewhere as well.

The eventual result of the political challenge from Europe was the onset of modern colonialism, which spread throughout the Arab world during the nineteenth and early twentieth centuries. It would be an exaggeration to argue that colonialism was the direct result of defensive modernization, that without indigenous programs of development the nations of Europe would have been content to leave the Arabs alone. At the same time, it was probably a contributing factor in Egypt and several other countries, influencing at the very least the mechanism and timing of foreign intervention. Finally, in any event, the introduction of colonial rule demonstrates that the Arab world failed to achieve the political objectives motivating its development efforts. Even in the countries where it was pursued most vigorously, defensive modernization did not make the Arabs strong enough to resist European domination.

The case of Tunisia under Khayr al-Din Pasha illustrates the limits of defensive modernization as a strategy for combating Europe's imperialist designs. By the time of his reign as premier, from 1873 to 1877, France had been a colonial power in neighboring Algeria for more than forty years and had given many indications of its desire to colonize Tunisia as well. England and Italy also displayed an interest in Tunisia at this time, and Khayr al-Din hoped rather vainly that a combination of diplomatic maneuvering and intensified modernization might stave off these foreign challengers. Powerful European diplomats in Tunis worked to undermine Khayr al-Din's authority, however, conspiring not only among themselves but with local conservatives, and securing his dismissal in a relatively short time. Bitter and humiliated, Khayr al-Din went to Turkey to live out his remaining years, where, ironically, he was much praised for his vision and accomplishments. In Tunisia, French forces invaded from Algeria in 1881 and forced the *bey* to sign a treaty accepting a French protectorate.

The case of Egypt also shows how programs of modernization encouraged the introduction of colonial rule, with especially significant roles played by the country's increased strategic importance and by its growing external debt. Egypt's strategic significance increased dramatically following construction of the Suez Canal, which opened a new trade route between Europe and the Far East and, in particular, gave Britain improved access to its colonies in India. As a result, Britain and other European powers viewed themselves as having a vital and legitimate stake in the affairs of Egypt and believed they could not afford to be indifferent to its rulers and their policies. Construction of the canal also initiated a period of steadily growing Egyptian indebtedness, with other development projects and many frivolous expenditures contributing further to the country's financial problems. During Ismail's sixteen-year reign, from 1863 to 1879, the country's external debt increased from 3 million to 94 million pounds. Not all of this debt was legitimately incurred. Unscrupulous European financiers persuaded the Egyptians to accept many loans carrying usurious rates of interest and all manner of fees and penalties. One source estimates that Egypt actually received less than half the amount for which it became indebted. Nevertheless, as with strategic considerations, this indebtedness brought a concern on the part of European powers, most notably Britain and France, that Egypt be governed by men who would recognize and respect their countries' "investments."[62]

The subordination of Egyptian to European interests entered a new phase as a result of developments during the late 1870s and early 1880s. In 1878, Britain and France secured the appointment of a new Egyptian cabinet, in which the

Ministry of Finance was supervised by an Englishman and the Ministry of Public Works by a Frenchman, and in 1879 they convinced the Ottoman sultan to dismiss Ismail because of his opposition to this government. In response, Colonel Ahmed al-Arabi led a rebellion of Egyptian army officers in 1881–82 and forced the new *khedive*, Tewfic, to install a nationalist government. Britain and France demanded the resignation of this government, however, and the British undertook military action when Egypt refused to yield. Alexandria was bombarded from offshore, and 30,000 British troops entered the country through the Suez Canal, killing as many as 10,000 Egyptian soldiers in a decisive battle at Tel al-Kebir. Following this defeat, al-Arabi surrendered and the British took Cairo, initiating an occupation that did not end completely until 1956. Beginning in 1883, the *khedive* was required to take advice from a British resident consul with virtually absolute power, and British advisors were given unofficial but effective administrative authority over all important government ministries. This arrangement, often described as a "veiled protectorate" since Egypt was not officially a colonial dependency, continued until the country was made a formal British protectorate on the eve of World War I.

Colonialism and Protonationalism in the Arab World

Although British occupation was not without some benefit for Egypt, as in other countries where European colonialism installed itself, Arab leaders insisted that good government was no substitute for self-government and that no contribution to the Arab world's development could justify the forced imposition of alien rule. Thus, while the British put Egypt's finances in order within a decade, invested in rural development, and even convinced a few knowledgeable and patriotic Egyptians that a short period of foreign rule might be beneficial, it was not long before there emerged a nationalist consensus in opposition to European domination. Describing the gloomy mood brought on by occupation, Tewfic's son, Abbas Hilmi, who was *khedive* from 1892 until 1914, wrote that British rule "spread confusion and dissension everywhere. . . . Everyone looked as if he had lost his way in the general chaos that prevailed."[63]

Arab intellectuals and nationalists also insisted that Europeans deserved only limited credit for whatever progress was made during the period of occupation. For example, when supporters of colonialism pointed out that roads, post offices, and other public works were constructed during the years of colonial rule, nationalists responded that these were in fact built by natives, many of whom were forced by colonial policies to sell their labor, and all of whom were miserably paid. Similarly, with respect to education, a significant proportion of those given an opportunity to pursue their studies attended schools for which Europeans were not responsible. They attended either religious institutions, schools established prior to the introduction of colonial rule, or private schools built at the initiative of the local population. Writing of Egypt, for example, an Arab historian reports that "the educational program of the British-controlled administration was limited for financial and political reasons alike, and private [Egyptian] committees were therefore set up to open schools."[64] By the end of the century, these schools, at which most of the students paid fees, were educating sixteen times as many primary school pupils as government institutions.

Reinforcing their contention that European colonialism was superfluous, nationalists added that roads, schools, and other civic improvements would have been constructed whether the Europeans were present or not. To the Arabs, this judgment was confirmed by both logic and the experience of nineteenth-century Egypt, which demonstrated clearly that modernization and development did not require the imposition of foreign rule. As expressed in 1906 by Mustafa Kamil, the leading Egyptian nationalist of his day, "All reforms would have been carried out [without the British], and even better carried out."[65] In addition, nationalists pointed out that the motives of the Europeans were totally self-serving. Rhetoric to the contrary notwithstanding, the colonial powers were not embarked on an altruistic venture to prepare the Third World for eventual independence; they were advancing their own interests, and any benefits that might accrue to colonized peoples were no more than chance byproducts.

This is not to say that dramatic advances *were* made under colonialism or that the life circumstances of most Arabs *did* improve significantly during the period of European rule. Although the situation varied from country to country, certain patterns were reasonably general. After decades of colonial rule, poverty was rarely less widespread than when the Europeans arrived. In Egypt, for example, male life expectancy (at age one) was only forty-seven years as late as 1947. In Algeria, which had the longest and most intense colonial experience of any Arab country, it was even lower. Educational gains were equally uninspiring. Literacy rates were rarely above 20 percent by the end of the colonial era, and usually much lower, and in few countries did the proportion of high-school graduates exceed 3 or 4 percent. Thus, quite apart from the question of who deserves credit for gains made during the period of European rule, nationalists pointed out that there was in fact far less progress than apologists for colonialism liked to pretend.

Finally, nationalists bitterly complained about economic distortions and deliberate exploitation. Colonial administrations, they charged, were hostile to industrialization and encouraged the export of unprocessed commodities, their goals being to remove competition for European products and to guarantee the metropole a stable supply of inexpensive raw materials. Expressing these and other grievances, a nationalist manifesto disseminated in Cairo declared that Egypt had become "a plaything in the hands of him who has no religion but to kill the Arabs and forcibly to seize their possessions." It went on to tell the Egyptian people that to the British "you are but a flock of sheep whose wool is to be clipped, whose milk is to be drunk and whose meat is to be eaten. Your country they consider a plantation which they inherited from their fathers. . . . "[66] In addition, in colonies where there were substantial numbers of European settlers, as in North Africa, these dislocations were compounded by massive land alienation and the influence of a *colon* lobby. In an unusually objective account, the British consul in Tunis wrote in 1899 that "there is a growing disposition on the part of the French to consider their possessions in North Africa as intended only for the occupation, profit and enjoyment of French citizens." The local European population, he continued, "clamors for increased protection against the natives, which means that the unscrupulous French [will] be allowed to cheat the native out of his lands by legal processes, or even to shoot him on sight if he objects, and yet to go scot free, acquitted by French courts."[67]

Although many of their grievances were obvious and immediate, the Arabs also saw in colonialism an interruption of their renaissance and a threat to its ultimate fulfillment. Instead of making steady if occasionally uneven progress toward their goals of cultural and political revitalization, they now found that domination was being exercised over them by a new oppressor. The periodization of Arab history thus helps to explain the psychology of nationalism and its response to colonization. A brilliant age of expansion and grandeur had been followed by a long period of stagnation and decline; and while the Arabs had, thankfully, awakened at last from the dark centuries of narrowness and slumber, European imperialism now brought fears that the age of *nahda* might end prematurely.

A related consideration is that colonialism demonstrated much more convincingly than could any amount of internal debate the limits of defensive modernization as a strategy of development. Conservatives found in European victories a confirmation of their judgment that the strategy had been flawed from the outset. They had predicted that currents of liberalism and cultural borrowing would end in disaster, and they believed their dismal forecasts had now been vindicated. They counseled that only by returning to the strict path of orthodox Islam could Arabs and Muslims hope for better times. Colonialism also strengthened the determination of a new class of Arabs who favored more sweeping changes than those envisioned by the original architects of defensive modernization. These radicals, whose numbers grew during the latter part of the nineteenth century, argued that the halfway- house approach of defensive modernization was inadequate, that progress and power demanded daring reform unencumbered by sentimental attachment to outmoded traditions or by romantic attempts to balance material change with cultural continuity. The inadequacy of such an approach to development was, in their eyes, confirmed beyond dispute by the ease of imperialism's victories, especially in Egypt, which had spent seventy-five years preparing for the confrontation. Finally, even those who had inherited the intellectual center, with its commitment to liberalism and to a revitalization of traditional society, could not deny that something was profoundly amiss. The shock of the British invasion in 1882 is sometimes compared in this connection to that which followed the invasion of the French in 1798. According to Hourani, "the fragile self-confidence of the nation, or at least its small educated class, was shattered" by the Egyptian defeat at Tel al-Kebir.[68]

Making the psychological impact of colonialism even more intense was the ideological context into which European nations sought to place their imperialist activities. Far from acknowledging that colonialism was but another instance of the strong exercising power over the weak, European politicians and intellectuals put forward an elaborate philosophy which divided the world into civilized and savage and spoke of the rights and obligations of the former with respect to the latter. The French stated explicitly that their colonial works were guided by a "civilizing mission," while the British often talked somewhat more vaguely of "the white man's burden." The content of these doctrines was an affirmation of Europe's moral duty to share the gift of its civilization with Africans and Asians endowed with "inferior" cultures and to rule over those who, in their present state, were unfit to rule themselves. As one French historian observed, the only liberty French imperialism offered was "the liberty to resemble us,"[69] the assumption being, in the words of an American scholar, that "no boon to be conferred on colonial protégés . . . could match being transformed into brown-skinned Frenchmen."[70] Approaching the matter somewhat differently, the first British resident consul in Egypt expressed his opposition to the nationalists' call for self-rule in Egypt by saying that it would be "a flagrant injustice, not only to the very large foreign interests involved, but also to those ten or twelve millions of Egyptians, to the advancement of whose moral and material welfare I have devoted the best years of my life."[71] The reason for this injustice, he stated on another occasion, is that "the progressive and reforming impulse [in Egypt] is supplied almost wholly by an alien race."[72]

Such views were fraught with evident cultural racism. Arabs and other colonized peoples were made to feel that they were only partly civilized and could be saved from themselves only by becoming more like Europeans or by entrusting their governance to those whose culture and temperament were better suited to the exercise of leadership. The literature of colonialism is replete with statements that express these sentiments, some more explicit and offensive than others. An interesting document, written when colonialism was already mature, is an account from the 1920s by Louis Bertrand, a French resident of Algeria who had recently visited Egypt. One of the Arabs' problems, Bertrand suggested, is the mental confusion produced by the Arabic language, which is "more of an encumbrance than an aid to the mind." Bertrand also undertook to explain the hostility toward Europeans that he encountered in Egypt, stating, "It is not only the hate of the poor for the rich, of the Muslim for the Christian, it is the hate of the barbarian for the civilized. He feels his inferiority much too cruelly."[73] While statements of this sort are more common in the context of French colonialism, they articulate assumptions of cultural superiority that were common among the British as well.

It would not be appropriate to present a unidimensional view of European attitudes toward the Arabs and other colonized peoples. There were certainly some Europeans who had praiseworthy intentions and who sincerely sought to better the lot of those who came under their care. A French resident general in Tunisia, for example, spoke with evident sincerity when he told an assemblage of Tunisians and Algerians in 1908, "We shall distribute to you everything that we have of learning; we shall make you a party to all that makes for the strength of our intelligence."[74] Nevertheless, sincerity and good intentions on the part of some, or even of many, could neither change nor justify the cultural racism in colonial ideologies. Statements about the superior culture of Europe and the inferior culture of the Arabs, and about the attendant need of the Arabs for foreign guidance in the managing of their affairs, could not but make any dialogue between the Occident and the Orient impossible. Communication was transformed into a one-way discourse between superior and subordinate, a situation that was clearly unacceptable to the Arabs.

Arab political thought and action addressed itself to two interrelated sets of issues in this ideological climate. One was intellectual and one was political, and both represented a new phase in preoccupations that had been central to the thinking of Arab intellectuals during the first three-quarters of the nineteenth century. A principal intellectual concern was to refute the cultural justifications of imperialism being offered, in order both to defend Arab and Islamic civilization and to undermine the legitimacy that colonialism sought to acquire. An equally important intellectual preoccupation was to carry forward the effort to define and construct a normative order that would be simultaneously open to progressive change and faithful to esteemed religious and cultural traditions. Overriding political concerns were, obviously, to articulate the desire for self-rule and to fashion movements capable of working for the realization of this goal. An important associated objective was to define the locus and character of the political community in whose name a nationalist platform was to be advanced.

Almost all of these themes came together in the ideas of Jamal al-Din al-Afghani (1838–1897), an intellectual of profound and widespread influence.[75] Al-Afghani's origins are obscure. His early education was in India but he claimed to be an Afghan, and some suggested he may have been Persian. In any event, he resided in Cairo in the 1870s and inspired many Egyptians with his lucid analysis of the Muslim world's weakness and his passionate opposition to European imperialism. Some of his followers took part in the al-Arabi rebellion of 1881–1882, although al-Afghani himself had been exiled in 1879, following the appointment of a new, pro-British *khedive*. Al-Afghani thereafter established himself in Paris, where he and his famous disciple, Muhammad Abduh, published a weekly Arabic-language newspaper in 1884–1885. Called *al-Urwa al-Wuthqa* (The Unbreakable Link), the newspaper inspired young men in many parts of the Arab world. Egyptian nationalists of the next generation attested to its impact upon their thinking. It also reached North Africa and the Arab East in substantial numbers.

Islam was central to al-Afghani's analysis, and, as with Tahtawi before him, an important part of his argument was that Arabs and Muslims must acknowledge the stagnation and inner decay of their civilization and then banish these through application of the once-legitimate principle of *ijtihad*. His thesis is summarized succinctly in the following passage from Hourani:

> Since reason can interpret, all men can interpret, provided they have sufficient knowledge of Arabic, are of sound mind, and know the traditions of the *salaf*, the first generations of faithful guardians of the Prophet's message. The door of *ijtihad* is not closed, and it is a duty as well as a right for men to apply the principles of the Quran anew to the problems of their time. To refuse to do this is to be guilty of stagnation (*jumud*) or imitation (*taqlid*) and these are enemies of true Islam.[76]

An episode that illustrates both al-Afghani's thinking and temperament and the character of the times in which he lived was his much-publicized exchange with Ernest Renan, a leading French student of history and religion. In a lecture on *L'Islamisme et la Science*, Renan had asserted that Islam constitutes a value system that is hostile to innovation and the spirit of science. The Muslim religion, in Renan's analysis, breeds fatalism and intellectual myopia, and those who practice it, especially the Arabs, are therefore condemned to weakness and stagnation. Al-Afghani published his refutation in 1883. Among the points he advanced, in this instance and in his writings and statements more generally, were an acknowledgment that a spirit hostile to rational inquiry had crept into Islam, an insistence that this spirit had nothing to do with the true character of Muslim civilization, an insistence that such rigidities and obscurantism were not unique to Islam but could be found as well in the institutionalized Christian Church, and a passionate affirmation that progress in the Arab and Islamic world required a rediscovery of authentic Muslim values and not submission to European rule.

According to al-Afghani, Islam held the key to achieving political as well as intellectual objectives, since it constituted a unifying force and a source of the solidarity needed to resist European expansion. Unity and solidarity were central elements in al-Afghani's political thought and, as with calls for restoring the legitimacy of *ijtihad*, they became and have remained concepts of pivotal importance to Arab modernists and nationalists. Solidarity, *asabiyya*, is the political cement that binds a community, giving it a national consciousness and making it capable of collective political action. The idea that *asabiyya* contributes to the rise and fall of civilizations is traced by Arab intellectuals to Ibn Khaldoun, the fourteenth-century scholar who explained how tribal solidarity enabled the early Arabs to fashion a powerful kingdom and construct a vast empire, and how the loss of that solidarity later helped to bring about the Arabs' political decline. The problem for al-Afghani and his contemporaries was to discover a source of *asabiyya* pertinent to their times, and al-Afghani's own contribution was first in reviving the principle and then in emphasizing that religion, as well as tribal ethnicity, could be an efficient machine for its production.[77]

Al-Afghani in effect transformed Islam into an ideology of nationalism, or protonationalism, conceiving of the religion as a temporal political force that would enable Muslims to unite against their enemies and for the common pursuit of other worldly objectives. He acknowledged that religion was not the only source of *asabiyya* relevant to Arabs and Muslims. For example, he recognized the utility of language in fostering the unity that must underlie any nation which aspires to self-rule and purposive political action, and in this he presented a view that would soon be championed by nationalists oriented toward pan-Arabism. Al-Afghani's own conviction, however, was that "the religious tie among Muslims is stronger than any racial or linguistic tie."[78] But whether the bonds of nationalism were to be built on Islam, pan-Arabism, or some other source of solidarity, a major part of al-Afghani's critical contribution was the link he established, via the concept of *asabiyya*, between the early accomplishments of the Arab world and the political needs of the Arabs of his day.

Muhammad Abduh (1849–1905), al-Afghani's former disciple and his associate in Paris, was the other leading intellectual of this period. Along with al-Afghani, he stands out as one of the seminal theorists of the Arab and Islamic renaissance. Abduh was Egyptian, and this is reflected in both his ideas and his activities, although he, too, influenced his contemporaries throughout the Arab world. His ideas were widely disseminated through *al-Urwa al-Wuthqa*, but his prominence is also based on his public life in Egypt. Having been exiled as well, he returned to his homeland in 1888 and was named mufti of Egypt the following year. This position gave him responsibility for the entire system of religious law, and he used it to work on behalf of the reform he preached.

Like al-Afghani, Abduh considered the Arab world's weakness to be the result of stagnation and inner decay and believed the path to revitalization lay in applying reason to matters of religion and to all human pursuits. His autobiography accordingly records a determination to reopen the door of *ijtihad*, in order, in his own words, "to liberate thought from the shackles of *taqlid* . . . to return, in the acquisition of religious knowledge, to [Islam's] first sources, and to weigh them in the scales of human reason."[79] Throughout Abduh's writings, emphasis is placed on the rationality and timeless relevance of the Islamic essence, the "true" Islam, and on a need to train Muslim jurists capable of discovering this essence and using it to adapt Islam to modern life. Abduh's efforts to achieve these goals included the reform of Islamic education, particularly at the mosque university of al-Azhar. "Reforming al-Azhar," he once stated, "amounts to reforming the Muslim world." Abduh hoped the *ulama* trained at al-Azhar and elsewhere would understand that *ijtihad* is a process without end, and that at no point in time is the consensus of the community complete and infallible.

Abduh was much loved and attracted many followers. Prominent among his disciples were Qasim Amin, who stirred controversy through his advocacy of women's emancipation; Saad Zaghlul, who was to lead the Egyptian nationalist movement after World War I; Ahmed Lutfi al-Sayyid, a respected newspaper editor and teacher whose concerns also included the emancipation of women; and Rashid Rida, an early contributor to Arab nationalism. These men and others possessed a vision of modern Arab society which was the product of nearly a century of social change and development. They carried forward a new version of the liberal philosophy articulated by Tahtawi and other early modernists, and they proposed what at the time was probably the only realistic program with hope of wide acceptance among the educated classes.

Despite his appeal, Abduh was cross-pressured by criticism from both sides of the ideological spectrum, to which he responded that part of his purpose was to bridge the gap between conservatives who resisted all change and radicals who would retain nothing. His autobiography discusses the quest for what might be called radical reconciliation, an effort to find the middle ground between "the opinion of the two great groups of which the body of the *umma* is composed— the students of the sciences of religion . . . and the students of the arts of this age."[80] In pursuit of his synthesis of tradition and modernity, Abduh responded to his critics with vigor. He told radicals and others who judged Arab and Islamic norms to be hopelessly outdated that stagnation was not intrinsic to Islam, that it was a passing illness rather than an incurable disease. Conservatives, who advanced the familiar charge that Abduh and his followers were undermining rather than revitalizing the culture and religion of the Arabs, were rebuked with equal or even greater force. An opponent of his program for the reform of al-Azhar once sought to demonstrate the adequacy of the ancient and venerable mosque university by observing that Abduh himself was among its graduates. "But didn't you study at al-Azhar, and find matchless wisdom there?" the mufti was sarcastically asked. Abduh's reply was scathing: "If I have had the good fortune to remember any worthwhile knowledge, I acquired it only after I spent ten years sweeping the filth of Azhar out of my mind. And even today I have not finished cleaning up."[81]

Debates among radicals, liberals, and conservatives about the appropriate mix of continuity and change did not take place in a political vacuum; they were strongly influenced by European colonialism and the ideology that accompanied it. It was difficult and often degrading to debate the validity of one's own civilization in the presence of a colonizing power, especially one that sought to justify its presence by issuing its own statements about Arab and Islamic backwardness. It was harder still to acknowledge that Europeans were partly correct in their criticisms of Arab society and Islam, even if their motives were known, and even if forward-looking Arab scholars had come to similar conclusions independently fifty years before. Exaggerated or not, European doctrines pierced to the root of Arab self-awareness and made it almost impossible to address questions of religion and culture with total objectivity. To prove that Europe's presence was not needed to bring about progressive change, modernists redoubled their efforts and intensified their attacks on conservatism and narrow-mindedness. Yet, lest they effect too great a transformation, thereby demonstrating that Arab society was after all unsuited to the modern age, they also reaffirmed with passion the timeless validity of Arab and Islamic civilization. The presence of these conflicting imperatives was not altogether unfamiliar, but colonialism raised the stakes and planted seeds of self-doubt that could not easily be denied. The troubled spirit of Arab modernists in the face of imperialist doctrines is captured by a noted French scholar, who writes, "Colonialism and expanding capitalism played in the Arab world, and in the Oriental world in general, the role played for us [in Europe] by the doctrine of original sin."[82]

Radical critics charge in this connection that colonialism actually retarded the social transformations in whose name it sought justification. The ease of Europe's penetration had initially bolstered the arguments of those who considered defensive modernization too timid a strategy of development, but colonial ideologies subsequently undermined the position of advocates of radical change. In order to demonstrate opposition to foreign rule, many who articulated the aspirations of colonized peoples felt compelled to mount a defense of the cultural and religious traditions disparaged by Europe, even though many of these individuals would themselves have been eager to criticize and modify at least some Arab and Islamic traditions were it not for the danger that this would be exploited by those seeking to justify colonial rule.

Another of imperialism's evils was thus the creation of an ideological climate that encouraged colonized men and women to cut themselves off from needed change, thereby engaging in self-destructive behavior and, in effect, participating in their own oppression. This point is forcefully advanced in a psycho-sociological analysis based on the experience of Algeria.[83] The psychology of resistance strongly encouraged denial of a need for new or foreign social codes, irrespective of whether Arab society might in some instances have profited from cultural adaptation. Further, the destruction did not stop even here. While a defense of tradition and affirmation of a unique and valid identity may have been motivated by a desire to "keep intact a few shreds of national existence," the colonizer insisted that these were but another instance of "religious, magical, fanatical behavior"[84] and offered them as additional evidence of the need for European rule. This is another dimension of the psychological and cultural trap of colonialism, and it was within this problematic ideological context that those who inherited the legacy of defensive modernization pursued the quest for a dynamic and authentic normative order.

The Locus of Political Solidarity

Currents of nationalism intensified in this environment, and questions about the locus of political solidarity, already addressed in the writings of al-Afghani, were particularly salient. The issue was also taken up by Abduh, for example, although attempts to define the affective boundaries of that natural political community whose *asabiyya* makes it a nation in the modern sense, and which thereby animates the struggle for self-determination, did not take place in Egypt alone. As opposition to foreign rule grew in both scope and intensity, the voices of the Arab East could be heard as well. Indeed, George Antonius records the presence of protonationalist sentiments in the eastern Arab provinces of the Ottoman Empire, in Syria, Iraq, and Arabia, as early as the 1880s. In *The Arab Awakening*, drawing upon both contemporary Arab witnesses and the reports of European travelers, he observes that a desire for liberation from Turkish hegemony was beginning to drift "in haphazard flight over the vast surface of the Arab world."[85]

In nationalist statements about the locus of political solidarity, sentiments that were Islamic, territorial and statist, pan-Arabist, and even pan-Ottoman could all be heard, with each having its supporters during the first years of the twentieth century. Abduh, for example, in contrast to al-Afghani, who had focused on Islam, judged Egypt to be the political unit of greatest significance. Abduh was deeply attached to Egypt, which he viewed as a separate nation with a unique heritage, and in 1907 his disciples founded a political party, the Umma Party, and a journal, *al-Jarida*, both of which sought to project Egypt's distinctive personality. *Al-Jarida*'s editor, Ahmed Lutfi al-Sayyid, later became one of the leading advocates of the position that Egypt is a natural political unit, united by a love of country among its citizens that supersedes all other loyalties.

This territorial and statist perspective is also visible in the life and thought of Mustafa Kamil, the most militant and influential Egyptian nationalist prior to World War I. In 1907, Kamil transformed his well-established movement of opinion into the National Party, whose principal objective was freedom from European rule. Kamil shared with Abduh, Lutfi Sayyid, and others a belief in the existence of the Egyptian nation, even though he also placed Egypt within a pan-Islamic and a pan-Ottoman political context. "Egypt is the world's paradise," he once wrote, "and the people which dwells in her and inherits her is the noblest of peoples."[86]

Pan-Arabist currents also emerged at this time. Moreover, an important contribution to the idea that the Arabs constitute a political unit possessed of *as-abiyya* was made by Abduh, despite the Egyptian scholar's emphasis on the territory of his own country in defining the locus of national solidarity. Although this contribution was not explicitly political, being limited to a concern for modernizing the language of the Quran, the central importance that Abduh attached to the Arabic language was incorporated into an ideology of pan-Arab nationalism by several of his followers, most notably Muhammad Rashid Rida. A Syrian from a village in the region of Tripoli, Rida had met Abduh during the Egyptian's travels in the area in the early 1890s, and in 1897 he moved to Cairo and began to publish *al-Manar*, a periodical that reflected many of Abduh's teachings. Rida was one of the first to assert that the Arabs constitute a natural political community, their solidarity resting on the pillars of their language and their historic centrality within the Islamic community. On the strength of this *asabiyya*, Rida declared himself to be a Muslim Arab, as well as an Arab Muslim.

Another early contributor to pan-Arabist thought was Abd al-Rahman al-Kawakebi, a Syrian who came to Cairo in 1898 and became an associate of Rashid Rida. He wrote two books which were widely read and discussed. Both were published anonymously in Egypt and then smuggled into Syria and distributed in secret. Al-Kawakebi expressed militant opposition to Turkish as well as European rule, arguing that the tyranny of the former had brought about the decline of Muslim civilization. The case against the Turks was advanced on behalf of the Arabs as well as Islam, however. Whereas Muslims "are now a dead people, with no corporate being or feelings,"[87] the Arabs are unified by bonds of language and ethnicity. One of his books lists twenty-six reasons for the "excellence of the Arabs," from which he draws the conclusion that reconstruction of the Muslim political community should be founded on Arab primacy. Al-Kawakebi's vision was of an independent and regenerated *umma*, led by Arabs and governed by an Arab caliph residing in Mecca.

Political sentiments that were at once pan-Arabist and anti-Ottoman were also articulated by Negib Azoury, a Christian Arab who had studied in France and then served in the Ottoman administration of Jerusalem. Azoury returned to Paris in the early 1900s to pursue his opposition to the Turks. In 1904 he founded a secret society called La Ligue de la Patrie Arabe, and the next year he published a book entitled *La Reveil de la Nation Arabe*. He called for a separation of civil and religious power and advocated creation of an independent Arab polity "stretching from the Tigris and the Euphrates to the Suez Isthmus, and from the Mediterranean to the Arabian Sea." Significantly, Azoury's league rejected the incorporation of Egypt into the Arab empire because "the Egyptians do not belong to the Arab race; they are of the African Berber family and the language which they spoke before Islam bears no similarity to Arabic."[88]

Pan-Ottoman and pan-Islamic sentiments were expressed by Mustafa Kamil, even though the influential Egyptian political activist is best known for his contribution to the territorially focused nationalism of his own country. On the one hand, reasoning that conflict between the sultan and the *khedive* had made it possible for Britain to enter Egypt, he urged Egyptians to support the sultan and declared that only so long as the Ottoman Empire remained viable and Egypt stood with it was there hope of checking European expansion. On the other hand, Kamil also believed in Muslim solidarity. Although he did not advocate creation of a single Muslim state and urged cooperation with non-Muslims, he asserted that the Muslim world possessed its own political unity, which was also to be tapped in the struggle against Europe. Finally, Kamil perceived a sort of moral affinity among the whole of the eastern world, united by common opposition to colonialism and by a similar need to balance continuity and change in the face of cultural challenges from Europe. In the latter connection, Japan's victory over Russia in the war of 1905 was an important symbol to Kamil and his followers; inspired by the strength of a modernized Japan, he wrote *The Rising Sun* to tell Egyptians about the new power in the east.

Pan-Ottoman inclinations were temporarily strengthened by the "Young Turk" Revolution of 1908. A coalition of army officers and exiles in Paris, united under the banner of the Committee of Union and Progress (CUP), forced Sultan Abdulhamid to restore the constitution he had suspended in 1876. The opening up of political life that accompanied the revolution included the formation of political groups, greater freedom for the press, and parliamentary elections. Under the constitution, representatives to parliament were elected from many Arab provinces, bringing men from Jerusalem, Jaffa, Damascus, Beirut, Baghdad, and other cities to Constantinople. Arab deputies were outnumbered in the assembly only by Turks, and the representatives were impressed by the freedom of debate and discussion they encountered in parliament. An Arab-Ottoman Friendship Society was created to institutionalize the new spirit of cooperation between Arabs and Turks, with local branches being opened in many cities in the Arab world.

Beyond its potential for direct Arab-Turkish cooperation, many modernists and nationalists in the Arab world were impressed by the Young Turk movement's success in forcing progressive change on an autocratic sultan and a conservative Muslim society. The symbolic value of these accomplishments was significant, and the advent of Ottoman democracy suggested to some Arab nationalists that their own country's interests might thus be best served by preserving rather than seeking to sever ties with the empire. As noted, this was the position of some in Egypt, including Mustafa Kamil. Pan-Ottoman sentiments of this sort were also expressed by some political leaders in the Fertile Crescent, including Palestine, and in Tunisia.

Pan-Ottoman tendencies in the Arab world were nonetheless short-lived. The Young Turk Revolution did not succeed in eradicating Turkey's weakness, and the democratic reforms of the CUP were soon abandoned. Even more important, tendencies of purely Turkish nationalism soon sprang up within the CUP, with Turks themselves stressing linguistic and racial ties to their cousins in central Asia and virtually abandoning the ideal of equality and unity among Ottoman subjects. Despite the brief duration of its importance, however, the pan-Ottomanist current in Arab political thought is significant for the light it sheds on the search for a political formula. Arab modernists and nationalists placed heavy emphasis on unity and solidarity. They sought to define the locus of a national community whose natural cohesion would make them strong enough to attain their political and cultural objectives, and Pan-Ottomanism was one of the political formulas with which some for a time experimented.

Ironically perhaps, the Turks contributed to pan-Arab currents of nationalist opinion. They gave Arabs throughout the Ottoman Empire a common enemy and, even more important, the Young Turk Revolution provided an opportunity for Arabs from different provinces to meet in Constantinople and forge inter-Arab political institutions. The Ottoman assembly was important in this connection, offering a structure within which Arab representatives communicated freely and began to work together. Contact among Arabs residing in or visiting the Ottoman capital was also promoted by the Literary Club, established in Constantinople in 1909. Although its program was not avowedly political, the Literary Club had a membership of several thousand, of whom the majority were students, and it opened branches in a number of towns in Syria and Iraq. Pan-Arabism was also championed by the Ottoman Decentralization Party, an important political organization established in 1912 by Syrians living in Cairo. The party's goal was to mobilize Arab support in favor of provincial autonomy within the empire. It had branches in many Syrian cities and towns and maintained close contact with other Arab associations in Syria and Iraq. According to Antonius, it became within a year the "best-organized and most authoritative spokesman of Arab aspirations."[89]

Several secret societies with a pan-Arabist orientation also appeared about this time. One was al-Qahtaniyya, founded in 1909 and named after Qahtan, a legendary ancestor of the Arabs. Among its carefully chosen leadership core were several Arab officers of high rank in the Turkish army, and in addition to its center in Constantinople, al-Qahtaniyya had branches in five other cities. The society proposed transforming the Ottoman Empire into a dual monarchy, with an Arab kingdom and a Turkish kingdom and with the Ottoman sultan wearing the crown of each. The Arab kingdom, which would be a unified political entity encompassing the Arab provinces of the Ottoman Empire, would have its own governmental institutions and make Arabic its official language.

Another secret society was al-Fatat (Youth), which was organized by Arab students in Europe. The society was established in Paris in 1911, and in 1913, when its founding members completed their studies, its headquarters was moved to Beirut and then Damascus, whereupon its membership grew substantially. Most of its activists were Muslim, although there were also some Christians within its ranks. Al-Fatat also took the lead in organizing an Arab Congress in Paris in 1913, working in collaboration with the Ottoman Decentralization Party based in Cairo. In 1914, al-Qahtaniyya's program of a dual monarchy became the basis for yet another secret society, al-Ahd (The Covenant). Army officers of Iraqi origin were among al-Ahd's most important leaders, and the society had branches in the Iraqi cities of Baghdad and Mosul.

Just as there is a periodization that gives structure and analytical meaning to the whole of Arab history, there are periods within the history of nationalism in the Arab world as well. The first period, which ended with World War I, was expressive in character, and it was the logical and necessary point of departure for efforts to promote change in societies that were largely unmobilized and suffering from centuries of autocratic and foreign rule. The tasks that modernists and nationalists set for themselves at this time were of necessity concerned more with ideas and principles than with mobilization and action, even though the latter were not entirely absent. More specifically, Arab scholars and political activists labored to give voice and coherence to inarticulate sentiments that something fundamental was amiss, to initiate debate and self-examination with a view toward discovering the causes of stagnation and toward sharpening the vision of a revitalized political community, and, finally, to examine critically the ideas and programs of action that might eventually make it possible to move from the former to the latter.

As expected during a period in which political activity is expressive in character, the vehicles for accomplishing these tasks were newspapers and periodicals, books, speeches, discussion groups, and congresses. Only later would nationalists build institutionalized mass movements and confront their political adversaries with more than words and symbols. When this occurred, however, during the interwar years, it would become clear beyond dispute, despite the claims of colonizers that they represented no one but themselves, that nationalists in the Arab world were in possession of ideas and progressive visions which commanded popular loyalty and were capable of moving men to action.

During this expressive phase of nationalist activity, there emerged no ideological consensus about the political formula that would best meet the needs of the Arabic-speaking world. As with the construction of institutionalized mass movements, such a consensus, even in individual countries, would have to wait until the interwar period. But while early Arab theorists and nationalists advanced competing definitions of nationalism and solidarity, and of the political community to which they belonged, elements of common concern and transcending importance were already fully apparent. Among these were the quest for self-rule and freedom from foreign domination, an insistence on the authenticity, validity, and dignity of Arab and Islamic civilization, and the desire for a political system which would permit the Arabs to struggle in honesty and without interference to define the boundaries of their political community and the content of their cultural future. It is therefore inappropriate to ask which nationalist platform or definition of *asabiyya* was most correct. What is important is that the search for a political vision and strategy was underway, and that this effort laid a foundation for the development of political identities as they appear in the Arab world at the present time.

The history of the interwar period is for the most part the history of individual Arab countries, since territorial and statist definitions of nationalism gained supremacy at this time, and since it was in the name of the territorial state that a right to self-determination was now proclaimed. In a few countries, most notably Egypt, Tunisia, and Syria, territorial nationalism was already somewhat familiar. More generally, however, and even in these three countries to a considerable degree, it was only after World War I that the political identity of particular societies began to evolve separately from that of the Arab world as a whole, and that there emerged particular "national" stories which also need to be told. It is for this reason, of course, that it has been necessary to present a general history of the Arabs in order to tell properly and fully the story of the Palestinians.

PART **II**

Emergence and History of the Conflict to 1948

B<small>Y THE END</small> of the nineteenth century, Zionists and Arabs had come into contact, and the results included instances of both cooperation and conflict. On the one hand, Jews were visible as they passed in increasing numbers through Beirut and other Arab cities on their way to the Holy Land, and inside Palestine the small but growing Zionist presence could hardly escape the notice of the indigenous Arab population. Indeed, many Jewish settlers took the initiative in establishing relations with Palestinian Arabs, making themselves known not only to the peasants who lived near their new communities but also to local merchants and landowners. On the other hand, on a political level, Zionist and Arab leaders took cognizance of one another, pondered the matter of the relationship between their respective movements, and in some cases established a dialogue. There were early warnings, especially from some Arabs, that Zionism and Arab nationalism were incompatible in Palestine. Moreover, the intensity of Arab complaints about Zionism increased as World War I approached. At the same time, there was also a belief in the potential for cooperation. Contacts were initiated by Arab organizations and Zionist representatives alike. They were based on a recognition that Jews and Arabs had similar aspirations and reflected a hope that the two peoples might therefore fashion an alliance of mutual benefit. There were even instances in which the symmetry of Jewish and Arab history was acknowledged.

Shaping the character of early contact between Zionists and Arabs was the fact that in the nineteenth century Palestine was among the less-developed regions of the Arab world. The circumstances of the country were by no means unique; the problems it faced, while serious, did not differ greatly from those confronting many other regions. Further, economic and political conditions improved noticeably during the last decades of the century, in ways, moreover, that had little to do with the arrival of the first Zionist settlers. Nevertheless, life in nineteenth-century Palestine was difficult and dangerous. Moreover, the country was not an important center of Arab political activity. None of its cities figured on the short list of Arab capitals from which radiated the intellectual currents and programs of defensive modernization that at the time were giving substance to the Arab reawakening.

Palestine was poorly governed and marked by a climate of broad insecurity, which contributed directly to its underdeveloped character. The Ottoman administration was for the most part corrupt and indifferent.[1] Also, local feuds were common, and in warfare among villages it was not unusual for fruit or olive trees to be cut down and crops to be uprooted. Bedouins, too, engaged in such practices, and they also sometimes carried off livestock or destroyed the wells and water reservoirs of villages they raided. These conditions forced land out of cultivation and disrupted agriculture, making hunger a serious problem in many areas. Trade and commerce were also discouraged by the unsettled circumstances of the territory, further reinforcing the country's impoverishment. These obstacles to development help to explain the small size of Palestine's population, which was approximately 300,000 during the latter part of the eighteenth century, or even less according to some estimates. As late as 1880, the country still had fewer than 590,000 inhabitants, roughly 96 percent of whom were Arabs.[2]

Palestine's underdevelopment was also reflected in widespread illiteracy and the absence of important urban centers. Among Muslims, who made up almost 90 percent of the country's Arab inhabitants, literacy rates could not have been above 5 percent. Although precise figures are not available, a census in 1931 reported that even then only 10 percent of the country's Muslims could read and write. The size and heterogeneity of the city-dwelling population were also extremely limited. Jerusalem, for example, the largest town in Palestine, had barely 10,000 inhabitants during the first decades of the nineteenth century. As late as 1860, the city still had only 18,000 residents and remained a traditional and generally impoverished community.[3] According to a traveler who visited the Jewish section of the town at this time, many homes "were like holes in the ground which Europeans would not have converted into living quarters even for their cattle."[4] The urban population of the entire country, including Jerusalem, totaled no more than 90,000 in 1860, and of this number approximately 20 percent were Jews. Gaza, Acre, and Nablus, with populations of 15,000, 10,000, and 9,500 respectively, were the only other cities with more than 8,000 inhabitants.

Still other problems confronting the population were indebtedness and disease. While land in some cases belonged to individual peasants or to the villages in which they lived, much was owned by absentee landlords and worked by indebted tenant farmers, whose financial burdens were passed on from one generation to the next.[5] To meet short-term obligations, many peasants also borrowed heavily from moneylenders, at interest rates sometimes approaching 50 percent. Under this feudal arrangement, neither peasant nor landlord had much incentive to work for agricultural betterment. In addition, such diseases as cholera, smallpox, and malaria were widespread, with epidemics common. In 1813–1814, for example, the northern city of Safad was devastated by an epidemic of malaria. An uncertain water supply helped to foster the problem, while swamps and dammed-up streams provided a fertile breeding ground for disease-carrying insects.

Finally, the lack of a modern economic sector and the virtual absence of a professional or bureaucratic middle class contributed to the lack of development. Beyond some ruling officials and a small and privileged landowning elite, the settled population was composed overwhelmingly of agriculturalists, artisans, and petty merchants. The elite was not only small, moreover, it was also ingrown and dedicated to preserving the traditional social structure.[6] Religious and administrative officials were usually drawn from the ranks of powerful landowning Muslim families, such that the British consul in Jerusalem could write in 1850 that "a close cooperation of Arab families, not recognized by law, but influential by position, usurped all the municipal offices among them."[7] This situation perpetuated a political order characterized by feudalism, conservative clientelism, and the central importance of patron-client relations, a pattern of political economy that goes a long way toward explaining the inability of Muhammad Ali's lieutenants to arouse nationalist feelings in Palestine, after Egypt invaded and took control of the country in the 1830s in an attempt to extend its own resistance to Ottoman domination.

The poverty, lawlessness, and chaos of life in Palestine began to decline under the reign of Abdul Hamid, the Ottoman sultan who ruled from 1876 until 1909. The government at long last took action to suppress intervillage warfare and Bedouin raids. This led to an increase in the amount of land under cultivation, both that controlled directly by the peasants who worked it and the large estates owned by absentee landlords, some of whom lived outside of Palestine. Moreover, this not only permitted a rise in the production of food, it was also accompanied by other agricultural improvements, such as the development of citrus cultivation in the coastal plain. In addition, the improved situation provided the security necessary for freer trade and travel. New roads were constructed and existing ones improved, including the important route linking Jerusalem with the coastal town of Jaffa. A rail link between the two cities was built as well, as was a spur making it possible to travel by rail from Acre to Damascus. Under these conditions, the standard of living gradually improved and the indigenous population began to increase. There was even a small amount of Arab immigration from northern Syria.

Although these developments did not bring about a radical transformation in the structure of Palestinian Arab society, material improvements and related increases in urbanization and education gradually led to the formation of new social classes. Further, while the country continued to be dominated by a few rival families, who were allied in loose confederations and who competed for influence through the formation of patron-client networks, new intellectual and political currents began to take shape as well. These developments indicate that Palestine was not unaffected by the onset of the modern age. The country shared in the important transformations that were making themselves felt in other parts of the Middle East and which were laying a foundation for even greater changes in the future.

Early expressions of nationalism accompanied these demographic and social-structural changes. For example, as noted earlier, Negib Azoury, a Christian Arab from Palestine, founded La Ligue de la Patrie Arabe in Paris in 1904. Azoury advocated independence from the Ottoman Empire and the construction of a unified Arab kingdom stretching from the Mediterranean Sea to the Indian Ocean. Some authors have cast doubt on the sincerity of Azoury's motives.[8] Nevertheless, he carried forward the pan-Arabist strain of nationalism that had been articulated by others, and he was one of the first to express publicly the sentiments of those elements within the Arab world desiring full independence from the Turks.

Notable among the political groupings in which Palestinians were active at this time is the Ottoman Decentralization Party, which was based in Cairo. The party advocated self-rule for the Arab provinces and, in Palestine as elsewhere, it maintained local branches in an effort to mobilize popular opinion in support of decentralization. The most important of the party's Palestinian members were Ali Nashashibi, an army officer from Jerusalem, Salim Abd al-Hadi from Jenin, and Hafiz al-Said from Jaffa. During World War I, all three were charged with treasonable nationalist activities and hanged by the Turks. All three were also the offspring of important Muslim families that later, after the war, assumed positions of leadership in Palestine national organizations. The Arab Literary Club, based in the Ottoman capital, also had a well-connected Palestinian within its inner circle. This was Jamal al-Husayni, the son of a leading Muslim family from Jerusalem. Al-Fatat, a secret and much more radical society based first in Paris and then in Syria, had several Palestinian members as well, including Auni Abd al-Hadi from Jenin and Rafiq Tamimi from Nablus. Finally, although information about them is limited, there were at least a few explicitly Palestinian organizations in existence during this period. One was the Nablus Youth Society, based in Beirut and composed of about one hundred students from Nablus. The movement's platform had a Syrian, Palestinian, anti-Zionist, and Arab nationalist orientation. Its goal was "to protect the rights of the Arabs, to agitate for the good of the Arab people and for the good of Syria."[9]

3 | The Conflict Takes Shape

Early Encounters inside Palestine

Against this backdrop may be seen the Arabs' early response to Zionism and Zionist attitudes toward the Arabs in the years before World War I. The record does not lend itself to simple generalizations. On the one hand, there were instances of dialogue, cooperation, and a recognition of mutual interests. On the other, there was indifference followed by suspicion and, eventually, active mutual antagonism.

Relations between the first Jewish settlers and neighboring Arab peasants appear to have been reasonably satisfactory. There were some early conflicts, but most grew out of the general insecurity of the area and do not seem to have had any lasting consequences. Thus, according to one of the most comprehensive and objective studies of the subject, after the Arabs recognized that Zionist settlements could not be dislodged, a *modus vivendi* was established and "day-to-day relations were generally close and good, especially as most [Zionist] colonies employed from five to ten times as many Arabs as Jews." [10]

Relations between Zionists and Arab officials and city dwellers were more complex. There were from the beginning some Palestinian notables who opposed Jewish immigration and land purchases. Their motives included fear of economic competition and resentment of the special privileges given to foreign residents, including unauthorized Jewish immigrants, under the capitulations granted by Constantinople to the powers of Europe. [11] Thus, for example, some Palestinian merchants from Jerusalem sent a telegram to the Ottoman capital in 1891 to express their fear that the Jews might monopolize trade and threaten local business interests. Similarly, in 1901, Arab notables in Jerusalem collected signatures on a petition in order to protest new Ottoman regulations giving foreign residents and subjects of the empire the same rights to buy land. On the other hand, many landowners were happy to sell their land to the Zionists, often at inflated prices. Also, more generally, local notables frequently maintained good personal relations with Jews, and many appear to have been willing for Zionists to settle in Palestine, adding only that they should regularize their status by becoming Ottoman subjects. Cooperation between Jews and prominent Arabs is revealed in the comment of a member of the Husayni family of Jerusalem. Insulted by a local Jewish official, he complained that such treatment was undeserved because "I have been working with the Jewish Colonization Association for three years with the most sincere and honorable intentions" and have shown "my loyalty to the sons of Israel."[12] The general conclusion about early Arab attitudes to which these contradictory fragments point is conveniently summarized by Mandel:

> By the eve of the Young Turk Revolution, which took place in the summer of 1908, it is clear that Arab anti-Zionism had not yet emerged. On the other hand, there was unease about the expanding Jewish community in Palestine, and growing antagonism toward it. . . . Thus, to the extent that Arab attention had been drawn to the Jewish newcomers by 1908, the issue was probably still seen in terms of immigration rather than Zionism. And in light of later expressions of opinion, one can speculate that the majority view was close to that contained in the report submitted by local notables in Jerusalem in 1899—that either the entry restrictions be made to work, or Jews be allowed to settle in Palestine, provided that they become Ottoman subjects.[13]

Between 1908 and 1914, from the Young Turk Revolution until the beginning of World War I, new political tendencies began to emerge among the Arabs of Palestine. Explicit anti-Zionism developed, and there were also the first significant stirrings inside the country of local Arab patriotism and nationalist political activity. Neither trend reached maturity until after the war. Nevertheless, the appearance of new newspapers, journals, and political associations showed that Palestine was affected by the same intellectual and political forces that were associated with the Arab awakening elsewhere. While the country continued to lag far behind Egypt and a few other centers of nationalist agitation, there was a clearly visible rise in political consciousness and concern about the future.

Palestinian Arabs were increasingly concerned at this time about the possibility that Zionism might threaten their political aspirations. Almost all of the Arab arguments against Zionism that were later to become familiar were expressed in Palestine in the years before World War I. There are admittedly additional dimensions to the story of this period, with popular opposition to the expanding Zionist presence growing incrementally rather than emerging as a full-blown phenomenon.[14] For one thing, the most militant anti-Zionist groups remained small, and Jews continued to enjoy good relations with at least some Palestinian notables. Further, some Jews took cognizance of increasingly hostile Arab opinion and sought to identify a basis for mutual cooperation. Finally, Arab organizations outside Palestine established contact with Zionists and worked for a time to fashion an alliance of mutual benefit. Nevertheless, as summarized by a careful Israeli scholar, "the Revolt of the Young Turks in July 1908 is to be viewed as the beginning of open Jewish-Arab conflict, as well as the cradle of the Arab national movement."[15]

New political tendencies were reflected in the appearance following the Young Turk Revolution of several Arabic-language newspapers. One was *al-*

Quds, published in Jerusalem, and another was *al-Asmai*, published in Jaffa. The latter frequently criticized Zionist settlers, resentful, in particular, of the privileges that foreign immigrants enjoyed under the legal capitulations granted by the Ottoman Empire. At the same time, *al-Asmai* concerned itself with the plight of the peasantry and urged that Arabs adopt Jewish agricultural methods. Yet another newspaper established in 1908 was *al-Karmil*, edited by Najib al-Khuri Nassar, a Protestant of Greek Orthodox origin who was raised in Tiberias and later moved to Haifa. The biweekly paper advocated a mixture of Ottoman loyalism and local patriotism and was also militantly anti-Zionist, principally on economic grounds. In 1913, *al-Karmil* proposed a second Arab congress, modeled on the one recently concluded in Paris. The venue proposed was Nablus, because that city offered "an enlightened Arab environment, youth with principles and ideas, and the most zealous of nationalists."[16] The purpose of the congress was to deal with the Zionist challenge, and though it was never convened, the proposal was endorsed by newspapers in Beirut, Damascus, and other parts of Palestine. Telegrams expressing support also arrived from Palestinians in Constantinople.

Among the other Arab newspapers in Palestine were *al-Najjah* and *Filastin*. The former, which was short-lived and had limited influence, was edited by Ahmed al-Rimawi, a Muslim from Jerusalem. *Filastin*, by contrast, had considerable influence. Founded in 1911 by Yusuf and Isa Daud al-Isa, Christian Arab brothers from Jaffa, *Filastin* devoted much of its attention to the affairs of the region's Greek Orthodox community. It also dealt with issues of concern to Palestinians more generally, however, including the growing Zionist presence. The paper used the term "Palestine" as a territorial designation, although the editors sometimes employed it in reference only to the administrative subdistrict of Jerusalem. Among the actions for which *Filastin* is remembered is its 1913 campaign to establish a "Palestinian Patriotic Society," composed of Arab notables from Nablus, Jerusalem, Haifa, Jaffa, and Gaza. A major purpose of the society was to purchase state land before this was done by Zionists. Later in the year the group held its first meeting in Nablus.

A number of local organizations sprang up about this time. Their platforms were varied, and few possessed more than limited institutional strength. Most met only intermittently, had a restricted radius of influence, and ultimately proved to be short-lived. Nevertheless, their presence was an additional indication of the Arab awakening inside Palestine. Among the groupings and committees that preceded the Palestinian Patriotic Party were the Orthodox Renaissance Society, the Ottoman Patriotic Society, and the Economic and Commercial Company. The first group, al-Nahda al-Urthuduxiyya, was concerned with the affairs of the Greek Orthodox patriarchate but also oriented toward Arab nationalism. It was led by educated young men who opposed the conservatism of their own community's leaders and who, after the war, formed even more militant political movements. Among its most active members were the al-Isa brothers, the editors of *Filastin*, who were known for their anti-Zionist views.

The Ottoman Patriotic Society, about which limited information is available, was established in Jaffa in 1911. Its most visible leader was Sulayman al-Taji, a blind sheikh from Ramleh with ties to important Muslim families. Although Palestine is not mentioned by name in al-Taji's writings, one scholar concludes that he was a local patriot first and an Ottoman loyalist second.[17] His platform was militantly anti-Zionist and, not surprisingly since he was a Muslim sheikh, it also had an Islamic orientation. After the war, the sheikh edited *al-Jamiyya al-Islamiyya*, an Islamic journal with a strongly anti-Zionist focus. The Economic and Commercial Company was also founded in Jaffa in 1911. Al-Taji was among its leading members, along with al-Hajj Haydar, a merchant originally from Nablus, and Muhammad Amin Sihyun, a pharmacist from Jaffa. The organization was concerned primarily with matters of business but also expressed itself on political and religious affairs, especially as they related to economic competition from Jewish settlers.

Another battery of political groupings was formed in 1914. One was the Literary Club, led by Najib Nassar, the editor of *al- Karmil*. Despite its name, the small club's interests were in fact political. Its platform blended local patriotism and Arab nationalism, Nassar having by now abandoned his earlier pro-Ottoman tendencies. Like Nassar and his paper, the Literary Club was also strongly anti-Zionist. Two additional societies, both of which were also concerned about the growing Zionist presence, were the Patriotic Economic Company and the Arab Palestinian Economic Company. Both of these associations were based in Jerusalem, and they had in common a fear of economic competition from Zionist immigrants. The former was generally pro-Ottoman, however, whereas the latter, as its name suggests, was more overtly nationalist.

The emergence of these newspapers and political associations demonstrates that Palestine was not unaffected by the currents of change sweeping over the Arab world. While the country was not an important center of modernist or nationalist activity, like Egypt or, to a lesser extent, Tunisia and Syria, it began in the years before World War I to experience at least some of the intellectual and political ferment that was underway in several other Arab provinces. In addition, the political programs of the groups that had emerged make it clear that opposition to Zionism was being vigorously articulated in certain Palestinian circles during the first decade and a half of the twentieth century. Arab arguments against the Zionist presence were based on several considerations. One was fear of economic competition and increasing Jewish influence in commercial activities. Another was resentment that Jewish immigrants retained their foreign citizenship instead of becoming Ottoman subjects. In addition to these practical considerations, there were fears that Zionism would undermine the Arab character of Palestine. Zionists were perceived to have vast resources available for the support of immigration and for the purchase of Arab land. The Arabs also complained that instead of integrating into the local population, Jewish settlers set up independent institutions and insisted upon the maintenance of their own language and culture.

While it is essential to take note of the significant increase in both political activity and opposition to Zionism among Palestinian Arabs in the years before the war, the magnitude of these two interrelated trends should not be exaggerated. So far as political change is concerned, the emergence of new voices and platforms did not bring meaningful discussion of domestic social and economic issues. Progressive or modernist ideas relating to development, such as those under discussion in Egypt, received scant attention. Not only was there no advocacy of the kind of far-reaching economic and social-structural transformation that might be necessary for the development of Palestine, there does not appear to have been any serious and sustained consideration of even small-scale reform, such as that which might be undertaken in education, jurisprudence, the status of women, and other similar areas. Even more important, most of the new voices and political organizations inside Palestine had little to do with elite politics, which remained conservative and dedicated to existing patterns of political economy. Leadership continued to be vested in a small number of wealthy and extended Muslim families, including the Husaynis, Nashashibis, Alamis, and Khalidis of Jerusalem and the Abd al-Hadis and Tuqans of Nablus. Although a few of their sons had become involved in nationalist politics abroad, these powerful clans had little reason to seek radical change. Having fared well under Ottoman domination, most remained loyal to the empire and sought no more than constitutional reform and greater local autonomy.[18]

So far as opposition to Zionism is concerned, its intensification during this period should not be minimized, but it must also be reported that a number of factors prevented it from growing more rapidly. One important consideration is the severe institutional weakness of almost all of the political groupings with anti-Zionist platforms. Most were short-lived, many had only a handful of members, and some were inactive for periods of a year or more. As a result, despite the increasingly harsh tone of their rhetoric, none was able to implement its program in a serious or meaningful fashion. In addition, the appeal of these groups' anti-Zionist rhetoric may have been at least somewhat diminished by the fact that many recognized and, in some cases, offered grudging praise for Jewish accomplishments in Palestine. For example, both *al-Asmai* and *Filastin* praised the agricultural achievements of Jewish settlers, and the latter paper also recorded admiration for Zionism's renaissance of the Hebrew language.[19]

Of equal or even greater importance during the years after 1908, anti-Zionism was articulated most vigorously by a narrow stratum of urban intellectuals whose political influence appears to have been limited. Further, the most active and militant of these individuals were Christians, notably Najib Nassar of Haifa and the al-Isa brothers of Jaffa, and this, too, almost certainly limited their influence among the predominantly Muslim population, including the leading families. Christian Arab professionals and merchants were particularly fearful of economic competition from Zionists, especially in the area of commerce and foreign trade. This was of less concern to other sectors of society, however. In addition, more generally, there were important ideological differences between the Muslim establishment and Christian intellectuals, with the former regarding the latter as a conduit for pernicious European influences, for anti-Ottoman sentiments, and for Arab radicalism. Though for different reasons, powerful and conservative Christian leaders were similarly opposed to the politics of young militants such as Nassar and the al-Isa brothers.

Opposition to Zionism was not unknown among other categories of Palestine's Arab population, including Muslim notables. Relations between Jews and Muslims, which from the beginning had been superior to those between Jews and Christians and which in many cases had in fact been cordial, deteriorated significantly as the war approached.[20] For example, most of the notables who represented Palestine in the Ottoman parliament at this time were staunch opponents of Zionism. In the elections of 1914, Raghib al-Nashashibi, the candidate from Jerusalem who subsequently received the largest number of votes, declared, "If I am elected as representative I shall devote all my strength, day and night, to doing away with the threat of the Zionists and Zionism." Another successful candidate, Said al-Husayni, promised to fight against land sales to the Jews.[21] Thus, according to the official correspondence of Zionist representatives in Palestine, Muslim rather than Christian Arabs had become the most important opponents of Zionism by the eve of World War I.[22]

On the other hand, prior to 1914, there continued to be Palestinian notables who were not opposed to the Zionist presence. One such individual was Asad Shuqayr, a member of the Ottoman parliament who represented the district of Acre. Shuqayr is reported to have believed that the Zionists would help to develop the country, and accordingly to have expressed a willingness to intervene on their behalf in Constantinople.[23] In addition, as a conservative Muslim concerned primarily about the European and Christian influences in his country, Shuqayr considered the Jews a useful ally against Western penetration. Another Muslim notable who maintained good relations with the Jews was Husayn al-Husayni, president of the Jerusalem municipal council. Husayni's friendship with and respect for Jews led him to assist the Zionists on a number of occasions, although it should be added that by 1914 he, too, had come to favor stricter regulation of Jewish land purchases.

A final consideration is that opposition to Zionism was not the only or in some cases even the most important item on the political agenda of various Arab groups in Palestine. Muslims were concerned about the future of the empire and were divided between the established supporters of Ottoman unity and newer elements oriented toward Arab nationalism. Christians not only had similar differences of opinion within their ranks, they were concerned as well about their status as minorities and their often unsatisfactory relations with the Muslim majority. For example, the Greek Orthodox constituted the largest Christian Arab community in Palestine, and its leadership at this time was probably more fearful of Arab nationalism than of Zionism.[24] Greek Orthodox religious leaders were worried about the trend to Arabize the patriarchate, and more generally, like many other Christian leaders, they sought the protection of European rule after the Ottoman collapse.

Thus, in sum, anti-Zionism was limited, though by no means absent, among the Arabs of Palestine prior to 1908; but it increased rapidly after the Young Turk Revolution and had reached serious proportions by the eve of World War I, even though its locus and intensity continued during this period to be at least somewhat constrained by a variety of social and political considerations.

Turning to Zionist attitudes toward the Arabs, there is a distinction to be made between the views of Zionist officials based in Europe and those of Jews residing in the *Yishuv*. As expressed by Yosef Gorny, the Arab question for the former was "essentially an academic issue, while for the latter it was a problem of daily existence. For Zionists abroad, principles did not have to face the acid test of reality, while settlers in Palestine were constantly faced with concrete challenges requiring solution."[25]

Some scholars have suggested that Zionists in Europe did not at the outset give adequate attention to relations with the Arabs of Palestine; being remote from the Middle East, they knew little of Arab culture or Arab political aspirations and were said to be unaware of the need to fashion a coherent and constructive policy toward Palestine's Arab population. This view is put forward by Yaacov Ro'i, for example, who states that "Zionist leadership, centered in Europe, was sufficiently removed from the scene to allow it to vacillate and procrastinate insofar as efficacious steps in the field of relations with the Arabs were concerned," a situation which "prevented the Zionist Head Office and executive from appreciating the real issues at stake and therefore from making, or even accepting, concrete suggestions as to the way in which to achieve the sought after friendship with the Arabs of Palestine."[26] Ro'i notes in this connection that many Zionist leaders regarded the reports of tension in Palestine as unnecessarily alarmist. As late as the Tenth and Eleventh Zionist Congresses, held respectively in Basel in 1911 and in Vienna in 1913, many delegates asserted that antagonism toward the Jews did not reflect the opinion of the majority and should not be exaggerated.[27] Also suggesting that a low priority was attached to improving Arab-Jewish relations is the failure of the Zionist Organization to place an official representative in Palestine until 1908, when it opened the Palestine Office in Jaffa.

In fact, however, early Zionists did concern themselves with the Arabs of Palestine, writing about and discussing their attitudes toward the Jews even before 1908, and considerations other than ignorance and disinterest are therefore responsible for the fact that they made only a limited effort to deal with the Arab question. One factor that prevented Zionists from addressing the issue of Jewish-Arab relations in a more coherent fashion is the institutional weakness of the Zionist Organization at this time. In particular, Arab perceptions to the contrary notwithstanding, the early Zionist movement was plagued by severe poverty and had few resources to devote to the problem. Also important are political motivations, especially a desire to deny legitimacy to Arab complaints. Since the Zionists were pursuing diplomatic initiatives and seeking international support for their cause, they had reason to emphasize the potential for Arab-Jewish cooperation in Palestine and to minimize the degree to which the Arab population of the country was fearful of the growing Jewish presence. Reluctance to acknowledge and address the Arab issue also reflected a desire to rebut the criticism of European Jewish opponents of Zionism, some of whom charged that Jewish-Arab coexistence in Palestine was impossible.

Perhaps most significant, many Zionist leaders saw the problem of the Arabs as transient and accordingly judged it to be of secondary importance. Although some, such as Ahad Ha'am, warned about a confrontation with the Arabs and urged action to prevent its emergence, Herzl, Nordau, Borochov, and others were convinced that Jews and Palestinian Arabs could live side by side, and that the latter would in fact benefit from the Zionist enterprise. These Zionist leaders believed in universal progress and the superiority of Western culture, which led them to assume that the institutions and values brought to Palestine by Zionism would eventually give rise to a "great, strong and open Jewish society [that] would absorb the Arabs into its midst in one way or another."[28] It is beliefs of this nature, as well as political calculations, that led many European Zionists to express confidence in the compatibility of Arab and Jewish interests in Palestine, and to assert that most Palestinian Arabs actually welcomed the material and other benefits they were said to derive from a Zionist presence.

It is thus clear that Zionist leaders based in Europe were not unaware of the Arabs in Palestine or unconcerned about their attitudes. Rather, the priorities of these Zionists lay elsewhere, in part because many believed, at least in the early years, that Arab opposition was not a pressing problem. As expressed by Shafir, these men "were not ignorant of the Palestinian Arabs, but in their assessment of the balance of forces estimated that the Palestinian Arab population could put obstacles in the way of Jewish rebirth in Eretz Israel but ultimately was not capable of arresting the process."[29] Similarly, according to the report of a historical symposium in Jerusalem, scholarly research has laid to rest the myth that "the Zionist movement—with the exception of small and marginal groups—supposedly, closed its eye to the Arabs living in Eretz Israel and to the 'Arab question,' thus precluding the possibility of mutual understanding between the two national movements. At the same time, there is no doubt that all the Zionist executives and almost all the currents in the Zionist movement underestimated the strength of Arab nationalism and the weight of its opposition to Zionist aspirations."[30]

Finally, after the Young Turk Revolution and especially in the years immediately before World War I, during a period when there was in fact a significant increase in anti-Zionism among the Arabs of Palestine, Zionist leaders began to acknowledge that the problem was more serious than they had previously realized, or had now become so, and that Arab hostility involved more than localized and episodic disturbances and was beginning to reflect a "national hatred and jealousy."[31] Shafir describes these changing perceptions as a "continuous sobering," which was most intense within the *Yishuv* but was beginning to characterize Zionist leaders in Europe as well, even if they did not often say so in their public statements.[32] It is this growing concern that led the Zionist Organization to open the Palestine Office in 1908, and subsequently to establish a bureau to translate articles from the local Arabic press.

In contrast to the Zionists based in Europe, Jews residing in the *Yishuv* were heavily exposed to Arab culture and buffeted directly by Arab discontent, and in this environment there were some who attached a high priority to the issue of Jewish-Arab relations and spoke publicly about the need for greater cooperation between Palestine's Jewish and Arab inhabitants. Indeed, as early as the 1890s, there was a small group of Jews in Palestine, men such as David Yellin and Israel Belkind, who studied and translated Arabic literature and discussed what they believed to be the common, pre-Islamic, cultural origins of the Jewish and Arab peoples. Among the writings of these individuals were statements to the effect that "the two peoples are one people, and these two branches belong to one stock, and the more we explore the roots, disposition, language and literature of the Arab people, the more we shall reveal Israel and the secrets of its language."[33] A few went so far as to urge that Jews "jettison their European outlook, enter into genuine partnership with the people of the country and learn from their ways and skills."[34] While these latter ideas were confined to a small group of men and were in no sense representative, they nonetheless contribute to an understanding of the differing experiences of Zionists based in Europe and Jews living in the *Yishuv*.

This positive orientation toward the Arabs, which Gorny describes as an "integrative outlook," was articulated in the years that followed by men such as Yitzhak Epstein, Yosef Luria, and Nissim Malul. Epstein wrote in 1907 that Arab-Jewish cooperation would foster "the renaissance of two ancient and gifted Semitic peoples with great potentialities, who complement each other," and in 1911 Luria argued that Zionism would not succeed without the agreement of the Arabs, and that this in turn "could only be attained if the Jews integrated into the East, aided the Arabs and won their trust."[35] Malul, a Palestinian-born Sephardi Jew educated at Cairo University, went even farther in urging the Jews to embrace Arab culture. He wrote in 1913, "We must consolidate our Semitic nationality and not obfuscate it with European culture. Through Arabic we can create a true Hebrew culture. But if we introduce European elements into our culture then we shall be committing suicide."[36] All of these men remained ardent

Zionists. Their admiration for the Arabs, and even the call for Jews to identify with the East rather than the West, did not connote anything less than a full commitment to Zionist immigration and to a Jewish renaissance in Palestine. It was simply their view that the success of the Zionist enterprise depended, more than anything else, on Jewish-Arab relations and Zionism's attitude toward the Arabs. As expressed by Epstein, these issues "outweigh all others" and are the questions "on the correct solution of which depends the realization of our national aspirations."[37]

The concerns of these men oriented toward Jewish-Arab integration were not limited to matters of culture and civilization. They also included recognition of Arab political ambitions and calls for the redress of Arab complaints about Zionist activities in Palestine. Epstein, for example, sparked public controversy in 1907 when he published an article entitled "The Hidden Question." On the one hand, he denounced some of the methods by which the Zionists acquired land, arguing that it was both morally unacceptable and politically damaging to cause the dispossession of poor Arab farmers. On the other, he also criticized the leadership of the Zionist movement in more general terms, complaining of its disregard for the fact "that there resides in our treasured land an entire people which has clung to it for hundreds of years and never considered leaving it."[38] There were also denunciations of Jewish separatism and aloofness, which were said to be a cause of Arab opposition to Zionist immigration, and related criticism of Labor Zionists who sought to prevent the employment of Arab workers in Jewish agricultural settlements. Finally, almost all who shared this integrative outlook called for recognition of the Arab nation, including its Palestinian component, and argued that Zionist cooperation with the Arabs was an ethical requirement as well as a political necessity.

Gorny's important study of Zionism and the Arabs identifies three additional schools of thought within the *Yishuv* during this period, one of which is a "separatist outlook" that stands in direct ideological opposition to the integrative perspective of men such as Epstein, Luria, and Malul. Those who championed this orientation spoke of the dangers of assimilating Jewish settlers into Arab culture, in most cases viewing this as a threat both to Zionist political aspirations and to the preservation of a high standard of morality and civilization. Moshe Smilansky, for example, a prominent *Yishuv* leader, wrote in an article published in 1907 that separation was a prerequisite for the attainment of a Jewish majority in Palestine, and in addition he urged Jews to "keep their distance from the fellahin and their base attitudes . . . lest our children adopt their ways and learn from their ugly deeds."[39] Some advocates of separation also asserted that intercommunal conflict in Palestine was unavoidable, and for this reason they opposed giving assistance to the Arabs. Such assistance would not produce Arab acceptance of Zionism, they argued; it would only make the Arabs stronger and thereby undermine the security of the *Yishuv*. Finally, many separatists denied the legitimacy of Arab political ambitions, asserting, for example, as did Smilansky, that the nationalism of the Arabs had no validity in Palestine, and that in fact the Arabs themselves were not even a nation, being nothing more than a collection of warring factions and tribes.

Support for a separatist outlook increased with the deterioration of Arab-Jewish relations during the years immediately before World War I. Among those identified with the separatist school of thought, in addition to Moshe Smilansky, were Ze'ev Smilansky, Moshe's cousin and a political activist; Yehoshua Barzilay, a Hebrew writer who had lived in Palestine since 1887; Avraham Ludivpol, a Russian-born journalist who settled in Palestine in 1897; and Yosef Chaim Brenner, a prominent writer who came to the *Yishuv* in 1909. These men and others insisted that mounting tension in Palestine showed the folly of the course proposed by advocates of integration, whom they characterized as naive and childish dreamers. Brenner, for example, writing in 1913, stated that there was already hatred between Jews and Palestinian Arabs, and "so it must be and will continue to be." As a result, he continued, the Jews must "be ready for the consequences of the hatred . . . [and] above all, let us comprehend the true situation, without sentimentality and without idealism." [40] In 1914, also denouncing advocates of closer Jewish-Arab relations, Barzilay published an article in which he rejected the study of the Arabs' language and culture. The former, he contended, had no utility other than routine commerce, and assimilation of the latter would bring a lowering of Jewish cultural standards. For these reasons, Barzilay urged the Jews to follow the example of German and other European settlers in Palestine: they "do not maintain close ties with the Arabs; their attitude is cool and impersonal; they study Arabic only in order to discuss essential needs and no more." [41]

Separation was advocated by a number of Zionist leaders in Europe, as well as some within the *Yishuv*, and among them were a handful who gave thought to removing the Arab population of Palestine. The most important of the latter was Israel Zangwell, an Anglo-Jewish writer who first visited Palestine in 1897 and subsequently concluded that *Eretz Yisrael* was too small to contain two peoples, who in any event could not coexist peacefully. In speeches in New York in 1904 and in Manchester the following year, Zangwell stated, "We must be prepared to expel [the country's non-Jewish population] from the land by the sword, just as our forefathers did to the tribes that occupied it." Later, displaying more restraint, he argued that force would be unnecessary because the Arabs could be persuaded "decorously to carry out a migration." [42] While others, including even Theodor Herzl, occasionally contemplated this sort of "transfer," the possibility of removing Arabs from Palestine was not taken seriously or even placed on the Zionist agenda during this period. [43] The foremost supporter of separation among Zionist leaders outside the *Yishuv* was Ze'ev Vladimir Jabotinsky, who later founded the Revisionist Zionist Party and distinguished himself as a militant defender of the Jews' right to settle on both sides of the Jordan River. Jabotinsky rejected the possibility of Jewish-Arab integration and urged cooperation with the Turks in their own struggle with the Arabs. On the other hand, he called for tact and moderation in dealing with the non-Jewish inhabitants of Palestine and told Zangwell in a conversation in 1916 that he opposed population transfer and did not believe in progress through coercion.[44]

In between the extremes of integration and separation is a school of thought that Gorny describes as a "liberal outlook." Among the Jews of Palestine associated with this orientation was Arthur Ruppin, head of the Zionist Organization's Palestine Office. Another was Ya'acov Thon, an associate of Ruppin, and a third was Moshe Smilansky, who had previously advocated separation but modified his views in the years before the war. These liberals, whose motives were at once self-interested and sincere, argued that good relations with the Arabs should be a central preoccupation of Zionist politics. Although they did not favor integration or call for Jews to identify with the East rather than the West, they stressed the importance of knowing more about the Arabs and their culture and urged Zionist action to redress legitimate Arab grievances, including land purchases that resulted in the eviction of peasants. They also called for the decent and fair treatment of Arab workers in Jewish settlements. According to Gorny, the views of these pragmatic liberals carried implicit recognition of the Arabs as a nation with a say in Palestine's future, even though they probably would not have conceded that this claim was equal to that of the Jews.[45]

With Ruppin as its director, the Palestine Office in Jaffa became the center of efforts to head off deteriorating Arab-Jewish relations during the period from the Young Turk Revolution until the outbreak of World War I. The office was under the administrative jurisdiction of the Zionist Inner Actions Committee, located first in Cologne and then in Berlin. Ruppin and his small staff brought together representatives of the various Zionist organizations and communities in Palestine in order to discuss the subject of relations with the Arabs and to solicit suggestions about how they might be improved, such as his own proposal that the Jews seek to buy land which was of limited use to the Arabs because of their methods of cultivation. Ruppin also sought to educate Zionists abroad. He repeatedly stressed the need for a positive attitude toward the Arabs, telling the 1913 Zionist Congress, for example, that friendly relations and understanding in everyday life were more important than propaganda. In addition, Ruppin stressed the importance of learning Arabic. On one occasion he responded to an inquiry from Russian Zionists by writing that unpleasant incidents keep occurring "simply because the Jew understands neither the language nor the customs of the Arab and the Arab views with animosity what in reality has to be ascribed to the Jew's ignorance."[46]

Ruppin and other liberals encouraged Jews to develop personal friendships with Arabs, especially those from leading families; and while they believed that this would be to the advantage of Arabs as well as Jews, they were fully aware of the practical value of assisting Arabs in various ways, including the provision of loans, medical help, and agricultural assistance. Benefits would be derived by rendering such assistance both to the common people and to Arab notables, although the highest priority, of course, was to gain the support of the leaders of Palestine. Further, in addition to establishing a foundation of friendship, or at least mutual interest, with the majority and its leaders, these Zionists also hoped to undermine the influence of their most militant critics. They paid particular attention to the Arabic-language press in this connection, both within Palestine and elsewhere, and in 1912 the Palestine Office established a special press division under the direction of Nissim Malul. This office monitored the Arab press closely, translated or prepared Hebrew and German résumés of selected articles, and conducted several systematic content analyses. The Palestine Office also encouraged replies to anti-Zionist newspaper articles.

The final school of thought identified by Gorny, which he characterizes as a "constructive socialist outlook," fits less easily on the ideological continuum ranging from integration to separation. Associated with Labor Zionism and reflected in the writings of men such as Yitzhak Ben-Zvi, David Ben Gurion, Ya'acov Zerubavel, Yosef Sprinzak, and David Blumenfeld, all leaders of the Second *Aliya*, this perspective attached central importance to the question of whether there was a contradiction between the requirements of Jewish workers and Zionist development on the one hand and socialist solidarity and the needs of an international proletariat on the other. Applied to Palestine, this concern expressed itself in debates about both the ethical and practical implications of struggling for Jewish employment at the expense of Arab workers, instead of permitting or even encouraging the hiring of Arab laborers by Jewish employers and promoting the formation of a labor movement in which Jewish and Arab workers would make common cause.

Differing points of view were put forward about these issues, but the common denominator among Labor Zionists was a belief that, should a choice be required, the national cause of the Jewish people must be given priority over considerations of social class with the potential to unite Jewish and Arab workers. The impact of Zionist employment practices on relations with the Arabs was noted by Zerubavel following a tour of Galilee in 1911: Arabs were attacking those Zionist settlements that had introduced Jewish labor and guard duty, whereas those still employing Arabs were being left in peace. Nevertheless, Zerubavel advocated the employment of Jewish workers and guards as a requirement for national redemption, even if this might lead to greater conflict with the Arabs. Ben-Zvi, concerned with ideological as well as practical considerations, sought to resolve the contradiction between national and class requirements by arguing in a 1913 article that the interests of the worldwide proletariat were not more important than those of the working class in any particular nation. Ben Gurion contributed to this debate as well, arguing that the employment of Arab workers in Jewish settlements would not bring peace and might even exacerbate tensions. Workers will always oppose their employers, he asserted, and the conflict between them will be even more intense if it involves a national difference as well as a clash of economic and class interests.[47]

On the other hand, many Labor Zionists acknowledged that the Arabs, like the Jews, had historical rights in Palestine, and in this connection at least some appeared to believe that their programs, though perhaps exacerbating tensions in the short run, would eventually form a basis for peaceful coexistence between Palestine's Jewish and Arab inhabitants. Ben-Zvi, for example, reasoned that policies favorable to Jewish labor would promote the growth and development of the *Yishuv*, which in turn would make the needs of the Jewish working class less pressing and create resources with which to promote the well-being of Arab as well as Jewish laborers. Ben-Zvi also argued that Arab hostility toward the *Yishuv* was the result, in part, of the economic and political weakness of the Jewish community in Palestine, which inclined the Arabs to scorn overtures of Jewish friendship.[48] Other Labor Zionists, including Zerubavel and Sprinzak, explicitly acknowledged that Palestine contained two peoples possessing equal national rights and urged the Zionist movement to pay more attention to improving relations with the Arabs, while continuing, of course, to give highest priority to the needs of Jewish labor. The dilemmas and contradictions associated with this prescription were very much on the minds of Labor Zionists during this period. Yet at least some insisted, as did Zerubavel shortly after the outbreak of World War I, that "since two nations, Jews and Arabs, have found themselves together in Palestine, and have been destined to weave the fabric of their national lives in the same geographical area, they must find a common denominator and a way to evolve a local policy common to Jews and Arabs."[49]

This constellation of Zionist outlooks and ideological orientations, reflecting a diversity of views within the *Yishuv* and still different perspectives among Zionists based in Europe, reveals the complexity of Jewish attitudes toward the question of relations with the Arabs during the years before World War I. But while there was no single Zionist response to this question, it is evident that Jews, especially in the *Yishuv* but to some extent elsewhere as well, were fully cognizant of the demands and grievances of Palestine's Arab population and were struggling to identify the implications for the Zionist enterprise of various strategies for dealing with the Arabs and their complaints. Moreover, as intercommunal tension increased during the years between the Young Turk Revolution and the onset of the war, at least some within the Zionist movement worked to improve relations between Arabs and Jews, calling for greater Jewish sensitivity toward the Arabs and clinging to the hope that, with such sensitivity, a way might be found for the two peoples of Palestine to cooperate in the development of their shared homeland.

Early Efforts at Cooperation outside Palestine

A different aspect of Arab-Jewish relations during these early years concerns the interaction between Zionists and Arabs outside Palestine. As late as 1913, only a small minority of Arab nationalists were opposed to Zionism or held the opinion that it threatened the Arab renaissance.[50] Zionist officials were in contact during this period with Arab representatives in Constantinople, and also with Arabs in Europe, Syria, and Egypt. The Arab press contained articles discussing Zionism, not only those that spoke of the danger it represented but also those which advocated Arab-Jewish cooperation. Malul's survey of the Arab press in Egypt and Syria, published in 1914, showed a considerable diversity in Arab opinion outside Palestine. Papers with a nationalist orientation tended to be more hostile than those favoring the unity of the Ottoman Empire, and in contrast to the situation inside Palestine, papers published by Christians were less hostile than those published by Muslims. Overall, however, there were papers in every category utilized by Malul that were not opposed to Zionism.

Another indication that Arabs were not uniformly hostile to the Zionist movement may be seen in the discussion of immigration to Palestine (which most delegates still regarded as part of Greater Syria) at the Arab Congress held in Paris in 1913. The major speech on the subject was made by Sheikh Ahmad Tabbarah, a newspaper editor from Beirut. Tabbarah avoided all references to Jewish immigration or to Jewish land purchases in Palestine. He noted that while some were opposed to non-Arab immigration, he personally agreed with those who believed that immigration could be of benefit. A resolution was then introduced expressing approval of immigration that would contribute to the economic well-being of the country, and in the ensuing discussion it was asserted without challenge that this was meant to indicate support for Jewish but not Turkish immigration. The resolution was not voted upon, and the entire discussion was later condemned by Arabs in Palestine. Nevertheless, these events provide another indication that the possibility of cooperation between Arabs and Zionists was under consideration. Moreover, the chairman of the congress, Abd al-Hamid al-Zahrani, later told a Zionist newspaper that the Jews of the world are "but Syrian émigrés," with an understandable "nostalgia for the country of their birth," and that Jews and Arabs should therefore "make common cause for the material and moral rehabilitation of our common land."[51]

Negotiations aimed at building a concrete alliance on this foundation took place on two fronts, one centered in Cairo and the other in Beirut. The first involved the Ottoman Decentralization Party, which was led by Syrian émigrés and which in fact took the initiative in seeking an entente with the Zionists. Formed in 1912, the party contained Christian as well as Muslim members and was concerned principally with reform and decentralization within the context of the Ottoman Empire. As indicated earlier, the Decentralization Party also had branches in Syria, Palestine, and Iraq.

The Decentralization Party's initiative took place in 1913, beginning with a comment published in *al-Ahram* by Daud Barakat, the paper's editor and a party member. Barakat wrote, "It is absolutely imperative that an entente be made between the Zionists and the Arabs. . . . The Zionists are necessary for the country; the capital which they will bring, their knowledge and intelligence, and the industriousness which characterizes them, will contribute without doubt to the regeneration of the country."[52] Another article was then published in *al-Ahram* by the party's secretary, Haqqi Bey al-Azm, supporting Jewish immigration to Palestine on the condition that the Jews become Ottoman subjects and refrain from political activity; and a month later yet another party member, Ibrahim Salim Najjar, wrote to the editor of *Le Jeune Turque*, a Zionist-sponsored newspaper in Constantinople, to request that the Decentralization Party be put in touch with a Zionist representative.

Although these sentiments were not shared by most Arab leaders in Palestine, the Syrians in Cairo looked at Zionism from a broader pan-Arab perspective and were inclined to believe that Jewish immigration could bring economic benefits without posing a challenge to the long-term political aspirations of the Arabs. Many decentralists placed conditions on the kind of Zionist presence they were prepared to welcome. There was general agreement that Jews must not seek to take over the country or to establish an independent state. Others, such as al-Azm, added that the Jews should learn Arabic and embrace the aspirations of the Arab peoples. Within this context, however, the Cairo-based party did more than express a kind of passive tolerance for the Jewish goal of a national home.

Decentralization Party leaders saw the Arabs as major beneficiaries of any entente with the Zionists, with some adding that such an alliance was in fact essential for their own purposes. Rashid Rida, editor of *al-Manar*, a founding member of the Decentralization Party, and one of the leading political theorists of this period, held the modernist view that the Arab world had to strengthen itself against the superior power of Europe. As a Syrian, he stated that his country of origin badly needed development projects, but that these were not possible without foreign capital and technical skills, both of which the Jews could provide. To reject this aid, in his view, would spell poverty and ruin.[53] In addition, although this cannot be proved, it is probable that the decentralists perceived the weakness of the Ottoman state and, fearing its collapse, sought Zionist support for eventual Arab independence. These are the considerations that led this group of intellectuals and nationalists in Cairo to take the initiative in seeking an entente with the Jews.

The first fruit of the initiative undertaken by the decentralists was a preliminary verbal agreement worked out with the editor of *Le Jeune Turque* in May

1913. The pledges given in this agreement, reproduced below, began to be implemented in the months that followed. Discussions were also begun with a view toward convening an Arab-Jewish congress in Cairo.

> 1. The Cairo Committee, being in principle in favor of Jewish immigration into Syria and Palestine and of an agreement with the Zionists, will make a point of working for a rapprochement between the Arab world and the Jewish world, and of dispelling by its word-of-mouth propaganda and by way of the Arabic press all prejudices which have been current until now in the Arab world as regards Jewish immigration and which have prevented an Arab-Jewish rapprochement.
>
> 2. In exchange, *Le Jeune Turque* will make a point of supporting the cause of the Arab movement while it remains compatible with the unity and integrity of the Empire. *Le Jeune Turque* will do all it can so that European newspapers (especially German ones), with which it has relations, will do the same.[54]

Centered in Beirut but including many contacts in Palestine as well, an entirely separate set of negotiations developed in the spring of 1914 in response to another Arab initiative. Under the original proposal, ten Arab and ten Zionist delegates were to assemble for a secret meeting in Brummana, a village near Beirut. The Arab most centrally involved in this project was Nasif Bey al-Khalidi, a native of Jerusalem who lived in Beirut and who sought to gain support for the project from the Arab notables in Palestine. Several of the other Arabs involved in preliminary discussions possessed anti-Zionist views; but, motivated in part by their antipathy toward the Ottoman government, they, too, appear to have been favorably disposed toward the idea of an entente, and a meeting was accordingly planned. Officials of the Zionist Organization's Palestine Office, including Ruppin, were among Jews who participated in planning the project.

Neither the Brummana meeting nor the proposed Arab-Jewish congress in Cairo was ever convened. Contacts between Arabs and Zionists continued, until interrupted by the outbreak of the war in August, but opposition from the Turks, Zionist hesitation, and Palestinian anti-Zionism increasingly made it clear that efforts to forge an alliance of Arabs and Zionists were destined to fail. Ottoman authorities had initially encouraged Arab-Jewish contacts, seeing themselves as beneficiaries of any Jewish contribution to the development of Palestine. As Arab opposition to Turkish rule intensified, however, they saw little value in permitting the Arabs to acquire the Zionists as allies. It is for this reason that the senior Ottoman official in Beirut withdrew his authorization for the Brummana meeting, which consequently never took place.

Zionist attitudes and behavior are also responsible for the fact that the Brummana meeting and the proposed Arab-Jewish congress never took place. One Zionist concern, especially relevant with respect to the gathering planned at Brummana, was that the presence of Arab critics would turn the session into an occasion for anti-Zionist rhetoric. These concerns were articulated by Jewish officials in Palestine and Europe alike. More generally, on a different level, Zionists were also disturbed by the magnitude of the "investment" in Arab development that some Arabs expected them to make. Finally, the most important factor constraining the Zionists was their participation in delicate negotiations with the Turks. Since 1909 there had been high-level discussions about the possibility of exchanging Zionist financial and diplomatic support of the Ottoman cause for more favorable Turkish policies toward Jewish immigration and land purchases in Palestine,[55] and the possibility that these talks might lead to an agreement placed obvious limits on the commitments that Zionists were prepared to make in their deliberations with Arab leaders. While they were happy to explore the option of an alliance with the Arabs against the Turks, most Zionist officials, especially those based in Europe, believed that an accord with the Turks was both more attainable and more beneficial to their cause.

In addition to Ottoman opposition and Zionist hesitation, growing anti-Zionism among the Arab population of Palestine also became an increasingly important obstacle to the conclusion of an Arab-Jewish entente. For example, it proved impossible to secure meaningful Palestinian participation in the Brummana meeting; only four of the ten proposed Arab delegates were from Palestine, and none of these was an individual of significant political stature. By 1914, no important member of the Palestinian political elite was willing to attend such a meeting. Even those on good terms with Zionists would adopt no more than a wait-and-see attitude. Such attitudes were also increasingly in evidence among Palestinians residing in Cairo and Beirut, where a number of anti-Zionist societies were formed on the eve of the war. In 1914, for instance, Palestinian students at al-Azhar University established a group that had opposition to Zionism "by all possible means" as the first of its official objectives. Also indicative of the increasing militancy of Palestinian anti-Zionism at this time was a political tract distributed in Jerusalem in July of 1914. Called "A General Summons to Palestinians," it was signed anonymously and combined anti-Zionist sentiment with expressions of Arab and Islamic nationalism. It read, in part:

> Countrymen! We summon you in the name of the country which is in mourning, in the name of the homeland which is lamenting, in the name of Arabia, in the name of Syria, in the name of our country, Palestine, whose lot is evil, in the name of everything which is dear to you. . . .

> Men! Do you want to be slaves and servants to people who are notorious in the world and in history? Do you wish to be slaves to the Zionists who have come to you to expel you from your country, saying that this country is theirs?[56]

Thus came to an end prewar efforts at cooperation between Arabs and Zionists. There would be another, short-lived attempt to fashion a common front after the war. More generally, however, these efforts, whatever their promise and potential, bore no tangible fruit. Nor did they check the deterioration of Arab-Jewish relations inside Palestine. Within a decade they would be all but forgotten, as intercommunal tension continued to mount and as Jews and Arabs found themselves set on a course of historical development leading inexorably toward confrontation and violence.

British Promises during World War I

The population of Palestine suffered greatly during the First World War. The Turks arrested both Arab nationalists and Zionist leaders, executing some of the former and giving most of the latter a choice between prison and exile. As a result, overt Arab nationalist activity in Palestine ceased and Zionist activists, such as David Ben Gurion and Yitzhak Ben-Zvi, went into exile. The general population suffered as well. Food was in short supply, for example, partly because of the consumption of the Ottoman army, which used Palestine as a base for the fighting in Sinai. Crops and livestock were commandeered for the troops, and trees were cut down to be used as fuel. Also, tens of thousands of Arab peasants were conscripted, adding to the dislocation and contributing further to a decline in agricultural production. Thus, by the time the Ottoman war effort collapsed and British forces took control of Palestine in the first half of 1918, the country was in a state of extreme disorder. Many people were on the brink of starvation, with hunger in the countryside as well as in the cities.

As a result of these developments, both the Arab and Jewish populations of Palestine declined during the war. In 1914 there were about 604,000 Arabs in Palestine and about 85,000 Jews.[57] Precise figures are not available for the Arabs, but with the expulsion of foreign citizens the number of Jews had declined to approximately 55,000 by 1918. Jewish immigration resumed after the war, however, returning the population of the *Yishuv* to its former level by the time a census was conducted in 1922. The Arab population had also resumed its pattern of growth by this period; in 1922 there were reported to be 668,000 Arabic-speaking Palestinians, including 589,000 Muslims, 71,000 Christians, and 7,500 Druze.[58]

An immediate postwar concern was, of course, the administration of the country and the provision of basic services. A major preoccupation of the British forces occupying Palestine in 1918 was the revival of food production and the reorganization of its distribution. Political concerns were not long in reappearing, however, and with them came a new agenda of issues and disagreements. On the one hand, there was the matter of Palestine's political status in the wake of the dissolution of the Ottoman Empire. Both Jews and Arabs hoped that the European powers would support their political aspirations in Palestine. Moreover, the situation was complicated by the promises that each people had received from the British during the war, and by the emergence of Britain's own interest in the country. On the other hand, it was also necessary to address the matter of Palestine's boundaries. The country was not a recognized administrative unit within the Ottoman Empire, being regarded simply as the southern part of Syria. As the international community organized itself to define and impose on the Middle East the terms of a peace settlement, Arab and Zionist leaders therefore increased the level of their political activity and, in one important instance, reestablished a dialogue in order to explore the possibility of creating an alliance of mutual benefit.

During the war Britain encouraged the Arabs to revolt against the Turks and to join in the fighting on the side of the Ottoman Empire's enemies. The most important contacts had in fact been initiated by the Arabs, however, when Husayn, the sherif of Mecca and founder of the Hashemite dynasty, sent his son to Cairo in 1914 for a secret meeting with Lord Kitchner, the British high commissioner. Although appointed by the Turks, Husayn was guardian of Islam's most holy cities and possessed considerable political stature in the Arab and Islamic world. Husayn was motivated both by immediate concerns, including Ottoman conscription and the harshness of the Turkish administration, and by a belief that European support might enable the Arabs to achieve independence. The course of an alliance with Britain was not without danger. As in Egypt and Palestine, opinion in Arabia was divided with respect to both the empire and the trustworthiness of European powers. Some continued to believe that the Arabs' best course was to stand by the Turks and to seek concessions from them. Nevertheless, the contacts continued, and in 1915, with the war already underway, they resulted in a formal agreement between Husayn and Sir Henry McMahon, Kitchner's replacement in Cairo. The British promised to support the emancipation of the Arabs if the latter would became their allies in the war.

Husayn and McMahon exchanged eight letters in which their agreements were specified. In his letter to Husayn of October 24, 1915, McMahon wrote that "subject to the above modifications, Great Britain is prepared to recognize and support the independence of the Arabs in all the regions within all the limits demanded by the Sherif of Mecca."[59] The sherif's limits included an area between Persia to the east and the Mediterranean and the Red Sea to the west. Britain's modifications included a few areas of no relevance to Palestine and, rather vaguely, "portions of Syria lying to the west of the districts of Damascus, Homs, Hama and Aleppo [which] cannot be said to be purely Arab." The Arabs were satisfied by this response to their demands and, led by Husayn's son, Faycal, they began their revolt against the Turks in June 1916. They were assisted by a number of British liaison officers, one of whom was T. E. Lawrence, who soon became known as "Lawrence of Arabia." The Arab campaign did not play a large role in the overall military effort, but it did render valuable assistance to the British by seizing the port of Aqaba, which made it possible to attack Ottoman forces in Palestine from the southeast, as well as from Egypt. The campaign also prevented the Germans from establishing a submarine base in the Red Sea, and later helped to encourage an Arab uprising in provinces farther to the north.

After the war there emerged a disagreement about whether Britain had intended that Palestine be excluded from the area specified by the Husayn-McMahon agreement. The British had told Husayn that the exclusion of portions of "western Syria" was in consideration of the interests of France, their wartime ally, and this fostered a belief that the reference was to the area of present-day Lebanon and did not involve Palestine. Moreover, this interpretation was consistent with the facts of geography. Palestine was regarded as southern, not western, Syria; and the territory lying directly west of Damascus, Homs, Hama, and Aleppo is all north of Palestine. Thus the Arabs were convinced, with reason, that they had received a promise of British support for their independence in Palestine, as well as elsewhere.

The British saw things differently, however. They asserted that the excluded areas should be defined in terms of prewar Ottoman administrative subdivisions. One of these was the District of Beirut, which lay directly west of Hama, Homs, and Damascus. The district encompassed modern Lebanon but extended southward as well, covering the northern half of Palestine. It was also argued by this logic that since the administrative district of Syria extended south to Aqaba, the territory to the west of it embraced all of Palestine. McMahon himself stated many years later that he had always believed Palestine to be part of the area excluded from his government's pledge to the Arabs. In response to this British logic it was pointed out that the Husayn-McMahon correspondence made no mention of Ottoman administrative districts, nor could it have done so since Damascus, Homs, and Hama refer only to cities.[60] Further, background papers prepared by the intelligence service of the British Foreign Office, which fell into the hands of the American delegation to the 1919 Peace Conference, clearly acknowledged that Palestine was part of the territory covered by Britain's promise to the Arabs.[61] Nevertheless, these reports were not official policy and Britain maintained that its interpretation was correct. It did not publish the Husayn-McMahon correspondence until many years later, although the letters were of course available through the Arabs.

The situation was made more complicated, and British motives were called into question further, by the revelation of a secret agreement between Britain and France that had been signed in 1916. Known as the Sykes-Picot agreement, the accord was worked out by Mark Sykes, a member of the British Parliament and an assistant secretary to the war cabinet, and Charles Georges-Picot, formerly the French consul general in Beirut. It called for Britain and France to divide much of the Arab Middle East into zones of influence after the war. In some of the areas in which each European country agreed to respect the influence of the other, the possibility of Arab independence was admitted, and the powers accordingly restricted their priority rights to "enterprise and local loans" and to the "supply of advisors and foreign functionaries." In other regions, however, they proclaimed their respective right "to establish such direct or indirect administration or control as they [Britain and France] desire and as they may think fit to arrange. . . . " Under this arrangement, France was to have authority in coastal and northern regions of Syria, and Britain in Iraq, Transjordan, and the port cities of Haifa and Acre. Parts of Palestine were to be placed under "an international administration, the form of which is to be decided upon after consultation with Russia, and subsequently in consultation with the other Allies, and the representatives of the Sherif of Mecca."[62]

Russia, a wartime ally, initially approved the agreement but then renounced it following the Bolshevik revolution of November 1917. Russia's subsequent publication of the Sykes-Picot accord, along with other secret documents, naturally stirred Arab doubts. Antonius expressed the Arab point of view when he described it as "a shocking document" and "a startling piece of double-dealing."[63] Nevertheless, the British were able to allay Arab fears by sending Husayn two telegrams in which their promises to the Arabs were reaffirmed. They asserted that the Sykes-Picot agreement was not a formal treaty and reflected only background talks designed to eliminate any possible tension between France and Britain. In retrospect, it is clear that Britain misrepresented its intentions. At the time these assurances were sufficient, however, and the Arabs rejected a peace overture from the Turks and remained in the war on the side of the Allies.

The third important pledge made by the British during the war was the Balfour Declaration of November 1917, in which an expression of sympathy for Jewish aspirations in Palestine was delivered in the form of a letter from Lord Balfour, the British foreign secretary, to Lord Rothschild, head of the Jewish community in Britain. The text of the letter had been reviewed at the cabinet level and in previous consultations with prominent Jewish leaders, and Rothschild was asked to convey its contents to the Zionist Federation. The letter read:

> I have much pleasure in conveying to you, on behalf of His Majesty's Government, the following declaration of sympathy with Jewish Zionist aspirations which has been submitted to, and approved by, the Cabinet.
>
> His Majesty's Government view with favor the establishment in Palestine of a national home for the Jewish people, and will use their best endeavors to facilitate the achievement of this object, it being clearly understood that nothing shall be done which may prejudice the civil and religious rights of existing non-Jewish communities in Palestine, or the rights and political status enjoyed by Jews in any other country.
>
> I should be grateful if you would bring this declaration to the knowledge of the Zionist Federation.

Like the Husayn-McMahon correspondence and the Sykes-Picot agreement, there is controversy surrounding the Balfour Declaration. Some Zionists had hoped for a stronger statement. Zionist policy did not at this time advocate creation of an independent Jewish state in Palestine and continued to concern itself with the immediate needs of immigration and land purchase. Nevertheless, some Zionists had urged that Britain make its declaration more specific and proposed that His Majesty's government endorse the idea of establishing "*the* national home *of* the Jewish people." On the other hand, the document was most welcome to the supporters of Zionism. It strengthened considerably the international political status of the movement and, coming at a time of great difficulty for the *Yishuv*, it provided a significant boost to Zionist morale.

The Arabs, of course, were disturbed by the declaration, all the more so when the Sykes-Picot agreement became public the following month. While the British could claim that they had taken into consideration the religious and civil rights of non-Jews, the Arabs must have wondered, as later writers have pointed out, why mention was not made of their political and economic rights as well. After all, had not Britain's recognition of these been made clear in pledges given to the sherif of Mecca? Again Britain succeeded in reassuring the Arabs, however, and Husayn sought to show his good faith by affirming that Jews would be welcome to settle in Palestine or any other Arab territory so long as the areas remained under Arab control. In March 1918, in an article in his official publication, *al-Qibla*, he even called upon the Arabs of Palestine to treat the Jews as brethren and to work with them for the common welfare of the country.[64]

Britain's motives in issuing the Balfour Declaration have been much discussed. Some in the cabinet and Foreign Office were not sympathetic to the Zionist plan, and this included Edwin Montagu, the only Jew in the cabinet. Also, some, including Balfour himself, were keenly aware that promises to the Arabs and Jews were at least potentially incompatible. Nevertheless, the declaration was made, and the reasons for it would seem to have more to do with Britain's war needs and long-term strategic interests than with the ability of Zionists to exert political influence. As expressed by one scholar, "It was not the Zionist leaders who taught the English how much they needed Palestine and not they who pulled them into the country."[65]

The relative weight of Britain's various goals is a matter of disagreement, but a long list of objectives has been enumerated by observers. One immediate goal was to rally the United States to the Allied war effort. Jews were believed to be influential in the U.S., and it was hoped that even non-Zionist American Jews, whose numbers at the time were considerable, would be moved by Britain's concern for their coreligionists. Beyond support in the war, a related consideration may have been to mute any possible American endorsement of Arab independence after the conflict, especially as the principle of self-determination had been articulated by the American president, Woodrow Wilson. Some British officials also expressed concern that should their country not offer support for Zionist aspirations in Palestine, Jews might exert their political influence on behalf of Germany in the years ahead. As expressed by Leopold Amery, another assistant secretary in the war cabinet, "It would be a fatal thing if, after the war, the interests of the Jews throughout the world were enlisted on the side of the Germans."[66]

Even more important were Britain's long-term strategic interests in Palestine, which grew out of its imperial presence in Egypt and India. On the one hand, some officials worried that a Turco-German alliance might survive the war and be capable of exerting influence in Palestine, especially if the Arabs controlled the territory. According once again to Amery, "the Jews alone can build up a strong civilization in Palestine which could help that country to hold its own against German-Turkish oppression."[67] On the other, Britain also feared that its communications with India might be threatened by a French presence in Syria unless it had a protectorate of its own in Palestine. This, too, made attractive the possibility that Palestine should possess a friendly and dependent colony, most of whose inhabitants were of European origin, particularly were this colony to seek protection from the British in preference to an internationally secured administration. Finally, support for the Zionist cause might give the British both a propaganda advantage and international allies should either France or Russia seek to challenge its preeminence in Palestine after the war.[68] Indeed, so far as the French were concerned, it was expected that intense rivalry for influence in the Middle East more broadly would follow the war, and, accordingly, Britain hoped that its general bargaining position would be enhanced by an opening to the Jews.

Postwar Zionist and Arab Diplomacy

These three conflicting British pledges, and the strategic interests that lay behind them, provided the background for postwar diplomacy aimed at determining Palestine's political status. Among this diplomatic activity, moreover, were new contacts between Zionists and Arabs. In March 1918, Dr. Chaim Weizmann, a distinguished chemist and leading British Zionist who had been deeply involved in the negotiations over the Balfour Declaration, went to Cairo and Palestine in an attempt to assure the Arabs that the Jews were interested in peaceful coexistence. He emphasized that Zionism's official goal was a national home for the Jewish people rather than an independent Jewish state. This point was technically correct at the time but potentially misleading, since most leading Zionists did hope the *Yishuv* would eventually acquire political autonomy. Weizmann, who later became president of the Zionist Organization and the Jewish Agency for Palestine, himself favored the creation of a Jewish state, although he saw this as a long-term goal which could be achieved only through patience, pragmatism, and accommodation with the Arabs.[69]

The leading spokesman for the Arab cause at the end of the war was Faycal

Ibn Husayn, Husayn's third son, who had commanded the Arab forces during the fighting. Weizmann traveled to Aqaba to meet Faycal in the summer of 1918 and the two men impressed one another favorably. They worked out an agreement for Arab-Zionist cooperation that was signed in January 1919, a few weeks prior to the opening of the Paris Peace Conference.[70] The agreement contained an introduction and nine articles and included language of remarkable cordiality. The introduction states that the signatories were "mindful of the racial kinship and ancient bonds existing between the Arabs and the Jewish people," and realized that "the surest means of working out the consummation of their national aspirations is through the closest possible collaboration." Article I declares that all Arab-Jewish relations and undertakings "shall be controlled by the most cordial goodwill," and subsequent articles make explicit what some of these undertakings will be. The most important are articles IV and VII, reproduced below:

> IV. All necessary measures shall be taken to encourage and stimulate immigration of Jews into Palestine on a large scale, and as quickly as possible to settle Jewish immigrants upon the land through closer settlement and intensive cultivation of the soil. In taking such measures, the Arab peasant and tenant farmers shall be protected in their rights, and shall be assisted in forwarding their economic development.

> VII. The Zionist Organization proposes to send to Palestine a Commission of experts to make a survey of the economic possibilities of the country, and to report upon the best means for its development. The Zionist Organization will place the aforementioned Commission at the disposal of the Arab State . . . and will use its best efforts to assist the Arab State in providing the means for developing the natural resources and economic possibilities thereof.[71]

Faycal's motives were obvious but nonetheless sincere. He had ample reason to be suspicious of British intentions and was particularly concerned about the ambitions of France, whose desire to control Lebanon and other parts of Syria was well known. In October 1918, Faycal had entered Damascus and received a tumultuous welcome from the local population, whereupon the flag of the Arabs was raised in Beirut. French protests caused Britain to remove it, however, and the subsequent anger of the Arabs led the British and French to issue a joint declaration promising "national governments and administrations deriving their authority from the . . . choice of the indigenous populations." Thus, though some historians have stressed the ease with which Britain was repeatedly able to allay Arab doubts, Faycal had logically reasoned that the case for Arab independence would be greatly strengthened by an alliance with the Zionists. Faycal also believed—and in this he was encouraged by Weizmann— that Zionism's financial resources and political influence would be helpful in securing international support for Arab self-determination. There is no evidence that Faycal was reluctant to commit himself to the establishment of a large Jewish presence in Palestine in return. After all, other Arab leaders had expressed support for this principle, and the possibility of Arab-Jewish cooperation was by no means unprecedented. Nonetheless, he took special precautions to make it clear that his agreement with Weizmann was conditioned upon the Arabs obtaining their independence. In an addendum, signed by both parties, Faycal wrote by his own hand:

> Provided the Arabs obtain their independence as demanded . . . I shall concur in the above articles. But if the slightest modification or departure were to be made, I shall not then be bound by a single word of the present Agreement which shall be deemed void and of no account or validity, and I shall not be answerable in any way whatsoever.[72]

As the Paris Peace Conference went forward, Faycal continued his contacts with Zionists. Late in January, for example, he sent emissaries to discuss with the Zionist delegation the possibility of a joint strategy against the European powers. Also, in an attempt to win the support of Zionists in the United States, Faycal in March exchanged letters with Felix Frankfurter, a distinguished American lawyer who was later to become a U.S. Supreme Court justice. Frankfurter was a leader of the Zionist movement in America, and the influence of the United States at the Paris conference was considerable. Faycal wrote to Frankfurter that both the Zionist and Arab movements were "national and not imperialist" and that "there is room in Syria for us both," adding, "I think neither can be a real success without the other." He opened the letter with a strong statement:

> We feel the Arabs and Jews are cousins in race, having suffered similar oppressions at the hands of powers stronger than themselves, and by a happy coincidence have been able to take the first step toward the attainment of their national goals together.
> We Arabs, especially the educated among us, look with the deepest sympathy on the Zionist movement. . . . We will wish the Jews a most hearty welcome home.

Frankfurter responded, in part:

> The Zionist leaders and the Jewish people for whom they speak have watched with satisfaction the spiritual vigor of the Arab movement. Themselves seeking justice, they are anxious that the just national aims of the Arab people be confirmed and safeguarded by the Peace Conference.[73]

These remarkable agreements and exchanges unfortunately had little impact. There were two reasons for this. First, they proposed an accommodation between Arabs and Jews that neglected the realities inside Palestine, where Arabs still constituted almost 90 percent of the population and where opposition to Zionism was growing steadily. Second, they did not produce an alliance capable of exerting any significant measure of pressure on Britain or France.

Many Zionists were sincerely interested in an accommodation with the Arabs. Indeed, Weizmann appears to have believed that Zionism could serve as a link between the Arabs and the Western world, a factor that would give the Jewish commonwealth in Palestine greater legitimacy and strategic importance in the eyes of European powers. The attention of Weizmann and most other Jewish leaders outside Palestine, however, was focused not on Palestinian Arabs but on Faycal, whom they regarded as the leader of an authentic national movement parallel to their own. Faycal was an ideal interlocutor; his orientation was truly pan-Arab, and he was capable of flexibility with respect to Palestine precisely because his interest was in the larger arena of the eastern Arab world—namely, Greater Syria, Iraq, and the Hejaz. Weizmann described Faycal in a 1918 letter to his wife as

> the first real Arab nationalist I have met. He is a leader! He is quite intelligent and a very honest man, handsome as a picture! He is not interested in Palestine but on the other hand he wants Damascus and the whole of northern Syria. He talked with great animosity against the French. He expects a great deal from collaboration with the Jews. He is contemptuous of the Palestinian Arabs and hardly regards them as Arabs at all.[74]

Thus, though Faycal had repeatedly stressed his demand for Arab independence and requested assurances that the Jews did not seek a state of their own, Weizmann found ample room for dialogue with the Arab leader.

On the other hand, Weizmann sought no more than proper economic relations with the Arabs of Palestine, and in fact was openly critical of the liberal attitude toward local Arab aspirations held by a number of Jewish notables in the *Yishuv*. In his judgment, Arab nationalism was exclusive, and there thus could be no accommodation with it in Palestine unless Zionism was prepared to abandon its dream of an independent Jewish existence, be it a national home or a state.[75] Further, in contrast to his genuine regard for Faycal, Weizmann held the Arab political class in Palestine in low esteem. On one occasion he described its members as "dishonest, uneducated, greedy and unpatriotic."[76] Finally, Weizmann believed that most Arab agitation in Palestine was not an expression of genuine nationalism but rather a product of local factionalism and the political infighting of a feudal elite.

In view of these considerations, the Weizmann-Faycal accord did not provide a meaningful basis for Arab-Jewish accommodation in Palestine. Faycal was gravely out of touch with local Arab sentiment. Although he had told the Jews frankly of his insistence that Palestine be part of the independent Arab kingdom he sought to establish, he had accepted that they might make of the country "a Jewish subprovince."[77] This led one British officer to write that the agreement would be a noose around Faycal's neck should its contents become widely known among the Arabs.[78] Weizmann, for his part, saw the agreement as exchanging support of Arab aspirations outside Palestine for an endorsement of Zionist goals inside the country. That none of this was a solid foundation on which to construct the political future of Palestine was recognized by the British, although the accuracy of their assessment should not obscure the self-interested character of their motives. In any event, as summed up later by Christopher Sykes, "If Faycal had been a Palestinian Arab of Jerusalem his treaty with Zionism might have had some feeble hope of acceptance, but since he was who he was, it had none at all."[79]

Faycal and Weizmann might have hoped for greater British sympathy. Both had received wartime promises of support from His Majesty's government and, perhaps more important, both had been clients whose entente Great Britain had encouraged for its own strategic reasons. By encouraging Faycal, the British not only endeavored to obtain Arab support during the war, they also sought to create a political situation which might later be used to contain French ambitions in Syria and, above all, to promote their own interests in the wider Arab East. Britain's political motives in supporting Zionism have been mentioned earlier, and to this it must be added that Weizmann was in no sense a reluctant partner. As early as 1914 he had conceived the idea that Jewish and British interests might both be served by installing a British protectorate in Palestine after the war. The Zionists would develop the country in accordance with their own aspirations but would, at the same time, integrate themselves into the British Commonwealth and undertake to protect Britain's strategic interests in the Middle East. Weizmann did not see this as injurious to the Arabs; the indigenous population of Palestine would benefit from modernization of the country and, more important, the Arabs would have obtained independence in the most important of their territories. The key point, however, is that Weizmann never sought an alliance with the Arabs *against* Britain. Nor is it likely that he ever entertained seriously the idea that Jewish interests in Palestine should be protected by the country's incorporation into a larger Arab kingdom. In any event, he ended any illusion that Faycal and other Arabs might have had on this point in February 1919, when he told the Paris Peace Conference that the Zionists favored a British trusteeship in Palestine.

Ultimately, however, both the Zionists and the Arabs were used by Britain for its own purposes. All of Weizmann's endeavors were encouraged by the British Foreign Office, which favored Britain's control of Palestine for military and strategic reasons but had little sincere interest in the development of Zionism. Indeed, while they had no hesitation about manipulating the Jewish leader's naive faith in an alliance with their country, some British officials secretly worried that Zionism might undermine England's interests in the rest of the Arab and Islamic world. In any event, for the most important architects of British policy, Zionism after the war was little more than a vehicle for ensuring their own country's entry into Palestine. Moreover, given the hostility to Zionism of local Arab opinion, there was little likelihood that the *Yishuv* would free itself from dependence on the English. Weizmann saw this only later, however, whereupon he would subsequently write that although cooperation with Great Britain had been the cornerstone of his policy, even when a different course was advocated by other Zionist leaders, "this cooperation remained unilateral—it was unrequited love."[80]

Nor were the British prepared to resist pressure from France in order to honor their pledges to the Arabs, to say nothing of sacrificing their own strategic interests in Palestine and other parts of the Arab world. When Faycal addressed the Paris Peace Conference, he condemned the Sykes-Picot agreement, demanded Arab independence, and sought to strengthen his case by proposing that a commission of inquiry be sent to Syria and Palestine to determine the wishes of the local population. This plan was endorsed by President Wilson and subsequently approved, it being suggested that there should be French, British, Italian, and American commission members. France vigorously opposed the project, however, knowing full well that the population of Syria did not want French rule. Britain, though it initially named its delegates, was not displeased to see French opposition undermine the project. The Arabs of Palestine might be opposed to foreign rule as well, and they would almost certainly express opposition to Zionism, all of which would complicate Britain's imperial design. When the Italians dragged their feet, Britain withdrew from the project, and only the Americans were left to carry out the investigation. Led by Henry C. King, president of Oberlin College, and Charles R. Crane, a businessman close to President Wilson, the commission toured Syria and Palestine in June and July of 1919 and solicited opinion from all segments of the population. It submitted a report in August, although this was not made public until several years later.

Meanwhile, political agitation in Palestine and Syria offered a clear demonstration of Arab aspirations. In Palestine, six patriotic and religious societies and over one hundred prominent individuals had in November 1918 addressed a petition to British military authorities in which they proclaimed their loyalty to the Arab government in Damascus and denounced the Balfour Declaration. In the latter connection, they stated that while they had "always sympathized profoundly with the persecuted Jews and their misfortunes in other countries . . . there is a wide difference between this sympathy and the acceptance of such a [Jewish] nation . . . ruling over us and disposing of our affairs."[81]

Similar sentiments were voiced by the majority of the delegates who attended a political meeting called by the Jerusalem and Jaffa Muslim-Christian societies and held in Jerusalem in February 1919. Sometimes referred to as the First Palestinian National Congress, or the First Palestinian Arab Congress, the meeting brought together about thirty politically active men from all parts of the country. Although there was not unanimity either on the issue of unity with Syria or on opposition to Zionism, the platform approved by the majority endorsed both positions and included a plank stating, "We consider Palestine as part of Arab Syria as it has never been separated from it at any time."[82] The congress also decided to send delegations to Paris and Damascus to communicate its resolutions; and in March, when British military authorities refused to allow a Palestinian delegation to leave for the Peace Conference, the Muslim-Christian Association of

Jerusalem sent Faycal a letter authorizing him to represent the Arabs of Palestine and to defend their interests in Paris.

Political activity in Syria was even more widespread. Faycal, who had proclaimed himself head of the Syrian state upon his entry into Damascus in the fall of 1918, returned to the country in May 1919. At the same time, former leaders of al-Fatat established the Arab Independence Party, and at their initiative elections were held for a general congress. Palestinian delegates also attended the meeting, most apparently having been chosen by various Muslim-Christian associations. In July, the General Syrian Congress passed a series of resolutions calling for the independence of Syria and all of its provinces, including Lebanon and Palestine. Although it made explicit its opposition to any formal trusteeship arrangement, the congress did express willingness to accept a foreign connection that would provide temporary and limited assistance. Its preference was that this assistance be provided by the United States or, failing that, Britain. It would accept no political arrangement involving France, however, and none at all that would compromise its independence. The congress also expressed opposition to the creation of a Jewish commonwealth in Palestine, and to all efforts to separate Palestine from the rest of Syria. According to Antonius, these resolutions were enacted "amidst an impressive display of patriotic fever." Also, as they became more widely known, the views of the congress were "echoed throughout the country. . . . Mass demonstrations were held in all those portions of Syria in which the French held no sway, and delegations flocked to the capital to cheer the Amir Faycal and acclaim the congress."[83]

In addition to making clear the Arabs' desire for independence from Europe, the General Syrian Congress represented a high point in efforts to realize Palestinian Arab aspirations within the framework of Greater Syria. Moreover, support for this aspect of the congress's program was passionately expressed by many political figures from Palestine itself, as well as by those from other Syrian provinces, although there were important intergenerational differences among the Palestinians that should be noted as well. According to one recent scholarly analysis, it was younger Palestinian politicians who were most enthusiastic about the program of the congress and about the unity of Palestine with Syria. Although some older Palestinian notables also accepted the idea of unity, this group was in general much less enthusiastic about the prospect. Many worried that a change in political and economic relationships would undermine the foundation of local interests on which their own positions of leadership were based, and some accordingly adopted a position of considerable ambiguity so far as relations with Syria are concerned.[84]

The King-Crane Commission witnessed these events and issued a report that incorporated some but not all of the ideas championed by the General Syrian Congress. It recommended that Palestine, Lebanon, and Syria remain united in a single state, with Faycal as its head, but it added that for a limited time this state should be placed under the mandatory authority of a foreign power. Following Arab opinion, it suggested that this authority be given to the United States or, if Washington refused, to Great Britain. It recommended against giving any portion of the mandate to France. With respect to Zionism, the King-Crane Commission found what later commissions of inquiry would also find, that the goals of Arab and Jewish nationalism in Palestine were by now quite incompatible. As a result, although the commissioners recorded in the text of their report an initial predisposition in favor of Zionism, they noted that the Zionist program could not be implemented without prejudice to the rights of the non-Jews of Palestine, and they accordingly recommended restrictions on Jewish immigration.

The Palestine Mandate and Its Boundaries

As indicated, none of this made much difference so far as British policy was concerned. It did not even persuade Britain to use its superior power to limit the actions of the French. Britain withdrew its troops from the zones of French occupation in the fall of 1919, and by the end of the year there was fighting between the Arabs and the French. In March 1920 the General Syrian Congress reiterated its call for unity and independence, and again these demands were rejected by Britain and France. The powers called a meeting of the Allied prime ministers at San Remo, Italy, the following month, whereupon the work of fashioning the political map of the postwar Near East resumed. In July, having by now obtained international recognition of their declared rights in Syria, the French seized Damascus and dethroned Faycal, who was forced to flee.

The Paris Peace Conference had reached no decisions so far as the Middle East was concerned, but at San Remo the Allies agreed upon the disposition of the territories they had stripped from the Turks. In an attempt to mollify the Arabs, and in order for Britain to claim fidelity to its pledge to the sherif of Mecca, the Hejaz region of the Arabian Peninsula was recognized as an independent kingdom.[85] The Arabs did not at this time obtain independence elsewhere, however. Greater Syria was dismantled, with Britain being accorded mandatory jurisdiction in Palestine and, as noted, France receiving this authority in the northern part of the country. Further, the area of Lebanon was given a special and separate status under the French, laying the foundation for its permanent detachment from Syria. Finally, Iraq was also declared a British mandate, and in 1921 Faycal was installed as its king. In order to find a home for the Arab leader, who had been driven out of Syria by the French, the British organized a hasty plebiscite in Iraq and then proclaimed Faycal monarch. The avowed purpose of all these mandates, which subsequently received formal approval by the League of Nations, was to promote the well-being and development of the indigenous population. The relevant paragraphs from Article 22 of the League Covenant read as follows:

> 1. To those colonies and territories which as a consequence of the late war have ceased to be under the sovereignty of the States which formerly governed them and which are inhabited by peoples not yet able to stand by themselves under the strenuous conditions of the modern world, there should be applied the principle that the well-being and development of such peoples form a sacred trust of civilization and that securities for the performance of this trust should be embodied in the Covenant.

> 4. Certain communities formerly belonging to the Turkish Empire have reached a stage of development where their existence as independent nations can be provisionally recognized subject to the rendering of administrative advice and assistance by a Mandatory until such time as they are able to stand alone. The wishes of these communities must be a principal consideration in the selection of the Mandatory.

Though they disappointed the Arabs, these arrangements were not unfavorable to the Zionists inasmuch as Weizmann had called for a British mandate in Palestine at the Paris Peace Conference. Moreover, while the mandatory instruments for Syria, Lebanon, and Iraq were highly similar, the one governing Palestine was very different and included many provisions respecting Zionist aspirations. Its text, based on the recommendations of the San Remo conference of April 1920 and formally approved by the League of Nations in July 1922, incorporated the Balfour Declaration into the preamble. The preamble also contained language giving explicit recognition "to the historical connection of the Jewish people with Palestine and to the grounds for reconstituting their national home in that country." Among the various articles of the mandatory instrument was a provision declaring that "the Administration of Palestine . . . shall facilitate Jewish immigration under suitable conditions and shall encourage . . . close settlement by Jews on the land, including State lands and waste lands not required for public purposes." [86]

At the same time, it was clear that Britain was pursuing its own interests in all these endeavors, and in fact the overall postwar settlement conformed closely to the imperial designs set forth in the secret Sykes-Picot agreement of 1916. The French had obtained their strategic objectives, and Britain was in control of the territory it deemed essential for the protection of its interests in India and Egypt. The Jewish presence in Palestine seemed likely to prevent the country from evolving into an independent Arab state, and in the meantime the terms of the mandate gave England extensive powers. These included legislative and administrative authority and responsibility for Palestine's foreign relations, domestic security, and defense. They also provided that the mandatory power "shall be entitled at all times to use the roads, railways and ports of Palestine for the movement of armed forces and the carriage of fuels and supplies."

Political activity leading up to the establishment of the mandatory system was concerned principally with questions about who would rule the former Ottoman territories, and in Palestine with questions about the degree to which the political rights asserted by Arabs and Jews would be respected. But while the issue of control was paramount, the matter of boundaries was also extremely important. The administrative divisions and subdivisions of the Ottoman Empire prior to World War I do not correspond to the geographical units known today, which permitted disagreement about the boundaries of Syria, Palestine, and Lebanon and about whether the countries should be united or ruled separately. Under the Turks, the eastern Arab world was divided into several large territorially defined regions, and on the eve of the war these included Syria, Iraq, and the regions of the Hejaz, the Nejd, and Yemen. The latter three occupied the territory of the Arabian Peninsula, with the Hejaz in the west, the Nejd in the east, and Yemen in the southwest corner. The general location of these major Arab territories is shown in Map 3.1. The term "Syria" at this time referred to the general land mass in the northwest portion of the eastern Arab world, extending from the Mediterranean in the west to Iraq in the east. This area is today occupied by the modern states of Syria, Lebanon, Israel, and Jordan. Under the Ottomans, the term "Syria" referred to the whole of this region, but it was also the name of one of the territory's internal administrative divisions, with the result that the area as a whole was also sometimes known as Greater Syria.

The administrative divisions inside Greater Syria were occasionally changed during the course of Ottoman rule, but by the end of the nineteenth century there existed within the territory three provinces, each of which was subdivided into districts, and two autonomous districts with an independent administration responsible directly to Constantinople. The Province (*Vilayet*) of Aleppo occupied the northern third of the country, the Province of Syria extended southward from it and covered the southeastern portion of the territory, and the Province of Beirut ran along the Mediterranean coast in the southwest. The Independent District (*Sanjaq*) of Lebanon was carved from the central mountain region of the latter province and was administered separately. The Independent District of Jerusalem, in the far southwest corner of the territory, was bounded in the north by a line running from a point just above Jaffa to the Jordan River and in the south by a line extending from Rafah in the direction of Aqaba. The boundaries of these administrative units, each of which had a governor responsible directly to the Turkish capital, are shown on Map 3.2a. The whole of the region encompassed by these five provinces and autonomous districts constitutes the territory within which the General Syrian Congress sought to establish an independent and unified state.

The southern portion of Greater Syria contained the territory generally recognized as Palestine, although there has been some disagreement about its precise location within this complex of administrative units. The Independent District of

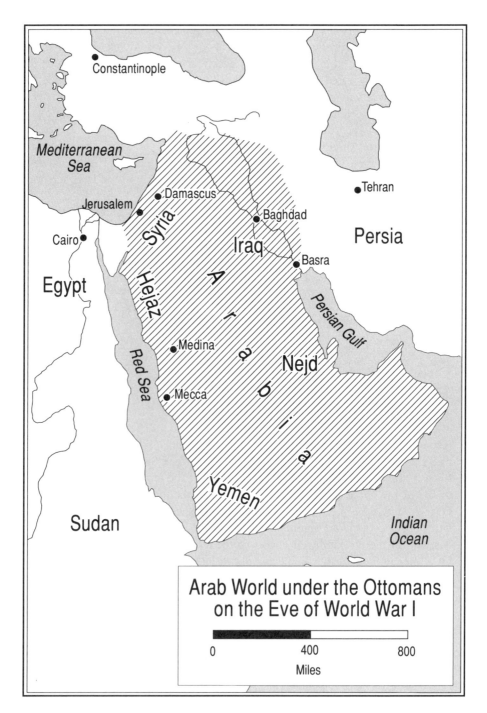

Arab World under the Ottomans
on the Eve of World War I

0   400   800
Miles

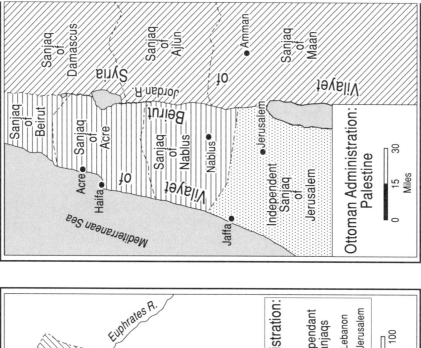

Ottoman Administration: Palestine

Sanjaq of Damascus
Sanjaq of Ajlun
Amman
Sanjaq of Maan
Syria
of
Jordan R.
Vilayet
Sanjaq of Beirut
Sanjaq of Acre
Beirut
Acre
Acre
Sanjaq of Nablus
Nablus
Jerusalem
Haifa
Vilayet
of
Independent Sanjaq of Jerusalem
Mediterranean Sea
Jaffa

0 15 30
Miles

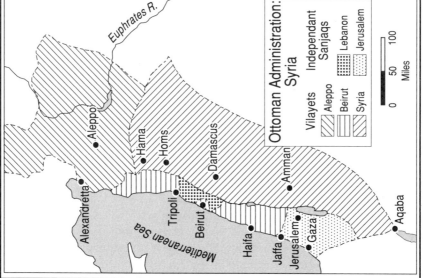

Ottoman Administration: Syria

Independant Sanjaqs

Vilayets
Aleppo
Beirut
Syria

Lebanon
Jerusalem

Euphrates R.
Aleppo
Hama
Homs
Damascus
Alexandretta
Tripoli
Beirut
Amman
Mediterranean Sea
Haifa
Jaffa
Jerusalem
Gaza
Aqaba

0 50 100
Miles

Jerusalem constituted most of southern Palestine, with an additional tract of territory between the Dead Sea and Aqaba, and the country's northern region was approximately coterminous with the southern section of the Province of Beirut. The latter contained two internal districts, Nablus and Acre, as shown in Map 3.2b. The disagreement concerns whether the whole of Palestine falls within this area, all of which lies to the west of the Jordan River, or whether territory to the east, comprising the southern districts of the Ottoman Province of Syria, should also be considered part of Palestine. These latter districts, lying east of the river, became known as Transjordan (or Transjordania) after the war. The significance of this issue lies in its implications about the extent of the territory within which Jews claim the right to construct their national home.

Zionists have historically argued that Palestine includes lands east of the Jordan River. At the time of World War I, this enabled them to assert that the country within which Britain had recognized their rights included both sides of the Jordan. Although territorial maximalists within their ranks argued that this meant everything up to the western border of Iraq, the boundaries of the Jewish national home proposed by the Zionist Organization at the Paris Peace Conference extended only as far east as present-day Amman. These boundaries are shown in Map 3.3. In any event, basing their claims on the extent of King David's Biblical empire, Zionists from the beginning saw the Ottoman districts of Jerusalem, Nablus, and Acre as constituting only the western part of Palestine. Indeed, some of the earliest Zionist settlements in Palestine were east of the Jordan River. Finally, more recently, by arguing that present-day Israel is located entirely within western Palestine, some Zionists seek to establish that current boundaries represent a reasonable division of the country between the Arabs and the Jews. They assert, in other words, that the Arabs already possess a considerable portion of historic Palestine and thus have no grounds for demanding border modifications in the name of territorial compromise.

Historical usage of the term does not resolve the matter definitively. The Roman provinces of Palaestina Prima, Palaestina Secunda, and Palaestina Tertia collectively covered the entire territory, including Transjordan. During the Umayyad and Abbasid periods, however, the region was divided into two military districts, or *jund*s, Jund Filastin and Jund al-Urduun (Jordan). Jund Filastin was the district west of the Jordan River, but in the tenth century it was expanded eastward and southward, extending to Amman in the former direction and to Aqaba in the latter. In the thirteenth century the name "Palestine" ceased to be an official designation, and later, during the Mamluk period, the *jund* was carved up into a number of smaller districts. As seen, additional administrative reorganizations took place under the Turks. Thus, although the term "Palestine" remained current in popular usage throughout this whole period, it lacked a precise territorial definition. To the extent that it was understood to apply roughly to the boundaries of Jund Filastin after the tenth century, which seems probable,

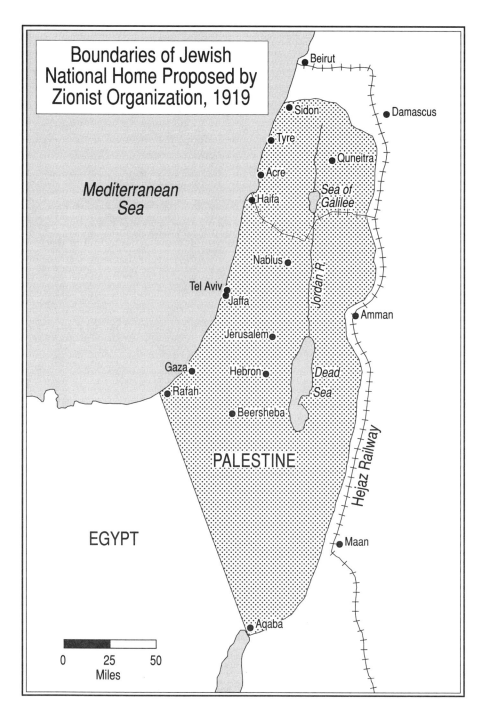

Boundaries of Jewish National Home Proposed by Zionist Organization, 1919

it encompassed some but not all of what later became Transjordan. It may be noted, too, that some Palestinian patriots writing before the war used the term in a more inclusive way, sometimes even applying it to the whole of Transjordan. Such, for example, was its usage in a 1913 booklet published by one of the leaders of the Orthodox Renaissance Society.[87] Nevertheless, while there has always been agreement that the most important part of Palestine is the more heavily populated and climatically hospitable region west of the river, whether or not the country also includes territory to the east remains, in the final analysis, a political judgment.

Boundaries became fixed in the years after the war. The mandate awarded to Britain at San Remo in 1920 included Transjordan, and it was sometimes referred to specifically as the Mandate for Palestine *and* Transjordan.[88] On the other hand, the mandatory charter ratified by the League of Nations in July 1922 appears to regard the separate political identity of Transjordan as still in the future. In this connection, Article 25 refers to "territories lying between the Jordan [River] and the eastern boundary of Palestine as ultimately determined." In any event, the matter was soon resolved by the British. Although the Zionists claimed that the Balfour Declaration recognized their right to construct a national home on both sides of the Jordan, the terms of the mandate specified that the provisions of the Balfour Declaration and of other clauses supportive of Zionism need not apply in the territory east of the river. In this way, Britain hoped to reduce opposition from the Arabs, and in 1921 the British did in fact close Transjordan to Jewish settlement. This decision was approved by the League of Nations in September 1922.

Even more important, by the time Britain's mandate for Palestine officially came into force, in September 1923, the British had completely severed the administration of Transjordan from that of Palestine and established the former as a semi-autonomous state under its general mandatory authority. Britain recognized as leader of the new state Abdullah Ibn Husayn, another son of the sherif of Mecca, and in this way sought to pay an additional share of its debt to the Hashemites. Britain also sought to mollify Abdullah, who in 1921 had marched north with an army from the Hejaz and was threatening to make war on the French in Syria. Although it is denied by the British, there is some evidence that Abdullah's arrival may have been prearranged with Great Britain. In any event, his authority in Transjordan was promptly recognized by Winston Churchill, at the time Britain's colonial secretary. As explained in one major study, establishment of the Transjordanian emirate was part of a general "Sharifian policy" being pursued by Churchill, "a policy of forming a number of small states in Arabia and the Fertile Crescent, all headed by members of the sharif's family and of course under British influence and guidance."[89]

Transjordan was reorganized as an autonomous state in May 1923, and in 1928 the Anglo-Jordanian Treaty gave Abdullah's government additional powers, although Britain still retained control over defense and external relations. The separation of Palestine and Transjordan brought renewed protests from the Zionists, and in 1925 some of them formed the militant Revisionist Party, which demanded that the mandate be revised to include Transjordan. Nevertheless, from 1923 onward, Transjordan and Palestine remained separate political units and evolved in very different ways. The latter became the scene of increasingly bitter confrontations between Jews and Arabs. The former, an impoverished and underpopulated desert kingdom, contained no Jewish inhabitants and remained on the periphery of the Arab-Zionist conflict for the duration of the mandate period, even though Abdullah himself participated actively in the diplomatic maneuvering associated with the evolving dispute. The boundaries of Palestine and Transjordan under the mandatory system that came into operation in 1923 are shown in Map 3.4.

Alternatives to Conflict?

These developments established the framework within which the Arab-Zionist conflict was to evolve in Palestine during the years between the two world wars. On the one hand, Jewish immigration and land purchases resumed, and the *Yishuv* grew in size, self-sufficiency, and structural complexity. On the other, political activity among Palestinian Arabs increased in scope and intensity and, although early meetings produced calls for independence as part of a unified Syrian Arab state, an explicitly Palestinian national consciousness soon took shape. Clashes between the two national movements resulted in violence as early as 1920. In April of that year, there was an Arab assault on the Jewish population of Jerusalem. After two days of rioting, there were 5 Jews killed and 211 injured. Four Arabs were killed and 21 injured. In May of 1921 there were much more serious disturbances. Anti-Jewish riots began in Jaffa and were followed by attacks in Rehovoth, Petah Tikvah, Hadera, and other Jewish towns. Forty-seven Jews were killed and 140 wounded; Arab casualties were 48 dead and 73 wounded, due mostly to British action to suppress the rioting.

From the vantage point of the present, it is instructive to ask whether violent conflict between Arabs and Jews in Palestine was inevitable. No definitive answer is possible, of course, and the matter today is of only limited analytical interest. Nevertheless, it is possible to envision circumstances under which, conceivably, matters might have worked out differently. It would be naive to argue that all conflict could have been avoided if only the parties to the dispute had displayed greater sensitivity and taken a more enlightened view of their own self-interest. There were both systemic obstacles to Arab-Jewish accommodation and fundamental political interests that, at least in part, were truly incompatible. A clash between Arabs and Jews in Palestine was thus probably inevitable. At the same

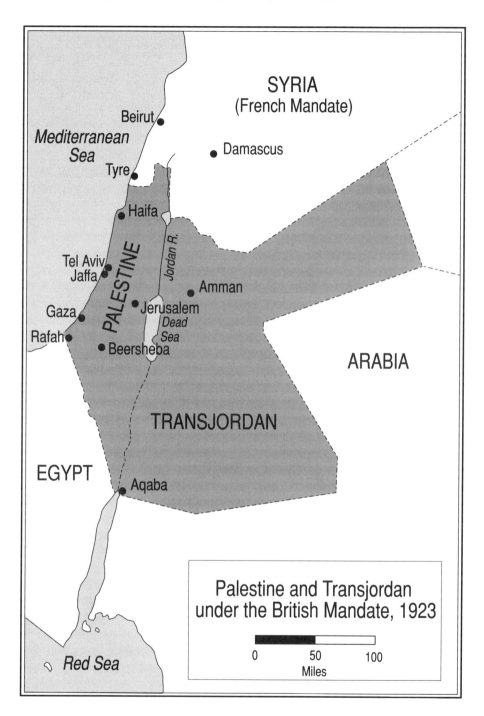

SYRIA
(French Mandate)

Beirut

Mediterranean
Sea

Tyre

Damascus

Haifa

Tel Aviv
Jaffa

Jordan R.

PALESTINE

Amman

Gaza

Jerusalem

Dead
Sea

Rafah

Beersheba

ARABIA

TRANSJORDAN

EGYPT

Aqaba

Red Sea

Palestine and Transjordan
under the British Mandate, 1923

0   50   100
Miles

time, it remains possible to theorize that under certain conditions the conflict taking shape might have evolved somewhat differently, with considerably less violence and with greater potential for compromise.

Peaceful coexistence would first have required that Britain honor its wartime pledges to the Arabs and pay serious attention to the political and economic rights of Palestine's indigenous population. Under these circumstances, Faycal's vision of an independent Arab kingdom with a region available for Jewish development might have been attainable. Arab opposition to Zionism, which existed even before the war, cannot be discounted. On the other hand, most Arabs did not at the time oppose a Zionist presence but, rather, feared that increased Jewish immigration would mean the loss of their political rights and the transformation of their country's Arab character. These fears might have diminished significantly had Palestine been incorporated into an independent Arab kingdom roughly coterminous with Greater Syria, since both the political rights and the cultural aspirations of the state's Arab inhabitants would then have been secure.

Under these conditions, Arabs and Jews might have worked together for the development of Palestine, and a Jewish national home might have developed under an Arab rather than a British umbrella. The attitude of such an Arab state toward the eventual independence of the *Yishuv* would probably not have been favorable. Yet it is also possible that a legacy of Arab-Jewish cooperation would have permitted the matter to be resolved through political means, with far less bitterness than turned out to be present. In any event, had a different political order been imposed upon Palestine after the war, Arab-Jewish relations might not have become a zero-sum game, wherein the gains of one community were (or were perceived to be) at the expense of the latter. As it turned out, however, the British determined that their own interests precluded such developments. They colluded with France to prevent Arab unity and to limit Arab independence, and they used Zionism as a vehicle to facilitate their own entry into Palestine.

For things to have worked out differently, it would also have been necessary for Zionist leadership to place less faith in Britain and more in the Arabs, especially the Arabs of Palestine. When Weizmann told the Paris Peace Conference that the Jews favored a British mandate, and then coupled this statement with his famous pronouncement that Palestine would ultimately become "as Jewish as England is English," all hope was probably lost. But a different attitude might have been possible, and Zionist opinion was in fact divided at the time. Some, such as Ahad Ha'am, who is identified with Cultural Zionism, recognized the legitimacy of Palestinian aspirations and urged that they be taken seriously. Others, such as Vladimir Jabotinsky, founder of the Revisionist Party, considered the Arabs to be of no political consequence and believed that an understanding with them was neither desirable nor possible. The debate among contemporary Zionists about relations with the Arabs is thoughtfully summarized by Walter Laqueur, who reports that there existed "healthy national egoism being urged on the one side and on the other the demand that Jewish settlement in Palestine should be based on the highest moral principles and proceed only in agreement with the Arabs."[90]

Interestingly, Weizmann appears to have shared Ahad Ha'am's view with respect to the Arabs in general, but that of Jabotinsky so far as the Palestinians were concerned. According to one prominent student of Zionism, "Weizmann's attitude toward the Palestinians was the gravest error of his political leadership." He was "heavily influenced by his British advisors" and "approached the Palestinians with a prejudice that blinded him to the most obvious facts" and caused him to listen to those who "viewed the Palestinians as backward, treacherous and corrupt."[91] More generally, many Zionist leaders based in Europe simply ignored the Arabs of Palestine, refusing to "consider the presence of half a million non-Jews an insurmountable obstacle."[92] For the most part they did not consider Arab rights when dealing with the British; and when they did concern themselves with the Palestinians, they argued only that Zionism would provide material benefits for the Arab population and ignored any question concerning Palestinian political aspirations.

If Zionists had seen the Palestinians as the latter saw themselves, however, as members of the Arab nation with the same political and cultural aspirations as other Arabs, at least some measure of accommodation might have been possible. This cannot be known with certainty, of course, and there undoubtedly would have been tension even had the Zionist leadership adopted a different posture toward the Arabs. Nevertheless, the tendency of Palestinian Arabs to regard Zionism as a mortal threat was in fact intensified by the refusal of most mainstream Zionist leaders to accept the legitimacy of Palestinian desires for self-determination and national independence. As expressed by Laqueur, a respected Zionist historian who assigns part of the responsibility for deteriorating relations to Jewish attitudes and behavior, "Undeniably the Zionist Executive in Europe is open to criticism for . . . showing little foresight in its relations with the Arabs, though from time to time it did press resolutions stressing the importance of making efforts to gain the sympathy of Palestine's Arab population."[93]

Finally, for events to have turned out differently the Arabs would have had to accept Zionism as a political movement, one whose struggle for a national home demanded political autonomy and, perhaps eventually, statehood. Arabs today often charge that Zionists see the Palestinians only as refugees, as unfortunate individuals whose principal needs are sympathy and humanitarian assistance. They reject this view, however, insisting that the Palestinians are a national community with political rights that must be acknowledged. Curiously, the Zionist attitude about which Arabs complain parallels their own view of the Jews during the early years of Arab-Zionist contact. They were unwilling or unable to accept that modern Zionism was by definition a political movement, and to understand that self-determination was as important for the Jews as they knew it to be for themselves. There were sincere and realistic Arab leaders prepared to come to terms with the Jews, but the price that Zionists were usually required to pay for cooperation was a denial of the national and political character of their movement.

It is also unfortunate that the political class in Palestine was dominated by conservative families whose fortunes were tied to feudal social and economic structures. These families were opposed to meaningful social transformation, and this attitude also made it difficult for them to appreciate the political dimension of modern Zionism. Although most had initially been pro-Ottoman in orientation, many prominent sons of these families were now sincere Arab nationalists. Their nationalism remained conservative, however, and was largely devoid of concern for genuine modernization. Thus they saw Zionism not only in terms of the conflict between Arab and Jewish interests but also as the spearhead of a social revolution with the potential to undermine the political order on which their own status was founded.

It would not be accurate to conclude, as some Zionists allege, that the Palestinian elite therefore created hostility toward Zionism among an Arab peasantry which otherwise would have been unconcerned about the growing Jewish presence in their country. Nevertheless, by discouraging any serious attention to issues of modernization and development, and by defining Palestinian aspirations in terms of their own narrow political interests, they, too, reduced any possibility that Zionism and Arab nationalism might seek to cooperate—not only in pursuit of immediate objectives but in the construction of a new and progressive political order. Influential and well-connected Palestinians at this time were for the most part uninterested in the construction of a socioeconomic system based on new values and institutions. Further, though they championed the principle of self-determination, they did not attach to the concept a concern for political accountability or popular control of national leaders. These ideological considerations encouraged them to view the program of modern political Zionism in the same unidimensional and uncomprehending manner in which they were themselves viewed by many Zionists. They might understand and sympathize with the plight of individual Jews, but they were unwilling to recognize Zionism as a legitimate political movement, one whose origins and objectives had much in common with similar movements in the Arab world.

Perhaps the results would not have been different if Palestinian Arabs had sought from the Jews a recognition of their right to self-determination and offered the Zionists the same in return. Perhaps this would only have hastened and intensified the confrontation by making more clear the incompatibility of what Weizmann himself once called "a conflict between two rights." On the other hand, again, if the British had not interfered and if Arabs and Zionists had been prepared to recognize one another's legitimate political rights, a measure of cooperation and mutual respect might have been possible, and out of this might have evolved a consensus and a formula for sharing the country. Under such circumstances, Arabs and Zionists would perhaps have been able to make of their joint presence in Palestine something other than a zero-sum competition. Whether any of this was possible in the years before and immediately after World War I is now entirely academic, of course. The necessary political course was not followed by any of the principal actors. The British manipulated both the Arabs and the Jews for their own purposes, at least initially, and each of the two latter parties found in the uncompromising posture of the other confirmation that its own militant stance was the only course available.

Incompatible Zionist and Palestinian Interests

Nothing was more important to the development of the Jewish *Yishuv* in Palestine than immigration, and nothing was more central to the Arabs' fear of Zionism. During the war the Jewish population of Palestine declined to approximately 55,000, and by 1918 the viability of the *Yishuv* had been placed in doubt. In 1919, however, Jewish immigrants once again began to arrive. Between 8,000 and 9,000 *olim* (new immigrants; those who make *aliya*) arrived each year between 1920 and 1923. Thereafter, as shown in the table below, the numbers were even larger. While the arrival of these Jews was of critical importance for Zionism, the newcomers intensified Arab fears that the whole of Palestine would soon be transformed into a Jewish colony. Over the long haul these fears might not have been unreasonable. At the time, however, they were based on wild rumors about massive invasions of immigrants, numbering 100,000 or more, whose arrival was held to be imminent. Thus, like the Jews, the Arabs of Palestine saw in the issue of immigration the matter of their political and cultural survival.

1919— 1,806 immigrants	1930— 4,944 immigrants
1920— 8,223 immigrants	1931— 4,075 immigrants
1921— 8,294 immigrants	1932—12,553 immigrants
1922— 8,685 immigrants	1933—37,337 immigrants
1923— 8,175 immigrants	1934—45,267 immigrants
1924—13,892 immigrants	1935—66,472 immigrants
1925—34,386 immigrants	1936—29,595 immigrants
1926—13,855 immigrants	1937—10,629 immigrants
1927— 3,034 immigrants	1938—14,675 immigrants
1928— 2,178 immigrants	1939—31,195 immigrants
1929— 5,249 immigrants	

The British were initially favorably disposed toward Jewish immigration, but their attitude soon became more restrained. Sir Herbert Samuel, the first British high commissioner of Palestine, took office in July 1920 and, consistent with the terms of the Balfour Declaration and the agreement signed at San Remo, he worked to facilitate the arrival of Jewish settlers. Samuel, a Jew, had been Weizmann's choice for the job. As early as 1915 he had submitted to the British cabinet a memorandum arguing that it was in England's interest to support a Jewish national home in Palestine, and as high commissioner his early statements indicated continuing support for Zionism. Upon taking up residence in Palestine, however, Samuel, like many British officials who came from London, gained a new understanding of the realities in the country, and this in turn tempered his enthusiasm for the Jewish cause. In the end, many Zionists were to complain about Samuel's policies, while many Arabs came to regard the high commissioner as a fair-minded and honorable man.[94] In any event, Samuel and the British soon became aware of and concerned about the rising tide of Arab opposition to Jewish immigration, especially following the riots of May 1921. A British Foreign Office report on these disturbances deemed it significant that Jaffa should have been the town to suffer from an explosion of Arab sentiment, stating that there was no cause for surprise since the city was a major port of entry for Jewish immigrants.[95] The riots had in fact begun with an attack by local Arabs on a group of Jews in an absorption center awaiting resettlement.

Samuel set up a commission of inquiry to investigate the disturbances and put it under the direction of Sir Thomas Haycraft, the chief justice of Palestine. The Haycraft Commission placed the blame on anti-Zionist sentiment among the Arabs and on a widespread belief among the latter that Great Britain was favoring the Jews and according them too much authority. The report denounced the Arabs as aggressors in the disturbances and strongly criticized the Jaffa police for failing to contain the violence. Nevertheless, the underlying problem on which the Haycraft Commission placed emphasis was of a different character. It concluded that "the fundamental cause of the Jaffa riots and the subsequent acts of violence was a feeling among the Arabs of discontent with, and hostility to, the Jews, due to political and economic causes, and connected with Jewish immigration. . . . "[96] Further, the commission criticized the Zionists for failing to give adequate consideration to the legitimate interests of the Arabs. It concluded that the Zionist Organization had "exercised an exacerbating rather than a conciliatory influence on the Arab population of Palestine, and has thus been a contributory cause of the disturbances."

The Zionists rejected these conclusions and asserted that the sentiments of uneducated Arabs were being artificially manipulated by self-serving Palestinian leaders. The latter, they charged, were fearful that the introduction of modern and Western ideas would undermine the feudal social and political structure which supported their privileged position. On the other hand, while there was probably a measure of accuracy in these contentions, the Haycraft Commission refused to draw from them any suggestion that the riots would not have occurred "had it not been for incitement by the notables, effendis and sheikhs." According to the commission's report, "the people participate with the leaders, because they feel that their political and material interests are identical."[97] In any event, the British viewed the disturbances with considerable concern, and even as the Haycraft Commission began its work, Samuel took action designed to respond to Arab opinion. On May 14 he announced the temporary suspension of Jewish immigration, pending new legislation. On June 3 he stated that Jewish immigration should be limited by the "numbers and interests of the present population" and declared that Jews should come to Palestine "in order to help by their resources and efforts to develop the country, to the advantage of all the inhabitants."[98] These pronouncements were also condemned by the Zionists, who accused Samuel of rewarding violence and appeasing Arab extremism. In his June statement, Samuel also indicated that Britain was considering a constitution which would establish a partially elected legislative council, in order that the inhabitants of Palestine might have a mechanism for the expression of their political views.

In August of 1921 the Arabs carried their protest to London, sending a delegation of Muslims and Christians led by Musa Kazim al-Husayni. Al-Husayni, head of one of Palestine's leading families, had been mayor of Jerusalem until April 1920, when he was dismissed for support of the anti-Jewish riots of that month. The delegation spent nearly a year negotiating with the British, and it also visited the League of Nations in Geneva to protest that Palestine's Arabs had not been consulted when their country's future was determined. The unswerving demand of the Palestinians was that the Balfour Declaration be annulled, and while in London the group set forth their arguments in a booklet entitled *The Holy Land: The Moslem-Christian Case against Zionist Aggression*. The British made it clear to the Palestinians that the Balfour Declaration would not be repudiated. On the other hand, they did acknowledge and invite discussion on "the real fear with which the Arabs regarded the idea of Jewish immigration" and "the real fear with which they regarded the contingency of Jewish political ascendancy in Palestine."[99]

In February 1922 Winston Churchill, then colonial secretary, presented the Palestinian delegation with a draft of the constitution which Samuel had promised the preceding summer. Among its provisions was a legislative council composed of the high commissioner, ten appointed British officials, and fifteen elected local representatives. Of the latter, nine were to be Muslim, three Christian, and three Jewish. Although Zionists were fearful that the new constitution would not be to their advantage, it was the Arabs who rejected it out of hand, stating that they would not discuss any constitutional arrangements which left the Balfour Declaration intact. Negotiations continued for a time. The British suggested, for example, that the elected representatives to the legislative council might be empowered to set up an advisory committee on immigration. No progress was made, however, and the proposed constitution was eventually shelved, with the high commissioner continuing to rule by executive decree.

Under growing pressure from both the Jews and the Arabs, Samuel visited London in May to urge that Britain offer an official interpretation of the Balfour Declaration, preferably one that would clarify British policy toward Jewish immigration in a manner acceptable to mainstream Arab opinion. A white paper was thus prepared for issuance over Churchill's signature and shown to the Palestinian delegation in London. It was also presented to the Zionist Organization. The Zionists responded that the document was acceptable to the Jews, although its virtues were decidedly mixed from their point of view and it was not received without some complaint. Many saw it as another instance of what they perceived to be Britain's policy of appeasing the Arabs. Nevertheless, Weizmann sent Churchill a carefully worded letter of approval on behalf of the Zionist Executive, writing that "the activities of the Zionist Organization will be conducted in accordance with the policy therein set forth." [100] The Arabs, for their part, flatly rejected the white paper, stating that its endorsement of the principles of the Balfour Declaration made it unacceptable, despite some provisions addressed to their grievances. In spite of this Arab response, Churchill issued the statement, and it was approved by the British parliament early in July. It provided the British government's official interpretation of the mandate on the eve of its formal approval by the League of Nations.

The white paper satisfied the Zionists by affirming that Jews were in Palestine "as of right and not on sufferance," and by asserting that "the existence of a Jewish National Home in Palestine should be internationally guaranteed" and "formally recognized to rest upon ancient historic connection." On the other hand, it dissociated Britain from such phrases as "Palestine is to become as Jewish as England is English," specifically stating that "His Majesty's Government regard any such expectations as impractical and have no such aim in view. Nor have they at any time contemplated . . . the disappearance or subordination of the Arabic population . . . [or the prospect] that Palestine as a whole should be converted into a Jewish National Home." Accordingly, the white paper continued, "When it is asked what is meant by the development of a Jewish National Home in Palestine, it may be answered that it is not the imposition of a Jewish nationality upon the inhabitants of Palestine as a whole. . . . " Finally, therefore, Jewish "immigration cannot be so great in volume as to exceed whatever may be the economic carrying capacity of the country at the time to absorb new arrivals," and "it is essential to assure that the immigrants should not be a burden upon the people of Palestine as a whole." [101]

The issue which followed Jewish immigration as a source of conflict in mandatory Palestine was the purchase of land by the Zionist Organization. The overall amount of land acquired by the Zionists was not extensive. The magnitude of Jewish landholdings at different times is shown below. [102] Figures are in thousands of dunams, with one dunam measuring approximately one-quarter of an acre. While steady growth may be noted, the total land area of mandatory Palestine exceeds 26 million dunams, and thus the figure for 1936 reflects only 4.6

percent of the total. The figure for 1947 is only 6.6 percent of the total. The geographical distribution of Jewish-owned land in 1947 is shown in Map 4.2, which is presented in the next chapter.

Total Holdings (in thousands of dunams) by Purchasing Agent

	JCA	JNF	Private	Total
1882	–	–	23	23
1900	145	–	73	218
1914	235	16	167	418
1927	323	197	345	865
1936	435	370	426	1,231
1947	435	933	366	1,734

As can be seen, much of the land purchased in the early years was acquired by private individuals. Increasingly, however, larger estates were purchased by the Jewish Colonial Association (JCA) and the Jewish National Fund (JNF), and these were held "in trust" for the Jewish people as a whole.[103] In addition, the sources from which land was obtained gradually changed. Much of the land acquired before 1900 had been owned by the Ottoman government or by small shareholders. Later purchases tended to be the larger estates of wealthy Arab landowning families, many of whom did not live in Palestine, and some of whom were branches of extended families prominently associated with the Palestinian Arab national movement. Among the latter were branches of the Dajani family of Jaffa, the Husayni, Nashashibi, and Alami families of Jerusalem, the Abd al-Hadi family of Nablus and Jenin, and the Shawwa family of Gaza.[104] Summary information about the changing character of Jewish land purchases is presented below.[105] Whenever possible, Jewish agencies sought to acquire contiguous properties. It was also Zionist policy that land once purchased was the inalienable property of the Jewish nation and should not be resold to non-Jews.

	Large Absentee-owned Estates	Large Local-owned Estates	Peasant Holdings	Government Holdings
1879–1890	–	28%	–	72%
1891–1900	40%	6%	43%	11%
1901–1927	68%	20%	3%	9%
1928–1936	36%	44%	20%	–

The acquisition of land was essential to construction of the Jewish national home for a variety of symbolic and practical reasons. Landownership, especially national landownership, represented the Jewish people's desire to give the *Yishuv* a territorial as well as a demographic foundation. It symbolized the Jews' physical repossession of a country which they believed had been promised to them, and toward which they had turned their prayers for centuries. Not only would Jews return to the Holy Land, but the land would be reclaimed and would itself once again become Jewish. Land's symbolic importance also reflected the fact that Jews had frequently been prohibited from owning land in the Christian countries of Europe, sometimes being required to live in ghettos and often restricted to the practice of certain professions. For this reason, too, an ability to live on and work the land represented freedom from oppression, a redemption and a liberation from the "rootless" existence in the Diaspora. These themes were expressed as early as 1904 by Menachem Ussishkin, a leading figure in the Hovevei Zion movement:

> In order to establish autonomous Jewish community life—or, to be more precise, a Jewish state, in *Eretz Yisrael*, it is necessary, first of all, that all, or at least most, of *Eretz Yisrael's* lands will be the property of the Jewish people. Without ownership of the land, *Eretz Yisrael* will never become Jewish, be the number of Jews whatever it may be in the towns and even in the villages, and Jews will remain in the very same abnormal situation which characterizes them in the diaspora.[106]

A related aspect of the drive for landownership was the emphasis that Zionism placed on self-sufficiency and agricultural development. The *Yishuv* was to become a complete and autonomous national community, not simply an aggregation of Jews who lived in a few urban centers, and it accordingly was to survive by the fruits of its own labor and productivity. Thus, the Zionist Organization founded as early as 1908 the Palestine Land Development Company (PLDC), whose mission was to train Jewish agricultural workers and to settle them on land acquired by the JNF and the JCA. During these early years the PLDC played a leading role in establishing various agricultural communities and cooperative settlements.[107]

Such views were central to the ideology of Labor Zionism and to such non-socialist writers as Yosef Chaim Brenner and Aaron David Gordon. Gordon, in particular, gave eloquent expression to the desire of the Jews to work the soil of Palestine. In 1920 he wrote, "We come to our Homeland in order to be planted in our natural soil from which we have been uprooted, to strike our roots deep into its life-giving substances, and to stretch out our branches in the sustaining and creating air and sunlight of the Homeland." Thus, as Gordon had written earlier, whereas "the Jewish people has been completely cut off from nature and imprisoned within city walls these two thousand years," the Jews should now bind themselves to their land and to their national culture by working the soil of Palestine. Without such labor, however, "the land shall not be ours and we shall not be the people of the land. Here, then, we shall also be aliens."[108]

In addition to this constellation of ideological and symbolic considerations, the Jews also sought to buy land in Palestine for more explicitly political reasons. First, they realized that the legitimacy of their claim to a national home would be immeasurably strengthened by the possession of extensive landholdings. This would give them a territorial as well as a demographic presence to lay alongside claims advanced by the Arabs. Second, should the day come when Palestine would be divided among its Arab and Jewish inhabitants, which is precisely what was proposed by commissions of inquiry investigating later disturbances, landholdings might well determine the extent and location of territory allocated to the Jews. Third, the construction of an integrated Palestinian Arab society, one which might effectively challenge the legitimacy of Zionism's claim to a national home in Palestine, could be slowed by carving out and gradually expanding blocks of Jewish territory in geographically strategic regions. Land purchase and immigration complemented one another in pursuit of these political objectives, and the Zionist movement set for itself the goal of creating a Jewish majority in as many districts as possible. Thus, according to Granott, the first priority in the selection of land for purchase was "its place in the upbuilding and the attainment of a Jewish majority."[109] This exceeded in importance the state of the land's readiness for colonization and agricultural exploitation.

The Jews faced important difficulties in acquiring land in Palestine, which is why the overall amount they purchased remained small. To begin with, the financial resources of the Zionist movement were decidedly limited. The Zionists were plagued by serious poverty in the years before the war, and in 1920 the Keren Hayesod (Foundation Fund) was established to raise additional funds for colonizing activities. The new fund set for itself the goal of raising 25 million pounds in five years, but in fact it took six years to raise only 3 million pounds, hardly enough to achieve its ambitions and not even enough to pull the Zionist movement out of debt.[110] In the years following the creation of the Keren Hayesod, between 1921 and 1939, for example, it is estimated that the Jews invested about 9 million pounds in land purchases, a sum that was considered extremely limited from the Zionist point of view.[111]

Equally important, the price of land rose steadily and dramatically for a variety of reasons, according to one estimate increasing as much as fifty times between 1910 and 1944.[112] In the early years, land prices were driven up partly by competition among would-be private and institutional Jewish purchasers.[113] Also, especially later, Palestinian nationalist opposition strongly discouraged the sale of land to Jews, and this in turn forced Zionists to provide more powerful economic incentives to landowners from whom they sought to make purchases. The Zionists were thus confronted with a strong "seller's market," which, in addition to driving up prices, also frequently forced purchasers to settle for land of inferior quality. The Jews made purchases in the coastal plain and in the Galilee, both of which were areas of potentially high productivity. But, especially in the early years, the holdings themselves were often "substandard, poorly developed or undeveloped tracts of marsh, swamp or sand dune, which [Arab] landlords were happy to sell at elevated prices to eager Jewish brokers."[114]

Having frequently acquired land of poor quality, Zionists rightly stressed the strenuous effort that was required to develop it for modern agriculture. Indeed, they had acquired land in the swamp-ridden Jezreel Valley as early as 1911 but had not succeeded in establishing a viable agricultural base. This changed with additional purchases in the 1920s, however, and Zionist historians point with pride to what was accomplished. As summarized by Sachar, "With JNF help, swamps were drained, water supplies installed, and roads built. Despite the crippling bouts of hunger and illness the settlers had to endure, twenty new collective and cooperative villages were functioning in the Emek [Valley] by 1925. Most of them were founded by youthful immigrants who regarded the presence of this virgin tract as a standing and romantic challenge to their Zionism. Ultimately the Emek was transformed from malarial waste into one of the glories of Jewish Palestine." [115]

Unfortunately, this "virgin" territory was not without inhabitants, and the intensification of Jewish land purchases accordingly brought protests from the Arabs about the displacement of Palestinian peasants. The first large land purchase to stir such concern took place in the early 1920s. An estate of approximately 240,000 dunams in the Jezreel Valley below the Galilee was sold to the Zionist Organization by its absentee landlords, primarily the Sursock family of Beirut. This was one of the largest estates in Palestine. Neither the Sursocks nor the Zionists made provisions for the Arab tenant farmers who worked the land, however, and the result was that several thousand peasants were evicted from the land on which the families of some of them had lived for generations. The precise number of peasants turned out in this manner was a subject of dispute. Not surprisingly, Zionist supporters tended to minimize the figure, while pro-Arab sources inflated its magnitude. At the time, according to Sykes, Arab activists also organized excursions to the scene to show how "peasant families had been turned out as beggars from the humble houses where they had dwelt as useful citizens for generations, so that they might make way for rich Jewish newcomers." [116]

Despite the differing assessments of Zionist and Arab sources, it is clear that a substantial number of peasants were being displaced by this and other land transfers, adding greatly to Arab fears of Zionism and intensifying the concerns of the British as well. One Arab source estimates that by 1935 about 30 percent of the Palestinian peasantry was landless,[117] a figure which seems greatly exaggerated but which nonetheless points to a problem of serious proportions. In the same year the British high commissioner wrote in a dispatch to the Colonial Office that "about one-fifth of Arab villagers are already landless." [118] A reasonable overall conclusion, both about the difficulty of precise estimates and about the magnitude of the issue of Arab displacement, is offered by Sykes:

> By the very nature of the case it is not open to precise documentary proof. Statistics must be largely guess-work. The Sursock deal is known to have involved the eviction of about 8,000 tenants "compensated" at three pounds ten shillings [about $17] a head, but this was a famous episode. There were many similar though lesser ones of which next to nothing is known. The governing principle is fairly evident but the details . . . remain obscure.[119]

In 1920, even before the Sursock land deal, the British considered the displacement of Palestinian peasants a serious enough problem to pass the Transfer of Land Ordinance. The ordinance required government approval for all sales of "immovable property" and specified that such agreement should not be given unless "any tenant in occupation will retain sufficient land in the district or elsewhere for the maintenance of himself and his family." The significance of this legislation lies more in Britain's recognition of the problem, however, than in its effectiveness as a solution. It did not prevent the displacement of the tenants from the Sursock estate, for example. On the contrary, according to one careful study, the Sursock land deal is significant, in part, precisely because it "proved how a tenant's rights could be circumvented under the pliant eye of subdistrict officials."[120] More generally, in the judgment of several other important studies, the fact that Arab families with prominent nationalist credentials were engaging in land sales to the Jews "supplied the British with an easy excuse not to intervene in the dispossession of Palestinian peasants."[121]

With both Arab landlords and Jewish officials eager for sales, mechanisms for circumventing the legislation were readily found. Zionist agencies were willing to pay prices considerably in excess of market value but demanded vacant land for settlement. Absentee sellers were usually more than willing to oblige and often used a small share of their substantial profits to pay tenants to vacate their homes. In this they sometimes worked through local moneylenders, to whom the peasants were frequently deeply in debt.[122] Although many peasants may have considered themselves adequately compensated at the time they vacated their holdings, they rarely realized the long-term implications of their actions, and many found themselves destitute within a short time. Further, peasants were sometimes deliberately deceived into believing their absence would be temporary. As a result, despite the Land Transfer Ordinance, the number of landless Palestinian peasants grew steadily during the 1920s.

In addition to immigration and land transfers, which were the major sources of tension between Arabs and Jews, relations in certain regions were further aggravated by the desire of some Zionists to hire only Jewish workers. As noted earlier, the ideological motivation behind the drive for Jewish labor was similar to that associated with working the land. It was strongest among the sectors of the *Yishuv* oriented toward Labor Zionism and reflected an understandable urge for self-sufficiency and for collective redemption through the literal, physical construction of the Jewish national home. Labor Zionists also argued that the moral stature and political legitimacy of the *Yishuv* would be undermined were it to be composed of Jewish employers overseeing a non-Jewish laboring class. The problem, as one Labor Zionist complained, was that in the agricultural communities established by early immigrants, the main task of Jewish capitalist planters was "to ensure that the Arabs worked properly."[123] As another had written in 1916, "Without Jewish Labor we will build on sand. We want to establish a national

Jewish entity in Palestine. But it is self-evident that this entity cannot be composed of a class of Jewish employers and one of non-Jewish workers."[124]

Nor was the demand for Jewish labor purely ideological. As many Zionist employers were quick to point out, Jewish workers demanded higher wages and shorter hours than the Arabs and, especially in agriculture, they were usually far less experienced and qualified. The demand for Jewish labor therefore had as a practical consequence the creation of jobs for new immigrants who might otherwise have had difficulty securing employment.

Labor Zionists and their unions sometimes organized demonstrations and boycotts in order to pressure Jewish employers to replace their Arab workers with Jews. The latter often resisted, however, stating that the Arabs were preferable as employees. In addition to the skills and lower wage demands of the Arabs, employers also sometimes complained about the attitude of Jewish workers. One agriculturalist wrote in 1918, for example, that "the Jewish worker tends to criticize, he is an extremist and rebellious, demanding an 8-hour day and the right to strike."[125] Arab laborers, by contrast, demanded little. They were unorganized, and most were hired on a short-term basis. In the important agricultural sector, for instance, it was common for Arabs seeking work to assemble in a village early in the morning, and from this pool employers would then select as many laborers as they needed.

Zionists also argued among themselves about the impact of Jewish hiring practices on relations with the Arabs. Labor Zionists asserted, with a measure of reason, that good relations could not be achieved on a foundation which equated religion and economic class. As Palestinian Arab society developed, they asserted from their socialist perspective, differences between employer and employee would become more important to the Arabs and would reinforce hostility to the Jews based on national and political grounds. Jewish employers took a less ideological view, however, observing, correctly, that by employing Arabs they had improved their relations with neighboring villages and had reduced the likelihood of attacks by the inhabitants of these communities. In the short run, at least, the latter of these two perspectives was the more accurate. Discrimination in favor of Jewish workers when hiring and calls for the displacement of existing Arab employees became an additional Palestinian grievance against Zionism. Although Labor Zionists directed their opposition at Jewish capitalists and employers, Arabs often believed that they themselves were the ones to suffer most. Sometimes they did not even perceive the inter-Zionist character of the issue. According to one objective analysis, the Arabs often interpreted Labor Zionism's struggle as an act of hostility against *them*, as a kind of economic boycott.[126]

Labor Zionists achieved their goals, but only to a degree. In the early years, especially, the supply of Jewish labor was not adequate to meet the demand. This was particularly true in the agricultural sector and, as discussed in chapter one, one Zionist response to the problem was an attempt to foster immigration among

Jewish agricultural workers in Yemen. Contributing to this situation was the fact that many Jewish workers oriented toward agriculture preferred to live on *kibbutzim* or in other types of cooperative settlements, thus eliminating them from the general labor market. Also, many postwar *olim* were middle-class merchants and professionals oriented toward urban life. As a result, the goal of an exclusively Jewish labor force was probably not even theoretically attainable until the 1930s. Nevertheless, the proportion of Arabs employed in the Jewish economy did diminish. The 1929 Jewish Agency constitution established that "in all works or undertakings carried out or furthered by the Agency it shall be deemed to be a matter of principle that Jewish labor shall be employed." By 1936, the overall proportion of Arab workers in the Jewish sector was only 14.6 percent, as the table below shows.[127]

	Total Employees in Jewish Economy	% Arab Employees
Agriculture	20,000	35.0
Construction	13,700	12.4
Industry and Handicrafts	21,900	8.7
Transportation and Ports	5,000	25.0
Commercial Services	6,400	6.7
Other Services	15,000	–
Total	82,000	14.6

That labor policies were an additional source of friction between Arabs and Jews was documented by several later commissions of inquiry. One determined, for example, that while the restriction of Arab labor on lands owned by Jews did not contribute to the primary economic problem faced by the Arabs, which was growing landlessness, it "has reduced the field of employment for [Arab] laborers and the means of livelihood of those cultivators who depend on work outside their [own] holdings to obtain an adequate income."[128] Thus, in sum, the labor practices of some Zionists generated grievances which reinforced Palestinian fears that the expansion of the *Yishuv* would inevitably be at the expense of their own political and economic welfare. The issue of employment was added to those of immigration and land transfer on the political agenda governing Arab-Jewish relations.

The Last Years of Tranquility

The explosive potential of this situation took several years to develop. Under Samuel and his successor, Field Marshal Lord Plumer, who served as high commissioner from 1925 to 1928, concessions to Arab nationalism seemed sufficient to give the Palestinians a measure of hope without being so sweeping as to cause more than grumbling from the Zionists. Although the Arabs and the Jews each voiced many complaints during these years, Samuel and Plumer demonstrated themselves to be fair-minded in responding to, or rejecting, the demands directed to them. Plumer, for example, recognized that the Transfer of Land Ordinance was ineffective and established a committee to devise new solutions to the problem of displaced and landless peasants. This action laid the foundation for new legislation, which was introduced by his successors. Some historians characterize the 1920s as a period of tranquility and hope, which is accurate to a degree but which should not be permitted to obscure the tensions building beneath the surface. Nevertheless, the years after 1921 were free from major outbreaks of violence. It was not until 1929 that this period of relative calm came to an end.

It is also notable that during the 1920s some Zionists made efforts to improve relations with the Arabs, although the emergence during this period of more militant Zionist factions should be reported as well. Weizmann himself addressed Jewish audiences about the need for reaching an accommodation with the Palestinians, sometimes receiving criticism for his moderation. He told a Jewish gathering in America in 1923, for example, "If, as I hope, there will be a Jewish majority in Palestine, it will nevertheless remain an island in an Arab Sea. We have to come to an understanding with this people which is akin to us and with which we have lived in concord in the past." Whereas Weizmann's reference here was to the Arab world in general, rather than to the Arab inhabitants of Palestine, he told the Fourteenth Zionist Congress, meeting in Vienna in 1925, that "Palestine must be built up without violating the legitimate interests of the Arabs. . . . [The Zionist Congress] has to learn the truth that Palestine is not Rhodesia and that 600,000 Arabs live there, who before the sense of justice of the world have exactly the same rights to their homes as we have to our National Home."[129] While such statements might be dismissed as Zionist propaganda, it is significant that they were directed not to Arab, British, or American audiences but to Jews and Zionists, not all of whom were being told what they wanted to hear.

There were also Zionists living in Palestine at this time who worked for a Jewish understanding of legitimate Arab rights and for Arab-Jewish cooperation. One of these individuals was Judah Magnes, an American-born rabbi who became president of the Hebrew University. Another was Arthur Ruppin, who was born in East Prussia and had come to Palestine in 1908 to head the Zionist Organization's Palestine Office and to direct the work of the PLDC. Magnes and Ruppin were part of a small group who championed the idea of a binational state in Palestine, by which they intended that Jews and Arabs should share Palestine and work together so that the two peoples might attain their respective national aspirations through mutual assistance and within a common political framework.

Underlying this perspective as well was a recognition that Arabs and Muslims, like Jews, were in a period of cultural renaissance and political ascendancy, which Zionism neither could nor should oppose. Ruppin wrote in 1922, for example, of the need for "a general understanding between Jews and Arabs with the aim in view of bringing about a new flowering of the whole East through common cultural endeavor." Also, "We [Jews] must integrate in the family of Eastern nations and form together with our racial brethren, with the Arabs [and the Armenians], a new cultural community in the Middle East." [130] To achieve this lofty goal, Ruppin argued, Palestine should become "a state of two nations." Magnes's view was similar. In a speech at the Hebrew University in 1929 he stated, "One of the greatest duties of the Jewish people is the attempt to enter the promised land, not by means of the conquest of Joshua, but through peaceful and cultural means." In the same year he wrote:

> "Immigration, Settlement on the Land, Hebrew life and culture." If you can guarantee these for me, I should be willing to yield the Jewish "state," and the Jewish "majority. . . . "
> Palestine can help this [Jewish] People perform its great ethical mission as a national-international entity. But this eternal and far flung People does not need a Jewish State for the purpose of maintaining its very existence. . . . Much of the theory of Zionism has been concerned with making the Jews into a "normal" nation in Palestine.[131]

The most important of the organized groups devoted to the binational idea was Brit Shalom, which made its appearance in the mid-1920s. The group's membership never exceeded two hundred, and it was criticized strongly by many mainstream Zionists. For the militant right wing of the Zionist movement, the group's name was a synonym for "traitor." Yet among its members were articulate and respected individuals, including a number of important and dedicated Zionist officials and leading scholars at the Hebrew University. The group's spiritual mentor was Martin Buber, the philosopher and scholar, who himself was greatly influenced by the ideas of Ahad Ha'am. Buber urged Jews to identify with "the spirit of the East" and denounced those Zionists who possessed a "dazed dream [of themselves] as emissaries of a West that is doomed to destruction." [132] His philosophy is sometimes characterized as "pan-Semitism." Other leading members of Brit Shalom included Ruppin; Ya'acov Thon, who succeeded Ruppin as director of the PLDC; Yosef Luria, head of the education department of the Zionist Executive; Chaim Margalit Kalvarisky, an agronomist with many personal Arab associations; Hugo Bergman, director of the National Library in Jerusalem; Gershon Scholem, a professor and leading student of Jewish mysticism; and Hans Kohn, an official of the Keren Hayesod who later migrated to the United States and distinguished himself as a writer and historian.

The importance of Brit Shalom and other, smaller groups should not be overemphasized. Although Susan Lee Hattis writes that "during the 1920s it had the attentive ear of Dr. Weizmann,"[133] the movement never struck a responsive chord among the Zionist public and remained a small and peripheral movement of opinion. Neither did it produce any meaningful response from the Arabs. As Ruppin was later to lament: "What we can get [from the Arabs] is of no use to us, and what we need we cannot get from them."[134] Nevertheless, at the time of its emergence in 1925, after the Zionist Congress in Vienna, it was an expression of hope that the chance for Arab-Jewish reconciliation was not yet definitively lost.[135]

A final sign that encouraged some observers in the 1920s was the cordiality that often characterized interpersonal relations between Arabs and Jews in Palestine. There were personal friendships among leaders and intellectuals within each community. Also, it was common for Arabs and Jews in rural communities to visit one another, attending weddings, circumcisions, and so forth in each other's villages. Even after renewed violence had broken out in 1929, such relationships did not entirely disappear. A 1930 commission observed, for example, that "it . . . is very noticeable in traveling through the JCA villages to see the friendliness of the relations which exist between Arab and Jew. It is quite a common sight to see an Arab sitting on the veranda of a Jewish house."[136] Thus, the conflict between the larger political and economic interests of Arabs and Jews did not always preclude the existence of friendly relations at the individual level, and this, too, fostered a measure of hope that cooperation between the two peoples was still possible. Indeed, as mentioned, one of the leaders of Brit Shalom was motivated by his many friendships with Arabs. This was Chaim Margalit Kalvarisky, a "hopeless optimist" who believed until the end that his personal experience could be replicated on a national scale.[137] Overall, then, the years of Samuel and Plumer were tranquil, at least on the surface. As an official Zionist document observed at the end of the Samuel era, the period was one of "peace and order and good government."[138]

Unfortunately, none of this should be permitted to obscure the incompatibility of Arab and Zionist aims, or the fact that the two peoples were on a collision course which sooner or later would express itself in the form of civil disorder or violence. The issues of immigration and land, and to a considerable extent jobs, were concerns on which the Zionists could not compromise. Even Magnes, whose vision of a binational state was unacceptable to all but a handful of Zionists, would not admit these as subjects for negotiation. They were *sine qua non* for a meaningful Jewish existence in Palestine, indeed for the survival of the *Yishuv*. To Palestinian Arabs, however, they represented the inevitable political and cultural transformation of their country. The Palestinians were thus concerned with survival as well. As a result, the country was moving inexorably toward a new and more intense confrontation, and this could not be changed by a fair-minded high commissioner, by noble sentiments about binationalism, or by personal friendships among individual Arabs and Jews.

Under these conditions, it is understandable that Sir Herbert Samuel, despite his accomplishments in keeping the peace, left Palestine with a firm conviction that there was little prospect for reconciling Arab and Jewish aspirations. During his tenure he had labored in the hope of finding an acceptable formula. He had sought reasonable compromise, reaffirming the Balfour Declaration while acknowledging and responding to Arab fears about immigration and land purchase. As described by one observer, British policy at this time "tried to reduce the Zionist program and to induce the Arabs to accept less than complete mastery of Palestine."[139] But while Samuel succeeded to a laudable degree in the short run, it proved impossible to harmonize the irreconcilable demands of the Zionists and the Palestinians. Plumer's legacy was similar. Although somewhat more rigid and detached than Samuel, he, too, was admired for his sense of fairness, and for the peace that prevailed during his tenure as high commissioner. Moreover, he left Palestine with less of a sense of personal frustration than did his predecessor, perhaps because Samuel, a Jew, had been subject to cross-pressures of a more personal nature. In any event, Plumer's departure in July 1928 was followed by the explosion of violence that in retrospect appears to have been inevitable. In less than two months there were disturbances in Jerusalem. The following year, widespread rioting in a number of cities brought extensive property damage and substantial loss of life.

In this environment, the political community of the Arabs and that of the Jews developed independently of one another. The evolution of each was to a considerable degree influenced by the threat it perceived in the other, but the two national units became increasingly unconnected on those dimensions that might have created common economic interests or a partially shared identity as citizens of Palestine. This pattern of segmentation, of juxtaposed autonomies developing separately within the common framework provided by the British mandate, has been aptly described as a "dual society."[140] The separateness of the Arab and Jewish communities of Palestine did not begin with the mandate, but it was greatly reinforced by events that took place during the period of British rule. Thus, as summarized by one important study of the *Yishuv* under the mandate, political development

> was characterized by steadily increasing tendencies toward separation between the Jewish and Arab population, beginning with *cultural* separation and continuing with *ecological* separation in the form of all-Jewish neighborhoods, at first in rural areas, and later in urban areas as well. Eventually the process included increasing *economic* separation and the emergence of separate *political* institutions which, at least in the case of the Jewish community, were characterized by considerable authority even in the absence of sovereignty.[141]

4 | The Dual Society in Mandatory Palestine

The Development of the *Yishuv* and the Zionist Organization

CONFLICT WITH THE Arabs was a fact of life for the *Yishuv* during the period of the mandate. Deteriorating relations with the British, whose policies sought without success to strike a balance between Jewish and Palestinian demands, was another political concern of the Jewish colony. Nevertheless, the *Yishuv* expanded and matured in the years between the two world wars, increasing in size and self-sufficiency and creating most of the social and political institutions that would later serve the independent State of Israel.

As noted earlier, Zionists chart the growth of the *Yishuv*'s population in terms of distinct waves of immigration, known as *aliyas*. The First and Second *aliyas*, which had ensured the viability of the Zionist colony in Palestine, took place in 1882-1903 and 1904–1914 respectively. During World War I, the *Yishuv* suffered greatly and its population declined by more than one-third. But growth resumed after the war, with the Third *Aliya* occurring between 1919 and 1923. Approximately 35,000 new immigrants arrived during these years, returning the Jewish population of the country to its prewar level of roughly 85,000. The character of this new wave of immigration did not differ markedly from that of the Second *Aliya*, which came from Eastern Europe, was socialist in character, and was stimulated by the failed Russian revolution of 1904–1905. The members of the Third *Aliya* came principally from Russia and Poland and were responding to both a push and a pull; they were alienated by the Bolsheviks' seizure of the Russian Revolution of 1917, and they were encouraged to make their way to Palestine by the Balfour Declaration and the British mandate, which seemed to promise new opportunities for Zionist development. The Third *Aliya* increased substantially the more modern and secular component of the Jewish community in Palestine, what was sometimes called the "new *Yishuv*" in order to distinguish it from the traditional Jewish community that existed in Palestine prior to the rise of modern Zionism. Its members, together with those who arrived during the Second *Aliya*, became the elite of the Zionist movement in Palestine. After the State of Israel gained independence in 1948, they assumed the most important positions of national leadership.

The Jews who arrived between 1924 and 1931 constituted the Fourth *Aliya*.

Swelled by almost 35,000 new arrivals in 1925 alone, this wave of immigration brought about 75,000 newcomers, more than doubling the size of the *Yishuv*. As a result, the 1931 census reported that the Jewish and Arab populations of Palestine were about 175,000 and 860,000 respectively, the former having grown from 11 percent of the total in 1922 to 17 percent in the latter year. The Fourth *Aliya* brought many middle-class elements, including merchants, artisans, shopkeepers, and professionals. The majority of these individuals came from Poland, where economic restrictions were being applied to the Jews. Indeed, the Fourth *Aliya* is sometimes called the "Grabski *Aliya*," after the Polish finance minister whose policies encouraged it. The fact that so many Jews came to Palestine at this time was also the result, in part, of new immigration restrictions introduced in the United States. Because this wave of new immigrants was less strongly oriented toward socialism and toward agriculture, the Fourth *Aliya* increased the heterogeneity of the *Yishuv* with respect to ideological orientation and economic structure. Settling principally in Jerusalem, Tel Aviv, and Haifa, these *olim* also expanded the urban sector of the Jewish colony. According to the 1931 census, only 46,000 Jews, about 27 percent of the total, lived in communities classified as rural. Additional information about the size and composition of the Third and Fourth *aliyas*, as well as subsequent waves of immigration, is provided in the appendixes to this chapter.

Many important institutions were established during these years. The Jewish defense force, the Hagana, was established in 1920, in the wake of the Arab attacks on Jews in Jerusalem that took place in that year. Although its origins were in the Jewish watchman's association formed before the war, the new force was organized for the purpose of self-defense because Jews judged that they could not rely on the British for protection. The Hagana eventually developed into the modern army of present-day Israel. In the 1920s, however, it was loosely organized, composed of volunteers, and strongly identified with the socialist wing of the Zionist movement. One author calls it a kind of working-class militia.[1] The Hagana became more disciplined and tightly organized in the 1930s, when conflict with the Arabs increased the need for a Jewish defense force, and during this period it operated branches for training and recruitment in almost all the localities of the *Yishuv*. The process of induction into one of these local cells is recalled in a biography of Shimon Peres, who would later become Israel's prime minister. As a teenager in a youth village at Ben-Shemen, the young Peres and his comrades were sworn into the Hagana in a solemn candle-lit ceremony before a pistol and a copy of the Bible. Thereafter they began training almost every night.[2] Although defense was the main concern of the Hagana, the militia also assisted in matters of immigration. During World War II, it helped to smuggle into Palestine thousands of Jews who had not received authorization to immigrate legally.

Another very important institution established in 1920 was the Histadrut, the general union of Jewish workers in Palestine. Known formally as the General Federation of Hebrew Workers in the Land of Israel, the Histadrut was another expression of the Labor Zionist orientation that dominated the *Yishuv* during this period. At the time of its creation, the Histadrut had about 4,400 members and was governed by an elected council of eighty-seven.[3] Its avowed purpose was the creation of a Jewish workers' society in Palestine, and among the practical considerations to which it devoted attention were the provision of health care and education and the management of consumer unions and employment exchanges. Although there were challenges to labor's dominance from the new immigrants of the Fourth *Aliya*, the workers' federation grew rapidly and reached a membership of approximately 22,000 by 1927. By 1930 its sick fund (Kupat Holim) had about 15,000 members, and by 1935 this number had more than doubled. The fund also had the largest registry of physicians and nurses in the country, maintained clinics in five cities and thirty-three rural centers, and operated two hospitals and two nursing homes. In yet another area, that of education, the workers' federation built an extensive network of schools. By the mid-1930s, 44 percent of all the institutions in the Hebrew educational system of Palestine were associated with the Histadrut.[4] After Israel gained independence in 1948, the organization became the national trade union of the country's workers and established a special section to incorporate non-Jewish Israeli laborers into its ranks.

Education was another important arena for institutional development during this period. Under an agreement worked out in London in 1920, a federated educational system composed of three semi-autonomous networks of primary and secondary schools was established. One of these networks, as noted, was affiliated with the Histadrut and was oriented toward the Labor trend within the Zionist movement. A second network was associated with the "General Zionist" trend, supported mainly by groups on the right or in the ideological center of the movement. A third network was controlled by the parties of orthodox Judaism. These interrelated educational networks were supported by the Zionist Organization and were independent of British authorities in matters pertaining to standards, curriculum, and budget. By 1934 there were 300 schools in this system, enabling the *Yishuv* to offer elementary education to almost all of its children. It was also able to provide specialized as well as general secondary education, there having been established a number of teacher-training, agricultural, and trade schools. Finally, institutions of higher education were established. The Technion was opened in Haifa in 1924. It was a technical university and eventually evolved into one of the world's leading institutions devoted to research in science and engineering. The Hebrew University was founded in Jerusalem in 1925, with Lord Balfour traveling to Palestine to attend the opening ceremonies. The campus was built on Mount Scopus, which overlooks the city and where land had been bought before the war for the purpose of constructing a university.

Institutions of still a different sort were those concerned with banking. The Zionists had established the Anglo-Palestine Banking Company in 1907, making it the first modern bank in the country. It was used by merchants throughout the *Yishuv* and soon opened branches in a number of towns. The bank continued to expand during the period of the mandate, and by the 1930s it was second in size only to Barclay's Bank, the bank of the British government in Palestine and agent for the Palestine Currency Board. The Anglo-Palestine Bank was the official bank of the *Yishuv*, and after Israeli independence it became known as Bank Leumi, the National Bank. It is at present controlled by the Zionist Organization and the Jewish Agency and is the largest bank in Israel. The second-largest bank in present-day Israel is Bank Hapoalim, the Workers' Bank, which was organized in 1926 under Histadrut auspices. Its purpose was to provide credit to rural settlements and to worker enterprises in the cities.

Another development that took place in the 1920s was an attempt to construct a unified system of *kibbutzim*, the collective agricultural settlements that had been established by Labor Zionists. Although the effort failed, it did result in the creation of three broad *kibbutz* federations, adding further to the institutional development of the *Yishuv*. Also, each of these federations eventually became affiliated with an independent political party. The Kibbutz Hameuchad group and the Kibbutz Artzi group were formed in 1927. The former favored large cooperative agricultural settlements and actively sought new members. It was less militantly socialist and its *kibbutzim* had something of a proletarian character. The Kibbutz Artzi group was more ideological and had a pro-Soviet orientation. Its settlements were more completely communal in character, with members sharing equally in all aspects of *kibbutz* life. In 1927 there were only four settlements in the Kibbutz Artzi federation, but by the time of World War II this number had increased to thirty-nine. The third group, Chever Kvutzot, was established in 1928. Composed of the first *kibbutzim* that the Zionists had created in Palestine, it was considered somewhat elitist by the other two federations. Chever Kvutzot resisted the loss of intimacy that characterized the large Kibbutz Hameuchad settlements, and also the ideological purity of those associated with Kibbutz Artzi. It gradually lost members, however, and became the smallest of the three federations. Nevertheless, together with the others, it constituted yet another dimension of the growing structural complexity of the *Yishuv*.[5]

The *Yishuv* experienced economic as well as institutional development, although there were also periods of economic difficulty. In 1923, for example, the *Yishuv* was in the grip of a severe crisis. Jobs were scarce, especially for new immigrants, and several thousand Jewish workers were unemployed. As a result, 3,200 Jews departed from Palestine in 1923. This was over one-third of the number of *olim* arriving in that year.[6] Another difficult period was 1926–27. Problems were caused, in part, by an economic crisis in Poland, which brought to a halt the flow of capital from that country's large Jewish population. In 1927 the number of unemployed reached 7,000, and more than 5,000 more Jews left the country.[7] Nevertheless, despite these problems, the economy of the *Yishuv* expanded steadily and development took place on many levels. Among the industries established in the 1920s were the Silicate Brick Factory, the Atlit Salt Works, the Grand Moulins Flour Mills, the Shemen Edible Oils Factory, and the Nesher Cement Works. In the domain of agriculture and rural development, citrus cultivation was expanded substantially in the coastal plain, and many new communities were established in this part of the country. Among them were Herzliya, Netanya, Pardes Hanna, and Benyamina, all of which lie on or near the Mediterranean coast along the route from Tel Aviv to Haifa. Some of these communities are today fashionable towns, but they all began as centers for agricultural development in the years between the two world wars.

A particularly important economic role was played by the Histadrut, which not only concerned itself with the welfare of Jewish workers but also participated actively in the development of the *Yishuv*. Much of the construction in the new cities of the Jewish colony was carried out by the Public Works Office of the labor federation. In 1925, for example, 45 percent of the work force of Tel Aviv was engaged in construction, a large proportion under Histadrut auspices. The city itself had grown to approximately 40,000 by this time. The Public Works Office, which was later reorganized under the name Solel Boneh, also built factories and quarries, as well as roads, buildings, and homes. Another Histadrut venture was the Chevrat Ovdim (the Workers' Association), which was established in 1923 as a semi-independent economic development corporation. Chevrat Ovdim was charged with carrying out entrepreneurial activity on behalf of the workers' movement. One of its creations was the Tnuva cooperative, set up in 1926 to market dairy products from *kibbutzim* and other agricultural settlements. Chevrat Ovdim also established a housing company to provide apartments to workers on a nonprofit basis. A partial picture of the Histadrut's wide-ranging contribution to the development of a Jewish workers' society in Palestine is offered by Laqueur:

> The Histadrut was the first to promote high-seas fishing, shipping and even civil aviation in Palestine. It set up cooperative retail stores, urban housing offices, a workers' bank, a big insurance company (*Hasneh*), and countless medium-sized enterprises in industry, transport and agriculture. *Solel Boneh* expanded rapidly after the depression of 1926–7. From modest beginnings it grew into a major concern even by international standards, eventually building up to fifty thousand houses a year. *Koor*, its industrial branch, controlled steel rolling mills, chemical plants, cement and glass factories, and held substantial interests in the timber and food-processing industries.[8]

In the years between the wars, large amounts of capital flowed into Palestine for the development of the *Yishuv*. The amount invested between 1919 and 1936 was in the area of $350–400 million, and during these years total imported capital almost always exceeded the sum actually invested. About 80 percent of the imported capital came from private sources, and after some debate about whether a labor federation should cooperate with private capitalists, the Histadrut sought to attract its share of these funds for worker enterprises. Approximately half of all monies invested in the Jewish economic sector were devoted to the construction of towns and agricultural communities. This included infrastructural investments in roads and transportation systems. Another 11 percent was devoted to the purchase of land. Of the remainder, two-thirds was spent for agricultural development, especially the expansion of citriculture, which by the 1930s was Palestine's largest category of exports. The remaining capital, about 15 percent of the total, was invested in industry and handicrafts.[9]

The results of these investments were visible in many areas. For example, the number of agricultural communities and workers grew rapidly under these conditions. There were 82 agricultural settlements by 1936. In the same year, there were about 32,000 Jews employed in agriculture, in contrast to fewer than 4,000 in 1921. A similar pattern of growth took place in the industrial sector. By 1936 there were 5,602 manufacturing establishments in the *Yishuv*, about 90 percent of which were small-scale handicraft operations. The number of industrial workers rose from fewer than 5,000 in 1921 to almost 29,000 in 1936, and the value of industrial output reached $42 million in the latter year. Most of the products of the *Yishuv*'s industries were consumer goods and construction materials, both of which were sold on the domestic market. The most important industrial export was chemical products derived from Dead Sea extractions. A good overall indication of the *Yishuv*'s expanding economic base during this period is the rapid acceleration that occurred in the consumption of electricity. The output of the Palestine Electric Company, whose largest shareholder was the Jewish Agency and whose principal consumer was the *Yishuv*, grew from 2 to 65 million kilowatt-hours between 1926 and 1936. Industry and irrigation each consumed about one-third of this total.[10] It should also be noted that the economy of the *Yishuv* was almost completely independent of the Arab economic sector. The monetary value of inputs from the Arab economy was only about 3 percent of all inputs. The value of inputs from the Jewish into the Arab sector was slightly higher but did not exceed 10 percent of all inputs into the Arab economy.[11]

The growing size and complexity of the *Yishuv* were also reflected in its political development. On the one hand, there were the Zionist agencies, which were international in character and which defined their mission as the construction of a national home in Palestine for the benefit of the Jewish people as a whole. On the other, domestic institutions were created for the conduct of political life inside the *Yishuv*. These latter institutions structured the activities of government and administration and helped to make the Jewish colony an autonomous and self-governing political community. As a result of these developments in the political domain, as well as those related to immigration, the creation of social institutions, and economic growth, the *Yishuv* evolved during the years of the mandate into an autonomous and self-sufficient national entity, fulfilling the dream of the founders of modern Zionism. When Israel became independent in 1948, its needs related to nation-building were therefore far less than those of most other countries that secured their freedom in the years following World War II. Whereas many had yet to create the structural foundations of a modern state, Israel inherited social, economic, and political institutions that had been performing effectively for twenty years or more.

The authority of international Zionist institutions was recognized in the mandatory charter approved by the League of Nations. Specifically, Article 4 stipulated that "an appropriate Jewish agency shall be recognized as a public body for the purpose of advising and cooperating with the Administration of Palestine in such economic, social and other matters as may affect the establishment of the Jewish national home and the interests of the Jewish population in Palestine." The Zionist Organization provided the institutional framework for the performance of this role.[12] The purpose of the organization had been fixed at its first meeting, held in Basel in 1897: "To create for the Jewish people a home in Palestine, secured by public law." All of the major Zionist institutions, including the Jewish National Fund, the Palestine Land Development Company, and the Keren Hayesod, operated under the administrative umbrella of the Zionist Organization.

As discussed earlier, these agencies played a critical role in the acquisition of land in Palestine and the settlement of new immigrants. The Zionist Organization also played the leading role in bringing Jewish immigrants to Palestine. The number of Jews who could enter the country legally in any given year was fixed by the British administration, and the authorized number of entry permits, known as "certificates," was then given to the Zionist Organization for distribution. Not surprisingly, there were often impassioned battles over the division of these certificates among Zionist groups scattered throughout the Diaspora.[13] Membership in the Zionist Organization was open to "all Jews who accept the Zionist program and pay the shekel,"[14] the Biblical name "shekel" being selected to denote the organization's membership fee.

Another goal of the Zionist Organization was to foster unity among the Jewish people and to create a consensus regarding the nature and purpose of modern political Zionism. To achieve these objectives, the Zionist movement established the practice of holding international congresses on a regular basis. Indeed, it was at the First Zionist Congress that the Zionist Organization was itself formally established. Theodor Herzl set forth two aims in connection with the congresses. The first was "to close the Zionist ranks, bring about an understanding between all Zionists and to unify their endeavors." The second was "to establish the national assembly of the Jewish people."[15] Congresses were held every year until

1901, and thereafter biannually until 1939. The only exception was the period of World War I, there being no congress between 1913 and 1921. There were also no congresses during the years of the Second World War. Since 1946 they have again been held on a regular basis, however, although the interval between meetings has varied. Early congresses were held in Europe, and this practice continued throughout the years of the mandate. One reason for this was a desire to stress the international character of Zionism, to emphasize that it was a movement not of Jews in Palestine but, rather, of the Jewish people throughout the world. A majority of the congresses convened through 1913 were held in Basel, and among the cities where later meetings were convened are Carlsbad, Vienna, Zurich, Prague, Lucerne, and Geneva. Following Israel's independence, Jerusalem became the permanent venue for meetings of the Zionist Congress, beginning with the Twenty-Third Congress, held in 1951.

As stated, the purpose of the congresses was to foster a consensus on the goals of Zionism, to "show what Zionism is and wants," as Herzl had put the matter at the first congress. It was also to consider and debate programs of action concerned with the construction of the *Yishuv*. Sessions were often heated, as Zionists of different ideological tendencies clashed over issues of policy and struggled to place their representatives in positions of authority. For example, at the Fourteenth Zionist Congress, held in Vienna in 1925, many delegates asserted that more private enterprise was needed to solve the economic problems of the *Yishuv*. There was both a strong attack on and a vigorous defense of the settlement methods of Labor Zionism. An even more heated debate took place at the Seventeenth Congress, which met in Basel in 1931. The militant Revisionist wing of the Zionist movement demanded that the congress clarify the definition of a national home by proclaiming that Zionism sought to establish a Jewish majority and an independent state in Palestine. The congress refused to declare these to be the official and final aims of Zionism, however, thereby deepening the split between the Revisionists and the majority. In the wake of this schism, the next congress, meeting in Prague in 1933, stipulated that "in all Zionist matters the duty of discipline in regard of the Zionist Organization must take precedence over the discipline to any other body."[16]

Under the constitution approved in 1921, members of the Zionist Organization were organized into both territorial federations and political parties, and each type of structure was permitted to send delegates to the Zionist congresses. Territorial federations were organized on a country basis, such as all Zionists in Britain, and were made up of the local Zionist groupings within each country. These federations brought together Zionists without regard to political or ideological orientation, and their members were accordingly known as General Zionists. Political parties, on the other hand, were formed by Jews having a common ideological perspective, representing, according to the 1921 constitution, "a special point of view." These parties, which were designated "separate unions," transcended national boundaries and had branches in a number of countries. In the early years most Jews affiliated with the Zionist Organization through territorial federations, but the relative size and weight of the separate unions increased over time. At the 1921 Zionist Congress, for example, nearly three-fourths of the 512 official delegates were General Zionists. At the 1939 congress, by contrast, 70 percent of the 557 delegates were from separate unions.[17]

The activities of the Zionist Organization and its various auxiliary associations were under the general administrative direction of the Zionist Executive. While broad directions of policy were established by decisions taken at the congresses, political and administrative leadership was exercised by the Executive on a day-to-day basis. The structure of the Executive was revised at a special Zionist meeting called by Weizmann and held in London in 1920. At that time, it was determined that authority would be vested in an eleven-member presidium and that six of these individuals would be assigned to Palestine.[18] The latter group was known as the "Palestine Zionist Executive," and one of its principal responsibilities was to represent the Zionist Organization in dealings with the British. Another component of the Zionist Organization's structure was the Zionist Actions Committee, a quasi-parliamentary forum that was elected biannually by the Zionist Congress. The Actions Committee met on a regular basis and was the political body to which the Executive was responsible during the interval between congresses. Presiding over this entire pyramid—Congress, Actions Committee, Executive—was the president of the Zionist Organization, a position which also involved chairmanship of the Executive. The name and tenure of each president who served prior to 1946 are listed below, along with the city in which the Executive was located under each individual. It will be noted that Weizmann was president of the Zionist Organization during most of the period of the British mandate, and that the Zionist headquarters remained in Europe until 1936. In that year the Executive was transferred to Jerusalem, although Weizmann continued to reside in London and a few other members of the Executive remained there as well.

> 1897–1905, Theodor Herzl (Vienna)
> 1905–1911, David Wolffson (Cologne)
> 1911–1920, Otto Warburg (Berlin)
> 1920–1931, Chaim Weizmann (London)
> 1931–1935, Nahum Sokolow (London)
> 1935–1936, Chaim Weizmann (London)
> 1936–1946, Chaim Weizmann (Jerusalem)

A final international Zionist institution is the Jewish Agency, a term that for a time was used interchangeably with the Palestine Zionist Executive. The term came into use following the establishment of the mandate. As noted, the mandatory instrument called for cooperation with "an appropriate Jewish agency," and the British then recognized the Zionist Organization for this purpose. Accordingly, the Palestine Zionist Executive, which represented and spoke for the Zionist Organization in Palestine, was often called the "Jewish Agency." In 1929, however, the Sixteenth Zionist Congress created a separate institution to which it gave the designation of Jewish Agency, assigning it explicit responsibility for "discharging the functions of the Jewish Agency as set forth in the Mandate." Further, on Weizmann's initiative, the new agency was structured so as to include "non-Zionists" as well as Zionists, the former being defined as "Jewish persons and bodies supporting the building of the national home, without identifying themselves with the political aspirations of Zionism."[19] In pressing for the creation of an enlarged Jewish Agency, Weizmann and his supporters had concluded that financial and political considerations required that the Zionist Organization no longer serve as the sole instrument of the Jewish people for construction of the national home. Nevertheless, the Zionist Organization and the new agency cooperated closely in pursuit of a common cause. Moreover, half the members of the governing bodies of the Jewish Agency were designated by the Zionist Organization, and the president of the latter institution also chaired the assembly and the executive council of the Jewish Agency, thereby minimizing any likelihood of serious policy differences or a lack of coordination between the two interconnected structures.[20]

First as the Zionist Executive in Palestine and then as a separate political institution, the Jewish Agency fused the international and Palestinian dimensions of Zionist activity. On the one hand, as an international institution, the Jewish Agency represented the Zionist Organization in on-the-spot dealings with the British. Further, its administrative structures had international connections and responsibilities. "Zionist" members of its assembly and council were chosen by the Zionist Organization, from within its own ranks. "Non-Zionist" members resided in many countries and were called upon to support philanthropic efforts and otherwise render material and moral assistance in the construction of the Jewish national home.

On the other hand, the agency also had major political and administrative responsibilities inside the *Yishuv*. From the time of its creation in the form of the Palestine Zionist Executive, it undertook to carry out and coordinate programs of internal development in a wide range of areas. Departments were established to manage political affairs, immigration, labor, colonization, education, and health. The political department, for example, maintained contact with the British high commissioner and his staff. The colonization department concerned itself with the development of agricultural settlements. Each department, which was headed by a member of the agency's executive council, coordinated its activities with British authorities, and also with autonomous institutions inside the *Yishuv*, such as the Histadrut. Most of these departments also carried out their own social and economic programs, using their own funds. As a result of this work, despite the international dimension of its character, the Jewish Agency became an important part of the internal political structure of the Jewish community in Palestine.[21]

Political Development inside the *Yishuv*

Although these international Zionist organizations played a critical role in the growth and development of the *Yishuv*, the steadily increasing autonomy and maturity of the Jewish community in Palestine were also reflected in the emergence of internal political institutions, those chosen by and responsible to the Jews living in Palestine. Agreement about the basic structure and functions of these domestic institutions was reached at a meeting of Palestine Jews held in Jaffa in December 1918. The purpose of the meeting was to adopt resolutions concerned with the "constitution" of the Jewish national home. The political structures created included an Assembly of Delegates, Asefat Hanivharim, and a National Council, Va'ad Leumi. Taken together, the political institutions of the *Yishuv* constituted Knesset Israel, the Assembly of Israel, a term used to denote the officially sanctioned and politically organized Jewish Community in Palestine. Knesset Israel and its constituent institutions were recognized by the British through the King's Order in Council of 1921, which granted the Jews, as well as other religious communities in Palestine, autonomy in their internal affairs. The mandatory government gave additional legal recognition in the Religious Communities Ordinance of 1926, which authorized all religious communities in Palestine to establish regulations for the conduct of their own affairs. The 1926 ordinance also granted the power to levy taxes.

Religious as well as secular communal institutions were given legal status by the British ordinances. The authoritative religious organs were the Chief Rabbinate and the Rabbinical Council, which had already been functioning for a number of years. Under procedures systematized in 1921, the Rabbinical Council was elected by a select group of rabbis and other qualified orthodox Jews. The council was headed by two chief rabbis, one representing each of the two major branches of Judaism—the Ashkenazi tradition, derived from the practice of Jews in Eastern Europe and Germany, and the Sephardi tradition, which traces its origin to the Jewish communities of Spain and Portugal. The council also contained associate rabbis and lay advisors, and one of its major functions was to appoint and supervise the work of jurists on rabbinical courts. The latter were responsible for the administration of Jewish law in the traditional areas of personal status.[22] It is notable that in accepting these religious institutions as part of Knesset Israel, the Zionist movement rejected any separation of religion and politics and acknowledged that "religion was not a private matter for the individual conscience but an essential component in the structure of leadership within the new Jewish society, and . . . a source of Zionist legitimacy."[23]

There was another important religious issue connected with the establishment of Knesset Israel. Ultraorthodox Jews had historically rejected modern political Zionism,[24] and those in Palestine therefore rejected the concept of Knesset Israel since it made explicit and gave legal status to the political character of the *Yishuv*. In the view of these pious Jews, no Jewish institution or political community was legitimate unless it derived the full measure of its authority from *Halakhah*, orthodox Jewish law. The ultraorthodox, of whom there were approximately 13,000 in Palestine at this time, accordingly placed themselves outside of Knesset Israel. Indeed, they defined departure from it as a religious obligation and demanded of the British that they be recognized as a separate and parallel political community, which in their eyes, of course, would be the only one that was legitimately Jewish. This position was particularly troublesome for the Zionist majority, which sought to create political institutions that represented the whole of the *Yishuv* and which asserted that membership in the community governed by these institutions was compulsory. Otherwise, Knesset Israel would not be coterminous with the *Yishuv*.[25] Moreover, any group which disagreed with government policy would then, in theory at least, be free to secede. The British responded with a compromise that was not fully satisfactory to either party, rejecting the ultraorthodox demand for parallel status but recognizing their withdrawal from Knesset Israel.

Secular political institutions played an important role in the *Yishuv*. They were a major step on the road to self-government, not only in terms of British recognition but also from the viewpoint of organizational development. They laid a foundation from which evolved some of the most important political institutions of present-day Israel. Providing a framework for consensus-building and unified action in the domains of public policy formation and programmatic political action was the Assembly of Delegates, Asefat Hanivharim, the elected plenum of the *Yishuv*. The Assembly, which became the parliament (Knesset) of the Jewish state following Israeli independence, was the comprehensive communal organization of the Jews in Palestine and supreme political arbiter in the domestic arena. Although its resources and powers were in fact quite limited, particularly in comparison to those of the Jewish Agency, it nonetheless functioned as a quasi–state institutional center and provided a framework for interaction among political parties and other political organizations.

The Assembly was elected at irregular intervals during the years of the mandate, with the first election taking place in 1920. The population of the *Yishuv* at that time was about 67,000, and ballots were cast by 22,000 out of 28,000 eligible voters. The Assembly itself had 314 members belonging to approximately twenty different political factions.[26] Balloting for the second, third, and fourth assemblies took place in 1925, 1932, and 1944 respectively. Seats were awarded on the basis of proportional representation, but several distinctive features characterized electoral competition. First, the principle of universal suffrage was not accepted by ultraorthodox Jews. Specifically, these Jews objected to women's participation in the electoral process. Separate, all-male polling stations were therefore set up for the ultraorthodox in the first election. By the next election, as noted, they had withdrawn from the institutions of Knesset Israel. Second, voters did not cast their ballots for individual candidates but rather for party lists. Voter choice was thus restricted to the expression of a preference among slates of candidates fielded by competing political parties, and the candidates themselves accordingly owed primary allegiance to their party and its platform and were not viewed as representing a particular territorial constituency. Finally, in the 1932 election, the country was divided along ethnic lines for electoral purposes, with separate party lists being presented to Ashkenazi and Sephardi voters, and also to Jews of Yemenite origin. These ethnic constituencies were abolished in 1944, however, and the entire *Yishuv* was thereafter treated as a single electoral district, with each party presenting the same list to all voters.

This system was retained for elections to the parliament of the Jewish state, the Knesset, after Israeli independence in 1948. The present Knesset contains 120 members, and each political party therefore presents voters with a list containing up to 120 ordered names. All voters choose among the same set of party lists, and each casts his or her ballot for one of them in its entirety, there being no opportunity to endorse some candidates of one party and some of another. Each party receives a number of the 120 Knesset seats being contested that is proportional to the percentage of votes it received in the election, and all candidates whose ordinal position on the party's list precedes that number then become its delegates to the Assembly.

In present-day Israel, supreme political authority is vested in the parliament. During the mandate, however, the power of Asefat Hanivharim was more limited. The major reasons for this are that the Zionist Organization and the Jewish Agency possessed far greater resources and also had responsibility for negotiating with the British high commissioner, and these institutions thus played the leading role in the construction of the *Yishuv*. In addition, the Assembly had few outstanding personalities and was convened only on special occasions, which gave considerable autonomy to the executive structures that in principle were responsible to it. Nevertheless, the Assembly of Delegates was the formal institutional center of Knesset Israel and the foundation of a multilevel governmental structure. It was required to meet at least once a year, and on these occasions it had final authority in matters of public policy.

Above the Assembly was the Va'ad Leumi, a thirty-six-member National Council elected by the parliament. The council met on a regular basis and was responsible for giving direction to political activity between meetings of the Assembly of Delegates, thereby functioning as a national executive committee. Further, the Va'ad Leumi chose a smaller executive from within its own ranks, adding yet another level to the government's institutional pyramid. Finally, below the

Va'ad Leumi and under its jurisdiction, there was a network of local community councils.

The Assembly and National Council were permitted to levy taxes for education, health, and welfare programs, and also for support of the Rabbinical Council and the Assembly itself. Local councils were permitted to collect taxes as well. The revenues raised were meager, however, which explains why the Zionist Organization and the Jewish Agency were much more influential in the fields of education and social welfare, to say nothing of immigration, resettlement, and community development. On the other hand, the Zionist Organization did gradually transfer some of its responsibilities to the National Council. In the field of education, for instance, the Zionist Organization in 1932 assigned authority for the Jewish school system in Palestine to the Va'ad Leumi and provided it with the financial resources to carry out its new responsibilities. In any event, despite their limitations, the creation and functioning of the Assembly and National Council helped the *Yishuv* to prepare for its political future and to begin its journey on the path toward self-government.

The world of Zionism, both in Palestine and abroad, was extremely heterogeneous so far as ideology is concerned, and this heterogeneity was reflected in the many political parties that structured participation in the *Yishuv*'s internal institutions and in the Zionist Organization. Some Zionist parties had their origins in Europe and some were created by Jews in Palestine. During the period of the mandate, most political parties were transnational in character. The *Yishuv* became the organizational center of a growing number of these factions, but most also maintained important branches in a number of countries in the Diaspora. As noted, the proportion of party-affiliated delegates to the Zionist congresses increased steadily during the 1920s and 1930s.

Political parties and factions may be grouped into three general categories, the first of which is composed of those groups oriented toward socialism and Labor Zionism. It will be recalled that socialist tendencies had been dominant during the Second and Third *aliyas*. Two intellectuals who played a leading role in converting many Russian Jewish socialists to Zionism after the turn of the century were Nachman Syrkin (1867–1924) and Dov Ber Borochov (1881–1907). Syrkin, a utopian socialist, believed that the Jews might construct a just society in Palestine, one that would offer opportunities to poor Jews as well as to the Jewish bourgeoisie. Such a state would solve the Jewish problem of Europe. Moreover, by showing how a just society might be created along socialist lines, this fusion of Zionism and socialism would also enable the Jews to fulfill their ancient destiny as the Chosen People. "Israel," Syrkin wrote in 1898, "will redeem the world which crucified him."[27] Finally, even should progressive and classless societies eventually be created in Europe, Syrkin doubted that this would bring an end to anti-Semitism and the marginal status of Jews. Borochov, a Marxist, held a similar view, believing that the class struggle in Europe would inevitably exclude the Jews, and that Jewish workers could join the universal movement of workers only if they resided in a state of their own. Within Palestine, Jewish workers would oppose Jewish capitalists, and the result would be both the "productivization" of the Jewish people and the integration of Jewish workers into a worldwide class struggle. Among the other intellectual contributors to labor-oriented Zionism was A.D. Gordon, whose advocacy of redemption through work (but not class struggle) was discussed earlier.

These ideas led to the creation of two socialist parties under the early Zionist umbrella, the largest of which was Poalei Zion, the Workers of Zion. Poalei Zion was a general Labor Zionist federation, established in the Diaspora in 1906 on the foundation of local groups in Russia, Poland, and other countries of Eastern Europe. At the time it was heavily influenced by the writings of Borochov. One of the early leaders of the Poalei Zion branch in Palestine was David Ben Gurion, who became Israel's first prime minister in 1948. Although Poalei Zion began as a Marxist movement, it gradually developed a more socialist orientation and devoted greater attention to uniquely Jewish problems. As a result, its left wing broke away in 1919 and formed a separate party dedicated to Marxist principles. The new faction initially called itself the Socialist Workers' Party, and in 1923 an offshoot took the name Poalei Zion Smol, Left Poalei Zion.

The other major socialist faction at this time, which opposed Poalei Zion, was Hapoel Hatzair, the Young Worker party, which was formed in Palestine in 1906. Hapoel Hatzair was a smaller and more moderate workers' party. Although its philosophy was socialist, it was preoccupied more narrowly with the needs of the Jews in Palestine and was influenced by Gordon's idea that the political and spiritual uplifting of the Jewish people could best be achieved through manual labor and by working the soil of the Holy Land to construct the Jewish National Home.

Although many new immigrants remained aloof from both parties upon their arrival in Palestine, Poalei Zion and Hapoel Hatzair contributed to the formation of a new generation of socialist-oriented parties that played an important role in the political development of the *Yishuv* and, later, became the parties of the left and center which dominated Israeli politics for nearly three decades after its independence. A new socialist party established in 1919 was Ahdut Ha'avoda, the Unity of Labor party. Among its founders were members of the more moderate wing of Poalei Zion; and following the creation of Poalei Zion Smol in 1923, Poalei Zion itself became associated with Ahdut Ha'avoda. In the 1920s, the new party became the largest labor party within the *Yishuv*, and in 1930 it merged with Hapoel Hatzair to form as yet another party dedicated to mainstream labor values. The new party was Mapai, an acronym for Mifleget Poalei Eretz-Yisrael, Party of the Workers of the Land of Israel. The movement also incorporated the Kibbutz Hameuchad federation of collective settlements, which had affiliated with Ahdut Ha'avoda in 1927.

On the strength of this merger of the two largest labor blocs, Mapai became the dominant party in the *Yishuv*, a position it continued to enjoy in the years after Israeli independence. It was led by Ben Gurion, who was also secretary-general of the Histadrut and who expressed the evolution of the party's philosophy with the slogan "From class to nation." Under Ben Gurion's leadership, Mapai worked aggressively to consolidate its preeminent political position and called for a strengthening of the institutions of Knesset Israel. Ben Gurion became chairman of the Jewish Agency Executive in 1935, and members of Mapai assumed other important positions of leadership. The party also advocated cooperation with nonlaboring classes in the construction of the *Yishuv*, although it saw itself as the dominant partner in all political alliances.[28] While it remained a workers' party, committed to the principles of Labor Zionism, Mapai gradually moved toward the political center and, as Ben Gurion's slogan suggested, gave the bulk of its attention to issues of Zionism rather than socialism.

The left wing of the socialist camp also remained important. The Socialist Workers' Party soon evolved into the Palestine Communist Party, joining the Comintern in 1924, and a new movement emerged three years later to fill the ideological space between Mapai on the one hand and the Communists and the remnants of Poalei Zion Smol on the other. The foundation of the new movement was Hashomer Hatzair, the Young Watchman, a youth movement that received much of its support from the Kibbutz Artzi federation and was influential among the young men and women of the Third *Aliya*. Hashomer Hatzair did not become a political party until 1946, the reason being, according to its leaders, that it wished to remain ideologically pure and avoid the political compromises that parties were inevitably forced to make. It was thus a cadre of intellectuals and activists, dedicated principally to preservation of the collectivist ideals embodied in the *kibbutz* experience, and this led some to view the movement as elitist. A.D. Gordon, for example, once stated that its members constituted "an intellectual bourgeoisie living in an intellectual salon."[29]

A final set of developments within the socialist stream began with the re-emergence of Ahdut Ha'avoda, a separate faction being established under that name in 1944 by a group of left-wing Mapai members who had become unhappy with the party's ideological drift. Most of these individuals were associated with the *kibbutz* movement within Mapai. In 1948, after Israeli independence, Hashomer Hatzair and Ahdut Ha'avoda merged to form Mapam, the United Workers' Party, which became an important political force in the new Jewish state. As Mapai moved closer to the political center, Mapam, though a smaller party, carried forward the ideological legacy of the Zionist left. A remnant of the Communist Party continued to function as well, but it was much smaller than Mapam and had little influence within Zionist ranks, especially after relations between Israel and the Soviet Union deteriorated in the mid-1950s.

A second ideological stream within which political parties emerged was religious in character. It included both Zionist and non-Zionist factions. The most important religious party was Mizrahi, an abbreviation for Merkaz Ruhani, meaning Spiritual Center. Although orthodox Jews had historically been hostile to modern political Zionism, Mizrahi embraced Zionism and participated in the Zionist Organization from the beginning. Indeed, it was an important partner within the coalition that led the Zionist Organization at this time. The party's origins lie among religious Jews within the Hovevei Zion (Lovers of Zion) group that initiated the First *Aliya*. To distinguish themselves from nonreligious elements within this early Zionist movement, they established a separate office in 1893. They called it the "spiritual center" and used it to organize religious Zionists. Mizrahi's platform was not only to work for the realization of modern political Zionism's goal of establishing a Jewish society in Palestine, it also sought to create a religious majority within the *Yishuv*, thus ensuring that the latter would be Jewish from a religious as well as a sociological point of view. Mizrahi's early leader, Rabbi Samuel Mohilever (1824–1898), told the First Zionist Congress in 1897 that "the Torah, which is the Source of our life, must be the foundation of our regeneration in the land of our fathers."[30] In 1902, Mizrahi established itself as a political party, and at the time it was the first group within the Zionist Organization to organize as a distinct political grouping. Interestingly, when the 1903 Zionist Congress debated Herzl's suggestion that the Zionist Organization explore with Britain the possibility of establishing a Jewish colony in Uganda, the Mizrahi faction voted to authorize Herzl to explore the British proposition.

Like other Zionist parties, Mizrahi was a transnational political movement and had sections in a number of countries. A branch was set up in the *Yishuv* by Mizrahi leaders who had immigrated to Palestine, and here it operated within the domestic political framework of Knesset Israel, as well as in the international Zionist arena. In 1922, the party established its own labor movement, Hapoel Hamizrahi, the Mizrahi Worker. Hapoel Hamizrahi received medical assistance through the Histadrut and cooperated with the dominant workers' federation in a number of other areas. At the same time, the religious union maintained its independence and sought to meet the special needs of orthodox Jewish workers. In addition, Hapoel Hamizrahi gradually took on a more explicitly political character, and in elections for the Assembly of Delegates it ran candidates independent of the parent Mizrahi party. Further, the number of its members and the size of its electoral following gradually surpassed those of the parent party, although both factions remained a part of the world Mizrahi movement and shared a commitment to orthodox Jewish goals.

In principle, Mizrahi and Hapoel Hamizrahi were dedicated to the construction of a Jewish national home governed by orthodox Jewish law. In practice, however, since most Jews in Palestine did not share this vision, the two religious parties concentrated on securing respect for *Halakhah* in critical areas, such as education and personal status. They were pragmatic and demonstrated their skills in the art of politics. They also displayed an active concern for issues of labor and of social welfare, fusing the preoccupations of Zionism and socialism as did the parties of Labor Zionism. Several years after Israel's independence, in 1955, Mizrahi and Hapoel Hamizrahi merged to form the National Religious Party (Mafdal), which became a powerful force in Israeli politics.

Although they cooperated effectively with nonreligious parties, Mizrahi and Hapoel Hamizrahi possessed an outlook that made them more than a lobby for religious interests in a secular society. They believed that modern political Zionism was not a movement of secular nationalism. It was rather the instrument God had chosen for the fulfillment of His plan for the Jewish people and for the world; whether nonreligious Zionists realized it or not, their political movement was but the first stage in the fulfillment of Biblical prophesy and the redemption of the Jewish people. Thus, to Mizrahi, the rebirth of Israel was not a routine and man-made political event. As expressed by Rabbi Meir Bar-Ilan (Berlin), who in 1926 became head of the Mizrahi world movement and immigrated to Palestine, "The State of Israel is something celestial, it is the divine world, our eternal destiny."[31]

The view that modern political Zionism is the instrument by which God is carrying out the Divine promise on which traditional Zionism is based was articulated most forcefully by Rabbi Avraham Yitzhak Hacohen Kook (1865–1935), who immigrated to Palestine in 1904 and first became head rabbi of Jaffa and then Ashkenazi chief rabbi of Palestine. Kook rejected the opposition to modern political Zionism articulated by ultraorthodox Jews. Whereas the latter saw Jewish nationalism as heresy, as supremacy of the political over the religious and as man's audacity to act in the Creator's stead in returning the Jews to Zion, Kook affirmed that the Messianic age had already begun. The proof of this was the growth of the *Yishuv*, however secular might be the orientation of most of its inhabitants. The breakup of the traditional Jewish communities of Eastern Europe was also, in Kook's view, evidence that the history of the Jews had entered a new era. Finally, Kook expressed confidence that the Jewish community in Palestine would ultimately turn to religious law for governance. Modern political Zionism was an instrument for the ingathering of exiles, but once in the Holy Land Jews would be reunited with their Divine law by another instrument of God's design. Kook's philosophy is summarized in the following passage:

> In our life in general, and in *Eretz Yisrael* in particular, we must feel that we are being reborn and that we are being created once again as at the beginning of time. Our entire spiritual heritage is presently being absorbed within its source and is reappearing in a new guise. . . . All of our people believes that we are in the first stage of the Final Redemption.[32]

This train of thought has remained an important intellectual current within the Mizrahi movement, and in the National Religious Party to which it later gave rise. In present-day Israel, it finds expression in the philosophy of Gush Emunim, the organizational and ideological foundation of the settler movement which is seeking to expand the Jewish presence in the occupied Arab territories of the West Bank and Gaza Strip. Many Gush Emunim activists believe that Israel's capture of these territories in 1967 is additional evidence that the Messianic age has begun, and also that their retention will deepen the spiritual character of the Jewish state and hasten the coming of the Messiah.

The ultraorthodox and non-Zionist element among religious Jews in the *Yishuv* was not completely organized. But while the most devout rejected any worldly political activity, the mainstream and more pragmatic wing of the ultra-orthodox organized itself into Agudat Yisrael, the Federation of Israel. Aguda, as it is usually called, was established in Eastern Europe in 1912 and remained the dominant political party among the orthodox Jewish communities there until World War II. In addition, it soon developed branches in many countries, including Palestine, and the entire movement called itself the Agudat Yisrael World Union. Aguda's principal preoccupation was to promote obedience to orthodox Jewish law. Direction of the party was placed in the hands of a rabbinical body known as the Council of Torah Sages, and the council's opinions were authoritative in matters of legal interpretation, as well as governance of the movement.

Aguda remained outside the Zionist Organization, and in the *Yishuv* it also placed itself apart from Knesset Israel. As noted, Aguda's general opposition to modern political Zionism was based on religious grounds. Its members believed that only upon arrival of the Messiah would the Jewish people be reestablished in the Promised Land, and for this Jews must wait with patience and faith. Moreover, the strength of Aguda's opposition was such that the movement contacted Britain and the League of Nations in order to denounce Zionism and to insist that the Zionist Organization's program was at variance with the wishes of the Jewish masses.[33] Inside the *Yishuv*, Aguda was initially prepared to cooperate with other parties in order to meet the social and economic needs of Palestine's growing Jewish population. It soon withdrew from Knesset Israel, however, arguing that it could not participate in a political community which sanctioned Jews living in violation of *Halakhah*. As noted, the issue that precipitated its withdrawal was women's suffrage. Even though all-male balloting was offered to Aguda, along with counting each male vote twice so as not to put the party at an electoral disadvantage, the ultraorthodox decided they could not support a political process which allowed any Jewish women to vote.

As also occurred in the ranks of Mizrahi, a workers' party spun off from Aguda in the 1920s. Known as Poalei Aguda (Workers of Aguda), it was more willing to cooperate with Zionism than the parent body. Also, though it in principle recognized the authority of the Council of Torah Sages, it was in practice more likely to disregard its rulings. Poalei Aguda remained a small faction, however, and after Israeli independence it eventually rejoined Aguda.

Aguda itself moved toward cooperation with the Zionists in the 1930s, as the position of Jews in Europe deteriorated. Tragically, this came too late to save many of the orthodox Jews trapped in the ghettos of Eastern Europe. According to one scholar, most of these Hassidic Jews would have followed their rabbis to Palestine, had the latter not continued to oppose the construction of the *Yishuv* until it was no longer possible to escape from the Nazis.[34] In the *Yishuv*, however, many members of Aguda were now willing to cooperate with Zionism on a practical basis, and in 1947 an agreement was reached whereby Aguda would take part in the political process of the new Jewish state.

To remove Aguda's refusal to join a Jewish polity whose laws were not based on *Halakhah*, the Executive of the Jewish Agency agreed in a letter to the Aguda World Union that in four critical areas the circumstances of Jews in Israel would be governed by regulations consistent with Jewish law. These areas are the sabbath, dietary regulations, marriage and divorce, and education. A few ultraorthodox elements, most notably the Neturei Karta, rejected this accommodation with modern Zionism and remained outside Knesset Israel. Even today, its members refuse to recognize the Jewish state. Aguda, however, accepted the arrangement. The party has participated in all elections since Israeli independence and its members accept citizenship in the State of Israel. They do not recognize Israel as *the* Jewish state, and hence, in their view, the country's security and welfare are of no significance so far as Judaism is concerned. Rejecting Mizrahi's belief that creation of the modern State of Israel is part of the Divine plan, Aguda sees these things as totally irrelevant from a spiritual point of view. On the other hand, since the majority of its citizens are Jewish, Israel is *a* Jewish state, and Aguda accordingly accepts that its fortunes are of critical importance to the well-being of Jewish people.

Parties of the political center and right constitute a third and final ideological stream within the Zionist framework. The center was occupied by General Zionists and the right by the Revisionists. General Zionists, as noted earlier, were those groups and individuals within the Zionist Organization that initially were not affiliated with any political party. Most General Zionists were from the middle class, and most affiliated with the Zionist Organization through its territorial structures, national federations that mobilized Jews within a single country without regard for ideological considerations other than a commitment to modern Zionism. By the 1920s General Zionists were operating as an organized caucus in elections at Zionist congresses, however, and in 1931 they established the World Union of General Zionists as an institutional foundation for their political efforts. In that year they also participated as a political party in elections for the *Yishuv*'s Assembly of Delegates.

In 1935 the General Zionists split into two wings, popularly known as A and B. This division occurred both within the World Union and among General Zionists in Palestine. General Zionists A was led by Chaim Weizmann and remained essentially nonideological. Its philosophy was to seek economic and cultural support from all sources in building the *Yishuv*. Accordingly, this faction cooperated with the Zionist Labor parties that had become dominant in Palestine (and, increasingly, in the Zionist Organization generally), and in 1936 this wing even formed its own section within the Histadrut. General Zionists B was more ideological, however. It was militantly opposed to the labor movement and socialism and insisted that only through private enterprise could Zionist development succeed in Palestine. Accordingly, it often allied itself with political parties emerging on the Zionist right. Seeking to represent the interests and philosophy of the middle class, General Zionism B clashed bitterly with Labor Zionism on many occasions. Between 1933 and 1935, for example, the party withdrew from the Zionist Executive rather than participate in a coalition with Labor. In 1944 it boycotted the election for the Assembly of Delegates. General Zionists B also remained outside the Histadrut and established its own labor organization.

General Zionism remained an important element within the broader Zionist Organization generally, but its political influence inside Palestine was limited throughout the mandatory period. This was a result of the divisions within its ranks, and also of the fact that its political organization and ideological coherence were not well developed. The two factions of the World Union of General Zionists reunited in 1946. They remained apart in Palestine until 1961, however. After Israeli independence, the A faction reconstituted itself as the Progressive Party and the B faction inherited the name General Zionists. When they merged for elections to the Israeli Knesset in 1961, the two groups formed the Liberal Party, whose philosophy was somewhat vague but which was dedicated generally to free-enterprise economic policies.

The right wing of this Zionist stream was occupied by the Revisionist Party, which was founded in 1925 by Ze'ev Vladimir Jabotinsky (1880–1940). The founding conference of the Revisionists took place in Paris and was immediately followed by the creation of a Palestinian branch. Jabotinsky, whom Laqueur describes as a "liberal anarchist"[35] and whom his enemies, including Ben Gurion, sometimes characterized as a fascist, was a controversial man of strong opinions and single-minded purpose. Born in Odessa, Jabotinsky joined the Zionist Organization at a young age, and in his early years he identified with the ideals of socialism. The most important of his early accomplishments were his success in persuading the British to establish a Jewish legion to fight in the Middle East during World War I and his organization of self-defense units in Palestine during the anti-Jewish Arab riots of 1920. Jabotinsky was appointed to the Zionist Executive in 1921 and was at first content to work within the political framework of General Zionism. He soon clashed with Weizmann, however, denouncing the Zionist president and other leaders for the vagueness of their program and for moderation toward the Arabs.

The Revisionists' program was characterized by territorial and political maximalism, as well as by discipline and calls for military preparedness in pursuit of these goals. As noted earlier, the Revisionists took their name from a demand that the mandate be revised to recognize Jewish rights on both sides of the Jordan River. Further, the Revisionists were uncompromising in their insistence that within this enlarged territory there must be a Jewish majority and an independent Jewish state. Weizmann and other mainstream Zionists were vague on these territorial and political issues. They preferred to work within the existing framework of the mandate and contented themselves with the idea of a Jewish "national home" and a sharing of Palestine between Jews and Arabs. In their view, it was neither timely nor useful to consider these matters further. This was unacceptable to the Revisionists, however. Thus, in an exchange at the Sixteenth Zionist Congress, held in Zurich in 1929, Jabotinsky told his critics that the notion of a national home "has simply one meaning for the soul of the Jewish people, and that is a National State with a preponderant Jewish majority, in which the Jewish will must decide the form and direction that the life of the community must follow." To achieve this goal, moreover, Jabotinsky stated that it was necessary "to found a colonization regime in Palestine, and to . . . open up territory on either side of the Jordan for the reception of great colonizing masses."[36]

These issues were of paramount importance to the Revisionist movement, whereas the parties of Labor Zionism focused attention on social and economic as well as political concerns. Moreover, the Revisionist Party was viewed by the British as an irrelevant lunatic fringe,[37] and after 1929 mandatory authorities prevented Jabotinsky from returning to Palestine. For these reasons, in part, the party was always stronger among Zionists outside of Palestine than among the Jews of the *Yishuv*. Nevertheless, Jabotinsky's followers delivered their uncompromising message in straightforward terms, and its monolithic and unsophisticated character did not prevent it from striking a responsive chord among some Zionists, especially younger elements. Its youth wing, Betar, was particularly successful in providing a steady stream of new recruits.[38] The party's strength inside the *Yishuv* was apparent in the 1931 election for the Assembly of Delegates, in which it captured 23 percent of the total vote and was awarded the second-largest number of delegates. The Revisionist movement's appeal, as explained by Laqueur, was that it "recognized certain basic facts earlier and more clearly than other Zionist parties: that without a majority there would be no Jewish state, and that in view of Arab opposition to Jewish immigration and settlement on even a relatively small scale, there was no solution but a Jewish state."[39] The Revisionists also stressed the need for discipline and military organization, celebrating such martial values as courage and preparedness and substituting for Labor's image of the Jewish worker and farmer their own image of the Jewish soldier defending his land.[40]

In the 1930s, the Revisionists withdrew from the established framework of the Zionist movement. In 1931 they established an autonomous underground paramilitary organization, the Irgun Zvai Leumi (IZL [Etzel]; National Military Organization). The Irgun was a right-wing militia that was loosely affiliated with the Revisionist Party and that rejected the authority of the Va'ad Leumi and the Jewish Agency.[41] After 1944 the Irgun carried out guerrilla warfare in an attempt to drive the British out of Palestine. In 1940, the Lohamei Herut Yisrael (Lehi; Fighters for the Freedom of Israel, also known as the Stern Group) seceded from the IZL and employed terrorist tactics in the struggle against the British, and later against the Arabs. On the political level, Jabotinsky took most Revisionists out of the Zionist Organization in 1933. Only a small minority faction, which called itself the Jewish State Party, did not follow his lead. Believing that mainstream Zionists were incapable of the necessary discipline and action, the Revisionists in 1935 established their own political structure, which they called the New Zionist Organization. This parallel structure continued to function until 1946, at which time the Revisionists reentered the Zionist Organization and once again attended Zionist congresses. During these years the Revisionists remained members of Knesset Israel, although they did boycott elections for the Assembly of Delegates of 1944. They also established a separate trade union organization, which they called the National Labor Federation. Following Israeli independence, the banner of right-wing nationalism was carried forward by the Herut Party, which was established in 1948. Its leader was Menachem Begin, who had assumed control of the Irgun in 1944 and convinced most Revisionists that he, not Jabotinsky's successors within the parent party, was the true spiritual heir to the Revisionist political legacy. Herut emerged as an important minority party in early Israeli politics. Its platform called for the exercise of Jewish sovereignty on both sides of the Jordan River.

An indication of the political strength of major factions within the Zionist movement can be seen in the proportion of votes that each received in elections for the Zionist congresses. The percentages for the congresses between 1931 and 1946 are given below, with each party's performance shown both among voters in Palestine and for the combined total of voters in Palestine and in the Diaspora.[42] The figures reveal the dominant position of Labor, both generally and, especially, inside the *Yishuv*. The figures may exaggerate the strength of the General Zionists after 1933, since the party probably picked up support among Revisionists, whose own party boycotted the elections of 1935, 1937, and 1939. Finally, it will be recalled that Aguda was not a part of the Zionist Organization, and that Mizrahi (both the parent party and Hapoel Hamizrahi) was the only religious faction within the Zionist movement.

	Labor	Mizrahi	Revisionists	General Zionists
1931				
Palestine	62	9	17	8
Combined	29	14	21	36
1933				
Palestine	68	8	12	7
Combined	44	12	14	28
1935				
Palestine	67	14	–	16
Combined	49	16	–	32
1937				
Palestine	70	15	–	15
Combined	46	17	–	35
1939				
Palestine	71	10	–	18
Combined	47	14	–	36
1946				
Palestine	61	12	14	12
Combined	40	15	11	33

The *Yishuv* continued to build upon this social, economic, and political foundation, moving toward the day when its political future would be determined. A fifth and final wave of immigration took place in the years between 1932 and 1939 and, much larger than any of the preceding *aliya*s, it more than doubled the Jewish population of Palestine. Stimulated by the rise of Nazism in Europe, and reflecting also the fact that entry into the United States was limited, especially during the first part of this period, approximately 200,000 legal Jewish immigrants made their way to Palestine as part of the Fifth *Aliya*. Thousands more entered illegally, without the required British certificates. Thus, by 1939 the *Yishuv* numbered about 445,000 and constituted 30 percent of the population of Palestine.

Many who came to Palestine during the Fifth *Aliya* were from Central Europe, and among their number were many middle-class Jews and well-educated professionals. Although 40 percent of the new *olim* came from Poland, about 20 percent were of German origin, and another 10 percent came from other Western and Central European countries. Immigration was also accompanied by a substantial influx of private capital, principally from Germany but also from other countries. The transfer of private German capital was greatly facilitated by the controversial Ha'avara agreement, which was concluded by Zionists and the German Economics Ministry in 1933. The agreement permitted departing German Jews to deposit their assets in a special account in Germany, which would then be used to purchase goods for export to Palestine. Later, when the goods reached Palestine, importers would make payment to the newly arrived German Jewish immigrants.[43] Thus, despite the tragic developments taking shape in Europe, the 1930s on the whole were years of growth and prosperity in the *Yishuv*.

Most who came with the Fifth *Aliya* settled in the cities of Palestine. Tel Aviv was the most rapidly growing of these urban centers. About half the new immigrants settled there, and by 1936 it had a population of approximately 150,000. Its annual budget was more than that of the country's twenty-two other municipalities combined. There were also important developments in Haifa and Jerusalem. Construction of the country's first modern port was completed in Haifa, and the city's population grew to about 100,000, half of which was Jewish. In Jerusalem the population reached 125,000 in 1936, and more than 60 percent of this total was Jewish. As discussed earlier, substantial growth also took place in industry, agriculture, education, and other fields, all of which made the *Yishuv* an increasingly complex and self-sufficient political community. For example, between 1931 and 1939 the export of citrus increased sixfold, from 2.5 million cases to over 15 million cases. By 1937 the Histadrut had 100,000 members.

The internal development of the *Yishuv* did not take place in a political vacuum, however, and, unfortunately, the Jewish community in Palestine was increasingly confronted with serious external problems. The most immediate of these was Palestinian Arab opposition to the rapidly growing Jewish presence. On the one hand, the Arab community was increasingly politically mobilized and was itself experiencing an important evolution of its ideology and institutions. Thus, on a political level, there was an increasingly clear conflict between Jewish and Arab nationalism in Palestine. On the other hand, there were also direct and violent confrontations between Arabs and Jews, including extensive anti-Jewish Arab rioting. The years between 1936 and 1939 marked the height of this violence. They were characterized by recurring disturbances and widespread civil unrest.

A second source of difficulty for the *Yishuv* was the deterioration of Zionist relations with the British. Concerned about the growing disorder in Palestine, and increasingly sensitive to Arab grievances, British authorities in the late 1930s took new steps to balance their support of Arab and Jewish interests. Most disturbing to Zionists was the substantial reduction in immigration quotas imposed in 1939, at the very time that Jews in Germany and other countries of Central and Eastern Europe were becoming desperate for a place of refuge. A limit of 10,000 new immigrants per year for five years was established by the British in 1939. After 1940, Britain began deporting immigrants who had entered Palestine illegally. The British also denied landing rights to a number of ships laden with refugees from Europe. Jews saw these policies as an attempt to appease the Arabs and believed they were motivated by Britain's strategic calculation about the need for Arab support in the war.

Most troubling of all was the rise of the Nazi movement in Europe. As early as the late 1930s, pogroms in Germany, Poland, and elsewhere drove tens of thousands of Jews from their homes, transforming them overnight into destitute and defenseless refugees. In the years that followed, nearly six million Jews perished in Nazi death camps, and at the end of the war there were hundreds of thousands of displaced European Jews. This included between 50,000 and 100,000 survivors of the concentration camps, who had been brought to relocation centers and for whom the Jewish Agency was demanding immigration certificates to Palestine. The terrible tragedy of the Holocaust was for the most part played out far from Palestine. Nevertheless, it was a catastrophe that affected Jews everywhere in the most profound manner. Among Zionists, it strengthened the determination that the Jewish people must have a country of its own. Among other Jews, the tragedy of World War II brought new support for the Zionist goal of a national home in Palestine. Even if they remained unpersuaded by the argument that a Jewish state would meet the needs of Judaism, thus enabling the Jewish people to fulfill its spiritual and cultural destiny, most agreed that the immediate and practical needs of Jews were justification enough for the Zionist program. The Jewish people required a state where any Jew seeking refuge could find it and where Jews could organize for their collective defense and survival.

Social and Economic Change among the Arabs of Palestine

Although the proportion of Jews among Palestine's population rose steadily during the years of the British mandate, the Arabs remained the overwhelming majority. In 1930 they still constituted more than 80 percent of the country's inhabitants, and as late as 1940 they accounted for fully 70 percent. Indeed, according to the census of 1931, Arabs remained the majority in all of the country's eighteen subdistricts; in only four of these districts—Jerusalem, Jaffa, Haifa, and Tiberias—did they account for less than 85 percent of the population, and in half they constituted either 99 or 100 percent of the total. Equally important, the absolute size of the Arab population grew steadily during this period. Although it increased at a slower rate than did the Jewish community, the Palestinian Arab population grew at an annual rate that averaged almost 3 percent between 1922 and 1945, enabling it to nearly double during these years. The growth rate itself also increased steadily as improvements in health care lowered the number of deaths each year. Among Muslims, for example, the annual rate of natural increase had risen to almost 4 percent by the end of the mandate.[44] As a result, the number of Arabs in Palestine grew from 668,000 in 1922 to slightly more than 1,000,000 in 1937 and to 1,256,000 in 1945.

At least some of the Arab population growth was the result of immigration from neighboring Arab countries. This immigration, most of which originated in Sinai, Lebanon, Syria, and Transjordan, was stimulated by the relatively favorable economic conditions of Palestine, not only in the Jewish sector but in the Arab sector as well. Most analysts report that this immigration was not of substantial magnitude. According to one scholarly estimate, for example, based on an analysis of census data from 1922 and 1931, Arab immigration represented only 7 percent of the 1922–1931 Arab population growth, and only about 4 percent of the settled Arab population in the latter year had been born outside the country.[45] A few scholars and other observers have challenged these figures, contending that they are much too low. For example, making reference to the same census data, another analyst asserts that Arab immigration represented as much as 38.7 percent of the 1922–1931 Arab population growth and, consequently, that approximately 11.8 percent of the 1931 Arab population was foreign-born.[46] The significance of this discrepancy lies, in part, in its implications for competing claims about Arab and Jewish rights in Palestine, with some supporters of Zionism asserting that heavy Arab immigration undermines the Arabs' claim to be the indigenous population of the country.[47] Israeli as well as Palestinian scholars have disputed this assertion, however, concluding that it is at best a theory and in all probability a myth. As expressed by a highly respected Israeli analyst, who writes in direct response to Zionist arguments about large-scale Arab immigration, "one cannot escape the conclusion that most of the growth of the Palestinian Arab community resulted from a process of natural increase."[48]

Most Palestinian Arabs were Sunni Muslims. They counted for about 88–89 percent of the population, a proportion that varied little during the course of the mandate. Most of the remaining Arabs were Christians. They constituted about 10–11 percent of the entire population, growing in number from 71,000 in 1922 to 100,000 in 1934 and about 140,000 in 1945. About half of the Christians were Greek Orthodox and were under the jurisdiction of the Greek Orthodox Patriarchate in Jerusalem. Another 43 percent of the Christians were Roman Catholic, and of these roughly half belonged to the Latin Church and had their own patriarchate in Jerusalem. The second-largest Roman Catholic denomination was the Greek Catholic community, whose members were also known as Melkites. A much smaller Roman Catholic group was the Maronite community. The rest of the population was composed of small Christian communities and Muslim sects. The largest of these was the Druze, an independent community that had split off from Shiite Islam in the eleventh century. Although the Druze made up only 1 percent of the total Arab population, they were recognized by the government as an autonomous political community. These divisions had sociological as well as religious significance. Each community had its own political and administrative institutions, and each was governed by its own legal codes.

There were also social norms discouraging intermarriage, especially between Muslims and Christians.

Patterns of residence and livelihood constituted another dimension that divided the Palestinian population. Peasants made up approximately two-thirds of the population. They lived in about 850 small villages, most of which were located either in the central hill district running between Hebron in the south and the Jezreel Valley in the north or in the coastal plain running from Gaza to the border of Lebanon. The vast majority of these *fellahin* were Muslims, and most were either landless or in possession of holdings inadequate to meet even subsistence needs. As mentioned earlier, many were also deeply in debt to their landlords or to local merchants and moneylenders. Another 10 percent of the population was composed of seminomadic Bedouins, all of whom were Muslim and most of whom lived in the Negev Desert south and east of Beersheba. Finally, by the latter years of the mandate, roughly one-quarter of the Muslims and almost 80 percent of the Christians lived in urban areas. Jerusalem, Jaffa, and Haifa contained many Arabs of both religions. Gaza, Hebron, and Nablus were important cities with a predominantly Muslim population. So too were Ramleh and Lydda, though these latter cities were smaller. The most important cities with a primarily Christian population were Nazareth and Bethlehem. In each of these cities and towns there gradually emerged an Arab proletariat and a small but growing middle class composed of merchants, businessmen, and professionals.

As noted previously, the political economy of Palestinian Arab society was dominated by a small corps of extended and wealthy families. At the national level, a few powerful Muslim clans constituted a kind of Palestinian aristocracy. These families were based in the major towns but had extensive landholdings and exercised influence in many parts of the country, thus sitting atop a national pyramid of patron-client relationships. It is estimated that the estates of these upper-class urban families occupied nearly one-quarter of the total land in Palestine at the beginning of the mandate. Patriarchal clan associations, known as *hamulas*, also dominated smaller towns and villages, and Ottoman law provided that each *hamula* be led by a headman, or *mukhtar*.[49] In order to gain access to land or to receive protection from Bedouin raids and intervillage warfare, most *mukhtars* allied their clans with a more powerful family outside of their community, and this in turn produced broader, district-wide hierarchies of authority relationships. Finally, at the local level, *hamula* ties transcended intravillage divisions based on social class, giving rise to smaller subsystems marked by clientelism and feudalism. Many villages had several major *hamulas* and several *mukhtars*, however, and rivalry among them was often intense. Most villages with 1,000 to 5,000 inhabitants had two *mukhtars*, and larger villages had as many as eleven.[50] The influence of the *mukhtar* derived from his role in securing land and protection for the members of his clan and its political supporters, and also from his participation in assessing property for purposes of taxation and in determining the distribution of government aid. During the mandate period, the *mukhtar* was also the major point of contact between the village and the British administration.

These patterns of patrimonial politics reinforced the generally conservative nature of political and economic life, and competition among families and clans also enhanced the segmented character of Palestine Arab society. The *hamula* system gave *mukhtar*s and other clan leaders numerous opportunities to enrich themselves and to increase their authority and social prestige. Also, more generally, the system in most villages tended to function as a conservative political machine, perpetuating dependence on a small and privileged elite and working to block the emergence of new groups which might threaten the prevailing political order. Finally, at the national level, the narrow and self-interested perspective of the elite worked against the emergence of an integrated political movement wherein the masses and their leaders might work together to achieve common goals. As summarized by one scholar, the subsequent failures of the Palestinian nationalist movement were in considerable measure the result of an "inability and unwillingness of the Arab leadership to co-opt the peasants. . . . The upper classes could not think in terms of *being obligated* to the lower classes in the context of a total national struggle; they could only feel *some* obligation *for* the lower classes insofar as this did not conflict with their own vital interests." [51] All of this limited the modernization and political development of Palestine Arab society, both in general and with respect to its ability to successfully confront the Zionists and the British.

In addition, the *hamula* system was marked by competition, clannishness, and parochialism. This further discouraged the development of a broader Palestinian political identity and, along with divisions based on religion and residence, added yet another dimension to the fragmented nature of Palestinian society. At the local level, the presence of multiple *mukhtar*s in a village usually did not satisfy the claims of competing *hamula*s. In most cases this served to intensify the rivalry among competing clans, which led a British study committee to recommend in 1941 that there be only one headman in a village. [52] Equally serious was the fragmented character of the overall Palestinian society. As summarized by Hurewitz, "The Muslim community was atomized by clannish separatism," and "the persistence of these clannish networks into the mandatory period enabled the Muslim oligarchy, even though surpassed in wealth by many middle class families, to retain its position of social dominance." Moreover, to this Muslim parochialism was added Christian sectarianism, and as a consequence progress toward "the integration of the Arab community and the development of a sense of community-wide social responsibility" was seriously retarded. [53] Thus, patrimonialism, elite parochialism, and social fragmentation reinforced one another and constituted for the Arabs of Palestine an important obstacle to political development.

Despite these constraints, Palestinian Arab society did modernize and develop in significant respects during the years of the British mandate. Education was one arena in which important gains were made. Whereas less than 11 percent of the primary-school-aged children were attending class in 1915, the percentage had doubled by 1931 and was in excess of 30 percent by 1936. The 1931 census thus reported that the overall Arab literacy rate was in the area of 18 percent, with important variations associated with religion, gender, and residence. The literacy rate among Christians was 58 percent, in contrast to a rate of 14 percent among Muslims. A considerable part of the difference between Muslims and Christians was the result of differing patterns of residence, however. Literacy rates were much higher among urban residents than among village dwellers, and in the cities the difference between Christians and Muslims was less pronounced. In addition, among both Christians and Muslims, men were much more likely to be educated than women. For example, the 1931 literacy rates for Christian and Muslim men were 71 percent and 25 percent respectively. Finally, there were differences with respect to the type of school attended; three-fourths of the Muslim children were enrolled in government institutions, while about one-half of the Christian pupils attended private schools, many run by foreign missions.[54]

These statistics were not impressive in absolute terms, and they contrasted sharply with the educational attainments of the Jewish *Yishuv*, where almost all boys and girls received at least some formal schooling. Moreover, opportunities for secondary schooling were even more limited, with most high schools being either indigenous or foreign-run private institutions. Finally, a university education could be obtained only by traveling to Lebanon or Egypt or by leaving the Middle East for Europe or America, a consideration which tended to limit higher education to the offspring of wealthy families. Nevertheless, the pattern of educational growth remained significant. The number of teachers and pupils climbed steadily during the years of the mandate, and by the mid-1940s the aggregate literacy rate was over 30 percent. The percentage of Arab children attending school at this time was around 40 percent, with increases most pronounced among Christians of both sexes and among Muslim men. These figures, despite obvious limitations, made Palestinians among the best-educated people in the Arab world, and far better educated than most other Third World communities at this time. As a further indication of Palestinian desire for education, it may be noted that many who applied to attend government schools were turned away for lack of space. Indeed, complaining that educational opportunities were not being expanded rapidly enough to meet the growing demand, some Arabs accused the British of having a deliberate policy designed to keep the Arabs ignorant.[55]

Palestinian society also experienced economic growth and became more professionally differentiated during this period. On the one hand, a variety of factors contributed to the emergence of an Arab working class. On the other, the Arab middle class expanded, as did the number of Arab commercial and business enterprises. Taken together, along with gains in education, these developments laid a foundation for the gradual transformation of Arab Palestine from a conservative and socially fragmented feudal society into a coherent national community with modern institutions and political aspirations. Progress was uneven and important problems remained, including the failure of Palestinian leadership to articulate a clear and comprehensive ideology of development. Nevertheless, the stagnation which had long made Palestine a backwater of the Arab world came to an end during the years between the two world wars. In contrast to the situation during the early years of the Arab renaissance, when Palestine was not among the handful of states where the most important educational, economic, and political gains were being made, Palestinian society at this time experienced change and modernization at a rate equal to or greater than that in many other Arab countries.

Some of the stimuli that contributed to the formation of a Palestinian proletariat had to do with the Zionist presence. Particularly important was Arab loss of land, which transformed many peasants into laborers and forced them to seek work outside the Arab agricultural sector. Zionist enterprises also offered employment opportunities to some Arabs, and, more generally, Jewish capital contributed to the expansion of public works projects for which many Arabs were hired. The role of the mandatory administration in expanding port, railway, and transport facilities was equally significant, and Britain's investment in the economy of Palestine increased substantially with the approach of World War II. These developments, too, provided opportunities for Arab employment and contributed to the proletarianization of a large segment of the Arab peasantry. Finally, the transformation of peasants into workers was accelerated by rapid population growth in the countryside and by the general stagnation of the Arab agricultural sector. As a consequence of all these developments, it is estimated that by the onset of the war there were an equal number of peasant farmers and peasant wage laborers.[56]

Work was not steady, and few jobs carried any social benefits. Some workers were recruited for public works projects directly from their villages, but thousands of others migrated to the cities in search of employment. On the other hand, while many stayed in the towns for extended periods, most did not become permanent city dwellers; they remained as long as employment was available, frequently returning home to visit their families, and during periods of recession they retreated to their villages and sought support from their extended kin networks. Another peculiarity of this process of proletarianization is that it was a stimulus rather than a response to broader structural changes within Arab society. It was not shaped in significant measure by Arab capital or Arab entrepreneurship. Rather, as noted, its principal determinants lay in Zionist and British activity, and secondarily in a failure to modernize Arab agriculture. But while these considerations reflected the difficulties and contradictions of Palestinian peasant life, the consequences of proletarianization remained important and had potentially far-reaching implications.

Among workers and their families, proletarianism created new attitudes and behavior patterns, including a heightened awareness of life beyond the village. Also, for rural Arab society as a whole, it deepened involvement in the cash economy and brought new demands for manufactured products, both of which modified traditional economic roles and the established division of labor. Another important development was the formation in many cities of new voluntary associations, including benevolent societies, religious organizations, and youth groups. Some of these associations sponsored classes to teach reading and writing, modern health care, and other subjects related to urban life. Some also lent money or provided other forms of assistance to members in times of difficulty, such as upon the death of a family member or during a period of prolonged illness. Still other groups, especially those frequented by more middle-class elements, organized social and cultural programs, many of which were open to the public. In addition to these social and self-help activities, a number of the new associations subsequently became vehicles for political mobilization and the diffusion of nationalist ideas.

There also developed the beginnings of an Arab labor movement. Some early unions, such as the Jaffa Lightermen's Association, were small guild-like organizations; others, including the Orthodox Labor Union, were sectarian in character. The first Western-style union, the Palestine Arab Workers Society, was founded in Haifa in 1925, and a few years later it opened branches in Jaffa and Jerusalem. The society remained small, and the Jerusalem and Jaffa branches soon declared their independence and formed the Arab Laborers' Federation. Nevertheless, overall, the movement of Arab workers in Palestine was another indication of the important social and economic changes taking place. Moreover, despite its limitations, it was more advanced than the labor movement in any neighboring Arab country except Lebanon.[57]

The proletarianization of the Palestinian peasantry also had an impact on the vigor and authority of the traditional *hamula* system. In some respects, the spread of peasant wage labor reinforced the role of traditional clan associations. The government's Public Works Department often used *mukhtar*s and other clan leaders to recruit laborers, thus enabling these individuals to maintain control over the livelihood of their traditional clients. A related consideration is that workers were frequently recruited from a single *hamula* within a village for nearby projects. These policies were designed not only to minimize costs but to prevent the development of "an uprooted labor army, dependent on public works for a livelihood."[58]

In other ways, however, the influence of clan leaders and their external patrons gradually diminished. Many peasants no longer depended on these leaders for land, and villagers who took up temporary urban residence usually obtained employment without their assistance. Peasant earning power gave greater independence in other areas as well, increasing the ability to purchase needed goods and services rather than to obtain them through established feudal connections. Also, in the cities, migrant workers formed new alliances and social networks. For example, the membership of many urban voluntary associations cut across *hamula* lines, even when an organization was established by immigrants from a single village. There were other factors, not directly related to the process of proletarianization, that also weakened the established pattern of patrimonial politics. One was the termination of raids and intervillage warfare, which reduced the security functions associated with traditional feudalism. Another was the government's appointment of new officials to collect village taxes, removing this responsibility from the functions of the *mukhtar*. A third was an end to the isolation of most villages, which gave rural residents more opportunities to learn about changes taking place in other parts of the country. Thus, overall, while the growth of an Arab working class reinforced traditional institutions in certain respects, it was also an important part of a broad movement of change. It laid a foundation for accelerated social mobilization and contributed to the eventual emergence of new patterns of political economy.

Change was also visible in the growth of the Palestinian middle class and in the expansion of Arab business enterprises. The middle class was composed of both highly educated individuals who pursued careers in such liberal professions as law, medicine, and teaching and entrepreneurs who engaged in trade, manufacturing, and commercial farming ventures. Christians had traditionally been preponderant in most middle-class professions, but during the period of the mandate they were increasingly joined by educated Muslims, many of whom were the sons of leading Muslim clans. The presence of these latter individuals, moreover, blurred the distinction between the professional and commercial middle class on the one hand and the established landowning upper-class families on the other. As among urbanized workers, new organizations sprang up in response to the expansion of the middle class. Among them were Arab chambers of commerce and the Palestine Arab Bar Association. There were also Arab women's societies in Jerusalem, Jaffa, Haifa, and a few other cities. These latter organizations were led by the wives of leading politicians; among their activities were programs aimed at helping the needy, at educational and cultural advancement, and, in addition, at building support for Palestinian political causes. The first Palestine Arab Women's Congress was convened in Jerusalem in 1929.[59]

The new middle class was concentrated in the cities, the Arab population of which grew from slightly less than 200,000 at the beginning of the mandate to about 300,000 in 1936, and urban society in Arab Palestine was an increasingly complex and heterogeneous environment. There were schools, hospitals, factories, labor unions, and other modern institutions. Thus, though developing more slowly than the Jewish *Yishuv*, Palestinian Arab society was experiencing important social and economic transformations, and the process of nation-building was well underway. These developments were also visible in the areas of manufacturing, business, and commerce. For example, the number of Arab factories, including both handicraft and industrial enterprises, grew from 1,000 to 3,000 between 1921 and 1943. The number of persons employed in these factories increased sixfold between 1921 and 1939, reaching 30,000 in the latter year, and during the same period the value of investments in these enterprises increased fourfold and annual output increased eightfold. The later figures are reduced somewhat if adjusted for increases in the cost of living. Nevertheless, as one scholar concludes, "All the indices demonstrate considerable growth, including an increase in the efficiency of manpower and capital."[60] The broad occupational distribution that resulted from these and other developments is shown below, with figures presented from the *Yishuv* and Egypt for comparative purposes.[61]

	Primary Sector Agriculture & Fishing	Secondary Sector Industry & Construction	Tertiary Sector Services & Commerce
Arabs (1939)	52.9	11.6	35.5
Jews (1939)	19.3	27.1	53.6
Egypt (1937)	62.0		38.0

A useful and concise summary of this broad constellation of changes at the upper and middle levels of Arab society is provided by Hurewitz, who describes the situation in the mid-1930s:

The most visible economic changes in the Arab Community occurred among the upper and middle classes. Investment in citriculture spiraled upward until the Arab-owned plantations covered 33,750 acres in 1936, as compared with a combined Arab-Jewish acreage of only 7,500 in 1918. Other newly acquired capital went into construction and the production of building materials to meet the demands of the enlarging population. By the mid-1930s Arab manufacturing had branched out from the traditional textile, soap and olive-oil industries to a variety of consumer goods. The bulk remained handicraft shops, but the number of firms using power-driven machinery multiplied from seven in 1921 to 313 in 1935. Home industries, common fifteen years before, were on the wane. Forward strides in commerce and finance were suggested by the growing percentage of the Arab national income attributable to trade and transport and by the appearance of the community's first two banks, which served as bankers to the local Arab national movement. Finally, opportunities increased noticeably in the liberal professions—education, medicine, law, white-collar government employment, and journalism.[62]

Political Development among the Palestinians

Along with this battery of demographic, social, and economic changes came important political developments, adding a critical dimension to the slow but steady transformation of Palestinian Arab society into a coherent national community. As noted earlier, organizations with explicitly political concerns emerged shortly after World War I, in response to the activities of the British, the French, the Zionists, and Emir Faycal.

Of the thirty to forty clubs that sprang up in Palestine after the war, three were of particular political importance during the formative period between the end of the war and the beginning of the mandate. The first was the Muslim-Christian Association, al-Jamiyya al-Islamiyya al-Masihiyya, which was led by older politicians associated with the most notable families of Arab Palestine. The MCA claimed more than two hundred members in 1919 and had branches in a number of cities. Among the most important planks in its political platform were firm opposition to Zionist immigration and to the creation of a Jewish national home in Palestine, unconditional independence for Greater Syria under the rule of Faycal, and internal self-government for Palestine as part of the broader Syrian state. Though Palestine was to rule itself under a Syrian umbrella, the MCA called for the creation of an independent Palestinian legislature to be elected by local inhabitants.[63] The local branches of the MCA were the mainstay of the Palestinian nationalist movement during this period. The Jerusalem MCA was headed by Arif Pasha al-Dajani, a member of one of the country's most influential families.

The other two major organizations were al-Muntada al-Adabi, the Literary Society, and al-Nadi al-Arabi, the Arab Club. Both were dominated by younger and well-educated activists and contrasted with the MCA in that they were not deliberately composed of leading notables. Rather than being dedicated to the representation of traditional elites, these organizations were based on definable ideologies. Also, again unlike the MCA, the groups were made up exclusively of Muslims. Although there were important differences between al-Muntada and al-Nadi, the groups were united not only by opposition to Zionism but also by a desire to see Palestine ruled by Faycal as part of Syria. They referred to Palestine at this time as "Southern Syria," and their Greater Syrian orientation contrasted notably with that of the MCA. Al-Muntada also urged that Faycal be named *khalif* in Friday prayers. By the end of 1919 al-Nadi claimed more than 500 members and al-Muntada claimed about 600, although these numbers are probably exaggerated and may also reflect a degree of overlapping membership.

Consistent with their more activist orientation, al-Muntada and al-Nadi maintained contact with several smaller and highly militant secret societies. These latter societies espoused direct action and had commoners as well as elites within their ranks. One such group was al-Fidaiyya, the Self-Sacrificers, which was organized in the slums of Jaffa early in 1919, for a time called itself "The Black Hand," and later established small cells in Jerusalem, Gaza, Nablus, Ramleh, Hebron, and Tulkarm. Another secret organization was al-Jamiyya al-Ikha wa-al-Afaf, the Society of Brotherhood and Purity, which distributed pamphlets and organized demonstrations. Al-Ikha wa al-Afaf also possessed weapons, considered the use of terrorism, and counted a number of policemen among its approximately 200 members.[64]

Al-Muntada was set up as an educational and cultural organization and was active in the Arab schools of Jerusalem. It sponsored intellectual and athletic programs, established an orchestra, and concerned itself with the dissemination of Arab literature. Al-Muntada was originally financed by the French, who sought to generate Palestinian support for their designs in Syria. In this connection al-Muntada also had ties with the Palestine Catholic Association, which was fully supportive of French imperialism in the Fertile Crescent. Under British pressure, however, al-Muntada installed new leadership in 1919, after which it came under the influence of the Nashashibi family, another of Palestine's leading clans. Although it remained strongest in Jerusalem, the organization established branches in a number of cities, including Jaffa, Tulkarm, and Gaza. Among its most active members were teachers, former army officers, and policemen.

Al-Nadi was dominated by the Husayni family, perhaps the most prominent Palestinian clan at this time. Six of the thirteen Jerusalem mayors since 1864 had been Husaynis. Al-Nadi was under the influence of younger Husaynis and had as its president al-Hajj Muhammad Amin al-Husayni, who in his early years was considered pro-British. Like al-Muntada, al-Nadi was strongest in Jerusalem but had branches in a number of towns, the most important being Gaza, Hebron, and Nablus. The members of al-Nadi were for a time willing to cooperate with the British, in the hope that Britain would limit its support of the Jewish cause and would render assistance to Faycal in Syria. Nevertheless, one of its members edited the first Arab nationalist newspaper to appear in Palestine, *Suriya al-Janubiyya* (Southern Syria), and more generally, as with al-Muntada, its program was the unification and independence of Syria. During this period al-Nadi maintained close contact with Faycal's regime in Damascus and received financial assistance from it. Despite early differences in their respective pro-French and pro-British orientations, al-Nadi and al-Muntada had nearly identical political programs. The main difference between the two was based on an intense rivalry between the Husayni and Nashashibi families, both of which aspired to leadership of the incipient nationalist movement.

A series of Palestine national congresses grew out of these early political institutions. An All-Palestine Congress, known also as the First Congress of the Muslim-Christian Societies, was organized by the MCA and convened in Jerusalem in February 1919. As discussed earlier, it sought to formulate a program to present to the Paris Peace Conference and, although there were differences of opinion on the matter, it concluded by supporting the "Southern Syria" position of younger activists and urging that Palestine remain an Arab country and be joined with Syria. The congress brought together members of various social and political organizations, as well as local branches of the MCA. For example, though it was chaired by al-Dajani, president of the Jerusalem MCA, the secretary of the congress was Izzat Darwazah, leader of the Nablus branch of al-Nadi al-Arabi. The congress named a delegation to carry its resolutions to Paris and sent another group, which included Darwazah, to Damascus.

Much of the political activity of the next year or so was centered in Damascus. A number of Palestinian activists, including some who had served in Faycal's army and administration, were already concentrated in the Syrian capital, and in 1919 they were joined by the delegation from the All-Palestine Congress and a number of others. In Damascus these Palestinians organized under the banner of al-Nadi al-Arabi, and they soon became the dominant political faction there, helping to organize a General Syrian Congress in July 1919 and another in March 1920. The first of these meetings was held in the al-Nadi al-Arabi club in Damascus. Both congresses affirmed the unity of Greater Syria, including its southern province of Palestine, and demanded creation of a constitutional monarchy under Faycal with no more than limited technical and economic ties to any Western power. Late in 1919 there was also a conference of pro-Syrian, pan-Arab Palestinians in Haifa; and in March 1920, following a proclamation of independence by the second General Syrian Congress, demonstrations were organized in Palestine by both al-Nadi and al-Muntada. In April 1920, al-Hajj Amin al-Husayni fled to Damascus, having been accused by the British of involvement in the anti-Jewish riots that took place in Jerusalem that month, and in May a new organization of Palestinians in Syria was established. It was known as the Palestinian Arab Society, al-Jamiyya al-Arabiyya al-Filastiniyya.

Most Palestinian politicians in Syria returned home following Faycal's ouster by French forces in July, after which the center of political activity shifted back to Jerusalem. Another important development was the end of the Husayni family's pro-British orientation. Not only had the British condemned al-Hajj Amin and charged al-Nadi in Jerusalem with responsibility for inciting the April disturbances, they also held responsible and dismissed the mayor of the city, Musa Kazim al-Husayni, another important member of the Husayni family. A related consideration is that the British then supported Raghib al-Nashashibi to replace Musa Kazim, so that while the Husaynis became bitter opponents of the British, the Nashashibis now allied themselves with Great Britain. The two most important consequences of these events were a deepening of the rivalry between the Husayni and the Nashashibi families and the former's emergence as the leading faction of an increasingly militant Palestine national movement. These developments also coincided with the collapse of the pan-Arabist "Southern Syria" orientation of Palestinian nationalism, in the wake of the French seizure of Syria.

Palestinian nationalists convened a congress in Haifa in December 1920, which they called the Third Arab Congress in order to establish continuity with the two conferences that had been held in Damascus. The meeting, which lasted six days and was attended by thirty-seven delegates, was preceded by meetings throughout the country in which local groups formulated recommendations and selected delegates to carry their views to Haifa. The delegates assembled in Haifa issued calls for Muslim-Christian unity and demanded self-rule for Palestine. Although they did not rule out a limited British presence, similar to that exercised by Britain in Transjordan, they were clear in their demand that Palestine should be an Arab country. The Balfour Declaration and the Zionist program were strongly and unequivocally condemned.

To give continuity and unified leadership to their movement, the delegates elected a nine-member executive committee. Originally called the Central Committee and later widely known as the Palestine Arab Executive, the committee elected in Haifa contained seven Muslims and two Christians and was composed of men from seven different subdistricts, including Jerusalem, Jaffa, Haifa, Acre, Ramleh, Nablus, and Tulkarm. The Arab Executive's president was Musa Kazim al-Husayni, the former mayor of Jerusalem who had also presided over the Haifa congress. Its vice-president was Arif Pasha al-Dajani, former head of the Jerusalem MCA, and its secretary was Jamal al-Husayni, who had assumed the chairmanship of the national Muslim-Christian Association.

These developments determined the structure and leadership of much of the nationalist movement through the 1920s and the early 1930s. Congresses were held annually through 1923. The fourth congress was convened in Jerusalem in May 1921, the fifth in Nablus in August 1922, and the sixth in Jaffa in June 1923. Congresses steadily increased in size, and it may be noted that by the Jaffa meeting the term "Southern Syria" had fallen completely into disuse and all discussions focused on Palestine alone.[65] There were about 115 delegates at the 1923 congress, roughly 15 percent of whom were Christian.

Each congress also elected a new Arab Executive, and like the congresses themselves, the executive expanded progressively in size and scope. The executive elected in 1923, for example, contained twenty-nine members, among them five Christians, representing sixteen of the country's administrative districts. After a hiatus of five years, the Seventh Palestine Arab Congress was convened in Jerusalem in June 1928. The executive it elected contained forty-eight members representing all the districts of Palestine. Seats were also reserved for all of the major religious communities, such that the 1928 executive included twelve Christians elected on a communal basis. Musa Kazim al-Husayni served as president of the executive during this entire period, except while he was in London in 1922 as head of the Palestinian delegation. To a considerable degree the work of the executive was also animated by the labors of its secretary, Jamal al-Husayni.

The Arab Executive depended heavily for grass-roots support on local chapters of the MCA. This was the structure through which politicians operating at the national level mobilized and exercised influence over the nonelite population. Zionist and British sources both estimate that about 3,000 Palestinians were mobilized directly into the ranks of these branches in 1919–20. Moreover, almost all MCA branches were under the influence of local notables prepared to participate in nationalist activity, including representatives of influential families, Muslim officials, and Christian leaders. The local structure of the MCA was thus ideally suited for motivating and organizing the general population. The societies planned and financed their own programs, but they also maintained regular contact with the MCA secretariat in Jerusalem and through it coordinated some of their activities, such as petition drives. Therefore, as expressed by Porath, "In places where branches of the MCA were set up, political-nationalist activity was more systematic and organized. In those places it was easier to gather funds to finance the country-wide activities, and the participation of those places in the development of the country-wide political framework was less problematic."[66]

The Supreme Muslim Council (SMC) was another important institution created during this period.[67] The council grew out of an attempt by the British in 1920 to establish an advisory council composed of Muslims and Christians with whom the high commissioner could consult. During 1921, however, Muslim leaders sought the formation of an independent council to supervise the affairs of their community, especially in matters pertaining to the administration of religious trusts (*awqaf*) and *Sharia* courts, and British acceptance of their proposals toward the end of the year resulted in creation of the Supreme Muslim Council. A prominent role in these developments was played by al-Hajj Amin al-Husayni, who, with British approval, had become mufti of Jerusalem earlier in 1921.

The first Muslim Council was elected in 1922, chosen by fifty-three former electors to the last Ottoman parliament. The SMC had five members, one each from the old Ottoman districts of Acre and Nablus, two from the district of Jerusalem, and a president, known as *rais al-ulama* (head of the *ulama*). Al-Hajj Amin was elected *rais al-ulama*, and among the council's other members was Muhammad Murad, the mufti of Haifa who was also known for his nationalist inclinations. Subsequent councils were elected in 1926, 1929, and 1930, although the 1926 elections were annulled by the High Court of Justice, and council members in that year were appointed by the mandatory government. Upon the death of a council member, the government also appointed a replacement until the next election. The authority of the council was defined somewhat vaguely, but its control over appointments to religious courts and revenues from pious trusts gave it considerable power.

Competition between the Husaynis and Nashashibis was reflected in events surrounding the creation of the Supreme Muslim Council. First, the Nashashibis had sought to make one of their number mufti of Jerusalem when the post became vacant in March 1921, upon the death of its occupant, Kamil al-Husayni. The British permitted al-Hajj Amin to assume the post, however, probably in an attempt to compensate the Husayni family for its loss of the mayoralty.[68] Second, the Nashashibis had originally sought to gain seats on the new SMC but were heavily outvoted by supporters of the Husaynis. Thus, in 1923, with both the Arab Executive and the SMC dominated by the Husaynis, the Nashashibis sought to form a political organization of their own, and in this they received support from other notables who resented the dominance of the Husayni family or whose own political aspirations remained unfulfilled. Though divisions were based principally on family or personal rivalries, there were also some overlapping political and ideological divisions. Some notables felt that Palestinian interests would be better served by less militant opposition to the British. For example, they were willing to join a government-sponsored advisory council, which was opposed by the Husaynis.

To give expression to these personal and political differences, the Nashashibis in November 1923 took the lead in forming the Palestine Arab National Party, al-Hizb al-Watani al-Arabi al-Filastini. They received strong support from the Jerusalem branch of the Dajani family, with Arif Pasha al-Dajani resigning from the Arab Executive. The National Party, whose members soon became known as *Muaradah*, "oppositionists," had some initial success. The party won about half the seats in the 1926 election for the Supreme Muslim Council, and its candidates also fared well in the municipal election of 1927. The 1926 SMC election, as noted, was annulled by the courts, but oppositionists were nonetheless given half the positions appointed by the government. Nevertheless, the National Party scored few other victories and its overall influence remained limited. Raghib al-Nashashibi had played a central role in organizing the opposition, but he was prevented from joining the party or supporting it openly because of his position as mayor of Jerusalem. Further, in an attempt to compete with the mainstream of the nationalist movement, the National Party adopted a platform that differed little from that of more militant factions. This caused some of the political moderates who had helped to found the new party to lose interest in it, and it caused many others to see the oppositionist movement as a superfluous and divisive element within a nationalist movement in need of unity.[69]

Two sets of developments led to an agreement between the opposition and the nationalist mainstream in 1928. The first was the growing weakness of the Arab Executive and the Muslim-Christian Association, from whose local branches the Executive received much of its support. The second was increasing dissatisfaction over the national movement's fragmentation, especially when the Husaynis went so far as to seek an arrangement with the Jews in their unsuccessful attempt to defeat Raghib al-Nashashibi in the 1927 Jerusalem municipal elections.[70]

Many local MCA branches disintegrated during the early 1920s, and the two most important chapters, in Jaffa and Nablus respectively, split into internal warring factions in 1924–25. Thus, according to Porath, what remained of the Arab Executive and the MCA during the period between 1924 and 1928 was "no more than an office run by Jamal al-Husayni." Further, this decline in activity meant that the financial resources of the executive were badly strained, "to the point where in 1926 there was not enough money left to cover its current expenses or to pay the secretary his much reduced salary."[71] One reason for this institutional atrophy at the grass-roots level was probably the dramatic (though temporary) decline in Zionist immigration. In 1927, for example, more Jews left than arrived in Palestine. This and other Zionist difficulties during these years led to a reduction in Palestinian fears, which in turn may have diminished the impetus for nationalist activity. In any event, there occurred a serious weakening of the MCA structure at the local level, with the result that in 1927 the office of the Arab Executive closed and Jamal al-Husayni took a position as secretary of the Supreme Muslim Council.

With both the Arab Executive and the National Party characterized by weakness, there were calls in 1927 for repairing the division within the nationalist movement. Complaints about the rivalry between the Husayni and Nashashibi camps were given particularly forceful expression by the small Liberal Party, which had been formed in Jaffa and Gaza in 1927. Among its founders was Isa al-Isa, the editor of *Filastin*.

The desire to forge a unified movement was a major stimulus to the convening of the Seventh Palestine Arab Congress, which met five years after the Sixth Congress in 1923. Following lengthy negotiations, agreement was reached concerning the composition of an enlarged Arab Executive, which was also charged with formulating plans to reorganize and unify the nationalist movement in other respects. The new executive was composed of forty-eight members. It included two Muslims—one allied with the Husaynis and one with the oppositionists—from each of Palestine's eighteen administrative subdivisions. It also contained twelve Christian delegates chosen on a communal basis. As noted, Musa Kazim al-Husayni remained president of the executive. The two vice-presidents were supporters of the opposition, however. These individuals were Tawfiq al-Hajj Abdullah, mayor of Acre, and Yaqub al-Farraj, deputy mayor of Jerusalem. Other oppositionists, as well as independents and Liberal Party members, were also added to the executive, thus increasing substantially the unity and institutional integration of the Arab national movement in Palestine. There were strains within this grand coalition, and the Arab Executive itself remained weak in the years after 1928. Nevertheless, unity was maintained until the executive collapsed following the death of Musa Kazim in 1934.

These developments breathed new life into the Arab Executive, but only temporarily and to a limited degree. Some local MCA branches revived. This was the case in Jaffa, for example, where local militants urged a more activist posture on the executive. It was also the case in Nablus, where the local branch reorganized under the name al-Jamiyya al-Arabiyya al-Wataniyya, the Arab National Society. In both Jaffa and Nablus, as well as elsewhere, younger and more activist elements came to the fore. These developments were not only the result of the Seventh Congress's efforts to unify the nationalist movement, they were also in response to the widespread disturbances that occurred in August 1929 and Britain's subsequent attempt to accommodate Arab demands.

By 1931, the circumstances of the executive had once again deteriorated. The organization experienced renewed financial difficulties and, more generally, there was a growing conviction among Palestinians of all political orientations that national institutions had failed in their fundamental objective, to halt the construction of the *Yishuv*. The Jewish presence in Palestine was once again expanding, and Palestinian grievances were accordingly felt with increasing intensity. Younger nationalists, in particular, lost faith in the executive, and by 1933 it may have lost faith in itself. In the months following Musa Kazim al-Husayni's death in March 1934, the structure that had provided a framework for nationalist activity during the 1920s therefore passed quietly out of existence.

The fate of the Supreme Muslim Council, the other major institution created in the 1920s, was different. Financially secure as a result of revenues derived from the administration of pious Muslim trusts, the council became a vehicle for the political advancement of its president, al-Hajj Amin al-Husayni, who was also mufti of Jerusalem.[72] During the 1920s the council concentrated on Muslim affairs and helped to organize the reconstruction and refurbishing of Islamic holy places in Jerusalem. Among its accomplishments were the repair of al-Aqsa Mosque and the Dome of the Rock and the construction of an Islamic art museum. Al-Hajj Amin also presided over local Muslim ceremonies, including the annual Nebi Musa celebration in Jerusalem. In this connection the mufti undertook to oppose Zionism by articulating the view that an expanding Jewish presence threatened the Muslim character of Palestine, seeking as well to mobilize international Muslim opinion in support of this position. The international dimension of the SMC's activities also increased al-Hajj Amin's visibility as a Muslim personality in other Arab countries.

One effort which combined these preoccupations was a drive in the mid-1920s to raise funds in neighboring Arab countries for restoration projects being carried out in Jerusalem. For example, ten thousand Egyptian pounds were raised in Egypt for the reconstruction of al-Aqsa, half of which came from King Fuad and half from the Egyptian Ministry of *Awqaf*.[73] Another effort was the convening of an international Islamic congress in Jerusalem in December 1931. Al-Hajj Amin invited *ulama* from all over the Arab world, including *Shia* leaders, and the gathering passed a number of resolutions condemning Zionism and the French and British mandates.[74] Although such international displays of Muslim solidarity were to an extent designed to compensate for the internal weakness of the Palestine national movement, they did increase public awareness and provide an ideological framework for opposition to Zionism. According to one analyst, they were also inspired in part by al-Hajj Amin's desire to emulate the Zionists' success in generating support for their cause among their own coreligionists throughout the world.[75]

The SMC was also active in attempts to prevent the sale of Arab land to Jews, as is explained in al-Hajj Amin's own account.

> Ever since the formation of the Supreme Muslim Council, which the Palestinians in 1922 elected for the management of the *Sharia* courts, the *awqaf* and Muslim affairs in Palestine, the Council has done much to safeguard lands in the face of the Jewish invasion. Through the *Sharia* courts, which were placed under the control of the SMC, it prevented the selling of lands in which legal minors had a share. The SMC also bought many lands which were offered for sale through the *awqaf* funds, and lent money to many landowners who were in need of cash, out of the orphans' funds, in order to prevent them from selling.[76]

The extent and effectiveness of SMC action are probably exaggerated in al-Hajj Amin's account and, in any event, the transfer of land to the Zionists did increase during these years. Nevertheless, a leading Israeli scholar has carefully reviewed the claims of the mufti and concluded that in some cases SMC efforts did result in the cancellation of projected sales, and that "some land was endowed as *waqf* and thus its transfer to the Jews forestalled."[77]

Although al-Hajj Amin became increasingly visible and the SMC was generally successful in its attempt to fuse Islamic and nationalist concerns, the council was affected by the same personal and family rivalries that plagued other organizations within the national movement. Both the main coalition and the oppositionists sought to increase their representation on the council, and both put pressure on the government when it became necessary to appoint the replacement for a deceased council member. The opposition also sought to reduce some of the SMC's powers, on the grounds that these were abused by al-Hajj Amin. For example, they tried in 1930 to persuade the government to revoke the SMC's power to appoint and dismiss *Sharia* court judges, proposing that this authority be transferred to the president of the *Sharia* Court of Appeals. A particularly bitter confrontation surrounded the 1931 Islamic Congress. Oppositionists traveled throughout the country to denounce the gathering to religious officials in the rural areas, and Raghib al-Nashashibi then called a counterconference to express the oppositionists' lack of confidence in al-Hajj Amin's leadership and to form a new opposition party. The rival gathering was called the Congress of the Palestinian Muslim Nation and was attended by approximately 1,000 individuals, including members of all the leading families opposed to the Husaynis. The opposition was also helped by the emergence at this time of a split within the Husayni camp, based on a disagreement between al-Hajj Amin and Musa Kazim.

Two kinds of developments characterized the national movement in the years that followed. First, there was an increase in the number of political parties and groupings. Second, a broader range of political opinion was encompassed by the new organizations. In addition to those associated with the Husaynis and the Nashashibis, there were groups that represented the views of younger and more radical Palestinians, some of whom had not previously participated in the nationalist struggle but were deeply frustrated by the rivalries and infighting that had sapped so much of the national movement's energies.

One new party was the pan-Arabist Istiqlal, or Independence Party. Formed in 1932 and known formally as Hizb al-Istiqlal al-Arabiyya fi-Suriya al-Janubiyya, the Istiqlal called for complete and unconditional independence and urged closer ties between Palestine and other Arab states. The party was composed largely of young professionals and did not attempt to construct a grass-roots base. Another new group was the Youth Congress, established at the end of 1932. Originally formed by Muslims who were dissatisfied with the job opportunities available to educated young men, it soon took on more explicitly political concerns and sought to coordinate activities with some Christian Palestinians. Youth Congress activists were involved in illegal demonstrations in 1933, leading to the arrest of some of its organizers. In 1934 its members patrolled the coast in an attempt to prevent the landing of unauthorized Jewish immigrants.[78] The formation of the Istiqlal and the Youth Congress was indicative of a new wave of militancy making its appearance. There were also more radical, secret societies that began to operate in the early 1930s.

Leading to the formation of a new party by the Nashashibis was a split within oppositionist ranks in 1934. An important ally of the Nashashibis had been the Khalidis, yet another of Palestine's leading families, but personal differences led the latter to run their own candidate for mayor in the Jerusalem municipal elections of 1934. They also formed a common electoral front with the Husaynis in an attempt to defeat the incumbent, Raghib al-Nashashibi; and indeed their candidate, Husayn Fakhri al-Khalidi, was successful. In June 1935, al-Khalidi formed the Reform Party, Hizb al-Islah, a small patron party that had little lasting impact on the nationalist movement but which further contributed to institutional pluralism. A second patron party formed in 1935 was the National Bloc, al-Kutla al-Wataniyya, which was organized by Abd al-Latif Salah, a lawyer from Nablus. The party was an attempt by Salah to provide himself with a local power base, although, like al-Khalidi, he defended his new organization on the grounds that it would transcend divisions between the Husaynis and Nashashibis. In the meantime, however, in December 1934, the Nashashibis took the lead in creating a new party, Hizb al-Difaa al-Watani, the National Defense Party. Its president was Raghib al-Nashashibi, whose defeat as mayor left him free to participate directly in partisan politics.

The National Defense Party was supported by the Dajani family in Jerusalem and gained the support of mayors and other notables in a number of towns, most notably Nablus, Jaffa, and Ramleh. It was also supported by some Christian leaders and included several of the latter among its officers. Its vice-president, for example, was Yaqub al-Farraj, a Greek Orthodox. Although the new party was a vehicle for advancing the interests of certain segments of the Palestinian elite, it was able to use the *hamula* system to construct a grass-roots base in some areas. The party condemned the militancy and aggressiveness of groups such as the Youth Congress. Its own platform, by contrast, emphasized moderation, in the hope that a less confrontational approach would win concessions from the British. There was a measure of realism in this tactic, since the weakness of the national movement had become quite evident. The party also sought to develop international linkages, and early in 1935 it sent delegations to Egypt and the Arabian Peninsula in order to explain its views and seek support. In addition, however, the National Defense Party was heavily motivated by considerations of self-interest. On the one hand, one of its goals was to undermine the position of al-Hajj Amin al-Husayni. The mufti was denounced by party delegates traveling abroad, and in Palestine he was vigorously attacked in local newspapers supportive of the Nashashibis. On the other hand, the party was concerned that the status and authority of the traditional elite were being undermined by the emergence of more radical political factions and by increasing social mobilization at the non-elite level. As expressed in one major study, "The party's leaders undoubtedly feared upheavals in the social status quo as much as they feared the British and Zionists."[79] This fear provided at least some of the motivation for the National Defense Party's moderation.

In March 1935, the Husaynis responded to these developments by establishing a new party of their own, the Palestine Arab Party, Hizb al-Arabiyya al-Filastiniyya. The founding conference in Jerusalem was attended by about 1,500 individuals. Al-Hajj Amin did not assume a position of leadership because of his official position, and Jamal al-Husayni thus resigned his post as secretary of the SMC and became the new party's president. Its vice-president was Alfred Rok, a Greek Catholic from Jaffa. The Palestine Arab Party adopted a platform and tactics which distinguished it from the National Defense Party led by the Nashashibis. Its rhetoric and ideology were much more militant and approached those which characterized the Istiqlal Party and the Youth Congress. Rejecting piecemeal and partial reform, it called for unconditional independence and abolition of the British mandate, for resistance to Zionism and the protection of Palestine's Arab character, and for close ties between an independent Arab state in Palestine and other Arab countries. The party was active at the grass-roots level. Jamal al-Husayni toured the country in 1935, and his efforts led to the establishment of local branches in many towns. The new party also paid considerable attention to the mobilization of young people, initially working with local Boy Scout troops and in 1936 creating its own young people's organization, the Youth Troops.

Newspapers favorable to the Palestine Arab Party strongly denounced the Nashashibis, and the propaganda battle between the two camps became extremely bitter, eventually producing several libel suits. The Palestine Arab Party conducted a vigorous propaganda campaign against Zionism and the British as well, however. As did the National Defense Party, it also sought to establish ties with neighboring Arab countries, and it asserted that these countries, too, might eventually be threatened by Zionist expansion. Some in the Husayni camp were influenced by the Nazis during this period, seeing in Nazi Germany both a model for constructing a mass organization and a potential ally against the Jews and Britain. Al-Hajj Amin met with the German consul in Jerusalem in 1933 and expressed support for the new regime in Germany. Several speakers at the founding conference of the Youth Troops praised the skill of the Nazis in organizing the German people in defense of their national interests.[80]

Although these developments left the national movement as fragmented as ever, pressure was building in response to the continuing growth of the *Yishuv*, and events pushed the various parties toward renewed cooperation and more radical policies in the mid-1930s. Jewish immigration and land transfers to Jews were again on the rise. This was also a period of economic difficulty, which raised both the general level of Arab frustration and Arab fears of landlessness and unemployment. The *Yishuv* was affected as well by the economic problems that gripped Palestine, and the failure of many small businesses led to a rise in Jewish unemployment. Labor Zionists responded by intensifying their calls for Hebrew labor, however, and this added further to Arab concerns. Finally, in addition to these continuing fears about the growth of the Zionist enterprise, the increasing militancy of Palestinian nationalism was a result of contact with anti-colonial national movements in neighboring Arab countries, most notably Syria, Egypt, and Lebanon.

Two important incidents in 1935 also contributed to the increasingly radical and confrontational mood of the Palestinians. One was the discovery in the port of Jaffa of a shipment of arms being smuggled into the country. Although the importers were never officially identified, the Arabs were probably correct in their assumption that the shipment had been arranged by Jewish agents and was destined for the Hagana. In any event, the episode intensified Arab anger. The other incident was the death of Sheikh Izz al-Din al-Qassam. Al-Qassam was president of the Haifa branch of the Young Men's Muslim Association, and after 1934 he devoted himself to organizing young Arabs for direct action against the *Yishuv*. In November 1935 he was undertaking organizational work in villages near Jenin, and in the course of their activities one of al-Qassam's group killed a policeman. A chase and battle then ensued, in which al-Qassam and several of his collaborators were killed. Al-Qassam's funeral was an occasion for passionate expressions of militant nationalism.

The situation deteriorated further in 1936, with outbreaks of communal violence during the first part of the year, and in this atmosphere Arab politicians in Nablus and Jaffa advanced the idea of calling a general strike. Support for the proposal quickly took hold, and in April the six existing Palestinian parties formed a committee to coordinate strike activities. This body had ten members and was known as the Higher Arab Committee, al-Lajnah al-Arabiyya al-Ulya. Al-Hajj Amin was chosen as president, and by assuming the position he abandoned the pretense of political neutrality that was associated with his position as mufti, and which had kept him from participating openly in the Palestine Arab Party. The secretary and treasurer of the Higher Arab Committee were both members of the Istiqlal Party. Among its remaining seven members were the president and vice-president of both the Palestine Arab Party and the National Defense Party and the president of the Youth Congress, the Reform Party, and the National Bloc. In addition to the Higher Committee, there was a largely autonomous network of "national strike committees," which were set up in almost every city and which carried out strike-related activities at the local level. In May, by which time the strike was underway, the Higher Committee organized in Jerusalem a congress of representatives of the national committees. The 150 delegates who attended this meeting resolved unanimously that the strike would continue "until the British Government introduces a basic change in its present policy which will manifest itself in the stoppage of Jewish immigration."[81] The congress also elaborated plans for civil disobedience and a refusal to pay taxes.

Support for the strike came from many quarters. It was endorsed by the Arab mayors of eighteen towns, who assembled in Ramleh at the end of May. Petitions of support were also submitted by hundreds of senior and middle-level civil servants. Although only six municipalities actually shut down, the effects of the strike were nonetheless widely felt. Thousands of workers left their jobs, and numerous businesses were closed. To provide food and other essential goods for strikers, some of the national committees opened special distribution centers. Workers also closed the port in Jaffa, and the Supreme Muslim Council shut its schools. In addition, there was considerable violence during this period. A May Day demonstration in Haifa turned into a riot, for example. The demonstrators then attacked police, who responded by firing into the crowd and killing several persons. By the middle of June, the British reported that they had arrested more than 2,500 persons in connection with various disturbances. The general strike formally ended in October, but the country had by this time entered a period of prolonged disorder. What became widely known as "the Arab Revolt" continued on an intermittent basis until 1939, and the pattern of civil conflict resumed after World War II.

British authorities responded to these developments by creating the Palestine

Royal Commission to investigate the causes of the disorder and, of more immediate significance, by mounting a vigorous campaign to suppress Palestinian resistance. In July 1937, the month in which the Royal Commission submitted its report, an order was issued for the arrest of al-Hajj Amin al-Husayni, although he eluded capture and later, together with Jamal al-Husayni, escaped to Lebanon. In October, the Higher Arab Committee—from which the two National Defense Party members had already resigned—was declared illegal and dissolved, as were the national committees. Other political parties were banned as well, the only exception being the Nashashibis' National Defense Party, which of course left it with no credibility in the eyes of a resentful public. Restrictions were also placed on the Arab press, and many political activists were put in detention camps. Finally, a number of leading politicians were deported, including members of the Higher Committee. As noted, these actions did not bring about the complete and immediate restoration of order. But while guerrilla groups continued to operate, the Palestinians advanced their cause little during 1938, and what remained of the resistance movement collapsed in mid-1939. The Palestinian banner was thereafter carried by al-Hajj Amin and a few others from positions outside the country, where they remained visible but exercised only slight influence on events inside Palestine.

While the failure of the nationalist resistance should not be attributed exclusively to the fragmented and conservative character of Palestinian leadership, these considerations were certainly harmful to the Arab cause. The political leaders of Palestine never successfully transcended their personal rivalries, and the most important factions never presented a coherent blueprint for the development of Palestinian society. The masses of the country were becoming increasingly educated and mobilized during the years of the mandate. There were also a growing number of well-trained and politically sophisticated young professionals. Finally, a national Palestinian consciousness crystallized during this period. But the political class continued to be dominated by representatives of an older order, men who had little ideology other than opposition to Zionism, who were motivated in large part by personal ambition and jealousy, and who continued to operate within the normative and structural framework of traditional clan politics.

The end of the Arab Revolt brought a suspension until after the war of Palestinian efforts at resistance. The Arabs had succeeded in calling attention to their grievances and to the fact that there was widespread opposition to Zionism among the indigenous inhabitants of Palestine, but they had not succeeded in constructing a national movement capable of forcing the Jews or the British to accede to their demands. Moreover, not only had its leadership been decimated, the rank and file of the Palestinian population was completely exhausted by 1939 as a result of the Arab Revolt's impact on the local economy and social order.

In the wake of the collapse of the nationalist resistance, it fell to Egypt and other Arab countries to speak out on behalf of the Palestinian cause. Arab leaders to a degree were successful in pressing Britain for a policy that respected Arab as well as Jewish rights in Palestine. In the late 1930s, Britain was genuinely fearful that its political relations with the Arab world would be impaired by an overtly pro-Zionist policy,[82] and pressure from Egypt and other Arab countries was thus "an important factor in Great Britain's evolving policy for Palestine between 1937 and 1939."[83] Nevertheless, the involvement of other Arab countries did not seriously retard the progress of the Zionist enterprise. Rather, as a leading scholar concludes, "The period 1937–1939 may be considered a watershed in the somber, disaster-strewn history of the Palestinians." The flight of al-Hajj Amin, he writes, symbolizes the change that took place during these years: "Self-appointed and self-seeking as he was, yet his policies, however unwise or undesirable, in their fashion were primarily concerned with the interests of the Palestinians. When the Arab states were invited at the end of 1938 to intervene in the Palestinian problem, Palestinian interests necessarily became a pawn or a weapon in the hands of these states in their pursuit of power and primacy."[84]

Cycles of Violence Prior to World War II

It is necessary to retrace some of this ground when charting the path that Zionists and Palestinian Arabs followed toward a violent collision. Although serious tensions were already evident at the end of the First World War, Palestine for the most part remained free of violence until 1929. Arab and Jewish society evolved side by side, but contact between the two communities was limited. Cordial and even friendly relations were not unknown at the individual level, especially in the early years of the mandate. In the aggregate, however, the attitudes of each national community were increasingly characterized by suspicion and fear.

Musa Alami, a widely respected Palestinian who became the high commissioner's private secretary and later government advocate, describes and laments the growing estrangement of Arabs and Jews in Palestine. The observations reported in his biography offer sad testimony to the steadily diminishing chances for cooperation between the two peoples; and, though Alami of course views the situation from an Arab perspective, his judgments are for the most part highly objective. Upon returning to Palestine after World War I, following several years of study in England, Alami found a change in Arab-Jewish relations. Whereas his family and others had once enjoyed warm relations with Jews, especially the "old school of Arabic-speaking Palestinian Jews," he now found that "the old friendliness and classlessness, the tolerance between races and creeds, had evidently gone for ever."[85] Moreover, though in the 1920s there was a certain amount of Arab-Jewish cooperation in such public bodies as municipal councils and local chambers of commerce, Alami rejected the optimistic view of the

British officials with whom he worked that a *modus vivendi* had been established. The following statement of his observations provides a useful summary of the situation in Palestine on the eve of the disturbances which broke out in 1929.

> But Musa Alami did not share these [British] hopes, for he could perceive, as no British official could, the dangerous fires smoldering beneath the surface. It was clear to him that far from an integrated society evolving in Palestine, the two communities were growing further apart. Their children had no contact, for the Jews were running their own educational system based on Hebrew, whereas the Arabs were dependent on either Quranic or Government schools, both based on Arabic. But it was on the social side that he felt most anxiety. . . . Now, as a direct result of Jewish immigration and land purchases, increasing numbers of [Arab peasants] were becoming landless and even more unemployed. His family had sold no land to Jews, but many Arabs, mostly absentee Syrian and Lebanese landlords, had done so; and much land had also been acquired by Jewish interests from moneylenders who foreclosed on the properties of smallholders unable to redeem their debts. The *Histadrut*, the powerful Jewish Federation of Labor, was now insisting that Jewish enterprises should employ only Jewish labor, and [Jews] were enforcing their edict by organizing the picketing of any who attempted to employ the far cheaper Arab labor.[86]

Zionist and Israeli sources have similarly emphasized the growing social distance between the *Yishuv* and Palestine Arab society during this period, and the fact that the political and economic circumstances of the two communities were increasingly independent of one another.[87] Social contact at the elite level became increasingly rare, and interpersonal relations at nonelite levels, though not completely absent, were not of a character or magnitude to produce any significant measure of understanding between the Jewish and Arab rank and file. The Jewish attitude toward the Arab masses is probably fairly similar to that expressed by Shimon Peres, who wrote of his encounters as a teenager in the late 1930s with the inhabitants of Arab villages surrounding Ben-Shemen Youth Village, where he lived and studied. Violent incidents between Jews and Arabs had by this time become common. The attitude reflected in the writings of the young Peres is not one of hatred, however, but of an unbridgeable social and cultural chasm. The Arab peasant appeared to Peres and his companions as the remnant of an earlier and more simple time, one with which they had nothing in common.

> The director of the village tried to get us acquainted with the Arab villages around Ben-Shemen. We would go out hiking in the Judean Hills almost every Saturday, picking wild anemones and narcissus, and sometimes we would go over to an Arab village and be treated to *pitta* and *hummous* (flat bread and a paste of chick peas). Our attitude toward the Arabs was mixed. They seemed so strange to us, so terrifying, and yet the creatures closest to nature.[88]

The social distance and political separation between Arabs and Jews did not permit the two communities to ignore one another. Far from going their separate ways with mutual indifference and only a minimum of contact, the resentments and tensions which Alami had noted soon burst forth. Communal violence erupted in August 1929, shattering whatever illusions the British and others may have had about peaceful coexistence and initiating an era of direct Arab-Zionist conflict that has yet to come to an end. For several months there had been minor clashes in Jerusalem between Jews and Muslim Arabs in the part of the city that both deemed most holy. Built on the remains of Solomon's ancient Temple were Islamic shrines that were under the control of the Supreme Muslim Council. These included the al-Aqsa Mosque, the third-holiest site in Islam. The Jews knew this area as the Temple Mount, however, and also considered it sacred. Moreover, the western wall of the Temple had been preserved, and Jews claimed the right to pray at this site. Known also as the "Wailing Wall," this remnant of the Second Temple is more holy than any other site to Jews.

In the increasingly tense atmosphere that prevailed in Jerusalem, both sides found ample provocation in the actions of the other. The Supreme Muslim Council under al-Hajj Amin al-Husayni goaded the Jews by suggesting that it might use the stones of the Wailing Wall to construct a highway.[89] Al-Hajj Amin also played on Arab sensitivities by accusing the Jews of a plan to seize the entire Temple Mount area. On the other hand, Muslim fears were fed by the militant tone of the Zionist press and by the actions of the Revisionist wing of the Zionist movement, led by Jabotinsky. On August 16, a group of Revisionists marched to the Wall, whereupon they held "an anti-Arab demonstration, with loud demands for [Jewish] ownership of the wall and the taking of an oath to defend it at all costs."[90] The next day was Friday, the day of Muslim prayers, and it was only with difficulty that police prevented the assembled Muslims from rioting.

Although the conflict between Arabs and Jews was not of a religious nature, these events intensified the antagonism between the two peoples and offered each an opportunity to express its growing frustration and anger. In the days that followed, a young Jew was stabbed by an Arab, the Zionists used the occasion of the boy's funeral to stage a major demonstration, and then, on August 23, an Arab mob armed with clubs and knives moved throughout the city, attacking Jews at random. The rioting lasted for several days and quickly spread to many other cities, with Jews being attacked in Tel Aviv, Haifa, Safad, Hebron, and elsewhere. British security forces, whose numbers had been reduced by Lord Plumer shortly before the end of his tenure as high commissioner, were unable to keep order. The security situation was made worse by the fact that Arabs in the police often refused to act against fellow Palestinians.

The Hagana succeeded in defending Jews in Tel Aviv and Haifa, and in launching a counterattack on one occasion, but 70 defenseless Jewish men, women, and children were killed in Hebron on August 24. Most Jews of Hebron were pious and belonged to the old *Yishuv*, the community being an ancient one centered on a Talmudic college. Eighteen Jews also were killed in Safed a few days later. Many more were wounded, and the Jewish quarter of the town was sacked while its terrified inhabitants took refuge in the police compound. Some of the attacks were particularly brutal, and accounts of these events are grisly and depressing. Sykes, an observer known for his impartiality, states that "the infection of murder spread so rapidly that it is difficult and even impossible to believe that this sudden outbreak of savagery was unplanned."[91] By the time order had finally been restored, 133 Jews had been killed and 339 wounded, almost all by Arabs. Casualties on the Arab side included 116 killed and 232 wounded, most by British security forces.

In the wake of these disturbances, the British established two successive commissions of inquiry. The first, headed by Sir Walter Shaw, was formed in September 1929 and charged with determining the "immediate cause" of the outbreak of violence. The Shaw Commission exceeded its mandate, however; rather than confining its inquiry to the events at the Wailing Wall and the riots to which they led, it commented on the underlying factors contributing to tension in Palestine. Among its major conclusions, most of which were disputed by the Zionists, were that the Arab attacks on Jews had been "unpremeditated" and that the fundamental cause of these attacks was "the Arab feelings of animosity and hostility to the Jews consequent upon the disappointment of their political and national aspirations and fear for their economic future." The Shaw Commission further concluded that Arab feelings were the result of a "landless and discontented" class being created by the expansion of the *Yishuv*, and it accordingly recommended that limitations be placed on Jewish immigration and land purchases.

The second commission, under the direction of Sir John Hope-Simpson, was charged with formulating proposals to deal with the problems that the Shaw Commission had identified. It submitted its report in the summer of 1930. Placing emphasis on the dislocation of the Arab peasantry that had been caused by the construction of the Jewish national home, the Hope-Simpson Commission reported that there was "no margin of land available for agricultural settlement by new immigrants." While it qualified this conclusion to a degree by adding that it applied under "existing methods of Arab cultivation," it took pains as well to deny that such methods might offer a justification for removing the Arab peasant from his land. "The *fellah* [Arab farmer]," the report stated, "is neither lazy nor unintelligent. He is a capable and competent agriculturalist, and there is no doubt that, were he to be given the chance of learning better methods and the capital which is a necessary preliminary to their employment, he would rapidly improve his position."[92] Finally, Hope-Simpson condemned Zionist practices in the field of employment, stating, "It is wrong that a Jew from Poland, Lithuania or the Yemen should be admitted [to the country] to fill an existing vacancy, while in Palestine there are already workmen capable of filling that vacancy."[93]

The recommendations of the Shaw and Hope-Simpson commissions were for a reduction in Jewish immigration to Palestine and for tighter control of land purchases by Jews. The Zionists rejected these conclusions, however, placing emphasis not on the underlying tensions between Arabs and Jews but rather on the role of al-Hajj Amin and other Arab leaders in provoking the disturbances. A pro-Zionist position was taken by one member of the Shaw Commission, Harry Snell, who expressed his disagreement with the opinion of the majority in the following terms:

> What is required in Palestine is, I believe, less a change of policy in these matters than a change of mind on the part of the Arab population, who have been encouraged to believe that they have suffered a great wrong and that the immigrant Jew constitutes a permanent menace to their livelihood and future. I am convinced that these fears are exaggerated and that on any long view of the situation the Arab people stand to gain rather than to lose from the Jewish enterprise.[94]

The Hope-Simpson Commission's recommendations concerning Jewish immigration, land purchases, and employment were incorporated into a British government White Paper, which the colonial secretary, Lord Passfield, issued in October. Hope-Simpson had proposed a British development scheme to increase the amount of cultivable land, but in the meantime it was proposed that there be a moratorium on Jewish land purchases. The Jews already had, it was argued, "a large reserve of land not yet settled or developed." Also, though Jewish immigration was to be permitted to continue, it was urged that there be established a mechanism to protect Arab farmers "against ejection or the imposition of excessive rental." Finally, the White Paper stressed the equality of Britain's obligations to Arabs and Jews in Palestine, affirming that it took seriously the clause in the Balfour Declaration stating that the construction of the Jewish national home must not prejudice the rights of the non-Jewish communities of Palestine. This latter affirmation particularly disturbed the Jews, who claimed that under the Balfour Declaration Britain's obligations to Zionism took precedence over its obligations to the Arabs of Palestine.

Weizmann and other Zionists pressed the government to repudiate the White Paper, and in this they were aided by influential pro-Zionist British officials. To dramatize his opposition, Weizmann announced his resignation as head of the Zionist Organization and the Jewish Agency. In November, the White Paper was debated in Parliament, and it soon became evident that it had many opponents. Under this combination of political pressures, the British prime minister, Ramsay MacDonald, sent a lengthy letter to Weizmann in which he provided an interpretation of government policy that had the effect of repudiating the Passfield White Paper, as well as the Shaw Commission and Hope-Simpson Commission recommendations on which it was based. The letter, which was read in Parliament in February 1931, stated, *inter alia*, that "His Majesty's Government did not prescribe and do not contemplate any stoppage or prohibition of Jewish immigration in any of its categories," and also that "the statement of policy of His Majesty's Government did not imply a prohibition of acquisition of additional land by Jews . . . nor is any such intended."[95]

The MacDonald letter deeply disappointed the Arabs of Palestine, to whom the White Paper and the commissions of inquiry had temporarily given a measure of hope. Many called it the "Black Letter." It was hailed as a great victory by the Zionists, however. Weizmann later wrote that the British government's change of attitude "enabled us to make the magnificent gains of the ensuing years. . . . It was under MacDonald's letter that Jewish immigration into Palestine was permitted to reach figures like forty thousand for 1934 and sixty-two thousand for 1935."[96] Thus, the disturbances of 1929, and whatever insights they may have produced about the causes of Arab-Jewish tension in Palestine, did not lead the British to modify their policies.

This pattern was similar to that which would be observed throughout the remaining years of the mandate, when new disturbances would at first portend a shift in Britain's attitude but would ultimately leave the situation unchanged. This rhythm is described by Sykes, who writes that the British continued to believe a solution could be found if only a clear statement of the problem might be obtained. In fact, he continues, this belief was never applicable in Palestine. "A royal commission goes out to the troubled land; its recommendations lead to the sending of a subsidiary commission to make definitive proposals on how to put the recommendations into effect; the proposals conflict with too much of settled opinion and involve too much political risk to be acted upon; both commissions prove to have been a waste of talent and time."[97] This pattern, already quite visible in 1929–1931, left Palestine more tense than ever. The country continued to drift toward civil war.

The six-year period from 1933 until the outbreak of World War II was characterized by steadily mounting unrest and disorder in Palestine. These years, and particularly the period from 1936 to 1939, are usually described as the era of the Arab Revolt, or Arab Rebellion. In March 1933, the Arab Executive Committee issued a manifesto denouncing the British for collaboration with Zionism and calling upon Palestinians to refuse all cooperation with the mandatory administration. The manifesto also urged a general boycott of both Jewish and British goods and institutions. The Arab press intensified its criticism of the government at this time as well. The goal of al-Hajj Amin and other Arab leaders was to mobilize Palestinian opinion against the British, in the apparent belief that Zionism could best be opposed by pressing the British to reduce their support of the Jewish cause.

A fresh outbreak of violence occurred several months later, in October 1933, when the Arab Executive called for an antigovernment demonstration in Jerusalem. Authorities denied permission for the rally, but it took place nonetheless, whereupon police used force to disperse the assembled Arabs. No one was killed but there were several serious injuries. There soon followed clashes between Arabs and police in Jaffa and several other Arab communities, including Haifa and Nablus. Twenty-seven Arabs were killed in these confrontations and more than 200 were wounded. Among the latter was Musa Kazim al-Husayni, who was then in his eighties and who died several months later as a result of his injuries. Jews were not involved in any of the disturbances, which the Arab Executive had organized in the hope of putting pressure on the British. In fact, Jewish and Arab leaders held several meetings in the spring and summer of 1934 in a futile effort to narrow the differences between them.[98]

After a year and a half of comparative calm, the Arab Revolt amplified dramatically in the spring of 1936. The Arabs were ever more fearful and angry, especially in the wake of the large-scale Jewish immigration that had taken place in 1934 and 1935, and in April there were riots which soon developed into a general uprising. Following the first disturbances, which broke out in Jaffa on April 19, the *Palestine Post*, an English-language Zionist daily, carried headlines reporting: "9 Jewish Dead, Scores Hurt in Arab Attacks" and "Pedestrians and Motorists Knifed and Stoned in Jaffa Streets." Arabs were killed and wounded, too. A number of rioters were shot by the police. In addition, following the funeral in Tel Aviv of two slain Jews, two Arabs were murdered by Zionist extremists. As noted earlier, the Arabs also called a general strike in April, which lasted until October and was finally ended in response to appeals from neighboring Arab states, who were themselves responding to diplomatic pressure from the British.

There was continuing violence during the period of the strike, and many atrocities were committed. In one case, for example, defenseless patients and nurses in a Jewish clinic were slaughtered. Children were also murdered in some instances. Overall, 80 Jews were killed during this period and approximately 300 were wounded. Extensive property damage occurred as well. The Arabs, for their part, suffered heavily, too, with 197 killed and nearly 1,000 wounded, the majority at the hands of British security forces. Finally, 28 British citizens lost their life during the same six-month period.

This pattern of disorder and violence did not end with the strike in October but continued on an intermittent basis into 1939. Armed Arab bands operated in the rural areas, and there were attacks on British police and security forces, as well as on Jewish settlements. Indeed, in the latter part of this period, some of the most intense clashes were between the Palestinians and the British. The general situation in the summer of 1938 is summarized by Yehoshua Porath, who describes a continuing cycle of violence. In some cases, Arab bands broke through the defenses of Jewish settlements and killed the residents of the houses they captured. Jewish workers in the fields or passengers on the roads were the most frequent targets. Some were murdered or kidnapped and then murdered. In turn, as Porath notes, "these outrageous attacks triggered off Jewish reprisals committed by the Irgun which were no less murderous. Bombs were planted in the Arab market-places of Jerusalem and Haifa and passengers on the roads were indiscriminately attacked. These Irgun reprisals further incited the Arab bands to attack Jews and drove more moderate elements to their fold, a fact from which the leaders of the Arab terror derived much satisfaction."[99]

The Arab Revolt was broad in scope and effective in disrupting the life of the country. Police stations in many parts of the country were seized by the rebels, providing a steady flow of arms and ammunition. Train service was severely disrupted, armed bands took control of many roads, and interurban telephone lines were destroyed in some areas. Most banks and post offices had also closed by the summer of 1938. Further, Arab civil servants often cooperated with the rebels, sometimes under coercion, and this permitted many official documents to fall into the hands of the revolt's leaders. By the end of August 1938, in the judgment of the general officer commanding British troops, "the situation was such that civil administration and control of the country was, to all practical purposes, non-existent."[100]

Though tainted by the atrocities associated with it, the Arab Revolt was a genuine popular uprising, devoted to the expression of authentic and deeply felt political aspirations. Its strength and leadership were in the rural areas, where it was fed by the frustration and anger of the Palestinian peasantry. In the words of one British observer, "although instigated, to some extent guided and certainly used by the political leaders of Arab Palestine, the Arab Rebellion was in fact a peasant revolt, drawing its enthusiasm, its heroism, its organization and its persistence from sources within itself."[101] This conclusion is confirmed by Porath, a careful Israeli scholar who has done a detailed empirical analysis of those who held office in the rebel movement. Porath's research group determined that only 22 percent of the 282 individuals about whom information is available were of urban origin. Moreover, he reports that not only was the urban population underrepresented in the leadership of the revolt, but its proportion among all rebels was even smaller. Porath also notes the underrepresentation of Christians in the ranks of the revolt and reports that among Muslim villagers it was persons "of the lower strata" who were most numerous. Conversely, contrary to what some Zionists argued at the time, Porath states explicitly that his group's findings do not corroborate the impression of those who believe the revolt was carried out by criminals or people with a criminal record. Finally, he reports that the rebellion was strongest in locations adjacent to the main areas of Jewish settlement, most notably the central coastal plain, the Haifa–Acre Bay region, and the Jezreel Valley. For the Arab population of these regions, "the Jewish National Home was a concrete reality."[102]

Although its main enemies were Zionism and the British, the revolt also challenged urban Arab notables and the monied interests of Arab Palestine. Leaders of the rebellion demanded contributions to the cause from wealthy urban families, and in this they appear to have been motivated, in part, by class antagonisms. Rebel forces took control in a number of important towns during the summer and fall of 1938, most notably in Jaffa but to a degree also in Nablus and the Arab sections of Haifa and Jerusalem. In these cities, the rebels identified themselves with the struggle of the urban poor against the propertied classes and took action on behalf of the former against the latter.[103] Such action included imposition of a moratorium on debt repayment and the reduction or cancellation of apartment rents. Under such conditions, some notable families fled when the rebels began to operate in their towns. The rich families of Haifa departed *en masse* in August 1938, and the property of departing families was sometimes seized and sold. The British high commissioner at this time was Sir Harold MacMichael, who summarized these aspects of the Arab Revolt by reporting that "something like a social revolution on a small scale is beginning. The influence of the landlord-politician is on the wane. He has done nothing but talk (and pay): others have taken the risks, and these others are disposed to take a line of their own."[104]

The disturbances of 1936 spawned another British commission of inquiry. Under the direction of William Robert Wellesley, Lord Peel, the six-member Palestine Royal Commission, also known as the Peel Commission, began its work in November and eventually held sixty-six meetings, half of them secret. Although it sought to collect information from all parties, the Palestinians boycotted the Peel Commission for several months. Only toward the end of its information-gathering activities were they persuaded by Arab leaders outside Palestine to meet with the commissioners. The Zionists, by contrast, made themselves readily available, and Weizmann himself gave extensive testimony. Jabotinsky, too, submitted "evidence" to the commission. Rejecting the assertion that the Jewish presence had been injurious to the Arabs, the Revisionist leader stated that "the economic position of the Palestinian Arabs, under the Jewish colonization and owing to the Jewish colonization, has become the object of envy in all the surrounding Arab countries, so that the Arabs from those countries show a clear tendency to immigrate to Palestine."[105]

The Peel Commission report, published in July 1937, was comprehensive and balanced. It also recorded the commission's judgment that many Palestinian grievances were genuine. Among its major findings were the conclusion that the disturbances of 1936 had been caused by "the desire of the Arabs for national independence" and by "their hatred and fear of the establishment of the Jewish National Home." The report added, moreover, that these were "the same underlying causes as those which brought about the 'disturbances' of 1920, 1921, 1929 and 1933," and also that they were the *only* underlying causes, all other factors being "complimentary or subsidiary."[106]

The Peel Commission made clear the implications of these findings and offered a bold proposal for the future of Palestine. "An irrepressible conflict has arisen between two national communities within the bounds of one small country," the commission report stated. "About 1,000,000 Arabs are in strife, open or latent, with some 400,000 Jews. There is no common ground between them." Moreover, the commission stated forthrightly, the British mandate had not only failed to achieve a reconciliation of Arab and Jewish aspirations, it had kept alive and even reinforced the antagonism between the two peoples. Therefore, in the judgment of the commissioners, the mandate should be terminated and, in order that each national community might govern itself, the territory of Palestine should be partitioned. More specifically, the Peel Commission proposed creation of a small Jewish state. The territory suggested for this state included the coastal plain, though not the port cities of Jaffa, Haifa, and Acre, and most of the Galilee, as shown in Map 4.1. The remaining territory, with the exception of a corridor from Jaffa to Jerusalem, which was to remain under British control, would be given over to the Palestinians. The commission also envisioned an exchange of populations in connection with partition, which for the most part would involve the resettlement of Arabs living within territory proposed for the Jewish state. In addition, the commission proposed that the territory allocated to the Palestinians be united with Transjordan, to create a single state.

Partition was a logical response to the deepening conflict, and since 1937 it has frequently been proposed by those charged with finding a solution to the dilemma of Palestine. The Peel Commission's report was rejected by the protagonists, however. Although awarded almost all of the most fertile land in Palestine, the Zionists judged that their state would possess an inadequate amount of territory. They also refused to accept the loss of Palestine's most important cities. Thus the Twentieth Zionist Congress, held in Zurich in August 1937, passed a resolution declaring that "the scheme of partition put forward by the Royal Commission is unacceptable."[107] On the other hand, the congress did not reject the principle of partition, and in fact welcomed the Peel Commission's recognition that creation of a Jewish state was desirable. Wisely choosing to regard this critical aspect of the commission's recommendations as an important opportunity, it empowered the Zionist Executive "to enter into negotiations with a view to ascertaining the precise terms of His Majesty's Government for the proposed establishment of a Jewish State."[108]

In formulating their response to the Peel Commission's partition proposal, some Zionists also discussed the possibility of transferring Arabs from that part of Palestine in which the proposed Jewish state was to be established. Ben Gurion wrote in his diary in July 1937, for example, "We should not assume that it [the Peel Commission's proposals concerning Arab resettlement] is definitely impossible. If it were put into effect, it would be of tremendous advantage to us. . . . For every transferred Arab, one could settle four Jews on the land."[109] Some also expressed interest in this kind of population transfer even before the Peel Commission rendered its report. In May 1936, for example, as the Jewish Agency

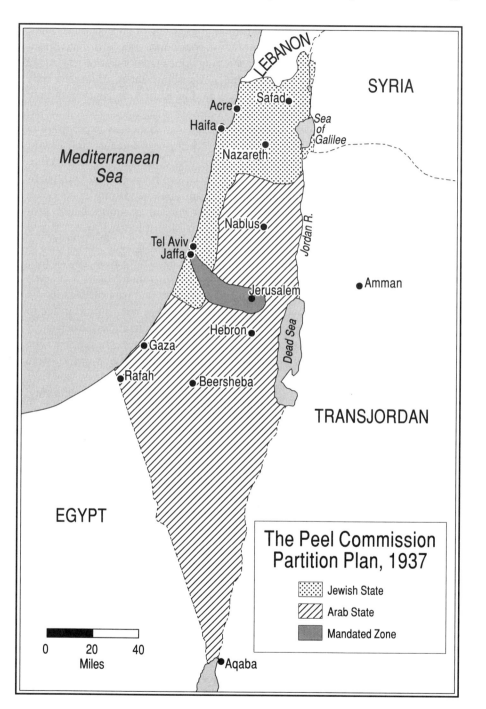

The Peel Commission Partition Plan, 1937

Executive prepared to present the Zionist case before the British commissioners, Menachem Ussishkin, head of the Jewish National Fund, proposed that consideration be given to the possibility of transferring Arabs from Palestine to Iraq. "I would certainly like the Arabs to go to Iraq," Ussishkin stated, adding, "I hope they will go there some time since . . . they would be in an Arab country and not a Jewish country."[110]

Zionist historians, as well as many others, insist that these expressions of support for a policy of transfer were not indicative of mainstream Zionist thought and must be seen in the context of the Peel Commission's own recommendations concerning the exchange of populations to be associated with partition. Teveth, for instance, states that Ben Gurion considered transfer to be an "immoral solution" and reports that the Peel Commission recommendations produced "a month of soul-searching," during which Zionist councils were marked by a debate between "the advantageous and the just, reality and illusion."[111] It is in this context, he notes, that some asserted the Peel Commission "is not proposing the dis-possession of Arabs, it is proposing to transfer them and settle them in the [independent] Arab state" to be created in one part of Palestine.[112] Teveth characterizes statements such as that of Ussishkin regarding transfer to Iraq as "wishful thinking" expressed "in the course of deliberations." Such statements bore no relationship to any actual or planned Zionist programs at the time and were in fact challenged by other Zionist leaders almost as soon as they were made.[113]

In contrast to the careful and politically calculated response of the Zionists, the Arab Higher Committee rejected the Peel Commission's proposals concerning territorial partition and an exchange of populations totally and unequivocally. It is probable that these proposals were advanced in the belief that they would receive a favorable response from neighboring Arab states, who in turn were expected to urge their acceptance on the reluctant Palestinians.[114] Any such possibility quickly disappeared, however, in the face of the Palestinians' firm opposition. Al-Hajj Amin and other Palestinian spokesmen proclaimed that Britain had neither the authority nor the right to partition *their* territory and, as noted, the Arab Revolt continued.

Britain explored the possibility of partition for another year but thereafter abandoned the idea in the face of continuing opposition from both protagonists. It sent the Woodhead Commission to Palestine in 1938 and charged it with making recommendations concerning the boundaries of the proposed Jewish and Arab states. None of the plans considered by the commission produced agreement, however. Early in 1939 Britain convened a round table conference in London in one last attempt to find common ground between the Jews and Arabs. This, too, produced no tangible results. Arab delegates refused to sit with those of the Zionist Organization, and the British were required to put them in separate rooms and carry messages back and forth.[115]

Since agreement could not be reached among the parties themselves, the government in London at this point determined that its responsibilities required the imposition of a settlement; and, with the partition scheme now a dead letter, the direction of British policy changed. His Majesty's government was acting in response to the mounting pressure upon Great Britain itself, of course. Twenty thousand British troops were bogged down in Palestine, attempting with only limited effectiveness to suppress the Arab rebellion. Even more, it was painfully evident that the outbreak of the Second World War was near. Attempts to appease the Germans had only encouraged Hitler, who in March sent his forces into Czechoslovakia. Under these conditions, Britain had a strong interest in placating the Arabs of Palestine and in satisfying the leaders of neighboring Arab states, whose assistance would be needed in the coming war.

New British proposals for Palestine were set forth in a White Paper issued by the colonial secretary, Malcolm MacDonald, in May 1939. The MacDonald White Paper observed that the Peel Commission's recommendations concerning partition had been found to be impractical, and that the objective of His Majesty's government was therefore "the establishment within ten years of an independent Palestine State in such treaty relations with the United Kingdom as will provide satisfactorily for the commercial and strategic requirements of both countries in the future." The polity envisioned by the White Paper was a binational state, "in which the two peoples of Palestine, Arabs and Jews, share authority in government in such a way that the essential interests of each are secured." The document stated further that Britain would take steps to implement its new policy "as soon as peace and order have been sufficiently restored in Palestine." Finally, in addition to repudiating the doctrine of partition, and with it Britain's acceptance of an independent Jewish state, the MacDonald White Paper proposed new restrictions on Zionist immigration and on land purchases by Jews. Jewish immigration was to be limited to 75,000 during the next five years—10,000 per year plus 25,000 refugees. After the five-year period, moreover, no further Jewish immigration was to be permitted "unless the Arabs of Palestine are prepared to acquiesce in it." With respect to land purchases, the White Paper stated that in some areas "transfers of land must be restricted if Arab cultivators are to maintain their existing standard of life and a considerable landless Arab population is not to be created." Accordingly, the high commissioner was empowered to "prohibit and regulate" any transfer of land that might be injurious to Palestine's Arab population.[116]

The White Paper was not very satisfactory to the Arabs. The main political factions inside Palestine rejected its authorization of continued Jewish immigration. Most also rejected the principle that Arabs and Jews should share in the government of Palestine, even in the context of a binational state. Nor were there endorsements of the White Paper from Arab leaders outside Palestine. The most angry denunciations came from the Zionists, however, whose reaction paralleled that of the Arabs to Ramsay MacDonald's letter of 1931. Weizmann is reported to have become physically ill when the colonial secretary informed him of the new policy. The Jewish Agency issued a statement accusing Britain of seeking to create "a territorial ghetto for Jews in their own homeland," then called the White Paper "a breach of faith and a surrender to Arab terrorism."[117] Thus, like earlier efforts, Britain's new policy initiative failed to define a course acceptable to both Jews and Arabs. The British were reaping the bitter harvest of their self-interested entry into Palestine; and indeed, by 1939, it is doubtful that any policy satisfactory to both Arabs and Jews could have been devised.

Jewish anger and frustration were greatly intensified by the dire situation in which European Jewry found itself at this time. The Jewish Agency statement declared, "It is in the darkest hour of Jewish history that the British Government proposes to deprive the Jews of their last hope and to close the road back to their Homeland."[118] Even some defenders of British policy, among them Sykes, suggest that the "morality of the White Paper cannot be judged without reference to the position of Jews in the world as a whole." Sykes adds that, whatever may have been the short-term justification, "nothing can disguise the fact that there was odious moral cruelty in inflicting so heavy a disappointment on millions of people to whom Palestine was the only hope left on this earth; [Britain's] policy limited yet further what little opportunity existed for Jewish escape from Nazi tyranny." Finally, he concludes, the White Paper can be defended "only as a necessary but ruthless war-measure, and experience and history show that all such measures have to be paid for dearly."[119] Nevertheless, British policy continued to be guided by the White Paper for the duration of the war.

The War Years

The period of World War II, which Britain formally entered in September 1939, saw no relaxation of the tensions in Palestine. Nor did the efforts of Great Britain to implement the policies set forth in the MacDonald White Paper produce any significant change in the conflict between Arabs and Jews. Land transfer regulations introduced in February 1940 divided the country into three zones and permitted the Jews to buy land without restriction in only one of them, that being the coastal plain between Zikhron Ya'akov and Rehovot.[120] The Zionists complained bitterly. They also continued to find Arabs willing to sell land, however, and from 1940 to 1946 the Keren Kayemet in fact nearly doubled the overall extent of its holdings. Moreover, the vast majority of the newly acquired land was in the two zones where Jewish land purchases were either restricted or prohibited.[121] The resultant pattern of landownership in Palestine in 1947, on the eve of Israel's independence, is shown in Map 4.2.

In the area of immigration, Britain not only limited the number of certificates provided to the Zionists, it also intensified efforts to intercept Jews entering Palestine illegally. The Jews, for their part, motivated both by a desire to establish their national home and by the deepening tragedy in Europe, vowed to

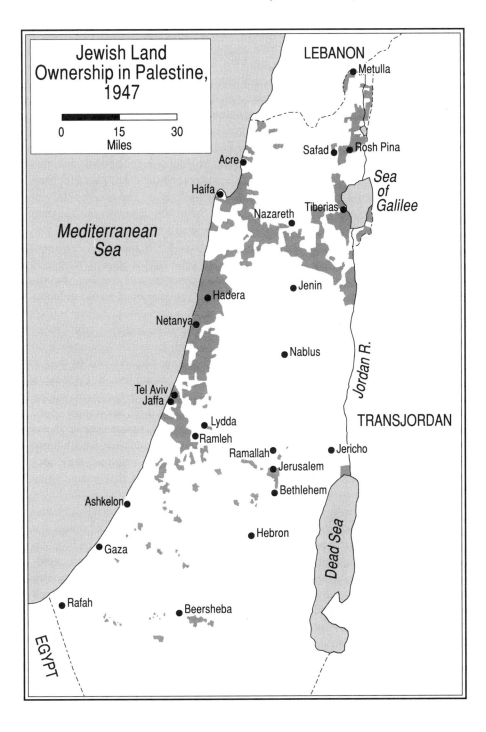

Jewish Land Ownership in Palestine, 1947

0   15   30
Miles

LEBANON

Metulla

Safad   Rosh Pina

Acre

Haifa

Sea of Galilee

Nazareth   Tiberias

Mediterranean Sea

Jenin

Hadera

Netanya

Nablus

Jordan R.

Tel Aviv
Jaffa

TRANSJORDAN

Lydda

Ramleh

Ramallah   Jericho

Jerusalem

Bethlehem

Ashkelon

Hebron

Dead Sea

Gaza

Rafah   Beersheba

EGYPT

fight the White Paper "as if there were no war." Under these circumstances, there were a number of deplorable incidents as Jewish refugees from Nazi barbarism struggled to make their way to Palestine.

One of the most dramatic and unfortunate of these incidents occurred in November 1940, when Britain intercepted two broken-down ships carrying 1,700 Jewish refugees without valid immigration certificates. The ships were brought to Haifa harbor and a third ship soon joined them. The refugees were not permitted to land, however. Instead, a French liner, the *Patria*, was commandeered to take all of the would-be immigrants to Mauritius. The high commissioner justified these actions with a cold declaration to the effect that His Majesty's government "are bound to see to it that the laws of the country are not openly flouted . . . [and] can only regard a revival of illegal Jewish immigration at the present juncture as likely to affect the local situation most adversely, and to prove a serious menace to British interests in the Middle East." [122] To prevent the *Patria* from leaving, the Hagana planned to blow up the ship's engines. Its agents miscalculated the strength of the charge, however, and the ship was destroyed, killing 240 refugees and 10 policemen. The surviving Jewish refugees were thereafter permitted to remain in Palestine. [123]

Seeking to escape responsibility for the tragic miscalculation, the Jewish Agency declared that the sinking of the ship had been an act of mass suicide on the part of the refugees on board, designed to protest Britain's odious policy. Though this account at the time was widely accepted among Jews in Palestine, a later investigation established that in fact the act was almost certainly carried out by a small team of operatives working from shore, without the knowledge of the refugees on the ship. In the larger sense, however, the unfortunate episode shows that the Jews, like the Arabs, were on a collision course with the British from which there was little chance of escape. Like the Arabs of Palestine, they, too, felt a need to take desperate measures in the defense of what they judged to be a matter of national survival.

Regrettably, the story of the *Patria* is not the only instance of refugees destined for Palestine being lost at sea, or even of a disaster taking place because the British would not permit unauthorized immigrants to enter Palestine and the Zionists would not accept an alternative destination. In February 1941, an explosion sank the *Struma*, an aging cattle boat crowded with Jewish refugees which had been anchored off the Turkish coast for more than two months while British and Zionist officials argued over the fate of its wretched cargo. Accounts differ with respect to the cause of the blast but, in any event, the ship quickly sank in the Black Sea and all but one of the 769 refugees on board were killed. [124] Overall, it is not known how many Jewish refugees from Hitler perished trying to make their way to Palestine. It is known only that the vessels carrying them were usually decrepit and unreliable and almost always overcrowded.

Although Jewish immigration to Palestine continued, even after the Nazis closed the door to Jews trying to flee the countries under their control, the number of new arrivals declined sharply after 1939. There was not only a ceiling on the total number of immigration certificates the British would provide, there were also limits to the number that could be obtained for Jews in certain categories or from certain countries, particularly those in the Balkans. Reflecting the arrogance and bigotry in the latter aspect of British policy is the allegation, reported by a leading scholar, that the high commissioner told Zionist authorities in 1940 that it might be wiser for them "to save up [immigration] permits for postwar use, when they might be allocated to Jews of a 'better type' than those from the Balkans."[125] In any event, whereas an average of 2,371 Jews were entering Palestine each month during the first part of 1939, the figure—based on both legal and illegal immigration—dropped to approximately 700 in 1940, 500 in 1941, and 300 in 1942. The numbers were higher in the next two years, but total immigration between 1939 and 1944 was still less than the 75,000 authorized by the White Paper. Moreover, roughly half of the new immigrants were "illegals," Jews who did not possess the proper entry papers and were smuggled into the country. On the other hand, Jews continued to enter Palestine (legally as well as illegally) after 1944, the date by which the White Paper had projected an end to Jewish immigration. In 1945, at the conclusion of the war, the population of the *Yishuv* was 554,000.

Although they had vowed to fight against the White Paper as if there were no war, the Zionist agencies in fact strongly discouraged any activity that might weaken Britain's war effort. In September 1939, upon Britain's declaration of war against Germany, the Jewish Agency Executive in Jerusalem made its position clear in a forceful statement of policy, affirming that opposition to the White Paper was not directed against Great Britain or the British Empire. The statement proclaimed that the Jewish community had three objectives: "the protection of the Jewish Homeland, the welfare of the Jewish people, the victory of the British Empire." In the latter connection, it continued, "the war which has now been forced upon Great Britain by Nazi Germany is our war, and all the assistance that we shall be able and permitted to give to the British army and to the British people we shall render wholeheartedly."[126] At the time, the sentiments reflected in this statement appear to have been those of most members of the *Yishuv*. Even the principal Jewish underground organization, the Irgun, for several years moderated its attacks against the British. Moreover, although Zionist policy may to a degree have been motivated by a hope that it would persuade Great Britain to abandon the hated White Paper, it was dictated above all by a commitment to destruction of the Nazi regime and to the rendering of assistance to those who were fighting the Germans.[127]

The Jews also sought to make a direct military contribution, both by volunteering for service in the British army and by urging creation of a Jewish military force which would fight under its own colors. During the course of the war, 136,000 Palestinian Jews volunteered for service with the British. By 1942 there were about 19,000 of these Jews, including some 2,000 women, fighting in His

Majesty's armed forces. The vast majority were in the army, and about 25 percent were in combat units. By the end of the war the number had risen to over 26,000, among them more than 4,000 women. Moreover, these Jews rendered valuable service in many instances. In 1942, for example, the British deployed a force of 1,500 specially trained Jewish guerrillas to fight the Axis forces in the Libyan desert. Officially known as the Jewish Rural Special Police, the group called itself the Palmach and later developed into the elite commando unit of the Hagana.

Efforts to establish a Jewish fighting force were more problematic. In September 1940, Weizmann had been informed that the British were prepared to organize such a force, which initially would contain 10,000 men (a division), of whom 4,000 were to be recruited in Palestine. This Jewish army was to have its own flag and to be led by Jewish junior officers, although it would fight within the structure of the British military and be under the general command of senior British officers. Implementation of the plan was repeatedly delayed by Britain, however, which claimed to have inadequate equipment and resources for the force but which in reality was heavily influenced by the political implications of the project. Nor were the Zionists unaware that an experienced and well-armed fighting force would be an invaluable asset in the struggle for Palestine that would take place after the war. In any event, it was only in 1944 that a special Jewish force, limited in size to a brigade, was finally established.[128]

A resumption of Jewish terrorist activity about this time, as well as the frustration of Zionist efforts to establish a Jewish army, contributed to a renewed deterioration in relations with the British after 1942. Under the direction of Menachem Begin, who had entered Palestine in 1942, the Irgun terminated its moratorium on operations against the British. The most notorious action of this period was carried out two years later by Lehi, a smaller and even more fanatical organization that was also known as the Stern Group.[129] In November 1944, two Sternists murdered Lord Moyne in Cairo. Moyne had served as British colonial secretary between 1941 and 1943, and in 1944 he had come to Egypt as British minister of state. Many Zionists held him responsible for upholding the provisions of the 1939 White Paper. Understandably, this and other terrorist actions greatly strained relations between the British and the Zionists. The murder of Lord Moyne had a particularly strong personal impact on Churchill and Amery, the two most important supporters of Zionism in the British cabinet.[130]

The press of events sharpened the resolve of the Zionists to create an independent state. Although it had once been possible for Zionists to debate the definition of the Jewish national home they sought to construct, there was now growing agreement that this could mean nothing other than a fully sovereign Jewish state. This position, which some Zionists had taken from the beginning, was dictated in part by a deepening loss of faith in the British, who continued to enforce the 1939 White Paper's immigration quotas and to resist calls for a Jewish army. It was also dictated by increasing alienation from the Western community of nations more generally. Nazi terror, coupled with complicity or indifference on the part of many other countries, convinced most Zionists that the Jews could count only on themselves.

These sentiments were expressed at an Extraordinary Zionist Conference, convened by American Zionists and held at the Biltmore Hotel in New York in May 1942. The conference was attended by about 600 American Jews and 67 Zionists from abroad, including Weizmann and Ben Gurion. The Biltmore conference is notable, in part, for the clash that it witnessed between Weizmann and Ben Gurion, a clash of generations within the Zionist leadership. Ben Gurion, the militant leader of the *Yishuv*, successfully challenged the gradualist approach of the aging Weizmann.

The 1942 conference in New York is best remembered for the "Biltmore Program," in which Zionist policy was reformulated and the objective of creating a Jewish state over the whole of Palestine was declared. With reports of Nazi atrocities beginning to reach the outside world, delegates were told that as much as a quarter of European Jewry might be lost in the war. The tragic truth, known only later, was that only 40 percent would survive the Holocaust. Thus, the conference placed emphasis not on Zionism's vision of a progressive national community devoted to Jewish laws and values, but rather on the desperate plight of the Jews in Europe and on the urgent need for a country of refuge. "This Conference," they declared, "offers a message of hope and encouragement to their fellow Jews in the ghettos and concentration camps of Hitler-dominated Europe and prays that their hour of liberation may not be far distant." The content of this message:

> The Conference urges that the gates of Palestine be opened; that the Jewish Agency be vested with control of immigration into Palestine and with the necessary authority for upbuilding the country, including the development of its unoccupied and uncultivated lands; and that Palestine be established as a Jewish Commonwealth integrated into the structure of the new democratic world.
>
> Then and only then will the age-old wrong to the Jewish people be righted.[131]

Within a few months, the magnitude of the terrible tragedy being experienced by the Jews of Europe began to come to light, even though the still-greater horrors that lay ahead in the Nazi gas chambers and ovens continued to defy imagination. Late in 1942 came the following dark statement by the Allied Powers:

> From all the occupied countries Jews are being transported, in conditions of appalling horror and brutality, to Eastern Europe. . . . None of those taken away are ever heard of again. The able-bodied are slowly worked to death in labor camps. The infirm are left to die of exposure and starvation or are deliberately massacred in mass executions. The number of victims of these bloody cruelties is reckoned in many hundreds of thousands of entirely innocent men, women and children.[132]

In the years that followed, there were only a small minority of Zionists who did not subscribe to the Biltmore program. Nevertheless, a few men and women did revive the ideal of binationalism, the most prominent among them being individuals who had long persisted in the hope that Jews and Arabs might cooperate in the development of Palestine. One such individual was Chaim Kalvarisky, who helped to found the League for Arab-Jewish Rapprochement and Cooperation in the summer of 1942. Kalvarisky, an early member of Brit Shalom, was now seventy-five. His league was founded in association with Hashomer Hatzair and had a socialist workers orientation. Also formed at this time was the Ihud, or Union, which was led by Judah Magnes and Henrietta Szold, president of the Hebrew University and founder of the Zionist Women's Organization of America respectively. None of these movements had much impact, however, even though the Ihud for a brief time was a source of some concern to mainstream Zionist leaders, who denounced Magnes as a Jew who had betrayed his people. The binational movement never won support among the Jewish rank and file. Nor, as with Brit Shalom, did it succeed in stimulating any significant response from the Arabs.

Far from moving toward an accommodation with the Arabs of Palestine, Zionist attitudes hardened in the wake of the Biltmore Conference and the events to which it was a response, with leadership of the Zionist movement gradually passing from Weizmann, the aging advocate of patient diplomacy, to a new generation of more militant Jewish leaders. Weizmann continued to urge a dialogue with Britain, and in this he was encouraged greatly by the belief that British support for the principle of partition could be revived. In the fall of 1943, he was informed by Winston Churchill that a cabinet committee on Palestine was prepared to recommend that Palestine be partitioned and that the Jewish people be granted full sovereignty over one sector. Weizmann also reported that Churchill was receptive to the idea of granting the Jewish state more territory than had the Peel Commission, including much of the Negev Desert. The mainstream of the Zionist movement was now opposed to partition, however, and Weizmann, despite the esteem and affection in which he continued to be held, could not obtain support for his negotiations with the British. Led by Ben Gurion and Moshe Sharett, the Jewish Agency in 1944 sent a memorandum to the British government declaring that it was opposed to establishing a Jewish state over only part of Palestine. Toward the end of the year the governing body of the *Yishuv*, the Va'ad Leumi, by a wide margin also passed a resolution reaffirming the Biltmore Program and rejecting the idea of partition.

A footnote to Weizmann's inability to contain Zionist militancy and to steer the movement on a more moderate course is that the British Labour Party at this time adopted a remarkable resolution that exceeded what even Ben Gurion was prepared to advocate. After stating that the Jewish case for Palestine was made compelling by "the unspeakable atrocities of the cold and calculated German

Nazi plan to kill all the Jews in Europe," the 1944 annual conference of the party proposed a transfer of populations in Palestine. "Let the Arabs be encouraged to move out as the Jews move in," their resolution declared. "Let them be compensated handsomely for their land and let their settlement elsewhere be carefully organized and generously financed. The Arabs have many wide territories of their own."[133] Ben Gurion and other Zionists did not call for the implementation of these resolutions. Nevertheless, the Labour Party's declaration of support for a Jewish Palestine aided their cause and contributed to the continuing political ascent of Ben Gurion and his program.

The war years found the Arabs of Palestine disorganized and leaderless. The Arab Revolt had come to an end, and the White Paper had removed some of the immediacy attached to Palestinian grievances. Nevertheless, the Arabs remained as determined as ever that Zionist aspirations should not be realized at their expense. Al-Hajj Amin, who had already emerged as the leading spokesman for the Palestinian cause, lived in Germany during much of the war. Like a number of other Arab leaders, Husayni supported the Axis powers, and like others, too, much of his motivation came from a desire to see Great Britain and France defeated. Britain and France were the major colonial powers in the Middle East, the countries whose imperial designs had denied the Arabs their independence after World War I. Britain was also guilty of breaking the promises it had made to the Arabs during the preceding war and, above all, of supporting Zionism's expanding presence in Palestine.[134]

In addition to these considerations, however, which were political in character and wholly understandable from the Arab point of view, much has rightly been made of al-Husayni's anti-Semitism and his tolerance or even approval of Hitler's policy toward the Jews. As mufti of Jerusalem, al-Hajj Amin had frequently blurred the distinction between political opposition to Zionism and condemnations of Judaism and the Jewish people. Under his influence, in the judgment of one objective study, to be a Jew became an offense in and of itself. Arab nationalism in Palestine adopted anti-Semitism "on the coarsest European model."[135] This dimension of the mufti's political orientation was also present during the war. In Germany he met with Nazi leaders, including Hitler, and made plans for Arab-Nazi cooperation. At a secret meeting in November 1941, Hitler and al-Husayni agreed that the Germans and the Arabs had the same enemies, the British, the Jews, and the Communists. Indeed, Hitler added, there was little difference between the capitalism of England and the communism of Soviet Russia, since both countries were citadels of Jewish power. The *Führer* stated that when German armies entered the Middle East, their objective would be "the destruction of the Jewish element residing in the Arab sphere under the protection of British power." It was also agreed that the mufti was to prepare a secret Arab operation to be set off at the same time in support of this objective.[136]

Inside Palestine, there were some efforts to revitalize the Arab nationalist movement. In 1943, by which time it was becoming clear that Arab hopes for a British defeat in the war were unlikely to be realized, several former leaders of the Istiqlal Party revived their organization and sought to unify the ranks of the nationalists under a new banner. The Istiqlalis demanded continued adherence to the White Paper, and in this context they were prepared to work with Britain for the realization of Palestinian political aspirations. But while the wisdom of al-Husayni's alliance with the Germans had temporarily cost him some popularity in Palestine, his supporters responded to the challenge of the Istiqlalis and founded a new party of their own, the Arab Palestine Party. The Arab Palestine Party adopted a harsher tone and called for Arab independence and the total dissolution of the Jewish national home. The new party kept the mufti in the forefront of Palestinian leadership, and its ability to retain a local following may have been due not only to the skill and prominence of its organizers but also to the contribution to renewed tension made by a revival of Irgun and Stern Group terrorism.

The result of these and related developments was continued fragmentation of the nationalist movement. Neither the Husayni nor the Istiqlali faction was able to achieve supremacy and establish a foundation for political unity. Moreover, this situation encouraged the continuing independence of a number of smaller prewar parties and groupings, thereby reinforcing further the tendency toward disunity. In 1945 there were six separate political parties. At the close of the war, with Britain preparing to reexamine its policies toward Palestine, and the United States now displaying a strong interest in the affairs of the region, the leaders of these various factions did begin to negotiate with one another and to coordinate their activities. Nevertheless, they did not succeed in reestablishing the kind of unified political structure that had earlier existed in the form of the Arab Executive and the Arab Higher Committee.

This did not mean that the intensity of Arab demands had lessened. Indeed, Palestinian political aspirations were sharpened by new currents on the international scene and by developments in neighboring Arab countries, where it appeared that colonialism was at long last receding. European and American support for the principle of self-determination had been loudly proclaimed during the war against Germany, and it was hoped that the victorious powers would not seek to apply the principle to Europe while denying it to colonial dependencies. The establishment of the United Nations in 1945 also raised hopes that the postwar period would see the creation of a new world order. The most immediate Middle Eastern consequences of this new spirit were in Syria and Lebanon. In contrast to what had happened after the First World War, the British sent troops to the two countries to prevent France from reasserting its hegemony; and in the spring and summer of 1946, after a year's residence, these forces withdrew so that Syria and Lebanon might obtain independence. Although these events restored some of Britain's credibility in Arab eyes, they also heightened expectations. Further, in Palestine, they deepened the anger directed at those who continued to stand in the way of Arab independence. As Palestinian representatives stated in 1946, "While the other Arab countries have attained or are near to the attainment of self-government and full membership in the U.N.O., Palestine is still under the Mandate and has taken no steps toward self-government. . . . While other Arab countries are working through the Arab League to strengthen their ties and coordinate their policies, Palestine cannot participate fully in this movement so long as she has no indigenous government." [137]

The Palestinians believed they were in danger of losing their country. In their eyes the issue was one of national survival. Yet the intensity of Arab demands and expectations was matched by the determination of the Jews, all of which merely served to introduce a new round of activity in what was by now a familiar and apparently irresolvable conflict. The horrors of the war led Zionists to conclude that the national survival of the Jewish people was also at stake, and that the only solution was the creation of a Jewish state in Palestine. Indeed, as explained by one historian, "At the conclusion of the war in Europe, and once the full scale of the Holocaust was universally understood, following the liberation of the concentration and death camps, the Zionists assumed, *ipso facto*, that enlightened world opinion would recognize the legitimacy of their demand for a Jewish state in Palestine." [138]

The story of the Holocaust, in which Jews were not alone among the millions who perished in Nazi death camps, properly belongs to a more general history of the Jews or of Europe. Yet the loss of nearly six million souls, perhaps the most tragic experience of the Jewish people's long history, had an effect on the thinking of Zionists and other Jews which cannot be overestimated. The magnitude of the tragedy defies description; all one can do is present the statistical distribution of human loss (see Appendix 3 at end of chapter) and observe, with Sachar, that "the simple figures speak so eloquently that embellishment is an anticlimax." [139] As the Jews' worst fears were confirmed and the enormity of the Holocaust became known, many overseas Jews who had once been indifferent to Zionism, or no more than apathetic supporters of its political program, rallied to the cause. This was especially true in the United States, which was now the center of world Jewry and which had emerged from the war as a dominant world power.

The Zionists aggressively pressed their case both on the world scene and inside Palestine. The Jewish Agency in June 1945 demanded that Britain immediately issue 100,000 new immigration certificates, so that the pitiful survivors of Hitler's death camps might be permitted to enter Palestine; and a positive response to this demand was anticipated when the Labour Party came to power the following month. The new foreign secretary, Ernest Bevin, took his party and government in a different direction, however, exacerbating the deterioration of British-Zionist relations and forcing the Zionists to intensify and expand their efforts at "illegal" Jewish immigration to Palestine. Also described as the "alternative" immigration, or "*aliya beth*," this illegal immigration brought roughly 70,000 Jews to Palestine between the end of the war and Israel's independence in 1948. Most traveled by sea in aging ships, and more than 2,000 drowned or otherwise perished en route. Many were intercepted by the British and for a time held in detention camps on the island of Cyprus.[140]

Zionist leaders also directed their diplomatic efforts at the American government, some of whose members had expressed support for the Jewish cause during the war. President Truman showed a keen and sympathetic interest in the plight of Jewish (and non-Jewish) refugees from the war, issuing a directive that procedures for admitting more of them into the United States be expedited. At the end of August, he also asked the British government to reconsider its refusal to issue the 100,000 immigration certificates sought by the Zionists, a request that produced a chilly response from London. On the other hand, Truman approached the refugee issue on humanitarian grounds and endeavored to avoid partisan positions in the Palestine conflict. From Roosevelt he had inherited a policy of seeking productive relations with both the Zionists and the Arabs, and this was a policy he struggled to maintain.[141]

Inside Palestine, tension between the Zionists and the British was mounting steadily. Local Jews sometimes taunted British soldiers and likened them to Nazis. The soldiers on a number of occasions entered Zionist settlements and scrawled swastikas or anti-Semitic slogans on walls. As one British sergeant explains, "I went out there [to Palestine] without any anti-Jewish feeling at all, but after a few months we were all very angry with the Jews, I admit it."[142]

Increased terrorism on the part of the Irgun and the Stern Group, most of it now directed at the British, played a particularly important role in heightening tension. Toward the end of 1945, the Irgun carried out a coordinated attack on two British police stations, killing nine. Ben Gurion and other mainstream Zionist leaders condemned the operation and informed the high commissioner that the Zionist movement did not support such activities, although some historians question the validity of these statements and suggest that the Hagana, too, was participating in a resistance campaign that "manifested all the features of political terrorism."[143] In any event, additional attacks followed. In April 1946 the Stern Group murdered seven British soldiers, and in July the most infamous episode occurred. The Irgun blew up a wing of the King David Hotel in Jerusalem, a portion of which was being used as a British military headquarters.[144] Ninety-one lives were lost, among them Jews and Arabs as well as British. By the end of the year the Irgun and the Sternists claimed to have killed 373 people, of whom 300 were civilians, and a number of additional terrorist acts were carried out by these organizations in 1947. In this atmosphere, with the political temperature rising and violence once again on the increase, both Arabs and Jews prepared for armed conflict.

Israel's Independence

The last round of diplomatic activity aimed at finding a way out of the Palestine impasse opened with the creation in November 1945 of an Anglo-American Committee of Inquiry. The committee's report was made public in April 1946. In many of its specific recommendations, the Anglo-American Committee issued proposals favorable to the Zionists. It recommended issuance of the 100,000 immigration certificates that the Zionists had been demanding, as well as a more permissive attitude toward future Jewish immigration. It also recommended removal of the restrictions on Jewish land purchases introduced by the 1939 White Paper. Only in the area of labor practices were concessions made to the Arabs, it being recommended that Zionist discrimination against Palestinian labor be made illegal. In the larger sense, however, the committee's recommendations about the political future of Palestine constituted an unrealistic compromise that satisfied no one. Based on the logic of binationalism, a noble ideal for which there was no more than marginal support on either side, the committee proposed that "Palestine shall be neither a Jewish state nor an Arab state." Nor was the country to be partitioned, for "Palestine must ultimately become a state which guards the rights and interests of Muslims, Jews and Christians alike and accords to the inhabitants, as a whole, the fullest measure of self-government."[145] Finally, the Anglo-American Committee recommended that the country remain subject to international supervision, which meant, since the United States was unwilling to participate in such an administration, that the British mandate would continue.[146]

The Anglo-American Committee's efforts were without practical consequence, and the publication of its report brought bitter condemnation from many quarters. The British government found the recommendations concerning immigration and land purchases unacceptable. The Zionists were satisfied with the report's provisions in these areas but remained committed to a larger political settlement based on the Biltmore Program. At a meeting in Paris at the end of July, the Zionist Executive did retreat from the Biltmore doctrine to the extent of moderating its opposition to the idea of partition. After lengthy discussion, the executive passed a resolution declaring its willingness to "discuss a proposal for the establishment of a viable Jewish state in an adequate area of Palestine."[147] Nevertheless, Zionist leaders remained as opposed as ever to the binational solution put forward by the Anglo-American Committee. Finally, the Arabs judged the committee's findings to be a disaster on all counts, taking solace only in the fact that the British shared some of their complaints and had rejected the proposals having to do with immigration and land transfer. Publication of the report was accompanied by strikes and violent Arab demonstrations in Palestine, as well as by vigorous protests in several other Arab countries.[148]

Beyond increasing tension in Palestine itself, publication of the report also strained American-British relations. As noted, the two governments had different views on the key issue of Jewish immigration, and they thus responded differently to the report's recommendations in this area. Another development was the formulation of the Grady-Morrison Plan, named for American and British officials who conferred in an attempt to resolve the policy differences between their two countries. This plan, issued in July 1946, was a modified version of partition. It recommended that Palestine be divided into two separate and autonomous political units, but added that the mandate should continue and both "autonomous provinces" should remain under international supervision. Sykes describes the fate of this plan in particular, and of efforts to solve the problem of Palestine in general, with the apt observation that "it followed its many predecessors and a few successors into limbo."[149] After more than a quarter-century of disturbances, commissions of inquiry, policy statements, and peace plans, the prospects for accommodation in Palestine were bleaker than ever, and Britain's painful and unrewarding experience in that country was approaching its end.

Meetings and consultations continued for several months, but little was accomplished. Thus, in February 1947, Great Britain finally acknowledged formally and publicly what had long been evident, that it was not within London's power to impose a settlement in Palestine. The British government then announced in Parliament that it had decided to turn the matter over to the United Nations, the League of Nations' successor on whose behalf Britain was, in theory at least, exercising the Mandate.

The UN accepted the return of the mandate, and in May the world body established an eleven-member Special Committee on Palestine (UNSCOP). To avoid Soviet participation, no Security Council member was represented on the committee, which was composed of delegates from Australia, Canada, Czechoslovakia, Guatemala, India, Holland, Iran, Peru, Sweden, Uruguay, and Yugoslavia. Charged with making recommendations concerning Palestine's future, the UNSCOP arrived in the country in June to take testimony and receive evidence from the Zionists and the Arabs, all of which was by now depressingly familiar. The committee also found itself in an increasingly chaotic and violent environment. Not only had Zionist terrorism continued, with the principal target being the British, but Arab terrorism had resumed as well and was directed against the Jews.

The UNSCOP submitted its report at the end of August. It contained both a majority and a minority proposal. The majority plan endorsed the idea of partition but added several new features. First, the territorial divisions proposed for the Arab and Jewish states were constructed so that each state would be composed of three noncontiguous regions, as shown in Map 4.3. The proposed boundaries contrasted with those recommended by the Peel Commission in that the Arabs were awarded the western part of Galilee and the Negev was now attached to the Zionist state, thereby giving the Jews 56 percent of the country. Most significant, however, was the overall territorial pattern, which allowed each state to intersect and separate the provinces of the other. This implausible and impractical geopolitical arrangement has been described by one British scholar as two fighting serpents entwined in an inimical embrace.[150] Second, the majority proposed that the two states establish by treaty a formal economic union, and then added that the independence of neither state should be recognized until such a treaty had been signed. Finally, the majority proposal envisioned the establishment of an international enclave surrounding Jerusalem and extending as far south as Bethlehem.

In contrast, the minority proposal submitted by the representatives of India, Iran, and Yugoslavia (with Australia abstaining) derived its inspiration from the idea of binationalism. It recommended that the Arab and Jewish political communities be united within a federal political structure. The federal government, which would be located in Jerusalem, would have full powers in such areas as defense, foreign relations, finance, and immigration. The Arab and Jewish polities, which the proposal calls "states" and whose suggested borders are also shown in Map 4.3, would have full autonomy in such areas as education, housing, public health, and so forth. It would also enjoy powers of taxation related to the performance of its responsibilities in these fields. The federal government would have two legislative chambers, one elected on the basis of proportional representation and one composed of an equal number of representatives from the Arab and the Jewish state. Legislation would be enacted when approved by a majority in both chambers.

The Arabs rejected both of these proposals. They adhered to their long-held position that Palestine was an integral part of the Arab world and that from the beginning its indigenous inhabitants had opposed the creation in their country of a Jewish national home. They also insisted that the United Nations, a body created and controlled by the United States and Europe, had no right to grant the Zionists any portion of their territory. In what was to become a familiar Arab charge, they insisted that the Western world was seeking to salve its conscience for the atrocities of the war and was paying its own debt to the Jewish people with someone else's land.

The Zionists, by contrast, after initial hesitation, declared their willingness to accept the recommendations of the majority. The Jewish Agency termed the Zionist state which would be created by their implementation "an indispensable minimum," on the basis of which the Jews were prepared to surrender their claims to the rest of Palestine. In responding to Arab charges, the Jews pointed out that their movement and its program neither began with the war nor derived their legitimacy from the Holocaust. Furthermore, they reasoned, whatever the history of the Palestine conflict, the point had now been reached when compromise was essential, and there was no body more capable of taking the lead in this

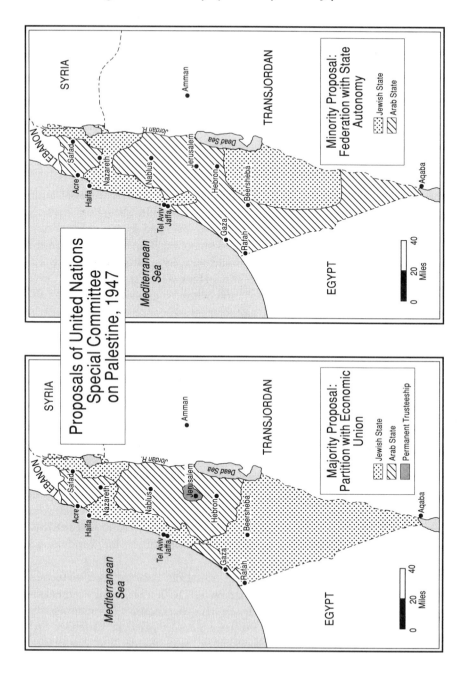

Proposals of United Nations Special Committee on Palestine, 1947

Majority Proposal: Partition with Economic Union
Jewish State
Arab State
Permanent Trusteeship

Minority Proposal: Federation with State Autonomy
Jewish State
Arab State

matter than the United Nations. Having taken this position, the Zionist Organization deployed what political influence it possessed in support of the partition plan recommended by the UNSCOP majority.

The United Nations General Assembly endorsed the partition resolution on November 29, 1947. The vote was thirty-three to thirteen with ten abstentions, a close vote since passage required a two-thirds majority. The Soviet Union, as well as the United States, was among the countries voting in favor of the resolution. Britain, claiming that the resolution was unworkable but also seeking to protect its interests in the Arab world, was among the abstentions.

Political negotiations went on for several weeks prior to the action of the General Assembly, with the Jews using all of their influence in the United States not only to secure an affirmative vote from the Americans but also to persuade the U.S. government to put pressure on other countries to support the resolution. Truman at first refused to make a public statement in favor of partition, in order not to antagonize the Arabs and the British, and he was strongly urged on this course by most of the Washington foreign-policy establishment.[151] Thus, as reported by Hurewitz, "The hesitant unfolding of United States support of partition suggested that Washington was experiencing difficulty in reconciling the traditional pressures."[152] Eventually, however, the president yielded to the urging of the Zionists and gave approval,[153] and thereafter the Americans worked as well to obtain an endorsement from several UN members initially opposed to the partition plan. Six countries were the recipients of special pressure—Haiti, Liberia, the Philippines, China, Ethiopia, and Greece—and all, with the exception of Greece, eventually either voted for the resolution or abstained.[154] After the United Nations vote, Britain announced that it would relinquish the mandate in about six months' time, setting the date of May 15, 1948, for its final withdrawal. The borders of the Arab and Jewish states envisioned in the UN partition resolution, which were to be recognized upon the termination of the mandate, are shown in Map 4.4. They differed only slightly from those proposed in the UNSCOP report.

War broke out in Palestine almost as soon as the UN had passed the partition resolution. On November 30, there were Arab attacks on Jews in many cities, including Haifa, Tel Aviv, Jaffa, Lydda, and Jerusalem. There were also anti-Jewish riots in Beirut, Aleppo, Damascus, Baghdad, and a number of other Arab cities outside Palestine. Al-Hajj Amin al-Husayni had reestablished the Arab Higher Committee in Cairo and then moved it to Beirut, and from the Lebanese capital he now declared that the Arabs considered the partition resolution to be "null and void," and that it accordingly would not be respected by the Palestine people. Similar statements were issued by the member states of the Arab League. With Britain preparing to withdraw its military forces from Palestine and no longer willing to commit its resources to the maintenance of order,[155] the Palestinians raised a guerrilla army to resist implementation of the partition resolu-

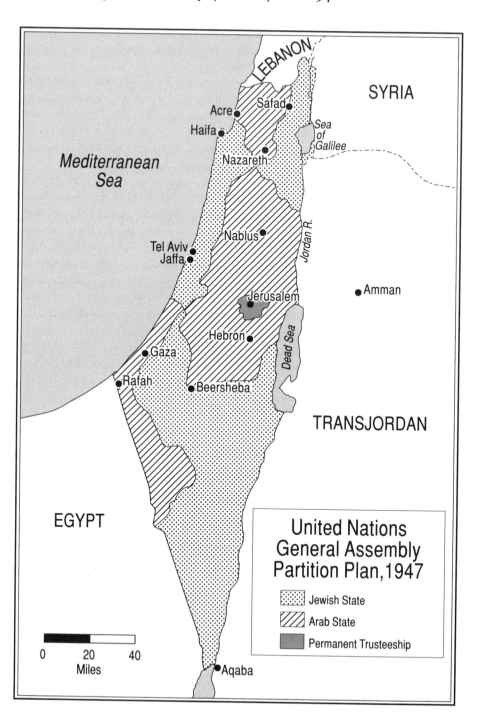

United Nations
General Assembly
Partition Plan, 1947

tion. It was supported by a network of local committees devoted to fund-raising and recruitment, and by March 1948 it had been augmented by the arrival of 6,000 to 7,000 volunteers from neighboring Arab countries. These forces constituted the Arab Liberation Army.

The Arab forces achieved a number of early successes. For example, they cut the road between Tel Aviv and Jerusalem and laid siege to the Jewish neighborhoods in the western half of the latter city. By the end of the winter the Jews of Jerusalem had run out of food, and dozens of Hagana troops had died in vain attempts to reopen the highway and break the siege. The tide of the war had turned by April, however. The siege of Jerusalem was broken and, following a succession of rapid victories, the Hagana gained control of most of the territory allocated to the Jewish state by the United Nations. In accordance with *Tochnit Dalet* (Plan D), the Hagana's master plan adopted in March 1948, Jewish forces also launched operations that eventually brought control of some of the areas the UN had allocated for an Arab state in Palestine.[156]

With the approach of the May 15 date for termination of the mandate, the Zionists assembled a provisional National Council, and this body in turn elected a thirteen-member provisional government, with Ben Gurion as its prime minister and defense minister. Then, on May 14, the council gathered in the Tel Aviv Museum and declared the *Yishuv*'s independence, proclaiming the establishment of the State of Israel in that portion of Palestine which the United Nations had allocated for a Jewish state. The new country was immediately recognized by the United States, President Truman having once again disregarded the advice of his advisors, most of whom had urged him to wait.

With these events the State of Israel came into existence, fulfilling a Zionist vision that in its modern and political form was nearly three-quarters of a century old. Yet the war by which Israel secured its independence continued for another eight months, and by the time it ended, both the political map and the demographic character of Palestine had changed dramatically. These changes spelled disaster for the Arabs of Palestine. On the one hand, the Palestine Arab state envisioned by the United Nations partition resolution did not come into existence, leaving Israel the only independent state in the territory. On the other, the bulk of the Palestinian population left the country. Under circumstances about which Arabs and Jews passionately disagree, hundreds of thousands of Arab men, women, and children either fled or were expelled from the country, making Jews the majority and transforming the Palestinians into stateless refugees.

Although the Palestinians' guerrilla army had collapsed, Israel was attacked on May 15 by the military forces of Egypt, Jordan, Iraq, and Syria. The leaders of Israel's Arab neighbors were unwilling to recognize the new state's existence and took steps to reclaim the country for the Palestinians. Israeli leaders appear to have been confident of their ability to defend the Jewish state, however, even though they depicted their country as a small nation surrounded by large and hostile powers.[157] The Jewish Agency also let it be known that it would regard an invasion by Arab armies as releasing Israel from the obligations of the UN resolution of November 29.[158]

There were three phases to the fighting that followed, each of which saw Israeli forces extend the territory under their control. The first phase lasted for about a month and was followed by a short truce. The second, sometimes known as the "Ten Days War," took place between July 8 and July 18. During this phase Israeli forces seized territory in the Galilee and in the Tel Aviv–Jerusalem corridor that the UN had allocated to the proposed Palestinian state. On the other hand, part of that portion of the Negev allocated to the Jews was under the control of the Egyptian army when a second truce was implemented. A final round of fighting began in October and continued until the following January. During these months the Hagana expelled Egyptian forces from the Negev, extending its control to the borders of Sinai and capturing additional territory previously allocated to the Palestinian state. Hostilities finally ended early in 1949, after which Israel and the Arab states began armistice negotiations on the island of Rhodes. By July the Jewish state had signed armistice agreements with all of its neighbors, Egypt, Lebanon, Jordan, Iraq, and Syria.

The area under Israeli control when the armistice agreements were signed became the official boundaries of the new state. These borders, shown in Map 4.5, left the State of Israel in possession of a large portion of the territory projected for an Arab state by the UN partition resolution. The fate of the remainder of the territory, and of the now-stateless Palestinian people, is a story to which attention will be turned shortly. In the meantime, the State of Israel had become an established fact, militarily secure and recognized by the international community.

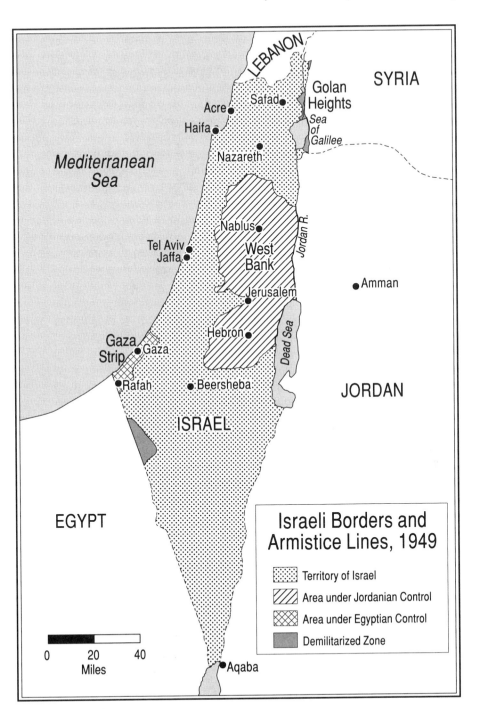

Israeli Borders and Armistice Lines, 1949

Appendix 1. Palestine Population by Religious Communities

Year	Date		Muslims	Jews	Christians	Others	Total	% of Jews
1922	(10/23)	Census	589,177	83,790	71,464	7,617	752,048	11.1
1923	(6/30)		599,331	89,660	72,090	7,908	768,989	11.7
1924	,		627,660	94,945	74,094	8,263	804,962	11.8
1925	,		641,494	121,725	75,512	8,507	847,238	14.4
1926	,		663,613	149,500	76,467	8,782	898,362	16.6
1927	,		680,725	149,789	77,880	8,921	917,315	16.3
1928	,		695,280	151,656	79,812	9,203	935,951	16.2
1929	,		712,343	156,481	81,776	9,443	960,043	16.3
1930	,		733,149	164,796	84,986	9,628	992,559	16.6
1931	(11/18)	Census	759,700	174,606	88,907	10,101	1,033,714	16.9
1932	(12/31)		778,803	192,137	92,520	10,367	1,073,827	17.9
1933	,		798,506	234,967	96,791	10,677	1,140,941	20.6
1934	,		814,379	282,975	102,407	10,793	1,210,554	23.4
1935	,		836,688	335,157	105,236	11,031	1,308,112	27.3
1936	,		862,730	384,078	108,506	11,378	1,366,692	28.1
1937	,		883,446	395,836	110,869	11,643	1,401,794	28.2
1938	,		900,250	411,222	111,974	11,839	1,435,285	28.7
1939	,		927,133	445,457	116,958	12,150	1,501,698	29.7
1940	,		947,846	463,535	120,587	12,563	1,544,530	30.0
1941	,		973,104	474,102	125,413	12,413	1,585,500	29.9
1942	,		995,292	484,408	127,184	13,121	1,620,005	29.9
1943	,		1,028,715	502,912	131,281	13,663	1,676,571	30.0
1944	,		1,061,277	528,702	135,547	14,098	1,739,624	30.4
1945	,		1,101,565	554,329	139,285	14,858	1,810,037	30.6

SOURCE: A. Gertz, ed., *Statistical Handbook of Jewish Palestine, 1947* (Jerusalem: Jewish Agency, Department of Statistics, 1947), pp. 46–47.

Appendix 2. Summary of Jewish Immigration by Periods

Citizenship	1919–23	1924–31	1932–39	1940–45	1919–45	%
Austria	497	294	5,623	892	7,306	2.2
Bulgaria	328	1,127	948	2,257	4,660	1.4
Czechoslovakia	112	363	4,779	1,181	6,435	1.9
England	180	173	806	89	1,248	0.4
Germany	469	660	35,980	2,022	39,131	11.7
Greece	158	696	5,280	797	6,931	3.1
Hungary	291	230	1,107	1,297	2,925	0.9
Italy	37	57	556	559	1,209	0.4
Latvia	401	858	3,212	86	4,557	1.4
Lithuania	901	3,014	5,208	180	9,303	2.8
Poland	9,158	37,387	83,847	6,833	137,225	40.9
Rumania	1,404	3,739	9,548	6,474	21,165	6.3
USSR	13,363	14,636	2,473	634	30,836	9.2
Yugoslavia	145	136	702	746	1,729	0.5
Iran	197	865	489	176	1,727	0.5
Iraq	171	2,617	124	627	3,539	1.0
Turkey	478	1,140	1,455	3,537	6,610	2.0
Yemen	184	2,317	6,416	5,537	14,454	4.3
USA	601	1,158	4,621	16	6,396	1.9
Other countries	886	882	6,704	2,037	10,449	3.1
Stateless	—	—	4,132	4,616	8,748	2.6
Unspecified	5,140	1,146	2,087	110	8,483	2.5
Total	35,101	73,435	186,097	40,433	335,066	100.0

SOURCE: A. Gertz, ed., *Statistical Handbook of Jewish Palestine, 1947* (Jerusalem: Jewish Agency, Department of Statistics, 1947), p. 100.

Appendix 3. Estimated Jewish Population of Europe in 1939 and 1947

Country	1939	1947
Albania	200	
Austria	60,000	42,300
Belgium	100,000	34,500
Bulgaria	50,000	46,500
Czechoslovakia	360,000	60,000
Denmark	7,000	5,500
England	340,000	345,000
Estonia (U.S.S.R.)	5,000	500
Finland	2,000	1,800
France	320,000	205,000
Germany	240,000	188,600
Greece	75,000	8,000
Holland	150,000	33,000
Hungary	403,000	180,000
Irish Free State	4,000	4,500
Italy	51,000	56,000
Latvia (U.S.S.R.)	95,000	12,000
Lithuania (U.S.S.R.)	155,000	20,000
Luxembourg	3,500	500
Norway	3,000	1,000
Poland	3,250,000	105,000
Portugal	3,500	4,000
Rumania	850,000	430,000
Soviet Union	3,020,000	2,000,000
Spain	4,500	3,500
Sweden	7,500	15,500
Switzerland	25,000	25,500
Turkey	80,000	80,000
Yugoslavia	75,000	11,900
TOTAL	9,739,200	3,920,100

SOURCE: *American Jewish Year Book*, 1947–48.
NOTE: 1947 figures for Austria and Germany include, respectively, 35,000 and 170,600 displaced persons in zones controlled by Allied Powers. 1947 figures for Italy include 26,000 displaced persons and refugees.

PART III

Routinization of the Conflict, 1948–1967

THE ARAB-ISRAELI War of 1947–48 resulted in the establishment of an independent Jewish state, one which, moreover, had proved capable of defending itself against the combined military might of the Arabs of Palestine and of neighboring Arab countries. As one Israeli leader later declared with pride, the military victory which secured Israel's independence resulted from the self-sacrifice and determination of a people fighting for its national existence.[1] Further, the new state received diplomatic recognition from an array of foreign powers, including both the United States and the Soviet Union. Indeed, the U.S. and the USSR initially competed with one another for leadership among Israel's diplomatic benefactors.[2] In May 1949, after several months of British-led opposition, the State of Israel became the fifty-ninth member of the United Nations.

May 14, 1948, the date of Israeli independence, saw the attainment by modern political Zionism of its nationalist ambitions and marked a turning point in the history of the Jewish people. David Ben Gurion, the Labor Zionist leader who provided the *Yishuv* with decisive leadership during its War for Independence, and who subsequently became Israel's first prime minister, called the achievement of Israeli statehood the "consummation of the Jewish revolution." Speaking to a group of youth leaders in Haifa in 1944, for example, Ben Gurion reaffirmed the Zionist vision and declared, "The meaning of the Jewish revolution is contained in one word—Independence. Independence for the Jewish people in its homeland!"[3] Ben Gurion concluded his 1944 address by declaring, "There is hope that many of us will live to see the consummation of the Jewish revolution."

The Declaration of Independence issued by Israel left no doubt about the Jewish character of the new state. Reflecting a Zionist conception of political normalcy that borrowed from both Herzl and Ahad Ha'am, the document asserted that "it is the natural right of the Jewish people, like any other people, to control their own destiny in their sovereign state." Affirming also the ancient and historic rights of the Jewish people in Palestine, the preamble declared, "The Land of Israel was the birthplace of the Jewish people. Here their spiritual, religious and national identity was formed. Here they achieved independence and created a culture of national and universal significance. Here they wrote and gave the Bible to the world." Thus, the document continued, "WE DO HEREBY PROCLAIM the establishment of the Jewish State in Palestine, to be called Medinath Yisrael," the State of Israel. Interestingly, the name "Israel" was selected at the last minute by the Jewish Agency, which had for a time been inclined to choose "State of the Jews," or "The Jewish State," the title of Herzl's book.[4]

In 1950, the Israeli parliament passed the Law of Return, which gave further substance to the Jewish character of the state. It declared that every Jew has the right to immigrate to Israel and become a citizen. Only in the case of "acts against the Jewish nation" or of a threat to public health or state security may citizenship be withheld. The Law of Return further specifies that "every Jew who migrated to the country before this law goes into effect, and every Jew who was born in the country either before or after the law is effective, enjoys the same status as any person who migrated on the basis of this law." The Law of Return thus made it clear that Israel was to be the state of the entire Jewish people, of Jews in the many communities of the Diaspora, as well as those in Palestine.

The Declaration of Independence and the Law of Return left unanswered many fundamental questions about the character of the Jewish state. For example, is Israel's mission to bring Jews throughout the world together in a single commonwealth? Is the establishment of the Jewish state therefore the first stage in an ingathering of the exiles? Or, alternatively, are the establishment of Israel and the permanence of the Jewish Diaspora fully compatible from the perspective of modern political Zionism? And if so, what is to be the relationship between Israel and Jews living elsewhere? Is the country to be the spiritual and cultural center of world Jewry, as well as a haven for Diaspora Jews periodically faced with persecution? There also remain fundamental questions about the kind of Jewish state envisioned by modern Zionism. Is Israel to be a modern and secular polity, Jewish in the national sense that it is of and for Jews but, beyond this, governed by legal and moral codes that resemble those of any Western society claiming affinity with Judeo-Christian ethics? Or alternatively, once again, should the country to some degree be organized and ruled in accordance with Biblical law, with the true believers of orthodox Judaism perhaps playing a dominant role in the interpretation and application of normative codes?

One of the many Israelis who have articulated such concerns is Amnon Rubinstein, a Member of Knesset and former dean of the Tel Aviv University Law School. Asking about the implication of these issues for the national identity of the state of Israel, Rubinstein refers to an "ever unsolved question" that has long preoccupied Zionist theoreticians: "Will the new Hebrew nation, on regaining sovereignty in its land, forsake all claims to Jewish exclusivist tradition and become a nation like every other nation?" "Will the new Jews," he wonders, eventually "differ from other peoples only as the French differ from the English, or will they retain some universal message, some uniqueness, some 'otherness'—the heirlooms of their past—in the world they seek to join?"[5]

Although questions of this sort had been explicitly raised and passionately debated by Zionist theoreticians since the early days of the movement, Israeli independence gave them practical as well as ideological significance. After 1948, the Jewish people possessed freedom and sovereignty in its own country, and questions about religion, culture, and identity accordingly became arenas for the formulation of public policy. So, too, did other critical issues, such as the relationship between Israel's Jewish citizens and the state's sizable non-Jewish minority. Indeed, although not a concern that received serious attention in the early years of statehood, it remained to be seen whether Israel could be a Jewish state, by any definition, without unavoidably imposing an inferior political status on its non-Jewish citizens. As expressed by one Zionist leader in 1948, "For the first time we shall be the majority living with a minority, and we shall be called upon to provide an example and prove how Jews live with a minority."[6]

With independence achieved, the moment had come to test Jewish wisdom and ethics against the complex problems of the present age, to demonstrate that Jewish values could indeed give prosperity and meaning to a modern nation-state and, perhaps, could themselves evolve and become enriched through their application. Moreover, this is precisely the test for which the Jewish people had historically longed, and herein lies a large part of Israel's significance for Jews. It is in this connection that a distinguished American Jewish scholar rhetorically asks, "What is the meaning of the State of Israel?" and then states that although there can be no single answer, one fact is clear: "In no other community do we witness such an intense, ongoing search, such an effort to understand itself in terms of a higher vision, as in Israel. Mere self-preservation is regarded as an inadequate motivation."[7]

5 | The Palestinian Disaster and Basic Issues after 1948

The Palestinian Disaster

THE 1947–48 WAR was a watershed event in the history of Palestine's Arabs, as well as its Jews. The war's meaning for the two peoples was completely different, however. With their nationalist aspirations thwarted, the results filled Palestinians with despair, rather than with hope and anticipation. Indeed, Palestinians refer to the defeat of 1947–48 as *al-naqba*, "the catastrophe" or "the disaster."

To begin with, ceasefire lines in place at the beginning of 1949 left Israel in control of much of the territory that the United Nations had in 1947 allocated for an Arab state in Palestine. As can be seen from a comparison of Maps 4.4 and 4.5, the territorial locus of the new Jewish state increased by roughly one-third as a result of the fighting. Moreover, Israel incorporated within its borders all of the territory under its control; no distinction was made between lands allocated to the Jews by the UN Partition Resolution and lands that fell into Israeli hands as a result of the 1947–48 War. Israel understandably defended its expansion by recalling that it was the Palestinians and other Arabs who had rejected partition and initiated the fighting. Abdullah of Transjordan was alone among Arab leaders in accepting the principle of partition in 1947; and he, too, joined in the war against Israel once the Jewish state declared independence. Nevertheless, from the Palestinians' viewpoint, the war not only was a military defeat but, equally important, it brought the loss to Israel of yet another large portion of their homeland.

The impossibility of reviving the idea of partition and of creating an independent Palestinian state alongside Israel was demonstrated by the course of mediation efforts that began even before the war had concluded. Within a week of Israel's declaration of independence, the UN appointed Count Folke Bernadotte as its mediator, and Bernadotte, who had been president of the Swedish Red Cross, soon formulated his own plan for a final settlement. Presented to the UN General Assembly in September, it proposed modifying the 1947 Partition Resolution by redrawing the boundaries between Jewish and Arab Palestine, such that Arabs would receive the Negev and the towns of Ramleh and Lydda, while the entire Galilee would become part of Israel. In addition, significantly, Bernadotte proposed that Arab Palestine be attached to Transjordan, stating that the creation of an independent Palestinian state was now unrealistic. Bernadotte found little receptivity to his plan among the Arabs. There was opposition to his proposal to unite Arab Palestine and Transjordan and, more generally, he met continued Arab rejection "of any suggestion of acceptance or recognition of the Jewish state."[8] On the other hand, somewhat ironically since he had strongly urged the Arabs to recognize the new Jewish state, Bernadotte was most bitterly denounced by the Zionists and their supporters, including the Soviet Union, which insisted that his plan threatened the security of Israel. On September 17, the UN mediator was murdered in Jerusalem by Stern Group fanatics, and thereafter, despite several months of additional discussion, Bernadotte's plan was deposited in the crowded archives of failed diplomatic efforts to find a solution to the problem of Palestine.

Another diplomatic initiative that revealed the futility of attempts to breathe new life into the notion of partition was the Lausanne Conference of 1949, convened in April and May under the auspices of the UN Conciliation Commission. The meeting was attended by representatives of Egypt, Lebanon, Syria, and Transjordan, as well as Israel, and on May 12 the Arabs and Israelis signed separate but identical protocols agreeing that the 1947 Partition Resolution was an acceptable "starting point and framework for the discussion of territorial questions." This was not the breakthrough that it appeared, however. The Israelis made it clear that they would not relinquish any of the territory they had captured, insisting that they had accepted the partition plan boundaries as only *a* basis, not *the* basis, for further discussion.[9] For their part, the Arabs rejected direct negotiations with representatives of the Jewish state and, more generally, "continued to show great reluctance to accept the very existence of Israel."[10] The Lausanne Conference also showed that by 1949 it was the Arab states, rather than the Palestinians, who were sought as bargaining agents. The Middle East conflict was increasingly being viewed as a dispute involving Israel and the Arab *states* of the region; the Palestinian Arab dimension, despite its historic centrality, was beginning to fade into the background.

Israel quickly gained international recognition of its post-1948 borders. Only with respect to the position of Jerusalem did the United States, the Soviet Union, and other foreign powers extending recognition to the Jewish state reject the territorial status quo that emerged at the end of the war. Although the Partition Resolution had called for Jerusalem to be an international enclave, a *corpus separatum*, the city was divided into a Jewish-controlled western sector and an Arab-controlled eastern sector at the conclusion of the fighting. The Israeli parliament began meeting in West Jerusalem in December 1949, and the following month the Knesset approved a resolution affirming that Jerusalem had been the country's capital from the first day of independence. The legitimacy of these actions was not recognized by the international community, and the U.S. and other countries therefore maintained their embassies in Tel Aviv. With this exception, however, Israel was accepted as an independent and sovereign state within the borders demarcated by the postwar armistice agreements. Such acceptance was made explicit, for example, in the Tripartite Declaration that the United States, the United Kingdom, and France issued in May 1950. In this statement of policy, the three powers declared their "unalterable opposition to the use of force or threat" to settle the Arab-Israeli conflict and added that they would take immediate action, both within and outside the United Nations, "should they find that any of these states was preparing to violate frontiers or armistice lines."[11]

Those parts of Palestine that were not incorporated into Israel fell under the control of neighboring Arab states. One area remaining in Arab hands was the Gaza Strip, a twenty-five-mile by four-mile sliver of land that extends northward along the Mediterranean coast from the Egyptian border below Rafah. Gaza was in the hands of the Egyptian army at the conclusion of the fighting, and Cairo's continuing control of the territory was recognized in the Israeli-Egyptian armistice agreement of February 1949, even though the Egyptian government maintained, consistent with the provisions of the agreement, that it had accepted ceasefire lines which did not constitute a political boundary and were completely without prejudice as regards the "ultimate peaceful settlement of the Palestine question."

With support from the Arab League, the Egyptians permitted the establishment in Gaza of a nominal Palestinian Arab government, led by the Arab Higher Committee under the direction of Ahmad Hilmi Pasha and al-Hajj Amin al-Husayni, the former mufti of Jerusalem. In July 1948, acting on Egyptian initiative, the Political Committee of the Arab League sanctioned creation of a Gaza-based All-Palestine Administrative Council. Then, with the approval of Egypt and other Arab states, this body in September declared itself to be the "Arab Government of All Palestine," and on October 1 it proclaimed Palestine's independence from its headquarters in Gaza. These actions did not significantly affect the political status of postwar Palestine, however. Despite its impressive name, the All-Palestine Government was not in a position to influence developments in other parts of the country, and even in Gaza its powers and autonomy were quite limited. Egypt kept effective control of the Gaza Strip firmly within its own hands and administered the territory as an unincorporated military district.

More damaging from the Palestinian point of view was the disposition of the West Bank, the remaining portion of Palestine that had not become part of Israel. Lying between the Jordan River and the central coastal plain of post-1948 Israel, dominated by a high ridge of hills running from Jenin in the north through Hebron in the south, the West Bank at the end of the war was largely under the control of the Transjordanian army, commonly known as the Arab Legion. The

West Bank contains many important Palestinian towns, including Nablus, Tulkarm, and Jenin in the north, Ramallah, Bethlehem, East Jerusalem, and Jericho in the central region, and Hebron and Halhoul in the south. Prior to 1948 it also contained important Jewish settlements, all of which were either abandoned or fell to the Arabs during the fighting.

The Arab Legion, generally considered the most effective Arab fighting force, had approximately 4,500 men in the field in May 1948.[12] It was led by John Glubb, a seasoned British officer. During the fighting, Israeli forces captured territory on the western slopes of the West Bank, in an area that the UN had assigned to the Arabs under the Partition Resolution. For the most part, however, the Arab Legion effectively limited Israel's eastward expansion. The legion held the Nablus-Tulkarm-Jenin triangle in the north and the Arab sector of Jerusalem in the central region. In the south, where it was the Egyptian rather than the Jordanian army that fought the Israelis, more of the territory proposed for a Palestinian state fell to the Jews. Nevertheless, the West Bank, containing about 80 percent of the central block of land that the UN had originally allocated to the Palestinians, was in the hands of the Arabs when the conflict ended and armistice lines were drawn.

The damage to the Palestinian cause was not that the West Bank remained in Arab hands but that in April 1950 it was annexed by Transjordan, which also changed its name to the Hashemite Kingdom of Jordan at this time. A new parliament was elected to give legal sanction to this action. It was composed of twenty representatives from the West Bank and twenty from the East Bank, and one of its first acts was to pass a resolution endorsing "complete unity between the two sides of the Jordan and their union into one state, which is the Hashemite Kingdom of Jordan, at whose head reigns King Abdullah Ibn al-Husayn."[13] Jordan's annexation of the West Bank brought to an end, at least for the foreseeable future, any possibility that an independent Arab state would be established in Palestine. Indeed, King Abdullah had issued a royal decree in March, more than a month before the election of the new parliament, forbidding the word "Palestine" to be used in official documents. By insisting upon the terms "East Bank" and "West Bank" rather than "Palestine" and "Transjordan," the king sought to make clear that there would be no separate Palestinian state.[14]

Abdullah was eager to expand the borders of his country, and thereby his own power and prestige, and his designs on Palestine were well established even before the outbreak of the 1947–48 War. The king had initially supported the idea of partition, and in this he was motivated by a view that those parts of Palestine allocated to the Arabs should and eventually would be incorporated into neighboring states. Transjordan would take control of the West Bank, the Western Galilee would be added to Lebanon, and Egypt would acquire the Gaza district and the northwest region of the Negev. Once the war began, however, Abdullah concluded that it was best to pursue his quest for the West Bank in a different manner. The king met with a Zionist delegation headed by Golda Meir shortly before the termination of the mandate but rejected its request that his country remain neutral.[15] Rather, he joined other Arab states in declaring war on May 15 and sent the Arab Legion into Palestine with the clear intention that it would remain there after the fighting. Abdullah's attitude toward Palestine was also encouraged by the British, who agreed that Jordanian forces should occupy areas of the country that had been designated for an Arab state.[16]

Although Abdullah's ambitions were strongly supported by a class of Palestinian notables with ties to the government in Amman, the Jordanian monarch was bitterly opposed by the Palestinian rank and file, and also by the All-Palestine Government based in Gaza. These Palestinian critics accused Abdullah of treason and charged that his "land grabbing" scheme would cost them most of what little remained of Palestine. Abdullah was also opposed by the leaders of virtually every other Arab state. In the Arab League, this opposition was led by Egypt, Syria, and Saudi Arabia, all of whom feared that an increase in Jordanian political influence would be at their expense. Egypt also worried that Abdullah might have designs on the Gaza Strip, as well as the West Bank, and the Hashemite leader in fact showed a keen interest in the disposition of Gaza. During secret talks with the Israelis in 1948 and 1949, for example, he first sought to enlist Zionist support for Gaza's incorporation into Jordan and then told the Israelis, "Keep it, or give it to the devil—so long as you don't leave it for the Egyptians."[17] Palestinian and Arab opposition to Abdullah's designs on the West Bank provided some of the motivation for the establishment in September 1948 of the All-Palestine Government in Gaza, as did that government's declaration of independence on October 1. Palestinian nationalists and the Arab states hoped the existence of an independent Arab state in Palestine would make the king reluctant to press ahead with annexation.

None of this deterred Abdullah, however. His government, alone among members of the Arab League, refused to recognize the All-Palestine Government in Gaza. In addition, responding to the declaration of independence issued from Gaza, the king convened a "Palestine Arab Congress" in Amman in October 1948 in order to challenge the Gaza government's claim to represent all of Palestine. The congress was attended by several thousand Palestinian notables who insisted they were the true representatives of the Palestinian people, who denounced al-Hajj Amin and the government in Gaza, and who asked that the Palestinian homeland be placed under Jordanian "protection." In December, a second conference of Palestinian notables sympathetic to the monarch was convened in Jericho. The delegates passed a resolution calling for an immediate union of the West Bank and the East Bank under Abdullah's leadership and then cabled their recommendations to the Arab League and the United Nations. The parliament in Amman approved the recommendations of the Jericho congress later in December, after which Abdullah's prime minister announced that the proposed unification would soon be implemented. In the spring of 1949, the separate administration of the West Bank was withdrawn and the Transjordanian parliament was dissolved.

Abdullah also sought to enhance his country's position by participating in secret negotiations with Zionist leaders, beginning a new round of talks in November 1949. He explored the possibility for a separate peace between Transjordan and Israel, and at one point, when a final settlement appeared out of reach, he proposed a five-year nonaggression pact between the two countries. The king also discussed various options for cooperation in Jerusalem, in defiance of the United Nations resolution calling for the city to be governed as a *corpus separatum*. In one proposal, for example, made in January 1950, he offered to give Israel access to sections of Jerusalem held by the Arab Legion in return for control of several former Arab neighborhoods that had been captured by the Hagana during the war. The Israelis responded that they would consider modifications of the present armistice line only on a "meter for meter" basis.[18]

Arab criticism of Abdullah continued to mount as his plans to annex the West Bank went forward during the first part of 1950, and it became even more intense when his secret talks with Israel became public knowledge in March of that year. Indeed, the Arab League threatened Jordan with expulsion at this time. In response, Abdullah called off talks with Israel and assured his critics that Jordan's annexation of the West Bank was not meant to preclude the eventual creation of an independent Palestinian state. His representative to the league specifically declared that Jordan's action was without prejudice to a final settlement of the Palestine question. Nevertheless, although these statements persuaded the Arab League to withdraw its threat of expulsion, they did little to diminish the general criticism of Abdullah. Opponents continued to insist that the king's deeds were more important than his words; and it was in this atmosphere that Abdullah was assassinated on the steps of Jerusalem's al-Aqsa Mosque in July 1951. He was shot at point-blank range by a Palestinian with ties to al-Hajj Amin al-Husayni. Although it has never been definitively established, it is widely believed the assassin belonged to an underground organization that had carefully plotted its campaign against the Jordanian monarch. In any event, few Palestinian tears were shed. In the words of the French consul in Jerusalem at the time, "There are 600,000 Palestinian Arabs who are delighted with the death of Abdullah."[19]

While the events of this period reveal much about the subsequent course of Palestinian-Jordanian relations, their significance in the present context lies in their implications for Palestinian statehood. As one Palestinian writer was later to observe, the state of Palestine "had disappeared from the map."[20] Israel had seized most of the territory proposed by the UN for a Palestinian Arab state, the Egyptians had thereafter installed themselves in Gaza, and the West Bank had now been swallowed up by Jordan.

All of this was only one part of the Palestinian disaster. Equally tragic was the dispersion of much of the Arab population of Palestine. During 1948 and the first part of 1949, hundreds of thousands of Palestinian civilians left their homes in the territory encompassed by the new Jewish state and made their way either to that part of Palestine remaining under Arab control or to neighboring Arab countries. The reasons for this mass exodus, to be discussed shortly, were and to some extent remain the subject of fundamental disagreement between Arabs and Israelis. For the present, it is sufficient to report, in the phrase of UN mediator Bernadotte, that these hapless Palestinians became refugees in response to "the hazards and strategy of the armed conflict" swirling around them.[21]

Approximately 300,000 Palestinians had already left their homes by the time that Israel declared its independence. According to UN figures, the number of refugees had risen to 750,000 by the beginning of 1949 and to 940,000 by June of that year.[22] Arab sources generally concur with these estimates and occasionally place them even higher. Israeli sources, by contrast, often contend that the UN statistics are grossly inflated. They argue, plausibly enough, that the heads of refugee households and the administrators of UN and other relief agencies frequently exaggerated the number of displaced persons in order to make a case for additional funds. One observer sympathetic to Israel thus puts the number of Palestinian refugees at only 500,000.[23] A realistic albeit rough estimate is provided by Benny Morris, an Israeli scholar whose important study draws upon a wide range of primary sources, including newly released documents from the Zionist archives. Morris reports that from December 1947 to September 1949, "some 600,000–760,000 Palestinian Arabs became refugees."[24] He also reports that these Palestinians came from 369 different Arab towns and villages, a figure which, again, is somewhat lower than that found in many Arab sources.

Disagreements between Israeli and Arab sources derive principally from dissimilar estimates of the number of Arabs in Palestine prior to 1948, and not from any argument about how many remained in their homes. Both sides concur that only about 150,000 Palestinians remained inside Israel by the end of 1949, and thus, despite their differing totals, there is agreement that the overwhelming majority of the indigenous Arab population was removed from the area of the new Jewish state. To the loss of Palestinian hopes for statehood and independence must consequently be added the physical uprooting and demographic dispersion of the Palestinian people. The table below, based upon figures of the United Nations, shows the distribution of refugees by city or region of origin and by place of relocation at the beginning of 1950. Not mentioned are several thousand additional refugees who established Palestinian communities in Iraq, the states of the Arab Gulf, and elsewhere. It should also be noted that a substantial number of the Palestinians who fled to the West Bank between 1947 and 1949 moved to the territory east of the Jordan River after 1950.

Place of Origin	Place of Relocation	Number of Refugees
Ramleh, Tiberias, and central region	West Bank	420,000
Jaffa and southern coastal region	Gaza Strip	220,000
Haifa, Acre, and Western Galilee	Lebanon	120,000
Beisan and Lower Galilee, Negev	Transjordan	80,000
Safad and Upper Galilee	Syria	80,000
Beersheba and Negev	Egypt	10,000

The circumstances of the Palestinians who left their homes added to the intensity of the crisis. There are conflicting accounts of the events of this period, suggesting that generalizations should be treated with caution. Nevertheless, most Palestinians left their homes and villages on short notice, and most assumed that their dislocation would be temporary. For both of these reasons, they usually took few of their possessions and were neither materially nor psychologically prepared for a prolonged absence. Yet they were consistently prevented from returning to their communities of origin, not only by the continuing uncertainties of a wartime situation but, in most instances, by deliberate Israeli policy. Israeli authorities explained and defended their position, arguing that the security of their country would be imperiled by the return of hundreds of thousands of Arabs sworn to the destruction of the Jewish state. Nevertheless, the effect on the displaced Palestinian population was devastating. With or without justification, it was not uncommon for Israeli forces to destroy abandoned Arab villages, both to limit the scope of any eventual repatriation and to prepare the land for settlement by Jews. In the judgment of Bernadotte, a contemporary observer, the property of many fleeing Palestinians was "wantonly destroyed," and within the areas controlled by Jewish forces there occurred "large-scale looting . . . and instances of destruction of villages without apparent military necessity."[25]

The refugees themselves, who often arrived in Arab-held territory after a difficult and perilous journey, for the most part found themselves in camps and other centers which, at the beginning at least, were poorly equipped to care for them. Relief efforts were initially handled by Red Cross and Red Crescent societies, as well as other charitable organizations. By 1950 the scope of the effort had increased, and the majority of the work was being carried out by the United Nations Relief and Works Agency for Palestine Refugees (UNRWA), which was established in December 1949 with an initial eighteen-month budget of about $55 million. By 1952, UNRWA's three-year budget had grown to $250 million, but the agency nevertheless reported in 1953 that "the economic, political and social obstacles to rehabilitation were much more serious than had been antici-pated."[26] A major problem was that most refugees not only were destitute but also lacked any formal education or job skill other than farming. A contributing factor was the attitude of the refugees, many of whom feared that participation in UN programs might carry with it a renunciation of their claims to repatriation or compensation.

Many of the approximately 150,000 Arabs who remained inside the area of the Jewish state also became refugees during 1948 and 1949. Although they had not left the country, they, too, abandoned their homes during or immediately after the war, and then either were prevented from returning, allegedly for secu-rity reasons, or found that their dwellings had been razed or occupied by Jews. As a result, they either resettled in neighboring Arab villages or were obliged to occupy the homes of others who had fled. The latter pattern was particularly common in the urban areas, most notably Acre, Jaffa, and Nazareth. Large num-bers of Palestinians fled from these cities, and refugees from adjacent rural areas eventually moved into some of the residences they left behind. The circumstances of these Palestinians, who became citizens of the State of Israel, were not the same as those of refugees elsewhere. Nevertheless, as *internal* refugees, they, too, found themselves in unfamiliar surroundings and were divorced from their traditional social and economic institutional connections. Also, in the cities, they were un-able to acquire legal title to the dwellings they occupied, which were considered absentee property and held in trust by the state.[27] Finally, and perhaps most im-portant, they were completely cut off from their families and countrymen who resided in states with which Israel remained at war. This situation contributed further to their alienation and, more generally, constituted another important di-mension of the overall fragmentation and dispersion of the Palestinian people.

The extent to which Palestinian psychology is marked by the events of this period cannot be overemphasized. Palestinian sources provide graphic and ago-nized descriptions of the exodus from Palestine, of the dispersion of the Palestin-ian people, and of the conditions of refugee life. Some of these reports draw con-clusions which are challenged by observers sympathetic to Israel, especially those bearing on the reasons that Palestinians left their homes in 1948 and 1949. While the Arabs contend that most Palestinians were driven out by a deliberate cam-paign of Jewish terror, Israeli spokesmen insist that the vast majority left of their own volition. Nevertheless, putting this important issue aside temporarily, one can readily find in Palestinian writings poignant accounts of those experiences which shaped, and continue to shape, Palestinian political consciousness. The quotations below are from a social survey carried out in 1973 among Palestinians who left the Galilee when Israel was established and were residing in Lebanon or Syria at the time of the study. The researcher is a Palestinian social scientist, and each quotation reports the experience of a different individual from a different Galilee village.

> It was too hazardous for us to stay in the village orchards. My family and I, accompanied by my younger brother, Mau'ad Muhammad Mau'ad, and his family, decided to go north to the village of Mash-had. . . . We were so panicked, confused and worried . . . we lost our way to Mash-had. We walked all night, and at dawn we ended up at the Deir Hanna–'Arraba road, to the north. We met the other villagers there, and together we left north to the villages of Er Rama, El Buqei'a, Suhmata, Deir el Qasi, and then to Bint Jubail in Lebanon.[28]

> My sixty-five year old grandmother, Fatimah 'Abid, remained in the village ten days after it had fallen to the Jews. She said that after the armored cars shelled the village, the Jews entered the village and shelled more houses. . . . A few Jewish soldiers stayed in the houses they did not destroy. The elderly took refuge in Umm Khanazir's cave. At night, she would go with Zuhrah al-Nuf to the village and bring food to the others. During the day, every time she tried to leave the cave, the Jews would stop her and force her back into it. On the night of the eleventh day, Zuhrah al-Nuf and she made their way out of the village, leaving behind the other elderly people in the cave. . . . She does not know what happened to them.[29]

> We were sure that we would return. . . . On our way to Lebanon we stopped at Beit Jann and stayed with Naif Abu Khaiya, a Druze friend of my family. We left the few things we had carried with us with him until we would return. . . . At the village of Hurfeish, we were stopped by the Jews; they searched us and decided to detain me. My mother started to cry, saying if they kept me, they would have to keep us all. They let me go. We have not to this day returned to our home; our personal belongings [left in 1948] with my father's friend, Naif Abu Khaiya, are still there.[30]

> We came to Lebanon and life was not what we expected it to be. Conditions were bad. We had nothing to live on. I became desperate, and one night I decided to leave my family and go back to the village to get some money I had buried outside my house before the Jews attacked. . . . But I never reached my village. I was caught by the Jews and put in jail.[31]

The loss of the Palestinian homeland and the dispersion of its indigenous Arab population are themes which pervade the art and literature of the Palestinian people, as well as their political writings. Even today, decades later, they remain a principal preoccupation and are subjects that generate strong and bitter emotions. Writing in the introduction to several short stories and poems by Palestinian authors, a leading American student of Palestinian affairs points out that the subject of physical and emotional separation is central to Palestinian literature. Ever since 1948, poets and novelists have focused on the longing to return from exile and to reunite the people with its homeland. This longing is expressed in images of tangible objects: olive trees, orange groves, pomegranates, grapes and stony fields. It is also expressed symbolically, most frequently with Palestine represented by the lover, father or mother from whom the writer is separated and with whom he longs to merge. A key theme is the difficulty or impossibility of becoming a complete person when one is living as an alien.[32]

In sum, 1948 was a turning point for both Zionists and Palestinians. For the former, it was the year in which age-old desires for the re-creation of a Jewish state in Palestine were finally realized. For the latter, however, it was a different kind of political and psychological watershed. The prospect of creating an independent Arab state in Palestine was lost, and the Palestinians themselves were scattered throughout the Middle East and elsewhere. Disappointment was undoubtedly intensified by the contrast between the Palestinians' own experience and the fate of other peoples residing in lands that had been colonized by European powers. The years after World War II saw growing acceptance of the principle of self-determination. Political freedom and national independence were demanded by Third World peoples, and though a few anticolonial wars remained to be fought, in Algeria, Indochina, and southern Africa, the legitimacy of these demands was increasingly recognized by the world community. Thus, like the Jews, many Arab peoples had achieved or were in the process of achieving independence and statehood. Among Palestinians, by contrast, the quest for self-determination not only remained unfulfilled, it had apparently come to an end. For the time being, at least, the Palestinians ceased even to be critical actors in the Arab-Israeli conflict. Although their cause continued to be championed by the Arab world, which remained in a state of belligerency with Israel, the conflict itself evolved into a dispute between Israel and the Arab states in the years after 1948.

The Basic Issues between 1948 and 1967

The signing of the armistice agreements between Israel and its Arab neighbors did not bring peace to the Middle East. The Arabs refused to accept the political consequences of their defeat in the 1947–48 War. While Israel's military victory required them to sign agreements promising to limit their struggle to nonviolent means, they in no sense renounced their claims against the Jewish state. There would not be real and permanent peace, they insisted, until the Palestinian problem was solved. Further, the outcome of the war brought psychological as well as political developments that propelled the conflict forward. As convincingly argued by Fred J. Khouri, both sides became more intransigent. "On the one hand, the extent of their victory caused such a great increase in the pride and self-confidence of the Israelis that they became less willing to make those concessions which were needed if there was to be any hope of reconciliation with the Arabs. On the other, the extent of the Arab defeat brought about such a blow to the pride and self-reliance of the Arabs that they became more opposed than ever to acknowledging the existence of an enemy who had so deeply humiliated them." [33] It is in the latter context that Gamal Abdul Nasser, who became president of Egypt in 1954, once referred to Israel's victory as a "smear on the entire Arab nation," adding that "the shame brought on by the battle of 1948" could not be forgotten. [34]

Two interrelated issues dominated thinking about the Arab-Israeli conflict after 1948, and they remained central preoccupations for the next nineteen years. They were at the top of the agenda for international peacemaking efforts and were of paramount concern in serious debates and discussions about the conflict. They were also central themes in the political rhetoric and propaganda churned out by various antagonists. Further, although the territorial and political status quo changed after 1967, modifying the way in which the Arab-Israeli conflict was perceived and addressed, these issues remain relevant to present-day efforts to understand and solve the lingering dispute. The first issue concerns the legitimacy of the State of Israel, and the second concerns the fate of the Palestinian refugees. In the years after 1948, the latter issue embraced arguments both about the causes of the Palestinian exodus and about the way to solve the refugee problem.

The Legitimacy of Israel

The Arab position was and for the most part remains that the establishment of a Jewish state in Palestine was an illegal and illegitimate act. Even most of the many Arabs who today are prepared to recognize and make peace with Israel continue to believe that this is the case; they may accept Israel as a reality and acknowledge that political compromise is the only way out of the present impasse, and hence is in their own best interest, but they nonetheless remain firmly convinced that a historical injustice was done to the indigenous inhabitants of Palestine by the founding of the Jewish state.

An image often presented by Arab spokesmen is that of an occupied house. They point out that Palestine had been an almost entirely Arab country for hundreds of years, until organized migrations of Jews began to arrive in the late nineteenth century. The Jews entered and then occupied the house of the Palestinians, as it were, against the will of the latter and with the aid of European colonial powers. Later, the Arab analysis continues, Zionist leaders sought to portray themselves as reasonable people who were open to compromise, who were willing to accept the partition of Palestine. The Arabs, by contrast, were called intransigent and even fanatic because they would not agree to a division of the country. But how, the Arabs ask, can someone pretend that he is reasonable because he is content to steal only half of another person's house, or label as fanatic the owner of the house who resists this theft? Palestinian representatives had used this image and called Palestine their "house" as early as 1937, when they rejected both the partition proposals of the Peel Commission and the argument that the indigenous population of Palestine had benefited from the Zionist presence: "You say we are better off; you say my house has been enriched by the strangers who have entered it. But it is *my* house, and I did not invite the strangers in, or ask them to enrich it, and I do not care how poor or bare it is if only I am master in it."[35]

There are numerous documents in which Palestinians and other Arabs express their view that the creation of Israel was illegal and that the state itself is therefore illegitimate. The two that follow, issued more than twenty years apart, are generally representative. The first is from a statement that Palestinian officials gave to the Anglo-American Committee of Inquiry in 1946. The second is from a 1967 book by Sami Hadawi, a Jerusalem-born Palestinian who at the time headed the Institute for Palestine Studies in Beirut.

> The whole Arab people is unalterably opposed to the attempt to impose Jewish immigration and settlement upon it, and ultimately to establish a Jewish state in Palestine. Its opposition is based primarily upon right. The Arabs of Palestine are descendants of the indigenous inhabitants of the country, who have been in occupation of it since the beginning of history; they cannot agree that it is right to subject an indigenous population against its will to alien immigration, whose claim is based upon a historical connection which ceased effectively many centuries ago. . . . The idea of partition and the establishment of a Jewish state in a part of Palestine is inadmissible for the same reasons of principle as the idea of establishing a Jewish state in the whole of the country.[36]

> The fundamental reason for Arab opposition to Zionism is based on the fact that the Muslim and Christian [Arab] inhabitants of the country could not be expected to yield to an ideology which sought to wrest—as events later proved—their homeland from them. The Arabs rejected absolutely and unanimously any attempt to destroy the Arab character of Palestine. They still do. The Arabs claim the right of a population to determine the fate of the country which they had occupied throughout history. To them it is obvious that this right of immemorial possession is inalienable; and that it could not be overruled either by the circumstances that Palestine had been governed by the Ottomans for 400 years, or that Britain had conquered the land during World War I, or that a "Jewish State" has been established in part of it by brute force.[37]

A forceful statement of the Arab case for Palestine, carefully reasoned and documented, is to be found in Edward Said's *The Question of Palestine*. Said, a prominent scholar and leading Palestinian intellectual, not only affirms that the right to self-determination in Palestine should be exercised by the indigenous population of the country, he also insists that Zionist leaders understood from the beginning that their own platform was incompatible with the exercise of this right, and that as a result they took actions which made Zionism the natural enemy of the Palestinian people. "Both in theory and in practice," he writes, the effectiveness of the Zionists "lies in how they Judaize territory coterminously with de-Arabizing it."[38] Among the many statements presented in support of his analysis of Zionism is an 1895 passage from Herzl's *Diaries*: "We shall have to spirit the penniless population across the border by procuring employment for it in the transit countries, while denying it any employment in our own country. Both the expropriation and the removal of the poor must be carried out discreetly and circumspectly."[39] Elsewhere he quotes from a 1940 statement by Joseph Weitz, the head of the Jewish National Fund:

> It must be clear that there is no room for both peoples in this country. . . . If the Arabs leave the country, it will be broad and wide-open for us. And if the Arabs stay, the country will remain narrow and miserable. . . . The only solution is Eretz Israel, or at least Western Eretz Israel, without Arabs. There is no room for compromise on this point. . . . There is no way besides transferring the Arabs from here to the neighboring countries, to transfer them all; except maybe for Bethlehem, Nazareth and Old Jerusalem, we must not leave a single village, not a single tribe. . . . For that purpose we'll find money, and a lot of money. And only with such a transfer will the country be able to absorb millions of our brothers, and the Jewish question shall be solved, once and for all. There is no other way out.[40]

Consistent with the essential nature of Zionism, both in theory and in practice, Jewish political rights have been achieved at the expense of the Palestinian people, and Israel's creation is therefore a triumph of "settler colonialism," meaning the substitution by force of arms of an alien people for an indigenous one. Yet, like other colonized peoples, the Palestinians cannot reasonably be expected to acquiesce in their own political extinction. This is the foundation of the Arab case against Israel. Palestine of right belongs to its indigenous Arab population, to the Palestinians, whose presence in their native land was undisturbed for centuries prior to the emergence of modern political Zionism and who, but for the creation of Israel, would have joined other Arab and Third World peoples in the exercise of self-determination and the attainment of national independence. In the years after 1948, these points were made repeatedly by Arab spokesmen who refused to accept the legitimacy of Israel and who insisted that there could be no peace until the inalienable rights of the Palestinians were restored. A good illustration is provided by the following passages from a booklet published in Beirut in 1965 by Fayez Sayegh, a leading Palestinian intellectual and political activist:

Many have been the self-appointed counselors of "realism," urging upon Palestinians acknowledgment of the new status quo in Palestine and acceptance of their exile "in good grace." . . . But the people which had remained for thirty years undaunted by the combined power of British Imperialism and Zionist Colonialism . . . knew very well how to resist those siren-calls.

The Zionist settler-state, therefore, has remained a usurper, lacking even the semblance of legitimacy—because the people of Palestine has remained loyal to its heritage and faithful to its rights. . . .

And the people of Palestine knows that the pathway to the future is the liberation of its homeland.[41]

Zionists see things differently, of course, and the foundation of their argument on behalf of Israel is that Jews, too, have legitimate and inalienable rights in Palestine. This point is stated categorically, though with hyperbole, in Gervasi's 1967 book *The Case for Israel*, which features an introduction by Abba Eban, at the time Israeli foreign minister.

Palestine, the Arabs claim, is theirs by right of prior possession. It is an argument which many decent people rightly concerned with the humanitarian aspects of the problem of the Palestine refugees accept as gospel. It happens to be false, or, at best, only partly true. . . . *There is no greater falsehood in history than that the Arabs are the sole, legitimate heirs to the lands of an Israel that once was Palestine and before that was Canaan* [emphasis added].[42]

Supporters of Israel maintain that Jewish rights are derived, in the first instance, from a historical connection with the land of Palestine that was established almost four thousand years ago, when God told Abraham, patriarch of the ancient Hebrews, that he and his descendants would have all of the land of Canaan "for an everlasting possession" (Genesis, XVII, 8). Thereafter, at least from the time of Moses, Canaan was the center of Jewish life until the Hebrews were driven into exile by the Romans in the first century. Finally, Jews preserved an unbroken affective tie to *Eretz Yisrael* during the centuries of their "exile," when only a handful of individuals remained to give Palestine a *physical* Jewish presence.[43] They regularly and ritually affirmed their remembrance of the Holy Land, praying that the day of their return might not be distant. In their own eyes, at least, the experience of the Biblical era and the salience of premodern, religious Zionism give Jews a claim in Palestine which is at least equal, and perhaps superior, to that of the country's Arab inhabitants.

Further, to accept that legitimate Jewish rights in Palestine flow from this historical record does not require belief in a Divine plan. While true believers, Jewish and other, may argue that Palestine should and does belong to the Jews because that is God's will, most supporters of Israel make a different argument. They contend that the *facts* of Jewish history, regardless of whether or not one believes this history to be Divinely guided, give Jews their legitimate rights. It is a fact, Zionists insist, that the Jews have been involved with Palestine for the

whole of their collective history, that even when few Jews lived there they retained a firm conviction that *Eretz Yisrael* was *their* country, and that for centuries this conviction guided and inspired Jewish attitudes and behavior. Jewish
national rights, therefore, cannot be exercised but in Palestine; and since the Jewish people, like all peoples, has an inalienable right to self-determination, its
claims in Palestine are fully valid and legitimate.

A frequent anti-Zionist response is that the Jews are not a people or a nation
at all, but rather a religious community. As expressed by Hadawi in a typical
passage, "Many people make the simple mistake in believing that Judaism and
Zionism are the same. This is not so. *Judaism* is a religion of universal values.
Jews are regarded as members of a religious fellowship, who have no national or
ethnic ties with their co-religionists of other lands. In the countries of their citizenship, Jews, like Christians and Moslems, have national ties with their fellow
citizens, regardless of their religious faith."[44]

Zionists and most Jews reject such arguments, however, calling them self-
serving half-truths. Zionism insists that the Jews are a religious *and* a national
community, that Jews outside Israel are loyal citizens of the countries in which
they reside *and* that they nonetheless possess a sense of Jewish peoplehood. These
and other national characteristics of the Jewish people are established beyond any
doubt by the objective historical record, supporters of Israel maintain. Further,
their acceptance is required by those who claim commitment to the principle of
self-determination, for certainly it is the Jews themselves, not others, and especially not their political adversaries, who must take the lead in defining the identity of the Jewish people.

This constellation of arguments is forcefully and consistently advanced by
Zionists in support of their insistence upon the legitimacy of Israel. The tone is
sometimes poetic and sometimes militant, but the point is always the same: the
Jews maintained an unbroken connection with the land of their forefathers, and
so they may justly lay claim to it today. Abraham Heschel, for example, writes
that Jerusalem "is the city of David, of the prophets of Israel—not of Titus, the
Roman Emperor; or of Godfrey of Bouillon, the Crusader; or of Saladin. The
descendants of Titus, of Godfrey, of Saladin never fasted, never mourned for her.
Jerusalem was not a part of their soul, their grief, an answer to their suffering."
More generally, he continues, "Throughout the ages we said No to all the conquerors of Palestine. We said No before God and man emphatically, daily. We
objected to their occupations, we rejected their claims, we deepened our attachment, knowing that the occupation by the conquerors was a passing adventure,
while our attachment to the land was an eternal link." Thus, in other words,
"The Jewish people has never ceased to assert its right, its title, to the land of
Israel. This continuous, uninterrupted insistence, an intimate ingredient of Jewish
consciousness, is at the core of Jewish history."[45]

As expressed by another Zionist author, "The consciousness of the Jew that

Palestine was his country . . . was a pervasive and inextricable element in the very warp and woof of his daily life. Jewish prayers, Jewish literature are saturated with the love and longing for and the sense of belonging to Palestine." Therefore, making explicit the conclusion to be drawn, "If ever a right has been maintained by unrelenting insistence on the claim, it was the Jewish right to Palestine."[46] Numerous additional quotations of this sort could be presented. There are count-less books, articles, and speeches in which supporters of Israel maintain that the Jews' historic and continuous attachment to the land of their ancestors estab-lishes the right of the Jewish people to pursue its national destiny in Palestine, which is also *Eretz Yisrael*, the Land of Israel.

The claims and counterclaims advanced after 1948 do not focus only on the history and political rights of Jews and Palestinian Arabs. The debate about Is-rael's legitimacy has also been carried out from the perspective of international law. Making the case against Israel, Mallison, for example, concludes after re-viewing the Balfour Declaration and later international agreements that they do not give juridical authority to Zionist claims to "constitute the 'Jewish people' nationality entity and to confer membership in it." One reason, in his judgment, is that "the safeguard clauses in these agreements are so unequivocal that they must be construed as prohibiting the claim." Another is that Israel exceeds the limits of international law by attempting to confer "nationality" on Jews who do not reside within its borders.[47] The report of a seminar of Arab jurists, held in Algiers in 1967, adds another legal argument to the case against Israel. Citing a resolution adopted by the League of Nations, and also Article 38, paragraph 3, of the Statute of the International Court of Justice, the report declares Israel's creation to be illegal because "the obligation to withhold recognition from new States falls upon all members of the international community when the creation of these new States is accompanied by manifest irregularities or by acts of vio-lence."[48]

Supporters of Israel again rebut these claims. Responding to the arguments of Mallison, for example, Halpern insists that, contrary to Mallison's accusation, Zionists neither intend nor claim to "constitute a 'Jewish people' nationality en-tity" and, accordingly, Israel does not in any way confer "nationality" on Jews who are citizens of other states. Halpern contends that not one of the documents cited by Mallison is properly interpreted. Discussing the Balfour Declaration by way of illustration, he reports that Zionists supported the inclusion of a safe-guard clause to the effect that the creation of a Jewish national home in Palestine was without prejudice to "the rights and political status enjoyed in any other country by such Jews who are fully contented with their existing nationality and citizenship." Indeed, he adds, the direct antecedent of this clause was a Zionist statement expressing respect for "the position or loyalty of the very large part of the Jewish people who have identified themselves thoroughly with the citizenship of the countries in which they live."[49]

The major legal focus of debates about Israel's legitimacy is the UN Partition Resolution of 1947. Opponents of Israel argue that (1) the UN probably exceeded its legal competence in adopting the resolution, and (2) even if it did not, it is illegal for Israel to exercise sovereignty over those parts of Palestine which the UN allocated to the proposed Arab state. In the first connection, one basis for questioning the competence of the UN is that in 1947 it had few African and Asian members and was in fact dominated by the United States and European powers. Thus, as the Arab jurists' seminar pointed out, the Partition Resolution "was not approved by the immense majority of Asian and African countries and certainly not by any country geographically close to Palestine."[50] Rather, it is often asserted, the Western world sought to salve its conscience for the treatment of Jews during World War II by paying its own debt to the Jews with the land of the Palestinians. Another argument, more legalistic in character, is that the General Assembly in 1947 acted contrary to the provisions of various articles of the Charter, an opinion which is supported by some non-Arab legal authorities.[51]

With respect to the second contention, Arab scholars cite various international legal conventions and treaties which specify that a conqueror "does not in any way acquire sovereign rights in the occupied territory but exercises [only] a temporary right of administration on a trustee basis."[52] Thus, it is argued, Israel's post-1948 borders cannot be recognized, since the Jewish state violated international law when it incorporated the territory it captured during the 1947–48 War.

One of the most thorough Israeli responses to these arguments is provided by Nathan Feinberg, professor emeritus of international law and relations of the Hebrew University. Feinberg contends, for example, that the assertion that the General Assembly exceeded its powers in 1947 is invalid since the International Court of Justice unanimously held, in its Advisory Opinion on Southwest Africa, that "competence to determine and modify the international status . . . [of a mandated territory] rests with the Mandatory, acting with the consent of the United Nations Assembly."[53] He notes that other legal authorities also conclude that the Court has recognized the Assembly's power to modify the international status of a mandated territory.[54]

Feinberg also addresses claims related to Israeli control of territory allocated by the UN for a Palestinian Arab state. He argues that the 1949 Armistice agreements, which Arab governments signed and pledged to respect, acknowledge the rights and claims in this area of each party to the conflict, that is to say of Israel as well as the Arabs of Palestine; and they also stipulate that the agreed armistice lines cannot be modified except in the context of a permanent peace settlement to which all parties, again including Israel, give consent.[55] A similar conclusion is advanced by Julius Stone, who deals in his brief with the Partition Resolution of 1947, rather than the armistice agreements of 1949. Citing various legal documents and authorities, he argues that since the Partition Resolution and plan "were prevented by Arab rejection and armed aggression from entering into legal operation, [they] could not therefore carry any legal effects binding upon Israel."[56] However, reinforcing arguments in support of the UN's competence to act in the matter, Stone adds that the resolution would indeed have been binding upon Israel under international law had it not been prevented from taking effect.

Causes of the Palestinian Exodus

All of these political and legal arguments about the legitimacy of Israel were advanced with regularity in the debates and exchanges that became common in the years after 1948. In addition, however, a second issue, closely linked to the first, was also central to the dispute between Israel and the Arabs during this period. This was the issue of the Palestinian refugees, with respect to which two specific questions were debated. First, why did hundreds of thousands of Palestinian civilians leave their homes during and immediately after the 1947–48 War? Second, what should be done to solve the refugee problem? It was the contention of the Arabs that the Palestinians had been deliberately driven out of their homes and, accordingly, that they possessed the right to return to their communities of origin. The plight of the refugees was therefore yet another part of the Arab case against Israel. It offered an additional basis for Arab insistence that Israel's creation had been illegal, and for the Arabs' refusal to make peace with the Jewish state.

With regard to the causes of the Palestinian exodus, it is the Arab position that large numbers of refugees were driven out of their homes by a deliberate Zionist campaign of intimidation and terror. The instance of such terror cited most frequently is that of Deir Yassin, a deplorable episode which most Israeli spokesmen acknowledge with regret, but which many also insist was an isolated and unrepresentative incident. Deir Yassin was a Palestinian village about five miles west of Jerusalem, and on April 9, 1948, forces of the Irgun and Stern Group entered the village and massacred 254 defenseless civilians, including about 100 women and children. Many of the bodies were then mutilated and thrown into a well.

Opponents of Israel, as well as some Israeli scholars and pro-Zionist authors, assert that the motivation for the Deir Yassin massacre was to incite panic among the Palestinian population, and thereby to frighten many Arabs into leaving their homes. They also note, in support of this contention, that the inhabitants of Deir Yassin were taking no part in the war, the village being one of several that had sought to avoid cooperation with Arab forces and signed a nonaggression pact with its Jewish neighbors.[57] According to one account, the Irgun command sent out a congratulatory message after the massacre, stating, "As in Deir Yassin, so everywhere. . . . Oh Lord, Oh Lord, you have chosen us for the conquest."[58] In addition, the leader of the Irgun, Menachem Begin, subsequently boasted about the contribution of the massacre to other military operations. He writes that as Jewish forces made their way through the city of Haifa, for example, "the Arabs began to flee in panic, shouting 'Deir Yassin.' "[59]

Israeli sources differ among themselves about the Deir Yassin episode. Some contend that the village was a legitimate military target, since it was blocking the road to Jerusalem at a time when Jewish sections of the city were under siege. Further, these sources claim that before the battle a sound truck had urged the village to surrender, and that residents who did so were escorted to safety without incident. Finally, those who defend the operation insist that Deir Yassin harbored armed Palestinian and Iraqi soldiers, that the village was taken only after fierce house-to-house combat, and that Jewish forces sustained a number of casualties in the fighting.[60] At least partial support for some of these claims is also provided by more objective analysts. For example, Sykes reports that Arab armed forces may have seized the normally neutral village and made plans to use it for an attack upon Jerusalem.[61] In addition, according to Morris, "the weight of the evidence suggests that the dissident troops did not go in[to Deir Yassin] with the intention of committing a massacre but lost their heads during the battle, which they found unexpectedly tough-going."[62]

At the same time, most pro-Israeli sources acknowledge and deplore the fact that unarmed Arab civilians were murdered at Deir Yassin. Further, they agree with critics who insist that it makes no difference whether or not a legitimate military operation preceded the massacre. Some suggest that Irgun and Sternist leaders may have been seeking to avenge a massacre of Jews that had recently occurred in Haifa. Again, however, they add that this in no sense justifies what took place. Nevertheless, along with these acknowledgments and condemnations, supporters of Israel stress that the atrocities were carried out not by regular forces of the Hagana but rather by extremist elements operating outside the command structure of the Jewish Agency. Indeed, they note, the Agency, the Hagana, and the Chief Rabbinate issued strong public condemnations of the episode as soon as it became known, and Ben Gurion himself sent King Abdullah a telegram expressing apologies and regret.

The major significance of Deir Yassin lies not in a dispute about what really happened or about whether there could be any justification for the massacre, it lies in bitter disagreement about whether or not there was a systematic and calculated Zionist campaign of terror designed to drive Palestinians from the area that became the State of Israel. The Arabs and their supporters insist that there was indeed such a campaign. They point to Zionist statements and the reports of foreign observers, as well as other incidents that terrified the civilian Arab population. John Glubb, for example, quotes a Zionist official as stating in December 1947, in response to a question about whether there would be many

Arabs in Israel, "Oh no! That will be fixed. A few calculated massacres will soon get rid of them."[63] Among the other incidents to which Arab sources point is a massacre in Nasr al-Din, a small village adjacent to Tiberias. Irregular Jewish forces entered the village on April 10 and, according to Arab accounts, destroyed all its houses, killed seven of its inhabitants, including several women and children, and expelled the remainder of its ninety citizens.[64] Glubb reports that in the wake of the massacre at Deir Yassin, and also at Nasr al-Din, members of the Jewish underground roamed the Arab quarters of Jerusalem and told residents through loudspeakers, "The Jericho road is still open. . . . Fly from Jerusalem before you are killed."[65]

Arab sources insist that the attempt to provoke flight was not limited to the Jewish underground. On the contrary, they charge that mainstream Zionist institutions were informed and involved. For example, they allege that the attack on Deir Yassin, although perhaps not the massacre, was carried out with the approval of senior Hagana officials.[66] Even more important, they point out that the Zionist General Council ratified an agreement for cooperation between the Hagana and the Irgun shortly after the Deir Yassin episode.[67] As expressed by one analyst who sets forth the Arab claim, "Although the dirty job [at Deir Yassin] was done by the Irgun, the official-Zionist Hagana knew of the planned attack; immediately afterward the Irgun, instead of being pilloried in horror by the Zionist movement, was welcomed by the Hagana into a new pact of collaboration. . . . Of course the Irgun was able to show the way . . . but the Hagana leaders learned fast."[68]

Arab and other sources also point to attacks against civilians carried out by the Hagana itself. For example, there was a massacre of Arab soldiers and their women by mainstream Jewish forces in Jerusalem at the end of April, following a successful Hagana attack on the Katamon quarter of the city.[69] Atrocities perpetrated by mainstream Zionist forces are also reported in the interviews with Palestinian refugees from the Galilee that Nazzal conducted in Lebanon and Syria. Respondents describe the exodus from twenty-five different communities, and incidents of terror are alleged in three of the accounts. One is summarized below. In a number of additional cases, one of which is also summarized below, the use of violence was limited but a deliberate attempt to intimidate the local population is nonetheless described. The following passages are taken from the longer accounts supplied by Nazzal's respondents. They refer, in order, to the villages of Ain al-Zeitoun and Er-Rama. It should be noted that in both cases, as well as the others where the use of terror is alleged, the villages fell after local armed resistance was overcome by Israeli forces.

Yusif Ahmad Hajjar suddenly stood up, addressing the soldiers. "Our village has been captured, we have surrendered, and we expect to be treated hu-

manely." . . . A Palmach soldier slapped Yusif in the face and ordered his soldiers to choose thirty-seven teen-aged boys at random, ordering the rest of the
villagers to move into the storage rooms of the mosque. . . . I do not know what
happened to our young men. We have been away from 'Ein ez-Zeitun now for
almost twenty-five years, and I still don't know what happened to them.[70]

The people of Er-Rama were ordered to assemble at the center of the village.
A Jewish soldier stood on top of a rise and addressed us. He ordered the Druze
present among us to go back to their homes. . . . Then he ordered the rest of
us to leave to Lebanon, threatening death to those taking any of their belong-
ings with them.[71]

Although acts of terrorism and deliberate intimidation are described in only
a minority of the accounts collected by Nazzal, most descriptions of the Palestinian exodus testify vividly to the fear that gripped the Arab population of Galilee. Villagers sometimes fled as soon as Jewish forces approached—and sometimes even before, upon hearing that neighboring villages had fallen. In other
instances, armed resistance was mounted but soon proved ineffectual, after which
men and their families retreated to the north. In a large number of these cases,
whether justified or not, residents feared the consequences of remaining in their
homes and therefore fled in panic. As described in the report of a refugee from
Kukeikat, for example, "We were awakened by the loudest noise we had ever
heard, shells exploding and artillery fire . . . the whole village was in
panic . . . women were screaming, children were crying. . . . Most of the villagers
began to flee with their pajamas on."[72] A few of Nazzal's respondents refer specifically to the Deir Yassin massacre as one of the sources of their fear, as do a
number of other accounts of the Palestinian exodus. Geoffrey Furlonge writes in
his biography of Musa Alami, for example, that following the news of Deir Yassin "fear gripped the countryside and the trickle of refugees became a flood."[73]

Arab spokesmen insist that these Palestinian fears did not result from the
disorder and confusion that occurs in any wartime situation but rather were the
products of a deliberate Zionist effort to drive Arab civilians from the territory
of the new Jewish state. Atrocities, they contend, even if limited in actual number
and scope, must therefore be understood not as individual excesses carried out
in the heat of battle but as part of a larger psychological and political campaign
directed against the Palestinian population. On the one hand, the use of violence
against unarmed or disarmed Arabs was tolerated, even as it was deplored by
some with evident sincerity, because it contributed to the attainment of a desired
political objective. On the other, the existence of such violence, whether premeditated or not, created a climate of fear in which it was possible to employ other
methods to stimulate the Palestinian exodus.

Many analysts place particular emphasis on the Zionists' use of psychological warfare. Edgar O'Ballance states, for example, that "it was deliberate Jewish
policy to encourage the Arabs to quit their homes, and they used psychological

warfare extensively in urging them to do so."[74] The same point is made by Rony Gabbay, who writes that "Jewish encouragement to the Arabs to flee took different forms. It was more often conducted by psychological methods than by open ejection."[75] An illustration of this kind of psychological warfare is given by Furlonge in connection with the town of Ramleh, where the Arab mayor is said to have received a secret message of warning from a prominent Jew with whom he was friendly. The message declared that "on the Israeli side things had got out of hand and the terrorists were in power," and then added that transport would be provided for those wishing safe conduct to Arab-controlled areas.[76]

Many of the actions and policies about which Arabs complain were associated with *Tochnit Dalet*, or Plan D, which was formulated by Hagana leaders in March 1948 as a military program for the defense of the new Jewish state. In the judgment of critics, however, Plan D had political as well as military significance, and some accordingly describe it as a blueprint for preventing the emergence of a Palestinian state and expelling the Palestinian population. They point out, as does one prominent Israeli critic, that Plan D provided for the capture by Jewish forces of areas in the Galilee and the Tel Aviv–Jerusalem corridor that had been allocated to the Arab state, and that it also dealt in detail with "the expulsion over the borders of the local Arab population in the event of opposition to our attacks."[77] Therefore, this Israeli analyst continues, "the aim of the plan was annexation—the destruction of Arab villages was to be followed by the establishment of Jewish villages in their place."[78] Plan D was not put into effect officially until Israel declared its independence on May 14, although some writers report that it guided the Hagana from the time it was formulated two months earlier.

The character and significance of Plan D are disputed by many Israeli sources, including some who are among its critics. Morris, for example, who has carried out extensive and systematic research on Israel's role in fostering the Palestinian exodus, emphasizes that the plan "was not a political blueprint for the expulsion of Palestinians: it was governed by military considerations and was geared to achieving military ends,"[79] the most important of which was defense of the territory assigned to the Jewish state. "It was not," he repeats elsewhere, "a grand plan of expulsion as Arab propagandists . . . have depicted it."[80] Nevertheless, even if it was formulated as a purely military strategy, the effect of Plan D was to legitimize and even encourage many of the actions that caused Palestinians to abandon their homes. As Morris himself reports,

> Given the nature of the war and the admixture of the two populations, securing the interior of the Jewish State for the impending battle along its borders in practice meant the depopulation and destruction of villages that hosted hostile local militia and irregular forces. . . . Plan D provided for the conquest and permanent occupation, or leveling, of Arab villages and towns. It instructed that the Arab villages should be surrounded and searched for weapons and ir-

regulars. In the event of resistance, the armed forces in the village should be destroyed and the inhabitants should be expelled from the State.[81]

Morris elsewhere states that the plan "allowed the expulsion of hostile or potentially hostile Arab villages (and 'potentially hostile' was, indeed, open to a very liberal interpretation)."[82]

Documentation offered in support of the Arab contention that Zionist actions and policies bear primary responsibility for the Palestinian exodus include many accounts by Israeli and Jewish sources. For example, discussing the May 1948 campaign in Safad, one Israeli author reports that the commander of Zionist forces in the north, Yigal Allon, admitted some years later that "it was not our intention to prevent the flight of the Arab population."[83] Another account deals with the fall of Haifa two weeks earlier, in late April. According to a 1949 report by Arthur Koestler, a Zionist sympathizer, Jewish armed forces used loudspeaker vans and Arabic-language radio broadcasts to urge Arab residents to accept safe conduct out of the city and into Arab territory, and then "hinted at terrible consequences" if the offer was disregarded.[84] Approximately 70,000 Arabs eventually fled from Haifa, accounting for roughly 10 percent of the total Palestinian exodus. Still another account describes the fall of Lydda and Ramleh in July 1948 to Israeli forces under the command of Moshe Dayan. Refugees from the two towns constituted another 10 percent of the total Palestinian exodus, and some of the conditions of their departure are reported in the following passage from a 1960 book by Jon and David Kimche:

> [Israeli forces] drove at full speed into Lydda, shooting up the town and creating confusion and a degree of terror among the population. . . . Its Arab population of 30,000 either fled or were herded on the road to Ramallah. The next day Ramleh also surrendered and its Arab population suffered the same fate. Both towns were sacked by the victorious Israelis.[85]

Writing of his country's policy more generally, an Israeli historian wrote in 1972 that "the operation in Deir Yassin was in line with dozens of attacks carried out at that time by the *Hagana* and *Palmach*, in the course of which houses full of elderly people, women and children were blown up."[86] The following statement by Yigal Allon describes some of the psychological warfare used by the Israeli forces to encourage the exodus from Arab villages in the Huleh Valley. The 1953 statement has been translated and published by a Palestinian scholar in support of the general argument made by Arab spokesmen.

> I gathered all of the Jewish Mukhtars, who have contact with Arabs in different villages, and asked them to whisper in the ears of some Arabs, that a great Jewish reinforcement has arrived in Galilee and that it is going to burn all the villages of the Huleh [Valley]. They should suggest to these Arabs as their friends, to escape while there is still time. And the rumor spread in all the areas of the Huleh that it is time to flee. The flight numbered myriads.[87]

In recent years, with the opening of the Zionist archives from the period of the 1947–48 War, Israeli analysts have provided much more extensive information about the actions of Jewish leaders and fighting forces. The most thorough research to date on the causes of the Palestinian exodus has been carried out by Morris, who makes extensive use of Israeli state and private papers, as well as archival material from Britain and the United States. One of his conclusions is that during certain critical periods, particularly in April-May and again in October, "the 'atrocity' factor played a major role in certain areas of the country in encouraging flight."[88] Another is that several of the most important expulsions of the war were undertaken in response to direct decisions by Israeli leaders. This was particularly clear in the case of Lydda and Ramleh, large Arab towns lying outside the territory assigned to the Jewish state by the United Nations. Morris reports that Ben Gurion, Allon, Yitzhak Rabin, and several others met while Lydda and Ramleh were under attack by the Hagana in July, and that when Allon asked what should be done with the towns' approximately 70,000 Arabs, "Ben Gurion made a dismissive, energetic gesture with his hand and said: 'Expel them (*garesh otam*).' "[89]

Morris presents a wealth of additional documentation and sheds light on the many aspects of Israeli behavior during this period toward the Arab population of Palestine. For example, he discusses a June 1948 report of the Israeli Defense Forces Intelligence Service which sought to assess the reasons that roughly 400,000 Palestinians left their homes between December 1, 1947, and June 1, 1948. The report concludes, "It is possible to say that at least 55 percent of the total of the exodus was caused by our [Hagana/IDF] operations and by their influence." The Intelligence Service document further concludes that the activities of dissident Jewish organizations directly caused an additional 15 percent of the emigration.[90]

In another study, Morris reports on the activities of Yosef Weitz, head of the Jewish National Fund. Weitz, according to Morris, "helped facilitate the exodus of Arab communities from various localities," and he also worked to influence national policy so as to ensure that Palestinian refugees would not return to their homes. In pursuing these objectives, he established two "transfer committees," one of which was semi-official and active during May and June of 1948, and the other of which had official status and operated from August to November of that year. Morris summarizes not only Weitz's efforts but the opposition he encountered among some Zionist officials. He notes, however, that Ben Gurion was sympathetic to the JNF leader's program, and he concludes more generally that "Weitz played a major role as executive, advisor and lobbyist in the emigration of Palestine's Arabs, in the takeover of Arab lands and villages, and in the crystallization of opinion and policy in the *Yishuv* against allowing a return of the refugees."[91]

The correspondence and diaries of Zionist leaders are among the many other documents examined in Morris's research, and some of these shed additional light on the degree to which there was support for Weitz and his proposals. For example, Israeli Foreign Minister Moshe Shertok, who later changed his name to Moshe Sharett, wrote to Weizmann in August 1948 in order to express his determination "to explore all possibilities of getting rid, once and for all, of the huge Arab minority which originally threatened us." Shertok stated, "What can be achieved during this period of storm and stress will be unattainable once conditions stabilize," and he added in this connection, referring to the transfer committee, "A group of people from among our senior officers has already started working on the study of resettlement possibilities [for the refugees] in other lands."[92]

Among the other Israeli authors who provide important information about Zionist attitudes and behavior at this time is Tom Segev, a veteran journalist whose powerful and controversial 1986 book became a best-seller in Israel. Drawing upon the minutes of cabinet meetings and the personal diaries of political leaders, Segev states that "tens of thousands of Arabs remained in their homes—only to be driven out by the Israeli army."[93] Segev also states that "reports of atrocities committed by Israeli soldiers during the course of the conquest, and also afterward, preoccupied the government in several of its sessions. The information which reached the ministers shocked them." Ben Gurion, for example, who for several months had been receiving reports of atrocities, including acts of "slaughter" and rape, declared in November, "I am shocked by the deeds that have reached my ears." Segev calls the following statement by Aharon Cizling, the minister of agriculture, one of the most severe ever made in an Israeli cabinet meeting.

> I've received a letter on the subject. I must say that I have known what things have been like for some time and I have raised the issue several times already here. However, after reading this letter I couldn't sleep all night. I felt the things that were going on were hurting my soul, the soul of my family and all of us here. I could not imagine where we came from or to where we are going. . . . I often disagreed when the term Nazi was applied to the British. I wouldn't like to use the term, even though the British committed Nazi crimes. But now Jews too have behaved like Nazis and my entire being is shaken. . . . Obviously we have to conceal these actions from the public, and I agree that we should not even reveal that we're investigating them. But they must be investigated.[94]

There is, again, another side to the story, and supporters of Israel usually begin their arguments with a reminder that there would have been no war in 1947–48, and hence no refugee problem at all, had the Arabs not rejected the UN Partition Resolution. As stated in a 1958 speech by Abba Eban, at the time Israel's representative to the UN and later its foreign minister, "Once you determine the responsibility for that war, you have determined the responsibility for the refugee problem." Eban also quotes from the 1948 statement of an official of the Higher Arab Committee, who is reported to have said: "The fact there are these refugees is the direct consequence of the action of the Arab states in opposing partition and the Jewish state."[95]

Israeli spokesmen also assert that Zionist behavior during the war, regardless of why it started, was not characterized by a deliberate campaign to drive Palestinians from the country. Zionist and some neutral analysts insist in this connection that charges about widespread Jewish atrocities have been wildly exaggerated by Arab propagandists. They acknowledge that there were indeed some regrettable incidents for which irregular and even regular Jewish forces bear responsibility. But they add that most of the allegations about "Zionist terrorism" are either false or grotesquely inflated, and they point out that some of the evidence for this conclusion comes from observers who do not hesitate to criticize Israel on other grounds. Bernadotte, for example, a UN official with whom the Jews bitterly disagreed on other matters and who can hardly be accused of having a pro-Israel bias, reported to the UN in September 1948 that accusations of Jewish terrorism were "greatly exaggerated."[96] Thus, most supporters of Israel are adamant that the excesses which did occur, however regrettable, in no way add up to an orchestrated campaign of intimidation and terror.

An equally important related contention is that most of the Israeli actions involving violence against Palestinian civilians were carried out by local commanders acting on their own initiative, and that there was consequently no grand Zionist design for the expulsion of Palestine's Arabs. This claim is at least partially supported by recent research, moreover, most notably by Morris's important study which documents many specific abuses by Jewish forces but nonetheless concludes that there was no explicit or official "expulsion policy."[97] Morris reports that until April 1948, by which time the first wave of refugees had departed, "there was no *Yishuv* plan or policy to expel the Arab inhabitants of Palestine, either from the area destined for Jewish statehood or those lying outside it."[98] Further, the continuing Arab exodus of the next two months "caught the *Yishuv* leadership, including the authors of Plan D, by surprise."[99] And even during the fighting in July that brought Arab departures from Lydda, Ramleh, and other areas, "there was no Cabinet or IDF General Staff–level decision to expel. . . . [There was in fact] an explicit IDF General Staff order to all units and corps to avoid destruction of Arab villages and expulsion of Arab communities without prior authorization by the Defense Minister."[100] Thus, despite his documentation of Zionist actions that contributed to the Palestinian exodus, Morris's general conclusion is that "the Palestinian refugee problem was born of war, not by design, Jewish or Arab. It was largely a by-product of Arab and Jewish fears and of the protracted, bitter fighting that characterized the first Israeli-Arab war."[101]

In discussing the issue of atrocities, Israelis often assert that the use of violence against civilians was actually more common among the Arabs during the

1947–48 War, and that instances of so-called Jewish terrorism were consequently limited in relative as well as absolute terms. Those who make the case for Israel note that Arab spokesmen in 1948 threatened to carry out massacres against the Jews. They also point out that these words were in some instances accompanied by deeds. As a result, such analyses conclude, it was in reality the Arabs who waged a campaign of psychological warfare and who both threatened and practiced terrorism. Eban cites the following statement by the secretary-general of the Arab League as an example of Arab rhetoric and, presumably, of Arab intentions: "This will be a war of extermination. It will be a momentous massacre to be spoken of like the Mongolian massacre and the Crusades."[102] An example of an act which gave tangible expression to such threats was the ambush of a Jewish convoy traveling to Hadassah Hospital and the Hebrew University, both in Jerusalem, under the protecting colors of the Red Cross. Seventy-seven Jewish doctors, nurses, teachers, and students were killed in the attack, which took place on April 12. Another was the massacre a month later of prisoners at Kfar Etzion, a Jewish community east of Jerusalem. According to one Israeli account, the Arab Legion's conquest of the area was followed by the arrival of Arab villagers, "who massacred [Jewish] prisoners, both men and women being lined up and shot in cold blood: three men and a girl, who managed to escape under cover of darkness, were all who survived from the entire population to tell the tale."[103]

Although some sources suggest that these attacks were an attempt to take revenge for the slaughter at Deir Yassin, there were atrocities committed by Arabs even before the Deir Yassin episode. A vivid account is given by Uri Avnery, an Israeli journalist and politician who is highly critical of Zionist policy on most accounts. Avnery, who was himself a soldier in 1948, writes that in the early stages of the fighting "Arab irregulars and primitive villagers . . . killed and mutilated every Hebrew who fell into their hands. We all saw the pictures of the severed heads of our comrades paraded through the alleys of the old city of Jerusalem. . . . No one can quite understand what happened later on without realizing the impact of these pictures on the small Hebrew community."[104] A related consideration is that such episodes may also have had a psychological impact on the Palestinians and heightened their own fears of Jewish terrorism, since Jews would naturally be expected to take revenge for real or threatened Arab atrocities. As Sykes suggests, "The terror was all the more since many Palestine Arabs had a bad conscience about atrocity toward the Jews."[105] This point is also emphasized by Morris, whose account includes the statement of an English sergeant about the surrender of Jaffa: "The Arabs were frightened to death when they imagined to themselves that the Jews would do to them half of what they would have done to the Jews were the situations reversed."[106]

Returning to the question of the Palestinian exodus, Israeli sources emphasize that the fear and panic which caused many Arabs to abandon their homes were to a large extent the result of rumors or exaggerated reports about Zionist atrocities that were circulated by the Arabs themselves, rather than by the Jews. This point is made by Sykes, among others, who adds that such behavior was highly counterproductive from the Arab point of view.

> The Arab radio-propaganda dwelt on atrocity stories and exaggerated them. Unknowingly, the Arab propagandists did the work of the Irgun and the Sternists for them. The aim was to inflame men with hatred of the Jews; the effect was to fill them with terror of the Jews. . . . The Arab readiness to take flight . . . became greater every day after the news of Deir Yassin had been first broadcast. It was repeated with inflated figures and invented vileness in excess of the vileness of the deed itself.[107]

A similar assessment is made by Furlonge, who writes from a viewpoint sympathetic to the Arabs. He notes that news of Israeli atrocities was disseminated "by word of mouth and through Arab radios." He states also that "Arab governments, by trying to raise world indignation against the Israelis by spreading word of their misdeeds, caused panic amongst the unwarlike Palestine peasantry."[108] This can be seen in the testimony of one of the refugees interviewed by Nazzal, for example. "We heard about the massacre of Deir Yassin," he recalled. "Arab newspapers and radios said a great deal. It encouraged us to arm ourselves, but it also scared us."[109]

The conclusion to be drawn, Israeli spokesmen reiterate, is that there was no grand Zionist design for the expulsion of Palestine's Arabs. Actions involving violence against Arab civilians were far less extensive than charged by Israel's enemies; those abuses which did occur, while serious, were in many cases carried out by local commanders acting on personal initiative; and the panic sown among Palestinians by exaggerated accounts of "Zionist terrorism" was the result of Arab propaganda much more than a Jewish campaign of psychological warfare. As noted above, the analyses of Morris, reflecting research rather than propaganda, are among the most serious attempts to demonstrate that there was no Israeli master plan for expelling the Arabs from Palestine. Morris repeats this conclusion in a recent exchange with critics, carried out, interestingly, in the pages of the *Journal of Palestine Studies*, and he supports his argument with an account of Israel's capture of the upper and central Galilee pocket in October 1948. The operation had been thoroughly planned weeks in advance, and upon its completion "the IDF had full control of the territory, the fog of battle thoroughly covered the whole area, and Israel/the IDF could have done . . . whatever it wanted with impunity." Accordingly, Morris asks, "Why is it, then—if a policy of expulsion was in place and being implemented—that more than half the pocket's [60,000 Arab] inhabitants, many of them Muslims, were left in place?"[110]

Supporters of Israel often add to their denials of a systematic expulsion policy the claim that Jews in some instances sought to prevent the Palestinian exodus. Zionists point out that Israel's very Declaration of Independence calls upon the Arabs to remain in the country. "Even amidst the violent attacks launched against us for months past," the document declares, "we call upon the sons of the Arab people dwelling in Israel to keep the peace and to play their part in building the state on the basis of full and equal citizenship and due representation in all its institutions." Zionists argue that they had every reason to work for the realization of these ideals. It was in Israel's interest to demonstrate that the United Nations had proposed a workable as well as a fair compromise, and that a Jewish state could be established without preventing Palestinians from realizing their own aspirations for independence and statehood. This was particularly important in light of the Arab world's rejection of partition and Israel's need for international recognition.

The case of Haifa is cited most frequently to support the claim that Jews sought to persuade Arabs to remain in their communities of origin. Three weeks before independence was declared, the Jewish Workers' Council of Haifa issued a proclamation urging the Arabs of the city not to flee. It stated, in part, "Do not fear . . . and do not bring upon yourself tragedy by unnecessary evacuation and self-imposed burdens. . . . In this city, yours and ours, Haifa, the gates are open for work, for life, and for peace for you and your family."[111] In addition, once Arabs began to flee, the city's Jewish mayor, Shabtai Levy, made a personal appeal to Palestinian authorities, urging them to call for a halt to the exodus. They refused, however, and Levy then went into the streets and implored the departing Arabs to remain, again without success.[112] An independent account of these events mentioned by pro-Israeli sources is a British police report which declares that "every effort is being made by the Jews to persuade the Arab populace to stay and carry on with their normal lives, to get their shops and businesses open and to be assured that their lives and interests will be safe."[113] Another account is an article in the *Economist*, from October 2, 1948. It states that "Jewish authorities . . . urged all Arabs to remain in Haifa and guaranteed them protection and security."[114]

Although they applaud the efforts of the city's mayor and a number of other local Zionist officials, pro-Arab sources insist that events in Haifa are not indicative of Zionist policy elsewhere. They also point out, correctly, that supporters of Israel tend to generalize from the case of Haifa without presenting comparable documentation pertaining to other areas. Nevertheless, there are at least a few other instances in which Jews sought to prevent the Palestinian flight. During the early stages of the war, Jews sometimes distributed leaflets calling upon Palestinians to remain in their homes. Indeed, according to a credible Israeli observer, the Hagana in some cases risked the lives of its soldiers to distribute these leaflets to Arab villagers.[115] A few of Nazzal's respondents also give accounts that support Israeli claims. According to a refugee from Hittin, for example, "We were not threatened by our Jewish neighbors at Kfar Hittin. As early as November . . . they approached us and assured us they did not want a war with us."[116] Another, from El Khalisa, reports that the Jews distributed leaflets saying they wanted peace and asking villagers to remain in their homes, although he adds that most Arabs thought this to be a trick.

Having rejected the charge that the refugee problem was created by a deliberate Zionist campaign of terror and psychological warfare, supporters of Israel usually advance two arguments when pressed to explain the Palestinian exodus. First, they contend that many Palestinians were simply uprooted by the wartime situation and the general climate of insecurity, and that the war for Israel's independence was no different from most other wars in that it produced a large number of refugees. Dislocations were made all the more likely, and perhaps inevitable, they add, by residence patterns which involved the close proximity and even intermingling of the two warring communities. That the unplanned and uncontrolled ravages of war caused many Palestinians to leave their homes does not, by itself, demonstrate the absence of a Zionist campaign to intensify the Arabs' flight. Nevertheless, it is difficult to deny that the fighting alone made a significant contribution to the refugee problem, and this appears to have been an especially important factor during the first months of the war.

The second Israeli argument is that many Palestinians departed in response to ill-conceived appeals by Arab leaders, who are alleged to have urged Palestinians to abandon their communities in order to facilitate a military campaign against the Jews. According to this analysis, such calls were disseminated in radio broadcasts and in oral and written declarations by both local Arab leaders and officials in neighboring states, most of whom are said to have promised that Palestinian civilians would soon return to their homes behind victorious Arab armies. Thus, while the Palestinian exodus may have involved more than the effects of war on a civilian population, Israeli spokesmen contend, again, that much of the responsibility lies with the Arabs themselves.

A recent Israeli account argues that Arab evacuation appeals were especially critical during the first months of the war, from the Partition Resolution through March or early April 1948. Roughly 75,000 Palestinians became refugees during this period, and most of this number were middle-and upper-class families who constituted a large part of the country's Arab elite. Among them were local officials and civil servants, businessmen and landowners, and doctors, lawyers, teachers, and other professionals. The departure of this leadership class was particularly important in that it sapped morale, rent the fabric of Palestinian society, and set the scene for an expanding exodus in the months ahead. As stated by Shabtai Teveth, who makes the Israeli case, this initial wave of refugees "set the flight in train, cast its pattern." But the origins of this flight, Teveth goes on to insist, are to be found in the orders of local Palestinian commanders and, by early March, in formal instructions from the Higher Arab Committee. He states, writing generally, that this early exodus "was all the work of [Arab] instruction, whether by personal example, by word of mouth or in writing, or even better, by the quickest telegraph of all, rumor." [117]

Supporters of Israel cite various accounts to buttress their claim that Palestinians were instructed to abandon their homes by local and external Arab leaders. Teveth, for example, cites an Israeli intelligence report from April 1948 which records rumors that the Arab Higher Committee in Jerusalem had ordered evacuations in several localities. According to the report, "Arab residents are advised to flee Palestine as soon as possible, and after its fall into the hands of the Arab governments, they will be returned as victors."[118] Another account is by an American correspondent who reported from Palestine in 1948. He writes that "the Arab exodus, initially at least, was encouraged by many Arab leaders, such as Hajj Amin al-Husayni. . . . They viewed the first wave of Arab setbacks as merely transitory. Let the Palestinian Arabs flee into neighboring countries. It would serve to arouse the other Arab peoples to greater effort, and when the Arab invasion struck, the Palestinians could return to their homes and be compensated with the property of Jews driven into the sea."[119] Still another account, cited by a number of Zionist sources, is by the Research Group for European Migration Problems. It states that the Arab League exhorted people to seek temporary shelter in neighboring Arab countries as early as the first months of 1948, telling them they would receive a share of abandoned Jewish property upon their return.[120]

Israeli sources assert that these evacuation instructions are acknowledged by many Arab writers. As an illustration, one Israeli leader quotes a statement from the memoirs of Khaled al-Azm, who was prime minister of Syria in 1948 and 1949: "Since 1948 we have been demanding the return of the refugees . . . but we ourselves are the ones who encouraged them to leave."[121] One of the interviews conducted by Nazzal also presents information consistent with this analysis. Villagers from El Khalisa, in the region of Safad, were apparently advised by the Arab Liberation Army to take their families to Lebanon for a week or so. They were told that the ALA was planning an attack to recapture Safad and that the Arab countries would be sending planes to bomb Jewish positions. Nazzal's informant adds that the villagers heeded this advice but decided only to move to a nearby village.[122] The following are two additional statements taken from Arab sources, one from the secretary of the Arab League and the other from the Arab Higher Committee.

> The wholesale exodus was due partly to the belief of the Arabs, encouraged by the boasting of the unrealistic Arab press and the irresponsible utterances of some of the Arab leaders that it would be only a matter of weeks before the Jews were defeated by the armies of the Arab states.[123]

> Some of the Arab leaders and their ministries in Arab capitals . . . declared that they welcomed the immigration of Palestinian Arabs into the Arab countries until they saved Palestine.[124]

Arab sources, a number of neutral observers, and even some serious Israeli analysts vigorously reject the assertion that appeals by Arab leaders played an important role in the Palestinian exodus. Erskine B. Childers, for example, insists that there is absolutely no truth to the allegation that Arab radio broadcasts urged Palestinians to depart from their communities of origin. After a careful review of transcripts prepared by the BBC, he reports that "there was not a single order, or appeal, or suggestion about evacuation from Palestine from any Arab radio station, inside or outside of Palestine, in 1948." [125] This is also the conclusion of Benny Morris, who strongly disputes the allegations advanced by some supporters of Israel. Morris reports that he has been unable to find any evidence of radio or other calls appealing to the Palestinian masses to leave, either by the Arab Higher Committee inside Palestine or by the Arab states. [126] He notes that Arab leaders did not always condemn the Palestinian flight, and to the extent that silence can be construed as consent, it might be argued that the Arabs bear some responsibility. This is very different from the kind of responsibility alleged by Israel, however. Simha Flapan, another Israeli analyst, also rejects the contention of an Arab "order from above" leading to the Palestinian exodus. He states that although this "proved to be particularly good propaganda for many years, despite its improbability . . . the recent publication of thousands of documents in the state and Zionist archives, as well as Ben Gurion's war diaries, show that there is no evidence to support Israeli claims." [127]

Arab and other sources also challenge the validity of many of the reports and statements presented in support of the Israeli case. These sources make the following assertions. First, the few genuine Arab calls for an exodus that can be cited are *ad hoc*, isolated, and unrepresentative. Moreover, they are usually a response to, rather than a cause of, the panic that took hold in many Palestinian communities. Second, passages quoted by Zionists have often been taken out of context and had their meaning distorted. The Childers study reviews a number of these quotations, including some reproduced above, and presents omitted passages which place major responsibility for the exodus on Zionist action. [128] Third, the Israeli case often utilizes Arab statements made after 1948. This point is emphasized by Sykes, an even-handed observer who in other instances provides information supportive of Israeli claims. Sykes notes that after the war "Arab journalists and broadcasters asserted on several occasions that the exodus was a planned Arab maneuver." While such assertions were probably a mixture of boasting and rationalization, the important point is that they were made after the refugees had left. Nevertheless, according to Sykes, "they gave Zionist propagandists their cue." [129]

Not only is the allegation that Arab leaders called upon the Palestinians to flee untrue, the rejoinder continues, it is in fact the case that many Arab spokesmen actively urged the Palestinians to remain in their communities of origin. Again according to the important study by Childers, "There is repeated monitored record of Arab appeals, even flat orders, to the civilians of Palestine to stay put." One example given by Childers is an April 1948 broadcast from Damascus, in which Palestinians were told to stay in their homes and continue at their jobs. Another is a broadcast three weeks later by the Arab Liberation Radio, which complained that "certain elements and Jewish agents are spreading defeatist news to create chaos and panic among the peaceful population. Some cowards are deserting their houses, villages or cities."[130] Childers adds that "even Jewish broadcasts [in Hebrew] mentioned such Arab appeals to stay put. Zionist newspapers in Palestine reported the same; none so much as hinted [in 1948] at any Arab evacuation orders." The same conclusion is put forward by Flapan and Morris. Flapan provides additional examples of Arab statements and actions which sought to prevent Palestinian flight.[131] Morris, citing IDF intelligence sources, discusses Arab attempts "to halt the flow out of Palestine, specially of army-age males . . . [and instances where] National Committees and local irregulars' commanders tried to fight the exodus, even setting up people's courts to try offenders and threatening confiscation of the property of departees." Morris also states that the magnitude of the refugee problem "quickly persuaded the Arab states—primarily Transjordan—that it was best to halt the flood tide."[132]

Overall, it seems necessary to conclude that there is no single cause of the Palestinian refugee problem and, accordingly, that there is a mixture of fact and propaganda in both Arab and Israeli arguments. The factors that led Palestinian civilians to leave their homes varied from one location to another. Even more, they varied from one phase of the war to the next. During the early months of the conflict, from the Partition Resolution through March or early April of 1948, it appears that Palestinians fled primarily in response to the fighting itself, although it is possible that encouragement from local Arab leaders was a contributing factor in some instances. Most of the Palestinians who left during this period were middle-and upper-class residents of major towns, including Haifa, Acre, Jaffa, Jerusalem, and several others. Possessing the resources to support themselves while away from home, and almost certainly believing that their absence would be temporary, most were apparently motivated neither by Zionist intimidation nor by Arab appeals, but rather by a straightforward desire to distance themselves from wartime perils. They preferred, and were able, to sit out the war in Beirut, Amman, or Cairo, or at least in the comparative security of less central Palestinian cities, including Nablus, Hebron, and Gaza. Departures during this period are thus largely attributable to the danger and uncertainty of the situation, rather than to any Zionist or Arab design.

The refugee story became more complex during the next few months, in the spring of 1948. Atrocities committed by Jewish forces, including the massacre at Deir Yassin in April, contributed greatly to Arab fears and were an important stimulus to the intensifying Palestinian exodus. On the other hand, such episodes were relatively few in number, they did not represent official Zionist policy, and accounts of them were often embellished and then disseminated by the Arabs themselves. The destruction of Palestinian communities and the departure of their inhabitants during this phase of the conflict were also a consequence of Zionist military offensives. The first goal of these operations was to block the advance of armies from neighboring Arab states. Yet IDF campaigns were guided to at least some extent by Plan D, which provided for the expulsion of civilian Arab populations in areas deemed to have strategic significance. On the other hand, again, at least in the case of Haifa, some local Jewish officials tried at this time to persuade Arabs to remain in their homes.

By the summer of 1948, Israeli leaders seem to have become more consciously aware of the benefits that would result from the departure of the Palestinians and, accordingly, at least some of them began to modify their policy. Expulsion of the Arabs was still not a consistent and coordinated policy. It was not the result of formal deliberations within the cabinet or other political bodies of the new Jewish state. Also, as in the case of Nazareth, the victorious Israelis sometimes permitted Palestinians who had surrendered but not fled to remain in their homes and guaranteed their safety. Nevertheless, decisions and actions by mainstream Zionist institutions and leaders, occasionally at the highest level, were now sometimes taken with the explicit intent of driving Palestinians from their towns and villages. The July campaign to expel the Arabs of Lydda and Ramleh illustrates this particularly clearly.

By the concluding stages of the conflict, in the fall of 1948, there appears to have been a more widespread and explicit understanding that it was in Israel's interest to facilitate the Arabs' departure. Thus, military operations in the south of the country, conducted in October and November under the command of Yigal Allon, left almost no Palestinian communities in place behind the advancing Israeli lines. This was not always the case, however, even at this late date. For example, Arab villages in the Galilee conquered in late October were left intact. In addition, more generally, the Palestinian exodus had by this time assumed its own dynamic, and strong-arm tactics were often unnecessary, the mere arrival of Jewish forces sometimes being sufficient to provoke Arab flight. In the face of incomplete evidence and conflicting claims, these are the most plausible conclusions to be drawn about the causes of the Palestinian refugee problem.

Solutions to the Refugee Problem

Equally bitter, though less elaborate, were Arab and Israeli arguments after 1948 about how the refugee problem should be solved. Consistent with their general insistence upon Palestinian rights, the Arabs argued that repatriation was the only acceptable solution. The refugees should be permitted to return to the homes from which they had been illegally expelled. The Israelis rejected this, however. They observed that many of the Palestinians' homes had been destroyed during the war and, much more fundamentally, they insisted that the State of

Israel could not realistically readmit hundreds of thousands of persons desiring its destruction. The Israelis therefore proposed that refugees be compensated for lost property and resettled in neighboring Arab countries. They also pointed out that several hundred thousand Jews living in Arab countries had migrated to Israel after 1948, and so there had actually been an exchange of populations between Israel and the Arab world. They added that war often brought on such exchanges, and that the Palestinian refugee problem was therefore not unique.

The Israeli case begins with the assertion that by demanding repatriation, the Arabs were knowingly and explicitly calling for the destruction of the Jewish state. Their insistence on the refugees' right of return was expressed in conjunction with a continuing refusal to recognize the State of Israel. Furthermore, they appear to have proceeded on the same assumption as the Jews in this matter, that repatriation would be a step toward the liquidation of the Zionist state. Thus, as early as July 1948, during the truce that followed the "ten-days war," the Israeli foreign minister sent the United Nations a note declaring that the return of thousands of Palestinian Arabs would "gravely prejudice our rights and position." [133] In the months and years that followed, Zionist leaders consistently reaffirmed that the return of the refugees was incompatible with the survival of the State of Israel, repeating that this was well understood by Israel's enemies. It is in this connection that an American Zionist quoted President Nasser of Egypt as saying in 1961, "If the Arabs return to Israel, Israel will cease to exist." [134]

In defense of their alternative, resettlement, supporters of Israel made a number of points. First, they argued that in every recent case, except that of the Palestinians, refugee problems resulting from war had been resolved within the countries to which the displaced population had fled. This point was stressed in a 1958 address to the UN by Abba Eban, for example, who supported his case with a Carnegie Endowment study which concluded that "no large scale refugee problem has even been solved by repatriation." [135] Next, the Israelis contended that the refugee status of the Palestinians was being deliberately maintained by the governments of the countries in which they now resided. With the exception of Jordan, no country had granted citizenship to the Palestinians, for example. The reason for this, in the Israeli view, was that Arab leaders sought to keep the issue of Palestine alive in order to deflect the attention of their citizens from domestic economic and political problems, including the corruption and authoritarianism of the regimes by which they were governed. Finally, supporters of Israel argued that religious, linguistic, and cultural affinities between the Palestinians and other Arabs were such that the refugees could be easily absorbed by neighboring Arab states. As expressed in a 1958 U.S. congressional study that recommended resettlement, integration would not be difficult because the Palestinians were in a "familiar environment." [136]

Supporters of Israel have frequently sought to buttress the case for Palestinian resettlement by emphasizing that roughly 450,000 Jewish "refugees" from the Arab world were resettled in Israel in the decade after 1948. More than half of these individuals arrived in the Jewish state between 1949 and 1951. As stated by Abba Eban, "These refugees from Arab lands left their homes, property and jobs behind. Their standards of physique and nutrition were in many cases pathetically low. They have had to undergo processes of adaptation to a social, linguistic and national ethos far removed from any that they had known before. Thus, integration in this case has been far more arduous than it would be for Arab refugees in Arab lands." Nevertheless, the newcomers were effectively absorbed by Israel, despite the country's small size and limited resources; and in the judgment of Eban and other Israeli spokesmen, the refusal of Arab governments to bring about an integration of the refugees in their own huge lands was all the more indefensible in view of what the Jewish state had achieved in the area of immigrant absorption and refugee resettlement.

While the arrival of these Jews from the Arab world played a critical role in shaping the character and evolution of Israeli society after 1948, the argument that their dislocation was comparable to that of the Palestinians is controversial and problematic. Israeli propagandists stressed the difficulties that confronted Jews in Arab lands and suggested that they had been forced to leave their homes. As one Zionist writer states of the Jews in Yemen, for example, "Though they were not expelled after 1948, the danger to their safety was so blatant that the exodus of the whole community was organized from Israel in one large scale operation in 1949, with the passive consent of Yemen authorities." Of the situation in Iraq, he writes, "The range of repression of the Jews, growing in intensity from 1948, compares only with the worst excesses of the Nazi regime."[137] In fact, however, such statements give a distorted impression of the complex and varied situation of the Jews in Arab countries and of the diverse reasons that led most to leave.

Scholarly Israeli and Jewish sources, as well as others, offer a more realistic appraisal. Segre, for example, states that while Jews in the Arab world often had a feeling of insecurity that was strong enough to set them on the path toward Israel, "no one can compare the Arab violence against the Jews in the Islamic world with the horrors of [even] the mildest Russian pogroms."[138] Comparisons with Nazi Germany are therefore totally irresponsible. Further, though Jewish insecurity was both real and justified in some Arab countries, it was far less significant in others, and, in any event, it was only one of the reasons that Jews chose to leave the Arab world at this time. Immigration to Israel was sometimes the result of a desire to participate in the building of the Jewish state. This motivation was most intense in the more traditional and religious Jewish communities, often located in rural areas. In these cases, and undoubtedly some others, it was the attraction of Israel, rather than a desire to flee persecution, that led Jews to leave the Arab countries in which they lived.

Socioeconomic factors may have been an even more important consideration.

In most Arab countries, Jews had for many years been better educated and more prosperous than the Muslim majority, but in many instances the attainment of independence brought the prospect of a decline in their prosperity and economic privileges, and this, in turn, led some to consider the possibility of seeking their future elsewhere. In Iraq, for example, again according to Segre, "the Jewish community—one of the oldest in the world—suffered heavily in social and political status first from the disappearance of Turkish, and afterward British rule, two administrations which had leaned heavily on the Jewish minority" and provided Jews with many opportunities and privileges. The same was the case in Egypt and the countries of the Maghreb, where colonial powers had often deliberately discriminated in favor of the indigenous Jewish population. Moreover, not only did an uncertain economic future lead some Jews to think about leaving, but the economic advantages and favoritism Jews had enjoyed in the past created resentment among the majority, a consideration that may also have encouraged Jewish emigration but which had nothing to do with the Arab-Jewish conflict in Palestine.

In some instances, cultural factors provided yet another stimulus to Jewish emigration. During the colonial period, many Jews in Morocco, Egypt, Iraq, and other Arab countries sent their sons and daughters to European schools, where they studied in English or French and began to identify with the civilization of those who ruled the states in which they lived. Indigenous Jewish communities were also to some extent marginalized by the Islamic orientation of the independence movements that emerged in some countries. All of this increased the social and cultural distance between the Jewish minority and the Arab majority and led many of the former to seek relocation when the colonial era ended. In fact, many of these Jews emigrated to Europe rather than to Israel.[139]

Finally, post-1948 Zionist efforts to promote Jewish emigration appear to have been an important factor in at least a few instances. The most clear-cut case is that of Iraq, from which more than 120,000 Jews departed during 1950 and 1951 under the terms of an agreement concluded between Israeli agents and the government in Baghdad. Although undisputed evidence is not currently available, it appears that the Israelis bribed senior Iraqi officials in order to secure the agreement, which not only gave Jews the right to leave but also permitted Zionists to organize the evacuation. It is also possible that the American government pressed Baghdad to accept this arrangement, presumably at Israel's urging. Finally, a number of bomb attacks were directed at Iraqi Jewish targets during 1950 and 1951, while the evacuation was taking place, and Iraqi authorities and some foreign observers charge that these attacks were the work of an underground Zionist network seeking to frighten local Jews into leaving for Israel.[140] Although Israeli spokesmen deny these allegations, they have received some support from recent archival research. In any event, when Zionist involvement is added to the socioeconomic, cultural, and other factors that helped to stimulate

Jewish departures, it becomes clear that it is highly oversimplified, and in many ways misleading, to equate the flight of Palestine's Arabs with the immigration to Israel of Jews from Arab countries.

Much of the international community in 1948 and 1949 was inclined to favor repatriation of the Palestinian refugees. Many observers were unmoved by Israel's arguments in favor of resettlement, not only those that emphasized an exchange of Arab and Jewish populations but others as well. In addition, there was broad agreement that the return of the Palestinians was a necessary ingredient in any peace plan. Such was the foundation of an accord that Bernadotte sought to hammer out between Israeli authorities and the Arab League in August 1948, for example. Bernadotte called upon the former to accept the principle of repatriation and asked the latter to recognize the Jewish state in return. For a brief moment, it looked as though agreement might be reached. In the end, however, the chances for a breakthrough disappeared because the Israelis insisted on peace talks prior to the return of any Palestinians, while the league stipulated that repatriation was a precondition for negotiations with Israel.

The United Nations proceeded along similar lines when it formally took up the refugee question at the end of the year. General Assembly Resolution 194 (III), adopted in December, created a UN Conciliation Commission for Palestine. It also affirmed that the Palestinians should be accorded the right of return. Specifically, Paragraph 11 of the resolution resolved "that the refugees wishing to return to their homes and live at peace with their neighbors should be permitted to do so at the earliest practicable date, and that compensation should be paid for the property of those not choosing to return." The United States government also urged repatriation on the Israelis during this period. In May 1949, President Truman sent Ben Gurion a note in which he expressed strong disappointment at Israel's continuing refusal to make any concessions on the refugee issue. He expressed the American view that such concessions were essential if the conflict was to be resolved. He also indicated that the U.S. might be forced to reconsider its positive attitude toward the Jewish state if the government in Jerusalem did not display greater flexibility.[141]

In responding to specific Israeli arguments against repatriation, UN representatives and others made it clear that the Jewish state was not being asked to repatriate a hostile Arab population. It was being asked only to accept the return of those Palestinians willing to live in peace with their Jewish neighbors. This condition was expressly stipulated by UN Resolution 194 (III), they pointed out, and machinery set up to implement the resolution would certainly provide for the screening of returning refugees in order to make sure that their intentions were indeed peaceful. UN officials also declared that the Palestinians remained attached to their communities of origin, thereby calling into question the Israeli claim that affinities between Palestinians and other Arabs were such that the refugees could be resettled in neighboring states with little or no loss of their national identity. UNRWA and the Conciliation Commission reported in the summer of 1950, for example, that Palestinian refugees "invariably displayed an extremely emotional and deep-seated desire to return to their homeland."[142] A later UNRWA report also disputed the claim that Arab governments had deliberately kept the Palestinians in impoverished conditions in order to serve their own political ends. The report stated that over the years these governments had "shown a deep concern for the well-being of the refugees . . . [and had] given substantial direct help to the refugee community in the form of education, health, administrative and other services."[143]

Nevertheless, Israel persisted in its opposition to repatriation. Its spokesmen questioned the objectivity of UN reports cited by those calling for the Palestinians' return. More fundamentally, the Israeli government maintained, as it had from the outset, that the refugee problem, like the larger conflict of which it was a part, derived from the consistent refusal of the Arabs to acknowledge that the Jewish people had legitimate rights in Palestine and to endorse the concepts of partition and territorial compromise. Therefore, any attempt to deal with the refugee problem and bring peace to the area had to begin with Arab recognition of the Jewish state. Israelis and other Zionists added that continuing Arab hostility also led them to question the validity of the supposed safeguards contained in Paragraph 11 of UN Resolution 194 (III). Ben Gurion made this point directly to the Conciliation Commission in 1949, saying that "so long as the Arab States refused to make peace . . . Israel could not fully rely upon the declarations that Arab refugees might make concerning their intention to live in peace with their neighbors."

A related issue raised by the Israelis was whether most refugees could make an informed and independent decision should they be asked to choose between repatriation and resettlement, as presumably they would be called upon to do under the UN resolution. First, many refugees probably had little idea of what life would be like inside Israel. In many cases, their homes had been destroyed or taken over by others. More generally, even if they could go back to the homes they had abandoned, Palestinians desiring repatriation would need to understand the implications of being part of an Arab minority in the modern Jewish state.[144] Second, many refugees might be influenced in their decisions by external pressures. Heavy pressure could be exerted by Arab officials and host governments, both in their dealings with individual refugee communities and by creating obstacles to resettlement in order to make the alternative of repatriation appear more attractive. International observers often acknowledged that there was some validity to these Israeli concerns but usually argued in response that steps could be taken to insulate the refugees from political pressures and to see that they were properly informed about the options available to them. One later plan, for instance, proposed that private interviews be conducted with the refugees.[145]

On the other hand, many observers also found validity in the response of the

Arabs, namely that Israel would not consider large-scale repatriation under any circumstances and was itself taking dramatic action to limit the refugees' options. The Arabs charged in this connection that many Palestinian villages had been destroyed almost as soon as their inhabitants left, and more generally that it was the policy of the government to obliterate the Palestinian presence. As early as June 1948, Ben Gurion told the Israeli cabinet that "no Arab refugee should be admitted back,"[146] and an American journalist on the scene at this time reported that the government was actively working to build a consensus against repatriation among the Israeli public.[147] One recent account that sets out to provide additional documentation in support of these Arab contentions quotes the following 1948 entries from the published diary of Yosef Weitz, the head of the JNF. The first entry summarizes a conversation between Weitz and the Israeli foreign minister, and the second describes Weitz's own visit to an abandoned Arab village.[148]

> Should we do something so as to transform the exodus of the Arabs from the country into a fact, so that they return no more? His answer: he blesses any initiative in this matter. His opinion is also that we must act in such a way as to transform the exodus of the Arabs into an established fact.
>
> I went to visit the village of Mu'ar. Three tractors are completing its destruction. I was surprised; nothing in me moved at the sight of the destruction. No regret and no hate, as though this was the way the world goes. So we want to feel good in this world, and not in some world to come. We simply want to live, and the inhabitants of those mud huts did not want us to exist here.

Against the background of these irreconcilable Arab and Israeli positions, the United States and the United Nations continued to press Israel to accept the return of at least some Palestinian refugees.[149] The United States indicated that it considered the figure of 200,000–300,000 to be reasonable, a figure that represented well under half the total refugee population but was a substantial number nonetheless. Pressure on Israel increased during the spring and summer of 1949, especially after both sides sent representatives to meet with the UN Conciliation Commission in Lausanne at the end of April. Negotiations were conducted on an episodic basis for the next five months, with one proposal considered briefly at this time calling for the Gaza Strip to be transferred to Israel so that Jerusalem would have direct responsibility for the territory's large refugee population.[150] By early summer, Israeli representatives had grudgingly agreed to accept the repatriation of a limited number of refugees as part of a family reunification plan. In August, Israeli officials offered a more inclusive repatriation package, stipulating that the number of returning Palestinians was not to exceed 100,000.[151]

In addition to placing a small upper limit on the number of refugees that would be permitted to return, the Israelis also insisted on two other conditions. First, refugees would not necessarily return to their homes but would settle in locations determined by Israel. In selecting such locations, Israel would seek to ensure that repatriated Palestinians "not come into contact with possible enemies" of the Jewish state, and also that they "fit into the general plan for the economic development of the country." Second, other displaced Palestinians would be resettled in the Arab world, and with the refugee problem thus resolved, the Arabs would agree to a general peace settlement.

The proposal to repatriate 100,000 refugees was extremely controversial in Israel. It had little public support and encountered fierce opposition in government circles as well. One Mapai Party official called it "a hair-raising proposal" and "a prescription for war." He added, "The front will adjoin every house in Israel. The refugees will not be a fifth column—they will be the first column." Ben Gurion himself stated that the decision to offer the plan had been made "against my judgment."[152] Yosef Weitz went even further. In September, as an additional precaution against the return of any Palestinians, he proposed a series of measures to drive refugees away from the border and deep into neighboring states. "They must be harassed continuously," he told Ben Gurion, who instructed him to study the matter further.[153] In view of this domestic opposition to repatriation, some observers wondered whether Israel had any real intention of permitting refugees to return, or whether, alternatively, the offer to accept 100,000 Palestinians had never been more than a tactic, made on the assumption that the Arabs would be unwilling to compromise. On the other hand, the scheme was vigorously defended by Sharett and some others, and plans proceeded to the extent that Foreign Ministry officials actually drafted the oath of allegiance that would be administered to returning Palestinians.[154]

The United Nations Conciliation Commission found Israel's proposal unsatisfactory but transmitted it unofficially to Arab representatives. The latter pointed out that it failed to respect UN Resolution 194 (III) but indicated that they were nonetheless prepared to consider it under certain conditions. Specifically, they said it would be an acceptable basis for discussing the return of refugees who had fled from those parts of Palestine which the UN had allocated for a Jewish state, if it was agreed that there should be no restrictions on the right of return for refugees from the territory originally designated for an Arab state.

While it might be argued that both sides had given some ground in this exchange, the Arabs and Israelis obviously remained far apart. Subsequent developments did little to narrow the gap between them. The Arab states most deeply involved—Egypt, Jordan, Syria, and Lebanon—gradually accepted the fact that the Palestinians were destined to become long-term residents in their societies.[155] Nevertheless, with the exception of Jordan, they took only limited steps to integrate the refugees. All, moreover, continued to affirm that the State of Israel was illegal, and that sooner or later Palestine would be restored to its rightful occupants. Israelis, for their part, insisted that they would go no further on the issue of repatriation, and that, in any event, there was nothing to talk about so long as the Arabs refused to recognize their state.

The parameters of the refugee problem thus remained unchanged in the years after 1948. In 1957 the director of UNRWA reported that "the passage of time has not improved the prospects for a settlement of the problem and the longer the refugee problem remains unsolved, the more dangerous would be the consequences for the countries of the Near East."[156] Two years later, in December 1959, the General Assembly renewed UNRWA's mandate with the sad observation that "no substantial progress has been made . . . for the reintegration of the refugees either by repatriation or resettlement and that, therefore, the situation of the refugees continues to be a matter of serious concern."[157]

Other Underlying Issues after 1948

Two other important issues were part of the Arab-Israeli conflict in the years after 1948. They did not go to the heart of Zionist and Palestinian political aspirations in quite so central a fashion as did arguments about Israel's legitimacy and the Palestinian refugee problem. Nevertheless, they were the subject of many of the charges and countercharges put forward by Israeli and Arab spokesmen during this period, and they figured prominently as well on the agenda of would-be peacemakers and others concerned with political and legal aspects of the dispute. The first of these issues concerned the status of Jerusalem. The UN had proposed in 1947 that the city be accorded international status and governed as a *corpus separatum*. In fact, however, Jerusalem was the scene of fierce fighting during the 1947–48 War and was divided into an Arab sector and an Israeli sector when hostilities finally ceased. The second issue concerned the Arab boycott against Israel, and in particular the status and use of two key waterways, the Suez Canal and the Gulf of Aqaba. The Arabs refused to allow Israeli ships to pass through these waterways, and they also took steps to prevent their use by the vessels of other nations traveling to or from the Jewish state.

Jerusalem

Jerusalem generates intense passions not only because both Israelis and Palestinians regard it as their political capital but also because the city holds deep spiritual significance for all three of the major religions that have shaped its history. To Jews, Jerusalem is the City of David. It was the center of the first and second Jewish commonwealths in Palestine; and in it the Jews built their Temple, in order to worship their God and affirm their faith that the presence of the Jewish people in the Holy Land had religious as well as earthly significance. After the destruction of the second commonwealth and the dispersion of the Jewish people in the first century C.E., Jerusalem became the most powerful and evocative symbol of the Jews' continuing tie to the Holy Land. Giving voice to their belief in the Biblical prophecy of a return to Zion, Jews in the Diaspora for centuries repeated the verse from Psalm CXXXVII: "If I forget thee, O Jerusalem, Let my right hand forget its cunning." During this entire period, and today as well, the holiest site for Jews throughout the world has been the one remaining wall of their ancient Temple. This is the Western Wall or, as it is more commonly known in English, the Wailing Wall.

Jerusalem is also the world's holiest city to Christians of all denominations. Jesus was born in Bethlehem, a few miles south of the city. He lived and preached in Jerusalem as a young man and was tried and crucified there by the Romans. Numerous Christian shrines mark the location of key events in his life. In addition to the Church of the Nativity in nearby Bethlehem, the list of Christian holy places includes the Cenacle, site of the Last Supper and the forerunner of all Christian churches; the nine Stations of the Cross, known collectively as the Via Dolorosa; and the Basilica of the Holy Sepulchre, which stands on Calvary, the site of the crucifixion.[158] Further, it was in Jerusalem that Christianity was established as an organized religion after Jesus' death, and the city has since that time remained the religion's most important spiritual center. Thousands of Christian pilgrims visit Jerusalem every year, and dozens of Christian denominations maintain orders and congregations there. Like most of the holy sites, the majority of these orders and congregations are located within the walls of the Old City. Almost all of the rest are in the Eastern, or Arab, sector of Jerusalem.

Less well known outside the Islamic world is the importance that Jerusalem holds for Muslims. Muslims call Jerusalem al-Quds, meaning "the Sanctuary." It is the third-holiest city in Islam, after Mecca and Medina. Part of Jerusalem's spiritual significance in Islam derives from that religion's relationship to Christianity and Judaism. Islam accepts the Divine messages of the Hebrew prophets and of Jesus, adding only that the revelations of God's final prophet, Muhammad, must be accepted as well. Accordingly, Islam embraces both Judaism and Christianity, just as the latter itself affirms the holiness of the Hebrew Bible but considers it incomplete. For the same reason, the holy places of Judaism and Christianity are also sacred to Muslims; indeed, during the first years after he began to reveal the word of God, Muhammad instructed his followers to turn toward Jerusalem when saying their prayers.[159]

In addition, Jerusalem is sacred to Muslims because it is the site of an important miracle that they believe took place during Muhammad's lifetime. Accompanied by the angel Gabriel and traveling on a miraculous donkey-like creature called al-Buraq, Muhammad is said to have traveled from Mecca to Jerusalem and back in a single night, having stopped en route to pray at the birthplace of Jesus in Bethlehem. Moreover, in Jerusalem Muhammad visited the former site of the Hebrew Temple, standing on a great rock located on the Temple Mount and from there ascending to heaven. This event is unique in the life of Muhammad, who is regarded only as God's messenger, and to whom supernatural qualities are not attributed by Muslims. Thus, the rock from which the prophet ascended to heaven is sacred, its holiness surpassed only by that of the Kaba in Mecca. The Umayyad caliph Abd al-Malik built a shrine over the holy rock of Jerusalem in 688–691. This shrine is known today as the Dome of the Rock or, more commonly, as the Mosque of Omar. The al-Aqsa Mosque was built a few yards away by Abd al-Malik's son. Whereas the Dome was meant to guard and glorify the holy rock, al-Aqsa was intended as a mosque for public prayer. As noted, these structures are located in the elevated enclosure where the ancient Hebrew Temple once stood, thus making the area of the Temple Mount (including the Western Wall) sacred to Muslims as well as to Jews. To the former it is known as Haram al-Sharif, "the Noble Sanctuary."[160]

Both Jews and Muslims emphasize that their attachment to the city is historic as well as religious. Zionists point out that Jews have always lived in the City of David; a small Jewish presence remained even after most Jews were forcibly evicted from Jerusalem by the Romans. Thus, the Jewish people has maintained an unbroken physical link with the ancient kingdoms of Israel. Further, in the modern period, Jews as early as 1844 were the largest religious community in the city; and by 1876 they constituted an absolute majority of the population.[161] Muslims, too, stress historic and demographic factors. They point out that Jerusalem, like the rest of Palestine, was an integral part of the Arab-Islamic world from the seventh century onward, and that it had a clear Muslim majority from the ninth to the nineteenth centuries. Muslims also sometimes observe that Jewish and Christian minorities living in Jerusalem during these centuries for the most part found Islamic rule highly tolerant.[162]

These religious and historic considerations, as well as those having to do with the confrontation between Zionism and Palestinian nationalism, led the United Nations to give particular attention to the status of Jerusalem when it addressed the Arab-Zionist conflict in 1946 and 1947. The UN Special Committee on Palestine included specific recommendations about the city in the report that it submitted to the General Assembly. Moreover, proposals about Jerusalem were contained in the minority as well as the majority report.

The minority report of the UNSCOP proposed that Palestine become independent as a single political entity. It was to be a federal state, and Jerusalem was to be its capital. The report further recommended that there be established in Jerusalem two separate municipal administrations, one Jewish and one Arab. These administrations were, of course, to cooperate in areas affecting the whole of the city, such as telephone service and the supply of water. Finally, the minority report called for the creation of a separate international jurisdiction charged with protecting and supervising the holy places in and around Jerusalem. The latter administration would operate under the general authority of the United Nations and would exercise sovereignty over the holy sites on behalf of the entire international community.

The report of the majority, which was adopted by the General Assembly on November 29, 1947, also recognized the special character of Jerusalem. In addition to recommending that Palestine be partitioned into a Jewish state and an Arab state, it proposed that Jerusalem be governed apart from both and treated as a *corpus separatum* under the supervision of the United Nations Trusteeship Council. Specifically, as provided in Part III of the Partition Resolution: "The City of Jerusalem shall be established as a *corpus separatum* under a special international regime and shall be administered by the United Nations. The Trusteeship Council shall be designated to discharge the responsibilities of the Administering Authority on behalf of the United Nations. . . . "

The Partition Resolution further specified that within five months the Trusteeship Council was to "elaborate and approve a detailed statute of the City." The statute was to contain the substance of measures pertaining, *inter alia*, to the city's governance and security and to administration of the holy places of all three religions. The Trusteeship Council began the work of drafting the required statute in February 1948 and completed the document two months later, although because of the war its formal ratification was postponed. Consistent with some of the recommendations of Part III of the Partition Resolution, the statute specified that Jerusalem should be demilitarized; that the chief executive of the city would be its governor, who was to be appointed by the Trusteeship Council and was not to be a citizen either of Jerusalem or of the Arab or the Jewish state; that under the governor would be a unicameral Legislative Council, composed of eighteen Jews, eighteen Arabs, and four others (e.g., Armenians); that the governor of Jerusalem would have responsibility not only for holy places in the city but also for those within the Arab and Jewish states; and that after ten years the residents of Jerusalem should decide by referendum whether or not they wished to modify the political status of the city.

As with other provisions of the Partition Resolution, the 1947–48 War prevented implementation of the UN proposals pertaining to Jerusalem. The city was the scene of some of the bitterest fighting of the war. Through the winter and spring of 1948, the western part of the city, inhabited by about 100,000 Jews, was under siege and, during certain periods, desperately short of food and water.[163] Nevertheless, Zionist forces managed at this time to take control of several Arab neighborhoods bordering the Jewish sector, notably Talbiya, Katamon, and Baqa. After Israel declared its independence, the Arab Legion of King Abdullah marched on Jerusalem, overrunning an Irgun force which sought to block its advance from the north through the Sheikh Jarrah quarter.

Despite the arrival of the disciplined Transjordanian army, Israel was able to retain control of the western part of the city. Several thousand locally mobilized Jewish troops defended West Jerusalem without serious challenge, and Hagana forces reached the city in June, lifting the siege and bringing reinforcements. On the other hand, the legion's presence prevented Israeli forces from expanding the area under their control and thus secured Arab hegemony in the neighborhoods of East Jerusalem, including the Old City within the walls. The legion also forced into surrender a small Hagana contingent defending the Jewish Quarter of the Old City and the roughly 2,000 orthodox Jews who lived there. Only the Hebrew University campus and Hadassah Hospital, located on Mount Scopus, remained as Israeli enclaves in the Arab-held areas. Thus, when the first truce was declared on June 11, the city was effectively divided into a Jewish sector in the west and an Arab sector in the east.

De facto division of the city did not prevent the United Nations from continuing to seek support for internationalization. A report submitted by Bernadotte shortly before his assassination urged that the city be placed under UN supervision. So, too, did General Assembly Resolution 194 (III) of December 11, 1948, which dealt with the Progress Report of the UN Mediator. The resolution instructed the Conciliation Commission to prepare detailed proposals for "a permanent international regime for the Jerusalem area which will provide for maximum local autonomy for distinctive groups consistent with the special international status of the Jerusalem area." Nevertheless, these efforts notwithstanding, the city remained divided after the war, and both Israel and Transjordan soon took steps to make the partition permanent.

The government of Israel formally declared its opposition to the establishment of an international regime for the city. In December 1949, for example, Ben Gurion told the Knesset, "We cannot lend ourselves to take part in the enforced separation of Jerusalem, which violates without need or reason the historic and natural rights of a people which dwells in Zion."[164] A few days later he reiterated the point, saying, "Jews will sacrifice themselves for Jerusalem no less than Englishmen for London." Israel did express a willingness to accept international control of the city's holy places, and in this it may have been influenced by the fact that most of the holy sites were in Arab hands at the conclusion of the fighting. In any event, beyond the status of the holy places, the Israelis were adamant that West Jerusalem was an integral part of the sovereign Jewish state, and that no other formula for governing the city would be considered.

Transjordan joined Israel in declaring to the United Nations that it would not permit an international regime to be established in Jerusalem, even though by 1949 other members of the Arab League had shifted their position and told the Conciliation Commission that they were now willing to see the city placed under UN supervision. Jordan also declared its opposition to internationalization of the holy places, most of which were located in the sector of the city it controlled, and thus went even further than Israel in rejecting the proposals of the United Nations. In 1949, the Jordanian government informed the General Assembly that "no form of institutionalization . . . would serve any purpose, as the holy places under Jordan's protection . . . were safe and secure without the necessity for a special regime."[165] The following year the Jordanian representative repeated his government's opposition to any form of international control, adding that the UN "had lost all moral justification for imposing its control over the city since it had failed to do so while Jerusalem was being menaced by destruction."[166] In the spring of 1949, a civilian administration was established in East Jerusalem, and the military rule of the Arab Legion was terminated. Then, along with the rest of the West Bank, East Jerusalem was formally incorporated into Abdullah's kingdom in April 1950, and residents of the city became citizens of Jordan.

These and other Israeli and Jordanian actions deepened the partition of the city. Moreover, the increasingly institutionalized division of Jerusalem was physical as well as political. With a state of belligerency still existing between Jordan and Israel, the border between the two sectors of the city was in effect a military front. Armed forces from the two hostile countries faced one another along a line running from north to south, and between them patches of "no man's land" laced with mines and covered with barbed wire separated the eastern and western sectors. This division is shown in Map 5.1, which also contains a detailed plan of the Old City. Only the Mandelbaum Gate permitted passage from one part of Jerusalem to the other. Its use was supervised by United Nations personnel and was restricted to consular officials, other diplomatic representatives, and a few Christian pilgrims.

In rejecting calls for internationalization, Israel not only insisted upon the unrestricted exercise of its sovereignty over the western part of the city, it also took steps to make Jerusalem its capital, accelerating a process that had begun even before the conclusion of the war. The first movement in this direction was in September 1948, when the High Court of Justice was established in the city. In February 1949, the first session of the Knesset was held in Jerusalem, and later that month the first president of the state, Chaim Weizmann, took his oath of office in the city. Then, on January 23, 1950, the Knesset formally proclaimed Jerusalem to be the capital of the Jewish state, declaring in its resolution that the city had in fact been Israel's capital from the day of the country's independence. Finally, almost all government ministries were transferred to the city at this time. Only the Foreign Ministry remained for a time in Tel Aviv, in deference to the United States and other Western powers who had their embassies there and who continued to favor the internationalization of Jerusalem.

With Jerusalem effectively functioning as the country's capital, there was pressure to move the Foreign Ministry there as well. The ministry's staff complained that it was inconvenient to be separated from the rest of the government, and many political forces within the country championed the move for ideological and nationalist reasons. For these reasons, Israel did move the Foreign Ministry to Jerusalem in July 1953, and in response the U.S. and its allies issued a strong protest. The Western governments not only declared that their own embassies would remain in Tel Aviv, they also instructed their diplomatic personnel

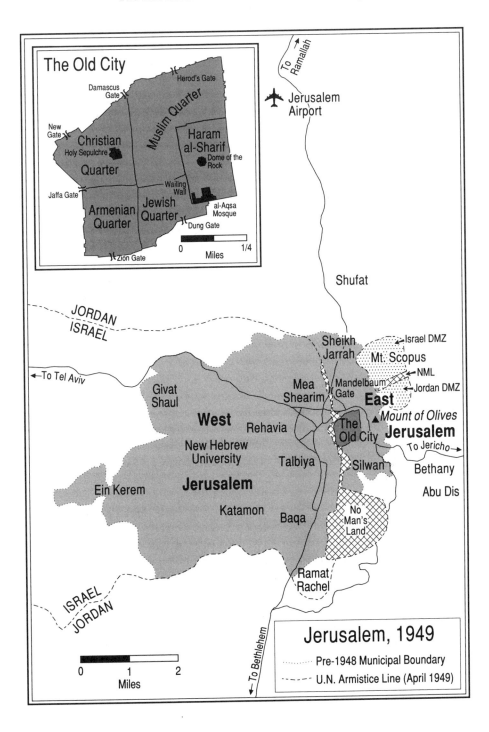

The Old City

Herod's Gate

Damascus Gate

Muslim Quarter

New Gate

Christian Quarter

Holy Sepulchre

Haram al-Sharif

Dome of the Rock

Wailing Wall

Jaffa Gate

Armenian Quarter

Jewish Quarter

al-Aqsa Mosque

Dung Gate

Zion Gate

0   1/4
Miles

To Ramallah

Jerusalem Airport

Shufat

JORDAN
ISRAEL

To Tel Aviv

Sheikh Jarrah

Israel DMZ

Mt. Scopus

NML

Jordan DMZ

Givat Shaul

Mea Shearim

Mandelbaum Gate

East

West

Rehavia

The Old City

Mount of Olives

Jerusalem

New Hebrew University

Talbiya

Silwan

To Jericho

Ein Kerem

Jerusalem

Bethany

Abu Dis

Katamon

Baqa

No Man's Land

Ramat Rachel

ISRAEL
JORDAN

To Bethlehem

Jerusalem, 1949

.... Pre-1948 Municipal Boundary

– – – U.N. Armistice Line (April 1949)

0   1   2
Miles

not to conduct official business in Jerusalem. This boycott ended late in 1954, however; the American, British, and French governments decided that although the location of their embassies would not be changed, their ambassadors would thereafter present their credentials in Jerusalem and be authorized to conduct official business there. Most other countries followed the same policy, and with these developments Israel gained *de facto* recognition for Jerusalem as its capital. In the years that followed, many new government buildings were erected. An impressive new Knesset building was opened in 1966. Five thousand guests attended the inaugural ceremonies, among them parliamentary delegations from more than forty countries.

West Jerusalem developed in other important ways in the years after Israel's independence. Its population expanded rapidly, swelled, in part, by new immigrants from abroad. The number of inhabitants increased from 100,000 to 140,000 between 1948 and 1952, and by 1967 the population of the city had grown to approximately 200,000. New residential areas were built to meet the needs of an expanding populace, as were parks, religious institutions, theaters, a national museum, and numerous other cultural centers. In the economic realm, commercial activity greatly increased during this period, and light industry was also brought to the city. Tourism became particularly important, leading to the construction of a large number of new hotels and stimulating the economy in other ways. Finally, since Israel had only very limited access to its enclave on Mount Scopus, the site of the Hebrew University and Hadassah Hospital, an entirely new university campus and medical complex were built in West Jerusalem. Thus, in sum, Israeli Jerusalem was a dynamic and prosperous city and soon became one of the country's most important urban centers.

Both Israel's exercise of sovereignty over West Jerusalem and the transformation of the city into the nation's capital were condemned by the Arabs, most of whom by 1949 were endorsing the UN proposals for internationalization that they had formerly rejected. In a progress report issued in 1950, for example, the Conciliation Commission recorded that conversations with Arab delegations had shown the latter, in general, to be "prepared to accept the principle of an international regime for the Jerusalem area, on condition that the United Nations should be in a position to offer the necessary guarantees regarding the stability and permanence of such a regime."[167] In taking this position, most Arab states were criticizing Jordan as well as Israel. Nevertheless, both in their discussions with UN representatives and in their general political statements, Israel was the target of their most bitter condemnations. Moreover, it was not unusual for representatives of Egypt, Syria, and other Arab states to put disagreements with Jordan aside and make common cause with the Hashemite regime when condemning the Zionists. For example, in May 1949, the Egyptian, Syrian, Lebanese, and Jordanian delegations meeting with the Conciliation Commission in Lausanne prepared a joint memorandum condemning the transfer to Jerusalem of Israeli government ministries. The memorandum demanded the immediate withdrawal of the "administration and services which have been installed in this city [by Israel] in contempt of the resolution of December 11, 1948."[168]

The charge that Israel showed blatant disregard for the United Nations and its resolutions has been advanced in both scholarly analyses and publications seeking to influence public opinion. Writing from a scholarly perspective, Henry Cattan argues that resolutions enacted in accordance with the principles of international law do not lapse by reason of their nonimplementation. Were it otherwise, it would be possible to defeat any resolution through simple disregard. Cattan asserts that this reasoning applies to the internationalization of Jerusalem, and that Israel's incorporation of the western part of the city is therefore a violation of international law: "The war of 1948 prevented its implementation but did not affect or impair its validity. Insofar as the *corpus separatum* of Jerusalem is concerned, the General Assembly made it quite clear that its military occupation by Israel and Jordan in 1948 did not affect the binding character" of the Partition Resolution.[169] A pamphlet designed to present the Arab case for Jerusalem to the American public makes a similar point, again arguing that Israel refused to abide by any of the pertinent UN resolutions enacted between 1947 and 1950.

> In the Partition Resolution . . . Jerusalem was set aside and given a separate international status of its own, in order that it might be outside the sovereignty of Israel as well as of the proposed Palestinian Arab state. But Israeli forces entered and occupied the greater part of it during the cease-fire, and in violation of the truce. . . . Israel's continued occupation and administration of Jerusalem are in violation of the following five UN resolutions: the *General Assembly* resolutions of November 29, 1947; December 11, 1948; and December 9, 1949; the *Security Council* resolution of August 9, 1948; and the *Trusteeship Council* resolution of December 20, 1949.[170]

Israelis respond to these charges by reminding observers that it was the Arabs of Palestine and neighboring states who in 1947 rejected the Partition Resolution. Israel, by contrast, accepted the resolution, including its provisions pertaining to Jerusalem. As stated in one booklet which sets forth the Israeli case and rebuts what it calls the myths of Arab propaganda, "The Jewish Agency in 1947 was willing to accept the plan in the hope that internationalization might preserve the historic city from conflict. The Arab states were as bitterly opposed to the internationalization of Jerusalem as they were to partition."[171] Israeli sources also stress that Arab opposition to the Partition Resolution of 1947 was expressed in military as well as political terms. It was the Arabs, not Israel, who initiated the 1947–48 War; and as a result it was Arab aggression that led to a new territorial status quo under which the Jewish state obtained possession of West Jerusalem. Finally, supporters of Israel point to what they charge is a glaring contradiction in the position of the Arabs. Even as they condemned Israel for its unwillingness to accept the internationalization of Jerusalem, they themselves continued to reject the most important element of the Partition Resolution: the principle of territorial compromise and the existence of an independent Jewish state in part of Palestine.

Several Israeli and other scholars also assert that the Jewish state's claim to West Jerusalem finds support in international law, principally because the Arabs initiated the 1947–48 War, whereas Israel acted in self-defense. As expressed by Blum, who also summarizes other legal opinion supportive of his argument, Israel has a legitimate title to West Jerusalem because it came into possession of the city "in lawful exercise of her inherent right of self-defense, which is recognized also under Article 51 of the United Nations Charter."[172] Blum argues that this principle also gives Israel legal title to the other parts of Palestine which the United Nations did not originally allocate for a Jewish state but which subsequently came under Israeli control as a result of the war initiated by the Arabs.

The circumstances of East and West Jerusalem were quite different in the years after 1948. In contrast to the experience of Israeli Jerusalem, the Jordanian half of the city did not undergo significant economic or political development. Nor did it become the country's capital, remaining instead in the shadow of Amman. Abdullah did originally entertain the idea of making Jerusalem his capital, or perhaps an alternate capital, but notions of this sort were quickly shelved in the wake of Palestinian and other Arab opposition to Jordan's annexation of the West Bank. Hussein revived the idea a few years later, partially in response to Israel's moves to transform West Jerusalem into the capital of the Jewish state, but again the results were limited. In 1953, the Jordanian cabinet held a session in Jerusalem, resolving to continue the practice on a periodic basis and declaring the city to be the country's second capital. The parliament also met there later the same year. In 1954, Hussein announced that he would build a palace in Jerusalem and reside there for a month every year, a practice that he did later follow with some degree of regularity. Nevertheless, there was little of real substance behind these symbolic gestures. Almost all of the central government's political and administrative machinery remained in Amman, which was the unchallenged center of policy and decisions-making.

The Jordanian government did make some investments in Jerusalem, principally in road construction and the expansion of tourist facilities. Tourism was a major source of foreign currency, and the Old City of Jerusalem was the country's premier tourist attraction. Moreover, the influx of tourist dollars, especially in the 1960s, enabled certain segments of Jerusalem's population to prosper, which in turn gave rise to a boom in private housing construction and to the growth of new suburbs. On the whole, however, East Jerusalem did not experience the kind of dynamic growth that marked the Israeli half of the city. It also stagnated in comparison with Amman. With the government devoting most of its development resources to the territory east of the Jordan River, and thus neglecting both East Jerusalem and the rest of the West Bank, Amman quickly became the economic and business center of the country, as well as its political capital.

Jordan, like Israel, was heavily criticized for its policies and actions with respect to Jerusalem. Moreover, some of this criticism came from Arab sources, who incorporated the issue of Jerusalem into their general condemnation of Abdullah's annexation of the West Bank. At the same time, at least so far as the Arab League was concerned, a face-saving formula acceptable to Jordan was soon adopted. Although Jordan told the league that its annexation of East Jerusalem and other parts of Arab Palestine was irrevocable, it added, somewhat contradictorily, that this was without prejudice to a final settlement of the Palestine question. Thus the League Council passed a resolution declaring that Jordan was holding part of the West Bank, including East Jerusalem, "as a trust in its hands until the Palestine case is fully resolved in the interests of its inhabitants."[173] Thereafter, the league invited Jordan to agree that the territory it controlled in Palestine would be relinquished should the frontiers as they existed under the British mandate be restored.[174] Jordan did not formally respond to this invitation, but the matter nonetheless ceased to be a serious preoccupation of the Arab League, and with few exceptions the Arab states refrained from challenging Jordanian sovereignty over Jerusalem and the rest of the West Bank.[175]

On the other hand, condemnation of the Hashemite regime continued to be expressed by Palestinians, and on a few occasions by Egyptian and Syrian officials seeking to take advantage of Palestinian frustration. Further, in addition to insisting that Jordan had no legitimate right to exercise sovereignty over Jerusalem, or any other part of Palestine, there was also much discontent with Hashemite neglect of Jerusalem and the West Bank. Palestinian leaders pointed out that the government was dominated by politicians from the East Bank, whom they charged with deliberate discrimination in favor of their own region of the country. East Bankers, for their part, were often suspicious of the Palestinians, whose loyalty to the Hashemite regime they rightly suspected. Jerusalem, in particular, was seen as a hotbed of radicalism and dissidence. Nevertheless, many of the complaints lodged against the regime in Amman were justified. The government did indeed favor the East Bank in the allocation of development funds. It also ruled Jerusalem and the rest of the West Bank with a heavy hand. The grievances of many Palestinians were well expressed by the vice-mayor of Jerusalem in 1953 when he complained of the government's "neglect, subjugation and humiliation of the Holy City."[176]

Supporters of Israel criticized Jordan on several grounds. First, like some Arabs, they challenged the legitimacy of Jordanian rule over East Jerusalem. Second, they complained that Jordan had failed to honor its pledge, contained in the armistice agreement it had signed, to grant Israel unimpeded access to certain areas in the eastern part of the city. Third, they bitterly denounced the Hashemite regime for failing to protect the holy places under its care. In this they were joined by some Christian leaders.

Israelis distinguished between their own rights in Jerusalem and those of Jordan. While they rejected Arab claims that the Jewish state had violated international law by refusing to accept internationalization of the city, they argued that such claims had validity in the case of Jordan, and that the legitimacy of Jordanian rule in East Jerusalem was therefore in dispute. This was not an issue with which Israelis were greatly preoccupied in the years after 1948. It became critical only after the war of June 1967, following Israel's capture of East Jerusalem and the city's subsequent reunification. Nevertheless, several arguments were advanced by those who insisted that Jordan did not possess proper title to East Jerusalem. To begin with, they pointed out that Jordan's occupation of the city was the result of aggression. Abdullah's government had rejected the UN's call for a *corpus separatum* and then deliberately sent the Arab Legion to the city in an attempt to prevent the implementation of this and other provisions of the Partition Resolution. In addition, according to this Israeli analysis, Jordan's formal annexation of Jerusalem and the rest of the West Bank violated the armistice agreement that the Hashemite regime had signed in April 1949. As argued by Blum, the effect of the agreement was to "freeze, as it were, the rights and claims of the parties as they existed on the day of the agreement's conclusion. . . . The purported annexation by the Kingdom of Jordan of the 'West Bank' in April 1950 was, therefore, from the point of view of international law, devoid of any legal effect."[177]

A major Israeli concern in the 1950s and 1960s was the question of access to holy places located in the eastern half of Jerusalem and to Mount Scopus, the Israeli enclave in Jordanian territory where the old Hebrew University campus and Hadassah Hospital were located. Officials of the Jewish state strongly criticized Jordan for failing to respect Article 8 of the armistice agreement it had signed. This article recorded "agreement in principle . . . [on] free movement of traffic on vital roads; resumption of the normal functioning of the cultural and humanitarian institutions on Mount Scopus and free access thereto; free access to the Holy Places and cultural institutions and use of the cemetery on the Mount of Olives. . . . " The article also provided for the establishment of a special committee "for the purpose of formulating agreed plans and arrangements" in connection with these and related matters. Yet Jordan refused to implement most of these provisions. Although the Hashemites did accept arrangements whereby Christian Arabs holding Israeli citizenship could cross into East Jerusalem for short stays during Christmas and Easter, Jewish and Muslim Israelis were completely barred from entering areas under Jordanian control. Jews could not pray at the Western Wall or visit the ancient cemetery on the Mount of Olives, where Jewish dead had been buried for 2,500 years. Similarly, Muslim Palestinians who had remained in Israel and become Israeli citizens were denied access to the mosques of the Haram al-Sharif. When Israel called for the formation of the special committee envisioned by Article 8, Jordan refused on the grounds that Israel had been unwilling to abide by the provisions of various UN resolutions.

Although Israel was given limited access to its institutions on Mount Scopus, Jordan refused to accept the resumption of their normal functioning. Abdullah's policy may initially have been, in part, an element of bargaining in the secret talks he was conducting with Israel. The king apparently sought to exchange use of the old Hebrew University campus and of Hadassah Hospital for border modifications that would give Jordan control of former Arab neighborhoods which were now in the Israeli half of the city. In any event, Article 8 of the armistice agreement notwithstanding, Israel's access after 1949 was limited to a 120-person staff of caretakers and lightly armed police, who would remain isolated on Mount Scopus for two-week periods. Under the escort of the United Nations Truce Supervision Organization (UNTSO), fortnightly convoys passing through Jordanian territory ferried these crews back and forth and brought a few supplies. Israel was not the only party to complain about this arrangement. Jordan charged that Israel was using the convoys to transfer military supplies and equipment to Mount Scopus, which was supposed to be a demilitarized area, and that for the most part it blocked UNTSO officials from investigating these charges. Moreover, it was later established that Jordan's complaints had validity.[178] From the Israeli perspective, however, the critical issue at the time was Jordan's refusal to permit the old Hebrew University and Hadassah Hospital to resume normal operations.

The most serious complaints lodged against Jordan concerned the fate of the holy places under its control. In rejecting calls for international administration of Jerusalem's religious sites, the government in Amman had insisted that the holy places of all religions were safe and secure under its protection. In fact, however, the Hashemite record with respect to administration of the holy places and protection of the city's unique religious character was decidedly mixed. Much attention was paid to the city's Islamic heritage. Also, an effort was made to establish good relations with Christian religious leaders, although Christians had many complaints as well. On the other hand, places sacred to the Jews were poorly maintained and protected, and indeed there was considerable desecration of Jewish holy places. Jews in Israel and elsewhere protested this desecration vigorously, often with considerable non-Jewish sympathy and support.[179]

Efforts to deepen the Islamic character of East Jerusalem intensified following Abdullah's assassination in July 1951. The king was succeeded by his son, Talal, and then in August 1952 Talal abdicated in favor of his own son, Hussein. The young monarch, who at the time was only seventeen years of age, almost immediately took steps to enhance the mosques of the Haram al-Sharif. He added a golden dome and ceramic exterior to the Mosque of Omar, for example, and he also repaired and embellished the al-Aqsa Mosque. Beginning in 1953, special celebrations of the Prophet's nocturnal journey and ascension to heaven were organized in East Jerusalem, and the event became the occasion for an annual pilgrimage to the city. A meeting of the World Islamic Congress was also convened in Jerusalem in 1953. Other meetings took place in 1960 and 1961. Part of Hussein's motivation for these efforts and activities was to obtain recognition for Jordanian rule of al-Quds, especially in the face of continuing opposition from Palestinians and a number of Arab states. In addition, however, like his grandfather, the king had a genuine attachment to the city. The Hashemite dynasty traces its origins to the Arabian Peninsula, where Hussein's great-grandfather had been the sherif of Mecca. Although the family had long since surrendered its role as custodian of the two most important Muslim cities, Mecca and Medina, Hussein took pride in the fact that the third-holiest city in Islam was under his care.

Some Christian leaders complained that too much emphasis was being placed on the Islamic element in Jerusalem's personality, and also that there was too much government interference in the administration of Christian holy places and charitable organizations. Thus, for example, Christians in Jordan and abroad protested vigorously in 1953 when laws were enacted which gave the government strict control of Christian institutions, making them subject to Jordanian regulation and inspection and restricting their right to acquire real estate. There were also more general complaints about bureaucratic interference and discrimination in favor of Muslims. In the words of one Christian scholar, Monsignor John Oesterreicher, "Petty restrictions were imposed on pilgrims, institutions were prohibited from acquiring new property, Christian schools were subjected to control of the education they offered." [180] In view of these considerations, many Christians left East Jerusalem after the establishment of Jordanian rule. The total population of the city increased from about 42,000 in 1948 to approximately 50,000 in the mid-1950s and then 70,000 in 1967. Jerusalem's Christian population declined during this period, however, not only as a percentage of the total population but in absolute terms as well. It went from roughly 17,000 in the mid-1950s to about 12,000 in 1967.

On the other hand, Christian holy places were consistently treated with respect, and no serious obstacles were placed in the way of their operation and maintenance. They also figured prominently in the efforts to promote tourism undertaken by the Jordanian government. In addition, Jordanian authorities consulted regularly with Christian leaders and worked effectively to resolve a number of long-standing interdenominational disputes. An important achievement in this regard was the conclusion of a 1961 agreement among competing confessional and institutional interests, which made it possible to begin restoration of the Church of the Holy Sepulchre. Finally, Jordan took great pride in a papal visit in 1964. Pope Paul VI was the first pontiff ever to make a pilgrimage to the Holy Land, and according to one account by an Israeli authority on Jerusalem, he was "the most honored guest ever to arrive in the city." [181]

Jordan's attitude toward Jewish holy places was much more negative, and this was the source of numerous complaints from Israel and Jews in other countries. Although the Western Wall (sacred also to Muslims) was not damaged, Jordanian authorities did nothing to stop the destruction of the synagogues of the Jewish Quarter in the Old City. Some of the buildings in which they had been housed were transformed into stables and garbage dumps. The most wanton destruction occurred in the ancient Jewish cemetery on the Mount of Olives, where many prophets and men of great religious learning are buried. Numerous tombstones were broken, and many were removed for use in construction elsewhere. In some cases, the graves themselves were desecrated. Much of the destruction took place when Jordan gave permission for a road leading to the new Intercontinental Hotel to be built through the cemetery. Jews charged that the road could easily have been constructed so as to avoid the cemetery. In addition, they charged that other instances of destruction were deliberately abetted by the Jordanian government and the municipality of Jerusalem. They reported, for example, that some of the gravestones had been taken by the Jordanian army and used to build fortifications, and also that the city had granted concessions to merchants who smashed the graves and then sold the stones to building contractors.[182] A vivid portrait of the situation is given by Oesterreicher, a Christian clergyman and scholar:

> During Jordanian rule, 34 out of the Old City's 35 synagogues were dynamited. Some were turned into stables, others into chicken coops. There seemed to be no limit to the work of desecration. Many thousands of tombstones were taken from the ancient cemetery on the Mount of Olives to serve as building material and paving stones. A few were even used to surface a footpath leading to a latrine in a Jordanian army camp.[183]

Amidst the battery of Arab and Israeli complaints and accusations, East and West Jerusalem developed separately through the 1950s and 1960s. The United Nations in the early years made several additional efforts to generate movement toward internationalization. None was of any practical significance, however. On September 1, 1949, the Conciliation Commission submitted a new plan for Jerusalem. Although charged by the General Assembly Resolution of December 11, 1948, with formulating proposals for an international regime, the commission sought to take into account the political and territorial status quo that existed at the end of the war. Thus it proposed that Jerusalem be divided into an Arab zone and a Jewish zone which would each have a high degree of local autonomy. Only matters of international concern, such as protection of the holy places and supervision of permanent demilitarization, would be placed under the jurisdiction of a United Nations commissioner. The commissioner was to be appointed to a five-year term by the General Assembly.

On December 9, 1949, the General Assembly again took up the Jerusalem question. It took note of the Conciliation Commission's report but ignored its recommendations. Instead, it reaffirmed its intention to establish Jerusalem as a *corpus separatum.* The Assembly also instructed the Trusteeship Council to complete preparation of the statute by which the international regime would be governed, adding that it should not allow any interested government to divert it from adopting and implementing this statute. The council completed its work and approved the statute on April 4, 1950. The document it ratified respected the General Assembly's insistence that Jerusalem be administered as a *corpus separatum* and drew heavily on the draft statute which the council had prepared in April 1948. Nevertheless, as seen, any possibility of implementing the recommendations of the United Nations had disappeared in 1948. Thus, though the actions of the General Assembly and the Trusteeship Council may have represented the views of the broader international community, they grew ever more removed from the realities of Israeli and Jordanian Jerusalem. In recognition of this fact, United Nations deliberative bodies did not again deal seriously with the question of Jerusalem until the Arab-Israeli war of June 1967. As expressed by one authority, the UN, "by its unconcern with the idea of territorial internationalization [in the years after 1951] . . . effectively acquiesced in the demise of the concept."[184]

The Arab Boycott and Use of Disputed Waterways

Arab opposition to Israel after 1948 was reflected in a general economic boycott directed against the Jewish state. Organized by the Arab League and managed from a full-time office in Damascus, the boycott sought first to prevent any contact between the Arab states and Israel. Not only was there to be no diplomatic or consular interaction, but all other forms of contact were barred as well. Borders between the Jewish state and its Arab neighbors were closed, and virtually all Arab countries refused to handle telephone, telegraph, and postal communications involving Israel. The league also sought to enforce a boycott of all goods produced in Israel.

In addition to these actions aimed directly at the Jewish state, the Arabs also attempted to wage economic war on Zionism by pressing non-Arab governments and companies to refrain from doing business with Israel. Foreign firms that did so were threatened with exclusion from Arab markets, and some of these threats were subsequently carried out. For example, Coca-Cola and Ford Motor Company products could not be sold in the Arab world because the companies had erected plants in Israel. Moreover, the boycott was not only aimed at companies who invested in Israel or traded with the Jewish state, it was also directed at those who sold patents or copyrights to Israeli enterprises or who contributed to the country's economic well-being in any way whatsoever. By 1962, approximately eighty companies had been placed on a blacklist and prohibited from doing any form of business in the Arab world.[185] Another aspect of the boycott was the refusal of Arab countries to admit tourists and other third-party nationals known to have visited Israel.

Although the Arab boycott was a nuisance to Israel, it had little significant impact on the economic or political life of the Jewish state. The country developed rapidly in the years after 1948. Thanks in part to generous assistance from overseas Jewish communities, the nation's GNP increased at an annual rate of almost 10 percent between 1949 and 1967. This was one of the highest growth rates in the world. During this period, Israel also succeeded in establishing important economic and financial relationships with many other countries. Imports doubled and exports increased sevenfold between 1949 and 1960. Between 1949 and 1967, the respective increases were threefold and eighteenfold. Moreover, Israel's trading partners were varied and included almost all of the nations of Western Europe. Less than half of the Jewish state's exports, for example, went to the United States, Great Britain, West Germany, and France, the four countries with which it had the most extensive commercial relations.

Several other factors further reduced the impact of the Arab boycott. For one thing, Israel benefited at this time from the payment of German war reparations. Under an agreement reached between Israeli and German officials in 1952, $862 million in cash and goods was paid to the government of Israel by 1965. The amount paid to individual Israelis who had survived the Nazi death camps was much larger, as much as $9 billion by the end of 1965, according to some German estimates. Another important consideration was Israel's deepening relationship with a number of Third World countries, especially in Sub-Saharan Africa. In the late 1950s and early 1960s, the Jewish state sought to counter the Arab boycott by providing packages of technological and developmental assistance to many newly independent African countries. It also brought many African students to Israel for advanced training in specialized fields. These efforts gave Israel a political presence and important diplomatic alliances in the Third World,[186] enabling it to "leap over the Arab wall," as it were.[187]

All of these considerations indicate that Israel's diplomatic and economic circumstances were generally favorable in the years after its independence, and as a result, supporters and critics of the Jewish state are in agreement that the Arab boycott did no more than minor damage. The boycott's most important consequences were probably symbolic and psychological. It kept the Palestinian issue alive in the eyes of the Arab world, thereby reducing the chances that Israel would gradually come to be accepted by the Arab public.[188] In so doing, it also helped to perpetuate a climate of "mutual ignorance, distance and hostility."[189]

The one area where restrictions imposed by the Arabs played a central role in the Arab-Israeli conflict in the years after 1948 was the status and use of two key waterways. The first is the Suez Canal. The second is the Gulf of Aqaba or, more precisely, the Strait of Tiran, which is the point of entry into the gulf from the Red Sea. Passage through the Suez Canal was controlled by Egypt, even though a legacy of British colonialism was that until 1956 Great Britain retained the right to station troops in the Suez Canal Zone. Egypt was also in a position to restrict shipping in the Gulf of Aqaba. The bluff at Sharm al-Sheikh, located at the southern tip of Egypt's Sinai Peninsula, commands passage through the narrow channel between the Egyptian coast and the islands of Tiran and Sanafir standing at the entrance to the gulf; and in 1949 Egypt placed guns at Sharm al-Sheikh. Although Egyptian policies and actions were not identical with respect to the two waterways, the government in Cairo in both cases used its strategic position to limit Israeli shipping, arguing that this was both politically justified and permissible under international law, since a state of war continued to exist between Egypt and Israel. Israel, by contrast, insisted that Cairo's action threatened its security and was thus in violation of the Israeli-Egyptian armistice agreement.

Israel's trade with the Far East was greatly hampered by the limits Egypt placed on use of the Suez Canal by ships sailing to and from Haifa, the country's main port. The canal permits passage between the Mediterranean Sea and the Indian Ocean via the Red Sea. Vessels wishing to make this voyage but unable to transit the canal are required to sail around the Horn of Africa, a journey that is much longer and more expensive. An alternative is to use Israeli port facilities at Eilat, located on the Gulf of Aqaba and giving access to the Red Sea and Indian Ocean. Eilat was little more than an isolated military outpost at the southern end of the country in 1948, but the Israeli government soon took steps to construct a port capable of handling oceangoing traffic. By 1965, Eilat was a small but bustling town of 14,000. Yet access to the port of Eilat depends on free passage through the Strait of Tiran, which, again, Egypt was in a position to control. As noted, the only entrance into the Gulf of Aqaba, which leads to Eilat, is a half-mile-wide channel between the Egyptian shore and Tiran Island. The gulf itself is about a hundred miles long and varies in width from seven to fourteen miles. The location of the Suez Canal and the Strait of Tiran in relation to the Israeli ports of Haifa and Eilat is shown in Map 6.1. Presented in the next chapter, this map also provides information about the war that was fought over these disputed waterways in 1956.

Egypt refused to permit Israeli ships to use the Suez Canal and threatened to confiscate any that tried to enter the waterway. It also refused to allow the passage of non-Israeli ships coming from or traveling to the Jewish state. The Cairo government established these policies from the time it entered the 1947–48 War in response to Israel's Declaration of Independence, and it immediately began searching ships suspected of carrying cargo to or from Haifa. The cargo itself, if discovered, was seized as war contraband. Israel, of course, complained about these practices, but Egyptian officials insisted they were perfectly legitimate since a state of belligerency existed between Cairo and Jerusalem. The

Egyptians argued that only hostile acts carried out by armed forces were prohibited under the armistice agreement their country had signed. As they told the Security Council in response to a complaint from Israel in 1951, "We are exercising a right of war. . . . An armistice does not put an end to a state of war."[190]

Egyptian officials cited various legal authorities and precedents in support of their position on use of the Suez Canal. For example, the Egyptian delegate to the UN quoted from Oppenheim's *International Law*, to the effect that armistices and truces provide only for a temporary cessation of hostilities and are "in no wise to be compared with peace." Therefore, "the right to visit and search over neutral merchantmen remains intact."[191] Egypt also observed that maritime search-and-seizure operations had been carried out by the Allied Powers during World War I and World War II. Finally, Cairo asserted that its regulation of shipping through the canal was sanctioned by the Suez Canal Convention of 1888, which authorized Egypt to take any measures needed to protect its own security.[192]

Israel challenged these Egyptian arguments and took its case to the United Nations Security Council in 1950 and in 1951, arguing that Cairo had violated the UN Charter and the armistice agreement. While acknowledging that Egypt's arguments about the limits of an armistice agreement were valid in the abstract, Israeli legal scholars asserted that the exercise of belligerent rights is not lawful under an armistice concluded in response to Security Council action.[193] Israeli spokesmen also disputed the claim that Egypt's action was permissible under the Suez Canal Convention of 1888. The convention, they pointed out, requires Egypt to keep the canal open to all traffic during war as well as during peace.[194] Finally, Israel argued that Egypt's behavior set a precedent which, if unchallenged, would threaten freedom of navigation generally and place in jeopardy the interests of all maritime nations. Persuaded by these arguments, the council in September 1951 passed a resolution calling upon Egypt to cease its interference in shipping through the canal. The resolution, submitted by Britain, France, and the United States, agreed that Egypt could not lawfully assert belligerent rights against Israel, concluded that Cairo's search-and-seizure operations were not necessary for self-defense, and concurred in the opinion that Egypt's actions did indeed pose a challenge to all maritime nations.

Egypt declared that it would not abide by the Security Council resolution, which in fact contained no enforcement provisions. But while Cairo continued to deny Israeli ships passage through the canal, the intensity of its interference in third-party shipping to and from Israel declined markedly. In response to an Israeli complaint to the United Nations in 1953, Egypt reported that no ship or cargo going to Israel had been confiscated since September 1951. It also reported that of 32,047 vessels transiting the canal during this period, only 55 had actually been inspected.[195] Indeed, it had even become common by this time for third-party vessels to pass through the canal in order to carry Israeli goods between

Haifa and Eilat. Nevertheless, there were a few instances of Israel-bound ships being temporarily detained, and these led Israel to continue its protests to the UN. In response, a resolution expressing "grave concern" that Egypt had not responded to the Security Council's 1951 request that it terminate restrictions on use of the canal was introduced in 1954, although this resolution died because of a Soviet veto. The moment of greatest tension came in September 1954, when Israel tried to send one of its own merchant ships through the Suez Canal. This was the *Bat Galim*, which Egypt promptly seized. Although the crew was released three months later, the incident made it clear that Egypt still had no intention of opening the waterway to vessels from the Jewish state.

Egypt also claimed the right to regulate shipping through the Strait of Tiran. Although Israel argued that the strait was an international waterway, and hence outside Egypt's lawful control, the government in Cairo rejected this view and insisted that the passage was part of its territorial waters. Cairo pointed out that all countries in the region, including Israel, considered their territorial waters to extend six miles from shore. This being the case, the whole of the strait (and part of the Gulf of Aqaba) was properly and legally under Egyptian jurisdiction. Another legal argument advanced by Egypt was that Israel's control of Eilat was in violation of international law, since the Jewish state had occupied the area after signing an armistice agreement with Egypt and in violation of several Security Council ceasefire resolutions. As a result, in the Egyptian view, Israel had no legitimate basis for demanding unimpeded maritime access to Eilat. Finally, repeating some of the arguments it had made in connection with the Suez Canal, Cairo asserted that the continuing state of war gave it both belligerent rights and a right to self-defense, either of which would permit restricting Israel's use of the Strait of Tiran.[196]

While some legal scholars saw validity in the claim that the Strait of Tiran is part of Egypt's territorial waters, others concurred with the assertion of those who judge it to be an international waterway. Writing in the *American Journal of International Law* in 1958, Charles Selak offers the following summary of the argument in support of the latter position:

> By the weight of international precedent the Gulf would seem clearly to be non-territorial and basically a part of the high seas, even though a considerable portion of the waters therein constitute the territorial seas of the coastal states. Not only is more than one coastal state involved, but also there is a belt of water along the center of the Gulf which is not included in the territorial sea of any of the coastal states (and, as we have noted, contiguous zones constitute a part of the high seas). Consequently, the straits at the entrance would appear clearly to constitute an international waterway, even though these waters comprise in their entirety the territorial seas of either Egypt or Saudi Arabia. . . . [197]

Legal scholars also disagreed about whether international adjudication was required to resolve the dispute about use of the Strait of Tiran. Selak, for example, judges the strait to be an international waterway but nonetheless acknowledges that this is a matter of legitimate dispute. He thus concludes that Israel's right of innocent passage should be settled by the decision or advisory opinion of an appropriate international body, such as the International Court of Justice. Leo Gross, on the other hand, does not consider this essential. He contends that Cairo would be required to permit unrestricted passage into the Gulf of Aqaba even were it not disputed that the strait is an Egyptian waterway. This argument rests on the proposition that Egypt cannot lawfully prevent passage between the high seas and either the nonterritorial waters in the center of the gulf or the territorial waters of Israel adjacent to Eilat. Gross reports that the 1958 Geneva Conference on the Law of the Sea confirmed general principles which give validity to this argument. Specifically, it determined that a state shall not suspend free and innocent passage through straits which are used for international navigation either between two nonterritorial waterways or between an international waterway and the territorial sea of a foreign state. This determination, Gross concludes, renders unnecessary any debate about whether the Strait of Tiran is an Egyptian or an international waterway.[198]

The importance of these legal disputes was more academic than practical between 1948 and 1955. In the early years, Eilat remained undeveloped and was the destination of very few ships. Traffic increased steadily after 1952, but it remained light in absolute terms. More significantly, on only a handful of occasions did Egypt choose to exercise its declared right to inspect ships en route to Israel. According to Egyptian figures, 267 vessels transited the Strait of Tiran between 1951 and 1955, but only 3 were actually visited and searched. And in no case was the cargo confiscated.[199] Indeed, as noted, in most cases Cairo not only permitted ships to sail to Eilat, it also allowed non-Israeli ships to carry supplies from Haifa by passing through the Suez Canal. The maritime connection between Haifa and Eilat assisted Israel greatly in its effort to develop the latter town and enhance its port facilities. Thus, though the Gulf of Aqaba was to play a critical role in the Arab-Israeli wars of 1956 and 1967, differences of opinion about the legal status of the Strait of Tiran were not accompanied by any important confrontation between Cairo and Jerusalem in the years immediately following Israel's independence.

6 | Israel and the Arab States through June 1967

Toward the Sinai-Suez War

T HE PALESTINIAN ARABS did not occupy center stage in the Arab-Israeli conflict between 1948 and 1967. The most significant patterns of interaction and confrontation were those involving Israel and neighboring Arab states, and in this connection the relationship between Israel and Egypt was particularly critical. Moreover, the relationship between Jerusalem and Cairo underwent important transformations in the years after 1948, especially between 1952 and 1956. The former year witnessed the Egyptian revolution, which brought a new political regime to power in Cairo. The latter year marks the date of the Sinai-Suez War, in which Israel invaded and occupied the Sinai Peninsula and the Egyptian-controlled Gaza Strip.

The corrupt and inefficient *ancien régime* in Egypt, led by King Farouq and the Wafd Party, was by 1950 under strenuous attack from many quarters. Critics included nationalist intellectuals, students, militant Islamic groups, and middle-level army officers. Most of these elements regarded the monarchy as a political anachronism. In their eyes, not only was it a symbol of the country's backwardness and stagnation but, more important, it perpetuated outdated conceptions of governance that were in large measure responsible for Egypt's economic and social decay. Most of these critics also bitterly resented the continuing influence in their country of Britain and other imperialist powers, with whom the Egyptian government was perceived to have formed a self-serving alliance against the true interests of the Egyptian people. The presence of British troops on Egyptian soil, for example, was an affront to the country's independence and pride. It was also a reminder of the conservative international alliance which, in the opinion of the government's critics, worked against the development of Egypt and the rest of the Arab world.

The regime was not only detested by politically conscious counterelites, it was increasingly unpopular with the masses as well. Popular grievances were in the first instance fueled by crushing poverty. Thereafter, resentment was generated by the contrast between the desperate lot of the average Egyptian on the one hand and the visible waste and indulgence of the privileged classes on the other. The alien character of the monarchy was yet another dimension of the psychological distance between the Egyptian people and the institutions by which they were ruled. A descendant of Muhammad Ali, Farouq belonged to a dynastic line that Egyptians rightly regarded as non-Egyptian and non-Arab. Finally, all of these sentiments of opposition were intensified by the rising expectations of the post–World War II era, with its concern for self-determination, economic development, and cultural reaffirmation in countries emerging from decades of colonial domination.

Mounting criticism of the monarchy and the Wafd soon expressed itself in the form of demonstrations, strikes, and worker protests. There were dozens of public disturbances of this sort in 1951, as well as a number of violent peasant uprisings; and as disorder spread, the government began to lose the support of the army. Then, on January 26, 1952, thenceforth known as "Black Saturday," extensive rioting broke out in Cairo. Mobs opposed to both elite privilege and Western influence marched through the city, looting and burning many neighborhoods. Dozens were killed and hundreds injured. The number of businesses destroyed also numbered in the hundreds.

The Wafd government fell in the wake of the Black Saturday riots, and six months later, on July 23, a group of young army officers seized power and Farouq himself was forced to abdicate. Between 1952 and 1954, Egypt was governed by "the Free Officers," the military group that had led the July 23 coup. The most prominent member of the Free Officers group was Major-General Muhammad Naguib, who became president of the Revolutionary Command Council (RCC) that was established to govern the country. Naguib was a veteran military leader who had not personally taken part in the coup of July 23. One of the most dynamic and powerful of the younger officers within the RCC, and a leading architect of the coup, was Colonel Gamal Abdul Nasser.

There were internal struggles for power as the Free Officers strengthened their hold on the reins of government. By the spring of 1954, however, Nasser had emerged as the dominant leader of the Egyptian revolution.[1] Born in Alexandria, Nasser was the grandson of an illiterate farmer from rural Upper Egypt, making him the first man of native Egyptian stock to exercise sustained and uncontested leadership of the country in two thousand years. This was highly significant in the Egyptian context and was part of the basis for Nasser's claim that his ascent to power heralded a true revolution. Even more important was the attention Nasser promised to pay to the political and economic needs of the Egyptian people. Indeed, the RCC had begun to implement reforms almost as soon as it was established. In September 1952, it introduced a land-redistribution scheme. It placed an upper limit (of 200 feddans) on the amount of agricultural land that an individual could own and then divided among small shareholders any land in excess of this limit.

Nasser had fought against Israel in 1948, and his participation in the war played a critical role in the formation of his political beliefs. In contrast to what might be expected, however, and in contrast to what was sometimes suggested by Zionist propaganda, the principal orientation that the young officer carried away from the conflict was not an unyielding enmity toward the Jewish state but rather a profound awareness of the needs of his own country. Nasser was deeply distressed by the backwardness of the Egyptian military and by the ineptitude of its commanders. Moreover, the army's disastrous performance on the battlefield was in his view the result of problems that pervaded all sectors of Egyptian political life.

It was thus a commitment to the Egyptian revolution, not to the struggle against Zionism, that was forged by Nasser's experience in the Palestine war. Both his priorities and his analysis of Egypt's requirements were shaped by this critical experience in his life. In later speeches, Nasser frequently quoted the admonition of a dying comrade: "The main battle is Egypt."[2] His bitter description of Egypt's senior officer corps, given below, was in fact an indictment of the corruption and indulgence that characterized the entire political elite prior to the Free Officers coup. Nasser herein expresses the frustration and anger that were widespread in Egypt in the early 1950s, and which finally burst forth in the Black Saturday riots.

> They were overfed, lazy, and selfish and they spent their time eating, drinking, gambling, carousing, smoking hashish, and engaging in many different forms of tyranny and corruption. They had the most unmilitary stomachs I ever saw on army officers anywhere. They were fawning and subservient to the British Military Mission, and a disgrace to the uniform they wore. They spent money that belonged to the Egyptian army on food and drink for themselves.[3]

Nasser's orientation produced an inclination to make peace with Israel, in order that the energy and resources of the Egyptian government might be devoted without distraction to the problems of domestic development. This was his predisposition between 1952 and 1954, when he shared leadership with other members of the Free Officers group, and also after he acquired unchallenged control of the government in the spring of the latter year. Many of those with political influence in Egypt did not share Nasser's view. For example, Mahmoud Riad, who later became foreign minister, reports that he feared military adventurism on Israel's part and urged Nasser in 1953 and 1954 to prepare for an armed confrontation with the Jewish state. He adds, however, that Nasser was totally preoccupied with Egypt's domestic revolution, and hence "adamant that priority in expenditure should be given to development projects." Riad also records that Nasser was prepared for peace with Israel on the basis of the 1949 armistice agreements.[4] Nasser himself wrote in an article that appeared in *Foreign Affairs* in January 1955:

> We do not want to start any conflict. War has no place in the reconstructive policy which we have designed to improve the lot of our people. . . . There is

much to do in Egypt. . . . A war will cause us to lose much of what we seek to achieve in Egypt.

A number of Israelis and supporters of Israel concur in this assessment of Nasser's orientation.[5] Yair Evron, an Israeli scholar, points out that Nasser's disinterest in a confrontation with Israel might be explained by other factors. These include a recognition of the weakness of the Egyptian military and a desire to delay the struggle with Israel until British troops had been removed from the Suez Canal Zone. Nevertheless, Evron observes that it is "just possible that he was interested in reaching a more permanent peace with Israel," and he then concludes that this "is further substantiated by the chronological evidence."[6] A similar conclusion about the sincerity of Nasser's desire for peace is reached by Richard Crossman, a British politician with pro-Zionist tendencies. Crossman interviewed the Egyptian leader during this period and wrote that "he [Nasser] judged that Israel ought not to distract him from the problems of Egypt, those of the social revolution."[7]

Although Nasser's disinterest in confrontation was a source of frustration for Palestinians, it led to a dialogue of sorts with the government in Jerusalem. There were private contacts between Egyptian and Israeli officials during 1954, and it appears that these took place in response to both Egyptian and Israeli initiatives. A leading force on the Israeli side was Moshe Sharett, who had replaced Ben Gurion as prime minister in September 1953 and who believed it was important to secure an accommodation with Israel's largest and most powerful Arab neighbor. Sharett's attitude toward Egypt was not universally shared in Israeli political circles. According to Evron, some Israeli leaders distrusted Nasser, and others "did not feel any great need for an immediate settlement."[8] In this there was a symmetry between Egypt and Israel, given that many in Cairo did not approve of Nasser's moderate stance toward Israel. In any event, although the documentation needed for a full account of Egyptian-Israeli relations during this period has yet to be made available, it appears that Nasser and Sharett maintained an intermittent dialogue through their respective embassies in Paris and, possibly, several other European capitals.

Egyptian and Israeli representatives discussed the possibility of a partial normalization of border relations and other outstanding issues, including Israel's use of the Suez Canal. Israeli press accounts, published seven years later, report that the Egyptians "expressed a willingness to reach a secret agreement with Israel on the normalization of relations without a formal peace agreement . . . [in order] to maintain a tranquil border, and to create direct contacts in a European capital as a base for clearing controversial matters or conflicts." In the context of such an accord, Egypt also agreed that Israeli cargoes would be permitted to transit the Suez Canal, although not in ships flying the Israeli flag.[9]

Any possibility that these contacts might have led to a breakthrough disappeared as a result of events in Israel, in Egypt, and in the Egyptian-controlled Gaza Strip. In Israel, internal political and ideological battles made it difficult to pursue a coherent policy toward Egypt and eventually produced provocative actions directed against the Nasser regime. In Egypt, the attention of the government gradually turned away from an accommodation with the Jewish state and toward issues deemed to be of higher priority, most notably the status of the Suez Canal. Finally, violent clashes between Palestinians and Israelis in Gaza created additional tension and eventually helped to bring Israel and Egypt to the point of war.

The political contest taking place in Israel at this time pitted Moshe Sharett, who was foreign minister as well as prime minister, against the defense establishment, which through the end of 1953 was headed by David Ben Gurion. Sharett and Ben Gurion had both personal and ideological differences. On the one hand, Ben Gurion nourished hopes of once again becoming head of the government, a position in which he had served for more than five years. On the other, he strongly disagreed with Sharett's moderation in matters of foreign affairs and defense. Sharett, a man of intellectual inclinations, was philosophically predisposed toward negotiation and compromise. His former service as head of the Jewish Agency's political department had given him much experience in the conduct of diplomacy. Ben Gurion, by contrast, was a political infighter, a militant patriot who was more concerned with action than with nuance.[10] On the eve of his departure from the cabinet, early in 1954, Ben Gurion appointed several of his political and ideological allies to key positions in the Defense Ministry, thereby attempting to ensure the continuity of his hard-line approach to issues of national security. The most important of these men were Moshe Dayan and Shimon Peres, respectively chief of staff and director of the Defense Ministry. Both would later become senior political figures.

The internal political situation in Israel was further complicated when Pinhas Lavon replaced Ben Gurion as defense minister. Lavon, a Labor Zionist veteran, had been a political moderate, by some accounts even a pacifist, before his appointment; and for this reason he was distrusted by Ben Gurion and his protégés within the defense establishment. In the case of the latter, especially that of Dayan, relations were also strained by personal rivalries and competing political ambitions. Yet Lavon did a political about-face following his appointment, adopting a hard-line stance toward the Arabs akin to that of Ben Gurion, and in the end pursuing policies that placed him in direct conflict with Sharett. The new defense minister's ideological conversion did not alter his poor relations with Dayan, Peres, and other Ben Gurion supporters in the Defense Ministry, however. On the contrary, there were intense and continuing battles over the control of resources and decision-making authority. There were thus two political confrontations taking place at this time. The first was a continuation of the clash between the prime minister and the defense minister, which had begun when the latter position was held by Ben Gurion. The second was a conflict *within* the Defense Ministry, between factions that possessed similar foreign-policy orientations but were bitterly opposed on personal and political grounds.[11]

This situation had serious implications both for Israel's relations with Egypt and for politics inside the Jewish state. With respect to the former, the Defense Department frequently acted in ways that undermined Sharett's effort to maintain a dialogue with Nasser. For example, Palestinian commando raids against Israel were occasionally launched from the Gaza Strip, and the Israel Defense Forces frequently responded with retaliatory strikes. The Defense Ministry did not always coordinate the planning and execution of these attacks with Sharett, however, and on some occasions it deliberately extended the scope of strikes authorized by the cabinet in order to embarrass Nasser and exacerbate tensions between Cairo and Jerusalem. So far as domestic Israeli politics is concerned, this situation raised important and potentially troubling questions about civilian-military relations. Both Lavon and Dayan, as defense minister and chief of staff respectively, displayed a willingness to defy cabinet directives and carry out policies of their own. The two colluded when it served their purpose. Each also sometimes acted without the knowledge of the other, compounding concern about lines of authority and control of the military.[12]

The Israeli action which did the greatest damage to hopes for an accommodation with Egypt was a sabotage scheme planned in secret by Defense Ministry operatives and put into operation in July 1954. Its specific goal was to undermine the increasingly cordial relations between Egypt and the United States, which Israeli hard-liners feared would reduce American support for their own country. In fact, however, to the satisfaction of Sharett's political opponents, the episode created great distrust between Cairo and Jerusalem.

The essence of this scheme was a plan to use Israeli agents and about a dozen locally recruited Egyptian Jews to plant bombs and set fires at various public buildings in Cairo and Alexandria, including libraries of the United States Information Service. The purpose was to create anti-Egyptian sentiment in the U.S. at a time when Nasser's government was seeking arms and assistance from Washington and was also hoping to enlist American support in negotiations with Great Britain over military bases in the Suez Canal Zone. A related objective was to persuade the British that their military presence was still needed in Egypt. The plot was uncovered, however, and the majority of the participants were captured and tried. Two of the Israeli agents were hanged. Six others received long prison sentences, and two of the Egyptian Jews were acquitted and released. Egypt was surprised and angered by this Israeli action and immediately terminated its contacts with the Jewish state. The affair also undermined Sharett's confidence in Nasser. Inadequately informed about the operation, which had been planned entirely within the Defense Ministry, the Israeli prime minister regarded Egypt's reaction as exaggerated and provocative. Sharett was also disturbed when Egypt hanged two of the conspirators in spite of the appeals his government transmitted to Nasser.

This episode, which later became known as the "Lavon Affair," had both immediate and continuing repercussions inside Israel. Defense Ministry officials described it as a "mishap," asserting rather unconvincingly that agents had somehow confused instructions to plan the scheme with an order to execute it. The most controversial aspect of the affair within the domestic Israeli context concerned the responsibility of the defense minister, a matter that was referred to a secret commission of inquiry in January 1955. Lavon insisted that he had not known of the plot in advance, and he bitterly denounced the commission of inquiry's report, which concluded that it was impossible to determine beyond a reasonable doubt whether or not the defense minister had ordered the operation in Egypt. Lavon also accused Dayan and Peres of giving false testimony. While he did not charge either man with responsibility for the campaign in Egypt, he insisted that both had lied to the commission of inquiry and thus conspired to engineer his downfall.[13]

Although these developments led to his resignation several weeks later, Lavon continued to profess his innocence, and many subsequently concluded that he may have been telling the truth. The issue surfaced again and caused a new political storm in the early 1960s. In fact, it was only at this time, in response to new investigations, that information about the secret diplomacy of Sharett and Nasser became public. So far as Lavon's involvement in the 1954 operation in Egypt is concerned, new questions were raised about the testimony of Dayan and Peres before the commission of inquiry in January 1955. More generally, some observers suggested that the deep divisions and intense personal rivalries which characterized the Defense Ministry in 1954, even among men who shared opposition to Sharett's foreign policy, lent credence to Lavon's claim that others had planned the operation without his knowledge and then misled the commission of inquiry about their own responsibility.

The most important political consequence of the Lavon Affair was that it returned Ben Gurion to a position of leadership, first as Lavon's replacement at the head of the Defense Ministry and later as prime minister. Ben Gurion gladly came out of retirement when supporters argued that he alone was capable of managing the defense establishment. He wrote in his diary at this time, "Lavon is definitely going, and there is no one [to replace him]. They propose that I return. I was overcome. I decided that I must accept and return to the Defense Ministry. Defense and the army precede everything."[14] Ben Gurion assumed the post of defense minister in February 1955, and in this position he ordered actions that soon brought increased tension with Egypt. In particular, he ordered harsh retaliatory strikes in response to guerrilla raids launched by Palestinians in the Gaza Strip, insisting that such reprisals were necessary to deter a larger military confrontation. These and other developments over the course of 1955 weakened the position of Sharett, and in November Ben Gurion once again assumed the premiership. A biography of Ben Gurion reports that the new prime minister was "in a warlike mood" when he mounted the Knesset rostrum to present the members of his cabinet. This mood was also reflected in his strong speech, which signaled "a change in the government's political and military policies."[15]

Egypt's own foreign-policy preoccupations, as well as the Lavon Affair and the changing political climate in Israel, are among the reasons that early contacts between representatives of Nasser and Sharett bore no fruit, and that tension between Cairo and Jerusalem increased during the latter part of 1954 and throughout 1955. The attention of the Egyptian government turned to the Suez Canal during this period, and specifically to an effort to remove British troops based in the Canal Zone. As noted, this was the subject of negotiations between Egypt and Britain during the summer of 1954.[16] Egypt benefited in these talks from the American posture. President Eisenhower had assumed an attitude of comparative neutrality and encouraged Britain to accommodate itself to Egyptian demands. In October 1954, an accord was reached. Great Britain agreed to evacuate all of its troops by June 1956, although it reserved the right to return them in the event of an armed attack on one of the states of the Arab League or on Turkey. Article 8 of the agreement reaffirmed the provisions of the 1888 Suez Canal Convention that guaranteed free passage through the waterway. Addressing concerns about the legal status of the Suez Canal, the treaty recognized that it was an integral part of Egypt, but added that it was also a waterway of international importance.

The Israeli government was not initially opposed to an agreement along the lines sought by the Nasser regime. This was in part a reflection of Sharett's general attitude toward Egypt. Israel also claimed to have received private assurances that Egypt would be ready for peace once the Suez Canal issue was resolved. Sharett thus told the Knesset in August that Israel understood Egypt's desire for uncontested control of the canal, adding only that the Jewish state wished this to be linked to peace. The left-wing Mapam Party went even further, declaring its full support for an end to all vestiges of British colonialism in Egypt.[17] On the other hand, there was also growing Israeli concern that the new agreement would not be accompanied by an end to the state of war between Egypt and Israel, or even by a modification of Cairo's policy toward Israel's use of the canal. The passage of Israeli ships had not been permitted when British troops were present, of course. Nevertheless, Israel continued to insist on its right of passage and worried that Egypt would oppose this more vehemently than ever once there was no longer a British presence. Israel also feared that Egypt might use its improved position to place new restrictions on the passage of non-Israeli ships bound for the Jewish state.

In the aftermath of the Lavon Affair, Israeli concerns mounted as negotiations between Cairo and London drew to a close. Thus, in September, the government in Jerusalem decided to test Egypt's intentions by sending the *Bat Galim* into the Suez Canal. The result, as noted earlier, was the seizure of the vessel by Egyptian authorities. Some argued that Israel's action was provocative, and that the Jewish state should have waited until the new agreement was formally signed and then given Egypt an opportunity to show its peaceful intentions in a timely fashion. From the Israeli perspective, however, or at least in the view of hard-liners in the Defense Ministry, it was Egypt that had behaved in a provocative manner, with the Nasser government giving a clear demonstration that it was not sincerely interested in peace. Coming in the wake of the Israeli-sponsored sabotage operation in Egypt, the *Bat Galim* affair pushed Egypt and Israel further along the road toward armed confrontation. One Israeli scholar notes that had it not been for these two episodes in the summer and early fall of 1954, the private dialogue between Jerusalem and Cairo might have continued, and thereby "created another constraint on Nasser's policy toward Israel and contributed to the creation of precedents for future behavior."[18] Unfortunately, this was not the case.

The Gaza Strip provided the arena for a third set of developments leading to the second Arab-Israeli war. Palestinian guerrillas had for several years occasionally crossed into Israel from refugee camps in Gaza in order to commit acts of sabotage and harassment. Pipelines were cut and roads were mined in typical operations. A number of Israelis were also killed by Palestinian infiltrators. Such acts were naturally of concern to Israelis, many of whom not only blamed Palestinians but also argued that Egypt's control of Gaza made Nasser at least partly responsible.

There is conflicting opinion both about the extent of guerrilla action during this period and about the degree to which Cairo encouraged and aided Palestinian infiltration. Yair Evron, for example, cites UNTSO reports which indicate that by October 1954 there had been a decline in both the number and the importance of raids from Gaza.[19] He also suggests that acts of infiltration did not appear to be part of a coordinated campaign carried out by Egypt or any other Arab government.[20] Thus, Sharett could report to the Knesset in January 1955 that the border with Gaza was "relatively quiet."[21] At the same time, others argue that the number and severity of guerrilla raids increased after the conclusion of the Egyptian-British agreement and during the first two months of 1955.[22] In addition, they charge that these raids were accompanied by clear and unambiguous statements in which Egyptian officials declared their commitment to the liberation of Palestine. Finally, a number of independent journalists report that the Egyptian government had given authorization for Palestinian raids inside Israel as early as the spring of 1954.[23]

Disagreements about the extent of Palestinian raids and Egyptian complicity notwithstanding, the pattern of infiltration and violence was intolerable to Israel, and the government in Jerusalem soon adopted a deterrent strategy based on retaliatory strikes that were far more severe than the original provocations. This policy was carried out with particular vigor when Lavon was minister of defense. Moreover, as noted, Lavon often acted on his own initiative and without specific instructions from the cabinet. This practice, as well as the Defense Ministry's sabotage operation in Egypt, led Sharett to record in his diary in October 1955 that Lavon "has constantly preached in favor of acts of madness and taught the army leadership the diabolic lesson of how to set the Middle East on fire, how to cause friction, cause bloody confrontations."[24] Yet the most massive Israeli retaliatory strike occurred on February 28, 1955, eleven days after Ben Gurion had replaced Lavon as minister of defense. Under cover of darkness, Israeli paratroopers carried out a bold mission designed to destroy military targets inside Gaza. During this operation, the Israelis also ambushed and destroyed an Egyptian convoy of reinforcements. According to Cairo, thirty-eight Egyptians were killed and sixty-two were wounded.

The Israeli raid on Gaza brought to a definitive end whatever remained of the possibility for a rapprochement between Nasser's government and leaders of the Jewish state. Israel insisted that the strike had been necessary and justified, and that it had been carried out in response to provocations which demonstrated conclusively that Egypt was uninterested in peace. Alternatively, from the vantage point in Cairo, the raid was but another example of Israeli provocation. Coming on the heels of clandestine operations in Egypt and the *Bat Galim* affair, the Gaza strike left Egypt completely convinced that Israel's leaders did not have peaceful intentions. In addition, the strike dealt a psychological blow to the Egyptians, demonstrating Israel's clear military superiority and indicating that the Egyptian army was as weak as it had been in 1948. In the words of the UNTSO chief of staff, this was a "stinging slap in the face of the Egyptian army—still sore from its defeats in 1948."[25] Thus, overall, the Gaza raid was a watershed in Israeli-Egyptian relations, not only ending any possibility of peace for the foreseeable future but putting the two countries squarely on the road to a more explosive confrontation. The ensuing developments are succinctly summarized by Robert Bowie, who writes that the strike "put Israel and Egypt on a collision course. Its consequences were inexorable: Nasser's decision to mount *fedayeen* guerrilla-type reprisals, the succession of raids and reprisals; the expanding arms race; and, finally, the Sinai war. Reacting to the [Israeli] raid, Nasser placed new restrictions on foreign-flag vessels entering the Gulf of Aqaba for the Port of Eilat."[26]

Although it was the deepening conflict between Egypt and Israel that led to the Sinai-Suez War of October and November 1956, the vicious cycle of Arab raids and Israeli reprisals had already intensified hostility between Israel and Jordan. Indeed, in the early 1950s, the largest number of Palestinian raids against Israel emanated from the West Bank rather than from Gaza. The moment of greatest tension came when Israeli forces attacked the Jordanian village of Qibya in October 1953. Sixty-six civilians were killed, among them a number of women and children. Although the strike was in response to various acts of sabotage and terrorism carried out inside Israel by Palestinians from the West Bank, including the recent murder of an Israeli woman and two Israeli children, the magnitude of Jerusalem's retaliation was widely judged to be excessive. It was strongly condemned both by the United States and by the United Nations Security Council. Nevertheless, as seen in the case of the Gaza raid, the Jewish state continued its policy of carrying out retaliatory strikes that were much more severe than the provocations to which they were a response.[27]

Israel argued that only major retaliatory strikes would have deterrent value, and this strategy of retaliatory deterrence was in fact largely successful in the case of Jordan. Demonstrations of Israeli military superiority did little to advance the cause of permanent Arab-Israeli peace. On the contrary, they contributed to the general climate of uncertainty and apprehension. Nevertheless, Israeli strikes did help to quiet the Jewish state's border with Jordan. In order to prevent future reprisals, the Hashemite government made a determined effort to patrol the frontier and prevent infiltration, instances of which accordingly declined significantly in 1954 and 1955.

The reaction to Israeli retaliatory strikes was different in Egypt. Determined to resist what it considered to be extremism and provocation on Israel's part, Cairo undertook to respond in kind. In the summer of 1955, it began to organize and equip squads of Palestinian commandos, known as *fedayeen*, and to send these units across the Gaza border into Israel. Guerrilla raids were often aimed at civilian targets. For example, seven small schoolchildren were murdered by *fedayeen* in the Israeli town of Shafrir. In this atmosphere, the vicious cycle of raid and retaliation intensified, and mounting losses on both sides continued the inexorable movement toward a full-scale confrontation. The table below, based on United Nations sources, shows the number of Arab and Israeli casualties during 1955. It confirms that while the border with Jordan was by now comparatively quiet, the Egyptian-Israeli frontier was the scene of escalating violence.[28]

Casualties	*Jordan-Israel Front*	*Egypt-Israel Front*
Israelis killed	8	47
Israelis wounded	30	118
Arabs killed	18	216
Arabs wounded	7	188

Israel undertook to increase its supply of arms from abroad during this period and developed a particularly close relationship of political and military cooperation with France. This relationship began to take shape in the summer of 1953, and French weapons began to arrive in Israel roughly two years later. France's motivation for a military partnership with Jerusalem lay in its anger over Egypt's active support for independence movements in Algeria, Tunisia, and Morocco, all of which had long been part of the French colonial empire. France was particularly concerned about the situation in Algeria, which contained approximately one million Frenchmen and which Paris considered to be an integral part of the French state. Algerian nationalists initiated an armed struggle for independence in 1954, and as Nasser himself confirmed in an interview,[29] Cairo provided the Algerians not only with political support but with arms as well. Thus, as Moshe Dayan revealed some years later, Paris delivered weapons to Israel with the clear understanding that they would eventually be used against Egypt.[30]

Israel was concerned at this time not only about the expanding scope of *fedayeen* raids but also about Cairo's intensified blockade of the Gulf of Aqaba. Egypt completely sealed the Strait of Tiran in September 1955, bringing to a halt all shipping in and out of the port of Eilat. This was a *casus belli* so far as Israel was concerned, and in response Ben Gurion instructed his subordinates in the Defense Ministry to prepare for war and brought to the cabinet a proposal to occupy Sharm al-Sheikh. The cabinet declined to act on the recommendation, but in November, amid growing fears that a major military confrontation was inevitable, Ben Gurion once again became prime minister. Early in 1956, the United States attempted to calm the situation by dispatching a mediator, Robert Anderson, to the region. Anderson shuttled between Cairo and Jerusalem for two months but was unable to work out a compromise on any of the issues separating the Israelis and Egyptians. In June, as the situation continued to deteriorate, Ben Gurion forced Sharett out of the cabinet, presumably because the former prime minister could not be counted on to support an offensive war.

Egypt's behavior during 1955 and 1956 was shaped by the changing circumstances of Middle Eastern and world politics, as well as by its steadily mounting concern about Israel. Nasser was a militant critic of Western imperialism, and under his charismatic leadership Egypt emerged in 1954 both as a major political force within the Arab world and as a leading advocate of Third World solidarity. As noted, this placed him in opposition to France, which was struggling to hold on to its colonies in the Maghreb. It also placed him in opposition to Great Britain, especially after London sponsored the Baghdad Pact, which Iraq and Turkey signed late in February 1955, several days before Israel's raid on Gaza. Britain itself joined the new alliance in April, as did Pakistan and Iran later in the year. The declared objective of the Baghdad Pact was to prevent Communist penetration into the Middle East by providing for a common defense of the region's "northern tier" states, all of which, with the exception of Iraq, shared a border with the Soviet Union. An additional, undeclared British goal was to preserve London's influence in the face of growing U.S. involvement in Middle Eastern affairs. In Nasser's view, however, the practical effect of the alliance was to strengthen conservative Middle Eastern regimes while simultaneously reinforcing Western and colonial influence in the region. In addition, Nasser feared that the pact would enable Iraq to rival Egypt for leadership within the Arab League.

In an attempt to counter the influence of both Britain and Iraq, Nasser concluded bilateral defense agreements with Syria, Saudi Arabia, and Yemen. The Egyptian president also sought to improve ties with King Hussein of Jordan, an important and long-time British ally; and partly as a result of warmer relations between Cairo and Amman, as well as opposition to the Baghdad Pact within Jordan itself, the Hashemite regime decided to remain outside the British-sponsored alliance. Further, in March 1956, Hussein dismissed General John Glubb, the British citizen who had commanded the Arab Legion for almost twenty-five years.[31] Although this development greatly embarrassed Great Britain, and contributed further to the deterioration of its relations with Egypt, London honored the 1954 agreement it had signed with the government in Cairo and removed the last of its troops from the Suez Canal Zone in June 1956.

There were also growing strains in Egypt's relations with the United States in 1955 and 1956. Cairo initially hoped that its increasingly militant foreign policy would not be opposed by the administration in Washington, from which it had received support in negotiations with Britain in 1954. But the U.S. declined an Egyptian request for military assistance in May 1955, and so Cairo turned to the Eastern Bloc, concluding an arms agreement with Czechoslovakia in September. This was the first time a major Arab country had received weapons from a Soviet-bloc country, and the event was treated with great seriousness by Western powers preoccupied with the Cold War. Similar developments took place in connection with Egypt's effort to secure international financial assistance for the construction of a major dam at Aswan, in Upper Egypt. Late in 1955, the United States (and Britain) expressed a willingness to make funds available through the IBRD. Negotiations dragged on, however, and on July 19, 1956, the American secretary of state, John Foster Dulles, announced that the U.S. would not support the project after all. Dulles was angered by Nasser's opposition to some of the financial safeguards required by the IBRD. Above all, however, the United States was motivated by Nasser's increasingly anti-Western posture, to which Dulles referred by stating, "Recent developments have not been favorable to the success of the project."[32]

Egypt subsequently obtained Soviet aid for the Aswan Dam, but Nasser's immediate response to the American rebuff came on July 26, when he took the dramatic step of nationalizing the Suez Canal Company.[33] The Egyptian president stated in an interview some years later that he took this action in response both to the substance of U.S. policy, "which was not at all willing for the development of our country," and to "the insulting attitude with which the [Aswan Dam loan] refusal was declared."[34]

Great Britain, historically the dominant Western power in Egypt, took the lead in expressing opposition to the nationalization of the Suez Canal Company. The British view was set forth in a telegram which Anthony Eden, the prime minister, sent to President Eisenhower on July 27. Eden wrote, in part:

> The canal is an international asset and facility, which is vital to the free world. The maritime powers cannot afford to allow Egypt to expropriate it and to exploit it by using the revenues for her own internal purposes irrespective of

the interests of the canal and of the canal users. . . . We should not allow ourselves to become involved in legal quibbles about the rights of the Egyptian Government to nationalize what is technically an Egyptian company, or in financial arguments about their capacity to pay the compensation which they have offered. I feel sure that we should take issue with Nasser on the broader international grounds. . . . We ought in the first instance to bring maximum political pressure to bear on Egypt. . . . My colleagues and I are convinced that we must be ready, in the last resort, to use force to bring Nasser to his senses. For our part we are prepared to do so. I have this morning instructed our Chiefs of Staff to prepare a military plan accordingly.[35]

As a result of these developments, Britain shared with France and Israel a desire to force Nasser to modify his policies, and the three countries soon undertook coordinated military action in an attempt to achieve this objective.[36] Early in August, Britain and France initiated planning for an invasion of Egypt—even though both countries at the time were also participating in diplomatic efforts to find a nonviolent response to Nasser's nationalization of the canal—and on October 16 the French and British prime ministers met in Paris and agreed to take action jointly with Israel. From the 22nd to the 24th, officials of the three countries met in Sevres to complete their planning, and then, on October 29, Israeli forces invaded Sinai and attacked positions of the Egyptian army. The next day, France and Britain vetoed Security Council resolutions calling upon Israel to leave Egypt without delay, and the day after that, French and British planes dropped bombs on Egyptian airfields.

By November 5 Israel had occupied the Gaza Strip and strategic locations throughout the Sinai Peninsula, including Sharm al-Sheikh. The three sequential offensive drives by which Israeli forces took control of the peninsula are shown in Map 6.1. At the same time, France and Britain moved to occupy the Canal Zone, which lay between the Sinai Peninsula and the rest of Egypt. The two European powers landed paratroops at Port Said and Port Fuad on November 5, and the next day Anglo-French seaborne forces invaded Port Said. The Sinai-Suez War, as this confrontation is usually called, ended in a complete military victory for Israel and its allies. For Egypt, which was forced to accept a ceasefire with foreign troops occupying large portions of its territory, the war was a bitter and humiliating defeat.[37]

Into the 1960s

Following French and British vetoes in the United Nations Security Council, the General Assembly undertook to act in response to the Sinai-Suez War of 1956. This was an important development in the constitutional evolution of the international body. Reinforcing a precedent established by the Uniting for Peace Resolution of 1950, the Assembly asserted its right to deal with matters reserved

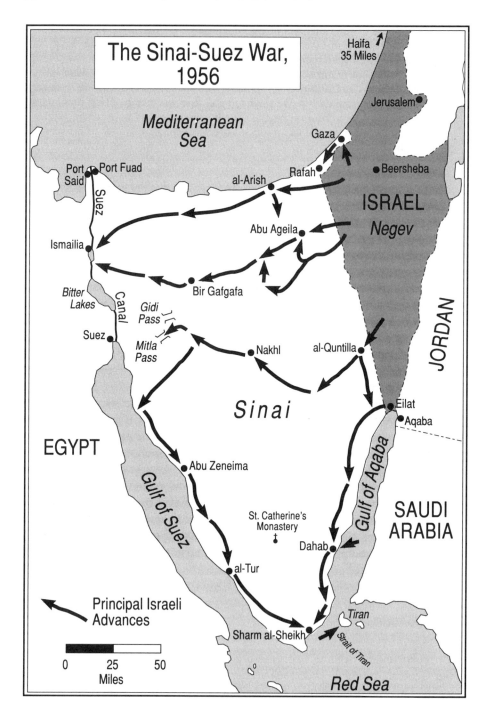

The Sinai-Suez War,
1956

Mediterranean
Sea

Haifa
35 Miles

Jerusalem

Gaza

Port
Said

Port Fuad

al-Arish

Rafah

Beersheba

ISRAEL

Suez

Negev

Ismailia

Abu Ageila

Bitter
Lakes

Bir Gafgafa

Canal

Gidi
Pass

Suez

Mitla
Pass

Nakhl

al-Quntilla

JORDAN

Sinai

Eilat

Aqaba

EGYPT

Abu Zeneima

Gulf of Suez

Gulf of Aqaba

SAUDI
ARABIA

St. Catherine's
Monastery

Dahab

al-Tur

Principal Israeli
Advances

Tiran

Sharm al-Sheikh

Strait of Tiran

0   25   50
Miles

Red Sea

under the Charter for the Security Council. On November 2, the Assembly called for a ceasefire, to be followed by the withdrawal of Israeli forces from Gaza and Sinai, and two days later it authorized the establishment of a special international peacekeeping force, the United Nations Emergency Force (UNEF). Details of the peacekeeping operation were worked out and approved by the General Assembly during the next few days.

On November 12, Egypt agreed to accept UN forces on its soil, subject to certain conditions. Cairo insisted that the United Nations presence must not infringe upon Egyptian sovereignty, which meant that the composition and tenure of the UNEF required Egypt's continuing approval. On November 15, the first troop contingents arrived in Egypt, and two weeks later France and Britain announced that they would soon withdraw their own forces from the Canal Zone. The evacuation of French and British forces was completed on December 22, and by the end of the year efforts to clear and reopen the Suez Canal had begun under United Nations auspices.

Israel, by contrast, did not immediately agree to a complete withdrawal of its troops from Egyptian territory. While it had pulled back from most of the Sinai Peninsula by the end of January 1957, it refused to surrender Sharm al-Sheikh, which overlooked the Strait of Tiran, and it also kept in place its forces in the Gaza Strip. This response to pertinent UN resolutions and to creation of the United Nations Emergency Force reflected Israel's strong conviction that there should not be a return to the *status quo ante*, a situation which, Zionist leaders argued, had been the cause of the Sinai-Suez War in the first place. Specifically, in return for the removal of its troops from Gaza and Sharm al-Sheikh, Jerusalem demanded an end to *fedayeen* raids launched from Egyptian territory and the removal of all restrictions on Israel's use of the Suez Canal and the Gulf of Aqaba.

Supporters of Israel stated that the world community had long turned a blind eye to the Jewish state's legitimate concern in these areas. For example, they pointed out that although the Security Council had called upon Egypt to permit Israeli use of the Suez Canal as early as 1951, Cairo's blatant and continuing defiance of the Council's resolution had in fact been met with widespread apathy. Thus, Israeli representatives concluded, their country could not be expected to relinquish the fruits of a decisive military victory unless and until its just requirements were met. This view was clearly spelled out by Abba Eban, who addressed the General Assembly on January 28, 1957, in the following terms:

> Our view is simple. . . . In the three outstanding issues—the Suez Canal, the Gulf of Aqaba and the Gaza Strip—our duty is not to reestablish but to prevent the reestablishment of the previous situation, for in each case the situation of 28 October 1956 was one of illegalities and not of law. . . . These three illegalities, more than any other factors, brought about the hostilities which we are now seeking to liquidate. In pursuing its policy for the withdrawal of non-

Egyptian troops, the United Nations surely has no duty to restore Egypt's blockading and raiding capacity to its former state.[38]

There was validity to these Israeli claims, as there had been to many of the complaints Jerusalem lodged against Egypt before the 1956 war. Yet there was also a widespread belief that Israel had pursued its objectives, however legitimate, in an unacceptable manner. Once again, as in the past, Israel was criticized for retaliatory action that was excessive in comparison with the provocation to which it was a response. In addition, Israel's invasion of Egypt was deemed to be inadmissible behavior on the part of a state claiming commitment to the rule of law. The case that was made against Israel is summarized succinctly and objectively by Robert Bowie, who was U.S. assistant secretary of state in 1956. Bowie writes, "Despite the violations of Israel's rights, it was still hard to square its resort to force with the provisions of the [UN] Charter. And in practical terms, Israel weakened its position by the collusion with France and Britain."[39] Thus, Israel's military victory was not without political costs. As expressed by another observer, "Israel sustained a setback in the intangible realm of its reputation as a law-abiding member of the community of nations. As had happened in connection with the [pre-1956] retaliation policy, the provocation was not of sufficient magnitude to keep the label of aggressor from being hung upon Israel."[40]

These charges against Israel, whether justified or not, led the United Nations to give priority to the removal of Israeli troops from Egyptian territory and to attach less importance to Jerusalem's concern that there be no return to the *status quo ante*. As a result, Israel's call for assurances that the withdrawal of its troops would not be followed by new Egyptian provocations was for the most part brushed aside by UN officials. For example, while Israel proposed that the Gaza Strip be placed either under a United Nations administration or under Israeli civilian control, in order to ensure that *fedayeen* raids would not resume, UN Secretary-General Dag Hammarskjold flatly rejected these suggestions. Hammarskjold, who was authorized by the General Assembly to implement its resolutions, insisted that control of Gaza would have to revert to Egypt before there could be any consideration of the Israeli proposals, and the secretary-general added that even then no change in the administration of Gaza would be possible without Egyptian consent.

In taking this position, Hammarskjold and other United Nations officials did not deny the need to deal with the underlying sources of tension identified by Israel, or, for that matter, with even broader issues of Arab-Israeli accommodation. They did, however, reject the view put forward by Zionist representatives that these concerns should be addressed *at the same time* as the matter of Israel's withdrawal and the restoration of Egyptian control over Sharm al-Sheikh and Gaza. To proceed otherwise, they argued, would be to negotiate under the pressure of Israel's illegal occupation of Egyptian territory, and thereby to give Israel a bargaining advantage derived through the illegitimate application of force.

This was also the view of most UN member states. The call for unconditional Israeli withdrawal was, of course, put forward forcefully by the Soviet Union. The USSR had emerged as a strong ally of the Nasser regime and had repeatedly vetoed UN attempts to condemn Egypt either for raids launched from Gaza or for restrictions placed on Israel's use of the Suez Canal. In addition, however, it was the general position of the UN Assembly that Israel should not derive benefit from an action the world community considered illegal, and hence that the removal of Israeli troops from Egyptian soil should be immediate and unconditional.

This view was formally expressed by the General Assembly on February 2, 1957. The Assembly called upon Israel to remove its forces from the Sinai Peninsula and the Gaza Strip and stipulated that withdrawal of Israeli troops behind the 1949 armistice lines was a prerequisite for UN attention to other Arab-Israeli issues. In a concomitant resolution, approved on February 2 as well, the Assembly also expressed its recognition of the need to deal with underlying sources of tension and acknowledged that the world body itself had responsibilities in this area. It stated, in part, that "withdrawal by Israel must be followed by action which would assure progress toward the creation of peaceful conditions," and it therefore requested the secretary-general, in consultation with the parties concerned, to take steps to bring about such progress. Yet the connection between the two resolutions was clearly understood to be sequential. The UN would make no effort to discharge its responsibility to work for a long-term settlement of the Arab-Israeli conflict until Israel's withdrawal had been completed. Only *after* Israel's withdrawal would it be possible to go on to the next stage of peacemaking.

Further complicating the situation was Egypt's attitude toward the UNEF. Cairo not only maintained that the invasion of its territory by Israel, France, and Britain had been illegal, a position in which the United Nations concurred, but it insisted as well that acceptance of UN troops on its soil did not imply a renunciation of belligerent rights against Israel. Egyptian spokesmen declared that their government did not seek conflict and remained committed to the rule of law; but, they added, Egypt neither accepted the validity of Israeli complaints nor offered any guarantees about its own future behavior. On the contrary, Egypt would tolerate no interference in the exercise of sovereignty over its territory and would decide for itself how best to respond to aggression. This view, which reinforced Israel's disinclination to withdraw from Sharm al-Sheikh and Gaza, was expressed to the General Assembly by Mahmoud Fawzi, Egypt's foreign minister.

> The United Nations Emergency Force is in Egypt not as an occupation force, not as a replacement for the invaders, not to resolve any question or to settle any problem, be that problem in relation to the Suez Canal, to Palestine or to freedom of passage in territorial waters. It is not there to infringe upon Egyp-

tian sovereignty in any fashion or to any extent but, on the contrary, for the sole purpose of giving expression to the determination of the United Nations to put an end to the aggression committed against Egypt and securing the withdrawal of Israel behind the armistice demarcation lines.[41]

Fawzi's statement was not intended as a threat against Israel. It was rather an affirmation that, in contrast to the policy of the Jewish state, Egypt did seek a return to the *status quo ante*. In other words, Cairo would continue to judge for itself how its interests might best be defended and would not be constrained either by the fact that an invasion had taken place or by the fact that Israeli troops occupying Sinai and Gaza had been replaced by a United Nations presence.

This situation led to an impasse early in 1957. Israel refused to remove its troops without guarantees that its vital interests would be protected, and the UN refused even to discuss Israel's concerns until the withdrawal of its troops had been completed. The UN did promise to deal with Israel's grievances after its withdrawal from Egyptian territory, but officials of the Jewish state pointed out that the United Nations had failed to take effective action in the past, even when its own resolutions had been violated, and they therefore reiterated Jerusalem's reluctance to surrender gains made on the battlefield without tangible evidence that Israel's security and shipping interests would be safeguarded. Finally, the deadlock was reinforced by Egypt's conditions for accepting the UNEF on its soil—namely, that the force was no more than a mechanism by which the Israeli withdrawal could be accomplished, that its presence on sovereign Egyptian territory would not be permitted to constrain in any way the Nasser government's behavior, and that the force could remain in Egypt only so long as it had Cairo's permission.

The deadlock was broken in February and March when the United States exerted pressure on Israel to withdraw its forces. The U.S. had condemned the Israeli invasion from the beginning and had supported the Security Council's resolution of October 30, 1956, which called for an immediate Israeli withdrawal. This was also an occasion for Washington to break with its European allies, since the resolution had been vetoed by Britain and France. Thus, early in November, President Eisenhower sent Ben Gurion a letter stating that Israel's action "might impair the friendly cooperation between our two countries." The United States did accept the validity of some of Israel's concerns, which were reiterated by Golda Meir, Israel's foreign minister, in a meeting with John Foster Dulles at the end of the year. For example, Washington had initially taken the position that the UNEF could be called upon to prevent Cairo from exercising belligerent rights. Nevertheless, areas of agreement with Jerusalem notwithstanding, Washington had by February decided that, if required, it would exert pressure on Israel to bring about the removal of its forces from Gaza and Sharm al-Sheikh.

The American position was set forth in an *aide-mémoire* that the U.S. government delivered to Israel on February 11, 1957. First, concerning the situation in the Gaza Strip, the document stated that "the United Nations General Assembly has no authority to require of either Egypt or Israel a substantial modification of the Armistice Agreement. . . . [Therefore] Israeli withdrawal from Gaza should be prompt and unconditional, leaving the future of the Gaza Strip to be worked out through the efforts and good offices of the United Nations." Second, with respect to Sharm al-Sheikh, the *aide-mémoire* reaffirmed the Jewish state's right of passage in the Gulf of Aqaba and reiterated the U.S. belief "that the Gulf comprehends international waters and that no nation has the right to prevent free and innocent passage in the Gulf and through the Straits giving access thereto." On the other hand, the document also stated that "the enjoyment of a right of free and innocent passage by Israel would depend on its prior withdrawal in accordance with the United Nations Resolutions." Third, and significantly, the *aide-mémoire* made no mention whatsoever of the Suez Canal. Finally, in conclusion, the document explicitly set forth Washington's view "that the United Nations has properly established an order of events and an order of urgency and that the first requirement is that forces of invasion and occupation should withdraw."[42]

On February 20, President Eisenhower dealt with these matters in a television broadcast. He acknowledged Israel's desire for firm guarantees as a condition for the withdrawal of its forces from Egypt but then added that Jerusalem should satisfy itself with American and UN calls for peacemaking efforts following the removal of Israeli troops. To accede further to Israeli demands, he stated, would be to turn back the clock of international order. "If we agree that armed attack can properly achieve the purposes of the assailant," the president reasoned, " . . . we will, in effect, have countenanced the use of force as a means of settling international differences and through this gaining national advantages." Emphasizing this theme throughout his speech, Eisenhower declared, "We cannot consider that the armed invasion and occupation of another country are 'peaceful means' or proper means to secure justice and conformity with international law." In concluding, the president alluded directly to his administration's willingness to put pressure on Israel. Drawing a comparison with the Soviet Union's recent invasion of Hungary, which the United States had forcefully condemned, Eisenhower ended his speech by saying, "It would indeed be a sad day if the United States ever felt it had to subject Israel to the same type of moral pressure as is being applied to the Soviet Union."[43]

All of this was sufficient to persuade Israel to remove its forces without the additional guarantees it had sought. Jerusalem announced withdrawal plans on March 1 and carried them out a week later. The removal of Israeli forces took place in conjunction with the deployment of the UNEF at Sharm al-Sheikh and in Gaza.

Israel realized some but not all of its strategic objectives in the months and years ahead. Nasser did not attempt to send Egyptian forces into Sharm al-Sheikh, and the UNEF presence there was thus sufficient to ensure that the Strait of Tiran remained open to Israeli vessels. This remained the case for the next decade, and the port of Eilat experienced significant growth and development as a result. On the other hand, Egypt never acknowledged Israel's juridical right to use the waterway and retained the option of dismissing the UNEF at any time, an option that it chose to exercise in spring 1967. So far as the Suez Canal is concerned, Cairo reopened the waterway on April 8 and soon after established the Egyptian Canal Authority to govern its use. The Egyptians promised to respect the rights of users as set forth in the convention of 1888 but declared that the blockade against Israel would continue. The United States and other powers reluctantly accepted this situation, acquiescing both in the nationalization of the canal and in the denial of passage to Israel.[44]

The postwar situation in Gaza was also generally but not completely satisfactory from the Israeli point of view. *Fedayeen* raids and other illegal border crossings did not return to their prewar levels after Israel's withdrawal and the entry of the UNEF. Indeed, there were virtually no serious incidents along Israel's southern frontier during the next decade, leading one Israeli author to write that "as time went by, the Sinai Campaign brought Israel rich dividends, first and foremost ten years of peace."[45] At the same time, the Egyptian government moved quickly to reestablish its political control of the Gaza Strip and secured UN recognition of its right to administer the district without interference from the UNEF troops stationed there. Israel protested this development, and in response the United Nations proposed that the UNEF's deterrent capability be enhanced by positioning its troops on the Israeli as well as the Egyptian side of the armistice line. Israel rejected this proposal, however.

Although it had made a number of significant gains, this was not as impressive a balance sheet as Israel might have wished. The Jewish state had proved itself to be the dominant military power in the region and, presumably, had given not only Egypt but other Arab states as well cause to hesitate before taking action against Jerusalem's interests in the future. As asserted by Moshe Dayan, "The military victory in Sinai brought Israel . . . a heightened prestige among friends and enemies alike."[46] Nevertheless, Israel had not been able to translate its military accomplishments into the kind of political settlement it sought. Egypt had not been compelled to make any juridical concessions, the Suez Canal remained closed to Israeli shipping, and Jerusalem's two major gains—use of the Gulf of Aqaba and a tranquil border with Gaza—both depended on the presence of UN forces which Egypt had the right to expel at any time. Finally, Israel had been branded as an aggressor by the world community. Its image in the Third World was damaged by collusion with France and Britain, which were acting in defense of their imperial interests. Israel also experienced a temporary strain in relations with its most important ally, the United States.

Nasser, by contrast, despite his country's military defeat, had made major political gains. He secured international recognition for his nationalization of the

Suez Canal, and his insistence that the canal would remain closed to Israel was not seriously challenged. Moreover, by presenting himself as one who had stood up to British and French imperialism, and who had in fact brought an end to the last vestiges of colonialism in Egypt, Nasser's position of leadership in inter-Arab and Third World politics was greatly enhanced. These latter accomplishments were emphasized by Nasser himself, who told an interviewer that "the meaning of Suez is that there is an end to the methods of the nineteenth century: that it was impossible to use the methods of the nineteenth century in the twentieth century."[47] It is therefore difficult to avoid the conclusion that, in spite of Israel's victory on the battlefield, Egypt and Nasser came away from the Sinai-Suez War with the most impressive political gains. The Egyptian president had become a hero at home and the preeminent political leader in the Arab world.

A final consideration is the psychological impact of the war. In contrast to the situation following Nasser's rise to power, when for a time it appeared that an accommodation might be reached between Jerusalem and Cairo, the Sinai-Suez campaign left the two countries more antagonistic toward one another than ever. Israel's anger at having been denied the fruits of victory was deepened by the indifference of the international community, especially in connection with the Suez Canal. Yet Jerusalem's bitterness was mixed with a measure of grudging respect for Nasser. The Egyptian president was recognized as a resourceful and potentially troublesome adversary, one who not only could challenge Israel from Egypt but whose increasing prestige would enable him to mobilize anti-Israel forces throughout the region.

Egypt, for its part, was humiliated by its military defeat and determined to rebuild its army in order to confront Israel from a position of strength in any future conflict. Toward this end it found a willing ally in the Soviet Union, and the delivery of Soviet arms soon enabled Nasser to increase the strength of his army considerably. Egypt also came away from the war with a firm conviction that Israel had expansionist impulses. It interpreted Jerusalem's reluctance to withdraw from Gaza as an indication that the Jewish state wished to control additional portions of Palestine, noting that Ben Gurion had in fact told the Knesset that "the Armistice Agreement with Egypt is dead and buried and will never be resurrected."[48] Egyptian officials also noted with grave concern that Ben Gurion had followed the invasion of Sinai with declarations to the effect that "our forces did not infringe upon the territory of the land of Egypt," and that the Sinai Peninsula "has been liberated by the Israeli army."[49]

This complex of costs, benefits, and psychological orientations is not only the concluding chapter in the story of the Sinai-Suez War, it is also an important part of the Middle Eastern political order out of which the next war would arise, in June 1967. In addition, the decade between 1957 and 1967 saw Syria emerge as an important element in the Arab-Israeli equation. On the one hand, Syria joined with Egypt in February 1958 to form the United Arab Republic. The experiment in political unification lasted only until September 1961. Nevertheless, Syria continued to be an active participant in inter-Arab politics. On the other hand, tensions along the Syrian-Israeli border gave rise to a number of incidents, reminiscent to a degree of the hostilities that had characterized the Israel-Gaza border prior to 1956. In February 1960, for example, Israel responded to an accumulation of raids from Syria with a major strike against Syrian military positions on the eastern shore of the Sea of Galilee.

Under the influence of the Baath Party, with its revolutionary ideology of secular pan-Arabism and socialism, Damascus had since 1955 pursued a foreign policy that aligned it with both Egypt and the Soviet Union. Led by its founders and principal ideologues, Michel Aflaq and Salah al-Din al-Bitar, both of whom were French-educated schoolteachers, the Syrian Baathists had pursued their doctrine of pan-Arab nationalism by establishing branches of their party in several neighboring Arab capitals. Then, in 1958, the Baathists secured Nasser's agreement to a merger between Syria and Egypt. As noted, the new political entity was called the United Arab Republic.

Leaders of Syria's Baath movement had several motivations for establishing a union with Egypt, including not only an ideological commitment to Arab unity but also a desire to gain Nasser as an ally in the struggle for power inside their own country.[50] In fact, however, Nasser was the principal political beneficiary of the merger, even though the Egyptian president had initially been hesitant about the proposed union. The United Arab Republic was ruled by a single, unified political party, the National Union, which was headed by Nasser. Moreover, the Baathists not only found themselves in a union dominated by Cairo, they also experienced an erosion of their position within Syria itself. Among their opponents were local Nasserists, who favored the union with Egypt but looked directly to Cairo, rather than to Baath ideologues, for inspiration and leadership. The opposition also included a coterie of conservative political figures, who disliked the socialist and reform-oriented program of both Nasser and the Baathists. Finally, since Syria was the weaker partner in the United Arab Republic, there was a measure of resentment which handed all of the Baathists' opponents an issue with which to rally support. As a result, despite the merger with Egypt, and to an extent because of it, Baath Party candidates fared poorly in the July 1959 elections for local committees of the National Union.

The Syrian-Egyptian union came to an end in September 1961. Chafing under its subordination to Egyptian officers, the Syrian military staged a coup and declared their country's secession from the United Arab Republic. In support of their declaration, the Syrian officers arrested and then sent back to Cairo the Egyptian military commander based in Damascus. The officers also installed a new government composed primarily of traditional notables, who in turn proceeded to abolish most of the social and economic reforms introduced during the period of the union. Not surprisingly, Cairo refused to recognize the new regime in Damascus, which it bitterly attacked through the Egyptian radio and press. As summarized by Kerr, the Egyptians painted the ideological contrast between themselves and the new Syrian government "in bold and simple strokes—the reactionary alliance pitted against the historic forces of Arabism and socialism."[51]

The situation changed again in 1963. In February, a military coup in Baghdad brought to power the Iraqi branch of the Baath Party, and the young leaders of the new Iraqi government soon opened talks with their Baath counterparts in Damascus. Then, exactly one month after the change of government in Iraq, a pro-Baath coup occurred in Syria, too. The existing Syrian government, by now demoralized and largely discredited, offered little resistance. Egypt reacted cautiously and did not restore full diplomatic relations with the government in Damascus. On the other hand, Nasser acceded to the Baathists' request for a new round of negotiations, after which Syrian officials promptly flew to Cairo and raised the possibility of reviving the Syrian-Egyptian experiment in Arab unity. Iraqi representatives were also present at these talks, and in April an agreement in principle was reached concerning the creation of a political union among all three states.

The prospects for the new Arab unity scheme evaporated during the latter half of 1963, in substantial measure because of the Syrian Baathists' machinations. Fearing that they would again be dominated by Nasser, the Baathists in Damascus sought to strengthen their domestic position by suppressing local Nasserists. In addition, seeking to put Nasser on the defensive, they opened an independent dialogue with Baghdad in order to explore the possibility of a separate union between Syria and Iraq. These actions, understandably, led to a rapid cooling of Egyptian-Syrian relations. In the meantime, in Baghdad, hostility between the civilian and military wings of the Iraqi Baath Party produced a new distribution of power late in 1963. This caused Iraqi politics to turn inward and, for the time being at least, diminished that country's own interest in any of the unification proposals under discussion.

The evolution of Syrian politics and of Syrian-Egyptian relations helps to place in context the increasing tension between Damascus and Jerusalem in the years after 1958. In contrast to the border between Israel and Egypt, where 3,400 UNEF troops were assigned to keep peace, the frontier between Syria and Israel was the scene of frequent clashes. From the Israeli point of view, it was not surprising that the border with Syria became tense during this period. Under Baath tutelage, Syria had become more politically militant and more ideologically opposed to compromise with Zionism. Hostility toward Israel was encouraged by the Baath's revolutionary philosophy, which called for struggle against the forces of imperialism and reaction. In addition, Damascus had become more closely allied with those Arab states, above all Egypt, which were now the greatest enemies of the Jewish state. Finally, as will be discussed presently, domestic challenges gave the Baath Party in Syria an instrumental reason to project militant opposition to Israel, in order to put its critics on the defensive and to enhance its legitimacy in the eyes of the Syrian public. As in its approach to the union with Egypt, Baath attitudes toward Israel thus reflected a blending of ideological factors and considerations of practical politics.

In light of these Syrian attitudes and motivations, Israeli Prime Minister David Ben Gurion viewed the 1963 unity talks between Damascus, Cairo, and Baghdad with particular alarm. Some Israeli analysts rightly saw little of lasting significance in the April agreement among the three countries. Others, however, including Ben Gurion, feared that a new, Nasser-led pan-Arabism was about to emerge. The Israeli prime minister sent urgent messages to Washington, London, and Paris, warning of the danger and seeking guarantees of Israeli security should a new Arab union in fact be established. Ben Gurion's letters indicate that although Nasser was still perceived to be Israel's most dangerous Arab adversary, there was mounting concern about Syria as well.[52] Jerusalem also worried that the regime in Damascus would be encouraged and emboldened by the Soviet Union, which was supplying ever-increasing quantities of military hardware to the Syrians. For example, during a twelve-month period in 1962 and 1963, the Soviets delivered forty MIG-17 fighter planes, a number of IL-14 transports and helicopters, eighty T-54 tanks, forty SU-100 assault guns, and six minesweepers. More equipment was delivered in 1964 and 1965.[53]

From the Syrian perspective, growing tension along the border with Israel was not the result of Baath militancy, domestic insecurity, or Egyptian and Soviet encouragement. It was rather the product of provocative actions taken by Jerusalem. Three sets of concerns were expressed by the Damascus regime. First, Syria charged that while Israel cultivated land in the demilitarized zone between the two countries, it frequently employed border police to prevent Arabs from doing the same. Indeed, according to the Syrians, Israeli farmers sometimes extended their own cultivation to areas assigned to the Arabs, or even, occasionally, to Arab-owned lands beyond the buffer zone. Damascus insisted that these Israeli actions not only were unacceptable but were frequently in direct violation of UNTSO recommendations, which generally sought to divide the territory equitably between Jewish and Arab farmers. Second, Syria charged that Israel was illegally denying use of the Sea of Galilee (also known as Lake Tiberias and Lake Kinneret) to Syrians and Palestinians. Although the lake lies wholly within the Jewish state, its northeastern shore defines the border between Israel and Syria; and Damascus claimed that Arabs living along the sea were therefore entitled to fish in the lake without interference from Jerusalem. Third, in what eventually became the most important source of tension, Syria objected vehemently to an Israeli plan to draw large quantities of water from the Sea of Galilee for irrigation and industrial development inside the Jewish state. This plan was of concern not only to Syria but to other Arab states as well, and in 1960 the Arab League called it "an act of aggression against the Arabs, which justifies collective Arab defense."[54]

Israel insisted that it was acting completely within its rights in each of these three areas and argued that Syria was simply seeking a pretext for attacks upon the Jewish state, whose legitimacy it of course still refused to recognize. All of these matters could be easily resolved, spokesmen for Jerusalem continued, if Syria and other Arabs would accept Israel's right to exist and agree to peace talks. Israel also repeated its contention that Syrian leaders were encouraging anti-Zionist sentiment in an effort to deflect attention from domestic problems and to enhance the Damascus regime's legitimacy among the Syrian masses.

Questions of legality and political motivation notwithstanding, border incidents became common under these circumstances, and Israel and Syria both took action that contributed to the tension. The Israeli strike of February 1960 has already been mentioned. It took place in response to Syrian attacks on Israeli farmers and border police who, illegally in the Arab view, had taken control of lands within the demilitarized zone. Partly on the basis of UNTSO recommendations, the Arabs claimed for themselves the territory being cultivated by the Israelis. Additional outbreaks of violence occurred in 1962 and 1963. In March of the former year, for example, Israel responded to Syrian attacks on its fishing and patrol boats in the Sea of Galilee. Following an exchange of fire between Israeli police boats and Syrian shore batteries, which each side accused the other of beginning, the Israel Defense Forces carried out a major retaliatory raid. Casualties were heavy as the IDF hit several villages, as well as Syrian military positions.[55] Another episode took place in December 1962, when Syrian forces again opened fire on Israeli farmers working land claimed by the Arabs. The Syrians also shelled several nearby Israeli agricultural settlements. In August of 1963, two Israelis working in a field north of the Sea of Galilee were killed in yet another attack.

Israel's needs in agriculture and industry led it to undertake schemes for the diversion of water resources that were an additional source of tension in relations between Jerusalem and Damascus, as well as in relations between Jerusalem and Amman. Israeli experts had conducted a hydrological survey of the Jordan River Valley as early as 1950. Then, in September 1953, the Jewish state began construction on a project to divert water from the Jordan River to a hydroelectric power plant and inland reservoir, from which it would subsequently be channeled to the Negev and other areas within the Jewish state. The diversion canal was to be built at Banat Yaqub (or Bnot Ya'acov) Bridge, about twelve miles north of the Sea of Galilee. This point, south of the confluence of the Jordan, Banyas, and Dan rivers, is approximately nine hundred feet above the Sea of Galilee, high enough to permit the waters of the Jordan to flow without assistance to other parts of the country. The Banat Yaqub area was in a demilitarized zone established by the 1949 Israeli-Syrian Armistice Agreement, however, and this gave Syria grounds to object to the Israeli project.

Following some small-scale military encounters that accompanied the beginning of Israeli construction, the Banat Yaqub project was discussed by the United Nations Security Council, and thereafter, partly in response to pressure from the United States, Jerusalem agreed to abandon the scheme. Instead, in 1956, it began construction of a pumping station and a conduit to carry water southward from the Sea of Galilee itself. The pumping station was located at the northwestern end of the lake, well within the borders of the Jewish state.

During this period the United States also addressed the question of water resources in connection with the Arab-Israeli conflict. In 1953, President Eisenhower sent a personal representative, Eric Johnston, to the area to work out and seek agreement on a water-sharing arrangement. The plan that Johnston laboriously put together during two years of consultation with technical experts and government officials in Israel, Syria, Jordan, and Lebanon called for the construction of a number of dams, canals, and other waterways and would have yielded about one billion cubic meters of water per year. Israel, which was to receive almost 40 percent of the water from the Jordan River and its tributaries, endorsed the scheme. Alternatively, although many Arab officials had previously expressed agreement with technical aspects of the project, the Johnston Plan was rejected by the Arab states. Syria, which would have received about 10 percent of the water produced by the project, took the lead in organizing opposition to the U.S.-sponsored initiative. At the insistence of Damascus, and with the active concurrence of Cairo, the plan was formally vetoed by the Arab League in October 1955.

There were several reasons for the opposition of Syria and other Arab states. First, and most important in the judgment of Israeli analysts, participation in a cooperative water-management scheme would imply recognition of the Jewish state and willingness to normalize relations with Jerusalem. The Arabs were not prepared to surrender their claims of belligerency, however, at least not so long as Palestinian rights continued to be abridged. In addition, as Israeli supporters of the Johnston Plan and other water-diversion schemes themselves pointed out, the provision of water to the Negev and other regions was important precisely because it would enable Israel to increase both its productive and its absorptive capacity. On the one hand, this would make Israel more powerful and self-sufficient and hence, in Arab eyes, a more formidable adversary. On the other, it would encourage many more Jews to immigrate to Israel, which the Arabs also considered a threat. Increased Jewish immigration was seen as diminishing the chance that Palestinian refugees would ever return to their homes, since more of the land inside Israel would presumably be needed for newly arriving Jews. Indeed, some suggested that an expanding population might even lead the Jewish state to seek additional land from its Arab neighbors.[56]

Although the Johnston Plan was officially shelved, both Israel and Jordan proceeded to implement some of its provisions. In 1958, the government in Amman received American assistance to begin construction of the East Ghor Canal, a forty-two-mile conduit carrying water from the Yarmouk River southward into the Jordan River Valley. The canal, completed in 1963, was not opposed by Israel. It gave Jordan a substantial portion of 480 million cubic feet of water that was to be its annual allocation under the Johnston Plan, and it enabled the Hashemite government to irrigate roughly 30,000 acres of land on the eastern bank of the lower Jordan. Amman also proposed to erect a dam on the Yarmouk at Mukheiba, in order to generate hydroelectric power for both Jordan and Syria and to provide additional water for irrigation.

As noted, Israel had in 1956 begun construction of a pumping station and conduit that would eventually remove water from the Sea of Galilee. Jerusalem defended this project, which was sanctioned by the Johnston Plan and which, Israel insisted, would take no more water than had been allocated to the Jewish state under the American initiative. Nevertheless, as reported, Syria and other Arab states had steadfastly opposed the Israeli scheme; and by the end of 1963, with construction nearing completion, the prospect that water would soon begin to flow through Israel's National Water Carrier produced increasing concern in Arab political circles. An Arab summit meeting was therefore convened in Cairo in January 1964, and the assembled delegates agreed on the outlines of a plan that they hoped would limit Israel's ability to pump water from the Sea of Galilee.

The Arab plan that was subsequently devised to outflank the Israelis proposed erecting dams on the Hasbani and Banyas rivers in order to divert the headwaters of the Jordan into an eighty-mile-long canal flowing southward to the Yarmouk River. The proposed canal would run east of the Sea of Galilee, thus bypassing Israel. The Arab scheme also proposed to divert an additional quantity of water into the Litani River in Lebanon by means of a tunnel running westward from the Hasbani River. If implemented, this project would to a very considerable degree reduce the amount and increase the salinity of water available to Israel.[57] In addition, the January summit called upon the members of the Arab League to help finance the project and recommended creation of a unified military command to protect the water-diversion scheme from attack by Israeli forces.

The Israeli pumping station was in full working condition and the conduit was carrying water southward from the Sea of Galilee by the summer of 1964. As a result, the Arabs held another summit in September and sought to press ahead with the water-diversion plan they had adopted in January. Jerusalem warned that it would use whatever means were necessary to prevent implementation of the Arab project, however, and Israeli strikes were indeed carried out in 1965 and 1966. In March 1965, for example, the IDF fired on Syrian equipment being used to construct an access road for work on the proposed Banyas-

Yarmouk Canal. A similar attack took place in May, as did an aerial attack in July 1966. These and other Israeli operations prevented Syria from making any meaningful progress on the Arab water-diversion scheme, and by early 1967 Syrian activity was limited to a handful of bulldozers working intermittently to level several stretches of land.

Tensions between Israel, Syria, and Palestinian Guerrillas

It is against this background that tension between Israel and Syria continued to mount. The respective Israeli and Arab water-diversion projects had added a new dimension to the conflict between the two states. Further, incidents associated with the cultivation of disputed lands remained common in 1965 and 1966, with Syria frequently firing on Israeli farmers working land claimed by the Arabs, and Jerusalem periodically launching a retaliatory strike. Israeli and Syrian forces also from time to time traded fire directly across the demilitarized zone. In addition, however, hostility between Damascus and Jerusalem during the middle 1960s was driven not only by the complaints of each against the other, but also by domestic circumstances within each country.

In Syria, the character of the Baath regime experienced significant changes in the months after the March 1963 coup. By 1964, a new leadership group had begun to emerge, dominated by younger military men and a few civilians with little commitment to the party's pan-Arabist ideology. The orientation of this new wave of Baath politicians was described as "regionalist," since its members' principal concern was the Syrian "region" rather than the larger Arab "nation" of which Syria was a part. In addition, there were structural as well as ideological changes. Previous Baath politicians had admittedly shown a tactical readiness to suppress their rivals with little hesitation or remorse. Nevertheless, the party and its leaders had remained committed to democracy, civil liberties, and civilian rule. By the mid-1960s, however, the ruling coalition presided over an increasingly authoritarian and militarized political system. A new constitution, introduced in 1964, provided for a facade of civilian and representative governmental institutions; but in fact these structures were totally subservient to the military-dominated National Revolutionary Council. Thus, as Hurewitz concludes, "The Ba'th Party became in effect the private property of the military junta."[58] The overall impact of these ideological and political changes is described by Malcolm Kerr, who states that the Baath Party suffered from a "serious moral impoverishment" as a result of its abandonment of early revolutionary principles.[59]

There was another important change in the character of the regime that emerged following the 1963 coup. Many of the younger men who achieved political primacy after the coup were members of Syria's religious minorities, especially the Alawis and to a lesser extent the Druze.[60] Alawis and Druze are both heterodox Muslim sects, being offshoots of Shiite Islam that established their doctrinal independence during the Fatimid period. The most prominent member of the new regime was General Salah Jadid, an Alawi, and Alawis were particularly dominant in the military. According to one estimate, perhaps exaggerated, 70 percent of the officer corps was drawn from Alawi ranks.[61] Therefore, overall, the coup of 1963 had set in motion an important transformation of the Syrian political elite. Although some of the older Baath politicians remained in the government through the end of 1965, Jadid and others of the younger generation effectively dominated the political scene.

A violent military coup in February 1966 solidified movement in this direction. It occurred in response to an attempt by old-guard Baath politicians to regain some of their former power; and, confirming that Syria still lacked a stable and institutionalized political system, it was the ninth change of government by force in seventeen years. The coup, in which several hundred persons were killed, completely removed the founders of the Baath Party from positions of influence. Many, including Aflaq and Bitar, were for a time placed under arrest and later sent into exile. Jadid, the mastermind of the coup, now exercised power from his position as secretary of the Syrian branch of the Baath Party. Another leader of the new regime was Nureddin al-Atassi, who left his post on the Presidential Council to become head of state.

The significance for the Arab-Israeli conflict of these developments within Syria lies in two interrelated areas. First, the regime was not popular inside the country, and as a result it was faced with a temptation, perhaps even a need, to pursue a foreign policy that would enhance its domestic position. Hostility toward Israel was one important dimension of such a foreign policy. Second, Syria repaired its relations with Egypt. The motivation for new overtures toward Cairo was not dissimilar to that which contributed to the regime's antipathy toward Jerusalem. Whatever might be its ideological appeal, an alliance with Nasser was above all a foreign-policy initiative that promised practical advantages. Moreover, these advantages were sought not only in the arena of domestic Syrian politics but also in the sphere of inter-Arab relations, where Damascus needed allies in the face of competition from Iraq and Jordan. As seen from Jerusalem, however, this meant the resurrection of an alliance between Israel's two most powerful and implacable Arab adversaries.

As discussed previously, old-guard Baathists had also found themselves in need of a foreign policy that would buttress their domestic political position. First, their socialist ideology had placed them in opposition to the notables of the traditional political class, which was based on once-powerful merchant and land-owning families located in the country's major urban centers. Even more important, the Baath Party's brand of secular pan-Arabism was alien to the country's Sunni Muslim majority, most of whom were pious and would oppose any ideology that left no room for religion. Still another factor contributing to the Baathists' limited popular appeal, and hence to their need for a foreign policy that would rally public support, was what one analyst calls its "clandestine mentality," meaning that the party had begun its political life as a subversive movement of opposition and had never completely abandoned its secretive character. Even after the Baathists came to power, party membership and organizational structure for the most part remained secret and revolved around the activities of a few hundred men.[62]

All of these considerations had figured prominently in the Baath Party's decision to seek a union with Nasser in 1958. They also contributed to the Baathists' hostile attitude toward Israel, transcending those substantive complaints that the Damascus regime had lodged against Jerusalem. In both cases, political circumstances encouraged the Damascus government to pursue foreign-policy initiatives that would put domestic opponents on the defensive, deflect public attention from local grievances, and above all enhance the Baath Party's legitimacy.

The distance between rulers and masses increased with the advent of a new coterie of leaders in 1963 and 1964, and especially after the coup of February 1966. For one thing, the increasingly authoritarian character of the government and the growing influence of the military reinforced the secretive and inbred character of the regime. For another, the new leaders were doctrinaire socialists, as much as if not more so than the men they had ousted; and their militant commitment to a collectivist, state-run economy rekindled the discontent of traditional and conservative political notables. Finally, and probably most important, the influence of religious minorities continued to grow. Alawis, who constituted only 11 percent of the total population, had become particularly influential. Also overrepresented were Druze, who made up no more than 3 or 4 percent of the overall population. Although Baath ideology proclaimed that distinctions based on religion and ethnicity were not important, it quickly became evident that the new government was placing a disproportionate number of Alawis in positions of importance, particularly within the military and also within the bureaucracy. In addition, it appears that a disproportionate amount of governmental assistance was being provided to the northern provinces of the country, especially in the region of Latikia, the area of greatest Alawi concentration.[63]

The unrepresentative character of the regime reinforced other factors which limited the popular base of the Syrian government, and this in turn contributed further to the tendency to regard foreign relations as an arena for shoring up domestic support. The implications of this situation for Syrian attitudes toward Israel are discussed by a number of scholars. Michael C. Hudson, for example, refers to the issue of Palestine in this context as a "legitimacy resource," reporting that the Baathists succeeded in exploiting this resource more effectively than any other political faction in Syria.[64] Evron, too, reports that considerations of legitimacy and domestic political competition encouraged successive Baath governments to adopt a militant posture toward the Jewish state. In particular, he argues, this inclination was reinforced by the minority character of the regime that came to power in the mid-1960s. Aggressiveness toward Israel was intensified by the new leaders' "feeling of insecurity inside Syria and their fear that precisely because they belonged to a minority group they were suspect, in the eyes of the majority, of being ready to compromise on pan-Arab nationalism." [65] Much the same point is also made by Gordon Torrey, who stresses the domestic as well as the foreign-policy consequences of the regime's failure to strike popular roots.

> The Ba'thist regime has never succeeded in attracting popular support. . . . Despite control of the press, radio and television, the party has been unable to project an image of real identity with the Syrian people. Its propaganda tends to concentrate on charges against the "imperialists" or Israel. The public has no sense of participation in the governing of the country and, if not alienated, is indifferent or disgusted. [66]

A second set of developments associated with the evolution of Syrian politics also had important consequences for the Arab-Israeli conflict. This was a rapprochement between Damascus and Cairo. Shortly after the 1966 coup, Jadid and Atassi undertook to improve relations with the Nasser regime in Egypt. In contrast to old-guard Baathist politicians, who were driven by an ideological commitment to pan-Arabism as well as by considerations of practical politics, the concerns of the new leaders in Damascus resided almost entirely in the latter domain, including a desire to obtain Cairo's support in their own country's competition with Jordan and Iraq. Nasser at first reacted with caution. Nevertheless, given the political demise of those in Syria whom he held responsible for the failure of the United Arab Republic, as well as the subsequent unity agreement of April 1963, the Egyptian president permitted the Syrian foreign minister to come to Cairo for consultations in June. This visit almost immediately led to a trade and payments agreement, and later in the summer the Egyptian foreign minister visited Damascus. This was the first visit to Syria by an Egyptian cabinet member since the breakup of the UAR in 1961. As a result of these and other exchanges, the two countries in November reestablished formal diplomatic relations, which also had been severed since the dissolution of the UAR.

Damascus and Cairo also signed a mutual defense pact in November 1966. Each country committed itself to come to the aid of the other in the event of an attack. The agreement also provided for a merger of the two armies and the establishment of a unified military command in the event of war. Nasser's motivation for the pact was, at least in part, to constrain the behavior of the Syrians, whom he considered reckless and unpredictable. He feared that Syria's provocative posture toward Israel might ignite another war in the Middle East, one for which, he was confident, the Arabs were as yet unprepared. Yet Damascus had sought the defense pact for its own purposes and, distrustful of Nasser, it refused to authorize the stationing of Egyptian troops and planes on its soil.

Israel was deeply concerned about the Syrian-Egyptian rapprochement, and especially about the mutual defense treaty concluded by the two countries. Despite Nasser's desire to exercise a moderating influence on the Syrians, Jerusalem feared, correctly as it turned out, that the agreement with Egypt would serve to encourage, rather than to temper, the aggressive attitude of the Baathists in Damascus. Yet a military alliance with Egypt might cause the Israelis to hesitate before retaliating against Syrian provocations, including the sponsorship of raids by Palestinian guerrillas or even, possibly, a direct attack on the Jewish state. Alternatively, should Israel believe it had no choice but to apply a strategy of punishment and deterrence, Egypt would be dragged into the conflict, and the confrontation could very well escalate. All of this heightened Israeli concerns and intensified the debates about military policy that were taking place in Jerusalem. As seen from the Israeli capital, the November defense pact had allied the Jewish state's two most dangerous enemies and, equally important, it had given the more aggressive and irresponsible of the two an ability to determine the behavior of the other, militarily stronger partner.

Israeli attitudes toward Syria, and toward the Arab world in general, were also affected by the Jewish state's own economic and political circumstances. The situation during the mid-1960s is summarized by Evron, who states that although pressures and uncertainties within Israel did not *cause* Jerusalem to favor war or to pursue adventurist policies, "the uneasy psychological situation was an added element in the decision to react strongly to Syrian provocations."[67] One factor contributing to this Israeli orientation was economic uncertainty, brought on by growing inflation, a rapidly increasing trade deficit, and eventually a sharp economic slowdown accompanied by a rapid rise in unemployment. Another factor was the changing political map of the country, including a split between Ben Gurion and the mainstream of the Labor Zionist movement.

Israel's economic problems were the result not of low productivity but rather, ironically, of overly rapid growth. GNP had continued to increase at an average annual rate of 11–12 percent, and national income had risen by 120 percent in the decade between 1955 and 1964. There had also been a steady growth in exports, which more than tripled during the same period. This situation had given rise to a serious labor shortage, however, which raised doubts about continued productivity in the future, and in the short run pushed up wages and fueled inflation. The government addressed the latter problems by placing a partial freeze on wages in 1963. Nevertheless, gross wages rose by 9 percent the following year, and per-hour wages increased by 11 percent. In 1965, gross wages rose by 16 percent, with workers in a number of industries negotiating contracts that guaranteed future increases of the same magnitude. These figures, while modest in comparison to the pattern of inflation that was to become common in Israel fifteen years later, drove up the cost of living and initiated a wage-price spiral that caused much concern. In 1965, the cost of foodstuffs increased by 15 percent, for example, and the overall cost of living increased by 9 percent.

A driving force behind inflation was the shortage of labor, particularly skilled labor; and, somewhat paradoxically, the excess of demand over supply in relation to labor had increased despite the steady growth of the Israeli population. By 1964, there were approximately 2.2 million Israelis, of whom almost 300,000 were Arabs. The former figure represents an increase of 211 percent in comparison with 1948. Roughly two-thirds of this increase, about 1.2 million individuals, was the result of immigration; and of this about 55 percent, or 650,000, were Jews who had immigrated from Muslim and for the most part Arab countries. Admittedly, the majority of the immigration to Israel had taken place in the years immediately following statehood. Nevertheless, population was growing at a rate of roughly 4 percent in the mid-1960s, and immigration still exceeded natural increase as a factor in this growth.

Despite the country's growing population, the supply of workers was not expanding rapidly enough to meet demand. Indeed, the labor force had grown by only 40 percent between 1955 and 1964, well under half the rate at which the economy had expanded. In addition, the situation was made worse by the poor occupational skills of many workers, especially those of immigrant origin, and by a concentration of too large a part of the labor force in the service sector of the economy.[68] The result of all this was the labor shortage noted earlier. Aggregate unemployment was only 3.4 percent in 1964, and competition for workers was intense in manufacturing and other occupations requiring professional skills. As expressed by one official of the Bank of Israel, "In certain skilled trades, the workman could almost name his own price."[69]

A steadily worsening balance of trade also contributed to Israel's economic problems. Between 1955 and 1964, the gap between exports and imports grew from about $250 million to about $450 million, an alarming deficit in a country of barely two million people. Moreover, the growth in imports was driven by rising levels of personal consumption, and also by arms purchases, rather than by the acquisition of industrial equipment and machinery that would contribute to the state's economic productivity in the future. One of the causes of this situation was rising inflation, which discouraged savings and hence stimulated personal consumption. Another contributing factor was the expansion of credit by the Israeli government.

The growing trade imbalance indicated that the Israeli economy, however productive, was unable to keep pace with the country's ever-increasing level of consumption, which one Israeli scholar called the "Achilles Heel" of the national economy.[70] In the immediate term, much of the deficit was offset by financial aid from abroad, including public assistance from the United States and private donations from Jews throughout the world. Nevertheless, by regularly eating up most of the growth in GNP and national income, and by forcing the expenditure of foreign-currency assets for goods and services that did not increase the level of economic productivity, the trade deficit was not only a problem of current accounts but also a threat to long-term growth and development.

Both inflation and a trade deficit driven by high levels of personal consumption pointed to the need for belt-tightening, and the government accordingly enacted various measures in order to bring about an economic slowdown. These included significant cutbacks in the state budget and a reduction in the money supply. Yet actions of this sort, whatever their long-term economic value, were highly unpopular. They lowered the standard of living of many Israelis and thus intensified the psychological pressure felt by much of the population. The mood had become particularly gloomy by the winter of 1966–67. A recession had set in, the effects of which were visible in rapidly rising unemployment and a deterioration of the circumstances of the country's poorer social classes. In dramatic contrast to the situation only two years earlier, unemployment climbed to 12 percent in January 1967, and the number of Israelis living in conditions of poverty reached 300,000. Also, principally because of the economic recession, the number of Jews emigrating from Israel exceeded the number of new arrivals at this time. According to one sympathetic observer, an "all-pervading malaise" gripped the Jewish state.[71]

Economic concerns became *political* issues in this environment. But there were other political concerns as well, some of which bore more directly on matters of foreign policy and on attitudes toward the Arabs. One was the Lavon Affair, which reemerged in the early 1960s as an important and divisive political issue. In December 1960, the Israeli cabinet accepted a ministerial committee report which exonerated Lavon of responsibility for the 1954 "mishap." Ben Gurion was dissatisfied with this report, however, and insisted on a full-scale judicial inquiry. Then, to emphasize his disapproval of the cabinet's action, he resigned the premiership in January 1961, forcing new elections in August.

Mapai, the party of Ben Gurion and the major political movement within the ranks of Labor Zionism, had dominated the political scene since independence, and this did not change with the elections of 1961. Moreover, differences between Ben Gurion and others in Mapai were almost immediately papered over; the veteran Labor Zionist leader headed Mapai's list of candidates in the 1961 elections, and after the balloting he was once more tapped by his party to head the government. Ben Gurion resigned again in June 1963, however, and in the year that followed he devoted much of his energy to his own study of the Lavon case.

Levi Eshkol became prime minister following Ben Gurion's resignation. Eshkol, who had previously served as finance minister, was known as a moderate and a conciliator. Also, initially at least, his flexible and restrained attitude toward the Arabs contrasted with that of the more militant Ben Gurion. In December 1964, the former prime minister took his report on the mishap in Egypt to the cabinet, but his renewed request for a judicial investigation was turned down by Eshkol and others. He then addressed the matter to the Mapai Central Committee, where he was supported by some, though not a majority, in a session so stormy that it led to the temporary resignation of Eshkol. After failing to obtain Mapai's endorsement, Ben Gurion determined to organize a new political movement and take his case directly to the electorate. Accompanied by Shimon Peres, Moshe Dayan, and a number of other followers, he founded Rishimat Poalei Yisrael (Rafi), the Israel Workers' List.

Ben Gurion's new party campaigned against Mapai in the elections of 1965, leading one analyst to characterize the competition between Ben Gurion and Rafi on the one hand and Eshkol and Mapai on the other as "waning charisma and increasing petulance versus monotonous competence and dreary efficiency."[72] Cast in such terms, the outcome of the 1965 election might have been difficult to predict. Also contributing to the uncertainty were the country's economic problems. Nevertheless, Mapai retained its dominant position. Establishing an alignment with Ahdut Ha'avoda, a small Labor Zionist party that had split off from Mapam in 1954, Mapai obtained 45 of the Knesset's 120 seats. This was only a modest decline, since Mapai and Ahdut Ha'avoda had obtained 42 seats and 8 seats respectively in the balloting of 1961.

Ben Gurion's new party received 10 seats, which was not enough to challenge seriously the preeminence of the Mapai–Ahdut Ha'avoda alignment but was an impressive showing nonetheless. Indeed, Rafi had fared substantially better than any other new party since the founding of the state. In the judgment of some analysts, the appeal of Rafi lay not so much in Ben Gurion but in Dayan, Peres, and other "Young Turks" of the defense establishment.[73] These men, like Ben Gurion, stood for a more hard-line attitude toward the Arabs. Rafi also represented a nonideological alternative to the increasingly inward-looking Mapai political machine. Finally, and perhaps most important, the formation of Rafi signaled the political emergence of younger, native-born Israelis, thus being the first important challenge to the generation of Labor Zionists who had immigrated to Palestine during the Second and Third *aliya*s and subsequently led the *Yishuv* to statehood.[74]

There was also movement on the right side of the Israeli political spectrum in 1965, among those parties which had since 1948 carried forward the traditions of General Zionism and Revisionism. The mantle of General Zionism was now borne by the Liberal Party, which had been formed in 1961 through a merger of the General Zionist Party and the Progressive Party. The Liberal Party stood for laissez-faire economic policies, in contrast to the socialism of the Labor Zionist establishment. It also championed individual rights in matters of religion, thus opposing the parties of orthodox Judaism. Leaders of the Revisionist wing of the Zionist movement had formed the Herut Party in 1948, and this party had grown modestly in the intervening years. Led by Menachem Begin, who had directed the Irgun prior to independence, Herut had a platform of militant nationalism and advocated hard-line policies toward the Arabs. In the 1961 elections, Herut and the Liberal Party had each received seventeen Knesset seats; and although this placed them well behind Mapai, which won forty-two seats, it put them comfortably ahead of the next-largest party, the National Religious Party, which captured twelve seats. Against this background, it was significant that Herut and the Liberals merged in 1965, forming the Herut-Liberal Bloc, or Gahal, in time for the elections of that year.

Gahal obtained only twenty-six Knesset seats in the 1965 balloting, substantially fewer than its two constituent parties had received separately four years earlier. In part, this was because one faction of the Liberal Party had remained outside Gahal, forming the Independent Liberal Party and presenting its own slate of candidates to the electorate. The Independent Liberal Party obtained five Knesset seats in 1965. Gahal's performance probably was also affected by the presence of Rafi, which may have attracted some who in the past had voted for either the Liberals or Herut.

Even though Gahal's performance was disappointing to its founders, the emergence of the party was highly significant. First, it unified the nonreligious opposition to Labor and created a sizable bloc on the right side of the political spectrum. Herut brought the vote-getting appeal of its ideology to the merger, whereas the Liberals provided access to financial resources and a number of seasoned political personalities. This coalition would challenge Labor for political preeminence in the years ahead, and even in the short run, coupled with the comparative success of Rafi, it tended to pull the political spectrum perceptibly to the right. Second, Gahal's creation conferred an important measure of legitimacy on Menachem Begin and the Herut political movement. Begin and other Revisionists whose origins lay in the Irgun or the Stern Group had long been regarded as fanatics, and accordingly treated as outcasts by mainstream Zionist politicians.[75] But a merger with the party of General Zionism, which traced its own roots back to Chaim Weizmann, conferred an important degree of respectability on these men. This, in turn, enhanced their ability to attract talented young men and women into party institutions. It would also enable them to broaden their popular appeal in future elections.

While these economic and political circumstances contribute to an understanding of the mood in Israel during the middle 1960s, it would be inappropriate to link them directly to the growing tension between the Jewish state and its Arab neighbors. From the Israeli point of view, it was clearly an objective threat, most notably from Syria, that was responsible for growing concern about the situation on the border. Moreover, Israel's conviction that strong retaliatory strikes were necessary to deter raids by the Syrians and other Arabs was by no means new, and thus not the product of contemporary domestic pressures.

On the other hand, domestic political and economic considerations almost certainly helped to condition Jerusalem's response to the challenges it faced, and added to the vigor with which it applied a deterrent strategy. Economic uncertainty created a climate of dissatisfaction and psychological insecurity, thereby heightening the country's determination to deal forcefully with the Arabs. Even more, the charge of weakness was continuously leveled at Eshkol by Ben Gurion and Rafi, and this in turn put pressure on the prime minister to act decisively in the realm of foreign policy. This pressure would appear to explain, in part, why the more restrained attitude Eshkol displayed upon assuming the premiership in 1963 gave way in less than a year to an increased readiness to authorize military strikes.[76] Further, what one author calls Eshkol's "credibility crisis," brought on by his quarrel with Ben Gurion and the attendant allegations of negligence in matters of national security, helped to shape his handling of the major Arab-Israeli confrontation that was to emerge in 1967.[77]

There is one more set of actors whose behavior during this period must be considered. Various Palestinian organizations appeared on the scene about this time and involved themselves both in the arena of inter-Arab politics and in the conflict between the Arab states and Israel. On the one hand, there were a number of clandestine and small-scale guerrilla movements. On the other, there was the Palestine Liberation Organization, established with much publicity and fanfare in 1964.

The most important of the guerrilla groups was Fatah, the Palestinian National Liberation Movement, whose name is an acronym from Harakat al-Tahrir al-Filastini (Palestinian Liberation Movement), the order of the initials being reversed. Palestinian sources disagree about the exact date of Fatah's founding. The movement began to take shape at a meeting held in Kuwait in October 1957 but apparently did not fully crystallize until 1962. The movement's publication, *Filastinuna* (Our Palestine), first appeared in Beirut in 1959.[78] Fatah and other guerrilla groups were seen as subversive and troublesome by Arab governments, especially by Egypt and Jordan, and they therefore operated in secret to avoid persecution from the Arab regimes.

The PLO, by contrast, not only was tolerated by the Arab states but in fact was their creation. Its origins lie in the Arab summit meeting convened in Cairo in January 1964, which was attended by thirteen Arab heads of state and whose principal objective, it will be recalled, was to formulate a reply to Israel's plan to remove water from the Sea of Galilee. In addition to making plans for the Arabs' own water-diversion scheme, the delegates assembled in Cairo called for the creation of Palestinian commando units that would carry out sabotage operations against Israeli water installations. Further, they empowered the Palestinian representative to the Arab League, Ahmad Shuqayri, to formulate plans for the establishment of a "Palestinian entity" that would contribute more broadly to the struggle against the Jewish state. Referring to these decisions, the report of the conference stated that "the necessary practical steps were taken . . . in the field of organizing the Palestinian people and enabling them to play their role in the liberation of their country and their self-determination."[79]

Despite the language of its report, the Arab summit's primary purpose in creating the PLO was not to give expression to Palestinian desires for self-determination. It was rather to co-opt and restrain the Palestinian resistance movement, in order to prevent existing guerrilla organizations from drawing the Arab states into a war with Israel. Fatah and other Palestinian groups were thus extremely cautious in their dealings with Shuqayri, whom they rightly viewed as Nasser's agent rather than an independent spokesman for the Palestinian cause. Further, perhaps partly for reasons of personal jealousy, Shuqayri was criticized strongly by al-Hajj Amin al-Husayni, who was then living in Beirut and continued to issue statements in the name of the Arab Higher Committee. Nevertheless, most Palestinian factions ultimately agreed to coordination with the new "entity" and its leader, reasoning that their interests could best be served by helping to shape the character of the new organization. Shuqayri spent several months shuttling throughout the Middle East early in 1964, and at the end of May he succeeded in bringing together 422 Palestinians from ten Arab countries. They met at the Intercontinental Hotel in Jerusalem, Jordan, and among their number were about a dozen Fatah delegates.

Shuqayri, who assumed the title of president of the First Palestine National Council, opened the Jerusalem meeting with a "Declaration of the Creation of the Palestine Liberation Organization." His statement defined the PLO as "a shield for the rights and aspirations of the people of Palestine." Thereafter, the delegates to the conference approved two key documents, both of which had been authored by Shuqayri. The first was the Palestine National Charter, also known as the Covenant, which contained twenty-nine articles and set forth the basic goals of the Palestinian people. As the following articles indicate, the charter was in effect a Declaration of Independence. It recorded the PLO's commitment to the liberation of the Palestinian homeland, and to the destruction of the Jewish state which occupied Palestine.

> ARTICLE 1. Palestine, within the boundaries it had during the period of the British Mandate, is an indivisible territorial unit.
>
> ARTICLE 6. Palestinians are those Arab citizens who, until 1947, had normally resided in Palestine, regardless of whether they have been evicted from it or have stayed in it. Anyone born after that date of a Palestinian father, whether inside Palestine or outside it, is also a Palestinian.
>
> ARTICLE 17. The partition of Palestine in 1947 and the establishment of Israel are entirely illegal, regardless of the passage of time, because they were contrary to the will of the Palestinian people and its natural right in its homeland, and inconsistent with the general principles embodied in the Charter of the United Nations, particularly the right of self-determination.

The second document approved by the delegates assembled in Jerusalem was the PLO's constitution, formally known as its General Principles of Fundamental Law. Among the key provisions of the constitution was the establishment of the

Palestine National Council, defined as the parliament of the Palestinian people and of which the Jerusalem meeting was deemed to be the first session. The constitution also provided for a fifteen-member Executive Committee, which was to be elected by the PNC and which in turn would elect the PLO's chairman.[80] Yet another body created by the constitution was the Palestine National Fund, which was charged with raising money.[81] With the PLO now formally recognized by the Arab League as the official representative of the Palestinian people, the organization sent delegates to various international meetings, including the Conference of Non-Aligned States held in Cairo in October 1964. The PNC held its second plenary session in Cairo in May and June of 1965 and its third session in Gaza in May 1966. Shuqayri remained chairman of the PLO Executive Committee throughout this entire period.

Although it would play a critical role after 1967, when the Palestinian dimension returned to center stage in the Arab-Israeli conflict, the PLO was not an important participant in the Arab struggle against Israel during the first three years of its existence. It did establish a Palestine Liberation Army, with units based in Egypt, Syria, and Iraq, but the force was kept under tight control and was not a major factor in the escalating tension between the Jewish state and its neighbors. Egypt would not permit the PLA to carry out raids from Gaza, and in fact the PLA was trained and equipped to be a conventional army rather than a commando force. PLA raids against Israel from other locations were strongly opposed by Shuqayri, at least partly because of his heavy dependence upon Cairo.

The PLO's passive orientation led to criticism in Palestinian circles, and to an extent within the organization's own ranks. Shuqayri had hand-picked the vast majority of the delegates to the Jerusalem convention at which the PLO charter and constitution were approved, and most were moderates or conservatives with little sympathy for the "revolution" advocated by some Palestinians. Similarly, as Shuqayri intended, the Executive Committee selected from the ranks of these delegates was dominated by middle-aged professional men whose outlook also tended to be conservative, leading critics to complain that the PLO would become "only an entity for propaganda and without any revolutionary meaning."[82] Shuqayri was criticized for his leadership style as well as his policies, and in particular for his heavy-handedness in dealing with other Palestinians while apparently obeying without question the orders he received from Cairo. This constellation of complaints led to bitter political and ideological battles within the PLO toward the end of 1966 and early in 1967. These complaints were also expressed in a steady stream of criticism directed at the PLO from Syria. The Damascus regime was particularly unhappy about the organization's close ties to Egypt, and Syrian officials accordingly denounced Nasser and Shuqayri for undermining the PLO's "revolutionary effectiveness and independence."[83]

Palestinian guerrilla movements played a different role in the period prior to 1967. A few men with links to one or another of these groups were active inside the PLO, pushing from within for a more revolutionary orientation. Yet the groups themselves remained independent, and with backing from Syria they pursued a very different political course. Fatah, as noted, had begun to take shape as early as 1957. An additional stimulus to the formation of commando organizations was the dissolution of the UAR in 1961, which led action-oriented Palestinians to conclude that the Arab states were unprepared to contribute meaningfully to their cause. So, too, was the formation of the PLO, which seemed to demonstrate that the Arab states, with the exception of Syria, actually sought to block any Palestinian action that might provoke a confrontation with Israel. In this environment, several new guerrilla groups appeared during 1965 and 1966. One was the Palestine Liberation Front, led by Ahmad Jibril. It had contacts with Fatah in 1965 but struck out on its own in 1966, carrying out its first commando raid against Israel late in the year. Another new group, under the leadership of Nayif Hawatmeh, called itself the Vengeance Youth. It appeared on the scene in 1966 and conducted its first commando operation in May 1967. A third group was the Heroes of the Return.

These three groups all had common origins in a radical movement of opinion dating from the 1950s, the Arab Nationalist Movement, led by George Habash. The ANM was ideologically oriented toward pan-Arabism but had lost its revolutionary character by the early 1960s, causing younger elements to break away and form semi-independent guerrilla organizations. In December 1967, however, six months after the third Arab-Israeli war, the ANM and its three offshoots merged to form a new organization, the Popular Front for the Liberation of Palestine. The PFLP came under the umbrella of the PLO the following year, and all three of its leaders, Habash, Jibril, and Hawatmeh, soon became influential within the Palestine Liberation Organization.

Fatah was larger and more active than any of the other guerrilla groups. Its leaders were Yasir Arafat, Khalil al-Wazir, Farouq al-Qaddoumi, Khaled al-Hassan, and Salah Khalaf. Fatah did not initially favor military raids against Israel, judging that it was as yet too weak to carry out such operations, but the group was nonetheless active in seeking support and building an organization. It forged important ties with the government in Damascus during the early 1960s, taking advantage of Syria's desire for Palestinian allies in its political and ideological competition with Nasser. It also sought support in several other Arab countries. In 1962, for example, the guerrilla group sent a delegation to Algeria, to meet with the president of the newly independent North African state. Finally, following the January 1964 Cairo summit meeting and the subsequent founding of the PLO, Fatah for a time cooperated with Shuqayri and sought to exercise influence through his organization.

By the end of 1964, Arafat and other Fatah leaders had concluded that cooperation with the PLO would not yield tangible results. Thus, despite some division of opinion within their ranks, they decided to break with Shuqayri's organization and launch commando raids against the Jewish state. Fatah established a militia, al-Asifa (The Storm), in January 1965. The name was selected in order to hide the institutional affiliation of the fighting force, in deference to those who feared that Fatah was still too fragile to engage in military action. Some al-Asifa commandos were trained at bases in Syria, and some, without revealing their Fatah membership, joined the PLA in order to receive training. By the end of 1965, according to Fatah's own claims, these fighters had carried out thirty-nine raids against Israel.[84]

The scope and effectiveness of early Fatah operations were limited. The organization acknowledged as much when it complained to the Arab League that Egypt and Jordan had been hampering al-Asifa activities. Nevertheless, Fatah succeeded in establishing a pattern of sustained armed struggle, which won it followers in the Palestinian diaspora, and which also contributed to the tension between Israel and its neighbors. The latter was in fact a specific Fatah objective. While the movement harbored no illusions about inflicting major damage on the Jewish state, it did hope to provoke Israeli retaliatory strikes to which the Arab governments would in turn be forced to respond.

Among the Arab states, Syria alone provided active support for Fatah's commando operations. Damascus also sponsored guerrilla raids against Israel by other Palestinian commando groups during 1966 and the first months of 1967. As noted, Baathist leaders were motivated in substantial measure by their rivalry with Nasser, and they were thus willing, indeed eager, to assist Palestinian fighters in order to draw a distinction between their own revolutionary orientation and the reaction and defeatism with which they charged the regime in Cairo. Fatah also acted independently, or semi-independently, on many occasions. Its ability to operate in Gaza, where the main PLA force was based, was restricted by the Egyptians. The Jordanian government, by contrast, was unable to prevent commando units from carrying out incursions into Israel, even though it did make an effort to do so. Thus, though its headquarters were in Syria, Fatah often preferred to launch raids across the Jordanian-Israeli frontier, which was much longer and more difficult to defend than the border between Israel and Syria. This also had the advantage of permitting Damascus to deny all responsibility for Fatah attacks, even though Syria was sheltering and supporting the Palestinian guerrillas.[85]

As intended, all of this had a significant impact in Israel. By themselves, Fatah's operations were no more than a minor irritant. But, reinforced by occasional Syrian military actions and a steady barrage of propaganda emanating from Damascus, guerrilla raids contributed to the climate of uncertainty already prevailing inside the Jewish state. Many Israelis became convinced that Syria was laying the foundation for a full-scale guerrilla war, and as public concern mounted, the government in Jerusalem debated the pros and cons of a major attack against Syria. In the meantime, driven by what one analyst called "a nearly irresistible determination to react,"[86] Israel carried out a number of strikes in response to Fatah raids launched from Jordan. In April 1966, for example, the IDF blew up fourteen houses in two Jordanian villages, in retaliation for acts of sabotage carried out by infiltrators who, it charged, had found shelter in these communities. In November, a much larger and more deadly Israeli strike took place. On the 13th, IDF armored columns invaded the West Bank in the region south of Hebron and carried out a major attack on the towns of Samu, Jimba, and Khirbet Karkay. This large-scale military operation, the most extensive since the Sinai-Suez War, resulted in the deaths of three Jordanian civilians and fifteen Arab Legion troops. Fifty-four more civilians and military personnel were wounded, and there was also extensive property damage, including 140 houses, a clinic, and a school. Israeli casualties included one killed and ten wounded.

Toward the War of June 1967

Growing tensions in the region were clearly visible long before Israel's November attack on Samu and two other West Bank towns. An escalating spiral of raid and retaliation had already been set in motion, reminiscent of the period before the Sinai-Suez War. As noted earlier, Israel's border with Syria, as well as with Jordan, was the scene of various military exchanges. In August 1966, for example, Jerusalem and Damascus fought a major battle in the region of the Sea of Galilee. Both sides sent planes into the exchange, while fire was traded between Israeli patrol boats and Syrian shore batteries. Each side accused the other of initiating the fighting, and each claimed to have inflicted heavy losses on its adversary. It is also significant that after the battle Syria declared that it would thereafter pursue a "new" strategy in dealing with Israeli "aggression." Rather than confine itself to "defensive action," Damascus proclaimed that it would now "attack defined targets and bases of aggression" inside the Jewish state.[87] Syria's motivations, as discussed, may to a considerable degree have been shaped by domestic political considerations. Nevertheless, Baath statements and actions reinforced the view that the Middle East was once again drifting toward war.

It is against this backdrop that Egypt's willingness to sign a mutual defense pact with Syria may be seen. Cairo entered into the agreement, concluded early in November 1966, largely in the hope of restraining Damascus and reducing the chances of a major Arab-Israeli confrontation. But the Syrians would not permit Egyptian troops to be stationed on their soil, thus leaving Cairo with only limited ability to control Syrian behavior. Indeed, in the judgment of many analysts, the practical consequence of the agreement was to give Damascus the ability to control Egyptian behavior. By sufficiently provoking Israel, the Baathists could elicit a military response from Jerusalem, and this in turn would drag Egypt into a war with the Jewish state. This was the situation when the IDF invaded the West

Bank on November 13, a few days after the conclusion of the Syrian-Egyptian pact.

Fallout from the Israeli invasion added to the tension. On the one hand, it produced a wave of violent protest inside Jordan and put pressure on the government of King Hussein. On the other, it brought a severe condemnation of Israel by the United Nations, one in which Jerusalem's allies joined other nations in supporting a resolution that Israel considered both one-sided and dangerous. Shortly after the IDF attack, Palestinian inhabitants in Nablus, Jenin, and other West Bank towns staged major protest demonstrations. Moreover, they took to the streets not only to condemn Israel but also to denounce the Hashemite regime for inaction. The protesters called for the Arab Legion to carry out reprisals against Israel, and they also demanded that arms be distributed to villagers living near the border. In the end, the Jordanian army had to be called out to restore order in several communities. Hussein's failure to act against Israel was also criticized by Egypt and the PLO, and Syria went so far as to offer aid to those Jordanians desiring to overthrow the government in Amman. Hussein responded to critics in other Arab countries by caustically observing that none of them had hastened to Jordan's aid during the Israeli invasion. And he taunted Nasser in particular by adding that it was easy to advocate military action when one's own troops were "hiding behind" the forces of the United Nations.

In the meantime, at Jordan's request, the Security Council took up the matter of the Israeli invasion. Amman urged the Council to condemn Jerusalem for aggression and called for economic sanctions against the Jewish state, to which Israel responded by insisting that it had acted in self-defense in the face of repeated instances of aggression and "terrorism" carried out against it by others. One of the many incidents about which Israel complained was an October bomb attack that wounded four civilians in Jerusalem. Another, which occurred the day before the Israeli invasion, was the explosion of a land mine placed on a road near the Dead Sea town of Arad, which caused the deaths of three Israeli soldiers and wounded six others.

Although many Security Council members acknowledged and deplored the provocations preceding Israel's attack, they nonetheless judged that the Jewish state's retaliatory strike had been excessive and was therefore unjustified. Accordingly, the Council passed a resolution condemning the Israeli strike but making no mention of the events to which it had been a response. The resolution also stipulated that the Security Council would consider "further and more effective steps envisaged in the Charter" should there be any additional attacks by Israel. The United States and several other countries may have been motivated to support this resolution by the hope that a strong and unqualified UN rebuke of Israel would relieve some of the pressure on the government of King Hussein. Israel, however, considered the Security Council's resolution not only to be unfair but, more important, to be worthless so far as peacekeeping was concerned. Repeating a point it had been making with regularity for some time, Jerusalem stated that so long as the UN was unwilling or unable to stop attacks upon it by Syria and the Palestinians, Israel would have no choice but to defend itself in whatever manner it deemed most appropriate.

Events within Jordan and at the United Nations intensified the debate over military policy that was already well underway inside the Jewish state. The IDF invasion had many supporters. A majority of Israeli analysts repeated that Jerusalem could not remain idle in the face of continuing provocations. Not to respond strongly and decisively, they insisted, would only encourage further attacks by Fatah and its backers. The absence of a meaningful response would also permit the civilian population of Jordan to conclude, with justification, that there was no price to be paid for the harboring of terrorists. Finally, supporters of Israel's retaliatory action argued that it had succeeded in further dividing the Arab world, showing that talk of Arab unity was without substance. In particular, it had embarrassed Nasser by demonstrating that the Arab world's would-be leader was unwilling to come to the aid of an Arab League member that had been attacked.

Other Israelis, however, questioned the wisdom of the IDF's massive strike. They observed that the invasion of the West Bank had created problems for Jordan, a moderate Arab regime that was committed to regional stability and did not seek a confrontation with the Jewish state. By contrast, Israel's action had left Syria, the real aggressor in the region, completely untouched. Further, they expressed doubt that it was in their country's interest to humiliate Nasser and create a situation in which the Egyptian leader might be goaded into action, perhaps removing UNEF troops from Sinai and Gaza. Finally, they pointed out that Jerusalem was handing Fatah an important propaganda victory by treating as major assaults terrorist actions that were in fact no more than minor incidents. Israel's harsh retaliatory strike, they reasoned, helped Fatah to perpetuate the myth that it was an effective fighting force and had inflicted serious injury on the Jewish state, and this could only embolden the guerrillas and bring new recruits into their ranks. For all these reasons, some Israelis argued that their country's security interests could best be served by the application of "static" defense measures. Such measures might include the construction of an electrified fence along the frontier, for which the U.S. had offered to supply special detection equipment, and an increase in the number of border patrols.[88]

Another key aspect of the debate taking place within Israel focused on the behavior and motivations of Prime Minister Eshkol. Even some members of the prime minister's own party, Mapai, suggested that Eshkol's motivation in ordering the strike against Jordan may have had less to do with rational calculations about defense than with a desire to show decisiveness in the face of domestic criticism. For example, one contemporary observer reported that some Israelis believed Eshkol had sent the IDF into the West Bank in order "to hide the weakness of his domestic economic policies" and "to take Israeli minds off problems at hand."[89] Others offered a similar analysis, but added that it was political rather than economic pressures that were of greatest concern to the prime minister. Ben Gurion and others had repeatedly accused Eshkol of hesitation and timidity in dealing with the Arab threat. Moreover, Ben Gurion had asserted that this was indicative of a more general flaw in Eshkol's character as a leader. As expressed in a March 1966 interview, for example, he accused the prime minister of "the moral failure of not being sure of himself and of not knowing what he really wanted to do."[90] Sentiments of this sort were echoed in various political circles, by men who were more objective than Ben Gurion and among individuals who took dissimilar positions on the matter of retaliatory strikes. Thus, such criticism was not only an additional source of pressure on Eshkol but also, and more fundamentally, a disturbing analysis of the current state of Israeli political life. A vivid picture of the disarray in leadership circles is provided by Jon Kimche, who quotes the following statement made by a senior civil servant the day after the attack on Samu:

> The present difficulties are only incidentally due to economic problems; what these have done is to intensify and to concentrate the basic problem which we have to overcome. At the root of everything is the lack of confidence in the Government, especially in Eshkol and in the Labor Party, Mapai. Moreover, after the most recent events, there is also some uncertainty about the soundness of judgment in the leadership of the armed forces. . . .

> The present crisis of confidence stems largely from Eshkol's failure to govern— his indecision, his lack of self-confidence which has been greatly increased by the insistent questioning of the soundness of his political judgment and intentions. This has concentrated primarily on the economic policy of the Government and also on important areas of foreign policy. . . .

> The result of this is the extraordinary state of national apathy and fatalism in the country. The general mood of the public is that there is nothing that can be done about it, nothing they can do. For the first time since the establishment of the state I have heard acquaintances [in their thirties and forties] who are considered to be pillars of the nation tell me that they were scared about the future.[91]

Whatever the motivation and justification for the actions of various parties during the latter months of 1966, the drift toward war continued in 1967. New Fatah raids against Israel were launched from Jordan in January. In addition, armed clashes took place along the Israeli-Syrian border. There were again exchanges of fire across the demilitarized zone, brought on by conflicts between Israeli and Arab farmers attempting to cultivate disputed lands, and there were also guerrilla activities in the area of the Syrian frontier. The most important incident occurred when a land mine placed at a soccer match killed one Israeli and wounded two others. Jerusalem responded with a stern warning to Damascus, and Eshkol also sent telegrams to the United States and France, stating that Israel would not exercise self-restraint indefinitely in the face of such provocations. The two parties thereafter agreed to submit their grievances to the Mixed Armistice Commission of the United Nations, but the MAC was unable to bring about any sustained reduction of tensions and within a few weeks there were new exchanges of fire and new instances of sabotage.

The final act of the prewar drama opened on April 7. Another conflict over the cultivation of disputed lands in the Israeli-Syrian demilitarized zone led to a major engagement between Jerusalem and Damascus. Following an exchange of fire between forces on the ground, Israel and Syria both sent planes into the air, and six Syrian MIG aircraft were shot down in a dogfight over Mount Hermon. Syria claimed that Israel had deliberately initiated the small incident with which the conflict began, adding that Jerusalem had sought to provoke a skirmish in order to justify the major attack it was planning. Syria also condemned Egypt for failing to come to its aid, although observers pointed out that the aerial battle was completed before Cairo could possibly have had time to act. For its part, Israel insisted that the clash had begun when Syrian forces fired on an unarmed tractor driver working land belonging to the Jewish state. In addition, however, Israeli officials made it clear that Jerusalem's reprisal was meant to deliver a general warning to the Baath government. Demanding the immediate cessation of Palestinian commando activity, for which Israel held Syria generally responsible, they declared that Israel would, if necessary, carry out additional strikes against Damascus. General Yitzhak Rabin, who had been chief of staff since 1964, bluntly stated that "while this time the action was in connection with a border dispute, the same lesson can be applied in other areas."[92]

The Arabs became convinced in the weeks that followed that Israel had determined to invade Syria, quite possibly with the intention of overturning the Baath regime. On May 8, two Syrian intelligence officers traveled to Cairo to advise Nasser that the IDF was preparing to attack, and Arab accounts report that Lebanese sources corroborated the movement of IDF troops in the area of the border with Syria.[93] On May 9 and again on May 12, Eshkol repeated the threat of reprisals against Syria if Damascus continued to support Fatah attacks against the Jewish state, and on the same day the *New York Times* reported that Israeli leaders had already decided that the use of force against Syria "may be the only way to curtail increasing terrorism."[94]

In another critical development, the Soviet Union informed Syria and Egypt on May 13 that its own intelligence assessments confirmed the presence of Israeli troops massing near the Syrian frontier.[95] This information heightened the Arabs' concern and helped to solidify their conviction that an invasion of Syria was imminent. The way in which Egypt responded to the Soviet intelligence report is described by Nasser in the following excerpt from a speech delivered on May 25:

On May 13 we received accurate information that Israel was concentrating on the Syrian border huge armed forces of about 11 to 13 brigades. These forces were divided into two fronts, one south of Lake Tiberias and the other north of the lake. The decision made by Israel at this time was to carry out an attack against Syria starting on May 17. On May 14 we took action, discussed the matter and contacted our Syrian brethren. The Syrians also had this information. Based on this information, Lt.-General Mahmoud Fawzi left for Syria to coordinate matters. We told them that we had decided that if Syria was attacked, Egypt would enter the battle right from the start. This was the situation on 14 May. Forces began to move in the direction of Sinai to take up their normal positions.[96]

The following account by Mahmoud Riad, Nasser's foreign minister, also makes clear that the unfolding of events during this period persuaded Syrian and Egyptian leaders that Israel was preparing a major assault.

Yitzhak Rabin, Israeli Chief of Staff, lent credence to Syrian apprehensions when he declared on 12 May 1967 that "we will carry out a lightning attack on Syria, occupy Damascus, overthrow the regime there and come back"; and two days earlier, Abba Eban, Foreign Minister of Israel, had instructed his ambassadors abroad to reiterate that Israel might be obliged to employ force against Syria. Reports received in Cairo confirmed Israeli concentrations on the Syrian borders. An Egyptian parliamentary delegation headed by Anwar el-Sadat, on a visit at the time to Moscow, received information to this effect.[97]

Additional insight into the view from the Arab world in May 1967 is provided by Muhammad Hassanein Haykal, a close confidant of Nasser and editor of the influential Cairo daily *Al-Ahram*. Haykal wrote on May 26 that Israel would attack because Jerusalem considered it essential to intimidate the Arabs, and because this "is the philosophy on which Israel has pivoted since its birth." Arguing that this is the way the Arab world is viewed by Zionists, with many believing the Arabs understand only the language of power, Haykal asserted that Israel would be pushed to war by its "psychological aim of convincing the Arabs that Israel could do anything and that the Arabs could do nothing; that Israel was omnipotent and could impose any accomplished fact, while the Arabs were weak and had to accept any accomplished fact." The implication of this Israeli approach to the Arab world, Haykal concluded, is that the Jewish state "must resort to arms . . . [and therefore] an armed clash between the UAR and the Israeli enemy is inevitable."[98]

Many Arab sources insist that these contemporary statements give an accurate reading of Israeli intentions, and that Jerusalem had indeed come to the conclusion that only a major offensive against Syria would bring an end to Fatah raids. Ibrahim Abu-Lughod, for example, concludes that Israel appears to have made a decision to go to war early in May.[99] He notes that as early as May 9,

Eshkol had stated, "We shall hit them when, where and how we choose. . . . Israel will continue to take action to prevent any and all attempts to perpetuate sabotage within her territory." Abu-Lughod also contends that "various [U.S. Jewish] groups sympathetically affiliated with Israel seem to have been informed" about this time that war was imminent.

Some Arab sources argue that Israel's hostile intentions toward Damascus reflected more than a concern about Syrian sponsorship of commando raids. For example, as explained by Hisham B. Sharabi, some were convinced that Jerusalem's attitude toward Syria was part of a larger and more ambitious design to remove "progressive" Arab regimes from the borders of the Jewish state. In this view, there had been an evolution of Israeli objectives: "it was no longer sufficient to teach its neighbors a lesson; it was now necessary for Israel to impose its explicit will on them." It followed from this proposition that Syrian support for Fatah guerrillas was "not the real issue but rather the symbol and the immediate cause of the confrontation," and that Israel could in fact be expected to extend its aggression to the territory of Egypt.[100] In another analysis of Israeli motivations, Riad states that in addition to its concern about Palestinian commando raids, "Israel needed war . . . to maintain the integrity and cohesiveness of the young State and the continued loyalty and support of diaspora Jews."[101] To the extent the Arabs believed that Israel was indeed driven by any or all of these various impulses, their fears of an imminent invasion of Syria were strengthened, as was their determination to position themselves for the inevitable confrontation.

The Israeli version of the situation in May 1967 is different. On the one hand, Zionist leaders dismissed analyses that attributed hidden motives to their statements threatening action against Syria. As they had done for many months, they declared that Syrian-sponsored attacks on Israeli lives and property were intolerable, and that Jerusalem's response to such acts of aggression was the same as would be that of any state in its position, an insistence on the right to use force against aggressors who refused to be deterred by any other means. On the other hand, while repeating that Israel was indeed prepared to use force against Damascus, officials in Jerusalem also insisted that many of the statements and actions attributed to them by the Arabs and their supporters were deliberate fabrications.

In particular, Israeli officials denied emphatically that there was an IDF buildup along the border with Syria. This point was made in the following terms by Abba Eban, the foreign minister, in an address delivered to a special session of the UN General Assembly on June 19:

> All that Syria had to do to ensure perfect tranquillity on her frontier with Israel was to discourage the terrorist war. . . . But the picture of Israeli troop concentrations in strength for an invasion of Syria was a monstrous fiction. Twice Syria refused to cooperate with suggestions by the UN authorities, and ac-

cepted by Israel, for a simultaneous and reciprocal inspection of the Israel-Syrian frontier. On one occasion the Soviet Ambassador complained to my Prime Minister of heavy troop concentrations in the North of Israel. When invited to join the Prime Minister that very moment in a visit to any part of Israel which he would like to see, the distinguished envoy brusquely refused. The prospect of finding out the truth at first hand seemed to fill him with a profound disquiet. But by May 9, the Secretary-General of the United Nations from his own sources on the ground had ascertained that no Israeli troop concentration existed. This fact had been directly communicated to the Syrian and Egyptian Governments. The excuse had been shattered, but the allegations still remained.[102]

Available evidence supports Eban's claim. The UN secretary-general's report of May 19 to the Security Council, based on communications from UNTSO field observers stationed along the Israeli-Syrian border, confirmed "the absence of troop concentrations and significant troop movements on both sides of the line." More recently, after an extensive examination of the documents and reports that have become available since 1967, a careful scholarly study reaches the same conclusion. "In spite of Soviet seriousness," the author writes, the report of IDF troops massing along the Israeli-Syrian frontier "seems to have been untrue. No evidence has been made public to date to support it, and there have been enough credible denials from a variety of sources to make it highly unlikely that Israeli troop concentrations actually existed as claimed."[103] This is not to say that Nasser had doubts about the Soviet reports at the time he received them. But while most observers concur that the Egyptian leader believed the information delivered by the Soviets, the information itself was almost certainly false. This has also subsequently been acknowledged by many who write about the conflict from the Arab point of view.[104]

Various explanations of the Soviets' behavior have been offered. One of the interpretations advanced most frequently is that the USSR knowingly and deliberately passed false information to Nasser in an effort to protect its Syrian ally. As explained by Churchill and Churchill, for example, the Soviets "wanted Nasser to commit his forces in Sinai in order to deter the Israelis from attacking" the regime in Damascus.[105] A similar interpretation is offered by Burdett,[106] as well as others.[107] On the other hand, some analysts suggest that the Soviets may have believed the reports they delivered to the Egyptians. Charles Yost, for example, states that the Soviets may simply have jumped to the wrong conclusion when Jerusalem itself told the USSR that there would be punitive action against the Syrians if Fatah raids continued.[108] The Israelis presumably stressed the urgency of the situation to the Soviets in the hope that Moscow would be able to restrain Damascus. Parker, too, suggests that "the Soviets may have believed what they were saying," and he reports in partial support of this hypothesis that "none of the former Egyptian officials with whom I discussed the report seemed to believe it was a deliberate Soviet fabrication."[109] Parker also notes the possibility that the USSR did not jump to the wrong conclusion but rather was deliberately misled by the Israelis, presumably for the purpose of intimidating Syria, but possibly in the hope of drawing Nasser into a fight.[110]

It is also difficult to draw tidy conclusions about Israeli intentions. Israel is capable of mobilizing its forces quickly, so the absence of troop concentrations does not necessarily demonstrate the absence of an intention to attack. Moreover, Israeli officials made many declarations affirming that they were ready, if necessary, to use force to bring an end to Fatah raids sponsored by Syria. The remarks of the UN secretary-general, U Thant, are helpful in this context. The secretary-general confirmed the accuracy of Israeli complaints. He stated on May 11, for example, that there had recently been an increase in Fatah activity in the vicinity of the Syrian and Lebanese borders, and that these incidents were "very deplorable . . . insidious, [and] contrary to the letter and spirit of the Armistice Agreements." At the same time, on May 19, U Thant called statements attributed to Israeli leaders "so threatening as to be particularly inflammatory in the sense that they could only heighten emotions and thereby increase tensions on the other side of the lines."[111]

An area of particular contention is whether there was ever an Israeli plan to overturn the Baath regime in Damascus, and whether Jerusalem was contemplating an attack on Egypt as well as Syria. The basis for accusations that Israel was thinking about removing the Baathists from power rests almost exclusively on a statement that may have been made by Yitzhak Rabin, to which a reference by the Egyptian foreign minister was noted earlier. According to Arab sources, Rabin declared on May 12, "We will carry out a lightning attack on Syria, occupy Damascus, overthrow the regime there and come back."[112] There is in fact some disagreement about whether Rabin actually made this statement. Some Israeli sources insist that he did not. Although they acknowledge that press reports attributing remarks of this nature to Rabin were taken very seriously in Damascus and Cairo, they claim that the reports themselves were based on garbled accounts and contained inaccurate quotations.[113] On the other hand, a number of Israeli analysts, as well as others, conclude that Rabin did make remarks in which the fall of the Syrian regime was mentioned. According to Herzog, for example, the IDF chief of staff warned that Jerusalem's reaction to continuing Fatah raids "would be such as to endanger the very existence of the regime in Damascus."[114]

Even if Rabin did threaten to topple the Syrian government, it is highly unlikely that this was intended to confirm the existence of a specific plan to overturn the Baath regime, and it is even less likely that the IDF's chief of staff sought to reveal that Israeli leaders had made a decision to put such a plan into operation. Rather, whatever may have been their specific content, Rabin's remarks are probably best understood as simply another of the many warnings issued by Israeli officials at this time, the purpose of which was to intimidate Syria. This

Israeli effort included verbal threats and also, as in April, displays of force. Moreover, reinforced by the Soviets' report of IDF troop concentrations along the Syrian border, Jerusalem's campaign of intimidation had a strong effect in both Syria and Egypt. But again, this does not mean that Israel was actually planning to remove the Baathists from power in May 1967.

So far as a planned Israeli attack on Egypt is concerned, this does not figure in the threats and warnings issued by Israeli leaders at this time. Nor does it figure in the press accounts which fueled Arab fears by reporting that Jerusalem had already decided to use force against Syria. The *New York Times* story of May 12, for example, reports that any military action taken in response to continuing guerrilla raids "would be of considerable strength but of short duration and *limited in area*" (emphasis added). In addition, frantic Syrian and Soviet attempts to involve Nasser would seem to indicate that they, too, believed Israel would be content to leave Egypt out of any fighting that might erupt. Finally, some light on the thinking in Jerusalem may be shed by Rabin's own memoirs. He writes, "1967 found us immersed in a mass overhaul of the Israel Defense Forces in anticipation of a presumably inevitable clash with our neighbors." He gives no hint that there existed a plan to overthrow the Damascus government, however, or even that a specific decision about invading Syria had been made in early or mid-May. Rather, he concludes, "as if out of the blue, the inevitable was upon us."[115]

In sum, analysts will continue to disagree about Israel's intentions during the early and middle part of May 1967. It is clear that Israel was indeed considering and talking about an attack on Syria. It is not clear, however, that this was to be any more than a sharp and punishing raid, similar to past retaliatory strikes. And it is at least reasonably likely that in mid-May Jerusalem was still hoping to restrain Syria by threats and had not yet definitively decided to exercise the military option for which it was preparing. Be this as it may, it is beyond dispute both that the Arabs genuinely believed an attack on Syria would be forthcoming shortly, and that Jerusalem's own rhetoric did much to foster this Arab belief. Encouraged as well by the erroneous information supplied to him by the USSR, Nasser thus responded to the situation as he saw it and made a move that pushed the region much closer to all-out war.

The Period of Waiting

On May 16 Egyptian authorities declared a state of emergency, and the Egyptian chief of staff, General Fawzi, instructed the UNEF to withdraw from Sinai in order that its positions might be occupied by the armed forces of Egypt. The UNEF commander transmitted this demand to the secretary-general, U Thant, and the latter immediately agreed that Cairo was fully within its rights in ordering the UN force out of Egyptian territory. Accordingly, the UNEF was withdrawn three days later, removing the buffer that had separated Egypt and Israel since 1956. This development instantly transformed the Israeli-Egyptian border into a second focus of concern. Regardless of what may or may not have been Jerusalem's prior intentions, the prospects for an armed conflict between Israel and Egypt, as well as between Israel and Syria, increased significantly with the departure of the UNEF.

There was little disagreement that Nasser's government was acting with proper authority in this matter. The UNEF's presence in Egypt had from the beginning been subject to the approval of the government in Cairo. Further, as was recognized by Israel as well as by the UN, Egyptian authorities had the right to place their own troops anywhere they pleased within their territory.

Alternatively, there was disagreement about whether the UN secretary-general should have so speedily complied with the demand he received. U Thant was criticized by many, especially in Israel. Israeli officials did not necessarily regard Nasser's call for removal of the UNEF as a serious threat. At least some initially viewed it as little more than another rhetorical expression of symbolic support for Syria. But U Thant's rapid compliance was another matter, in their judgment, with the potential to accelerate significantly the drift toward war. Israeli and some other analysts thus argued that although the secretary-general was legally required to comply with the Egyptian directive, he should have temporized, perhaps insisting that he needed time to consult the Security Council about a possible threat to international peace.[116] Had he done so, these analysts continue, the flow of events that led toward war might have been slowed, or possibly even turned in another direction.

But others defended the action of the secretary-general, pointing out that he had relatively little room for maneuver. For one thing, Egyptian troops had already moved into Gaza and Sinai to replace the UNEF. Indeed, in the strategically important area of Sharm al-Sheikh, they had in fact taken up positions; and thus, despite the continuing presence of the UNEF's small contingent, there was in fact no longer a UN barrier to Egypt's control of the Strait of Tiran. In addition, and more generally, the UN force could easily have been attacked had they tried to remain in Egyptian territory without proper authorization. U Thant stated that under these conditions the UNEF would be considered an "army of occupation"; and thus, given the escalating tensions in the region and the bellicose language that was by now being employed by Nasser, the secretary-general expressed "deep anxiety for the security of UNEF personnel."[117]

Another consideration which reduced the secretary-general's options is that key contributors to the UNEF indicated unilaterally that they would comply with Egypt's demand, regardless of U Thant's decision. Almost half of the UN force was provided by India and Yugoslavia, both of which had strong ties to the Nasser government.[118] These two countries indicated that they had supplied soldiers to the force in the first place only because this had seemed to be the desire of their Egyptian allies. Perhaps these states could have been persuaded to join U Thant in temporizing, had the secretary-general believed this to be a viable strategy, but this is by no means clear.

Concluding that he had no choice but to remove the UNEF from Egypt, U Thant then urged Israel to accept the force on its side of the frontier. In this he was repeating an offer that had been made to Jerusalem in 1956, and which Jerusalem had at the time rejected. Such a move in May 1967 would not have addressed all of Israel's security concerns. Most notably, it would not have prevented Egypt from reestablishing its control of Sharm al-Sheikh, overlooking the Strait of Tiran. On the other hand, it would have preserved at least some of the UN buffer between Israel and Egypt. Israel again rejected the offer, however, calling the secretary-general's proposal "completely unacceptable."

In addition to disagreements about Israeli intentions and about the wisdom of U Thant's prompt reply to the demand he received from Cairo, there are also differing opinions about the intentions and motivations of Nasser himself.[119] Some pro-Israeli and other sources assert that the Egyptian leader was eager to confront Israel, both to avenge the military defeat his country had sustained in 1956 and also to solidify his claims to leadership in the Arab world. Those who take this position quote heavily from Nasser's speeches, which at this time were indeed highly bellicose. Others, including both neutral and pro-Arab analysts, argue that the Egyptian president was for the most part overtaken by events, and perhaps to a degree by his own rhetoric, and that he thus found himself moving inexorably toward a confrontation he in fact would have preferred to avoid. As one careful student of Egypt suggests, "It is very probable that Nasser himself believed he would have more time to think out his next move and was surprised by U Thant's quick compliance."[120] In this view, the Egyptian president's principal sin was a failure to anticipate properly the reactions produced by his demand for removal of the UNEF.

Some who advance the latter set of arguments add that Nasser might even have preferred to see the UNEF remain in place. This possibility is consistent with the observation, mentioned above, that the Egyptian president was probably surprised by U Thant's prompt removal of the UN force. It is also supported by the suggestion that one of Nasser's objectives was a desire to respond to the taunts of King Hussein and other Arab rivals, who had mocked him for advocating a firm stance against Israel while "hiding behind" the UNEF. Hussein had caustically observed, for example, that while Nasser criticized Amman for failing to act in the face of Israeli retaliatory strikes, most notably after the IDF attack on Samu in November 1966, Egypt and the UNEF prevented Palestinian guerrillas from even carrying out raids from positions under Cairo's control. By issuing an order for the withdrawal of UN forces, even if it was not carried out, Nasser may have hoped to diminish these criticisms.

Even more important, Egypt's call for removal of the UNEF must be seen in the context of Nasser's determination that Cairo should honor its commitments under the Egyptian-Syrian mutual-defense agreement. Further, this was not merely a propaganda move, meaning that the Egyptian president sought to do more than *express* support for Damascus. Convinced that the IDF was indeed preparing to attack Syria, Nasser reasoned that Israel might be deterred by the prospect of having to fight on a second front, and it is with this in mind that a redeployment of Egyptian forces in Sinai had been initiated on May 14. If Israel did invade Syria, moreover, the intensity of its strike would perhaps be weakened by a need to hold forces in reserve for action on the southern front, and in any event the Egyptian military would be in a position to launch a counterattack in support of Damascus.

All of these possibilities emphasize the defensive character of Nasser's intentions and assert that Egypt was acting so as to reduce the possibility of war. This interpretation of Egypt's behavior, which Yost attributes to "reliable Arab sources," is also deemed plausible by a number of non-Arab analysts and would seem to be at least part of the reason the UNEF was ordered to leave Sinai on May 16.[121] This analysis is further supported by reports which indicate that Egypt had determined not to initiate hostilities and planned to fight only if attacked, a position that was communicated at the time to both the United States and the Soviet Union.[122]

This line of reasoning deems it highly significant that Egyptian troops began to redeploy in Sinai two days before a call for the UNEF's removal was issued, and this in turn leads to two important and interrelated observations. The first is that Cairo's demand for removal of the UNEF may in part have resulted from a lack of coordination between Egypt's military and civilian leadership concerning the redeployment of Egyptian forces, which thereby became yet another critical link in the chain of events and miscalculations leading toward war. The second observation is that Egyptian authorities did not seek a withdrawal of all UN forces in Egyptian-controlled territory, but rather called only for the removal of UNEF contingents in areas where Cairo wished to deploy its own forces.

The call for UNEF's withdrawal was contained in a telegram sent to the UN field commander, General Rikhye, by Egyptian Chief of Staff Fawzi. This telegram stated, in part, "I gave my instructions to all UAR armed forces to be ready for action against Israel the moment it might carry out any aggressive action against any Arab country. . . . For the sake of the complete secure [*sic*] of all UN troops . . . I request that you issue orders to withdraw all these troops immediately."[123] But Fawzi received his orders from Field Marshal Abd al-Hakim Amer, commander general of the Egyptian armed forces, rather than from Nasser, and there is at least the possibility that Amer exercised considerable independence in deciding how to implement the broad instructions he had received from the Egyptian president. Riad describes Amer's action as "an indiscreet and uncalculated measure" and states that he was concerned as soon as he read Fawzi's telegram.[124] Somewhat more specifically, Egyptian sources quoted by Yost report that "implementation of the redeployment [of Egyptian forces in Sinai] was left to military leaders, who failed to consult civilian authorities, including the president, about either the scope of the redeployment they intended to carry out or the demand addressed to General Rikhye on May 16." As a result, "when the Secretary General confronted the UAR government with the naked choice between reversing the redeployment, to which its military leaders had publicly committed it, and requesting the withdrawal of the UNEF, it felt obliged to choose the latter."[125]

Concerning the scope of the UNEF withdrawal sought by Cairo, the Egyptian government's principal concern appears to have been limited to the removal of several UN contingents along the Sinai border, in order that Egyptian armed forces might without interference take up positions in support of the defense-related objectives summarized earlier. Conversely, Nasser appears to have been prepared to leave UN forces at Sharm al-Sheikh, in order to communicate to Israel that he was not seeking to take offensive action against the Jewish state. He may also have been willing to leave the UNEF in Gaza, which would allay Jerusalem's fears about a resumption of guerrilla raids from lands administered by Cairo. To the extent that this analysis of Egyptian intentions is accurate, Nasser not only was surprised by the promptness with which U Thant withdrew the UNEF, he was also caught off guard by the secretary general's view that the removal of UN forces from certain positions was incompatible with the maintenance of UNEF posts in other areas.

Riad, the foreign minister, asserts that Egypt did indeed seek this kind of limited withdrawal. He states that Fawzi's telegram to Rikhye specifically asked the UN commander to "give orders to pull them back from *these positions*" (emphasis in original). He also states that Cairo's desire for a partial withdrawal of the UNEF is confirmed by the unfolding of events. When informed of Fawzi's telegram, U Thant told Rikhye that such a communication should be addressed directly to him by the Ministry of Foreign Affairs, whereupon Riad sent a letter which did not ask for the withdrawal of UN troops from Gaza and Sharm al-Sheikh. As Riad states, "My request was restricted to a withdrawal from our international borders. [But] when U Thant refused to effect a partial withdrawal, Egypt could not back down on its demand and had to accept a complete withdrawal."[126]

Once the UNEF had left, Egyptian troops moved up to the frontier. They were also now in unrestricted control of Sharm al-Sheikh, and Nasser on May 23 used his forces there to close the Strait of Tiran to Israeli shipping. Those who believe Cairo was not seeking war assert that Nasser took this step without the guidance of a master plan, or even careful premeditation, having in effect been pressured to do so by the escalating tension in the region more generally. He had not foreseen that the redeployment of Egyptian troops in Sinai would lead to such a situation. Now, however, as leader of the most powerful Arab state, the Egyptian president could hardly refrain from imposing a blockade on Israel at a time when Jerusalem was thought to be planning an attack on his Syrian allies, to whose defense he was committed by formal treaty obligations. As expressed by one senior Egyptian commander, "[were we] to abstain from exercising Egypt's legal right to control its territorial waters and to close the Gulf of Aqaba to Israeli navigation . . . our attitude would be characterized as weak and would be subject to political and propaganda attacks by some of the Arab states." [127]

Yet in taking this step, Nasser and other Egyptian leaders understood that it would be considered a *casus belli* by Israel. This is acknowledged by both Egyptian and foreign observers. Indeed, a number of senior Egyptian officials rightly concluded at the time that closing the strait to Israel made war inevitable. An Egyptian general writes that as early as May 17, almost a week before the closure of the strait to Israeli navigation, there was a meeting at which the commanders of land, air, and naval forces and the directors of military intelligence and operations recommended against such action because it "would mean cutting off the political line of retreat and make war inescapable." [128] And after the closure there were indications that the Egyptians now expected war. Haykal wrote on the 26th, for example, "As from now, we must expect the enemy to deal us the first blow. But as we wait for that blow we should try to minimize its effect as much as possible. The second blow will then follow. But this will be the blow we deliver against the enemy in retaliation and deterrence. It will be the most effective blow we can possibly deal." [129]

Although some Israeli analysts agree that the Egyptian president may not initially have been seeking war with the Jewish state, others saw little restraint in Nasser's words and actions. Israeli Foreign Minister Abba Eban articulated his government's official position in an address to the UN when he charged that Cairo had from the beginning displayed an intention to commit aggression. The redeployment of Egyptian forces in Sinai could be only for offensive purposes, he insisted, since Egypt (and Syria) knew that allegations about an Israeli troop buildup were false. Further, Eban continued, when Egypt mobilized its reserves on May 21, any possible doubt that Cairo was bent on war vanished. [130]

Nor was there much doubt about Cairo's intention on the part of the Israeli public. The removal of the UNEF and the closing of the Strait of Tiran were compared in the local press to the German invasion of Czechoslovakia on the eve of World War II. Parallels with the failed policy of appeasement were also drawn, it being asserted that each gain by Egypt would simply encourage its leader to take additional aggressive action. To large numbers of Israelis, Egypt's closure of the Strait of Tiran was thus final proof of what they had been sure all along were Nasser's true warlike intentions. And almost all of the rest agreed that Nasser was now committed to war, even if they might acknowledge that the course bringing him to this point had not been fully charted in advance. The Egyptian president told a British interviewer at this time that the problem was not the Gulf of Aqaba but rather "Israel as such." [131] To Israel and its supporters, such a statement could have been made only by one firmly committed to the destruction of the Jewish state; and therefore, in the final analysis it mattered little whether the prospect of taking action to realize this objective crystallized in Nasser's mind before or after removal of the UNEF and closure of the Strait of Tiran.

Israeli and Zionist sources cite many statements by Nasser and other Arab leaders in which a desire for war is expressed. Cairo Radio announced on May 25, for example, that "the Arab people is firmly resolved to wipe Israel off the face of the earth and to restore the honor of the Arabs of Palestine." The next day Nasser made a speech to Arab trade unionists in which he stated that "the Arab people wants to fight. . . . Sharm al-Sheikh implies a confrontation with Israel. Taking this step makes it imperative that we be ready to undertake a total war with Israel." On May 28, Nasser told a press conference, "We will not accept any possibility of coexistence with Israel," and on May 29 he made an oft-quoted speech in which he spoke of turning back the clock not only to 1956 but also to 1948. Addressing the members of the Egyptian National Assembly, he received prolonged applause when he defined the gains that had already been realized and then spoke of the larger victory that lay ahead.

> [By closing the Strait of Tiran] we are restoring things to what they were in 1956. This is from the material aspect. In my opinion this material aspect is only a small part, whereas the spiritual aspect is the great side of the issue. The spiritual aspect involves the renaissance of the Arab nation, the revival of the Palestine question, and the restoration of confidence to every Arab and to every Palestinian. This is on the basis that if we were able to restore conditions to what they were before 1956 God will surely help us and urge us to restore the situation to what it was in 1948. [132]

There were also similar statements by other Arab officials, all of which reinforced the fears and convictions of the Israelis. For example, the PLO's Ahmad Shuqayri coined a famous phrase by asserting that the Arabs would throw the Jews into the sea. [133] The president of Iraq expressed the same idea. On May 31 he stated, "The existence of Israel is an error which must be rectified. This is our opportunity to wipe out the ignominy which has been with us since 1948. Our goal is clear—to wipe Israel off the map." That Israelis had heard such statements before only deepened their assurance that the Arab world was unwilling to accept the existence of the Jewish state and would, if possible, use the opportunities and crises of May 1967 to pursue an objective to which it had long been committed. As expressed by one Zionist writer, "In the three weeks before the war broke out, the full meaning of Arab intentions was made clear to the world." [134]

As with Israeli intentions and with the behavior of U Thant, Nasser's motivation in ordering Egyptian troops into Sinai and in calling for removal of the

UNEF will remain a subject of controversy. But after May 23, following the closure of the Strait of Tiran to Israel, prior motivations and intentions mattered little. The point of no return had almost certainly been reached. Developments occurring on other fronts were also important, both reflecting and further stimulating the inexorable march toward war. Iraq and Kuwait had announced the mobilization of their forces on May 18, and on the 22nd Cairo reported that Nasser had accepted an offer by Iraq to supply army and air force units in the event of war. Also, on May 21, Ahmad Shuqayri had announced that 8,000 fighters of the Palestine Liberation Army, based in Gaza, were being placed under Egyptian command. Saudi Arabia stated on the 23rd that it, too, had ordered its troops to prepare for war against Israel. Jordan took steps to participate in the general mobilization on the 24th, by which time, as noted, war seemed inevitable. The Hashemite government both announced the mobilization of its own forces and gave permission for Iraqi and Saudi troops to enter its territory, in order that they might join in the battle against the Jewish state. Sudan mobilized on the 28th, and the next day Algeria announced that it would send military units to fight alongside the Egyptians.

On May 30, King Hussein flew to Cairo. The surprise visit, which had not been expected by the Egyptians, lasted only six hours. Nonetheless, it ended the tension that had persisted in Egyptian-Jordanian relations and led to the conclusion of a mutual defense agreement. Under this agreement, Jordanian forces would be placed under Egyptian command in the event of war. As with the closure of the Strait of Tiran, the rapprochement between Cairo and Amman was viewed with great alarm in Jerusalem. Israel is most vulnerable along its border with Jordan. The country's densely populated coastal plain is susceptible to attack along its entire length from the hills of the West Bank. In places, moreover, the distance from the border to the Mediterranean is less than ten miles. Thus, confronted by superior numbers of Arab troops and weapons, and by the prospect of having to fight simultaneously on three different fronts, Israel girded for war while the cabinet examined the case for striking first.

The Israeli public's mood was one of deepening anxiety, shaped by long days of waiting without relief for some resolution of the crisis. But the political situation inside Israel was much more complex.[135] The scene within leadership circles was marked by both heightened levels of activity and intense debate. There were many expressions of confidence, and even some suggestions that Israel would emerge from the crisis with important gains, which would enhance the country's postwar political and territorial position. In addition, however, there were deep and often bitter divisions among the Jewish state's leaders. On the one hand, opinions differed about the relative value of diplomacy and military force in dealing with the Arab threat, particularly the closure of the Strait of Tiran. On the other, there were important political conflicts. Considerations of personality, partisan loyalty, and civilian-military relations complicated decision-making as the country passed through this tense period of waiting.

The cabinet met in emergency session on May 23. Despite agreement that closure of the Strait of Tiran could not be tolerated, there was disagreement about how to reopen the waterway. Some, led by Foreign Minister Eban, favored a diplomatic effort. They reasoned that the world's maritime powers would be concerned over Nasser's move and could be persuaded to put pressure on the Egyptian president. This position was also taken by Chief of Staff Rabin, who stated that since "the political echelon judges that it can solve the problems by political means, one should let it exhaust all the possibilities."[136] Others, however, including most of the country's military leaders, saw the matter differently. Opening the strait, they argued, was not the only goal. Nasser had not only challenged Israeli shipping, he had also challenged Israel's ability and determination to defend itself. Thus, if Israel relied on others to bring about a resolution of the crisis, Egypt and other Arab states might conclude that Jerusalem lacked resolve and become further emboldened. For the deterrent power of Israel's military strength to remain credible, in other words, it was necessary that the Jewish state *itself* reopen the Strait of Tiran.

On May 27, after several days of inconclusive diplomatic initiatives, the cabinet voted on the question of whether to go to war. The result was a nine-nine tie, which meant that the country's diplomatic efforts would continue. Prime Minister Eshkol, who at this time held the defense portfolio as well as the premiership, was among those voting in favor of war. Those voting against war included Eban and other Labor Alignment ministers committed to diplomacy. In addition, however, considerations of personality and partisan politics were a factor in Israeli thinking and decision-making. Several cabinet members voted against going to war not because they favored a diplomatic approach but because they had serious reservations about Eshkol's capacity to lead the nation. In particular, they doubted his ability to manage the defense establishment, and so they judged that the country should not initiate an armed conflict until a new defense minister had been named. This view was expressed by, among others, the three cabinet members belonging to the National Religious Party, Labor's partner in the ruling parliamentary coalition.[137] Concerns about Eshkol's leadership were partly the result of criticism directed at the prime minister by Ben Gurion and the Rafi Party. But in addition, as noted earlier, several years of economic problems and Syrian-sponsored guerrilla activity had undermined confidence in Eshkol in other political circles and among much of the public.

The situation was further complicated by the pattern of civilian-military relations. The military was disturbed by the cabinet's May 27 decision and made its discontent known. There was a bitter exchange when Eshkol met with IDF leaders the following day. Accounts of this session have never been made public, but the language used was apparently extremely harsh. Also, the prime minister was told that since war was inevitable, the only result of the cabinet's procrastination would be an increase in Israeli casualties. In a separate encounter, Brigadier General Ezer Weizman confronted Eshkol in his office, throwing his IDF insignia on the prime minister's desk and saying, "Jewish history will never forgive you if you do not declare war."[138]

IDF leaders, and civilian officials who shared their sentiments, offered various arguments in support of their calls for military action. As noted, they argued that the credibility of Israel's strategy of deterrence required a military response to Egyptian provocations. They also argued that if Israel did not strike first, the Arabs would. Thus, by waiting, Israel's enemies would be permitted to improve their military positions before attacking and would also have the advantage of tactical surprise, all of which would prolong the eventual confrontation and increase the number of Israeli casualties. Finally, some advocates of war suggested that there were political and territorial gains to be made, so that Jerusalem might acquire bargaining chips to be used after the conflict.

Although the decision to go to war had not yet been definitively made, there were moves at this time to force Eshkol to surrender the defense minister's portfolio. Even the Labor Alignment, composed of Ahdut Ha'avoda and Eshkol's own Mapai Party, called for such action at a meeting on the 29th. The two men deemed most suitable for the post were Yigal Allon and Moshe Dayan, heroes respectively of the 1948 and 1956 Arab-Israeli wars. Allon, who belonged to Ahdut Ha'avoda, was serving as minister of labor and had been among the cabinet members voting in favor of war. Strong support for making him defense minister came from his own party. He was also Eshkol's choice, after the prime minister finally acknowledged that he could no longer hold the portfolio himself. Dayan, however, was the candidate preferred by the largest number. Although he was a political ally of Ben Gurion and a leader of the Rafi Party, which had opposed Labor in the elections of 1965, he nonetheless had support among a majority belonging to Mapai. He was the choice of NRP ministers as well, and military leaders also lobbied on his behalf.

For several days there was intense political maneuvering, but on June 1, in the evening, the cabinet determined that Dayan should be made minister of defense. The new defense minister quipped that it had taken 80,000 Egyptian soldiers to get him into the government. The cabinet also decided at its meeting of June 1 to invite the opposition Gahal Bloc, composed of Herut and the Liberals, to join in the formation of a national unity government. Thus, the cabinet contained two new ministers when it assembled on June 2. Not only had Dayan, representing Rafi, been added as minister of defense, but Menachem Begin, representing Gahal, had been made minister without portfolio.

Begin's entry into the cabinet was an important development, even though its significance was not appreciated at the time. The stimulus for the formation of a national unity government was provided solely by the crisis of the moment, the goal being to ensure that the country would face the challenge before it with closed political ranks. Viewed in this context, Begin's inclusion in the cabinet was not particularly notable. Seen from a more long-term political perspective, however, this was a highly significant occurrence that would enable the former Irgun leader to establish his legitimacy in mainstream political affairs, especially those bearing on security and defense. Begin, reviled by old-guard Labor Zionists, the man whom Ben Gurion would not even address by name in the Knesset, had been called into the cabinet to share the burden of preparing for war. According to Yoram Peri, this was "a revolutionary change in Israeli political history." [139]

But all thought of revolutionary political change lay in the future. When the new cabinet met on June 2, attention was focused exclusively on the crisis at hand. Accounts differ as to whether by making Dayan defense minister and establishing a national unity government the cabinet had consciously and explicitly decided to go to war. Many argue that the debate within Israel was effectively resolved by the Nasser-Hussein agreement of May 30, and that the cabinet changes approved on June 1 were thus a virtual declaration of Jerusalem's intent to initiate hostilities, even if there had not been a formal vote on the matter. Alternatively, some contend that there was still a slim possibility that the decision to attack would not be taken. In any event, it was only a few more days before the period of waiting came to an end. On June 5, Israel carried out a devastating strike against its Arab neighbors.

Although the outside world was at first kept in the dark about the course of the fighting, the certainty of an Israeli victory was clear within hours. With awesome precision, Israeli planes attacked the airfields of Egypt and other Arab states. More than 350 Arab bombers and fighter planes were knocked out within the first two days of the war, along with several dozen transport aircraft. On the ground, also beginning on June 5, the IDF pushed into Sinai and Gaza on the Egyptian front and into East Jerusalem and the West Bank on the Jordanian front. The main battles with the Syrians were fought on the Golan Heights, overlooking Lake Tiberias and the Upper Galilee, on June 9–10. Despite stiff resistance in some areas, the IDF quickly pushed forward on all fronts and was soon in control of large stretches of Arab territory.

By June 10, the Arab states had agreed to ceasefire arrangements and the war was over, leading Israelis to call the conflict the Six Day War. The Arabs, by contrast, prefer to speak of the June War when discussing the conflict, since the former designation signifies the rapidity as well as the extent of their crushing defeat. Arab losses were not limited to territory and prestige. Some sources put the number of Arab soldiers killed as high as 20,000, although estimates vary widely and are often unreliable. The largest number of casualties was sustained by Egypt; and in a report to the National Assembly, Nasser told the delegates that 11,500 Egyptian soldiers had fallen, of whom 1,500 were officers. There were 766 soldiers killed on the Israeli side, of whom 45 percent were lost on the Egyptian front and 40 percent in the fighting with Jordanian forces.

PART IV

The Palestinian Dimension Reemerges
From the June War through Camp David

THE IMPACT OF the war of June 1967 cannot be overstated. It introduced critical new elements into the Arab-Israeli conflict, including a revival of concern with its central Palestinian dimension. It also had far-reaching consequences for the internal political dynamics of both the Arab world and Israel, and many of these consequences continue to be felt more than a quarter-century after the war.

Since Israel's victory left it in possession of land that had previously been part of Egypt, Jordan, or Syria, or controlled by Egypt in the case of the Gaza Strip, the most immediate result of the June War was a change in the territorial status quo. Map 7.1 shows the area under Israeli control at the end of the fighting and identifies the five Arab territories occupied by the Jewish state. Two of these territories, the Sinai Peninsula and the Gaza Strip, were captured from Egypt. The Sinai is a vast area by the standards of the region, encompassing roughly 20,000 square miles and being about two and one-half times the size of pre-1967 Israel. On the other hand, principally because of its inhospitable mountainous and desert terrain, the peninsula is sparsely populated. Its population in 1967 was no more than 45,000–50,000, perhaps even less, and roughly one-fifth of this number were nomadic Bedouins living in the barren and forbidding southern part of the territory. The remainder of Sinai's inhabitants resided either in its principal town, al-Arish, or in smaller towns and villages along the flat and sandy Mediterranean coast.

Although the Sinai's mineral resources give it economic significance, the peninsula's importance in the context of the Arab-Israeli conflict is primarily strategic. It serves as a huge land buffer between Israel and Egypt, and its strategic value in this regard is enhanced by its topography. The southern half of the peninsula is composed of rugged granite mountains that are nearly impassable by modern military vehicles. The central region, though more hilly than mountainous, offers only two axes that can be readily traversed by military convoys. Both, moreover, are commanded by narrow passes. From the Israeli point of view, Sinai's defensive value is also enhanced by the Suez Canal and Great Bitter Lake, which separate the peninsula from the rest of Egypt. Egyptian troops bound for Israel would have to cross the canal before beginning their march toward the Jewish state; and after the June War, with the IDF in control of both the canal's eastern bank and the key Mitla and Gidi passes, the security of Israel's border

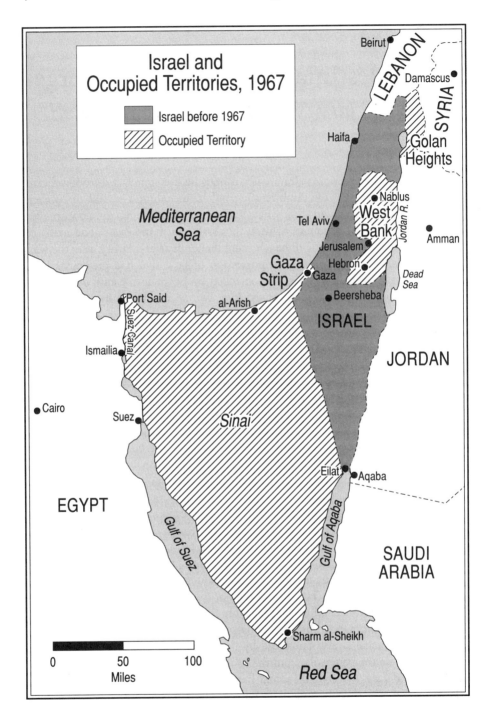

Israel and
Occupied Territories, 1967

Israel before 1967

Occupied Territory

with Egypt did indeed appear immensely improved. Finally, the Sinai Peninsula offers access to the Gulf of Aqaba. Through its commanding position overlooking the Strait of Tiran at Sharm al-Sheikh, the Sinai gives those who hold it an ability to control shipping in and out of the Israeli port of Eilat.

Unlike Sinai, Gaza was not an integral part of Egypt but rather a portion of Palestine that had come under Cairo's administrative control as a result of the 1947–48 War. Small and densely populated, Gaza is the precise opposite of Sinai. Its land mass is only 140 square miles, but in 1967 a population of about 360,000, or even more according to some estimates, was crowded into the narrow coastal strip running north from the Israeli-Egyptian border. The vast majority of these Palestinians were refugees. By 1949, Gaza's 80,000 indigenous inhabitants had been joined by about 200,000 men, women, and children from the territory now encompassed by Israel, and a combination of natural increase and out-migration caused this population to grow slowly over the next eighteen years, at an average annual rate of about 1.1 percent. In 1967, slightly over half of Gaza's population was still living in refugee camps. Most of the remaining inhabitants resided in the district's two major towns, Gaza and Khan Yunis, which in 1967 had populations of approximately 115,000 and 50,000 respectively. The history and demography of the Gaza Strip, along with the neglect of the Egyptian military administration by which it was governed between 1948 and 1967, left the region without a viable economic base. Poverty and related social ills were widespread, with most residents being heavily dependent on support from the United Nations and various international and local charitable societies.[1]

Another territory that came under Israeli control as a result of the June War is the West Bank, which some Israelis prefer to call by the Biblical names of Judea and Samaria. Judea refers to the southern part of the West Bank; it stretches from the area around Jerusalem to the northern reaches of the Negev desert, in the vicinity of Beersheba. Samaria is the territory lying north of Jerusalem, extending up to the Jezreel Valley and the cities of Afula and Beit Shean, both of which lie inside pre-1967 Israel. The West Bank, which is 2,100 square miles in size and thus about one-quarter as large as pre-1967 Israel, was left in Jordanian hands at the conclusion of the 1947–48 War. It was formally annexed by the Hashemite kingdom in 1950, and Israeli officials insist that it would have remained a part of Jordan had King Hussein not entered the 1967 War in support of Egypt and Syria. They point to a last-minute plea for Jordanian neutrality, which Levi Eshkol sent to the king through United Nations representatives, and maintain that the IDF did not invade the West Bank until Hussein had disregarded this appeal and ordered the Arab Legion to shell positions in the Jewish section of Jerusalem.[2]

Capture of the West Bank, along with Gaza, gave Israel control over all of the territory that had been allocated for Jewish and Palestinian states under the

United Nations Partition Resolution of 1947. Some Israelis maintain that the historic boundaries of Palestine encompass not only the land between the Jordan River and the Mediterranean Sea but also the territory to the east of the river, meaning the country of Transjordan where, with British help, the Hashemite dynasty had been installed after World War I. It is this larger land mass, these Israelis assert, that should have been the basis for partition and attempts at territorial compromise. This was not the position of the United Nations, however, which saw competing Zionist and Palestinian Arab claims as applying only to the territory west of the Jordan River. Nor has it been the position of the Palestinians themselves, who do not regard Transjordan as part of their ancestral homeland. In any event, with the territory of Gaza and the West Bank added to that of pre-1967 Israel, the 1967 War left the Jewish state in control of all of the land from which the international community had once sought to carve both a state for Jews and a state for Palestinian Arabs.

As in the case of the Gaza Strip, Israel's capture of the West Bank had demographic as well as territorial implications. It not only extended the Jewish state's control over the land of Palestine, it also placed hundreds of thousands of additional Palestinian Arabs under Israeli military administration.

Estimates of the West Bank population in the early 1950s vary considerably, complicated not only by disagreement about the number of refugees but by the absence of a census until 1961 and by the movement of many Palestinians from the West Bank to the East Bank during this period. According to Jordanian authorities, the West Bank in 1952 contained about 380,000 indigenous inhabitants, who had not left their homes as a result of the 1947–48 War, and approximately 360,000 more who had fled from other parts of Palestine. At the time this constituted about 56 percent of Jordan's total population, of which roughly two-thirds was Palestinian since an estimated 140,000 refugees were then residing in the territory east of the Jordan River. Approximately 70 percent of the West Bank's refugee population, which some estimates place at no more than 300,000 in 1952, or even less, was absorbed into the territory's towns and villages. The remainder was forced to settle in refugee camps.

The population of the West Bank grew very slowly between 1950 and 1967, with natural increase largely offset by the substantial number of Palestinians who left the territory for the East Bank or elsewhere. Indeed, at least 300,000 persons emigrated from the West Bank to the East Bank during this period, the majority in the early and mid-1950s, and some estimates place the number as high as 400,000. The Jordanian census of 1961 thus reported a total of 800,000 West Bank residents, reflecting an average annual growth rate of only .8 percent. This was about 47 percent of Jordan's total population, and about two-thirds of its 1.2 million Palestinian inhabitants. By 1967, on the eve of the June War, the West Bank's population had grown to approximately 900,000, of whom about 80,000 lived in East Jerusalem.

About one-quarter of the West Bank's population fled across the Jordan River during and shortly after the June War, many becoming refugees for the second time, and this left only about 670,000 inhabitants under Israeli occupation.[3] According to an Israeli census conducted in September, the territory had a population of 665,000, including the 66,000 Palestinians residing in East Jerusalem. In the years immediately following, the region's population grew slowly but steadily, averaging slightly more than 2 percent per year and attaining a total of 700,000, or 620,000 without East Jerusalem, in 1971. Perhaps 10 percent of these persons lived in refugee camps. The remainder resided in the region's well-established municipalities, including Nablus, Hebron, Bethlehem, Ramallah, and Jericho, and in its numerous smaller towns and villages.

The West Bank's importance for the Arab-Israeli conflict is also strategic. While its territorial and demographic significance make it central to the Palestinian dimension of the lingering dispute, its location and topography raise additional concerns, especially in Israel, about its military value. To begin with, the West Bank runs parallel to Israel's narrow coastal plain, which extends south from Haifa to Tel Aviv and on to Ashkelon, and which at some points is no more than nine or ten miles in width. This central coastal region is the most densely populated and heavily industrialized part of the country. It also divides the Negev and the south from the Galilee and the north, all of which makes any threat to its security a cause for alarm in Israel. In addition, the unifying geographic feature of the West Bank is a mountainous ridge running its entire length in a north-south direction, and these heights dominate Israel's coastal plain and offer a clear military advantage to those who would use them to attack the Jewish state. Finally, the West Bank surrounds the Israeli capital of Jerusalem on three sides; and prior to 1967 Jordan had heavily fortified the high ridges which flank the corridor linking the city to the rest of Israel.

East Jerusalem, though an integral part of the West Bank prior to 1967, must be considered independently when enumerating the Arab territories that came under Israeli control as a result of the June War. The reason is that Israel almost immediately gave the city a legal status different from that of other occupied territories and took action to separate it from the rest of the West Bank. Indeed, the distinction is reflected in and reinforced by Israeli terminology, since the terms "Judea" and "Samaria" refer to the West Bank without East Jerusalem.

Following the IDF's capture of East Jerusalem in June 1967, thousands of Jews from West Jerusalem and elsewhere in Israel rushed to the Western Wall, celebrating their first opportunity in nineteen years to pray at Judaism's holiest cite. To make room for the crowds and to facilitate access to the wall, the Israeli government in fact evacuated and demolished the homes of several hundred Arabs living nearby. Amidst the outpouring of emotion in Israel that accompanied the capture of the Old City, many Jews called for the annexation of East Jerusalem and for unification of the city under Israeli rule. Some orthodox Jews argued that conquest of the Old City offered additional evidence that the Messianic era had begun, and some also asserted that religious law forbade Jews from surrendering control over any part of Jerusalem. Many secular Israelis, including men of prominence such as Moshe Dayan, defense minister and hero of the recent war, also urged that East Jerusalem be made a permanent part of the Jewish state. Among the additional justifications they offered was the significant abuse that Jewish holy places had sustained during the period of Jordanian rule.

Although a number of foreign powers, including the United States, spoke out against any permanent change in the legal and political circumstances of the occupied territories, Israel was determined that there should be no return to the *status quo ante* so far as East Jerusalem was concerned. Thus, without debate, the Knesset on June 27 passed legislation empowering the minister of the interior to apply Israeli law and administration "in any area of Palestine to be determined by decree," and the next day the government used this power to proclaim the unification of Jerusalem. The Israeli and Jordanian sections of the city were merged into a single municipality under Israeli control, and the borders of the new municipality were themselves enlarged to include Mount Scopus, the Mount of Olives, and several adjacent Arab villages. All of the barriers and military installations that had separated the two halves of the city since 1948 were thereafter removed.

Unified Jerusalem at this time had a population of about 260,000, of whom roughly one-quarter were Arabs. The latter included about 55,000 Muslims and 12,000 Christians. Both Christians and Muslims, as well as Jews, were guaranteed access to their holy places by legislation which the Knesset passed in tandem with the law empowering the government to unify the city. On the other hand, East Jerusalem's juridical status as part of the West Bank was terminated, and the city's Arab residents were transformed into a minority in a city governed by Israeli law and possessing a clear Jewish majority.

The Golan Heights, captured from Syria, is the final piece of territory that Israel occupied as a result of the war. The Golan is a forty-five-mile-long plateau which lies immediately to the east of, and rises sharply above, Lake Tiberias and the Hula Valley of Israel's Upper Galilee. An integral part of Syria, the Golan had a population of about 120,000 before the war, the vast majority of whom were Syrian citizens, but about 16,000 of whom were Palestinian refugees from the war of 1947–48. The major town of the region was Kuneitra, a community of about 60,000 lying on the road to Damascus near the eastern perimeter of the territory captured by the Jewish state. By the end of 1967, however, all of the Palestinians and all but a handful of the Syrians had been displaced, having fled from occupied to unoccupied Syria and leaving the area under Israeli control with dozens of abandoned towns and villages. Israeli sources put the population of the Golan at this time at only 6,400. Virtually all were Syrian citizens belonging to the Druze minority and living in and around the village of Majdal Shams, located in the northeast corner of the territory near the Lebanese border.

Not being a part of Palestine, the Golan Heights, like the Sinai Peninsula, derives much of its significance for the Arab-Israeli conflict from strategic considerations. At its southernmost point, below the Sea of Galilee, the Golan is only about 600 feet above the floor of the Yarmouk River valley; but the height of its western escarpment increases steadily as it extends toward Mount Hermon, whose 7,000–9,000-foot peaks bound it to the north. Thus, from a height averaging 2,000 feet, the Golan plateau dominates the entire northern "finger" of Israel stretching up to the border with Lebanon.

In the years between 1948 and 1967, Syria constructed extensive military fortifications on the Heights, both along the principal routes leading eastward toward Damascus and on the western ridges overlooking Israel; and from the latter positions Syrian artillery could hit targets inside Israel as far away as Safad. Further, in addition to the obvious threat this posed to the security of the Jewish state, the Golan's importance to Israel also derives from the access it gives to the headwaters of the Jordan River. The Banyas River rises on the Golan, and the Wazzani River rises near Mount Hermon and flows southward along the Lebanese-Syrian border. So far as Syria is concerned, the topography of the Heights makes them no less important for the defense of the country. After the June War, IDF positions on the Golan were only forty miles from the Syrian capital, and from the abandoned town of Kuneitra the road to Damascus is free of any natural obstacles that might help the Syrians to defend against an Israeli attack.

Despite its strategic importance, Israel did not invade the Golan until June 9, the fifth day of the war. The Israelis delayed in part out of a reluctance to fight on three fronts at once, and in part out of concern that an action against Syria might draw the Soviet Union into the conflict. By the 9th, however, the Egyptians had been defeated in Sinai and Jordanian forces had been pushed out of the West Bank, and at this point the IDF decided to attack. Following a day and a half of intense fighting, which included a difficult Israeli assault up the Golan's western slopes, the Syrians were defeated and the Heights were added to the other Arab territories occupied by the Jewish state. As a result, Israel substituted its own strategic advantage for that which the Damascus government had enjoyed prior to the war.

7 | Postwar Diplomacy and the Rise of the Palestine Resistance Movement

Obstacles to a Settlement

THE JUNE WAR gave the world community new determination to address the Arab-Israeli conflict, and international activity involving consultation and efforts at mediation began within days of the cessation of hostilities. On June 19, for example, the American president, Lyndon Johnson, delivered an important speech in which he set forth five general principles for peace in the Middle East. Among these principles were the right of every nation in the area to live in peace with its neighbors, assistance to the homeless and justice for the refugees, freedom of legitimate maritime passage, an end to the arms race in the Middle East, and respect for the territorial integrity of all states in the region.[4] Johnson also discussed the Middle East situation with Soviet Premier Aleksei Kosygin several days later, when the two leaders met on June 23 and 25 at Glassboro College in New Jersey.

The United States and the Soviet Union were in fundamental disagreement, however, and so the Glassboro Summit reflected not only a concern for international mediation but also the wide political gap that would have to be bridged if progress was to be made. The USSR, like the Arabs, believed that the immediate need was "to achieve the prompt withdrawal behind the armistice lines of the forces of Israel, which has committed aggression against the Arab states." Kosygin added, "This question is of signal importance for the restoration of peace in the Middle East."[5] The U.S., by contrast, shared the Israeli view that occupied Arab land should be returned only in the context of a meaningful peace settlement. Although Israel had fired the first shot in the recent war, the Johnson administration held Egypt responsible for the outbreak of fighting because of its closure of the Strait of Tiran; and the American president accordingly concluded that there could be no permanent peace until Egypt and other Arab states recognized Israel's right to exist. As explained by William Quandt, "Johnson and his advisors were mindful of how Eisenhower had dealt with the Israelis after the Suez war. They were determined not to adopt the same strategy of forcing Israel to withdraw from conquered territories in return for little in the way of Arab concessions."[6]

The focus of diplomatic activity soon shifted to the United Nations, where a deadlock in the Security Council had led the Soviet Union to request an Emergency Special Session of the General Assembly on June 13.[7] On July 4, responding to Israel's annexation of Jerusalem at the end of June, the Assembly passed a resolution declaring any alteration of the city's status to be without validity and calling upon the Jewish state to rescind the measures it had already taken.[8] More generally, however, the Emergency Special Session provided but another forum for expression of the apparently irreconcilable positions held by Israel, the Arabs, and their respective supporters. On June 30, a draft resolution was circulated by a group of Latin American countries. It called for Israeli withdrawal from Arab territories captured in the war, an end to the state of belligerence, freedom of navigation in international waterways, and a full solution to the refugee problem. Both Israel and the United States opposed the resolution, however, because it did not call for Arab recognition of the Jewish state. The Arabs were also dissatisfied, because, as explained by Mahmoud Riad, the Egyptian foreign minister, they "felt strongly that Israel should not be rewarded for its aggression and its withdrawal should consequently be unconditional."[9]

A compromise proposal was worked out in mid-July by Arthur Goldberg and Andrei Gromyko, American ambassador to the UN and Soviet foreign minister respectively; but this, too, failed to win agreement. The American-Soviet draft called for withdrawal without delay from territories occupied in the recent war, "in keeping with the inadmissibility of conquest of territory by war," and for acknowledgment that each member state of the United Nations enjoys the right "to maintain an independent national State of its own and to live in peace and security." This resolution remained unsatisfactory to the Israelis, however. They complained that the U.S. had virtually embraced the Soviet position by abandoning "not only the call for a lasting peace but even the demand for the termination of the state of war, while supporting a precipitate withdrawal by Israel."[10] Yet the Arabs were equally vehement in their opposition. Led by the more militant governments of Syria and Algeria and by Ahmad Shuqayri of the Palestine Liberation Organization, they again rejected any concessions which would in effect reward the Jewish state for starting the June War. As a result of this Arab opposition, to the relief of the Israelis, the American-Soviet compromise resolution was never formally submitted; and with this, amidst deep disappointment that an unusual opportunity had been missed, the Emergency Special Session of the UN General Assembly concluded its efforts at peacemaking.[11] On July 21, the session began a prolonged recess.

Despite their opposition to the U.S.-Soviet resolution, the Arabs were actually deeply divided about the proper course of action. The more hard-line states continued to reject any form of political accommodation and called for guerrilla warfare against Israel, arguing that only by military means could the Jewish state be forced to relinquish the territory it had captured. Moreover, for these hard-line Arabs, the goal was the liberation of all of Palestine, not merely the reconquest of territories lost in the June War. As expressed by the Syrian newspaper *al-Baath*, for example, "The occupied Arab territories will be evacuated by the enemy only through armed struggle. The Israeli enemy will be liquidated only by means of force."[12] Others, however, particularly Hussein of Jordan and Nasser of Egypt, called for a more realistic approach. King Hussein had already sought to initiate an indirect dialogue with the Jewish state about its price for withdrawal from the West Bank and East Jerusalem; and available reports indicate that Hussein was prepared to make sweeping concessions.[13] Nasser, for his part, argued that the Arabs were too weak to have a realistic military option and joined the Jordanian monarch in urging the Arabs to pursue their objectives by diplomatic means. Noting that there were already calls in Israel for permanent retention of the West Bank, as well as East Jerusalem, the Egyptian leader argued that the Arabs should move quickly and added, "We have only one way before us by which to regain the West Bank and Jerusalem: political action."[14]

Inter-Arab diplomacy assumed increasing importance under these circumstances, and at the end of August, after several months of diplomatic jockeying and two preparatory foreign ministers' conferences, an Arab summit meeting was convened in Khartoum, Sudan. The kings, presidents, and representatives of other Arab heads of state assembled in the Sudanese capital issued a declaration which some interpreted as a victory for the hard-liners and an emerging consensus around their advocacy of continuing belligerence. The resolution adopted at Khartoum contained the famous "three noes": no peace with Israel, no recognition of Israel, and no negotiation with the Jewish state. The resolution also affirmed "the rights of the Palestinian people in their own country" and reported that in defense of these rights "the participants have agreed on the need to adopt the necessary measures to strengthen military preparation to face all eventualities."[15]

From the perspective of Israel and its supporters, the Khartoum conference was an important indication of continuing Arab intransigence. Yehoshafat Harkabi, former director of Israeli military intelligence, reported that an unshakable commitment to the destruction of Israel had been reaffirmed at Khartoum. He stated that the Arabs had rejected negotiation "not because they prefer another procedure leading to peace but because . . . negotiations imply a renunciation of politicide."[16] Similarly, telling his country's cabinet that the Khartoum conference was an event of great significance, Abba Eban, then foreign minister, concluded that the Arab governments not only had refrained from exploring a peace settlement but "had closed every door and window that might lead to one in the foreseeable future."[17] This Arab attitude could not but lead to a resumption of hostilities, insisted Chaim Herzog, an Israeli analyst who was later to become president of the Jewish state; and Herzog judged his assessment to be confirmed when Egyptian forces opened fire in September on Israeli ships in the Gulf of Suez.[18]

While a number of independent analysts also interpret the Khartoum resolution as an expression of Arab intransigence,[19] the Arabs themselves, as well as some other observers, see the summit in a very different light. To begin with, the meeting was dominated by the more moderate Arab leaders, and since it had been clear in advance that this would be the case, the more militant presidents of Syria and Algeria in fact refused to attend.[20] Ahmad Shuqayri of the PLO did attend in order to represent the Palestinians, but he was displeased by the decisions reached, as well as by the fact that Nasser disagreed with him in public, and he therefore boycotted the concluding session. Thus, with the leaders of Egypt, Jordan, and Saudi Arabia playing a dominant role, there were repeated statements about the need for political rather than military action, and even declarations by Nasser to the effect that the Jordanians and Saudis should use their ties to the United States to pursue a diplomatic solution.[21]

In addition, Arab sources insist that the summit rejected negotiation with Israel but not political compromise.[22] First, there were no calls for the destruction of Israel, nor were efforts at conflict resolution based on UN or other third-party mediation ruled out. Indeed, the Khartoum resolution specifically called for unified political efforts at the international and diplomatic level and, further, it stipulated that the objective of such political action would be "to ensure withdrawal . . . from the Arab lands which have been occupied since the aggression of 5 June." Second, refusal to hold direct talks with Israel was justified on tactical rather than strategic grounds; face-to-face talks would give Israel an opportunity to negotiate with each Arab country separately, and so divide the Arab world, and it would also allow the Jewish state to achieve *de facto* recognition without making concessions in return.

Seen from this perspective, the Khartoum resolution did not represent a victory for Arab hard-liners. On the contrary, the summit facilitated and gave legitimacy to the efforts of Hussein, Nasser, and other Arabs who appeared ready for compromise. To these Arab leaders, the three noes simply reflected a belief that the Jewish state would be less willing to relinquish captured territory after it had gained a measure of recognition through negotiations with the Arabs, and a corresponding judgment that the Arab cause would therefore be best served by making withdrawal a precondition for peace talks.

Despite the willingness of some Arabs and Israelis to work for a political settlement, the obstacles to accommodation remained formidable. One important difficulty was the continuing intransigence of hard-line Arabs and the opposition to concessions that was articulated as well by certain political forces in Israel. On the Arab side, although placed outside the main Arab consensus by the Khartoum conference, Syria, Algeria, and Palestinian groups sought to hinder progress toward peace by making it difficult for Arab moderates to repeat in public what they were saying in private, and by limiting their ability to build support for political accommodation among the Arab masses. These rejectionist elements issued forceful condemnations of Hussein, Nasser, and others whom they accused of betraying the Palestinian cause and capitulating to the enemy, and their harsh pronouncements were not without effect.

As a result of pressure from rejectionists, Arab leaders seeking compromise, particularly Nasser, often felt obliged to reiterate the Arab world's traditional case against Israel in order to counter the charge that they had sold out to the Jewish state and its American allies. This in turn made them look duplicitous to Israel and the U.S., and the contrast between private assurances of moderation and public statements of a more militant sort also gave political ammunition to Israel's own hard-liners. Equally important, or perhaps even more so, this situation reinforced the constraints that public opinion placed on the behavior of Arab leaders. Those seeking compromise found it difficult to take their case to the masses, whose thinking about Israel continued to be shaped by rejectionists, and so the former were required to proceed cautiously and to justify unpopular concessions with face-saving formulas.[23]

On the Israeli side, there was an emerging consensus among virtually all sectors of the electorate that Jerusalem should not be restored to its prewar status; and, more generally, there were some who spoke out forcefully against withdrawal from some or even any of the other territories Israel had captured in the recent fighting. With respect to Jerusalem, there was broad agreement that the city would remain united under Israeli rule, with the entire city serving as the capital of the Jewish state. Very few Israelis regarded as a subject for negotiation either the city's redivision or the restoration of Arab sovereignty over East Jerusalem.

There were also calls within Israel for the permanent retention of other territories captured during the June War. Although not yet constituting a major constraint on the behavior of the government, which continued to be led by the Labor Alignment, the Herut wing of Gahal was particularly vocal in its opposition to territorial compromise. Reaffirming its historic advocacy of Jewish sovereignty over the entire territory of *Eretz Yisrael*, Herut called for formal annexation of those parts of the Land of Israel that had recently been "liberated," meaning the West Bank (Judea and Samaria) and Gaza.[24] Younger elements within the National Religious Party, which carried forward the Mizrahi tradition of religious Zionism, also began to call for retention of the West Bank. Fusing concerns of nationalism and religion, the NRP's Young Guard faction said that Judea and Samaria made up the central core of the Holy Land, and they insisted that withdrawal from these territories was therefore prohibited by Jewish law.[25] Some religious Zionists also proclaimed that the restoration of Jewish sovereignty over the Biblical Land of Israel would deepen the spiritual character of the country and hasten the coming of the Messiah.

In addition to this opposition to territorial compromise on the right side of the political spectrum, there were also some prominent Labor Zionists who believed Israel should retain substantial portions of the territory it now occupied. These individuals included Yigal Allon and Moshe Dayan, the former of the left-leaning Ahdut Ha'avoda party and the latter of Rafi. Although motivated by strategic rather than nationalist or religious considerations, both men believed that Israel's security required a significant modification of the country's pre-1967 borders.[26]

The extent and significance of hard-line Israeli opinion at this time is in dispute. Many observers assert that the dominant political sentiment in Israel was a willingness to make major territorial concessions in the context of a peace settlement. According to this view, Israel would have accepted, in return for a complete and unconditional peace with its Arab neighbors, a return to the pre-1967 boundaries with no more than minor modifications. A willingness to withdraw from occupied territory almost certainly did not apply to Jerusalem, a qualification which is significant, but this characterization of Israeli political attitudes nonetheless affirms that the views of Herut and NRP militants remained peripheral, and that Labor stalwarts such as Allon and Dayan constituted a distinct minority within government circles.

Yet, even leaving aside the question of Jerusalem, and as much as the views of Herut and the NRP Young Guard may indeed have had only limited influence in the summer and fall of 1967, it is difficult to find official Israeli statements in which a commitment to near-complete withdrawal in return for peace is proclaimed unambiguously to be government policy. Much more common are general declarations reaffirming Israel's readiness to meet with Arab representatives in order to discuss the requirements of peace.[27] Moreover, at least some Zionist leaders stated openly during this period that the Jewish state sought "freely-negotiated new frontiers [in order to assure] peace and security in the area."[28] Thus, in the judgment of at least one careful observer, a former Indian ambassador to the United Nations, by mid-October "the Israelis seemed increasingly reluctant to accept a formula which would require their complete withdrawal from territories occupied in the war, even if their objectives of secure frontiers, nonbelligerency, and freedom of navigation were conceded."[29]

As serious as opposition from Arabs and Israelis opposed to compromise was the profound distrust with which even Arabs and Israelis seeking political accommodation continued to regard one another; and, accordingly, each side was unwilling to take the lead in making concessions and demanded demonstrations of the other's good faith before it would act. Arab reluctance to enter into negotiations was reinforced by Israel's vagueness in speaking about territorial issues and by the pronouncements of some Zionist officials to the effect that there would be no return to the pre-1967 frontiers, all of which convinced the Arabs that the Jewish state preferred territorial expansion to peace with its neighbors. Contributing further to Arab hesitation was a belief that the United States could not be counted on to press for complete Israeli withdrawal should negotiations in fact begin. Mahmoud Riad, Egypt's foreign minister, reports in this connection that there was a striking difference in the way that U.S. statements specified very precisely what would be required of the Arabs in any peace settlement but spoke much more ambiguously and indecisively about the issue of Israeli withdrawal from occupied Arab lands.[30]

Arab thinking about negotiations and movement toward a resolution of the conflict was also strongly influenced by perceptions of what had taken place following the 1947–48 War. The Arabs argued that their participation in the armistice negotiations had not led Israel either to return to the borders proposed by the UN Partition Resolution or to deal meaningfully with the Palestinian problem. The talks had given tacit recognition to the Jewish state, and thereby increased its legitimacy, but had not produced anything equivalent for the Arabs. With this unsatisfactory experience in mind, the Arabs were fearful that Israel would not withdraw from the West Bank, Gaza, and the other occupied territories but would instead use any movement toward peace to press for a settlement based on the "new reality" prevailing after the June War. For all these reasons, Arab leaders seeking peace called for evidence that Israel was looking for compromise rather than capitulation and took the position that the Jewish state must relinquish control of the occupied territories before negotiations could begin.

Israeli perceptions produced the same kind of reasoning but the opposite conclusion. Zionists asserted that if some Arabs were now willing to speak of accommodation, it was only because they sought the return of territory held by Israel. Were Israel to voluntarily and unilaterally withdraw from this territory, however, the Arabs would have much less incentive to compromise and would probably return to the militancy by which their attitude toward the Jewish state had been characterized prior to the June War. According to Zionist officials and others supportive of the Jewish state, Israel had been forced into a war by Arab belligerency and could not reasonably be expected to surrender any gains it had made until the Arabs demonstrated their readiness for a full and definitive peace. Otherwise, not only would Israel's enemies be undeserving of concessions from the victor in the war, but the victor itself, Israel, would eventually be forced to fight again and would need the lands it had captured because of their strategic and military significance. Reversing the logic of the Arabs, the Israelis therefore rejected the proposition that withdrawal was a precondition for peace and insisted that, on the contrary, it was peace which was a prerequisite for any modification of the postwar territorial status quo.

It was not logic alone that led the Israelis to this view. Distrust of the Arabs was widespread in the Jewish state and was based on a belief that the notion of Arab moderation was largely a myth. Their perceptions reinforced by the inflammatory rhetoric that continued to be heard in Arab capitals, including Cairo and Amman, as well as Damascus, most Israelis doubted that the Arab world had abandoned its determination to wipe their country off the map. These beliefs and perceptions would probably have persisted even had Arab leaders agreed to enter peace talks prior to an Israeli withdrawal from the occupied territories. Given the depth of their fears, many Israelis would have interpreted such action as a political move designed to weaken and isolate their state before resuming the struggle against it by more traditional means; and under these circumstances, ambivalence and hesitation would undoubtedly have characterized Israel's response to any Arab agreement to begin face-to-face negotiations and exchange peace for land. The Arabs' own hesitation made it unnecessary to face this situation, of course, but this only served to intensify Israel's conviction that the enemy was not sincerely interested in peace, even should it be able to achieve a settlement on the basis of the pre-1967 borders. In sum, just as most Arabs were convinced that Israel preferred territorial expansion to peace with its neighbors, most Israelis believed that the Arabs would be satisfied with nothing less than all of Palestine.

These mutual fears and suspicions, destined to hinder attempts at peacemaking for many years to come, were a source of frustration to the diplomatic community in the summer of 1967. The efforts of the UN General Assembly's Emergency Special Session had been unsuccessful, and little had been accomplished elsewhere after the Assembly recessed on July 21. The Emergency Special Session therefore reconvened on September 18 with no more on its agenda than to declare itself officially adjourned. Prior to adjournment, which came shortly after noon, a resolution transferring consideration of the Arab-Israeli conflict to the regular session of the UN General Assembly was introduced and approved.

United Nations Resolution 242

Diplomatic activity resumed in the fall, with the United Nations Security Council now becoming the principal arena for consideration of the Arab-Israeli dispute. The pace at the outset was unhurried. Also, reflecting the failures of the Emergency Special Session, the mood in the Council was not one of optimism. Yet there remained a determination to act and, even more important, a consensus about the form that a peace settlement should take had begun to develop among the members of the international community.

The resolutions considered by the Emergency Special Session of the General Assembly, as well as the principles set forth by Lyndon Johnson on June 19, had already identified the logical meeting point of Arab and Israeli demands: an exchange of land for peace. There was growing agreement that Israel should relinquish the lands it had captured during the June War, thereby allowing the Arabs to recover their lost territories; and in return the Arab world was expected to make peace with Israel, ceasing all acts of belligerency and recognizing the legitimacy and sovereignty of the Jewish state. The creation of a peace process based on this formula remained elusive, of course, obstructed by hard-line sentiments in both the Arab world and Israel, and by the distrust that Arabs and Israelis harbored toward one another. But it is nonetheless significant that the nature of a settlement judged to be durable and just had become increasingly clear to most members of the United Nations. From this point of view, despite the gaps remaining to be bridged, there was at least the possibility that an accommodation could be reached. The outline of a solution that might prove workable had begun to emerge.

In late October, a new outbreak of hostilities in the Gulf of Suez introduced an element of urgency into the behind-the-scenes deliberations of the members of the Security Council. On October 21, Egyptian vessels fired on and sank the Israeli destroyer *Eilat*. Israel claimed that its ship had been on a routine mission in international waters, more than thirteen miles off the Egyptian coast. Cairo, on the other hand, insisted that the *Eilat* was less than ten miles off shore and hence well within its twelve-mile territorial sea. The Egyptians also charged that the *Eilat* had been heading for Port Said in a provocative manner. In response, following an exchange of gunfire across the Suez Canal on October 24, Israeli artillery blew up two large oil refineries in the Egyptian city of Suez. The Security Council was thereupon called into urgent session, and both the U.S. and the USSR introduced draft resolutions. The draft submitted by the Soviet Union condemned Israeli aggression in the area of the city of Suez and demanded that the Jewish state pay compensation to the United Arab Republic. The more general American proposal condemned any and all violations of the ceasefire and called on the governments concerned to instruct their military forces to refrain from all firing. On the following day, the 25th, a resolution borrowing heavily from the U.S. draft was approved by the Council.[31]

Mindful that the October 25 resolution addressed only the most recent outbreak of fighting, six members of the Security Council delivered speeches following its passage, and all spoke of the need to bring about a long-term settlement of the conflict. Taking the lead in calling for such action was the United Kingdom's permanent representative to the United Nations, Lord Caradon, who for several weeks had been patiently attempting to construct a resolution based on the principle of exchanging land for peace. Lord Caradon had pulled together and adapted elements of the resolutions considered in the Emergency Special Session of the General Assembly, to which he had added the idea of a special UN representative who would act as mediator, and he had then quietly circulated draft resolutions to the various interested parties. Now, during the deliberations of October 24–25, he told the Security Council, "No one can claim that we should hesitate any longer." He also stated, "I cannot remember a greater sense of common purpose, common impatience and general agreement amongst us."[32] The translation of these common sentiments into language acceptable to the warring parties and their respective supporters was a task that Lord Caradon had thus far failed to complete. Following the sinking of the *Eilat* and the shelling of

Suez, however, the British diplomat approached this task with renewed determination and found his sense of urgency shared by a growing number of Security Council members.

The Council was encouraged at this time by reports from both Soviet and Western sources to the effect that most Arab governments were now prepared to accept the substance of the Goldberg-Gromyko compromise resolution, which they had rejected when it was discussed in the Emergency Special Session in July. Thus, when India, Mali, and Nigeria jointly introduced a draft resolution on November 7, Jordan, Egypt, and other Arab states indicated their willingness to go along with this as well. The three-power draft affirmed that "occupation or acquisition of territory by military conquest is inadmissible under the Charter of the United Nations and consequently Israel's armed forces should withdraw from all the territories occupied as a result of the recent conflict." In addition, or in exchange, the draft also affirmed that "every State has the right to live in peace and complete security free from threats or acts of war," and that as a consequence "it is obligatory on all Member States of the area to respect the sovereignty, territorial integrity and political independence of one another." Other provisions proclaimed the need for a just settlement of the question of Palestinian refugees and for freedom of navigation through international waterways.[33]

While the willingness of moderate Arab states to accept the three-power draft constituted an important evolution of their diplomatic posture, Israeli representatives complained that, for the most part, the Arabs continued to limit their expressions of a readiness for peace to private discussions and behind-the-scenes consultations. A cause of even greater Israeli concern, however, was the extent of territorial concessions called for by the three-power draft. The resolution's language dealing with territorial issues embodied the specificity demanded by the Arabs and explicitly instructed the Jewish state to withdraw completely from the lands it had captured the preceding June. This was more than Israel was prepared to accept, and Zionist officials accordingly opposed the resolution, complaining that they had not been fully consulted by its Asian and African sponsors. The latter replied that they had borrowed heavily from resolutions considered in the General Assembly, which had been thoroughly discussed with Israeli representatives, and that their present draft was based on principles which by now had gained wide acceptance among the member states of the United Nations.

Israel also raised questions about rightful ownership of the territory from which it was being instructed to withdraw, and argued that some of these lands had in fact come under the control of neighboring Arab states as a result of military conquest. As Abba Eban told the Security Council during the ensuing debate, "If territorial dispositions based on military considerations are 'inadmissible,' then the inadmissibility applies to territories occupied by Egypt and Jordan in defiance of cease-fire and truce resolutions in May 1948."[34]

The situation in the Security Council was made more complex by the introduction of a second draft resolution on November 7. Following submission of the draft by India, Mali, and Nigeria, the United States tabled a somewhat different formulation based on the principle of exchanging land for peace. The American resolution spoke in much more general terms about the need for Israeli territorial concessions, calling only for "the achievement of a state of just and lasting peace in the Middle East embracing withdrawal of armed forces from occupied territories. . . . " This language reflected apparent U.S. agreement with Israel's claim that a peace settlement need not necessarily be based on the armistice lines in effect prior to the June War, but rather that the determination of permanent boundaries should be a subject for negotiation in the context of an overall settlement. Indeed, the U.S. permanent representative, Arthur Goldberg, told the Council a few days later that there was no reason to consider the ceasefire lines resulting from the 1947–48 War to be any more satisfactory and legitimate than those resulting from the recent conflict. Permanent borders, he stated on November 15, "have to be established by the parties themselves as part of the peace-making process."[35]

In other respects, the U.S. draft of November 7 was broadly similar to that submitted by India, Mali, and Nigeria. It declared that the charter requires "mutual recognition and respect for the right of every State in the area to sovereign existence, territorial integrity, political independence, secure and recognized boundaries, and freedom from the threat or use of force." Like the three-power draft, it also affirmed the need to guarantee freedom of navigation through international waterways and to achieve a just settlement of the refugee problem.[36]

The Arabs, as well as most members of the Security Council, preferred the three-power draft to that of the Americans, arguing that the latter offered peace to the Jewish state while specifying in only the vaguest terms what Israel's neighbors would acquire in return. The U.S. replied to this criticism with the argument that it was not the intent of the American resolution to make peace on behalf of the combatants. This could be done only by the Arabs and Israelis themselves, Arthur Goldberg insisted. The American goal was rather to articulate general principles and to set forth flexible guidelines, which, despite five months of diplomatic activity, were not yet embodied in any United Nations resolution. Asserting that the language of the U.S. resolution "takes into account and in no way prejudices the positions or the vital interests of the States concerned," Goldberg sought to convince the Council that his country's draft was more likely than that of India, Mali, and Nigeria to prod the warring parties to action in the pursuit of a political solution.

American officials insisted that the U.S. resolution was even-handed, as well as more practical than the three-power draft, and Goldberg made a special effort to reassure the Arabs on this point. The U.S. permanent representative to the UN declared that, despite its belief that an open-ended peace process was the best way to break the current diplomatic stalemate, Washington remained committed to the principle of exchanging land for peace and hoped that negotiations would indeed result in a settlement involving the Arabs' recovery of their land. Mahmoud Riad, Egypt's foreign minister, reports in this connection that he received private assurances from the American representative to the effect that "there is no problem concerning Israel's complete withdrawal. Our draft [resolution] seeks to achieve this goal even without a clear statement, because Sinai is a part of Egypt, the West Bank is part of Jordan, and the Golan part of Syria."[37]

There was validity to the U.S. claim that a resolution which would be ignored by one or more of the parties would carry no political weight and might even damage the credibility of the United Nations. Yet the U.S. resolution failed to win much support and was seen by many, especially by the Arabs, the Soviet Union, and some Third World delegations, as little more than an attempt to legitimize Israel's territorial expansion. Lord Caradon contributed to the evolving debate with the observation that both the U.S. and the three-power draft were flawed, after which he recommended that the council allow some time for private consultations before voting on either resolution. The council did recess from November 9 to 13, and on the 15th Lord Caradon again addressed the council and attempted to introduce a spirit of reconciliation into its sometimes-acrimonious deliberations. He summarized the case of both the Arabs and the Israelis and asserted that each deserved to be taken seriously. "The Arab countries insist that we must direct our special attention to the recovery and restoration of their territory," he stated. "The issue of withdrawal to them is of top priority." On the other hand, "the Israelis tell us that withdrawal must never be to the old precarious truce; that it must be to a permanent peace, to secure boundaries. . . . "[38] Then, exercising his considerable diplomatic skill, Lord Caradon advanced two important conclusions. First, the Arab case and that of the Israelis are of equal right and necessity. Second, the aims of the two sides converge rather than conflict.

Lord Caradon now completed the drafting of his own resolution, revising it several times during private consultations with Arab and Israeli delegations and then, with the support of the United States, presenting it to the council late on November 16. Characterized by what is often called "constructive ambiguity," the British diplomat's formulation was purposely vague and deliberately employed language that would permit both Israelis and Arabs to interpret the resolution in a manner consistent with their own requirements.

On the key issue of occupied lands, Lord Caradon's draft once again emphasized the inadmissibility of the acquisition of territory by force, but thereafter sought to patch over Arab-Israeli differences by calling for the "withdrawal of Israeli armed forces from territories occupied in the recent conflict." By specifically mentioning Israel and by calling upon the Jewish state to relinquish captured territory, the British draft was closer to the resolution submitted by India, Mali, and Nigeria than to that introduced by the United States. Yet it also differed significantly from the former resolution by refusing to give specific instructions about the extent of the Israeli withdrawal. Other provisions of the British draft called for, again, acknowledgment of the sovereignty, territorial integrity, and political independence of every state in the area; the guaranteeing of freedom of navigation through international waterways; and the achievement of a just settlement of the refugee problem. Finally, incorporating an idea that Lord Caradon hoped would expedite the achievement of a settlement, the resolution requested the secretary-general to designate a special representative who would "proceed to the Middle East to establish and maintain contacts with the States concerned in order to promote agreement. . . . "

In formulating the critical passage about Israel's withdrawal, Lord Caradon had made several attempts to obtain Zionist acceptance of the addition of the definite article, so that the resolution would call upon the Jewish state to withdraw "from *the* territories occupied in the recent conflict." Israeli officials refused to accept this additional degree of specificity, however, recalling their argument about territories occupied by Jordan and Egypt as a result of the 1947–48 War and expressing disappointment that the British draft called upon their country alone to relinquish territory acquired by conquest. The Arabs, for their part, continued to prefer the three-power draft and at first pressed for an even greater amendment of Lord Caradon's text, insisting that they would support it only if called for Israel's withdrawal from *all* of the territories captured in the June War. By the 17th, however, the principal Arab states concerned had concluded that their interests would be best served by adoption of the resolution, rather than by holding out for the three-power draft that had no prospect of passage in the face of American and British opposition. The Arabs also abandoned their efforts to see the language of the British resolution modified. Lord Caradon, who had himself been informed that U.S. support would be withdrawn should there be any changes in his draft, told the Arabs that his text was a delicate balance which could not be altered. The choice was therefore between the British resolution and no resolution at all.[39]

Most other members of the Security Council saw the situation in this way as well, and therefore, encouraged by the deliberate ambiguity which permitted differing views about the proper interpretation of the text, broad support for Lord Caradon's resolution quickly developed. A brief detour was encountered when the permanent representative of the Soviet Union announced on November 19 that his country wished to introduce a new draft for consideration by the council, and this was duly submitted the following day. Two days of consultations showed that the British draft continued to be preferred, however; and on the 22nd Lord Caradon's text, thereafter known as United Nations Resolution 242, was unanimously adopted by the fifteen members of the Security Council.

The text of UN 242 is reprinted in full below. Despite its ambiguity, it ranks, along with the Partition Plan of 1947, as one of the most important United Nations resolutions addressed to the Arab-Israeli conflict.

> *The Security Council,*
> *Expressing* its continuing concern with the grave situation in the Middle East,
> *Emphasizing* the inadmissibility of the acquisition of territory by war and the need to work for a just and lasting peace in which every State in the area can live in security,
> *Emphasizing further* that all Member States in their acceptance of the Charter of the United Nations have undertaken a commitment to act in accordance with Article 2 of the Charter,
> 1. *Affirms* that the fulfillment of Charter principles requires the establishment of a just and lasting peace in the Middle East which should include the application of both the following principles:
>
> (i) Withdrawal of Israeli armed forces from territories occupied in the recent conflict;
>
> (ii) Termination of all claims or states of belligerency and respect for and acknowledgment of the sovereignty, territorial integrity and political independence of every State in the area and their right to live in peace within secure and recognized boundaries free from threats or acts of force;
> 2. *Affirms further* the necessity
>
> (a) For guaranteeing freedom of navigation through international waterways in the area;
>
> (b) For achieving a just settlement of the refugee problem;
>
> (c) For guaranteeing the territorial inviolability and political independence of every State in the area, through measures including the establishment of demilitarized zones;
> 3. *Requests* the Secretary-General to designate a Special Representative to proceed to the Middle East to establish and maintain contacts with the States concerned in order to promote agreement and assist efforts to achieve a peaceful and accepted settlement in accordance with the provisions and principles in this resolution;
> 4. *Requests* the Secretary-General to report to the Security Council on the progress of the efforts of the Special Representative as soon as possible.

Constructive ambiguity had been an effective device for breaking the diplomatic stalemate in the United Nations. Through its application, the efforts of Lord Caradon had resulted in passage of a resolution that was acceptable to both supporters of Israel and those allied with the Arab world; and there was thus cautious optimism in November 1967 that United Nations Security Council Resolution 242 would be a positive stimulus to new attempts at peacemaking. Several considerations contributed to this hope. First, the resolution gave formal and legal expression to principles that, in the judgment of the international community, constituted the basis of a just and lasting settlement. In this respect, by enshrining the principle of an exchange of land for peace, UN 242 established a coherent framework within which peace could be sought. Second, passage of the resolution offered the possibility of a psychological breakthrough. Since it appeared that both Israel and its most important Arab neighbors were willing to support the resolution, even if they retained some important reservations and continued to insist on widely differing interpretations, there appeared at last to be a basis for discourse between the protagonists in the Middle East conflict.

In addition, UN 242 provided a mechanism by which the United Nations could take specific steps to achieve the goals set forth in the resolution. This was yet another basis for a measure of optimism in November 1967. UN 242 calls for a special representative to be sent to the Middle East to assist the parties in reaching a settlement, and this provision was implemented only one day after the Security Council resolution was adopted. On November 23, U Thant announced that he had given this assignment to Gunnar Jarring, a seasoned Swedish diplomat with prior experience in the Middle East.

Jarring, who at the time was serving as Swedish ambassador to the Soviet Union, had been selected by U Thant a full month before the passage of UN 242. In October, the secretary general had requested and received the Swedish government's agreement for Jarring's appointment as UN special representative. The Jarring mission began almost immediately, with the Swedish diplomat in the service of the United Nations traveling to Egypt, Jordan, and Israel for consultations. Only Syria, declaring its opposition to the political compromise on which UN 242 was based, refused to receive the Jarring mission. Jarring's mandate was renewed in May 1968 and again in November, so that it had spanned three successive six-month periods by the time he returned to his post in Moscow in April 1969. One of Jarring's first tasks was to facilitate arrangements for an exchange of prisoners, and here his efforts contributed to the desired outcome. On the other hand, he failed to make progress on another early objective, the release of ships that the June War had trapped in the Suez Canal; and, unfortunately, this was a portent of the disappointment that soon came to characterize his mission as a whole.

It is to Jarring's credit that his efforts did contribute to a meaningful narrowing of the political distance between Israel and its Arab neighbors. By early 1968, Egypt and Jordan appeared to have abandoned their insistence that Israel withdraw from captured Arab territory before peace talks could begin, and also to have agreed that there could be indirect talks as soon as Jerusalem declared its willingness to implement the United Nations resolution. These Arab countries also accepted the idea that the exchange of peace for land envisioned in UN 242 could be carried out simultaneously, rather than in stages which must begin with an Israeli withdrawal.[40] Israel, for its part, moved from a noncommittal response to UN 242 to public endorsement. Whereas Abba Eban had told the Security Council that his government would determine its attitude toward Resolution 242 "in light of its own policy, which is as I have stated it,"[41] an unqualified statement of acceptance was made in the Security Council on May 1, 1968, by Yosef Tekoah, Israel's permanent representative to the United Nations. Though it led to an acrimonious debate within the Israeli cabinet, this statement remained an authoritative expression of Jerusalem's policy. Israel also eventually moved away from opposition to any alternative to direct negotiations with the Arabs and accepted the UN special representative as a third-party mediator. In October 1968, for the first time, Israel agreed to discuss substantive as well as procedural issues with Jarring.

More generally, however, the Jarring mission came to an end in April 1969 having made almost no real progress toward a resolution of the conflict. Although constructive ambiguity had temporarily papered over the gap between the positions of Jerusalem on the one hand and those of Cairo and Amman on the other, thus enabling the passage of UN 242, critical differences between the parties remained, and these had come to the fore as soon as consultations began.

The critical obstacle to progress was, predictably, the extent of any Israeli withdrawal from occupied Arab territory. The Arabs remained adamant that this withdrawal must be complete, whereas the Israelis continued to argue that this was an area where agreement had not yet been reached. Noting the vagueness of UN 242, which specified only a withdrawal "from territories occupied in the recent conflict," Eban declared, "For us, the resolution says what it says. It does not say that which it has specifically and consciously avoided saying."[42] The Israelis thus resisted Jarring's effort to extract from the parties a commitment to implement UN 242. While Egypt and Jordan gave such assurances in February 1968, Israel declared that such a commitment could be given only after Jarring had succeeded in fostering agreement about the substantive content of the resolution to be implemented, and specifically about its proper interpretation with respect to the establishment of permanent boundaries. This deadlock remained unbroken when Jarring returned to Moscow in April 1969, at which time the Swedish diplomat explained the termination of his mission by declaring that "there was no further move which he could usefully make at that stage."[43]

The New PLO

Even had Jarring been able to make more progress, a critical and necessary ingredient in any formula for a comprehensive and durable peace settlement would still have been missing. By focusing on an exchange of land for peace, UN Resolution 242 assumed that a resolution of the conflict could be achieved by returning, either completely or in meaningful measure, to the situation prevailing before the June War. But the question of territory and borders failed to address the circumstances of the Palestinian people, whose unfulfilled political aspirations remained at the core of the Arab-Israeli conflict.

The Palestinian question had in recent years come to be understood as a refugee issue, as a problem involving displaced individuals in need of relief and rehabilitation; and thus, consistent with its reliance on constructive ambiguity, UN 242 had contented itself to call in the vaguest possible terms for a just settlement of the refugee problem. To the Arabs, however, and especially to the Palestinians themselves, the problem was in reality one of statelessness. Mahmoud Riad called this the "greatest fallacy" of the UN resolution. He added, "It would not have helped the Palestinian cause to be debated at a time when we had just suffered a total military defeat, and we [therefore] preferred at this juncture to concentrate on the liberation of Arab territories occupied by Israel."[44] Nevertheless, Riad correctly observed that UN 242 confined itself to the consequences of the June War and pointed out that "the inalienable rights of the Palestinian people, recognized and continually reaffirmed by the United Nations," were completely ignored.

In the wake of the Arabs' crushing defeat in the June War, even before the failure of the United Nations to address the problem of the Palestinians, Fatah and other Palestinian guerrilla groups had come to the conclusion that they alone could carry on the struggle for the reconquest of their homeland. The governments of Egypt, Jordan, and Syria had been thrown into disarray, the humiliating demonstration of their impotence having dealt a severe blow not only to their military capabilities but to their morale and self-esteem as well. Furthermore, however much the Israelis might point to the Khartoum declaration as evidence of continuing Arab intransigence, the Palestinians saw in Egypt, Jordan, and most other Arab governments a willingness to compromise which seemed to spell an end to the struggle for Palestinian rights. All of this led, inescapably, to the conclusion that the Palestinians could rely on no one but themselves.

The circumstances of Nasser in Egypt epitomized the orientation to which Palestinians were responding. Although the guerrilla groups had criticized Cairo for seeking to control their liberation movement, having created the subservient Palestine Liberation Organization in 1964 and installing Nasser's puppet, Ahmad Shuqayri, at its head, Egypt in a larger sense had been the hope of the Palestinians. Beyond the fact that Egypt was the most populous and powerful Arab state, Nasser, like revolutionary Palestinians, possessed a vision born of the Arabs' defeat in 1947–48, one which proclaimed that corrupt and feudal Arab leadership deserved most of the blame for the Arab world's stagnation and weakness. In June 1967, however, the deeply demoralizing conclusion was that two decades of progressive reform and sincere attempts at modernization and development had accomplished little. Egypt under Nasser was defeated more easily and decisively than Egypt under Farouq had been twenty years earlier. Nor had the Baath regime in Syria fared much better, despite its pursuit of development in accordance with the modern principles of socialism and secularism.

Nasser himself recognized and acknowledged the blow that had been dealt by the June War to the prestige of so-called progressive regimes in the Arab world. On June 9, before the war on the Syrian front had even concluded, the Egyptian president broadcast his resignation to his countrymen, stating that while the victory of the enemy was due in part to "imperialist collusion," he himself was "ready to bear the whole responsibility."[45] He withdrew his resignation the next day, in response to massive popular demonstrations and a unanimous call issued by the National Assembly. Nevertheless, Nasser and Egypt, and indeed men and women throughout the Arab world, remained profoundly demoralized by the June War. Offering a characterization that might be applied to the Arab world in general at this time, the Egyptian leader described himself as "a man walking in the desert surrounded by moving sands not knowing whether, if he moved, he would be swallowed up by the sands or find the right path."[46]

While the PLO and Shuqayri seemed as impotent as their Arab League patrons in the months following the June War, Fatah and other independent Palestinian guerrilla groups began to organize new efforts at resistance in the summer of 1967. On the one hand, a number of Fatah leaders visited Arab capitals in an effort to raise funds and obtain diplomatic support; and, led by Khalil al-Wazir, Salah Khalaf, Farouq al-Qaddoumi, and Khaled al-Hassan, these missions achieved substantial results. Particularly significant was Khaled al-Hassan's success early in 1968 in persuading the monarch of Saudi Arabia to levy a "liberation tax" on Palestinians working in his kingdom. This levy soon brought 50 to 60 million riyals a year to the guerrilla movements.[47] Additional funds were raised in Libya, as well as elsewhere, with contributions being obtained both from a number of governments and from wealthy individuals. The Fatah representatives also received expressions of diplomatic support from various Arab governments.

On the other hand, during the same period, Yasir Arafat and a few other guerrilla organizers slipped into the Israeli-occupied West Bank and began to explore the possibility of initiating an armed uprising. Arafat established his headquarters in the old section of Nablus late in August, then later moved to a one-story villa in Ramallah. For the next few months he traveled in disguise throughout the occupied territories, and reportedly inside Israel as well, attempting to organize commando operations and to create a network of local resistance cells. An American journalist who interviewed Arafat about his activities during this period reports that the Palestinian leader told of passing his childhood home in Jerusalem on one of these clandestine trips and of finding in the doorway a brother whom he had not seen for many years. Arafat did not identify himself or speak to the man, however, for the disguised Fatah leader could not run the risk of being discovered.[48]

Arafat and other Fatah activists continued their organizational efforts until the end of the year but made little headway, thwarted in part by a local leadership class which retained its ties to the Hashemite regime in Amman, and even more by Israel's tough and effective security apparatus. The latter, aided by informants and by captured Jordanian intelligence files, imposed severe economic sanctions on villages suspected of harboring Fatah members and gradually rounded up the guerrillas themselves. Arafat himself barely escaped capture, fleeing to Jordan early in 1968 and, according to an Israeli journalist, leaving behind a decimated movement which had sustained losses of approximately 1,000 captured and 200 killed.[49]

Fatah's inability to organize an effective resistance network in the occupied West Bank did not prevent it from attracting new recruits. Along with smaller resistance movements, it continued to offer hope to young Palestinians in the wake of the Arabs' defeat, and there are even reports to the effect that many non-Palestinian Arabs volunteered for service in one or another of the guerrilla organizations. The Palestinians were at least taking action, refusing to accept the consequences of defeat.

In addition, Fatah's reputation and popularity were greatly enhanced by a confrontation with Israeli forces in the Jordanian village of Karameh on March 21, 1968. Having crushed attempts at resistance in the West Bank, the IDF now began to attack guerrilla positions east of the Jordan. Its raid on Karameh, four miles across the river, was this sort of operation. The Israelis were determined to prevent Fatah from organizing raids from East Bank communities which had come under its control; and Karameh in particular, where the guerrilla movement had established a major command center following its ouster from the West Bank, was a likely IDF target. The Israelis understandably viewed Fatah's commando operations not as acts of resistance but as cowardly acts of terrorism, and Jerusalem's determination to suppress such activities was strengthened when an Israeli school bus was blown up by a mine on March 18, three days before the Battle of Karameh. Two people were killed and twenty-eight were injured.

Although accounts of the Battle of Karameh differ with respect to important details, it seems clear that the heavily outnumbered Fatah defenders fought bravely and well and inflicted a relatively large number of casualties on the invading Israelis. Indeed it is significant that the Palestinians fought at all, since the Jordanian intelligence service had learned of Israel's plan to attack Karameh in advance, possibly from an American CIA source, and had advised the guerrillas to abandon their positions. But Fatah decided to stay and fight, despite Jordan's warning that an especially heavy assault was anticipated; and, because of their preparations, as well as assistance from Jordanian forces, 300 Palestinian guerrillas were able to engage 1,500 or more Israelis in a battle that ranged all day and into the evening.[50] When the fighting finally stopped, the Palestinians had killed 28 of the attackers and wounded 90 more.

Karameh's Palestinian defenders sustained much heavier losses— as many as 170 of their number may have been killed, in addition to about 100 Jordanians— but the battle was nonetheless considered a major victory by Fatah and its supporters, and the name "Karameh," which means "honor" in Arabic, has accordingly assumed a place of distinction in the folklore of the resistance. Moreover, the encounter almost immediately had consequences which were practical as well as symbolic. One Palestinian leader, Abdallah Frangi, labeled it "the political and military turning point in the Palestinian resistance, especially for al-Fatah." Frangi states that "only a few hours after it ended, the battle of Karameh was a legend," and he reports as well that it "restored the dignity and self-esteem of the Palestinians and of the entire Arab world."[51] Whether or not the facts of the March 21 encounter justify the impact that it had on young Palestinians is largely beside the point, for Frangi is correct in his assessment of both the psychological and the practical significance of the "victory" at Karameh. Thousands of new recruits now applied to join Fatah, aspiring to become commandos or *fedayeen* (literally, "those who sacrifice themselves for a cause"). Khalaf reports that 5,000 would-be guerrillas showed up within forty-eight hours, and Frangi adds that only about one-fifth of the new volunteers could be accommodated at existing training camps. The ranks of other Palestinian guerrilla organizations, most notably George Habash's Popular Front for the Liberation of Palestine (PFLP), also grew substantially in the wake of Karameh.

Fatah and, to a lesser extent, other guerrilla organizations used their growing popularity to establish a political presence in the towns and especially in the refugee camps of the East Bank.[52] Fatah first established a political department to coordinate its activities and to produce newspapers and booklets for distribution through its growing network of grass-roots committees, the latter serving additionally as vehicles by which the resistance movement could participate in the administration of local affairs. Thereafter, both to render genuine service to the Palestinian rank and file and to increase its own support at the grass-roots level, Fatah undertook to provide an expanding range of social services to local communities. A number of clinics and health-care projects were established, for example, most of which treated Jordanians as well as Palestinians. In 1969, these local facilities were organized into the Palestine Red Crescent Society, which was thereafter granted observer status by the International Red Cross.

A related development was the expansion and reorientation of activities undertaken by the Palestinians' general unions, including the General Union of Palestine Workers, the General Union of Palestine Students, and the General Union of Palestinian Women. Although affiliated with the PLO, these organizations were led by activists from Fatah and other guerrilla groups at the local level, and as the influence of these groups increased, the unions themselves began to do more work at the grass-roots level, particularly in the refugee camps. The General Union of Palestinian Women, for example, sought to improve the circumstances of women from poorer social classes, and also to prepare these women for participation in the struggle against Israel. Thus, according to Brand's important study, the union used funds from membership dues and contributions to establish "vocational training centers, literacy programs, and military training sessions for women . . . [as well as] educational sessions ranging in topic from health care and women's issues to the latest developments in the national struggle." [53] Brand also reports, with respect to the organization of Palestinian workers, that if a worker had a problem, he often would go not to his particular trade union but instead to the "workers' bureau" of Fatah or another guerrilla organization.[54]

Although the scope and effectiveness of these programs should not be overstated, the period from 1968 to 1970 nonetheless witnessed a significant expansion of activities that helped to mobilize the Palestinian population and which gave substance to the guerrillas' claim that their movement was one of true emancipation. These activities also contributed to the political and institutional development of the resistance movements themselves, enabling them to gain strength for the struggle not only against Israel but against those in the Arab world who opposed an independent effort on behalf of the Palestinian cause.

Led by Fatah, the guerrilla organizations were now in a position to challenge the existing leadership of the Palestine Liberation Organization for control of the movement dedicated to the reconquest of their homeland. Encouraged by their growing popularity among the Palestinian rank and file, and also by the favorable reception they were now receiving in many Arab capitals, the leaders of Fatah and other groups issued denunciations of the PLO and its leader, Ahmad Shuqayri. They charged, correctly, that the former was the artificial creation of Arab governments seeking to prevent meaningful resistance, and that the latter had been selected not for his nationalist credentials but for his subservience to Nasser and other Arab heads of state. In December 1967, following passage of United Nations Resolution 242, the guerrilla groups feared that Shuqayri would adopt the Egyptian and Jordanian position toward the resolution and thus demanded that he be repudiated as spokesman for the Palestinian cause. On December 9, for example, Fatah sent a memorandum to a meeting of Arab foreign ministers taking place in Cairo, asking that Shuqayri's statements no longer be disseminated by the official Arab media. Shuqayri was also publicly criticized at this time by several members of his own Executive Committee, and on December 24 the PLO leader bowed to mounting pressure and submitted his resignation.

Shuqayri is reported to have recommended that Fatah take control of the PLO, but the guerrilla movement chose to disregard his recommendation, preferring to see the organization transformed into a comprehensive political front uniting all resistance groups. Yahya Hammouda, a veteran activist with a wide range of political connections, was therefore chosen as Shuqayri's interim replacement; and about the same time, in January 1968, Fatah invited all of the various resistance organizations to assemble in Cairo and establish a unified political strategy. With only Habash's PFLP refusing to attend the meeting, the Palestinians in Cairo created a Permanent Bureau to coordinate their activities. In April, in the wake of Karameh and amidst plans to convene the Fourth Palestine National

Council, the Fatah Central Committee appointed Yasir Arafat as its official spokesman and representative, and Arafat then took the lead in articulating the demands of Fatah and the Permanent Bureau for increased representation at the forthcoming PNC meeting. May 1968 was a time of hard bargaining between the various resistance groups and those who remained loyal to the existing PLO.

The Fourth PNC, which took place in Cairo on July 10–17, saw Fatah and the other guerrilla movements consolidate their gains and move closer to taking undisputed control of the PLO. In response to their demand for greater representation, thirty-eight of the council's one hundred seats had been allocated to the Permanent Bureau, and another ten had been given to the PFLP, giving the guerrillas almost half of the entire number. Almost all of the remaining seats went to persons active in the PLO, including representatives of the PLA and previous PNC members, but among these individuals were representatives of the affiliated Palestinian unions, such as the General Union of Palestine Students and the General Union of Palestine Workers, which by now had become sympathetic to the resistance movements.

The delegates meeting in Cairo amended the PLO charter and constitution in ways that reflected further the influence of Fatah and other commando organizations. They introduced a provision into the charter, for example, to the effect that "armed struggle is the only way to liberate Palestine" (Article 9), and then stipulated in a second provision that "the Arab Palestinian people, expressing themselves by the armed Palestinian revolution, reject all solutions which are substitutes for the total liberation of Palestine" (Article 21). The delegates also revised key provisions of the constitution, abolishing, for example, the chairman's ability to appoint the Executive Committee and requiring instead that its members be elected by the PNC, which was in effect the National Assembly of the Palestinian people. The Executive Committee, in turn, was given responsibility for electing its chairman, thus making the PLO's chief executive officer much more responsible to the organization's membership than had previously been the case.[55]

Despite these important manifestations of the guerrilla movements' growing influence, it was not until the next meeting of the Palestine National Council, held in February 1969, that these groups were able to capture a majority of seats on the PLO Executive Committee and see one of their own leaders installed as chairman. The Fourth PNC had been unable to reach agreement on the composition of a new Executive Committee, and so, with only one modification, the term of the existing Executive Committee had been extended. But political maneuvering continued as preparations were made for the Fifth PNC, once again to be convened in Cairo, and the intensification of existing trends was visible to all engaged in the bargaining. On the one hand, the resistance groups continued to gain influence relative to the pre-1967 PLO. On the other, Fatah continued its emergence as the dominant force among these groups. Both of these trends were reflected in the allocation of seats for the Fifth PNC; the total number was increased to 105, and of these 33 were allocated to Fatah and 24 more were divided equally between the two next-largest resistance organizations, the PFLP and the Syrian-sponsored Saiqa. Fatah's preeminence at the February 1969 meeting was further enhanced by the support it received from many independent delegates, and by the fact that some of its major rivals claimed to be inadequately represented and boycotted the meeting in protest. Among those who refused to participate were Habash's PFLP and the PLO's military arm, the Palestine Liberation Army.

Under these circumstances, Fatah easily dominated the Fifth PNC and emerged from the meeting with control of the PLO's key institutions, completing the guerrilla groups' capture of the organization. In effect, a new, more representative and more authentic PLO had been created. The Executive Committee elected at the Fifth PNC contained eleven members, of whom four were Fatah delegates. These individuals were Yasir Arafat, Khaled al-Hassan, Farouq al-Qaddoumi, and Muhammad Youssef al-Najjar. The Executive Committee elected in 1969 also included three Fatah sympathizers, as well as two Saiqa members, one Saiqa sympathizer, and one holdover from the old PLO. Fatah's leader, Yasir Arafat, was elected chairman of the new Executive Committee, and Khaled al-Hassan was given an important post as well, becoming head of the Political Department, the PLO's foreign ministry.

Under Fatah's leadership, the PLO set out to establish organizational unity within Palestinian ranks, and by summer 1970 it had largely succeeded. Early in 1968, Fatah had declared its commitment to making the PLO a comprehensive political front, representing the Palestinian people in its entirety, but the achievement of this objective remained difficult in the face of personal jealousies, disputes about representation, and the formation of several new guerrilla groups, such as the Iraqi- sponsored Arab Liberation Front set up in April 1969. Particularly troublesome was opposition from the PFLP, which maintained its boycott when the Sixth PNC meeting convened in September 1969. On the other hand, the Popular Democratic Front for the Liberation of Palestine, an offshoot of the PFLP led by Nayif Hawatmeh, did agree to come under the PLO umbrella, and eight seats at the congress were accordingly allocated to the PDFLP. In addition, outside the institutional framework of the PLO, Fatah, the PLA, and a number of other organizations had by this time formed a unified military structure, the Palestine Armed Struggle Command.

The process of unification was completed in 1970. Aided by a common desire to preserve their political independence in the face of Jordanian efforts to regulate commando groups operating in the East Bank, the PFLP for the first time in two years agreed to cooperate with Fatah and other members of the PLO. Although it sent only one representative to the Seventh PNC meeting, held in late May and early June 1970, PFLP participation signified the achievement of unity within the ranks of the Palestinian resistance. Habash's group, like others, now accepted the authority of the PLO Central Committee, and the PLO itself emerged as the comprehensive and representative organization envisioned by Fatah.

As shown in the table on the following page, the groups brought together within the framework of the PLO were a heterogeneous lot with respect to size, ideology, and source of support. Fatah, the largest, had little ideology beyond that of Palestinian nationalism and received financial assistance from a wide range of Arab sources. The same was true of the Palestine Liberation Army, which had been established by the PLO prior to 1967 and which received most of its support from the Arab League. Saiqa, the next-largest group, was sponsored by Syria and espoused the general philosophy of the Baath Party, although, like Fatah, it was not a particularly ideological movement. Each of these three groups had a fighting force that in 1970 was estimated to consist of 5,000-10,000 men.

Somewhat smaller, with perhaps 1,000–3,000 men in arms, were PFLP and PDFLP, the latter having been established by dissidents within the former. Despite their relatively small size, however, these groups had considerable influence because of the presence in their ranks of intellectuals with important educational, professional, and media connections. PFLP and PDFLP were both noted for their Marxist orientation, and for their conviction that the goal of the resistance movement should be not only the liberation of Palestine but a political revolution throughout the Arab world. Both were also characterized by heavy dependence on an Arab government sponsor. Habash's PFLP received most of its aid from Iraq, whereas Hawatmeh's PDFLP was supported by Syria; and though there were genuine ideological disagreements between the two movements, these were abetted by the rivalry between the Syrian and Iraqi wings of the Baath Party. This rivalry also led the Iraqis to create the Arab Liberation Front in April 1969, largely as a counterweight to Saiqa. With fewer than 500 fighters, the ALF typified the smaller groups which rounded out the PLO's institutional membership in the summer of 1970. Other groups of this magnitude included the Popular Front for the Liberation of Palestine–General Command, led by Ahmad Jibril, the Action Organization for the Liberation of Palestine, and the Popular Organization for the Liberation of Palestine.

The PLO sought to achieve a high level of institutionalization and structural development, as well as comprehensiveness with respect to membership, and the organizational chart presented below shows the eventual result of efforts in this direction. The major policy-making bodies, as noted, were the Palestine National Council and the Executive Committee; and the Seventh PNC also created a twenty-seven-member Central Committee to serve as an intermediate advisory organ. The Central Committee consisted of all Executive Committee members, a representative of each commando group belonging to the PLO, and several in-

Major Palestinian Groups in 1970[56]

	Resistance Group	Major Source of Support
	I. Larger Groups (5,000–10,000 armed men)	
1.	Palestine National Liberation Movement (Fatah) (Military forces: al-Asifa)	Saudi Arabia, Kuwait, Libya, Algeria, Syria, private Palestinian sources
2.	Palestine Liberation Army (PLA)	Arab League
3.	Vanguards of the Popular Liberation War (Saiqa)	Syria
	II. Middle Groups (1,000–3,000 armed men)	
4.	Popular Front for the Liberation of Palestine (PFLP)	Iraq
5.	Popular Democratic Front for the Liberation of Palestine (PDFLP)	Syria
	III. Smaller Groups (100–500 armed men)	
6.	Popular Front for the Liberation of Palestine–General Command (PFLP-GC)	Syria
7.	Arab Liberation Front (ALF)	Iraq
8.	Organization of Arab Palestine (OAP)	Egypt
9.	Action Organization for the Liberation of Palestine (AOLP)	Egypt, Kuwait
10.	Popular Organization for the Liberation of Palestine (POLP)	Egypt

dependents. The most important elements of the PLO's permanent bureaucracy were the Secretariat, the Political Department, the Military Department, and the organization's fund-raising arm, the Palestine National Fund. The Military Department, in theory at least, supervised and coordinated activities of the resistance forces of Fatah, the PLA, and other groups that in 1969 had come together

Organizational Structure of the PLO[57]

Palestine National Council
|
Central Committee
|
Executive Committee —— General Secretariat

Chairman of the
Executive Committee

—Department of —— PLO Information
Political   Offices
Affairs

—Department
of Education

—Department —— Palestine
of Health   Red Crescent

—Department of
the Palestine
National Fund
(Finance)

—Information —— Palestine
and National   News Agency
Guidance   (WAFA)

—Department of —— General Union of Palestinian
Popular
Organizations

—Department of
the Occupied
Homeland

—Department of
National
Relations

—Military Forces
and Unified
Command

—Planning Center

—Research Center

—Workers
—Students
—Women
—Peasants
—Writers and
Journalists
Teachers
—Lawyers
—Doctors
—Engineers
—Artists

to form the Palestine Armed Struggle Command. Finally, as noted earlier, there were a number of well-developed affiliated syndicates, such as the General Union of Palestine Workers and the General Union of Palestine Students. Additional departments, unions, and specialized units were established in the years after 1970, although some for a time existed mostly on paper, and the eventual result was the elaborate organizational network shown in the chart.

Ideological Developments

The institutional development of the PLO was accompanied by an important evolution of the organization's ideology. Despairing of effective assistance from Arab governments and determined that the Palestinian people should in any event speak for itself in international affairs, the PLO sought a political formula that not only would articulate the rights of the Palestinians but also would offer a positive vision on the basis of which the conflict with Israel might be resolved.

The PLO's search for a new political formula was in the first instance motivated by one overriding consideration. In contradistinction to the provisions of UN Resolution 242, the organization sought to make clear that the Palestinians required more than "a just settlement of the refugee problem." Although developments after 1948 had tended to obscure the political dimension of the Palestinian problem, such that Palestinian statelessness often appeared to be a secondary aspect of what at its core was a confrontation between Israel and the Arab states, the PLO sought in late 1967 and early 1968 to reestablish a proper and historically accurate understanding of the conflict, to make clear that the essence of the Arab-Israeli conflict was the struggle between Zionism and Palestinian nationalism and the fact that the Zionists had displaced the Palestinians and taken possession of their ancestral homeland. Thus, while UN 242 defined the Palestinians as refugees and employed language suggesting a need for humanitarian aid, including assistance aimed at rehabilitation, resettlement, and perhaps compensation for lost property, the PLO insisted that the problem was of a very different order. Insofar as their conflict with Israel was concerned, the Palestinians are not a collection of displaced individuals requiring assistance. They are, rather, the PLO maintained, a people and a nation that has been deprived of its land and had its aspirations for statehood thwarted. The Palestinian problem is thus a political problem, one requiring a political solution.

These sentiments are reflected in the revised National Charter adopted by the fourth session of the Palestine National Council in July 1968. Over and over again, the articles of the charter place emphasis on the political and national rights of the Palestinian people, insisting that these rights transcend the disasters which have befallen the Palestinians. The charter also asserts that these political and national rights can be exercised only in Palestine, the Palestinians' legal and legitimate homeland; and that it is for the Palestinians themselves, led by the PLO, to determine the character of the political system to be established in that homeland.

> Article 1. Palestine is the homeland of the Palestinian Arab people. . . .
>
> Article 2. Palestine, with the boundaries it had during the British Mandate, is an indivisible territorial unit.
>
> Article 3. The Palestinian Arab people possess the legal right to their homeland and have the right to determine their destiny after achieving the liberation of their country. . . .
>
> Article 4. The Palestinian identity is a genuine, essential and inherent characteristic. . . . The Zionist occupation and the dispersal of the Palestinian Arab people do . . . not make them lose their Palestinian identity. . . .
>
> Article 7. That there is a Palestinian community and that it has material, spiritual and historical connection with Palestine are indisputable facts. . . .
>
> Article 9. . . . The Palestinian Arab people assert . . . their right to normal life in Palestine and to exercise their right to self-determination and sovereignty over it.
>
> Article 24. The Palestinian people believe in the principles of justice, freedom, sovereignty, self-determination, human dignity, and in the right of all peoples to exercise them.
>
> Article 26. The Palestine Liberation Organization, the representative of the Palestinian revolutionary forces, is responsible for the Palestinian Arab people's movement in its struggle to retrieve its homeland . . . and exercise the right of self-determination in it. . . .
>
> Article 28. The Palestinian people assert the genuineness and independence of their national revolution and reject all forms of intervention, trusteeship, and subordination.
>
> Article 29. The Palestinian people possess the fundamental and genuine legal right to liberate and retrieve their homeland.
>
> Article 30. The Organization shall have a flag, an oath of allegiance, and an anthem.

PLO thinking was shaped not only by the circumstances of Palestinians themselves but also by the situation in the Arab world more generally, and particularly by the profound crisis of confidence that emerged in the wake of the June War. The Arabs' rapid and humiliating defeat produced a loss of faith in established ideologies, or at least in their application, and this led many Palestinian and other Arab intellectuals to call for a new approach to the problems of the Arab world. Abdallah Laroui, a leading Moroccan scholar, described the mood of the Arabs at this time as a "moral crisis," which he said "culminated in a period of anguished self-criticism, a searching reappraisal of postwar Arab culture and political practice."[58] Observed in retrospect, the political and intellectual consequences of this deep malaise make the 1967 War appear as a watershed in the Arab world's continuing ideological evolution, comparable in many ways to the Arab-Israeli war of 1947–48 and the Egyptian revolution of 1952.

Within a few years, one result of this soul-searching would be renewed interest in the political role of Islam and growing support for movements contending that the way to end stagnation and weakness is to reorganize Arab polities in accordance with Muslim law. Indeed this tendency was fueled by a perception of Israel that gained currency in some Arab circles in the years after 1967; Israel's power was held to be the result, at least in part, of an openly proclaimed identification with Judaism and a refusal to abandon its religious character in the name of modernization and development. Expanded support for Islamic-tendency movements was still several years away, however, and in 1968 and 1969 the most compelling ideological and political analyses came not from Muslim activists but from radicals favoring leftist solutions, a central component of which was secularism. This tendency, too, found support in the Arabs' view of the victorious Israelis. As expressed by Laroui, "All found in the enemy that which justified their argument,"[59] and for Laroui himself it was Israel's open, democratic, and scientific orientation that accounted for its strength. Specifically, he wrote, "The principal factor was the enemy's social organization, his sense of individual freedom, his lack of subjugation, despite all appearances, to any form of finalism or absolutism."[60]

A key contributor to radical Arab thought during this period was Sadeq al-Azm, an American-educated Syrian intellectual teaching at the American University of Beirut. His *Self-Criticism after the Defeat*, published in 1968, as well as *The Criticism of Religious Thought*, published in 1969, asserted that the Arabs' continuing weakness was primarily the result of psychological and cultural factors, particularly a fatalism born of conservative interpretations of Islam and a preoccupation with ancient glories that prevented the Arabs from wholeheartedly embracing the scientific and political culture of the modern world. Al-Azm's contribution is discussed by the American political scientist Malcolm Kerr, who describes his work as "the most scathing of all indictments of Arab society and culture";[61] and by Fouad Ajami, a scholar of Lebanese origin, who states that *Self-Criticism after the Defeat* "must surely go down as one of the most impressive and controversial pieces of Arabic political writing in recent times."[62] Reviewing his harsh judgments about the inadequacy of the Arabs' social and moral order, Ajami quotes al-Azm as asking whether it is possible "for a people to wage war with such obsolete notions . . . to enter a war that requires movement and initiative when the society is permeated by passivity and reluctance to initiate decisions?"[63]

The anger of al-Azm and others was focused in particular on the regimes of Nasser and the Baathists. While little had been expected from the Arabian monarchies and other conservative governments, the failure of the more progressive regimes in Cairo, Damascus, and Baghdad was highly significant; it revealed the depth of the Arab world's attachment to its traditions and led al-Azm and those who shared his views to the inescapable conclusion that only a truly radical approach could rid the Arabs of their stagnation and weakness. As explained by Ajami, the political experiments of Egypt and Syria were judged to have been no more than "halfhearted and ambiguous." The Arabs were said to be afflicted with "a middle-of-the road orientation" and, more generally, to be incapable of deciding what they wanted. Did the Arab revolution seek to preserve the past and to control men and women with laws that had been codified fourteen centuries earlier, or did it want "a new legislative order derived from scientific, socialist thought"?[64] These themes were echoed by other Arab intellectuals as well, such as Adonis, the Syrian poet and essayist. Responding to a 1968 speech by Nasser, Adonis wrote, "We must realize that the societies that modernized did so only after they rebelled against their history, tradition and values. . . . We must ask our religious heritage what it can do for us in our present and future. . . . If it cannot do much for us we must abandon it."[65]

This radical perspective was shared by many Palestinian intellectuals. Indeed, with its emphasis on guerrilla activity, direct action, and grass-roots organization, the new PLO became a source of hope and pride to young men and women throughout the Arab world. With defeatism reigning in the capitals of the Arab world, the dynamic Palestinian leaders became popular heroes, and their movements were regarded, temporarily at least, as the very embodiment of the radical vision to which many young Arabs now looked for inspiration.

So far as ideology is concerned, the PLO's philosophy was at once conditioned by and a prime contributor to emerging normative currents, and the central notion on which its focus was fixed in this regard was that of secularism. A separation of religion and politics appealed to the Palestinians for a variety of reasons. Few in the Arab world had suffered more as a result of Arab weakness than had the Palestinians; and, consistent with the radicals' judgment about the needs of Arab society, secularism held out the prospect of a social order that was forward- rather than backward-looking and that was liberated from medieval Muslim codes which were alleged to constrain behavior and to discourage creativity and original thinking. Secularism, in other words, being a key plank in the radicals' platform of revolutionary social, cultural, and political change, was an essential part of the treatment prescribed for the Arab world's illness. In addition, secularism appeared to fit particularly well the special circumstances of the Palestinians themselves. With a substantial Christian minority in its ranks, the conduct of politics without reference to religion would both promote the unity of the Palestinian people and encourage the emergence of political processes that were egalitarian in character.

The attractiveness of secularism was also directly tied to the Palestinians' conflict with Zionism. On the one hand, the notion was held to have public-relations value. It was hoped that calls for a dissociation of religion and politics would expose what Palestinians regarded as the true nature of Zionism, laying bare its contradictions and undermining the legitimacy of the state to which it had given rise. In this connection, first, the Palestinians asserted that the Jews do not need or deserve a country of their own because they are a religious group rather than a national community. As stated in Article 20 of the revised PLO charter, "Judaism, being a religion, is not an independent nationality. Nor do Jews constitute a single nation with an identity of its own; they are citizens of the states to which they belong."

In addition, however, in the analysis of the PLO at this time, the State of Israel is anachronistic, even tribalistic, as well as superfluous, and here the Palestinians sought a propaganda advantage by charging that Zionism is a form of racism. Israel was alleged to be out of step with the twentieth century, having turned its back on the lessons of the United States and other secular democracies, and to be discriminatory in at least two important ways. First, with about 13 percent of its population being either Muslim or Christian, a consequence of Israel's official and declared identification with Judaism was said to be the unavoidable denial of full and equal rights to the state's non-Jewish citizens. In one contemporary account setting forth this contention, Sabri Jiryis, a Palestinian who had lived in Israel, wrote that the policy of the Jewish state toward its Christian and Muslim citizens was one of "racial discrimination and repression."[66]

Further, some Palestinians and others who criticized Israel's rejection of secularism charged that the state places a claim on the loyalty of Jews in other countries, whether they wish such a claim or not, and thereby undermines the status of these Jews in the countries where they live. This is implied in Article 23 of the revised PLO charter, which states that "right and justice require all states . . . to consider Zionism an illegitimate movement in order that . . . the loyalty of citizens to their respective homelands may [be] safeguarded." As expressed by Clovis Maksoud, at the time a prominent Arab journalist, Israel not only discriminates against its own non-Jewish citizens but also "establishes a permanent polarity between the Jew and man" in the rest of the world.[67] A more general articulation of the case against Israel's fusion of religion and politics is provided by Naseer Aruri, an American scholar of Palestinian origin who summarizes the charge that "the ideal of Zionism in Israel is racial and exclusionist." Expressing the view put forward by Palestinians after 1967, Aruri asserts that "the very concept of a Jewish state precludes the notion of pluralism and coexistence," and that "the rise of the Palestinian resistance was the single most important factor that exposed Israel as a colonialist oppressor, its enterprise based on legal discrimination between Jews and non-Jews."[68]

Although supporters of Israel often charged that the PLO advocated secularism in the Middle East solely because of its perceived propaganda value, it would appear that many Palestinians were also motivated by a sincere commitment to progressive values, as they conceived them, and by a genuine belief that the sepa-

ration of religion and politics might provide a suitable alternative to the peacemaking formula enshrined in United Nations Resolution 242. While insisting on
their right to self-determination, and thus rejecting the return to the *status quo
ante* advocated by the Security Council resolution of November 1967, progressive Palestinians suggested that Jews and Arabs might both live in Palestine and
might share in ruling the country on a nondenominational basis. As explained
by Aruri, these conceptions would replace "Israel's zero-sum solution," so that
"Israelis could no longer claim they were in danger of being pushed into the sea"
by Palestinians seeking to return home.[69]

These notions, fusing contemporary Arab thinking on the issue of stagnation
and weakness with the Palestinians' determined insistence that their own statelessness was at the core of the Arab-Israeli conflict, led the PLO to call for the
creation in Palestine of a democratic and secular state, where Arabs and Jews
would live together on the basis of equality. The revised PLO charter appeared
to acknowledge that Jews as well as Arabs had rights in Palestine. Specifically,
Article 6 declared that "Jews who were living permanently in Palestine until the
beginning of the Zionist invasion shall be considered Palestinians." Moreover,
although Article 6 raised important and hotly debated questions about exactly
which Israeli Jews were entitled to citizenship in the Palestinians' proposed state,
subsequent declarations went further and repeated that the PLO was indeed committed to the construction of an open, pluralist, and nonsectarian political order.
Thus, according to an account of PNC deliberations during this period, the plan
for a democratic and secular state in Palestine was not put forward as a negotiating proposal or bargaining chip, but rather as "a strategic objective" of the
Palestinian resistance movement.[70]

A January 1969 meeting of the Central Committee of Fatah, the largest and
most powerful of the guerrilla organizations united under the PLO umbrella,
adopted a seven-point declaration which explicitly and solemnly proclaimed that
"the final objective of its [Fatah's] struggle is the restoration of the independent,
democratic State of Palestine, all of whose citizens will enjoy equal rights regardless of their religion."[71] This is in direct contrast to the provisions of UN 242,
which the Fatah declaration called a "pseudo-political solution" because it failed
to recognize Palestinian political rights, and which therefore "is in no way binding on the Palestinian people." Several months later, in August of the same year,
Fatah's chairman, Yasir Arafat, repeated the same points, saying that the PLO
offered an enlightened alternative to the Jews in Palestine: "the creation of a democratic Palestinian state for all those who wish to live in peace on the land of
peace . . . an independent, progressive, democratic State of Palestine, which will
guarantee equal rights to all its citizens, regardless of race or religion."[72] And as
stated yet again in a PLO handbook published in Beirut in 1972, "The Palestinians will keep on struggling, as they have always done, for the liberation of Palestine and for the erection of a progressive democratic state where everyone can
live and enjoy equal rights and privileges, regardless of race or religious belief."[73]

The Palestinians' proposal was an alternative to the United Nations Partition Resolution of 1947, as well as to UN 242. In contrast to the latter document, the Partition Resolution recognized the political rights of the Palestinian people and called explicitly for the creation of a Palestinian state, which was to occupy a portion of Palestine and exist alongside the Jewish state of Israel. The revised PLO charter was specific in rejecting this kind of two-state solution; although the PLO mainstream would substantially modify its position on this issue a decade or so later, the organization was unwilling in the late 1960s and early 1970s to consider trading its claims in one part of Palestine for political recognition and the establishment of a Palestinian state in the remainder of the territory. Thus, as noted, Article 2 refers to Palestine as "an indivisible territorial unit," and Article 19 declares directly that "the partition of Palestine in 1947 and the establishment of the state of Israel are entirely illegal, regardless of the passage of time. . . . " This being the case, the democratic and secular state proposal appealed to Palestinians not only because it recognized their right to self-determination but also because it held out the possibility of an accommodation with the Jews that did not require the Palestinians to abandon their claim to the whole of their ancestral homeland.

PLO calls for a democratic and secular state involved what their spokesmen sometimes called the "de-Zionization" of the Middle East. The State of Israel, the political expression of Zionism, was to be dismantled, and a state conforming to the PLO's vision was to be established on the whole of Palestine, as that territory had come to be defined during the British mandate. Yet, consistent with their progressive vision of a secular Middle East, Palestinian spokesmen declared that their proposals were addressed to the needs of Jews as well as Palestinians. "We wish to liberate the Jews from Zionism," Arafat told an interviewer in August 1969, "and to make them realize that the purpose behind the creation of the State of Israel, namely to provide a haven for persecuted Jews, has instead thrown them into a ghetto of their own making."[74] The alternative to this ghetto, he stated in February 1970, was for Jews in Israel to abandon their Zionist ideology and "agree to live with us" in a democratic Palestinian state.[75]

Palestinians attempted to demonstrate the intellectual honesty of their progressive vision by insisting that they opposed Zionism but not Judaism. Fatah's 1969 seven-point declaration stated that the PLO "is not struggling against the Jews as an ethnic and religious community . . . [but against Israel as] a theocratic, racist and expansionist system."[76] Clovis Maksoud stressed in a 1970 article that "the survival of the Zionist entity is at stake, but most definitely not the survival of the Jews in Palestine." On the contrary, he continued, the proposed Palestinian state would be truly nonsectarian, such that "neither Hebrew nor Arabic would be coterminous with a particular racial or religious group."[77]

Some Palestinians went further and insisted that their distinction between Zionism and Judaism brought an obligation to root out the anti-Semitism that had become common in some Arab circles. Thus, in 1969, Yasir Arafat declared that one immediate objective of the Palestinian revolution was "the destruction of any racial or sectarian notion that might exist among the Arabs";[78] and about the same time, according to the *Christian Science Monitor*, Palestinian leaders associated with the PLO toured the West Bank to condemn the anti-Jewish character of some Arab propaganda. A 1970 article in *The Militant* was both frank and hopeful on this subject, forthrightly acknowledging the problem of Arab anti-Semitism. "[We] Palestinians learnt to hate the Jews and everything Jewish," it reported with disarming honesty. But now, it went on to assert, "a new, humane image of the Jew is being formed. . . . Palestinians are redefining their objectives and finding the goal of creating a new Palestine that compasses them and the present Jewish settlers a very desirable one."[79]

In sum, proclaiming the progressive and egalitarian character of their vision, Palestinians and other Arabs argued that the proposal to establish a democratic and secular state in Palestine should be welcomed even by those who might disagree with its substance. It was creative, revolutionary, and consistent with the canons of the modern age. Equally important, if not more so, it turned attention from tiresome and perhaps irresolvable debates about the past to a meaningful discussion of how Arabs and Jews might in the future live together in Palestine.[80]

Israelis and supporters of the Jewish state responded to the PLO's de-Zionization proposal in a predictable manner. Many argued that the Palestinians were not sincerely committed to their vision of Arab-Jewish rapprochement, but rather had deliberately devised a strategy of propaganda and public relations calculated to appeal to Western audiences. Charging that the Palestinians sought to influence public opinion in the United States and other countries governed by principles of secularism, in order to reduce international support for Israel, Zionists contended that the PLO had proposed the establishment of a democratic and secular state in large part because it believed such a proposal would win friends for the Palestinian cause.

Many also asserted that the PLO vision was fraught with ambiguities and contradictions, making it, whether put forth with sincerity or not, an unsatisfactory foundation for thinking about peace. For one thing, supporters of Israel argued that it is for Jews, not Palestinians, to decide whether the Jewish people is a religious group or a political community, and whether in this connection there is a need for the Jews to be "liberated from Zionism." If the PLO was sincere in its insistence that every people has a right to self-determination, which was the basis for its repeated claim that this right could not be denied to the Palestinians, then surely it is for Jews themselves to define the political requirements of the Jewish people and to answer any questions that might arise about the relationship between Judaism and Zionism. Palestinians might reasonably complain that their own political rights had been abridged as a consequence of Zionism. But Palestinians could not plausibly assert that they know better than the Jews how Jewish life should be conducted, or that they, the enemies of Zionism, have the right to determine whether concepts of Jewish nationalism and Jewish statehood are or are not legitimate. Such an assertion runs directly counter to the principle of self-determination, in whose name the PLO had rejected not only Israeli efforts to deny the legitimacy of Palestinian nationalism but even attempts by the United Nations to specify the just requirements of the Palestinian people.

The most thorough Israeli critique of the revised PLO charter was offered by Yehoshafat Harkabi, who raised many other objections to the Palestinians' call for a democratic and secular state. One of Harkabi's arguments was that the PLO failed to specify exactly which Jews would have the right of citizenship in a de-Zionized Palestine.[81] The 1968 charter refers to those Jews "living permanently in Palestine until the beginning of the Zionist invasion," and a literal interpretation of this passage might mean the small minority of Israeli Jews whose ancestors were there before 1917, the year of the Balfour Declaration, or even before 1882. Other Arab statements suggest a broader interpretation, although they do not necessarily indicate that the State of Palestine would welcome all Israeli Jews. For example, Arafat declared in 1969 that the proposed PLO state would contain approximately 1.25 million "Arabs of the Jewish faith who live in what is now the State of Israel,"[82] a number that at the time constituted roughly half of Israel's Jewish population. Harkabi and others correctly pointed out that the vague and contradictory statements which Palestinians issued on this point did little to inspire confidence in their proposals, or to rebut Jewish charges that the true goal of the PLO was an Arab rather than a nondenominational state.

Harkabi and others also complained about the Palestinians' failure to criticize the absence of secularism in the Arab world, where every state, with the exception of Lebanon, had made Islam its official religion. Some Arab states had also adopted constitutions based on Muslim law or made it a legal requirement that the president be a Muslim. Revolutionary Palestinians frequently did assert that they considered their vision to be universal and were committed to the construction of a Middle East in which all states are democratic and secular. For example, the platform of the Popular Front for the Liberation of Palestine, led by George Habash, condemned the reactionary and bourgeois regimes of the Arab world, who have "used the question of Palestine to divert the Arab masses from realizing their own interests," and then proclaimed that "the Palestine struggle is part of the whole Arab liberation movement."[83] Nevertheless, Harkabi and others argued that the mainstream of the PLO paid no more than lip service to such revolutionary principles, if even that, and insisted that calls for a critical look at Israel would remain hypocritical so long as there was no meaningful movement toward secularism or even democracy in the Palestinians' own political arena, the Arab world.

There is also an alleged conflict between the universal principles espoused by the PLO and the parochialism of the organization's specific political conclusions. For example, Harkabi saw an unresolved tension between universalism and parochialism in the PLO's claim that Zionism undermines the loyalty of Jews out-side Israel to the countries in which they reside. He wrote that "Arabs apparently do not sense the contradiction in this claim. Despite the prevalence of supranational tendencies among circles in the progressive world, with which the Palestinians claim to have an affinity, a narrow, formal nationalistic approach is stressed here, which maintains that a man cannot cherish a loyal attachment to any factor apart from his own state."[84]

Harkabi sees a similar contradiction between the PLO's call for unity among Arabic-speaking peoples on the one hand and an emphasis on Palestinian nationalism on the other. Although Article 13 of the charter proclaims that "Arab unity and the liberation of Palestine are two complementary aims," he finds unpersuasive the PLO's contention that "the Liberation of Palestine leads to Arab unity" and argues that the PLO cannot advocate a reduction in the political and cultural distance among the Arab peoples while simultaneously demanding recognition of the Palestinian political community's distinctive character.[85] Moreover, for a genuine revolutionary, even Arab unity should be superfluous. It should be enough to be a human being. But the PLO's proposals not only stipulate that it is necessary to be an Arab as well as a man or a woman, they insist that it is also necessary to be a Palestinian and demand acceptance of a more narrow, Palestinian national identity.

Even though some critical analyses of the PLO's ideology may be persuasive, it does not follow that the Palestinians' proposals were put forward with duplicity and cynicism. Like any similar document, the 1968 PLO charter reflected the political environment within which it was drafted; and in this case the tensions and contradictions identified by the PLO's critics are in large measure a result of the organization's deliberate use of constructive ambiguity. Specifically, given a need to tolerate some ideological tension between the more explicitly nationalist views of Fatah and the Palestinian mainstream on the one hand and the more revolutionary sentiments of the PFLP, the PDFLP, and several additional guerrilla groups on the other, the Fourth PNC found it necessary to paper over philosophical differences with language sufficiently general to be acceptable to all factions. This was not very different from what had taken place when the UN Security Council adopted Resolution 242.

Support for this assessment is offered by independent scholarly observers, who point out that the circumstances of the PLO in the late 1960s of necessity discouraged thinking in depth or with precision about the character of the proposed Palestinian state. Quandt, for example, reports that this inevitably produced statements marked by vagueness and ambiguity. Writing in 1973, he states that it is not an accident that "no authoritative document or set of statements can be taken as representing Palestinian thinking with respect to the nature of the envisaged democratic state," and therefore, as a result, "most Palestinian *fedayeen* leaders would probably agree that little attention has been paid thus far to the nature of a future Palestinian state."[86] Another indication that the PLO platform was not intended principally as a public-relations device is the fact that the tensions and ambiguities identified by critics, as well as the philosophical differences of opinion to which they were a response, are not unique to the Palestinian case. They are present in the ideological debates taking place in almost every Arab country. As Hisham Sharabi reports with respect to the unresolved tension between territorial identities and pan-Arabism, "This dichotomy is reflected today—both politically and psychologically—in the insurmountable contradictions in every Arab nation-state between the reality of national sovereignty and the idea of greater Arab unity."[87]

Nor should any merit that criticisms of the PLO may have obscure what was constructive in the organization's progressive vision. Despite its deliberate ambiguity, there was indeed something positive and sincere in the Palestinian ideology that took shape after the June War. It denounced anti-Semitism, looked to the future, and called for cooperation between Arabs and Jews, to say nothing of rightly demanding that the Palestinian problem be recognized as the core of the Arab-Israeli conflict. Thus, as stated, even some who might disagree with the logic or substance of the revised PLO charter could accept the contention of those who, like Clovis Maksoud, asserted that the Palestinians' progressive vision had "detonated new and healthy forces in the overall Arab society."[88]

There was also a modest but nonetheless significant evolution of Palestinian thinking between the 1968 PNC meeting and the end of the decade. Palestinian statements in 1969 and 1970 increasingly asserted that *all* Jews presently living in Palestine would be entitled to full citizenship in the PLO's democratic state. For example, a Fatah statement proclaimed in February 1969 that "all Jewish Palestinians—at present Israelis—have the same rights, provided of course they reject Zionist racist chauvinism and fully accept to live as Palestinians in the new Palestine." Further, this statement added, "It is the belief of the revolution that all present Israeli Jews will change their attitudes and will subscribe to the new Palestine, once they are aware of its ideology."[89] The inclusiveness of the Palestinian state was also proclaimed by Yasir Arafat. In February 1970, he declared that "every Jew who will give up . . . the Zionist ideology" would be welcomed by the Palestinians,[90] and in December of that year he told *Time* magazine that if Zionists would accept the principle of a democratic state, "we would not insist on having an Arab majority."[91] Indeed, there were even a few public declarations at this time to the effect that the Jews had *national* as well as individual civil rights, and that democratic Palestine would offer political rights to both Arabs and *Israelis*.[92]

In addition, it is reliably reported that in private conversations Palestinian leaders often expressed a willingness to discuss alternative political formulas and to consider proposals that might satisfy demands for Israeli sovereignty. According once again to the careful study by Quandt, who interviewed key Palestinian figures in Beirut and Amman, "Palestinian leaders in the Spring of 1970 were willing to consider political arrangements similar to the Swiss canton system, Czech federalism, and virtually any form of loosely knit political system of a federal nature."[93] These public and private declarations were summarily dismissed by those Israelis and others who saw the 1968 PLO charter as little more than a confused propaganda ploy, and even if taken seriously these declarations did not propose political arrangements that would be acceptable to most Zionists. Nevertheless, they displayed considerable flexibility regarding the form that a political settlement in Palestine might take and reflected an evolution of Palestinian thinking which, as Quandt put the matter, it would be "premature and intellectually unfounded" to disregard.[94]

For better or worse, there was little prospect that the Palestinians would go further until there was a meaningful response from the international community, including general recognition of their right to self-determination. The PLO would probably need to be convinced as well that more specific proposals and additional movement in the direction of accommodation with Israel would improve its bargaining position and enhance the prospects for an acceptable solution to the Arab-Israeli conflict, one giving due consideration to the Palestinians' political requirements. These conditions were not fulfilled in the late 1960s and early 1970s, however, and so the PLO's secular state proposal remained vague and continued to be vigorously denounced by Israel and its supporters. Indeed, Israel countered the PLO's political and ideological thrusts with public statements to the effect that Palestinian Arabs had never conceived of themselves as a separate nation, as had the Egyptians and the Syrians, for example, and that consequently there was no such thing as Palestinian nationalism. It is in this context that Israel's new prime minister, Golda Meir, issued her much-publicized June 1969 declaration that the Palestinians do not exist, asserting that the recent and artificial political claims advanced by the PLO were in no way comparable to the ancient and historically legitimated national rights of the Jews.

But while ideological developments within the ranks of the PLO did not move the Arab-Israeli conflict nearer to a solution, or convince many Israelis that the road to peace lay in the creation of a democratic and secular state, they did alter international perceptions of the conflict in significant ways. They returned the attention of diplomats and would-be peacemakers to the Palestinian dimension of the conflict and forced an awareness, and ultimately an acceptance, of the Palestinians' demand that they be represented by men and women of their own choosing. These developments also contributed to a modified perception of the Palestinians themselves, who, as the PLO intended, were now increasingly viewed as a stateless people with a legitimate political agenda rather than a collection of displaced individuals requiring humanitarian assistance. This important evolution in the way the world saw the Arab-Israeli conflict, which became ever more pronounced in the 1970s and 1980s, can be traced directly to the political and ideological transformations that took place in the Palestinian community after the 1967 War. And, judged with hindsight, these developments loom much larger than the failure of the revised PLO charter to offer a convincing and workable formula for Arab-Jewish cooperation in Palestine.

Military and Political Confrontations

Although the restructuring of the PLO and the organization's ideological evolution were reviving interest in the Palestinian problem and laying the foundation for a renewed recognition that this problem formed the core of the Arab-Israeli dispute, the confrontation between Israel and the Arab states remained a pressing concern from the fall of 1968 through the summer of 1970. This period witnessed new hostilities between the Jewish state and its Arab neighbors, most notably Egypt; and in March 1969, by which time there had already been dozens of armed exchanges, Nasser publicly acknowledged that his country had initiated a "War of Attrition" against Jerusalem.

Egypt's declared objective in the War of Attrition was to destroy the Bar Lev Line, the defensive fortifications that Israel had built on the eastern side of the Suez Canal, at the edge of occupied Sinai. An additional goal, unstated, was to create a sense of urgency which would encourage international diplomatic efforts to bring about Israel's withdrawal from the territory it had occupied in 1967. The common element in both of these objectives was Egypt's unwillingness to remain passive in the face of Israel's continuing occupation of the Sinai Peninsula. Several related factors influenced Nasser's thinking as well. One was a desire to demonstrate to the Palestinians and other Arabs, especially in the wake of the Battle of Karameh, that Arab governments still had the will and capacity to confront the enemy. Another was to relieve growing domestic frustration, which had been building since the June War and was reflected in student demonstrations and other domestic disturbances.[95] As noted, this frustration was fueled by a sense that the modernizing regimes in Cairo and Damascus had failed, and by a widely perceived contrast between the dynamism of the new PLO and the defeatism said to reign in most Arab capitals.

Israeli forces stationed along the Suez Canal were severely outgunned and were subject to regular and heavy shelling by Egyptian artillery. At the end of October 1968, however, the IDF undertook a major retaliatory strike inside Egypt, attacking bridges over the Nile and electricity plants in Upper Egypt; and this in turn brought several months of quiet, during which construction of the Bar Lev fortifications was completed. The War of Attrition began in earnest in March 1969, when several Egyptian reconnaissance planes penetrated Israeli air space and one of them was shot down, and for the next seventeen months, with only brief periods of calm, Cairo and Jerusalem attacked one another with a vengeance. Egypt reasoned that its superior artillery and manpower would result in steadily mounting Israeli casualties, and that the Jewish state would soon find this too high a price to pay for its positions along the canal. Cairo also judged that Israel's commitment to the Bar Lev line would reduce the IDF's mobility and require it to fight the kind of static war that worked to Egypt's advantage.

Israel responded to Nasser's challenge by striving to make the price of the conflict unacceptable to the Egyptians. Through the summer and fall of 1969 and into the early months of 1970, the IDF, aided by newly acquired U.S. Phantom jets, carried out increasingly punishing retaliatory operations. In January 1970, for example, Israeli bombers launched raids deep into Egyptian territory, dropping bombs only a few miles from Cairo. Later in the month, the IDF captured and temporarily occupied Shadwan Island at the entrance to the Gulf of Suez near Sharm al-Sheikh. Thirty Egyptian soldiers were killed in the attack, with many more wounded and taken prisoner, whereas the IDF's losses were three killed and six wounded. Two Egyptian torpedo boats were also destroyed.[96]

As the War of Attrition dragged on and intensified, Israel's retaliatory action succeeded in reversing the tide of the conflict. By the beginning of 1970, the Egyptians were taking losses that could not be sustained. Thus, eager for weapons with which to counter Israel's air superiority, Nasser made a secret trip to Moscow to appeal for assistance. About a month later, in February, approximately 1,500 Soviet personnel arrived in Egypt with advanced anti-aircraft equipment, including new SAM-3 missiles.[97] Israel responded with attacks of even greater intensity, but these only encouraged Nasser to expand the Soviet military presence in his country. Russian combat personnel entered Egypt in the months that followed, and Soviet pilots soon began to fly in defense of Egyptian positions, forcing Israel to suspend its deep penetration raids and encouraging Egypt to step up its own attacks on Israeli positions.

With the involvement of the Russians, the momentum of the conflict once again began to favor the Egyptians, as it had in the spring of the preceding year. In March, April, and May of 1970, 64 Israelis were killed, 155 more were wounded, and 6 were taken prisoner.[98] In response, despite the Soviet presence, the Israeli air force resumed its activities, developing new evasion tactics and in the first week of June dropping more than 4,000 bombs on Egyptian positions. Several days later, IDF ground forces crossed the canal and destroyed Egyptian installations near Port Said.

Israel received support from the United States during this period, but there were also important complications in relations between Jerusalem and Washington. Both the U.S. and Israel had new leaders, Richard Nixon having been elected to the American presidency in 1968 and Golda Meir, the Labor Party secretary-general, having assumed the Israeli premiership following the death of Levi Eshkol in February 1969.[99] Nixon and his secretary of state, William Rogers, met with representatives of the new Israeli government and reaffirmed the United

States' commitment to the security of the Jewish state, and they repeated these assurances when Golda Meir traveled to Washington and met with Nixon in late September and early October. According to Yitzhak Rabin, then serving as Israeli ambassador to Washington, Nixon showed rare warmth in his dealings with Meir, for whom he felt genuine personal affection. He also told the Israeli leader that "as long as he was president of the United States and made the decisions, Israel would never be weak militarily."[100] In addition, the American president repeated a statement he had made during the election campaign, to the effect that if he were an Israeli he would find it truly difficult to give up the Golan Heights.

At the same time, the Nixon administration began to take a more balanced approach to the Arab-Israeli conflict and to press Jerusalem on the matter of the occupied territories. Abba Eban, the foreign minister, visited Washington in March 1969 and was disturbed by the shift he perceived in the position of the U.S. government. He reports that while "the most Lyndon Johnson had ever said about withdrawal was that it should be to 'secure and recognized boundaries' which should not 'reflect the weight of conquest,' " Nixon's secretary of state "now added the stipulation that any changes agreed upon in the 1967 boundaries should be 'minor.' "[101] Rogers also told Eban that while this did not require the redivision of Jerusalem, the U.S. did favor Jordanian participation in the administration of the city.

In April, the United States joined the Soviet Union, France, and Britain in a series of consultations, known as the Big Four Talks. These meetings continued throughout the course of the year, and with the War of Attrition raging and the Jarring mission having collapsed, they sought to foster agreement among the major powers about the proper interpretation of United Nations 242 and about the modalities of its implementation. There were also bilateral talks between the U.S. and the USSR during this period, for the most part focused on bringing an end to the hostilities between Egypt and Israel. It is against the background of these diplomatic initiatives that Nixon coupled the assurances he gave to Golda Meir in the fall of 1969 with the observation that Washington and Jerusalem might have to disagree about the best way to advance the cause of peace in the Middle East. The Israelis were also disturbed by the president's refusal to make any commitment about the delivery to Israel of new American weapons, including some that had been promised in an agreement of December 1968.

On October 28, three weeks after Golda Meir returned to Jerusalem, U.S. Secretary of State Rogers gave the Soviet Union a proposal for a joint U.S.-Soviet position regarding the conflict between Israel and Egypt, and in a speech on December 9, 1969, Rogers outlined his recommendations in public. Reflecting a more even-handed approach to the Middle East, the Rogers Plan, as the proposals quickly became known, called for a settlement in which Israeli forces would return to the international border between the two countries. The Rogers Plan also called for a binding commitment to peace on the part of both parties and guarantees that neither would permit its territory to be used for hostile acts against the other.[102] A few days later, on December 18, the U.S. submitted to the four-power talks a parallel proposal for a settlement between Israel and Jordan, reiterating many of the general principles set forth in its October 28 recommendations and calling for permanent borders which would approximate the Israeli-Jordanian boundary existing before the 1967 War.

The U.S. proposals were denounced by the more militant Arab governments but received praise from Egypt, Jordan, and other moderate regimes, even though these endorsements, especially that of Nasser, were not without important qualifications. Cairo welcomed American support for Israel's withdrawal from captured Egyptian territory and observed with satisfaction that the U.S. appeared to be seeking a return to the Israeli-Egyptian border that had existed prior to the June War, meaning that the U.S. plan called for a total rather than a partial Israeli withdrawal. On the other hand, Cairo worried that Washington might attempt to broker a separate accord between Israel and Egypt, rather than the comprehensive settlement to which the Nasser government was committed. Mahmoud Riad, the Egyptian foreign minister, accordingly writes, "I did not reject the Rogers proposals; rather my acceptance depended on the position of the US on the fronts in Jordan and Syria." In his response to Rogers, Riad stated, "I am sure you will appreciate that our final position cannot be defined until we examine the integrated formula for implementing the Security Council resolution of 22 November 1967."[103]

Israel, for its part, swiftly and unequivocally rejected the Rogers Plan, which even more moderate members of the Labor Party found unacceptable, and Jerusalem reiterated its rejection of the American initiative following the introduction of the December 18 proposal. On the 22nd, the cabinet issued a forceful denunciation, calling the Rogers Plan "an attempt to appease [the Arabs] at the expense of Israel" and stating that "Israel will not be sacrificed by any power or interpower policy and will reject any attempt to impose a forced solution on her. . . ."[104] The following week, in Washington, the Israeli ambassador told Henry Kissinger, Nixon's national security advisor, "I personally shall do everything within the bounds of American law to arouse public opinion against the administration's moves."[105] In addition to its substantive objections, Jerusalem also complained that U.S. intentions had deliberately been kept from it, even though the relevant documents were being readied for presentation at the very time that Golda Meir was visiting Washington. Rabin wrote in his memoirs that he was "genuinely appalled" at the lack of consultation.

The Rogers proposals introduced temporary strains into Israeli-American relations but did not have any long-term effect on the evolution of the Arab-Israeli conflict. The U.S. remained officially committed to the Rogers Plan for the duration of the Nixon presidency, but the American president and his secretary of state were reluctant to push for its implementation in the face of both Egyptian hesitation and determined Israeli opposition. Thus, like the efforts of Gunnar Jarring, the 1969 American initiative became but another name on a lengthening list of unsuccessful Middle East peace proposals. Moreover, American concerns shifted, and Washington's relations with Jerusalem improved, as a result of Nasser's overtures toward Moscow in the early months of 1970. The U.S. at this time gave renewed consideration to Jerusalem's request for the delivery of new weapons, including additional Phantom jets. After some hesitation, Nixon decided in March that no new weapons would be delivered until the situation in the area became more clear. He offered an economic-assistance package instead. In May, however, following another trip to Washington by the Israeli foreign minister, Nixon decided that the delivery to Israel of American jets and other equipment would resume. In return, the president asked for and received a public Israeli statement declaring that Jerusalem continued to regard UN 242 as the basis for any peace settlement.

The evolution of the War of Attrition and of U.S.-led diplomacy came together in the summer of 1970. In mid-June, the United States proposed to Israel, Egypt, and Jordan that they accept a ceasefire of three months' duration and agree to a new round of talks under the auspices of Gunnar Jarring. The Nixon administration hoped that a reduction in hostilities between Egypt and Israel would check the growing Soviet influence in the region and would offer a foundation for improving the United States' own position in the Arab world. By including Jordan, the U.S. also hoped to commit King Hussein to putting an end to raids by Palestinian guerrillas, who opposed any settlement based on UN 242. President Nasser accepted the U.S. proposal after returning from a visit to Moscow in July, and Jordan gave its approval a few days later. Shortly thereafter, Israel agreed to the plan as well, after having received assurances that the U.S. would not pressure the Jewish state to accept the Arabs' interpretation of UN 242 in any subsequent negotiations.[106] With these developments, the diplomacy of Nixon and Rogers scored a limited albeit significant success, and the costly and prolonged War of Attrition came to an end.

While the War of Attrition was a major focus of international attention through the summer of 1970, there were also important conflicts involving both Lebanon and Jordan, and in these arenas a central role was played by the Palestinians. In the Lebanese case, although Israel was involved, the most significant disturbances resulted from tensions between the Beirut government and the increasingly large and restive Palestinian population of the country. More than 100,000 Palestinians had fled to Lebanon as a result of the 1947–48 War,[107] which meant that in 1949 Palestinians constituted roughly 10 percent of the country's total population. By the late 1960s, their numbers had grown to approximately 250,000.

In the political and ideological context of the post–June War period, the Palestinian community in Lebanon was increasingly influenced and led by the Palestine Liberation Organization. Operating in the crowded refugee camps where most Palestinians in Lebanon were to be found, groups under the PLO umbrella built political bases in 1968 and 1969 and drew a steady stream of recruits for their guerrilla activities. As summarized by Rosemary Sayigh, "The freeing of Jordan for guerrilla action after the battle of Karameh had an effect on the situation in Lebanon, by increasing the flow of recruits for training. There were no arms in the camps in Lebanon, but the mass mood was growing steadily more defiant." One young commando interviewed by Sayigh stated, "We saw our young men eager to go to training camps. . . . The whole nature of talk changed, as if there had been a deep psychological change among our people. Because the Arab states were defeated, we Palestinians had a chance to be active, and we felt we had to use it to the ultimate extent."[108]

Equally important, the PLO, and especially Fatah, began in the fall of 1968 to establish a semi-autonomous political and military operational zone in southern Lebanon, on the western slopes of Mount Hermon. Israelis soon started to refer to this region as "Fatahland," and the PLO's supply route running west from Damascus and then southward through the Beqaa Valley to the village of Marjayoun, west of the mountains, was sometimes called "the Yasir Arafat Trail." This region of southern Lebanon was attractive to the PLO for several reasons. First, with mountains, caves, and thick brush, the area possessed a topography favorable to the guerrilla warfare. It was much better suited to commando operations than was the more open terrain of Jordan or the West Bank. Second, the region was adjacent to the Israeli Galilee, which, though not the most heavily populated or industrialized part of the Jewish state, contained important development towns and agricultural communities. Moreover, far from the center of the country, these towns and communities felt a sense of isolation and vulnerability that would be intensified by guerrilla activities. The Galilee also contained most of Israel's Palestinian Arab population, from whom the PLO may have believed it could obtain assistance. Finally, the south of Lebanon was inhabited by the country's Shiite Muslim population. The Shia were at once the largest confessional community in the Lebanese political mosaic and the most impoverished, underrepresented, and alienated component of the population. Ruled by a local landowning elite allied with the remote and neglectful Lebanese government, itself dominated by Maronite Christians and Sunni Muslim notables, the Shia of southern Lebanon offered a receptive audience for the Palestinians' message of resistance and revolution.

It was not long before there were clashes between the PLO and the Lebanese government. Indeed, there was a lethal confrontation between the *fedayeen* and Lebanese security forces almost as soon as the PLO began to establish itself in southern Lebanon, in October 1968. Three soldiers and one commando were killed in this early skirmish, which took place on October 28. There were two major sources of tension between Lebanese authorities and the PLO. One was a specific disagreement about whether Palestinians should be permitted to attack Israel from bases inside Lebanon. The other involved a more general dispute about the degree to which Palestinians in Lebanon should be permitted to run their own affairs, without interference from the Lebanese government. Fueled by both considerations, clashes between Palestinian and Lebanese forces increased in number and intensity in 1969, with results that for the most part were favorable to the Palestinians. While the latter proved to be strong enough to pursue their own political agenda, despite Lebanese opposition, the weakness of the Beirut government was exposed and enhanced.

The Lebanese government strongly opposed PLO attacks against Israel from positions inside Lebanon. It reasoned that an intensifying cycle of PLO raids and Israeli retaliation, no matter what might be the consequences for the combatants, would result in the loss of Lebanese life and property. Lebanese officials also worried that this situation would inevitably call into question the government's ability to police its borders and protect its citizens, and possibly force it into military operations against Israel for which it was unprepared. For these reasons, Beirut had faithfully respected the armistice agreement it signed with the Jewish state in 1949; it had even refused to participate in the 1967 War and, consequently, was the only one of Israel's neighbors not to lose territory as a result of the fighting.[109]

The Palestinians had different priorities, however, and were unwilling to respect the preferences of the Beirut government. Some guerrilla groups accordingly used their political strongholds in the Palestinian refugee camps to plan commando operations, including airline hijackings. For example, PFLP agents, believed to be operating from Lebanon, hijacked an El Al airliner in July 1968 and forced the plane to land in Algiers. In addition, constituting an even greater danger from the Israeli point of view, the PLO used its positions in southern Lebanon to launch commando raids against the Jewish state, carrying out its first attacks on northern Israel in November and December of 1968.

As expected, consistent with its policy on other fronts, Jerusalem responded with retaliatory strikes, and thus, despite its desire to remain apart from the conflict, Lebanon was soon caught up in an escalating cycle of Palestinian challenge and Israeli response. The most spectacular Israeli strike of this period came on December 28, 1968. Responding to the PFLP's hijacking of an Israeli aircraft, as well as raids from southern Lebanon, the IDF blew up thirteen planes at Beirut International Airport. This constituted the greater part of Lebanon's fleet of civilian aircraft. Palestinian incursions did not cease with the raid on Beirut Airport, however, and retaliatory actions by Israel continued as well. According to the *Middle East Record*, published in Israel,[110] there were 560 incidents initiated from the Lebanese side of the border in 1969–70, almost all directed against towns and *kibbutzim* rather than military installations, and the Israelis responded on a regular basis. Retaliation usually involved returning fire and shelling the

452 | *The Palestinian Dimension Reemerges*

locations from which an attack had come, although it sometimes took the form of an armed incursion by IDF units of considerable strength. Both types of Israeli action brought death and destruction to Lebanon, often taking a heavier toll on Lebanese civilians than on Palestinian guerrillas. Indeed, some of the damage inflicted on the Lebanese may have been deliberate. Following the logic it had employed in Jordan, Jerusalem apparently reasoned that only by punishing the local population could it compel the Lebanese government to suppress guerrilla activity.[111]

The government in Beirut condemned the PLO but was unable to force the Palestinian organization to terminate its commando operations, which took place not only without Lebanese consent but often without even the knowledge of Lebanese authorities. Nor were the Palestinians deterred by military clashes with Lebanese armed forces, which occurred with particular intensity in the spring of 1969. Palestinian positions were by now heavily fortified, both in the refugee camps and in the south, and the government soon discovered that it was unable to impose its will upon the guerrillas by force. Indeed, the *fedayeen* not only offered stiff resistance in the face of government efforts to restrict their military activities, they sometimes cooperated with Lebanese leftists and initiated attacks against government installations.

Under these conditions, confronted with its own weakness, the government had little choice but to accept the painful dilemma that had been imposed upon it. If it did nothing, it would be criticized by Israel, and Lebanon would suffer from Jerusalem's punishing reprisals, which would then bring condemnation from the Lebanese as well. Yet fighting with the PLO did not change the situation; it rather brought additional casualties and highlighted further the weakness of the government. Predictably, the response of the government was to muddle through as best it could, sometimes ordering the army to carry out limited operations that would give the impression of action without seriously engaging the Palestinians.[112]

The impotence of the Beirut government was to a considerable degree the result of the domestic political equation in Lebanon. To begin with, effective political power rested with the leaders of the country's confessional communities, including the Maronites, Sunnis, Shia, Druze, and others. National political institutions for the most part provided a structure for competition among these communities; each was allocated a quota of senior government positions, which it filled with its own chieftains and their clients. Thus, government officials represented and were responsible to their coreligionists, rather than to a national constituency, and the central government itself possessed little independent power.

In addition, significantly adding to this weakness so far as the Palestinians were concerned, different confessional communities took different attitudes toward the Palestinian problem, and some sectors of the Lebanese population were actually more sympathetic to the Palestinians than to the government. Specifically, Maronite Christians, who were given disproportionate influence by existing political arrangements, were most opposed to Palestinian commando activity and most concerned about the threat that it posed to the established political order. Alternatively, Sunni and Shiite Muslims, and especially the more disadvantaged elements within their ranks, were more favorably disposed toward the Palestinian cause and to a considerable extent looked with favor on the PLO's challenge to the government. Indeed, on a number of occasions during this period, tens of thousands of these Lebanese Muslims took to the streets to demonstrate in favor of the Palestinians. In view of these latter considerations, clashes between the government and the PLO threatened to exacerbate the already considerable tension associated with Lebanon's religious and economic cleavages, sharpening the dilemma confronting the government.

The implications of this situation became clear in April and May of 1969 and led to a historic agreement between the Lebanese and the PLO in November of that year. In April, the army laid siege to the community of Bint Jbel, in the extreme south of the country, in an attempt to capture a commando group that had just returned from a raid inside Israel. The town refused to hand over the Palestinians, however, and after a three-day standoff the army threatened to bomb Bint Jbel, at which point the commandos surrendered to avoid damage to the town. News of the Palestinians' imprisonment led to demonstrations in Beirut and a number of other communities, organized by Lebanese opposition parties as well as Palestinian organizations; and these protests spread as the government attempted to suppress the disturbances, sometimes firing on unarmed demonstrators. A vivid account is provided by Sayigh, who contends that these events discredited the government in the eyes of an important segment of the Lebanese public by showing that authorities were prepared to use force not only against Palestinians but against their own people as well.[113]

These developments also produced dissension within the Lebanese government itself, thereby complicating the situation further. On May 6, President Charles Helou declared a state of emergency and proclaimed that Lebanon would thereafter support the Palestinians only if they submitted to the authority of the government and curtailed actions against Israel. But the Sunni prime minister, Rashid Karami, immediately opposed Helou's statement and tendered his resignation, declaring that guerrilla activities should continue despite the danger to Lebanon. Karami also proposed that the PLO and the Lebanese army cooperate in order to reconcile the Palestinians' campaign against Israel with the country's security interests. It is against this background that one may understand the danger to the Lebanese political system of the government's inability either to impose its will on the Palestinians or to fashion a response which would end Israel's retaliatory strikes. By fostering antigovernment sentiments among some sectors of the Lebanese public and by widening the gap between competing sectors of the ruling elite, its collision with the Palestinians had not only revealed but actually increased the weakness of the Beirut government.

These events also highlighted the second source of tension between the Beirut government and the Palestinian organizations. By 1969, the demands of the latter were not confined to the right to carry out guerrilla warfare against Israel. Palestinian leaders insisted as well that they should control the camps where most Palestinians resided. On the one hand, they called for the "liberation" of the camps, affirming the right of the Palestinian people to be governed by men and women from within their own ranks. On the other, they demanded an end to harassment by Lebanese authorities, especially the Deuxième Bureau, the intelligence agency of the Lebanese army. The arbitrary arrests and harsh interrogations carried out by the D. B., they claimed, had encouraged a climate of random brutality.[114]

In August and September of 1969, there were confrontations with police in a number of refugee camps over the issue of Palestinian autonomy, with guerrilla groups gradually forcing the withdrawal of Lebanese authorities. As described by one Palestinian fighter,

> The *fedayeen* entered Nahr al-Bared and the Lebanese authorities tried to confront them. They fought for four days with very simple weapons and little ammunition. The result was victory for the Revolution. The next camp was Rashidiyyeh, on September 10. After that the camps fell one after another, and the forces of oppression began to withdraw. . . . They felt afraid because the people had started to confront them, and they didn't know from where the next blow would come.[115]

Palestinian sources also report that their struggle received encouragement and support from many Lebanese Muslims, who held demonstrations in favor of the Palestinians and, in areas where the refugee camps were adjacent to Muslim neighborhoods, prevented the army from attacking the Palestinians. In the wake of these developments, the police and the D. B. withdrew from most camps. Sometimes, as in Shatilla, a large Palestinian community on the outskirts of Beirut, the PLO took over the former D. B. office.

Fighting between the Lebanese army and Palestinian guerrillas continued in the south, but the Lebanese soon felt compelled to negotiate with the PLO. Hesitant and divided, the government had been almost paralyzed since the resignation of Rashid Karami, who now denounced all actions designed to restrict Palestinian activities. Beirut was also denounced at this time by many Arab governments. The regimes in Damascus, Cairo, and elsewhere, though restricting PLO action in their own countries, sought to pressure the Lebanese into giving the PLO more freedom. Syria closed its border with Lebanon as a protest measure, for example, and the Egyptian parliament passed a resolution declaring that "in fighting the battle for Palestine the Palestinian commandos are in fact also fighting the battle for Lebanon."[116] In the face of all these pressures, General Bustani, the Lebanese army commander, undertook to negotiate an agreement with the PLO and called upon the president of Egypt for assistance. Early in November, Bustani and Yasir Arafat flew to Cairo and worked out a secret accord under the auspices of President Nasser.

The Cairo Agreement, as the accord was called, gave the Palestinians most of what they wanted. Although the PLO promised to consult with the Lebanese before conducting operations against Israel, the accord left the Palestinians in undisputed control of their fortified positions in the south, from which they could continue their guerrilla war against the Jewish state. Equally important, if not more so, the Cairo Agreement gave the PLO rather than the Lebanese government the right to administer and police the Palestinian camps. By the end of 1969, the PLO had thus forced the Lebanese government to accede to both of its major demands, the right to attack Israel and the principle of Palestinian autonomy. The PLO in Lebanon had in effect become a state within a state, possessing the right to bear arms, to conduct its own military and foreign policy, and to rule over a subset of the country's population. As noted, these developments undermined the moral authority of the Beirut government and reinforced the divisions existing within Lebanese society, both of which in turn moved the country in the direction of civil war.

The conclusion of the Cairo Agreement did not bring quiet to the south of Lebanon. Despite the accord, there were bitter and sometimes lethal confrontations between Lebanese and Palestinian forces through the spring of 1970. These clashes were encouraged by the actions of the Maronite Christian Phalangist militia, which in March began to attack *fedayeen* positions in support of the Lebanese army. They were also encouraged by the actions of Saiqa, the PFLP, and several other commando groups, who adhered only loosely to PLO discipline and sometimes deliberately provoked the encounters with Lebanese forces.[117]

Continuing exchanges with Israel brought even greater turmoil to southern Lebanon. Guerrilla groups continued and even stepped up their raids against the Jewish state after the signing of the Cairo Agreement, usually without bothering to seek the consent of the Lebanese army,[118] and the air strikes that Jerusalem carried out in response did extensive damage. Israel also sometimes invaded southern Lebanon. On May 12, 1970, for example, the IDF crossed the border and, according to its own account, destroyed nineteen guerrilla bases and killed about a hundred commandos. A number of Lebanese soldiers and civilians were also killed. Palestinian sources give a different picture, claiming that the Israeli advance was checked and that the invaders sustained heavy losses before being forced to retreat.[119] No matter what the accuracy of these competing accounts, however, it is clear both that the pattern of raid and reprisal continued after the Cairo accord and that the consequences for Lebanon were serious. The general situation in 1970 is described by David Gilmour, who reports that many Lebanese villagers left the south as conditions deteriorated. "Air raids [by Israel] were directed against refugee camps and villages suspected of being friendly to the Palestinians. Assaults by land usually led to the blowing up of houses and bridges, the destruction of roads and crops, and the seizure of villagers who were often taken back to Israel for interrogation."[120]

The Civil War in Jordan

The Palestinians were equally active in Jordan in the period following the June War, with guerrilla groups affiliated with the PLO launching numerous raids against the Jewish state from their bases in the East Bank. Indeed, one Israeli source reports that such raids accounted for almost half of all the hostile acts carried out against the Jewish state in 1968 and 1969.[121] Moreover, as noted in connection with the June 1968 El Al hijacking, guerrilla groups had also begun to hit Israeli targets abroad during this period, planning operations from strongholds in Lebanon and Jordan.

The political and military dynamics flowing from these *fedayeen* activities were similar to those observed with respect to Lebanon. First, consistent with its policy on other fronts, Israel responded to PLO actions with retaliatory strikes, which Jerusalem insisted were designed to deter further aggression. Second, as in Lebanon, these strikes proved to be as troublesome for the Jordanian government as they were for the Palestinians, perhaps more so. Finally, as a result, King Hussein judged it necessary to exercise greater control over the commando groups operating within his country. The first serious confrontation between Jordanian forces and Palestinian fighters occurred in November 1968, when elite Hashemite troops entered two refugee camps in Amman and killed twenty-eight people. Palestinian sources describe the event as a massacre.[122] Other important clashes occurred in the early months of 1970; and in the summer of that year, King Hussein told his government that Jordan's acceptance of peace proposals put forward by U.S. Secretary of State William Rogers would undoubtedly bring additional confrontations, since Amman would be expected to prevent attacks on Israel by *fedayeen* based on the East Bank.[123]

Though seriously aggravated by Israeli retaliatory strikes, the escalating conflict between the Jordanian government and Palestinian organizations operating within the Hashemite kingdom was also the product of a much more complex set of factors. Indeed, these factors were even more important than Israeli raids in convincing Hussein that it was necessary to restrict the activities of the PLO. On the one hand, the political and demographic character of Jordan created a basis for disagreement about the country's national identity and about its place in the Arab-Israeli conflict. The tension inherent in this situation, which for the most part had been latent prior to the June War, came to the fore in the late 1960s and had a dynamic that was independent of the situation on the Israel-Jordan border. On the other hand, the Palestinians at this time, led by the newly restructured PLO, became a symbol of resistance and revolution that constituted a challenge to many Arab regimes. Although this by no means applied to Jordan alone, the government of King Hussein shared with other Arab leaders a concern about the growing popular appeal of the Palestine Liberation Organization. In view of these considerations, which reinforced one another in the Jordanian case, Hussein recognized that the PLO posed a threat to the stability of the country in general and to the Hashemite monarchy in particular; and this recognition, even more than a desire to end Jerusalem's retaliatory strikes, gave the king reason to be concerned about guerrilla activities in Jordan.

History and demography had conspired to associate Jordan and the Palestinians in a variety of ways, some of which involved a convergence of interests but many of which laid a foundation for the tension between the Hashemite regime and the PLO that emerged after the June War. Between 1950 and 1967, after Transjordan annexed the West Bank and reconstituted itself as the Kingdom of Jordan, the country had been in possession of a part of historic Palestine and had had a population of which approximately two-thirds was Palestinian.

In contrast to the situation in every other Arab country, Palestinian refugees who found themselves in Jordan were granted full and unconditional citizenship, and in many instances were able to rise to positions of political and economic importance. As explained by Arthur R. Day, writing of the Palestinian elite of the West Bank prior to 1967, "The notable families that supported Abdullah [and later Hussein] were well rewarded with economic and political power. Some major West Bank families expanded their lucrative economic enterprises to the East Bank. Some formed links with leading East Bank families to dominate certain areas of trade or commerce. For these Palestinians, the post-1948 years brought economic prosperity."[124] Further, this prosperity was not confined to Palestinian notables. Many middle- class elements, better educated and more enterprising and sophisticated than Jordanians of East Bank origin, became dominant in the liberal professions, the state bureaucracy, and many fields of business and commerce, including banking, insurance, manufacturing, construction, shipping, and food processing. As a result of these considerations of demography, geography, and political economy, Jordan before 1967 was a country whose very character and identity were Palestinian in important respects.

But while the Hashemite government could claim credit for the important opportunities it had provided to Palestinians, opportunities which were unmatched in any other Arab country, the Palestinian citizens of Jordan also had serious grievances. For one thing, Amman's investment policies tended to favor the East Bank at the expense of the West Bank. No universities were established in the former territory, for example, and, more generally, almost all of the government's development projects were located in the territory to the east of the Jordan River.

This situation encouraged an internal migration from the West Bank to the East Bank, especially among young people, with an estimated 300,000–400,000 Palestinians moving from the former territory to the latter between 1950 and 1967. Many West Bankers, and some East Bankers, also left the country during this period to seek employment in the oil-producing states of the Persian Gulf. Consequently, while the East Bank contained only 44 percent of the total Jordanian population in 1950, this number had increased to about 53 percent in 1961 and was over 56 percent on the eve of the June War. This pattern of migration also changed significantly the demographic character of the East Bank. Taken together, Palestinian refugees who settled in the region after 1948 and those who relocated after 1950 accounted for about 45 percent of all East Bank residents by 1967, giving the area a social and political identity that was almost as much Palestinian as it was Transjordanian. Further, with more than 200,000 additional refugees passing from the West Bank to the East Bank as a result of the June War, Palestinians became the majority in the latter territory in the late 1960s.

An even more important set of grievances concerned the circumstances of hundreds of thousands of impoverished Palestinians who remained in refugee camps. As noted, about one-third of the West Bank's refugee population lived in camps in the early 1950s, although the number declined in subsequent years as a result of out-migration and absorption into the general population. In the East Bank, by contrast, where refugee absorption was largely offset by the continuing Palestinian influx, the proportion of camp-dwellers remained substantial, being estimated by various sources at 40 percent or more of the territory's Palestinian population at the time of the June War.

Residents of the camps were poorly integrated into the mainstream of Jordanian society, being alienated both from the Hashemite government and from the Palestinian notables and middle-class elements associated with the regime in Amman. Also, most of those living in the camps had received little education and possessed limited professional skills; and accordingly, with few opportunities to better themselves, most remained dependent on international assistance. The difficult conditions in which these men and women lived understandably gave rise to resentment and bitterness, which in the period following the June War would strengthen the appeal of the guerrilla groups operating in Jordan. In the meantime, as Hurewitz put the matter, "the regime was beleaguered by a discontented mass, larger than the kingdom's original society, which the new citizens, though still substantially unassimilated, threatened to overwhelm."[125]

Still another significant Palestinian complaint concerned restrictions on political discourse and on political activity. Freedom of the press was severely limited, and there were also controls on sermons in mosques, in both cases making any criticism of the Hashemite regime impossible. Nor were independent political organizations permitted. Palestinian elites who sought to maintain a political base that did not depend on a connection to the regime or who worked to redirect the priorities of the Jordanian state were systematically pushed to the periphery, steadily losing their power and influence during the 1950s. Moreover, even Palestinian notables who did collaborate with Amman were subject to rigid political controls. According to one careful scholar, they were, together with opposition groups, "objects of surveillance, oppression and manipulation by external forces rather than independent elements controlling their own resources"; and thus, during the period prior to 1967, "Amman successfully prevented Palestinian rivals and supporters from forming or joining political bodies that would threaten Amman's control of the loci of power, so the Palestinians remained in an inferior political position."[126]

Mechanisms of political control aimed at the poorer classes were even more direct and intrusive. The Jordanian army and secret police operated efficiently; and, according to a researcher critical of the Amman regime, "popular discontent was ruthlessly suppressed and the camps kept under close surveillance."[127] Not only was political activity in general prohibited, moreover, there was even an attempt to suppress demonstrations of Palestinian nationalism, for fear they might turn into anti-Hashemite protests. Similarly, Jordanian officials strove to isolate the population from such radical Arab ideologies as Nasserism and Baathism. A resident of one refugee camp during the early and mid-1960s summarizes some of the political controls to which Palestinians were subjected, describing a milieu from which would come support for the PLO during the confrontation between the guerrillas and the king in the period following the June War:

> The camps were always more supervised on certain dates, for instance May 15 (the establishment of Israel). When we were children in school, before 1967, the tanks would surround the camp so that no demonstration could take place against the Uprooting. On those days they would make the school children walk in single file, three or four meters apart, and we were forbidden to talk together. . . . We weren't allowed to listen to the Voice of the Arabs from Cairo or to Damascus (Saudi Arabia, Amman and Israel were permitted). Soldiers filled the camp all the time and used to listen at the windows to hear which station we were listening to. People used to put blankets over their windows to stop the sound going out.[128]

Against the background of these tensions in the Amman government's relationship with many of the Palestinians over whom it ruled, the PLO established a strong presence in Jordan after the June War and was soon quite explicit about its challenge to the regime of King Hussein. Jordan was the operational center of PLO activity at this time, its political infrastructure in 1968 and 1969 surpassing even that which it had created in Lebanon. Many of the social and political institutions set up by the reorganized PLO had their headquarters in Jordan, for example, and the Palestinian organization took control of the refugee camps in the country more rapidly and with less opposition than had been the case in Lebanon. In addition, not only did the PLO assume responsibility for organizing and administering life in the camps, but well-armed commando militia units patrolled the streets of Amman where, in order to demonstrate the power and independence of the guerrilla groups, they stopped pedestrians to examine identity papers and sometimes even directed traffic.[129] As described by one analyst, the Palestinians were steadily encroaching on the prerogatives of the state. "They had formed their own police force. They had initiated armed clashes with the army. They had started their own radio station. They had organized mass demonstrations and . . . were appealing to the people over the head of the government, with alarming success."[130]

The PLO was not only striving for political autonomy by these actions. In what represented a departure from the established ideology of Fatah, the largest and most powerful of the guerrilla groups, the Palestinian movement consciously and deliberately sought to undermine the regime of King Hussein and to change the very character of the Jordanian state. Fatah had in the past favored nonintervention in the affairs of Arab states, and in mid-1969 Yasir Arafat had explicitly declared in a published interview, "We will not interfere in the internal affairs of any Arab country that will not in its turn put obstacles in the way of our Revolution or threaten its continuation."[131] Though prepared to oppose regimes that sought to restrict its activities, Fatah had thus been willing to coexist with any Arab government offering support, including Jordan, and had in fact paid little more than lip service to the revolutionary slogans articulated by the PFLP, the Democratic Front (formerly the PDFLP), and other, more radical groups. But these latter groups were also active within the PLO in Jordan and they strongly denounced the doctrine of nonintervention. George Habash and Nayif Hawatmeh, leaders of the PFLP and the Democratic Front respectively, openly called for the "overthrow of the oligarchy" in Amman and stated that the king deserved "a well-earned exile" in the United States.[132] More broadly, as summarized by Cobban, "For all these [radical] groups, a confrontation with Hussein, whom they variously saw as 'reactionary,' 'a puppet of imperialism' or 'a Zionist tool,' was considered not only desirable, but also ideologically necessary."[133]

The message of revolutionary intervention put forward by the PFLP, the Democratic Front, and others was striking a responsive chord among the Palestinian rank and file in Jordan, and this in turn exerted pressure on Fatah to put aside whatever inclination it might otherwise have had to seek an accommodation with the Amman government. Again according to Cobban, "the Fatah core's own ideology [of nonintervention] was trickling down only slowly to the movement's thousands of new recruits, some of whom, influenced by the revolutionary outpourings sweeping through Palestinian communities in those days, may have felt inclined to join with the 'subversive' groups in calling for Amman to be turned into a Palestinian Hanoi from which to assail the Israeli Saigon in Tel Aviv."[134]

As a result of this situation, although Fatah would perhaps have preferred to avoid a direct attack on the Jordanian regime, the group found itself moving in precisely this direction. Unable or unwilling to oppose those who believed such an attack was necessary, and inevitable, Fatah in 1970 joined the more radical commando groups in calling for the installation of a "national authority" in Amman and began to prepare for the possibility that the Hashemite government might be overthrown.[135] A development that helped to consolidate this trend was King Hussein's endorsement in July 1970 of the peace proposals put forward by U.S. Secretary of State William Rogers, which called for an end to the War of Attrition and for negotiations based on UN Resolution 242 to resolve the Arab-Israeli conflict. These proposals, and Hussein's support for them, were vehemently denounced by the Palestinians at an emergency session of the Palestine National Council, held in Amman the following month.[136]

The king for a time seemed uncertain about how to respond to this challenge from the PLO. Throughout 1969 and the first half of 1970, his government avoided an all-out military confrontation with the *fedayeen* and pursued policies that one scholarly observer characterized as "weak and hesitant,"[137] which undoubtedly emboldened the PLO and gave additional vigor to groups calling for a more interventionist posture. According to the memoirs of Henry Kissinger, at the time President Nixon's national security advisor, Hussein remained reluctant to take on the Palestinians as late as June 1970, even after he had foiled an assassination plot and assumed personal command of the Jordanian army.[138] On the other hand, the regime did not remain passive in the face of the mounting threat. There were numerous small-scale armed exchanges between Jordanian and Palestinian forces, with ceasefire agreements repeatedly reached and then broken by one side or the other. The Jordanians also sought to disrupt guerrilla activities in other ways. A Palestinian source describes the character of these efforts, reporting that "the Jordanian secret service operated very skillfully, smuggling *agents provocateurs* into the Palestinian ranks; and the Jordanian security services provoked incidents whenever this appeared to be to the king's tactical advantage."[139]

All hesitation came to an end in September. The Palestinians, led by the PFLP, dramatically escalated the stakes in what had been a war of increasing but still relatively low intensity, and Hussein then responded with an assault designed to put a definitive end to the challenge from the PLO. PFLP agents made two unsuccessful attempts to assassinate Hussein early in September. Then, on the 6th, the same organization carried out a spectacular series of four airline hijackings. In an action intended as a symbolic attack on Jordanian sovereignty, two of the planes, one American and one Swiss, were flown to a little-used airstrip in the Jordanian desert near Zarqah, where their crew and passengers were held hostage for four days. The third plane, a Pan Am jumbo jet, was flown to Cairo and blown up as soon as its passengers were permitted to disembark. The fourth hijacking, involving an Israeli aircraft en route to London, was foiled after a mid-air exchange of gunfire between one of the hijackers and an Israeli security agent. Three days later yet a fifth plane, a British aircraft flying out of Bahrain, was hijacked and forced to land alongside the two that were still on the ground at Zarqah. Adding to the drama being played out at this time, the PFLP demanded and obtained the release of Palestinian comrades charged with crimes and held by Britain, Switzerland, and West Germany, after which they set free the crew and passengers detained in Jordan. Finally, with Hussein's army unable to inter-vene, the hijackers blew up the three planes sitting on the runway at Zarqah.

These actions were not the result of a plan agreed to by the PLO, which in fact denounced the hijackings and suspended the PFLP. Nevertheless, the latter organization had accomplished its objectives, at least in the short run. It had laid down a challenge which could not be ignored and made it impossible for either Hussein or PLO moderates to postpone a showdown very much longer. The level of fighting escalated during the following week, and although there were also negotiations during this period, both sides made preparations for the major bat-tles that lay ahead. By the middle of the month, the guerrillas had seized control of several important Jordanian installations, including the oil refinery at Zarqah, and had created a unified military command with Yasir Arafat at its head. The PLO had also made plans for a general strike and a campaign of civil disobedi-ence. On the Jordanian side, the king was pressed not only by the Palestinians but also by his own army, which had become increasingly frustrated by the government's hesitation. On the 15th, Hussein dismissed his civilian cabinet and replaced it with a military government; and on the 16th, with Arafat now refus-ing further negotiation, he named a new commander-in-chief. Then, on Sep-tember 17, the king ordered an all-out attack on the camps, the guerrillas' bases, and the PLO headquarters in Jordan.

The fighting lasted for eleven days and resulted in a bloody and disastrous rout for the Palestinians. Despite the long buildup to the confrontation, and the guerrillas' growing confidence and boldness during 1969 and 1970, the Pales-tinians with their light weapons and commando training had no chance against the disciplined, tank-backed troops of the Jordanian army. Also, assistance prom-ised to the guerrillas by a number of Arab countries never materialized. Only Syria made an effort to render support, and the column of tanks it sent into northern Jordan was quickly withdrawn in the face of warnings that Israel would intervene if the invasion continued. The guerrillas, unable to mount a serious de-fense, thus were soon at the mercy of the Hashemite troops, who fought with a fury that reflected the frustration which had been building in their ranks.

Thousands of *fedayeen* were killed, leading Palestinians to refer to this pe-riod as "Black September." The official Jordanian estimate was 1,500 killed, although this figure is almost certainly too low, and some Palestinian sources place the number as high as 30,000.[140] The latter also emphasize the brutality of the Hashemite forces, claiming that "civilians in the refugee camps were cold-blood-edly murdered or crushed by Jordanian tanks" and that "thousands of wounded died on the streets because the Jordanian army would not allow any medical aid."[141] The fighting finally came to an end on the 27th, when, in response to the PLO's desperate situation, Nasser persuaded Jordan to accept a ceasefire. The agreement which he brokered between Hussein and Arafat was the last political undertaking of the Egyptian president, who, adding to the bleakness of September 1970, died the next day.

The ceasefire brokered by Nasser led to the signing two weeks later of a fourteen-point agreement between Jordan and the PLO. Moreover, somewhat surprisingly given the weak position of the Palestinian organization, the agreement gave PLO commandos considerable freedom of movement inside the country and even contained a clause in which Hussein declared his "unreserved support for the Palestinian revolution." In fact, however, this agreement had little effect on the policies of the king, who was now determined to rid his country of the Palestinian challenge. Hussein entrusted this task to Wasfi Tal, whom he named prime minister and minister of defense, and in the spring of 1971 Tal ordered a new assault on the guerrillas. The *fedayeen* were driven from Amman and a number of other cities in April, and in mid-July the Jordanian army advanced against their remaining positions. Then, on July 19, the Jordanian prime minister announced that all PLO bases in the country had been taken and that there were no longer any guerrilla groups operating in Jordan. With 2,300 commandos taken prisoner and another 3,000–5,000 having fled to Lebanon, many with their families, Radio Amman announced, "We completely rejected . . . any dialogue with these organizations, which represent nobody but themselves."[142]

The next two years were dark ones for the Palestinians. Although the PLO still had a solid base of operations in Lebanon, from which the organization gradually rebuilt itself, there was a possibility in the wake of the civil war in Jordan that the resistance movement might disappear altogether. Palestinians acknowledged that the PLO was on the verge of collapse. "Not only were its military units defeated and fragmented," wrote one, "but the political and social work of the previous three years was practically destroyed."[143]

One response to this situation was an increase in the Palestinians' use of terrorism, the most immediate example of which was the formation following the PLO's ouster from Jordan of a secret organization intending to seek revenge. It took the name "Black September," and its first act, in November 1971, was to assassinate Wasfi Tal, who was shot at close range as he entered the Sheraton Hotel in Cairo. Other terrorist actions followed, some of which were intended to bring about the release of Palestinian prisoners in Jordan and some of which can be characterized only as acts of pure revenge born of hatred and despair. As described by one Fatah leader, Black September "expressed the deep feelings of frustration and anger felt by the whole Palestinian people toward the killings in Jordan and the complicities that had made them possible." [144]

There was also another response to the situation in which Palestinians found themselves after July 1971. More constructive, and eventually embraced by the mainstream of the PLO, this response placed emphasis on international diplomacy and the establishment of political relations with major governments and international organizations. But while this trend would later assume significant proportions and introduce important new elements into the Israeli-Palestinian conflict, enabling the PLO once again to display initiative and dynamism, the mood of most Palestinians in the winter of 1971–72 remained dark and depressed. As reflected in the commentary of one Palestinian during this period, "The people here, they feel now that whatever they do it's no use. We tried petitions, demonstrations, strikes—nothing worked. We tried grenades and sabotage—no use. We are punished and nothing changes." [145]

During the period between the June War and the civil war in Jordan, the Palestinian resistance movement became a significant actor on the Middle Eastern political scene and made an important start at reshaping the way the Arab-Israeli conflict was viewed. The PLO established the political and national agenda of the Palestinian people and forcefully articulated the right of this people to self-determination, which included a right to be represented by men and women of its own choosing. Moreover, and most important, these were gains that would prove to be irreversible. For the moment at least, the heady days of 1968 and 1969 came to an end in the summer of 1970. Also, there was no longer much appeal in the vivid distinction that Palestinians had sought to make between their own revolutionary élan and the defeatism and ideological bankruptcy of the Arab regimes, a situation that helped to lay the groundwork for new developments in the the Arab world's ideological evolution. Nevertheless, despite the somber mood that settled over the Palestinian community in the early 1970s, the dynamics of the Arab-Israeli conflict had been fundamentally altered by the transformation of the PLO in the wake of the June War and by the organization's political and ideological achievements during this critical period.

8 | Israel, the Palestinians, and the Occupied Territories in the 1970s

DURING THE COURSE of the 1970s, the central focus of the Israeli-Palestinian conflict gradually shifted to the occupied territories of the West Bank and Gaza Strip, territories that had been administered by Israel since the war of June 1967 but which in the early 1970s were inhabited by approximately 700,000 and 360,000 Palestinians respectively. Given the failure of postwar diplomatic efforts to resolve the conflict, or even to foster negotiations between Israel and the Arabs, Jerusalem retained control of these areas, and under these circumstances the nature and evolution of its policies toward the territories became a critical dimension of the Israeli-Palestinian dispute.

An equally significant consideration during this period was the revival of the Palestine Liberation Organization and the related emergence of new political and ideological currents among the Palestinians now living under Israeli control. By the mid-1970s, the PLO had once again become an important actor in the Middle Eastern political arena; and a particularly critical development, both reflecting and contributing to the improvement of the PLO's fortunes, was the ascendancy of a new generation of West Bank political leaders who identified openly with the Palestinian resistance movement.

Relations between Israel and the Arab states also remained important, and this provided a measure of continuity with the conflict as it had taken shape after 1948 and evolved through June 1967. Under the press of events, however, tensions between Israel and its Arab neighbors diminished in relative importance, and by the end of the decade they constituted the background against which the primary struggle, between Israelis and Palestinians, was being played out. At the center of this struggle were the West Bank and Gaza. It was within these occupied territories that Israelis and Palestinians confronted one another on a daily basis, and it was to questions about the present and future political status of these areas that the most important diplomatic initiatives were addressed.

Israeli Policy toward the Territories in the Early 1970s

There were competing tendencies in Israeli attitudes toward the occupied territories from the very beginning. Jerusalem maintained that its acquisition of the

West Bank, Gaza, and other territories had been the result of a war forced on it by Arab belligerency; it was not, Israel insisted, the consequence of any deliberate plan to expand the borders of the Jewish state. Yet the government of Israel took steps almost immediately to alter the territorial status quo. First, and most important, there was a deliberate effort to divide East Jerusalem from the rest of the West Bank, of which it had been an integral part prior to the June War.[1] The part of the city formerly belonging to Jordan was merged with West Jerusalem shortly after the war, creating a unified municipal administration governed by Israeli law, and the borders of the new municipality were then expanded to the north, east, and south. The government also began to construct Jewish neighborhoods in former Arab areas, some of which were explicitly designed to give newly acquired sections of the city a more Jewish character, and some of which were intended to create a physical barrier between East Jerusalem and the rest of the West Bank.

A second set of modifications in the prewar territorial situation involved the construction of Jewish settlements in the occupied territories, in addition to those associated with Israel's annexation of East Jerusalem. On the one hand, beginning in 1968, Israeli settlements were established along the eastern perimeter of the West Bank, in the Jordan Valley.[2] These small communities, created with the assistance of the Israeli army, were paramilitary in character, and their construction was motivated by perceived security considerations, being part of the IDF's effort to prevent infiltration by *fedayeen* units based on the East Bank. Eventually, however, though they remained small, the Jordan Valley settlements developed a solid foundation based on commercial agriculture and became highly profitable economic units, providing a rationale for their maintenance and expansion which transcended the military objectives that had led to their creation.

The construction of these Jordan Valley settlements, known as *nahalim*, or outpost villages, was heavily influenced by a document submitted within three weeks of the June War by Yigal Allon, a Labor Party leader who served as minister of education in the Eshkol government and minister of labor under Eshkol's successor, Golda Meir. The essence of the "Allon Plan" was that Israel should establish a permanent defensive perimeter along the eastern border of the West Bank but should not settle in the heavily populated heartland of the territory, which would be returned to Jordan in the context of a peace settlement.[3]

On the other hand, settlement activity after the June War was also undertaken by Israelis committed to permanent retention of the West Bank and Gaza. These Israelis referred to the former territory by the Biblical designations of Judea and Samaria, terms employed for the deliberate purpose of asserting that the territorial claims of the Jews predate those of the Arabs, and also to create a subtle but important symbolic distinction between East Jerusalem and the rest of the West Bank. In contrast to the Jordan Valley settlements, which were established for purposes relating to military security, these Israelis sought to construct civilian communities that would create a Jewish demographic presence in the occupied areas and lead eventually to the exercise of Israeli sovereignty over Judea, Samaria, and Gaza.

In the immediate postwar period, orthodox Jews played a leading role in the establishment of settlements motivated by these demographic and political considerations. Their first and most important initiative was the construction of Qiryat Arba, a religious community adjacent to the West Bank city of Hebron. Work on Qiryat Arba began in the spring of 1968 and was technically illegal at the time, since the government had refused to authorize the settlement. Indeed, some Israeli sources argue that work on Qiryat Arba would never have been tolerated had Defense Minister Moshe Dayan not been seriously ill at the time. When the new town was later given official recognition and authorized to continue construction, in February 1970, it was after a long conflict with militant Jewish settlers and in the context of a compromise by which the government sought to prevent the latter from establishing settlements *inside* Hebron.[4]

Jerusalem's initial refusal to grant authorization for the construction of Qiryat Arba was a reflection of the fact that, despite an important division of political opinion on the subject, the Israeli government was not thinking about annexation of the West Bank and Gaza in the years following the June War. Some prominent politicians did call for permanent retention of the territories, of course. In the October 1969 Knesset elections, for example, Gahal, the right-wing opposition party headed by Menachem Begin, campaigned on a platform calling for retention of Judea, Samaria, and the Gaza District. Begin and his associates criticized the Labor-led government both for its failure to deepen Israel's presence in the territories and for putting obstacles in the way of private settlement groups, like those associated with Qiryat Arba, who were prepared to organize their own initiatives. The preamble to Gahal's 1969 platform, as summarized by Isaac, thus "announced that the central historical question before Israel was whether the liberated patrimony was to be entirely under its sovereignty," and the party then answered its own question in the affirmative by calling for the imposition of Israeli law in the territory "liberated" in 1967.[5] Despite the ardor of its campaign rhetoric, however, Gahal's performance in the 1969 election was not impressive. The party won only twenty-six Knesset seats, the same number it had obtained in the election of 1965.

The victor in the 1969 balloting was the Labor Alignment, a recently formed union of the Israel Labor Party, the foundation of which was Mapai, and the much smaller and more left-leaning Mapam Party. The Alignment, which received fifty-six seats and won the 1969 election handily, remained faithful to Labor's traditional advocacy of territorial compromise and expressed a willingness to make significant concessions in return for peace. The Alignment did declare that it would not accept a complete return to the armistice lines used before the June War; asserting that changes were dictated by security considerations, it called for a negotiated peace settlement based on limited though not inconsequential modifications of the pre-1967 boundaries. But while the territorial concessions advocated by Labor appeared insufficient to most Arabs, even to those now thinking seriously about an accommodation with the Jewish state, the Alignment's position was vehemently denounced by right-wing politicians. Moreover, the latter were correct in their assertion that even relatively conservative Labor leaders, such as Golda Meir and Moshe Dayan, did not share their own view that the Land of Israel was indivisible and, consequently, that no part of the West Bank and Gaza should be returned to "foreign" rule.[6] As noted, Labor's thinking was reflected in the unofficial but highly influential Allon Plan, which called for the retention of areas deemed vital for security purposes, but which also envisioned Israel's eventual withdrawal from most of the West Bank.

In the late 1960s and early 1970s, Israeli leaders sometimes described themselves as waiting for a telephone call from Arab heads of state.[7] The annexation of East Jerusalem and some settlement activity in the Jordan Valley and elsewhere notwithstanding, the policies of the Jerusalem government reflected a belief that the Arabs would eventually recognize that their lost territories could be regained only by seeking an accommodation with the Jewish state, and that they would then agree to negotiations and eventually accept a settlement involving the kind of limited territorial modifications advocated by the Labor Alignment. The metaphorical telephone call referred to by Israeli leaders represented an expected announcement that, in the wake of their crushing defeat in the 1967 War, the Arabs had at last reached this point and were now ready for compromise; and, until this announcement was made, the government of Israel judged that its own country's interests were best served by patience. The West Bank and Gaza were sometimes said to be held in escrow during this period. They were being held in trust for the Arabs, as it were, to be returned at some unspecified time in the future when, from the Israeli point of view, a fair bargain had been struck and a comprehensive peace agreement reached.

The Labor-led Israeli government believed that this understanding was clearly reflected in United Nations Security Resolution 242. Debates about the resolution and its proper interpretation had focused on the extent of Israeli withdrawal, about whether Israel should relinquish all or simply most of the West Bank and Gaza; but the Israeli government had never argued that all or most of the territory should be retained permanently by the Jewish state. As expressed by Abba Eban, at the time Jerusalem's foreign minister, the UN resolution gave Israel international justification for maintaining its control of the territories, but only so long as the Arab governments persisted in their refusal to make peace.[8] Similarly, according to a report prepared by the Ministry of Defense, UN 242 "confirmed Israel's right to administer the captured territories *until* the cease-fire was superseded by a 'just and lasting peace' arrived at between Israel and her neighbors" (emphasis added). The Defense Ministry report went on to observe that the key to changing the status quo lay in Arab hands, adding that "the moment they were ready . . . to negotiate a final political settlement with Israel, they would be met more than halfway." In the meantime, the report also noted, proper planning for the administration of the occupied territories was in fact being hampered because "the present situation is therefore to be regarded as temporary."[9]

Israeli advocates of territorial compromise were motivated by two very different kinds of factors. On the one hand, of course, they recognized that peace with the Arabs required their country's withdrawal from lands captured in the war of June 1967. Moreover, they judged this an acceptable price to pay for a resolution of the long-standing Arab-Israeli conflict, provided that the Arabs' commitment to peace was genuine, and so long as their own country's territorial concessions did not involve a return to borders which would be costly to defend should renewed hostilities nonetheless occur. In other words, in contrast to supporters of Gahal and other advocates of territorial maximalism, they judged peace with their neighbors to be more important than Jewish sovereignty over as much of the Land of Israel as possible. Though Israel would maximize its security from a purely geo-strategic point of view by retaining all of the occupied territories, they recognized that such a policy would increase the likelihood of future wars, and they therefore concluded that Israel's long-term welfare would be much better served by embracing the land-for-peace formula contained in UN 242. Put differently, they recognized that true security lay not in territorial buffers but in open borders and good relations with their Arab neighbors, and they accordingly judged it desirable and proper that their own country accept a meaningful territorial compromise in the West Bank and Gaza in order to obtain this kind of security.

In addition, however, there was a second, entirely different battery of arguments advanced in support of territorial compromise. Labor Zionists and others who shared their orientation asserted that there was a "demographic" as well as a military threat to the existence of the Jewish state and argued that it was necessary to pursue policies which would defend against this threat, too. Specifically, to the extent that Israel was indeed to be a Jewish state, dedicated to serving the needs of Jews and of Judaism, it was essential to preserve the Jewish demographic majority that had been built up with so much effort during the mandatory period and in the years immediately after independence. Israelis and Jews may disagree among themselves about the proper definition of a Jewish state, but almost all believe that struggling to provide such a definition is central to the mission of the state, and also that Israel's Jewish character, however defined, cannot be preserved unless most of its population is Jewish.

Given the importance of preserving a Jewish majority, permanent retention of the West Bank and Gaza would threaten Israel's existence as a Jewish state just as surely as any military challenge, since it would add a million or more non-Jews to the country's population. It is in this context that Moshe Dayan was asked in December 1970 whether he preferred a larger binational state to a smaller state with a Jewish majority. Dayan was one of Labor's hard-liners, and the territory he considered important for purely military purposes exceeded that deemed essential by many other Laborites. Nevertheless, although stating that he preferred a larger country for reasons of defense, he concluded by saying, "If it threatens the essence of our Jewish state, then I prefer a smaller one with a Jewish majority."[10] Demographic considerations, as well as factors bearing on military security, were accordingly reflected in Labor's proposals concerning territorial compromise. The Allon Plan, for example, proposed retaining the eastern part of the West Bank for strategic purposes but advocated withdrawal from the central highland regions which are home to most of the territory's Palestinian population.

There was also another dimension to these demographic considerations. Retention of the occupied territories, or at least of those areas where the bulk of the Palestinian population resides, had the potential to threaten the democratic as well as the Jewish character of Israel. Full rights of citizenship are enjoyed, at least in principle, not only by Jews but also by Arabs living within the borders of Israel prior to 1967. But it is not clear that these same political rights would be granted to Arabs in the West Bank and Gaza were these territories to become a permanent part of Israel.

Many Arab citizens of Israel complain that principles which emphasize equality are not always translated into practice and, accordingly, that they are frequently the victims of unofficial but nonetheless significant discrimination. Even more important, they often assert that Israel's official and self-conscious definition of itself as a Jewish state means that non-Jewish citizens are of necessity second-class members of the national political community. They do not share in the normative basis of statehood and political association in the same way, or to the same extent, as do Jews. Also, many policies and resource allocations undertaken by the government are irrelevant or even antithetical to their interests, having world Jewry rather than the citizens of Israel as their intended constituency. Although Jewish Israelis sometimes reject these charges, or insist that they are highly exaggerated, many objective observers acknowledge that Arab complaints are accurate in important and fundamental respects.[11]

Nevertheless, no matter how valid and serious may be the grievances of Israel's Arab citizens, it remains the case that their basic political rights are guaranteed both in principle and in practice. Arabs in Israel vote in all national and local elections, and they regularly elect some of their number to the Knesset. In addition, the Israeli political system includes non-Zionist as well as Zionist political parties, with the former articulating and addressing Arab grievances and receiving most of their electoral support from non-Jewish Israelis. Thus, while the complaints articulated by Arabs in Israel deserve to be taken seriously, they do not lead to the conclusion that Israel is not a democracy, as critics of the Jewish state sometimes charge.

But this situation might change should the West Bank and Gaza be permanently retained and incorporated into Israel, as advocated by Gahal and other factions on the right side of the political spectrum. Should the West Bank and Gaza be annexed, their Palestinian inhabitants would of course become part of Israel's permanent population, and under these conditions Israel's democratic character would indeed be compromised if these Palestinians were not given the same rights of citizenship as Jews and Arabs in pre-1967 Israel. Were this to occur, a large proportion of Israel's permanent inhabitants, as many as 30 percent or more, would be unable to vote in national elections and would be without representation in the parliament by which they are governed. This would be a totally different situation from that of the Arab citizens of Israel, whose political circumstances, however imperfect, are regulated by legal codes that declare them to be full and equal citizens, with the same rights and duties as Jewish Israelis. In this case, with full and equal rights denied to Palestinians in the West Bank and Gaza, political discrimination would become legal and officially sanctioned, and Israel would begin to resemble states such as South Africa, which explicitly and formally tie an individual's political status to his or her race, religion, or nationality.

To avoid this undesirable situation, Israel could of course extend full rights of citizenship to Palestinians in the West Bank and Gaza, but this would only exacerbate other problems associated with retention of the territories. These new Israeli Palestinians would undoubtedly vote for political parties and public policies that would weaken the state's Jewish and Zionist character, and they might also oppose policies associated with military preparedness. Given their numbers, such legal challenges to the basic interests of the Jewish state would be of significant magnitude, and they would be more serious still should the million or more West Bank and Gaza Palestinians form, as would be probable, a political alliance with the Arab citizens of pre-1967 Israel. In this case, Israel's non-Jewish citizens would have almost enough political strength to vote the Jewish state out of existence. At the very least, they would be able to press effectively for political changes that would move the country toward the kind of secular and binational state advocated by the PLO, an outcome even more unacceptable to most Jewish Israelis than the undermining of the state's democratic character.

These kinds of concerns were not the subject of widespread public debate in the late 1960s and early 1970s, principally because the vast majority of Israelis did not entertain thoughts of annexing the West Bank and Gaza; but the dangers of annexation were nonetheless articulated forcefully by a number of intellectuals. Yehoshua Arieli, for example, sternly warned against the debasing of Israeli democracy, quoting Abraham Lincoln's statement to the effect that "a democratic government cannot remain for a long time half democratic and half oppressive." Moreover, Arieli added, whether Israel chose to sacrifice its Jewish character or to abandon democratic principles, the consequences of retaining the West Bank and Gaza would be equally disastrous: "We would have lost our souls for some additional territory."[12] Arguments of this sort reinforced the position of the Labor-led government and its supporters in the years after the June War. Territorial compromise was not only the key to peace with the Arabs, it was in the interest of the Jewish state for other important reasons as well.

The Israeli government's declared willingness to withdraw from most of the West Bank and Gaza did not mean that Jerusalem was indifferent to the behavior of the territories' Palestinian inhabitants. In particular, Israel sought to prevent the emergence of Palestinian leaders who identified with the PLO or who otherwise appeared too radical and intransigent. Such elements had to be suppressed, Israeli authorities argued, both because they might provide support for *fedayeen* attacks against the Jewish state and because they might organize opposition to the occupation that Israel considered necessary until the Arab world sued for peace. Israel also faced a need to deal with Palestinian opposition to its annexation of East Jerusalem, which emerged among prominent residents of the city in the summer of 1967. To contain these challenges, Israel deported East Jerusalem notables whom it considered particularly troublesome and used its security forces to infiltrate and destroy PLO guerrilla activities in other areas. In the West Bank, for example, the IDF rounded up more than 1,000 suspected guerrillas in late 1968 and imposed economic sanctions on villages suspected of providing shelter to the *fedayeen*.

The Israelis also took action against Palestinian commando units in Gaza, forcefully suppressing armed resistance in 1970 and 1971, for example. According to the dark portrait painted by Rafik Halabi, an Israeli Arab who had served in the military, "Gaza's rebellion went on for eighteen months, and day in and day out the IDF kept up its searches and patrols. Eventually, the tug-of-war completely paralyzed life in the area." [13]

Operations during 1971, which were led by General Ariel Sharon, commander-in-chief of the Southern Command, were particularly severe. [14] Sharon's crackdown began in January with the dismissal of the mayor and removal of the Municipal Council. The Israelis also placed refugee camps under round-the-clock curfew and conducted house-to-house searches. Men were often rounded up during these operations, and they sometimes were forced to stand waist-deep in the Mediterranean Sea for hours. In addition, approximately 12,000 members of families of suspected commandos were sent to detention camps in the Sinai Peninsula. In July, Sharon decided that refugee camps should also be "thinned out," such that an additional 13,000 residents were transferred during the two months that followed. [15] Finally, large numbers of guerrillas were killed in gun battles in the camps during July and August, after which the *fedayeen* in Gaza were increasingly fragmented and ineffective, although scattered incidents continued. Israel kept up the pressure in the months that followed in order to prevent any resurgence of commando activity, often employing measures of collective punishment in an attempt to prevent the population from giving assistance to efforts at resistance. Sharon's actions, which were praised by some and condemned by others in political debates inside Israel, succeeded in "pacifying" the area until, according to Halabi, all that "remained of the harrowing year and a half of violence was the festering resentment of the people of Gaza."[16]

Israeli policy involved a carrot as well as a stick.[17] In addition to its crackdown on supporters of the PLO and other opponents, Jerusalem also took steps designed to regularize the conditions of occupation and bring a reasonable measure of normalcy to everyday Palestinian life. One important policy aimed at achieving these objectives was the opening of the bridges spanning the Jordan River, which enabled the population of the West Bank to maintain economic and cultural relations with Jordan and the rest of the Arab world. Another involved arrangements for civil servants, teachers, and other state employees to receive their salaries from Jordan and to carry out their functions in accordance with Jordanian law.

In pursuing these policies, which were initiated by Defense Minister Moshe Dayan in the summer of 1967, Israel for the most part found itself able to work with the West Bank's traditional leadership class, notable families who had forged close connections to the regime in Amman during the years between 1948 and 1967.[18] The cooperation of these Palestinians was sometimes secured by offering direct political and economic incentives. More often, however, traditional Palestinian notables, despite their strong opposition to the Israeli occupation, believed that their cause was best served by cooperating with the Jewish state. Both to maintain their own political status and to give order and continuity to life on the West Bank, they sought to establish a *modus vivendi* with Zionist officials in day-to-day affairs while maintaining their traditional ties with the Kingdom of Jordan, to which, like many Israelis, they believed the West Bank would eventually be returned. Also encouraging this kind of cooperative attitude was the fact that most Palestinian notables had little sympathy for the PLO and the radical political order it proposed to establish, and that whatever inclination these traditional leaders might have had to reexamine their assumptions and commitments largely disappeared after the PLO was ousted from Jordan.

It is against this background that Israel permitted municipal elections in the West Bank in March and May of 1972. The PLO called for a boycott, but the turnout was nonetheless extremely heavy, reflecting both the weakened position of the Palestine Liberation Organization in the wake of the civil war in Jordan and the fact that the West Bank's traditional leaders saw the elections, as the Israelis intended, as an opportunity for the local population to exercise greater control over its own affairs. Traditional West Bank politicians may also have benefited from a proposal introduced by King Hussein at this time. Making his announcement less than two weeks before the first round of balloting, the king called for the creation of a United Arab Kingdom, which would reunite the West Bank and East Bank but, in contrast to the pre-1967 situation, would give each region a significant measure of autonomy. The West Bank, moreover, would be formally designated as the Region of Palestine.[19]

Whether or not Hussein's proposal had any impact on the elections in the

West Bank, which is certainly what the king intended, politicians allied with Jordan and opposed by supporters of the PLO were victorious. Most of the 23 mayors and 192 municipal councillors elected in the spring of 1972 were conservative members of the traditional pro-Jordanian elite. Three-quarters were either landowners, merchants, or businessmen, for example. In addition, only 10 percent had received any postsecondary education, another indication of their traditional orientation.[20]

From the Israeli point of view, the 1972 election appeared to give a measure of normalcy to the occupation. It also enabled Jerusalem to claim that its occupation was in most respects benign, that the West Bank was being governed, for example, in accordance with the democratic principles which were applied inside Israel itself. Thus, the Israelis argued, as a short- or intermediate-term arrangement, to be terminated at such time in the future that the Arab world recognized the Jewish state's right to exist, Jerusalem's administration of the territories captured in 1967 posed few serious problems either for Israelis themselves or for the Palestinians living under occupation.

It followed from this Israeli analysis that Jerusalem's strategy of diplomatic patience was a good one. With the external Palestinian challenge greatly diminished and the situation in the occupied territories deemed satisfactory by the Israeli government, most Zionist leaders saw no reason to do anything other than wait for the Arabs to accept the consequences of their defeat in the June War and signal their readiness to trade unconditional peace for meaningful territorial concessions. The right side of the Israeli political spectrum denounced this policy of patience and moderation, of course, declaring that Jerusalem's control of the West Bank and Gaza should be made permanent, and calling for the state to take action which was consistent with this nationalist vision. Israeli policy was also denounced by most Palestinians, who saw nothing moderate in the IDF's brutal pacification campaign in Gaza and who insisted, more generally, that occupation by definition could be neither normal nor benign. Neither of these criticisms had much immediate impact, however. In the early 1970s, the Labor-led Israeli government was content to bide its time, believing that it was pursuing a policy toward the occupied territories which had few immediate costs and many potential benefits.

The 1973 War and Its Aftermath

Although the situation in the West Bank and Gaza appeared to be under control from the Israeli perspective, the Jewish state soon received a severe shock from an unexpected quarter, one which indicated that the Palestinian dimension of the Arab-Israeli conflict had not yet made the attitudes and behavior of the Arab states a secondary consideration. On October 6, 1973, which was Yom

Kippur, the Day of Atonement, the holiest day in the Jewish calendar, Egypt and Syria launched coordinated attacks on Israeli positions in the Sinai Peninsula and on the Golan Heights, taking the IDF completely by surprise and scoring important victories in the early days of the fighting. Thus began what Israelis call the Yom Kippur War, which is often called the Ramadan War by the Arabs, since it occurred during Ramadan, the holiest month in the Islamic calendar and a month of fasting. The success of the Egyptian and Syrian attacks reflected careful and effective planning, as well as coordination between the two Arab countries and the skill and bravery with which both Egyptian and Syrian soldiers fought. Also, on both fronts, Arab fortunes were significantly enhanced by the failure of Israeli intelligence to give advance warning and, in some instances, by the complacency and inadequate organization that characterized Israel's forward bases.[21]

In the south, Egyptian forces crossed the Suez Canal and overran the IDF's extensive fortifications at the western edge of Sinai, pushing the Israelis back into the peninsula. The operation had been planned to the smallest detail. After initial air attacks and several hours of artillery fire, the first wave of 8,000 Egyptian infantrymen crossed the canal in the afternoon. These forces landed between the lightly manned Israeli fortifications, which were strung out at intervals of roughly seven or eight miles along a seventy-mile perimeter on the eastern bank of the canal, while the strongpoints themselves were pinned down by concentrated shelling. This phase of the attack was completed by sundown on the 6th, and for the next two days, with ten bridges now thrown across the waterway, Egyptian infantry and armored units continued to cross. They established new bridgeheads four or five miles inside the Sinai Peninsula and then organized for defense against expected Israeli counterattacks. Israeli resistance was limited in many areas, and Egypt's casualties, only 208 during this initial phase of the fighting, were in fact much lighter than the Egyptians themselves had expected. Roughly two-thirds of the 290 Israeli tanks along the canal when the fighting started were put out of action by the Egyptians, and the remainder were presented with the impossible task of both defending the IDF's forward positions and checking the Egyptian advance.

In the north, IDF positions in the eastern Golan fell to the advancing Syrian army, which threw huge quantities of men and armor against the Israelis. In contrast to the situation in Sinai, the opposing armies confronted one another directly and immediately in the more restricted arena of the Golan Heights, with the result that there were fierce battles and heavy casualties on both sides from the very beginning. Although the IDF offered determined and sometimes effective resistance, superior numbers enabled the Syrians to achieve a complete breakthrough in the southern sector. In this area, the Syrians had been able to move six hundred tanks into position, whereas Israeli forces had only sixty to throw into the battle. Moreover, all but fifteen of these had been knocked out of action by the night of October 6. So far as troops were concerned, Israeli units of platoon strength were ranged against, but were unable to check, battalions or even brigades on the Syrian side.

Under these conditions, the IDF was authorized to withdraw from many of its fortified positions in the southern sector of the Golan Heights, but some of these were by now surrounded and besieged, making evacuation impossible. Elsewhere, soldiers from abandoned forward positions straggled away from the front while the remaining Israeli tank units continued to fight, hoping to slow the Syrian onslaught until reservists could be mobilized. Defense Minister Moshe Dayan visited the area at this time and concluded that the very existence of Israel was in danger. He called the commander of the Israeli air force and told him that the fate of "the Third Temple" was at stake.[22]

Although these Arab military accomplishments were without parallel in any of the previous Arab-Israeli wars, and were a justifiable source of pride to the Egyptians and the Syrians, the Israel Defense Forces were able to contain the threat on both fronts within several days, and thereafter to initiate a series of successful counterattacks. Many Israeli soldiers displayed bravery and even heroism during the difficult early days of the fighting. In addition, Israel was aided during the critical early stage of the war by Egypt's decision to consolidate its positions in western Sinai rather than to advance eastward, which enabled the IDF to utilize more of its resources against the Syrians on the Golan. The Syrian attack was accordingly broken on October 9, and thereafter it was the Israelis who were moving forward. After this point, with Syria on the defensive, Israel was also able to concentrate more of its forces in the Sinai. Another important factor contributing to the eventual turning of the war's tide was the superior tactical flexibility of Israeli field commanders, including an ability to improvise when it became necessary to depart from established plans of battle. This was particularly true of the massive tank engagements fought in the Sinai Peninsula a week after the war began, where in one day, on October 14, the IDF knocked out 264 Egyptian tanks while losing only 6 itself. The fighting in Sinai on the 14th turned out to be the decisive battle of the war on the Egyptian front.

Israel received critical assistance from the United States in the form of a full-scale airlift of military equipment, and this, too, played a major role in the eventual outcome of the October War. Responding to urgent Israeli appeals for arms, and also to the fact that the Arabs were being resupplied by the USSR, the United States on October 10 dispatched a number of F-4 Phantom jets to Israel and authorized El Al planes to pick up preassembled cargoes at Oceana Naval Station. By October 14, an "air bridge" capable of delivering nearly one thousand tons per day was in place. It consisted of four or five flights of giant C-5 transport planes and twelve to fifteen flights of C-141s. El Al planes also continued to transport military supplies and, in addition, a number of C-130 transport planes were flown to Israel and made available to the Israeli air force.[23] With its stock of weapons thus replenished, and in the wake of recent victories on both the Syrian and Egyptian fronts, Israel resisted calls for a ceasefire, which it had earlier been prepared to accept, and sought to improve further the position of its forces on the ground.

As a result of all these factors, the situation had changed completely by the time the fighting ended on October 24. The IDF had transformed what very nearly had been a disaster for the Jewish state into a total military victory. Israel recaptured most of the territory in Sinai from which it had been forced to retreat. It also crossed the Suez Canal and established positions to the west of Sinai, in the process encircling the Egyptian Third Army, which remained on the eastern side of the canal.[24] Similarly, in the north, the IDF retook the territory on the Golan Heights from which it had been expelled and then drove deeper into Syria, moving eastward along the road to Damascus.

Although the 1973 War left Israel in an advantageous military position, the country was nonetheless badly shaken. The intelligence failures of the IDF and associated battlefield losses during the first days of the fighting raised deep doubts about the country's military establishment. Further, the somber mood in the Jewish state was greatly intensified by the heavy casualties that had been sustained.[25] Much public anger was directed at Golda Meir and Moshe Dayan, prime minister and defense minister respectively, and these sentiments were clearly visible during the Knesset elections that took place in December. The principal opposition party in 1973 was the Likud Union, formed at this time through the merger of Gahal and two small political factions, and in the December balloting Likud captured 50 percent more Knesset seats than had Gahal in 1969, bringing its total to thirty-nine. The Labor Alignment, by contrast, experienced a decline of almost 10 percent over its 1969 total, giving it only fifty-one seats and narrowing very substantially the gap between the major parties of the government and the opposition.[26]

Nor was the dark and angry mood of the country visible only in the electoral arena. The commission of inquiry established after the war, the Agranat Commission, felt compelled before presenting its substantive findings in 1974 to observe that "the tense—and even ugly—atmosphere [in the country] made our mission, which was sufficiently difficult as it was, almost impossible."[27] The commission, like many in Israel more generally, was full of praise for the courage and resourcefulness of junior officers and the men they commanded. Many regarded them as genuine heroes, without whose bravery the war might have ended in disaster. On the other hand, the Agranat Commission report was highly critical not only of the IDF's inadequate intelligence but also of problems associated with military discipline and training. The presentation of the report also brought renewed public outrage directed at civilian politicians, especially Moshe Dayan, with the specific complaint that the Agranat Commission had found fault with the military but had failed to address the culpability of those political leaders who bore ultimate responsibility for Israel's losses.[28]

Against the background of public uncertainty and grief over casualties exceeding those sustained in any of Israel's previous wars, these concerns and criticisms contributed to the country's dispirited mood and reinforced doubts about general military preparedness and, more specifically, about the competence of senior IDF officials and the civilian politicians to whom they were responsible. This situation, and resultant feuding within the Labor Alignment, led Golda Meir to resign the premiership in April of 1974. Moshe Dayan also resigned as minister of defense at this time, amidst public outrage that while the Agranat Commission report had strongly criticized the IDF intelligence service and senior military officials in other areas, it had not addressed itself to the responsibility of Dayan, who was not only the civilian official with final responsibility for the country's defense but also the proud and self-proclaimed architect of Israel's powerful military machine.

Meir was succeeded by Yitzhak Rabin, a Laborite with little prior involvement in partisan politics. Rabin had been chief of staff during the 1967 War and subsequently served as ambassador to the United States and then minister of labor. Dayan was replaced by Shimon Peres, who had challenged Rabin for the premiership and lost only narrowly. Peres, a protégé of David Ben Gurion, was at the time affiliated with the more conservative Rafi wing of the Labor Party. Adding to the impact of these changes of government in April 1974 was the fact that Rabin and Peres were bitter rivals. The animosity between the two men soon became a permanent fixture of political life inside the Alignment, and in mid-1974 it added to public doubts about the country's present and future course.

The mood in the Arab states was different. Despite the fact that they had been defeated militarily, the political benefits of the war were reaped by the Arabs rather than by Israel. Indeed, recognition of this apparent anomaly was yet another factor contributing to the gloom in Israel. Political gains were made in particular by Anwar Sadat, Nasser's vice-president, who had become president of his country following the Egyptian leader's death in 1970. Prior to the 1973 War, Sadat, like other Arab leaders, had been derided for inaction and charged with a failure to end the humiliation imposed on his country by its disastrous defeat in the war of June 1967. During and after the 1973 War, by contrast, the Egyptian president was hailed at home for taking action to end the defeatism and *immobilisme* that had reigned in Arab capitals since 1967. In the months that followed, Sadat was also welcomed on the international scene as an effective political strategist who had designed and implemented a plan to break the deadlock in the Arab-Israeli conflict.

The contrast between the political and psychological climate in Egypt before and after October 1973 reveals much about Sadat's reasons for going to war.[29] In 1971 and 1972, Sadat himself became the subject of ridicule and derision. While he had promised his countrymen that 1971 would be a "year of decision," the year came and went with no important accomplishments, and the Egyptian president's transparent excuses were satirically lampooned in Cairo. In 1972 Sadat pursued a diplomatic strategy designed to restore Arab lands lost in 1967, but this, too, was without any apparent consequences, which only intensified the complaints and bitter jokes heard in Egypt at this time. In an attempt to win American support and put pressure on Israel, Sadat expelled thousands of Soviet advisors from Egypt in July 1972.[30] Moreover, this move followed an attempt by Hafez al-Assad, who had become president of Syria in November 1970, to signal the United States that his country was also ready for a political settlement. Whereas Syria had not formally accepted United Nations Resolution 242 at the time of its adoption by the Security Council, Assad declared in March 1972 that Syria would now accept the resolution, provided that Israel withdraw from all Arab lands captured in the June War.[31] Nevertheless, from the Arab point of view at least, the United States did little in response to these overtures and made no attempt to encourage meaningful Israeli movement in the direction of territorial compromise, leading a disillusioned Sadat to issue threats of war that by this time few took seriously.[32] Finally, Sadat was under increasing pressure as a result of Egypt's mounting economic troubles, underscored by student riots in Cairo in January 1973.

Praise was heaped on Sadat after the October War, however, it now being evident that Egypt's accomplishments had been the result of careful planning and preparation. Sadat had shown himself capable of sound strategic thinking and effective political action. For example, while his removal of Soviet advisors from Egypt in July 1972 was undertaken in the hope that it would produce more favorable policies from the United States, the move also served to clear the way for military action without any possible interference from the Soviets. Sadat had become convinced that the Soviets sought to dissuade him from initiating hostilities following a sudden invitation to visit Moscow two months earlier;[33] as he told aides a month after the Soviets departed, "The Soviet Union does not want us to go to war."[34] Furthermore, since it gave the impression of diminishing both Egypt's military capacity and Sadat's intention to wage war, the departure of the Soviet advisors also had the effect of misleading Israel about Egyptian thinking.[35] So far as military operations are concerned, even Israeli analysts were forced to admit that Egypt's attack across the Suez Canal had been extremely well planned and executed, and that Cairo had devised an excellent strategy which effectively combined both offensive and defensive elements.

It was also recognized that Sadat had carefully related his military actions to political objectives and that, from the Egyptian point of view, the October War had been part of a more elaborate plan which at its core was political and diplomatic. The Egyptian president had never intended more than a limited military operation; he sought only to recapture enough Egyptian territory to show the Israelis that their forces were not invincible and, accordingly, that the Jewish state's security lay not in maintaining a territorial buffer but in seeking good relations with its neighbors. It is for this reason that Egyptian troops had not sought to drive westward after their successful invasion of Sinai. Sadat continued this strategy in the immediate postwar period by improving relations with the United States and by working with the U.S. to secure a partial Israeli withdrawal from the Sinai Peninsula, hoping to obtain through political action the break-through he had failed to achieve by military means. Having emerged from the war as a man of initiative and vision, a world statesman, he sought to consolidate and further enhance his new political status by demonstrating that his strategy would produce movement in the direction of a return to the pre-1967 borders.

Arab political fortunes were also significantly enhanced at this time by the actions of petroleum-exporting Arab countries.[36] Western consumption of Arab and Middle Eastern oil had been rising steadily for some time, and since 1970 the Organization of Petroleum-Exporting Countries had succeeded in raising the price of oil dramatically. Then, following the outbreak of the 1973 War, the Arab members of OPEC declared a total ban on petroleum exports to the United States and the Netherlands, which were deemed to be overtly sympathetic to Israel, and took steps to limit oil supplies more generally by reducing production in successive decrements. The Arabs had attempted to implement a similar policy after the war of June 1967, but the West was far less dependent on Arab oil at that time and the embargo had therefore had little effect. The United States was able to satisfy its own needs from domestic and other sources and was also able to assist those Western European countries whose supplies had been threatened. This was not the case in 1973, however, and the Arab oil embargo thus proved highly effective. U.S. imports of Arab oil, for example, dropped from about 1.2 million barrels a day in September 1973 to fewer than 20,000 barrels a day in January 1974.[37] This situation provided Washington with an additional reason to undertake diplomatic action aimed at resolving the Arab-Israeli conflict.

The major international diplomatic initiative of the immediate postwar period was undertaken by Henry Kissinger, at the time both the U.S. secretary of state and Richard Nixon's national security advisor. On October 22, the United Nations Security Council adopted Resolution 338, which called for a ceasefire and then reaffirmed the provisions of UN Resolution 242, and two weeks later Kissinger left for the Middle East to begin an extended mission that subsequently came to be known as shuttle diplomacy.[38] Kissinger not only believed that Egypt and Syria were now ready for compromise, he also reasoned that Israel's postwar political and economic troubles might lead Jerusalem to be more flexible on the issue of territorial withdrawal. This possibility was reinforced by the fact that Egyptian troops remained in eastern Sinai at the end of the 1973 War, meaning that Cairo had already regained some of the territory it had lost in 1967 and that Israel no longer possessed the elaborate defensive fortifications it had established along the Suez Canal.

Since progress toward a comprehensive settlement had proven to be impossible after the June War, Kissinger's strategy was to seek implementation of the land-for-peace formula set forth in UN 242 on a step-by-step basis. The U.S. diplomat tirelessly shuttled back and forth between Jerusalem, Cairo, and Damascus in an attempt to arrange a limited Israeli pullback in Sinai and on the Golan in return for a modest reduction in Egyptian and Syrian belligerency toward the Jewish state. Kissinger encouraged the Arabs by telling them that a bargain of this sort would establish a precedent for future Israeli pullbacks, initiating a disengagement process that would eventually enable Egypt and Syria to regain almost all of the territory they had lost in 1967. Taking a very different tack with the Israelis, he argued in Jerusalem that a partial withdrawal of Israeli forces would reduce international pressure for more sweeping territorial concessions in the future and would lead eventually to an accommodation involving a more limited Israeli withdrawal.

Although his arguments to the Arabs and to the Israelis were contradictory in important respects, Kissinger's persistence and negotiating skill led to two disengagement-of-forces agreements between Israel and Egypt and one between Israel and Syria. Under the first agreement between Jerusalem and Cairo, signed in January 1974, three adjacent territorial bands approximately five miles in width were created in western Sinai between the Mediterranean Sea and the Gulf of Suez. Egypt took control of the one farthest to the west, the middle band became a buffer zone under the control of United Nations forces, and Israel agreed to limit the strength of its forces in the band farthest to the east. This agreement was implemented during February and March, resulting in the territorial situation shown in Map 8.1. In May 1974, Israel and Syria agreed to a similar arrangement on the Golan Heights, with President Hafez al-Assad also pledging in a private memorandum to prevent Palestinian guerrillas from using Syrian territory to attack Israel.

In September 1975, a second Israeli-Egyptian disengagement agreement brought another pullback of IDF forces and enabled Cairo to regain more of the Sinai Peninsula. One part of the *quid pro quo* that Jerusalem received in return for its second pullback was a provision in the disengagement agreement specifying that nonmilitary cargoes destined for or coming from Israel would be permitted to pass through the Suez Canal. In return for agreeing to the second Sinai disengagement, Israel also obtained from Kissinger a promise that the United States would not recognize or negotiate with the Palestine Liberation Organization unless that organization explicitly accepted United Nations Resolution 242 and thereby recognized the Jewish state's right to exist.

Palestinian Political Initiatives

An equally important factor in the Arab-Israeli political equation that took shape following the 1973 War was a dramatic improvement in the circumstances of the PLO. In the wake of its ouster from Jordan in 1970 and 1971, the main-

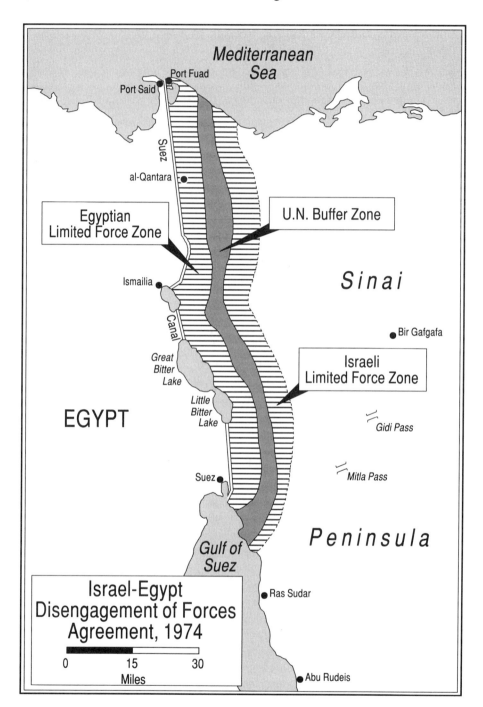

Israel-Egypt
Disengagement of Forces
Agreement, 1974

0   15   30
Miles

stream of the Palestinian organization had reduced its use of commando operations and begun to fashion a political and diplomatic strategy designed to win international support for the Palestinian cause. This strategy evolved and brought tangible results in 1974 and 1975, which was one important reason that Israel sought to use Kissinger's pursuit of a second disengagement agreement in Sinai to prevent the United States from talking to the PLO.

The character of the new currents in PLO thinking became visible during the first half of 1974, when Palestinian leaders debated possible changes in the organization's near-term goals and tactics; and at the twelfth meeting of the Palestine National Council, which convened in Cairo early in June, this thinking was incorporated into a ten-point program calling for the Palestinian revolution to be implemented in stages.[39] The ten-point program, which was overwhelmingly approved, contained language that was widely understood to mean that the PLO would now set as its immediate objective the creation of a Palestinian state in the West Bank and Gaza Strip. Specifically, the PLO endorsed an intermediate stage in the Palestinian struggle, and, although the occupied territories were not mentioned by name, Point Two declared that the goal of this stage would be the establishment of "the people's national, independent and fighting authority on every part of Palestinian land that is liberated."[40]

Although Israelis argued that the idea of stages and of a "fighting authority" showed the PLO to be as committed as ever to the destruction of the Jewish state, Palestinians themselves considered the ten-point program adopted in Cairo to be highly significant, and their assessment was shared by many outside observers. Moreover, the impression that an important change in PLO thinking was taking place persisted even when some Palestinian leaders who had supported the ten-point program declared that the establishment of a democratic state over the whole of Palestine did indeed remain their long-term objective. To begin with, the resolutions adopted by the PNC in June 1974 were the first official expression of a willingness to accept anything less than the liberation of all of Palestine, leading many to conclude that a basis for compromise had been established. Indeed, observers pointed out that the phrase "liberation of Palestine," so prominent in the PLO's national charter, was totally absent from the text of the program adopted in Cairo, having been replaced with the much more ambiguous "liberation of Palestinian land."[41] Accordingly, some analysts argued, what was declared to be an intermediate stage today might well be accepted tomorrow as the basis for a permanent solution.

In another significant departure from earlier PLO thinking, the Twelfth PNC also placed considerable emphasis on the possibility of political dialogue between a Palestinian state in the liberated territories and progressive and peace-oriented forces in Israel. One PLO leader, Nayif Hawatmeh of the Democratic Front for the Liberation of Palestine (previously the Popular Democratic Front for the Liberation of Palestine), had called for such a dialogue in a historic interview granted to the Israeli newspaper *Yediot Aharonot* two months before the PNC meeting.[42] Others voiced similar sentiments in Cairo, saying that after the establishment of a Palestinian state alongside Israel the struggle should be carried out by peaceful means and might even involve political alliances between certain Israeli and Palestinian elements. Thus, although armed struggle was not repudiated in Cairo, there was an explicit recognition of the value of political action.

The PLO's efforts during this period also included a highly successful diplomatic campaign aimed at securing international recognition, carried out first in Arab and Islamic circles and then in the broader international arena. In November 1973, the Arab summit conference meeting in Algiers recognized the PLO as the sole legitimate representative of the Palestinian people, even though the Jordanian delegation expressed reservations about this action. The PLO was accorded similar recognition by the summit meeting of the Islamic Conference Organization in February 1974; and a month later, in March, the PLO made additional gains within the Non-Aligned Movement. The movement's Coordination Bureau, at a meeting in Algiers, adopted a resolution expressing "full recognition of the Palestine Liberation Organization as the sole legitimate representative of the Palestinian people and its struggle."[43] The resolution, which also called on members of the Non-Aligned Movement to break off diplomatic relations with Israel, was important not only because it consolidated earlier gains but also because it showed support for the PLO outside Arab and Islamic circles. Yet another diplomatic accomplishment was Yasir Arafat's first official visit to the Soviet Union in August of the same year, with Moscow, too, agreeing that the PLO alone represented the Palestinians.

Particularly important to the PLO was the Arab summit that convened in Rabat, Morocco, in October 1974. The Rabat summit reaffirmed that the PLO was the sole legitimate representative of the Palestinian people, and, most significant, this time the decision was supported by Jordan. Jordan's action was a contribution to Arab unity on the Palestinian question. Even more important, however, were its implications for the Palestinian inhabitants of the Israeli-occupied West Bank. Although these Palestinians remained Jordanian citizens, and in many cases received their salaries from Amman, the government of King Hussein agreed at Rabat that the PLO, not the Jordanian monarch, was their legitimate and only political representative. More generally, with respect to both the West Bank and Gaza, the Rabat declaration meant that the PLO would have to be included in any negotiations aimed at resolving the status of these territories and their inhabitants. Finally, taking its cue from the PNC meeting of the preceding June, the Rabat summit affirmed the right of the Palestinians to set up an independent national authority under the direction of the PLO in any part of Palestine liberated from Israeli occupation.[44] In addition to these public pronouncements, embodied in the five-point resolution adopted by the Arab summit on October 29, there were also a number of secret clauses agreed to at Rabat, the most important being that the PLO would have veto power over any Arab peace proposal.[45]

The culmination of the PLO's impressive diplomatic gains during 1974 came in November, when Arafat was invited to address the United Nations General Assembly, the decision to invite the PLO to participate in its deliberations of the Palestine question having been taken by a vote of 105 to 4, with 20 abstentions. Arafat was given an enthusiastic welcome in New York, and his appearance at the UN was also accompanied by several days of pro-PLO demonstrations in the West Bank and Gaza. The PLO chairman was introduced to the General Assembly by Suleiman Franjieh, who had been president of Lebanon for four years. The choice of Franjieh, a Christian politician from pro-Western Lebanon, was intended to symbolize both the growing respectability of the PLO and the nondenominational character of Palestinian nationalism. Arafat himself told the assembled delegates that the PLO represents the Palestine people "legitimately and uniquely" and then spoke of his dream to return from exile and share in the building of a state "where Christian, Jew and Muslim live in justice, equality, fraternity and progress."[46] Nine days after Arafat's speech, which took place on November 13, the General Assembly passed two important resolutions dealing with the Palestinian question, one granting UN observer status to the PLO and a second giving international recognition to the "inalienable rights" of the Palestinian people, including "the right to self-determination without external interference" and "the right to national independence and sovereignty."[47]

In the months that followed, the UN was the scene of other important demonstrations of international support for the Palestinian cause. One was a nearly successful drive in summer 1975 to strip Israel of its membership in the United Nations, which failed only after the sternest of American warnings. Another was passage by the UN General Assembly in November 1975 of a controversial resolution declaring Zionism to be "a form of racism or racial discrimination." A third was the UN's creation, at the same time it passed the resolution equating Zionism with racism, of a permanent Committee on the Exercise of the Inalienable Rights of the Palestinian People. Established by a General Assembly resolution, which was passed by a margin of 93 to 18, with 27 abstentions, the committee was given the mandate of formulating recommendations for the realization of those Palestinian political rights that the United Nations now claimed to recognize. The committee submitted its first report a year later, at which time it was approved by a vote of 90 to 16, with 30 abstentions, and among its contents were statements declaring that "the question of Palestine is at the heart of the Middle East problem," and that "no solution in the Middle East can be envisaged which does not fully take into account the aspirations of the Palestinian people."[48]

Although there was more form than substance to many of these United Nations actions and resolutions, they nonetheless offered important additional evidence of how much the PLO had been able to accomplish through its diplomatic initiatives, and of the extent to which the Palestinian question was now regarded as the core of the Arab-Israeli conflict. Grudgingly acknowledging these Palestinian achievements, the veteran Israeli statesman Abba Eban wrote that the PLO "leaped forward to broad international recognition," whereas United Nations resolutions "in favor of the PLO and against 'racist Zionism' . . . would have been inconceivable a year or two before."[49]

Israel responded to the PLO's diplomatic initiatives with a political and public-relations offensive of its own. For example, Jerusalem made a determined effort to block any possibility of a dialogue between the PLO and the United States, as evidenced by its insistence on a pledge to this effect from Henry Kissinger when negotiating the second Sinai disengagement agreement. In addition, Israeli spokesmen issued numerous statements to the effect that the PLO did not deserve recognition because it was committed not to compromise but rather to the destruction of the Jewish state, and also because it did not in reality represent the Palestinian people. As Foreign Minister Yigal Allon told the UN General Assembly in September 1975, Israel was "categorically negative about the absurd pretensions of the so-called Palestine Liberation Organization," which he described as no more than "a congeries of feuding terrorist gangs whose principal victims are the Arabs of Palestine themselves, and whose primary aim is the annihilation of the State of Israel and the genocide of its people." Similar pronouncements were issued by other Israeli officials, including Prime Minister Yitzhak Rabin, who charged that the United Nations had little genuine interest in the Palestinian cause but was instead simply caving in to pressure from oil-rich Arab states. Rabin also asserted that the relationship between Israel and Egypt, not the Palestinian problem, was at the heart of the Middle East conflict.

Israelis and Jews were particularly disturbed by the passage of the UN resolution equating Zionism and racism, which was based on the allegation that Israel is a discriminatory state that explicitly denies political rights to its non-Jewish minority. Although passage of the resolution was largely symbolic, and had little substantive significance, supporters of Israel considered it an outrage. They pointed out that whatever might be the legitimate grievances of the country's non-Jewish citizens, the latter are equal before the law and enjoy numerous political and civil rights, not only in principle but in practice as well. For this reason, they continued, Israel bears no resemblance to the racist states, such as South Africa, with which it was being equated.

Even Israelis genuinely concerned about tension between their state's avowed desire to be both Jewish and democratic denounced the UN resolution, stating that it was an inflammatory action which discouraged, rather than encouraged, reasoned examination of the matter. In addition, most Israelis noted with bitterness and a sense of irony that their own country's democracy, however imperfect, stood in marked contrast to the political systems of the Arab world, where, with few exceptions, brutal and repressive regimes were in power. Finally, supporters of Israel charged that the resolution branding Zionism as a form of racism showed the United Nations to be less interested in accuracy and diplomatic leadership than in political expediency. In the minds of these critics, who included many in the United States, the international community had willingly acquiesced in what most of its members knew to be a blatant and politically motivated lie. This in turn raised fundamental questions, destined to linger for many years to come, about the UN's ability to act as an honest broker in the Arab-Israeli conflict.

Although public denunciations of the PLO and of UN resolutions may have suggested a unanimity of views within the Jewish state, there were in fact important differences of opinion in Israel on questions pertaining to the Palestinians. On the one hand, a number of Israeli leaders advocated a flexible and positive response to the Palestinians' diplomatic challenge. Indeed, even some who vigorously denounced the PLO in international gatherings took a much more restrained position in the debates taking place inside the Jewish state. Allon, for example, was a strong voice for flexibility and moderation within the Israeli cabinet. Similarly, Abba Eban, who had been foreign minister until May 1974 and remained influential in Labor Party circles, argued for recognition that the Palestinian problem lay at the core of Israel's conflict with the Arabs. Some politicians and intellectuals on the left went even further, not only echoing calls for attention to the Palestinian dimension of the Arab-Israeli dispute but adding that this was all the more important since growing sections of the PLO now appeared ready for a political settlement.[50]

On the other hand, while the Labor Alignment remained committed to the principle of territorial compromise in the West Bank and Gaza, the center of gravity within the Labor-led government drifted to the right in the mid-1970s, pushed in this direction, in part, by Israel's deepening international isolation. The National Religious Party, increasingly under the influence of its militant and nationalistic "young guard" wing, joined the governing coalition during this period. In addition, there were resignations by two of the most "dovish" ministers in the cabinet, Shulamit Aloni and Aharon Yariv, and Ariel Sharon, the hard-line general who had suppressed Palestinian commando activity in Gaza in 1971, was made the prime minister's national security advisor.

Both hard-liners and moderates in Israel recognized that the PLO's diplomatic strategy had succeeded in placing their country on the defensive, and many Israelis accordingly worried that the Palestinian organization might soon score even greater political victories. Of particular concern to Jerusalem, as noted, was the possibility of a dialogue between the PLO and the United States. Israel was successful in preventing such a dialogue, having extracted a pledge to this effect from the United States during the Sinai disengagement negotiations, and the Jerusalem government was also cheered by forceful American denunciations of the

UN resolution equating Zionism and racism.[51] Yet support for the Palestinian cause continued to grow, not only on the international scene in general but in the United States as well. For example, the prestigious Brookings Institution issued a report in late 1975 that spoke of the Palestinians' right to self-determination and of the need to involve "credible" Palestinian representatives in Middle East peace talks.[52] Moreover, much of the report was endorsed by "academics, congressmen, journalists, State Department officials, and prominent politicians."[53] Among the authors of the Brookings Institution report were Zbigniew Brzezinski and William Quandt. Both men favored contact with the PLO, and both would become influential in the next American administration.

Another indication that the United States was taking a new look at the Palestinian question was a policy statement that Harold Saunders, deputy assistant secretary of state for Near Eastern affairs, delivered to a Senate subcommittee in November 1975. The Saunders document stated that the Palestinian question was "in many ways . . . the heart of the conflict" between Israel and the Arabs, adding that "the legitimate interests of the Palestinian Arabs must be taken into account in the negotiating of an Arab-Israeli peace" and must be "expressed in the final settlement."[54] Saunders also reported that while the PLO remained officially committed to the establishment of a single state over all of Palestine, a growing number of Palestinians were prepared to accept "coexistence between separate Palestinian and Israeli states," and that the United States should therefore remain open to this prospect. The possibility that Washington was reexamining its traditional thinking about the Palestinians was also suggested by the absence of any more than token American opposition to PLO attendance of UN Security Council meetings in December 1975 and January 1976. Although these developments were quite modest in the view of most Palestinians, they were a source of serious concern in Israel and, more generally, they showed how much the climate of world opinion had changed so far as the question of Palestine was concerned.

Whereas the PLO had been defeated and disorganized following the civil war in Jordan, the Palestinians were now in the midst of an increasingly successful political and diplomatic campaign, bringing both increased international recognition of the PLO and growing condemnation of Israel. Even more important, the PLO's political victories were producing new thinking in international circles about the nature of the Arab-Israeli conflict. Between 1948 and 1967, observers had placed emphasis on relations between Israel and neighboring Arab countries; and, though the Palestinian dimension of the conflict had reemerged after the Arabs' defeat in June 1967, the PLO's ouster from Jordan and the war of October 1973 suggested continuity rather than change in the character of the dispute and made it possible to argue that the rise of the Palestine Resistance Movement in the late 1960s had been but a brief deviation from the well-established and continuing pattern of conflict between Israel and the Arab states. As a result of the events that took place in 1974 and 1975, however, it was increasingly difficult to make this argument.

In the wake of the PLO's victory at the Rabat Arab summit and Arafat's appearance before the United Nations, there was a growing appreciation that the unresolved Palestinian problem constituted the core of the Arab-Israeli conflict. Although the land-for-peace formula set forth in UN Resolution 242 remained persuasive to the international community, the General Assembly resolutions of November 1974 reflected widespread recognition that UN 242's call for a just settlement of the Palestinian refugee problem was no longer adequate. The governments voting for the 1974 resolutions, as well as for the November 1975 UN resolution establishing a Committee on the Exercise of the Inalienable Rights of the Palestinian People, in effect affirmed what the PLO had proclaimed in its revised charter of 1968 and repeated at every subsequent meeting of the Palestine National Council: the Palestinians are a nation, not a collection of refugees, and the problem requiring a solution is accordingly Palestinian statelessness. As a result, despite the United States' preoccupation with relations between Israel, Egypt, and Syria in 1974 and 1975, it was becoming evident to most observers that the emergence of the new PLO after 1967 was not a deviation at all, and that continuing concern with the Palestinian problem would indeed show the June War to have been a critical turning point in the evolution of the Arab-Israeli conflict.

PLO Gains in the Occupied Territories and Lebanon

These developments in the international diplomatic arena were matched by an evolution of the political situation in the West Bank and Gaza Strip. Despite Israeli efforts to limit its influence, the popularity of the PLO was growing steadily among the Palestinian inhabitants of the occupied territories. Moreover, in the West Bank, a new generation of pro-PLO political leaders emerged to rival the class of notables tied to Amman who had been dominant in the period before 1967 and whose status had been unaffected by the municipal elections of 1972.[55]

These changes were the result of a number of factors. On the one hand, the expansion of quasi-political associations outside the control of the traditional elite, such as labor unions and student movements, provided an institutional foundation for those oriented toward Palestinian nationalism. The members of these associations, and especially the youth, had been influenced by the PLO's ideological thrusts in the late 1960s and were encouraged in the mid-1970s by the organization's diplomatic successes. On the other hand, ironically, Israel's policies in the territories also helped to undermine the traditional elite and to promote the emergence of more nationalist-oriented political forces. For example, by restricting the activities of elected officials in order to prevent the emergence of an all–West Bank leadership, Jerusalem limited the power base of traditional leaders and created something of a political vacuum. Also contributing to this vacuum was Israel's deportation of numerous Palestinian politicians critical of its policies, many of whom in the late 1960s and early 1970s were members of the traditional pro-Jordan elite.

In addition, in the economic realm, expanding opportunities for Palestinians to work in Israel weakened the position of established notable families. By 1974, approximately one-third of the West Bank labor force was employed in Israel; and, whatever the balance of benefits and disadvantages of such employment for the individual worker, one important consequence was a reduction in dependence on West Bank landowners and businessmen, the backbone of the traditional political class.

The importance of these trends was evident to many observers in 1974 and 1975 and was confirmed beyond dispute by the West Bank municipal elections of April 1976, in which pro-PLO candidates defeated incumbents and gained control of the mayor's office and the Municipal Council in Nablus, Hebron, Ramallah, and eleven other towns. As early as 1973, pro-PLO activists had formed the Palestine National Front to fill the gap created by the declining influence of traditional elites,[56] and in October 1974 the PNF sent the Arab summit in Rabat a petition affirming that the PLO was the sole legitimate representative of the Palestinian people. The petition, signed by 180 West Bank and Gaza dignitaries, strengthened the position of the PLO at Rabat considerably and played a role in Jordan's decision to accept the summit's resolution in favor of the Palestinian organization.

In taking these and other actions, the PNF was not only seeking to lend credibility to the PLO's claim to represent the Palestinian people, and thereby to contribute to the organization's drive for international recognition, it was also working to advance its own political agenda. The activists who formed the PNF sought to use the PLO's name to improve their position in the struggle for political supremacy taking place among Palestinians in the occupied territories, and especially to establish the legitimacy of their challenge to the traditional elite. In addition, more broadly, the PNF was attempting to influence the development of PLO thinking and, specifically, to encourage the organization to pay greater attention to the West Bank and Gaza. Indeed, in the latter connection, some associated with the PNF urged the PLO to concentrate on the establishment of an independent Palestinian state in the West Bank and Gaza, and it is probable that their views contributed to the movement in this direction that took place at the PNC meeting in June 1974.

A related dimension of the changes taking place in West Bank political life at this time involved the emergence of the Palestine Communist Organization. West Bank Communists increasingly asserted their independence from the Jordanian Communist Party after 1973, identifying with the PLO and then, in

1975, establishing the quasi-autonomous PCO. Although technically a branch of the Jordanian Communist Party, the PCO did not take directions from the JPC and, like the PNF, asserted that the PLO was the sole legitimate representative of the Palestinian people.[57] Also like the PNF, and like Communist parties elsewhere, the PCO advocated the creation of an independent Palestinian state alongside Israel; and, consistent with this position, the organization's newspaper, *al-Watan*, in February 1976 called on the PLO to abandon its demands for an independent state in the whole of Palestine.[58] Taken together, the PNF and the PCO showed not only that new, pro-PLO political forces were emerging in the West Bank, but also that Palestinians in the occupied territories clearly favored and indeed sought to encourage the more moderate political orientation toward which the mainstream of the PLO had been moving for several years.

So far as the 1976 elections are concerned, candidates oriented toward the PLO and toward Palestinian nationalism won about 75 percent of the municipal council seats—153 of 205—and 14 of the 24 mayoralty races.[59] The latter included the largest and most important West Bank towns, the only significant exception being Bethlehem, where Elias Freij, a moderate pragmatist with strong links to Jordan, was elected mayor. In contrast to its call for a boycott of the elections in 1972, the mainstream of the PLO had favored participation in the balloting of 1976. Although there was opposition from the PFLP and several other hard-line factions, Fatah and others, encouraged by the PLO's diplomatic achievements and by increasingly frequent demonstrations of nationalist sentiments inside the occupied territories, were confident that pro-PLO figures would be swept into office.

Israel, for its part, was to at least some degree surprised by the results of the balloting. Jerusalem's reasons for permitting the scheduled election included a hope that by demonstrating its commitment to a measure of democracy in the territories it would be able to reduce international and local criticism, both of which had become intense by 1976. Israel may also have underestimated the strength of the nationalist movement in the West Bank and, mistakenly believing that traditional notables would be returned to power, viewed the elections as an opportunity to undermine the position of pro-PLO political figures who had recently gained prominence. In this connection, some members of the defeated pro-Jordan camp bitterly complained about Israeli negligence in permitting pro-PLO candidates to organize. Some critics even went so far as to allege that Israel welcomed the victory of PLO supporters because it enabled Jerusalem to claim that "radicals" had come to power, and that "there is no one to talk to" about the future of the occupied territories.[60]

The 1976 election, confirming the emergence of a new generation of West Bank leadership, was won by men who were very different from those who had been victorious in 1972. They were much better educated, for example, with almost 30 percent of the new municipal council members having had a university education. This was three times the proportion among those elected in 1972. In addition, the men elected in 1976 were much younger, 60 percent of the municipal council members now being under the age of fifty. There were occupational differences, too. Although landowners and businessmen still constituted an absolute majority, 40 percent of those elected to positions of urban leadership in 1976 were white-collar workers or members of the liberal professions.

As expected, the newly elected mayors and municipal council members began almost immediately to express not only their opposition to Israeli occupation but also their attachment to Palestinian nationalism and the PLO.[61] In September 1976, for example, a group of West Bank mayors sent a message to the Arab League protesting Syria's intervention in the Lebanese civil war against the PLO and its allies; and in January 1977, the mayors addressed a petition to U.S. Secretary of State Cyrus Vance, demanding an end to occupation and calling for the establishment of a Palestinian state in the West Bank and Gaza. All twenty-four also sent a joint message endorsing the formation of such a state to the thirteenth meeting of the Palestine National Council, which took place in Cairo in March 1977. As a matter of fact, about fifty political leaders from the occupied territories had planned to attend the meeting in Cairo, but they were prevented from leaving by Israeli military authorities.

The program adopted at the Thirteenth PNC reflected a growing convergence of mainstream PLO thinking on the one hand and the political orientation of the West Bank's new leadership class on the other. The session reaffirmed and clarified decisions taken at the PNC's 1974 meeting by calling for the creation of an independent Palestinian state, even though, as in the past, the West Bank and Gaza were not mentioned by name. The program adopted by the PNC in 1977 was thus consistent with the wishes of Palestinian nationalists in the occupied territories, who had become dominant at home and whose political orientations were increasingly influential outside the territories as well. Indeed, to an extent, it is likely that the emergence of a new generation of West Bank leaders contributed to the evolution of the PLO's political program after 1973 and assisted those factions seeking an alternative to the radical ideology that had emerged and become dominant following the war of June 1967.

In sum, the emergence of a new leadership class in the occupied territories between 1973 and 1977 was another important dimension of the dramatic improvement in the Palestinians' political fortunes. As with gains in the international diplomatic arena, developments in the territories brought increased visibility, status, and influence to the Palestine Liberation Organization. In addition, more broadly, they also contributed to the recognition in many world capitals that the Palestinians did indeed see the PLO as their sole legitimate representative, and that the question of Palestine was indeed at the core of the Arab-Israeli conflict.

The PLO's base of operations during this period was in Lebanon, where developments in the mid-1970s, including the 1975–76 civil war, also served to enhance the status and influence of the Palestinian organization. As noted earlier, the PLO had by 1969 forced the Beirut government to grant it substantial autonomy. In November of that year, Lebanese officials signed an agreement with Yasir Arafat in Cairo that left the Palestinians in undisputed control of their front-line positions in the south of the country, from which military operations against Israel could be launched. Even more important, the Cairo agreement recognized the right of the PLO to administer and police without interference the refugee camps where most of Lebanon's 250,000-300,000 Palestinian civilians resided.[62] These arrangements led many observers to regard the PLO in Lebanon as a state within a state; and, using the opportunities this situation provided, especially after being driven from Jordan in 1970 and 1971, the PLO had built up its political and institutional infrastructure and then coordinated its drive for international recognition from its new base in Lebanon.[63]

Some observers believe that challenges from the PLO in the late 1960s and early 1970s played a critical role in weakening the central government and, by upsetting the delicate balance among competing confessional communities, in exacerbating political tensions and pushing Lebanon toward civil war. According to one knowledgeable and objective analyst, Palestinian influence "destroyed the national consensus among the Lebanese. The PLO, by sheer numbers and resources, gradually established ideological and military links with Lebanese domestic groups, as allies and as clients."[64] Other observers, by contrast, believe that the influence of the PLO was the result rather than the cause of Lebanon's political problems; and they accordingly argue that the authority of the government, and the consensus on the basis of which it had traditionally operated, were eroded primarily by the sectarian character of Lebanese political and social life. Indeed, some believe the Lebanese political system was fatally flawed, and thus probably doomed, because individual political attachments were to confessional communities rather than to the nation as a whole.[65] In any event, regardless of the degree to which the Palestinian presence in Lebanon contributed to the country's problems, intercommunal conflict intensified in the early 1970s and led to civil war in 1975–76.

Although there were many Lebanese factions contending for political and ideological influence at this time, the civil war was preceded by the division of the country into two grand coalitions opposing one another. On the one hand, supporting the status quo and dominated by Maronite Christians, were the Lebanese Forces. This constellation, which included some Sunni Muslim elites and is usually described as a coalition of "rightists," favored preservation of the existing political system. It also represented those who opposed active Lebanese involvement in the Arab-Israeli conflict and, more broadly, who tended to see Lebanon as a Mediterranean country with links to the West as well as the Arab world.

Opposed to the status quo was the Lebanese National Movement, made up of factions which were primarily Muslim and nonelite in character. The LNM is frequently referred to as a "leftist" movement. One scholar describes the opposition groups out of which the LNM was subsequently constructed as "an untidy amalgam of Muslim traditionalists (Sunni and Shiite), Muslim radicals (left and right), secularists (left and right), pan-Arabists of every brand, socialists, student activists, trade unionists and a tiny sprinkling of Marxists."[66] The LNM, which received important support from the increasingly well-organized and well-armed forces of the PLO, sought a new political system, one which would distribute power and influence more equitably among confessional communities and, even more important, would reduce the gap between masses and elites. The LNM also sought a stronger Lebanese identification with Arab nationalism, including support for the Arab and Palestinian struggle against Israel.

Observers disagree about whether the PLO sought active involvement in the civil war or was reluctantly drawn into the fighting by its allies in the LNM. While there is no doubt that Lebanese opposition elements endeavored to enlist the PLO in their cause, it appears that the Palestinians themselves were divided about the course they should follow, with the most important leaders of Fatah, the dominant PLO faction, taking the position that local political entanglements were not in the Palestinians' interest. As stated by one of these leaders, Salah Khalaf, "It is in our interest to have the whole of Lebanon standing with us. . . . Our hope lies with dialogue and through dialogue, the only language that can pervade the whole of Lebanon."[67]

Be this as it may, any prospect that the PLO would resist full-scale participation in the fighting ended when the Lebanese Forces attacked Tal al-Zaatar and other Palestinian refugee camps early in 1976. As stated by another senior Fatah official, Khaled al-Hassan, "When they besieged Tal al-Zaatar, we couldn't but go in."[68] In the weeks that followed, the bulk of the PLO forces in Lebanon moved northward from their bases near the Israeli border and joined the LNM in an offensive against Christian and rightist positions in the Maronite heartland. Moreover, the LNM-PLO alliance scored important victories during this period.

The course of the 1975–76 civil war was shaped by Israeli and especially Syrian involvement, as well as by the relative strength of Lebanese participants and the military contribution of the PLO. Israel provided clandestine support in the form of arms and training to the Lebanese Forces;[69] and, since the National Movement was allied with the PLO, some were inclined to view the fighting in Lebanon as a proxy Israeli-Palestinian war. Israel's contribution was of secondary importance, however, and made only after the LNM and the PLO had taken the offensive early in 1976.

Syria's role, by contrast, was substantial and direct. It also eventually proved to be decisive. Syria had initially been providing support to the LNM, but Damascus shifted to a more neutral stance in spring 1976, and then, in late May and early June, Syrian President Hafez al-Assad sent 6,000 troops into Lebanon in an effort to contain the increasingly successful advance of LNM and PLO forces. The latter responded by forming a joint command and engaging the Syrians, with the immediate result being a general standoff. By September, however, Assad's forces had broken the stalemate and were able to carry out successful operations against the joint forces of the LNM and the PLO.

The evolution of the fighting during this period also included a military offensive by the Lebanese Forces, beginning late in June and continuing through the summer. With the attention of the LNM and the PLO directed toward the Syrians, a number of Muslim and Palestinian areas fell to Christian militias. This included the besieged Palestinian refugee camp of Tal al-Zaatar, which finally surrendered on August 12. The siege of Tal al-Zaatar had been a gruesome ordeal of human suffering in which hundreds of civilians lost their lives, including babies and children who had died of dehydration. In addition, 2,000 or more of Tal al-Zaatar's inhabitants were killed when the Lebanese Forces stormed the camp in the final assault.

Most of the fighting came to an end in fall 1976. The Syrians proclaimed a ceasefire on October 15, and the next day an Arab mini-summit was convened in Riyadh, Saudi Arabia, to consider the turmoil in Lebanon. Assisted by the leaders of Egypt, Saudi Arabia, and Kuwait, an agreement for ending the war was worked out by Yasir Arafat, Hafez al-Assad, and the Lebanese president, Elias Sarkis. Following the recommendations of the summit, Syria reconstituted its armed forces in Lebanon as an Arab Deterrent Force, which was charged with keeping the peace and, among other things, enforcing the 1969 Cairo Agreement governing relations between the PLO and the Lebanese government.[70]

In an additional development, Damascus now departed from its tacit alliance with the Lebanese Forces and, reestablishing its ties with the PLO and the Lebanese opposition, moved back to a position of comparative neutrality. Moreover, although there continued to be distrust between Damascus and elements of the LNM, the Syrians and the PLO within a year had gone a long way toward reestablishing their former alliance. Among the factors pushing them back together was shared concern about developments in southern Lebanon, where Israel had used the opportunity provided by the war to create a surrogate militia under the leadership of former Lebanese army major Saad Haddad. Haddad's forces, who were charged with preventing Palestinian commandos from infiltrating into Israel, controlled a buffer zone six or seven miles deep directly north of the Israel-Lebanon frontier.

While the civil war had been punishing from the Palestinian point of view, it also enhanced the circumstances of the PLO in Lebanon and initiated a period that was to be the heyday of Palestinian political and military strength. The war had not resolved any of Lebanon's underlying problems. On the contrary, not only had there been great human suffering and physical destruction,[71] but the country's confessional and class antagonisms were deeper than ever in the wake of the fighting. So far as the PLO is concerned, however, reduced external interference and greater freedom of maneuver were among the consequences of Lebanon's weakness and division, and the Palestinian organization was also able to expand its popular support in the postwar period through the provision of vital services that could no longer be ensured by the government in Beirut. In a related development, the Lebanese civil war also left Fatah, the mainstream faction headed by Yasir Arafat, in a stronger position relative to more radical groups within the PLO. Overall, as summarized by Rashid Khalidi, a Palestinian scholar who formerly lived in Lebanon: "For the Lebanese, the crisis which had begun in 1975 was the worst period in their history. On the other hand, in spite of the dangers facing them . . . Palestinians could look on their situation in Lebanon as marking a high point in the re-creation of their national identity." Khalidi adds that it is "ironic that the 1975–76 war waged against the PLO by its Lebanese and foreign foes was a primary impetus to the expansion of its presence in Lebanon."[72]

The administrative operations of the PLO in Lebanon expanded both during and after the civil war. Not only had the Lebanese government ceased to provide many important social services, but the work of the United Nations Relief and Works Agency among Palestinian refugees had been disrupted as well, creating an additional need for the PLO to fill the gap. Lebanese as well as Palestinians benefited from some of these actions, such as the PLO's efforts to ensure the maintenance of electricity and telephone service in certain areas. These activities sometimes provoked resentment among Lebanese civilians, who, though beneficiaries of PLO action, frequently complained of petty bureaucratic corruption and occasionally charged, more grandly, that the Palestinians seemed to be taking over Lebanon. Nevertheless, the PLO extended its authority as a result of these developments, retaining and continuing to expand much of its administrative infrastructure even after Lebanese and United Nations authorities resumed their work at the conclusion of the war.

An example is the growth of the Palestine Red Crescent Society, which had operated a single hospital prior to the civil war but by 1980 ran nine hospitals and twelve clinics in Lebanon alone. These institutions treated hundreds of thousands of persons every year, a substantial proportion of whom were not Palestinian. According to one account, the operations of the PRCS represented "a major social achievement" and "attracted many visitors, including foreign doctors and nurses from all over the world."[73] In addition, the PLO expanded its network of workshops and factories, of which thirty-two were in operation in the period after the war. Roughly 3,000 Palestinian and Lebanese men and women were employed in these enterprises. Among their products were blankets and furniture, most destined for export to other Arab countries or Eastern Europe.

The PLO also benefited from the inflow of large amounts of financial aid, especially in the wake of the 1974 Arab summit in Rabat. Much of this assistance came from Arab oil-producing states, whose revenues increased dramatically during this period, enabling them to respond generously to the Rabat decision to recognize and support the PLO as the sole legitimate representative of the Palestinian people. In addition, some of the funds that flowed to the PLO came from voluntary taxes on Palestinians in Kuwait and other Gulf states and from donations by wealthy Palestinians residing abroad; and here, as with the money from Arab states, most of the incoming revenue went directly to Fatah, the largest and most influential faction under the PLO's political umbrella. Not all of these funds were used for public-service enterprises, such as the Palestine Red Crescent Society, or for investments in factories and other business ventures. Significant sums were also wasted, or spent to support the luxurious lifestyles of some PLO leaders. This in turn generated considerable resentment in both Palestinian and Lebanese circles, "among people who were being asked to accept sacrifices in the name of the Palestinian cause, and could not understand how some were not only exempt from such sacrifices, but actually prospered."[74] Nevertheless, these valid complaints notwithstanding, the substantial growth of its financial base was another key dimension of the increasing power and influence of the PLO in the mid-1970s.

Finally, in addition to its expanding administrative infrastructure and its increasingly secure financial base, the PLO's position in Lebanon was also reflected in its growing military power, particularly in the southern part of the country. Although the area immediately north of the Israeli border was under the control of the proxy militia that Israel had created, which was led by Saad Haddad, the region between this area and Beirut was dominated by PLO forces who operated with little interference from either the Lebanese or the Syrians. Roughly 15,000 Palestinian fighters were based in the south, for the most part concentrated in four coastal and another four inland zones, the former spread out along the Mediterranean from Tyre to Beirut, and the most important of the latter around the towns of Nabitiya, Rashaiya, and Hasbaiya. According to Israeli estimates, the PLO's arsenal in this region, in addition to the weapons it maintained in Beirut, included about eighty tanks, about fifty 130mm and 155mm long-range cannons, roughly eighty Katyusha rocket launchers, sixty 100mm and 160mm mortars, and seventy-seven antitank cannons.

As with PLO activities in the fields of administration and finance, there was no shortage of Lebanese complaints about the actions of Palestinian fighters operating in the south of the country. Populated primarily by Shiite Muslims, whose fighting units had been allied with the PLO during the civil war, many of the towns and villages in this part of Lebanon now found themselves under the often heavy-handed influence of PLO forces. Despite their strained relations with substantial segments of the Lebanese population, however, including their former Muslim allies, the Palestinians' strong military presence in Lebanon gave power and additional substance to what Arafat at the time described as "the microcosm of our future mini-state."[75]

In sum, the position of the PLO was radically different than it had been only five or six years earlier. It had been possible to argue in 1970 and 1971, in the wake of the Jordanian civil war, that the revival of the Palestine Resistance Movement after June 1967 had run its course, and that the PLO would now return to the periphery of the Arab-Israeli conflict. By 1976 or 1977, and perhaps as early as 1974 or 1975, it was evident that such assessments had been extremely premature. The PLO had achieved wide recognition in the international diplomatic arena, a new generation of political leaders identified with the Palestinian organization had emerged in the West Bank and Gaza, and the PLO was governing a large Palestinian population in Lebanon, presiding over what some described as an autonomous mini-state.

The ideological orientation of the PLO as it emerged in the wake of these important political gains was reflected in the decisions of the Thirteenth PNC, which convened in Cairo in March 1977. As noted earlier, the program adopted by the PNC reaffirmed that the PLO's goal was the creation of an independent Palestinian state, thereby extending and further clarifying decisions taken at the PNC's meeting in 1974. Even though important details were left unspecified, the program represented a clear victory for Fatah and its supporters, including the nationalist mainstream in the West Bank and Gaza Strip. These elements favored the pursuit of Palestinian goals through political rather than military action, placed emphasis on the establishment of an independent state alongside Israel, and were beginning to conceive of a democratic and secular state over all of Palestine as a distant objective which would be achieved only, if at all, through natural historical evolution. Thus, as summarized by one analyst, the significance of the Thirteenth PNC meeting is that "after a three-year struggle, it was the 'moderates' who had won in the PLO. By agreeing to participate in the peace process and endorse the idea of a Palestinian state [alongside Israel], the PLO appeared to be taking its full place in an international settlement."[76]

This was not the conclusion drawn by most supporters of Israel, of course, who challenged the view of many observers that the PNC meeting had produced an unstated but implicit understanding that the Palestinian state would be established in the West Bank and Gaza Strip, rather than over the whole of Palestine. In this connection, Israeli officials correctly noted that the PLO had not amended its charter, and they also pointed out that the so-called "moderate" program adopted by the PNC in 1977 made no mention whatsoever of an accommodation with the Jewish state. Nevertheless, the accuracy of these Israeli complaints notwithstanding, most observers concluded that there had indeed been an important evolution of Palestinian thinking since 1973; and many also judged that the PLO had deliberately given itself room to maneuver and bargain, presumably laying a foundation for additional compromise in the future. Seen in historical perspective, the Thirteenth PNC therefore confirmed that improvement of the PLO's political fortunes had been accompanied by an important evolution of its ideological orientation. Accordingly, again, the PLO looked very different in 1976 and 1977 than it had only five or six years earlier. It was now politically established and secure, recognized and taken seriously in the world of international diplomacy, and in possession of a platform that many judged to be pragmatic and a basis for serious negotiation.

Israel's Earthquake Election of 1977

Two critical events took place in 1977, both of which set in motion developments whose impact on the Israeli-Palestinian conflict would be felt for many years to come. The first was the Israeli parliamentary election of May 17, in which the Likud Union of Menachem Begin defeated the Labor Alignment led by Yitzhak Rabin and Shimon Peres. Likud won forty-three seats to Labor's thirty-two, and Begin was then asked to form a cabinet and assume the premiership. This was the first time since the founding of the state that the government had not been under the control of Labor, leading some to describe the election results as a political earthquake;[77] and Likud's historic advocacy of territorial maximalism, as well as its specific calls during the campaign for retention of the West Bank and Gaza, portended a major shift in Israel's policies toward the occupied territories. Many Israelis characterized the coming to power of Begin and Likud as the most important change in the political scene since 1967, probably even since 1948.[78]

The other critical event, equally or even more dramatic, was the November visit to Israel of Egypt's president, Anwar Sadat. Several months of behind-the-scenes diplomacy, with King Hassan II of Morocco acting as intermediary, resulted in an agreement for Sadat to come to Jerusalem and address the Knesset. Sadat's visit held out the possibility of a dramatic breakthrough in the Arab-Israeli conflict, being the first instance of direct, official, and public contact between Israeli and Arab leaders since the State of Israel was formed. Moreover, Sadat told the Israeli parliament of his vision for peace and set forth the basis for a compromise in which his country, the largest and most powerful Arab state, would recognize Israel and accept its existence as a Jewish state. Both Likud's electoral victory and Sadat's visit to Jerusalem were completely without precedent, and neither would have been predicted a year or two earlier. Further, the significance of these events was increased by their historical juxtaposition, leading to what would become a major change in the character of the Arab-Israeli conflict.

The differing foreign-policy planks in the electoral platforms of Likud and Labor offered voters a clear choice in the 1977 Israeli elections. Likud issued a straightforward call for retention of the West Bank and Gaza Strip, whereas Labor, as in the past, reaffirmed its commitment to United Nations Resolution 242 and championed the principle of territorial compromise. Likud emphasized the strategic significance of the West Bank and Gaza, discussing the Sinai Peninsula and Golan Heights in this context as well and stating that its approach to all of the occupied territories was guided by Israel's need for secure and defensible borders. But its attitude toward the former areas clearly reflected other considerations, too, ones which in fact were the more central preoccupations of Begin and his associates. Affirming that Judea and Samaria (the West Bank) and the Gaza District were integral parts of the historic Land of Israel, Likud also justified its insistence on retaining these territories on historical and religious grounds and rejected returning to the Arabs even those regions that do not possess military value. The party maintained that foreign, meaning non-Jewish, sovereignty should not be reestablished over any part of the West Bank and Gaza, adding as a corollary that the right of Jews to live in any part of these territories was not a subject for negotiation.[79]

By contrast, Labor repeated its belief that Israel should withdraw from most of the territory captured in 1967 in return for peace. With the exception of Jerusalem, Labor attached no importance to these areas beyond that resulting from strategic considerations and declared itself ready to negotiate a comprehensive settlement in which Israel would insist only on those territorial modifications dictated by the country's security needs. Indeed, some Laborites added, the party had already demonstrated its commitment to territorial compromise by signing and implementing disengagement-of-forces agreements with Egypt and Syria.

Although there was some disagreement about exactly which parts of the West Bank a Labor government would insist on retaining for purposes of security, the position of the Alignment mainstream was reflected in a plan that had been drafted shortly after the June War by Yigal Allon, a senior party official who had served in the cabinets of Levi Eshkol and Golda Meir and then become foreign minister under Yitzhak Rabin. The elements of the Allon Plan were publicly clarified in a 1976 *Foreign Affairs* article: as shown in Map 8.2, Israel would retain the Jordan Valley and the Judean Desert, including the eastern slopes of the West Bank's central mountain ridge; the rest of the West Bank, including its heavily populated highland core, would be returned to Jordan in the context of a comprehensive peace settlement and would be linked to the East Bank by a corridor along the Jericho-Ramallah axis.[80] Beyond the West Bank, many in Labor also addressed the status of the other occupied areas and repeated their commitment to territorial compromise.

The crystallization of this central tendency in Labor's definition of territorial compromise did not eliminate important differences of opinion within the Alignment. Some advocated more sweeping concessions in return for peace, while others urged holding on to greater amounts of territory, particularly in the West

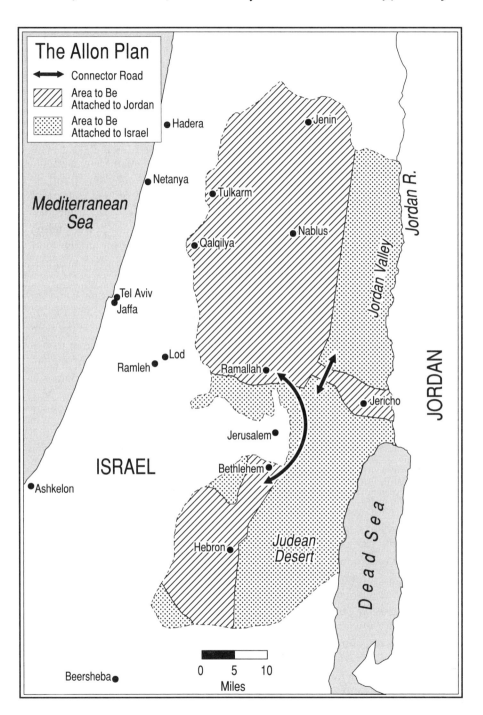

Bank. In the latter connection, some, such as Golda Meir and Moshe Dayan, considered the entire West Bank to be necessary for the security of the state and thus had serious reservations about the Allon Plan.[81] In addition, believing that anything less than complete Israeli withdrawal would be unacceptable to King Hussein, these elements within Labor may also have regarded the building of Jewish settlements, even if only in specified security locations, at least partly as a device for preventing movement toward a settlement, with the result that Israel would retain *de facto* control of the entire West Bank. Some Alignment leaders also took the position that neither the Gaza Strip nor the Golan Heights should be returned to foreign rule, and that Jerusalem should also retain Sharm al-Sheikh, which would be linked to the country by an unbroken land strip along the eastern edge of Sinai.[82] On the other hand, the influence of relative hard-liners such as Meir and Dayan declined after Yitzhak Rabin became prime minister in 1974. Indeed, when Rabin named a cabinet containing many of the more "dovish" members of the Alignment, Dayan wrote that he had never imagined such a cabinet "in his darkest dreams."[83]

In any event, despite both the differing views existing within Labor and the very substantial distance between mainstream Alignment thinking and the demands of Jordan and other Arab governments willing to seek peace on the basis of UN 242, Labor's 1977 platform remained sharply differentiated from that of Likud, whose own attitudes were shaped by considerations of history and nationalism and which insisted on no compromise whatsoever in Judea and Samaria. Overall, as repeatedly stated by Alignment officials in the weeks before the May 1977 balloting, a Labor government would neither return nor retain all of the West Bank.

While Likud insisted that its clear victory at the polls showed a strong voter preference for its own attitude toward the West Bank and Gaza, opposition to territorial compromise was probably no more than a secondary factor in the party's electoral success. Much more important was voter dissatisfaction with the Alignment, which for several years had been racked by rivalries and feuds among its most prominent leaders, and which in 1976 and 1977 was also tainted by scandal. In the latter connection, public concern was compounded by the dramatic suicide of Avraham Ofer, the housing minister, whom press reports accused of corruption and who left a suicide note proclaiming his innocence. This was followed six weeks later by the conviction on charges of soliciting bribes and income-tax evasion of Asher Yadlin, director of the National Sick Fund. Yadlin, like Ofer, was a respected Labor insider, who in fact had been nominated by the party to become governor of the Bank of Israel. Moreover, Yadlin testified at his trial that other Labor leaders, including two cabinet ministers, had been engaged in illegal fund-raising for the party. Finally, in March 1977, less than two months before the elections, Prime Minister Rabin was forced to admit that his wife had maintained an illegal foreign-currency account in Washington. Following this admission, he relinquished leadership of the Alignment to Shimon Peres and took a leave of absence from the premiership.[84]

Many analysts believe that these leadership problems within the Alignment, rather than a preference among voters for Likud's electoral platform, account for Labor's defeat in 1977. Many Israelis simply concluded, these analysts argue, that Labor had been in power too long and that it was time for a change. The results of the balloting, involving a large decline in the number of Knesset seats obtained by Labor (from 51 to 32) but only a small increase in the number won by Likud (from 39 to 43), lend additional credibility to such judgments. Also, most defectors from the Alignment did not vote for Likud but instead gave their support to the Democratic Movement for Change, a newly formed party that campaigned on a platform of clean government and electoral reform. The DMC obtained fifteen seats in the Knesset elected in 1977, a stunning accomplishment that far exceeded what a new party had achieved in any previous election. Foreign-policy considerations did not figure prominently among the issues raised by the DMC during the campaign, but the views of the party's most important leaders were in fact closer to those of Labor than to those of Likud.[85]

Another factor also played a critical role in Likud's victory at the polls, although in this case the implications for voter attitudes toward the West Bank and Gaza are subject to competing interpretations. The growing strength of Likud, which in fact had become visible in the elections of 1973, reflected a strong preference for the party among Jews of Afro-Asian origin, those whose families had emigrated to Israel from Muslim countries of the Middle East and North Africa in the 1950s and 1960s. Such individuals constituted roughly half of Israel's Jewish population in 1977, and their relative demographic weight was increasing steadily as the result of a birthrate exceeding that of Jews of European origin. So far as partisan preferences are concerned, surveys and electoral studies revealed that Israelis of Afro-Asian origin were disproportionately likely to vote for Likud, and this tendency was particularly pronounced among the second generation within this population category. Voters born in Israel of Afro-Asian parents were almost three times as likely to report a preference for Likud as a preference for Labor.[86]

Afro-Asian support for Likud is based on a number of factors, although there is disagreement about the relative importance of each. To begin with, compared to other Israelis, those whose families once lived in Muslim and especially Arab countries were disproportionately likely to regard Arabs as untrustworthy, to think peace with the Arab world is impossible, and to favor retaining most or all of the territory captured in 1967. Public opinion polls had confirmed the existence of these attitudinal tendencies for more than a decade by the time of the election in 1977, showing anti-Arab sentiments to be characteristic of Afro-Asian Jews in general, and to be especially prevalent among those whose families had come from Morocco, which is the largest single subcommunity in this category of the population.[87] The significance of these observations, according to some analysts, is that Afro-Asian Jews gave their votes to Likud in 1977 primarily because of an affinity between their own views on the one hand and the party's militant nationalism and commitment to territorial maximalism on the other; and this, these analysts continue, means that Likud's electoral victory gave the government led by Menachem Begin a specific mandate to implement new policies in the occupied territories.

The origins of anti-Arab attitudes among Israeli Jews of Afro-Asian origin are less clear than their existence. Afro-Asian Jews themselves sometimes attribute their views to the persecution of Jews in their countries of origin, saying they know from firsthand experience, or at least from that of their parents and grandparents, just how strong and widespread is Arab hatred of the Jews and of Israel. Such historical recollections are often at variance with the relatively satisfactory circumstances of Jewish life in Arab lands, although harassment and persecution were by no means unknown in Jewish communities of the Arab world.[88] Nevertheless, whether accurate or not, the existence of these historical recollections has been documented by public opinion polls and other studies.

Alternatively, many analysts point out that negative attitudes toward the Arabs may in fact be a response to the situation of Afro-Asian Jews in Israel, rather than to any real or imagined suffering in these Jews' countries of origin.[89] Since most Afro-Asians came to Israel only after independence, they may have adopted hard-line attitudes toward the Arabs upon their arrival either to demonstrate that they are committed Zionists or to compensate for the fact that they did not participate in the struggle to build the *Yishuv* during the difficult prestate years. Even more likely may be a desire born of low socioeconomic status to feel superior to another category of the population, in this case Israel's Arab citizens and the growing number of Palestinians from the West Bank and Gaza working in the Jewish state. This possibility reflects practical as well as symbolic considerations, moreover, since Arabs hold many of the menial jobs once filled by Afro-Asians and create pressure for upward mobility among the latter population category.[90]

Whatever their origins, the anti-Arab sentiments of Israel's Afro-Asian Jewish population, which in 1977 included not only negative views of Arabs in general but support for hard-line policies toward Arab governments as well, were consistent with the long-standing nationalism of Likud and led many to see Israel's Afro-Asian Jews as the party's natural constituency. Yet other observers argue that antipathy toward Labor, rather than an attraction to Likud, was the primary determinant of Afro-Asian partisan attachments. This antipathy is well documented and, moreover, it has little to do with ideology.

Many immigrants from African and Asian countries believe they were looked down upon and treated unfairly by the Labor Party that was in power at the time of their arrival in the 1950s and 1960s. Many claim they were shunted to development towns in regions where other Israeli Jews did not wish to live and, more generally, were made to feel like second-class citizens in their new homeland. Even more important, they deeply resent the fact that Labor leaders often responded to their complaints by calling them culturally inferior, or "*primitivim* in common Hebrew parlance," and by saying that their most important problem was thus their own backwardness. Ben Gurion once remarked about Jews from Morocco, for example, that "their customs are those of the Arabs. They love their women, but beat them. . . . Maybe in the third generation something will appear from the Oriental Jew that is different. But I don't see it yet," after which he added, "The culture of Morocco I would not like to have here. . . . We do not want Israelis to become Arabs. We are duty bound to fight against the spirit of the Levant, which corrupts individuals and societies."[91]

It is probable that these bitter experiences, far more than a preference for one ideology or another, turned Afro-Asian Jews against Labor and led them to embrace the major alternative, the opposition party led by Menachem Begin. Also, extending this analysis, some raise the possibility that only after their unhappy experiences with the Labor Party led them to Likud did Afro-Asian voters acquire hard-line political attitudes, perhaps to provide a philosophical justification for behavior that was in fact based primarily on symbolic considerations and perceptions of self-interest.

Whatever the relative merits of these competing explanations of the attitudes and behavior patterns of Israelis of Afro-Asian origin, their votes for Likud in 1977, as well as the leadership crisis in Labor that drove many voters to the DMC, resulted in the formation of a government that not only was committed in principle to Israel's permanent retention of the West Bank and Gaza but also was determined to implement policies that would make it impossible for a withdrawal to be effected should Labor return to power in the future.[92] Likud may not have won the election *because* of its posture toward the occupied territories. In addition, since the party had obtained only forty-three Knesset seats, Begin was able to form a government only after establishing a fragile parliamentary coalition with the DMC, the National Religious Party, and several smaller parties; and some of these coalition partners, most notably the DMC, did not share Likud's philosophy of territorial maximalism and joined the government only after great hesitation and protracted bargaining. Nevertheless, with or without a clear national mandate to change the direction of the country's foreign policy, Menachem Begin, the new prime minister, saw himself as having a historic opportunity to make progress toward the achievement of his party's long-standing goals.

Consistent with this ideological commitment, the new Likud-led government set out almost immediately to establish a vastly expanded network of Jewish settlements and interests in the West Bank and other occupied territories. This was often described as "creating facts," meaning that the political and demographic situation in the territories was deliberately being transformed in order to establish a new set of realities, to create a situation that would reduce, and hopefully eliminate, any chance of an Israeli withdrawal in the future. Begin proclaimed in this connection that there would never again be a political division between the Jordan River and the Mediterranean Sea. He told the Knesset in December 1977, for example, "We do not even dream of the possibility—if we are given the chance to withdraw our military forces from Judea, Samaria and Gaza—of abandoning these areas to the control of the murderous organization that is called the PLO. . . . We have a right and a demand for [Israeli] sovereignty over these areas of Eretz Yisrael. This is our land and it belongs to the Jewish nation rightfully."[93]

The Begin government's efforts to deepen and make permanent Israel's presence in the West Bank and Gaza received powerful support from Gush Emunim, or Bloc of the Faithful, a settler lobby formed in 1974 and composed primarily of religious Jews.[94] Gush brought together nongovernmental groups that had been working for some time to intensify settlement activity, not only attempting to influence government policy by lobbying but frequently operating by means of direct action as well, including the recruitment and transfer of settlers, the construction of both authorized and unauthorized settlements, and the harassment of Palestinians whose land they sought to acquire. Gush's militancy and organizational effectiveness had enabled the movement to exert pressure on the Labor-led government of Yitzhak Rabin, contributing to a significant increase in the number of settlements approved by the cabinet between mid-1975 and the elections of May 1977.

Gush Emunim also added an important religious justification to the ideological arguments advanced by those seeking to retain the West Bank and Gaza. Deriving their normative orientation from the stream of religious Zionism that believes the Messianic era has begun, and that the modern Zionist movement is thus the instrument God has chosen to fulfill His plan for the Jews and for mankind, Gush Emunim supporters assert that Israel's reconquest of the West Bank and Gaza shows the age of redemption to be unfolding and claim that retention of these territories will accordingly hasten the coming of the Messiah. In the meantime, they add on a more mundane level, settlement activity in the territories will deepen the spiritual character of Israel, and, in any event, Jewish law prohibits the surrender of any part of the Land of Israel.

Although not all religious Jews hold these views, such thinking had by 1977 become dominant within the National Religious Party, the oldest and largest religious party in Israel.[95] The NRP, a perennial coalition partner in Labor-led governments, had initially attached no religious significance to the West Bank and Gaza and had willingly given Labor a free hand in the occupied territories, seeking only in return for its support on issues of domestic and foreign policy the passage of legislation mandating public respect for Jewish law, such as the prohibition of public transportation on the sabbath and the observance of Jewish dietary codes in state-run kitchens. In the mid-1970s, however, a new generation of leaders came to prominence within the NRP. Known as the "young guard," these men shared the spiritual assumptions of Gush Emunim and sought to use their party as a vehicle for advancing its cause. After the 1977 election, the NRP, which had won twelve Knesset seats, joined Likud in forming a government coalition and used its influence inside the cabinet and the parliament, just as Gush Emunim continued to exert pressure from without, to push for an intensification of Israel's settlement drive in the West Bank and Gaza.

The Egyptian Peace Initiative

Like Israel's earthquake election, the other dramatic event of 1977, Anwar Sadat's November visit to Jerusalem, set in motion a series of developments which were to have far-reaching implications for the Arab-Israeli conflict, including its central Palestinian dimension. Sadat's policies during the period following the 1973 War had reflected a desire for an accommodation with Israel. Indeed, the Egyptian president was strongly criticized by Syrian, Palestinian, and other Arab leaders for agreeing to a second disengagement of forces in Sinai. Fearing that he would attempt to recover the Sinai Peninsula by seeking a separate accord with the Jewish state, these Arab leaders accused Sadat of undermining Arab unity and thereby playing into Israeli hands. Only by working together, they maintained, could all of the territory lost in 1967 be regained; and indeed, as confirmed by some Israeli analysts, Jerusalem was in fact attempting to give itself a freer hand in the eventual disposition of the occupied territories by dividing the Arabs, and also by weakening their bargaining position through the elimination of a military threat from Egypt.[96] Sadat replied to his critics by insisting that he was not seeking a separate peace with Israel, even though he also gave increasingly clear indications that he was indeed interested in a settlement and believed that this could be achieved only by political means.

During the course of 1977, key events leading up to Sadat's visit to Jerusalem included domestic unrest in Egypt, a meeting in Washington between Sadat and the new United States president, Jimmy Carter, and a secret meeting between Israeli and Egyptian representatives arranged by King Hassan II of Morocco. Sadat's inclination to seek a peace settlement was given a strong boost by the outbreak of rioting in Egypt in January 1977.[97] In response to mounting economic pressure, Cairo announced that government subsidies on foodstuffs and other basic commodities would be reduced, in effect raising prices, and this in turn touched off widespread protest demonstrations, which in many locations turned violent. There were disturbances in numerous cities along the Nile, but the rioting was most intense in Cairo and Alexandria, where there were attacks upon police stations, shops, hotels, and the homes of government officials. Order was restored only after the army was called out, this being the first time it had been used for such purposes since the Egyptian revolution of 1952. By official estimates there were seventy-seven people killed in Cairo alone.

These events left both the country and the government badly shaken and gave Sadat a pressing additional reason to look to Egypt's domestic needs, even if, vis-à-vis Israel, they were not completely identical to those of other Arab actors. Specifically, Sadat reasoned that movement toward peace would make it possible to reduce military expenditures and increase development-related spending, to obtain expanded assistance from the United States and also to attract more private foreign investment, and to complete the rebuilding of Ismailia and other Egyptian cities along the Suez Canal. In the latter connection, hundreds of thousands of residents had fled these cities in the aftermath of the June War and during the artillery battles that developed into the War of Attrition, contributing greatly to overcrowding and unemployment in Cairo; and many still had not returned even though Israeli forces were no longer along the canal. With these objectives flowing from an agreement with Israel clearly in mind, Sadat told workers and trade union leaders in his May Day address of 1977, "Wait until 1980 . . . to relieve the workers of the pressures of life and living conditions."[98]

In April 1977, Sadat traveled to Washington for a meeting with Jimmy Carter, the new American president, who had indicated that working for peace in the Middle East would be one of his administration's principal foreign-policy objectives.[99] Sadat was the first Arab leader Carter had met and the two men got along well. The Egyptian president urged the United States to work on behalf of a Middle East settlement and hinted that his country might be flexible on the issue of normalizing relations with Israel, although he also stated that decisions about normalization were a matter of national sovereignty and not a subject for international negotiation. Carter, for his part, encouraged Sadat by suggesting that in ten years Washington's economic, military, and political ties to Egypt might be as strong as those between the United States and Israel. Finally, the two men turned their attention to Yasir Arafat and the PLO, with Carter raising the possibility of a meeting with the Palestinian leader and Sadat speaking in generalities but giving no indication that he would accept an agreement with Israel that did not include a solution to the Palestinian problem. Following the meeting, American officials concluded that Sadat was indeed ready for peace talks, which they hoped would convene in Geneva, and in October Carter sent the Egyptian president a handwritten note stating that he was "deeply impressed and grateful" for Sadat's promise of help "in our common search for peace in the Middle East."[100]

Early in September, Moshe Dayan, now foreign minister in the recently formed Begin government, flew to Morocco to ask King Hassan II for help in establishing direct and high-level contact with Egypt. In sending Dayan to Morocco, Israel was responding to the diplomatic signals coming from Cairo and

Washington. It was also seeking to deal with Egypt directly in order to reduce the possibility of pressure from the United States, which Jerusalem feared would push for conformity to an American-led mediation effort directed toward a comprehensive peace agreement and, possibly, involving a role for the PLO. In pursuit of help in establishing direct contacts with Egypt, Begin himself had visited Rumania in August; but it was Dayan's trip to Morocco in September that produced the desired response.

Dayan's visit took place in strict secrecy, with the veteran Israeli politician disguising himself with a wig, sunglasses, and false mustache while traveling, and then following a complicated itinerary before being received by the Moroccan monarch in a six-hundred-year-old palace in Marrakesh. Even the United States was unaware of Dayan's purpose and destination, knowing only that he had dropped out of sight while in Europe and had returned to Israel instead of proceeding to the United States as planned. Hassan received Dayan with impressive hospitality and agreed to investigate the possibility of a meeting between Israeli and Egyptian leaders, and just eleven days later Dayan was invited to return to Morocco for talks with General Hassan Tohami, deputy prime minister of Egypt and Anwar Sadat's personal emissary.[101] Although specific arrangements for the Egyptian president's visit to Jerusalem two months later were not made by Dayan and Tohami, both men left Morocco convinced that a deal between their countries was possible.

Sadat was now eager to receive an invitation from the Israelis, and for the next few weeks the U.S. ambassadors in Egypt and Tel Aviv transmitted messages between the Israeli prime minister and the Egyptian president until arrangements were made for the latter to come to Jerusalem on November 19 and address the Knesset the next day, thus setting the stage for the first visit by an Arab head of state in Israel's almost three decades of statehood. Sadat showed himself to be both open and politically astute upon his arrival in Jerusalem, and his speech to the Israeli parliament, though containing no surprises, clearly articulated his desire for peace. Indeed, since Sadat was president of the largest and most powerful Arab country, which only four years earlier had launched a surprise attack and inflicted heavy casualties on the Jewish state, his presence before the most important political body in Israel was a symbolic gesture that spoke for itself, making the text of the Egyptian leader's address almost irrelevant.

Sadat's carefully constructed speech to the Knesset presented his formula for a fair and lasting settlement.[102] He declared that he did not seek a separate peace between Israel and Egypt and emphasized that a settlement required Israel's complete withdrawal from Arab territories captured in 1967. "There is no peace that could be built on the occupation of the land of others," he insisted. But such a withdrawal would bring acceptance by the Arab world, Sadat asserted, and he called it "logical" that Israel should live amongst its Arab neighbors in security and safety. Acknowledging, too, Israel's preoccupation with security, Sadat added to this passage a promise to accept any international guarantees requested by Jerusalem.

Although he decided at the last moment to delete a planned reference to the PLO, at U.S. urging, Sadat also dealt at length with the rights of the Palestinians in his address to the Knesset. "Even if peace between Israel and all the confrontation states were achieved," he stated in one early passage, "in the absence of a just solution of the Palestinian problem, never will there be that durable and just peace upon which the entire world insists." Nor could anyone deny that the Palestinian problem remains the crux of the Arab-Israeli conflict, he stated elsewhere, and here he went on to condemn Israel's unwillingness to recognize the existence of the Palestinian people: "The Palestinian people and their legitimate rights are no longer denied today by anybody; that is nobody who has the ability of judgment can deny or ignore it. It is an acknowledged fact, perceived in the world community, both in the East and in the West." And in still another passage, Sadat told the Israeli assembly that "it is no use to refrain from recognizing the Palestinian people and their right to statehood as their right of return."

Sadat's visit to Jerusalem set off a new round of diplomatic activity, in which the United States as well as Egypt and Israel was heavily involved, and which eventually led to a historic summit meeting at Camp David in September 1978. On Christmas Day 1977, Begin responded to Sadat's gesture and made his first visit to Egypt, traveling to Ismailia with a small team of advisors to meet the Egyptian president. Little of substance was agreed to, however, and Sadat expressed disappointment that Israel had not responded more fully and positively to his offer of peace. Strains between the two men were intensified, moreover, when Israel began work early in January on four new settlements in the occupied Sinai Peninsula, an action that also drew strong protests from the United States. About the same time, Jimmy Carter undertook a trip throughout the Middle East, and early in January, during a brief stopover in Aswan, he included in his calls for a settlement of the Arab-Israeli conflict a statement to the effect that this solution should recognize the legitimate rights of the Palestinian people and enable the Palestinians to participate in the determination of their own future. This in turn produced a protest from the Israelis.

Upon his return to Washington, Carter and his advisors decided to invite Sadat to the United States in order to coordinate their diplomatic efforts, and also to put pressure on Israel, which both men felt had offered little in response to Sadat's dramatic peace overture. Sadat accordingly spent two days at Camp David early in February, with talks between the two men revealing general agreement on both substantive and procedural matters. Six weeks later, Begin came to Washington to meet with Carter, and this session was far less cordial than had been the American president's meeting with Sadat. Carter urged Begin to be more flexible but was discouraged by the Israeli premier's response and subsequently complained that the main obstacle to an agreement between Cairo and

Jerusalem was Israel's insistence on retaining complete control of the West Bank and Gaza, not only during a transitional period but indefinitely, and even if the price of its actions was the loss of a chance for peace in the region.

Diplomatic activity remained intense during the spring and early summer of 1978, but little progress was made, and matters came to a head in late July when Sadat informed U.S. officials in Cairo that further contact with the Israelis would be impossible in view of Begin's continuing intransigence. Upon being notified of the Egyptian leader's statement, Carter decided that the only possibility of breaking the impasse and making progress toward peace lay in inviting both Begin and Sadat to a summit meeting in the United States. Carter sent his secretary of state, Cyrus Vance, to the Middle East to issue invitations for such a meeting, instructing him to keep the mission secret until both leaders had been contacted, and early in September Begin and Sadat and their respective advisors thus assembled at Camp David for the historic summit meeting.

The Camp David summit convened on September 5 and lasted until the 17th of the month, much longer than had been expected by any of the participants.[103] Moreover, the bargaining was intense and, during the first week and a half, almost completely without issue. Carter's notion that Begin and Sadat would learn to trust one another at Camp David quickly showed itself to be naive. Indeed, the two men were not even on speaking terms by the tenth day. With almost all of the participants believing that the talks had reached an impasse, the mood at this time was grim, and the pressure on Sadat seemed particularly intense, since it would have been harder for the Egyptians than for the Israelis to leave the summit without an accord.

Although agreement had been reached on a number of minor points, there were two fundamental issues on which no progress had been made. One, predictably, concerned the West Bank and Gaza. Begin had consistently rejected all draft resolutions calling for an Israeli withdrawal from these territories. The other issue, somewhat surprisingly, was Israel's refusal to abandon either the airfields that the IDF had constructed in Sinai or the Jewish settlements that had been established in the northern part of the peninsula, declaring in effect that it was unwilling to withdraw from Sinai completely. On the 15th, claiming to have concluded that Israel did not want peace enough to make meaningful concessions, a dispirited Sadat informed the Americans that he was breaking off the talks and preparing to leave. Only a strong appeal from Carter, involving both assurances of U.S. support and a warning that collapse of the summit would end the relationship between Egypt and the United States, persuaded the Egyptian president to remain.[104]

Renewed efforts finally produced a breakthrough with respect to the issue of Sinai. The Israelis agreed to relinquish their military bases upon receiving assurances that the U.S. would help to pay for new ones, to be constructed in Israel's Negev Desert. This would require about $3 billion in concessional loans from the United States. The Israelis then gave in on the matter of the Sinai settlements, with Begin agreeing to accept this as the price of peace with Egypt after receiving a phone call endorsing the idea from Ariel Sharon, the hard-line minister of agriculture who was one of the most forceful personalities in the cabinet.

With these matters resolved, the way was cleared for a formal agreement calling for the return of Sinai to Egypt and, in exchange, the normalization of relations between Jerusalem and Cairo. Specifically, as embodied in the "Framework for the Conclusion of a Peace Treaty between Egypt and Israel," which was one of two documents to result from the Camp David summit, the two countries agreed to negotiate in good faith with the goal of concluding a peace treaty within three months; agreed that the withdrawal of Israeli armed forces and the reestablishment of Egyptian sovereignty over the whole of Sinai should be completed within three years of the signing of the peace treaty; approved the right of free passage by Israeli ships through the Gulf of Aqaba and the Suez Canal; concurred on arrangements governing the use of airfields and the stationing of armed forces in Sinai, so as to ensure the security of the parties involved; and agreed that the signing of a peace treaty and the first stage of Israel's withdrawal from Sinai should be followed by the establishment of full and normal relations between the two countries.

The last days of the summit also produced agreement on a document dealing with the rights of the Palestinians and the future of the West Bank and Gaza. Entitled "A Framework for Peace in the Middle East," this document, along with the one concerning bilateral Egyptian-Israeli issues, was signed at a public ceremony at Camp David on September 17. Begin and Sadat signed the two documents, with Carter adding his signature as witness, and in his opening remarks the American president declared, "We are privileged to witness tonight a significant achievement in the cause of peace, an achievement none of us thought possible a year ago, or even a month ago, an achievement that reflects the courage and wisdom of these two leaders." Making only brief reference to the tensions and difficulties that had characterized the summit, or to the important ambiguities and differences of opinion that remained, Carter gave the impression that a new era of peace had begun in the Middle East. "Together with accompanying letters, which we will make public tomorrow," he stated, "these two Camp David agreements provide the basis for progress and peace throughout the Middle East." And again, the president concluded, "I hope that the foresight and the wisdom that have made this session a success will guide these leaders and the leaders of all nations as they continue the progress toward peace." Addressing a joint session of Congress the next day, Carter stressed the same theme. He stated that President Sadat and Prime Minister Begin have "exceeded our fondest expectations and have signed two agreements that hold out the possibility of resolving issues that history had taught us could not be resolved."[105]

Bilateral relations between Egypt and Israel evolved satisfactorily during the months following Camp David, indicating that personal animosity between Begin and Sadat would not be a stumbling block and suggesting that Carter's remarks about a new era of peace were justified in at least some important respects. Although negotiations for the Egypt-Israel peace treaty were difficult and protracted, exceeding by a considerable margin the three months envisioned at Camp David, a formal peace between the two countries was nonetheless signed on March 26, 1979.

A major sticking point during the negotiations had been Egypt's initial insistence that the normalization of relations envisioned in the peace treaty be tied to progress in implementing the second Camp David framework, that concerned with the West Bank and Gaza. Israel had adamantly refused such a linkage, however, and Egypt eventually relented, with Article VI of the treaty accordingly stipulating that its provisions were to be implemented independent of any external instrument. As a concession to the Egyptians, and to allay fears that the Israelis had bargained in bad faith at Camp David, agreed-upon minutes appended to the peace treaty specified that "Article VI shall not be considered in contradiction to the provisions of the Framework for Peace in the Middle East agreed at Camp David"; and in a joint letter to Jimmy Carter, also dated March 26, 1979, Begin and Sadat pledged to "proceed with the implementation of those provisions relative to the West Bank and Gaza."

Following the signing of the peace treaty, Israel completed the first stage of its withdrawal from Sinai on schedule, such that about two-thirds of the peninsula, including the economically important Alma oil fields, had been returned to Egypt by November 1979. During this period there were also important developments in the normalization of relations between the two countries. As early as the summer of 1979, for example, Egypt was visited by leaders of the Israel Broadcast Authority, the Histadrut, and the Israeli Manufacturers Association, as well as by delegations of businessmen, university professors, and others. The first group of Israeli tourists also traveled to Egypt at this time, and they were met upon their arrival by a welcome sign in Hebrew. Travel in the other direction brought Egyptian businessmen, industrialists, and senior government officials to Israel; and, in addition, the two countries coordinated tourist exchanges, made plans to establish a joint agricultural development company, agreed in principle to reopen the Lod-Cairo rail link, and initiated talks designed to produce cooperative ventures in many other areas. The culmination of these developments came early in 1980, when Israel and Egypt exchanged ambassadors.

These were stunning accomplishments, and their importance, indeed their revolutionary character, suggested that the promise of Camp David was being fulfilled. To be sure, there were also some problems and misunderstandings in relations between Israel and Egypt. Jerusalem complained, for example, that Cairo often failed to deliver visas to Israelis seeking to visit Egypt. Israel also asserted that Egyptian ambassadors, except in Washington, frequently remained hostile to diplomats from the Jewish state. Egypt, for its part, complained of Israeli obstinacy in reaching agreement on the military forces to be stationed in Sinai, claiming to be particularly perplexed by Jerusalem's opposition to a United Nations presence. Overall, each country sometimes accused the other of adhering to the letter rather than the spirit of the Camp David accords and the peace treaty. Specifically, Israel was charged with being too difficult on territorial issues, while Egypt was accused of dragging its feet on the full normalization of relations. On balance, however, these were decidedly minor and short-term problems. Having made far more progress toward peace than virtually anyone had thought possible barely two years earlier, the initiative that began with Sadat's trip to Jerusalem in 1977 had yielded impressive results and brought what was by far the most dramatic breakthrough in the entire history of the Arab-Israeli conflict.

Unfortunately, although not unexpectedly, the story of the Camp David framework dealing with the West Bank and Gaza is unlike that of the framework dealing with peace between Egypt and Israel. Indeed, the two documents themselves are radically different. Whereas the latter is precise, presenting a detailed formula for resolving bilateral issues and arriving at a peace treaty between the two countries, the former is no more than a general blueprint, characterized by broad guidelines, deferred decisions, and language amenable to differing interpretations. Moreover, whereas Israel had made the most important concessions so far as Sinai was concerned, enabling Sadat and the Egyptians to recover the peninsula in exchange for peace, Begin had bargained effectively and obtained an agreement concerning the West Bank and Gaza that left the future of these territories undecided. There was no mention of East Jerusalem whatsoever; and, though they agreed on the procedures that would govern negotiations about the final status of the territories, the Israelis made no firm commitment about an eventual withdrawal either from the rest of the West Bank or from Gaza.

The provisions of the Camp David document dealing with the West Bank and Gaza are not unreasonable in and of themselves. Although the Egyptians and Americans had obtained few concrete concessions from the Israelis, leading to the charge that Sadat had abandoned the Palestinian cause in order to recover the Sinai Peninsula, the Egyptians could claim with some credibility that negotiations about the West Bank and Gaza required Palestinian and Jordanian participation, and that Egypt could therefore do no more at Camp David than secure agreement on a satisfactory framework for the conduct of such negotiations. Furthermore, the Framework for Peace in the Middle East endorsed at Camp David was not one-sided; nor did it by any means preclude an outcome that would be unacceptable from an Arab and Palestinian point of view. It was agreed that negotiations about the final status of the West Bank and Gaza would be based on the provisions and principles of UN Security Council Resolution 242, and also that the solution resulting from these talks must recognize the legitimate rights of the Palestinian people and their just requirements.

More particularly, the Framework for Peace in the Middle East signed at Camp David envisioned a transitional period, not to exceed five years, during which the final status of the West Bank and Gaza would be determined. The inhabitants of these territories were to have "full autonomy" during this period, with the Israeli Military Government and its Civilian Administration being withdrawn as soon as "a Self-Governing Authority (Administrative Council)" could be freely elected by the inhabitants of the West Bank and Gaza. Jordan would be invited to join with Egypt and Israel in negotiating the modalities for establishing the Self-Governing Authority, it being specified that the delegations of Jordan and Egypt could include Palestinians from the West Bank and Gaza or other Palestinians as mutually agreed. These negotiations would also be charged with defining the powers and responsibilities of the Self-Governing Authority, which were to give due consideration both to the principle of self-government by the inhabitants of the territories and to the legitimate security concerns of the parties involved.

The transitional period would begin as soon as the Self-Governing Authority was established and inaugurated; and as soon as possible thereafter, but not later than three years, negotiations would be conducted among Israel, Egypt, Jordan, and the elected representatives of the inhabitants of the West Bank and Gaza in order to determine the final status of these territories and their relationship to their neighbors. These negotiations, again, would be based on the principles of UN 242 and would recognize both the legitimate rights of the Palestinians and the security requirements of the various parties. In addition, the agreement resulting from these negotiations would be submitted to a vote by the elected representatives of the inhabitants of the West Bank and Gaza, which, along with the other provisions, would enable the Palestinians to participate in the determination of their own future. Finally, although its principal focus was the West Bank and Gaza, the second Camp David framework also provided for negotiations leading to a peace treaty between Israel and Jordan.

But while the Camp David framework dealing with the West Bank and Gaza did not preclude an Israeli withdrawal or the granting of political rights to the Palestinian people, these possibilities were set forth in language that was deliberately vague and which, for the most part, did no more than identify these issues as subjects for future negotiation. Egypt could claim, as it did, that there was a spirit which transcended the specifics of the Camp David accord, an intent that was made clear by references to UN 242 and to Palestinian rights. Cairo also argued that there was no ambiguity about what the Arab world expected from the Jewish state in return for the peace; and the Egyptians added that the Americans tended to see things the same way, to believe that surrender of the West Bank and Gaza was a fair price to pay for Arab recognition of Israel. Thus, according to Egypt, the Camp David framework dealing with the West Bank and Gaza was designed to bring an end to Israel's occupation of these territories and to see them become the geographic focus for the exercise of Palestinian self-determination, and in so doing to create the conditions for a final resolution of the Arab-Israeli conflict.

The Begin government, on the other hand, in a manner reminiscent of the debates following the adoption of UN 242 in 1967, rebutted these Egyptian interpretations by insisting that the Camp David accord said only what it said, that it contained no additional, implicit meaning. The Israelis pointed out that their representatives at Camp David had promised only to participate in negotiations about the future of the West Bank and Gaza; they had not committed their country to any particular outcome of the so-called autonomy talks. Moreover, Israeli spokesmen added, the Egyptians knew very well what kind of a document they had signed at Camp David and could not now pretend otherwise. Having failed to obtain the provisions for which they pressed, Sadat and his advisors had contented themselves with Israeli concessions in Sinai and had decided that the bargain being offered to them, whatever its limitations, was preferable to no agreement at all. Thus, while Jerusalem would, of course, honor its pledge to negotiate, Begin and his associates made clear that in these talks Israel would naturally and properly hold to positions that were consistent with the goals of the Jewish state in general and the Likud-led government in particular, meaning, in other words, that Jerusalem had no intention of surrendering control over any part of the Land of Israel.

An early indication that it would be difficult, perhaps impossible, to bridge this gap involved a disagreement between the Israelis and the Americans about a moratorium on the construction of new Jewish settlements in the West Bank and Gaza Strip. Carter and Begin agreed in a private meeting at Camp David that "after the signing of the framework and during the negotiations, no new Israeli settlements will be established in this area. The issue of future Israeli settlements will be decided and agreed among the negotiating parties." But the two men had fundamental differences about the meaning of this statement, with Carter insisting that the moratorium was to be linked to negotiations over the West Bank and Gaza, and hence of open-ended duration, and Begin claiming it applied only to the three-month period during which Israel and Egypt were to negotiate a peace treaty.

Despite some differences of opinion among the other Israelis present at the meeting, Begin stuck to his position, and the Israeli government subsequently waited only three months before resuming the construction of new settlements, continuing a drive to deepen Israel's presence in the West Bank and Gaza that had been initiated when Likud came to power in 1977. It is possible that Begin's interpretation of what took place at the meeting with Carter is correct. Quandt suggests, for example, that the Israeli prime minister may have encouraged the president to believe an agreement was near without actually promising that the moratorium would be coterminous with negotiations about the West Bank and Gaza.[106] In any event, regardless of whether one places emphasis on the fact that

Begin made no firm commitment or on the fact that he apparently encouraged a misunderstanding on the part of the American president, the episode provides a clear indication both of Israel's determination to retain the West Bank and Gaza and of the difficulty this posed for the negotiations envisioned in the Camp David agreement pertaining to these territories.

Jordan and the PLO followed the Camp David summit with both interest and skepticism, their growing concern reinforced by Israel's attitude toward the question of settlements in the West Bank and Gaza and, more generally, by the fact that Jerusalem had given no indication it was prepared to withdraw from these territories in return for peace. The Jordanians and the Palestinians also worried that any possibility of pressing Israel to soften its position would be significantly diminished by what appeared to be a separate peace between Jerusalem and Cairo, adding that this would also give Israel a freer hand to carry out aggressive actions on other fronts.[107] Both King Hussein and Yasir Arafat nonetheless approached the Americans for clarification, seeking to learn whether there might be more to the Camp David accords than had been revealed. Arafat made inquiries through intelligence channels, and in October Hussein gave the Americans a list of fourteen questions in order to request more information. For example, the Jordanians asked whether East Jerusalem was included in the definition of the West Bank for purposes of the Camp David framework; they sought a clarification of the status of Israeli settlements in the occupied territories during and after the transitional period; and they asked what would be the U.S. position in the event of conflicting interpretations of UN 242.[108]

The U.S. response to Hussein's questions—in essence, that none of these matters had been settled at Camp David, and that all should be the subject of future negotiations—failed to resolve the doubts of the Jordanians, the Palestinians, and other Arabs and resulted in a Jordanian decision not to take part in the talks regarding transitional arrangements for the West Bank and Gaza, popularly known as the autonomy negotiations.[109] This decision reinforced the position of those in Israel who were determined to retain the West Bank and Gaza, enabling them to assert that Israel could hardly be expected to make concessions when the Arab government most directly concerned with the West Bank was not even willing to come to the bargaining table. From the Jordanian point of view, however, this logic was self-serving and contradictory, involving a deliberate confusion of cause and effect. Although the Egyptians had come to the negotiating table, there had been no change whatsoever in Israel's firm insistence that it would not withdraw from any part of the West Bank and Gaza. Indeed, Jerusalem would not even suspend its drive to create facts and thereby tie the hands of future Israeli governments.

Most Palestinians articulated the same sentiments, arguing that Israeli intransigence robbed the Camp David accords of any possible value as a formula for peace. For example, Amin al-Khatib, head of the East Jerusalem–based Palestinian Association of Charitable Societies, stated, "I do not believe that any plan for a solution to the Palestinian problem which does not include the establishment of an independent Palestinian state in the territory of Palestine will be successful, no matter how skillfully its sponsors choose names for it."[110] And the problem with the Camp David proposals, as explained more specifically by a representative of the PLO, is that "Israel's major and publicly stated goal is to use this [Camp David] autonomy plan as a means of preventing the establishment of a Palestinian state and extending its domination of the occupied territories."[111]

Despite Jordan's decision not to participate and continuing Palestinian criticism, Israel and Egypt pressed ahead with negotiations aimed at determining and implementing transitional arrangements for the West Bank and Gaza. Two working committees were formed, one charged with examining the modalities by which a Self-Governing Authority would be elected and the other with responsibility for producing agreement on its powers and duties. Neither committee made much progress, however. In the committee on elections, Egyptians argued that all Palestinians were entitled to vote, asserting that this included Palestinians outside the West Bank and Gaza, and being particularly adamant that voting rights be granted to those living in East Jerusalem. They argued that East Jerusalem's Arab population could not be considered anything other than an integral part of the population of the West Bank. Israel, by contrast, opposed participation by external Palestinians and contended that residents of East Jerusalem were not part of the West Bank's Palestinian population, since their place of residence was Israel and they already participated in Israeli municipal elections. After approximately eighteen months of on-again off-again negotiations, this disagreement remained unresolved and the committee on elections was still unable to complete the task assigned to it.

The gap in the committee on powers and responsibilities was even wider, reflecting the fundamental nature of the disagreement between Egypt and Israel about the future of the territories. Egypt pointed out that Israel had agreed to "full autonomy" at Camp David, and its negotiators accordingly maintained that the Self-Governing Authority should have broad powers, such as the authority to levy taxes, regulate land use, control water rights, and so forth. They also argued for the establishment of a Palestinian legislature. If substantial executive and legislative powers were not granted, they contended, the Palestinians would possess no more autonomy during the transitional period than they did under Israeli occupation. Their activities, some added with cynicism, would be limited to garbage collection and similar activities. These sentiments were echoed by Palestinian leaders in the occupied territories, even though they were not taking part in the autonomy negotiations. For example, Ibrahim Tawil, the mayor of al-Bireh, stated that "what is called 'autonomy' [by the Israelis] is nothing more than a creation of the occupation. Agreeing to this autonomy means conferring legitimacy on the occupation."[112]

Israel nonetheless remained resolutely opposed to a more powerful Self-Governing Authority. Its representatives insisted that the Camp David agreement called only for creation of an administrative council, thus precluding the granting of legislative powers, and Jerusalem opposed giving even executive authority in many of the areas that Egypt believed should be regulated by the Palestinians. Making no secret of their determination to remain in the West Bank and Gaza, Israeli representatives contended that broad powers would enable the Palestinians to act in ways that were detrimental to Jewish interests, and that the duties of the Self-Governing Authority must accordingly be limited. As a result, as with the committee on elections, virtually no progress had been made after almost eighteen months of negotiations.

The West Bank and Gaza after Camp David

As the impasse in the autonomy talks clearly showed, the Begin government had no intention of allowing the Camp David accords to lead to an Israeli withdrawal from the West Bank and Gaza. Begin himself had made this explicit almost as soon as he returned from the summit. Responding to the criticism of some Israelis that he had in fact given away too much at Camp David, the prime minister issued an eighteen-point interpretation of the accords that reaffirmed his traditional opposition to territorial compromise and contained a promise to oppose any political boundary between the Mediterranean Sea and the Jordan River that would divide the Land of Israel. Similar sentiments were expressed by Yosef Burg, minister of the interior and head of the Israeli delegation to the autonomy negotiations. As Burg, who was also head of the National Religious Party, told an Israel Bonds conference in August 1979, "There is a danger of a Palestinian state growing out of autonomy, and it is my task as chair of the Israeli delegation to the autonomy talks to prevent that possibility absolutely." Such statements were not enough to reassure all of the hard-line elements in Israel. In 1979, for example, several members of Likud resigned and established a new political party, Tehiya, charging that the government was making too many concessions on Palestinian issues. In general, however, the government's firm statements and its consistent refusal to accept any compromise in the autonomy negotiations convinced most observers, both inside Israel and elsewhere, that the Camp David accords, for better or worse, would not be associated with a change in Israel's policy toward the West Bank and Gaza.

There was also much more tangible evidence of the Begin government's attitude. Though the protracted stalemate in the autonomy negotiations might have suggested a lack of movement, a period of drift during which nothing was being resolved, Israeli authorities were in fact taking deliberate action to transform the political, economic, and demographic character of the occupied territories, especially the West Bank. Under the leadership of Likud and its political allies, Jerusalem was busily creating a new set of realities, placing physical as well as political obstacles in the path of those who argued that the Jewish state should explore seriously the opportunity for a comprehensive peace that Camp David appeared to offer.

As discussed, the policies of the Begin government were opposed by many Israelis. Although some who advocated territorial compromise in the West Bank and Gaza expressed doubt that the Arab world was truly ready for an accommodation with the Jewish state, these Israelis nonetheless argued that Camp David had created an opportunity to test Arab intentions and stated that Israel had nothing to lose, and potentially much to gain, by exploring this opportunity. Many were optimistic that, with patience, a solution involving both justice for the Palestinians and Arab recognition of Israel could be obtained. Alternatively, in the event that negotiations were unsuccessful because Arab intransigence showed that such a solution was not attainable after all, Israel would gain in the court of world opinion and be relieved of the pressure to make concessions beyond those that it had already accepted in Sinai. Analyses of this sort were also put forward in U.S. diplomatic circles, as well as by Israelis affiliated with the Labor Alignment and parties further to the left.

Likud had no interest in testing Arab intentions, however, or, above all, in discovering that land in the West Bank and Gaza might indeed be traded for peace. Thus, dedicated to movement in a very different direction, the Begin government had set out almost immediately to increase substantially the number of Israeli settlers and settlements in the West Bank, and to a lesser extent in the other occupied territories, too. There had been settlement activity under previous Labor governments, of course, primarily in the Jordan Valley but on a limited scale in other areas as well, most notably in the Etzion Bloc south of Jerusalem. By the time Likud came to power in 1977, the West Bank, excluding East Jerusalem, contained about 4,000 Jews living in thirty-four communities, four of which were in areas that, under the Allon Plan, the Alignment had indicated a willingness to relinquish.[113] By the end of 1977, however, there were more than 5,000 Jewish settlers in the West Bank, and the numbers rose to 7,500, 10,000, and 12,500 respectively during the following three years, with the actual number of settlements more than doubling by the end of 1980.[114] The numbers increased for the other occupied territories as well. By late 1980, there were twenty-six Jewish settlements on the Golan Heights, with 6,500 people; thirteen in the Rafah salient in northern Sinai, with approximately 6,000 settlers (scheduled for removal under the treaty with Egypt); and 700 Israelis in another three settlements in the Gaza Strip.

In the West Bank, the Begin government expanded the geographic locus as well as the extent of its settlement activities. Whereas Labor had deliberately discouraged the construction of Jewish communities in the central hilly areas where most Palestinians live, Likud made the heavily populated highlands the principal focus of its colonization efforts. Almost all of the new settlements constructed following Likud's ascent to power were in these areas, causing the number of Israelis living in this part of the West Bank to increase fivefold in a little more than three years.[115] The differing locations of the settlements established under Labor and Likud are shown in Map 8.3.

In addition, Israel pursued its drive to lay a foundation for permanent retention of the West Bank and Gaza by applying Israeli law to Jews residing in these areas. In 1979, all settlements were incorporated into five regional councils, whose jurisdiction was based on Israeli municipal and district law; in 1980, the Knesset underscored the annexation of East Jerusalem by voting that unified Jerusalem was the capital of Israel; and in 1981, Israeli municipal and rabbinical courts opened in the town of Qiryat Arba, at the time the largest Jewish community in the West Bank. The intent of these actions, and their net effect within the Israeli context, was to undermine the territories' legal status as occupied land.

Israel deepened its presence in the West Bank and Gaza in still other ways, too, some of which were even more important than its immediate settlement activities. It took control of large amounts of land, for example, ostensibly for military purposes but in some cases with projected settlement activity clearly in mind. Although there are conflicting estimates regarding the proportion of West Bank land to which Israel acquired legal title, figures run as high as 65 percent and are rarely below a quarter of the area's total land surface. Israel also took over approximately one-third of the land in the Gaza Strip. Moreover, according to one objective observer, since most restraints and restrictions on land acquisition were removed after 1979, the Israeli government in effect had the authority to seize virtually any area it considered desirable for settlement purposes.[116]

Israel also took control of water resources. It is estimated that by 1980 Israeli agricultural and other settlements were using as much as 20 percent of the water consumed in the West Bank, with the added effect that in some areas the diversion of water to Jewish settlements was causing the wells used by local Palestinians to dry up or drop much lower.[117] Further, Palestinians charged that the diversion of water was sometimes carried out not only to meet the needs of Israeli settlements but also in a deliberate attempt to make farming difficult for the Arabs and thereby encourage the Palestinians to sell their land.

In yet other areas, including transportation, communication, and economic activity, the Begin government took steps to link the West Bank and Gaza ever more closely with Israel and to reduce day-to-day awareness of the country's pre-1967 boundary, which is routinely called the "Green Line." In carrying out these policies, it was to a considerable extent possible to build on a foundation laid by previous Labor governments. For example, the integration of the West Bank and Gaza labor force into the Israeli economy had reached substantial proportions by the mid-1970s. More generally, however, in contrast to previous governments,

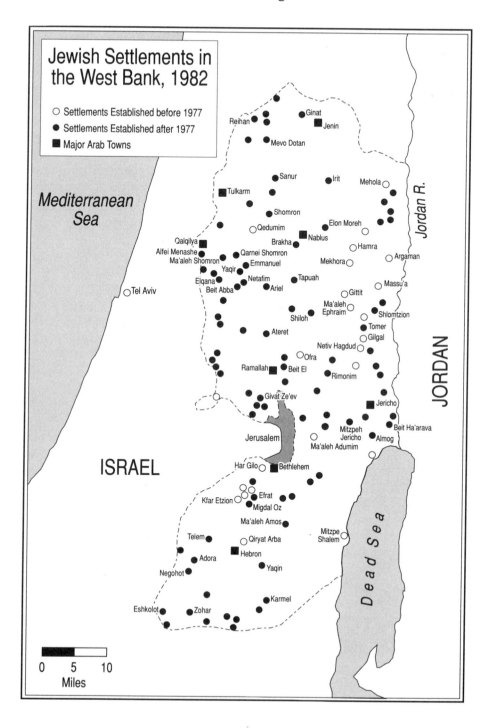

Jewish Settlements in the West Bank, 1982

○ Settlements Established before 1977
● Settlements Established after 1977
■ Major Arab Towns

Mediterranean Sea

Jordan R.

JORDAN

ISRAEL

Dead Sea

Reihan
Ginat
Jenin
Mevo Dotan
Sanur
Irit
Mehola
Tulkarm
Shomron
Elon Moreh
Qedumim
Qalqilya
Brakha
Nablus
Hamra
Alfei Menashe
Qarnei Shomron
Ma'aleh Shomron
Emmanuel
Mekhora
Argaman
Yaqir
Elqana
Netafim
Tapuah
Massu'a
Beit Abba
Ariel
Gittit
Tel Aviv
Ma'aleh Ephraim
Shlomtzion
Shiloh
Tomer
Ateret
Gilgal
Netiv Hagdud
Ofra
Ramallah
Beit El
Rimonim
Givat Ze'ev
Jericho
Jerusalem
Mitzpeh Jericho
Beit Ha'arava
Ma'aleh Adumim
Almog
Har Gilo
Bethlehem
Kfar Etzion
Efrat
Migdal Oz
Ma'aleh Amos
Mitzpe Shalem
Telem
Qiryat Arba
Adora
Hebron
Negohot
Yaqin
Karmel
Eshkolot
Zohar

0   5   10
Miles

Likud's explicit goal was to erase the Green Line, and its activities aimed at creating facts were vigorously pursued with this objective in mind. In any event, as a result of developments that occurred both before and after Likud came to power, the economic and administrative ties between Israel and the occupied territories, especially the West Bank, were strong and getting stronger by the end of the decade. Israel was the West Bank's most important trading partner, for example, being the source of 88 percent of its imports and constituting the market for 54 percent of its exports in 1980.

The Israeli drive into the West Bank and Gaza was a coordinated affair, with a leading role inside the government being played by Ariel Sharon, at the time minister of agriculture. Sharon, a staunch nationalist and a man whose belief in action exceeded his respect for conformity to rules and regulations or to established hierarchies of command, had administrative responsibility for much of the government's settlement activity. Critical, too, was the contribution made by the Israeli Military Government in the West Bank, which acquired large amounts of land for supposedly military purposes, and in many instances relinquished portions of it to the Agriculture Ministry for the construction or expansion of civilian Jewish settlements. As summarized by Peretz, under Sharon and then Chief of Staff Rafael Eitan, "The Military Government played an active role in the wholesale transfer of West Bank land from Arab to Israeli control. Military orders closing areas for security purposes were used to reserve land for current and future settlement. Military tribunals enforced strict interpretations . . . as a means to circumvent the [Israeli] Supreme Court's [1979] ruling against expropriation of private lands for settlement rather than security purposes."[118] Still other important contributions to Israel's settlement drive were made by international Zionist agencies. For example, the Jewish National Fund undertook to raise money for Jewish land purchases in the West Bank and other occupied territories.

The work of Matityahu Drobles of the Jewish Agency and the World Zionist Organization should also be noted in this context. In 1978, Drobles was appointed head of both the Jewish Agency's Land Settlement Department and the Rural Settlement Department of the WZO; and in October of that year he published *The Master Plan for the Development of Settlement in Judea and Samaria*, which offered a blueprint for Israel's settlement activity in the West Bank during the five-year period between January 1979 and December 1983.[119]

The Drobles plan, accepted by the Begin government as a general guide for its own action, called for raising the number of Jewish settlers in the West Bank to 100,000 by 1983. This would be approximately 27,000 families, about 10,000 to be accommodated through the expansion of existing settlements and the remainder to be located in some fifty new settlements specifically proposed by the plan. Several different kinds of new settlements were envisioned by the Drobles document, including urban settlements, community settlements, agricultural settlements, and others, and projections relating to size, location, and economic activity were put forward in each instance as well. In addition, Drobles outlined plans for raising funds for this settlement drive through the Jewish Agency and the JNF, estimating that it would cost an average of two million Israeli pounds to put each new Israeli family in the West Bank.[120]

The Drobles plan was judged at the time of its appearance to be unrealistically ambitious, and indeed this turned out to be the case. On the other hand, it is important as an expression of the kind of thinking that became prominent in government circles following the election of 1977. Further, in more practical terms, it was also an important contributor to the more limited but nonetheless highly significant increase in the number of Israelis who settled in the West Bank after Begin and Likud came to power.

There was both domestic and foreign criticism of Likud's settlement drive, and the Begin government responded with two kinds of arguments. First, blurring the distinction between its own actions and those of previous Labor governments, it asserted that Israel's occupation of the West Bank and Gaza had produced economic development and a higher standard of living, and therefore was actually in the interest of the inhabitants of these areas. Second, it insisted that its actions were consistent with Israel's international obligations, maintaining not only that it had broken no promises made at Camp David but also that retention of the West Bank and Gaza was not precluded by UN Resolution 242, the key international document addressing the disposition of the occupied territories.

So far as the former argument is concerned, Israeli authorities claimed with some justification that the material circumstances of the inhabitants of the West Bank and Gaza had improved significantly since the beginning of the occupation. In particular, they pointed to gains in personal income and a related rise in levels of personal consumption. For example, whereas only 13 percent of the Palestinian households in the Gaza Strip had had electric or gas stoves in 1967, 71 percent possessed such appliances in 1981.[121] Ownership of refrigerators and television sets had grown in a similar fashion. Moreover, the purchase of these conveniences had been made possible not only by increased earnings but also by the availability of electricity from the Israeli national grid, which enabled the proportion of Gaza households with electricity to grow from 18 percent in 1967 to 89 percent in 1981. Israeli officials also claimed credit for other benefits, including improvements in education and health care, the expansion of vocational training, and an increase in women's participation in public life. As summarized by a pamphlet published by the Israel Information Center, "The rapid economic growth that has taken place in Judea-Samaria and the Gaza district since 1967, coupled with the substantial expansion of infrastructure and public services, has brought a significant rise in the standard of living, resulting in a greatly improved quality of life for the inhabitants of both areas. While personal consumption has risen with the steady increase of real wages, the expanded infrastructure has made modern conveniences such as running water, electricity, indoor toilets and telephones available to more and more residents."[122]

A number of more scholarly Israeli analyses also called attention to advantages for the West Bank and Gaza of economic ties to Israel, occasionally describing the relationship between the Jewish state and the occupied territories as a sort of common market.[123] Although most did not deny that there were negative aspects as well, these Israeli studies generally argued that the latter were much less important than the gains which had been registered since 1967. Among the economic advantages deemed particularly important were the promotion of free trade between Israel and the territories; the near-eradication of unemployment in the West Bank and Gaza, since their inhabitants were now able to take jobs in labor-hungry Israel; the opportunities for capital formation that accompanied a decline in unemployment and a rise in personal income; and direct access to superior Israeli technology, particularly in the field of agriculture but to some extent in industry as well. Some scholars also placed emphasis on the fact that Israeli occupation had not forced the West Bank to sever its links to Jordan, noting that this gave the territories yet an additional outlet for their products.

Within the framework of a so-called common market among the economies of Israel, the West Bank, and Gaza, the latter territories had experienced significant economic growth in the years after 1967, greater, in fact, than had Israel itself. Between 1968 and 1978, GNP increased at an average annual rate of 12.9 percent for the West Bank and 12.1 percent for the Gaza Strip, whereas for Israel it increased at a rate of 5.5 percent. Thus, according to one account, "The impact of the Israeli economy promoted the expansion of the territories' domestic economies." More precisely, a substantial rise in personal income brought "significant increases in levels of consumption, which in turn spurred domestic economic activity," and "contact with a vastly superior technological environment resulted in innovations in virtually all sectors of the economy."[124]

Palestinians and their supporters tended to see things differently, however. To begin with, they asserted that conditions in the occupied territories were often far less favorable than suggested by Israeli apologists. With respect to housing, for example, a 1980 study by two Birzeit University economists reported that most housing units were substandard, that more than half the population lived in homes where the occupation density exceeded three persons per room, and that there had been an actual decline in the total number of housing units because of the low number of new starts and the high rate of deterioration and abandonment of older structures.[125] Palestinian scholars advanced similar conclusions with respect to education. For example, a study of the West Bank during the first ten years of occupation reported that new school construction was very limited, that existing school buildings were in a poor state of repair, and that most schools lacked adequate facilities, including library materials and laboratory equipment.[126] While critics of occupation acknowledged that these inadequacies were attributable in part to Jordanian discrimination in favor of the East Bank prior to 1967, and to Egypt's neglect of Gaza during the same period,[127] they insisted that Israeli rule was also a major cause of the problems in such areas as housing and education. According to the previously mentioned study of educational conditions, for example, the circumstances of occupation had contributed directly to poor teaching conditions, a high dropout rate, deteriorating school facilities, and limited school budgets—in sum, to the generally low standard of education that prevailed in the West Bank a decade after the introduction of Israeli rule.[128]

In addition, although many Palestinians acknowledged that there had also been gains since 1967, they asserted that most could have been achieved without occupation and, more fundamentally, that dependency and distortion, not economic development, had been the principal consequence of Israeli rule. The starting point for structural analyses undertaken from this perspective was the observation that the economies of the West Bank and Gaza were based largely, and increasingly, on the export of unskilled labor.

Both Israeli and Palestinian sources, as well as others, agree that the area where economic conditions had shown the greatest improvement was in the income, and hence the level of personal consumption, of unskilled and semiskilled West Bank and Gaza workers who commuted to Israel to do manual labor.[129] In 1976, at least 65,000 workers from the territories, roughly 32 percent of the total labor force, were formally registered as working in Israel. About half were in the field of construction. By 1980, the number had increased to 72,000, or 34 percent of the total; and as many as 20,000 more, another 9.5 percent, may have been working in Israel illegally.[130] Although the conditions of employment were often difficult, involving menial or physically demanding jobs that most Israelis were unwilling to perform, work was available to those with poor educational and professional qualifications, who might otherwise have been unemployed. Further, salaries in Israel were high in comparison to those in the territories, thus permitting a measurable improvement in the standard of living of many who had traditionally been socially and economically disadvantaged. Salary differentials were particularly pronounced in Gaza, where in the mid-1970s wages paid for construction work were only about one-fifth as high as those paid in Israel.

But while some Israeli and other analysts called attention to the multiplier effect of income earned in Israel and spent in the territories, arguing that the injection of this capital stimulated economic activity and thus promoted growth and development,[131] most Palestinians reached a different conclusion. In their view, the fact that labor was the most important export of the occupied territories, and that exporting labor was in fact the principal economic activity of the West Bank and Gaza, was a clear indication of weakness rather than strength. It showed that the occupied territories were not experiencing economic development at all; they were instead moving in the direction of deepening dependency. As stated by one Palestinian scholar, who also noted that approximately 90 percent of West Bank and Gaza imports came from Israel, "Unequal exchange in terms of trade, direct exploitation of Palestinian cheap labor, and the dislocation and subordination of the Palestinian pre-capitalist economy to the needs of the advanced Israeli economy are the mechanisms by which surplus is transferred from the occupied territories to Israeli capitalism."[132] The magnitude of this transfer, according to a second Palestinian source, was reflected in a trade surplus of more than \$500 million in favor of Israel between 1967 and 1974.[133] As expressed by yet another Palestinian analyst, "The vast majority of goods are imported from Israel. The West Bank exports labor and produces only a limited range of agricultural goods, which are promptly bought up and exported by Israeli companies. The deformation and dependence of the West Bank and Gaza economies are the result of Israeli occupation."[134]

There were other bases, too, for asserting that the West Bank and Gaza had experienced little economic development since 1967. For one thing, Israeli rule had not been accompanied by construction of the infrastructure necessary for significant and sustained economic development. This was evident in the field of transportation, for example, where there had been no investment in airports, port facilities, railroads, or even modern highways serving the Arab population. Nor had there been any meaningful measure of infrastructural development in telecommunications, banking, and a number of other critical areas. A related indication of underdevelopment was the low and declining level of industrial production. Whereas the industrial sector had accounted for 9 percent of the West Bank's GDP in 1968, that figure had declined to 8.2 percent by 1975 and was only 6.5 percent in 1980.[135] As a result of this situation, local enterprises were incapable of meeting the demand for employment. Nor, with the partial exception of agriculture, were they able to produce very much of what was consumed by the inhabitants of the West Bank and Gaza.

It is this situation that forced many West Bank and Gaza Palestinians to seek work in Israel, meaning that the income gains associated with this pattern of employment were not an indication of development at all but, on the contrary, a sign of the continuing underdevelopment of the occupied territories. Indeed, according to some Palestinian analysts, the economic relationship between Israel and the occupied territories was "not dissimilar to the relationship between a metropolitan economy and its colonial satellite."[136] Given the dependent and underdeveloped state of the economy in the territories in which they lived, many Palestinians had no choice but to sell their labor to Israel in order to earn the money to buy needed goods, many of which it was then necessary to import from the Jewish state.

This conclusion is reinforced by the fact that even much of the income that was not earned in Israel was derived from the export of labor. Specifically, many Palestinians left the territories to work in other Arab countries, most notably in the oil-exporting states of the Arabian Gulf, and the remittances they sent to family members remaining in the West Bank and Gaza were equal in 1980 to roughly 40 percent of the value of wages earned by inhabitants of the territories working in Israel. Taken together, foreign wages from all sources exceeded $300 million and contributed almost one-quarter of the combined GNP of the West Bank and Gaza.[137] Thus, again, whether from remittances or from wages earned in Israel, it was this "imported income" that had financed the improved standard of living which supporters of Israel claimed, incorrectly, to be the result of economic development brought about by occupation.[138]

Concluding their response to Israeli claims about the economic advantages of occupation, Palestinians pointed out that no matter what might be the ratio of associated costs and benefits, their economic relationship with Israel was not one into which they had entered voluntarily. This point became particularly important after Likud came to power in 1977, for it no longer pertained to the effectiveness of Israel's provisional management of the territories, until such time as the Arabs sued for peace. In the late 1970s and early 1980s, it concerned the Begin government's assertion that Israel's permanent retention of the West Bank and Gaza was actually in the interest of their Palestinian inhabitants, and should accordingly be welcomed even by those who might not share Likud's belief about the supremacy of Jewish rights in the historic Land of Israel.

Palestinians denounced the fact that inhabitants of the occupied territories played no meaningful role in formulating the economic policies by which their lives were governed and were forced to accept these policies whether they wished to do so or not. Despite a rise in the standard of living of some Palestinians, and even, for that matter, if it could be shown that their complaints about dependency and underdevelopment were flawed, or exaggerated, this was an arrangement that few Palestinians would accept willingly. Like other peoples, Palestinians in the West Bank and Gaza demanded the right to govern themselves and to assume responsibility for their own collective welfare, even in the unlikely event that a decline in their standard of living would be the result.

In addition to its claims about the economic benefits brought by occupation, the Begin government defended its efforts to lay a foundation for permanent Israeli control of the West Bank and Gaza by arguing that its actions in these territories were consistent with the international accords to which Israel had agreed. This included both the Framework for Peace in the Middle East signed at Camp David and United Nations Resolution 242. So far as the Camp David accords are concerned, Likud and its supporters pointed out that the language agreed to at Camp David offered autonomy not to the West Bank and Gaza but rather to their inhabitants, which meant, these Israelis insisted, that the "full autonomy" promised to the Palestinians was personal and local rather than territorial. In other words, while Palestinian communities were to be granted a meaningful measure of self-rule, the Israeli government asserted that the framework approved at Camp David said nothing about the exercise of sovereignty over the territories in which these communities were located, leaving this question to subsequent negotiations about the final status of the West Bank and Gaza.

The Begin government also argued that Palestinian autonomy should be permanent rather than provisional and declared that this, too, was consistent with the language adopted at Camp David. Autonomy was to be granted to the Palestinians during the transitional period envisioned at Camp David. But Begin and his supporters maintained that the accords did not require autonomy to be superseded by a different political arrangement when the transitional period came to an end, and they asserted that personal and local autonomy should in fact be the permanent status of West Bank and Gaza Palestinians. Since the disposition of the territories themselves had been left open at Camp David, it having been agreed only that there should be negotiations about final status issues, the Likud-led government insisted that nothing prevented it from demanding Israeli control of the West Bank and Gaza, with provisions for Palestinian autonomy, at the conclusion of the transition period. Thus, asserting that this would indeed be Israel's position in all future negotiations, and that in working for this outcome Jerusalem was not violating the commitments it had made in good faith at Camp David and elsewhere, Israeli leaders told critics that their country's actions in the occupied territories were both logical and completely legal. These actions were designed to lay a foundation for the permanent exercise of Jewish sovereignty over the West Bank and Gaza, a political arrangement which, they repeated, was in no way precluded by the Camp David accords.

Although Likud was correct in stating that the Camp David summit had deliberately left the final status of the West Bank and Gaza unresolved, the Begin government's interpretation of those provisions pertaining to autonomy was called into question not only by Egypt and the United States but also by important political elements inside the Jewish state. The Labor Alignment, for example, had from the beginning expressed reservations about the Framework for Peace in the Middle East precisely because it appeared to call for the creation of a Palestinian state. In 1979 and 1980, most Alignment politicians recognized that eventual Palestinian control of the West Bank and Gaza was implicit in the Camp David accords. They agreed, in other words, with Begin's foreign critics who argued that the prime minister had signed at Camp David a document that envisioned not only Palestinian responsibility for matters of local government but also, following the transition period, Palestinian self-determination in a national sense, with control over land as well as people and over a corporate society rather than multiple, atomized individual communities.[139]

For this reason, many in Labor complained that Israel had placed itself in a disadvantageous position. If taken seriously, the framework signed at Camp David would bring about the establishment of an independent Palestinian state, something that Labor did not favor. Alternatively, if the Begin government continued to empty the autonomy agreements of their intended content and to insist that self-determination meant little more than administrative control over local affairs, Israel's international credibility would suffer and the prospects for peace would diminish. Either way, in the Alignment's view, the result would be detrimental to the interests of the Jewish state.

These kinds of reservations were also expressed by several important individuals within the Israeli government. One was Moshe Dayan, who had previously served in Labor governments but had been Begin's foreign minister since 1977. Another was Ezer Weizman, a Likud politician who had managed Begin's successful election campaign in 1977 and thereafter became minister of defense. Although the views of Dayan and Weizman were strongly opposed by most others in Begin's cabinet, their thinking is of particular interest because it was these two men, along with Begin, who had led the Israeli negotiating team at Camp David. Dayan and Weizman, as well as a few others associated with the government, rejected the argument that autonomy applied to people but not to land. They also stated that by accepting the principle of Palestinian self-determination, Israel had committed itself to a solution involving more than Palestinian local government under permanent Israeli rule. In other words, these two men who had helped to fashion the language agreed to at Camp David did not believe that autonomy should characterize the political circumstances of the Palestinians even after the transition period came to an end. Because of their views, Dayan and Weizman were effectively isolated within the Begin cabinet, and this in turn led each man to resign, Dayan in October 1979 and Weizman in May 1980.

So far as UN 242 is concerned, the Begin government sought to refute claims that this document required Israel's withdrawal from the West Bank and Gaza by offering a new and controversial interpretation of the key UN resolution. The Israeli Labor Party had long rejected the claim that UN 242 calls for Israel's complete withdrawal from Arab lands captured in 1967, insisting that the resolution's framers had deliberately chosen not to employ language that would require such an interpretation; and in 1978 Likud extended this reasoning by pointing out that the text of UN 242 also says nothing about a withdrawal on all fronts. In other words, just as UN 242 had deliberately failed to specify the precise amount of territory to be relinquished by Israel, it also remains silent on the matter of exactly which areas are to be returned to Arab rule.

Likud argued on the basis of this logic that an accurate reading of UN 242 can be said to make mandatory only an Israeli pullback on at least one front, such as on the Golan Heights or in the Sinai Peninsula; and indeed, Likud added, Israel had already agreed to and implemented a partial withdrawal in both of these areas. By insisting that demands for an Israeli withdrawal on additional fronts were based on interpretations which are inconsistent with the actual language of the UN resolution, the Begin government maintained that there was no contradiction between Israel's declared willingness to seek an accommodation with the Arabs on the basis of UN 242, a willingness it had reaffirmed at Camp David, and its own solemn declarations to the effect that Arab sovereignty would never be reestablished over any part of the West Bank and Gaza.

This reasoning, which even many Israelis found contrived, was rejected not only by the Arabs but by the United States as well. For example, in its written answers to the questions about Camp David submitted by King Hussein of Jordan, the Carter administration stated that according to its own interpretation of UN 242, "the withdrawal provision of that resolution applies on all fronts." Nevertheless, Jerusalem's statements and actions showed that the Begin government worried little about whether its arguments were judged to be persuasive. From its point of view and that of its supporters, Israel's policies in the West Bank and Gaza derived all the legitimacy they needed from considerations of history, religion, and Jewish nationalism. If the standard of living of the Palestinians in the occupied territories had improved, and if retention of these territories could be justified by a particular reading of the Camp David accords and UN 242, so much the better. But these arguments were not put forward for serious scrutiny, and Israel's claim to the West Bank and Gaza was not, in Likud's view, dependent on their accuracy.

With the autonomy negotiations hopelessly deadlocked and Israel's presence in the West Bank and Gaza expanding steadily, it was only a matter of time before Egypt abandoned its efforts to implement the provisions of Camp David addressed to a comprehensive peace. In fact, Cairo displayed considerable patience and flexibility during 1979 and 1980, professing to understand the domestic political constraints in Israel and suggesting that Israeli thinking about the Palestinian problem needed time to mature. This maturation, Egyptian officials added, was the purpose of the negotiations. Sadat and Begin also held a number of summit meetings during this period, with the Egyptian president hoping that differences between Cairo and Jerusalem could be narrowed and that at least something could be salvaged from the autonomy talks. But while these sessions produced statements that the parties would not abandon their efforts to reach an accommodation, and would in the meantime press ahead with the improvement of bilateral relations, nothing of real substance was accomplished at any of the meetings.

Following the January 1980 Aswan summit between Begin and Sadat, the fifth such session since the signing of the Egypt-Israel peace treaty less than ten months earlier, the Egyptian minister of state for foreign affairs, Butros Ghali, observed with a mixture of bitterness and resignation that time was now running out for the autonomy negotiations. And indeed, on May 8, 1980, Sadat bowed to the inevitable and unilaterally suspended the talks. Although he cited as his immediate reason the introduction in the Israeli Knesset of a motion to legalize further Israel's annexation of East Jerusalem, the principal and obvious motivation for Sadat's action was his recognition that there was no longer any hope that the Camp David accords would provide a basis for solving the Palestinian problem. The Begin government had succeeded in emptying these accords of what Egypt regarded as their proper content, and it was clear that Israel's effort to lay a foundation for its permanent control of the West Bank and Gaza would not be changed by Egyptian diplomacy.

PART V

The High Price of Stalemate

Confrontations between Israel and the Palestinians in the 1980s

THE CAMP DAVID accords of 1978 held out the hope of movement toward a peaceful resolution of the Arab-Israeli conflict, and there was indeed significant progress with respect to the important relationship between Israel and Egypt. A peace treaty was signed in 1979, and plans for the completion of Israel's phased withdrawal from the Sinai Peninsula were proceeding on schedule in 1980 and 1981. There were also expanding contacts between Israelis and Egyptians, at the level of private citizens as well as government officials. In 1980, the first year in which the border between the two countries was open for tourism, 14,000 Israelis visited Cairo and other destinations in Egypt. The number increased to 38,000 in 1981 and to 45,000 in 1982. Israeli businessmen also participated in Cairo's annual international trade fair in the spring of 1981, and again in spring 1982.

Although there continued to be strains in relations between Israel and Egypt, giving rise to what analysts frequently described as a "cold peace," the break with the past was nonetheless dramatic. Both states were firmly committed to the principle that disagreements between them should be openly discussed and dealt with by peaceful means. In addition, there were important practical steps on the road to a normalization of bilateral relations. Not only was there an exchange of ambassadors and the establishment of standard connections in the areas of telecommunications and transportation, there were also agreements for cooperation in the fields of agriculture, commerce, tourism, cultural and academic exchange, and scientific research. The projects resulting from these agreements were for the most part modest, and in addition they were sometimes cumbersome or productive of friction. For example, Israel sold only $10 million worth of goods to Egypt in 1980 and only $13.7 million in 1981. Also, reflecting another limitation on the trade between the two countries, Israeli trucks carrying goods bound for Cairo were required in 1980 and 1981 to reload their cargoes onto Egyptian lorries at the al-Arish crossing point. Nevertheless, judged in comparative terms and from the perspective of history, these limitations and difficulties appeared insignificant when contrasted with the radical difference between the situation before and after the Camp David accords and the Israel-Egypt peace treaty.

Developments with respect to the Palestinian dimension of the Arab-Israeli conflict were of a decidedly different order. Relations between Israel and the Palestinians not only failed to improve after the Camp David accords, they in fact continued to deteriorate, giving rise to violent confrontations that began in the early 1980s and continued throughout much of the decade. Some Arabs charged that peace with Egypt had made Israel more aggressive in its dealings with Palestinians: with the danger of a military conflict with Egypt eliminated, Israel was said to face fewer risks and thus to be less constrained in its actions on other fronts, particularly in the West Bank and Gaza but also, possibly, in Lebanon or on the Golan Heights. Israeli government spokesmen, by contrast, insisted that surrender of the large and mineral-rich Sinai Peninsula represented a major territorial concession and indicated beyond any possible doubt the good faith of their country in the search for a just and lasting peace. Thus, they added, it was now up to the Arabs to recognize Israel's right to exist and to offer full and unconditional peace to the Jewish people living in its ancestral homeland.

Regardless of whether there is any connection between the Israel-Egypt peace treaty and the increased tension associated with the Palestinian dimension of the Arab-Israeli conflict, the latter was characterized in the early 1980s by an entrenched political stalemate, by agitation and unrest in the West Bank and Gaza, and by a steady drift toward violent confrontations of significant intensity and scope. Moreover, the events of this period set the tone for the remainder of the decade. The mid-1980s saw the failure of successive diplomatic initiatives aimed at fostering movement toward peace, and the latter years of the decade, beginning in December 1987, witnessed the emergence of a sustained rebellion by Palestinians in the occupied territories.

9 | Violent Confrontations in the Early 1980s

Propaganda, Stalemate, and the Drift toward Violence

THE PLO ESTABLISHED itself on the international scene during the 1970s, and by the end of the decade, in the aftermath of Camp David, it was increasingly recognized as the sole legitimate representative of the Palestinian people. In the summer of 1979, for example, Chancellor Bruno Kreisky of Austria and West German socialist leader Willy Brandt both met with Yasir Arafat, chairman of the PLO, thereby extending the visibility and legitimacy of the Palestinian organization in political circles outside the Third World and Communist bloc. Moreover, both Kreisky and Brandt later issued statements expressing the opinion that the PLO should be included in the search for Middle East peace, and that, in their judgment, it could be trusted and would accept a solution to the Palestinian problem that did not involve the destruction of Israel. Arafat and other PLO leaders also met with top officials in Spain, Italy, Belgium, Portugal, and Greece during this period, obtaining additional expressions of support and, in some cases, formal political recognition for the PLO. Such recognition was accorded by Italy in November 1979, for example, and by Austria in March 1980.

The PLO and the Palestinian cause scored another important diplomatic victory in 1980, when the nine members of the European Council, meeting in Venice in June, declared their recognition of the "legitimate rights of the Palestinian people." The statement of the council, which became known as the Venice Declaration, distanced itself from provisions of UN Resolution 242 pertaining to the Palestinians by stating that the Palestinian problem "is not simply one of refugees." Further, more positively, it affirmed that "the Palestinian people, which is conscious of existing as such, must be placed in a position . . . to exercise fully its right to self-determination." In addition, the Venice Declaration offered explicit, or nearly explicit, recognition of the PLO, stating, "The Palestine Liberation Organization . . . will have to be associated with the negotiations" aimed at resolving the Arab-Israeli dispute. Although the council sought to balance its expressions of support for the Palestinian cause with language reaffirming "the right to existence and to security of all states in the region, including Israel," the Venice Declaration was criticized by Israel and welcomed by the PLO, both of whom correctly saw it as extending international recognition of Palestinian rights and offering support for a two-state solution to the conflict. Israel was also disturbed by a paragraph which proclaimed that "the Nine . . . will not accept any unilateral initiative designed to change the status of Jerusalem."

In the propaganda battles taking place during this period, Israeli representatives continued to insist that the PLO was a terrorist organization dedicated to the destruction of the Jewish state, whereas PLO officials repeated their readiness for a political settlement based on compromise. Evidence that the latter position was indeed that of the PLO was summarized about this time by Walid Khalidi, a leading Palestinian intellectual and member of the Palestine National Council, who argued in an important *Foreign Affairs* article that "if the resolutions adopted by successive [meetings of the PNC] are read in sequence, a movement away from maximalism and in the direction of accommodation is unmistakable."[1] This movement, Khalidi stated, was visible on four distinct levels: (1) the discarding of statements calling for liberation of the whole of Palestine; (2) a deemphasis on the objective of establishing a secular democratic state in all of Palestine; (3) a declared willingness to attend international peace conferences and to meet with "progressive" elements in Israel, thereby acknowledging that armed struggle is not the only way to secure Palestinian rights; and (4) an "implied though conditional" acceptance of a Palestinian political entity, or mini-state, in only part of Palestine. Khalidi also asserted that most Palestinians were ready to carry this movement forward to its logical conclusion and recognized that it was in their interest to do so. Specifically, he wrote, "a sovereign Palestinian state on the West Bank, in the Gaza Strip, and in East Jerusalem in coexistence with Israel—the terms on which the PLO would settle—means a haven from their diaspora and a repository for their vast potential for constructive achievement. The endorsement by Fatah, the mainstream PLO group, of a settlement along these lines will isolate and contain the Palestinian and Arab dissidents."

This alleged softening of the PLO's platform continued to be strongly disputed by Israel and its supporters, however, who insisted that Palestinian calls for compromise remained vague, ambiguous, and highly conditional. Critics of the PLO also pointed out that its representatives said different things to different audiences, noting, for example, that Arafat's 1979 meeting with Bruno Kreisky had been followed by a press conference in Damascus at which PLO officials articulated maximalist positions. Similarly, according to a "media abstract" which was prepared for general distribution by the Israeli prime minister's office and which cited PLO Radio in Lebanon as its source, Arafat told a meeting in Beirut in December 1980, "When we speak of the Palestinians' return, we want to say: Acre before Gaza, Beersheba before Hebron. We recognize one thing, namely that the Palestinian flag will fly over Jaffa."[2]

In the view of many supporters of Israel, statements of this sort demonstrated that PLO interest in a political entity reflected no more than a strategy of seeking to destroy the Jewish state in stages, first to acquire a Palestinian state in the West Bank and Gaza, and thereafter to struggle for a final solution based on the 1968 PLO charter. For example, the media abstract quoted above reported that Khaled al-Hassan, a senior PLO official "who is termed a 'moderate' by European countries," told a Kuwaiti newspaper in November 1980 that "the Covenant expresses the national unity which is attained by permanent strategic objectives and not by changing phased political goals." It also reported that al-Hassan told an American correspondent about this time that "an independent state on the West Bank and Gaza is [only] the beginning of the final solution. That solution is to establish a democratic state in the whole of Palestine."[3]

While there was validity to the arguments advanced by both Israeli and PLO spokesmen, diplomatic opinion was increasingly lining up on the side of the Palestinian organization, judging the evolution of PLO thinking during the 1970s to be more significant than a failure to remove all ambiguities and conditionalities from recent PNC declarations. Also persuasive, apparently, were Palestinian claims that hard-line statements by Fatah and other mainstream PLO leaders were increasingly rare and, in any event, designed only to fend off extremist critics and create room to maneuver.

Contributing further to support for the Palestinian cause in the court of world opinion were both Arab political initiatives and developments in the occupied territories. With respect to the former, Arab governments were increasingly indicating their support for the kind of two-state solution advocated by the PLO. This was clearly the position of Egypt, for example, even though the governments of Sadat and his successor, Hosni Mubarak, had angered the Palestinians by continuing to deal with Israel despite its opposition to any movement in this direction. It was also the position of conservative Arab states such as Morocco, which had worked behind the scenes to facilitate the Egyptian-Israeli contacts that led to Camp David. Indeed, the Moroccan king, Hassan II, invited Israeli Labor Party leader Shimon Peres to Morocco on two occasions during this period. In July 1978, Peres spent two days with the Moroccan monarch in Rabat, and early in 1981 he visited Morocco again and stayed in the same Marrakesh palace where Hassan had welcomed Moshe Dayan in 1977.[4]

A political initiative launched by Saudi Arabia in August 1981 offered support for a two-state solution from an Arab actor that had not previously declared itself willing to recognize Israel, thereby enhancing the credibility and plausibility of calls for a solution based on the establishment of a Palestinian state alongside the Jewish state of Israel. Put forward by the Saudi crown prince, Fahd ibn Abd al-Aziz, and known as the Fahd Plan, the Saudi proposal declared itself to be based on a recognition that "the Palestinian figure is the basic figure in the Middle Eastern equation." The Fahd Plan contained eight points, among them a call for Israel to dismantle Jewish settlements in the occupied territories and to withdraw from all Arab territory captured in 1967, including East Jerusalem. It also affirmed the right of the Palestinian people to return to their homes or to receive compensation if they did not wish to do so. The Saudi plan further proposed that following Israel's withdrawal from the occupied territories, and after a short transition period under UN auspices, an independent Palestinian state should be set up with East Jerusalem as its capital. Finally, the Fahd Plan declared that all states in the region should be able to live in peace, and that the United Nations should guarantee respect for this principle.

Many supporters of the Jewish state saw the Saudi proposal as no more than another Arab propaganda effort. Pointing out that it did not even mention Israel by name, they charged that the plan was but another ambiguous statement fed to a gullible Western public searching desperately for Arab moderation.[5] Nevertheless, in the judgment of many outside observers, the Fahd Plan contributed to an accumulation of evidence that the Arab world, like the PLO, was indeed ready for a solution to the Palestinian problem which did not involve the destruction of Israel, and that the major obstacle to progress was in fact the refusal of the Israeli government to consider any peace proposal requiring withdrawal from the West Bank and Gaza.

Developments in the occupied territories lent additional credibility to the PLO's claim to be ready for a political settlement, and also to the PLO's insistence that it was the sole legitimate representative of the Palestinian people. As discussed, Palestinians in the West Bank and Gaza were now being led by a new generation of men with an explicitly nationalist orientation, men who openly identified with the PLO and who declared their opposition both to the Israeli occupation and to the hollow autonomy scheme that had emerged from the Camp David summit. Moreover, these men had come to power in the relatively democratic election of 1976, which gave them an important measure of legitimacy and made it possible to gauge the political preferences of Palestinians in the territories more generally. Within the context of Palestinian politics, the most visible figures in the occupied territories identified with and supported the moderate mainstream of the PLO. Though they saw no prospect of a solution emerging from the Camp David accords, many stated without hesitation that they were prepared to accept the existence of Israel, as a Jewish state, in return for the exercise of Palestinian self-determination and the establishment of an independent Palestinian state alongside Israel.

West Bank mayors thus endorsed the political strategy being pursued by the PLO, as did Rashad Shawwa, the more conservative mayor of Gaza; and they also expressed satisfaction at the gains that had been registered through international diplomacy. For example, the mayor of Hebron, Fahd Qawasmeh, defended Arafat's 1979 meetings with Kreisky and Brandt against criticism from Palestinian and Arab rejectionists, stating that the meetings would be helpful in the search for a comprehensive Middle East peace. More generally, voicing sentiments which most observers believed to be widespread among West Bank and Gaza Palestinians in the late 1970s and early 1980s, the head of the Palestinian

Women's Federation stated, "All of us here agree that there should be an independent Palestinian state. Anything other than that will only meet with rejection and indifference on the part of the Palestinian people." Similarly, a petition drafted and circulated in 1979 declared, "We aspire to establish a just and lasting peace in the region, which can only be on the basis of our people's exercising their right to self-determination and national independence, after the complete withdrawal [of Israel] from all the territories [captured in 1967] and the establishment of the Palestinian state." The petition was signed by sixty mayors, municipal and village counselors, and heads of charitable societies.[6]

Ranged against the PLO and the Palestinians of the West Bank and Gaza was the Israeli government, led by Likud and supported by other nationalist and religious groupings on the right side of the Israeli political spectrum. No matter how vigorous might be Palestinian opposition, and no matter how plausible in the eyes of outside observers might be the political solution for which Palestinians and other Arabs now claimed to be ready, these Israelis were determined that the future of the West Bank and Gaza would be shaped exclusively by their own ideological vision. Further, they were in the midst of an intense campaign to transform the political, economic, and demographic character of the West Bank and Gaza, and from their point of view they were having considerable success in their drive to translate vision into reality.

Israel's drive into the West Bank and Gaza involved not only the settlement policies of the Begin government but also the provocative actions of Gush Emunim and the organized settler movement. Though tolerated, and to an extent even encouraged, by the government, militant settlers, many of whom believe that Jewish law requires Israel to exercise sovereignty over the territories, took initiatives of their own to deepen the Jewish state's presence in the West Bank and Gaza.

Perhaps the most important effort of this period was an attempt by Gush Emunim to establish a Jewish community in the center of Hebron. Jews had been massacred and driven from Hebron during the intercommunal violence of 1929; and in 1979, the wife of Gush Emunim's leader, Rabbi Moshe Levinger, claimed that she had been told in a dream to reestablish a Jewish presence in the large Arab city. Mrs. Levinger subsequently led a small group of women in a sit-in at the building that had been a Jewish medical center prior to 1929, and in the weeks and months that followed, protected by Israeli soldiers, a small Jewish community grew up in the heart of Hebron. The number of buildings controlled by Jewish militants soon increased, with Gush activists, aided by the government, beginning the reconstruction of the city's old Jewish neighborhood. In addition, settlers frequently flaunted their presence in Hebron in ways that were deliberately designed to provoke the local population. Indeed, sending the message that Arabs were simply the temporary inhabitants of a land that God had given to the Jewish people, Gush Emunim organized tours in Hebron for its supporters from other areas. Assembling in the central square and announcing their political goals with bullhorns or loudspeakers, while the city's Arab residents looked on, Levinger or others would then lead their followers on a walk through those parts of the city which they deemed to have Jewish significance.

Likud and Gush Emunim did not represent all Israelis, of course, and those with a different vision for the West Bank and Gaza strongly denounced the developments taking place in the occupied territories. Particularly important in this connection was the Labor Alignment. As noted previously, Labor challenged the official Israeli interpretation of the framework signed at Camp David, stating that Jerusalem should accept a meaningful definition of Palestinian autonomy in the short run and seek a comprehensive peace based on territorial compromise in the long run. Most Labor leaders accordingly opposed the government's settlement drive in the West Bank and Gaza and declared that by taking steps to prevent Israel's eventual withdrawal from these territories, Likud was in fact working against the interests of the Jewish state.

Alignment spokesmen advanced a number of arguments in support of their position. To begin with, some Labor politicians bitterly denounced the spending of millions of dollars for Jewish settlements in the occupied territories at a time when capital for essential development projects within Israel proper was in critically short supply. Even more important, according to Labor, Likud's settlement policies were undermining the peace process and strengthening the position of Arab rejectionists opposed to negotiations with Israel. Finally, and most important of all, permanent control of the West Bank and Gaza would create serious new security problems for Israel and would increase the number of Arabs living under Israeli rule to the point where the country's Jewish character would be diluted and its democratic political system threatened. Labor did not advocate total Israeli withdrawal from the West Bank and Gaza, insisting that retention of the Jordan Valley and several other areas was necessary for purposes of defense. Nor did Labor favor the establishment of an independent Palestinian state in the remainder of the territories, proposing instead that areas relinquished by Israel be incorporated into Jordan. Nevertheless, under these conditions, Labor believed it was appropriate and even desirable to exchange land for peace, and the party's leaders therefore condemned Likud's efforts to create facts in the West Bank and Gaza in order to limit the options available to future Israeli governments.

Israeli political factions to the left of Labor were even more vigorous in condemning the policies and practices of the Begin government.[7] Particularly vocal at this time was Peace Now, a broad movement of opinion that had been formed in 1977, in the wake of Sadat's visit to Jerusalem, and which in 1979 and 1980 was attempting to mobilize and give direction to opponents of Likud's program of "creeping annexation." Estimates of the number of Peace Now supporters varied widely, from 50,000 to 250,000. At some of the movement's biggest rallies, organized to demonstrate opposition to the settlement policies of the Likud-led government, 80,000 to 100,000 Israelis turned out to march. One such rally took place in Tel Aviv in October 1979, for example; and in 1979 Peace Now also claimed to have gathered more than 200,000 signatures on petitions to the prime minister in opposition to his settlement campaign. The movement carried out small-scale projects, too. On one occasion, for instance, some of its members traveled to a West Bank village near Hebron in order to replant Palestinian vineyards that had been uprooted by militant Jewish settlers associated with Gush Emunim. On another, some of its supporters from a *kibbutz* in the Negev joined in preparations to rebuild a house in Beit Sahour that had been demolished by the IDF, even though the army subsequently prevented them from carrying out the work.

There were religious as well as nonreligious Jews associated with the Israeli peace movement. Reacting against the fundamentalism of Gush Emunim and important elements within the National Religious Party, which asserted that withdrawal from the occupied territories was prohibited by Jewish (*Halakhic*) law and that settlement in these areas would deepen Israel's spiritual character, a number of religious individuals and groups strongly denounced the equation of Judaism and nationalistic chauvinism. One such group was Oz VeShalom (Strength and Peace), which operated under the Peace Now umbrella and concerned itself in particular with what it regarded as a corruption of Jewish ethics and the disservice done to Judaism by Gush Emunim and NRP militants.

Oz VeShalom and other religious factions within the peace movement also challenged the theological assumptions of these Jewish fundamentalists, citing the principle of *pikuach nefesh*, the saving of lives, and arguing that Jewish law permits the return of territories taken during war if to do so brings peace and security.[8] In the latter connection, they noted that one of Israel's two chief rabbis, Rabbi Ovadia Yosef, who at the time headed the Sephardic tradition of Israel's Afro-Asian Jews, had stated at a conference in Jerusalem in 1979 that, in his opinion, Jewish law does permit withdrawal from the occupied territories if this results in a true peace. These arguments were not those of a majority of the country's orthodox Jews. More widely held, it seemed, was the opinion of Israel's other chief rabbi, Rabbi Shlomo Goren of the Ashkenazic Jewish tradition, who responded to Rabbi Yosef in 1980 by declaring, "*Halacha* prohibits returning the territory of *Eretz Yisrael*, even in cases where lives are in danger if it is not handed over."[9] But while such matters continued to be passionately debated among orthodox Jews, at least some within Israel's religious community, including some NRP members disturbed by the party's drift to the right, added their voices to those within Labor and the secular left that were vigorously denouncing the government's settlement drive in the West Bank and Gaza.

Although their political weight was considerable, Labor, Peace Now, and other domestic opponents of the Likud-led government were unable to bring about a modification of Israel's policies in the occupied territories. The Begin government's parliamentary coalition had only a slender majority; it controlled but 65 of the Knesset's 120 seats following the 1977 election, and there were repeated predictions in 1979 and 1980 that defections and internal conflicts would cause the government to fall. Further, the popularity of the government declined steadily in the eyes of the public, from over 50 percent early in 1979 to about 35 percent later in the year and only 21 percent in the spring of 1980. As stated by one Israeli journalist late in 1979, there was a widespread belief that "something has gone wrong with the workings of government."[10] Yet none of this led the Begin government to reexamine its actions in the West Bank and Gaza. While some might have expected caution in addressing so vital an issue in the absence of a clear national mandate, the prime minister and his supporters saw themselves as having a historic window of opportunity, one which was not to be missed. Indeed, if anything, the precariousness of the ruling coalition intensified their determination to deepen Israel's presence in the occupied territories. Fearful that the government could fall at any time, they labored to use their days in power to the fullest, to create a network of Israeli interests that would make it politically and economically impossible ever to withdraw from the West Bank and Gaza, even should some future government wish to do so.

Under these conditions, with both international diplomacy and domestic Israeli politics failing to slow the Begin government's settlement drive, the political and propaganda battles between Israelis and Palestinians were soon accompanied by more violent confrontations. Nor is it surprising that the violence began in Hebron, the large West Bank town where a small Israeli settler community had been established in the center of the city. In May 1980, unknown Palestinian assailants shot and killed six religious Jews who were walking through Hebron. In response, Israel greatly tightened military security, stepping up police patrols which, according to many West Bank residents, often insulted local Palestinians and treated them harshly. Israel also deported three prominent, pro-PLO leaders at this time—Mayor Fahd Qawasmeh of Hebron, Hebron religious leader Rajab Tamimi, and Muhammad Milhem, the mayor of nearby Halhoul.

These developments set in motion an escalating cycle of violence. In June, exactly one month after the Hebron shooting, Jewish extremists associated with Gush Emunim and the Israeli settler movement placed bombs in the cars of Nablus mayor Bassam Shaka and Ramallah mayor Karim Khalaf, seriously wounding both. A bomb was also placed in the garage of al-Bireh mayor Ibrahim Tawil, and an Israeli officer sent to warn Tawil was injured when he opened the garage. Claiming credit for these incidents was an underground Jewish organization calling itself "Terror against Terror," a group which said that its goal was not only to take revenge for Arab terrorism but also to drive Palestinians out of the West Bank. There were other violent confrontations as well during the month of June. An Israeli soldier patrolling the Old City in Jerusalem was wounded by a sniper, a Palestinian student at Bethlehem University was subsequently wounded by an

Israeli policeman, and, still in June, an Israeli soldier was shot near the spot where the Bethlehem student had been wounded.

The events of this period provided additional fuel for the political debates taking place inside Israel. Indeed, political opinion in the Jewish state was increasingly polarized on the issue of the occupied territories, with Likud and Labor drawing very different conclusions from the escalating spiral of violence. Likud and other parties advocating permanent retention of the West Bank and Gaza stated that Palestinian agitation reflected hatred of the Jews and showed that the Palestinians would never make peace with the Jewish state. Thus, Israel could not afford to think about withdrawal from the territories because to do so would make it possible for their inhabitants to organize even more attacks against Israeli citizens; it would permit them to work without interference for the destruction of the Jewish state. Advocates of territorial compromise, on the other hand, argued that the escalating violence in the territories, Jewish as well as Arab, showed that retention of the West Bank and Gaza was not in Israel's interest. It increased rather than reduced the country's security concerns by placing hostile Arab elements inside the state's *de facto* borders. It also weakened the moral and democratic character of Israeli society by making many Jews insensitive to the rights of those Palestinians over whom their government exercised control, and even leading some Jews to employ the kinds of terrorist activities for which Israel had long condemned its enemies.

The Second Begin Government and Its Approach to the Territories

These disagreements loomed large with the approach of new elections in June 1981, although Israel's increasing economic problems were of major concern, too, in the minds of many voters. With triple-digit inflation and a mounting external debt, Finance Minister Yigal Hurewitz had been calling for new austerity measures, including a reduction in government subsidies on basic commodities, and this, as much as or even more than Likud's controversial policies in the occupied territories, had contributed to the sharp decline in the government's popularity. Moreover, economics and politics were understood to be connected, given that spending on settlement-related activity not only contributed to the country's economic crisis but also had been made immune from the belt-tightening measures proposed for other government programs. As a result of these considerations, public opinion polls taken during the first months of 1981 suggested that the coming election might well return the Labor Alignment to power.

To improve its political fortunes, Likud adopted a new set of economic policies designed to give the average Israeli a short-term windfall. Although the government was accused of fiscal irresponsibility and of mortgaging the country's economic future, Begin accepted the resignation of Hurewitz and replaced him

544 | *The High Price of Stalemate*

with Yoram Aridor, who then suspended all talk of austerity. To control inflation, Aridor used the short-term and essentially artificial device of pumping the country's modest foreign currency reserves into the banking system. Even more important, he sought to make people feel as good as possible about their economic circumstances by slashing the excise taxes that had been placed on many imported products in order to protect the country's dollar and Common Market currency reserves. Making such goods as color television sets, video recorders, and freezers much more affordable, the latter action produced a buying frenzy. Though transparent, these policies, which one analyst called "the most startling example of economic interference" in any Israeli election,[11] were highly effective. They played a major role in changing the subjective mood in the country and appeared to give substance to Likud's campaign slogan, "The right direction."

Likud was also aided as the electoral campaign went forward by continuing doubts about Labor fostered by the ongoing feud between Shimon Peres and Yitzhak Rabin, who had been fighting each other for leadership of the party for several years. In his memoirs, published in 1979, Rabin had offered a highly unflattering characterization of his rival, charging that Peres was unfit for national leadership, and also casting aspersions on the latter man's prior record as minister of defense. Many viewed Rabin's charges as irresponsible, and the party in general lined up behind Peres, reaffirming his position as party chairman at its convention in December 1980. Yet Rabin, a war hero and former prime minister, remained more popular than Peres with many voters and could not be ignored by the party. Also, at least some within Labor believed that there was substance to Rabin's allegations, regardless of the former prime minister's motivation, and that Peres's qualifications to lead the party and the nation did indeed need to be examined. All of this was reminiscent of the election campaign of 1977, in which scandals and bitter feuds within the ranks of Labor led many voters to conclude that the party had become self-absorbed and was out of touch with the needs of the country.

Finally, early in June, just three weeks before the election, the Israeli air force bombed a nuclear reactor being constructed in Iraq, and this action, too, enhanced the domestic political standing of Begin and Likud. Iraq's Osiraq reactor was being built with French assistance and was said to be intended for peaceful purposes only. Nevertheless, there was concern not only in Israel but in the United States and even France that it would be capable of producing weapons-grade plutonium, leading some analysts to predict that the regime in Baghdad would have a small stockpile of atomic weapons within a few years. To avert this possibility, Israel made political overtures to France and succeeded in persuading the Paris government to lower the quality of the nuclear fuel to be delivered to Iraq. Jerusalem also took direct action to upset Baghdad's plans. In April 1979,

Israeli agents broke into a warehouse in France and destroyed casings destined for the Iraqi reactor, and in June 1980 they assassinated the Egyptian-born physicist directing Baghdad's nuclear research program.[12] Then, on June 7, 1981, Israeli F-16 and F-15 jets flew more than a thousand miles to Iraq and back, carrying out a precision bombing raid that devastated the Osiraq reactor and killed a French technician working at the site.

It is unclear whether the timing of the Israeli strike was influenced by the forthcoming election. There is no firm evidence that this is the case, although, on the other hand, even some who feared Iraq might indeed acquire nuclear weapons pointed out that there was no need for immediate action and suggested that France could probably have been persuaded to limit further the Osiraq reactor's capability. In any event, while the Israeli strike brought broad and vigorous international condemnation, including harsh criticism from the United States, it did turn out to be of benefit to the prime minister and his party in the domestic political arena. As stated by one scholar, "The sheer audaciousness of the raid, no less than the brilliance of its execution, enhanced the prime minister's political standing only a few days before the election."[13]

All of these economic and political considerations, in addition to the fundamental division of political opinion about the West Bank and Gaza, resulted in an election which was much closer than that of 1977 but which, in the end, left Begin and Likud in power. While Labor recovered a large proportion of the votes it had lost in the preceding election, winning a total of forty-seven Knesset seats, Likud also did better than in 1977 and captured a total of forty-eight Knesset seats.

This outcome was particularly significant in that it showed that Likud's tenure in power would not be short-lived. Although the results of the 1977 Knesset election had been described as a political earthquake, it had nevertheless been possible to argue that many voters were protesting what they judged to be the lethargy and inadequacy of Labor party rule, and that these results should accordingly be described as an Alignment defeat rather than a Likud victory. But the 1981 election demonstrated that a fundamental realignment had taken place in the Israeli partisan arena, with Likud now an established political force and, for the foreseeable future, a leading contender for political preeminence. Despite the party's manipulation of economic issues and the continuing dissatisfaction among some of Labor's traditional constituency, an Israeli scholar could credibly observe that the 1981 election reflected "no less a positive choice *for* Likud than a negative vote *against* Labor."[14] Regardless of whether the earthquake election of 1977 had been influenced by particular and transitory circumstances, Likud's constituency had now come into its own, and there was every reason to believe the party would remain influential in the years ahead. Rather than a return to the pattern of Labor dominance that had characterized political life between

1948 and 1977, it appeared after the 1981 balloting that the division of the country into two large and antagonistic blocs had become a permanent feature of politics in the Jewish state.

Despite the political significance of Likud's emergence as a permanent contender for power, the party's electoral victory in 1981 could not have been more narrow, and the ruling coalition formed by Begin after the election in fact had but a single-seat majority in the 120-member parliament. To the forty-eight Knesset seats captured by Likud were added thirteen from three religious parties, for a total of sixty-one. Six of the thirteen seats belonging to Likud's partners had been won by the National Religious Party, whose platform fused religious orthodoxy and militant Jewish nationalism, and which in recent years had identified itself with Gush Emunim and the organized settler movement. Four more seats were provided by the ultraorthodox Agudat Yisrael party, which, though not ideologically committed to territorial maximalism, was willing to trade its support on foreign-policy issues for Likud's promise to work for the enactment of legislation extending the influence of orthodox Jewish law. Finally, the remaining three seats in the coalition belonged to a new party, Tami, which had recently been formed by defectors from the NRP who charged the latter party with insensitivity to the needs of religious Jews of Afro-Asian origin. Though it was not a member of the ruling coalition, an additional three seats had been captured by Tehiya, an ultranationalist party formed in 1979 by a group of Likud politicians opposed to the Camp David accords. With this most slender of majorities, even should the votes of Tehiya be added to the coalition in the future, Likud's domestic political position was thus even more precarious than it had been before the election, indicating once again that deep division was the result of the realignment taking place in Israeli politics.

Its precariousness notwithstanding, the prime minister was able to keep his parliamentary coalition intact and, reaffirming the principles of the first Begin government, Likud used its continuing hold on the reins of power to carry forward Israel's drive into the West Bank and Gaza. The intentions of the new government were formally recorded in the agreement that Begin negotiated with his party's coalition partners. According to this statement of policy guidelines, which Likud and the other members of the ruling coalition pledged to respect and implement, "the right of the Jewish people to the land of Israel is an eternal right that cannot be called into question" and, so far as the Palestinians were concerned, "the autonomy agreed upon at Camp David means neither sovereignty nor self-determination." Further, the coalition agreement continued, the Camp David autonomy agreements are "guarantees that under no conditions will a Palestinian state emerge in the territory of western Eretz Yisrael." Finally, "At the end of the transition period, set down in the Camp David agreements, Israel will raise its claim, and act to realize its right of sovereignty over Judea, Samaria and the Gaza Strip," and therefore, in the meantime, "settlement in the land of Israel is a right and an integral part of the nation's security."[15]

Consistent with his government's continuing commitment to territorial maximalism, Begin made Ariel Sharon minister of defense following the election of 1981. Sharon had been proposed for the position after the resignation of Ezer Weizman in 1980, but the hard-line former general was not acceptable to all factions within the government's parliamentary coalition, leading Begin to assume the Defense Ministry himself. Nonetheless, as minister of agriculture, Sharon had emerged as a powerful force within the government, and in 1978, 1979, and 1980 he had played a leading role in formulating and implementing Israel's policies in the occupied territories. Now, at the Defense Ministry, Sharon became the most influential member of the cabinet more generally. His new position enabled him to dominate the army as well as government policy[16] and gave him responsibility for the Military Government that ruled the West Bank and Gaza on a daily basis.

In addition, the foreign minister at this time was Yitzhak Shamir, who had been named to the post following the resignation of Moshe Dayan in 1979. A long-time ally and close confidant of Begin, Shamir had been a leader of the irregular Jewish underground in the prestate period. He was opposed to the Camp David agreements when they were signed in 1978, but, unlike those who formed Tehiya, he remained within Likud and continued to support the prime minister. Thus, in the summer and fall of 1981, Shamir was another influential figure within the second Begin government, joining the prime minister and the defense minister in their determined efforts to lay a foundation for the permanent exercise of Jewish sovereignty in the West Bank and Gaza.

To encourage the movement of Jewish settlers into the West Bank, Begin and Sharon poured huge amounts of resources into a new strategy that placed emphasis on practical rather than ideological incentives. This "pragmatic" formula had actually been proposed by Sharon the year before. Acknowledging that Likud's goal of placing hundreds of thousands of Jews in West Bank settlements could not be accomplished with the use of ideologically motivated settlers alone, the government sought ways to mobilize other Israelis for settlement purposes, and in 1981, even before the election, the outlines of the new strategy began to take shape. Begin and Sharon reasoned, logically and essentially correctly, that Israelis who did not share an ideological commitment to Greater Israel would consider relocating in the occupied territories only if it were to their personal advantage. To attract such individuals, the government therefore began to construct new communities within commuting distance of Tel Aviv and Jerusalem and to offer housing in these "bedroom" communities at artificially low prices.

The most important of the new commuter communities were Ma'aleh Adumim, which offered a ten-minute commute to Jerusalem, and Ariel, which served Tel Aviv and was designed to be the Jewish capital of Samaria. Residences in these and other suburban communities located in the West Bank were offered at extremely attractive prices, with subsidized financing available not only to homebuyers but to private developers as well. As a result, according to one analyst, "it was possible for a Jewish family to build a four-bedroom villa in the West Bank, on a spacious plot of land, with well-equipped schools and stunning views, for the price of a small apartment in a crowded neighborhood in Tel Aviv."[17] For several years beginning in 1981, more than four-fifths of all public funds invested in the territories were directed to the construction of commuter communities such as Ma'aleh Adumim and Ariel, for which some industry was planned but which were designed principally as residential suburbs for families employed in Tel Aviv or Jerusalem. According to one estimate, expenditures related to this settlement activity, including investments in infrastructure, administrative expenses, and the cost of tax exemptions for companies and individuals doing business in the West Bank, consumed roughly 8 percent of the total government budget.[18]

The growth of Ma'aleh Adumim, Ariel, and other commuter communities, as well as the continuing settlement activity of Gush Emunim and other ideologically motivated factions, brought thousands of new Jews to the West Bank and made Sharon's vision of 300,000 Israeli settlers in Judea and Samaria by the end of the decade appear at least somewhat less implausible than it had a year or two earlier. By the end of 1981, the number of Jewish settlers in the West Bank exceeded 16,000, nearly 30 percent more than a year earlier; and by the end of 1982 the number stood at 21,000, another 30 percent increase.[19] At this time there were a total of 103 Jewish settlements in the West Bank, 70 of which had been built since Likud came to power in 1977. The optimism of the government and the settler movement during this period is illustrated by the remarks which Mordechai Zippori, minister of communication in the new Likud-led government, delivered in an address in October 1982 to residents of a new Jewish settlement near Nablus: "Don't worry about the demographic density of the Arabs. When I was born in Petah Tikvah, we were entirely surrounded by Arab villages. They have all since disappeared."[20]

Israel's actions in the occupied territories were not concerned only with Jewish settlers and settlements. The new government also addressed itself to the political circumstances of the Arab inhabitants of the territories and took steps in the fall of 1981 to implement its version of autonomy for the Palestinians. Specifically, it adopted two new approaches to the Palestinian population at this time. First, the civil and security functions of the Military Government administering the territories were divided, and special Israeli civilian administrators were appointed for the West Bank and Gaza.[21] This move corresponded with the Israeli position in the Camp David negotiations that the Military Government should be withdrawn but not abolished. Second, many elected municipal and village councils were disbanded and replaced with more compliant Palestinian political structures, including a network of village leagues staffed by Arabs but appointed and funded by Israeli authorities. By mid-1982, the Begin government had dissolved nine Palestinian municipal councils, arguing that this action was being taken not in response to unrest in the territories but to correct the fundamental error made by previous Labor governments in permitting these bodies to be elected in the first place. The functions of the dissolved municipalities, and of a number of Palestinian mayors who were dismissed during the first half of 1982 as well, were turned over to Israeli administrators and the village leagues. In addition, local officials in many towns, villages, and refugee camps were replaced by individuals willing to cooperate with the civilian administrator and the leagues.

The man whom Begin and Sharon chose to head the new Civilian Administration in the West Bank was Menachem Milson, a professor of Arabic literature at the Hebrew University of Jerusalem and the author of a plan for dealing with the Palestinians that had inspired creation of the village leagues. Milson, though not himself an advocate of territorial maximalism, had argued in a 1981 article in *Commentary* magazine that most Palestinians in the occupied territories would be willing to deal with Israel were they not prevented from doing so by PLO threats and intimidation. The article, entitled "How to Make Peace with the Palestinians," therefore recommended that Israel attempt to limit the activities of West Bank and Gaza leaders tied to the PLO and foster the emergence of an alternative leadership class, which Milson asserted would be not only more compliant but also more representative of the Palestinian masses, especially those residing in the villages of the West Bank.[22] The idea of suppressing nationalist activities and creating an alternative Palestinian leadership appealed to Ariel Sharon, who now had responsibility for the occupied territories, and despite political and ideological differences between the two men, the minister of defense thus appointed Milson civilian administrator for the West Bank on November 1. In addition, a month later, Brigadier General Yosef Lunz was named civilian administrator for the Gaza Strip.

Encouraged by Sharon, and with a mandate to implement Milson's plan for undermining PLO influence in the occupied territories, the Military Government and the new Civilian Administration took steps to silence Palestinian voices articulating nationalist sentiments. Universities in general, and Birzeit University near Ramallah in particular, were among their first targets. In November 1981, Israeli authorities charged that Birzeit students were engaging in political activities and ordered the university closed.

The closure was based on Military Order No. 854, which had been issued by the military commander of the West Bank in July 1980, and which extended the regulations then governing lower-level educational institutions to universities, including private universities. Among other things, Order No. 854 required West

Bank universities to obtain annual operating permits and gave the Military Government the right to regulate the appointment of faculty, the admission of students, the selection of textbooks, and the development of curricula. Later, in the summer of 1982, this law would be used as a basis for demanding that foreign faculty teaching at Palestinian universities sign an oath declaring that they did not support the PLO. In November 1981, however, the Military Government cited it as the legal foundation for its decision to close Birzeit. Following several days of student protests commemorating the anniversary of the Balfour Declaration, a Defense Ministry spokesman stated that the university's administration had disregarded repeated warnings to curtail demonstrations on or near the campus and announced that, by the authority of Order No. 854, the institution was therefore being shut down.

Israelis as well as Palestinians condemned the closure of Birzeit, asserting that it was a political act unrelated to genuine security considerations, and also that it was a form of collective punishment which penalized students and faculty members who had not even taken part in the protest demonstrations. West Bank and Gaza residents correctly understood the symbolic significance of the university's closure, seeing it as the opening salvo in a new campaign against PLO influence and Palestinian nationalism in the territories. Israelis, on the other hand, tended to condemn the action for its violation of academic freedom, with more than one hundred instructors from Israeli universities denouncing Milson and Sharon in a paid ad that demanded: "Open Birzeit immediately. Stop all collective punishment. Abolish Order No. 854, the basis for the restriction of academic freedom in the territories."[23] Birzeit nonetheless remained closed for two months, until early January, and there were also instances of interference in the affairs of other West Bank universities during this period. For example, according to the Bethlehem University Information Committee, a December meeting of faculty and students was broken up by Israeli soldiers, who claimed that youths in the street had thrown stones at them, and who then fired tear gas onto the campus.

Another aspect of the campaign against Palestinian nationalism was the censorship of newspapers published in East Jerusalem and the banning of newspapers and books from entry into the West Bank and Gaza. With respect to newspapers, *al-Fajr*, considered to be nationalist in orientation, was closed for nine days early in November 1981 and then, later in the month, was closed for another thirty days by order of the minister of the interior. According to a spokesman for the ministry, the paper was guilty of publishing information liable to endanger the public welfare, including "words of praise for acts of terrorism and murder and encouragement for their commission."[24] In addition, *al-Fajr*'s editor, Mamoun Sayyid, was placed under town arrest, as was Bashir Barghouti, editor of the Communist weekly *al-Taliyya*. In a related development, another Palestinian editor, Akram Haniyya of *al-Shaab*, was arrested and held in detention for fifty days. Although the case against Haniyya concerned his own alleged political activism, rather than his activities as a journalist, forty-five journalists from various East Jerusalem newspapers protested his detention with a sit-in strike and declared that he, as well as Sayyid and Barghouti, was a victim of military censorship of the Palestinian press.

Beginning in April 1982, distribution of *al-Fajr* and *al-Shaab* was prohibited in the West Bank and Gaza, and there was also a significant increase in the number of books which were banned from sale or distribution in the territories. Some Arab sources claim that 2,000 or more works were banned. IDF figures, released in March 1982, put the number at 1,100 but acknowledged that even this was almost twice what it had been a year earlier. Moreover, although some books were banned because of their anti-Semitic content, the list of outlawed volumes included many political works by Palestinian and other Arab authors. It also contained a book on the Israeli army by Yigal Allon and a volume critical of Israel by Maxime Rodinson, a Jewish scholar from France who is a well-known authority on the Middle East.[25]

The other half of Milson's strategy for combating PLO influence in the territories was an attempt to create an alternative leadership structure in the West Bank and Gaza. As Milson told interviewers in December 1981, "We're giving a chance to people who want to organize in institutions other than those guided by the PLO,"[26] and soon thereafter the new Civilian Administration intensified efforts to identify Palestinians willing to participate in the network of village leagues the Israelis sought to create. Israeli officials had in fact spent several months in 1980 trying to persuade Palestinian notables to join in such an effort, only to meet with no success in the districts of Nablus, Tulkarm, Jenin, and Jericho and winning the cooperation of only marginal figures in the districts of Bethlehem and Ramallah. In late 1981 and early 1982, however, under Milson's direction, a new effort was made.

To enable the village leagues to function, the Israelis agreed to provide modest financial resources for development projects designed to increase public support. The Israelis also delegated administrative powers to the leagues, thereby giving them authority in their own communities, and in many instances requiring the local population to bypass elected Palestinian officials. In Dura village near Hebron, for example, where Milson sought to work with an existing political organization, the Israelis offered to pay half the cost of mutually approved projects and authorized the Dura league to process requests for exit permits, pilgrimage permits, government jobs, and the like. The logic of this approach was based on clientelism, which Milson saw as the traditional Middle Eastern political style that Israel should understand and utilize in its administration of the West Bank and Gaza. The village leagues would be clients of Israel and would use the connections and resources provided by this relationship to gain clients of their own, who, in return for benefits received, would offer loyalty to the leagues and their Israeli patrons.

Although the Begin government hoped that the creation of alternative leadership structures would reduce PLO influence in the occupied territories, and for a time claimed that progress toward this goal was being made,[27] the village leagues were not the authentic and representative political institutions Milson had sought. According to Israeli theory, the leagues were supposed to speak for rural Palestinians, who were said to be resentful of neglect and discrimination on the part of urban-based nationalist politicians. In practice, however, the village leagues were unable to strike roots; aside from gaining the support of some members of their immediate families and clans, the leagues could not claim any substantial constituency. The one possible exception was the league in Dura village, which had been established in 1978 by Mustapha Doudin, a minister in the Jordanian cabinet before 1967. Doudin had established the Dura league in order to promote modernization and development in his agricultural village; and its generally apolitical nature, as well as the fact that Doudin himself was a conservative and traditional politician, with ties to Jordan rather than the PLO, made it precisely the kind of local-level structure sought by Milson. More generally, however, the leagues came into existence not as a result of indigenous efforts but through initiatives fostered by Israel.

Since the leagues lacked legitimacy in the eyes of the local population, Israeli officials often had great difficulty in persuading Palestinians with any social standing to organize or participate in the new administrative structures. In the district of Bethlehem, for example, a senior Israeli officer asked twelve local notables to join a league based in Beit Sahour before one finally agreed.[28] As a result, the village leagues tended to attract elements from the social and political margins of Palestinian society, individuals who not only were viewed as collaborators and quislings by most other Palestinians but, in some cases at least, were deemed to be social misfits, thus adding further to the artificial nature of the Israeli-sponsored institutions. One Israeli commentator accordingly described league members as "questionable types . . . unsavory characters who are ready to work for anyone."[29]

The village leagues were frequently used in ways that discredited them further and removed whatever legitimacy they might otherwise have been able to build. For example, given responsibility by Israel for municipal services, local development projects, and a variety of essential administrative functions, such as renewing identity cards and issuing permits for travel, building, and various commercial activities, those in control of the leagues frequently flaunted their newfound influence and used their administrative power to settle scores with their enemies. Later, when the head of the Ramallah league was assassinated and threats were made against the increasingly unpopular leaders of other leagues, the Israeli-sponsored organizations were issued jeeps and weapons which, on at least some occasions, were then used to harass rivals and intimidate the local population.[30] Finally, undermining their credibility in perhaps the most critical way of all, the village leagues were no more able than the political structures they replaced to offer protection from Israel's settlement drive, including the confiscation of village land. Even 5,000 acres belonging to Dura village, most of the remaining land available for grazing and cultivation, was seized by the Israelis for purposes of Jewish settlement.[31]

All of this meant that the village league program made little progress toward achievement of the goal for which it had been established. Most Palestinians rejected the logic underlying the leagues, insisting that they did not represent an authentic expression of the views of a significant sector of West Bank society—denying, in other words, that they were a legitimate alternative to the PLO. Most of the remainder, including those who, like Doudin, looked to Jordan rather than the PLO for political leadership, agreed that the village leagues behaved in ways that won little support for their Israeli patrons. Indeed, the leagues were strongly condemned by Jordan as well as the PLO. Although the Hashemite kingdom had initially been indifferent to their creation, Jordanian Prime Minister Mudar Badran announced in March 1982 that his government would view those who supported the village leagues as collaborators with the Israeli occupation authorities.[32]

Within a year or two, Israeli officials recognized these flaws and contradictions in the village league policy and acknowledged the generally artificial nature of the leagues themselves. In the spring of 1984, for example, the Defense Ministry's coordinator for the occupied territories, General Benyamin Ben Eliezer, referred to leaders of the leagues as "quislings," and the Federation of Village Leagues, which had been established in the fall of 1982, was officially disbanded.[33] In 1981 and 1982, however, many Israelis committed to territorial maximalism defended Milson's thesis and rejected complaints about the leagues, insisting that they were being put forward by pro-PLO Palestinians who correctly saw the new political structures as a serious challenge to their authority. As summarized by one observer, "By early 1982, Israeli and foreign observers sensed that the PLO's grip on the West Bank, while far from broken, appeared at least to be increasingly contested."[34] Some supporters of the Begin government went even further, claiming that the PLO was now on the defensive and that unrest in the West Bank and Gaza would soon diminish as a result. Thus, as with its settlement drive and its other efforts to deepen Israel's presence in the West Bank and Gaza, the Begin government pushed forward at this time with its attempt to undermine nationalist political activity in the occupied territories and to create alternative and compliant Palestinian political institutions.

The logic and application of Likud's policies were challenged not only by Palestinians but also by Likud's political opponents in Israel, with Labor and parties further to the left making a determined effort to turn the government from what they believed to be a dangerous and counterproductive course. In addition to political debates and protest activities organized by Peace Now and other groups, several motions of no confidence were introduced in parliament in late 1981 and early 1982. Indeed, in March 1982, there were fifty-eight votes for and fifty-eight votes against a motion specifically expressing no confidence in Likud's policies in the West Bank and Gaza, which caused the motion to fail for lack of a majority but showed that the government's base of support in parliament could not have been more narrow. Moreover, the result of this tie might easily have been different. Although a tie vote on a motion of no confidence does not require the prime minister to resign, Begin's announcement that he would remain in power constituted a break with precedent, and it also violated his own earlier pledge to resign if the motion was not defeated.

Nevertheless, while public opinion polls showed that more than half of the Israeli population had reservations about the government's settlement policies and favored the exchange of land for peace, domestic opposition in the end was not any more effective in 1981 and 1982 than it had been in 1979 and 1980, before the election of the second Begin government. The prime minister was once again able to hold his parliamentary coalition together and, as in the past, the Likud-led government worried little about the precariousness of its political position or the absence of a national mandate to bring about change in the occupied territories. As long as it remained in power, Likud had an opportunity to shape the future in accordance with its own ideological vision, and Begin, Sharon, and Shamir had no reservations whatsoever about taking full advantage of this opportunity.

The Tension-Ridden Spring of 1982

As the situation in the occupied territories became increasingly tense and moved steadily toward a new round of violent confrontations, there were several other important developments in the fall of 1981 and the winter and spring of 1982 that shaped the evolution of the Arab-Israeli conflict. While not concerned directly with Israeli-Palestinian relations, these developments contributed in significant ways to the general political climate within which these relations evolved. First, on October 6, 1981, the anniversary of the outbreak of the 1973 War, Anwar Sadat of Egypt was assassinated while reviewing a military parade in the Cairo suburb of Nasser City. Second, in December of 1981, Israel took action to annex the Golan Heights, which it had captured from Syria in the war of June 1967. Third, in the winter and spring of 1982, Israel confronted fierce and sometimes violent internal opposition as it moved to implement the last phase of its planned withdrawal from the Sinai Peninsula. All of these developments, as well as the outbreak of new violence in the West Bank and Gaza, made late 1981 and early 1982 a time of growing uncertainty.

By fall 1981, there was widespread opposition in Egypt to the government of Anwar Sadat. In part, this was the result of growing disillusionment with the

Camp David accords. Most Egyptians were not opposed to peace with Israel. On the contrary, despite the complaints of some intellectuals, most believed their country had made its contribution to the Arab cause, and therefore, in 1978 and 1979, there had been genuine popular enthusiasm at the prospect of a peaceful resolution of the Arab-Israeli conflict. But the solution to the Palestinian problem promised by Camp David had not been realized, and in 1980 and 1981 Sadat was increasingly criticized for continuing to deal with an Israeli government that, in the Egyptian view, had not kept its promises with respect to the West Bank and Gaza. Egyptians had also been stung by their country's ouster from the Arab League, which in 1979 moved its headquarters from Cairo to Tunis, and by Egypt's general isolation within the Arab world following the signing of a peace treaty with Israel. After 1979, only two other Arab countries, Sudan and Oman, maintained diplomatic relations with Cairo. Exclusion from the Arab world was unnatural for Egypt and painful for many Egyptians, who in turn directed their frustration against the Sadat government.

Yet these complaints about Camp David were clearly of secondary importance, except to the extent that Sadat had raised expectations for an improved standard of living by promising his countrymen a "peace dividend." At the core of the growing antipathy to the government in Cairo were domestic economic and political considerations. Sadat's economic policy was known as the *infitah*, or "opening," a strategy based on seeking extensive aid and investment from the West and on the promotion of indigenous capitalism. This policy was not a total failure. Considerable sums of money flowed into Egypt, including roughly $2 billion a year in direct American assistance, and aggregate economic measures revealed substantial growth as a result. But the circumstances of the average Egyptian improved little, if at all, creating a situation in which the gap between rich and poor grew significantly and the latter became increasingly resentful of the regime by which they were governed.

Mass discontent, slow to emerge but widespread at the time of Sadat's assassination, was intensified by several concomitant factors. Inflation rose rapidly as money poured into the Egyptian economy at the top, and this in turn eroded the purchasing power of ordinary citizens. Equally important, if not more so, middle- and especially upper-class Egyptians prospered greatly in an economic environment that emphasized foreign connections above productive investment, to say nothing of distribution,[35] and the highly visible consumption of the rich, and of their increasingly numerous foreign associates, generated rising anger among the less favored categories of the population. Finally, favoritism and corruption had become widespread in government and elite circles, and this added further to popular resentment of the ostentatious consumer society that had grown up in the midst of Egypt's deepening poverty. According to a 1980 article in *al-Ahram al-Iqtisadi*, "The scope of what is afoot has come to alarm even some of the staunchest proponents of *infitah*. There is a feeling that there is so much money around, and so many projects approved, that development strategy has been cast to the winds and a scramble among well-placed Egyptians to get in on the action has begun." [36]

Tensions rose even further in September 1981 when Sadat instituted a sweeping political crackdown in response to the growing criticism of his government. Approximately fifteen hundred opponents of the regime, including both Islamic militants and leftists, were arrested. Prominent as well as more obscure political figures were detained, among them journalists, the leaders of established political parties, and even the pope of the country's Coptic community. Further, following these arrests, which were said to be aimed at both Islamic and Coptic extremists, ten Muslim and three Christian associations were dissolved and seven publications were suspended. [37]

This political repression added to discontent already fostered by economic and, to a lesser extent, foreign-policy considerations, and it provides the backdrop against which Sadat was assassinated on October 6. The assassination itself was carried out by four Muslim fundamentalists who belonged to the army and used the opportunity provided by their participation in ceremonies commemorating the October 1973 war to fire directly at the president as their unit passed the reviewing stand. The men, belonging to a small extremist organization calling itself al-Takfir wal-Higra [38] and led by a twenty-four-year-old lieutenant named Khalid Islambouli, apparently acted on their own initiative. Islambouli himself, while sharing the generalized grievances against Sadat that had become widespread, was also motivated by the fact that his brother had been arrested in the crackdown of the preceding month.

In a sense, given the immediate motivation of Islambouli and his associates, there was no direct connection between Sadat's assassination and the economic and political discontent that was widespread in Egypt at this time. Indeed, veteran observers were quick to point out that even those Egyptians who most disliked the president rarely had any sympathy for his assassins. On the other hand, as one analyst wrote at the time, mass discontent must have encouraged Islambouli and his collaborators to believe that their action would bring an end to Sadat's policies, since "the more pervasive the underlying domestic problems and the more visible they are, the larger will be the number of individuals who believe that such an act will initiate momentous change." [39] Further, since there were bloody clashes between police and Muslim fundamentalists in several locations within hours of the assassination, it appeared in October 1981 that additional confrontations might well lie ahead.

In any event, quite apart from Islambouli's motivation and questions about its connection to the country's problems, Sadat's death was not greatly mourned in Egypt. On the contrary, whereas the Egyptian president had enjoyed wide popularity after the 1973 War and, later, after the signing of the Camp David accords, he had been the target of mounting anger in the fall of 1981. His unhappy position in his own country also contrasted with the prominence and popularity he had enjoyed on the international scene, where he had been hailed as a peacemaker and statesman.

Following Sadat's assassination, the presidency passed to his vice-president, Hosni Mubarak, who had sat next to Sadat on the day of his murder but had not been injured in the attack. Mubarak announced that he would attempt to correct some of the abuses associated with Sadat's economic policies, particularly with respect to the corruption and other excesses that had accompanied *infitah*. Thus, early in 1982 he dismissed Abd al-Razzaq Abd al-Magid, the deputy prime minister for economic and financial affairs who had been the principal architect of Sadat's open-door strategy. The government also brought several prominent Egyptians to trial on charges of corruption, hoping to show that the favoritism and privilege of the Sadat era would no longer be tolerated.

Mubarak also sought to distance himself from Sadat's political crackdown. He released many of the more prominent political prisoners, and then, in January 1982, he dismissed Nabawi Ismail, the interior minister who had aggressively carried out the arrests of Sadat's opponents the preceding September. These actions were popular and bought time for Mubarak, inclining most Egyptians to give their new president an opportunity to fashion his own political and economic style. At the same time, those who thought seriously about the future recognized that there were no easy or short-term solutions to Egypt's pressing economic problems, and that political challenges would almost certainly remain as well. Six months after Sadat's assassination, the majority of those arrested in September 1981 were still in prison, and Mubarak had rejected, for the time being at least, a Council of State request that he rescind the order of Sadat on the basis of which dissidents had been rounded up. Further, as many as 2,500 additional Muslim extremists had been arrested in the wake of the assassination.

Among Mubarak's early statements were expressions of a strong commitment to the peace process begun at Camp David. Indeed, he stated this specifically in his inaugural address of October 14, proclaiming that "Egypt, the state and the people, is continuing along the road to a lasting and comprehensive peace based on the framework that has been agreed upon at Camp David and that is based on the peace treaty between Egypt and Israel in letter and in spirit."[40] Most observers were of the opinion that Mubarak's statements to this effect were sincere, at least partly, perhaps, because the new Egyptian president had strong incentives to continue the foreign-policy course set by his predecessor. Egypt was highly dependent on the U.S. aid it was receiving as a result of its accommodation with Israel. Further, as Sadat's vice-president, Mubarak was himself closely associated with existing policies, and any abrupt change of course would undoubtedly have raised questions about his own past actions.

At the same time, some Israeli and other analysts suggested that the situation might change in the future, and that it would be some time before the intentions of the new Egyptian president were clear. With Israel scheduled to withdraw in April 1982 from those portions of the Sinai Peninsula that it still controlled, Mubarak had no reason to do anything other than bide his time, leading some to argue that only after Cairo's recovery of the Sinai was complete would it be possible to form judgments about what might be expected from the Mubarak government. Thus, while continuity was the order of the day so far as foreign policy was concerned, at least in the near term, both continuing domestic pressures in Egypt and the passing of the only Arab leader to have concluded a peace treaty with the Jewish state were sources of uncertainty late in 1981 and early in 1982.

Israel's annexation of the Golan Heights in December 1981 contributed further to the tension and uncertainty of this period. The Golan had been captured from Syria in the June 1967 war; and, although the territory had no ideological significance for the Jewish state, not being considered part of the historic Land of Israel, it was judged to be of major strategic importance, and both Labor and Likud governments had accordingly built settlements in the territory. By 1981 there were about 6,000 Jews living in these settlements. Nevertheless, despite this strategic significance and the presence of Israeli settlements, the future of the Golan had been considered negotiable by most Israelis. The position of the Labor Alignment was that in the context of a comprehensive peace settlement, and with suitable guarantees to ensure that the territory would not be used for aggression against Israel, most or even all of the territory would be returned to Syria. Likud, although it maintained that Israel's obligation to withdraw from territory captured in 1967 had already been fulfilled, had no official policy opposing territorial compromise on the Golan and rarely even mentioned the area when proclaiming its unshakable commitment to Israel's permanent retention of the West Bank and Gaza.

Israel's annexation of the Golan had not been expected. With Syria scrupulously respecting the disengagement-of-forces agreement negotiated in May 1974, and with United Nations truce observers serving on the Golan with the approval of both the Israeli and Syrian governments, most observers were caught by surprise when, on December 14, the prime minister introduced a bill in the Knesset specifying that "the law, jurisdiction and administration of the State shall apply to the Golan Heights." The bill was passed by a vote of 63 to 21, with eight Alignment members supporting it. According to one scholar, the Labor opposition was caught totally unprepared and was in total disarray.[41]

Although the Golan itself had been quiet for some time, and was consequently almost forgotten as attention focused on Israel's relations with Egypt and the Palestinians, there had been a few moves designed to ensure that the Golan would remain under Israeli control. In 1979 and 1980, for example, Jewish settlers circulated a petition opposing any future withdrawal from the territory and eventually collected 750,000 signatures on the document. Prominent Labor Alignment leaders were among the signatories, including Shimon Peres, Yitzhak

Rabin, and Yigal Allon, and this led some left-oriented critics to charge that Labor had "its own Gush Emunim," hawkish elements who preferred land to peace
and were prepared "to sacrifice national political strategy to the sanctity of territory."[42] In reality, however, despite their belief that the Golan had strategic significance, most Labor leaders probably signed the petition for political reasons,
hoping to compete with Likud for conservative voters and to identify their party
with policies that would make its advocacy of territorial compromise in the West
Bank and Gaza more broadly acceptable.[43] In any event, the petition drive helped
to keep the Israeli government aware of the Golan issue. The issue was also raised
early in 1981 by the right-wing Tehiya Party. In March, Tehiya introduced a bill,
which was only narrowly defeated, to annex the Golan Heights.

An important motivation for the Begin government's action in December
1981 was a desire to demonstrate its commitment to territorial maximalism in
the face of challenges from parties to both its left and its right. Of even more
immediate concern, Likud sought to defuse criticism from Gush Emunim and
other right-wing elements who had recently formed a "Stop the Withdrawal from
Sinai" movement and were pressing the prime minister to renege on his promise
to relinquish those portions of the Sinai Peninsula that Israel still controlled. Begin himself, of course, gave different reasons for wishing to annex the Golan,
including an unsubstantiated and essentially inaccurate charge that Damascus
had decided to "revert to its hostile and bellicose posture."[44] Although there was
no evidence of change in either the policy or the actions of the Syrian government, the Israeli prime minister told the Knesset of a recent speech in which Hafez al-Assad, the president of Syria, had reportedly declared that he would "not
recognize or even negotiate with Israel, even if the PLO does so."[45]

Motivations apart, the extension of Israeli law to the Golan Heights was
another source of tension and uncertainty in the winter and the spring of 1982,
and the situation grew more problematic when, in February, the Druze residents
of the Golan proclaimed a general strike to protest Israel's annexation of the
territory in which they lived. Although still citizens of Syria, most of these Druze
had previously offered little resistance to the Israeli occupation. Indeed, many had
maintained friendly relations with Israelis. Now, however, residents of the Golan
assembled in local mosques and decided to cut off all relations with Israel. They
militantly refused the new Israeli identity cards which the army had ordered them
to accept and, more generally, initiated a comprehensive strike that persisted for
several months. Workers did not go to their jobs, businesses were closed, and
schools were shut down. The Druze also refused to pay taxes to Israel and declared that they would not accept any payments or favors from the Israeli government.

The IDF's use of coercion and collective punishment in an effort to break
the strike and to force the Druze to accept Israeli identification cards added to
concern about the situation on the Golan and intensified the political debates

taking place inside the Jewish state. In particular, there was an outcry when the army cited emergency regulations dating back to 1945 and imposed a state of siege on the area. This action was denounced by many Israelis. For example, *Ha'aretz* editorialized in March that "the Druze are learning on their very flesh that the hand of oppression can be many times worse under civil rule than under military government.... Twelve thousand residents—non-violent up till now, politically passive until annexation to Israel was forced upon them ... are imprisoned in their villages without food supplies (excepting foodstuffs sold by the IDF), without regular medical services, medicines and other vital commodities."[46] In mid-May, retired Supreme Court Justice Chaim Cohn, who was also chairman of the Association for Civil Rights in Israel, issued a powerful statement in which he characterized IDF actions on the Golan as "barbarism" and publicly detailed the bases for his charge. But criticism from Cohn and others also brought strong rebuttals from the government and its sympathizers, in the end reinforcing the political divisions in the Jewish state.

Also contributing to the uncertainty of this period were confrontations between the IDF and activists of the Stop the Withdrawal from Sinai Movement, which had recently been formed by elements from Tehiya, Gush Emunim, and the National Religious Party. Hoping to prevent the Begin government from completing the last phase of its withdrawal from the Sinai Peninsula, which was to be implemented by April 26, anti-withdrawal forces were active on many fronts. They sought to raise money and support among overseas Jews, and to obtain endorsements of their cause from prominent political and even military figures in Israel. In January and February 1982, they also announced plans to erect several new Jewish settlements in northern Sinai before April 26. Most important, the movement sent squatters to take over the apartments of Jewish residents who were leaving the communities they had built in Sinai. Many of the departing settlers had initially denounced the Camp David accords, arguing that the government had previously encouraged them to settle in Sinai and could not now ask them to abandon the communities they had worked so hard to develop. Most of these settlers subsequently accepted the generous compensation offered by the government, however, and thus willingly, if sometimes sadly, they took their movable property and returned to Israel. It was into the vacant residences of these departing settlers that Stop the Withdrawal activists now moved.

The IDF was charged with preventing Stop the Withdrawal forces from hindering the evacuation of the Sinai, and this led to numerous, and sometimes violent, clashes. As early as February, for example, the IDF had to employ considerable force to subdue right-wing militants attempting to prevent the removal of water pipes serving northern Sinai. Activists also confronted the IDF at army checkpoints, sometimes wearing yellow Stars of David and denouncing as "Nazis" the soldiers charged with blocking their entry into the territory scheduled to be returned to Egypt.

As the date of the final withdrawal approached, most clashes centered on efforts to limit the infiltration of would-be squatters and to remove those already present, especially in Yamit, a former settlement town where Stop the Withdrawal diehards had made their headquarters, and inside which three to four thousand of their number had barricaded themselves by mid-April. Yamit squatters included many women and children, and following the eviction of anti-withdrawal activists from other Sinai settlements, they vowed to resist by all means at their disposal the government's effort to remove them.[47] Among their number were also members of the supernationalist Kach Party, who threatened to commit suicide rather than permit the army to remove them. Both physical and rhetorical violence accompanied this prolonged confrontation, although the demonstrators at the last minute agreed to leave Yamit peacefully, and the IDF showed great restraint in the face of intense provocation as it carried out the remaining militants on April 22 and April 23. The army then ended the unhappy saga of Yamit by razing the town with giant bulldozers.

Israel completed its withdrawal from the Sinai Peninsula two days later. Although many Egyptians had feared that the Begin government would find some pretext to postpone the implementation of its promised withdrawal, the transfer of territory was accomplished on schedule, on April 25, in a simple ceremony in which the Israeli flag was lowered for the last time in Sinai and Egyptian authority was reinstated. In the picturesque southern Sinai town of Sharm al-Sheikh, which the Israelis had called Ophira, Israeli soldiers sang the national anthem and their commander declared, "We are leaving Sinai for our own sake, for the sake of our children, and for future generations, to try to find a way other than the way of war."[48] Later in the day, Begin and Mubarak broadcast remarks simultaneously to television audiences in Israel and Egypt, with the Israeli prime minister stating that there would be "no more war, no more bloodshed," and the Egyptian president telling viewers that "tomorrow a new dawn will break and the banner of peace will be hoisted forever."

While these developments were greeted with sighs of relief in both Israel and Egypt, and with expressions of hope for the future, the felicitous pronouncements issued in Jerusalem and Cairo were more of a plea than a conviction that good times lay ahead. Malaise and apprehension consistently competed with the hope spawned by the peace process, and nagging fears remained, perhaps even intensified, as the Sinai withdrawal brought the first phase of the Camp David peace process to an end. As noted, there were doubts about the course that the new government in Cairo would follow, there was continuing unrest and agitation on the Golan Heights, and many in Israel had been shaken by the domestic violence that accompanied the evacuation of Yamit and other Sinai settlements. All of this made Israel's withdrawal from the Sinai Peninsula an occasion not only for rejoicing but for sober reflection as well.

Confrontations between Israelis and Palestinians were played out against this backdrop during the difficult spring of 1982. Moreover, the deteriorating situation in the West Bank and Gaza frequently overshadowed concerns related to Sinai and the Golan, such that the festering Palestinian problem not only appeared more worrisome in light of the difficulties on other fronts but was itself a major cause of the tense and uncertain mood that hung over Israel and the occupied territories during this period.

A new round of disturbances began when an Israeli official was beaten by Palestinian students at Birzeit University near Ramallah on February 15, after which Israeli authorities closed the school for two months, and protest demonstrations were then organized at other West Bank universities. Agitation grew more intense in the weeks that followed, and in addition to demonstrations and protest marches, there were general strikes in many areas, including East Jerusalem, and incidents in which young Palestinians threw stones at Israeli soldiers and Jewish civilians traveling in the occupied territories. The clashes that erupted during this period were the most intense and prolonged of any that had occurred since Israel took control of the West Bank and Gaza in 1967. As Palestinians reaffirmed their opposition to occupation and demanded recognition of their right to self-determination, even many Arab citizens of Israel were caught up in the Palestinian struggle, making support for resistance in the occupied territories the theme of their annual "Land Day" protests on March 30.

The violent character of the disturbances that took place during March, April, and May can be seen in the reports of the Palestinian press. Though heavily censored, newspapers published in East Jerusalem gave broad coverage to Palestinian efforts at resistance and to the resultant clashes between Israelis and Palestinians. The following list of incidents, which gives a sense of the widespread unrest that prevailed in the West Bank and Gaza during the spring of 1982, represents a sampling taken from *al-Fajr Jerusalem* in mid-April.[49] It is a partial list of the clashes that occurred in a single day.

> A mass demonstration broke out at An-Najah University in Nablus, in which Palestinian flags were hoisted and national slogans were chanted. Israeli forces surrounded the campus, used tear gas and opened fire inside. Military roadblocks were erected on the streets leading to the campus.
>
> Several student demonstrations broke out in Tulkarm and in nearby Anabta. Demonstrators set tires afire and Israeli troops used force to quell the demonstration.
>
> Additional student demonstrations took place in Jenin and in the nearby villages of Silat el-Thaher, el-Ymoun, Tamoun and Tubas. Demonstrators stoned Israeli forces and several youths were detained. Israeli forces broke into the village of Silat el-Thaher and opened fire and used tear gas to break up demonstrating students.
>
> In the Ramallah area, residents of Jalazoun camp erected road barriers with stones and burning tires.

In the Bethlehem area, a demonstration broke out in the village of Husan. Barriers were erected and a Palestinian flag was hoisted. The soldiers opened fire, injuring a 16 year old student.

Student demonstrations broke out in several towns and villages near Hebron, particularly Dura, Beit Awwa and the refugee camp of Arroub. Several residents, including students, were arrested and classes were disrupted in several schools.

In the Gaza Strip, people are searched by soldiers and several students and other persons were beaten up by the soldiers. Curfews are still imposed on Abasan, Jabalia, and the refugee camp of Khan Yunis.

One week later, *al-Fajr Jerusalem* reported that "fighting between Palestinian civilians and Israeli troops erupted again, on April 25, in the confrontation which is now almost two months old. Several people were shot and scores were arrested, following demonstrations in the north, center and south of the West Bank, as well as the Gaza Strip."[50] The following are a few of the nearly two dozen incidents reported for April 25 alone, with the paper adding that five more Palestinians were shot and wounded in disturbances on April 26.

Three people were hospitalized and several others received emergency first aid when soldiers opened fire on demonstrators in the Qalandia refugee camp. All entrances to the camp were sealed by soldiers. Students at the al-Bireh girls secondary school threw stones at Israeli military cars. Soldiers fired tear gas and shot in the air to disperse the demonstrating students. Several hundred people from Tubas stormed the police station and hoisted the Palestinian flag over it, after taking over the building. Four policemen, including the station commander, were injured during the attack. The protesters remained in the building for more than half an hour before they were forced out. One girl was injured by bullets. More than 70 people were detained and the village was placed under curfew. One woman student from Arroub refugee camp was shot in the leg as soldiers fired on demonstrating students on the main road between Hebron and Jerusalem.

The accuracy of these reports is ensured by the heavy censorship to which the Palestinian press was subjected. Indeed, *al-Fajr* at the time followed the practice of reporting how many of the articles it had submitted to the Israeli censor were either disallowed or substantially modified. Moreover, the Israeli press provided detailed accounts of these clashes as well, featuring articles in April and May with titles such as "Boy dies as violence sweeps Gaza, W. Bank," "Two Arabs killed as troops disperse riots," "Youth shot after stonings in Bethlehem area village," "2 killed, 9 hurt in West Bank disturbances," and "Girl pupil killed during Gaza Strip school riot."[51] These and many other reports, which tell of incidents in which as many as twenty Palestinians may have been killed, led the *Jerusalem Post* to editorialize that "from all but official reports, the image of this little war has emerged as nasty, brutish and hopeless."[52] Further, the editorial was prompted by a press conference at which six IDF reserve officers recounted their experiences while serving in the occupied territories, giving an account, according to the *Jerusalem Post*, which "was depressing when it was not hair-raising." Thus, with a scope and intensity unmatched during the previous fifteen years of Israeli occupation, the West Bank and Gaza exploded in the spring of 1982, making it all the more evident that even a positive evolution of relations between Israel and Egypt would not bring peace in the absence of a resolution of the Palestinian dimension of the Arab-Israeli conflict.

The Israeli actions to which Palestinians in the West Bank and Gaza were responding in the spring of 1982 included not only the settlement drive of the Begin and Sharon government but also the lawlessness and vigilantism of Gush Emunim and other elements of the organized settler movement. Further, not only were there a number of incidents in which Palestinians were attacked by Jewish settlers, but the lenient treatment which Israeli authorities gave to the perpetrators of these acts was an additional source of Palestinian anger. In March 1982, for example, an Arab teenager from the village of Sinjal was shot and killed by an Israeli resident of a nearby settlement. The settler was detained briefly but released a few days later, and the case against him was subsequently dropped. Also in March, settlers shot and killed another Palestinian youth from a village near Hebron, after young men from the village had thrown stones at the settlers' car. As in the earlier incident, no one was brought to trial and the case was dropped after a cursory investigation.

According to an Israeli government inquiry into settler violence against Palestinians in the West Bank, headed by Deputy Attorney General Yehudit Karp, there were a total of fifteen such incidents during April and May, all of which involved either death or injury as a result of shootings.[53] There were also instances of Jewish settlers throwing hand grenades at Arab homes, automobiles, and even schools in several locations.[54] The Israeli government claimed that these and other charges contained in the Karp report were greatly exaggerated, and the document was shelved when it was submitted on May 25, 1982. When the report was made public twenty months later, however, the *Jerusalem Post* wrote in a powerful editorial that it "bears out the initial suspicion that a systematic miscarriage of justice is being perpetrated in the West Bank. Jewish settlers, wishing to assert their rights in the area, take the law into their own hands . . . [after which the] files are closed without anyone being booked."[55]

As noted, the problem of settler violence was seriously compounded by the complicity of Israeli authorities, including the IDF. Most of the incidents that took place during this period were not properly investigated, and in no case were those responsible for the violence arrested and placed on trial. Moreover, according to the conclusions of the Karp report, this situation appears to have been mainly the result of "external interference on the part of Military Government personnel, in giving orders [to police] concerning the actual opening of investigations and related matters such as release from detention."[56] Not only did this interference raise constitutional questions, the report continued, but intervention by Military Government personnel had "the direct consequence of making [police] investigations more difficult . . . [and was] naturally interpreted as backing for suspects."[57] The IDF also contributed to vigilantism by allowing settlers to do their military reserve duty by patrolling Arab communities near their West Bank settlements. Whether intended or not, this gave many settlers an opportunity to harass and intimidate the local population while claiming to be acting in self-defense.

In an effort to contain Palestinian agitation and restore order in the occupied territories, Israeli authorities instituted a crackdown that included a relaxation of the circumstances under which soldiers could shoot at demonstrators in the West Bank and Gaza. While there do not appear to have been any formal orders to this effect, a number of Israeli analysts reported in the spring of 1982 that senior military commanders, especially the minister of defense, had let it be known that they would not deal harshly with soldiers who opened fire when seeking to put down protest demonstrations, and whose actions resulted in the death or injury of Palestinians. According to a prominent journalist, writing in April 1982, "Junior officers have been given to understand that if they are quick to give the order to fire [when confronted by protesters], they will not run too much risk of being reprimanded by their supervisors, and certainly not of being court martialed." Thus, he continued, "there has been a change in the conceptions at the top of what the army may and may not be used for in democratic Israel. The change has been for the worse, and is associated with the dominating role played by Minister of Defense Ariel Sharon."[58]

Israeli authorities responded to unrest in the territories not only by confronting demonstrators in the streets but also by intensifying their attack on institutions serving the Palestinians of the West Bank and Gaza, particularly those judged to be vehicles for PLO influence. On March 11, invoking emergency regulations dating back to 1945, the defense minister outlawed the National Guidance Committee. The committee, which included representatives from Fatah, PFLP, and DFLP and which the Israeli Defense Ministry called "a *de facto* arm of the PLO" in the occupied territories, had been formed several years earlier to coordinate Palestinian opposition to the Camp David autonomy proposals. Several of the NGC's leading members had been deported in 1980, and a number of others had been under house or town arrest since that time, thus restricting their activities and, the Israelis hoped, preventing them from organizing resistance to occupation. Nevertheless, Israeli authorities accused the committee of encouraging the political unrest in the West Bank and Gaza and explained that it was now being outlawed for this reason.

Banning of the National Guidance Committee was followed by removal of the pro-PLO mayors and municipal council members who had come to power in many West Bank towns in the elections of 1976. As noted earlier, the Begin government stated that this action was prompted only secondarily by unrest in the territories and, more fundamentally, was designed to correct an error of the previous Labor government in permitting these individuals to be elected in the first place. In fact, however, the government's action in the spring of 1982 was a response to the growing resistance to occupation, including the fact that some mayors were refusing to discuss the affairs of their city with Menachem Milson, head of the Israeli Civilian Administration in the West Bank. It was also part of a more general struggle for influence in the West Bank and Gaza, with the Israelis hoping that by dismissing pro-PLO officials they might reduce opposition to the village leagues.

On March 18, the mayor of el-Bireh, Ibrahim Tawil, was escorted from his office by a Military Government official who handed him a dismissal order signed by Milson. The city's municipal council was ordered to disband as well, after which the Defense Ministry announced that Tawil and his council had been sacked for refusing to cooperate with the Israeli Civilian Administration, and "because this situation had seriously harmed the interest of the city and its inhabitants." In response to these Israeli actions, including Milson's appointment of a special committee of IDF officers and civilians to run the town, the inhabitants of el-Bireh called a three-day general strike. Strikes in support of el-Bireh were also called by the municipalities of Ramallah, Nablus, Hebron, and at least four other West Bank towns.

A week later, the Israelis fired Bassam Shaka and Karim Khalaf, the mayors of Nablus and Ramallah respectively, both of whom had been wounded by Jewish terrorists in 1980. As in the case of Tawil, the Israelis said that the mayors' refusal to cooperate with the Civilian Administration provided a legal basis for their removal. In addition, however, Shaka and Khalaf, who were outspoken supporters of the PLO and members of the National Guidance Committee, were also accused of inciting strikes and demonstrations, and this was undoubtedly the principal reason for the action against them. Indeed, especially since sustaining their injuries, the two men had been the most prominent symbols of Palestinian nationalism and resistance to occupation in the territories; and thus, in defending the firing of the two mayors, Milson specifically told reporters at a press conference in Ramallah that "Israel is engaged now in a very serious struggle against the PLO," and that "if people are pro-PLO they are terrorists, anti-Semites and committed to the destruction of Israel." [59] For their part, Shaka and Khalaf both refused to accept their dismissal, or even to sign documents confirming they had received the order, but were nevertheless prevented from continuing their duties. The Civilian Administration appointed Israeli officers to run the Nablus and Ramallah municipalities.

Predictably, banning the National Guidance Committee and firing Tawil, Shaka, and Khalaf, all of which took place in March, neither reduced the intensity of agitation in the West Bank and Gaza nor undermined the influence of the PLO in these territories. As noted, demonstrations and clashes with Israeli soldiers continued and grew more intense during April and May. Also, a poll commissioned by *Time* magazine and conducted in April revealed overwhelming support for the PLO and its goal of establishing an independent Palestinian state. The survey of 441 residents of fifty-eight towns and refugee camps in the West Bank and Gaza was carried out by the Pori Institute of Tel Aviv, with assistance from Israeli sociologists at the Hebrew University. It found that 98 percent favored the creation of a Palestinian state, and 86 percent believed this state should be governed solely by the PLO. Conversely, only 0.2 percent expressed support for Mustafa Doudin, the most prominent leader of the village leagues.[60] Similar findings were reported in a poll taken about the same time by Palestinians from An-Najah National University in Nablus. Based on a sample of 3,000 West Bank respondents, the survey found that 86 percent of those interviewed considered themselves to be represented by the PLO, with another 8 percent not responding to the question. Only 3 percent considered themselves to be represented by King Hussein of Jordan, although another 17 percent suggested that Jordan could be a partner of the PLO in representing the Palestinians.[61]

While a few Israelis called upon the government to accept the fact that Palestinians in the occupied territories considered themselves to be represented by the PLO, and accordingly urged that Israel confront the PLO with an intelligent negotiating position, the government of Begin and Sharon pushed ahead with its efforts to change the political equation in the West Bank and Gaza. In late April, the mayor and municipal council of Anabta were dismissed. In June and July, four more West Bank municipalities were dissolved, and the mayor of Gaza was also fired. The reason given for dismissing the mayor and council in Jenin, for example, was "the on-going strike and the continuing work-stoppage led by the Mayor and his council." In Gaza, Mayor Rashad Shawwa, a political moderate who had been appointed by the Israelis in 1975, was dismissed following his refusal to comply with an order from the Military Government to restore full municipal services and refrain from political activity. In still other actions designed to suppress independent Palestinian voices, Israel also attempted to exercise greater control over journalists in East Jerusalem. As noted earlier, authorities in March charged two Palestinian dailies with incitement and banned their distribution in the West Bank and Gaza.

Once again, all of these actions were opposed by many Israelis. Following the ouster of Shaka and Khalaf, for example, tens of thousands of Peace Now supporters from all over the country assembled in Tel Aviv's Habimah Square to protest government policy in the occupied territories. Organizers estimated that there were 50,000 participants. In addition, indicating that opposition was not confined to the political left, the Knesset came within a single vote of passing a motion of no confidence in the government's policies in the West Bank and Gaza, a motion which, had it passed, would have required the prime minister and his cabinet to resign. Both the contradictions and the brutality of the government's approach to the territories were also denounced in editorials and speeches. For example, *Ha'aretz*, Israel's leading daily, editorialized in March that the government, "which thought it ought to give the Defense Minister an opportunity to break Arab resistance, would do well to call a halt to this path: 'Greater Israel' is not worth the brutalization which will spread within us as a result of pursuing the methods of repression required to attain it."[62] According to another commentator, writing in May, "Never has there been such brutalization. . . . Arab blood is cheap. Sometimes it seems that Ariel Sharon is the greatest recruitment officer the PLO ever had."[63]

The divisions in Israel, as well as the unswerving commitment of the government to its vision of Greater Israel, are nicely illustrated by the events that took place on Independence Day. The government chose the theme "One Hundred Years of Jewish Settlement" for the festivities it had planned, which took place on April 28, three days after the withdrawal from Sinai. It also announced that eleven new military settlements would be inaugurated to mark the occasion, eight of which were to be in the West Bank. One of these, Nahal Telem, near Hebron, was to be formally dedicated by the defense minister, and the government publicized the event widely and even offered free transportation to the ceremonies. Some of the buses did not reach Nahal Telem, however, for a roadblock had been set up by supporters of Peace Now. At the site itself, Peace Now also succeeded in disrupting the ceremonies. Although about 600 demonstrators had been prevented by the army from reaching Nahal Telem, roughly 150 others eluded the army and sat quietly with the rest of the crowd until Sharon began to speak. They then rose, waved flags and banners, and chanted slogans opposing the defense minister and his policies, whereupon they were attacked by members of Betar, the youth movement of the Herut wing of Likud. To many Israelis, the fact that Jews not only were clashing with Palestinians in the West Bank and Gaza but were fighting among themselves, too, as they had done in connection with the withdrawal from Sinai, was a sign that something fundamental was amiss. It was also a reflection of the tension and uncertainty that filled the difficult spring of 1982.

The Israeli Invasion of Lebanon

A logical extension of Israel's campaign against PLO influence in the West Bank and Gaza was a desire to inflict damage on the PLO itself through an attack on the organization's political and military bases in Lebanon. As noted, most members of the Begin government, including its leading personalities, the prime minister himself and Defense Minister Ariel Sharon, considered the PLO to be the source of most of Jerusalem's troubles in the occupied territories. As an American State Department official put the matter at the time, "The Israeli government believes it has a Palestinian problem because of the PLO; not that it has a PLO problem because of the Palestinians."[64] The conclusion which Begin and Sharon deduced from their analysis was that if Israel could force the PLO to curtail its encouragement of resistance in the West Bank and Gaza, either by weakening the organization or by teaching it that its actions were not cost-free, notables in the territories would accept Jerusalem's overtures, participate in the village leagues or other alternative leadership structures, and seek an accommodation with Israel within the framework of the government's autonomy proposals. Suppressing Palestinian nationalism in the West Bank and Gaza and inflicting a military and political defeat on the PLO in Lebanon were thus two interrelated aspects of a single vision shared by Begin, Sharon, and other Israeli supporters of territorial maximalism.

The possibility of an Israeli offensive against the PLO was also raised in the spring of 1982 by Jerusalem's claim that the Palestinian organization was using its Lebanese bases to launch direct attacks upon the Jewish state. There had been periodic exchanges of fire between Israel and the PLO a year earlier, with the former carrying out air strikes against Palestinian targets in southern Lebanon and the latter occasionally shelling towns and *kibbutzim* in the Galilee region of northern Israel. A related source of tension at this time was Syria's installation of sophisticated SAM-6 missiles in Lebanon's Beqaa Valley, which threatened IDF surveillance flights over southern Lebanon and which Jerusalem viewed as a violation of its tacit agreement with Damascus to preserve the status quo in the area. Following a series of Israeli air attacks on PLO positions in May and June of 1981, American diplomatic intervention calmed the situation briefly. Then, in July, Israel launched additional air strikes and initiated a new and much more intense round of hostilities. The PLO responded by shelling the northern Israeli city of Nahariya, after which Jerusalem escalated the fighting and bombed the PLO's headquarters in Beirut, killing at least 100 persons and wounding many more;[65] and this was then followed by a blistering PLO rocket attack that disrupted life in the Galilee and inflicted considerable damage. This spiral of violence is sometimes described as the "Two-Week War."

The hostilities of July 1981 left Israel acutely aware of the firepower the PLO had amassed in Lebanon. Even though PLO shelling had been in response to an escalation initiated by Jerusalem,[66] the Israeli government and others in the Jewish state were deeply concerned about the ability to rain destruction on northern Israel that the PLO now appeared to possess, and as a result security in the Galilee became an important issue on the country's political agenda. So far as the Two-Week War itself is concerned, the conflict was brought to an end through the efforts of American mediator Philip Habib, who contacted the PLO through the good offices of Saudi Arabia and arranged a ceasefire. The Begin government accepted the ceasefire as well. Indeed, Jerusalem welcomed and encouraged the American mediation effort, even though it did not result in victory from the Israeli point of view. Not only did it leave intact the PLO arsenal in Lebanon that was a source of Israeli concern, it also, as Begin's domestic critics were quick to point out, involved both Israel and the United States in indirect negotiations with the PLO, and this gave additional international legitimacy to the Palestinian organization.

It is against the background of unrest in the occupied territories and the Two-Week War of the preceding summer that Israel massed troops on its northern border in April 1982 and threatened to take whatever action was necessary to clean out PLO strongholds in southern Lebanon. The PLO denounced the Israeli action, of course, insisting that it was without justification since Palestinian guerrillas in Lebanon had respected the ceasefire agreement negotiated by Habib. The PLO also declared that it would "teach Israel a lesson" if Jerusalem insisted on sending troops across the border, and this led residents of the Upper Galilee to urge the government to avoid a confrontation. Indeed, recalling the devastating attacks of July 1981, some circulated a petition opposing an invasion of Lebanon. Restraint was also urged by senior Labor Alignment politicians and by two former Israeli chiefs of staff, both of whom accused the Begin and Sharon government of looking for an excuse to go to war.

Calls for restraint notwithstanding, many observers thought Israel would act on its threat to send IDF ground forces into southern Lebanon at this time, calculating that world criticism would be muted so as not to provide Jerusalem with a pretext for postponing its evacuation of the Sinai Peninsula. Expectations of an invasion intensified as the date of the Sinai withdrawal approached, and on April 21, while the IDF was preparing to remove squatters from Yamit, Israeli bombers launched major strikes against PLO bases and also downed two of the Syrian MIG-23 fighters sent to deter them. No ground assault followed, however, and the Lebanese-Israeli border remained tense but quiet as the withdrawal from Sinai was carried out on schedule.

Although predictions of an Israeli invasion of Lebanon had proven incorrect in April 1982, the IDF sent thousands of troops across the border six weeks later, on June 6, launching what the government in Jerusalem termed "Operation Peace for Galilee." The immediate catalyst for the invasion was an attack by Palestinian extremists on Israel's ambassador to Great Britain, Shlomo Argov, on the night of June 3. A Palestinian gunman fired at Argov from close range and gravely wounded the Israeli diplomat as he emerged from a banquet at London's Dorchester Hotel. The Israeli cabinet met the next morning, with Begin telling its members, "We will not stand for them attacking an Israeli ambassador. An assault on an ambassador is tantamount to an attack on the State of Israel, and we will respond to it."[67] There were no dissenting voices, and later in the day Israel did respond, launching major air strikes against PLO positions both in southern

Lebanon and in Beirut. Several hours later it was the turn of the PLO, which, with Yasir Arafat in Baghdad attempting to mediate in the Iraq-Iran War, undertook sporadic shelling of settlements in the Galilee. The PLO's attacks did comparatively little damage. Eight Israelis were wounded and one man died of a heart attack, whereas IDF raids earlier in the day had killed 45 and wounded about 150 Palestinians and Lebanese.[68] Nevertheless, the PLO shelling gave Israel an additional incentive to act.

These events led directly to the Israeli invasion. Sharon, on a visit to Rumania, hurried home for a cabinet meeting on the evening of the 5th, at which he and Begin convinced the government to authorize a ground assault on PLO positions in southern Lebanon. The IDF attack began the next morning, and Begin later stated in a speech to the National Defense College that had Jerusalem not gone to war against the PLO in Lebanon, it would have had to reconcile itself to "the ceaseless killing of our civilians . . . [and] gone on seeing our civilians injured in [the northern towns of] Metulla or Qiryat Shmona or Nahariya."[69]

While the attack on Argov and the latest round of PLO shelling were described by Israel as actions which showed the true colors of the PLO, and which demanded a response, it was not the case that PLO aggressiveness left the Jewish state no choice but to go to war. On the contrary, the PLO had shown considerable restraint during the eleven months between June 1982 and the ceasefire agreement signed the preceding July; and it was Israel's determination to clean out PLO strongholds in southern Lebanon, rather than any recent aggression by Arafat's guerrillas, that provided the impetus for the invasion. Begin had been convinced since the hostilities of the preceding summer that Israel should drive the PLO out of south Lebanon once and for all, and with the lead taken by Sharon and Chief of Staff Rafael Eitan, both military and political preparations for an eventual invasion had gone forward steadily during late 1981 and early 1982. Military preparations were considerably advanced by the early spring of the latter year, well before Jerusalem's threatened invasion in April.

An important part of the political groundwork that Israel sought to lay was the removal of any possible opposition from the United States. As early as December 1981, Sharon began telling American officials that "if the terrorists continue to violate the ceasefire, we will have no choice but to wipe them out completely in Lebanon."[70] In February, the IDF's chief of military intelligence, Major General Yehoshua Saguy, visited Washington and received a sympathetic hearing from American Secretary of State Alexander Haig. Begin and Sharon believed that Saguy's visit resulted in significant progress toward obtaining tacit American approval for an Israeli ground operation in Lebanon.

Sharon himself visited Washington in May and made sure that the U.S. understood Jerusalem's intentions; and following the defense minister's own meeting with Alexander Haig, the American secretary of state had no doubt that Israel would respond to a serious PLO violation of the ceasefire with military action in Lebanon. Even more important, the Israeli government was convinced that Haig would not oppose such an operation. Whether Haig actually gave Sharon the green light remains a matter of some dispute. The former secretary of state denies that this is the case, and it seems that no statement explicitly approving an Israeli attack was given. On the other hand, in the absence of a clear expression of opposition from Haig, the Israelis believed they had at least tacit approval for a limited ground assault carried out in response to a genuine provocation on the part of the PLO.[71] One analyst concludes that Haig gave Sharon a "dim yellow light," and then quotes a U.S. State Department official to the effect that "it doesn't really matter what Haig gave him, Sharon has been known to run lights of all colors."[72]

Israeli claims to the contrary notwithstanding, the PLO had been observing the ceasefire negotiated the preceding summer, and Jerusalem thus required an attack by the Palestinian organization to justify the implementation of its planned invasion. Although radicals under the PLO umbrella wanted to shell settlements in northern Israel, Arafat labored to hold them in check through the spring of 1982, and the PLO accordingly did not shell Israel in response to IDF air raids in April. The Palestinians did retaliate when the IDF carried out additional air strikes early in May, but they deliberately aimed their artillery barrage away from towns and settlements, hoping to show that while they had the ability to inflict punishment if Israel insisted on an escalation, they in fact wished to avoid war.[73] Indeed, about a week later, Arafat sent Begin a letter through the United Nations in which he made explicit his desire to avoid war with Israel. "You of all people must understand that it is not necessary to face me on the battlefield," he wrote. "Do not send a military force against me."[74]

In the meantime, however, the Israelis had learned that the PLO could be maneuvered into giving Jerusalem the justification it needed for an invasion of Lebanon. Israeli intelligence confirmed in May that a political struggle between Arafat and PLO radicals seeking a more aggressive policy had produced a compromise: the Palestinians would not unilaterally violate the ceasefire but would automatically respond to any Israeli artillery attack in the sector from which it emanated. This information was not widely disseminated in Israel. It is possible that it had not even been shared with the Israeli cabinet when, at its meeting of June 4, it authorized new strikes against the PLO. But Israeli sources make clear that it was understood and utilized by Begin and Sharon. In the words of an important and objective study by leading Israeli journalists, "Once the Israelis discovered that an appropriate provocation would elicit a shelling of the Galilee, they could dictate the plays that would lead to war."[75]

Even though the PLO had nothing to do with the terrorist attack on Shlomo Argov in London, Israel characterized the attack as yet another provocation which showed the need to remove the PLO from southern Lebanon. In fact, Argov was shot by Palestinian extremists of the terrorist group led by Abu Nidal, an Iraqi-sponsored dissident who was a sworn enemy of Yasir Arafat, as well as Israel, and whose followers had also carried out operations against PLO officials and institutions. In June 1982, Abu Nidal sought to provoke an Israeli offensive against the PLO, and, whether or not he understood that this was also the Begin government's objective, his action in London did bring movement in this direction. Israeli intelligence knew that Abu Nidal was almost certainly responsible for the attack on Argov, but Begin dismissed the information, saying, "Abu Nidal, Abu Shmidal. . . . They're all PLO." He also declined to share the information with the cabinet.[76] As noted, the cabinet responded to the attack on Argov by authorizing new IDF air strikes against PLO positions in Lebanon, and, armed with the knowledge that the PLO would automatically reply by shelling the Galilee, Begin and Sharon had exactly what they needed to initiate a series of events that would justify an invasion of Lebanon. Within two hours of Israeli air raids carried out on the afternoon of June 4, towns in northern Israel had been hit by PLO shells coming from southern Lebanon. War was now only thirty-six hours away.

In discussions inside the cabinet and in their communications with the Americans, Begin and Sharon repeatedly stressed that Operation Peace for Galilee would be a limited initiative, with precise military objectives. The cabinet meeting on the evening of June 5, at which the decision to go to war was taken, discussed only an operation that would push back PLO artillery. When one government minister expressed concern about entanglements farther north, he was told by Sharon that the IDF's sole mission was to move PLO rockets and artillery out of range of Israeli settlements. "Beirut is outside the picture," the defense minister stated categorically. "We're talking about a range of forty kilometers. That is what the cabinet has approved."[77] Begin and Sharon also assured the cabinet that Israel would not attack Syrian forces in Lebanon. The United States was given similar assurances about the limited nature of Operation Peace for Galilee. When Philip Habib telephoned the Israeli prime minister on June 6, Begin told the American diplomat that the operation would take no more than seventy-two hours, and that the IDF would stop at forty kilometers, a figure that Begin also communicated in writing to the U.S. president, Ronald Reagan.

In addition, Begin and Sharon emphasized the limited nature of Operation Peace for Galilee in their discussions with senior officials of the Labor Alignment. The government had briefed Alignment leaders about plans for a ground operation in Lebanon as early as mid-May, and although the figure of forty kilometers was not specifically mentioned, Begin and Sharon had stressed that Israel's objectives in Lebanon were limited. On June 6, just as the first Israeli troops were crossing the border, Labor leaders were again told that the IDF would confine itself to southern Lebanon, and also that it would do everything possible to avoid a confrontation with the Syrians. As expressed by one analyst, Begin made it clear that he envisioned only "an expanded Operation Litani that would avoid a war with the Syrians and would avoid entry into Beirut."[78] Based on these assurances, most top Alignment leaders shelved the opposition that had characterized their attitude toward a possible invasion in April and expressed a willingness to support Operation Peace for Galilee. Despite their awareness of PLO restraint, most agreed with the prime minister that the growth of the Palestinians' arsenal in Lebanon was a threat that could not be ignored. A typical view was that expressed by Chaim Bar Lev, a Labor Party leader and former chief of staff. As Bar Lev later stated in a speech to the Knesset, military action was "necessary and justified" in order to free Israel's northern towns from the threat of PLO artillery.[79]

Israeli troops entered Lebanon in force on June 6, attacking in three different zones, as shown in Map 9.1. In the west, along the coast, the IDF deployed 22,000 men and 220 tanks, pushing past Tyre and crossing the Litani River before the first day was over. On the second day of the invasion, a large amphibious force was landed north of Sidon, and Israeli troops penetrated to the outskirts of Damour. The IDF also attacked Tyre and Sidon on the 7th and, with assistance from the Israeli air force, overran these two PLO strongholds. In the central region, IDF columns containing a total of 18,000 men and 220 tanks entered Lebanon from Metulla, crossed the Litani River, and headed for the important junction town of Nabitiya, which they captured on the 7th. Beaufort Castle, the Crusader fortress with a commanding view of northern Israel, was taken during the night of June 6, and by the end of the next day IDF forces in the central region had crossed the Zahrani River and engaged Syrian and PLO units near Jezzine. In the eastern zone, four divisions, consisting of 38,000 men and 800 tanks, advanced toward Syrian positions in the Beqaa Valley. Their objective was to prevent the Syrians either from reinforcing their own positions or from moving to assist Palestinian forces farther to the west. The town of Hasbaiya fell to the IDF columns advancing in the east, and by the end of the second day Israeli ground artillery was within range of Syrian missile batteries.

Thus, with a huge force of almost 80,000 men and 1,240 tanks, as well as 1,520 armored personnel carriers, the IDF swept through southern Lebanon in less than forty-eight hours. On June 8, at almost the same time that Begin was repeating to the Knesset that Israel's objectives in Lebanon were limited, Israeli forces reached a line forty kilometers from the country's northern border.

Despite the success of the Israeli sweep, there was fierce fighting in some areas, with the stiffest resistance to the IDF's advance offered not by the PLO's semiregular units but by the home-guard forces of a number of Palestinian refugee camps.[80] The fighting at Ain al-Hilweh Refugee Camp near Sidon was particularly intense. Indeed, the battle for Ain al-Hilweh was perhaps the most savage of the entire war. The Israelis could not bypass the camp, which straddled the road leading north; and despite heavy bombardments as well as a ground assault, its defenders refused to surrender and held up the Israeli advance past

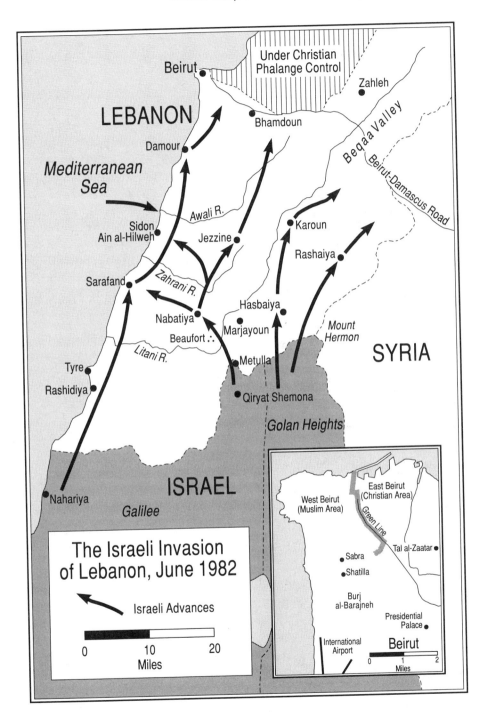

The Israeli Invasion of Lebanon, June 1982

Sidon for two days. Determined to resist at all cost, Ain al-Hilweh itself held out until June 14, and in the end paid a terrible price. Hundreds of civilians were killed and the camp was completely destroyed. According to an Israeli journalist who visited after the attack, "Words lose their significance when one walks through Ain al-Hilweh. . . . It is virtually a symphony of destruction and annihilation. Between and above the debris, women, children and old people are strolling like ghosts, like shocked shadows."[81] Although the fighting at Ain al-Hilweh was by far the most intense, other refugee camps, including Rashidiya, al-Bass, and Burj al-Shemali, also offered determined resistance and suffered greatly in the ensuing battles. According to a UNRWA report, the three camps lost 70 percent, 50 percent, and 35 percent of their homes respectively.[82]

Israeli and Palestinian sources give widely differing casualty figures, but there is no doubt that the human toll in these encounters was extremely heavy. One British journalist, using informed estimates from Lebanese medical sources, suggests that 600 Palestinian guerrillas and civilians may have died at Ain al-Hilweh alone.[83] The head of the International Committee of the Red Cross declared on June 12 that a total of 10,000 Palestinians and Lebanese had died as a result of Israel's invasion, although Israeli spokesmen called this figure "preposterous," and a subsequent report in the *Guardian* concluded that "a round sum of 3,000 is beginning to look more accurate."[84]

The semiregular units of the PLO in southern Lebanon, hopelessly outnumbered and outgunned, offered far less resistance than did Palestinians in the camps. With only 7,000–8,000 armed men and a few dozen outdated tanks and field guns in the south, PLO guerrillas in most areas preferred to retreat rather than confront the invaders who had been sent to destroy them. The Palestinians had also been left to meet the Israeli onslaught alone. The PLO's traditional Lebanese allies, the Druze and the Shiite Muslims, offered no assistance and, most important, the Syrians also endeavored to stay out of the fighting. Finally, both Israeli and Palestinian sources attribute the lack of effective resistance by guerrilla units to inadequate preparation and poor field coordination on the part of the PLO, although the Palestinians did fight well in the limited encounters that took place.[85] Thus, despite the heavy fighting that had taken place in the refugee camps, the IDF accomplished its assigned mission in less than seventy-two hours. By June 8, the PLO had been pushed beyond artillery range of the towns and *kibbutzim* in northern Israel.

The Israeli victory, though rapid and decisive, was not without limits. The IDF failed to destroy or capture most of the PLO forces in southern Lebanon. Two-thirds or more of the guerrillas escaped, avoiding the Israelis and making their way either to Beirut or to the Syrian-controlled Beqaa Valley. The Israelis also failed to kill or capture any senior PLO civilian or military leader.[86] Thus, although it had been pushed away from Israel's northern border, the Palestinian organization did not sustain losses of the magnitude sought by the architects of Operation Peace for Galilee.

There were also important costs, both human and political, associated with the Israeli victory. About 130 Israeli soldiers were killed and as many as 600 wounded during the army's sweep through southern Lebanon, with the greatest number of casualties occurring in fighting for control of the refugee camps around Tyre. Though modest in comparison to the losses sustained by Palestinians and Lebanese, these casualty figures represented a significant cost from the Israeli point of view.

Another important cost was political in nature. In the wake of reports that thousands of Palestinians and Lebanese had been killed or wounded, and tens or even hundreds of thousands rendered homeless, Israel was vigorously condemned in European as well as Arab and Third World capitals. As noted, Israel responded to this criticism by insisting that most reports of death and destruction in Lebanon were greatly exaggerated. In addition, Jerusalem claimed that its soldiers had taken great pains, and sometimes even placed themselves in danger, in order to minimize civilian casualties.[87] Yet accounts in the Israeli as well as the international news media left no room for doubt about the widespread destruction that had accompanied the Israeli invasion, and this in turn led to increasingly sharp denunciations and a deepening of Israel's international isolation. As expressed by one Israeli journalist, Operation Peace for Galilee "was certainly not planned by 'The Committee for the Improvement of Israel's Image.' The sight of the gutted towns of Tyre and Sidon is numbing; it would provide grist for propaganda mills so long as pictures of devastated cities have impact."[88]

Despite these limitations and costs, Operation Peace for Galilee was a clear military success from the Israeli point of view, and, of almost equal importance to Begin and Sharon, it was a success in the domestic political arena as well. Even with heavy Israeli casualties and mounting international condemnation, most Israelis, including most supporters of the Labor Alignment, approved of the government's decision to send troops into southern Lebanon. A few Israelis forcefully condemned the operation, arguing that it was neither necessary nor justified. These Israelis pointed out that the PLO had respected the ceasefire negotiated in July 1981 and that it did not bear responsibility for the attack on Shlomo Argov. Some also rejected the government's claim that the PLO's military buildup in southern Lebanon could not be tolerated; in their view, the IDF's easy victory showed how exaggerated had been the portrait of PLO strength painted by Begin and Sharon before the invasion. Finally, some Israelis on the political left, such as Victor Shemtov of the Alignment's Mapam wing, criticized the invasion because "only an existential threat to Israel warrants going to war."[89] All of these arguments were rejected by the overwhelming majority of Israel's citizens, however. A poll taken in late June found that 93 percent of the Jewish public considered Operation Peace for Galilee to be justified. The polls also showed a substantial rise in the popularity of the government, and of Begin and Sharon personally, reversing a decline that had taken place over the course of the difficult spring of 1982.

Expansion of the Israeli-PLO War in Lebanon

Israeli forces did not stop upon achieving the objective set for Operation Peace for Galilee; rather, with officials in Jerusalem beginning to defend the invasion in more elaborate terms and to articulate additional goals for the operation, the IDF undertook to engage the Syrians in the central and eastern zones and to encircle Beirut in the west. Labor Alignment officials and other opposition elements, including many who had supported the invasion only a few days earlier, condemned these "rolling" war aims. Some wondered whether Israel was developing a new military doctrine, since it had never before added political objectives during the course of a war. Some also debated whether the government's intentions had indeed evolved or whether, alternatively, they had been present from the very beginning, in which case the country had been misled. Finally, some knowledgeable Israelis suggested, correctly as it turned out, that the cabinet itself, and to an extent even the prime minister, had been manipulated by Sharon. In any event, after achieving its initial objective of pushing the PLO out of a forty-kilometer zone in South Lebanon, the IDF continued to push forward.

In the center and the east, despite repeated assurances that the IDF would not initiate conflict with the Syrians, clashes instigated by Israel began as early as June 7. Moreover, while Damascus responded with signals that it did not want war, Sharon convinced the cabinet to authorize an advance into the Beqaa Valley that he knew would almost certainly bring additional conflict with the Syrians.[90] Thus, from June 7 to June 11, war raged between Israel and Syria, as well as between the IDF and the PLO. The Israeli air force also attacked Syrian positions during this period. IDF planes destroyed Damascus's SAM missiles on June 9 and 10 and shot down as many as ninety of the Syrian jets sent to intercept them. These jets represented about 15 percent of the total Syrian air force, and perhaps 25 percent of its first-line fighter fleet. The destruction of Syria's missiles and planes, which Sharon later called the turning point of the war, gave Israel unchallenged ability to strike enemy forces from the air. In response to strong pressure from the Americans, who complained that the Israelis had gone far beyond their original announced objectives, Jerusalem agreed to a proposal for a ceasefire, which Damascus also quickly accepted and which took effect at noon on June 11. Arafat announced that the PLO was also willing to observe the June 11 truce, but his offer was ignored by Jerusalem.

In the west, the IDF continued to bomb Beirut, and from the 9th to the 13th ground troops moved into the southern and eastern suburbs of the Lebanese capital. This advance was ordered by the defense minister, possibly with Begin's approval, but it had not been formally authorized by the cabinet. Only on the 15th did the cabinet decide that Beirut should be a central focus of the war effort, issuing an official demand that the PLO withdraw from the city. The cabinet determined at this meeting that the IDF would not enter the Muslim neighborhoods of Beirut, but Sharon made it clear that this limitation applied only to the army's method, not to its objective: "Beirut itself, as the terrorist organizations' political and military center, is an objective which cannot be left as it is. As long as terrorist headquarters remain in Beirut, it cannot be said that the IDF's mission has been completely accomplished."[91]

By the 26th, the IDF had driven PLO and Syrian forces from Bhamdoun and other mountain towns overlooking the Lebanese capital, and also taken control of the highway leading from Beirut to the Beqaa Valley and Damascus. The Israelis were now poised for an all-out assault on Beirut, and at this time, on the 27th, the cabinet removed its earlier limitation on entry into the city. Agreeing that the PLO enclave in Beirut could not be left intact, the ministers determined that all members of "the fifteen organizations operating under the so-called PLO . . . without exception must leave Lebanon." Thus, although Begin had previously told the Knesset Foreign Affairs and Defense Committee that "Israel has never entered an Arab capital and will not do so in the case of Beirut," and had repeated these assurances to Ronald Reagan as late as June 22, Sharon now told the same Knesset committee that the cabinet had decided "neither to enter Beirut nor not to enter it."[92] The government had now formally put behind it the objectives originally announced for Operation Peace for Galilee, and with the elimination of Syria from the fighting and the IDF's capture of Bhamdoun, the Israeli-PLO war in Lebanon entered its final phase, the siege of Beirut.

The Israelis articulated two broad goals for the expanded operation now in progress: installation of a friendly, unified, and Christian-dominated government in Lebanon, and elimination of the PLO as both a military and a political threat. With respect to the first of these two objectives, Begin and Sharon called for the removal of all foreign forces from Lebanon, meaning the PLO and the Syrians, and for the formation of a new national government in Beirut. This government would naturally be friendly to Israel, and would perhaps even sign a peace treaty with the Jewish state. In the rhetoric of the day, it was said that "an arc of peace and stability" would stretch from Cairo to Jerusalem and on to Beirut.[93]

The Begin government insisted that Lebanon as well as Israel would benefit from a new status quo, and Israeli authorities in fact found a substantial number of Lebanese civilians willing to express support for the invasion, including members of the Shiite Muslim community that was presumed to be allied with the PLO.[94] Actually, while Shia and others may have been pleased to see Palestinian guerrillas driven out of southern Lebanon, the political changes for which these elements had fought in the 1975–76 civil war were antithetical to the Israeli government's conception of a stable and unified Lebanon. Jerusalem saw removal of the Syrians and the PLO, allies of the Lebanese left, as leading to the restoration of Maronite Christian domination and a return of the political order that had existed before the civil war. Nevertheless, in seeking to justify the expanded operation, spokesmen for the Begin government insisted that most Lebanese supported the Israeli invasion and welcomed the political transformation to which it would lead.

There were indications as early as fall 1981 that Sharon aspired to transform the political equation in Lebanon; and since this could not be achieved so long as the PLO controlled southern Lebanon and two-thirds of Beirut and the Syrians dominated other sections of the country, the defense minister envisioned Israeli action to bring about the new political order he sought.[95] As a result, preparation for an eventual invasion of Lebanon actually involved the planning of two military operations, one confined to the south and another, designed to remove Palestinian and Syrian forces from Lebanon, which would carry the IDF beyond the Beirut-Damascus highway. The plan for a more ambitious operation, which bore the code name "Big Pines," was specifically intended to reestablish Maronite power in Lebanon. Indeed, when Sharon met Alexander Haig in May and told the American secretary of state about the existence of a second plan, he described it as an operation that would "redraw Lebanon's domestic politics in favor of the Christian Phalangists."[96] As part of his preparations, the defense minister also established direct contact with the Maronite Christian community in Lebanon during this period. Sharon himself made a secret trip to Beirut in January 1982 to consult with Maronite leaders, and in February and March Chief of Staff Eitan visited Lebanon for more detailed discussions about possible Israeli-Maronite military cooperation.

Despite Sharon's repeated statements that only the plan for a limited operation in southern Lebanon would be implemented, these actions led some analysts to believe that the defense minister had never intended to order the IDF to halt when it reached a line forty kilometers from Israel's northern border. Indeed, even before the invasion, several Israeli journalists had revealed Sharon's grand design to the public and warned that "whoever reads Sharon correctly knows that his purpose in Lebanon is not another Operation Litani . . . [but rather] to create the conditions for the emergence of a new [Lebanese] government."[97]

Yet Sharon succeeded in deceiving not only the public and the opposition but his own party as well, and some suggest that he and Eitan may even have taken in the prime minister.[98] The defense minister had been surprised and disappointed by strong opposition when the plan for Operation Big Pines was first presented to the cabinet, in December 1981, and thereafter he and Eitan disclosed as little as possible about the military preparations they were making. Nor did they again bring the plan to the cabinet for discussion, even as it became *de facto* government policy during the latter part of June. On the contrary, they endeavored to convince the Alignment, the Americans, and even the cabinet that Operation Big Pines was a contingency plan that would not be implemented, at least for the time being, and that the sole objective of IDF ground action in Lebanon was to push PLO artillery away from the towns and *kibbutzim* of northern

Israel. Thus, as noted, Israeli ground troops moved into the southern and eastern suburbs of Beirut without cabinet authorization. Only on the 15th did the cabinet agree that the Lebanese capital should be a focus of the war effort, and only on the 27th did it remove the limitations it had previously placed on the IDF's entry into the city.

With Operation Big Pines already in progress, the intentions of the defense minister and the chief of staff became unmistakable during the last days of June, and at this point, whether they had previously approved of the action or not, the prime minister and other government officials acknowledged what was taking place and defended the expanded operation. Responding to critics, Begin and others emphasized the importance of redrawing the political map of Lebanon. On at least one occasion, in a speech to the Knesset on June 29, the prime minister also sought to give the impression that the goals of what he called "the maximum plan" had been among the original aims of the war.[99]

The other objective that Israel now articulated, in addition to the establishment of a new political order in Lebanon, was to crush the PLO. With its fighting forces either captured, killed, or dispersed, and with its independent political base in Lebanon destroyed, the organization would no longer be able to carry out operations against the Jewish state. Nor, in the Israeli analysis, would it be able to impose its will on the Palestinian people and, most critically, the inhabitants of the occupied territories. Israeli spokesmen had long maintained that PLO intransigence was the major obstacle to a resolution of the Palestinian problem and an expansion of the peace process begun at Camp David. The Begin government also blamed the PLO for the disturbances which rocked the West Bank and Gaza in spring 1982, alleging that it directed resistance to occupation and intimidated Palestinians interested in compromise. Israel's expanded operation in Lebanon was designed to change this situation. The Palestinian organization would be defeated militarily and deprived of its virtually autonomous base of operations in Lebanon, and this in turn would undermine its ability to intimidate Palestinian "moderates" or otherwise influence developments in the West Bank and Gaza.[100]

Once Begin and Sharon had decided that the IDF's invasion of Lebanon would seek to do more than remove the PLO from southern Lebanon, the link between Operation Big Pines and the situation in the occupied territories was stressed by Israeli officials. On June 28, for example, Sharon stated, "We are seeking a solution allowing peaceful coexistence with the residents of the territories who would no longer be subjected to the fear of PLO terrorism."[101] A month later, he repeated that "it is quite possible that following the elimination of the PLO in Beirut the road will be open for real negotiations with the Arabs of Eretz Israel."[102] Real negotiations and peaceful coexistence were, of course, to be based on the Israeli government's notion of autonomy for Palestinians living in territories permanently controlled by Israel; and Begin and Sharon argued late in June that the expanded operation in Lebanon would eliminate most Palestinian opposition to this political formula. Israeli leaders repeated this assertion over the course of the summer, with Sharon stating candidly in August, for example, that after the departure of the PLO from Lebanon, "I believe Palestinians will come forward prepared to negotiate with Israel on the autonomy plan proposed by Prime Minister Menachem Begin."[103]

As these and other statements by Israeli leaders indicated, and as a prominent Palestinian scholar correctly observed, the government in Jerusalem in a very real sense conceived of the expanded operation in Lebanon as "a war for the future disposition of Palestine."[104] The ambitious objective of this war, according to another knowledgeable analyst, was "to annihilate the PLO, douse any vestiges of Palestinian nationalism . . . [and] cripple, if not end, the Palestinian nationalist movement."[105]

Israeli concern with the Palestinian problem was not limited to the West Bank and Gaza; an important related objective of the expanded operation in Lebanon was to damage the PLO's international legitimacy and its status as an important actor in the arena of Middle Eastern international relations. In a narrow sense, the PLO's credibility would be undermined by the fact that Arab and other allies had failed to come to its defense. This, it was said, would show that the Arab-Israeli dispute remained an interstate conflict and, as the government in Jerusalem claimed, that the Palestinian problem was of secondary importance. More broadly, the Begin government asserted that robbing the PLO of its Lebanese base would cripple the organization's ability to wage a diplomatic campaign in favor of the Palestinian cause and would reduce the pressure on Israel to accommodate itself to Palestinian nationalism.

In recent years, the PLO had registered important diplomatic gains, while Israel had become increasingly isolated on the world scene. Removal of the PLO from Lebanon offered the possibility of reversing this situation, forcing the Palestinian organization to devote its energies to matters of internal reconstruction, or perhaps even survival, and reducing the danger that negotiations with the PLO might eventually be forced on the Jewish state. Summarizing the thinking of Begin and Sharon in this regard, an Israeli journalist wrote in the spring of 1982 that these Israeli leaders support confrontation with the PLO in Lebanon because "Israel does not want the PLO as a partner for talks . . . [and because] with the loss of its physical strength, in their opinion, the PLO will lose not only its hold over the territories but also its growing international status."[106]

While some Israelis were persuaded by the government's case for an expansion of the war, others doubted the wisdom of such action, and a full-fledged political debate was accordingly raging in the Jewish state by the latter part of June. In contrast to the debate which accompanied the initial phase of the Israeli-PLO war in Lebanon, wherein the forceful criticisms of the political left were rejected by the overwhelming majority of the country's citizens, political opinion in Israel was now deeply divided.

As early as three weeks after the initial invasion, at a time when the siege of Beirut was just beginning, many expressed doubts that Israel would be able to translate its military accomplishments into political gains and thus achieve the objectives put forward for the expanded operation. Many also argued that the balance sheet of the war would in the end contain more costs than benefits from the Israeli point of view. A poll taken at this time found that such sentiments were held by more than half of those supporting the Labor Alignment, even though most had approved of the original invasion, and even by one-quarter of the pro-Likud respondents. Moreover, reservations and criticisms were expressed by the most important leaders of the Alignment. For example, Shimon Peres, Yitzhak Rabin, and Chaim Bar Lev, all of whom had been willing to accept government arguments in favor of the first phase of the operation in Lebanon, declared that peace with the Palestinians and other Arabs could not be achieved through military means, and that an expansion of Operation Peace for Galilee was thus not in Israel's interest.

More militant expressions of dissent appeared over the course of the summer, as the battle for Beirut went forward; and the significance of this opposition, and of the uncertainty that reigned among the public at large, will be appreciated only if it is kept in mind that the Jewish state had never before experienced mass opposition to the government while a war was in progress.[107] Criticism was expressed in numerous op-ed articles in the independent Israeli press, and in many statements and declarations issued by opposition politicians. Former Foreign Minister Abba Eban, for example, accused Begin and Sharon of not waging the war for which they had received Knesset approval, and asserted that the expanded operation in Lebanon was reducing, not increasing, the chances for peace. Opposition was also organized by Peace Now, which held a protest rally in Tel Aviv and drew a crowd estimated at 100,000. In addition, protest activities were undertaken by several new antiwar groups that sprang up at this time, including Mothers against Silence, the Committee against the War in Lebanon, and Yesh Gvul (There Is a Limit).

Military correspondents reported that there was also strong opposition to the war among many soldiers at the front. For example, Hirsh Goodman of the *Jerusalem Post* described how three Israeli correspondents in Lebanon were surrounded by officers and men from top IDF units and berated for not reporting the mood of those who were fighting the war. "We were accused by the overwhelming majority of men—including senior officers—of allowing this war to grow out of all proportion," Goodman wrote in a forceful article published late in June, and "of mindlessly repeating official explanations which we all knew to be false." Goodman also reported that the soldiers "made us promise we would tell the public and the cabinet."[108]

Critics of the expanded operation in Lebanon raised two particular concerns, one relating to costs associated with the war and a second about the feasibility of Israel's expanded objectives. With respect to costs, the greatest preoccupation was the steadily growing number of Israeli casualties. More than 300 soldiers had been killed by August 1982, and the number climbed to more than 600 before the IDF was finally withdrawn from Lebanon, with about 4,500 wounded. These are extremely large numbers in a country as small as Israel, leading Abba Eban to observe bitterly that the war against the PLO in Lebanon took more Israeli lives "than all the world's terrorists had been able to inflict on Israelis in all the decades."[109] Others lamented that the "wasteful adventure" in Lebanon had cost the IDF many of its finest men "in a vain effort to fulfill a role it was never meant to play."[110] Many Israelis were also deeply troubled by the war's toll on Palestinian and Lebanese civilians. Even some who insisted that the international news media had greatly exaggerated the loss of life and property acknowledged that there had been extensive destruction and deplored the fact that their own country was responsible for so much suffering. Some called it a crime and a national shame. Finally, Israeli opponents of the war worried about political as well as the human costs, pointing out that the consequences of the invasion included deepening international isolation, a potentially serious strain in relations with the United States, and a sharp slowdown in the normalization of ties with Egypt.

Costs aside, opponents argued that the expanded operation would achieve far less than its architects promised. With respect to the establishment of a new political order in Lebanon, the expulsion of foreign forces would not be accomplished by driving the PLO out of Beirut. Even after the siege of the Lebanese capital, there would still be a large Syrian force in the east and additional PLO guerrillas in the north. In addition, approximately 400,000 Palestinian civilians would also remain in Lebanon, the overwhelming majority of whom supported the PLO. Most important, tensions among competing Lebanese confessional communities, almost all with heavily armed private militias, would persist even should all foreign forces somehow be driven out of the country, as would the feudal and anachronistic patterns of political organization that governed the relationships among them. Thus, critics charged, it was naive in the extreme to believe that removing a few thousand Palestinian guerrillas from Beirut would permit Maronite Christians to reestablish their dominant position, and thereby bring stability and progress to Lebanon.

So far as the PLO and the Palestinian problem are concerned, the Begin government's domestic critics argued even more vigorously that Israel would not achieve the objectives in whose name the expanded war in Lebanon was being waged. Some, such as Hebrew University professor Yehoshafat Harkabi, pointed out that the PLO is an idea as well as an institution, and that adherence to this idea among Palestinians in the occupied territories, Lebanon, and elsewhere would not diminish as a result of the war. Further, as an institution, the PLO would be damaged but not destroyed by an Israeli victory. Though deprived of its base in Lebanon, it would continue the struggle for Palestinian rights from

other Arab countries or elsewhere; and while this struggle might be purely political in nature, with no significant military dimension, it was in the political
arena that the PLO had concentrated its efforts, and had its greatest successes,
for almost a decade.

Many of Begin and Sharon's critics also repeated what they had been saying
for some time about the situation in the West Bank and Gaza: it was Israel's
policies, as much as or even more than PLO rejectionism, that had produced the
recent unrest and prevented Jerusalem from reaching an accommodation with the
Palestinians. Without Israeli recognition of Palestinian rights, these critics asserted, resistance in the territories would continue, regardless of the outcome of
the fighting in Lebanon. With such recognition, on the other hand, many Palestinians would accept the principle of reconciliation with Israel, thereby making
the war irrelevant in bringing mainstream Palestinians to the bargaining table.

Spokesmen for the Israeli government naturally rejected all these criticisms.
They claimed that the cost of the war was greatly exaggerated or, in the case of
IDF casualties, a price that Israel had no choice but to pay. They argued further
that their invasion was an essential first step in putting Lebanon back on the road
to independence and stability, with most Lebanese therefore supporting the invasion, and that any defeat inflicted on the PLO could not but advance the cause
of Israeli-Palestinian peace. In short, they insisted that while it was unreasonable
to expect immediate and definitive solutions to long-standing problems, the
IDF's victories in Lebanon were creating new opportunities and removing major
impediments to peace and stability.

By the end of the summer of 1982, Israelis were deeply divided between
those who accepted these arguments advanced by the government and those who
found the critics of Begin and Sharon more persuasive. Like the government's
actions in the West Bank and Gaza, the war in Lebanon had thus set off competing political trends in the Jewish state. On the one hand, Operation Peace for
Galilee galvanized the right side of the political spectrum, increasing the government's popularity and reducing difficulties associated with its weak parliamentary position. On the other, as the war continued after its initial objectives
were achieved, opponents of government policy became more numerous and determined, and there was a deepening of the tension that had characterized the
first half of 1982.

Despite increasing domestic opposition, Sharon remained determined to
carry out his grand design, and the battle for Beirut thus raged on throughout
July and August, providing additional fuel for the political debates taking place
in Israel. The siege of Beirut, the final phase of the Israeli-PLO war in Lebanon,
was also the longest and most brutal of the bitter conflict; Jerusalem's efforts to
oust the PLO from Beirut persisted for seven weeks, until a combination of military pressure and diplomatic maneuvering finally resulted in the PLO's departure
during the last ten days of August. During the seven-week siege of the Lebanese
capital, the IDF regularly subjected West Beirut and Palestinian strongholds on

the southern outskirts of the city to intense air, naval, and artillery bombardments. Indeed, to underscore its determination to eradicate the PLO at all costs, and oblivious to the impact on world opinion that its devastating attacks were having, Israeli officials frequently took delegations from abroad to an observation point in East Beirut to watch IDF planes drop bombs from high altitudes.[111]

The IDF also formulated plans to send troops into West Beirut. Sharon told fellow ministers in mid-July that a ground assault was unavoidable, and despite strong opposition from a minority in the cabinet, a decision was taken giving a small committee of ministers the power to order such an assault. A few days later, a plan for the conquest of West Beirut was presented by senior military officials. To tighten the noose around the city, and also to prepare for possible entry into West Beirut, the IDF continued to advance northward in the weeks that followed. The Israelis also moved westward from positions they had taken up in Christian East Beirut. Although PLO forces offered stubborn resistance, fighting much more effectively than they had in southern Lebanon, Israel gradually succeeded in placing men and artillery in positions adjacent to Palestinian-controlled areas. On August 1, the IDF occupied the airport and, exchanging artillery fire with PLO units, approached the edge of Burj al-Barajneh, a large Palestinian refugee camp on the southern outskirts of Beirut. On the 4th, coming from the east rather than the south, the Israelis moved closer to the Sabra and Shatilla refugee camps.

Israeli actions exerted psychological as well as military pressure on the Palestinians. To undermine the morale of both PLO fighters and civilians, the Israelis frequently cut off water and electricity and limited food supplies to certain areas. The desperate circumstances of Palestinians huddled in their shelters were made all the more vivid, moreover, by the fact that life in Christian East Beirut proceeded as if conditions were normal; stores and cafés on fashionable avenues were full, and young men and women were swimming or sunning themselves on beaches just a mile or two from neighborhoods being shelled by the IDF. Adding to Palestinian fears was the rhetoric of Ariel Sharon and like-minded Israeli officials. During July, Sharon began calling not only for removal of the PLO from Beirut but also for the destruction of Palestinian neighborhoods in the southern part of the city. "The northern part of the city should be pampered with electricity, water, food, every possible comfort," the defense minister declared, "but the southern part of the city must be destroyed, razed to the ground." Not the city but its terrorist quarters were to be leveled, Sharon went on to explain, but "to my mind, we mustn't leave a single terrorist neighborhood standing."[112]

Equally worrisome for the Palestinians, if not more so, was the possibility of attacks on civilians by Israel's Maronite allies. In late June, for instance, Christian forces had entered Druze areas in the Shouf Mountains overlooking Beirut and killed unarmed civilians, and, recalling the massacre at Tal al-Zaatar during the Lebanese civil war, Palestinians expressed the fear that this was a sign of things to come. Indeed, they pointed out that Bashir Gemayel, commander of the

Maronite-dominated Lebanese Forces, had for some time been calling for the destruction of Lebanon's refugee camps and the mass deportation of as many as 200,000 Palestinian civilians. Thus, discussing the impact of the incident in the Shouf Mountains, a Palestinian scholar reported that since "the history of the Lebanese war was replete with massacres of defenseless civilians," the June incident was understandably perceived by many in Beirut "as a harbinger of what could be expected in the wake of an Israeli victory, a PLO withdrawal and a Phalangist takeover."[113]

Diplomatic maneuvering during the siege of Beirut began with calls for the PLO to withdraw from the city, and subsequently gave rise to negotiations concerning both conditions for the guerrillas' departure and the protection of Palestinians remaining in Lebanon. In late June, Israeli officials sent messages to Arafat through both Lebanese and American channels, offering not to molest PLO fighters leaving Beirut. "I'll give you better conditions of surrender than the British gave the Argentinian soldiers in the Falklands," Sharon stated in a message to Arafat on June 27.[114] Further, although the PLO chairman at the time insisted that he would not surrender, the leadership of the PLO, after intense internal debate, had by the beginning of July accepted in principle the idea of an evacuation from Beirut.[115] The terms proposed by Israel remained unacceptable, especially Jerusalem's demand that PLO guerrillas lay down their arms. Also, some PLO leaders, as well as some middle-level cadres, continued to argue in favor of resistance. Nevertheless, a clear majority of the PLO's top leadership had come to the conclusion that they had no alternative but to withdraw from Beirut, and therefore they now turned their attention to the conditions under which this would take place.

Initially, the Palestinians hoped there would be support for a plan put forward by France and Egypt, which urged that the PLO be given political compensation for its withdrawal, and also called for Israeli as well as PLO forces to remove themselves from the Lebanese capital. Under this plan, moreover, PLO troops would be required only to withdraw to Palestinian refugee camps, not to leave the country, and a peacekeeping force composed of Lebanese and United Nations units would be established to police the separation. Determined opposition from Israel and the United States killed this plan, however, and during July the PLO was under increasing pressure to accept the terms of an American evacuation plan, which was put forward by Philip Habib. For a brief moment it appeared that U.S. policy might change. Alexander Haig, the staunchly pro-Israeli secretary of state, was dismissed at the end of June and replaced by George Shultz, a man with connections in the Arab world. Nevertheless, despite the differences between Haig and Shultz, the Americans continued to insist upon the removal of PLO armed forces from Lebanon, not merely from Beirut, and in return offered only guarantees for their safe departure and for the protection of the Palestinians they would leave behind.

Contributing to the PLO's conclusion that it had no choice but to accept the

Habib plan was the failure of any Arab state to provide meaningful diplomatic support. Indeed, not only did an Arab League delegation sent to Washington during the latter part of July fail to modify the U.S. position, but the leaders of the delegation, the foreign ministers of Syria and Saudi Arabia respectively, did not seek to obtain for the PLO a *quid pro quo* for its exit from Beirut, and in fact tacitly accepted the terms being put forward by the Americans. This acquiescence was also evident in a six-point plan adopted at an Arab League conference in Jedda, Saudi Arabia, at the end of July. The plan did urge implementation of UN Resolution 509, which had been adopted by the Security Council on the day Israel invaded Lebanon and which called for Israel's complete, immediate, and unconditional withdrawal from that country. On the other hand, the Arab League plan called for the removal of PLO forces from Beirut and, like the Habib plan, offered the Palestinians nothing in return except guarantees for their safety. Thus, as summarized by Khalidi, "By the end of July, the Arab states—or at least the leading powers among them—had adopted the view of the United States, Israel and the Sarkis government [of Lebanon] that all the issues raised by the war could be addressed by solving the technical problem of the PLO's evacuation from Beirut. In a certain sense, the decision had thus been made for the PLO by its 'brethren.' "[116]

Exchanges between the U.S. and the PLO focused on American guarantees for the safe passage of the PLO forces that would leave Beirut, and above all for protection of the hundreds of thousands of Palestinian civilians who would remain in Lebanon, in the refugee camps around Beirut and elsewhere. With the PLO's armed forces removed, the inhabitants of these camps would be defenseless if attacked by Israel or its independent-minded Maronite allies. The U.S. addressed these Palestinian concerns in several diplomatic exchanges with the PLO during the first ten days of August, after which Washington recorded its commitment to Palestinian safety in a note to the Lebanese government. This memorandum, prepared on August 11 but not made public for another week, stated that the U.S. was making its commitment "on the basis of assurances received from the government of Israel and from the leaders of certain Lebanese groups with which it has been in contact." The tangible expression of the guarantees and commitments contained in the Habib plan was to be a multinational peacekeeping force, which would include U.S. Marines. This force would oversee the PLO's departure from Beirut and ensure the safety of Palestinians remaining behind.

The Israelis, for their part, expressed some reservations about the Habib plan, even though they did accept its broad outlines in principle. In particular, they were initially opposed to the PLO's withdrawal under the protection of an international force, especially one that included U.S. Marines. Their concern in this regard was that once the international force was in place, the PLO might refuse to withdraw from Lebanon, or at least might seek to leave some of its fighters behind, and that the IDF would then be prevented from taking military action in response to these developments.

In addition, still hoping that the application of force might drive the PLO from Beirut, Ariel Sharon ordered an escalation of the IDF's attacks on PLO positions beginning on August 1. Israeli ground forces moved forward, as noted earlier, and saturation bombing by the air force grew more intense. The Israeli navy also began to shell PLO positions at this time. On August 11 and 12, after ten days of punishing raids and at the very moment the Americans were committing themselves to the safety of the Palestinians, Sharon decided to make one last attempt to use force, rather than diplomacy, to remove the PLO from the Lebanese capital. Without cabinet approval, the defense minister ordered some of the most devastating air attacks of the entire war, focusing Israeli firepower not only on buildings used by the PLO in the center of Beirut but on Palestinian refugee camps as well. On the 12th, for reasons that one generally sympathetic observer calls "inexplicable," the Israeli air force carried out seventy-two uninterrupted bombing raids from 6:00 A.M. until 5:30 P.M., killing 128 and wounding 400, most of them civilians.[117] This attack brought a sharp protest from the Americans, including a blunt message to Begin from Ronald Reagan himself. It also produced anger in the Israeli cabinet, where even Sharon's supporters condemned the gratuitous attacks, and which then stripped the defense minister of the authority to order air raids.

Following these developments, the Israelis gave final approval to the Habib plan on August 19, and two days later the siege of Beirut came to an end. On August 21, 350 French paratroopers landed and the first contingent of PLO fighters left by ship, their immediate destination being Cyprus. Subsequently they would be dispersed among those Arab countries that had agreed to receive them, including Tunisia, Jordan, Syria, and Yemen. Each day that followed brought the departure of another group of Palestinian guerrillas, their withdrawal being supervised by an international peacekeeping force that included Italians as well as French and, after August 25, a contingent of U.S. Marines. Yasir Arafat left Beirut on August 30, sailing for Athens, where he was given a hero's welcome by Greek premier Andreas Papandreou, and on August 31 and September 1 the last two PLO contingents departed. Altogether, about 8,000 PLO guerrillas left by sea, for the most part without incident. On one occasion, however, American intervention was necessary to resolve a dispute with Israel about whether departing PLO forces would be permitted to take some jeeps with them. A contingent of about 6,000 additional men, including both Syrian soldiers and members of the Palestine Liberation Army, left by land. Loaded onto trucks, these men traveled along the Beirut-Damascus highway to Syria; and as they passed through East Beirut at the beginning of their journey, thousands of Maronite Christians lined the highway to observe the evacuation and shout their anger and hostility at the departing troops.

With the departure of the PLO and the lifting of the siege, the streets of West Beirut were soon jammed with civilians. Electricity, which had been shut off for months, was restored on the 22nd, and the following day Bashir Gemayel, the Maronite leader, was elected president of Lebanon. To the Israeli architects of the expanded IDF operation in Lebanon, Operation Big Pines, events were unfolding as planned. Indeed, in an expression of Israeli optimism about the future of Lebanon, Begin sent Gemayel an exceedingly cordial telegram on the occasion of his election, offering "Warmest wishes from the heart" and stating, "May God be with you, dear friend, in the fulfillment of your great historic mission, for the liberty of Lebanon and its independence."[118]

Yet many felt it was premature to declare that Lebanon had begun a new era and put its problems behind it. On the one hand, the outpouring of Maronite hate that accompanied the PLO exodus intensified fears about the fate of Palestinians remaining in Lebanon. On the other, there remained important and troubling questions about the future of the country more generally, about whether the departure of the PLO and the election of a new Lebanese president would reduce intercommunal strife or, alternatively, bring a new round of violent confrontation among Lebanon's antagonistic confessional communities. But at the beginning of September, with the siege of Beirut over, these were seen as questions for the future. Its work done, the international peacekeeping force departed, the Americans on September 10, the Italians on the 11th, and the French on the 13th.

With these developments, the Israeli-PLO war in Lebanon came to an end. Though costly, the war constituted a decisive military victory from the Israeli point of view. Yet it remained to be seen whether Jerusalem would reap political advantage from its military accomplishments. Consistent with the Palestinians' own pronouncements, many knowledgeable Israelis, most of whom had opposed the war in Lebanon once it moved into its second stage, warned that the PLO would continue to be a critical actor in the Middle Eastern political arena and asserted that the unresolved Palestinian question would remain as much as ever at the core of the Arab-Israeli conflict. Some also repeated what they had been saying for several months, that the military defeat of the PLO in Lebanon would not reduce opposition to Israeli occupation among Palestinian inhabitants of the West Bank and Gaza.

Sabra and Shatilla

A tragic postscript to the Israeli-PLO war in Lebanon was written from September 16 to September 18. During this period, with Israeli knowledge and possibly approval, forces of the Phalange Party entered Sabra and Shatilla, two large, adjacent Palestinian refugee camps on the outskirts of Beirut, and carried out the massacre of hundreds of civilians, many of them women and children. The Phalange Party is a militant political movement led by the Gemayel family and dedicated to the principle of Maronite primacy in Lebanon. It is also known for its hatred of the Palestinians, whose activities in Lebanon, many of its adherents insist, are largely responsible for the demise of the political order in which Maronites had enjoyed supremacy. In addition, in the latter connection, the Phalange and their Maronite leaders had been consulting and cooperating with Israel since the Lebanese civil war,[119] Ariel Sharon having met with Pierre Gemayel, the Maronite patriarch, as recently as the day before the events at Sabra and Shatilla began. So far as the Phalange militia is concerned, it was constructed and operated independently of the regular Lebanese army, even though the latter force was dominated by Christians and under the control of the Maronite-led government.[120] Joining the Phalange forces in the massacre at Sabra and Shatilla may have been a small number of soldiers from the militia of Saad Haddad, a proxy army from southern Lebanon that the Israelis had created and with which they continued to work closely.[121]

About 150 Phalangist soldiers, divided into three units of roughly 50 men each, entered the camps at approximately 6:00 P.M. on Thursday the 16th, and almost immediately there were reports that a massacre was in progress. According to one summary, based on a number of journalistic and eyewitness accounts, "The Israeli soldiers who had encircled and sealed off the camps were besieged by hysterical, screaming Palestinian women running from the refugee neighborhoods and telling of the massacre. These women were prevented from leaving the camps by the encircling Israeli army."[122]

According to the report of the Kahan Commission, the Israeli commission of inquiry established after the massacre, the first indication of the barbarism taking place came only an hour or so after the Phalange had entered Sabra and Shatilla. This occurred when an IDF officer at a rooftop observation post shared by Israeli and Phalangist personnel overheard a radio conversation between a soldier inside the camps and Elie Hobeika, the chief intelligence officer of the Phalange forces, who was also at the rooftop post. According to the Israeli officer, Lieutenant Elul, the Phalange soldier asked what he should do with the fifty women and children he had rounded up, whereupon Hobeika replied over the transmitter, "This is the last time you're going to ask me a question like that, you know exactly what to do." According to the Kahan Commission's description, "raucous laughter then broke out among the Phalangist personnel on the roof [and] Lieutenant Elul understood that what was involved was the murder of the women and children."[123] Elul immediately reported what he had heard to his own commanding officer.

Despite the abundance of eyewitness testimony[124] and the extensive inquiry of the Kahan Commission, many details of the Sabra and Shatilla massacre remain unclear. The Kahan Commission concluded that the number killed was probably 700–800, although some contend that it may have been significantly higher, perhaps as high as 1,500 or 2,000.[125] There is also uncertainty about exactly when the killing took place. The Kahan Commission concluded that "it is impossible to determine precisely when the acts of slaughter were perpetuated; evidently they commenced shortly after the Phalangists entered the camps and went on intermittently until close to their departure."[126] On the other hand, another account, citing eyewitness reports, suggests that most of the killing took place between the night of the 17th and the morning of the 18th.[127]

Nevertheless, imprecision about important aspects of the tragedy notwithstanding, there is little disagreement about the barbarism involved. Describing the Phalange actions as "butchery," Israeli journalists Ze'ev Schiff and Ehud Ya'ari give a chilling account of some of the killing: "In addition to the wholesale slaughter of families, the Phalangists indulged in such sadistic horrors as hanging live grenades around their victims' necks. In one particularly vicious act of barbarity, an infant was trampled to death by a man wearing spiked shoes. The entire Phalangist action in Sabra and Shatilla seemed to be directed against civilians."[128] Still other accounts speak of those raped or mutilated rather than killed. For example, an American researcher describes a Palestinian woman who succeeded in fleeing with her two infants only because nearby soldiers were too busy raping two other women. Further, she reports, "We were shown these two women, and as you can see they have chopped off the fingers of the woman in front. We have had many accounts of women raped, pregnant women, their fetuses cut out afterward, women with hands chopped off, earrings pulled."[129]

A particularly forceful firsthand account is provided by Ryuichi Hirokawa, a Japanese journalist and photographer who managed to enter Shatilla Camp on the morning of the 18th. Hirokawa describes his walk through the empty streets, which were littered with bodies. One old man had been shot in the head with a single bullet; ten bodies were lying on top of each other in a garage; an entire family, including a two-year-old child, had been shot in their garden; in an adjacent alley were the bodies of a boy and a girl about five years of age, next to their mother's body, which had been partly covered with rubble. Hirokawa stated, "I saw approximately fifty corpses with my own eyes in the streets and alleys I explored. Considering how the camps are hundreds of times larger than the area I visited, I can imagine that the number of dead must be staggering."[130]

Questions about Israeli complicity arose as the facts of the massacre became known, and it eventually emerged, partly as a result of Israel's own Kahan Commission investigation, that Israel did bear some responsibility for the tragic events at Sabra and Shatilla. Although the Kahan Commission asserted that no Israelis were "directly" responsible, in that "no conspiracy or plot was entered into between anyone from the Israeli political echelon or from the military echelon in the IDF and the Phalangists, with the aim of perpetrating atrocities in the camps,"[131] the commission vigorously affirmed that some key Israeli officials were "indirectly" responsible. It also emphasized the gravity of this responsibility, declaring that guilt falls not only on the perpetrators but also on "those who could and should have prevented the commission of those deeds which must be condemned." [132]

More specifically, the Kahan Commission found that Israeli authorities permitted Phalange forces to enter Sabra and Shatilla without giving proper consideration to the danger of a massacre, which, under the circumstances, they "were obligated to foresee as probable." [133] Indeed, the commission stated in this regard that "everyone who had anything to do with events in Lebanon should have felt apprehension about a massacre in the camps, if armed Phalangist forces were moved into them without the IDF exercising concrete and effective supervision and scrutiny of them." [134] Even more important, the commission concluded that "when reports began to arrive about the actions of the Phalangists in the camps, no proper heed was taken of these reports . . . and no energetic and immediate actions were taken to restrain the Phalangists and put a stop to their actions." [135]

An additional perspective is provided by the report of the International Commission to Enquire into Reported Violations of International Law by Israel during its Invasion of Lebanon. Constituted in August 1982 and chaired by Sean MacBride, a former assistant secretary-general of the United Nations, the International Commission harshly condemned Israel's involvement in the events of September 16–18 and placed special emphasis on Jerusalem's failure to fulfill its international legal obligations as an occupying power in West Beirut. Asserting that civilian residents of West Beirut, including those in the Palestinian camps, were "protected persons" under the terms of the Geneva Convention, the commission found Israel to be in violation of international law, since "an Occupying Power is responsible for the actions of its agents toward protected persons." [136] Further, the commission noted, a failure to prevent measures that cause "the physical suffering or extermination" of protected persons is regarded as a "grave breach" of the Geneva Convention. Finally, moving beyond the purview of international law, the commission called attention to the impact of what it termed Israel's "dehumanization" of the Palestinians. Noting the pejorative way in which Palestinians were routinely portrayed by Israeli political and military leaders, the commission expressed the opinion that this terminology "was an additional factor in creating conditions in which the massacres could occur, as well as the conditions in which they could be tolerated, for a period of time extending over thirty-six hours." [137]

Events leading up to the massacre provide a clearer and more vivid picture of Israeli involvement, as well as the general circumstances that contributed to the tragic developments of September 16, 17, and 18. To begin with, Sharon and Chief of Staff Eitan began asserting even before the PLO evacuation from Beirut was complete that a number of Palestinian fighters would be left behind, and that it would be necessary to find and disarm these "terrorists," who undoubtedly would seek to hide themselves among the civilian population of Beirut's refugee camps. PLO fighters had thus been sought inside Burj al-Barajneh refugee camp as early as August 23, with 230 men arrested in an operation carried out by the IDF and the regular Lebanese army. Later, defending the need to send forces into Sabra and Shatilla, Sharon charged that the PLO had left behind more than 2,000 fighters, with huge arms supplies, and Eitan added that these "armed terrorists" were indeed hiding in the camps.[138] Although these assertions are rejected as either false or grossly exaggerated by Israeli as well as Palestinian sources,[139] Sharon insisted that action was necessary, and for this reason, in order to give the IDF a free hand in making whatever moves it deemed necessary, he pressed for the departure of the international peacekeeping force as soon as possible after September 1.

During this period, Sharon, Eitan, and other senior IDF officials met with Phalange leaders and coordinated their strategy for dealing with the PLO guerrillas who were alleged to be hiding in Sabra and Shatilla. Sharon and Bashir Gemayel, the Maronite leader and Lebanon's president-elect, also reached agreement about the need for a military operation to track down these PLO fighters, although for a time it was unclear whether this would be carried out by the IDF itself, the Phalange militia, or the regular Lebanese army. From the Israeli point of view, the Phalange were seen as an appropriate partner in this effort not only because of their hatred of the Palestinians but also because of what the Kahan Commission described as "their skills in identifying terrorists and in discovering arms caches." Indeed, Elie Hobeika, the Phalange intelligence chief, had worked closely with the IDF during the siege of Beirut to collect information about the movements of senior PLO officials. In addition, as the Kahan Commission pointed out, the Israeli decision to involve Phalange forces in operations against the Palestinians was also taken in response to domestic public opinion, which "was angry that the Phalangists, who were reaping the fruits of the war, were taking no part in it."[140] The final decision that Phalange forces, rather than the IDF, would carry out the operation appears to have been made by Sharon and Eitan early in the evening of September 14. Six hours later, in the middle of the night, Eitan and Amir Drori, head of the IDF's Northern Command, traveled to Phalange headquarters at Qarantina to arrange the details, and the next morning Sharon himself went to Qarantina for additional discussions with Phalange leaders.

Also contributing to the unfolding of events was the assassination of Bashir Gemayel late in the afternoon on September 14. A bomb blast in the Phalange branch office in Ashrafiya killed Gemayel, along with fifty or sixty others. The bomb was planted by a member of the clandestine Syrian National Party, a small radical faction that had once been part of the Phalange Party but which now advocated union between Lebanon and Syria. The assassination not only further inflamed the passions of the Maronites, whom even Eitan now described as "thirsting for revenge,"[141] it also helped to determine the timing and dynamics of the drama being played out.

Following confirmation that Bashir had been killed in the blast at Ashrafiya, Sharon talked to Begin by phone and obtained his agreement that Israeli troops should be sent into West Beirut, telling the prime minister, who had himself expressed concern about the situation, that this action was necessary to prevent chaos and to protect Lebanese Muslims from the vengeance of the Phalange. At the same time, Sharon did not at this point inform the prime minister about the decision to send Phalange forces into the camps, even though he had announced this to the IDF's senior command earlier in the evening, before it was certain that Gemayel had been killed. In fact, Begin did not learn of this until almost two days later, on the evening of the 16th, when Phalange troops were already in Sabra and Shatilla.

The IDF takeover of West Beirut, code-named "Operation Iron Brain," began at dawn on September 15. The action was controversial in several respects. To begin with, Sharon had ordered the IDF to advance following consultation with the prime minister and foreign minister, but without informing other ministers or seeking cabinet approval. Thus, when the cabinet convened some thirty-six hours after the operation had begun, many of its members expressed anger that the defense minister had once again acted unilaterally and exceeded his authority.

In addition, Operation Iron Brain was in clear violation of the evacuation plan worked out by Philip Habib, and accordingly brought a strong protest from the United States. Morris Draper, an American official who had worked with Habib, met with Begin a few hours after the IDF began to move forward, and later in the day he joined Samuel Lewis, the U.S. ambassador to Israel, in a meeting with Sharon, Eitan, and several others from the Israeli Defense Ministry. Both Draper and Lewis strongly protested the Israeli operation and pointed out that Jerusalem had promised that the IDF would not enter Beirut, only to be curtly told by Sharon that circumstances had changed. Sharon also insisted that "we went in because of the 2000–3000 terrorists who remained there. . . . We even have their names." Draper challenged this assertion, telling the Israeli defense minister, "I asked for those names and you said there was an enormous list, but what you came up with was a minuscule one."[142] Nevertheless, the Americans, like the Israeli cabinet, were in the end forced to accept Sharon's coup and the resultant *fait accompli*. By the morning of the 16th, Israeli troops had encircled Sabra and Shatilla and the scene was set for the entry of Phalange forces.

Although they vigorously denied any intention of seeking to perpetuate a massacre, and while there is no evidence that they deliberately and specifically incited the Phalange to violence against civilians,[143] Israeli officials were fully aware that sending Phalange troops into Sabra and Shatilla could well have disastrous consequences. Eitan's assessment of the Phalange state of mind following

Bashir's assassination has already been noted, and it is significant that the Israeli chief of staff added to this characterization the observation that "there could be torrents of blood."[144] Nor was this a possibility that IDF officials came to recognize only in the wake of Bashir's assassination. More than a month earlier, Major General Yehoshua Saguy, the director of military intelligence, had stated in a meeting in the defense minister's office that PLO fighters would remain in Beirut after the evacuation of the PLO, and that "the Phalangists will find a way to get them and settle old scores. . . . One day the murders will start, and they will just go on and on without end."[145] A slaughter was also predicted by an intelligence and research officer in Tel Aviv who had served in Lebanon, and even a cabinet minister, David Levy, expressed similar concerns when he learned of the Phalange entry into the camps. "I know what vengeance means to them, the kind of slaughter [that could be involved]," Levy is reported to have stated.[146]

Among the other evidence that IDF officials fully realized the danger of sending Phalange forces into the Palestinian refugee camps are not only additional predictions of this sort but also the efforts of some, most notably Amir Drori, to have responsibility for the projected operation transferred to the regular Lebanese army. Drori sought this change precisely in order to avoid the kind of tragedy that subsequently took place. In addition, reflecting these same concerns, Brigadier General Amos Yaron issued explicit and repeated warnings to Phalange leaders, to the effect that civilians should not be harmed. While commendable, these actions not only proved to be an inadequate response to the disaster looming on the horizon, they constitute yet another clear indication that knowledgeable and responsible IDF officials were under no illusions about what was at least reasonably likely to occur if Phalange forces were turned loose against the Palestinians. Sharon, Eitan, and several other senior Israeli officials thus were not guilty of faulty intelligence, of authorizing an operation that they *should* have known had a high probability of leading to disaster, they were guilty of setting in motion a military action that they *did* know might result in the killing of defenseless civilians.

There is no doubt that Israeli military and political leaders learned of the massacre while it was still taking place. It is true that reports from the camps at first came out slowly and in a piecemeal fashion, enabling many Israeli officials to claim with credibility that for a time they did not realize what was occurring in Sabra and Shatilla. Yet the IDF's general staff was aware that something was seriously wrong by the morning of September 17, barely twelve hours after Phalange forces had entered the camps, and confirmed reports of specific incidents, as well as indications of the scope of the killing, were circulating widely by the afternoon of the same day.

Nevertheless, despite the presence of Israeli troops outside Sabra and Shatilla, the IDF senior command did not respond to the information it received with immediate and energetic action designed to put a stop to the killing. A few officers did take limited action in response to the information that was becoming available. For example, Yaron issued a strong protest to Phalange leaders when the first reports of atrocities were received, on the evening of the 16th, and he obtained assurances from Hobeika and others that the massacre would stop. Also, on the morning of the 17th, Yaron met with Drori, the senior officer of the Northern Command, and recommended that the entire operation be terminated. No further action was taken, however, even as the gravity of the situation became increasingly apparent in the hours that followed. Indeed, on the afternoon of the 17th, Yaron and Drori joined Eitan and his deputy for a meeting with Phalange leaders, including Hobeika, at which no mention was made of the killing of civilians, and the Israeli chief of staff in fact authorized Phalange forces to remain in Sabra and Shatilla until the morning of the 18th.[147]

Reports of the situation were also transmitted to senior political officials by Israeli journalists, and these, too, failed to elicit a meaningful response. Late in the morning of the 17th, Ze'ev Schiff, military affairs editor of *Ha'aretz*, relayed stories about the killing to Foreign Minister Yitzhak Shamir, only to learn later that Shamir ignored his request to investigate these reports. Even more specific information was transmitted to Sharon on the night of the 17th. Israeli Television's military correspondent, Ron Ben-Yishai, telephoned the defense minister in an effort to inform him directly of the atrocities taking place in Sabra and Shatilla. Again, however, even though Ben-Yishai provided details of murders and executions witnessed by Israeli soldiers, the information was ignored.

As the Kahan Commission concluded, this situation has clear implications for Israeli responsibility, and it is against this background that Schiff and Ya'ari offer the following forceful but accurate summary of the situation on the night of September 17:

> Eitan, Drori, Levi, Yaron and other officers knew that the Phalangists would be in the camps all night and that they were using bulldozers [to dispose of corpses]; they also knew about the flight of panic-stricken civilians northward. Yet there was no attempt to get to the bottom of all the "buzzing"—whether out of sheer indifference or because the reports were discredited or because the key men in the field were distracted by their own problems. . . . Nor were steps taken to hasten the departure of the Lebanese Forces or put an end to the wanton bloodletting. And outside the army, the two attempts by journalists to get around the usual channels by direct approaches to ministers had failed to elicit the intervention that might have been expected, either by Shamir or Sharon. And so a second night of bloodshed and terror settled over the streets and alleys of the two hapless camps.[148]

As the full scope of the tragedy became known in the days that followed, there was widespread anger and dismay, in Israel as elsewhere. On September 29, an estimated 400,000 Israelis, almost 10 percent of the country's population, gathered in a mass rally in Tel Aviv and demanded that those who shared responsibility for the massacre at Sabra and Shatilla be identified and punished. It was in response to these protests that Begin, reluctantly, appointed the commission of inquiry headed by Chief Justice Yitzhak Kahan. In presenting its findings and conclusions, the Kahan Commission employed judicious language designed to calm passions. Also, to some, the conclusions it reached appeared much too restrained given the enormity of the crimes that had been committed, and in Israel such sentiments were expressed at a Peace Now rally called to protest what was seen as the commission's excessive caution.[149] Nevertheless, the report of the commission, published in February 1983, did establish the culpability of a number of senior military and political leaders.

Although it judged a determination of responsibility to be sufficient in most instances, the Kahan Commission also saw fit to make recommendations concerning punishment in several cases. It recommended that Saguy be dismissed from his post as director of military intelligence, and that Yaron no longer be permitted to serve as an IDF field commander. The commission made no recommendation in the case of Eitan, noting that this would have no practical effect since he was about to complete his term as chief of staff and an extension was not under consideration. On the other hand, the language it employed in discussing Eitan's "acts and omissions" suggested that under other circumstances it would probably have recommended his dismissal.

The Kahan Commission did make a recommendation in the case of Ariel Sharon. Indeed, its harshest judgments were reserved for the defense minister, whom it found to bear "personal responsibility," since he had not ordered "appropriate measures for preventing or reducing the chances of a massacre." As a consequence of his responsibility, the commission called upon Sharon to draw "the appropriate personal conclusions arising out of the defects revealed with regard to the manner in which he discharged the duties of his office," meaning that the defense minister should resign, and it added that if he refused to do so the prime minister should consider removing him from office. In the end, these recommendations were only partially implemented, however. Sharon refused to resign, and the prime minister hesitated to remove him, both because of his own indecision and because the defense minister was a formidable political opponent. A compromise formula was eventually adopted: Sharon would relinquish the defense portfolio but remain in the cabinet, and perhaps this messy conclusion is a fitting end to the story of Israel's involvement in the Sabra and Shatilla massacre. As stated by Schiff and Ya'ari in 1984, in their award-winning account of Israel's war against the Palestinians in Lebanon, "If there is a moral to the painful episode of Sabra and Shatilla, it has yet to be acknowledged" by the government of Israel.[150]

More generally, while it is of course the Palestinians who were the victims at Sabra and Shatilla, the massacre that concluded Israel's war against the PLO in Lebanon may also be an appropriate symbol for the damage the Israeli architects of that war did to their own country. With high casualties of its own, negligible political gains, and the wrath of the world directed at the Jewish state, the Israeli public was both divided and disillusioned in the fall of 1982. Many Israelis were also deeply resentful, expressing their anger at Sharon, Begin, and other leaders in the huge rally protesting the massacre in Beirut and in the additional demonstrations that followed release of the Kahan Commission report. Yitzhak Rabin of the Labor Alignment thus spoke for many Israelis when he called the country's Lebanon adventure "a mistaken war . . . inspired by political and strategic delusions."[151]

Public opinion polls indicate the extent to which Israeli disillusionment became widespread in the aftermath of Sabra and Shatilla. Whereas the popularity of the government and its leaders had risen sharply during the first stages of the war, reversing what had been a steady decline in public support, opinion surveys in the fall of 1982 and the spring of 1983 showed a dramatic increase in the view that it had been wrong for Israel to go to war in Lebanon. In June 1982, polls found that only 13 percent opposed the decision to invade Lebanon, but by March 1983 more than 60 percent opposed the war as it had taken shape.[152]

Begin himself began to have serious doubts following publication of the Kahan Commission report, in February 1983, and knowledgeable Israelis suggest that this was probably a major factor in his decision to resign from office the following September, in the middle of his term, and then to retire from public view. The death of his wife was an important consideration as well, but in any event, following his resignation, Begin remained withdrawn, almost reclusive, and many believed he had become seriously depressed. Finally, so far as the IDF and Israeli military power are concerned, the war seemed to introduce a degree of hesitation and self-doubt and, in the short term at least, to limit the country's willingness to deploy its military might in pursuit of political goals. As stated by a seasoned American analyst of foreign affairs, "An Israel deeply disillusioned by the outcome of the 1982 war and the casualties from it, and under heavy economic strains, was simply a lot less powerful, or at least less willing to use its power, than it had seemed up to 1982."[153]

10 | Futile Diplomacy in the Mid-1980s

The Reagan Plan and the Fez Plan

On SEPTEMBER 1, 1982, the day that the last PLO guerrillas were departing from Beirut, U.S. President Ronald Reagan introduced a peace initiative designed to build on what he believed to be the momentum created by Israel's military victory in Lebanon. Called simply "September 1" by many U.S. officials, the Reagan Plan was presented in a televised address to the nation, with the president telling the American public, "I want to report to you on the steps we have taken and the prospects they can open up for a just and lasting peace in the Middle East."[1] The day before Reagan's televised address, the substance of the president's peace initiative had been communicated to the Israeli government by Samuel Lewis, the U.S. ambassador in Tel Aviv.

In putting forward his initiative, Reagan appeared to embrace the analysis advanced by the Israeli government, to the effect that the Palestine Liberation Organization was a major obstacle to peace, and that its military defeat could be an important step on the road to Arab-Israeli accommodation. "The Lebanon war, tragic as it was, has left us with a new opportunity for peace in the Middle East," the president stated. Reagan's negative view of the PLO extended to that organization's role in Lebanon, moreover, with the president declaring that in the wake of the PLO's evacuation from Beirut, "we can now help the Lebanese to rebuild their war-torn country." In this connection, although Lebanon was not the major focus of his address, Reagan appeared to be in agreement with those Israeli and Maronite Christian analysts who had long argued that the presence of foreign forces in Lebanon was the principal cause of that country's troubles, rather than a response to weakness and instability brought on primarily by internal confessional conflicts. Assuming that conditions for the reconstruction of Lebanon had therefore been created by Israel's defeat of the PLO, Reagan asserted that a foundation had been laid for peacemaking on other fronts as well. "In the aftermath of the settlement in Lebanon," he stated, "we now face an opportunity for a broader peace. . . . The opportunities for peace do not begin and end in Lebanon."[2]

One key element of the Reagan peace plan was the emphasis it placed on continuing American support for Israel. The president spoke repeatedly of Israel's "legitimate security concerns," declaring, "The State of Israel is an accomplished fact; it deserves unchallenged legitimacy within the community of nations . . . [and] has a right to exist in peace behind secure and defensible borders." Reagan also called on the Arab states to recognize this right, "to accept the reality of Israel and the reality that peace and justice are to be gained only through hard, fair, direct negotiation." Elsewhere, the president told his audience, "I have personally followed and supported Israel's heroic struggle for survival ever since the founding of the state 34 years ago." Underlining his awareness that prior to 1967 "the bulk of Israel's population lived within artillery range of hostile Arab armies," Reagan reaffirmed American support for the Jewish state's security by concluding, "I am not about to ask Israel to live that way again." Finally, toward the end of his address, Reagan declared, "America's commitment to the security of Israel is ironclad. And, I might add, so is mine."

While Reagan's view of the PLO and his strong reaffirmation of U.S. support for Israel might have suggested a lack of balance in the September 1 initiative, the president in fact acknowledged the legitimacy of Palestinian political claims and juxtaposed these claims to the rights and requirements of the Jewish state. At one point, for example, he declared that "the question now is how to reconcile Israel's legitimate security concerns with the legitimate rights of the Palestinians." Further, making it clear that these Palestinian rights were political in character, the president specifically recorded his agreement with the Palestinians' insistence "that their cause is more than a question of refugees." He also acknowledged that "the military losses of the PLO have not diminished the yearning of the Palestinian people for a just solution of their claims," and he added later that "the departure of the Palestinians from Beirut dramatizes more than ever the homelessness of the Palestinian people."

By placing emphasis on the Palestinian dimension of the Arab-Israeli conflict, the president distanced himself from the Israeli government's assertion that the Middle East dispute was first and foremost an interstate conflict, rather than a clash between the claims of Israelis and Palestinians to the same piece of land. On the contrary, the president seemed to be saying, while it was indeed the American view that the Arab states must accept Israel's right to exist, a solution to the problem of Palestinian homelessness was also a critical requirement for the achievement of a just and durable peace. This fundamental point was reiterated by Secretary of State George Shultz ten days later, when he stated in remarks to the Senate Foreign Relations Committee, "It is time to address, forcefully and directly, the underlying Palestinian issues" of the Arab-Israeli conflict.[3]

Deliberately departing from the principle of constructive ambiguity, the Reagan initiative made specific recommendations about the way in which Israeli and Palestinian rights might be reconciled. This was in contrast to United Nations 242 and the Camp David accords, which had deemed it productive to avoid specifics and had instead concentrated on general formulations or frameworks concerned with procedure. The logic of these efforts, based on constructive ambiguity, was that seeking agreement on broad principles was the best way, and perhaps the only way, to generate momentum and get the parties to the bargaining table. Only then, this logic continued, might it be possible to narrow the gap on critical issues that it had previously been impossible to address. Concluding that this approach had not led to progress on the Palestinian problem, however, Reagan addressed himself to substance as well as procedure and outlined the settlement his administration considered just and which he hoped could now be achieved. There remained issues to be negotiated, of course, but Reagan nonetheless spelled out with considerable specificity the American position on major points. Indeed, he explicitly stated that while the U.S. had in the past avoided public comment on major substantive issues, he now believed that "some clearer sense of America's position on the key issues is necessary to encourage wider support for the peace process."

The U.S. president began by reaffirming the call issued at Camp David for a five-year transition period during which Palestinians in the West Bank and Gaza would have full autonomy over their own affairs. He emphasized the transitional nature of these arrangements, however, placing himself in direct opposition to the Begin government's position that autonomy constitutes a permanent solution to the Palestinian problem. "I want to make the American position well understood," Reagan declared. "The purpose of this transition period is the peaceful and orderly transfer of authority from Israel to the Palestinian inhabitants of the West Bank and Gaza." The president did add that this transfer of authority must not interfere with Israel's security requirements, but he then went on to insist both that this did not provide a justification for Israel's settlement drive, which was "in no way necessary" for the defense of the Jewish state, and, more generally, that Israeli security was not incompatible with the principle of territorial compromise. Therefore, as the president sought to look to the future, beyond the transition period, he expressed the view that "peace . . . is not achievable on the basis of Israeli sovereignty or permanent control over the West Bank and Gaza." Elsewhere, in an additional slap at the policies of the Begin government, he not only repeated that the principle of land for peace "remains wholly valid as the foundation stone of America's Middle East peace effort," but stated as well that this principle "applies to all fronts, including the West Bank and Gaza."

A list of "talking points" accompanying the Reagan Plan was sent to the Israeli prime minister, as well as to Arab leaders, and the clarification provided by this document also showed a huge gap between the thinking of the U.S. administration and that of the government of Israel. In these talking points, Reagan indicated that the U.S. would support participation by the Palestinians of East Jerusalem in elections for the Self-Governing Authority in the West Bank, that he viewed the concept of autonomy as offering Palestinians in the occupied territories "real authority over themselves, the land and its resources, subject to fair safeguards on water," and that the U.S. would also support "progressive Palestinian responsibility for internal security based on capability and performance." The talking points also called, as did the text of the initiative itself, for a freeze on Israeli settlements in the occupied territories.[4]

With respect to each of these concerns, Reagan not only sought to remove any doubt about American thinking, he also weighed in against the Israeli position on an issue that had separated Israelis and Egyptians during the Camp David autonomy talks. Departing from its prior strategy of avoiding public comment and leaving these matters to negotiations between the parties, the American administration now made clear its view that not only was Palestinian autonomy to be a temporary rather than a permanent political arrangement, but even during the transitional period it applied to land as well as people and was relevant to the Palestinian inhabitants of East Jerusalem as well as other occupied areas.

Beyond seeking to dispel any possible ambiguity about the nature of Palestinian autonomy and about the requirement that Israel must withdraw from the West Bank and Gaza at the end of the transition period, the president also sought to articulate a clear American position regarding the subsequent disposition of the occupied territories. The final status of the territories must be determined through "the give and take of negotiations," Reagan acknowledged, and the United States accordingly would not seek to dictate the outcome of peace talks. Nevertheless, the Reagan Plan differed from previous initiatives in that it did not merely articulate the principles that should guide negotiations but instead presented substantive suggestions in response to final status questions.

Specifically, reflecting distrust of the PLO and Palestinian nationalism, Reagan not only expressed his opposition to annexation or permanent control of the West Bank and Gaza by Israel, he also declared that "peace cannot be achieved by the formation of an independent Palestinian state in those territories." "There is, however, another way to peace," the U.S. president continued, and, more precisely, "it is the firm view of the United States that self-government by the Palestinians of the West Bank and Gaza in association with Jordan offers the best chance for a durable, just and lasting peace." In calling for the exercise of Palestinian self-determination in association with Jordan, the U.S. president hoped that Israelis, Palestinians, and Jordanians would all accept this formula as a sound basis for resolving the conflict among them and for reaching agreement on such outstanding issues as the status of Jerusalem and the final border between Israel and Jordan.

The Israeli cabinet discussed the Reagan Plan in a special session the day after it was introduced and had little difficulty in formulating Israel's sharp and unequivocal response: despite its strong reaffirmation of America's commitment to Israel, its denial to the PLO of any role in the peace process, and its declared opposition to a Palestinian state, the Reagan initiative of September 1 was unacceptable to Israel both in its specifics and as a point of departure for any and all negotiations. In rejecting the American initiative, the Begin government stressed that the plan was at variance with the Camp David accords on many important points, including the status of East Jerusalem, Jewish settlements in the occupied territories, the definition of autonomy, ties with Jordan, and Israeli sovereignty. In most of these instances, the Israelis accused the Americans either of violating agreements reached at Camp David or of providing specificity with respect to matters the Camp David accords had deliberately chosen to leave open. The Israelis also pointed out that Jordan, once in possession of the West Bank and Gaza, might permit the Palestinians to establish an independent state in these territories. Despite Reagan's declared opposition to such a state, they argued, "there would be nothing to prevent King Hussein from inviting his new found friend, Yasir Arafat, to come to Nablus and hand the rule over to him."[5] The Israeli statement insisted that "it is inconceivable that Israel will ever agree to such an 'arrangement' whose consequences are inevitable."

While these arguments were accurate as far as they went, at the heart of the official Israeli response was Jerusalem's rejection of the Reagan Plan's insistence on territorial compromise. The Likud-led government was firmly committed to the eventual imposition of Israeli sovereignty over the West Bank and Gaza. In addition, the Jewish state had just fought a war in the hope and expectation that victory over the PLO in Lebanon would reduce Palestinian opposition to Israel's definition of autonomy, as a concept that applied to the inhabitants of the occupied territories but not to the territories themselves, and as a permanent rather than provisional arrangement for Palestinian self-rule. Thus, not only in light of its established ideological convictions but also in the wake of its success on the battlefield in Lebanon, Israel found the Reagan Plan wholly unacceptable.

With the gap between the September 1 initiative and Israel's position unbridgeable, Jerusalem issued a communiqué which reported, in particularly blunt and undiplomatic language, that "the Government of Israel has resolved that on the basis of these [American] positions it will not enter into any negotiations with any party."[6] The Israeli government communiqué also declared, in response to specific points in the U.S. initiative that it found objectionable, that "Jerusalem is one city, indivisible, the capital of the State of Israel [and] thus it shall remain for all generations to come," that the creation of Israeli settlements in the West Bank and Gaza "is an inalienable Jewish right . . . [and] we shall continue to establish them in accordance with our natural right," and that "there is nothing in the Camp David agreement that precludes the application of Israeli sovereignty over Judea, Samaria and the Gaza district following the transitional period." In the days that followed, the Reagan Plan was also denounced in forceful statements by senior Israeli officials, as when Sharon declared on Israeli radio that "not only will Israel not accept [the U.S. plan], it will not discuss it," and on September 8 the Knesset formally rejected the American peace plan by a vote of 50 to 36.

The Begin government's rejection of the Reagan initiative was coupled with the announcement of an accelerated settlement drive, which included a reaffirmation of the program formulated several years earlier to put more than one million Jews in the West Bank and Gaza during the next three decades, in planned cities and towns. Israel also took immediate action to demonstrate its continuing commitment to Jewish settlement in the occupied territories. Four days after the introduction of the Reagan Plan, it allocated $18.5 million for the construction of three new settlements and approved plans for the establishment of seven more, and in December the Israelis announced that forty-two additional Jewish communities would be constructed in the West Bank during the next four years. In addition, Israel launched a major media campaign in an attempt to persuade more Jews to take up residence in the occupied territories and to encourage private developers to increase the number of housing units available to would-be settlers. Further, in a parallel move, an Israeli judge ruled at this time that companies registered in Israel but doing business primarily in the West Bank and Gaza were exempt from taxation.[7]

Some spokesmen for the government asserted that these moves had no special connection to the Reagan Plan, and it is certainly correct that they reflected the continuation of a settlement drive which was well developed before the introduction of the American initiative. At the same time, both Israelis and Americans understood that these actions were part of the Likud government's answer to the U.S. initiative of September 1, and indeed this was made explicit by others in the government. For example, Yehuda Ben Meir, the deputy foreign minister, stated that Jerusalem's response to the Reagan Plan should be the construction of even more Jewish settlements in the occupied territories, "as this is the best proof that no force will be able to uproot us from our homeland."[8]

Likud's was not the only Israeli response to the American initiative, however; Labor and parties further to the left gave the Reagan Plan a much more positive reception, as did many Jews in the United States. Expressing concern about a number of points, including the status of Jerusalem and the precise definition to be given to Palestinian self-government, Labor shied away from an all-out endorsement of the September 1 initiative. More generally, however, the Alignment saw much that was worthwhile in the Reagan Plan and took strong exception to the government's conclusion that it was unfit even for discussion. Indeed, with its call for territorial compromise and for Palestinian self-rule in association with Jordan, as well as its rejection of Palestinian statehood, the American initiative had a great deal in common with Labor's own approach to the territories, which advocated returning most of the West Bank to Jordan.

Commonalities between the Reagan Plan and the position of the Alignment produced suspicion that the U.S. president had crafted his proposals with Israeli domestic politics in mind. Some commentators suggested that Reagan hoped to enhance Labor's position and increase the pressure on the Begin government, or even, perhaps, to bring about the latter's demise. Some went so far as to suggest that Reagan may have consulted with Labor Party leader Shimon Peres before presenting his plan, an allegation that Peres denied.[9] In any event, whether or not such consultation took place, Labor asserted that the U.S. plan had merit and deserved a favorable response. Peres characterized it as "a basis for dialogue with the U.S.," for example,[10] and this attitude was also reflected in the votes of many Alignment MKs when the initiative was considered by the Knesset. Moreover, following the vote, Peres and other Alignment leaders lamented the Knesset's endorsement of the government's attitude and asserted that the Reagan Plan was in fact favored by a majority of the electorate, which caused Begin to state that he would welcome early elections to demonstrate that this was not the case.

The depth of Alignment enthusiasm for the Reagan initiative should not be overstated, however. As noted, there were important substantive differences between Labor's "Jordanian option" and the specifics of the plan put forward by the U.S. president. In particular, Labor advocated Israeli retention of the Jordan River valley and adjacent areas, a program known as the Allon Plan, which was wholly unacceptable to King Hussein of Jordan. In addition, rather than conceiving of withdrawal from the rest of the West Bank as a mechanism for addressing the legitimate rights of the Palestinian people, Labor, like Likud, tended to see Israel's conflict with the Arabs as an interstate dispute, and the Alignment favored an arrangement with Hussein in large part because its leaders believed the Jordanian monarch could be counted on to contain Palestinian nationalism. Labor also shared Likud's view that the status of Jerusalem as the undivided capital of Israel was nonnegotiable, although the party's position was somewhat more vague concerning participation by East Jerusalem Arabs in the autonomy scheme advanced in the Camp David accords.

Given these points of disagreement, some called Labor's positive response to the Reagan Plan "superficial," or in some cases even "hypocritical," and noted that a number of Alignment spokesmen openly expressed reservations about the September 1 initiative.[11] Some analysts also argued that Labor's attitude toward the Reagan Plan was shaped by political considerations. For example, Samuel Lewis, U.S. ambassador to Israel when the Reagan Plan was introduced, suggests that Labor's response was influenced by its status as an opposition party. Lewis notes that in the fall of 1982, with troops still in Lebanon and the results of the war in the north not yet digested, no Israeli government "would have been ready or able to tackle the toughest political nut of all, the future of the West Bank." Thus, he adds, while Shimon Peres could afford the luxury of welcoming the Reagan initiative, "his diplomatic room for maneuver would have been far more restricted" had he been Israel's prime minister.[12]

The Reagan Plan was fashioned with a view toward the Arabs, as well as Israel, and in this connection it was designed at least in part to blunt Arab criticism of American support for Israel during the war in Lebanon, and more broadly to rebuild U.S. prestige in the Arab world. Arab states, including Egypt,

Jordan, and other American allies, were angry that U.S. Secretary of State Alexander Haig had apparently given Jerusalem the green light for an operation in Lebanon. They were also deeply disturbed that the U.S. had taken no action in response to Israel's use in Lebanon of American-made cluster bombs, which was a violation of the agreement under which these munitions had been purchased from the United States. The Reagan Plan was intended to mute some of these criticisms, which had become particularly intense during the siege of Beirut. Moreover, to increase the chances of a positive Arab response, the U.S. had consulted in advance with Jordan, the Arab state most directly concerned, and Reagan had in fact gone forward with his initiative only after being assured by American envoys that it would draw a favorable reaction from King Hussein.[13] This prior consultation incensed Begin, since Jerusalem had not been consulted in advance, and the Israeli prime minister was also angry that after introducing its peace plan on September 1, the U.S. did not wait for Israel's reaction before beginning discussions with Egypt, Saudi Arabia, and other Arab states.

By putting some distance between itself and Jerusalem and by articulating proposals displaying sensitivity to the Palestinians, Washington succeeded in eliciting a generally positive response from the Arabs. Jordan and other key Arab actors, including the mainstream of the PLO, welcomed the plan and described it as a meaningful step in the right direction. Arafat, for example, issued a carefully worded statement on September 3 in which he declared, "We do not reject [Reagan's proposals], nor do we criticize them."[14] Farouq al-Qaddoumi, head of the PLO's political department and often described as the organization's foreign minister, characterized the U.S. initiative as possessing "some positive elements" and "not altogether bad."[15] In particular, the Arabs praised the American president's call for Israeli withdrawal from the occupied territories and lauded as equally important the emphasis that Reagan placed on the Palestinian dimension of the Arab-Israeli conflict. Less satisfactory to the Arabs, of course, were the failure of the Reagan Plan to assign a role in the peace process to the PLO, and the fact that the American administration had formally declared its opposition to the establishment of an independent Palestinian state. But while these latter considerations were deemed to be important, most Arab leaders, including senior officials of the PLO, saw the September 1 initiative as a significant evolution of U.S. policy and deemed its positive features adequate to justify further discussion. Indeed, according to one student of the PLO, Washington's recognition of the Palestinian people's need for a homeland constituted a potential "turning point" in American-Palestinian relations, "at least in comparison with the traditional position of the U.S."[16]

On September 6, Arab leaders assembled for a summit meeting in Fez, Morocco, and three days later they issued their own eight-point peace plan, thereby offering a collective response to the Reagan initiative and carrying forward the new round of diplomatic activity set in motion by the U.S. president. The Fez summit, chaired by King Hassan of Morocco, was attended by almost every member of the Arab League, with the PLO represented by Yasir Arafat. The only Arab states not in attendance were Libya, which boycotted the summit, and Egypt, whose membership in the league had been suspended after Cairo signed a peace treaty with Israel. The summit was convened in the hope of building on the foundation laid by the Reagan Plan and encouraging the United States to deepen its involvement in Middle Eastern peacemaking, and in this spirit a deliberate effort was made to avoid all criticism of the American initiative during the meeting in Fez. Rather, making no mention of the Reagan Plan in its final statement, the summit offered a peace plan of its own in order to show that the Arabs were ready for an accommodation with Israel and that the gap between the American proposals and Arab requirements was not too large to be bridged. Moreover, despite some private opposition, most notably from Syria, this peace plan was approved unanimously by the twenty Arab heads of state assembled in Fez.

The Fez Plan, as the proposals adopted at the Arab summit came to be known, implicitly recognized Israel within its pre-1967 borders and offered a "two-state solution" to Israeli-Palestinian conflict. To begin with, the plan called for Israeli withdrawal from all Arab territories occupied in 1967 and for the removal of Israeli settlements in these territories. The Arabs here went further than the Reagan Plan in attaching specific meaning to the notion of territorial compromise. On the other hand, the principles they put forward were not qualitatively different from those of the American initiative. There were qualitative differences between the Fez Plan and the Reagan Plan with respect to the issue of Palestinian rights, however. While U.S. recognition of the centrality of the Palestinian problem was applauded by the Arabs, the Fez Plan called for the Palestinian people not only "to exercise their firm and inalienable national rights" but to do so "under the leadership of the PLO, its sole legitimate representative." In addition, showing no interest in the Jordanian option that was at the heart of Reagan's approach to final status issues, the Fez Plan called for "the creation of an independent Palestinian state with Jerusalem as its capital." The Fez Plan also called for compensation for Palestinians who do not wish to return to their homes.

The Fez formula thus embraced the notion of partition, committing the Arabs to the proposition that both a Jewish state and an Arab state should be established in Palestine. To supervise Israeli withdrawal from the occupied territories and the establishment of a Palestinian state, the Fez Plan advocated placing the West Bank and Gaza Strip under UN supervision, for a period "not longer than several months," and then added that the UN Security Council should draw up "guarantees for peace for all states of the region, including the independent Palestinian state."[17] In adopting these principles, the statement of the Fez summit observed that several Arab leaders had put forth similar proposals in the past.

The statement cited the Fahd Plan of 1981 and a plan for peace based on the partition of Palestine that Tunisia's president, Habib Bourguiba, had attempted to launch in the 1960s.

The Limits of American and Arab Diplomacy

The Fez Plan, with its implied Arab recognition of Israel and its advocacy of a two-state solution to the question of Palestine, emerged after the 1982 Arab summit as the consensus position of the Arab mainstream. It was endorsed by Jordan, whose attitude was critical given the substance of the American initiative and the view of the Israeli opposition that territories relinquished by Israel should be turned over to the Hashemite kingdom. The Fez Plan was also agreed to not only by Egypt, which had already made peace with Israel, but by Saudi Arabia, Morocco, and most other Arab actors, including the dominant Fatah faction of the PLO. The only significant exceptions were Palestinian splinter groups and the rejectionist regime in Libya, the former now on the defensive and the latter having little influence or credibility in inter-Arab political circles. Syria expressed some opposition, too, although, recognizing its political isolation, Damascus had in fact felt obliged to vote with the others in Fez to make endorsement of the eight-point peace plan unanimous. Moreover, the pragmatic Syrian regime was not opposed to peace with Israel along the lines of the Fez Plan; rather, Damascus was angry that its claim to the Golan Heights had been ignored by the Reagan initiative, and that Washington seemed to be deliberately excluding it from the Arab-Israeli peace process and attempts to bring about the political reconstruction of Lebanon.[18] Thus, although it could rightly be argued that the principles put forward at Fez were not new, being contained in the Fahd Plan of 1981 or even, so far as recognition of Israel is concerned, in Arab acceptance of UN Resolution 242, the Fez Plan was intended both to send a clear signal that there existed an Arab consensus in support of peace and to lay out what its authors hoped Washington and others would regard as a credible and constructive bargaining position.

Significantly, the PLO, and Arafat in particular, played an important role in helping to forge this mainstream and moderate Arab consensus. Arafat himself helped to write the eight-point Fez Plan, working closely with the Saudi royal family, and a senior PLO representative was included in the seven-member Arab League delegation that visited the permanent members of the UN Security Council in order to explain and seek support for the proposals adopted at Fez. Among the factors animating PLO diplomacy at this time were the dangers facing Palestinians after the war in Lebanon and the fact that, ironically perhaps, the war had strengthened moderate elements and weakened rejectionist factions inside the PLO. Also important, as indicated, was the American diplomatic initiative. Despite its obvious and important limitations, the PLO mainstream saw the Reagan Plan as a potentially significant departure from past American policy. Thus, Arafat and other PLO leaders turned with greater determination than ever to the diplomatic campaign they had been waging since the mid-1970s, devoting attention to the Arab world as well as the U.S. and the broader international community, and seeking to reestablish a moderate Arab consensus along lines that would isolate rejectionists, accept negotiations with Israel, and bring Egypt back into the Arab fold.

Having suffered a profound blow as a result of its military defeat in Lebanon, with its cadres and fighters now scattered over a dozen countries, the PLO ran the risk of permanent fragmentation. At a minimum, it was confronted by serious new problems relating to communication, political coordination, and the collection and distribution of resources. Further, deprived of its base in Lebanon, the Palestinian organization had become more vulnerable to interference by Arab governments, and particularly to attempts by Syria and Libya to utilize rejectionist groups within the PLO to divide the Palestinian national movement, undermine Arafat's authority, and discredit the political line that Fatah and the PLO mainstream had been pursuing since the mid-1970s.[19] Finally, apart from the possibility of interference by Arab governments, PLO losses in Lebanon left Palestinians in the West Bank and Gaza feeling more isolated and vulnerable to Israeli pressure, and the withdrawal of the PLO from Beirut also left Palestinian civilians in Lebanon unprotected. All of these pressures motivated Arafat and the PLO mainstream to work for the construction of a broad inter-Arab alliance, of which they would, of course, be an integral part. This alliance would marginalize rejectionist elements, both within the PLO and in the broader Arab arena, and would have an interest in the continued dominance of the political orientation championed by Fatah and Arafat.

Also bearing on PLO diplomacy at this time was the diminished influence of rejectionist groups within the PLO, including the Popular Front for the Liberation of Palestine (PFLP) and the Democratic Front for the Liberation of Palestine (DFLP). Although these groups accepted Arafat's leadership, they were strongly critical of his policies and openly expressed the view that his diplomatic and political initiatives were based on flawed assumptions. The rejectionist camp also included three smaller factions, the Popular Front for the Liberation of Palestine–General Command, the Palestine Popular Struggle Front, and Saiqa. These groups were even more militantly opposed to the orientation of PLO moderates and rejected any political settlement of the conflict with Israel. They were also prepared to challenge the PLO's current leadership, to the point, in the summer of 1983, of offering military support for a rebellion inside Fatah.[20] Even taken together, the five rejectionist groups were a distinct minority within the PLO. According to Emile Sahliyeh, about 80 percent of the organization's fighting force and about 90 percent of its political positions were filled by supporters of Fatah, which also had direct control of about two-thirds of the funds provided to the PLO by Arab states.[21] On the other hand, despite their small size and the differing political tendencies among them, rejectionist factions were an important part of the PLO's institutional structure as it functioned in Lebanon before the Israeli invasion. As explained by Sahliyeh, the exercise of their influence served "as a system of checks and balances inside the PLO's political institutions, limiting Fatah's range of policy options."[22]

While it is true, as noted, that the PLO mainstream was itself greatly weakened by the war in Lebanon, and hence more vulnerable to interference by Arab governments allied with Palestinian rejectionists, PLO losses in Lebanon dealt an even harsher blow to the rejectionist camp. Prior to the war, rejectionists within the PLO enjoyed a solid base of support in Lebanon. Indeed, in the judgment of Khalil Shikaki, another careful Palestinian scholar, they possessed "something approaching veto power over PLO decisions, a power incommensurate with their actual size or with the limited support they had enjoyed from the Palestinian people."[23] But this situation changed as a result of Israel's military victory in the summer of 1982. The demise of the PLO's independent political and military base in Lebanon put an end to many of the institutional arrangements that had been the power base of radicals and leftists, bringing a sharp diminution in the political and financial resources directly controlled by rejectionist factions and, as a consequence, reducing their ability to impose limits on the policies pursued by Fatah and the PLO mainstream.

A related consequence of the PLO's defeat in Lebanon, which not only reduced the influence of rejectionist factions but also simultaneously strengthened the PLO's moderate mainstream, was the enhanced political weight of the West Bank and Gaza in intra-Palestinian politics. At the grass-roots level, Palestinians in the occupied territories became the PLO's most important and politically influential constituency, and this in turn brought greater support for the more moderate ideological orientation that had long been dominant among these Palestinians. At least in part, the PLO had launched diplomatic initiatives and moved toward acceptance of an accommodation with Israel in the 1970s in response to calls for a two-state solution emanating from the West Bank and Gaza; and now, in the fall of 1982, these calls were more salient than ever. Even had he wished to do so, Arafat would have found it difficult to disregard the views of West Bank and Gaza Palestinians. With its cadres dispersed and deprived of its Lebanese base, the Palestine national movement, especially Fatah, was highly dependent on Palestinians in the territories for political support. At the same time, the views prevailing in the occupied territories constituted a political resource for Arafat, as well as a political interest that he was required to take into consideration. Despite Israeli attempts to suppress expressions of nationalism, inhabitants of the West Bank and Gaza continued to articulate both their identification with the PLO in general and their preference for the political line espoused by Arafat and Fatah in particular.

These developments did not leave the PLO's hard-line factions powerless, particularly so long as they received support from Damascus and Tripoli, but they did for a time alter the balance of power between the organization's moderate mainstream and its rejectionist minority. As explained by Shikaki, "The rejectionists' strength within PLO institutions deteriorated to reflect the extent of their actual presence in the occupied territories and among Palestinians in general," whereas, alternatively, "groups which enjoyed greater grass-roots support in the occupied territories and among Palestinians [in general], such as Fatah, were able to maintain and increase their influence in PLO institutions in the post-1982 period."[24] Thus, as a result of the PLO's defeat in Lebanon, there was a reduction in internal opposition to Arafat's efforts to engage the PLO in a new round of diplomacy and to work for the emergence of an Arab consensus in favor of a political solution to the conflict with Israel.

In addition to these institutional and political considerations, the relative decline in the rejectionists' fortunes was also due to the fact that, beyond ineffective and counterproductive acts of terrorism, there was no meaningful sense in which armed struggle against Israel remained a viable option for Palestinians. The PLO's concentration of men and weapons a few miles from Israel's northern border had enabled hard-liners to argue before the war that Palestinians possessed the military capacity to inflict damage on the Jewish state and should utilize this capacity. It was much more difficult to make this argument in the fall of 1982. In addition, Palestinian recognition that a military option no longer existed was enhanced by the failure of virtually every Arab state to come to the aid of the PLO in Lebanon. This inaction was bitterly denounced by Palestinians everywhere, and anger was directed with special force at Syria, since Damascus had long argued in favor of a military dimension to the struggle against Israel and, even more important, was militarily positioned to challenge the Israelis in Lebanon. The emptiness of Arab rhetoric, and particularly that of Syria, served to further weaken and isolate those PLO factions that denounced diplomacy and asserted that only armed struggle would enable Palestinians to secure their rights. Thus, while hard-liners and rejectionists might credibly assert that Arafat's past diplomatic efforts had produced little, having been met not with Israeli policies designed to test the PLO's declared readiness for compromise but with unprovoked military adventurism on the part of the government in Jerusalem, it remained the case that Palestinian radicals opposed to continued diplomacy were not seen as offering any feasible alternative.

Finally, PLO diplomacy at this time also reflected a desire to take advantage of the Reagan administration's apparent recognition of Palestinian political rights. Its important limitations notwithstanding, Arafat and other mainstream PLO leaders welcomed the Reagan initiative's focus on the Palestinian dimension of the Arab-Israeli conflict and judged it worthy of exploration precisely because they believed American military, political, and financial support for Israel made U.S. participation indispensable if progress toward Middle East peace was to be made.[25] Accordingly, an important PLO goal at this time was the establishment of a dialogue with the United States without preconditions. As explained by Sahliyeh, the PLO, like Jordan, Saudi Arabia, and most other Arab countries, intended their positions at Fez to be an indication of diplomatic flexibility and an expression of their desire to achieve a political solution to the Israeli-Palestinian conflict.[26] It was first and foremost for the American administration that this message was intended. Some hoped, too, that the Fez Plan and its acceptance by the PLO mainstream might influence the political debate inside Israel and strengthen the position of the Labor Alignment and other advocates of territorial compromise. In any event, not only the dangers confronting Palestinians but also the possibility of a new relationship with the United States was a stimulus to PLO diplomacy in the months following the war in Lebanon.

Late in 1982 and early in 1983, Arab diplomacy worked to counter Israeli government efforts to brand the Fez Plan as a propaganda ploy and undertook to offer additional evidence that Arabs and Palestinians were truly ready for peace. For example, the host of the Fez summit, King Hassan of Morocco, termed the Arab peace plan a first step toward nonbelligerency with Israel, and King Hussein of Jordan told the BBC on September 13 that the Fez meeting had re-created an Arab consensus in support of a just and durable peace. In addition, the Jordanian monarch stressed that the Fez Plan was compatible with the Reagan Plan, which he welcomed as "very constructive" and "very positive," and this led U.S. Secretary of State George Shultz to return the compliment by declaring that the Fez Plan was a genuine breakthrough.[27] So far as the PLO is concerned, Arafat on September 15 announced his willingness to meet with Israeli civilian and military leaders who opposed their government's policies in Lebanon and endorsed the notion of an accommodation with Palestinian nationalism.[28] Further, in January 1983, Arafat met three representatives of Israeli peace groups. The meeting took place in Tunis, where the PLO had now established its headquarters, and was intended as a sign that the PLO was prepared for deeds as well as words in the pursuit of peace.

Arab diplomacy at this time also sought to narrow the distance between the Reagan Plan and the Fez Plan, and in particular, if possible, to move the American administration beyond its general interest in the Palestinian problem toward acceptance of a two-state solution to the Middle East conflict. Toward this end, in October, King Hassan led an Arab League delegation to the United States to explain the Fez Plan and urge support for it, seeking also to discuss with administration officials concrete steps that might be taken to promote peace. Representatives of Algeria, Jordan, Saudi Arabia, and Tunisia joined the Moroccan monarch in this delegation. In presenting the Arab case, Hassan also attempted to respond to those in Washington and elsewhere who complained that the Fez Plan did not offer unambiguous Arab recognition of Israel, and in this connection he made a number of statements that blurred the distinction between the Arab and

American initiatives and emphasized the fact that there existed a basis for making progress toward peace. In one public declaration, for example, Hassan expressed confidence that a settlement of the Arab-Israeli conflict could be achieved "on the basis of the American and Arab proposals and the U. N. Security Council resolutions." In another, he stated that "the Arab nations will recognize Israel if it returns to its pre-1967 borders."[29] These and other statements by Hassan sought to make it clear that Morocco was prepared to recognize the Jewish state, and to communicate that this was also the position of the other Arab countries that had attended the Fez summit.[30]

Although Arab diplomatic efforts were received with cordiality by the Reagan administration, they brought no appreciable change in the American position. On the contrary, the Reagan administration made clear its unwillingness to move beyond the positions of its own September 1 peace initiative and, though praising the Fez Plan for its positive and constructive tone, began pressing the Arabs to abandon their calls for PLO participation and the establishment of an independent Palestinian state. An indication of U.S. resistance to Arab diplomacy was Washington's insistence that the visiting Arab League delegation led by King Hassan contain no members of the PLO. Senior PLO officials were included in the Arab League delegations that visited other major capitals after the Fez summit, but U.S. opposition forced Hassan to abandon his proposal that a representative of the PLO also be included in the mission to Washington. Moreover, Washington now urged friendly Arab governments to embrace the American view that Palestinian political rights should be exercised in association with Jordan. For example, the delegation that Hassan brought to Washington was specifically told upon its arrival in the United States that the Reagan administration hoped the Arab League would authorize Jordanian participation in Palestinian autonomy negotiations, which were called for in both the Camp David accords and the Reagan Plan, and which denied to the PLO any role in representing the Palestinians.

American diplomacy during this period focused on King Hussein of Jordan, both because of the centrality of Jordan to the U.S. peace plan and because Reagan had launched his initiative only after being told by his envoys that it would be favorably received in Amman. Thus, the Americans now urged Hussein to endorse the U.S. plan formally and publicly and, in particular, to agree to negotiate with Israel even if not authorized to do so by the Arab League or the PLO. The Jordanian monarch was pressed on these points when he visited Washington in December, with American officials telling him that this was the only possibility for securing Palestinian rights. Reagan himself urged the king to endorse the American initiative in two private meetings, repeating prior offers of military assistance and other concrete inducements if Hussein would agree to take part in restarted autonomy talks.[31] Hussein was apparently tempted by these offers, all the more so in view of his strong desire to strengthen Jordan's political influence in the West Bank. As both Palestinians and outside observers have frequently noted, acceptance of the PLO's role in representing the Palestinian people did not mean that the king's interest in recovering the occupied territories had waned.[32] In the end, however, Hussein told his American hosts that he was not prepared to act without PLO and Arab League approval, and he informed them that further consultation would be necessary before Jordan could officially state whether or not it would accept the Reagan Plan.

With the gap between Arab and American positions as wide as ever, both the PLO and Jordan formally declared their opposition to the Reagan Plan early in 1983. The PLO's decision came at the sixteenth meeting of the Palestine National Council, which took place in Algiers in February. Several months of behind-the-scenes maneuvering preceded the session, much of it involving work by Fatah and independents associated with the PLO mainstream to counter the efforts of Syria, Libya, and their client groups within the PLO to force a postponement of the PNC session.[33]

Rejectionist elements had sought to delay the Sixteenth PNC meeting for fear that it would provide Arafat with an opportunity to consolidate his leadership position. In addition, many were angry that the PLO chairman had been seeking to work out a common negotiating strategy with King Hussein of Jordan, even though the PNC had not authorized this action. Arafat's supporters responded to this charge by arguing that consultation with Jordan had been necessary to ensure that Hussein did not give in to American pressure and agree to peace talks which excluded the PLO. They also insisted that the PLO leader had made no commitments and was only developing proposals for consideration by the council. As stated by one sympathetic PNC member, "Arafat is off on his own. If he comes up with something he will try to sell it to the rest of the leadership. If not, you will hear him singing a very different song very soon."[34] In any event, although it is unlikely that their critics were persuaded by these rebuttals, Arafat and Fatah had the power to convene the PNC meeting on schedule. Moreover, not only were they fully in control, but all of the rejectionist factions, fearful that their influence would diminish further, had felt compelled to attend.

In their speeches at the PNC meeting, PLO leaders affirmed the independence of the Palestinian movement. On the one hand, they denounced attempts at interference by Syria and Libya. Salah Khalaf, for example, the second-highest-ranking official in Fatah, delivered an official address on behalf of Fatah and declared his readiness to go to Damascus and tell the Syrian president personally that "our decision is not for you." He also complained of Syrian inaction during the siege of Beirut and bitterly criticized Libyan radio for labeling as "sheep and cattle" those PLO guerrillas who left Beirut rather than fight to their death. "They are men and the best of men," the Palestinian leader stated.[35] Further, in yet another slap at the rejectionist regimes in Damascus and Tripoli, Khalaf indicated in his address that Fatah would continue and intensify diplomatic coordination with Egypt, with which it had been in contact since the siege of Beirut. He also indicated that Fatah favored stepped-up consultation with Jordan, including continuing discussions devoted to the possibility of establishing a Palestinian-Jordanian confederation.

On the other hand, mainstream PLO leaders also declared their opposition to the Reagan Plan and their unwillingness to authorize either Jordan or non-PLO Palestinians in the occupied territories to negotiate with Israel on behalf of the Palestinian people. Just as the Syrians would not make decisions for the Palestinians, neither would the Jordanians or anybody else; this would be done by the PLO, the sole legitimate representative of the Palestinian people. "The Fez resolutions represent the end of Palestinian concessions and not the beginning," Khalaf accordingly declared in his speech; and he also stated that any future moves toward the establishment of a Palestinian-Jordanian confederation would be on the basis of cooperation between two equal partners, the Kingdom of Jordan and an independent Palestinian state led by the PLO.

So far as the Reagan initiative itself is concerned, its rejection by the PLO was incorporated into the political program formally adopted at the Sixteenth PNC. According to this program, arrived at through discussion and bargaining that continued while the public sessions of the meeting were taking place, "Reagan's plan, in style and content, does not respect the established national rights of the Palestinian people since it denies the right of return and self-determination and the setting up of the independent Palestinian state and also the PLO—the sole legitimate representative of the Palestinian people." Because of these inadequacies, the statement continued, "the PNC rejects the considering of this plan as a sound basis for the just and lasting solution of the cause of the Palestine and Arab-Zionist conflict."[36] With the adoption of this declaration by the Sixteenth PNC, it thus became clear that recent diplomatic maneuvering had not succeeded in bridging the gap between the Reagan Plan and the Fez Plan. To the disappointment of the United States, and of King Hussein as well, the PLO would not authorize Jordan or non-PLO Palestinians to enter into negotiations under the auspices of the American initiative.

An understanding of the PLO's position requires attention to the political dynamics of the Sixteenth PNC, as well as to the content of the political program it adopted. Although Fatah was in a dominant position, PLO leaders felt that unity in Palestinian ranks was essential in the wake of the war in Lebanon, both because of the PLO's vulnerability and in order to demonstrate that the PLO remained an inclusive and representative organization. Therefore, as explained by Sahliyeh, "The overreaching goal for the PLO after Beirut was to survive in a new, unfavorable environment, surrounded by formidable challenges . . . [and for this reason] participants in the PNC were under immense psychological pressure to project a unified position and a sense of viability. . . . "[37] As a consequence of this situation, calls for national unity were pervasive at the Algiers meeting, and the discussion of substantive issues was characterized by hard bargaining which, in most instances, produced either contradictory statements or compromise formulations designed to permit both moderates and hard-liners to claim that their views had prevailed. This ambiguity was reflected in the collection of statements about PLO relations with Jordan, Syria, and Egypt, for example. In addition to the previously noted denunciations of Syrian interference in Palestinian affairs and the calls for intensified consultation with the regime in Cairo, there were also resolutions urging the consolidation of ties with "brotherly Syria" and with those "progressive and democratic" forces in Egypt that opposed the Camp David accords.[38]

The PNC's statement on the American peace initiative was also the result of compromise, and several of its key passages were thus deliberately constructed so as to permit competing interpretations. For instance, making a subtle linguistic distinction, the political program adopted by the PNC rejected consideration of the Reagan Plan, rather than the plan itself. In addition, the PNC statement declared the American initiative to be an inadequate basis for "solving" the Palestinian problem, leaving open the possibility that "discussions" toward that end might be based on the Reagan Plan. Even without a need to accommodate rejectionists, there is little likelihood that Fatah leaders would have endorsed the American peace plan without reservations. After all, the Reagan administration not only had refused to accept the principle of Palestinian statehood but was unwilling even to meet with representatives of the PLO. Yet moderate Palestinian leaders sought to leave the door open for additional diplomacy aimed at establishing a dialogue with the United States, and they had insisted upon a political statement in Algiers which, in their view, gave them this flexibility. As explained by Helena Cobban, the ambiguity of the political program adopted by the PNC left most Fatah leaders convinced that "they had won enough room to continue, in the months which followed, their exploration of the value of the U.S. initiative."[39]

Taking all of this together, it may be concluded that the Sixteenth PNC showed both the possibilities and the limits of PLO diplomacy in the period following the war in Lebanon. Fatah and the moderate PLO mainstream were in a dominant position. In addition, they had managed to keep rejectionist factions within the PLO without sacrificing their own political program. Yet a need for unity within the ranks of the PLO had forced them to accept political formulations that were deliberately vague, and the Reagan administration's refusal to go beyond its Jordanian option left mainstream Palestinian leaders with little choice but to bide their time and try to preserve their options.

King Hussein of Jordan had hoped to be able to give a less ambiguous and more positive response to the Reagan Plan. Hussein calculated that he had much to gain by participating in the American initiative. In addition to the prospect of reasserting Hashemite authority in the West Bank and securing the economic benefits promised by Washington, there was also the likelihood of an increase in Jordan's regional stature. As the central Arab player in the American design, as well as a pivotal member of the emerging bloc of mainstream Arab states, Jordan would see its political fortunes improve should the peace process go forward. Furthermore, dangers to be avoided, as well as benefits to be obtained, led Hussein to conclude that it was in his interest for the American initiative to succeed. In particular, the king was deeply concerned that Israel's rapid absorption of the West Bank might compel many of its Palestinian inhabitants to leave for the East, overwhelming Jordan's resources and destabilizing its political system. He was also alarmed by the Israeli government's frequent reference to Jordan as the Palestinian state and feared that Israel might try to depose him in order to implement this view, as Ariel Sharon had suggested on several occasions.[40] Finally, more generally, a failure of the mainstream Arab consensus to achieve political gains might lead to the fragmentation and radicalization of the Palestinian movement, and this, too, could threaten the stability of the monarchical regime in Jordan.

For all these reasons, Hussein worked with Arafat to fashion a coordinated diplomatic strategy which, he hoped, would enable him to tell Washington that Jordan would take part in restarted autonomy talks. Participation in the American initiative offered an attractive mechanism for reducing the danger from Israel, and if sanctioned by the PLO, it would also enhance his influence among Palestinians in the occupied territories while simultaneously providing a cover for any concessions he might be required to make during negotiations. In addition, Hussein believed that he had maximum leverage over a weakened PLO, and that Jordan would therefore be the stronger partner in an alliance with the Palestinian organization.

Consultation between Hussein and Arafat began at the Fez summit in September 1982 and intensified when the PLO chairman visited Amman the following month. By late November, the two leaders had agreed that their goal should be a confederation, although, as noted, PLO spokesmen insisted it would be a confederation of two equal and independent states under a single presidency. By January 1983, Hussein and Arafat had also agreed in principle to form a joint negotiating team for peace talks with Israel, with the understanding that this joint delegation would be led by Jordan and include Palestinians approved by the PLO but not PLO officials. The Americans, fully briefed, encouraged these discussions and expressed the hope that a Jordanian-Palestinian negotiating team of this sort would in fact be constituted. The dialogue between Arafat and Hussein was strongly endorsed as well by Palestinians in the West Bank and Gaza. This support was expressed in several statements and petitions signed by prominent West Bank and Gaza personalities in October, following Arafat's trip to Amman. It was also reflected in a poll taken in February 1983, shortly before the PNC meeting in Algiers. Of the 750 respondents interviewed, only 15 percent opposed the Jordanian-PLO dialogue, with its calls for a confederation between the West Bank and the East Bank and a joint Jordanian-Palestinian delegation to negotiate with the Israelis.[41]

Despite both the potential benefits to his regime and the establishment of a dialogue with Arafat and the PLO, Hussein did not feel himself able to endorse the Reagan Plan. He had stalled when the Americans pressed him for a positive response in December 1982, and then, on April 10, 1983, less than two months after the PNC meeting in Algiers, he made a public statement announcing that Jordan, like the PLO, would not accept the American initiative. The king's statement ruled out Jordanian participation in autonomy talks backed by the U.S., declaring, "We in Jordan, having refused from the beginning to negotiate on behalf of the Palestinians, will neither act separately nor in lieu of anybody in Middle East peace negotiations."[42]

At least three sets of factors contributed to Hussein's decision. First, although probably least important, Hussein was pressed to reject the Reagan Plan by the Soviet Union. The USSR opposed the American initiative in part because it neglected the interests of Syria, the Soviet Union's most important client state in the Arab world. As noted, the Reagan Plan gave Damascus no role in the peace process it sought to fashion and made no mention of Israeli withdrawal from the Golan Heights. Of even greater importance to the Soviets, however, was the danger that they themselves would be excluded from the Middle East peace process, and for this reason, too, they insisted that a settlement should be brokered by the superpowers or the United Nations, rather than the United States. So far as Hussein is concerned, the Russians accordingly let the Jordanian king know that they would exert as much pressure as they could to prevent him from playing the role assigned to him by Washington. When Hussein visited Moscow in December 1982, for example, he was told by General Secretary Yuri Andropov, "We shall use all our resources to oppose [the Reagan Plan]. With due respect, all the weight will be on your shoulders, and they aren't broad enough to bear it."[43] In addition to issuing this and other warnings to Hussein, Moscow pursued its policies in the region by shipping a substantial quantity of sophisticated new weapons to the Damascus regime and by increasing the number of Soviet military advisors in Syria.

Second, and more important, the PLO refused to give formal approval to the common negotiating position that Hussein and Arafat had worked to define. Their proposal for a joint Jordanian-Palestinian negotiating team was strongly opposed by all five rejectionist factions within the PLO; and despite their reduced power after the war in Lebanon, these groups were still able to challenge Arafat's policies, even those, like his dialogue with Hussein, that had broad support in the occupied territories. As noted previously, Arafat and Fatah believed that unity within the PLO was essential in view of the organization's vulnerability following its ouster from Beirut, and for this reason they were extremely reluctant to impose decisions they could not persuade others to accept. In addition, even some within Fatah had serious reservations about the proposed Jordanian-Palestinian delegation, especially since Hussein had made public statements to the effect that the Arab-Israeli conflict could be settled only on the basis of the Reagan Plan and UN resolutions 242 and 338.

In view of these concerns, the PNC meeting in February 1983 authorized Arafat to pursue his dialogue with Hussein but placed strict limits on the kind of agreement he might conclude. The political program adopted at Algiers made it clear that Jordan would not be permitted to represent the Palestinians and ruled out the possibility of a joint Jordanian-Palestinian negotiating team that would have this effect.[44] It also stressed that establishment of an independent Palestinian state was a precondition for the construction of a confederation with Jordan. After the PNC meeting, with uncertainty about what his dialogue with Hussein would be able to achieve, Arafat postponed several scheduled trips to Jordan.

Although Arafat and Hussein worked out a draft agreement when they met again in early April, the failure of the PLO to ratify this agreement led the Jordanian king to abandon any hope of developing a joint negotiating position with the PLO and set the stage for his public statement declaring that Jordan would not take part in autonomy talks sponsored by the U.S. Immediately following his visit to Amman, Arafat traveled to Kuwait to present the draft agreement he and Hussein had fashioned to a special session of the Fatah Central Committee and the PLO Executive Committee. This meeting refused to endorse the agreement, however, and instead sent emissaries to Jordan to continue negotiations, and in particular to urge that Palestinian-Jordanian diplomatic efforts be based on the Fez Plan rather than the Reagan Plan. The special session in Kuwait also reaffirmed that any negotiating team representing the Palestinians would have to contain prominent members of the PLO.

It was at this point, with the Jordanians and Palestinians no closer to bridging the gap between the Reagan initiative and the Fez Plan than they had been the previous October, that a disappointed and somewhat embittered Hussein called off his dialogue with the PLO and declared that Jordan would not participate in the American peace initiative. In announcing his decision, Hussein reaffirmed his commitment to the 1974 Rabat resolution, which recognized the PLO as the sole legitimate representative of the Palestinian people. Thus, he said, his government would now "leave it to the PLO and the Palestinian people to choose the ways and means for the salvation of themselves and their land, and for the realization of their declared aims in the manner they see fit."

A third factor contributing to Hussein's decision was the inadequate assurances he received from the United States. In many ways this was the most important consideration of all. Understandably enough, the king reasoned that the American initiative would be stillborn if Washington was not prepared to exert pressure on the Israeli government. Yet, in late 1982 and early 1983, he watched in vain for some sign that such pressure was likely to be forthcoming.

Events in Lebanon provided one opportunity for Jordanians and other Arabs to gauge the resolve of the Reagan administration. Like other Arab leaders, Hussein believed that unless the Americans could arrange for a withdrawal of Israeli forces from Lebanon, there was not much likelihood they would be able to persuade Jerusalem to accept territorial compromise in the West Bank and Gaza. Accordingly, the IDF's continuing presence in Lebanon in April 1983 left Hussein and other Arabs with serious doubts about how much pressure the U.S. was prepared to exert in support of its own peace plan,[45] and this in turn led the Jordanian monarch to conclude that there was little reason to run the risks associated with acceptance of the Reagan Plan.

This Jordanian analysis was also supported by the Americans' own sequential linking of the situation in Lebanon and the Palestinian problem. The U.S. assigned top priority to negotiating an Israeli-Lebanese agreement that would bring about the withdrawal of both Israeli and Syrian troops, and Reagan himself had stated publicly that movement on the Palestinian problem would have to await such an agreement.[46] Initially, the American president had believed the departure of the PLO would enable rapid progress to be made in Lebanon, thus generating momentum for dealing with the West Bank and Gaza. But in reality this linkage was counterproductive from the U.S. point of view. Not only was it based on naive assumptions about the nature of the Lebanese conflict, but it also enabled the Israelis and the Syrians, at once the most determined opponents of the Reagan initiative and the political actors best able to dictate events in Lebanon, to place obstacles in the way of the American design. In any event, it was difficult for the U.S. to persuade Hussein that the continuing IDF presence in Lebanon was irrelevant when Washington itself had stated that movement toward a solution of the Palestinian problem would begin with the withdrawal of foreign forces from that country.

Nor were Jordan's doubts about American resolve based entirely, or even primarily, on Israel's continuing presence in Lebanon. Although Ronald Reagan had concluded the presentation of his September 1 peace initiative by declaring that "the United States will stand by these principles with total dedication" and that "I have made a personal commitment to see that they endure," neither the Israeli government's unequivocal rejection of the Reagan Plan nor its continuing settlement drive in the West Bank and Gaza brought the kind of forceful U.S. response that would have given credibility to the president's declaration. According to one analyst, the introduction of the Reagan Plan was followed by a statement from Washington condemning Jerusalem's decision to build new settlements in the occupied territories, and this "was virtually the end of overt U.S. efforts to promote Israel's acceptance of the new peace initiative." Thereafter, according to the same scholar, "the striking thing about the Reagan initiative was its ghostlike character."[47] The same point has been made by other observers. A senior Israeli scholar notes, for example, that the introduction of the Reagan initiative did not lead to an internal contest between its supporters and opponents in Israel because of "Reagan's reluctance to press for the acceptance of his plan."[48]

As a result, there appeared to be little prospect in the spring of 1983 that Washington would put pressure on Israel to accept the principles of the Reagan Plan. Following the Hussein-Arafat meeting in April, for example, while the PLO Executive Committee was still meeting in Kuwait, two days before King Hussein's announcement of his decision, a U.S. State Department spokesman reaffirmed American opposition to Israeli actions designed to change the status quo in the occupied territories, but then added that this should not be interpreted as "a threat to cut off aid or take any other action against Israel."[49] Such statements, as well as the administration's past inaction, increased Jerusalem's confidence that it could defy Washington with relatively little cost and gave Hussein yet another reason to conclude that little would be accomplished even were he to accept the risks of a break with the PLO and agree to participate in American-sponsored peace talks.

Finally, since debates within the PLO were also influenced by American inaction, it is possible that Arafat would have had more success in gaining support for an agreement with Hussein had he and other mainstream Palestinian leaders been convinced that there was some possibility of achieving the territorial and political compromises called for by the U.S. president. While it is also possible that the PLO would have remained unwilling to go beyond the Fez Plan, which it considered its minimum program, it can at least be reported that a central concern of PLO leaders during the dialogue between Arafat and Hussein was the likelihood that a modification of the nationalist position would produce American willingness to press Israel on the issue of withdrawal from the occupied territories. Yet even the PLO chairman's closest advisors, including Farouq al-Qaddoumi and Khalil al-Wazir, believed that such a gesture would be a useless concession since the U.S. could not be expected to undertake a confrontation with Israel.[50] Al-Wazir stated in a radio interview in April, "What we want are new factors and new developments that will give us confidence and trust in the American attitudes," adding that the PLO should not be "rushing into decisions without signs of improvement in American policy stands." Earlier, Arafat himself had declared, "Our own experiences tell us not to trust American pledges and promises."[51]

Had there been more reason to expect meaningful American support, it is at least possible that Hussein, perhaps even with the approval and participation of the PLO, would have been willing to move beyond the Fez Plan and thereby enable the American-sponsored peace process to go forward. This was not to be the case, however, for whatever combination of reasons, and Hussein's April declaration to this effect was an occasion for disappointment not only on the part of Jordan and the PLO but on the part of the Reagan administration as well. Reagan and American Secretary of State George Shultz believed they had been left dangling by both Israel and Jordan, the two key participants in the peace process they sought to construct, and they were particularly unhappy with Hussein, since Reagan had presented his initiative only after being told that Jordan would support it.

Following Hussein's declaration, the administration shelved its efforts to deal with the Israeli-Palestinian conflict and turned its attention to other world problems, including the situation in Lebanon. According to Samuel Lewis, Reagan and Shultz also learned some hard lessons about Middle Eastern realities, at least as seen from Washington. The presentation of specific American proposals had not been any more effective in generating movement toward peace than had earlier efforts based on constructive ambiguity, and for this reason, the next time the U.S. undertook to play the role of peacemaker in the Arab-Israeli conflict, "it would be in support of initiatives generated from within the region, not from Washington."[52] Arab diplomatic efforts also came to a halt in April 1983. It would be almost a year before Hussein and Arafat would meet again, despite efforts by King Hassan of Morocco to bring the two men together. In the meantime, Israel continued its drive into the West Bank and Gaza, and the PLO was soon confronted with new challenges from Syria and from dissidents within its own ranks. In addition, events in Lebanon during the remainder of 1983 became an important focus of attention for those concerned with the Arab-Israeli conflict and with U.S. policy toward the Middle East.

More Problems in Lebanon

Having refused even to discuss any diplomatic initiatives calling for Israeli withdrawal from the occupied territories, and with a large number of IDF troops remaining in Lebanon, the attention of the Begin government late in 1982 and during the spring of 1983 was focused on the pursuit of a Lebanese-Israeli peace treaty. Such an accord, it was hoped, would enhance Israeli security and lead to normalized relations between the Jewish state and a second Arab country. A treaty with Lebanon would have symbolic as well as substantive value, moreover, and was also sought by the Israeli government in order to buttress its claim that the war in Lebanon had yielded tangible results and was therefore justified, despite its high cost in both human and political terms. Specifically, a treaty with Lebanon would enable the Israeli government to claim that it had succeeded in constructing the "arc of peace" between Cairo, Jerusalem, and Beirut that had been promised by the architects of Operation Peace for Galilee and Operation Big Pines. For these reasons, Jerusalem pressed Lebanon's new president, Amin Gemayel, the brother of Bashir, to conclude an agreement.

The Reagan administration, too, had been hoping for a treaty between Israel and Lebanon, viewing this as leading to the withdrawal of foreign forces from the latter country and accordingly, as noted, placing it at the top of its agenda for Middle Eastern diplomacy. Following the massacre at Sabra and Shatilla, American Marines had returned to Lebanon as part of a new international peace-keeping force, thereby involving the U.S. directly in the situation on the ground. There were also consultations and negotiations in the diplomatic arena during the fall of 1982, beginning with an October trip to Washington by Amin Gemayel for talks with the U.S. president and other administration officials.

By the spring of 1983, American interest in an Israeli-Lebanese agreement was being spurred not only by a desire to bring peace to Lebanon but also by the price the U.S. was paying for its involvement in the affairs of that country. To begin with, there was friction between U.S. Marines and IDF forces in Lebanon, with the Americans complaining that Israeli patrols were operating in unauthorized areas, using excessive firepower, and harassing U.S. units that attempted to restrict their activities.[53] Of even greater concern were challenges from Syria and Lebanese opposition groups. As the Americans gradually abandoned the role of neutral peacekeeper and became an uncritical ally of the Lebanese government, and with it the Phalange, these elements charged that Washington was propping up an unrepresentative regime and thereby working against reform of the Lebanese political system.

Some Lebanese factions also employed violence to register their discontent with U.S. policy, and in an attempt to force Washington to remove its troops from their country. For example, Islamic Jihad, a shadowy Lebanese Shiite organization backed by Iran, claimed responsibility for a series of attacks on U.S., French, and Italian peacekeeping forces in February and March. The most serious episode of this period took place on April 18, when a Shiite suicide driver detonated a truckload of explosives at the entrance to the American embassy in Beirut. The embassy was destroyed and some sixty individuals were killed, among them seventeen Americans. In response to these events, as well as the unsettled situation more generally, the Americans intensified their efforts to persuade Gemayel to conclude an agreement with Jerusalem in the expectation that such an accord would be a significant step toward resolving the crisis in Lebanon. Indeed, later in April, Secretary of State Shultz traveled to the Middle East to deal personally with the negotiations between Israeli and Lebanese officials.

With the help of Shultz's intervention, an agreement between Israel and Lebanon was signed on May 17, 1983. Although not the formal peace treaty that had been sought by Jerusalem, the accord declared an end to the state of war between the two countries and recorded Israel's commitment to withdraw all of its armed forces from Lebanon. Unbeknownst to the Lebanese, Israel also signed a secret memorandum of understanding with the United States at this time. This memorandum stipulated that Israeli troops would be removed from Lebanon only when Syrian and the remaining PLO forces were withdrawn as well, and it also recorded U.S. recognition of Israel's right to retaliate against any attacks emanating from Lebanese territory.

The May 17 agreement committed Israel and Lebanon to respect the existing international boundary between them and to abstain from hostile propaganda against one another. The accord also contained many articles dealing with security considerations, including a pledge that the territory of one state would not be used as a base for hostile acts against the other. Special security arrangements pertaining to southern Lebanon were dealt with in an annex, in which the Lebanese government committed itself to enforcing measures that would prevent hostile activities and the introduction of unauthorized armed men or military equipment. The annex also provided that the Israeli-sponsored militia headed by Saad Haddad would operate in the area and be integrated into the regular Lebanese army. Finally, the agreement called for the establishment of a Joint Liaison Committee, which would settle disputes pertaining to the interpretation and application of the accord and, within six months following the removal of Israeli armed forces, undertake negotiations aimed at establishing peaceful relations between the two countries.[54]

Neither the Israelis nor the Lebanese were satisfied with the agreement. The day before the accord was signed, the Israeli Knesset approved it by a vote of 58 to 8 with 46 abstentions, most of the abstentions being cast by Alignment MKs. Even many MKs who voted for the agreement found it less than fully satisfactory, however. Some complained that the accord did not deal adequately with Israel's security requirements. To break a deadlock in negotiations with the Lebanese, Jerusalem had reluctantly dropped its demands for a direct presence and for surveillance stations in southern Lebanon. Jerusalem did win agreement that there should be joint Lebanese-Israeli military patrols in the area. Also, more generally, many shared the opinion of the Israeli general who asserted, "There's more security with an agreement than in military control without one."[55] Nevertheless, the accord did not give Israel the degree of control over southern Lebanon that had been sought by the Begin government, and some Israelis condemned it for this reason.

The political dimension of the agreement was even less satisfactory in the view of many Israelis. Although ending the state of belligerency between them, the agreement made no commitment to the establishment of full diplomatic relations between Israel and Lebanon, or even to an open border between the two countries, leaving these matters to future negotiations through the Joint Liaison Committee. Nor did the agreement promise that a full and formal peace treaty would be signed in the future. Indeed, as a further indication that the accord itself should not be construed as such a treaty, it was signed, at Lebanese insistence, by Israeli and Lebanese representatives rather than the two countries' heads of state.

The need for a secret memorandum of understanding with the United States was a further reflection of the inadequacies of the Israeli-Lebanese agreement from the Israeli point of view. This memorandum was concluded in recognition of the fact that an accord with Israel was strongly opposed by Lebanese Muslims and Druze, and even by many Lebanese Christians, and would also be forcefully condemned by the regime in Damascus. Thus, although both the Israelis and the Americans had pressed Gemayel to conclude an agreement in spite of this opposition, they had been willing to assign certain controversial provisions to a private and separate protocol in the hope of limiting this opposition and enabling Gemayel to preserve the fragile Lebanese consensus over which he presided.

All of this clearly demonstrated that the May 17 accord was not the foundation for peace and stability that Jerusalem and Washington had sought. As stated by Schiff and Ya'ari, "In Israel everyone knew that the outcome [of Israeli-Lebanese negotiations] bore only the faintest resemblance to the dreams that had fueled the whole foray into Lebanon a year earlier."[56] Moreover, not only did it fail to provide the kind of political settlement to which the Begin government could point as a justification for its invasion of Lebanon, it did not even mean that Israeli troops would soon be coming home. According to Schiff and Ya'ari, again, "Even before the ink on it was dry, the May 17 agreement had become a sterile, unenforceable document because it was conditional upon a Syrian withdrawal from Lebanon, and the Syrians did not regard themselves as obliged to uphold any terms that had been agreed upon without their prior consent."[57]

In Lebanon, the May 17 agreement was criticized not for inadequacy in promoting peace with Israel but because it involved unacceptable concessions and appeared to offer little in return. While Israeli spokesmen argued that an end to the state of war was of value to both countries, and that peace by definition must be seen as a benefit rather than a concession, many Lebanese insisted that the accord had been imposed on their country, not freely negotiated by equal and consenting parties. Indeed, they continued, it was the result of Israel's illegal and unjustified invasion of Lebanon, an action which had brought death and destruction to their country and was now rewarding the aggressor with an agreement that forced Lebanon to share sovereignty over a significant portion of its territory.

Such views were held by Muslim and Druze leaders, and also by some Christian and even anti-Phalange Maronite personalities, most of whom not only complained about the conditions imposed by Jerusalem but also charged Gemayel with using the agreement to enhance the position of his government. As expressed, for example, by Walid Jumblatt, leader of the Druze community and a close ally of President Assad of Syria, "We have given Israel more than it expected, which means that certain internal parties, namely the Phalange, wanted more for their own ends."[58] According to one scholarly assessment, Lebanese opposition to the agreement with Israel was so intense that it became a major obstacle to reconciliation among Lebanon's competing political factions.[59] Indeed, because of this opposition, Gemayel never submitted the agreement to the Lebanese parliament for formal ratification. The assembly had given its consent for the conclusion of a treaty, thus enabling Gemayel to claim that it had a legal foundation, but the document itself was never presented to parliament for consideration and approval.

Syria added its own concerns to the list of complaints about the Israeli-Lebanese agreement. It asserted that the accord transformed Lebanon into a client state of Israel, and thus detached it from the rest of the Arab world. It also strongly rejected the notion of symmetry between its own forces in Lebanon and those of Israel, as well as the attendant Israeli assertion, accepted by Washington, that removal of Syrian troops was a necessary precondition for withdrawal of the IDF. Damascus pointed out that its troops had entered Lebanon at the invitation of the Lebanese government during the 1975–76 civil war, and that their presence had in fact helped the Maronite-led government to remain in power. Moreover, Syria's entry had been sanctioned by the Arab League and was even welcomed at the time by the government in Washington; and thus, even if one did not fully agree that Syria's contribution had been a positive one, there could be no basis for claiming comparability between its military presence in Lebanon and that of Israel.

In view of these considerations, Assad declared that Syrian troops would remain in Lebanon until all Israeli forces had been withdrawn without preconditions. The Syrian president also stated that the accord with Israel would prevent his government from assisting in the political reconstruction of Lebanon. As an additional expression of his discontent, and of his anger over U.S. support for the accord and its refusal to recognize Syria's interests in Lebanon and the region, Assad at this time refused to receive the Reagan administration's special envoy, Philip Habib. He later met with George Shultz, who visited Damascus in July, but this meeting did not produce any change in the Syrian president's attitude toward the May 17 agreement.[60]

It is against this background that Lebanese opposition leaders, with active encouragement from Syria, formed the loosely organized National Salvation Front shortly after the announcement of the Israeli-Lebanese accord. The three founders of the Front were Jumblatt, the Druze chieftain; Suleiman Franjieh, a former Lebanese president and Maronite Christian who was opposed to the dominance of the Gemayel family and the Phalange; and Rashid Karami, a Sunni Muslim notable and former prime minister of Lebanon. The Front was also supported by the mainstream of Lebanon's Shiite community, led by Nabih Berri. One avowed purpose of the National Salvation Front was to force the Gemayel government to abrogate the May 17 agreement. Of equal or even greater importance, however, the Front sought to work for the acceptance of a new political equation in the governance of Lebanon, and in particular to press Gemayel to curb the growing intransigence and militancy of Phalange extremists, who refused to consider any meaningful reform of the Lebanese political system.[61] But while formation of the Front was a clear indication of the depth and breadth of Lebanese opposition to the Gemayel government, its political activities during the summer of 1983 did little to bring about the reconstruction of the country. On the contrary, this challenge served to illustrate further the fragility of the consensus that held the Lebanese political system together and was accompanied over the course of the summer by renewed fighting between the government and its opponents, particularly the Druze.

In a move that angered both the Phalange and the Syrians, and which also reflected the confusing complexity of the region's tangled web of rivalries and alliances, Israel responded to this situation by establishing a dialogue with Lebanese Druze leaders in the summer of 1983. In part, Jerusalem undertook this dialogue in order to communicate to the Gemayel government its dissatisfaction with the May 17 agreement, and thereby to let the Lebanese president know that a partnership with the Maronites was not Israel's only option in Lebanon. Of possible salience as well was a belief that Israel's relatively satisfactory relationship with its own Druze community might be replicated in the north, and thus serve as a model for building bridges to a second confessional community in Lebanon; and a corollary of this proposition was the possibility that a confrontation with the Druze of Lebanon might anger their coreligionists in Israel, many of whom were serving in the IDF. In the view of some observers, this line of thinking was particularly persuasive to Moshe Arens, who had recently replaced Ariel Sharon as Jerusalem's minister of defense.[62] Most important, however, the Begin government's overtures to the Druze of Lebanon, carried out with Israeli Druze leaders acting as intermediaries, were undertaken to lay the groundwork for removal of the IDF from the Shouf Mountains region east of Beirut, a traditional stronghold of both the Druze and the Maronites. In this context, Israel hoped it would be possible to arrange an accommodation between Gemayel and Walid Jumblatt, so that its pullback would not lead to additional confrontations between the two Lebanese communities contending for control of the area.

In the weeks following the conclusion of the May 17 agreement, the Begin government was under mounting pressure at home to remove its forces from Lebanon. The war had been opposed by many Israelis once it entered its second and expanded phase; and more recently, with IDF troops still stationed outside Beirut three-quarters of a year after the PLO had been ousted, involvement in Lebanon had become even more unpalatable to most Israelis. Disappointment in the agreement negotiated with the Gemayel government reinforced such feelings, fueling the popular view that Israel was propping up an ungrateful Lebanese government and receiving nothing in return for its efforts to preserve peace among Lebanon's warring factions.

Even more important in shaping public opinion in the Jewish state was the fact that Israelis continued to be killed and wounded in Lebanon, and that these losses were now the result of attacks by Lebanese rather than Palestinians. Six Israeli soldiers had been killed and 22 wounded in an ambush outside Beirut in October 1982; and the following month, in the single worst military disaster in the nation's history, an explosion at the IDF's headquarters in Tyre had taken the lives of 74 soldiers and civilians. Twenty-seven more were wounded. These losses continued during the first half of 1983. Between September 1982 and June 1983, during the nine months following the departure of the PLO from Beirut, about 180 additional Israeli soldiers had lost their lives, bringing to approximately 500 the total number of Israelis killed in Lebanon. In response to the vocal protests that this situation produced, the new defense minister, Moshe Arens, announced in June that Israeli forces would unilaterally withdraw from the Shouf Mountains around Beirut and redeploy along the Awali River, some twenty miles to the south.

The announced Israeli pullback from the Shouf was postponed twice at the request of the Americans. One U.S. concern was that withdrawal of the IDF would enable the Druze to achieve undisputed control of the strategically important mountain area overlooking Beirut, and also overlooking the international airport that was being guarded by U.S. Marines. Druze militia units under Jumblatt's command had in fact used positions in the Shouf to shell the airport early in August, taking this action to put pressure on the Gemayel government but in the process threatening the Marines as well. Accordingly, Washington worried that an Israeli pullback followed by a Druze advance would increase the risk to its forces in Lebanon.

The Reagan administration was also opposed to any extension of the Druze military capability because it regarded Jumblatt and his militia as vehicles for Soviet penetration into Lebanon. The Druze were clients of the regime in Damascus, which was itself a client of the Soviet Union; and Secretary of Defense Caspar Weinberger had stressed this connection when he told an American Jewish audience in May that obstruction of the "Lebanese peace process" by the Soviets and "any proxies they might have in Syria . . . would be met by a retaliatory force that would make the aggression totally unworthwhile."[63] Although more scholarly observers pointed out that the Soviets were actually urging caution on Assad and telling Damascus they did not want to be dragged into the Lebanese quagmire,[64] Reagan and Shultz continued to emphasize the Russian threat, and some administration officials accordingly described Druze efforts to gain control of the Shouf as "a plot originating in Damascus and orchestrated in Damascus."[65]

None of this made much difference to the Israelis, however. Although it shared the American view that an IDF withdrawal would almost certainly result in the Druze taking control in the Shouf,[66] the Begin government in the end responded to domestic political pressure rather than to American appeals. Thus, after several postponements over the course of the summer, Jerusalem carried out its announced pullback at the beginning of September.

Announcement of Israel's intention to withdraw from the Shouf brought renewed conflict between Druze and Phalange forces, in effect reigniting the Lebanese civil war. Ironically, both factions had alliances with Israel at this time, leading one observer to describe the Shouf in the late spring and summer of 1983 as "a battleground between Israeli-armed Druze and Israeli-armed Phalangists."[67] Further, although the fighting was fierce while the IDF still controlled the region, it became even more ferocious after the Israeli pullback was carried out at the beginning of September. Nevertheless, as the Israelis had expected and the Americans had feared, the Druze routed their Maronite adversaries within a few days and effectively placed almost all of the Shouf outside the authority of the Gemayel government. Maronite losses included approximately sixty villages, rendering some 50,000 individuals homeless. They also included the deaths of roughly 1,000 Phalange fighters and civilians, some of them slaughtered in operations that Israeli commentators compared to the massacre at Sabra and Shatilla.[68] Among the factors contributing to the Druze victory was a failure of the regular Lebanese army, commanded by Gemayel, to come to the aid of the Phalange. The Druze also benefited from some Syrian logistical and artillery support, although there is no evidence that either Syrian or Palestinian forces entered the fighting on the side of the Druze.

Both the battles in the Shouf and the subsequent Druze victory were an indication that the reconstruction of Lebanon required more than the ouster of the PLO. Indeed, despite the rout of the Palestinian organization, the Lebanese civil war had clearly resumed, with the Gemayel government not only losing control in the Shouf region but also under attack from Shiite militia units operating in and around Beirut. The warring factions agreed to a ceasefire at the end of September and established a National Reconciliation Committee, which convened in Geneva a month later. Nevertheless, despite these hopeful developments, tensions remained high through the remainder of 1983 and fighting continued on an intermittent basis.

These events brought intervention on behalf of Gemayel and the Maronites from the United States, which had declared itself to be a neutral peacekeeper when its forces first arrived in Lebanon, but which thereafter had steadily drifted into the Lebanese civil war on the side of one of the protagonists. By the middle of September, the U.S. had called in naval and air support; and though these actions were initially undertaken in defense of Marine positions at the airport, American warships were soon firing in support of the Lebanese army, and American planes at this time began to provide cover for Lebanese government air strikes against Druze and Shiite units.[69] Particularly notable was American intervention in the battle for Souq al-Gharb, a resort town in the foothills of the Shouf where forces of the Lebanese army were under siege at the end of September. U.S. officers were sent to the town to help organize its defense, while American ships bombarded nearby Druze and Syrian positions from offshore.

The direct and partisan military involvement of the United States helped to set in motion a new spiral of violence, in which Americans, as well as others, were prominently represented among the victims. On October 23, a week before Lebanon's National Reconciliation Committee convened in Geneva, Shiite extremists from Islamic Jihad drove a truck laden with explosives into the American Marine barracks at the airport, killing 241 U.S. servicemen. A similar attack was carried out at almost the same time against French peacekeeping forces, killing 59 soldiers, and a little more than a week later yet a third suicide lorry was driven into the Israeli military headquarters in Tyre, taking an additional 60 lives, half of them Israeli.

Although this tragic loss of life led to a questioning of U.S. policy toward Lebanon back in the United States, and to calls for bringing the Marines home, the Reagan administration insisted both that it would not capitulate to terrorism and that a precipitous U.S. disengagement would harm American interests by enabling Lebanese radicals backed by Syria and the Soviet Union to gain the upper hand. As asserted by the president at this time, keeping the Marines in Lebanon was "central to U.S. credibility on a global scale" and to preventing the entire Middle East from being "incorporated into the Soviet bloc."[70] The administration thus decided to stay in Lebanon and fight, and in the weeks and months that followed, U.S. shelling and bombing raids against Druze, Shiite, and Syrian positions intensified. Almost all of the other armed forces in Lebanon joined in the fighting as well. In November, Israeli planes retaliated for the attack on the IDF by bombing a suspected Islamic Jihad command post, and the French also carried out retaliatory air strikes at this time. These operations did not suppress attacks by Lebanese opposition elements, however. The Druze continued to shell the airport and other targets in Beirut from their stronghold in the Shouf Mountains, and forces of the Shiite Amal militia continued to confront the Lebanese army in various locations around Beirut.

The first months of 1984 brought an end to this round of the Lebanese conflict, and with it the collapse of American and Israeli designs in Lebanon. Early in February, in what many regard as the most compelling symbol of the Reagan administration's failed policy in Lebanon, the huge sixteen-inch guns of the battleship *New Jersey* unleashed a devastating artillery barrage against Druze positions in the Shouf, laying waste to a large area and killing civilians as well as Druze fighters. As summarized by George Ball, U.S. undersecretary of state during the Kennedy and Johnson administrations, the barrage was not only inaccurate but "fantastically destructive," displaying an "unconscionable disregard for civilian casualties."[71] However, whether justified or not, the punishing operation had little practical effect, serving only to demonstrate further that any pretense of U.S. neutrality in the Lebanese civil war had long since been abandoned, and that balanced diplomacy, not a display of firepower in support of the Gemayel government, was the only way the U.S. might contribute to Lebanon's political reconstruction.

As it turned out, the *New Jersey*'s fiery but unproductive contribution to the

Lebanese civil war was a parting shot by American forces. Within a few days, with Druze and Shiite militias continuing to make gains in Beirut and moving to establish a corridor between the Lebanese capital and the Shouf, Reagan responded to the virtual collapse of the Lebanese army and the prospect of chaos in Beirut by withdrawing the U.S. Marines, initially announcing that they would be "redeployed" to ships waiting offshore. Unwilling to deepen its involvement in the fighting, and perhaps realizing that its military efforts would in any event contribute little to solving Lebanon's political problems, the Reagan administration chose the only course available, to pack up and leave, declaring that it had done what it could and the rest was up to the Lebanese themselves.

Associated with these developments was the Gemayel government's abrogation of the May 17 agreement, and this in turn marked the end of Israeli as well as American designs in Lebanon. Gemayel was confronted with a rapidly deteriorating military and political situation in February 1984. The Lebanese army was on the verge of disintegration, with some of its members fleeing to areas in the south under Israeli control and others defecting to rival Lebanese militias. Gemayel was also forced to accept the resignation of his prime minister, Shafiq al-Wazzan. Thus, with his palace at Baabda coming under fire and few remaining options, the Lebanese president flew to Damascus early in March for discussions with Assad and, in return for Syrian support, accepted a peace proposal that included abrogation of the May 17 agreement with Israel. Taking this step on March 5, the cabinet issued a statement declaring that the Lebanese government would carry out whatever measures were necessary to "ensure sovereignty, security and stability in southern Lebanon" and to "achieve the withdrawal of the Israeli forces from all Lebanese territory."[72]

The Gemayel government's abrogation of the May 17 agreement delivered the final blow to any lingering Israeli illusions about deriving political benefits in Lebanon from the IDF's military victory in the summer of 1982. In the winter and spring of 1984, Lebanon was no more peaceful, stable, or close to a meaningful accommodation with the Jewish state than it had been before the invasion, when Begin, Sharon, and Shamir were insisting that everything in Lebanon would fall neatly into place if only the PLO presence in that country were eliminated. Nor had the interests and involvement of the Syrians been seriously undermined. If anything, with Gemayel now dependent on the support of Damascus, the Assad regime was in a stronger position than ever. Thus, as Schiff and Ya'ari wrote at the time, "It was as if close to 600 Israeli and [more than] 250 American lives had been lost in Lebanon just to bring the situation full circle."[73] Although Israeli troops would not be withdrawn from South Lebanon until June 1985,[74] and even thereafter would help to police a narrow security zone immediately north of the Israeli-Lebanese border, Israel, like the U.S., put behind it the political designs it had so boldly announced when entering Lebanon in June 1982. Indeed, as Israel soon found itself in the midst of a new election campaign, domestic political debates focused not on gains but on losses flowing from the invasion of Lebanon, and on the need to bring home those IDF troops remaining north of the border.

The Mutiny in Fatah

During the year in which Israeli and American designs in Lebanon were working their way toward an eventual dead end, that country was also the site of serious new difficulties for Yasir Arafat and the Palestine Liberation Organization. Following the PLO's withdrawal from Beirut in August 1982, Arafat had been actively involved in the formation of a moderate Arab consensus and had worked closely with King Hussein of Jordan and other Arab leaders to fashion a diplomatic strategy that would make gains on behalf of the Palestinians. These diplomatic efforts collapsed in the spring of 1983, however, and in the months that followed, Arafat and the PLO mainstream were beset by important challenges from Syria and Palestinian dissidents. In April, as if signaling the troubles that lay ahead, Issam Sartawi, a close advisor and confidant of the PLO chairman, was assassinated by Palestinian extremists. Sartawi, who openly advocated recognition of the Jewish state and had established contact with Israeli peace groups,[75] was gunned down by agents of the Abu Nidal faction, a Palestinian splinter group not connected to the PLO. As noted earlier, Abu Nidal had also been responsible for the attack on Shlomo Argov in June 1982.

In May 1983, a mutiny took place within the ranks of Fatah, the largest and most powerful PLO faction, which was led by Arafat, and this development undermined the unity and organizational cohesion that the PLO had worked so hard to preserve in the aftermath of its defeat in Lebanon. The mutiny was led by Abu Musa, a member of Fatah's Revolutionary Council and a commander of Fatah's forces in northern Lebanon, in an area controlled by Syria. Other prominent rebel leaders included Abu Khaled, a Fatah commander in central Lebanon, and two members of the Fatah Central Committee, Samih Quayk and Nimr Saleh. Abu Musa and the others not only had opposed the PLO's dialogue with Hussein but had denounced its endorsement of the Arab peace plan adopted at Fez, accusing Arafat and other PLO leaders who supported these policies of cowardice and capitulation to the Zionist enemy. Moreover, their opposition to the PLO chairman became even more intense in April, when Arafat removed Abu Musa and Abu Khaled from their military commands and appointed two of his own followers to direct Fatah's forces in northern and central Lebanon. Arafat's action was part of a series of personnel changes intended to ensure that PLO forces in Lebanon were under the control of his supporters.

The criticism directed at Arafat's leadership by Abu Musa and other leaders of the rebellion included charges that Fatah had ceased to be run in a democratic fashion, with decisions made by Arafat and a few others and with little regard for the views of the rank and file; that the PLO had followed a flawed military strategy in southern Lebanon during the 1970s, having transformed commando units into a semiconventional army that was vulnerable to Israeli air and ground attacks; and, above all, that Arafat had repudiated the PLO charter and various PNC resolutions calling for the liberation of all of Palestine and the use of armed struggle in pursuit of this objective.[76] In the latter connection, Arafat's opponents rejected the distinction that Palestinian moderates sought to make between "reactionary Zionism" and "progressive Zionism," declaring that Zionism by definition is "racist, expansionist and colonialist in its objectives, methods and techniques."[77] In addition, they argued that Arafat's policies not only had betrayed the Palestinian cause but had abandoned the revolutionary struggle against "reactionary Arab regimes," including the Maronite-dominated government in Beirut. Whereas Arafat and other Fatah leaders sought to normalize relations with the Gemayel government and instructed Palestinians in Lebanon not to interfere in the country's internal affairs, Abu Musa argued that it was impossible to have normal relations with a government that had cooperated with Israel during the war and then permitted the massacre of defenseless Palestinian civilians.[78]

The followers of Abu Musa and the other rebel leaders fought a series of battles with Arafat loyalists in those parts of Lebanon controlled by Syria. Fatah leaders had initially assumed they would have little difficulty suppressing this challenge, but the rebels received assistance from Syria, and armed clashes continued over the summer and into the fall of 1983. Whether Syria was involved from the beginning is a matter of some dispute. Fatah officials charged that this was indeed the case, pointing out that Assad had been giving political and logistical support to Palestinian rejectionists since the Israeli invasion, and insisting that at the very least Damascus had chosen not to use its superior military capability to separate the warring Palestinian factions. The Syrians and Fatah dissidents, by contrast, argued that Arafat had fabricated these allegations in order to hide the fact that the rebellion was based on genuine dissatisfaction with his leadership. In any event, citing Arafat's "continuous lies and slander against Syria" as the reason for his action, Assad abandoned his proclaimed neutrality late in June and publicly sided with Abu Musa and the rebels. Arafat himself was expelled from Syria and prohibited from returning to the country or to Lebanese territory under Syrian control.

Efforts at reconciliation were undertaken by some members of Fatah's Central Committee in the weeks that followed, but these actions failed either to end the fighting or to heal the rift between Syria and the PLO mainstream. Leaders of the most important rejectionist groups within the PLO, the Popular Front and the Democratic Front, also sought to mediate, up to a point. In addition, the PFLP and the DFLP in June established a joint leadership structure in order to coordinate their political and military activities. As in the past, the two factions criticized many of Arafat's policies. They also disputed his charges against Syria.

Nevertheless, they did not seek to aid the dissidents within Fatah, instead declaring themselves to be neutral in Fatah's internal struggle and calling for a ceasefire and the formation of a military committee to separate the combatants. This stance satisfied neither Arafat loyalists nor the rebels, however, and, more important, it did nothing to bring the mutiny to an end. Moreover, while the Popular Front and the Democratic Front remained neutral, the dissidents were encouraged and actively aided by other PLO rejectionist factions, most notably the PFLP–General Command, financed by Libya, and the pro-Syrian Saiqa.

Arafat returned to northern Lebanon in the middle of September, at a time when battles between contending Lebanese factions were becoming particularly intense, and his presence was accompanied by a similar intensification of the campaign against his own forces by Fatah dissidents and their Syrian supporters. Declaring that he had come back "when I found my people exposed to a definite massacre . . . to stand by their side in this crisis,"[79] Arafat attempted to rally his forces and, in the hope of bringing political pressure to bear on Syria, to focus Arab and international attention on the attacks against his followers. He also sought military support from several available but unlikely sources. He obtained weapons and ammunition, some of it of Israeli origin, from the Phalange.[80] In addition, he received direct military assistance from the Islamic Unification Movement, a Sunni Muslim faction opposed to the conservative political establishment in northern Lebanon, and also to the regime in Damascus, which the preceding year had ruthlessly suppressed an Islamic protest movement inside Syria.[81]

None of this enabled Arafat's forces to reverse their losses, however. By November, loyalist Fatah troops had been forced to retreat from most of their military strongholds and, along with Arafat himself, they were under siege in the northern Lebanese city of Tripoli, with shelling by Syrian and rebel forces producing many casualties among Palestinian and Lebanese civilians.[82] Indicative of the increasingly desperate situation was Salah Khalaf's statement that Assad's cruelty and his crimes against the Palestinian people during the previous few months had even "surpassed those of the Israeli enemy."[83]

Arafat's losses on the battlefield were accompanied by increasing political pressure. The PLO chairman's return to Lebanon was criticized by the PFLP and the DFLP, both of which now moved away from their previously neutral posture toward the rebellion inside Fatah. Arafat's presence in Tripoli was also condemned by Rashid Karami, a Sunni Muslim notable and the city's leading political figure. These denunciations were in part the result of pressure exerted by Damascus. They were also motivated by the new alliances that the PLO chairman had formed. Arafat's opponents called cooperation with the Phalange offensive to the PLO's nationalist Lebanese allies, and to the memory of those Palestinians who were murdered at Sabra and Shatilla. They also stated that Arafat was "offending the Palestinian revolution" by working with the fanatic and reactionary Islamic Unification Movement.[84]

The crisis ended in December 1983 when diplomatic intervention by Saudi Arabia led to an agreement with Syria, and this in turn resulted in the departure from Tripoli of Arafat and approximately 4,000 of his followers. The Saudi-Syrian agreement, which sought to offer Arafat an honorable departure, called for a ceasefire and emphasized the need to solve disputes inside the PLO in a peaceful and democratic manner. Both Fatah loyalists and Fatah dissidents accepted the agreement, and arrangements were then made for Greek ships to evacuate Arafat's forces and transport them to PLO camps in Tunisia, North Yemen, Iraq, Algeria, and Sudan. The evacuation was delayed for about three weeks as a result of Israeli interference. The Israelis blockaded the coast in order to prevent the arrival of the Greek ships, and also declared that they would not guarantee the safe passage of Arafat and his men. Under pressure from the U.S. and European states, however, the Israeli navy withdrew from Lebanese territorial waters and the evacuation took place on December 21.

Arafat's second forced exodus from Lebanon in little more than a year left the PLO chairman feeling more vulnerable than ever and demonstrated that, despite his diplomatic efforts and the construction of a moderate Arab consensus in the fall of 1982, Palestinian and Arab rejectionists had not been effectively isolated and the PLO itself remained in danger of fragmentation. After having been driven from Lebanon by the Israelis, who accused him of being a fanatic and intransigent enemy of the Jewish state, the PLO chairman had now been dealt a similar blow by Syria and Palestinian dissidents who, ironically, denounced him for being too ready to compromise. Arafat could reply that events might have unfolded in a very different fashion had the U.S. responded positively to Arab diplomatic overtures late in 1982, either by accepting elements of the Fez Plan or, following up on the principles of its own peace initiative, by pressing Jerusalem to withdraw its forces from Lebanon and slow its drive into the West Bank and Gaza. Under these conditions, with evidence that their political strategy was producing tangible results, Palestinian and Arab moderates might have succeeded in advancing the peace process and isolating the rejectionists in their midst. Now, however, with Arafat on the defensive and Syria and PLO dissidents flush with victory, it remained to be seen whether the Palestinian organization would remain intact and, if so, whether it would abandon the political and diplomatic strategy that its leaders had fashioned in the wake of the 1973 Arab-Israeli war and pursued since that time.

Leadership Changes in Israel

Important developments were taking place in the Israeli political arena during 1983 and 1984, and one of the most notable events of this period was the retirement of Menachem Begin. Late in August 1983, despondent over the country's losses in Lebanon and the death of his wife the preceding spring, Begin announced that he would step down as the country's prime minister. He formally submitted his resignation two weeks later, and then retired from public view as well as public life, remaining in his Jerusalem apartment, refusing all requests for interviews, and playing no part in the affairs of either the nation or the political party he had previously led.

With Begin's retirement came numerous assessments of the man and his legacy, many reflecting the strong opinions that the former prime minister had always generated. Predictably, conservatives and supporters of territorial maximalism regretted his retirement and offered high praise for his contributions to the nation. In the words of one such commentary, Begin had "retrieved and reasserted the Israelis' national self-confidence and their confidence that they can, at least partly, determine historical circumstances." Also, Begin was said to have "a mysterious and magnetic link with his followers, who trusted him like they never trusted any man."[85] On the other hand, a noted Israeli writer spoke for many when he characterized Begin as "the High Priest of Fear" who constantly emphasized the threat of another Holocaust;[86] and this theme was echoed by a leading scholar who wrote that while his tenure in office was associated with increased polarization and the shattering of public morale, "Begin's indiscriminate evocation of the Holocaust may have been his most flagrant transgression . . . [since he] politicized, and thereby trivialized, the single most tragic chapter in Jewish history."[87]

Begin's successor as prime minister would be the person chosen to lead Likud, a position that fell naturally to the chairman of the party's dominant Herut wing, and the Central Committee of Herut met at the end of August and selected Foreign Minister Yitzhak Shamir to fill this position. Although a strong campaign was mounted by Housing Minister David Levy, a Moroccan-born politician with a large following among Likud voters of Afro-Asian origin, Shamir was a close and long-time ally of Begin and was undoubtedly chosen, at least in part, because of his ties to the retiring prime minister. He assumed the premiership on September 15.

Shamir differed from Begin with respect to style, but he was similar to his predecessor with respect to substance. He possessed neither Begin's charisma nor his effectiveness as an orator. Also, whereas Begin's political style was brash and confrontational, Shamir was quiet, even-tempered, and affable. Nevertheless, the new prime minister was a dedicated and proven supporter of Revisionist Zionism, having been a partisan in the illegal Jewish underground in the prestate period and belonging to the right wing rather than the ideological center of Herut in the years after independence. Shamir's hard-line orientation had also led him to oppose the Camp David accords, even though, unlike several other prominent critics within Likud, he did not break with the party and the prime minister over this issue. Following Likud's electoral victory in 1977, Shamir became speaker of the Knesset, and in the fall of 1979, after the resignation of Moshe Dayan as foreign minister, Begin's confidence in his long-time political ally led him to appoint Shamir to the position. During the invasion of Lebanon in 1982, Shamir's influence in the cabinet was inferior only to that of Begin and Sharon, and, as noted, he had been criticized by the Kahan Commission for failing to act when information about the massacre taking place in Sabra and Shatilla was presented to him.

One of the leading personalities in the cabinet led by Shamir was Moshe Arens, who had replaced Sharon as defense minister following publication of the Kahan Commission report in February 1983. The difference between Arens and Sharon was in some ways similar to the difference between Shamir and Begin, being significant with respect to style but of secondary importance with respect to substance. Raised and educated in the United States and later a professor of aeronautical engineering at Haifa's Technion University, Arens was as smooth and polished as Sharon was tempestuous and coarse. Arens had also demonstrated his considerable diplomatic skill as Israel's ambassador in Washington. Yet the new defense minister was a staunch Herut conservative who fully supported retention of the West Bank and Gaza and who had also been highly critical of the Camp David accords. Although some Israeli moderates suggested that he would ultimately prove to be flexible on territorial issues, and in the meantime praised him for taking a tough stand against Jewish settler vigilantism, Arens allied himself closely with Shamir in both intraparty feuds and the broader arena of Israeli party politics, and he worked with the new prime minister to carry forward Israel's drive into the West Bank and Gaza.

During 1983 and the first half of 1984, under the leadership first of Begin and then of Shamir, the Israeli public was concerned primarily with the unresolved political and military situation in Lebanon and also, or perhaps even more, with the deteriorating economic circumstances in which the Jewish state found itself at this time. Questions about the future of the West Bank and Gaza, while as critical as ever in the long run, were to a considerable extent put on the back burner in the face of problems that most Israelis considered more pressing. The issue of the territories did not disappear from the political agenda, of course. Nevertheless, concerns about Lebanon and the economy were dominant during this period, and they were accordingly of greater salience to most voters when the nation went to the polls to elect a new Knesset in July 1984.

So far as the situation in Lebanon is concerned, the war itself had added an important new dimension to existing political divisions in the Jewish state, and this in turn produced bitter and sometimes violent confrontations when the Kahan Commission report was published in February 1983. A particularly disturbing incident, which symbolized both the unhappy mood of the country and its dangerous polarization with respect to questions about Lebanon, took place in Jerusalem shortly after the report was released. A group of thugs harassed Peace

Now demonstrators marching to the prime minister's office to demand that the recommendations of the Kahan Commission be fully implemented, and then, as the marchers were dispersing, a hand grenade was thrown into the crowd, killing one young man, Emile Grunzweig, and wounding several others. Additionally, several Peace Now leaders were assaulted when they went to the hospital to visit the wounded. This and other incidents, including the increasing vitriol that had entered into Knesset debates, led the president of the country, Yitzhak Navon, to tell journalists that Israel could face the prospect of civil war if the direction of increasing polarization did not change.[88]

As noted, there were additional concerns in the months that followed as both the political and the military situation in Lebanon began to deteriorate. Israelis were disappointed in the agreement negotiated with the Gemayel government in May 1983, and they were even more disturbed when this accord, modest as it was from Jerusalem's point of view, was repudiated in March 1984. Most important of all, the IDF remained in Lebanon and continued to sustain losses. With the total number of Israeli soldiers killed in Lebanon approaching 600 in the spring of 1984, even many who had supported the invasion now agreed that the remaining troops should be brought home, especially since it appeared that keeping them in Lebanon served no legitimate military or political purpose.

Israel's serious economic problems were evident in a number of domains. The government had massive expenditures, related in part to the cost of its operation in Lebanon,[89] and also to both its continuing settlement drive in the West Bank and Gaza and the program of economic benefits that had helped Likud to win the election of 1981. Yet another major expense at this time was Israel's attempt to develop a new fighter aircraft, the Lavi, a project which was strongly supported by Moshe Arens.[90] Lacking the resources to pay for these and other activities, the state printed huge amounts of new money, and this in turn set in motion a rapidly accelerating inflationary spiral. Inflation was approaching 400 percent by the summer of 1983, and with the country's currency rapidly losing its value, Israeli financial institutions were rocked as funds were withdrawn from investments and savings accounts in order to purchase durable goods or foreign currency. Additional problems included a soaring national debt and the decline to critically low levels of the country's foreign-currency reserves, all of which led to several sharp drops in the Tel Aviv stock exchange during the first half of 1983. The situation grew even worse in October of that year, shortly after Shamir became prime minister, when the rapid and widespread liquidation of investments in bank shares, no longer considered secure, led to a near-panic in the banking and financial community.[91]

The government responded to the deepening economic crisis with a 23 percent devaluation of the nation's currency, the shekel. To reduce government expenditures and further curb inflation, it also increased the price of state-subsidized goods by 50 percent. Finance Minister Yoram Aridor resigned a few days later and was replaced by Yigal Cohen-Orgad, a strong critic of Aridor's liberal economic policies who then introduced additional austerity measures, including new taxes. All of this only partially halted the country's economic slide, however, causing public uncertainty to remain high. In mid-November, Israelis heard the worrisome news that foreign-currency reserves had dropped below $3 billion, a "red line" that defined what economists considered a danger zone. In addition, much of the public was unhappy about the austerity measures that had been imposed, and some also complained that government action had come too late to prevent the value of their savings from significantly declining. Thus, reflecting growing discontent, a public opinion poll conducted in January 1984 found that Labor would have scored a decisive victory over Likud had Knesset elections been held at that time.

It is against this background that the country did move toward new parliamentary elections two months later. In March 1984, exploiting a division within the ranks of the ruling coalition, the Labor Alignment was able to bring down the government approximately a year before the expiration of its scheduled term of office, and thereby to force the country to schedule a new round of balloting. The faction that broke ranks with Likud was Tami, a small religious party that was discontent with some of the government's social and economic policies; and although Tami held only three seats in the Knesset, the parliamentary position of the Likud-led government was sufficiently precarious that the loss of these seats deprived it of its majority. Following the fall of the government, new elections were set for July 23. The Knesset to be elected would be the eleventh since Israel had become independent in 1948.

The onset of the campaign, in April, brought political contests inside both of Israel's major parties. In Likud, Shamir, Ariel Sharon, and David Levy vied for leadership of the party, with Shamir and Sharon the front-runners in what proved to be a bitter and divisive fight. Shamir was supported by Arens and other members of the Herut and Likud establishment, whereas Sharon, despite the war in Lebanon and the findings of the Kahan Commission, remained popular with many Likud voters and drew his strength from the party's rank and file. Shamir's continuing stewardship was eventually endorsed by 56 percent of the Herut Central Committee, a slender majority that gave him a mandate to lead Likud in the forthcoming election campaign, but which indicated that new challenges to his leadership of the party could be expected in the future. In Labor, the by-now-familiar contest between Shimon Peres and Yitzhak Rabin was replayed once again, with the same results as in 1981. Peres would remain the leader of the party.

In May, just as the electoral campaign was moving into high gear, the nation was stunned by the news that twenty-seven Israelis had been arrested by the government and charged with membership in a secret terrorist organization. The organization, known as Terror against Terror, was composed primarily of Jewish settlers living in the West Bank. Most of its members were active in Gush Emunim, and their number included many reserve officers, some with distinguished military records.[92] Among the specific acts with which these individuals were charged were the 1980 bombings of several West Bank mayors and the 1982 shooting and hand grenade attack on the Islamic University in Hebron. The news that alleged Jewish terrorists had been arrested and indicted added to the apprehension the public already felt about IDF troops remaining in Lebanon and economic difficulties at home; and, coming barely two months before the Knesset election, it provided another important focus for political debate as the electoral campaign went forward.

The accused terrorists were respectively condemned and defended by various sectors of political opinion in Israel. They were vigorously denounced by Labor and the left, of course. An ad placed in *Ha'aretz* by Peace Now declared, for example, "We have been warning for years about Jewish terror and the soil for its growth. . . . The Jewish terrorist movement is not a deviation or a coincidence. It is the price of Greater Israel, it is the bitter fruit of fanatical nationalist ideology, an ideology of power. The settlements—the seeds of expropriation—become the hothouse of terror." More surprising, some individuals on the political right, including some supporters of Gush Emunim, appeared to be genuinely dismayed by the revelations about Jewish terrorism. For example, Shubert Spero, holder of the Stone Chair of Jewish Thought at Bar Ilan University, wrote, "Grim foreboding took hold of many of us who saw ourselves in the ideological camp of Gush Emunim. . . . The discovery [of a Jewish terrorist organization] has posed a very serious challenge to Gush Emunim and those who identify with its philosophy."[93] Spero went on to state that it is a tragic distortion of Torah Judaism and religious Zionism to believe that there is any justification for the premeditated and indiscriminate killing and maiming of Arabs or for the destruction of Muslim religious institutions.

Yet the terrorists were also defended, not only by members of the settler movement but also by prominent Israelis from the political mainstream. There were also many calls for leniency. Among the highly visible Israelis who subsequently testified on behalf of particular defendants were Ariel Sharon, Yigal Cohen-Orgad, and Benyamin Ben Eliezer, all Members of Knesset. Cohen-Orgad was the newly appointed minister of finance at the time of the arrests. Ben Eliezer was a senior IDF officer who later joined the Labor Alignment, and during the trial he praised one defendant by stating that his "personal heroism and courage as a soldier" had made him "a revered figure in the army ever since he joined my [elite] unit in 1968."[94]

In addition to these statements on behalf of individual defendants, many on the political right put forward a broader defense of the accused. Moreover, this was the position of the vast majority of those who identified with Gush Emunim, making it clear that the kind of soul-searching described by Shubert Spero was not widespread. Some argued, for example, that violence against Arabs would not be necessary if the government gave adequate support to Jewish settlers in the occupied territories and if it were more vigorous in suppressing Palestinian resistance. Others condemned the government for putting the defendants on trial in the first place. One extremist leader later stated, for example, that Syria's capture of Israeli soldiers in Lebanon in 1984 was divine retribution for the arrest of Jews who were advancing the cause of Zionism in Judea and Samaria.[95]

As these reactions suggest, the discovery and arrest of alleged Jewish terrorists added yet another worrisome and divisive issue to the nation's political agenda. Moreover, although the fate of the accused could not be known in May 1984, as the country geared up for the July election, the issue remained divisive during a lengthy series of trials, and passions then flared again when verdicts were finally handed down in the summer of 1985. While most of the defendants were found guilty and several were sentenced to life in prison, both those who had condemned the accused and those who had supported them agreed that in a majority of instances the sentences were "surprisingly lenient."[96] For example, one defendant convicted of "weapons possession, membership in a terrorist organization and causing grievous bodily harm" received a four-month sentence.[97]

With the arrest and trial of alleged Jewish terrorists adding to the concerns of the Israeli public, the 1984 election campaign went forward during June and the first three weeks of July. One prominent feature of the campaign was an increase in the number of political factions competing for seats in the Knesset. Twenty-six parties presented lists to the electorate, thirteen of which were new. Moreover, a substantial number of these parties were successful; whereas only ten had received enough votes in the 1981 election to capture at least one seat in parliament, fifteen received enough votes, roughly 20,000, to win at least one seat in 1984. This increasing heterogeneity was visible in virtually all sectors of society, including the political right, the political left, among ultraorthodox voters, and in the Arab sector of Israeli society.

In what was something of a surprise given the underlying tensions in the country, the campaign was also marked by a decrease in the level of bombast and confrontation. Indeed, the chairman of the Election Commission called the 1984 campaign "the cleanest election in [Israel's] thirty-six year history."[98] This relative civility may have been attributable, in part, to Begin's retirement and his replacement by Shamir, whose political style was much more low-key. It was probably the result to an even greater degree of deliberate efforts by both Labor and Likud to avoid any increase in the tensions that had characterized the preceding year. Also setting the tone for the campaign were appeals for calm and restraint issued by the president of the country, the chairman of the Election Commission, and other public figures. Finally, the seriousness and immediacy of the problems facing the country undoubtedly contributed to the relatively sober and responsible tone that characterized the electoral campaign.

The election took place on July 23 and produced several interrelated sets of results. To begin with, the map of partisan affiliations became significantly more fragmented and heterogeneous. Not only did the number of parties represented in parliament increase, as noted, but there was also an appreciable increase in the number of Knesset seats held by these parties and, correspondingly, a decrease in the number controlled by Labor and Likud. Taken together, the two large blocs won only eighty-five Knesset seats in 1984, whereas they had captured ninety-five seats in the balloting three years earlier.[99]

Furthermore, fragmentation was visible across the political spectrum, with representatives from thirteen small parties now sitting in the Knesset alongside delegates from Likud and Labor, and with growing diversity both to the right of the former and to the left of the latter. Whereas there had been one party to the right of Likud after the 1981 election, or two if the National Religious Party is placed in this category because of its strong ties to Gush Emunim, three parties of the far right, in addition to the NRP, captured one or more seats in the 1984 balloting. These parties were Tehiya, which now held five Knesset seats; Morasha, with two seats; and Kach, with one seat. The NRP won four seats in the 1984 election, giving parties affiliated with the settler movement a total of twelve mandates. There was also fragmentation in the partisan alignment of ultraorthodox voters. Many pious Jews of Afro-Asian origin withdrew their support from Agudat Yisrael, traditionally the dominant political movement among ultraorthodox Israelis, and instead gave their votes to a new party, the Sephardi Torah Guardians, or Shas.[100] Shas captured four seats in the 1984 election, whereas the number of seats controlled by Aguda declined from four to two.

Additionally, on the left, the party most closely identified with Peace Now, the Citizens' Rights Movement, increased the number of Knesset seats it held from one to three. Holding three additional seats in parliament was Yahad, a new party that was more centrist than CRM but which frequently identified with the peace camp as well. Yahad was established and led by former defense minister Ezer Weizman, who had served in the first Begin government until his resignation in May 1980. A new party also emerged in the Arab sector, taking votes from Rakah, the Israeli Communist Party, which had in recent years been the dominant political force among Israel's Arab citizens. This was the Jewish-Arab Progressive List for Peace, which won two Knesset seats, half as many as were captured by Rakah. These and three other small parties, Shinui, Tami, and Ometz, defined the parameters of a heterogeneous and fragmented political environment, within which Israel's major parties were now required to operate.

A second result of the 1984 election, of even more immediate significance, was the virtual standoff between Labor and Likud. Labor did slightly better than Likud, capturing forty-four seats to Likud's forty-one, but this was a disappointment, since preelection polls had predicted a clear Alignment victory and since, in absolute terms, Labor won three fewer Knesset seats than in 1981. As explained by one Israeli scholar, Likud had lost but Labor had not won; although the trend of steady growth in support for Likud had been arrested, with the party capturing seven fewer seats than in the preceding election, this did not mean Labor had begun to reestablish its once-dominant position.[101] Rather, with neither party performing significantly better than the other, the 1984 election confirmed the increasing importance of the division between hard-liners and moderates, commonly referred to as hawks and doves respectively.

The nearly equal strength of Labor and Likud, combined with the general fragmentation of the new Knesset, made it extremely difficult for either of the two large parties to form a ruling coalition. No party other than Labor and Likud controlled more than five Knesset seats, and the distribution of these small parties across the political spectrum meant that neither of the two large parties had much chance of establishing a parliamentary majority unless it was able to conclude an agreement with several ideologically antagonistic political factions. For a brief moment it appeared that Labor might succeed in forging such a coalition, bringing religious parties together with center and leftist factions advocating a reduction in the influence of orthodox Jewish law. In the end, however, the Alignment was unable to reach an agreement with the religious parties. Labor might also have been able to form a coalition had it been willing to include Rakah and the Progressive List for Peace, non-Zionist parties that received almost all of their votes in the Arab sector. But neither the Alignment nor most of its potential coalition partners were prepared to depart from a tradition which specifies that only Zionist parties should share in governing the Jewish state. Similar or even greater obstacles confronted Likud, in part because it ruled out any agreement with the openly racist and antidemocratic Kach Party of the extreme right.

To deal with this situation, Likud proposed that Labor and Likud join together in a government of national unity, and in September, after nearly two months of inconclusive bargaining, the Alignment accepted this suggestion. Shimon Peres of the Alignment had initially rejected the idea of a national unity government, but then agreed to the compromise when it became evident that Labor would be unable to form a government on its own. Since Peres had never before served as prime minister, he also reasoned that by at least sharing in the direction of the country he would be able to demonstrate his leadership skills and thereby improve his chances in future electoral contests. Under the terms worked out between Labor and Likud, Peres would serve as prime minister and Yitzhak Shamir of Likud would serve as foreign minister for twenty-five months, after which the two men would reverse roles. Yitzhak Rabin of Labor would serve as defense minister during the new government's entire term of office.

Since the national unity government was conceived as a "wall-to-wall" coalition, other parties were invited to join with Labor and Likud in governing the country. The NRP, Tami, Agudat Yisrael, and Shas, all religious parties, accepted this invitation and brought eleven additional seats into the ruling coalition. So did Yahad and another centrist faction, Shinui, each of which added three more seats. Finally, one additional seat was brought into the coalition by Ometz, a new party founded by Yigal Hurewitz, who had previously served as Likud's minister of finance but had broken with his party over issues of economic policy. The formation of this grand coalition was applauded by most Israelis, who believed it would offer the country strong leadership and the unity of purpose necessary to address challenges pertaining to the economy and the situation in Lebanon.

Despite widespread public support for the national unity government, a number of parties declined the invitation to join the ruling coalition. One was Mapam, which together with the Labor Party had constituted the Labor Alignment. Mapam declared in the summer of 1984 that it would not participate in a government which included Likud, and the party accordingly withdrew from the Alignment and took its six Knesset seats into the opposition. It was replaced by Yahad, Ezer Weizman's electoral list, which joined with the Labor Party at this time to reconstitute the Labor Alignment. Like Mapam, the Citizens' Rights Movement also rejected cooperation with Likud and refused to join the government; and Tehiya and Morasha took a similar stance from their position on the right side of the political spectrum, stating that they would not participate in a coalition that included Labor or other parties committed to territorial compromise. Finally, the new government did not include Rakah and the Progressive List, non-Zionist parties that drew most of their votes from the Arab sector, or Kach, whose ideological extremism made it unacceptable to Likud as well as to Labor. All of these parties together controlled only twenty-three Knesset seats, however, leaving the national unity government established in September 1984 with an extremely comfortable ninety-seven-seat majority in parliament.

A third consequence of the 1984 election was the growing strength of the political right in Israel. Specifically, 12 of the Knesset's 120 seats, fully 10 percent, were now occupied by political factions to the right of Likud. Although marginalized for the time being by the national unity government, Knesset members from these parties represented the settler movement, and many of them not only condemned the platform of the Alignment, they also strongly criticized Likud for being too cautious and moderate. Moreover, the numerical importance of the far right raised the possibility that in the not-too-distant future the most plausible axis on which to base a ruling coalition would be an alliance between Likud and parties tied directly to Gush Emunim and the settler movement. Taken as a whole, the right side of the political spectrum had not gained strength. The 1984 balloting had rather given evidence of the country's ideological polarization, with a decline in the number of Israelis voting for Likud leading, overall, to a more equal balance in the relative strength of the moderate and hard-line camps. But there had been a shift *within* the latter political bloc, with some of Likud's losses offset by the gains of parties on the far right. As noted, this category of parties included Tehiya, Morasha, and Kach. It also included the NRP, despite some lingering internal differences on issues pertaining to the fusion of religious orthodoxy and militant Jewish nationalism.

Tehiya, which means "Revival" or "Rebirth," captured five seats in the 1984 balloting, making it the third-largest party on the Israeli political scene at this time. It was formed in 1979 by Geula Cohen and Moshe Shamir, Knesset members who resigned from Likud because they opposed the return of Sinai to Egypt.[102] They also opposed the idea of Palestinian autonomy, arguing that it was inconsistent with Israel's right to exercise permanent sovereignty over the West Bank and Gaza. Cohen was a long-time associate of Menachem Begin, and Shamir was a prominent novelist and former leftist who now headed the Land of Israel Movement. In 1980 and 1981, Cohen and Shamir were joined by several other well-known conservative figures, including Yuval Ne'eman, a nuclear physicist and former president of Tel Aviv University, and Hanan Porat, a leader of the religious settler movement. Tehiya declared at this time that it would accept only Jewish members. This contrasted with the policy of Likud which, despite its hawkish stance toward the Palestinians, had usually included a small number of Israeli Arabs on its Knesset list.

Tehiya won three Knesset seats in the elections of 1981, indicating that the new party had become institutionalized and found a constituency among Israeli voters in the two years since its creation, and public opinion polls showed that Tehiya's following continued to grow during 1982 and 1983. Support among voters of the political right was further enhanced in 1984 by the addition to the party's leadership of Rafael Eitan, former chief of staff and architect, along with Ariel Sharon, of the 1982 invasion of Lebanon. Eitan had formed his own political movement, Tzomet, which merged with Tehiya in time for the 1984 elections. Tehiya's position at this time was that Israel should formally annex the West Bank. As explained by Ne'eman, the party's platform also specified that "the only 'legitimate rights' of the Palestinian Arabs are the right to live in peace [as resident aliens] with the Jewish majority in Israel."[103]

The growth of the extreme right was further enhanced by the emergence of Morasha, a party established by Rabbi Chaim Druckman, a former NRP Member of Knesset. Druckman is a militant supporter of Gush Emunim who in 1979 and 1980 criticized the Begin government for lethargy in the expansion of settlements in the West Bank and Gaza, and also for agreeing to a withdrawal from Sinai. He supported the settler movement in its conflicts with the government, even though his own party belonged to the ruling coalition at this time. Druckman broke with the NRP after the 1981 election and established Morasha in time for the 1984 balloting. Among the new party's cofounders was Hanan Porat, a Gush Emunim leader who had been elected to parliament in 1981 on the Tehiya list. In the 1984 election, Morasha obtained two seats in parliament, one of which was occupied by Druckman and the other by Avraham Verdiger. While some analysts described Morasha as a single-issue party, dedicated to "unimpeded Jewish settlement in the occupied territories and no withdrawal by Israel,"[104] the party was also concerned with the same religious issues that preoccupied other orthodox and ultraorthodox parties. Its commitment to the fusion of religious orthodoxy and militant territorial maximalism thus appealed to those NRP voters who identified with Gush Emunim, intensifying the declining fortunes of the latter party. Indeed, to many of these voters it was Morasha, not the NRP, that best represented the vision and goals of Gush Emunim.[105]

The most extreme and controversial party of the far right was Kach. Led by Meir Kahane, an American-born rabbi who founded the Jewish Defense League in the United States and who retained his American citizenship until September 1985, Kach had run candidates for the Knesset since 1973 but consistently failed to win enough votes to obtain a seat. In 1977, for example, the year that Likud came to power, Kach received only .25 percent of the popular vote. Nevertheless, the party was active on behalf of extremist causes, challenging the government by means of direct action, and often using violence and breaking the law. Kach's declared objective was the breakdown of communication between Jews and Arabs and the exacerbation of hostility and violence to the point where all prospects for peace, or capitulation from Kach's point of view, would be destroyed. Thus, for example, after the attack by Jewish terrorists on West Bank Arab mayors in May 1980, a Kach leader, Yossi Dayan, stated that while his group was not responsible for the action, he was confident it had been carried out by "good Jews." Looking to the future, Kahane and Kach advocated the expulsion of Palestinians living in the West Bank and in Gaza. They also sought to rescind the rights of citizenship enjoyed by Arabs living inside Israel. According to Kahane, "No non-Jews can be citizens of Israel." If Arabs nonetheless chose "to live there in tribute and servitude, then they must be treated charitably, Never as equals, though." And if the Arabs refuse to accept this situation, Kahane continued, "We'll put them on trucks and send them over the Allenby Bridge. . . . We'll use force. And if they fire at our soldiers, we'll kill them."[106]

Although Kach was strongly condemned by Israeli authorities and could for a time be dismissed as a group of the "lunatic fringe," this became increasingly difficult after the 1984 elections. The party received almost 26,000 votes, 1.4 percent of the total cast, and Kahane accordingly became a Member of Knesset. Moreover, Kahane had declared in his campaign that he sought Knesset membership in order to acquire parliamentary immunity and thereby circumvent the restrictions that authorities had placed on his activities; and after the elections he sought to use his immunity to lead provocative demonstrations in several large Arab villages, including Um el-Fahm and Shefa Amr. Public opinion polls conducted in the months that followed suggested that support for Kahane was continuing to grow, with a mid-1985 poll indicating that as much as 10 percent of the nation's youth intended to vote for Kach in the next election and that the party would accordingly win four or more Knesset seats.[107] This was at a time when the trial of Jewish terrorists was arousing public passions, leading some Israelis to deplore the fanaticism and extremism that had emerged in certain political circles, but causing a greater number than ever before to defend and support politicians of the extreme right.

Thus, as Israel looked toward the second half of the decade and prepared to address its problems under the stewardship of a national unity government, politics in the Jewish state was marked by ideological and institutional fragmentation, by increasing polarization between supporters and opponents of territorial compromise, and by growing strength on the right side of the political spectrum. To many observers, Israeli politics appeared to be in a state of transition. But while the 1984 elections had increased its fluidity and raised important questions, some of them deeply troubling, the overall direction of change, the most likely outcome of competing trends, and the prospects for coping successfully with new challenges and conflicts were not yet fully clear and remained the subjects of intense debate.[108]

The Jordanian-Palestinian Agreement

The mutiny within Fatah late in 1983 and the Israeli elections of mid-1984 set the stage for a new round of diplomacy that continued until 1986. This time, however, initiatives came not from Washington but from the protagonists themselves. The opening act of this new diplomatic drama focused on the PLO and Jordan, and to a lesser extent on Egypt. Following his ouster from Lebanon in December 1983, Yasir Arafat traveled to Cairo to meet with Hosni Mubarak and seek support from Egypt, the only Arab country to have made peace with Israel. Arafat then sought enhanced cooperation with Jordan, eventually concluding an agreement with King Hussein for a joint Jordanian-Palestinian negotiating strategy. This agreement, which had proved elusive in 1982 and 1983, was formally concluded in February 1985.

Arafat's trip to Cairo in December 1983 was a bold and calculated move. All but a handful of Arab countries had broken off diplomatic relations with Egypt following the signing of its peace treaty with Israel in 1979. In addition, the headquarters of the Arab League had been moved from Cairo to Tunis at this time. The PLO chairman thus realized that his reconciliation with Egyptian president Hosni Mubarak would be strongly criticized by Palestinian and other Arab hard-liners, who would accuse him of betraying the Palestinian cause and violating resolutions of the Palestine National Council. Nevertheless, Arafat traveled to Cairo on December 22, telling Egyptian journalists the next day, "My trip sought to unite those Arab countries that were trying to resolve the Palestinian problem through political means." Attempting to lay the groundwork for Cairo's return to the Arab fold, he also stated that "the continued isolation of Egypt was harmful to the Palestinian question."[109]

In making this overture to Egypt, Arafat reasoned that it mattered little whether the Palestinian and Arab radicals who had attacked him in Lebanon were given additional ammunition for their denunciations of his leadership. With or without such criticism, the PLO chairman concluded, his own survival, as well as that of the political orientation he represented, required the construction of a powerful countervailing alliance; and in this connection he believed that Egypt alone had the political weight to neutralize Syria. Arafat also hoped that Egyptian support would strengthen his position in future dealings with Jordan and make it more difficult for King Hussein to exploit the PLO's weakened position. As expressed by one Palestinian scholar, "Cairo's support would be instrumental in preserving a separate Palestinian national identity and ensuring a role for the PLO in any political settlement."[110]

Egypt, for its part, saw Arafat's visit as an important opportunity and followed up with steps of its own to break out of the diplomatic isolation that had been imposed upon it. Since Cairo had been condemned by other Arabs for concluding a partial peace with Israel, for implementing the Camp David accords even though Jerusalem had disregarded those provisions addressed to the Palestinian problem, the PLO was better able than any other actor in the Middle East to confer legitimacy on the Mubarak government and to help reestablish Egypt's credibility as an important and trustworthy member of the Arab political community. As a result, even though the Israelis strongly condemned Mubarak for meeting with Arafat and charged that this constituted a violation of the Egyptian-Israeli peace treaty, the Egyptian president, like Arafat himself, reasoned that he had little to lose and potentially much to gain.

Moreover, although not solely because of its reconciliation with the PLO, Egypt did indeed score important political gains in the months that followed. The Islamic Conference Organization, meeting in Casablanca in January 1984, voted to readmit Egypt, taking this action even though Palestinian rejectionists had sent a petition stating that Arafat no longer represented the PLO. Even more important, diplomatic relations between Cairo and Amman were reestablished in October 1984, with King Hussein making a state visit to Cairo at the end of November. Although Egypt continued to be strongly condemned by a number of Arab states, most notably Syria and Libya, there were now major cracks in the wall of isolation that the Arab world had placed around Egypt five years earlier.

Reconciliation with Egypt was supported by many Palestinians. While bitter condemnations were issued by the Popular Front, the Democratic Front, the Palestine Communist Party, and other hard-line Palestinian factions, and also by the regime in Damascus, it was not the case that Arafat had defied the wishes of most Palestinians. Most members of the Fatah Central Committee recognized that contact with Egypt was important, and indeed such contact had been taking place with regularity and in the open since the Israeli invasion of Lebanon. The Central Committee and the Fatah Revolutionary Council therefore did not condemn Arafat's trip to Cairo, even though they did feel compelled to describe it as a personal initiative that had not been properly authorized. Further, although there was more division within the PLO at large, Arafat also had the support of a majority of both the organization's Executive Committee and the members of the PNC.[111]

In addition, and in some ways most important, Arafat had broad support among Palestinians in the West Bank and Gaza, who had in fact become the PLO's most important constituency in the aftermath of the war in Lebanon. Indeed, in a poll carried out in the West Bank and Gaza two weeks before Arafat's forced departure from Tripoli and his subsequent visit to Cairo, 95 percent of those surveyed declared their attachment to the PLO chairman.[112] Thus, while leftists in the territories agreed with their counterparts elsewhere and condemned the meeting with Mubarak, expressions of satisfaction with Arafat's action were much more common, as was the view that ties with Egypt would improve the PLO's position and ensure that it was not bypassed should peace negotiations eventually take place. In the meantime, Arafat's supporters added, such ties might help to distance Egypt from the Camp David accords, and they would certainly encourage Cairo to use its contacts in the U.S., Europe, and Israel to promote an appreciation of the Palestinian cause.

With active encouragement from both Egypt and Palestinians in the West Bank and Gaza, Arafat proceeded to reestablish the PLO's dialogue with Jordan. Mubarak had urged this course of action during Arafat's visit, telling the PLO chairman to seek negotiations based on the 1982 Reagan Plan, and Rashad Shawwa, the mayor of Gaza, spoke for many Palestinians in the occupied territories when he called on Arafat "to cooperate in our name with both Jordan and Egypt in any effort that will guarantee an end to Israeli military occupation."[113] In fact Arafat needed little encouragement. As in the case of his reconciliation with Egypt, the PLO chairman sought enhanced cooperation with Jordan in order to offset the support that leftist Palestinians were receiving from Syria and, more generally, to ensure the survival of his approach to the Palestinian problem and prevent the PLO from becoming a marginal force in the Arab political arena. As stated by a leading Israeli authority on the PLO, Arafat sought to maintain contact with Jordan, even at the risk of deepening the split within the PLO, because he refused to "turn away from the political process" or to "embrace the . . . hard-line insistence on armed struggle as the only way to liberate Palestine."[114] As expressed by one of Arafat's own advisors, it was in the interest of the PLO to be involved in political activity and not to exclude the possibility of a settlement through political means.[115]

In pursuing these ends through a dialogue with Jordan, Arafat was also attempting to ensure that King Hussein would remain faithful to the pledge he had made at the 1974 Arab summit in Rabat, that the PLO was the sole legitimate representative of the Palestinian people and, accordingly, that Jordan did not represent the Palestinian inhabitants of the West Bank. In addition, PLO cooperation with Jordan would facilitate contact with Palestinians in the occupied territories, on whom Arafat and the PLO mainstream were now increasingly dependent.

King Hussein's interest in a renewed dialogue with the PLO was based on two broad considerations, one defensive and the other involving an expansion of Jordanian political influence in matters bearing on the Palestinian problem. On the one hand, Hussein was eager to protect himself against the challenge of Arab radicalism, which was represented by the alliance between Syria and PLO leftists and which would undoubtedly have grown stronger among Palestinians living in Jordan had the mainstream of the PLO fallen under Syrian control. As explained by the king early in 1984, "there are definite efforts by a sister Arab country to extend its control over the PLO, and this is unacceptable and illegal."[116] On the other hand, Amman also aspired to the eventual reassertion of its political influence in the West Bank, and possibly to the extension of this influence to Gaza as well. To a degree, these aspirations were also defensive in nature. Hussein was eager to prevent leftists from mobilizing Palestinians in the occupied territories and thereby gaining additional power, and this concern was particularly pronounced in the fall of 1983, when Arafat's fate was uncertain. At the same time, Jordan was alert as well to the possibility that it might eventually emerge as the dominant Arab actor in the West Bank and Gaza, gaining legitimacy from cooperation with a weakened PLO and then presenting itself as champion of the Palestinian cause in negotiations aimed at determining the final status of the occupied territories.

In an important move designed to demonstrate that the future of the occupied territories concerned Jordan as well as the PLO, Hussein reconvened the Jordanian parliament in January 1984. This legislative body, which had not met in almost ten years, was structured so as to give equal weight to the West Bank and the East Bank, each of which had thirty deputies in the lower house. In addition, since some members of parliament had died during the period since the last legislative elections, nearly two decades earlier, by-elections were organized in March 1984 to replace eight deceased East Bank representatives.[117] Direct popular elections could not be held to select replacements for the four deceased West Bank deputies, however, so these vacancies were not filled until November 1985, when four new representatives from the West Bank were chosen by the parliament itself.

By reviving political and constitutional arrangements that represented Jordan's historic connection with Palestinians in the occupied territories, Hussein raised the possibility of a softening in Amman's commitment to the 1974 Rabat declaration, especially since suspension of the Jordanian parliament had taken place one month after the Rabat summit and had been justified on the grounds that sole responsibility for representing Palestinians in the West Bank now rested with the PLO. Also, although considerations of foreign policy were the king's primary motivation, the revival of parliamentary life allowed Hussein to respond to those who criticized Jordan for the absence of democracy and who, for this reason, might be responsive to the ideological appeals of Arab leftists. As stated in an editorial in the *Jordan Times*, most Jordanians hoped the step "would be a precursor to real democratic life in the country and a true attempt at popular participation in shaping our political and social life as well." [118]

Both Arafat and Hussein proceeded cautiously during the course of 1984, recognizing that any new diplomatic initiatives would have to wait until after the elections that were taking place in Israel and the United States. Caution was also dictated by opposition from Syria and the divisions this created in the arena of inter-Arab politics, making it necessary for Jordanian and Palestinian leaders to reconstruct a moderate Arab consensus that would give backing to new diplomatic efforts. Finally, and perhaps most important, Arafat could not get too far ahead of the PLO, which remained divided between moderates and hard-liners. In recognition of these challenges, Hussein took care during this period to affirm that Jordan remained committed to the 1974 Rabat resolution, and that his principal objective in cooperating with the PLO was an end to Israel's occupation of the West Bank and Gaza. The king also reaffirmed his commitment to United Nations 242, adding that he did not seek a separate accommodation with Jerusalem, and that peace required Israeli withdrawal from the Golan Heights, as well as the West Bank and Gaza.

Gradually, however, the outlines of a substantive agreement between Hussein and Arafat began to emerge. Reflecting a loss of confidence in the United States, particularly after the U.S. signed a strategic cooperation agreement with Israel in November 1983 even though Jerusalem had rejected the 1982 American peace initiative and failed to withdraw its military forces from Lebanon,[119] Jordan and the PLO ignored the Reagan Plan and called for peace talks in the context of an international conference sponsored by the permanent members of the UN Security Council, including the Soviet Union. Hussein and Arafat also agreed that Palestinians would be represented at this conference by a joint Jordanian-Palestinian delegation which would include members of, or individuals acceptable to, the Palestine Liberation Organization. Finally, following Israeli withdrawal from the occupied territories, a confederation would be established between Jordan and liberated Palestine, and the relationship between these two territories would be determined through direct negotiations between Jordanians and Palestinians.

Having built bridges to Egypt and Jordan, Arafat now sought to ensure that his actions had the backing of the PLO. His goal was to convene another session of the Palestine National Council in order to have his leadership confirmed, but such a meeting would not be fully authoritative if boycotted by the PFLP, the DFLP, and other leftist factions, and this possibility led to protracted bargaining with these groups during much of 1984. Joined by the Palestine Liberation Front and the Palestine Communist Party, the Popular Front and the Democratic Front formed the Democratic Alliance early in 1984 and sought to establish a common position on issues confronting the PLO, including Arafat's leadership and relations with key Arab countries. Also participating in debates inside the PLO was the National Alliance, made up of four groups that not only were critical of Arafat but were closely tied to Syria as well. These included Fatah dissidents led by Abu Musa, Saiqa, the PFLP–General Command, and the Popular Struggle Front.

Following meetings in Algiers and Aden, and in response to pressure from Algeria and South Yemen, an agreement between the Fatah mainstream and the Democratic Alliance was reached in June 1984. Known as the Aden-Algiers Agreement, this accord placed several limitations on Arafat's power and offered mild criticism of the PLO chairman's trip to Egypt, stating that normalization of relations with Egypt would be a subject for discussion by the PNC. On the other hand, the accord expressed support for a dialogue with Jordan and, more generally, it reaffirmed the primacy of Palestinian unity and appeared to clear the way for convening the PNC, which was then scheduled to meet in September. Internal bickering continued, however, principally because of opposition to the Aden-Algiers Agreement from Syria and its clients in the National Alliance, but also because of lingering dissatisfaction among some members of the Democratic Alliance, especially the Popular Front led by George Habash. This continuing dissension forced several postponements of the PNC meeting, since members of the Democratic Alliance, as well as the National Alliance, were now refusing to attend.

Although Fatah's differences with the Democratic Alliance and the National Alliance had not been resolved, Arafat finally convened the seventeenth session of the Palestine National Council in Amman on November 22. The meeting was boycotted by members of the two alliances, and participation was further reduced by the refusal of both Syria and Israel to allow PNC members residing in their territories to travel to Amman. Nevertheless, 261 of the PNC's 374 members attended, and overall the meeting was judged to be a triumph for Arafat and Fatah. It showed that the PLO chairman had the support of a wide majority. Also, by holding the meeting in Amman, the PLO signaled its independence from Syria, affirmed the importance of cooperation with Jordan, and strengthened its ties to the Palestinian rank and file in Jordan and the territories occupied by Israel. As summarized by Sahliyeh, convening the PNC was "a personal victory for the PLO chief and an opportunity to vindicate his policies. It also meant that Arafat continued to enjoy majority support within the Palestinian community and that his opponents were a small and isolated group."[120]

The resolutions of the Seventeenth PNC were deliberately phrased in general rather than specific terms, but they nonetheless gave Arafat the authority he needed to continue his cooperation with Jordan and Egypt. The vagueness of many formulations reflected a desire to avoid any deepening of the rift within the PLO, as well as some differences of opinion among the delegates assembled in Amman. There were also conciliatory gestures toward Damascus, with the PNC's final statement calling for improved relations with Syria on the basis of mutual respect and noninterference in one another's affairs. Overall, however, the meeting's political statement was highly favorable to Arafat and the Fatah mainstream. The authority of the PLO chairman was not reduced. The limits on Arafat's power proposed in the Aden-Algiers Agreement were ignored; on the contrary, Arafat and his supporters on the PLO Executive Committee were given new authority to make decisions on key issues without consulting the PNC in advance. Further, several of Arafat's prominent supporters in the West Bank were elected to the fourteen-member Executive Committee, not only directly enhancing the chairman's position but also signaling the growing importance to the PLO of the West Bank and Gaza, areas where support for Arafat and Fatah was particularly high.[121]

On substantive issues, the PNC communiqué called for deepening the special relationship between the PLO and Jordan and authorized Arafat to continue his dialogue with King Hussein in order to fashion a joint Jordanian-Palestinian diplomatic strategy, specifying only that Jordan and the PLO should be considered equal partners and that the PLO would not participate in any peace initiative that did not recognize the Palestinian people's right to self-determination. In the latter connection, the PNC rejected the call to endorse UN Security Council Resolution 242 that Hussein had delivered in his welcome address to the delegates. As an East Jerusalem newspaper editorialized at the time, the PNC could not possibly accept a resolution that characterizes the Palestinian problem as a refugee problem, when in reality this "is only one secondary aspect of the Palestinian question." To accept 242, the editorial continued, would be "to ignore the existence of a Palestinian people with inalienable and resolute national rights."[122] Nevertheless, while refusing to accommodate Hussein on the issue of UN 242, the Seventeenth PNC had clearly given Arafat the backing he needed to conclude an agreement with Jordan, backing it had denied him in 1983. Indeed, the newly elected Executive Committee decided at its first working session to remove all PLO institutions from Damascus and to transfer the PNC headquarters to Amman. Finally, with respect to Egypt, the PNC did not condemn Arafat's trip to Cairo, and in fact affirmed the importance of Egypt's return to the Arab fold. It also declared that "recent political developments in Egypt and its support for the Palestinian people demand that relations between the Palestinian and Egyptian peoples be strengthened."

The path to a formal agreement between Arafat and Hussein was now open, and a pact between the PLO and Jordan was accordingly concluded on February 11, 1985.[123] The agreement first endorsed a settlement based on the exchange of land for peace "as established in United Nations and Security Council resolutions," indicating that this required Israel's withdrawal from all Arab land occupied in 1967, including East Jerusalem. Despite the resolutions of the recent PNC meeting, this provision of the accord enabled Jordanian officials to assert that the PLO had now implicitly accepted UN Security Council Resolution 242, thereby satisfying a condition that the United States had imposed for a dialogue of its own with the PLO. Indeed, when Hussein traveled to Washington the following June, he declared that a historic breakthrough had been achieved, and specifically told American officials that "the Palestinians are willing to accept United Nations Security Council Resolutions 242 and 338, and the principles they contain, as the basis for a settlement."[124] At the same time, in an effort to remain within the framework of recent PNC decisions and to make fully clear that provisions of 242 describing the Palestinian problem as a refugee problem continued to be unacceptable, the February 11 agreement also proclaimed that its principles were being advanced in the spirit of the 1982 Fez Plan, and then reaffirmed the Palestinian people's inalienable right to self-determination.

The Arafat-Hussein agreement also proclaimed that Palestinian self-determination was to be exercised through the formation of a Palestinian state in the occupied territories that would be linked to the Hashemite Kingdom of Jordan in a political confederation. Specifically, it declared that "Palestinians will exercise their inalienable right to self-determination when Jordanians and Palestinians can do so within the context of an Arab confederation, to be established between the two states of Jordan and Palestine." In addition, the February 11 agreement called for peace negotiations to implement the principles it espoused, and indicated that such negotiations should be conducted under the auspices of an international conference in which the five permanent members of the UN Security Council and all parties to the conflict would participate. Finally, the accord declared that among these parties to the conflict was the Palestine Liberation Organization, the sole legitimate representative of the Palestinian people, and that the PLO would attend the international conference within a joint Jordanian-Palestinian delegation. In a subsequent clarification, it was stated that this delegation would contain an equal number of representatives from both the Jordanian government and the PLO.

Although the February 11 agreement deepened existing divisions within the PLO, it also raised hopes that the Jordanian-Palestinian diplomatic offensive which had proven elusive in 1983 might now go forward and generate momentum toward a settlement. Arafat had accepted an accord that provided for a political connection with Jordan, rather than a totally independent Palestinian state. He had also put his name to an agreement that endorsed the kind of solution to the Arab-Israeli conflict envisioned by UN 242, even if the PLO had not accepted the resolution itself. It was hoped that these concessions, which were formally approved by the PLO Executive Committee on February 20,[125] would be sufficient to elicit a positive response from the United States, or possibly even the

Israeli government led by Shimon Peres. Hussein, for his part, had made concessions, too, having accepted an agreement which affirmed that the PLO remained the sole legitimate representative of the Palestinian people, which in substance was as close to the Fez Plan as the Reagan Plan, and which specified that Jordan and the PLO would be equal partners both during and after the negotiation of a peace settlement.

The agreement between Arafat and Hussein was welcomed by most Palestinians, even though, in the judgment of some, Jordan had given too little and the PLO had given too much. Particularly disturbing to Arafat's critics was the chairman's willingness to allow Jordan to join with the PLO in representing the Palestinians during peace talks, and his agreement that Palestinian self-determination should find expression not in a fully independent state but rather in a confederation with Jordan. Nevertheless, especially in the West Bank and Gaza but to a considerable extent elsewhere as well, the consensus of the Palestinian mainstream was that these concessions were necessary to bring about Israel's withdrawal from the occupied territories. In the spring of 1985, the prevailing view thus appeared to be that the February 11 agreement deserved a chance, and that debates about its wisdom should be suspended until it was possible to determine whether or not there would be a constructive response from the United States and Israel. Expressing the view of many, an editorial in *al-Fajr Jerusalem* told readers to "wait and see if this Palestinian move is going to further the Palestinian cause."[126]

Israeli, Palestinian, and Jordanian Diplomacy

Israel was not a passive bystander while Jordan and the PLO were conducting their dialogue; the national unity government headed by Shimon Peres had spent the fall of 1984 putting a package of economic reforms in place, and by early 1985 a revival of the peace process was nearing the top of Peres's political agenda. Likud, as an equal partner in the government, was not without power, of course. For example, in cabinet negotiations concerning the construction of new settlements in the West Bank, Labor had been forced to agree in January 1985 to the erection of six additional settlements, three of which were in areas the Alignment was willing to trade for peace. Although this constituted a significant break with the intense settlement drive that had been pursued by the two previous governments, enabling Labor to assert that it had not been bested in the coalition bargaining, it was considerably less than the settlement freeze advocated by the Alignment, and this in turn led observers to wonder whether the new prime minister would be able to gain government backing for any compromise he might eventually work out in negotiations with the Arabs. But Peres told supporters that he would go to the electorate if an agreement with the Arabs was in sight, and that he was confident Labor would then be given a clear majority and an opportunity to lead the country toward peace. In the meantime, he would devote his efforts to the launching of peace talks aimed at an interim agreement consistent with the Camp David accords, an intermediate-range goal that he hoped would produce the outlines of a broader settlement he could take to the Israeli people.

Peres's vision of peace was consistent with the "Jordanian option" that Labor had championed since 1967, and in January 1985 he thus sent a message to King Hussein, indicating that Israel was prepared for negotiations based on the principle of territorial compromise as set down in United Nations Resolution 242. In sending this message, Peres went well beyond the provisions of the coalition agreement that Labor and Likud had worked out the preceding September. This agreement specified only that Israel would "call on Jordan to begin peace negotiations, in order to turn over a new leaf in the region . . . [and that] the Israeli Government will consider proposals raised by Jordan in the negotiations." Peres also signaled Hussein at this time that he was prepared to have Palestinians participate in the peace talks, although he made it clear that these could not be Palestinians who were publicly identified with the PLO.

In the weeks and months that followed, Peres followed up with numerous additional overtures to Hussein. As summarized by Samuel Lewis, "Public compliments, private emissaries and messages, consultations by American, other foreign and Palestinian intermediaries, and, according to hints in the press, secret Israeli-Jordanian encounters all played their parts." In addition, there was "a de facto freeze on new West Bank settlements, defended to suspicious Likud partners on grounds of economic stringency." Finally, "technical discussions to resolve various practical issues along the Jordan boundary, such as Yarmuk River water sharing, received more sympathetic attention from Peres than from his predecessors." All of these efforts, according to Lewis, were part of a persistent campaign "to persuade Jordan that after years of confrontation with Likud governments a wide-ranging process of negotiations, which could eventually culminate in formal peace talks, was now possible."[127]

Peres also moved at this time to improve Israel's relations with Egypt, his goal being both to thaw the "cold peace" that had characterized relations with Cairo since the Israeli invasion of Lebanon and to secure Egyptian support for peace talks dealing with the future of the West Bank and Gaza. Consistent with the Camp David accords, the negotiations envisioned by Peres would include Egyptian participation. Thus, beginning in the fall of 1984, Peres pushed for a resolution of the status of Taba, which had become one of of the most important outstanding issues between the two countries. The tiny parcel of beachfront property, located just below the Israeli city of Eilat, had been part of the Egyptian Sinai prior to 1967, but Likud-led governments had nonetheless refused to include it in the territory returned to Egypt under the Camp David accords. Now, however, at Peres's urging, previously abandoned talks addressed to the status of the disputed territory were resumed in Beersheba in January 1985. Peres also pressed the Israeli government to agree that the dispute should be submitted to international arbitration, as Egypt had demanded, even though it was not until January 1986 that Peres was finally able to persuade the inner cabinet to accept the "arbitration and normalization package" that had been proposed by Mubarak.[128] In response to Peres's efforts, and also because Israel was now beginning to withdraw its forces from Lebanon, relations with Egypt began to improve in the spring of 1985.

While Peres and other Alignment leaders were prepared to confront the Israeli right in order to move closer to an accommodation with Jordan and Egypt, they remained adamantly opposed to including the PLO in the peace process, their views in this regard differing little from those of Likud. Peres's attitude, summarized in an October 1983 newspaper article, was that "there is no greater obstacle to the solution of the Palestinian problem than the PLO itself." Had the Palestinian organization recognized the existence of Israel, abandoned terrorism, and declared its readiness for peaceful negotiations, it would immediately have been accepted as a legitimate bargaining agent, the Israeli prime minister stated. Instead, unfortunately, the PLO preferred "to remain faithful to the letter and spirit of the Palestine National Covenant, which calls for the destruction of Israel."[129] Labor had thus agreed without hesitation to an article in the September 1984 coalition agreement which stated simply and bluntly that Israel would not negotiate with the PLO.

Nor had the February 11 agreement between Arafat and Hussein changed the thinking of Peres and most other Israelis. While the Jordanian monarch was telling Americans and others that a breakthrough had been achieved, and while PLO rejectionists and even some mainstream Palestinians were criticizing Arafat for having made too many concessions, most Israelis, including the majority of those committed to territorial compromise, insisted that the PLO had not transformed itself into an acceptable negotiating partner. It had not endorsed UN 242, they pointed out, and nothing in Arafat's agreement with Hussein indicated that the PLO recognized Israel's right to exist. Indeed, the agreement did not even accept direct talks with Israel, calling rather for negotiations within the framework of an international conference. The February 11 agreement also demanded creation of an independent Palestinian state, which from Jerusalem's point of view would remain a serious threat even if linked to Jordan in a loose confederation. Finally, many Israelis charged that the PLO continued to engage in terrorism.[130] Thus, Peres pressed Hussein not only to agree to negotiations but to form a delegation which, in violation of his agreement with Arafat, would not include Palestinians who were members of the PLO.

Peres delivered a formal statement of the peace process he envisioned in an important address to the Knesset on June 10, 1985. Reporting that Israel was currently completing the withdrawal of its armed forces from Lebanon and had resumed a dialogue with Egypt after a freeze of several years, the prime minister now proposed direct negotiations, without preconditions, among "the parties interested in peace rather than the parties interested in continuing the conflict." He then suggested that negotiations be undertaken in several stages: first, continued talks between U.S. representatives, Israel, Jordan, Egypt, and Palestinians not affiliated with the PLO; second, establishment of a small Jordanian-Palestinian-Israeli team that would prepare an agenda for a Jordanian-Palestinian-Israeli summit with U.S. participation; and finally, an opening conference to initiate direct talks among all of the parties. These negotiations would include "Palestinian representatives from the territories . . . acceptable to all parties" and would be supported by the permanent members of the United Nations.

Peres restated his plan, with slight variation, in an address to the General Assembly of the United Nations on October 21, 1985. Calling upon the Palestinian people to end rejectionism, he again proposed direct negotiations without preconditions, specifying only that these talks should be based on UN resolutions 242 and 338. The object of these negotiations, he added, was to reach a peace treaty between Israel and the Arab states, as well as to resolve the Palestinian issue. Peres also stated that negotiations with Jordan should involve an Israeli delegation on the one hand and a joint Jordanian-Palestinian delegation on the other, "both comprising delegates that represent peace, not terror."

Even before Peres's address to the Knesset in June, Israel, Jordan, the PLO, Egypt, and the United States were all engaged in active diplomatic maneuvers generated by the Arafat-Hussein agreement on the one hand and the initiatives of Shimon Peres on the other. Egypt and Jordan were urging the PLO to accept UN 242 as the price to be paid for a substantive dialogue with the United States and subsequent entry into the peace process. At the same time, Mubarak was telling the Israelis that the PLO should be included in West Bank and Gaza negotiations, thereby strengthening Arafat's position in his own bargaining with Jordan; and Hussein was telling Washington that Arafat and Fatah were ready to accept 242 and further distance themselves from PLO radicals, but given the concessions they had already made and the divisions within Palestinian ranks, they could not do so without a clear indication that there would be a meaningful *quid pro quo*. Most important, perhaps, Israel and the United States were pressing Jordan to name an acceptable Jordanian-Palestinian delegation for possible peace talks, stressing to Hussein that Peres and the Alignment needed a positive Arab response to fend off their own increasingly powerful hard-line critics.

Many months were devoted to tedious and exhausting negotiations over the Palestinians to be included in a joint Jordanian-Palestinian negotiating team. Unable to satisfy the conflicting demands of Israel and the PLO, Hussein repeatedly delayed naming such a delegation, even after Washington and Israel suggested that independents belonging to the PNC but not formally affiliated with the PLO might be acceptable.[131] In July, the East Jerusalem newspaper *al-Quds* published the names that Hussein had finally submitted, but all of these names were subsequently rejected by Peres on the grounds that they were too close to the PLO. Peres later reversed himself, however, approving two residents of the occupied territories that had been proposed by Hussein and who were also acceptable to the PLO. The two were Hanna Siniora, a resident of East Jerusalem and the editor of *al-Fajr*, and Fayez Abu Rahmeh, a prominent lawyer from Gaza. Interviewed about their selection by Jordan and the PLO and their acceptance by Israel, Siniora said that he may have been chosen because Peres was under pressure from his coalition partners to approve only Palestinians from the occupied territories, and also because of his own belief that an end to Israeli occupation could be achieved only by political means and not through armed struggle. Asked whether he considered himself a member of the PLO, Siniora replied, "No Palestinian in the occupied territories can say that he is a member of the PLO. If I acknowledged being a member of the PLO, I might go to jail. But as a Palestinian journalist, I do not see any difference between the PLO and the Palestinian people. All Palestinians consider the PLO to be their representative."[132] Similar comments were made by Abu Rahmeh, who stated, "The PLO is the sole legitimate representative of the Palestinian people. Membership is not needed."[133]

Even with some agreement on the composition of the Jordanian-Palestinian delegation, both additional procedural issues and intervening political events prevented any real progress toward peace talks during the remainder of 1985 or the first part of 1986. An important procedural problem was a stalemate about the framework for discussions. Whereas both Israel and the U.S. adamantly refused to hold negotiations within the framework of an international conference, Jordan and the PLO refused the direct talks upon which Israel and the U.S. insisted. A possible compromise explored during this period involved holding "preliminary and informal" talks between the U.S. administration and a delegation of Jordanians and Palestinians acceptable to Jerusalem, but in the end this proved inadequate since the U.S. would meet with such a delegation only if it were agreed that direct negotiations with Israel would follow.

The possibility of reaching agreement was also seriously undermined by a series of events in the fall of 1985 that began with an Israeli air raid on PLO headquarters in Tunisia on October 1. IDF planes hit their target with accuracy, but in addition to damaging several buildings used by the PLO, the strike also killed approximately sixty persons and wounded many more, some of them Tunisian civilians. Jerusalem insisted that the operation had been undertaken in retaliation for PLO-instigated terrorism in the occupied territories and elsewhere, and particularly for a Palestinian attack in September that had killed three Israelis in Larnaca, Cyprus. There were conflicting reports about whether the Israelis killed in Larnaca were tourists or secret service agents, and also about whether the attack had been carried out by dissident Palestinians seeking to undermine the peace process or by a special PLO force under Arafat's control, although the PLO chairman himself condemned the operation and disavowed any connection with it. In any event, Israel responded with the raid on Tunis, the strike having been approved by all members of the inner cabinet except Ezer Weizman; and this in turn brought condemnations in most world capitals, Washington being a notable exception, and an outpouring of anger in much of the Arab world. In Egypt, for example, there were anti-Israel demonstrations, and the Mubarak government canceled a negotiating session devoted to the Taba dispute that had been scheduled to begin in Cairo on October 1. There were also protests and denunciations by Palestinians in the occupied territories, although one of the men named to the joint Jordanian-Palestinian delegation stated that he would not allow events to prevent him from proceeding with peace efforts.

Relations between Israel and Egypt were further strained when an Egyptian border guard shot and killed seven Israeli tourists at Ras Burqa in Sinai four days later. Egyptian authorities strongly denounced the incident, calling it the solitary act of an individual who had gone berserk and insisting that it was unrelated to external political developments. They also reported that the border guard, Suleiman Khater, had disarmed four other Egyptian policemen and killed one Egyptian officer before firing on the Israelis. Khater himself was promptly arrested and subsequently tried and sentenced to death by a military court. Yet Israelis were angered and deeply disturbed by the incident, and their concern was heightened by the fact that Khater became an instant folk hero to many Egyptians, some apparently judging his action to be fair revenge for the raid on the PLO headquarters in Tunisia.[134] At the time of the incident, partially in response to pressure from his coalition partners in Likud, Peres declared that efforts to settle the Taba dispute would not go forward until there had been a full investigation of the Ras Burqa affair.

There was also Palestinian anger at this time, with protests in the West Bank and Gaza following the Israeli raid on Tunis and a major terrorist episode shortly thereafter. On October 7, declaring that they were taking revenge for the IDF strike, four members of a small pro-Arafat faction of the PLO, the Palestine Liberation Front, hijacked an Italian cruise ship, the *Achille Lauro*. The hijackers demanded the release of a number of Palestinian prisoners held in Israeli jails and demonstrated that they were serious by killing an elderly American tourist and throwing his body overboard. While this brought scathing denunciations of the PLO from both Israelis and Americans, the denouement of the affair also led to important strains in the relationship between Egypt and the United States. With the terrorists still in control of the *Achille Lauro*, the Egyptian government began negotiations to free the passengers and persuaded the gunmen to surrender to Egyptian authorities at Port Said in return for safe passage to Tunis. According to Egyptian and Palestinian sources, the hijackers were to be turned over to the PLO, which had condemned the attack and promised to investigate and punish those responsible. The Egypt Air plane carrying the four Palestinians to Tunis was intercepted by American fighter aircraft, however, and forced to land at a NATO base in Sicily, whereupon Egypt complained that it had been betrayed and humiliated by the very government it was trying to assist. Also fueling the tension between Washington and Cairo were American boasts about the decisive action it had taken to combat terrorism. The Egyptian media complained of American arrogance, piracy, and ingratitude, and several popular demonstrations called for abrogation of the Camp David accords.[135]

In the wake of these developments, both Hussein and Arafat faced difficult dilemmas and as a result appeared indecisive. With Israel more adamant than ever in its refusal to accept the PLO as a negotiating partner, Jerusalem and Washington put additional pressure on Jordan to break with Arafat and enter negotiations alone. For example, three days before Peres presented his peace plan to the UN General Assembly, the Israeli Foreign Ministry issued a white paper charging that the PLO had planned or carried out 380 terrorist attacks since signing the February 11 agreement; and two days after Peres's address to the UN, the U.S. declared that it would postpone a promised arms sale to Jordan unless Amman began "direct and meaningful" peace talks with Israel. In addition, according to press reports about this time, Peres had recently urged the same course on Hussein during a secret meeting with the king in London. Yet the Jordanian monarch judged himself too vulnerable to begin peace talks without the participation of credible and legitimate Palestinian representatives and so increased his own pressure on the PLO, calling on the Palestinian organization to accept UN 242 and issue a clear denunciation of terrorism.

On the Palestinian side, Arafat and his supporters worried that Jordan, despite its vulnerability, might decide to go ahead without them. This would marginalize the PLO and, from their perspective, deny the Palestinian people any benefit from the diplomatic opening that Arafat himself had helped to create. Yet most Palestinians remained wary of Hussein and were fearful that the compromises he was urging on them would undermine the PLO's role as their sole legitimate representative. Even among Arafat supporters and moderates in the West Bank and Gaza, Peres's plan was thus greeted with near-unanimous rejection and resolute affirmations that "there is absolutely no substitute for the PLO."[136]

The political differences between Jordan and the PLO, as well as the cross-pressures on both Hussein and Arafat, were reflected particularly clearly in a failed attempt by the Jordanian monarch, still in October, to arrange for the joint Jordanian-Palestinian delegation to meet with the British foreign secretary in London. Hussein had hoped this would be a major step in legitimizing PLO participation in the peace process and, coordinating his efforts with Arafat, he had arranged with the British for the two Palestinian members of the delegation to sign a statement renouncing terrorism and recognizing Israel's right to exist as a precondition for the meeting. The Palestinians refused to sign the statement, how-

ever, insisting they had not seen it before and could not endorse it unless authorized to do so by the PLO Executive Committee, whereupon the foreign secretary
canceled the meeting. A planned meeting between European Community officials and the Jordanian-Palestinian delegation was subsequently canceled as well.

The failure of this initiative was a severe embarrassment for Hussein and
added greatly to the tension between Arafat and the king. In addition, in the
judgment of an objective Palestinian scholar, the PLO had missed an important
opportunity "that would have provided it with British and West European diplomatic backing, which was urgently needed to neutralize Israel's relentless efforts to discredit the organization."[137] Further, coming in the aftermath of the
Achille Lauro affair, this scholar notes that failure to meet with the British foreign secretary also led the pragmatic Palestinian elite in the West Bank and Gaza,
while continuing to support the PLO, to cease giving "automatic and unconditional approval" to what they regarded as errors in judgment by the PLO leadership.[138]

Responding to charges of indecisiveness and poor judgment, Arafat and the
PLO struggled to repair the political damage their cause had recently sustained,
including both setbacks resulting from missed diplomatic opportunities and accusations of support for terrorism on the one hand and the strains these developments had produced in the PLO's relations with Jordan and Egypt on the other.
Ten days after cancellation of the meeting with the British foreign secretary,
Hanna Siniora, editor of *al-Fajr* and one of the Palestinian members of the Jordanian-Palestinian delegation, traveled to Amman in the hope of repairing some
of the damage in relations between Jordan and the Palestinians. Arafat and Hussein, accompanied by their aides, met a few days later to discuss further the future of their relationship, with the PLO promising that it would avoid repetition
of incidents such as the *Achille Lauro* hijacking or "any act that would hurt the
11 February agreement."[139] Arafat traveled to Cairo the following week, seeking
to heal the rift with Egypt that had been caused by the *Achille Lauro* affair, and
after being pressed by Mubarak to remove the ambiguities in his position and
demonstrate that the PLO would be a responsible negotiating partner, the Palestinian leader delivered a carefully worded statement on terrorism over Egyptian
Radio.[140]

Despite these efforts, it was beginning to appear that the coordinated diplomacy of Hussein and Arafat might not last much longer. Although denied by
both parties, there were reports at this time that the king was secretly making
arrangements with the Israelis for joint control of the West Bank in the event of
a settlement. More clear cut was the dramatic improvement in relations between
Jordan and Syria. As discussed, the Damascus regime had in recent years devoted
considerable energy to undermining Arafat's leadership of the PLO. Assad had
also opposed the February 11 agreement; and now, seeing it begin to come apart,
he worked to establish an alliance with the government in Amman in order to

exert additional pressure for a break between Jordan and the PLO. Assad and Hussein issued a joint statement in response to Peres's address to the United Nations, declaring that their countries would not accept a "partial and unilateral" settlement and affirming that they would seek peace within the framework of the plan adopted at the 1982 Arab League summit in Fez. The two leaders also announced that diplomatic relations between their two countries, suspended for four years, would soon be reestablished, and an exchange of ambassadors indeed took place in January 1986.

Hussein made one final attempt to achieve progress on the basis of the February 11 agreement, reiterating his call to the PLO to endorse UN 242 and seeking to arrange for the United States to accept PLO participation in peace negotiations in return. Arafat and other senior PLO officials held intensive discussions with Hussein during the last five days of January 1986, this being the first time that Arafat and the king had met in more than three months, and at the conclusion of these talks the Palestinians announced that the PLO would accept UN 242 and 338 on two conditions. First, the U.S. would have to guarantee that this would enable the PLO to participate in a Middle East peace conference. Second, and even more important, the U.S. would have to declare its recognition of the Palestinian people's right to self-determination within the context of a Jordanian-Palestinian confederation, thereby enabling the PLO to endorse the land-for-peace formula in UN 242 without agreeing that the question of Palestine could be understood and addressed as a refugee problem.

To offer additional evidence that the Palestinian organization was prepared to play its part in the bargain being put together by Hussein, PLO officials in Amman also announced that they were now willing to endorse the statement renouncing terrorism and recognizing Israel's right to exist that had earlier been proposed as a precondition for meeting with the British foreign secretary. They explained that this was not so much a change of policy as a case of the PLO receiving in return something much more substantial than a British handshake with individual Palestinians. In any event, with the PLO apparently on board, Hussein let the Americans know that Jordan would not enter the peace process alone, and he urged them to provide the Palestinians with the required guarantees.

While the Americans were willing to move some distance toward an accommodation with the PLO, they were unwilling to issue a clear statement recognizing the Palestinian people's right to self-determination, and this caused Hussein's effort to fall apart. Significantly, the U.S. dropped its objections to the Jordanian-Palestinian proposal that negotiations be conducted within the framework of an international conference attended by the permanent members of the UN Security Council. In addition, although it remained unclear whether the U.S. would be able to persuade Israel to attend such a conference, with or without a PLO presence, the Americans promised that they would invite the PLO to participate in the international peace conference once the Palestinian organization had accepted UN 242 and 338. Hussein obtained a written statement to this effect and, judging this to be a major accomplishment, he told Arafat that this was an acceptable compromise and urged him not to miss this opportunity for a diplomatic breakthrough. But the PLO leader insisted that he could not go forward unless the U.S. also recognized the Palestinians' right to self-determination, and when the king took this response to the Americans he was told that Washington was unwilling to go beyond inviting the PLO to an international conference, and that further discussion of the subject would be futile. Arafat then stated that he needed more time to discuss the matter with other PLO leaders, and he left Amman for Cairo.

On February 19, 1986, as the Israelis looked on with satisfaction, a weary and frustrated Hussein delivered an emotional three-hour radio and television address in which he blamed Arafat for the failure to work out an agreement with the Americans and suspended all further political coordination with the PLO.[141] The king reviewed Jordanian diplomatic efforts to achieve a just peace and insisted that he had labored diligently and in good faith to normalize American-Palestinian relations. He added that PLO leaders had in fact acknowledged that his "extraordinary effort" had "caused a change in the U.S. position," which made their continuing hesitation and refusal to accept UN 242 all the more problematic. But since this was the case, Hussein stated that he had no choice but to discontinue political coordination with the PLO and accept the fact that another chapter in the search for peace had come to an end, that "an extremely important and significant round of Jordanian-Palestinian action was terminated—after a full year of serious and persistent efforts to transform the PLO's role." Although the king's speech focused on the hesitation of the PLO, he privately placed much of the blame on Washington as well, noting that the U.S. had chosen not to accept an offer from the PLO that may have fallen short in terms of political symbolism but which in fact gave the Americans virtually all of what they had demanded from a substantive point of view.

Palestinian reaction to the suspension of Jordan-PLO coordination included strong criticism of both Hussein and the United States. The king had suggested in his speech that Palestinians in the occupied territories and elsewhere might now dissociate themselves from the PLO and join with Jordan in seeking progress toward peace, and a few citizens' delegations from the West Bank did indeed travel to Amman at this time in order to express support for the Jordanian monarch. The members of these delegations were strongly criticized upon their return, however, and, more generally, it seemed clear that only a handful of Palestinians would respond positively to Hussein's appeal. Palestinians agreed that the king had been correct in identifying the PLO's refusal to endorse UN 242 as the crux of the problem. But most saw no reason why the PLO should be blamed for this, since both Hussein and the United States fully understood that the Palestinian position did not reflect a refusal to recognize Israel's right to exist or to accept the principle of land for peace. In the spring of 1986, these sentiments were reflected in the statements of prominent Palestinians in the West Bank and Gaza, and also in the local press. As expressed by the editor of *al-Shaab*, for example, "King Hussein blames the PLO because it refused to commit suicide instead of blaming the U.S. which wants to kill the PLO. . . . For the PLO, UN 242 means political liquidation."[142] A statement issued by the PLO Executive Committee in March charged that the United States had attempted to delude the Palestinian people and, in more moderate language, expressed deep regret that Hussein had chosen to blame the PLO when actually the U.S. was responsible for the failure to reach an agreement.

Anger at Hussein and support for Arafat and the PLO were visible not only among prominent political figures but also among the population at large in the West Bank and Gaza. For example, the assassination in March 1986 of Zaafer al-Masri, the Israeli-appointed mayor of Nablus, offered an opportunity to gauge popular sentiments. Al-Masri's appointment had been approved by the PLO, as well as Jordan; and his death, apparently at the hands of Syria-based Palestinian rejectionists, was followed by widespread demonstrations in support of nationalist aspirations. Thousands of Palestinians from throughout the territories marched in al-Masri's funeral procession, which was characterized by a mixture of grief and political militancy and which provided residents of the West Bank and Gaza with an occasion to express both their support for Palestinian self-determination and their opposition to Israeli rule. In addition, there were expressions of militant opposition to King Hussein of Jordan and to programs designed to increase Jordanian influence in the occupied territories, with young men chanting slogans such as "Down with King Hussein" and "Hussein is deceitful."

A few months later, in the summer of 1986, a public opinion poll conducted by a Palestinian political scientist provided broader and more systematic evidence for these clearly visible tendencies. Based on face-to-face interviews with 1,024 respondents in the West Bank and Gaza, the survey found that 93.5 percent of those interviewed declared the PLO to be the sole legitimate representative of the Palestinian people, whereas only 1 percent considered themselves to be represented by Jordan and only 3.4 percent selected Hussein as their preferred political leader. Most also agreed with Arafat and the PLO in refusing to endorse UN 242. Only 16.8 percent judged the resolution to be a satisfactory basis for resolving the Palestinian problem, although, significantly, 90.2 percent of those who thought otherwise said they opposed the resolution not because it recognizes Israel but because it ignores Palestinian rights. Turning to the breakdown of political coordination between Jordan and the PLO, only 5.3 percent judged Arafat to be primarily responsible. On the other hand, respondents were slightly more likely to blame the United States than Hussein. Also, more generally, only 3.4 percent judged that the U.S. was playing a positive role in Middle East peacemaking efforts.[143]

Israeli opinion welcomed Hussein's break with the PLO, and Shimon Peres hoped that it would now be possible for Jerusalem and Amman to come to some agreement. Moreover, Hussein did announce an ambitious five-year development plan for the occupied territories in August 1986; and while it was unlikely that much of the promised $1.5 billion in investment funds would actually materialize, there were at least some administrative moves that would benefit Palestinian inhabitants while simultaneously providing a basis for Israeli-Jordanian cooperation. For example, Amman and Jerusalem agreed to reopen the Nablus branch of the Cairo-Amman Bank which, like other Arab banks in the occupied territories, had been closed since 1967.

Nevertheless, despite these initiatives designed to deepen Hashemite involvement in the occupied territories, Peres was unable to fashion any political agreement with Hussein or to seriously advance the peace process by finding a mechanism for implementing the Jordanian solution championed by Labor. It is possible that the king would have been more responsive to Peres's calls for direct negotiations had a change of prime minister under the rotation agreement of Israel's national unity government not been fast approaching, with Yitzhak Shamir of Likud scheduled to replace Peres in October. But in fact this probably would not have made much difference, since Hussein apparently believed that even with an agreement to take to the Israeli electorate, Peres was unlikely to receive enough support to negotiate his country's withdrawal from the West Bank and Gaza. Thus, as summarized by Lewis, "The risks for Hussein exceeded the possible benefits," and "the Jordanian king decided to play for the longer run."[144] In the short term, he limited his goals to strengthening relations with Syria, defending himself from PLO criticism, and above all working for stability in the occupied territories in order to reduce tensions that might spill over into Jordan and undermine his own regime.

With his tenure as prime minister coming to an end, Peres explored other options for a diplomatic breakthrough and eagerly accepted an invitation in July to visit King Hassan in Ifrane, Morocco. Arrangements for Peres's visit were worked out on July 11 during a secret meeting in Paris between Moroccan and Israeli officials, and ten days later the Israeli prime minister and his party arrived in Ifrane. It is notable that Hassan had consulted with other Arab actors about receiving Peres. At an Arab League summit in March 1986, he had recommended exploring Israeli willingness to negotiate on the basis of the Fez Plan, and he had subsequently contacted key Arab states about his own intention to do this. It is also significant that moderate Arab leaders reacted with comparative restraint to the Hassan-Peres summit. Indeed, Saudi Arabia permitted Hassan's forty-five-minute speech to his countrymen about the meeting to be broadcast live in that country as well. Thus, potentially at least, Peres's visit with the Moroccan monarch would enable him to tell the Israeli electorate with more credibility that Arab leaders will respond to moderation on the part of the Jewish state, and that Labor's advocacy of territorial compromise in fact holds promise for movement toward peace.

But there was no agreement in Ifrane on a formula to advance the peace process, leaving Peres without the diplomatic breakthrough he had sought. Indeed, since the meeting in Morocco showed how great remained the distance between Arab and Israeli leaders committed to compromise, there was even a danger that Peres's trip would be counterproductive, reinforcing the belief of some Israelis that peace at an acceptable price was not an option after all. The unresolved issues, once again, were the Palestinian problem and the future of the occupied territories, which Hassan insisted upon making the focus of his substantive conversations with Peres. Specifically, the king told Peres that he had two questions to ask. First, in return for peace with the Arab world, would Israel agree to withdraw from all Arab territories captured in the 1967 War? Second, would the Israeli government agree to negotiate with the Palestine Liberation Organization? By asking these questions, Hassan placed his dialogue with Peres squarely within the framework of the Fez Plan, explicitly stating that recognition of the Palestinians' right to self-determination and acceptance of the PLO as their sole legitimate representative was the price Israel must pay for peace with the Arab world.

Peres, for his part, was compelled to answer Hassan's inquiries in the negative, thereby precluding any breakthrough that might have led to a substantive agreement between the two leaders. "How could it have been otherwise," a veteran Israeli journalist asked rhetorically: "Could Peres, without cabinet consultation, without party approval, without the presence of a legal advisor or non-partisan senior government official, and without any national mandate, have committed Israel to any of the basic assumptions of the Fez Plan—direct negotiations with the PLO; a pre-commitment to return all of the territories; the creation of an independent Palestinian state; and the renegotiation of the status of Jerusalem?"[145] Thus, as the Hassan-Peres talks ended with only a short communiqué summarizing the disagreement between the two leaders, it was clear that any benefits to be derived from the meeting would have to come in the future.

Peres's last hope for a diplomatic coup lay with Egypt, and the Israeli prime minister accordingly traveled to Alexandria for a summit meeting with Hosni Mubarak in September, only a month before he was scheduled to relinquish the premiership to Yitzhak Shamir. It was the first meeting between top Israeli and Egyptian leaders in five years, Mubarak having rejected Peres's previous requests for a summit because of the situation in Lebanon and the Taba dispute. Now, however, with the IDF out of most of Lebanon and agreement to submit the Taba matter to arbitration, Mubarak not only met with Peres but agreed that an Egyptian ambassador, absent since 1982, would return to Tel Aviv. The declaration issued by the two leaders at the conclusion of the twenty-four-hour Alexandria summit was limited to the expression of general principles but nonetheless encouraging. It proclaimed that the meeting marked a new era in bilateral relations between Egypt and Israel,[146] as well as in the search for a just and comprehensive peace in the Middle East. It also affirmed that 1987 would be a year of negotiations for peace and pledged that "President Mubarak and Prime Minister Peres, together with other concerned parties, will continue their efforts toward a solution of the Palestinian problem in all its aspects and the establishment of a comprehensive peace in the region."

The Peres-Mubarak summit did not lead to any important developments with respect to the Palestinian problem, but it did enable the Israeli prime minister to complete his term of office with a sense of accomplishment. A foundation had been laid for ending the cold peace with Egypt, and this was a major foreign-policy achievement for which Peres could justifiably take credit. Peres's meeting with King Hassan of Morocco, even though it yielded no tangible results, enabled the outgoing prime minister to assert that he had also generated momentum in the pursuit of a wider peace. He could claim a foreign-policy victory in Sub-Saharan Africa, too, having traveled to Cameroon in August to attend ceremonies marking the reestablishment of diplomatic relations between that country and Israel.

While Israelis might disagree about the importance of these and other accomplishments, Alignment supporters insisted that progress had been made in addressing problems on the country's foreign-policy agenda, and Peres himself, who would become foreign minister under the rotation with Shamir, pledged to continue his pursuit of peace and threatened that Labor would pull out of the coalition and bring down the government if Likud tried to prevent him from doing so. It is in the context of this pledge that Peres, as foreign minister, held a secret meeting with King Hussein in London in April 1987. Although the agreement reached at this meeting for the most part restated general principles that had already been accepted, such as negotiations based on UN 242 and 338 between Israel and a joint Jordanian-Palestinian delegation, it did record Peres's willingness for peace talks to be conducted within the framework of an international conference convened under United Nations auspices.[147]

In the end, however, for all his efforts, Peres fared no better than Arafat or Hussein in generating movement toward a solution to the Palestinian problem or the status of the occupied territories. Neither his numerous overtures to the Jordanian monarch, his political coordination with Washington, nor even his willingness to accept a Jordanian-Palestinian delegation that contained men from the West Bank and Gaza who supported the PLO produced the breakthrough for which he had tirelessly worked. Some of Peres's problems were undoubtedly the result of constraints imposed by his partners in the national unity government. As expressed by Samuel Lewis, who served as U.S. ambassador to Israel during this period, the diplomatic impasse confronting Israel and the Palestinians "required political daring well beyond the capabilities of any Labor Party leader of a national unity government." In addition, as was precisely the case with Hussein and Arafat as well, the limitations on Peres's accomplishments may also reflect the fact that he is a man of caution and a political survivor rather than a man of flare with an inclination toward bold initiatives. "Talented though he is," according to Lewis, "Peres is not a man to risk everything on one throw of the dice." Neither is the king of Jordan, which is "why they have survived so long in their respective jungles,"[148] and the same certainly applies to Arafat. In any event, whatever the relative weight of these and other explanatory factors, Peres was no more able or willing than the Jordanian monarch or the chairman of the PLO to make the radical moves that would have been necessary to break the stalemate that had settled over Arab-Israeli diplomacy addressed to the Palestinian problem.

Deepening Anger in the Occupied Territories

With Arafat on the defensive and at least temporarily excluded from the diplomatic mainstream, and with a cautious and wary Hussein now refusing to be drawn into any ambitious diplomatic initiatives, Peres's surrender of the Israeli premiership to Yitzhak Shamir of Likud in October 1986 brought to a disappointing conclusion the chapter in Middle East diplomacy that had opened when Ronald Reagan presented his peace plan in September 1982. While there had been some narrowing of the political and ideological distance between various interested parties, four years of active American, Arab, Jordanian-Palestinian, and Israeli diplomatic efforts had been unable even to get peace negotiations started. Although many observers perceived a genuine sense of urgency, and while Arafat, Hussein, and Peres had all labored tirelessly and with sincere dedication from their respective and differing perspectives, none of the various initiatives, plans, dialogues, and agreements of the preceding four years had produced a formula for peace acceptable to all major parties. The failed diplomacy of this period thus left knowledgeable observers in the region and elsewhere deeply worried. Israeli and Arab advocates of compromise had had their moment and, unable to achieve a breakthrough, they would in the future find it increasingly difficult to fend off hard-line critics who had insisted all along that the other side was not seriously interested in a just and lasting peace.

Four years of diplomacy also had done nothing to improve the situation on the ground in the occupied territories, where Israel's settlement drive continued unabated, and where violent confrontations between Israelis and Palestinians had become so common that they almost ceased to be newsworthy. In the spring of 1987, for example, there was a spiral of violence that began when a petrol bomb thrown at an Israeli vehicle in the West Bank town of Qalqilya resulted in the death of a Jewish woman. Settlers took revenge by carrying out a rampage through the town, breaking windows and uprooting trees in what the *Jerusalem Post* described as a "vigilante orgy."[149] In the weeks that followed, there were additional raids by Jewish settlers and numerous clashes between stone-throwing Palestinian youths and Israeli soldiers. Palestinian agitation was in one sense a manifestation of growing isolation among West Bank and Gaza residents, who were now without any hope that diplomatic efforts might bring movement toward the realization of their national aspirations. In addition, however, and in a much more immediate sense, tensions and unrest were a response not only to drift, stalemate, and failed diplomacy in the international arena, but also to the active advance of Israel's presence in the occupied territories and to resultant changes in the demographic and political circumstances of the West Bank and Gaza.

Although the construction of new settlements had slowed after the 1984 Israeli elections, the size and population of existing settlements continued to grow, as a result of both government-supported activity in the West Bank and Gaza and efforts by Gush Emunim and the private settler movement. The number of Jewish settlers in the occupied territories stood at almost 60,000 at the time of the rotation between Peres and Shamir, whereas it had been about 20,000 in the fall of 1982 and about 35,000 when the national unity government was elected in July 1984. These figures do not include East Jerusalem. Meron Benvenisti, an Israeli analyst whose West Bank Data Project is considered the most reliable source of information about the occupation, described the situation at the time of the rotation as follows: "All forces operative on the ground since Begin assumed power in 1977 have continued to operate with tremendous drive under Peres. In the last two years the government has spent $300 million in order to advance Israeli interests in the territories. We are not only talking about settlements but perhaps even more so about infrastructure."[150] Not surprisingly, settlement activity also continued at a rapid pace following Shamir's return to the premiership. By early 1988, there were approximately 64,000 Israelis living in 125 Jewish communities in the West Bank and another 2,600 living in 18 Jewish settlements in Gaza. The magnitude and distribution of both the Arab and Jewish populations of the territories at this time are shown in Maps 10.1 and 10.2.

Equally significant, the replacement of Likud's Moshe Arens by Labor's Yitzhak Rabin as minister of defense had not brought any reduction in the intensity of efforts by the Israeli military administration to suppress Palestinian nationalism in the occupied territories. On the contrary, even though he shared the willingness of his party to exchange land for peace, Rabin had almost immediately established himself as a tough-minded guarantor of order in the West Bank and Gaza. Palestinian universities were frequently closed, for example, on the grounds that instead of pursuing their education, students were engaging in political activities and organizing opposition to the occupation. Other Israeli actions, which by summer 1985 were routinely described as an "iron fist" policy, included deportations, press censorship, and such forms of collective punishment as curfews and the demolition of homes.

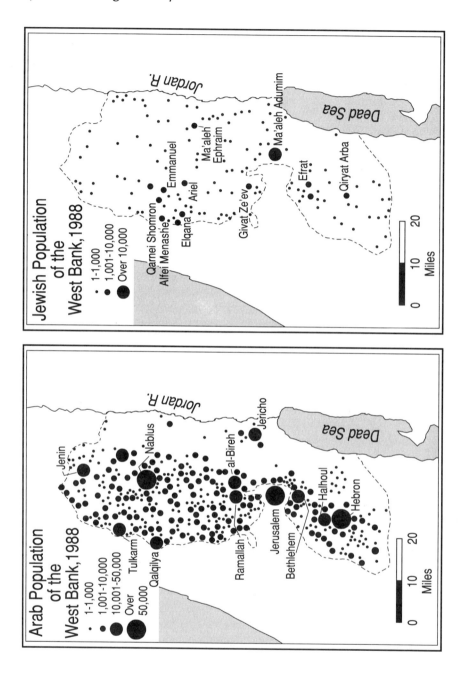

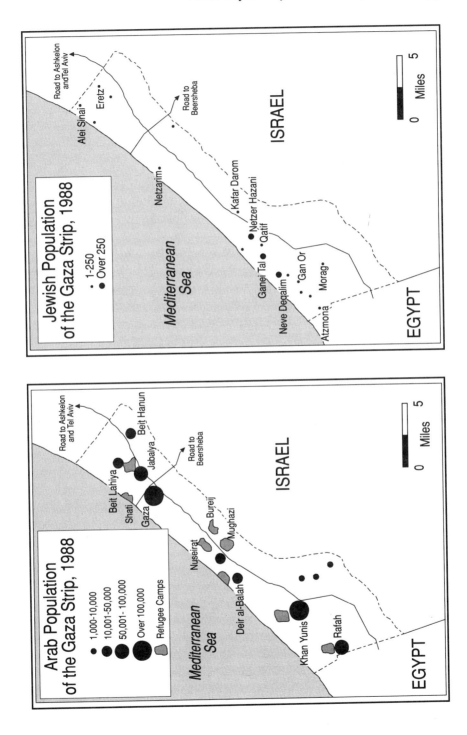

Measures of control became even harsher in the spring of 1986, with some attributing this to a tacit understanding reached between Jerusalem and Amman after the collapse of political coordination between Jordan and the PLO.[151] In fact, in the opinion of a number of observers, among them Israelis associated with the peace camp, Rabin's rule of the territories was actually more oppressive than that of his predecessors from Likud, including Sharon as well as Arens, and was itself a cause of heightened tension among Palestinians in the West Bank and Gaza.[152] Thus, overall, in the judgment once again of Benvenisti, both the steady increase in the number of Jewish settlers and the harsh mechanisms of control employed by the Israeli military administration meant that "nothing has changed in the running of the occupied territories since Peres came in except the style of the announcements. . . . The occupation is all-pervasive and quasi-permanent."[153]

Provocative and confrontational activities organized by the increasingly emboldened Israeli settler movement put yet additional pressure on Palestinians in the occupied territories. For example, as noted, Jewish settlers in the West Bank carried out raids and demonstrations in the spring of 1987, smashing bottles, overturning garbage bins, and sometimes breaking windows and uprooting trees as they marched through several Arab towns. Many of these vigilante efforts were led by Gush Emunim's secretary-general, Daniella Weiss, and in the editorial judgment of the *Jerusalem Post* their purpose was "to coerce the military authorities . . . into putting the screws on the local Arab population so painfully that they would either meekly subject themselves to Israel's rule forever—or get out."[154] Some segments of the settler movement criticized the rampages of Weiss and others, saying that these activities created an image problem for Gush Emunim and, more important, that they produced hysteria which served no useful purpose. Weiss and like-minded settlers responded that efforts to intimidate the local Arab population would be unnecessary if the government and the army would ensure the safety of Jews living in the West Bank and Gaza. None of these debates made much difference to Palestinians, however, who found themselves under attack from yet another quarter as settler violence against Arab towns and refugee camps continued during 1987.

All of this produced a steadily deteriorating and increasingly hopeless situation from the viewpoint of the 1.5 or 1.6 million Palestinians residing in the West Bank and Gaza. Under pressure in many aspects of their daily lives, and in the absence of any prospect that diplomatic efforts by either the PLO, Jordan, or Israeli advocates of territorial compromise would bring an end to the occupation of their homeland, these Palestinians were searching in the waning months of 1986 and in 1987 for ways to resist the expansionist forces within Israel.

Some Palestinians were joining militant Islamic groups in order to express their anger, and in the hope that the growing Islamist movement in the West Bank and Gaza would be able to slow the Jewish state's drive into these territories. Adherents of these groups drew inspiration from the 1979 Islamic revolution in Iran, and from the campaign that had been waged by militant Islamic groups in Lebanon against IDF forces in that country. In addition, the organizational efforts of Muslim activists in the West Bank and Gaza, particularly the Muslim Brotherhood and the Islamic Liberation Party, had benefited a few years earlier from the relative tolerance of Israeli authorities. Especially in 1979 and 1980, before turning their attention to the village leagues and before the war in Lebanon, some Israeli leaders had seen the Islamic trend as a potential counterweight to the PLO and as a useful mechanism for increasing the division in Palestinian ranks.[155] Jordan, too, had pursued this strategy, channeling resources to Islamic groups in the hope of enhancing its own influence in the territories.

Although a response not only to local grievances and opportunities but also to broader political and ideological trends, the Islamist movement had thus assumed significant proportions by 1986 or 1987, especially in Gaza but to a considerable extent in the West Bank as well. The public opinion survey carried out in the occupied territories in the summer of 1986, for example, reported that 26.5 percent of those interviewed said that if a Palestinian state was established, it should be based on Islamic law. The only political formula selected more often was "a state based on Arab nationalism and Islam," which was preferred by 29.6 percent. Only 10.4 percent, by contrast, favored the establishment of a "democratic and secular" state.[156] A Palestinian journalistic investigation published a year later, in July 1987, reported similar findings, concluding, "It is impossible to ignore the political weight of the Islamic student blocs at local universities and academic institutions, and in charitable and other societies in the towns, villages and camps of the West Bank and Gaza Strip."[157]

There was diversity in the political stands of various Islamist movements and their followers. Also, the growing strength of these movements could not be understood without reference to the ideological currents that had been fueling an Islamic resurgence throughout the Arab and Muslim world for almost two decades. Nevertheless, frustration and anger over the deteriorating circumstances of Palestinians in the West Bank and Gaza, as well as the apparent inability of Palestinian and Arab leaders who do not identify with Islam to work effectively for an end to Israeli occupation, contributed significantly to the growth of Islamic militancy in the territories and made religion an increasingly important framework for thinking about and expressing opposition to Israeli rule.

Whether under the banner of Islam or, as was more common, within the framework of mainstream Palestinian nationalism, the inhabitants of the West Bank and Gaza were seeking to be a force for change, to identify and pursue a course of action that would be effective in halting, or at least slowing, Israel's drive into the territories. They were thus continuing to stage strikes and protest demonstrations, hoping on the one hand to discourage Israelis from settling in the occupied territories, and on the other to draw world attention to the annexationist actions of the Jewish state. It remained to be seen whether these efforts would be effective, however, or whether they could even be sustained. Noting that the inhabitants of the territories bore signs of physical and psychological exhaustion in the mid-1980s, some observers wondered whether Israel's employment of school closings, censorship, and collective punishment, as well as the dissolution of Palestinian political institutions and the use of force to control demonstrations, would not succeed in undermining the Palestinians' capacity to resist. But while such assessments were plausible enough in 1986 and 1987, the world was soon to discover that these analyses had seriously underestimated the political will of West Bank and Gaza residents. At the end of 1987, at a moment in time when it appeared that events had conspired to leave these Palestinians on their own to face those in the Jewish state dedicated to permanent control of their homeland, their anger and determination burst forth in a way that had the potential to transform the political equation in the Israeli-Palestinian conflict more profoundly than had any series of events since the Camp David accords, or possibly even since the war of June 1967.

11 | The Intifada and Beyond

The Road to Rebellion

WHILE THERE HAD been predictions during 1986 and the first part of 1987 that Palestinians in the West Bank and Gaza were exhausted and would soon lose the will to resist Israel's continuing drive into these territories, spontaneous and widespread protest demonstrations erupted in December 1987, showing that Palestinians under occupation had in fact lost neither the political will nor the capacity to challenge Israeli government policies. Assessments stressing the exhaustion of the Palestinians were not without plausibility, of course. As discussed earlier, the Israeli military administration was pursuing an "iron fist" policy in the occupied territories, employing deportations, press censorship, and such forms of collective punishment as school closings, curfews, and the demolition of homes in its attempt to suppress Palestinian nationalism. These actions, along with the dissolution of Palestinian political institutions and the use of force to control public demonstrations, made it reasonable to suggest that unrest would be contained and that a somber and sullen calm would settle over the West Bank and Gaza. Nevertheless, such assessments were soon shown to be inaccurate. Large demonstrations took place in December 1987, and in the weeks and months that followed there were protests and civil disobedience on a scale that exceeded anything seen in the territories since the beginning of the occupation in 1967. Spontaneous outbursts of anger and efforts at resistance rapidly coalesced into a coordinated uprising embracing virtually all sectors of Palestinian society, a rebellion that some compared to the revolt of 1936–39 and which soon became known as the *intifada*, literally translated as the "shaking off."[1]

The spark that ignited the intifada was an accident at the Israeli military checkpoint at the north end of the Gaza Strip. On December 8, an IDF tank transport vehicle crashed into a line of cars and vans filled with men from Gaza who were returning home after a day of work in Israel. Four were killed and seven others were seriously injured, and the the funerals that night for three of the deceased quickly turned into a massive demonstration. Fueled by rumors that the crash had been deliberate, allegedly in retaliation for the stabbing of an Israeli businessman in Gaza the day before, thousands of Gaza residents went into the streets to express their grief and demonstrate their anger. Protests continued the next day and brought direct confrontations with the Israeli military, with IDF forces killing one young Palestinian and wounding many others as they fired tear-gas and live ammunition into the crowds in an attempt to restore order. There were additional demonstrations in the days that followed, and protests soon spread to the West Bank as well, expanding in both scope and intensity to a degree that caught most Israelis and even many Palestinians by surprise. Indeed, initially believing that these disturbances represented nothing more than the normal pattern of unrest in the occupied territories, Israeli Defense Minister Yitzhak Rabin departed on a trip to the United States.

Two different kinds of pressures were impinging upon the occupied territories at this time, fueling the protests that burst forth at the end of 1987 and producing a determination among Palestinians to sustain the intifada. The first, by now familiar, was the result of Israeli actions in the West Bank and Gaza. The second resulted from events on the international scene that deepened the sense of isolation among Palestinians in the territories and contributed to a belief among inhabitants of the West Bank and Gaza that they could rely only on themselves in the struggle to end occupation and secure their political rights.

So far as conditions in the territories are concerned, the Israeli settlement drive was continuing unabated. There were now roughly 63,000 Jews living in some 125 Israeli settlements in the West Bank, and another 2,500 or so residing in 18 communities in Gaza. This was in addition, of course, to developments in East Jerusalem, where Jewish neighborhoods and satellite communities ringing the city to the north, east, and south continued to expand. Moreover, beyond the long-term implications of this growing settler presence, through which the Zionist right sought to ensure that the West Bank and Gaza would remain under permanent Israeli rule, the increasingly provocative actions of some Jewish settlers also intensified the immediate abuses associated with occupation. Settlers frequently sought to harass and intimidate Palestinians, apparently believing that at least grudging acceptance of Jewish rule in the territories could be produced by displays of determination and power. Palestinians were particularly resentful of settler participation in IDF operations conducted in the name of security, including the daily car searches at numerous checkpoints. Many of these searches, which Palestinians judged to be mechanisms of control and intimidation rather than genuine security functions, were carried out by settlers, including civilians as well as military reservists doing duty near their places of residence. As one Palestinian observer complained, searches were often conducted by teenagers, "brandishing their weapons while the police watch. Indeed, one always sees a police car parked close to where these settlers search cars and check identity cards."[2] Some Israelis also condemned the abuses associated with these alleged security operations, and with the growing aggressiveness of Jewish settlers in the West Bank and Gaza more generally.[3]

Related to the settlement drive, and equally worrisome for the Palestinians, was Israel's expanding control of water resources in the occupied areas. Many

Palestinian towns and villages, particularly in the regions of Bethlehem and He-bron, suffered acute shortages because water was being diverted for Jewish set-tlements and other Israeli needs. Agriculture in both the West Bank and Gaza was also severely affected, with the amount of irrigated West Bank land declining by 30 percent between 1967 and 1987.[4] Water-related concerns mounted in the summer of 1987, moreover, when Israeli authorities announced a plan to drill a major new well in the vicinity of Bethlehem in order to divert 18 million addi-tional cubic meters of water to Jerusalem and surrounding Jewish communities. The scheme was abandoned, or at least shelved, in October as a result of mount-ing criticism from the U.S., the European Community, Egypt, and Jordan.[5] Nevertheless, as with other aspects of Israel's deepening presence in the West Bank and Gaza, the proposed drilling project increased Palestinian fears about the future of the territories.

Events at Jerusalem's al-Aqsa Mosque, Islam's third-holiest shrine, were an-other source of tension at this time. Although the mosque is located on the Tem-ple Mount, site of the ancient Israelite Temple and a place revered by Jews throughout the world, Israeli authorities had since 1967 respected the Islamic character of the area and restricted unsupervised worship by Jews to the Western Wall of the ancient Temple, which is below the Temple Mount. Newspapers re-ported in October, however, that this policy was about to change, and in particu-lar that Israeli authorities had responded positively to a request by an extremist Jewish group, the Temple Mount Faithful, for a permit to conduct prayer services on the grounds of al-Aqsa. These press reports were denied by Israeli police spokesmen following a protest by Muslim officials, it being explained that, con-sistent with existing practice, only small groups of Jews accompanied by a police escort would be permitted to pray on the Temple Mount. Tensions nevertheless continued to rise, stimulated, in part, by reports that members of the Temple Mount Faithful were planning a visit to the holy site on October 11.

Protests and clashes between Palestinians and Israeli forces took place on the 11th and continued for two days thereafter, ending what had been several months of relative calm. As many as 2,000 Muslims assembled on the grounds of al-Aqsa to prevent the anticipated visit by Jewish extremists, and this led to a violent confrontation with Israeli soldiers seeking to clear the area so that a small group of waiting Jews might enter. There were many injuries on both sides, as soldiers fired tear-gas into the crowd and Palestinians retaliated with stones and bottles, and it was only after three hours of fighting that a large police contingent was able to escort five members of the Temple Mount Faithful on a quick tour of the contested area. In the wake of the violence on the al-Aqsa grounds, Palestinians declared a commercial strike in East Jerusalem and organized protests in the Old City, Ramallah, and other parts of the West Bank and Gaza. Demonstrators hoisted Palestinian flags and clashed with Israeli soldiers, who sometimes used live ammunition, as well as tear-gas, to disperse them.

There were many other disturbances and manifestations of mounting tension during this period. Early in October, for example, a few days before the confrontations at al-Aqsa Mosque, four Palestinians and an Israeli security officer were killed in a shootout in the Gaza Strip, after which there were demonstrations at the Islamic University of Gaza. The Palestinians belonged to a cell of the Islamic Jihad organization, and according to the Israeli version of events, they were preparing to carry out military operations against Israeli targets in the region. Three weeks later, at the end of October, IDF forces killed one Palestinian student and seriously wounded another while dispersing demonstrators at Bethlehem University, and the next day occupation authorities issued an order closing the university for three months. In November, two East Jerusalem daily newspapers, *al-Fajr* and *al-Shaab*, were banned from distribution in the West Bank and Gaza because they had published a signed statement expressing support for the PLO.

An important event that further inflamed passions was an attack on November 25 by two Palestinian commandos who flew motorized hang-gliders from Lebanon into northern Israel. One of the Palestinians, landing near the town of Qiryat Shimona, managed to evade Israeli security forces and enter an IDF military base, whereupon he killed six soldiers and wounded seven others before being shot himself. Credit for the attack was claimed by a small Palestinian rejectionist group supported by Syria, the Popular Front for the Liberation of Palestine—General Command. This incident was highly troubling for Israelis, who not only mourned their losses but also criticized the military and wondered how terrorists could have penetrated the state's sophisticated defenses in the northern part of the country. Indeed, disciplinary action was subsequently taken against several IDF officers. Among Palestinians, by contrast, news of the hang-glider attack was received with satisfaction, and some described the attack itself as "a heroic operation."[6] It demonstrated that Israel was not invincible and brought Palestinians the satisfaction of knowing that for once they were not on the receiving end of a violent exchange with the IDF. According to one observer, "The sheer audacity of the raid—and the acute embarrassment that it caused for Israel—kindled the imagination of Palestinians in the territories."[7]

A final event that merits mention in this chronology leading to the outbreak of the intifada, even though it occurred during rather than before the first days of the uprising, was Ariel Sharon's move into an apartment in the Muslim quarter of the Old City of Jerusalem. Protected by a large contingent of police and border guards, Sharon, then Israel's minister of industry and trade, held a housewarming reception for three hundred guests on December 15, with Prime Minister Yitzhak Shamir and various Knesset members reportedly among those in attendance. Sharon's action was welcomed by Israelis favoring an expanded Jewish presence in all parts of the Old City. Indeed, the ruling Likud Party sent a congratulatory telegram, declaring that "the setting-up of a new home in such a crucial location is the best possible proof that the people of Israel have come to remain in the land for all eternity."[8] Palestinians, on the other hand, viewed Sharon's move as an important symbolic act and a deliberate provocation, and their anger helped to fuel protest marches inside the walls of the Old City and elsewhere in East Jerusalem, including a demonstration by women in the vicinity of Sharon's new residence.

In addition to these and other sources of tension in the West Bank and Gaza during the summer and fall of 1987, there were a series of developments on the international scene that also helped to shape the attitudes of Palestinians living under occupation. These developments increased the Palestinians' determination and unity of purpose, as well as their anger and alienation, and thus contributed directly to the widespread disturbances that erupted at the end of the year.

One set of developments concerned the circumstances of the PLO, particularly following the eighteenth meeting of the Palestine National Council, which took place in Algiers in April 1987. On the one hand, the PNC brought a reconciliation between Fatah and the most important factions that had been challenging Arafat's leadership of the Palestinian movement, with the Popular Front and the Democratic Front now retaking their seats on the PLO Executive Committee. Organizational unity was further enhanced by the addition of a Communist Party representative to the committee, reflecting the strength of the Communists in the West Bank and Gaza. These PNC actions are credited with reducing factionalism among Palestinians in the occupied territories, where, according to the report of a careful scholarly observer, "social and unionist organizations sponsored by the different movements were beginning to work together" and "a common sense of purpose was beginning to emerge." This observer also notes that for the first time "the Islamic movement began to participate alongside the nationalist groups."[9] The importance of these developments became clear early in 1988, when a unified leadership structure emerged to sustain and give direction to the Palestinian uprising.

On the other hand, the position of the PLO in some ways became more confused and precarious following the Eighteenth PNC meeting, reducing confidence in the organization's leadership among many West Bank and Gaza Palestinians. In order to achieve unity and bring radical factions back into the fold, Arafat had been required at Algiers to break with Jordan and Egypt, even though he almost immediately thereafter sent emissaries to Amman and Cairo in an effort to achieve a rapprochement. The PLO also at this time rejected calls by King Hussein and Israeli Foreign Minister Shimon Peres for an international conference to deal with the Arab-Israeli conflict, although there was again uncertainty about the PLO's position since Arafat and several of his deputies later in the summer offered conditional support for such a conference. According to a Palestinian political scientist writing at this time, "These conflicting statements and actions have created a certain degree of confusion among West Bank and Gaza leaders and have led to varying interpretations of the PLO's true position."[10] Even more important, while continuing to insist that the PLO is the sole legitimate representative of the Palestinian people, and also to express support and affection for Arafat himself, some in the territories began to voice disappointment with the policies and leadership of the Palestinian organization. Some questioned whether PLO leaders were sufficiently in touch with the day-to-day realities of occupation and wondered whether the organization itself was capable of doing anything to alter the situation in the territories. As expressed with hyperbole by one frustrated West Bank academic, Arab and Palestinian leadership outside Palestine "does not care whether Palestinians under occupation survive or not."[11]

A related development that further contributed to the growing sense of isolation among Palestinians in the West Bank and Gaza was a move by the United States to close the PLO's information office in Washington, D.C. Declaring that its objective was "to demonstrate U.S. concern over terrorism committed and supported by organizations and individuals affiliated with the PLO," the State Department in mid-September designated the PLO's Palestine Information Office a foreign mission and ordered it to cease operations and divest itself of all property within thirty days. This order was challenged by various Palestinian, Arab-American, and other organizations in the U.S., who insisted that the Palestine Information Office was duly registered and that the American citizens on its staff were entitled to protection under the First Amendment to the Constitution. Palestinians and others also charged that the principal purpose of the action was to placate American supporters of Israel, who had been campaigning for closure not only of the PLO office in Washington but of its observer mission at the United Nations as well. But while these protests did lead the State Department to accept a six-week delay in the implementation of its order, a court challenge seeking to overturn the closure decision was turned down by a U.S. federal judge early in December. Further, although not supported by the State Department, a bill was introduced in the U.S. Senate at this time calling on the government to close the PLO mission to the U.N. and to reveal all PLO investments in the U.S.

Perhaps the most disturbing development on the international scene from the Palestinian point of view was the failure of an emergency summit meeting of Arab states, convened in Amman, Jordan, in mid-November, to devote any serious attention to the situation in the occupied territories or to the Palestinian struggle more generally. The meeting gave priority to the seven-year-old Iran-Iraq War and reached a consensus condemning Iran's conduct in the lingering conflict. Indeed, Jordan's King Hussein and a number of other Arab leaders indicated that they now considered Iran, rather than Israel, to be the most serious threat to the Arab world. The summit also endorsed the resumption of diplomatic relations with Egypt, which almost all Arab countries had severed following the 1979 Egyptian-Israeli peace treaty and which, except in the case of Jordan, had not been restored. Motivated by a desire to increase Egyptian support for Iraq in the Gulf War, the Amman meeting authorized each Arab state to decide for itself about the restoration of diplomatic relations with Cairo, in effect declaring that Egypt should no longer be punished for making peace with Israel while the Palestinian problem remained unsolved. The United Arab Emirates reestablished diplomatic relations with Egypt almost as soon as the summit ended, and within a few weeks Saudi Arabia and the other Gulf states had also sent their ambassadors back to Cairo.

Although there were reports of a reconciliation between Yasir Arafat and King Hussein during the November summit, and also that a meeting in Amman between Arafat and Hafez al-Assad might soon bring an improvement in the PLO's relations with Syria, the summit was a major disappointment for the Palestinians. Arafat played only a minor role and was in fact treated with disdain by Hussein and other Arab leaders, reflecting the low priority that most Arab states appeared to be assigning to the Palestinian problem. Indeed, the PLO leader boycotted a dinner hosted by Hussein in order to protest the Jordanian monarch's behavior toward him, complaining that the king had personally welcomed the heads of all Arab delegations except the PLO. Even more important, the conference issued only superficial statements about the rights of the Palestinian people and did not even make reference to the 1982 Fez Plan calling for the establishment of an independent Palestinian state. Many in the West Bank and Gaza thus felt betrayed and abandoned. As expressed in a bitter editorial in *al-Fajr*, "The summit came out way short of the expectations of many people in the Arab world, particularly the Palestinians and Lebanese. . . . The Arab governments once again exposed their impotence and proved they are not fit to deal with fast moving developments in the world. This is very regrettable."[12]

The Profile of the Intifada

These developments in the territories and on the international scene during the summer and fall of 1987 help to explain why the accident at the Gaza checkpoint on December 8 produced disturbances of such intensity, and why these disturbances soon coalesced into a general uprising. In the words of Emile Nakhleh, a Palestinian-American scholar who had visited the area a few months earlier, "Gaza resembles a pressure-cooker ready to explode. In this 'forgotten corner of Palestine,' one witnesses overcrowding, poverty, hatred, violence, oppression, poor sanitation, anger, frustration, drugs and crime. The Palestinian population is daily becoming more resentful and rebellious. The military occupation responds by becoming more insecure and oppressive."[13] The situation in the West Bank was only slightly less grim, with Israeli as well as Palestinian analysts reporting that the tension had become palpable. As expressed in October by a correspondent for the *Jerusalem Post*,

You can feel the tension. Worshipers—Jews and Muslims alike—scurry rather than walk. Tourists cluster together and are protected by armed soldiers. Shopkeepers keep one hand on their shutters in anticipation of the next riot. In Gaza, you drive a car with Israeli plates at peril. . . . The atmosphere is reflected throughout Judea and Samaria and even some parts of Galilee. . . . Suspicion has become endemic in our lives. . . . Fear, suspicion and growing hatred have replaced any hope of dialogue between Israelis and Palestinians.[14]

Palestinians in the territories were not only angry, they apparently had also come to the conclusion that they were increasingly alone and could depend only on themselves in their struggle with occupation authorities and Jewish settlers. According to Nakhleh, more and more Palestinians in the territories were now persuaded that only their own efforts offered any hope for a change in the status quo. "Reliance on outside help has proven futile," he noted following his visit, and hence "it has become apparent to West Bank and Gaza Palestinians that outside actors—Arab and foreign—have been unable either to resolve the conflict or to end the occupation."[15] The same point is made by Ann Mosely Lesch, who also visited the occupied territories at this time. "Palestinians felt they had reached a dead end: they were not living as free human beings and they had no hope for the future. That sense of total blockage internally combined with the sense that no help could be expected from the outside. The PLO was too fragmented and distant, and the Arab states had lost interest. Europe and the Soviet Union lacked leverage and the U.S. was too committed to Israel to comprehend the Palestinian situation, much less broker a satisfactory accord."[16]

One of the Palestinian attitudes that this situation helped to produce is characterized by Nakhleh as a new form of *sumud*, or steadfastness, in which self-reliance is emphasized and the element of passivity is removed from a form of struggle that encourages Palestinians to remain on the land and construct viable community institutions in order to survive under occupation. Another Palestinian scholar, Salim Tamari, also discusses the impact of these events on the concept of *sumud*. Steadfastness, he notes, represents "a development strategy of survival and communal preservation until the unfavorable political conditions allow for an external intervention."[17] He adds, however, that while *sumud* began as an ideology of passive resistance, it gradually degenerated into "a form of passive non-resistance (some would say aggressive non-resistance)." Arab inaction was accepted as the norm, so long as the Arab states paid "guilt money" to help Palestinians maintain themselves in the occupied territories. Further, according to Tamari, the traditionalism and inequality of Palestinian society were defended in the name of conservation, even though this "unwittingly corresponded to the Israeli onslaught against the radical political forces of Palestinian nationalism." Populism, activism, and an emphasis on self-reliance, by contrast, were the hallmarks of the new *sumud*, which both the accumulated weight of occupation and a growing sense of abandonment helped to foster in response to this degeneration among Palestinians in the West Bank and Gaza.

So far as the intifada is concerned, this emerging attitude contributed to a new assertiveness on the part of the Palestinians, producing a posture that combined determination, militancy, and a sense of desperation, and which was clearly visible during the disturbances in December 1987 marking the start of the uprising. In effect declaring by their actions that they had nothing more to lose, the protesters, most of them teenagers, often refused to disperse when Israeli soldiers fired tear-gas and live ammunition. As one analyst concluded with respect to the unrest in Gaza, expressions of anger and grief "seemed more determined and fierce" than in the past.[18] According to a Palestinian journalist, writing a few months earlier about the attitudes crystallizing among Palestinians born after 1967, whose only experience was that of occupation, they had "grown up under the nose of the Israeli war machine . . . [and] come to the conclusion that, in the world they inhabit, might is right and the only way to survive and flourish is to be strong and violent."[19]

Israelis, too, seemed to acknowledge that there was a new spirit and daring among the youthful protesters taking to the streets in the West Bank and Gaza. According to one report, based on two visits to Israel and the occupied territories during the first half of 1988, "Even Israelis with little sympathy for the Palestinian cause sometimes say they have a new respect for their enemy . . . and one occasionally hears comments [from Israelis] to the effect that these are not the craven and cowardly Arabs described in our propaganda but young men with the courage of their convictions, willing to stand before our soldiers and risk their lives in order to give voice to their demands."[20]

This new assertiveness was repeatedly displayed as protest activities expanded in both scope and intensity during the weeks that followed. Demonstrations began in the refugee camps but soon spread to major towns, and thereafter to the roughly five hundred villages of the West Bank. Village participation in the intifada was particularly important; since villages are widely scattered and in many cases accessible only with difficulty, the IDF was able to confront protesters and maintain order in only a minority of these communities at any given time.[21] Demonstrators chanted slogans, raised Palestinian flags, and threw stones at Israeli soldiers who sought to disperse them. Young Palestinians also frequently threw stones at Israeli vehicles, including those of Israeli civilians traveling in the occupied territories. Makeshift roadblocks were erected in a further attempt to disrupt normal circulation, especially at the entrances to villages or in urban neighborhoods that the Palestinians sought to prevent Israelis from entering. These roadblocks were constructed of rocks, or occasionally of burning tires; and though they sometimes inconvenienced the local inhabitants as much as the Israelis, they represented an effort to wrest control of the streets from occupation authorities and were accordingly left in place.

A Palestinian journalist working in the occupied territories provides an instructive portrait of the organization of certain protest activities, giving particular attention to the stoning of Israeli vehicles and reporting that age often determined the task a young demonstrator performed. Children in the seven-to-ten age group, he reports, were often assigned the job of "rolling tires to the middle of the road, pouring gasoline on them, and setting them afire." Those in the next group, between the ages of eleven and fourteen, were usually "assigned the task of placing large stones in the road to slow down or stop traffic," and those in this category were also frequently seen "using homemade slings and slingshots." Palestinians between the ages of fifteen and nineteen are described as veteran stone-throwers: "Normally masked with *kufiyyahs* to hide their identity, this group can inflict the worst damage on passing cars. Using large rocks and standing relatively near the road, this group is the heart of the team . . . [and] consequently they are the most sought after by the Israelis." Finally, those over the age of nineteen assumed "key positions in order to lead the entire team. They are in contact with observers on the hillsides and on high houses and they help determine which cars are to be attacked and which are to be let go." In addition, those in this group "direct the stone throwers as to when and how far to retreat when the soldiers advance." This pattern of age-based role assignments, which appears to have emerged spontaneously rather than in response to a formal directive, was reported to be widespread throughout the West Bank and Gaza.[22]

Another instructive account, focusing on a different aspect of the intifada, describes the efforts of young Palestinians to prevent the IDF and Israeli settlers from entering villages in the north of the West Bank. Lesch, a seasoned observer, offers the following picture of one of the villages she visited in March 1988, during the fourth month of the uprising.

> As we turned west from the main highway onto a narrow road, our path was blocked by boulders. Only a bicycle could weave between them. Youths from the next village had blocked the way so that army vehicles and settlers' cars could not pass. The army used to enter the village with a convoy of jeeps and busses. . . . Settlers drove through the village late at night, honking the car horns, shouting curses. . . .
>
> The villagers' stone barrier thus kept out—or at least slowed down—the intruder. Once their youthful outpost decided that we had friendly intentions, they helped us remove enough boulders so that our bus could pass. Then they rolled the rocks back into place. . . . Hand-painted Palestinian flags fluttered from the electricity wires, and graffiti were scrawled on the walls—"Down with the Occupation" and "Palestine Lives." Behind their makeshift barricades, the villagers viewed themselves as a liberated island.[23]

The uprising was also clearly visible in East Jerusalem, a development that further differentiated the intifada from earlier protests of Israeli occupation. In working to isolate East Jerusalem from the rest of the West Bank, Israeli authorities had in the past sought an accommodation with the city's Arab residents, offering them considerable freedom of expression and fewer political restrictions than those placed on Palestinians in other occupied areas, and requiring in return that they keep the city quiet and confine their protests to oral and written statements. Moreover, this strategy had been largely successful from the Israeli point of view, permitting Jews and tourists to frequent all parts of Jerusalem without hesitation and enabling Israelis to think of their country's capital as a unified city. East Jerusalem Palestinians participated fully in the uprising that began at the end of 1987, however. They declared a general strike that suspended commercial life on an unprecedented scale, and they maintained their refusal to resume business as usual as the uprising continued, reopening shops only for the conduct of essential business and only for short periods prescribed by the emerging leadership of the intifada. Throughout 1988, and thereafter as well, East Jerusalem's commercial life thus remained far from normal, with many stores normally frequented by Israelis or tourists doing almost no business whatsoever.

Equally significant, if not more so, East Jerusalem became the scene of numerous clashes between Israeli police and Palestinian demonstrators, some of which were violent. With Palestinians blocking roads and stoning soldiers and police, and with tear-gas in the air and several of the city's neighborhoods under intermittent curfew, there were confrontations of the sort that in the past had taken place only in other areas, enabling Palestinians to claim success in bringing their resistance to the Israeli capital. As acknowledged by Yehuda Litani, Middle East correspondent for the *Jerusalem Post*, "The latest Palestinian achievement is the redivision of United Jerusalem." Writing when the intifada was barely two months old, Litani noted that "both Jews and Arabs living here know that for the last few weeks the city has been practically redivided. Many ask themselves if it was ever united. Jews are going out of their way to avoid passing through Arab neighborhoods, and fewer Arabs are shopping in [the Jewish areas of] Talpiot and Rehov Jaffa."[24]

Emerging patterns of organization and leadership constituted a particularly important feature of the intifada, and one which also helped to set the uprising apart from prior Palestinian efforts to arrest Israel's drive into the West Bank and Gaza. The political institutions that crystallized to give direction to the intifada and to deal with the problems and opportunities it created included both popular neighborhood committees and a unified national leadership structure. Furthermore, both at the local level and beyond, the new institutions were to a large extent led by the members of a new political generation.

Local committees established themselves in neighborhoods and villages throughout the West Bank and Gaza, their purpose being not only to carry forward the intifada but also to assume responsibility for a wide range of social services. Initially, these committees were formed in response to the hardships caused by the uprising. For example, it was necessary to organize the delivery of food to refugee camps and villages placed under curfew and to arrange for the care of Palestinians wounded in clashes with Israeli security forces. The local committees soon expanded their work, however, assuming responsibility for a wide range of basic needs. Activities included the organization of food production as well as distribution, at least to the extent of supervising the planting of vegetable gardens in backyards and vacant lots. They also included the provision of health and hygiene-related services and the establishment of educational programs after schools were closed by Israeli authorities. Observers report many additional activities as well, noting, for example, that in some localities teams were assembled to clean old wells and cisterns, for use in the event that Israel shut off water supplies. According to Lesch, "Even the illiterate woman with several children, who has a weak sense of self-worth, is assigned a task—perhaps to bake bread for the neighbors or to watch a group of children—if the district is besieged."[25] Thus, although the magnitude of what local committees were able to accomplish should not be overstated,[26] the intifada gave rise to a vast organizational network serving, and incorporating, tens of thousands of ordinary men and women. It is estimated that there were as many as one hundred local committees in each of the major towns, and up to ten in every refugee camp and village.[27]

Although the local committees to an important extent emerged spontaneously during the first weeks of the intifada, Palestinian scholars point out that they built upon the mass-based organizations that had developed during the 1980s, and that they also carried forward the populist ideology of these organizations. Following Israel's crackdown on nationalist institutions in the early 1980s, prior to the invasion of Lebanon, syndicates, women's societies, youth groups, labor committees, and other organizations expanded their activities in order to continue the nationalist struggle.[28] Further, a notable feature of these organizations was a kind of radical populism that emphasized mobilization of the more marginal and disadvantaged sectors of Palestinian society, and which also, in the judgment of some analysts, signified a conscious rejection of the more "elitist and nepotistic" aspects of the traditional nationalist movement in the West Bank and Gaza.[29] The local committees of the intifada continued this emphasis on populism and mobilization from below, holding out the promise that they would eventually be a force for revolutionary change. Their contribution during the first months of the intifada was to enhance communal solidarity, bring large numbers of previously uninvolved Palestinians into the nationalist movement, and, overall, make the average citizen a participant in, rather than merely a target for, organized social and political action.

This populist orientation was also reflected in the contribution local committees sought to make to the development of an independent administrative structure at the grass-roots level. Emphasizing self-reliance and self-sufficiency, they organized themselves with a view toward enabling communities to meet basic needs without external assistance. In addition, although they cooperated with one another and rendered assistance to needy Palestinians in neighboring communities, most also maintained a high degree of structural autonomy. Indeed, in response to Israeli charges that they were being established with funding from the PLO, some of their leaders declared that "the popular committees are not being funded by anyone. . . . Rather they are responding to the lack of funding for community services by trying to organize on their own."[30] Disengagement from Israel was a related goal of this organizational effort and of the drive for self-sufficiency, and in this connection there were also calls for Palestinians to boycott Israeli products, to refuse to pay taxes, and to avoid working in Israel.

The work of the local committees soon fostered the emergence of a broader leadership structure, initially to coordinate the provision of food and medicine to besieged communities, but shortly thereafter for the explicit purpose of guiding the evolution of the intifada. Known as the Unified National Leadership of the Uprising (UNLU), this structure remained underground; its members were unknown and it communicated through leaflets, *bayanat*, that were printed in secret and distributed at night throughout the occupied territories. At the time the first leaflet appeared, on January 4, 1988, the UNLU was composed only of individuals from the West Bank, although within a few weeks the command structure had been expanded to include representatives from the Gaza Strip as well.

As its name implied, the UNLU was broadly representative and inclusive of the diverse political tendencies found among Palestinians in the West Bank and Gaza. Composed of individuals identified with Fatah, the Popular Front, the Democratic Front, the Palestine Communist Party, and Islamic Jihad, it incorporated both the various factions that had reunited at the Eighteenth PNC the preceding April and, in addition, representatives of the Islamic movement that remained outside the organizational umbrella of the PLO. According to one scholar, citing "some authoritative Palestinians," the structure of the UNLU was based on rotating membership in a fifteen-person committee, with three members provided by each of the five constituent groups. If any of the fifteen members of the UNLU was captured by the Israelis, a replacement was provided by the organization to which that individual belonged.[31]

In addition, although precise information was lacking, Palestinian and other observers reported that the most important members of the UNLU were not professionals, academics, journalists, or other well-known veterans of Palestinian political life, but individuals who did not belong to the traditional elite and who, in at least some cases, were young enough to remember only vaguely, if at all, the period before Israel's occupation of the West Bank and Gaza. As in the case of popular committees, the emergence of the Unified National Leadership thus reflected the changing patterns of political recruitment that had taken shape in recent years and contributed to the ascendancy of a new political generation, one marked by its own experience and possessing its own political style.

Changes in the social origins of Palestinian leadership were particularly important. Wealthy notable families, which had traditionally been aligned with Jordan but subsequently established ties to the PLO, remained dominant in the 1970s and continued to exercise influence during the early and mid-1980s. These families identified with Palestinian nationalism but, in general, showed little interest in social and economic change and continued to operate on the basis of traditional clientelist politics. Activists and leaders of more modest origin, by contrast, possessed a different political orientation. They favored socioeconomic as well as political change, they were less directly dependent on external economic support, not only from Jordan but to an extent even from the PLO, and they devoted much of their energy to mobilizing the disadvantaged sectors of Palestinian society that traditional elites had largely neglected. The importance of a change in the age distribution of Palestinian leadership lay in the fact that younger individuals, too, had fewer ties to Jordan, especially to the Hashemite regime, and that they possessed little or no recollection of the 1967 defeat that had so strongly marked the thinking of their parents. The latter characteristic, some argued, made them more daring and self-confident.

As noted, the UNLU shunned any visible political role; it operated covertly, concealed the identity of its members, and issued instructions through leaflets printed and distributed in secret. In contrast to earlier nationalist coordinating bodies, such as the National Guidance Committee formed following the Camp David accords of 1978, the UNLU left public pronouncements to the PLO, with which it claimed affinity.

Others accordingly took the lead in calling a press conference in Jerusalem in mid-January to articulate the goals of the uprising. At this press conference, convened in the name of "Palestinian nationalist institutions," a fourteen-point memorandum setting forth the Palestinians' demands was presented by Birzeit University professor Sari Nusseibeh. Accompanying Nusseibeh were Gabi Baramki, acting president of Birzeit, former Hebron mayor Mustafa al-Natshah, and Mubarak Awad, director of the Palestinian Center for the Study of Non-Violence. Several other Palestinian personalities had also planned to take part in the press conference but were prevented from doing so by Israeli authorities. The preamble to the memorandum presented by Nusseibeh affirmed that the PLO is the sole legitimate representative of the Palestinian people and repeated that Palestinian aspirations include the right to self-determination and national independence. Most of the memorandum's fourteen demands addressed the abuses of occupation, setting forth what might be called interim goals. These included the release of political prisoners, the cessation of settlement activity and land confiscation, the cancellation of various Israeli taxes, and the removal of restrictions on industrial and agricultural products exported from the occupied territories.[32]

Leaving interviews and press conferences to others, the UNLU addressed itself to Palestinians under occupation rather than to the international community. Its goal was not to generate sympathy and support for the Palestinian cause but to bring direction and organization to the uprising in the territories. The leaflets through which the UNLU communicated were initially printed at a single location, but Israeli interference soon required that the process be decentralized. Thus, beginning sometime early in 1988, it became the practice to transmit the centrally composed text of each new directive by telephone, fax, or other means to many different locations for retyping, duplication, and distribution by local committees operating independently of one another. Leaflets were numbered and dated, and during the first half of 1988 they appeared at a rate of about one every week and a half, such that twenty-four had been issued by the end of August 1988. After this period they continued to appear with regularity but at somewhat greater intervals.

The directives issued by the UNLU brought a shift from spontaneous to organized resistance as the intifada went forward. The leaflets, usually two pages in length and giving instructions for the coming week or fortnight, announced commercial strikes, transportation strikes, mass demonstrations, and other protest activities. According to Daoud Kuttab, writing in the spring of 1988, the new command "quickly succeeded in establishing its political presence and credibility." It seemed to have "both the wisdom to correct irregularities . . . and the sophistication to request from Palestinians only those things that are possible."[33] Although support for the UNLU appears to have been broad and compliance with its directives largely voluntary, youthful activists also played a role in seeing that instructions transmitted through the leaflets were fully implemented. Palestinian teenagers in the larger towns and in many other communities organized themselves into small "strike forces," patrolling their neighborhoods in order to ensure that businesses closed when so directed and that other instructions were obeyed.[34] In addition to issuing directives about protest activities, many of the UNLU's leaflets also articulated the general platform of the Palestine national movement. They demanded recognition of the PLO, insisted upon the Palestinian people's right to self-determination and upon the right of return for its members living in the Diaspora, and called for the creation of an independent Palestinian state alongside Israel.

Most of the directives issued by the UNLU advocated civil disobedience and called for action of a nonviolent character. According to an analysis prepared by the Palestinian Center for the Study of Non-Violence in Jerusalem, dated May 31, 1988, "In the seventeen leaflets to date, 163 actions were called, the overwhelming majority of which were specifically non-violent in nature. Of the twenty-seven methods of demonstrating resistance to the occupation, twenty-six of these are non-violent." The report also lists these categories of protest activity, among which are strikes (19.6 percent); expressions of solidarity, including financial contributions and participation in community work projects (10.4 percent); demonstrations and marches (8.5 percent); prayer and fasting (6.7 percent); and flag raising (4.9 percent). Many of the other calls involved disengagement from Israel, rather than protest per se, and these, too, are nonviolent in nature. They include withholding taxes (4.9 percent), boycotting Israeli products (4.9 percent), and refusing employment in Israel (4.2 percent). Directives that specifically called for action involving violence, primarily stone-throwing and the use of petrol bombs, constituted 8 of the 163 instructions given in the leaflets, 4.9 percent of the total.[35] The content of the leaflets was generally responsible and moderate in other respects as well. As noted, the political platform articulated by the UNLU was that of the Palestinian mainstream, not that of rejectionists opposed to any accommodation with Israel. Also, while there were strong condemnations of Israel and its supporters, primarily the United States, there were no denunciations of Judaism or the Jewish people.[36]

The outbreak of the intifada and the emergence of a local leadership structure provided both challenges and opportunities for the PLO. The Palestinian organization, which commanded the allegiance of people in the territories but whose leaders and tactics had become the focus of considerable criticism, was taken by surprise by the events of December 1987. The PLO thus sat on the sidelines during the initial phase of the uprising. This did not signify any political competition between the UNLU and external Palestinian leadership, however, and a satisfactory partnership between "inside" and "outside" Palestinians soon developed. The UNLU continued to have wide discretion with respect to decisions about the day-to-day course of the intifada. Moreover, this led some analysts to conclude that Palestinians in the West Bank and Gaza would acquire greater influence within the organization's internal councils. On the other hand, there was never any thought that the PLO should not benefit from the accomplishments of the uprising. The UNLU issued its directives in the name of the organization, consulted regularly with its leaders based in Tunis, and recognized the primacy of the latter in articulating broad political themes. And at the popular levels, young protesters declared, even as they sometimes continued to assert that Palestinian leadership in Tunis had been guilty of lethargy and corruption, "We support the PLO because we are the PLO."

Islamic groups played a role in mobilizing participation in the intifada, giving the uprising yet another of its distinctive features. As discussed earlier, the Muslim Brotherhood and other Islamic organizations had gained strength in the occupied territories over the course of the 1980s, most notably in Gaza but to some extent in the West Bank as well. The Islamic resurgence among Palestinians was fostered in substantial measure by the diffusion of ideological currents taking shape in other parts of the Muslim world, especially in Egypt, home of the Muslim Brotherhood. The success of the Iranian Revolution was also an important stimulus; it seemed to demonstrate that militants organizing under the banner of Islam could defeat a powerful regime supported by the United States. In addition, however, developments related to the particular circumstances of Palestinians also enhanced the position of Islamic groups. On the one hand, Islamists benefited from declining confidence in the policies of the PLO, whose failure to dislodge Israel from the occupied territories was sometimes alleged to be the result of its preoccupation with secular nationalism. On the other, Muslim groups were assisted by both Jordan and Israel, which during the 1980s shared the goal of undermining PLO influence in the West Bank and Gaza. Jordan provided financial assistance, and Israel, for a time at least, granted a measure of latitude that enabled Muslim groups to organize and extend their influence.[37] There is evidence that on at least some occasions Israel also provided direct financial support.[38]

As a result of these developments, and also because the ability to congregate in mosques gave legal protection and institutional resources to Muslim activists seeking to organize and recruit followers, groups operating in the name of Islam were a visible presence in Gaza and in some West Bank locations, including university campuses. Eight or more factions affiliated with the Muslim Brotherhood were active in Gaza. The largest of these was al-Mujaama (the Community), with an estimated 2,000 members. It was led by Sheikh Ahmed Yassin, who was jailed by the Israelis in 1984–85 on charges of possessing weapons and plotting against the state, but who since that time had avoided conflict with occupation authorities and pursued a strategy of incrementalism that assigned priority to the struggle for religious rather than political change.[39] This evolutionary approach, with its emphasis on religious transformation through the steady infusion of Islamic thought and behavior into public life, was typical of the Muslim Brotherhood at this time. But while focusing on religion rather than politics, Brotherhood militants sometimes went beyond education and persuasion in their efforts to instill respect for Islam among the local population. Women were frequently pressured to wear Islamic dress, for example, and there were occasional attacks on stores selling liquor. Muslim activists also sometimes clashed with leftist organizations and attacked charitable societies headed by leftists or Communists.

A more direct and immediate challenge to the occupation was advocated by the Islamic Jihad organization, a clandestine society that seems to have come into existence in 1985 or 1986, and whose members were said to include men recruited while in Israeli prisons. Although Israeli sources estimated prior to the intifada that there were probably no more than several dozen hard-core activists in Islamic Jihad, grouped into independent cells of four or five individuals,[40] its emergence suggested that Islamic militants might turn away from the Muslim Brotherhood's emphasis on religious rather than political goals and call upon Palestinians to rise up against the Israeli occupation. Indeed, as noted, there had been a lethal confrontation between Israeli security forces and the members of an Islamic Jihad cell in October 1987, two months before the beginning of the uprising. A knowledgeable Israeli scholar predicted at this time that more Islamic Jihad cells would be established in the future, and that "Islamic activists may decide to mobilize the Palestinian masses in repeated waves of riots, disturbances and the disruption of public order." Further, he concluded, "it seems quite certain that the West Bank–Gaza population would respond to such a call."[41]

Islamic Jihad claimed credit for bringing Palestinian youth into the streets in

December 1987, and the society does appear to have played a major role in organizing protest demonstrations at this time, especially in Gaza. Appealing to the population in the name of Islam, activists employed mosques for organizational purposes and broadcast appeals and instructions from loudspeakers that normally call the faithful to prayer. Islamic Jihad's political activism also led it to join the UNLU at the beginning of the intifada, displaying a willingness to cooperate with nationalists and leftists that further distinguished its orientation from that of the Muslim Brotherhood, and which in return brought praise from some leftist organizations. For example, George Habash, leader of the Popular Front for the Liberation of Palestine, told an interviewer, "I would like to express my deepest appreciation for the phenomenon of the Islamic Jihad in occupied Palestine." [42]

Despite this willingness to make common cause against the Israelis, the ideological distance between Islamic Jihad and the PLO factions with which it shared membership in the UNLU remained substantial, and as a result Islamic Jihad soon began to operate independently of the unified leadership structure. It published a number of its own leaflets, for example, which were similar to those of the UNLU in that they contained directives concerning strikes, demonstrations, and other forms of protest. Islamic Jihad further set itself apart from the nationalist leadership of the uprising by appealing to the population in the name of Islam, and by insisting that the campaign to achieve Palestinian self-determination should be regarded as part of a larger Islamic revolution. In addition, its leaflets and other publications were much more militant than the statements issued in the name of the UNLU. The organization rejected the two-state solution championed by the PLO mainstream and demanded instead the liberation of all of Palestine. Its proclamations also frequently blurred the distinction between Zionism and Judaism, declaring the enemy to be the Jewish people, as well as the State of Israel. [43]

A new Islamic organization, Harakat al-Muqawama al-Islamiyya, the Islamic Resistance Movement, was established in January 1988 and quickly became the most important Islamic group working to sustain and amplify the intifada. Known by its acronym, Hamas, which is also the Arabic word for "zeal" or "ardor," the organization officially described itself as a wing of the Muslim Brotherhood in Palestine. One of its leaders was Sheikh Ahmed Yassin, who, as noted, was the head of a large Brotherhood faction in Gaza. Another was Dr. Abd al-Aziz al-Rantisi, an instructor at the Islamic University of Gaza. Hamas's ability to seize the mantle of Islamic activism was due in part to its ties to the Muslim Brotherhood, which had always been the largest and most influential Islamic organization in the occupied territories. Hamas also assumed a more important role in the intifada following an Israeli crackdown in the spring of 1988 that brought the arrest or deportation of key Islamic Jihad leaders and thereby diminished the operational capacity of that organization.

Although affiliated with the traditional Muslim Brotherhood organization, Hamas distinguished itself in two important ways. First, it renounced the quietist approach and religious priorities that had characterized the Brotherhood in recent years. Thus, while remaining outside the unified leadership structure of the intifada, it endorsed and sought to extend the uprising, issuing statements, like Islamic Jihad, that in fact were much more militant and uncompromising than those of the UNLU. Second, it did not address itself to the notables and merchants who were traditional Brotherhood supporters, and who in many instances had ties to Jordan, but instead sought recruits among younger and better-educated individuals without ties to the Palestinian establishment. Hamas's activism and anti-establishment orientation initially strained its relationship with the mainstream of the Brotherhood, especially at the beginning of 1988, before it was certain that the initial disturbances in the occupied territories would give rise to a sustained uprising. On the other hand, some Palestinians point out that Hamas's creation served the Brotherhood by directing Israeli reprisals away from the parent organization, and some suggest that this may even have been one of the original motivations for establishing Hamas as a movement with a distinct identity. In any event, in February 1988, the Brotherhood adopted Hamas as its military arm.

Hamas extended its influence in both the West Bank and Gaza during 1988 and became an important voice giving direction to the uprising, second only to that of the UNLU.[44] Its popularity was a result of the same factors that were fueling the Islamic resurgence more generally. In addition, the new organization had the benefit of financial support from Saudi Arabia and other oil-rich Gulf Arab states, which enhanced its ability to build a presence and expand its activities in many communities. By the second half of 1988, leaflets distributed by Hamas were appearing with approximately the same frequency as those of the UNLU. Like the UNLU, it issued calls for strikes, demonstrations, and other protest activities, and it appears that in most instances its directives, as well as those of the nationalist leadership, were respected by the local committees of the intifada.

Hamas's ideology was formally set forth in a charter published in August 1988, a document of thirty-six articles that spelled out the movement's Islamic orientation and showed its attitude toward Israel to be much more uncompromising than that of the PLO and the nationalist mainstream.[45] One theme of the Hamas charter is the centrality of Islam as a framework for all Palestinian nationalist efforts, as expressed, for example, in the declaration that "Hamas regards nationalism as part and parcel of religious faith." A related theme is that Palestine is an Islamic land, "an Islamic waqf throughout the generations until the Day of Resurrection," and that accordingly no portion of it may be ceded to Jews or other non-Muslims. A third theme is distrust of the Jews and their designs, often expressed in anti-Semitic terms that allege the existence of a Jewish-led international conspiracy. For example, Article 22 declares that "the enemies have been scheming for a long time. . . . Their wealth permitted them to take over control of the world media. . . . They also used the money to establish clandestine organizations which are spreading around the world, in order to destroy societies and carry out Zionist interests." Another theme, which follows logically, is rejection of "the so-called peaceful solutions," including international conferences, and the affirmation that "there is no solution to the Palestinian problem except by Jihad." Indeed, the charter states that "when our enemies usurp some Islamic lands, Jihad becomes a duty binding on all Muslims." Two final themes are the importance of social as well as political justice, expressed as a commitment to helping the needy and looking after the interests of the masses, and a willingness to coexist in friendship with Palestinian nationalists and the PLO. Nationalists are assured of Hamas's support, and the PLO is said to constitute "a father, a brother, a relative, a friend," although the charter also looks forward to the day "when the PLO adopts Islam as the guideline for life."

Propelled forward by popular determination, with organization and direction provided both by the Unified National Leadership of the Uprising and by Islamic movements, most notably Hamas, the intifada emerged as a full-blown rebellion early in 1988. It continued to increase in scope and intensity throughout the remainder of the year and during 1989 and 1990 as well. There were scores of strikes, bringing a severe disruption of the routines of work, commerce, transportation, and other public activities in the occupied territories. There were also hundreds of demonstrations and other protest activities, many bringing a strong response from Israeli security forces, and some leading to violent confrontations between Israelis and Palestinians. Virtually no sector of Palestinian society was untouched by the intifada, which to a large extent succeeded in sweeping away whatever degree of normalcy had characterized life under occupation. The course of events in the West Bank and Gaza was increasingly determined by Palestinians themselves, rather than by occupation authorities.

Israeli Efforts to Contain the Intifada

As soon as they recognized the coordinated and sustained character of the Palestinian uprising, Israeli leaders declared their intention to suppress the intifada. Primary responsibility for achieving this objective fell to Yitzhak Rabin, the minister of defense in the national unity government that had been established after the inconclusive parliamentary elections of 1984. As discussed earlier, the centrist Labor Alignment and the right-wing Likud Union were the principal factions in this coalition government; and under a rotation agreement between the two parties, the prime minister in December 1987 was Yitzhak Shamir of Likud. Rabin, by contrast, was from Labor. As a former military commander who was unaffiliated with any of Labor Zionism's internal ideological camps, Rabin had long been regarded as a nonideological pragmatist. Further, in prior service as Israeli ambassador to the United States, and then as his country's prime minister from 1974 to 1977, he had earned a reputation as a centrist and a supporter of territorial compromise. Nevertheless, even as he continued to profess commitment to an exchange of land for peace, the official position of the Labor Alignment, Rabin instructed the IDF to take vigorous action to bring the intifada to an end. If the uprising continued, he declared, Palestinian violence would be met by force on the part of Israel.

In addition to detaining and deporting suspected activists, Israel undertook to suppress Palestinian protest demonstrations, and when necessary it dispersed demonstrators by firing live ammunition. Rabin and most other Israeli leaders justified these actions by saying that the Palestinians had left them no alternative. In defending his policy, Rabin also predicted that Israel's use of force would bring an end to the uprising within a matter of weeks, perhaps even sooner.[46] Yet the intifada continued and, if anything, grew more intense, even as the number of Palestinian demonstrators shot by Israeli soldiers increased. Between December 8, 1987, and January 15, 1988, for example, Israeli security forces killed at least thirty-seven Palestinians taking part in protest activities, more than half of whom were under the age of twenty.[47] In late December 1987, with the United States abstaining, the United Nations Security Council passed a resolution deploring Israeli policies and practices and, in particular, calling for an end to the use of live ammunition against unarmed Palestinian civilians.

In response to both international and domestic criticism, Rabin announced on January 22, 1988, that a new policy had been developed to contain protest activities, and that the use of live ammunition was now limited to situations in which the lives of Israeli soldiers were at risk. This new policy, which the defense minister publicly characterized as "force, might and beatings," was less lethal than the one it replaced but brutal nonetheless.[48] Under the procedures now in force, Israeli troops used clubs to subdue protesters, often beating demonstrators indiscriminately, even when they were attempting to flee. Moreover, Israeli soldiers were encouraged to break the bones of young Palestinians, to break either their legs so they would be unable to run or their hands to prevent them from throwing stones. Hundreds of Palestinians were subsequently injured, and about a dozen Palestinians died from beatings administered by Israeli soldiers in the two months following the introduction of Rabin's new policy.

The use of live ammunition to put down demonstrations and other protest activities continued as well. This occurred with less frequency than in the past, but roughly twenty-five young Palestinians were nonetheless shot while participating in demonstrations during February and March 1988, and almost twice that number were shot by Israeli soldiers while inside their homes or walking in the street. Taking together all categories of intifada-related deaths, including those resulting from the use of tear-gas in closed spaces,[49] the number of Palestinians killed by Israelis since the beginning of the uprising had reached 160 by the end of March 1988 and 324 by August of that year.[50] Moreover, even though Israeli troops began in the fall of 1988 to use plastic bullets, which IDF spokesmen claimed are not lethal when fired at seventy meters or more, the Palestinian death count rose steadily throughout 1988 and 1989. It stood at 574 by June of the latter year, as the intifada entered its nineteenth month.[51] During this period, the uprising also resulted in seventeen Israeli deaths.

Israel's willingness to employ violence in its attempt to suppress the intifada also included an effort to reach beyond the West Bank and Gaza and to strike at PLO leaders in Tunis who were believed to be giving direction to the uprising. Specifically, a plan to assassinate Khalil al-Wazir, one of Arafat's closest aides and the PLO official that Israeli intelligence charged with coordinating resistance activities in the territories, was developed and presented to the inner cabinet in March and April 1988. According to subsequent reports, only Shimon Peres and two other members of the inner cabinet opposed the plan, which was accordingly carried out on April 16. On that day, a group of unidentified men shot al-Wazir, also known as Abu-Jihad, in his home in Tunis. His chauffeur and two body guards were killed as well. Although the operation drew praise from most leaders of Likud and also from some in Labor, including Rabin,[52] it did not have the effect of undermining the uprising in the West Bank and Gaza. If anything, in the short run at least, the assassination of al-Wazir increased the intensity of the intifada, giving rise to a new wave of strikes and demonstrations.[53]

All of this violence was in addition to the severe administrative measures that Israel employed in its effort to contain the intifada. For example, universities were closed until further notice by Israeli authorities, although several institutions managed to hold some classes in secret. Many primary and secondary schools were also shut for prolonged periods. Dozens of homes were blown up by Israeli troops, usually because it was believed that young men who lived in the houses had thrown stones at Israeli soldiers. In addition, entire communities were placed under curfew, sometimes for a week or more, preventing people from leaving their homes at any time, even to obtain food. As with school closings and the demolition of homes, curfews were a form of collective punishment that fell heavily not only on protesters but also on men and women who had not taken part in protest-related activities. The 55,000 residents of Jabalya refugee camp in Gaza, for example, spent about two hundred days under curfew between the beginning of the intifada and June 1989.[54]

The continuing deportation of suspected activists was another administrative measure designed to suppress the uprising. Although this contravened the Fourth Geneva Convention, about thirty-five Palestinians had been deported by December 1988, and in response the United Nations Security Council unanimously passed a resolution condemning Israel's action.[55] Israeli actions also included the censorship of Arabic-language newspapers published in East Jerusalem, closure of a number of Palestinian charitable societies, and the imposition of restrictions on the transfer of currency into the occupied territories.

Yet another aspect of Israel's test of wills with the Palestinians was the IDF's attempt to prevent or suppress expressions of protest even when they took place in remote areas or inconvenienced Arabs more than Jews. For example, military patrols were on the lookout for barricades of stones or burning tires, even when these were placed across urban alleyways utilized only by Palestinians or in the streets of out-of-the-way villages. In these cases, as elsewhere, Israeli soldiers usually confiscated the identity cards of anyone in the vicinity, even if it was obvious they were not responsible for the offending action, and then held these cards until their owners had removed the barricades. Similar methods were used to force Palestinians to paint walls laden with objectionable political graffiti and to remove Palestinian flags that had been displayed. Although these expressions of protest and nationalism were not violent, and had no immediate potential for inflicting injury on soldiers or other Israelis, they were regarded as part of an effort to mobilize support for the intifada, and they were thus intolerable from the viewpoint of the Israeli government.

Finally, thousands of Palestinians were arrested and detained, some for prolonged periods and the overwhelming majority without trial. In February 1989, Rabin announced that 22,000 Palestinians had been detained since the beginning of the intifada, and that 6,200 were being held in administrative detention at that time. Palestinian and some U.S. sources put the figures even higher. Under military regulations in force in the occupied territories, an individual suspected of illegal activities, such as membership in an organization supporting the uprising, could be held without trial for a period of up to six months, and administrative detention was also renewable without trial at the end of this period. Indeed, the U.S. State Department reported that 20 percent of the detentions completed in 1988 were renewed for a second six-month period.[56]

Many of these Israeli efforts to contain the intifada are described in the 1988 Human Rights Survey published by the United States Department of State in February 1989.[57] The survey, which devotes about eleven pages to Israeli policies and practices in the occupied territories, was strongly criticized by the government of Shamir and Rabin. Nevertheless, it provides a useful summary of much that had been reported by the world media since the beginning of the intifada, and it is particularly credible since the United States is Israel's most important ally, and since the U.S. had vetoed a number of UN resolutions condemning Israeli efforts to suppress the intifada. Among the conclusions of the U.S. Human Rights Survey: most Palestinians killed in 1988 were shot by Israeli soldiers using standard service bullets, in incidents involving stone-throwing, firebombing, and fleeing suspects; the number of Palestinians held in administrative detention or in prison increased from 4,700 in December 1987 to roughly 10,000 at the end of 1988; 154 homes were demolished, affecting more than 1,000 people;[58] suspects and detainees were frequently beaten or otherwise mistreated, with five Palestinians dying under "questionable circumstances" while in detention; and Israeli personnel who mistreated Palestinians in violation of regulations were frequently, although by no means always, dealt with leniently or not punished at all.[59]

There was mounting international and domestic criticism of these Israeli efforts to contain the intifada, and in response the government in Jerusalem put forward a vigorous defense of its policies and practices. Israeli spokesmen characterized the Palestinian uprising as an extreme and threatening provocation that could not be permitted to continue. They also pointed out that Palestinians could easily remove themselves from harm's way. As Chief of General Staff Dan Shomron told the Knesset Foreign Affairs and Defense Committee in October 1988, "[Only] Arabs who deliberately choose to go out and demonstrate are getting injured." The violence will stop when, eventually, these Palestinians "realize that it is not in their interest to get involved in riots."[60] In this connection, Israelis also rejected Palestinian claims that most intifada-related protests were nonviolent in nature. As expressed by Zvi Poleg, IDF commander in the Gaza Strip, "In a confrontation with a 12 year old boy with a stone and a 20 year old soldier with a rifle, sympathy naturally goes to the boy. But it is not justified, because a stone thrown by a boy of 12 can kill." Further, Poleg continued, "The local people ask me why the soldiers hit. I ask them the opposite question: what is your purpose when you throw stones or metal bars or petrol bombs at me? They're not embarrassed to say 'in order to kill you.' They're not embarrassed to say that."[61]

In the debates and discussions taking place within the Jewish state, some prominent Israelis expressed the view that the way to end the intifada was to seek a political accommodation with the Palestinians. In this, their analysis approached that of the Palestinians, who had insisted from the beginning that the uprising would continue until Israel agreed to negotiate a definitive end to its occupation of the West Bank and Gaza. Shomron himself said as much in a series of highly visible newspaper and television interviews in January 1989, acknowledging that the intifada was a genuine popular resistance movement and explicitly comparing it to the Algerian revolution and other anticolonial struggles in the Third World.[62] Similar sentiments were expressed by others, including many prominent Labor Alignment leaders. Even Rabin declared early in 1988, "You cannot saddle the IDF with a mission that is outside its proper function. The unrest in the areas reflects a problem that can only have a political solution."[63] Similarly, speaking almost a year later, the defense minister told students in a lecture at a Tel Aviv high school that the riots in the West Bank and Gaza "express a sense of frustration that no one in the Arab world, in the international community or in Israel had created any expectation of a political settlement."[64]

But this is not to say that Rabin, Shomron, and others were willing to see the intifada continue until a political accommodation was reached. If territorial compromise remained the key to solving the problem of the West Bank and Gaza, the key to negotiations aimed at achieving this goal was, in their view, the restoration of order, by military means if necessary. They may have agreed with the former member of the Israeli military establishment who wrote, "The Palestinians do not need to throw any more stones to convince us. They have made their point and sensible people in Israel and the rest of the world have got the message."[65] Nevertheless, as long as there continued to be disturbances in the occupied territories, these Israeli leaders supported and defended the use of force to suppress the uprising. Their belief in the need for a political solution did not lead them to embrace the Palestinian view that meaningful progress toward this solution must be made *before* the uprising could end.

The Israeli government thus remained determined to crush the Palestinian uprising, and this determination did not diminish as the intifada entered its second and then its third year. "The nation can bear the burden no matter how long the revolt goes on," Rabin declared in December 1989. Further, he specified, "We will continue with all the measures that we used for the first years, including the confrontations, the hitting, the arresting, the introduction of the plastic bullet, the rubber bullet and the curfews on a large scale."[66] At the time Rabin made this statement, at least 615 Palestinians had been killed by Israelis since the beginning of the intifada. Injuries, as opposed to deaths, also remained high. IDF figures reported that 15,000 to 20,000 Palestinians had been wounded in incidents related to the uprising, and arrests and imprisonments associated with the intifada totaled about 50,000 by the end of its second year. Of the latter figure, roughly 13,000 Palestinians remained in detention in December 1989.[67] In concluding his assessment, Rabin acknowledged that the IDF had thus far failed to suppress the intifada, but asserted that his government's policies would eventually succeed. "We have reached a war of attrition," the defense minister stated, "but I think they feel more attrition than we do."[68]

While the harshness of Rabin's policies drew strong criticism from overseas, and from some in Israel as well, the rapid expansion of the intifada brought calls from the Israeli political right for the application of even greater force. Such calls were particularly pronounced in the summer and early fall of 1988, with the approach of elections for a new Knesset, scheduled for November. Right-wing politicians repeatedly expressed the view that the uprising was continuing because the defense minister and the IDF were unwilling to employ the force needed to suppress it. For example, Geula Cohen, a leader of the right-wing Tehiya Party, complained that Israel should have deported "not just dozens" but hundreds of Palestinian activists, and that this should have been done years ago.[69] Similarly, Ariel Sharon, a contender for the leadership of Likud and minister of industry and trade when the uprising began in December 1987, denounced Rabin for timidity and misplaced moderation and challenged a declaration by Chief of General Staff Shomron to the effect that IDF operations must remain scrupulously within the law. Sharon stated that this was precisely the problem and insisted that "the law should have been changed if it does not empower the IDF to take sufficiently effective measures."[70]

Rabin and his supporters responded to this criticism, of course. For example, Likud spokesmen asserted during the 1988 Knesset election campaign that a homogeneous right-wing coalition would be able to suppress the uprising within one week, and on one occasion Rabin sarcastically told reporters in response that at least Likud leaders had become a little less unrealistic. They have "made progress from when they were going to solve the terrorist problem in Lebanon in forty-eight hours," he quipped, adding, "Six years later the problem [of Lebanon] is still with us."[71] Further, Rabin and other Alignment leaders parried the actions as well as the verbal assaults of the political right, working to prevent the government from adopting policies that would have made clashes in the occupied territories even more violent than they already were. Early in September, for example, with the election campaign in high gear, they headed off an attempt by Prime Minister Shamir to have the cabinet consider authorizing soldiers, and possibly even settlers, to fire on Palestinian stone-throwers, thereby extending the "open-fire" policy that was already in effect against those who threw petrol bombs. Rabin sent Shamir a strongly worded message declaring that he and all other ministers from Labor were opposed to such a policy, and Labor Minister Moshe Shahal stated in a cabinet meeting that this policy would be against the law and would "in effect constitute a license to kill." It would bring "something resembling the Phalangist anarchy of Lebanon," Shahal added, all of which was sufficient to cause Shamir to back away from the idea.[72]

The November election was a virtual standoff, with Likud capturing forty Knesset seats and Labor thirty-nine, and the result was another national unity government and continuation of the policies guiding Israel's efforts to suppress the intifada. In contrast to the national unity government formed in 1984, Likud was the senior partner in the new coalition. Thus, Shamir retained the premiership, and there was no requirement of a rotation. On the other hand, to the disappointment of some in Likud, including Sharon, Shamir agreed that Rabin should continue to serve as defense minister. The distribution of cabinet posts in the new government also included moving Shimon Peres from the Foreign Ministry to the Finance Ministry, thereby distancing him from policy-making bearing on the Israeli-Palestinian conflict. Replacing Peres as foreign minister was Moshe Arens, a Likud hard-liner and close political ally of Shamir.

In the months that followed, as the intifada continued to defy Israeli efforts at containment, there were additional calls by right-wing politicians and others for harsher measures against Palestinians in the West Bank and Gaza. For example, Rafael Eitan of the small Tsomet Party, which had once been a partner of

Tehiya, demanded the expanded use of collective punishment, telling the Knesset Foreign Affairs and Defense Committee in January 1989 that this would take care of the Palestinian uprising. A few weeks later, a prominent intellectual associated with the settler movement published an article urging the deportation of more Palestinians. Shubert Spero, a professor of Jewish thought at Bar Ilan University, wrote, "Henceforth anyone found guilty of throwing stones or gasoline bottles should be deported, regardless of his age or the success of his efforts. . . . [And] minors should be accompanied by their parents."[73]

Sentiments of a very different nature were also expressed in Israel at this time. In contrast to those who accused Rabin of timidity and called for harsher measures, some Israelis deemed the defense minister's methods to be excessive and were in fact deeply troubled by IDF behavior in the occupied territories. Moreover, much of this criticism was accompanied by assertions to the effect that the use of violence by the IDF was unacceptable for moral as well as practical reasons and was consequently harming Israel, as well as the Palestinians. For example, there were challenges to Rabin's claim that the IDF beat Palestinians only to break up demonstrations, not for purposes of intimidation or harassment. One left-wing Member of Knesset, Yossi Sarid, publicly called Rabin a liar and stated, "Grave incidents have taken place, involving extreme cruelty and violence against persons and property. The violence was not the result of soldiers defending themselves, but was applied as a punishment."[74] In response to the same charges, Attorney General Yosef Harish wrote a letter to the defense minister in which he demanded that it be made clear to soldiers that it is illegal to beat demonstrators after they have been arrested, and that "it is forbidden to use force to punish or humiliate."

An incident in the West Bank town of Halhoul in February 1988 illustrates the kind of behavior that was producing criticism, and the manner in which some of this criticism was articulated. According to testimony given by several IDF reservists serving in the West Bank, seventeen Palestinian men between the ages of seventeen and twenty were caught and bound and made to sit together on the road, and soldiers from the Golani brigade then beat them with rifle butts and truncheons. When they were severely bruised and could no longer walk, the reservists' report asserted, "fifteen of the bound youngsters were loaded onto a lorry and driven to a wadi filled with refuse and dumped into the valley . . . [and] it was only after argument and discussion among the soldiers that the prisoners' hands were unbound."[75] The letter containing this testimony was given to two Members of Knesset, Chaike Grossman of Mapam and Ran Cohen of the Citizens' Rights Movement, who praised the reservists for speaking up, released their letter to the press, and also sent it on to Rabin. A few days after the Halhoul incident, another leader of the left-oriented Mapam Party, Yair Tsaban, told a Peace Now rally that "orders to beat in order to break bones are unlawful and should be refused," adding that his quarrel was not with the soldiers serving in the territories but "with Rabin and the government for having put the IDF in an impossible position."[76]

There were similar expressions of concern in response to other reported abuses, some even more troubling than the incident in Halhoul. In one of the worst, which also took place in February 1988, soldiers buried alive four Palestinians in Salem village near Nablus. Further, the action was defended by some extremists. This incident brought forceful denunciations not only from civilian leaders but from many in the IDF. For example, General Amram Mitzna, OC Central Command, declared it unthinkable that such actions should be defended and stated, "Even in my worst dreams, I couldn't imagine it."[77] Mitzna also promised that officers would speak to their soldiers and do everything possible to prevent such incidents from recurring in the future. The brutal behavior of an IDF tank unit in the village of Qalqilya in October 1988 was yet another of the incidents that brought protest from those within the military. A group of reservists serving in Qalqilya filed a complaint, addressed to Rabin and passed on to leftist politicians, alleging that the medic in the group had been threatened at gunpoint not to reveal that Palestinians were routinely beaten by both officers and soldiers, that he had also been prevented from giving aid to Palestinians who were badly beaten, and that some detainees were kept in "dehydration facilities."[78]

In still another denunciation by soldiers that received wide public attention, Shamir was told by troops serving in Nablus in January 1989 that they were very disturbed by the IDF's behavior. Accompanied by reporters, whom military officials had tried in vain to convince the prime minister not to invite along, Shamir was inspecting IDF operations in the northern West Bank city and stopped to talk to a group of soldiers, whereupon, to his consternation, he was told in extremely strong terms that young Israelis were not raised on universal values and respect for human rights only to be sent to the occupied territories to commit violence unrestrained by the rule of law. The political and military establishments "have no idea what really goes on in the territories," one soldier told the prime minister, while another stated, with reporters present, that he had to "beat innocent people" every day.[79] As one of the reservists serving in Nablus later wrote, "The sunny morning Mr. Shamir visited our unit in Nablus, I would have liked to scream and cry about how our army is being sullied, corroded and undermined by the impossible task the government has given it."[80]

Similar criticism was directed at other IDF policies designed to contain the intifada. For example, Dedi Zucker, a Knesset member from the Citizens' Rights Movement, criticized the use of tear-gas in closed spaces and commissioned a study of the effects of this policy. In the study, released in June 1988, a team of Israeli doctors and toxicologists confirmed the charges of Zucker and other critics of IDF actions, finding that the use of tear-gas in closed spaces was extremely dangerous and could even be fatal, especially to babies, children, the elderly, and persons with heart and respiratory diseases. There were also condemnations of the IDF's use of plastic bullets against Palestinians, a policy that was instituted in the fall of 1988. Politicians affiliated with Labor, as well as others, charged that these bullets were being employed for purposes of harassment as well as for the control of demonstrations, thereby turning noninvolved Palestinians into enemies. A similar protest was lodged by the Association for Civil Rights in Israel (ACRI), with Judge Eli Natan, ACRI's chair, declaring that plastic bullets were in fact widely employed not only for riot control but also for punishment and deterrence, and that "there is no doubt [this] is an illegal act."[81]

Most of these complaints about the excessive use of force focused on human-rights violations and a disregard for the rule of law, which were seen as undermining Israeli democracy and the country's commitment to universal humanistic values. Although the IDF's use of violence in the West Bank and Gaza was obviously injurious to Palestinians, it was thus seen as doing serious damage to Israel as well. In making this argument, those advocating greater restraint insisted that the end does not justify the means. They stated that the goal of order in the territories, however desirable and necessary, fails to provide a justification for many of the actions taken in pursuit of this objective. Indeed, some rejected any distinction between means and ends in this context. Preserving the moral integrity and civilized character of the State of Israel is the only true goal, they insisted, and if this is lost in the pursuit of some more instrumental objective, such as the restoration of order in the West Bank and Gaza, then it is meaningless even to ask whether the end justifies the means.

A striking illustration of this kind of critical assessment, expressed in terms that carry special weight in Israel, was a discussion in May 1989 of the differences and similarities between the Nazi persecution and annihilation of Jews during World War II and the repressive measures being carried out by Israel in the occupied territories. The discussion took place at a Holocaust Memorial Day program organized by the Center for Holocaust Studies of Ben Gurion University.[82] Many speakers, and the majority in the audience, found the comparison not only unconvincing but offensive as well. "There is no room for spurious and idiotic comparisons between Auschwitz and the suppression of the intifada," declared one scholar, even though she herself was actively involved in opposition to Israel's occupation of the West Bank and Gaza. On the other hand, referring to the "dehumanization of the enemy" and to the different value systems that govern IDF behavior in Israel and the occupied territories, another speaker told a silent audience that "the intifada helps us to understand the human infrastructure that made Nazism possible."

It was highly significant that such a discussion could take place. Breaking a taboo, it was tolerated by the audience and reported in the press, being called "an amazing evening" by veteran journalist Tom Segev.[83] In his account of the program, Segev offered his own view, that the attempt to draw an analogy between the Holocaust and Israel's suppression of the intifada is "unintelligent and . . . infuriating, and for these reasons ineffective." Yet, Segev continued, "The attitude of Israeli society toward the repression in the territories, and the repression itself, are terrible and horrid . . . [so] perhaps I am mistaken." That Segev and others could entertain such thoughts revealed just how deeply disturbing and morally offensive some Israelis considered their government's policies to be.

With some political leaders and intellectuals urging greater restraint and others calling for harsher measures to contain the intifada, it is not surprising that Israeli public opinion was also divided on the subject. During 1988 and the first half of 1989, a substantial number of Israelis, possibly a majority, not only approved of the containment methods authorized by Rabin but in fact agreed with the defense minister's right-wing critics that greater force should be employed to suppress the Palestinian uprising.[84] Public opinion appears to have shifted during 1989, however, with more Israelis coming to the conclusion that greater force was not the answer to the problem in the territories, and that even current levels of force were excessive. A national survey conducted in May 1990, when the intifada was already well into its third year, reported that only 18 percent of the Jewish public advocated the application of more repressive measures. By contrast, 38 percent of those interviewed, and fully 30 percent of the respondents identifying themselves as supporters of Likud, indicated a preference for greater restraint and agreed that force should be employed "very cautiously" and "only against terrorists, inciters to violence and the leaders of the disturbances."[85] Another 8 percent rejected the use of any military force and called for Israel's immediate withdrawal from the territories, and the remaining respondents, about one-third of the total, expressed satisfaction with the policies in effect at that time.

Messages and Reactions

Palestinians under occupation were seeking by the rebellion that began in December 1987 to send a message to Israel and the world. The content of this message, made explicit in the conversations between Palestinian intellectuals and the large number of foreign journalists who flocked to the region to report on the spreading disturbances, can be summed up simply: "We exist and have political rights, and there will be no peace until these rights are recognized." The Palestinians' message also proclaimed that occupation was unacceptable, and that continued Israeli rule over the West Bank and Gaza, even with provisions for Palestinian autonomy, would be met with continuing resistance.

The Israeli public was the most important audience to which the Palestinians' message was addressed. In the debates and discussions inside Israel, Prime Minister Shamir and others on the right side of the political spectrum had frequently argued that most Palestinians in the occupied territories were actually content to live under Israeli rule. Asserting that the material conditions of most inhabitants of the West Bank and Gaza had improved significantly since 1967, Likud leaders told the Israeli public that only a few radicals affiliated with the PLO called for Israeli withdrawal. The vast majority of the Palestinian population, by contrast, was said to recognize and appreciate the improvement in their standard of living that had accompanied occupation, and accordingly, for the future, to seek no more than local or regional autonomy under continuing Israeli rule. To see the basis for these claims, territorial maximalists often added, one need merely travel through the occupied territories. The Palestinians had never lived better; television antennas were everywhere, there were more new cars than ever, and many new homes had been constructed.

A related Likud claim was that continuing occupation of the West Bank and Gaza was without significant costs from the Israeli point of view. Shamir and like-minded Israelis insisted that the Palestinian inhabitants of these territories did not constitute a serious obstacle to their development in accordance with the design of Israelis committed to territorial maximalism. Palestinian acquiescence, they asserted, meant there would be few burdens associated with the maintenance of order, and little to prevent ordinary Israeli citizens from conducting themselves in the West Bank and Gaza as if they were in their own country. According to one veteran Israeli analyst, these politicians "viewed the territories as though they were unpopulated. They viewed local Palestinians as either lacking political aspirations or lacking any desire to fulfill them. . . . The possibility that they might one day rebel against Israeli rule was completely discounted."[86] Although the assertions of Israeli government officials were not new, and had been challenged by Palestinians in the past, they were articulated repeatedly and forcefully by the Israeli political right during 1986 and 1987, and prior to the intifada they appear to have been accepted at face value by substantial segments of the country's Jewish population. As expressed by an Israeli journalist and politician opposed to Likud's policies, "The illusion was that Palestinian docility under occupation would go on forever."[87]

The intifada was intended to show these assertions to be myths in a way that could not possibly be explained away by apologists for occupation. In other words, the Palestinian uprising sought to send the Israeli public a message to the effect that the parties of the right were either ignorant about the situation in the West Bank and Gaza or, more probably, deliberately seeking to mislead the people of Israel. Palestinians sought to leave no room for doubt about their implacable opposition to occupation, and also to foster in Israel a recognition that the course charted by the country's leaders was a costly one, which was not in the interest of the Jewish state. This message was particularly important in view of the deep political divisions that existed within Israel, with the public bombarded by conflicting claims from Labor and Likud, and with many ordinary Israelis trying to determine which party's vision of the country's future was the wisest and most realistic.

Evidence that the Palestinians' message was having an impact in Israel was offered by a significant change in the way that most Israelis looked at the West Bank and Gaza after December 1987, a change often described as the resurrection of the "Green Line" in Israeli political consciousness. The Green Line refers to the pre-1967 border separating Israel from its Arab neighbors, and in the twenty years between the June War and the outbreak of the intifada, those parts of the Green Line running between the West Bank and Gaza on the one hand and Israel on the other had become nearly invisible to many Israelis. Even supporters of territorial compromise frequently found themselves in the occupied territories, traveling through the West Bank to get from one part of Israel to another, taking their cars to garages in Gaza, driving to Jericho for a casual meal in one of the city's oasis restaurants, and much more. These contacts, as well as the many important economic and institutional linkages established between Israel and the territories since 1967, gave many and perhaps most Israelis a feeling that there was a natural connection between their country and these areas. Indeed, by the end of 1987, a majority of Israel's population was too young even to remember a time when the West Bank and Gaza were not under their country's control.[88] As a result, while the West Bank and Gaza were not quite seen as Israel itself, neither did they appear to be part of another, foreign country.

The intifada transformed these perceptions, however, leading most Israelis to regard the West Bank and Gaza as zones of insecurity that should be avoided as much as possible. As Yitzhak Rabin himself explained in September 1988, when asked to comment on the fact that the number of Israelis killed in the territories had actually declined since the beginning of the uprising, "Jews simply don't visit the territories as they used to. No one's wandering around the garages of Gaza any more these days."[89] The resurrection of the Green Line was similarly evident in the effective redivision of Jerusalem, discussed earlier, a consequence of the Palestinian uprising that had an especially significant influence on the thinking of many Israelis. In the words of an authority on walking tours in the Israeli capital, for example, "Before the intifada, all the routes of the hikes I wrote about were over the Green Line. . . . [But] today the Green Line is my map of fear."[90] Thus, in the judgment of yet another Israeli analyst, writing in December 1989, "Perhaps the most conspicuous result of the intifada has been the restoration of Israel's pre-1967 border, the famous Green Line, which disappeared from Israeli maps and consciousness as early as 1968. . . . [Today] the West Bank and Gaza are seen as foreign territories inhabited by a hostile population, whose stone-throwing youngsters are ready to die—and do—in their quest for freedom."[91]

While Israelis increasingly recognized that what they had been told about Palestinian political sentiments and the cost-free character of occupation was not correct, they did not necessarily conclude that their country should withdraw from the occupied territories and accommodate itself to Palestinian nationalism. Indeed, those committed to the permanent exercise of Jewish sovereignty over the West Bank and Gaza in many cases drew a very different conclusion.

In particular, some Israelis on the right side of the political spectrum began to think about removal of the Palestinians from the West Bank and Gaza, which was a disturbing but nonetheless logical response to the Palestinian uprising from the perspective of those committed to territorial maximalism. If Israel was indeed to retain the territories, and if it was the case, as the intifada itself proclaimed, that the Palestinians would never submit to Israeli rule, then it was not a very big logical leap to the view that the Palestinians should be removed from the occupied areas. This is the policy of "transfer," and though it was not the official position of Likud or any other established party of the political right, the notion was the principal plank in the platform of a new party, Moledet (Homeland), which succeeded in capturing two seats in the Knesset elections of November 1988.[92] Moreover, partly as a result of Moledet's campaign, and in response more generally to developments in the occupied territories, the idea of transfer acquired a measure of acceptability in Israeli political discourse. Whereas it had previously been considered too outrageous to discuss, even though it was undoubtedly on the minds of a few extremists,[93] the possibility of removing Palestinians from the West Bank and Gaza had by mid-1988 become a legitimate subject for political discussion and debate.

Public opinion polls revealed that interest in the notion of transfer extended well beyond those Israelis who voted for Moledet or other political parties of the extreme right. For example, a survey conducted for the *Jerusalem Post* in August 1988 found that fully 49 percent of those interviewed, including 30 percent of those identifying themselves as supporters of Labor, leaned toward this approach to the problem of the occupied territories. Thus, as the *Jerusalem Post* wrote when reporting the results of its poll, "Virtually unmentionable (and unaskable) until a few months ago, except by the tiny minority that supports Rabbi Meir Kahane's Kach Party, the subject of transfer is no longer taboo; it has gained legitimacy, become a focus of public discussion and swept through the right."[94]

This was not the intifada's only impact on Israeli political discourse, however. The Palestinian uprising also reinforced the views of many committed to territorial compromise, giving new vigor to their arguments that it was not in Israel's interest to retain the West Bank and Gaza, and in particular leading some to reexamine commonly held assumptions about the strategic importance of the occupied territories. Challenges to the view that Israeli security required retention of the West Bank and Gaza were not completely new. For example, an important study by a scholar at Tel Aviv University's Center for Strategic Studies, published in 1983, argued that withdrawal from the West Bank and Gaza and the creation of an independent Palestinian state in these areas would "probably leave Israel in a better overall position than would a continuing political stalemate or any of the other potential outcomes. . . . [And if this independent Palestinian state] were created with appropriate risk-minimization provisions for Israel and within the context of a broad Israeli-Arab detente, it would probably result in a significantly less tense and dangerous environment for Israel."[95] But analyses along these lines became much more common following the outbreak of the intifada, and it was especially notable that many in the IDF now spoke out in support of the proposition that withdrawal from the West Bank and Gaza was acceptable from a security point of view.

Reflecting the strength of such sentiments in Israeli military circles, a group of senior reserve officers formed the Council for Peace and Security in the spring of 1988. The council maintained that withdrawal from the West Bank and Gaza is acceptable from a military point of view and, more specifically, one of the planks in its platform was that "the development of military technology, including missiles, precision-guided munitions and combat helicopters, can give the IDF a relative edge over the Arab armies and will lessen the need for continual and full occupation of the territories."[96] Composed of roughly three hundred generals and other high-ranking officers, as well as prominent scholars and business leaders, the Council for Peace and Security worked to influence both government policy and public opinion by issuing position papers and organizing conferences and seminars.

IDF officers and others who shared the perspective of the Council for Peace and Security were widely quoted in the Israeli and international press during the spring and summer of 1988, and some among them not only argued that Israel is fully capable of compensating for the loss of the West Bank and Gaza but went so far as to declare the military value of these territories to be quite limited. For example, former air force commander Amos Lapidot stated that "from the standpoint of Israel's defense, the territories have no value,"[97] and Brigadier General (res.) Ephraim Sneh, former head of the Civil Administration in the West Bank, asserted that three AWACS radar aircraft would provide Israel with better early warning than the country's current stations on the mountain ridges of the West Bank.[98]

Among the statements and writings of prominent Israelis outside of military circles was a powerful *New York Times* article by Abba Eban, in which the former Israeli foreign minister rebutted the charge that withdrawal from the West Bank and Gaza, even if accompanied by the establishment of a Palestinian state in these territories, would pose a threat to Israeli security. Citing figures from the Center for Strategic Studies at Tel Aviv University, Eban noted that Israel has a mobilizable manpower of 540,000, with some 3,800 tanks and 682 aircraft. The PLO, according to the same study, has "8,000 men in scattered places, zero tanks and aircraft, a few guns and no missiles, but a variety of hand grenades, mortars, stones and bottles." Thus, Eban concluded, in response to specific charges by some American supporters of Israel, "It takes a great effort of imagination to envision this array of forces flanking our cities from three sides and the sea, while inflicting 100,000 casualties."[99]

Some analysts even called the territories a security liability, arguing, among other things, that the intifada had transformed the IDF into a police force charged with keeping order in the occupied territories, and that this in turn was undermining Israel's military preparedness. According to this argument, military operations in the West Bank and Gaza had lowered morale, disrupted training, and undermined the IDF's organizational coherence, thereby making Israel weaker vis-à-vis Syria and other external challenges, the only real threats to its security of a properly military nature. As stated in the platform of the Council for Peace and Security, continued occupation "will devour our resources and divert the army from its main mission, preparation for war."[100] Such concerns were also articulated by others. For example, some soldiers complained about a loss of confidence in their commanding officers, and about confusion over which orders to follow when seeking to suppress the intifada.[101] In addition, psychologists sent into the field by the IDF found that confrontations with Palestinian demonstrators sometimes produced "inner agonies," particularly among new recruits, and gave rise to depression, nightmares, and a propensity to disobey orders.[102] Taking all of these considerations together, General (res.) Shlomo Gazit, one of the country's most respected strategic analysts, thus concluded in the fall of 1988, "Although the territories have some strategic value, in the end they are a burden."[103]

As with increased attention to the notion of transfer, formation of the Council for Peace and Security, and new thinking about the strategic significance of the West Bank and Gaza more generally, were in large part a response to the Palestinian uprising. According to an Israeli journalist who attended a gathering of retired army officers shortly before some of them established the council, the conversation focused on the intifada and the damage it was causing Israel at home and abroad. "We have to cut ourselves loose [from the West Bank and Gaza] quickly," said a veteran officer whose political orientation was described as middle-of-the-road.[104] There is also evidence that this kind of thinking gained wide acceptance within the military during the first half of 1988. According to an informal survey conducted by *Yediot Aharonot*, a prominent Israeli newspaper, "One can estimate that among the current general staff a clear majority of seventy-five to eighty percent believe that the security risks associated with Israel's continuing to rule the territories are greater than the security risks which Israel will assume if it relinquishes the territories."[105]

Perhaps the most fully developed account of the thinking that gained currency at this time, and of the role of the Palestinian uprising in fostering these attitudes, is a monograph published in 1989 by Ze'ev Schiff, the highly respected military affairs editor of *Ha'aretz*. According to Schiff,

> As a result [of the intifada], for the first time since 1967, many Israeli strategists have reoriented their approach to West Bank and Gaza security concerns. Israel has learned that the strategic importance of the area is not only a function of territorial depth, but also of the activities of the populace. The uprising has taught Israel that ruling the West Bank and Gaza does not automatically provide greater security to the rulers. What was once considered a security belt may now be a security burden. Israel has learned that one nation, particularly a small one, cannot rule another nation for long; that 3.5 million Israelis cannot keep 1.5 million Palestinians under perpetual curfew.[106]

The message that Palestinians sought to send by means of the intifada was addressed to a variety of audiences, and in addition to Israel these included American policy-makers and the U.S. public. In the immediate context, Palestinians were angry that the U.S. had closed the PLO information office in Washington, and that in this instance, as in many others, U.S. policy toward the Middle East appeared to be heavily influenced by the wishes of the Israeli government and its American supporters. Palestinians were also angry that the Reagan administration had in 1986 rejected a Jordanian-Palestinian plan under which the U.S. would recognize the Palestinian people's right to self-determination in exchange for PLO acceptance of United Nations Resolution 242.

More generally, Palestinians were disturbed by Washington's apparent indifference to the deteriorating situation in the occupied territories. Whereas the U.S. president had in September 1982 launched a peace initiative calling for Israeli withdrawal from the West Bank and Gaza, Jerusalem's formal rejection of the Reagan Plan and the subsequent intensification of its settlement drive in the occupied territories had brought few complaints from American officials. On the contrary, cooperation between Washington and Jerusalem had deepened. The Reagan administration also appeared to be fully in accord with Jerusalem's view of the Middle East conflict, agreeing both that the PLO was an obstacle to Arab-Israeli accommodation, and hence deserved no role in the search for peace, and that the core of the conflict itself was Arab intransigence rather than the continuing abridgment of Palestinian political rights.

Against this background, Palestinians hoped the intifada would force Americans to look at the Israeli-Palestinian conflict in a new light. Moreover, they had at least some success with respect to these objectives, even though, in a larger sense, there was more continuity than change in American attitudes and foreign policy. For one thing, a number of U.S. congressmen expressed concern about Israel's approach to containment of the Palestinian uprising.[107] In February 1988, for example, a dozen members of Congress met privately with the Israeli ambassador to warn that Israel's harsh treatment of demonstrators in the West Bank and Gaza had the potential to harm U.S.-Israeli relations. The following month, thirty senators, including both Republicans and Democrats, sent the Israeli prime minister a letter expressing "dismay" at his rejection of U.S. calls for peace based on an exchange of land for peace.

The intifada also helped to motivate the Reagan administration to undertake new diplomatic efforts to foster movement toward Middle East peace. In March 1988, Secretary of State George Shultz proposed that the U.S. sponsor peace talks between Israel and its Arab neighbors, which would include negotiations between Jerusalem and a joint Jordanian-Palestinian delegation. The talks would be based on United Nations resolutions 242 and 338 and, as stated in identical letters from Shultz to Prime Minister Shamir of Israel and King Hussein of Jordan, the objective of the new American initiative was to provide for the security of all states in the region and for "the legitimate rights of the Palestinian people." As with the formula adopted at Camp David a decade earlier, talks were initially to focus on provisions for limited Palestinian self-rule during a transition period, three years in this instance, and were to be followed by negotiations aimed at determining the final status of the West Bank and Gaza. Prior to the start of negotiations, according to the U.S. plan, there was to be an international peace conference convened under the auspices of the secretary-general of the United Nations.

Although little progress was made on the basis of the U.S. plan during 1988, the uprising could at least claim credit for a revival of American diplomatic activity and for an increase in U.S. attention to the Palestinian dimension of the Arab-Israeli conflict. This is not to say that Shultz's proposals won support among the Palestinians. Many prominent Palestinians in the West Bank and Gaza found "nothing new" in the Shultz initiative and complained that there could be no progress so long as the PLO was excluded from the diplomatic process. Further, in the latter context, Palestinians were particularly disturbed by renewed U.S. efforts in the spring of 1988 to close the PLO observer mission at the United Nations. Nevertheless, with the American secretary of state making several trips to the Middle East during 1988 in order to promote a peace plan that was disliked by the Israeli government precisely because of its emphasis on territorial compromise and Palestinian political rights, it was evident that the U.S., too, was responding to political messages sent by the intifada.

In addition, while continuing to resist all formal contact with the PLO, Shultz met in March 1988, over strenuous Israeli objections, with two prominent Palestinian-American professors who were members of the Palestine National Council. The two were Edward Said and Ibrahim Abu-Lughod, whose names had been proposed for inclusion in a Jordanian-Palestinian negotiating team during the Hussein-Arafat diplomatic initiative of 1985. Prior to the meeting with Shultz, Said and Abu-Lughod had consulted with Arafat and were instructed to report that the PLO was prepared to participate in any peace process that would lead to the establishment of an independent Palestinian state in the West Bank and Gaza.

With Americans seeing violent Israeli-Palestinian confrontations on their television sets virtually every evening, the intifada also appears to have had an impact on public opinion in the United States. In January 1989, by which time the PLO had launched a diplomatic initiative of its own, a *New York Times*–CBS poll found that 64 percent of the Americans surveyed favored contacts with the Palestinian organization, in contrast to 23 percent who opposed such contacts. The same poll also found considerable skepticism about Israel's desire for peace; only 28 percent judged Israel to be willing to make "real concessions" for peace, whereas 52 percent did not think that Israel was genuinely interested in compromise.[108] There was an approximately equal degree of skepticism about PLO willingness to make concessions in order to achieve a peace settlement, but given past and continuing U.S. support for the Jewish state, it is significant that a majority of Americans deemed Israeli attitudes, as well as Palestinian militancy, to be an obstacle to Middle East peace.[109]

In addition to sending messages to Israel and the United States, the intifada also had something to say to the rulers of Arab states. As noted, Palestinian actions in the West Bank and Gaza were partly a response to disappointment with PLO leadership and confusion about the organization's policies following the Eighteenth PNC, and even more to anger that the Palestinian problem had received no serious attention at the November Arab summit meeting in Amman. Thus, by seizing the initiative and launching their own attempt to shake off the occupation, Palestinians were in effect declaring that the lethargy and self-absorption of Arab leaders left ordinary men and women with no choice but to take matters into their own hands.

Implicit in this message to the leaders of Arab states was a reminder that Palestinians were not the only Arabs unhappy with the status quo, and a warning that popular rebellions might therefore break out elsewhere and bring additional challenges to established patterns of governance. More specifically, with many Arab countries ruled by inefficient, corrupt, or authoritarian regimes, and with leaders and elites largely preoccupied with their own power and privilege, or at least widely perceived to be thus preoccupied, the intifada demonstrated that there were limits to the patience and passivity of the Arab rank and file. Seen from this perspective, the uprising in the West Bank and Gaza, which was all the more remarkable in view of Israel's strenuous efforts at containment, offered compelling evidence that popular grievances could not be ignored indefinitely and put Arab leaders on notice that it was in their own interest to address unresolved problems, including the plight of the Palestinians.

The Arab states taken together responded to events in the occupied territories by convening an emergency summit in Algiers in June 1988. Seventeen heads of state attended, demonstrating that Arab leaders had indeed received the Palestinians' message and wished to protect themselves against the charge of being interested only in their own welfare. The Algiers summit gave prominence to Arafat and the PLO delegation and reaffirmed the PLO's status as sole legitimate representative of the Palestinian people. The summit also established a special committee to coordinate Arab action and mobilize support for the intifada, and the assembled Arab leaders agreed in addition to provide financial assistance to help sustain the uprising, even though the precise amounts and timing of these payments were left to future negotiations.[110] Finally, the summit criticized the United States for its pro-Israeli bias and declared the Shultz initiative to be ineffective and one-sided, calling instead for an international peace conference under UN auspices in which Palestinians would participate on a footing equal to that of other delegations.

Among individual Arab states, Jordan is the most sensitive to developments in the occupied territories, and it was indeed King Hussein who took the most dramatic action in response to the intifada. On July 31, 1988, the king made a televised address in which he officially relinquished his country's claims to the West Bank, declaring, "The independent Palestinian state will be established on the occupied Palestinian land, after it is liberated, God willing." He added that this action was being taken in response to the wishes of the PLO, and also because "there was a collective conviction that the struggle for liberating Palestinian land will be enhanced by legal and administrative disengagement between the [East and West] Banks." Palestinians viewed Hussein's disengagement speech as a major victory for the intifada, and on August 3 the PLO issued a statement declaring that it was prepared to carry out its responsibilities as the sole legitimate representative of the Palestinian people.

Hussein's decision was reflected in deeds as well as words. Indeed, the king's July 31 speech followed several days of activity during which he began to sever ties between Jordan and the West Bank. On July 28, Jordan's Council of Ministers announced cancellation of the $1.5 billion development plan for the occupied territories that the king had introduced in 1986, explaining that this was being done in order to "enable the PLO to shoulder its full responsibility as the sole legitimate representative of the Palestinian people." On July 30, Hussein dissolved the lower house of the Jordanian parliament, half of whose sixty seats were occupied by representatives of Palestinians in the West Bank. A few days after the king's speech, the Jordanian government abolished the Ministry of Occupied Lands and replaced it with a political department within the Ministry of Foreign Affairs.

Although Jordan's disengagement from the West Bank was a direct consequence of developments set in motion by the intifada, three more specific sets of factors also influenced Hussein's decision to sever connections with the West Bank. Of most immediate relevance were the king's strained relationships with West Bank and Gaza Palestinians and with the PLO. During 1986 and 1987,

Palestinians in the West Bank and Gaza found many opportunities to express their support for the PLO and their opposition to Jordanian influence in the occupied territories. Similarly, leaders of the intifada gave no indication of looking to Jordan for assistance in articulating Palestinian demands, which in fact left Hussein in an awkward position when George Shultz visited the Middle East in the spring of 1988 to seek support for his peace initiative. The king's unhappiness at this rebuff to what he insisted had been Jordan's significant and continuing efforts on behalf of the Palestinian cause intensified during the Arab summit in Algiers, especially when the assembled heads of state agreed to allocate funds for the occupied territories but ignored Jordan's request for assistance in recognition of its own special position in the Arab-Israeli conflict.[111] Following the summit, Hussein thus decided that the Palestinians and the PLO should be left, as they and other Arabs apparently wished, to fend for themselves in dealing with Israel and responding to the U.S. diplomatic initiative.

A second factor that contributed to Hussein's decision was the Shultz peace plan. Inspired by the Camp David accords of 1978 and the Reagan Plan of 1982, the U.S. sought to exclude the PLO from the peace process it hoped to set in motion, and Washington looked to Amman to provide the framework for a Jordanian-Palestinian delegation which would negotiate with Israel over the future of the occupied territories. The U.S. also hoped that its focus on a "Jordanian option," coupled perhaps with conciliatory gestures from Amman, would enhance the Labor Party's position within the domestic political arena in Israel. Hussein was in no position to play the role Washington sought to assign him, however, since he had no mandate from the PLO, and since the intifada had made the opposition of West Bank and Gaza Palestinians more clear than ever. Thus, with his room for maneuver even more restricted after the Arab summit, the king found disengagement from the West Bank a convenient mechanism for extricating himself from the no-win situation in which he had been placed by the Shultz initiative. Hussein may also have hoped that his action would exert some pressure on the U.S. and Israel, who seemed to expect much from the king while offering little in return.

The third set of considerations bearing on Hussein's decision concerned the king's calculations about the political mood inside Jordan itself. On the one hand, the king and his supporters were worried about growing activism among Jordanians of Palestinian origin. For example, between December 1987 and August 1988, there were at least 117 demonstrations in Jordan in support of the intifada, ranging in size from 100 to 2,500 participants.[112] This activism was of concern to the government, and even produced speculation that there could be a "second intifada" on the other side of the Jordan River, especially if Hussein appeared ready to join the U.S. peace initiative and substitute himself for the PLO. On the other hand, complaints about mounting economic and social problems *inside* Jordan were also fostering discontent and political alienation, raising once again the possibility that some in Jordan, inspired by the intifada, might rise up against a regime deemed unresponsive to their needs. Contributing to the plausibility of this analysis were the declining value of the Jordanian dinar, growing unemployment, and a rising crime rate, as well as the charge by some Jordanians that Hussein's preoccupation with the Palestinian issue was contributing to the severity of these problems. Writing at this time, a Palestinian scholar knowledgeable about Jordan thus concluded that while the intifada was "basically a call for liberation and national independence on Palestinian soil," it was also "a call to liberate Arab identity and thought from the repression and tyranny of the ruling Arab regimes." This latter interpretation, he added, "started [during the first half of 1988] to spread through the Amman Arab media, the Friday sermons in the mosques, and the church sermons on Sunday." [113]

Implementation of the disengagement decision made it clear that there was an element of anger, or even vindictiveness, in Hussein's action, and that the king was in effect sending the Palestinians a message in return. In early August, the Jordanian government, acting on instructions from the palace, dismissed about 21,000 civil servants, teachers, and others in the West Bank who had been employed by various ministries based in Amman, the only major exception being the employees of Islamic courts and the Department of Religious Endowments (Waqf). Jordanian citizenship was also withdrawn from West Bank residents, it being stipulated that expired passports would not be renewed, that new passports would not be issued, and that valid Jordanian passports would now serve only as identification and travel documents for Palestinians living in the occupied territories. By these and other actions, the king was seeking to demonstrate to residents of the territories that they received much more assistance from Jordan than they were willing to acknowledge, and he was also declaring to the PLO that filling the vacuum created by Jordan's disengagement would require more than rhetoric, and might in fact be beyond the organization's administrative and financial capabilities. Some Palestinians accordingly complained of Hussein's "pressure tactics," even as they called his disengagement speech a major victory for the intifada. As expressed by one Palestinian analyst, "Hussein was challenging the PLO to pick up the task of running daily life" in the West Bank and Gaza and, in addition, he "must be betting on the PLO falling short of this challenge." [114] Were this to occur, Hussein would of course be pleased should the inhabitants of the occupied territories, now chastened and properly appreciative, petition for reestablishment of their important relationship with the Hashemite kingdom.

The PLO Peace Program

While the intifada was designed to send the message that there could be no peace so long as Israel continued to occupy the West Bank and Gaza and refused to come to terms with Palestinian nationalism, Palestinians also sought to send a second, more positive message. They sought to tell Israelis and others that there was an alternative to continued conflict, that they did not seek destruction of the Jewish state but merely to realize their own national aspirations within the framework of a "two-state" solution to the Israeli-Palestinian dispute.

This second message was essential if there was to be a meaningful increase within Israel of support for territorial compromise. Although the intifada was forcing Israelis to change the way they looked at the West Bank and Gaza, and in particular to recognize that retention of these territories was not without significant costs from the viewpoint of the Jewish state, Israelis also needed to be persuaded that continuing to bear these costs was not their only option. In other words, Israelis needed to be convinced that withdrawal from the West Bank and Gaza would satisfy the Palestinians and make it possible to end the Arab-Israeli conflict. Only under these conditions would any recognition of the costs of occupation fostered by the intifada lead to decreased support for political parties committed to the concept of "Greater Israel." On the other hand, if convinced that relinquishing the occupied territories would indeed bring Arab recognition, and with it peace and security, even many who had in the past voted for Likud might in the future give their support to parties and leaders that advocate territorial compromise. As expressed in the spring of 1988 by Moshe Amirav, cofounder of the Council for Peace and Security and a former member of the Likud Central Committee, "nine out of ten Likudniks will compromise on territory if their questions about security are satisfied." [115]

Palestinians had in the past indicated a willingness to recognize Israel within its pre-1967 boundaries. Inhabitants of the occupied territories and other Palestinians had shown serious interest in a two-state solution since the mid-1970s, and the mainstream of the PLO had since the 1982 Arab summit in Fez been officially committed to mutual recognition between Israel and a Palestinian state located in the West Bank and Gaza, with East Jerusalem as its capital. Support for a two-state solution had also informed PLO diplomacy in the mid-1980s, when Yasir Arafat worked with King Hussein in an effort to persuade the United States to recognize the Palestinian people's right to self-determination in return for PLO acceptance of UN 242.

Most Israelis were nonetheless unpersuaded by these and other previous indications of a willingness to compromise on the part of the Palestinians, and some on the political right in fact argued that the intifada was itself evidence that Palestinians remained committed to Israel's destruction. Some Israeli hard-liners asserted in this connection that the uprising was not about the status of the West Bank and Gaza. It was not a struggle for Nablus and Hebron, they asserted, but a struggle for Haifa and Jaffa, the Palestinians' historic and continuing objective, a struggle for the end of the Jewish state. In advancing this argument, Likud and parties further to the right often used their pre-intifada assessment of conditions in the territories as a point of departure for the case they sought to make. Reaffirming their belief that occupation had significantly improved the life circumstances of most inhabitants of the West Bank and Gaza, they insisted that Palestinians in these territories had only ideological reasons to oppose Israeli rule, and therefore must logically be motivated by opposition to any realization of Zionist aspirations and by a continuing and unshakable commitment to Israel's destruction. Some Israeli officials also argued passionately, if inaccurately, that the uprising had been planned by PLO leaders in Tunis and thus, again, had nothing to do with conditions in the occupied territories.[116]

These arguments were the subject of political debate within Israel during much of 1988. Some Israelis dismissed the notion that occupation had been beneficial for the Palestinians and should thus logically be welcomed, and they accordingly rejected as well the assertion that the intifada must in reality be about something else, since rational men or women would not disrupt their lives so thoroughly and sustain such significant losses simply to drive Israel from the West Bank and Gaza. On the other hand, poorly informed about the conditions of life under occupation, many others found the reasoning of the political right to be plausible, or perhaps even convincing. Indeed, fully 36 percent of a sample of Israelis interviewed in August 1988 reported that they were more likely than before to believe West Bank and Gaza Arabs had fared well under Israeli occupation, whereas only 17 percent said they were less likely than before to hold this opinion.[117]

Against this background, many Palestinian leaders came to the conclusion that it was essential to put forward a clear and forceful message about their readiness to recognize Israel and make peace with the Jewish state. Such sentiments were expressed both by prominent Palestinians in the occupied territories and by senior PLO officials in Tunis, with many in both categories having come to believe, in the words of a knowledgeable Palestinian scholar, that "the situation demanded a moderate position and a practical program capable of capitalizing on, and dealing with, the changes and dynamics unleashed by the intifada."[118] As a result, whereas the fourteen-point memorandum presented by local Palestinian leaders at a Jerusalem press conference in January 1988 had addressed the abuses of occupation and set forth interim goals, Palestinian attention had by mid-1988 shifted to strategic objectives and the conditions under which peace could be achieved.

Also helping to foster this kind of thinking within PLO leadership circles was the changing position of the Soviet Union, which had long been the PLO's most important international patron. On the one hand, the USSR reduced military and financial support to Syria, another traditional Soviet client and the most important of the Arab "rejectionist" states. Alternatively, relations between the USSR and Israel improved significantly during the year leading up to the intifada. On the other hand, and even more important, the Soviets used their influence with the PLO to prod the Palestinian organization to take steps that might produce movement toward peace. For example, Soviet leaders publicly encouraged the PLO to accept UN Resolution 242 without preconditions in order to establish a dialogue with the United States. They also urged the PLO to recognize Israel's right to exist, prodding Yasir Arafat on this issue when he visited Moscow in April 1988.[119] In addition, and in some respects most important of all, the Soviets played a critical role later in 1988 in persuading George Habash and Nayif Hawatmeh, leaders of the Popular Front and the Democratic Front respectively and two of Arafat's most important critics on the PLO Executive Committee, to go along with a "realistic" and "flexible" Palestinian peace program.[120]

One of the first expressions of the PLO's peace program was a short position paper prepared and distributed in June 1988 by Bassam Abu Sharif, one of Arafat's closest political advisors. Abu Sharif's statement, which was presented to the international media on the eve of the Emergency Arab Summit, called for direct Israeli-Palestinian negotiations in order to achieve a two-state solution to the conflict. It also stated that Palestinians not only would accept but in fact would insist on international guarantees to ensure the security of all states in the region, including Palestine and Israel.[121] Abu Sharif's statement was to some extent a trial balloon. It was designed to signal the direction of PLO thinking and to open a discussion within the Palestinian organization about the merits of putting forth a more fully developed peace plan based on explicit recognition of Israel. It also sought to demonstrate PLO moderation and flexibility to Israelis, Americans, and others whom the Palestinians hoped to influence, and it is notable in this connection that Abu Sharif's position paper was reprinted in Jerusalem and Tel Aviv newspapers and hence was readily accessible to the Israeli public.

Another important Palestinian statement, this one emanating from the occupied territories, was the so-called Husayni Document presented early in August, following the announcement of Jordan's disengagement from the West Bank. Drafted by Faycal Husayni, head of the Arab Studies Society in Jerusalem and a prominent personality with close ties to Yasir Arafat, the document called for a two-state solution and a Palestinian declaration of independence based on the original United Nations partition plan. The Husayni Document also offered a detailed plan for the establishment of a Palestinian state, proposing, for example, that Arafat be its president, that members of the PLO Executive Committee constitute its government, and that the Unified National Leadership of the Uprising nominate personalities from the West Bank and Gaza for a general legislative body. In addition, the document urged formation of an interim government which would proclaim, on behalf of the PLO, a readiness to negotiate a final settlement with Israel, including agreed-upon boundaries between the two states.[122] During the month of August, Arafat also received from the occupied territories several other documents and letters urging the PLO to issue a declaration of national independence.

Although these and other expressions of support for a two-state solution were condemned by Palestinian rejectionists, including those associated with Hamas, they reflected the thinking of a growing number of senior PLO officials and soon coalesced into an effort by the Palestinian organization to regain the political initiative after weeks of responding to, rather than directing, events in the occupied territories. Members of the PLO Executive Committee praised the Husayni Document, for example, calling it important and stating that the PNC would soon authorize the establishment of a provisional Palestinian government. By September, Arafat was issuing calls in Europe and elsewhere for a peace conference that would include Israel and the PLO and be based on UN Resolution 242, as well as other UN resolutions.[123] Late in October, Arafat met in Aqaba, Jordan, with Hosni Mubarak of Egypt and King Hussein in order to discuss the prospects for peace. Arafat and Hussein were reported to have put their differences aside and agreed to cooperate in pursuit of a settlement; and, although it was officially denied by the three Arab leaders, observers judged that the timing, location, and focus of the meeting reflected an effort by the PLO to communicate its readiness for peace to the Israeli public on the eve of elections for a new Knesset.[124]

The culmination of these Palestinian efforts to break the diplomatic stalemate and foster movement toward a two-state solution arrived with the convening in Algiers in mid-November of an emergency meeting of the Palestine National Council. After several postponements, the nineteenth session of the PNC, described by some as the "intifada meeting," opened on November 12, and three days later heard Yasir Arafat issue a "Declaration of Independence for the State of Palestine." Arafat asserted that the Palestinian people derives its right to self-determination and statehood not only from its history as a nation but also from the UN Partition Resolution of 1947, which "still provides those conditions of international legitimacy that ensure the right of the Palestinian Arab people to sovereignty and national independence." Therefore, he declared, "The Palestine National Council, in the name of God, and in the name of the Palestinian Arab people, hereby proclaims the establishment of the State of Palestine on our Palestinian territory with its capital holy Jerusalem."[125] Arafat's statement also affirmed that the State of Palestine was a peace-loving state, committed to the settlement of regional and international disputes by peaceful means in accordance with the charter and resolutions of the United Nations.

The declaration of independence put forward by Arafat was reaffirmed in the political communiqué issued at the close of the Nineteenth PNC. Formally committing the PLO to a two-state solution to the conflict with Israel, the communiqué also called for an international peace conference to be convened on the basis of UN resolutions 242 and 338; for Israeli withdrawal from all Palestinian and Arab territories occupied in 1967, including Arab Jerusalem; for settlement of the question of Palestinian refugees in accordance with relevant UN resolutions; and for UN guarantees for security and peace between all states in the region, including the Palestinian state. Among the other notable features of the PNC communiqué were an affirmation of the "distinctive relationship" between the Jordanian and Palestinian peoples, who in the future were to be given the option of establishing a confederation between their two states; an expression of concern about the growth of extremism in Israel, including support for the mass expulsion of Palestinians from the West Bank and Gaza; and a message to the American people urging recognition of the national rights of the Palestinian people.[126]

A flurry of diplomatic activity followed the PNC meeting, with dozens of countries recognizing the newly created Palestinian state, while the Palestinians themselves devoted most of their energy to opening a dialogue with the United States. Within two weeks of the PNC meeting, at least fifty-five nations, including states as diverse as the Soviet Union, China, India, Greece, Yugoslavia, Sri Lanka, Malta, and Zambia, had recognized the Palestinian state. The U.S. response to the Palestinian declaration of independence and peace program was initially less positive, however. The Reagan administration insisted that Arafat and the PLO had still not adequately demonstrated their readiness to recognize and make peace with Israel, and the Americans also charged that the PLO "knows of, condones and lends support to" international terrorism. For these reasons, the U.S. announced late in November that it would deny Arafat's request for a visa to enter the United States in order to address the United Nations General Assembly during its annual session on Palestine. Despite reports of a State Department finding that Fatah had not in recent years taken part in terrorist acts, the U.S. refused to reconsider the PLO chairman's visa request, whereupon the General Assembly voted to move its session to Geneva in order to enable Arafat to attend.

By the middle of December, however, the PLO had restated its position in a manner the U.S. deemed acceptable, and Washington accordingly agreed to enter into a "substantive dialogue" with the Palestinian organization. Robert Pelletreau, Jr., the American ambassador in Tunis, was authorized to hold talks with PLO representatives, and on December 16 Ambassador Pelletreau led a U.S. delegation that met in Tunisia with Yasir Abed Rabbo and several other PLO officials. Clearing the way for this breakthrough were Arafat's address to the UN General Assembly in Geneva on December 13 and his remarks at a press conference the next day. Contributing, too, was a statement the PLO chief had issued in Stockholm a few days earlier, after meeting under the auspices of the Swedish foreign minister with a delegation of prominent American Jews committed to Israeli-Palestinian reconciliation. In all of these statements, Arafat offered clarifications and assurances with respect to the PLO's acceptance of UN 242 and 338, recognition of Israel's right to exist, and condemnation of terrorism, the three issues with respect to which Washington deemed previous PLO pronouncements to be ambiguous. During this period, similar clarifications were given by

Bassam Abu Sharif in a meeting with senior officials of the British Foreign Office, after which Britain declared itself to be satisfied and upgraded its own contacts with the PLO.

The American-PLO dialogue continued through 1989 and into 1990, but it produced little in the way of a tangible contribution to peace. The Palestinians, who had anticipated contact at a higher level, complained that Ambassador Pelletreau was the highest-ranking U.S. official with whom they had met. They also complained that discussions were often superficial and, more generally, that the PLO peace initiative did not appear to be having any meaningful impact on U.S. Middle East policy. Despite the PLO's own concessions, U.S. Secretary of State James Baker declared in March that the United States continued to oppose the establishment of an independent Palestinian state.[127] In addition, in response to the PLO's application for membership in the World Health Organization, the American administration announced in April that it had launched a campaign to prevent the PLO from gaining full membership in United Nations agencies. U.S. officials argued that this would exceed the PLO's status as a UN observer, and Baker stated in May that he would recommend terminating U.S. aid to any UN agency that supported the Palestinians' application. In explaining its continuing distrust of the PLO, the United States questioned the organization's declared renunciation of terrorism and suggested that Arafat was either unwilling or unable to control the more radical factions operating under the PLO umbrella.[128] As a result, the U.S.-PLO dialogue had reached an impasse by mid-1989, to the point, in fact, that the Swedish government undertook mediation efforts in an attempt to break the stalemate.

While the results of the U.S.-PLO dialogue were meager from the Palestinian perspective, the discussions in Tunis were nonetheless a source of concern to the Israeli government, which also rejected calls from Egypt, the Soviet Union, and others to the effect that the Jewish state should establish its own dialogue with the PLO. Despite the resolutions of the Nineteenth PNC and Arafat's subsequent declarations and clarifications, Israeli spokesmen insisted that the Palestinian organization was sincere neither about renouncing terrorism nor about recognizing Israel. In the latter connection, many Israelis, including many who did not support the government, pointed out that the PLO had not amended its charter so as to remove those provisions that reject the principle of partition and call instead for the establishment of a single state in Palestine. Thus, in January 1989, the Knesset passed a resolution affirming that Israel would not negotiate with the PLO, and in the months that followed, Prime Minister Yitzhak Shamir successfully opposed all formulas calling for Israel to talk to the PLO or otherwise give the Palestinian organization a formal role in peace negotiations. So far as the American-PLO dialogue is concerned, Israeli government officials repeatedly expressed their displeasure to Washington, charging that the PLO remained a "terrorist organization" and urging the U.S. to put an end to the talks in Tunis.

The PLO, for its part, pressed forward with its diplomatic initiative and sought, in particular, to communicate its message about territorial compromise and mutual recognition to the people of Israel, hoping thereby to reduce public support for politicians and parties committed to territorial maximalism. In February 1989, for example, PLO leader Salah Khalaf delivered a videotaped speech at a Jerusalem symposium on Middle East peace and called on Israel to begin talks with his organization in order to resolve all outstanding issues, including the PLO charter and security arrangements. About the same time, Yasir Arafat held an unprecedented news conference for Israeli journalists in Cairo, telling reporters that he wished to carry his message of peace directly to the Israeli public. Early in March, in order to offer evidence of his good intentions, Arafat ordered Fatah guerrillas in South Lebanon to halt anti-Israel operations. In the weeks that followed, Arafat and other PLO officials made additional statements challenging the Israelis to respond positively to their peace program. Arafat told Italian journalists in March, for example, that he was prepared to go to Jerusalem to meet with Israeli leaders. Early in May, he met with President François Mitterand of France, and then told French television that the PLO charter had been rendered obsolete by recent PNC resolutions. "As for the 25-year old Palestinian National Charter," Arafat told interviewers, "I believe you have an expression in French, 'C'est caduc,' it's null and void."[129] In response to these and other declarations, some officials in Europe and elsewhere called on Israel to begin talks with the PLO in order to test the intentions of the Palestinian organization.

Although there was little or no change in the official position of the Israeli government, the PLO's diplomatic initiative reinforced and amplified the challenge to the status quo put forward by the intifada, and taken together these two critical developments did appear to be having an impact on political thinking in the Jewish state. By late 1988 and early 1989, in a significant departure from their pre-intifada thinking, many in Israel had begun moving toward the conclusion that the Palestinian problem is at the core of the Arab-Israeli conflict, and that in order to deal with this problem it would be necessary for Israel to negotiate with the Palestine Liberation Organization.

Opinion polls conducted at this time documented a growing willingness to consider talks with the PLO. A December 1988 poll taken by *Yediot Aharonot*, a leading newspaper, reported that 21 percent of those sampled were "definitely in favor" of such talks, and another 33 percent were "in favor." Alternatively, 20 percent were "against," 24 percent were "definitely against," and 2 percent had no opinion.[130] Similarly, in a March 1989 *New York Times* survey, 58 percent said Israel should negotiate with the PLO if that organization recognizes Israel and ceases terrorist activity,[131] and 59 percent said the same thing in another *Yediot Aharonot* poll conducted a month later.[132] It is correct that most Israelis doubted the PLO had as yet fulfilled these conditions, which made it possible for hard-liners to argue that a majority actually opposed talks with the PLO. Yet earlier surveys, with the same conditionalities attached, had reported lower levels of support for an Israeli-PLO dialogue,[133] suggesting that a shift in public opinion was indeed taking place. It is also significant that 58 percent of those surveyed for the *New York Times* poll disagreed with the proposition that Palestinians want "a Palestinian state plus all of Israel in the long run," meaning that much of the Israeli public believed there to be a basis for negotiating with the PLO; and accordingly, 62 percent said they expected Israeli-PLO talks within five years. Yet another survey, conducted in May 1990, sought to assess attitude change and reported that the Israeli public, taken as a whole, had moved to the left in its thinking about the Palestinian problem, the PLO, and other aspects of the Arab-Israeli conflict.[134]

Support for negotiations with the PLO was most pronounced among Israelis who identified with Labor or leftist parties, but this was also the position of many having a preference for Likud. In the March 1989 *New York Times* survey, for instance, such negotiations were favored by 49 percent of the respondents describing themselves as Likud voters, as well as 78 percent of those identifying with Labor and 94 percent of those preferring parties to the left of Labor. In the May 1990 poll, which asked about talks with the PLO but did not attach conditions, support was expressed by 68 percent of those who had an opinion and identified with Labor, and by 89 percent of those who had an opinion and identified with parties further to the left. In addition, however, the authors report that 41 percent of the Likud supporters sampled were "in favor of typical dovish permanent solutions" to the Israeli-Palestinian conflict, whereas the "typical hawkish solutions of transfer and annexation" were endorsed by only 25 percent of the Likud voters interviewed.[135]

Public opinion polls were not the only indication of new Israeli thinking about the PLO and the Palestinian problem. Changing attitudes were also reflected in the statements of many politicians and intellectuals, including a few affiliated with parties of the right, and in a number of public encounters between Israelis and PLO officials. The clearest statements, predictably, emanated from the left side of the political spectrum. For example, Peace Now responded to the nineteenth session of the PNC with rallies and other activities as part of a campaign to "Speak Peace with the PLO Now." More striking, however, were the statements of some Labor Alignment and other officials who in the past had opposed negotiations with the PLO and advocated a "Jordanian option" for resolving the status of the West Bank and Gaza. Shimon Peres, leader of the Alignment and at the time minister of finance, stated that Israel should talk to the Palestinians "as they are—as they are organized." A less ambiguous expression of this prescription, calling for direct negotiations between Israel and the PLO, was offered by Yossi Beilin, a Peres confidant and deputy finance minister. Even Yitzhak Rabin, defense minister and architect of Israel's campaign to suppress the intifada, declared that whereas he had formerly believed "the best path for Israel was to keep the conflict and the solution within the framework of Israel's relations with the Arab states . . . the reality today is that the only partner with whom Israel can, perhaps, enter into a political process is the Palestinians . . . and whoever does not see this is not reading the map correctly." [136]

Among the other expressions of this kind of thinking was the report of a leading Israeli strategic studies center, made public in March 1989, which concluded that Jerusalem had no choice but to talk to the PLO if it wished to end the uprising and make progress toward peace. The report also concluded that the Palestinian organization was sincere in its calls for an accommodation with the Jewish state. [137] At this time, *Ha'aretz*, Israel's leading independent newspaper, also called for a new approach to the Palestinian problem and, more specifically, published an editorial urging the prime minister to drop his opposition to talks with the PLO.

Finally, the growing salience and legitimacy of the PLO as a negotiating partner, or at least a potential partner, was reflected in some well-publicized meetings between Israelis and PLO leaders and, equally, in the increased public and political tolerance that characterized reactions to these meetings. In January 1989, for example, four Israeli MKs joined PLO officials in Paris for a discussion-debate on Middle East peace, which both sides characterized as a step toward formal and high-level dialogue. Furthermore, the Israelis attending the session included two MKs from the Labor Alignment, as well as two from parties further to the left. Another meeting took place the following month, when seven Israelis, including politicians and academics, traveled to the Netherlands to participate in a conference with PLO representatives and other Palestinians. One of the Israelis was Abba Eban, veteran Labor politician and foreign minister from 1966 to 1974. At both meetings, the Israelis addressed their remarks to the audience rather than the Palestinians in order to respect a 1986 Knesset law making contact with the PLO illegal. On the other hand, subsequent criticism of this law provides yet another indication of changing Israeli attitudes. [138] Also, in a related and equally significant development, the Knesset failed to pass a bill proposing to lift the parliamentary immunity of MKs who violated the law banning contact with the PLO. The bill was introduced by right-wing politicians but was opposed by Labor, as well as the left, and so failed on a tie vote.

Although increased Israeli willingness to consider talks with the PLO undoubtedly reflected the evolution of that organization's attitude toward Israel, and especially its declarations in the fall of 1988 accepting a two-state solution to the Israeli-Palestinian conflict, the impact of the Palestinian peace program can be understood and evaluated only in the context of the new political circumstances created by the uprising in the occupied territories. The intifada demonstrated to many Israelis that there is a high price to be paid for retention of the West Bank and Gaza, not only in terms of hostility from the Arab world but also in the form of a threat to Israel's Jewish and democratic character, and possibly to its military security as well. In addition, the intifada brought increased recognition that Israel's conflict is with the Palestinians, and only secondarily with the Arab world in general. Thus, while new declarations by the PLO helped to convince Israelis that it may be possible to negotiate with the PLO about territorial compromise and mutual recognition, it is the intifada which persuaded many that it is desirable and important to exercise this option.

Both Israeli and Palestinian analysts have also stressed the central importance of the intifada in this context. According to Ze'ev Schiff, one of Israel's most highly regarded analysts of military and security affairs, "The Palestinian uprising against Israel has shattered a static situation that Israel has consistently sought to preserve . . . [and] removed any lingering suspicions that the Palestinians could be sidestepped in the search for an Arab-Israeli settlement. It has led to the unavoidable conclusion that there can be no end to the Arab-Israeli conflict without a resolution of the conflict between Israel and the Palestinians." As a result, Schiff adds, writing in mid-1989, "the possibility of Israeli-Palestinian negotiations is immeasurably closer than it was before December 9, 1987, the day the uprising began. The uprising, after all, has opened a new chapter in the political relationship between Israelis and Palestinians." Schiff also credits decisions taken by the PLO in fall 1988 with creating a new opportunity for Israel-Palestinian negotiations; but he observes as well that "it was only as a direct result of the uprising that the Palestine National Council met in Algiers in November 1988, to adopt resolutions reversing a more than 40-year-old rejection of U.N. resolution 181. . . . And it was only as a result of the uprising that PLO chairman Yasir Arafat, at a press conference in Geneva, formally renounced terrorism and extended virtual recognition to the state of Israel."[139] Among the Palestinian analysts who advance similar conclusions about the primary importance of the intifada is Philip Mattar, associate editor of the *Journal of Palestine Studies*. According to Mattar, also writing in mid-1989, "Unquestionably, the intifada, or uprising, in the West Bank and Gaza is responsible for the new situation."[140]

Additional Diplomatic Efforts

The focus of Middle East diplomacy shifted away from the peace initiative of the PLO during the second half of 1989 and the first half of 1990. The PLO's peace campaign, in combination with the intifada, had had a significant impact both on the international scene and on political thinking and discourse within the Jewish state. But the government of Yitzhak Shamir launched a diplomatic initiative of its own in the spring of 1989, and this effort competed with the PLO program and soon led to its displacement as the principal focus of political debate and diplomatic maneuvering.

In April 1989, Shamir proposed holding elections in the occupied territories to select a Palestinian delegation with which Israel would negotiate in order to establish a self-governing authority in the West Bank and Gaza during an interim period, to be followed by additional negotiations to determine the final status of these territories. These elections, Shamir added, would take place after the Palestinians called a halt to the intifada and calm was restored in the occupied areas. According to the Israeli prime minister, only under these conditions would it be possible to hold "free democratic elections, free from an atmosphere of PLO violence, terror and intimidation."

Shamir presented his proposals during a trip to Washington, where he met with U.S. President George Bush and obtained an expression of "cautious support" for his plan. In particular, Bush expressed approval of the plan's focus on Palestinian self-rule during an interim phase while postponing any discussion of the permanent status of the West Bank and Gaza. A two-stage approach of this sort had been the cornerstone of the 1978 Camp David accords, which the U.S. continued to believe offered the best chance for breaking the impasse between Israelis and Palestinians. Shamir's plan also borrowed freely from proposals that Yitzhak Rabin, the Israeli defense minister, had put forward several months earlier. In January 1989, as the intifada entered its second year, Rabin had called upon Palestinians to terminate the uprising and promised that Israel would then, three to six months later, permit residents of the West Bank and Gaza to elect representatives to negotiate with Israel and administer daily life in the occupied territories. In May, the national unity government led by Shamir formally adopted the prime minister's plan for elections in the territories.

Various aspects of Shamir's proposals made them unacceptable to Palestinians in the West Bank and Gaza. First, these Palestinians refused to lend their support to any initiative that did not give a role to the PLO. They also stated in this context that the Israeli plan was unacceptable because it attempted to divide Palestinians in the occupied territories from those living in other countries and, accordingly, did not recognize the national existence of the Palestinian people. Second, Palestinian spokesmen declared that they would negotiate with Jerusalem about interim arrangements for the territories only if these arrangements were understood to be part of a larger peace process leading to Israel's eventual withdrawal from the West Bank and Gaza. This was not the case, however, as statements and actions by the Israeli government continued to make clear. Indeed, with Shamir and other Israeli officials reaffirming their country's rejection of all peace formulas based on land for peace, Palestinians insisted that the Israeli plan was not a sincere effort to resolve the conflict but rather an attempt to divert attention from the PLO's peace program. Third, Palestinians rejected Israeli calls for an early end to the intifada, arguing that the uprising was necessary to press Israel to make concessions, and therefore that it would cease only when Jerusalem agreed to deal with the PLO and negotiate a comprehensive solution based on territorial compromise and mutual recognition.

Arab leaders, as well as Palestinians, rejected Shamir's proposals. Hosni Mubarak of Egypt visited Washington in early April and met with George Bush a few days before the Israeli prime minister. But Mubarak rejected an Israeli suggestion that he and Shamir hold a joint meeting with Bush, stating that he was declining in order to make clear his opposition to the peace proposals Shamir had put forward. Mubarak subsequently repeated to the American president that there could be no peace without an end to Israel's occupation of the West Bank and Gaza, and he also told Bush that Egypt was willing to participate in an international conference at which there would be negotiations based on the land-for-peace formula contained in Security Council Resolution 242 and other UN resolutions. King Hussein of Jordan, the other Arab leader with whom the United States was coordinating its efforts to deal with the Middle East conflict, also announced his opposition to the Shamir proposals. Hussein visited Washington later in April and declared that he welcomed American efforts to advance the peace process. He added, however, that the idea of holding elections in the occupied territories would have value only in the context of a comprehensive solution based on the principle of territorial compromise.

While Palestinians and many other Arabs regarded the Shamir plan as a cynical ploy, designed to mask Israeli intransigence in the face of compromises proposed by the PLO, elements within Shamir's own Likud Union worried that the prime minister might unwittingly have laid a foundation for far-reaching Israeli concessions. Despite Shamir's many public statements and private assurances to the effect that Israel would never relinquish control of the West Bank and Gaza, Likud hard-liners feared that Israel might come under increasing pressure from both domestic opponents and the international community, and they accordingly wished to remove any possibility that the plan for elections in the territories could be used to generate movement toward negotiations requiring territorial compromise. Among the recent developments that these hard-liners found worrisome were reports of unofficial but substantive contacts between Israeli officials and PLO representatives.[141] Also disturbing were continuing PLO gains on the international scene. In June, for example, the European Community passed a declaration which for the first time called for PLO participation in the peace process. About the same time, the U.S. State Department announced that the Bush administration had expanded its contacts with the PLO.

To tie the hands of the prime minister in any future bargaining, the Likud Central Committee held an emergency meeting in July and voted to impose four conditions on the election plan that Shamir had put forward and which the Israeli government had subsequently adopted. The move was led by Ariel Sharon, David Levy, and Yitzhak Moda'i, cabinet ministers whose motivations probably included their rivalry with Shamir and their own political ambitions, as well as their concern about retention of the occupied territories. The four conditions imposed by the Likud Central Committee included a ban on electoral participation by Palestinians residing in East Jerusalem, insistence that the intifada end before elections take place, reaffirmation that Israel would not relinquish any land (and hence opposition to a two-state solution), and a pledge to continue building Jewish settlements in the West Bank and Gaza.

The decision of the Likud Central Committee further reduced any possibility that the Israeli plan for elections in the occupied territories would become a vehicle for advancing the cause of peace. The conditions imposed on the Shamir initiative made it much more difficult to argue, as had some Israelis and Americans, that the prime minister's election plan contained useful elements and should be accepted as a point of departure for serious bargaining. The view of most Palestinians was summed up by Faycal Husayni, president of the Arab Studies Society in East Jerusalem and a leading personality in the occupied territories. According to Husayni, "This proves what we had been saying all along, Shamir was never serious in his proposal and he is not honest in pledging a free and democratic election. . . . [The four conditions are] merely a death certificate to a scheme that was born dead." [142]

With the diplomatic process having reached a stalemate, President Mubarak of Egypt undertook during the latter part of the summer to devise a formula that would win support from the United States while narrowing the gap between Palestinians and Israelis committed to territorial compromise. Late in July, he privately transmitted to the U.S. and Israel his suggestions for elections in the West Bank and Gaza, taking the Shamir plan as his point of departure but proposing ten additional points that not only clashed with the conditions established by the Likud Central Committee but also went far beyond the proposals Shamir himself had originally put forward. Some of Mubarak's ten points dealt with purely procedural matters, specifying, among other things, that Israel commit itself to accepting the election results, that international observers monitor the voting, that Israeli troops be withdrawn from balloting areas during the election, and that there be complete freedom of speech for all candidates. In addition, however, several of the Egyptian president's points were more substantive in character. These included a call for freezing Israeli settlement activity, for the inclusion of East Jerusalem Palestinians in the voting, for Israeli acceptance of the principle of trading land for peace, and for the setting of a date for the start of final status negotiations. [143] Mubarak hoped that his ten points might be the basis for direct Israeli-Palestinian negotiations in Cairo. He made his proposals public in September, and in October he traveled to Washington to discuss them with the U.S. administration.

Mubarak's plan brought favorable reactions from Israeli moderates and from the United States. Reflecting the attitude of most leaders of the Labor Alignment, Yitzhak Rabin met with the Egyptian president in mid-September and encouraged Mubarak in his efforts to mediate between Israelis and Palestinians. Rabin and other Alignment ministers, including Shimon Peres, also expressed strong support for the Egyptian plan in a variety of public and private forums in Israel, including meetings of the inner cabinet. Indeed, Peres and Rabin said they were prepared to pull the Alignment out of the national unity government if the cabinet did not respond positively to Mubarak's initiative. The U.S. position was expressed by Secretary of State Baker a few days before the Egyptian president visited Washington early in October. Baker warned that the Middle East peace process would collapse unless the government in Jerusalem either endorsed the Egyptian plan or found another formula for bringing Palestinians to the negotiating table.

Mubarak's initiative brought a more mixed response from Palestinians. Both the PLO and Palestinians in the occupied territories expressed appreciation for Mubarak's efforts but refrained from giving a full and unconditional endorsement to the Egyptian president's ten-point program. They complained, in particular, that Mubarak's plan gave no role to the PLO and made no mention of the Palestinians' right to self-determination. Nevertheless, Palestinians left the door open for further discussions and for the possibility that the Egyptian plan might be amended to remove its shortcomings. Arafat met with Mubarak on several occasions during this period and endorsed the principle of "open talks" with Israel. In addition, the PLO chairman asked Israeli journalists at a press conference in Cairo to carry the message that the PLO continued to seek talks with Israel and remained open to "a total and just peace." Palestinians also provided Mubarak with a list of twelve individuals who might participate in negotiations with Israel, a list that included Palestinians from outside as well as inside the occupied territories and which, according to press reports, had been approved by leaders of the Israeli Labor Alignment. Mubarak carried this list of potential Palestinian negotiators to Washington for his October meeting with the U.S. president.

In contrast to these more or less positive reactions, Likud leaders and other hard-line elements in the Jewish state bitterly denounced the ten-point Egyptian plan and eventually succeeded in securing its rejection by the Israeli government. Although Shamir for a time encouraged the cabinet to delay a formal decision, both to preserve its flexibility and in the hope of avoiding a Labor-Likud split that might bring down the government, the prime minister himself was among those who vigorously condemned the Mubarak initiative and insisted that it was a totally unacceptable basis for negotiations. Even stronger statements were issued by Ariel Sharon and others who had voted to impose conditions on Shamir's own proposal for elections in the territories. Then, on October 6, the six Likud ministers in the inner cabinet voted against the Mubarak plan, thereby removing any possibility that it would become an agreed basis for Israeli-Palestinian negotiations. The six Labor ministers in the inner cabinet supported the ten-point plan, but inner cabinet regulations stipulate that the position of the prime minister shall prevail in the case of a tie vote. Thus, once again, the diplomatic process appeared to have reached a dead end.

U.S. Secretary of State James Baker opened the next round of diplomatic maneuvering a few days later, introducing a "Five-Point Framework for an Israeli-Palestinian Dialogue" that he hoped would break the impasse. Among Baker's proposals: Israeli and Palestinian delegations should hold talks in Cairo; the U.S. understands that Egypt cannot substitute itself for Palestinians in any dialogue and must consult with Palestinians, as well as Israelis and Americans, in organizing negotiations; the U.S. also understands that Israel will attend the dialogue only after a satisfactory list of Palestinians has been worked out; the U.S. further understands that Israel will enter the dialogue on the basis of the Shamir election plan and that Palestinians will come to Cairo prepared to discuss this plan, although they may also raise any other issues they deem pertinent; and, to advance these proposals, the U.S. suggests that the American, Israeli, and Egyptian foreign ministers meet in Washington in the near future. Although presented by Baker in mid-October, the text of the secretary of state's five points was not officially released by the State Department until December.

Baker's five points, like the ten points of Mubarak, were viewed differently by the various parties to the conflict. They were accepted by the Israeli Labor Party, which subsequently also agreed that the Palestinian delegation could contain residents of East Jerusalem and several individuals who did not live in the occupied territories. Egypt, too, accepted the Baker plan, although the Mubarak government added that its approval rested on three "assumptions." These assumptions, designed to make the Baker proposals more acceptable to the PLO, specified that Palestinians from both inside and outside the occupied territories would be included in the delegation, that the agenda of the talks would be open, and that the dialogue in Cairo was the first step toward an international peace conference that would include participation by the PLO.

Although Palestinians once again expressed important reservations, they subsequently agreed to take part in the dialogue proposed by the American secretary of state. The PLO Executive Committee, meeting in Baghdad in October, initially denounced the U.S. proposals as a thinly veiled attempt to promote the Shamir plan. Early in December, however, PLO officials in Tunis delivered to U.S. Ambassador Robert Pelletreau a memorandum that accepted Baker's five points, subject to several conditions. These conditions, which were in fact the basis for the "assumptions" of the Egyptian government, called for a Palestinian delegation composed of individuals from both inside and outside the occupied territories, and for an open dialogue that had no preconditions and would foster movement toward an international peace conference. The Palestinians also called for the dialogue in Cairo to be held under the supervision of the United Nations and the permanent members of the Security Council.

In the weeks that followed, the PLO worked with Egypt to reach agreement on the composition of a Palestinian delegation. Arafat met with Mubarak on three occasions in January 1990, for example, and PLO officials also consulted indirectly with senior members of the Israeli Labor Alignment.[144] In February, both Egyptian and American officials announced that agreement had been reached on a Palestinian delegation that contained residents of the occupied territories and two deportees and would not require Israel to talk directly to the PLO, and at the end of the month Arafat confirmed this agreement in a letter sent by telefax to the International Center for Peace in the Middle East in Jerusalem.

As in the case of the Mubarak initiative, it was opposition from Israeli hardliners that ultimately derailed the Baker plan. Initially, some in Likud displayed tactical flexibility. In November, for example, three Likud members of the inner cabinet joined six Alignment ministers in giving conditional approval to the Baker plan, the conditions being that Israeli-Palestinian talks be limited to the issue of elections and that the PLO not be involved in these talks. The U.S. rejected these conditions, however, and diplomatic exchanges throughout the remainder of 1989 and the first part of 1990 failed to resolve the gap between the Israeli and American positions. Baker consistently told Israeli officials that Jerusalem would have to show greater flexibility both on the composition of the Palestinian delegation, including the kind of indirect involvement the PLO would have, and on the subjects that Palestinian negotiators might raise. Then, in late February, by which time Egypt had obtained PLO agreement on compromises acceptable to the Labor Party, Baker announced that he had done all he could and it was now time for a positive response from the Israeli government. Pointing out that the major purpose of an Israeli-Palestinian dialogue was to discuss Shamir's own proposals for elections in the occupied territories, the secretary of state also hinted that without a satisfactory response from Jerusalem, the U.S. might cease its efforts to bring Israelis and Palestinians together. Early in March, Bush himself sought to put pressure on the Israelis by declaring in a speech that U.S. opposition to Jewish settlements in the occupied territories also applied to East Jerusalem.

Differences between Likud and Labor over the American peace plan brought down Israel's national unity government on March 15, 1990. After several stormy cabinet meetings, Labor's Central Committee gave its Knesset members permission to withdraw from their coalition with Likud, if they determined that this would advance the cause of peace. Shamir, for his part, dismissed Shimon Peres, the Alignment leader who had been serving as deputy prime minister as well as minister of finance, whereupon the other cabinet ministers from Labor announced that they would resign from their posts. It is against this background that the Knesset voted on March 15, by a margin of 60 to 55, to dissolve the government because of Likud's refusal to accept U.S. proposals for talks with the Palestinians. Several Members of Knesset from religious parties either voted against Likud or abstained, enabling the no-confidence motion to pass.

While the collapse of the Shamir government was initially seen as a victory for those who supported peace based on territorial compromise, Israeli hard-liners eventually emerged in a stronger position than ever, and with this development came an end to the diplomatic maneuvering that had begun when Shamir presented his election plan in April 1989. Shimon Peres was given the first opportunity to form a new government, and the Labor leader bargained aggressively with religious and other parties in an attempt to put together a coalition that would exclude Likud but still control a majority of the seats in parliament. Peres was unable to construct such a coalition, however, and the opportunity to form a government then passed to Shamir, who by mid-June had succeeded in forming a ruling coalition from which Labor was excluded. Shamir's new government was based on the forty Knesset seats of Likud and twenty-two additional seats controlled by religious parties and two of the small nationalist parties to the right of Likud. The new coalition did not include Moledet, the ultranationalist party that had campaigned in 1988 on a platform of "transferring" Palestinians from the West Bank and Gaza.

The new Israeli government was the most right-wing in the history of the Jewish state. Shamir retained the premiership, and the Defense portfolio, the Foreign Ministry, and the Housing Ministry were given to Moshe Arens, David Levy, and Ariel Sharon respectively, all Likud stalwarts. Several of the other cabinet posts were assigned to the leaders of small ultranationalist parties in the coalition, and these parties also enjoyed considerable leverage in intracoalition bargaining because of the government's slender parliamentary majority. Shortly after the new government came to power, it formally rejected the plan for elections in the occupied territories that Shamir himself had introduced more than a year earlier. Its priorities, Shamir and others declared, would be to crush the intifada, to absorb new immigrants, principally from the Soviet Union, and to increase Jewish settlement activity in the West Bank and Gaza.

The United States responded to these developments with disappointment and anger. Baker expressed his frustration in testimony before Congress given in mid-June, strongly condemning Israel for rejecting his proposals for an Israeli-Palestinian dialogue. The secretary of state's testimony also included a forceful statement addressed to the Israelis: "The White House number is 202–456–1414," Baker declared, "and when you are serious about peace, call us." Palestinians and other Arabs praised Baker's harsh language, insisting that it was fully justified and long overdue. At the same time, they added that actions are more important than words and expressed regret that the U.S. government still appeared to be giving uncritical support to the Jewish state. Among their recent complaints was American opposition to a Security Council proposal to send an international team to investigate conditions in the West Bank and Gaza. Introduced in late May, following an escalation of violence against Palestinians in the territories, the proposed Security Council resolution was supported by all fourteen of the Council's other members.[145]

In yet another critical blow to the peace process delivered at this time, the United States on June 20 suspended its dialogue with the Palestine Liberation Organization. The issue on which this decision turned was terrorism. As recently as March 1990, the U.S. State Department had certified in a report to Congress that the PLO was honoring its December 1988 pledge to renounce terrorism. Although Palestinians had carried out a number of border and rocket attacks against Israel since that time, the State Department report said there was no evidence that any of these had been planned or even approved by Yasir Arafat or the PLO Executive Committee.[146] The attitude of the American administration changed in June 1990, however, following an attempted Palestinian attack on the Tel Aviv coast on May 30. The seaborne assault involved sixteen individuals in six speedboats, all of which were intercepted by the IDF, and was ostensibly undertaken to avenge the recent killing of Palestinians in the West Bank and Gaza. Responsibility was claimed by the Palestine Liberation Front, a small faction of the PLO based in Iraq and led by Abu al-Abbas.

Since the May 30 attack had been carried out by a faction of the PLO, and since Abu al-Abbas himself was a member of the PLO Executive Committee, American officials declared that doubts now existed about the sincerity of the organization's pledge to renounce terrorism, and that these doubts would have to be removed in order for the U.S.-PLO dialogue to continue. To accomplish this, the U.S. demanded that PLO leaders condemn the attack of May 30 directly and without reservation, and that the PLO also discipline those who had planned it and remove Abu al-Abbas from the Executive Committee. The PLO refused to meet these conditions, however, presumably so that Arafat would not be charged by his followers with allowing the U.S. and Israel to interfere in Palestinian affairs. In any event, whatever the reason, the response of the PLO was limited. Beyond insisting that Arafat and Fatah had neither participated in planning the attack nor known about it in advance, the Palestinian organization issued only a general statement reaffirming its declared policy, which was to condemn any and all military operations that target civilians, regardless of their nature. The State Department expressed disappointment at the PLO's response, calling it inadequate, and Baker accordingly used his mid-June appearance before Congress not only to denounce the intransigence of the Israeli government but also to question the PLO's commitment to peace. A few days later, in the absence of any additional response from the PLO, the U.S. suspended the dialogue. American officials added that talks could be resumed in the future, but only after the PLO had met Washington's conditions and thereby demonstrated that its opposition to terrorism was sincere.

In the wake of these developments, the summer of 1990 found Israeli hardliners operating from a position of strength, whereas mainstream Palestinians were increasingly on the defensive. In spite of whatever changes the intifada and the PLO peace program had introduced into the ranks of Israeli public opinion,

Likud had successfully outmaneuvered Labor in the arena of partisan politics, and Yitzhak Shamir now presided over a homogeneous right-wing government that was united in its opposition to territorial compromise and in its determination to intensify Jewish settlement in the West Bank and Gaza. Shamir had also successfully resisted efforts by the United States, Egypt, and others to establish an open-ended Israeli-Palestinian dialogue. Indeed, the peace initiatives of the PLO, Egypt, and the United States had exhausted themselves one after the other, with the Israeli government having had neither to make concessions nor to pay a price for its intransigence.

Palestinians, by contrast, had lost the initiative that the intifada and the PLO peace program had given them through the first half of 1989, and by summer 1990 most found it difficult to avoid the conclusion that their political and diplomatic efforts since December 1987 had failed to bring meaningful change in the policies and behavior either of the Israeli government or even of the United States. It remained possible that history would yet record that the uprising in the territories and the PLO diplomatic initiative had fostered movement toward a negotiated settlement based on territorial compromise and mutual Israeli-Palestinian recognition. The intifada, in particular, appeared to have had a significant impact on political thinking and discourse within the Jewish state, raising the possibility that a change in public attitudes would contribute to a change in government policy in the future, perhaps after the next Israeli elections. But such possibilities offered little comfort to Palestinians in the summer of 1990. Nor even were they central to Palestinian thinking at this time. Leaders of the PLO and mainstream nationalists in the occupied territories were increasingly under attack from rejectionist factions, including those operating under the banner of Islam, all of whom argued that diplomacy and moderation had failed to secure Palestinian rights, and that only a meaningful military challenge would force Israel to the bargaining table.

The Gulf Crisis and Its Aftermath

The year between summer 1990 and summer 1991 saw world attention shift from the Israeli-Palestinian conflict to the crisis in the Persian Gulf, beginning with Iraq's invasion of Kuwait on August 2, 1990, and followed first by diplomatic efforts to deter further aggression and restore Kuwaiti sovereignty, and then, early in 1991, by a massive U.S.-led military campaign to oust Iraq from Kuwait. Yet Israelis and Palestinians, too, were caught up in the tumult of this period. The circumstances of the PLO and of Palestinians in the occupied territories were strongly marked by the crisis in the Gulf. Israel was affected as well, although the Gulf crisis ultimately left unchanged the country's deep divisions on questions relating to the Israeli-Palestinian conflict.

Many Palestinians supported Iraq and its leader, Saddam Hussein, during the crisis in the Gulf. Palestinian leaders insisted that they did not approve of the Iraqi invasion and occupation of Kuwait, sometimes adding that no people understands the evils of occupation better than do the Palestinians. Some also argued that the PLO was attempting to play a mediating role and thereby bring about an "Arab solution" to the conflict, and indeed Yasir Arafat presented a peace plan early in August that called for the withdrawal of Iraqi forces from Kuwait. Nevertheless, there was an outpouring of popular support for Saddam Hussein throughout the West Bank and Gaza, and also among Jordanians of Palestinian origin. In addition, there were visible displays of solidarity with Iraq by Arafat and other PLO leaders. For example, when an Arab summit in Cairo voted on August 10 to send troops to help defend Saudi Arabia and other Gulf states against a possible Iraqi attack, the PLO was one of only two delegations to back Iraq at the meeting, the other being Libya. Arafat also traveled to Baghdad early in January 1991 and stated publicly that the PLO would side with Iraq in the event of a war with the U.S. and its coalition partners, and several days later, after the fighting had begun, the PLO called for a mobilization of its forces in Lebanon and warned them to be ready to strike at U.S. interests.[147]

The reason that many Palestinians supported Saddam Hussein lay partly in a generalized opposition to the political and economic status quo shared by ordinary citizens in many Arab countries, and partly in the growing belief among Palestinians that attempts to engage Israel in a peace process had been futile and, as a result, that only the presence of a credible Arab military challenge would force the Shamir government to the negotiating table. With respect to dissatisfaction in general, ordinary men and women in many Arab countries were deeply discontent with existing patterns of political economy and were directing their anger at corrupt and autocratic Arab regimes and the foreign governments believed to be supporting them. These sentiments were particularly strong among the poorer classes, who believed the resources of the Arab world were being squandered, who saw little prospect of a better future for themselves and their families, and who permitted themselves to hope, mistakenly and naively, that Saddam's attack upon the Kuwaiti monarchy might be the beginning of a revolution in the Arab world. Saddam encouraged such beliefs, of course, portraying himself as an opponent of privilege and excess and of the alliance between indulgent Arab regimes and the foreign interests that wished to keep them in power. The existence of such sentiments forced the leaders of a number of Arab countries to reject participation in the anti-Iraq coalition being constructed by the United States and, instead, to strive for neutrality in the Gulf crisis. This is the principal reason that only twelve of the twenty states attending the August 1990 Arab summit in Cairo voted to send troops to defend Saudi Arabia against a possible Iraqi attack.[148]

All of this had relevance for Palestinians, many of whom shared the view that Arab regimes and their foreign partners were more interested in business as usual than in meeting the needs of ordinary citizens, and who also believed that many Arab leaders were similarly indifferent to the plight of the Palestinians. This attitude toward Arab regimes was evident in the period leading up to the intifada, particularly after the Palestinian problem was neglected at the emergency Arab summit meeting convened in Amman in November 1987. During the fall of 1990, Palestinian frustration was readily apparent during an Arab League ministerial meeting in Tunis in mid-October, where the PLO led a walkout after failing to get support for a draft resolution condemning United States policy toward the Palestinians.

Palestinians were also deeply frustrated that PLO efforts to negotiate an end to the Israeli-Palestinian conflict had consistently been rebuffed by the government in Jerusalem. In the view of many Palestinians, concessions and expressions of moderation had proven futile and, if anything, brought more-aggressive Israeli policies. This seemed especially clear after June 1990, following the formation of an ultranationalist government in Israel and Washington's suspension of the American-PLO dialogue. Many Palestinians accordingly reasoned that the Shamir government was not interested in good-faith bargaining and would accept a settlement based on territorial compromise and mutual recognition only if forced to do so, and this in turn produced further support for Saddam Hussein, commander of the most powerful army in the Arab world and an Arab leader who declared himself ready to fight on behalf of Palestinian rights. Some Palestinians saw Iraq as an alternative to Egypt in this context. Cairo had sought to allay Israeli security concerns in order to persuade the Jewish state to accept the principle of territorial concessions; but this approach had achieved little or nothing for the Palestinians, and many thus concluded that they had nothing to lose, and possibly much to gain, by breaking with the moderate diplomatic approach represented by Egypt and pursuing instead the more confrontational approach represented by Iraq.

Finally, Palestinians and other Arabs were disturbed by what they regarded as a double standard in the world's swift and forceful response to Saddam's aggression against Kuwait, on the one hand, and, on the other, its unwillingness to display the same resolve in the face of Israel's continuing occupation of the West Bank and Gaza. The mobilization of the United Nations against Iraq, for the purpose of resisting aggression and enforcing respect for international law, showed that the international community was capable of decisive action when sufficiently provoked. Palestinians were angered that the world community apparently did not see as equally provocative Israel's prolonged occupation of the West Bank and Gaza and, indeed, its unilateral efforts to alter the character of these territories. This apparent double standard was also emphasized by Saddam, who won additional praise from Palestinians and other Arabs by arguing that those calling for Iraq's withdrawal from Kuwait could demonstrate the sincerity of their declared concern for international law only by pressing with equal determination for Israel's withdrawal from the West Bank and Gaza.

A few PLO officials and other prominent Palestinians pointed out as early as August 1990 that support for Saddam Hussein, whether understandable or not from the Palestinians' own perspective, would be injurious to the PLO and detrimental to the Palestinian cause more generally,[149] and subsequent developments demonstrated the accuracy of these assessments. This was evident in two areas in the fall of 1990. First, the attitude of the PLO disrupted relations between the Palestinian organization and some of its most important Arab backers, especially those Gulf Arab states that had long provided critical financial assistance to the PLO. The Saudis expressed their displeasure and called for a change of PLO leadership. Saudi financial aid was terminated as well, and in September the Riyadh government also restricted the residency and employment privileges enjoyed by Palestinian workers in Saudi Arabia. Other examples include the expulsion of twenty PLO officials from Qatar and a communiqué denouncing the PLO issued in October by the Kuwaiti Popular Congress.[150]

The other political arena in which the Palestinians suffered a setback involved relations with Israeli advocates of territorial compromise, particularly those in the peace camp. While PLO support for Saddam Hussein brought predictable denunciations from officials of the Israeli government, who stated that the organization had shown its true colors and that all should now understand why Jerusalem had refused to accept it as a partner for peace talks, there were also expressions of anger from Israelis on the left side of the political spectrum. Moreover, some of these statements were particularly intense, coming, as they did, from Israelis who had vigorously defended the Palestinian cause, and who felt betrayed by PLO and Palestinian sympathy for a man who threatened to launch missile attacks against Israeli population centers. For example, as one member of the peace camp wrote in *Yediot Aharonot* in August, "I now know what the Palestinians think: the vast majority want a modern-day Saladin, a leader who will unite the Arab world and banish the non-Arabs from the Middle East. . . . This week you [Palestinians] proved to me that for many years I was a great fool, and I pretentiously supported your aspirations, which are not your aspirations at all. When you ask once again for my support for your 'legitimate rights,' you will discover that your shouts of encouragement to Saddam have clogged my ears."[151] Among those who had been advocates of an Israeli-PLO dialogue but now expressed outrage at Palestinian support for Saddam Hussein were several Members of Knesset, including Dedi Zucker and Yossi Sarid of the Citizens' Rights Movement.

Events inside Israel and the occupied territories also fostered increased tension between Israelis and Palestinians during the fall of 1990. Of particular significance was another incident on the grounds of al-Aqsa Mosque in Jerusalem's Old City, this one even more serious than the confrontation in October 1987.

As in 1987, disturbances were precipitated by the Temple Mount Faithful, an extremist Jewish group that calls for rebuilding the Jewish Temple, and which in October 1990 was once again seeking to hold a prayer service on the grounds. On the 8th, several thousand Palestinian Muslims assembled to prevent the group from carrying out its plans, and this quickly led to a confrontation with Israeli police in which seventeen Palestinians were killed. Riots followed in a number of West Bank and Gaza locations, and this resulted in the deaths of several more Palestinians. Israeli and Palestinian accounts of the incident differ, with the former alleging and the latter denying that the violence began when Palestinians threw stones at Jews worshiping at the Western Wall, which is below the grounds of al-Aqsa.[152]

Contributing further to the mounting tension, and in particular to the rising anti-Palestinian sentiment among Israelis, were a number of attacks on Jews by Palestinians from the territories employed in Israel. For example, a Palestinian worker stabbed his former Israeli employer in Rishon Le-Zion early in November, leading to the roundup of several hundred Palestinians by Israeli police. Early in December, one Israeli was killed and several others were wounded when three Palestinians stabbed passengers on a bus in Ramat Gan. In still another incident, in mid-December, three Israelis were stabbed to death by unidentified Palestinians in a Jaffa aluminum factory, which provoked anti-Arab demonstrations by Jews and the arrests of hundreds of Palestinians by the police.

These and other attacks by Palestinians, as well as mounting tensions more generally, brought calls from many Israelis to reduce the number of West Bank and Gaza residents working in the Jewish state. Moreover, the government responded to these calls during the latter months of 1990. As many as 20,000 Palestinians in the territories were given special identity cards, which deny the holder the right to enter Israel, and there was also a crackdown to prevent Israeli employers from hiring Palestinians without proper authorization. In addition, in mid-December the *Jerusalem Post* reported that all institutions of the Jewish Agency and the World Zionist Organization had decided not to employ Palestinians from the occupied territories.

Although fears of violence played a large part in Israeli desires to reduce the number of West Bank and Gaza Palestinians working in the Jewish state, a concern for making more jobs available to the growing number of Jews immigrating to Israel from the Soviet Union at this time was also an important consideration. Further, apart from its implications for Palestinian employment, the arrival of an unprecedented wave of Soviet Jewish immigrants encouraged some on the Israeli right to argue that the West Bank and Gaza were needed to absorb the flood of arriving Jews, which contributed still further to the heightened tension of this period and gave Palestinians yet another reason to believe that concessions and moderation would be of little value in persuading the Shamir government to enter peace talks based on the principle of territorial compromise. Soviet immigrants were arriving in Israel at the rate of more than 20,000 a month in the fall of 1990. The number of new arrivals reached 35,000 in December, and by January 1991 the total who had immigrated to the Jewish state during the preceding year reached approximately 175,000.

The War in the Gulf unfolded against this background early in 1991, and with it came yet another rise in anti-Palestinian sentiment in Israel. Fearful that Iraq would attack their country with missiles carrying chemical weapons, large numbers of Israelis prepared a sealed room in their homes and spent long hours in that room during January and February, until the fighting came to an end with Iraq's surrender on February 26. Also, although they were not armed with warheads carrying chemical weapons, Iraq did fire thirty-nine SCUD missiles at Israel over the course of the war, and many succeeded in hitting neighborhoods around Tel Aviv and elsewhere. These attacks caused extensive property damage, as well as many injuries to civilians and some loss of life. Israelis were understandably outraged by these attacks, and their anger was increased by U.S. insistence that the IDF take no retaliatory action in order to avoid any risk of disrupting the alliance between Washington and its Arab partners in the anti-Iraq coalition. So far as attitudes toward Palestinians are concerned, these experiences increased Israeli anger at the support for Saddam Hussein displayed by both PLO leaders and ordinary citizens in the occupied territories. Further, anti-Palestinian sentiment increased when, during Iraqi SCUD attacks, some Palestinians assembled on the rooftops of their West Bank and Gaza homes and then cheered when incoming missiles hit targets in the Jewish state. Although Palestinians insist that reports of such behavior were greatly exaggerated, accounts of celebrating Palestinians intensified Israeli anger during the first months of 1991.

While Israeli passions ran high during this period, it does not appear that the Gulf crisis had any permanent impact on aggregate Israeli thinking about the Palestinian question. With Iraq experiencing a crushing defeat after only six weeks of war, attitudes that had prevailed before the crisis began to reappear in the months that followed, and, overall, the country remained as divided as ever on issues pertaining to the occupied territories. This conclusion is supported not only by impressionistic reports but by the results of a systematic comparative analysis of public opinion data collected in May 1990 and June 1991. The research was carried out by three Israeli scholars, whose specific goal was to examine differences and similarities in Israeli attitudes before and after the fighting in the Gulf. According to the authors' summary, "The general picture of public opinion in June 1991 was quite similar to that of the previous year. Some observers might be surprised that the Gulf War had no radical impact on Israeli views about the Arab-Israeli conflict."[153]

The Gulf crisis rather gave encouragement and rhetorical ammunition both to hard-liners and to advocates of territorial compromise, and so far as the former is concerned, it provided a number of new arguments that were vigorously put forward by the Israeli political right. For one thing, the Shamir government and its supporters asserted that Israel could hardly be expected to deal with the PLO when even many Arab states now recognized the duplicitous character of the Palestinian organization. Opponents of territorial compromise also insisted that the war showed the West Bank and Gaza to be essential for security purposes, since there could and almost certainly would be future Arab leaders who, like Saddam Hussein, would not hesitate to launch unprovoked attacks against the people of Israel. The Middle East is a hostile and dangerous part of the world, these Israelis added, where dictators and despots readily use violence against one another and even against their own people. Accordingly, Israel's preoccupation with security is wholly legitimate; it is not, as critics sometimes charge, the result of an obsession derived from Jewish history but is in fact based on an accurate assessment of present-day Middle Eastern reality. Finally, Israelis on the political right argued that the crisis in the Gulf made it clear that the Palestinian problem is not the only or even the primary cause of instability in the Middle East, and that the Shamir government was thus correct to insist that the central concern of any peace process must be the relationship between Israel and neighboring Arab states.

Many Israelis apparently found these arguments convincing in the spring and summer of 1991. The country continued to be ruled by the most right-wing government in its history. Indeed, Moledet, the ultranationalist party advocating the removal of Palestinians from the West Bank and Gaza, had been invited to join the government in February 1991, and the head of the party, Rehavam Ze'evi, had been made a minister without portfolio. Nevertheless, despite the claim of its critics that it was highly unrepresentative, opinion polls and the analyses of many knowledgeable observers indicated that the government was popular with voters, and that Likud would have improved its parliamentary position relative to that of Labor had the country held elections at this time.

Yet there also continued to be widespread Israeli support for territorial compromise and an accommodation with the Palestinians, and those who thought in these terms, like those on the political right, also had new arguments to put forward in the aftermath of the fighting in the Gulf. Most compelling, perhaps, was the assertion that Israel's vulnerability to missile attacks from Iraq showed the defense of the Jewish state to reside primarily in technology, and only secondarily in territory. According to Ze'ev Schiff, an independent Israeli journalist and an expert on military affairs, "In looking to the future, Israel cannot ignore the fact that more sophisticated missiles will be far more accurate and can be directed at strategic targets such as airfields and other vital facilities." Thus, whereas capture of the West Bank in 1967 gave Israel "a security zone that would help to delay an Arab armored assault . . . the missile firings during the Gulf War showed that Israel's existing strategic depth does not provide protection against all types of attack." As a result, Schiff concluded in an article published in *Foreign Affairs* that "the importance of territory (in this case the West Bank) for Israel's defense cannot be dismissed, but territory does not always enhance security. Under certain conditions, like those prevailing in the West Bank and Gaza Strip, the risks posed by additional territory are greater than the benefits they accord."[154]

An extension of these arguments in favor of territorial compromise was a recognition that Israel was potentially more militarily and politically vulnerable, which meant that a peace settlement, if indeed attainable, should not be sacrificed because of an ideological commitment to retain the West Bank and Gaza. One consideration, of course, is the possibility that future wars fought with advanced missile technology would bring a much greater number of civilian casualties. Despite considerable damage to property, Israel was extremely fortunate that only a few deaths were caused by Iraqi SCUD attacks early in 1991. Another consideration, as Schiff pointed out, is that almost all of Israel is vulnerable to missile attack from a country such as Iraq, whose western border is less than four hundred miles from Tel Aviv, whereas Israel would need missiles capable of traveling much greater distances to hit the Iraqi capital and regions of the country farther to the east.[155] A different but equally important concern involves the possibility of a change in Israel's important relationship with the United States. The end of the Cold War and the formation of Washington's Gulf War alliance with Syria and other Arab states hostile to Israel led many to wonder whether the United States would continue to regard the Jewish state as a valuable strategic asset.

These arguments, too, like those advanced by the government, appeared to strike a responsive chord among a substantial number of Israelis. Indeed, in spite of Likud's popularity and the anti-Palestinian sentiment that had accompanied the crisis in the Gulf, support for territorial compromise and an accommodation with Palestinian nationalism was as strong as or perhaps even stronger than it had been a year earlier. For example, according to the previously mentioned study comparing survey data from May 1990 and June 1991, the proportion of Israelis favoring territorial compromise had increased from 40 to 43 percent, and among these the proportion favoring the establishment of either a Palestinian state or a Palestinian-Jordanian state had increased from 12 to 24 percent. By contrast, support for annexation of the West Bank and Gaza and transfer of the territories' Arab population increased only from 10.3 percent in May 1990 to 11.2 percent in June 1991, and the proportion preferring Palestinian autonomy in conjunction with permanent Israeli rule of the West Bank and Gaza, the final status arrangement favored by Likud, actually declined slightly, from 18.5 percent to 16.7 percent.[156]

In addition, providing further evidence that the crisis in the Gulf had not brought a lasting rightward shift in Israeli political attitudes, members of the peace camp and many Labor Party moderates began to reassert their traditional positions and reestablish their contacts with Palestinian nationalists. While their anger over Palestinian support for Saddam Hussein had been genuine and intense, many had apparently concluded by mid-1991 that the case for peace based on territorial compromise and mutual recognition between Israelis and Palestinians was as compelling as ever. Thus, for example, a group of well-known Israeli scholars and political figures held discussions in California in July 1991 with a Palestinian delegation that included not only prominent personalities from the occupied territories but also a ranking member of the PNC. The report issued by the group urged Israel to return to its pre-1967 borders, with only minor modifications, and called for mutual recognition involving the Israeli state, the Palestinian state, and the Arab states.

Looking further ahead, elections for a new Israeli Knesset were scheduled for November 1992, and, given all that had transpired during the last three years, some predicted that this round of balloting, not that of 1988, would be the real "intifada elections." With the country aware of both the direct and the opportunity costs associated with retention of the West Bank and Gaza, and with the electorate finally being asked to decide how high a price it was prepared to pay in order to hold on to these territories, it seemed plausible to conclude that Palestinian resistance on the ground coupled with the possibility of peace offered by the PLO and other Arabs might significantly improve the fortunes of the Labor Party and movements further to the left. Moreover, although most observers writing in mid-1991 had suggested a different outcome, this turned out to be the case when elections were held in June 1992, five months ahead of schedule. Labor won forty-four Knesset seats, twelve more than did Likud, and, with Yitzhak Rabin now at its head, it succeeded in forming a government without the participation of Likud. It is also significant that Labor's principal coalition partner was Meretz, a new bloc of three leftist and peace-oriented parties which had captured twelve seats in the 1992 balloting. Composed of the Citizens' Rights Movement, Mapam, and Shinui, Meretz had campaigned on a platform of withdrawal from the West Bank and Gaza and recognition of Palestinian political rights.

In the meantime, however, from the end of the war until the elections of 1992, Israeli policies in the occupied territories continued to be made and implemented by the homogeneous right-wing government led by Yitzhak Shamir. Furthermore, even when Israelis turned back to Labor for the leadership of their country, Likud officials and other advocates of Greater Israel would be consoled by the fact that they had put their time in power to good use. They had succeeded in building a foundation of Jewish settlements and other Israeli interests in the West Bank and Gaza that would survive their own control of the government. These settlements and interests would be extremely difficult to dismantle, and accordingly, precisely as intended, they would pose problems for, and limit the options of, any future government oriented toward territorial compromise.

So far as the Palestinians are concerned, the PLO emerged from the Gulf crisis in a weakened position, with elements of its leadership bitterly condemned by many Arab governments and criticized even by some Palestinian intellectuals. Even more important, events in the West Bank and Gaza were following their own dynamic course and moving in a decidedly disadvantageous direction in the aftermath of the war against Iraq.

Of particular concern was a major effort to expand the number of Jewish settlers in the West Bank and Gaza. Under the direction of Ariel Sharon, the minister of housing, 13,000 new residential units, and possibly more, were under construction in Jewish settlements in occupied territories in 1991, at a cost of approximately $1 billion. This contrasts with a total of only 20,000 settler housing units built between 1968 and 1990. As a result, whereas settlement activity had declined somewhat during 1988 and 1989, primarily because of the intifada, the Jewish population of the territories, and especially the West Bank, had increased by approximately one-quarter over the course of 1990 and by almost that much again during 1991, even before many of the new units were ready for occupancy. By the end of 1991, according to government figures, at least 112,000 men, women, and children were residing in 157 Jewish settlements in the West Bank and Gaza, exclusive of East Jerusalem.

Further, the quality and character of Jewish life in the West Bank were being transformed in ways that tended to insulate settlers from Palestinian resistance activities. Writing of Ariel, for example, the second-largest Jewish town in the West Bank, a September 1991 article in *Ha'aretz* offered the following description:

> Ten thousand residents, 1,000 new immigrants, almost 3,000 housing units under construction, a community college, a deluxe hotel, a soccer field, a cemetery, a few dozen factories, two supermarkets, three commercial centers, an internal bus line, a pirate cable television station, 50 playgrounds, five schools, two pools, ethnic dancing on Friday night, the national arm wrestling championship on Saturday night.[157]

The article also reported that the concern of Ariel residents with the intifada and security had greatly diminished. "The intifada and the Arabs are gradually becoming a dim memory. The path of the road passes less and less through Arab villages, and soon the Trans-Samaria [Road] will bypass all of them. There is almost no more stone-throwing, and [residents] go down to Tel Aviv or Petah Tikvah day and night, with children or without."

Another concern of importance to Palestinians was the continuing arrival in Israel of large numbers of Soviet Jewish immigrants. This was a development of potentially monumental significance from the Israeli perspective. Hundreds of thousands, and by some projections as many as one million, Soviet Jews were expected to immigrate to Israel over the next five to ten years. The arrival of these new immigrants would lift the spirits and increase the self-confidence of the Jewish state, and would potentially transform the country's demographic and political character to an extent that had not been seen since the early days of statehood. But while Israelis looked to these possibilities with great anticipation, Palestinians and other Arabs worried that many of the new immigrants would settle in the occupied territories, thus creating yet another obstacle to an eventual Israeli withdrawal. Palestinians also worried that the arrival of the Soviet Jews would lessen Israeli fears of a demographic challenge from the Arab inhabitants of the West Bank and Gaza, a prospect to which Likud and its supporters readily called attention. Whereas some Israelis advocated withdrawal from the occupied territories in order to ensure that their country would retain a substantial Jewish majority, the arrival of half a million or more new Jewish immigrants would reduce the salience of this argument in favor of territorial compromise.

Beyond these fears that the course of events was in the direction of making permanent Israel's control of the West Bank and Gaza, Palestinians in the occupied territories also experienced a significant deterioration in the circumstances of their daily lives in the spring and summer of 1991. The economic and social pressure on their communities was particularly intense at this time, creating a situation in which Palestinian worries about Jewish settlements and the long-term future of the West Bank and Gaza were rivaled by a preoccupation with the mounting difficulties of day-to-day living.

Contributing to this situation were the political and economic consequences of the War in the Gulf, including those flowing from Palestinian support for Saddam Hussein, and diminishing opportunities for Palestinians to work inside Israel. With regard to the former, there was a drastic reduction in the remittances and financial aid from the Gulf on which Palestinians in the territories depended heavily. Palestinian workers now found fewer employment opportunities in Saudi Arabia and other Gulf states, which meant that less money was returned to relatives in the occupied territories. Even more important, the large and wealthy Palestinian community in Kuwait had been decimated, first as a result of the Iraqi invasion and subsequently by the actions of Kuwaitis angry at what they believed to be Palestinian support for the invasion of their country. As a result, the Palestinian population of Kuwait dropped from approximately 400,000 before the war to less than 100,000 by the end of 1991, with departures continuing in 1992.[158] Most of these Palestinians relocated in Jordan. This, too, meant that an important source of funds for Palestinians in the territories no longer existed. Finally, the governments of Saudi Arabia, Kuwait, and other oil-rich states in the Gulf terminated or severely curtailed their financial assistance to the Palestinians, including their payments both to the PLO and to institutions serving the population of the West Bank and Gaza.

With respect to employment in Israel, the number of West Bank and Gaza residents working in the Jewish state declined to roughly half of its pre–Gulf War total of 150,000. As noted, Israel encouraged this reduction, in part for fear of attacks against Jewish civilians and in part to reserve available jobs for Soviet Jewish immigrants. As a consequence of these developments, including a shrinking of the Palestinian economy because of reduced funding from abroad, there was a significant rise in unemployment, which was estimated in mid-1991 to be at least 30 percent and possibly much higher.

Perhaps the most important aspect of the grim situation that prevailed in the occupied territories in the aftermath of the Gulf crisis is the loss of direction that had come to characterize the intifada. This was both a consequence of the various pressures impinging on Palestinians in the West Bank and Gaza and a factor that was itself an additional cause of the deteriorating situation. In the spring and summer of 1991, and throughout the remainder of the year, inhabitants of the territories frequently complained about increasing disorganization and mounting pressures within their own community. Among the most important of their complaints were competition and infighting among rival political factions, rather than cooperation in pursuit of common objectives; behavioral constraints enforced by one segment of the population on another, such as the harassment by Muslim activists of women who do not wear Islamic dress; and rising crime and delinquency, reflecting a breakdown of the social order and diminished respect for authority inside the Palestinian community. Most Palestinians insisted that the origins of these problems were to be found in the conditions of occupation and in Israeli efforts to suppress the uprising. Nevertheless, many also acknowledged that elements of their own community had contributed to the intifada's loss of direction, and to the fact that the uprising in the territories was in danger of becoming, or indeed had already become, more injurious to Palestinians themselves than to the Israelis who occupied their homeland.

The intifada's loss of direction was also reflected in Palestinian-against-Palestinian violence, which was an especially troubling development. Much of this violence was the result of action taken against collaborators, especially those who allegedly had helped Israel to infiltrate Palestinian organizations or to identify and locate wanted activists. On April 1, for example, suspected collaborators were shot and killed by unknown assailants in Qalqilya and Gaza, and the next day another suspected collaborator was found dead in Ramallah. Killings of this sort had begun on a small scale during the second year of the uprising and increased the following year. Subsequently, after the crisis in the Gulf, these attacks continued, reflecting a broader decline in the ability of the intifada's leadership to maintain discipline and control. Indeed, more Palestinians were killed by other Palestinians (about 150) than by Israelis (about 100) in 1991.

Few Palestinians defended the killing of collaborators. On the contrary, action of this sort was explicitly condemned in a number of UNLU leaflets. Moreover, some Palestinians acknowledged, and lamented, that at least some of those labeled as collaborators were in fact falsely accused. In these cases, charges of collaboration were often a cover for Palestinian-against-Palestinian violence that in reality involved personal rivalries and the settling of old scores by feuding clans and families. Yet many also insisted that Israel bore much of the responsibility for this violence, since occupation authorities and intelligence units frequently used coercive methods to force Palestinians to collaborate, and since Palestinian society was denied the law-enforcement mechanisms by which it might defend itself in a less violent manner.[159]

The implications of these various developments from the perspective of the uprising are spelled out clearly by a leading Palestinian scholar, who wrote in spring 1991 that the Gulf War is associated with a turning point in the intifada. According to Salim Tamari, a sociologist at Birzeit University, the crisis in the Gulf brought "a fundamental break with the initial strategy and tactics of the intifada, indicating the need for rethinking those strategies." And in the meantime, while the leaders of the intifada and other Palestinians were searching for ways to give new direction to their efforts at resistance, "there is a general malaise in the Palestinian street affecting people's attitude to the daily routine of the intifada. . . . There is no doubt that the vast majority of the Palestinian people in the occupied territories are behind the intifada and its political objectives. . . . What is being questioned here are those tactics whose efficacy has been depleted. What people need today is a reprieve, a breathing space that allows them to rebuild their economy while waging a protracted political struggle of disengagement with Israel."[160]

Nevertheless, even if the intifada did not regain its earlier dynamism and coherence, as seemed most likely, Palestinians in the West Bank and Gaza could be expected to display a continuing commitment to steadfastness in one form or another, meaning that they would remain on the ground and continue to struggle against the occupation of their homeland. Moreover, if it turned out that mass protest and nonviolent agitation were no longer viable options, it was probable that acts of aggression and terrorism would increase, carried out not only or even primarily by organized political factions, but by individuals seeking revenge for their unfulfilled aspirations and the difficult conditions of daily life. The choice before Israel was thus, as it had been for some time, between territorial compromise and accommodation on the one hand or, on the other, confrontation and an open-ended struggle to suppress efforts at resistance. After the Gulf crisis, as before, despite the setbacks experienced by the PLO and the deteriorating circumstances of Palestinians in the occupied territories, few observers saw any meaningful prospect that the Israeli government, the United States, or the Arab regimes could ignore the rights of the Palestinians and still make progress toward peace.

Into the 1990s

After more than four years of sustained unrest in the West Bank and Gaza, as well as the peace initiative launched by the PLO and then the crisis in the Gulf, it remained to be seen whether there would at long last be movement toward a resolution of the Israeli-Palestinian conflict, or whether the 1990s would instead witness a replay of the violent confrontations and diplomatic failures that had characterized the 1980s. Neither scenario was implausible, and in 1991 and 1992 it was possible to argue that either one of these two opposing tendencies might become the more important during the decade that lay ahead.

On the one hand, there is nothing about the essence of either Zionism or Palestinian nationalism that makes resolution of the conflict impossible. For example, a settlement founded on the principle of partition, involving the establishment of two states in Palestine, one for Jews and one for Palestinian Arabs, with mutual recognition and peaceful relations between them, would fulfill the basic requirements of both protagonists in the lingering dispute. Indeed, although it would not give either party all that it desires, such a solution has long been proposed by objective observers as a reasonable basis for compromise and accommodation. Thus, perhaps, in response to recent events, Israelis and Palestinians might finally be ready to accept this or some other formula for a just and durable peace, thereby ending the struggle between them and laying a foundation for cooperation in the development of the territory they share.

On the other hand, the evolution of the conflict over more than three-quarters of a century had produced a legacy of anger, bitterness, and above all distrust, and this legacy, along with the intransigence of some Israelis and Palestinians, continued to propel the conflict forward and hinder efforts to make peace. Eventually, perhaps, distrust will be eroded by dialogue and confidence-building measures, pushing rejectionists on each side to the periphery and bringing an end to recurring cycles of violence. As noted, there is no a priori reason why this should not occur; there is nothing about the existential character of either Zionism or Palestinian nationalism that makes compromise impossible. But what is possible and what is likely are not the same, and more years of turmoil might well be required before Israelis and Palestinians find the political will to break with the past and overcome the mutual distrust that has long made compromise so difficult.

While the future remained uncertain, there were a number of encouraging developments in 1991 and 1992. To begin with, there was hope early in 1991 that diplomatic efforts by the United States would narrow the gap between Israelis, Palestinians, and other Arabs and make possible a new round of diplomacy aimed at reaching agreement both on the future of the West Bank and Gaza and on relations between Israel and neighboring Arab states. U.S. President George Bush had declared that the campaign to contain Iraqi aggression and force Baghdad to withdraw from Kuwait should be understood in the context of a "New World Order," in which international disputes would be settled through peaceful means and governments in the Middle East, as elsewhere, would become more responsive to the aspirations of ordinary citizens. Thus, in a speech before a joint session of Congress early in March, the American president coupled his announcement of an end to hostilities against Iraq with a declaration of four objectives for U.S. Middle East policy: security in the Persian Gulf, regional arms control, economic development, and Arab-Israeli peace, the latter to be achieved on the basis of UN Resolution 242 and through an exchange of land for peace. Several days later, setting out on an eleven-day trip to the Middle East, Secretary of State Baker stated that the U.S. would soon propose a series of "confidence-building measures" as a prelude to Arab-Israeli peace talks to be held under the joint sponsorship of the U.S. and the Soviet Union.

Baker made several additional trips to the Middle East in the months that followed, and in late October, after intense bargaining about the composition of the Palestinian delegation, his efforts led to the opening of an international peace conference in Madrid. Taking part in the Madrid conference were Israeli, Egyptian, Syrian, and Lebanese delegations, as well as a joint Jordanian-Palestinian delegation in which the Palestinian team was for all intents and purposes independent. Also present, although not seated at the negotiating table, were the Saudi Arabian ambassador to the United States and the secretary-general of the Gulf Cooperation Council. These peace talks continued in Washington and elsewhere on an intermittent basis throughout 1992 and the first half of 1993, and while no agreements were reached on significant matters of substance, the fact that Israeli and Arab representatives were meeting face to face and discussing substantive issues was itself a development of potentially great significance. Particularly encouraging was the spectacle of Israeli officials negotiating with Palestinians from the occupied territories who were in direct contact with PLO leaders in Tunis.

Hopes for progress in the ongoing peace talks, as well as for movement toward peace more generally, increased after the Israeli election of June 1992. As noted, Labor's principal coalition partner was the peace-oriented Meretz bloc, with the relatively dovish Shas party supplying the remaining votes necessary for a parliamentary majority. Further, the new prime minister, Yitzhak Rabin, explicitly committed his government to a successful resolution of the peace process. Rabin told an interviewer early in July, for example, that his "immediate goal" would be "advancing the peace talks first and foremost with the Palestinian delegation from the territories." Labor leaders also declared that no new Israeli settlements would be established in the occupied territories while peace negotiations continued; and although they added that the status of existing settlements would for the present remain unchanged, Rabin and other party officials also pointed out that they had long opposed the politically motivated settlements which previous Likud governments had constructed in densely populated Palestinian areas. Yet another encouraging sign was the government's introduction of a bill removing the ban on unauthorized meetings with members of the PLO. The bill passed its first reading in the Knesset in December 1992.

Nevertheless, it remained to be seen whether a new chapter was opening in the evolution of the Israeli-Palestinian conflict. The accomplishments of the in- tifada, the PLO peace plan, the convening of an international conference followed by continuing peace talks, and the coming to power of a new government in Jerusalem all raised hopes that the decade of the 1990s would at last bring move- ment toward a resolution of the conflict, and would consequently look very dif- ferent from the decade of the 1980s. These were not the only important events of this period, however. Balanced against these encouraging developments were continuing tension and escalating violence in the West Bank and Gaza, suggest- ing that the confrontations which had marked the 1980s might continue through the 1990s, and that it would in fact be several more years, or possibly much longer, before Israelis and Palestinians would be able to agree on a formula for peace involving compromise and mutual recognition.

A major source of tension in the West Bank and Gaza, and an important impediment to peace based on territorial compromise, was the network of Jewish settlements and other Israeli investments in the occupied areas that had been built up during Likud's years in power. Equally productive of anger and unrest, or even more so in the short run, was a new round of clashes, some of them lethal, between Israelis and Palestinians. Arab sources reported in December 1992 that a total of 1,135 Palestinians had been killed by Israelis since the beginning of the intifada, five years earlier. Israelis, too, complained of rising casualties. The Ra- bin government charged Hamas and Islamic Jihad with responsibility for a ter- rorist campaign aimed at civilian as well as military targets, and then arrested 1,600 Islamic activists, subsequently deporting 415 of them. These developments were accompanied by additional clashes between the IDF and Palestinian protest- ers early in 1993, leading the army to seal off the territories and prohibit their Palestinian inhabitants from entering Israel. The IDF also imposed protracted curfews on much of the Gaza Strip and on selected West Bank locations.

In order to put an end to these destructive confrontations, which not only cause immediate suffering but also deepen distrust and strengthen the position of rejectionists on both sides of the conflict, it will probably be necessary for Israelis and Palestinians to alter their perceptions of one another, and of the con- flict between them as well. Face-to-face negotiations in the diplomatic arena may provide a mechanism for achieving some of the progress that is necessary. In the end, however, a more profound psychological and emotional transformation is likely to be required. A majority of Israelis and a majority of Palestinians will have to accept that their adversary has legitimate national rights, rights which do not call into question their own valid claims and aspirations but which nonethe- less are genuine and deserve recognition. Majorities on both sides must similarly embrace the view that the Israeli-Palestinian conflict is not, or need not be, a zero-sum struggle, such that one party can achieve its rights only at the expense of the other. Finally, to effect this transformation of attitudes and perceptions, both Israelis and Palestinians will have to approach their adversary with the same empathy and open-mindedness for which they quite rightly call when they themselves are being judged.

Israelis and Palestinians can effect these transformations if they have the political will to do so, but when or even whether there will be enough movement in this direction to make peace a near-term prospect rather than a vague hope for the future was impossible to determine in 1991 and 1992. The political landscape of Israel and Palestine was marked at this time both by encouraging and potentially significant new developments, and also by an all-too-familiar pattern of confrontation and violence. Both dimensions of the situation deserved to be taken seriously, even though their relative importance in shaping the evolution of the conflict would be known only in the future. And if neither tendency should push aside the other, appeared likely in the judgment of many observers, hope and opportunity would intermingle with disappointment and continuing tension during the 1990s, meaning that the struggle between Israelis and Palestinians would persist as the parties made incremental but nonetheless limited progress toward the day when both sides would finally agree to the compromises necessary for peace.

Epilogue
The Beginning of the End?

Late in August 1993, the world learned that secret negotiations between officials of the Israeli government and the Palestine Liberation Organization had been taking place in Norway for many months. Even more dramatic was the news that the two sides had reached agreement on a Declaration of Principles which held out the possibility of a revolutionary breakthrough in the long-standing Israeli-Palestinian conflict. The declaration's preamble recorded the parties' hope for the future; it stated that it was time for Israelis and Palestinians "to put an end to decades of confrontation and conflict, recognize their mutual legitimate and political rights, and strive to live in peaceful coexistence and mutual dignity and security to achieve a just, lasting and comprehensive peace settlement and historic reconciliation."

The secret Israeli-PLO meetings had been sponsored and hosted by Norwegian Foreign Minister Jorgen Holst and his wife, Marianne Heiberg, a scholar who had conducted research in the occupied territories. In September 1992, with a new government in power in Israel, the Norwegians offered to serve as a bridge between the Israelis and Palestinians, and in the following months there were fourteen meetings at hotels, estates, and a union hall outside Oslo. Progress was uneven, and on several occasions it appeared that a dead end had been reached. Nevertheless, with the Israelis and Palestinians housed in close proximity, meetings took place in an informal atmosphere and discussions often lasted far into the night, creating a climate that eventually enabled the two sides to conclude an agreement.

The Declaration of Principles was sealed on September 13, 1993, at a ceremony at the White House in Washington. In order to give maximum visibility to the new accord, and also to set the stage for an international effort to raise funds for Palestinians in the West Bank and Gaza, the Norwegians were not only willing but eager to see the focus of international diplomacy shift to the United States. Thus, in a scene reminiscent of the signing of the Camp David accords, where the stage was shared by Menachem Begin of Israel, Anwar Sadat of Egypt, and Jimmy Carter of the United States, an audience of approximately three thousand crowded onto the sunny South Lawn of the White House to witness the signing of the Israeli-Palestinian agreement and to hear speeches by Israeli Prime Minister Yitzhak Rabin, PLO Chairman Yasir Arafat, and U.S. President Bill Clinton. Rabin and Arafat both spoke movingly, and following Clinton's brief remarks the agreement was signed and Rabin accepted the hand extended to him by Arafat.

These developments, revolutionary under any circumstances, were all the more impressive in view of the unrest that had continued to build in the West Bank and Gaza and the deepening stalemate in the peace talks being brokered by the United States. In the latter connection, even though it remained significant that face-to-face negotiations were continuing, the impasse had become so serious that the head of the Palestinian delegation, Haydar Abd al-Shafi, in May 1993 called for the suspension of Palestinian participation, and in August a survey of Palestinians in the West Bank and Gaza found that 50 percent also favored withdrawal from the peace talks. In Israel, citing the stalemate in the negotiations, as well as other complaints, the Knesset factions of Likud and two other right-wing parties in July introduced motions of no confidence in the Rabin government.

But the mood was radically different after the signing of the Israeli-PLO accord. While there was opposition in some quarters both in Israel and among Palestinians, the agreement was endorsed by substantial majorities on both sides. Palestinians celebrated throughout the West Bank and Gaza, flying flags that had previously been banned and displaying T-shirts and posters with pictures of Yasir Arafat over slogans calling for peace. A poll commissioned by CNN and French Television reported that 66.4 percent of the 1,500 Palestinians surveyed in the West Bank and Gaza supported the accord, whereas only 29.3 percent expressed opposition. Polls in Israel reported similar attitudes among the Jewish public, with support for the agreement in the range of 60–65 percent. It is also notable that right-wing political parties appeared to be having troubling attracting secular, working-class Israelis to the protest demonstrations they called.

A variety of considerations pushed Israel and the Palestine Liberation Organization toward the historic accord. The PLO, of course, had been seeking an agreement for several years, giving indications for more than a decade of its readiness for territorial compromise and formally launching its own peace initiative in November 1988. At the same time, more recent developments had increased the desire of the organization for an agreement that would produce tangible benefits for Palestinians. Particularly significant was the PLO's diminished international backing. The end of the Cold War and the collapse of the Soviet Union deprived the organization of a valuable patron. Equally important, the extensive financial and diplomatic support that had long been provided by Saudi Arabia and Kuwait disappeared as a result of Palestinian sympathy for Saddam Hussein during the Gulf crisis of 1990–91. These developments tended to isolate the PLO in international and inter-Arab diplomatic circles, and the loss of financial support not only put pressure on PLO leaders but also contributed to the disastrous economic situation in the occupied territories.

In addition, Palestinian nationalists were under pressure from Hamas and other Islamist groups, whose organizational strength and popularity in the West Bank and Gaza had assumed substantial proportions by the early 1990s. There were differing assessments of the actual strength of these groups, which had substantial influence in Gaza but were judged by some observers to have the support of relatively few West Bank Palestinians. Further, the reasons that Palestinians supported these groups were varied. For example, noting that many Christian Arabs voted for Hamas in the March 1992 Chamber of Commerce elections in Ramallah, observers asserted that Palestinians who do not favor an Islamist platform may nonetheless support Muslim groups in order to register their dissatisfaction with the meager results obtained by advocates of political compromise, and perhaps also with the lethargy and corruption of some nationalist politicians. In any event, with Islamists mounting a strong challenge for the loyalty of the Palestinian rank and file, the PLO was in need of a breakthrough in order to rebut the charge that its political strategy was bankrupt, and that advocates of armed struggle thus had a better chance of securing Palestinian rights.

Critical in Israel was the election of June 1992, which removed Likud from power and led to the formation of a government that was led by Labor and included coalition partners committed to territorial compromise. As discussed earlier, the Israeli election was held against the background of the uprising in the occupied territories and the crisis in the Gulf, both of which reinforced existing divisions in the Jewish state but also, more generally, persuaded a growing number of Israelis that retention of the West Bank and Gaza involved greater costs and fewer benefits than claimed by opponents of territorial compromise. This trend in Israeli public opinion, sometimes described as "creeping dovishness" but primarily one of greater realism, was marked by a decline in the belief that the status quo in the territories was satisfactory, a decrease as well in the conviction that the Arab world was unalterably opposed to Israel's existence, and an increase in the belief that Israel should and soon would be negotiating with the PLO.

Labor's electoral victory was widely interpreted in Israel as giving the new prime minister a mandate to seek an accord with the Palestinians, and this in turn gave Rabin and his party a strong interest in breaking the stalemate that had settled over the U.S.-sponsored peace talks by summer 1993. Indeed, many analysts argued that Labor's fortunes in the future would depend heavily on its ability to demonstrate that an emphasis on compromise and accommodation had produced tangible results. Some also noted that an agreement with the Palestinians could be concluded only with mainstream nationalists affiliated with the PLO, and that delays which strengthened the appeal of Islamist groups thus diminished the likelihood that Labor would be able to deliver an agreement showing the wisdom of its policies.

Whatever the combination of factors that led to the Declaration of Principles signed in Washington on September 13, the agreement itself was of historic significance. Even though it left substantive issues unresolved, making a contribution that was essentially symbolic and emotional, the accord gave each party the recognition it had long sought from the other and confirmed before the world that there is nothing about the essence of either Zionism or Palestinian nationalism that makes a solution to the conflict impossible. The accord demonstrated that the obstacles to peace are not insurmountable, that the parties can reach an accommodation based on territorial compromise and mutual recognition if they possess the political will to do so. In this respect, it introduced a revolutionary and perhaps irreversible change into the relationship between Israel and the Palestinians.

Revolutionary as it was, the Israeli-PLO accord deliberately deferred decisions on difficult substantive issues, including the status of Jerusalem, the future of Israeli settlements in the West Bank and Gaza, the right of return of Palestinians living in the diaspora, security arrangements, borders, and relations with other states in the region. The agreement, rather, set forth a timetable for the implementation of an interim solution, with its most notable feature being a plan for Palestinians to assume administrative responsibility for Gaza and the Jericho area within ninety days.

Under the "Gaza and Jericho First" plan, Israel and the Palestinians were to conclude by December 13, 1993, an agreement on withdrawal of the IDF and on arrangements for these areas then to be governed by Palestinians. A Palestinian police force was also to be built up during this initial period. Israeli troops were to undertake their withdrawal during the next four months, completing it by April 13, 1994, and thereafter domestic security and public order were to be the sole responsibility of the Palestinians. Palestinians were to assume responsibility in other domains as well, with only external security, settlements, Israeli citizens, and foreign relations to remain under Israeli jurisdiction. The accord also called for the establishment of a joint Palestinian-Israeli Coordination and Cooperation Committee for mutual security purposes, and for arrangements for the safe passage of persons and transportation between Gaza and the Jericho area.

The Declaration of Principles also outlined provisions for Palestinian self-rule in other parts of the West Bank during an interim period. Specifically, it called for the establishment of a Palestinian Interim Self-Government Authority, which would take the form of an elected council and would govern during a transitional period not to exceed five years. This Palestinian Council was to be elected no later than July 13, 1994, prior to which the modalities of the balloting were to be negotiated, as were the Council's structure, size, and powers and the transfer of responsibilities from the Israeli military government and its Civilian Administration. Prior to the Council's election, Israeli military forces, already withdrawn from Gaza and Jericho, were to be redeployed outside Palestinian communities in other parts of the West Bank, with their responsibilities then limited to external security and the protection of Israeli settlers. Significantly, the accord also specified that Palestinians from East Jerusalem would have the right to participate in the elections for the Interim Self-Government Authority.

Although the powers of the Palestinian Council remained to be negotiated, the Declaration of Principles specified that it should be able to enact legislation and should establish appropriate administrative and regulatory agencies, including a Palestinian Development Bank, a Palestinian Land Authority, a Palestinian Water Administration, a Gaza Sea Port Authority, and other institutions. After the inauguration of the Council, which would subsume the provisional administration in Gaza and Jericho, the Israeli Civilian Administration would be dissolved and the military government would be withdrawn. Following the Gaza-Jericho pattern, Israel would then retain responsibility only for external security, settlements, Israeli citizens, and foreign relations. In preparation for these developments, the accord further stipulated that Israel's withdrawal from Gaza and Jericho should immediately be followed by the transfer to "authorized Palestinians" in other localities of authority in the spheres of education and culture, health, social welfare, direct taxation, and tourism. An Israeli-Palestinian Economic Cooperation Committee was to be established as well, its goal being to promote coordination in such areas as water, electricity, energy, finance, transport, and communications.

Finally, the Israeli-PLO accord specified that negotiations to resolve final status issues should commence no later than two years after the withdrawal from Gaza and Jericho, at which time the transitional period would begin. These negotiations were to cover all outstanding issues, including Jerusalem, refugees, settlements, security, borders, and relations with other neighbors. The transitional period, which was not to exceed five years, would end with the conclusion of a "permanent settlement based on Security Council Resolutions 242 and 338."

Looking to the future, it became clear within a few weeks of the signing of the Declaration of Principles that important obstacles remained on the road to peace, but also that the historic agreement had generated broad momentum and was introducing significant changes into the international relations of the Middle East. The most serious problem confronting the agreement was the opposition of some Palestinians and Israelis. Palestinian critics included some, like Haydar Abd al-Shafi, who were not opposed to compromise but viewed the accord as one-sided and flawed. One of Abd al-Shafi's complaints was that Israel had not promised to withdraw from the occupied territories at the end of the transitional period. Another was that the agreement did not require an end to Israeli settlement activity. Pointing out that the accord "is phrased in terms of generalities that leave room for wide interpretations," Abd al-Shafi told interviewers in September, "It seems to me that we are trying to read into it what is not there."

Of more immediate concern was the opposition of rejectionist elements within the Palestinian community, particularly, but not only, those operating under the banner of Islam. Moreover, much of this opposition was violent, involving attacks on Israeli soldiers and civilians and also on Palestinian supporters of the accord with Israel. In October, for example, Islamic Jihad took responsibility for the murder of two Israelis who were touring in the Jericho area, members of Hamas kidnapped and murdered two IDF soldiers in the Gaza Strip, unidentified Palestinians kidnapped and killed a Jewish settler in the region of Beit El, and there were many other attacks, particularly in Gaza, in which Israelis were injured with varying degrees of severity.

Attacks on Palestinian supporters of the accord with Israel included the assassination in mid-October of Assad Saftawi, one of the founders of Fatah and a senior PLO official in Gaza. He was the third Fatah official to be murdered in recent weeks. Hamas denied that it was responsible for Saftawi's assassination, which was carried out by masked assailants, and some Palestinians speculated that it might have been the result of a feud within Fatah.

These developments posed serious problems for the implementation of the Israeli-PLO accord. Observers pointed out that terrorist activities, disturbing as they were, had actually diminished in recent months. They also pointed out that most attacks were carried out with the deliberate aim of creating an atmosphere in which the peace process could not go forward, and that this was understood by responsible Israelis and Palestinians who would not permit the terrorists to achieve their objectives. Nevertheless, the perpetrators of violence were making gains from their point of view. Their activities led some Israeli officials to criticize the PLO, charging that it was not doing enough to halt terrorism. The violence also complicated the IDF's planned release of Palestinian prisoners, leading some to be excluded and raising the possibility that the release of others might be delayed. Most important, the attacks produced doubts in Israel about the wisdom of withdrawing the IDF from Gaza and Jericho, making it possible that this would not be accomplished in accordance with the agreed timetable.

Unrest and violence were not the result of Palestinian actions alone. The vigilante activities of Israeli settlers also contributed to the tension and unrest. Settlers staged demonstrations, blocking roads in the West Bank and Gaza and attempting to prevent Palestinians from commuting to work in Israel. They also assaulted Palestinians and destroyed Arab property, leading Rabin to state early in November that while he did not equate the activities of terrorists with the disturbances perpetrated by Jewish settlers, the latter were also guilty of using violence to foster a climate in which the peace process could not go forward. Later in the month, the Israeli minister of justice issued an equally stern warning. Complaining of continuing disturbances, including a recent settler rampage in the center of Hebron, the minister stated that no one is above the law and that Jews as well as Arabs must express their views in an acceptable manner. The Justice Ministry also announced that it was studying ways to handle violence committed by Jewish settlers.

IDF operations were another factor in the continuing violence, with undercover soldiers tracking down and killing Palestinians deemed responsible for attacks on Israelis. In late November, Israeli agents assassinated a Hamas commander, and this led to riots which brought additional casualties. Soldiers shot and wounded dozens of Palestinian protesters, one of whom, as shown on Israeli television, was shot in the head after taunting Israeli troops. These developments also led the Israeli prime minister to announce that security requirements might necessitate a delay in the scheduled withdrawal from Gaza and the Jericho area, raising fears that the peace process would be interrupted.

Serious as were these threats to the peace process, the Declaration of Principles signed on September 13, 1993, marked a critical turning point in the Israeli-Palestinian conflict. Moreover, not only were there important and perhaps irreversible symbolic gains, reflected in the handshake between Arafat and Rabin, aging leaders who had been mortal enemies all of their adult lives, there was also practical movement in the direction of peace.

One particularly encouraging set of developments concerned the apparent willingness of a number of Arab countries to deal with Israel now that it had been recognized by the PLO. Rabin visited Morocco in September, on his way home from the signing ceremony in Washington, and his visit included a press conference and other events designed to show Moroccan readiness for peace with the Jewish state. More striking, or at least more unprecedented, were reports in October of Israeli negotiations with Qatar for the purchase of natural gas, much of it intended for reexport to Europe; an announcement about the same time that Israel's deputy foreign minister had visited Tunisia, followed by reports that Israeli tourists would now be welcome in that country and that an Israeli travel agency had been authorized to organize tours; Israeli support for a bid by Oman for a seat on the UN Security Council, this being the first time Israel had supported an Arab country seeking membership on the council; reports in November that Israelis would also soon be permitted to visit Qatar; and press accounts, also in November, of a visit to Morocco and Tunisia by an Israeli economic delegation composed of prominent industrialists and the governor of the Bank of Israel.

Developments in Jordan were similarly encouraging, beginning with a statement by King Hussein expressing full support for the Israeli-PLO accord and including a public meeting in Washington between Shimon Peres and Crown Prince Hassan. Despite years of private meetings and secret contacts, this was the first time Israeli and Jordanian leaders had appeared together in public. Notable, too, was a November meeting in Rome at which the Israeli and Jordanian ministers of agriculture discussed areas of possible cooperation, and yet another development was the creation of a joint Israeli-Jordanian apparatus to handle pollution in the Gulf of Aqaba. Most important, perhaps, the Jordanian parliamentary elections, held early in November, were won by candidates who supported the Israeli-Palestinian agreement. The Muslim Brotherhood, which opposed the accord and had previously been the largest bloc in parliament, control-ling 32 seats, captured only 16 seats in the 1993 balloting.

Among the encouraging developments on still other fronts was a successful fund-raising conference in Washington, at which delegates from 43 countries pledged to provide approximately $2 billion over the next five years for economic development in the West Bank and Gaza. Notable, too, was the participation of Saudi Arabia, which put aside its anger at the PLO and promised to contribute to the common fund. A development of a different order, but one which also showed the psychological change introduced by the Israeli-PLO accord, was an announcement in late October that several members of the Likud central committee would travel to Tunis for a meeting with Arafat. Still another hopeful sign was an Israeli-Palestinian agreement to establish a desalination facility in Gaza.

Against the background of these encouraging and for the most part unprec-edented developments, as well as the uncertainty produced by continuing violence in the West Bank and Gaza, the peace process went forward in the fall of 1993. Rabin and Arafat met in Cairo in early October, and other senior Israeli and PLO officials met in Tunis and Cairo in the weeks that followed. Israelis and Palestinians also established a steering committee and several subcommittees to oversee the implementation of the Declaration of Principles, and the main group met in Taba and then Cairo on a regular basis throughout October and Novem-ber. In the meantime, Israel began to release Palestinian prisoners, freeing the first of the roughly 10,000 individuals it held in late October, and Palestinians at this time began to assemble and train the police force that would be charged with maintaining order in Gaza and Jericho.

All of this lent credibility to competing predictions about how events would unfold, making it impossible late in the fall of 1993 to determine whether the peace process would break down, as it had so often in the past, or whether some-thing fundamental had changed and movement toward peace was now irrevers-ible. The Israeli-PLO accord had not put an end to unrest in the West Bank and Gaza, and it was probable that the unsettled situation in the territories would delay the IDF's withdrawal from Gaza and Jericho and the start of the five-year transitional period. But while the clashes between Israelis and Palestinians were disturbingly familiar, suggesting that the euphoria of September may have been premature, the signing of the Declaration of Principles had been followed by rev-olutionary developments. Senior Israeli and PLO officials were now meeting reg-ularly to plan for the implementation of principles to which they had both agreed. There was also an expanding array of contacts between Israel and a num-ber of Arab governments. This situation was unprecedented in the long history of the Israeli-Palestinian conflict.

Most important, Israelis and Palestinians had taken a step that held out the possibility of ending a dispute which many had come to believe could not be resolved, confirming that conflict is not inevitable and that a peace settlement based on territorial compromise and mutual recognition is available to the parties if they have the political will to embrace it. Further, with each side acknowledging that the other has legitimate rights and valid aspirations, Palestinians and Israelis had created a context within which there could be meaningful bargaining over substantive issues, rather than a hollow negotiating process in which the major objective of each party is to expose the alleged intransigence of the other. It remained to be seen whether these gains would be sufficient to bring peace, but there could be little doubt that at a minimum they were necessary; without them there could be no serious and sustained progress toward a settlement, no matter what the diplomatic formula or context. These are the considerations that led both Israeli and Palestinian analysts to describe the agreement as a landmark, a historic breakthrough which, no matter what the difficulties and disappointments that lay ahead, constituted a turning point in the Israeli-Palestinian conflict, and in this sense, just maybe, the beginning of the end.

Notes

Part I. Jews and Arabs before the Conflict

1. Jewish History and the Emergence of Modern Political Zionism

1. James Parkes, *A History of the Jewish People* (Baltimore: Penguin Books, 1964), p. 7.

2. Hanoch Reviv, "Until the Monarchy," in *Israel Pocket Library: History until 1880* (Jerusalem: Keter Publishing House, 1973), pp. 14–15.

3. Henri Daniel-Rops, *Israel and the Ancient World* (Garden City: Doubleday Image Books, 1964), p. 217.

4. Abram Leon Sachar, *A History of the Jews* (New York: Knopf, 1964), p. 48.

5. For discussions, see ibid., pp. 85ff.; Daniel-Rops, pp. 234–235; Bernard J. Bamberger, *The Story of Judaism* (New York: Union of American Hebrew Congregations, 1957), pp. 5–7 and 26ff.; and Solomon Goldman, "The Hebrew Bible," in Samuel Caplan and Harold U. Ribalow (eds.), *The Great Jewish Books and Their Influence on History* (New York: Horizon Press, 1952), p. 19–23.

6. Simon Federbush, "The Talmud," in Caplan and Ribalow, pp. 60–61.

7. A. L. Sachar, pp. 148ff. Sachar notes that this was a regrettable development in the opinion of some rabbis, for the *Mishnah* was never intended as an authoritative source of law. In this view, the compilation of the *Mishnah* "marked a turning-point in Jewish history," with the unfortunate consequence that "even the obsolete laws which it preserved—laws of sacrifice, of Temple ritual, of agrarian procedure—became sacred and were discussed and expounded as if they still had validity. No attempt was made to distinguish between fundamental laws and petty regulations" (p. 148). Further, more generally, "The Talmud faithfully reflected the beliefs and notions of its people. In close proximity were the crassest superstitions and the most commendable ethical ideals" (p. 153).

8. See Federbush, p. 63. As with the laws and traditions of other religions, there are debates about the degree to which orthodox Jewish law is indeed progressive and humanistic in character. For example, as in Islam, there are strong disagreements about both the intended and the actual impact of *Halakhic* codes on the circumstances of women. A summary of the status of women in rabbinic law is provided by Bamberger, who defends the position that "woman did not attain equality with man, but she had a dignified status and a large measure of protection. Her degree of independence was far greater than that possessed by American women up to a few generations ago" (p. 121). For a different point of view, focusing primarily on the interpretation and application of religious law in present-day Israel, see Natalie Rein, *Daughters of Rachel: Women in Israel* (New York: Penguin Books, 1980), pp. 139–142. According to Rein, "Of all the Jewish laws created to oppress women, the laws of Halacha are the worst. Implicit in them is the fact that the woman is the man's property" (p. 140).

9. Arthur Hertzberg, *The Zionist Idea* (New York: Atheneum, 1970), p. 21.

10. Guenter Lewy, *Religion and Revolution* (New York: Oxford University Press, 1974), p. 91.

11. Don Peretz, *The Government and Politics of Israel* (Boulder, Colorado: Westview Press, 1979), p. 13. Peretz adds that Jewish ties to Palestine, heightened by the conditions of exile, were "more intense and deeper than the attachments of the average Muslim or Christian."

12. R. J. Zwi Werblowsky, "Jewish Messianism," in *Encyclopedia of Religion* (New York: Macmillan, 1987), vol. 9, p. 475. Werblowsky also discusses Jewish opposition to Messianic speculation. He notes, for example, that the renowned philosopher-theologian Moses Maimonides warned in the twelfth century that "what scripture says on the subject is very obscure . . . and one should not waste time on their interpretation or on the computation of the date of the Messianic advent, since these things are conducive neither to the love of God nor to the fear of God."

13. Solomon Grayzel, *A History of the Jews* (New York: New American Library, 1968), pp. 75 and 124–129.

14. Abba Hillel Silver, *A History of Messianic Speculation in Israel* (New York: Macmillan, 1927); and A. L. Sachar, p. 129. Messianic fervor among the Jews of Palestine also appears to have been widespread at the time of the rise of Islam. See Moshe Gil, *A History of Palestine, 634–1099* (Cambridge: Cambridge University Press, 1992), pp. 60–64. Gil states, "One can assume that great messianic hopes were aroused among the Jews of Palestine." Many considered the Muslims a harbinger of salvation, perceiving the Muslim conquests "as an essential stage determined in advance by Providence for the coming of the Messiah" (p. 61).

15. Ibid.

16. This connection is also discussed by Norman Cohn, "Medieval Millenarianism: Its Bearing on the Comparative Study of Millenarian Movements," in Sylvia Thrupp (ed.), *Millenarian Dreams in Action* (New York: Schocken Books, 1970). Cohn observes that the coming of the Messiah was usually considered a distant and vague event but often became a matter of tense and urgent expectancy during times of major disaster.

17. Silver, p. 151.

18. Ibid., p. ix.

19. Norman Cohn, *The Pursuit of the Millennium* (London: Mercury Books, 1950), p. 61.

20. Ibid.

21. Shlomo Avineri, *The Making of Modern Zionism: The Intellectual Origins of the Jewish State* (New York: Basic Books, 1981), pp. 3–4.

22. Menashe Harel, "The Jewish Presence in Palestine throughout the Ages," in John M. Oesterreicher and Anne Sinai (eds.), *Jerusalem* (New York: John Day, 1974), p. 147. Harel's sources include the *Encyclopedia Brittanica, Calendar of Palestine*, and *Palestine Government Yearbook*. See also Yehoshua Ben-Arieh, "The Population of the Large Towns in Palestine during the First Eighty Years of the Nineteenth Century According to Western Sources," in Moshe Ma'oz (ed.), *Studies on Palestine during the Ottoman Period* (Jerusalem: Magnes Press, 1975), p. 51. Ben-Arieh presents and concurs with an estimate that in 1806 Jerusalem had a total population of 8,800, including approximately 2,000 Jews. For a fuller account, summarizing available Christian, Jewish, and Ottoman sources, see Jacob Barnai, *The Jews in Palestine in the Eighteenth Century* (Tuscaloosa: University of Alabama Press, 1992), pp. 170–177. Barnai reports that Hebron, Tiberias, and Safad taken together contained 1,500 to 2,000 Jews during the eighteenth century, and that a few dozen Jews lived in each of a number of other cities, including Gaza, Jaffa, Acre, and Nablus.

23. Ludwig Borne; quoted in Walter Laqueur, *A History of Zionism* (New York: Schocken Books, 1976), pp. 3–4.

24. A. L. Sachar, pp. 206ff.

25. Parkes, *A History of the Jewish People*, p. 172. See also David Vital, *The Origins of Zionism* (Oxford: Oxford University Press, 1975), p. 44. Referring to the stable Jewish communities of Eastern Europe, Vital describes a people "remarkable for social and ideological uniformity," for whom even local conflicts "never touched on the essentials of religious observance and principle, still less on the unique character of the Jewish people or the primacy of religious over secular affairs." For an account of religious and social life inside these communities, see Mark Zborowski and Elizabeth Herzog, *Life Is with People: The Culture of the Shtetl* (New York: Schocken Books, 1952).

26. Vital, *The Origins of Zionism*, p. 25.

27. Ibid. See also Arthur Hertzberg, *The French Enlightenment and the Jews* (Philadelphia: Jewish Publication Society, 1968), pp. 359–361.

28. Laqueur, *A History of Zionism*, pp. 3–5.

29. Vital, *The Origins of Zionism*.

30. Ibid., p. 43.

31. Ibid.

32. Raphael Mahler, *A History of Modern Jewry: 1780–1815* (New York: Schocken Books, 1971), pp. 152–163.

33. Hertzberg, *The Zionist Idea*, pp. 26–27.

34. Laqueur, *A History of Zionism*, pp. 9–11.

35. A. L. Sachar, p. 332.

36. Ibid., p. 329.

37. Laqueur, *A History of Zionism*, p. 17.

38. R. Mahler, p. 165.

39. Jacques Bigart, "L'Alliance israelite et son action éducatrice," presentation at a conference on February 6, 1900; quoted in André Chouraqui, *L'Alliance israelite universelle et la renaissance contemporaine juive* (Paris: Presses Universitaires de Frances, 1965), pp. 163–164. A fuller and more recent account of the AIU's "conquête morale" in the Mediterranean basin is provided by Aron Rodrigue, *De l'instruction a l'émancipation: les enseignants de l'alliance israelite universelle, 1860–1939* (Paris: Calmann-Levi, 1989). For additional information about the work of the AIU, see Michael Laskier, *The Alliance Israelite Universelle and the Jewish Communities of Morocco: 1862–1962* (Albany: State University of New York Press, 1983); and Aron Rodrigue, *French Jews, Turkish Jews: The Alliance Israelite Universelle and the Politics of Jewish Schooling in Turkey, 1860–1925* (Bloomington: Indiana University Press, 1990).

40. "She came from France in 1862. She captivated generations of Moroccan students. She is called l'Alliance Israelite Universelle,'" *Les Cahiers de l'Alliance Israelite Universelle* 184 (April 1973).

41. *Décisions doctrinales du Grand Sanhedrin* (Paris, 1812), p. 8; as discussed in Hertzberg, *The Zionist Idea*, pp. 22ff.

42. Hertzberg, *The Zionist Idea*, p. 25.

43. Ibid., p. 26.

44. R. Mahler, p. 154.

45. Vital, *The Origins of Zionism*, p. 44.

46. Avineri, pp. 14ff.

47. A. L. Sachar, p. 335.

48. Quoted in Hertzberg, *The Zionist Idea*, p. 154.

49. A. L. Sachar, p. 334.

50. Quoted in Jacob S. Raisin, *The Haskalah Movement in Russia* (New York: The Jewish Publication Society of America, 1913), pp. 231–232; as discussed in Laqueur, *A History of Zionism*, p. 63.

51. Vital, *The Origins of Zionism*, p. 45.

52. Ibid.

53. Ibid., p. 46.

54. Hertzberg, *The Zionist Idea*, p. 147.

55. A. L. Sachar, 335; see also Avineri, pp. 56–64.

56. Hertzberg, *The Zionist Idea*, p. 32.

57. Avineri, p. 52; Hertzberg, *The Zionist Idea*, p. 114.

58. Avineri, p. 45.

59. Ibid., p. 86; Hertzberg, *The Zionist Idea*, p. 165.

60. Vital, *The Origins of Zionism*, p. 51. Vital provides a useful summary of documentary evidence bearing on the question of whether anti-Jewish violence was officially sanctioned. He concludes that while it is clear "that at the provincial and local level the pogroms had been facilitated and even encouraged in a multitude of cases" (p. 53), the question of whether the pogroms were "deliberately instigated and orchestrated at the direct behest of the government in St. Petersburg . . . is less easily answered" (p. 54). Vital also emphasizes that a secret society, known as the Sacred Band of Warriors, deliberately exploited peasant discontent and channeled it against the Jews. The Sacred Band was a "consciously counter-revolutionary organization, enjoying, at the very least, access to, and the sympathy of, a great many highly-placed persons" (p. 55).

61. Ibid., pp. 59 and 51.

62. Ibid., pp. 53–54.

63. Ibid., p. 52.

64. Ibid., pp. 52–53.

65. Avineri, p. 69.

66. Ibid., p. 67.

67. Howard M. Sachar, *The Course of Modern Jewish History* (New York: Dell Publishing Company, 1977), pp. 245–246.

68. Ibid., pp. 305ff.

69. Vital, *The Origins of Zionism*, p. 82.

70. Walter Laqueur and Barry Rubin (eds.), *The Israel-Arab Reader: A Documentary History of the Middle East Conflict* (New York: Penguin Books, 1984), pp. 3–4.

71. A. L. Sachar, p. 342.

72. Theodore Herzl, *Palais Bourbon: Bilder aus dem franzosischen Parlamentsleben* (Leipzig, 1895); quoted in Avineri, p. 92.

73. "The New Ghetto," in Ludwig Lewison (ed.), *Theodore Herzl: A Portrait for His Age* (Cleveland and New York: World Publishing Company, 1955), p. 165.; quoted in Avineri, p. 92.

74. Vital, *The Origins of Zionism*, p. 267.

75. Ibid., p. 273.

76. Laqueur, *A History of Zionism*, p. 86.

77. Ibid., p. 91.

78. For a discussion, see David Vital, *Zionism: The Formative Years* (Oxford: Oxford University Press, 1982), pp. 125–126. Vital also provides a thorough account of Herzl's other diplomatic efforts and travels. For a useful summary, see also Howard M. Sachar, *A History of Israel: From the Rise of Zionism to Our Time* (New York: Knopf, 1979), pp. 47ff.

79. Ibid., p. 3. For a fuller discussion of the First Zionist Congress, see also Vital, *The Origins of Zionism*, pp. 354–370.

80. Vital, *The Origins of Zionism*, pp. 362–364.

81. Avineri, p. 89.

82. Ahad Ha'am, *Nationalism and the Jewish Ethic*, edited with an introduction by Hans Kohn (New York, 1962), pp. 78–79; quoted in Avineri, p. 116.

83. Hertzberg, *The Zionist Idea*, pp. 71–72.

84. Ibid., p. 68.

85. Laqueur, *A History of Zionism*, p. 108.

86. Isaiah Friedman, *Germany, Turkey and Zionism: 1897–1918* (London: Oxford University Press, 1977), p. 47.

87. David Ben Gurion, *Regards sur le passé* (Monaco: Editions du Rocher, 1965), p. 19; quoted in Jacques Soustelle, *The Long March of Israel* (New York: American Heritage Press, 1969), p. 37.

88. Soustelle, p. 37.

89. A thorough discussion of the Uganda scheme is provided by Vital, *Zionism: The Formative Years*, pp. 267–347. A good summary is provided by H. M. Sachar, *A History of Israel*, pp. 59–63.

90. Ahad Ha'am, "Those Who Weep" (HaBochim); quoted in H. M. Sachar, *A History of Israel*, p. 62.

91. Vital, *Zionism: The Formative Years*, p. 344.

92. Ibid., p. 345.

93. Quoted in Haim Z'ew Hirschberg, "The Ottoman Period (1517–1917)," in *Israel Pocket Library: History until 1880* (Jerusalem: Keter Publishing House, 1973), p. 246.

94. Ibid.

95. Laqueur states that there were twenty-one agricultural settlements in Palestine by the end of the century and that they contained about 4,500 inhabitants, of whom two-thirds were employed in agriculture. *A History of Zionism*, p. 78. Slutsky gives slightly different figures, reporting that there were 6,000 Jewish farmers living in twenty villages. See Yehuda Slutsky, "Under Ottoman Rule (1880–1917)," in *Israel Pocket Library: History from 1880* (Jerusalem: Keter Publishing House, 1973), p. 14. Much lower figures are given in Leonard Fein, *Politics in Israel* (Boston: Little, Brown, 1967), pp. 16–17. Reporting that only a dozen villages had been established, Fein cites David Ben Gurion, "First Ones," in *Israel Government Yearbook: 1962–63* (Jerusalem, 1963), pp. 63–64. He also cites a 1900 census which reported that there were only 473 Jewish agricultural workers.

96. A thorough discussion of labor patterns in Jewish agricultural settlements during this period is provided by Gershon Shafir, *Land, Labor and the Origins of the Israeli-Palestinian Conflict, 1882–1914* (Cambridge: Cambridge University Press, 1989), pp. 50ff.

97. For details, see ibid., p. 54. The quotation is from a Jewish yearbook published in Warsaw in 1901.

98. Laqueur, *A History of Zionism*, p. 59.

99. An instructive account of Degania's establishment and early history is provided in a biography of Moshe Dayan, written by Israeli author Shabtai Teveth. Dayan, who became an important military and political leader following Israeli independence, was born at Kibbutz Degania in 1915, and Teveth's account of his parents' life there following the settlement's creation effectively communicates both the spirit of early Labor Zionism and the many hardships that confronted new agricultural settlements. See Shabtai Teveth, *Moshe Dayan* (London: Quartet Books, 1974), pp. 15ff.

100. Shafir, p. 65.

101. Ibid., pp. 70–71.
102. Ibid., p. 106.
103. Ibid. The quotation is from an article published in October 1912.

2. Arab History and the Origins of Nationalism in the Arab World

1. For details, see Richard Bulliet, *Conversion to Islam in the Medieval Period: An Essay in Quantitative History* (Cambridge: Harvard University Press, 1979), pp. 104ff. For a comprehensive account of the impact of the Muslim conquest on the indigenous population of Palestine, including the country's Jewish population, see Gil, especially pp. 139–223 and 279–334. Gil also takes note of Islamic sources that speak of the assistance rendered to Muslims by local Jews in the conquest of several Palestinian towns, including Hebron and Caesarea. In addition, as discussed, he reports in this connection that the arrival of Islam appears to have intensified Messianic fervor among the Jews of Palestine (pp. 60–64).

2. See Bernard Lewis, *The Arabs in History* (New York: Harper, 1966), pp. 10ff.

3. The fact that the number of Arabs living outside the Arab world is beginning to assume sizable proportions, and that the children of these individuals in most cases do not have Arabic as their mother tongue, raises as yet unanswered questions about both the meaning and the operational definition of Arabism among men and women of Arab origin who reside permanently outside the Arabic-speaking world.

4. Albert Hourani, *Arabic Thought in the Liberal Age: 1798–1939* (London: Oxford University Press, 1962), p. 33.

5. Ibid., p. 308.

6. Gustav E. Von Grunebaum, *Modern Islam* (Berkeley: University of California Press, 1962), p. 224.

7. Hisham B. Sharabi, *Nationalism and Revolution in the Arab World* (Princeton: Van Nostrand, 1966), p. 5.

8. Sylvia G. Haim, "Introduction," in Sylvia G. Haim (ed.), *Arab Nationalism: An Anthology* (Berkeley: University of California Press, 1962), p. 64. See also James Bill and Carl Leiden, *Politics of the Middle East* (Boston: Little, Brown, 1979), pp. 290ff.

9. William Polk, *The United States and the Arab World* (Cambridge: Harvard University Press, 1969), p. 28.

10. See Carl Brockelman, *History of the Islamic Peoples* (New York: Capricorn Books, 1960), pp. 11–12. See also Ilse Lichtenstadter, *Introduction to Classical Arabic Literature* (New York: Schocken Books, 1976), pp. 20ff.

11. Hourani, pp. 6–7.

12. Abd al-Rahman al-Bazzaz, "Islam and Arab Nationalism," in Haim, p. 173. See also Isma'il al Faruqi, "Islam as Culture and Civilization," in Salem Azzam (ed.), *Islam and Contemporary Society* (London: Longman and the Islamic Council of Europe, 1982).

13. For general accounts of the life of the Prophet, written from differing perspectives, see Montgomery Watt, *Muhammad: Prophet and Statesman* (London: Oxford University Press, 1961); and Maxime Rodinson, *Mohammed* (New York: Vintage Books, 1974). For an excellent summary discussion, see John L. Esposito, *Islam: The Straight Path* (New York: Oxford University Press, 1988), pp. 3–36.

14. Some analyses of Muhammad's earthly motives suggest that he was influenced in these matters by the conservativism and traditionalism of his environment, recognizing the limits of reform that could be introduced as legislation and preferring in some areas, such as personal status and family life, to influence behavior by precept and personal example. See, for

example, H. A. R. Gibb, *Mohammedanism* (New York: Oxford University Press, 1962), pp. 32–34.

15. Frithjof Schuon, *Understanding Islam* (New York: Roy, 1963), p. 49. See also Philip K. Hitti, *Islam and the West* (Princeton: Van Nostrand, 1962), p. 14.

16. Marmaduke Pickthall, *The Meaning of the Glorious Koran* (London: Knopf, 1930), p. vii.

17. Gibb, *Mohammedanism*, p. 42.

18. B. Lewis, *The Arabs in History*, p. 68.

19. Doctrinal elements that eventually became associated with the Shiite political movement, and which today distinguish Shiism from orthodox (Sunni) Islam, include a belief that the religious as well as the political mission of the Prophet continues; a related insistence that leadership of the Muslim community be based on descent from Muhammad traced through the family of Ali; repudiation for these reasons of the first three caliphs, including a rejection of customs and legal interpretations established during their reign; increased political importance accorded to religious leaders; and the doctrine of the Imamate, which attaches to the community's leader, the Imam, superhuman qualities (which Muhammad never claimed and which other Muslims do not attribute even to the Prophet himself). For an account of the nature and evolution of orthodox views on some of these issues, see H. A. R. Gibb, "Some Considerations on the Sunni Theory of the Caliphate," in H. A. R. Gibb, *Studies on the Civilization of Islam* (Boston: Beacon Press, 1962).

20. Jacques Berque, *Les arabes d'hier à demain* (Paris: Editions du Seuil, 1960), p. 25.

21. Gibb, *Mohammedanism*, p. 7.

22. B. Lewis, *The Arabs in History*, p. 91.

23. For a wide-ranging account of the intellectual contributions of Islamic civilization, particularly in the natural sciences and philosophy, see Seyyed Hossein Nasr, *Science and Civilization in Islam* (Cambridge: Harvard University Press, 1968). For a summary, see Seyyed Hossein Nasr, "Islamic Education and Science: A Summary Appraisal," in Yvonne Yazbeck Haddad, Bryon Haines, and Ellison Findly (eds.), *The Islamic Impact* (Syracuse: Syracuse University Press, 1984).

24. For a selection of scholarly writings from this period, as well as other components of classical Arabic literature, see Lichtenstadter.

25. For a comprehensive account, see Noel J. Coulson, *A History of Islamic Law* (Edinburgh: Edinburgh University Press, 1964). A more general account is provided by Joseph Schacht, *An Introduction to Islamic Law* (Oxford: Clarendon Press, 1964). For useful summaries, see John Esposito, "Law in Islam," in Haddad, Haines, and Findly; and Aziz al-Azmeh, "Islamic Legal Theory and the Appropriation of Reality," in Aziz al-Azmeh (ed.), *Islamic Law: Social and Historical Contexts* (London: Routledge, 1988).

26. Gibb, *Mohammedanism*, p. 49.

27. Lichtenstadter, pp. 70ff. and pp. 257–258; also Gibb, *Mohammedanism*, pp. 78ff.

28. Lichtenstadter, pp. 259–262; also Gibb, *Mohammedanism*, p. 51.

29. From the Moroccan nationalist and reformer Allal al-Fasi; quoted in Hourani, p. 372. See also Michael Hudson, "Islam and Political Development," in John Esposito (ed.), *Islam and Development* (Syracuse: Syracuse University Press, 1980), p. 5.

30. Berque, pp. 40–43 and 226. See also Noel J. Coulson, *Conflicts and Tensions in Islamic Jurisprudence* (Chicago: University of Chicago Press, 1969), pp. 43ff.

31. Polk, *The United States and the Arab World*, p. 66.

32. George Kirk, *A Short History of the Middle East: From the Rise of Islam to Modern Times* (New York: Praeger, 1964), p. 34.

33. Thomas Naff, "Toward a Muslim Theory of History," in Alexander S. Cudsi and Ali

E. Hillal Dessouki (eds.), *Islam and Power* (Baltimore: Johns Hopkins University Press, 1981), p. 25.

34. Gibb, *Mohammedanism*, p. 97.

35. Coulson, *Conflicts and Tensions*.

36. Malise Ruthven, *Islam in the World* (New York: Oxford University Press, 1984), pp. 237–242; James Kritzeck (ed.), *Anthology of Islamic Literature* (New York: Meridian, 1964), pp. 170ff.; Gibb, *Mohammedanism*, pp. 134–139.

37. Ruthven, p. 241.

38. R. A. Nicholson, *A Literary History of the Arabs* (Cambridge: Cambridge University Press, 1969), p. 460. See also Peter Mansfield, *The Arabs* (Middlesex: Penguin Books, 1978), pp. 114–117.

39. B. Lewis, *The Arabs in History*, pp. 164–165.

40. Polk, *The United States and the Arab World*, pp. 66–67.

41. Anthony Nutting, *The Arabs* (New York: Mentor, 1964), p. 212.

42. Wilfred Cantwell Smith, *Islam in Modern History* (Princeton: Princeton University Press, 1957), p. 100. For other discussions see, for example, Mansfield, *The Arabs*, pp. 76–77, and Polk, *The United States and the Arab World*, pp. 55–56.

43. H. A. R. Gibb, *Arabic Literature* (Oxford: Oxford University Press, 1926), p. 159.

44. Habib Bourguiba, *Introduction to the History of the National Movement* (Tunis: Ministry of Cultural Affairs and Information, 1962), p. 9.

45. Quoted in Hourani, p. 49.

46. Bourguiba.

47. For a useful account of the work undertaken by Muhammad Ali and the dynasty he founded, see F. Robert Hunter, *Egypt under the Khedives, 1805–1879: From Household Government to Modern Bureaucracy* (Pittsburgh: University of Pittsburgh Press, 1984). See also P. M. Holt, *Egypt and the Fertile Crescent, 1516–1922: A Political History* (Ithaca: Cornell University Press, 1966), pp. 176ff.; and Nadav Safran, *Egypt in Search of Political Community: An Analysis of the Intellectual and Political Evolution of Egypt, 1804–1952* (Cambridge: Harvard University Press, 1961), pp. 26ff.

48. Quoted in Mansfield, *The Arabs*, p. 121.

49. Polk, *The United States and the Arab World*, p. 81.

50. J. M. Ahmed, *The Intellectual Origins of Egyptian Nationalism* (London: Oxford University Press, 1960), p. 10. Although accounts differ about the number of missions and the year in which the first student delegation was sent to Europe, all are in agreement about the importance of these educational activities.

51. Leon Carl Brown, *The Tunisia of Ahmed Bey* (Princeton: Princeton University Press, 1974), pp. 46–47.

52. Chedley Khairallah, *Le Mouvement Jeune Tunisien* (Tunis: Bonici, n.d.), pp. 12–14. See also Brown, pp. 292–295.

53. Polk, *The United States and the Arab World*, p. 82. See also William Polk, *The Opening of South Lebanon* (Cambridge: Harvard University Press, 1963).

54. Hourani, p. 53.

55. Jasper Yates Brinton, *The Mixed Courts of Egypt* (New Haven: Yale University Press, 1968), p. 6.

56. Quoted in Khairallah, p. 193. See also Mohamed-Salah Mzali and Jean Pignon (eds.), *Kheredine, homme d'état: mémoires* (Tunis: Maison Tunisienne de l'Édition, 1971).

57. Leon Carl Brown, "Stages in the Process of Change," in Charles A. Micaud et al., *Tunisia: The Politics of Modernization* (New York: Praeger, 1964), pp. 9–10.

58. Ibid.

59. Ahmed, p. 11.

60. Ibid., p. 14.

61. Hourani, p. 75.

62. For details, see David Landes, *Bankers and Pashas: International Finance and Economic Imperialism in Egypt* (Cambridge: Harvard University Press, 1958).

63. Quoted in Ahmed, p. 27.

64. Ibid., p. 30.

65. Quoted in Hourani, p. 203.

66. "Announcement to the Arabs, Sons of Qhatan," quoted in Haim, pp. 83–84.

67. Quoted in Nicola Ziadeh, *Origins of Nationalism in Tunisia* (Beirut: American University of Beirut Press, 1962), p. 57.

68. Hourani, p. 197.

69. Paul Mus, *Le destin de l'union française: de l'Indochine à l'Afrique* (Paris, 1954), p. 25.

70. David Gordon, *North Africa's French Legacy* (Cambridge: Harvard Middle Eastern Monograph Series, 1962), p. 12.

71. Quoted in Kirk, p. 116.

72. Ahmed, p. 27. For additional information, see Afaf Lutfi al-Sayyid, *Egypt under Cromer: A Study in Anglo-Egyptian Relations* (London: John Murray, 1968), pp. 62–63 and 79–80. See also Hourani, p. 198.

73. Louis Bertrand, *Devant l'Islam* (Paris: Plon, 1926), pp. 43 and 53–54.

74. René Millet, quoted in *Congrès de l'Afrique du Nord* (Paris: Comité d'organisation du congrès, 1908–1909).

75. For a comprehensive account, see Nikki Keddie, *An Islamic Response to Imperialism: Political and Religious Writings of Sayyid Jamal ad-Din al-Afghani* (Berkeley: University of California Press, 1983). An excellent summary is also provided by Hourani.

76. Hourani, p. 127.

77. Haim, p. 13.

78. Ahmed, p. 28.

79. Hourani, pp. 140–141.

80. Ibid., p. 141.

81. Osman Amin, *Mohammed Abduh* (Washington: American Council of Learned Societies, 1953), p. 85.

82. Berque, p. 27.

83. Frantz Fanon, *A Dying Colonialism* (New York: Grove Press, 1965). These points are also made in Albert Memmi, *Portrait du colonisé, précédé du portrait du colonisateur* (Paris: Gallimard, 1957).

84. Fanon, p. 41.

85. George Antonius, *The Arab Awakening* (New York: Capricorn Books, 1965), p. 91.

86. Quoted in Hourani, p. 206.

87. Haim, p. 26. See also Antonius, pp. 95ff.

88. Quoted in Haim, p. 81.

89. Antonius, p. 109.

Part II. Emergence and History of the Conflict to 1948

1. For a useful overview of the Ottoman administration in Palestine, see Muhammad Y. Muslih, *The Origins of Palestinian Nationalism* (New York: Columbia University Press, 1988), pp. 11–24.

2. For details about the population of Palestine during this period, see Stanford Shaw,

"The Ottoman Census System and Population, 1831–1914," *International Journal of Middle Eastern Studies* 9 (August 1978): 325–338; Alexander Scholch, "The Demographic Development of Palestine, 1850–1882," *International Journal of Middle Eastern Studies* 17 (November 1985): 485–505; Janet L. Abu-Lughod, "The Demographic Transformation of Palestine," in Ibrahim Abu-Lughod (ed.), *The Transformation of Palestine: Essays on the Origin and Development of the Arab-Israeli Conflict* (Evanston: Northwestern University Press, 1971), pp. 139–165; and Ben-Arieh, "The Population of the Large Towns in Palestine."

3. For an excellent account of the Jewish population of Jerusalem prior to the first organized Zionist migrations, see Jeffrey Halper, *Between Redemption and Revival: The Jewish Yishuv of Jerusalem in the Nineteenth Century* (Boulder, Colorado: Westview Press, 1991). See also Arnold Blumberg, *Zion before Zionism, 1838–1881* (Syracuse: Syracuse University Press, 1985); and Yehoshua Ben-Arieh, "The Growth of Jerusalem in the Nineteenth Century," *Annals of the Association of American Geographers* 65 (1975): 252–269.

4. Quoted in Ze'ev Vilnay, "Jerusalem in the Modern Era: 1860–1967," translated from the Hebrew by Claire Remba, in Oesterreicher and Sinai, *Jerusalem*, p. 20. For additional firsthand accounts, see Arnold Blumberg (ed.), *A View from Jerusalem, 1849–1858: The Consular Diary of James and Elizabeth Anne Finn* (Cranbury, New Jersey: Associated University Press, 1980).

5. James Parkes, *Whose Land: A History of the Peoples of Palestine* (Middlesex: Penguin, 1970), p. 220.

6. A useful account of urban notable families is provided by Muslih, *The Origins*, pp. 24–37. For additional discussion of the conservative character of Palestine's elite, see David Waines, "The Failure of the Nationalist Resistance," in I. Abu-Lughod, *The Transformation*, pp. 217–218.

7. Quoted in Yehoshua Porath, *The Emergence of the Palestinian-Arab National Movement: 1918–1929* (London: Frank Cass, 1974), p. 14. See also Geoffrey Furlonge, *Palestine Is My Country: The Story of Musa Alami* (London: John Murray, 1969), pp. 9ff.

8. Haim, p. 30.

9. Quoted in Neville J. Mandel, *The Arabs and Zionism before World War I* (Berkeley: University of California Press, 1976), p. 219.

3. The Conflict Takes Shape

10. Ibid., p. 37. A similar conclusion about early Arab-Jewish relations is drawn by John Ruedy, "Dynamics of Land Alienation," in I. Abu-Lughod, *The Transformation*, pp. 126–127.

11. For an introduction to the system of capitulations, see chapter 2. For additional information about the effects of the system on Palestine, see I. Friedman, *Germany, Turkey and Zionism*, pp. 32ff.

12. Quoted in Mandel, p. 43.

13. Ibid., pp. 55–56. See also Muslih, *The Origins*, pp. 78–79, who concludes that "before the Young Turk coup of 1908, the Arab reaction against Zionism had not been full-fledged." For a summary of the Young Turk Revolution and its implications for the Ottoman Empire, see David Fromkin, *A Peace to End All Peace: Creating the Modern Middle East, 1914–1922* (New York: Henry Holt, 1989), pp. 39–50.

14. For a review of scholarly research bearing on this point, see Shafir, pp. 202–210. Detailed studies include Rashid Khalidi, *British Policy towards Syria and Palestine: 1906–1914* (London: Ithaca Press, 1980), and Eliezer Beeri, *The Beginnings of the Israeli-Arab Conflict, 1882–1911* (Hebrew) (Tel Aviv: Sifriat Poalim, 1985).

15. Shafir, p. 202.
16. From *al-Muqtabas*, a Damascus paper which endorsed the proposed congress; quoted in Mandel, p. 173.
17. Ibid., p. 175.
18. See C. Ernest Dawn, "The Rise of Arabism in Syria," *Middle East Journal* 16 (1962): 145–168; see also Ann Mosely Lesch, *Arab Politics in Palestine, 1917–1939: The Frustration of a Nationalist Movement* (Ithaca: Cornell University Press, 1979), pp. 25ff., and Furlonge, pp. 37–38.
19. Porath, *The Emergence*, p. 29; based on articles which appeared in 1912 and 1913.
20. Mandel, p. 226. See also Yaacov Ro'i, "The Zionist Attitude to the Arabs 1908–1914," in Elie Kedourie and Sylvia G. Haim (eds.), *Palestine and Israel in the 19th and 20th Centuries* (London: Frank Cass, 1982), p. 44.
21. Porath, *The Emergence*, p. 27.
22. Shafir, p. 203.
23. Ro'i, p. 45.
24. Porath, *The Emergence*, pp. 295–296.
25. Yosef Gorny, *Zionism and the Arabs, 1882–1948: A Study of Ideology* (New York: Oxford University Press, 1987), p. 26.
26. Ro'i, pp. 35 and 38.
27. Ibid., pp. 20–22.
28. Gorny, p. 38. Gorny presents a thorough discussion of the images and conceptions about Arab-Jewish relations in Palestine held by the founders of the Zionist movement.
29. Shafir, p. 204.
30. Quoted in ibid. The conference was held at the Zalman Shazar Center in Jerusalem.
31. Ibid., p. 203.
32. Ibid.
33. Emile Marmorstein, "European Jews in Muslim Palestine," in Kedourie and Haim, *Palestine and Israel*, p. 9.
34. Ibid., p. 10.
35. Quoted in Gorny, pp. 44 and 46–47.
36. Ibid., p. 48.
37. Ibid., p. 43.
38. Ibid.
39. Ibid., p. 50.
40. Ibid., p. 55.
41. Ibid.
42. Shabtai Teveth, "The Evolution of 'Transfer' in Zionist Thinking," Occasional Papers of the Moshe Dayan Center of Tel Aviv University, no. 107 (May 1989), pp. 2–3. A fuller account of Zangwell's ideas, both during this period and after World War I, is presented in Chaim Simons, *International Proposals to Transfer Arabs from Palestine, 1895–1947: A Historical Survey* (Hoboken, New Jersey: Ktav Press, 1988), pp. 34–48.
43. According to Teveth, writing in 1989, "Here and there members of the Zionist Organization or its friends—some of them well known—were given to contemplating the possibility of an Arab transfer. But we probably would not even remember them had they not been cited as authorities of the highest repute by those who, over the past decade, and particularly during the last year, have advocated the solution of Israel's security and identity problems by means of transfer by agreement." "The Evolution," p. 2. A different view is presented by Simons, whose volume seeks to show that many Zionist leaders and others advanced proposals, usually in private, for either the compulsory or the voluntary transfer of Arabs from Palestine.

Most, though not all, of the writings and statements summarized by Simons are from the period following World War I.

44. Gorny, p. 271. See also Simons, pp. 35–36 and 50. There is some evidence that in the 1930s Jabotinsky moved from opposition to cautious acceptance of the idea of transfer. For discussions, see Teveth, "The Evolution," pp. 15–21; and Simons, pp. 48–54.

45. Gorny, p. 66.

46. Quoted in Ro'i, p. 39. See also Laqueur, A History of Zionism, pp. 217–219.

47. For a fuller account, see Gorny, p. 68.

48. Ibid., p. 73.

49. Ibid., p. 75.

50. Mandel, p. 226.

51. Ibid., p. 162.

52. Ibid., p. 150.

53. Ibid., p. 153.

54. Quoted in ibid., p. 157.

55. These negotiations are discussed in I. Friedman, Germany, Turkey and Zionism, pp. 143ff., and Mandel, pp. 141–149.

56. Quoted in Mandel, pp. 220–221.

57. Population estimates vary widely. See, for example, Lesch, Arab Politics, p. 27, and Parkes, Whose Land, p. 242. The former reports 75,000 Jews in Palestine in 1914, while the latter puts the number at 90,000–100,000.

58. Cited in Porath, The Emergence, pp. 16–20.

59. The full text of the letter appears in Laqueur and Rubin, pp. 15–16. The entire correspondence is reproduced by Antonius, pp. 413–427. A very useful summary of British promises made to the Arabs at this time is also provided by Fromkin, pp. 173–187.

60. The District of Syria was also sometimes called the District of Damascus, although this was not its official designation. A fuller account of these territorial issues is provided later in this chapter.

61. Yahya Armajani, Middle East, Past and Present (Englewood Cliffs: Prentice-Hall, 1970), p. 294. Useful discussions of these arguments are also to be found in Richard Allen, Imperialism and Nationalism in the Fertile Crescent (London: Oxford University Press, 1974), pp. 228–232; Fred J. Khouri, The Arab-Israeli Dilemma (Syracuse: Syracuse University Press, 1985), pp. 6ff.; Antonius, pp. 164–183; and Kirk, p. 146. The matter was raised again by a Palestinian Arab delegation which came to London in 1921. Although the delegation correctly pointed out that the promise to Husayn could not reasonably be interpreted so as to exclude Palestine, a June 1922 white paper issued by Winston Churchill, the colonial secretary, reaffirmed the British position that Palestine was not included in its pledge to the sherif of Mecca.

62. The entire text is provided in Laqueur and Rubin, pp. 12–15. For a discussion of British and French diplomacy leading up to the conclusion of the Sykes-Picot agreement, see Fromkin, pp. 188–203.

63. Antonius, p. 248. See also Sami Hadawi, Bitter Harvest: Palestine 1914–1967 (New York: The New World Press, 1967), pp. 15–17.

64. Quoted in Khouri, p. 9. See also Antonius, pp. 244–270.

65. Mayir Vereté, "The Balfour Declaration and Its Makers," in Kedourie and Haim, Palestine and Israel, p. 64.

66. John Barnes and David Nicholson (eds.), The Leo Amery Diaries, Vol. 1: 1896–1929 (London: Hutchinson, 1980), p. 170; quoted in Fromkin, pp. 290–291.

67. Ibid.

68. Additional discussions of the motives behind the Balfour Declaration are to be found

in Christopher Sykes, *Crossroads to Israel, 1917–1948* (Bloomington: Indiana University Press, 1965), pp. 3–15, and Vereté. The most authoritative work is Leonard Stein, *The Balfour Declaration* (London: Valentine, Mitchell, 1961).

69. An excellent account of Weizmann's political orientation is available in Simha Flapan, *Zionism and the Palestinians* (London: Croom Helm, 1979), pp. 17–95. Also highly informative is Jon Kimche, *Palestine or Israel* (London: Secker & Warburg, 1973), pp. 93–158.

70. For a valuable discussion of the Weizmann-Faycal negotiations, see Neil Caplan, *Futile Diplomacy, Volume I: Early Arab-Zionist Negotiation Attempts, 1913–1931* (London: Frank Cass, 1983), pp. 36–46. Caplan also appends pertinent documents, including Weizmann's reports of his meetings with Faycal.

71. The full text may be found in Laqueur and Rubin, pp. 18–20.

72. Antonius, p. 439. See also Caplan, *Futile Diplomacy, I*, p. 147.

73. Laqueur and Rubin, pp. 21–22. For a fuller account, see Caplan, *Futile Diplomacy, I*, pp. 149–151.

74. Flapan, *Zionism and the Palestinians*, p. 39. See also Kimche, *Palestine or Israel*, p. 153.

75. Kimche, *Palestine or Israel*, p. 157.

76. Ibid., p. 146.

77. From an October 1919 interview with the *Jewish Chronicle*; quoted in Flapan, *Zionism and the Palestinians*, p. 49.

78. Lt.-Colonel L. R. E. Waters-Taylor; quoted in ibid., p. 47.

79. Sykes, p. 35.

80. Chaim Weizmann, *Trial and Error* (New York: Schocken Books, 1966), pp. 783–784. See also the discussion of Weizmann's relations with the British in Flapan, *Zionism and the Palestinians*, pp. 20–31.

81. For details see Lesch, *Arab Politics*, pp. 85–86.

82. Porath, *The Emergence*, p. 81. For a general discussion see pp. 79–85. Porath notes that the British had permitted the congress to convene because they believed their behind-the-scenes efforts would result in a majority of delegates favorable to local autonomy under British trusteeship. This position was defeated by a coalition of pan-Arabists, most of whom were Muslim, and pro-French Christians. For another useful account of the congress, see Muslih, *The Origins*, pp. 178–185.

83. Antonius, p. 294.

84. Muslih, *The Origins*, pp. 193–194.

85. The Kingdom of the Hejaz was under the control of Husayn, but the Hashemite leader was challenged by Abd al-Aziz Ibn Saud, a follower of the puritanical and militant Wahhabi movement within Islam. Saudi forces were in control of the eastern part of the peninsula and inflicted successive military defeats on the Hashemites. By 1925 Ibn Saud had overcome all resistance from Husyan's son, Ali, and the following year he was proclaimed king of the Hejaz. His kingdom was recognized by the British in 1927 and changed its name to Saudi Arabia in 1932.

86. The entire text of the mandatory instrument is presented in Laqueur and Rubin, pp. 34–42. A useful summary of British thinking and actions in connection with the establishment of the mandate in Palestine is provided by Fromkin, pp. 515–529. Fromkin gives particular attention to the role of Winston Churchill, who became colonial secretary in February 1921, and he notes in this connection that Churchill "believed in trying the Zionist experiment, and thought that it would benefit everyone" (p. 519).

87. Khalil al-Sakakini, *Al-Nahda al-Urthuduksiyya fi Filastin* [The Orthodox Renaissance in Palestine]; discussed in Porath, *The Emergence*, p. 7. The Greek Orthodox Patriarchate

in Jerusalem at this time had authority over a district that encompassed Transjordan as well as the territory west of the Jordan River. For a useful summary of the changing administrative boundaries of Jund Filastin and Jund al-Urduun following the Muslim conquest, see Gil, pp. 110–114. Gil, an Israeli scholar who reviews both Arab and Jewish sources, notes that Jund Filastin initially encompassed the coastal region, Judea, and Samaria, stretching eastward to Jericho; and that Jund al-Urduun originally included the Jordan Valley along its entire length, south to Eilat, as well as the upper and lower Galilee and the territory east of the Sea of Galilee. More generally, Gil concludes from early sources that "by the name Filastin the Muslims meant only a part of Palestine," and that "also among the Jews [of this period] there was the awareness that Filastin is none other than the 'land of the Philistines' [a term which some Jewish writers used when] referring to Jund Filastin" (p. 113).

88. See, for example, *An Encyclopedia of World History* (New York: Houghton Mifflin Company, 1940), p. 1100.

89. Avi Shlaim, *Collusion across the Jordan: King Abdullah, the Zionist Movement, and the Partition of Palestine* (London: Oxford University Press, 1988), p. 27. For additional discussion of the reasons behind Britain's separation of Transjordan from the Palestine mandate, see Mary C. Wilson, *King Abdullah, Britain and the Making of Jordan* (New York: Cambridge University Press, 1987).

90. Laqueur, *A History of Zionism*, p. 217.

91. Flapan, *Zionism and the Palestinians*, pp. 78–79.

92. Laqueur, *A History of Zionism*, p. 218.

93. Ibid. Indifference or hostility toward the Arabs of Palestine characterized many rank-and-file European Zionists as well. For example, Musa Alami, a Palestinian Arab studying in Cambridge in 1920, describes how a group of local Zionists mistook him for a Jew and asked "how soon you people in Palestine are going to finish with the dirty Arabs." Reported in Furlonge, p. 78.

94. Furlonge. See also Neil Caplan, "The Yishuv, Sir Herbert Samuel, and the Arab Question in Palestine, 1921–1925," in Elie Kedourie and Sylvia G. Haim (eds.), *Zionism and Arabism in Palestine and Israel* (London: Frank Cass, 1982), pp. 17ff.; and Sykes, p. 94. Although Samuel's growing political estrangement from the *Yishuv* was painful for both, it was not uncommon for British officials who had been pro-Zionist while in England to gain their first understanding of the Arab cause only upon their arrival in Palestine. Weizmann once called it "an almost universal rule that such British administrators as came out to Palestine favorably inclined to the Jews turned against them in a few months." Quoted in John Bagot Glubb, *Peace in the Holy Land: An Historical Analysis of the Palestinian Problem* (London: Hodder and Stoughton, 1971), p. 281. On the other hand, although many Zionists considered Samuel's liberal attitude toward the Arabs misguided, some Jews later came to appreciate the degree to which his response to Arab grievances gave Palestine several years of peace. See Laqueur, *A History of Zionism*, p. 455.

95. Doreen Ingrams, *Palestine Papers 1917–1922: Seeds of Conflict* (London: John Murray, 1972), p. 122.

96. Quoted in Paul L. Hanna, *British Policy in Palestine* (Washington: American Council on Public Affairs, 1942), p. 73.

97. Quoted and discussed in Waines, p. 219.

98. Quoted in Sykes, p. 53.

99. Sir John Shuckburgh, Assistant Under Secretary of State; quoted in Ingrams, p. 148.

100. Quoted in Sykes, p. 69.

101. The entire text is printed in Laqueur and Rubin, pp. 45–50.

102. The table is from A. Granott, *Agrarian Reform and the Record of Israel* (London:

Eyre and Spottiswoode, 1956), p. 28. There are minor variations in the figures reported by different sources. See also Government of Palestine, *A Survey of Palestine* (Jerusalem: Government Printer, 1946), vol. I, pp. 141, 144, 185, 200ff., 244, 373; J. C. Hurewitz, *The Struggle for Palestine* (New York: Schocken Books, 1976), p. 28; Ruedy, pp. 125–129.

103. See H. M. Sachar, *A History of Israel*, p. 143. A thorough discussion of issues related to Jewish land purchases from 1917 to 1939 is provided by Kenneth W. Stein, *The Land Question in Palestine, 1917–1939* (Chapel Hill: University of North Carolina Press, 1984). Stein notes that prior to 1929 there was "an absence of coordination in establishing land-purchasing objectives," coupled with "fierce competition among Jewish purchasing organizations for areas and parcels of land" (p. 65). Additional information is provided in Yehoshua Porath, *The Palestine Arab National Movement: From Riots to Rebellion* (London: Frank Cass, 1977), pp. 80–108.

104. See Shafir, p. 42.

105. See Baruch Kimmerling, *Zionism and the Economy* (Cambridge: Schenkman, 1983), p. 23. Figures, based on data available for approximately half the total amount of land purchased, are from A. Granott, *The Land System in Palestine: History and Structure* (London: Eyre and Spottiswoode, 1952), p. 307.

106. Quoted in Shafir, p. 42.

107. Laqueur, *A History of Zionism*, p. 153. See also H. M. Sachar, *A History of Israel*, pp. 140ff.

108. Gordon's work is quoted in Hertzberg, *The Zionist Idea*, pp. 369–386, and H. M. Sachar, *A History of Israel*, pp. 74–76.

109. Granott, *Agrarian Reform*, p. 32.

110. Laqueur, *A History of Zionism*, pp. 460, 464. Debates about the character of the fund preoccupied the Zionist leadership for several years. Some wanted monies raised to be devoted principally to immigration and settlement and opposed any investment in ventures which were not economically productive. Accordingly, they complained of the fact that about 30 percent of the fund's revenues were employed to support Jewish education in Palestine. The latter position, which did not prevail, was championed by American Zionists under Brandeis.

111. Kimmerling, *Zionism and the Economy*, p. 21.

112. See Baruch Kimmerling, *Zionism and Territory: The Socio-Territorial Dimensions of Zionist Politics* (Berkeley: University of California, Institute of International Studies, 1983), p. 11. See also Shafir, p. 42.

113. K. W. Stein, *The Land Question*, p. 65.

114. Ruedy, p. 126. See also Granott, *Agrarian Reform*, p. 29.

115. H. M. Sachar, *A History of Israel*, p. 143.

116. Sykes, p. 89. The JNF had been negotiating for this estate for some time, and portions of it were acquired before 1920. A recent scholarly study reports that about 45 percent of the Sursock estate was unoccupied or unused by permanent tenants, and that there were 668 tenant families cultivating the remaining 130,000 dunams. These families, with an average of perhaps eight or nine members, received limited compensation as part of the land-sale package. See K. W. Stein, *The Land Question*, p. 56.

117. Hisham B. Sharabi, *Palestine and Israel: The Lethal Dilemma* (New York: Pegasus, 1969), p. 186.

118. Quoted in Lesch, *Arab Politics*, p. 70.

119. Sykes, p. 93. K. W. Stein's important study *The Land Question* makes a significant contribution to reducing some of the imprecision about which Sykes complained. For example, Stein's research shows that Sykes's report of 8,000 Arabs displaced as a result of the Sursock land sale may in fact be too high.

120. K. W. Stein, *The Land Question*, p. 59.

121. Shafir, p. 42. See also Yehoshua Porath, "The Land Problem as a Factor in Relations between Arabs, Jews and the Mandatory Government," in Gabriel Ben-Dor (ed.), *The Palestinians and the Middle East Conflict* (Ramat Gan: Turtledove, 1978).

122. See Sykes, p. 92. These aspects of land transfer are discussed further in Albert M. Hyamson, *Palestine under the Mandate* (London: Methuen, 1950). A useful discussion is also to be found in Kenneth W. Stein, "Legal Protection and Circumvention of Rights for Cultivators in Mandatory Palestine," in Joel Migdal (ed.), *Palestinian Society and Politics* (Princeton: Princeton University Press, 1980), pp. 238ff.

123. H. M. Sachar, *A History of Israel*, p. 73.

124. N. DeLima, "On Labor in Palestine," in *The Jewish National Fund: From the Beginnings of Its Activities in Palestine until the Purchases of the Valley* (Jerusalem: Initiating Committee, 1939), p. 17 (Hebrew); quoted in Kimmerling, *Zionism and the Economy*, p. 48.

125. Quoted in Kimmerling, *Zionism and the Economy*, p. 48.

126. Ibid., p. 51.

127. Ibid., pp. 49–50. Other sources include Zvi Sussman, *Wage Differentials and Equality within the Histadruth* (Ramat Gan: Massada, 1947), p. 40 (Hebrew), and M. Ettinger (ed.), *Book of the Economy of the Yishuv, 1947* (Tel Aviv: Hava'ad Haleumi, 1947), p. 277 (Hebrew).

128. The Peel Commission, to be discussed in chapter 4.

129. Quoted in Sykes, pp. 94–95.

130. Quoted in Susan Lee Hattis, *The Bi-National Idea in Palestine during Mandatory Times* (Haifa: Shikmona, 1970), pp. 39–40.

131. From *Like All the Nations?* (Jerusalem, 1930); quoted in Hattis, p. 70.

132. Quoted in H. M. Sachar, *A History of Israel*, p. 180.

133. Hattis, p. 38. For details on Brit Shalom, see ibid., pp. 38ff.; and Laqueur, *A History of Zionism*, pp. 251–255. Magnes supported the movement but was not a formal member. The movement also had important supporters among Zionists outside of Palestine, including Robert Weltsch, editor of *Judische Rundschau*, the organ of the Zionist movement in Germany.

134. Quoted in Caplan, *Futile Diplomacy*, I, p. 65.

135. For an account of other efforts to foster dialogue between Arabs and Jews in Palestine during the 1920s, see ibid., pp. 62–79.

136. From the Hope Simpson Report; quoted in Ruedy, p. 129.

137. Hattis, p. 41.

138. Report of the Executive to the Fourteenth Zionist Congress; quoted in Laqueur, *A History of Zionism*, p. 455.

139. Hanna, p. 86.

140. Dan Horowitz and Moshe Lissak, *Origins of the Israeli Polity: Palestine under the Mandate* (Chicago: University of Chicago Press, 1978), pp. 16–18.

141. Ibid., p. 18.

4. The Dual Society in Mandatory Palestine

1. Laqueur, *A History of Zionism*, p. 329.

2. Matti Golan, *Shimon Peres: A Biography* (London: Weidenfeld and Nicholson, 1982), p. 7.

3. Laqueur, *A History of Zionism*, p. 306.

4. H. M. Sachar, *A History of Israel*, p. 158.

5. Laqueur, *A History of Zionism*, pp. 320–325.

6. Yehuda Slutsky, "Under British Rule (1917–1948)," in *Israel Pocket Library: History from 1880* (Jerusalem: Keter Publishing House, 1973), p. 53.

7. Ibid., p. 57.

8. Laqueur, *A History of Zionism*, p. 325.

9. Figures are from Kimmerling, *Zionism and the Economy*, pp. 19–29. See also Horowitz and Lissak, pp. 62–63; and A. Getz (ed.), *Statistical Handbook of Jewish Palestine, 1947* (Jerusalem: Jewish Agency, 1947), pp. 370–371. The latter sources provide information about the Jewish Agency's expenditure of funds collected by the Keren Hayesod.

10. Figures are from Hurewitz, *The Struggle*, pp. 30–31.

11. Horowitz and Lissak, p. 31.

12. In 1960 the official name of the institution became the World Zionist Organization, although the older designation, Zionist Organization, continued to be widely used.

13. Certificates were awarded on the basis of proportional representation. Complaints were voiced in particular by the right-wing Revisionist Party, which charged that it was not receiving its rightful share. For details, see Arthur Hertzberg, "Ideological Evolution," in *Israel Pocket Library: Zionism* (Jerusalem: Keter Publishing House, 1973), p. 39.

14. Aharon Zwergbaum, "Zionist Organization," in ibid., p. 130.

15. Getzel Kressel, "Zionist Congresses," in ibid., p. 237.

16. Zwergbaum, p. 131.

17. Ibid., pp. 133–135. The structure of the Zionist Organization was transformed in 1960. Emphasis was placed on the autonomy of local federations and unions operating under the Zionist umbrella. It was stipulated that "every member shall determine the conduct of his affairs, the form of his organization and procedure." The Zionist Organization was "to act for and on behalf of the movement and all the members for the implementation of the Zionist program."

18. H. M. Sachar, *A History of Israel*, pp. 138–139.

19. Zwergbaum, p. 142. See also H. M. Sachar, *A History of Israel*, pp. 728–729.

20. Since Israeli independence there have been several changes in the relationship between the two organizations, but a similar pattern of overlapping directorates prevails at present and a functional division of responsibilities has been determined. The Zionist Organization works mostly with Jews outside of Israel to promote the ideals and programs of Zionism. The Jewish Agency works principally inside Israel, continuing the work of immigration, absorption and resettlement, and community development. The present arrangement came into existence under legislation introduced in 1971. From 1948 until 1971, the Jewish Agency and the Zionist Organization were merged; structural separation was eliminated and the distinction between the two institutions became solely one of function.

21. H. M. Sachar, *A History of Israel*, p. 139.

22. Ibid., p. 135.

23. Real Jean Isaac, *Party and Politics in Israel: Three Visions of a Jewish State* (New York: Longman, 1981), p. 183. The Zionists had practical as well as ideological motivations, since the British were prepared only to recognize religious communities. If religious institutions had been placed outside of Knesset Israel, the British might not have accorded legal status to the internal political institutions of the *Yishuv*.

24. See chapter 1.

25. Isaac, *Party and Politics*, pp. 167–168, 183.

26. See Horowitz and Lissak, p. 42. See also M. Atias, *The Book of Documents of the National Council of Knesset Israel, 1918–1948* (Jerusalem: R. H. Cohen, 1953), p. 13.

27. Hertzberg, *The Zionist Idea*, p. 350. See also Isaac, *Party and Politics*, pp. 19–21,

and Yehuda Slutsky, *Preface to the History of the Israeli Labor Movement* (Tel Aviv: Am Oved, 1973), chapter 12 (Hebrew). Syrkin's views for a time led him to the idea that the construction of a Jewish state did not necessarily have to take place in Palestine, and that any "colonizable" territory would be acceptable. He later abandoned this view, however.

28. Horowitz and Lissak, p. 40.

29. See the discussion in Isaac, *Party and Politics*, pp. 30–31. The ideology of Hashomer Hatzair otherwise differed little from that of Hapoel Hatzair and Ahdut Ha'avoda.

30. Hertzberg, *The Zionist Idea*, p. 403.

31. Quoted in Zalman Abramov, *Perpetual Dilemma: Jewish Religion in the Jewish State* (Rutherford, New Jersey: Fairleigh Dickinson University Press, 1976), p. 164. See also Isaac, *Party and Politics*, p. 66.

32. Hertzberg, *the Zionist Idea*, p. 430.

33. Isaac, *Party and Politics*, p. 39.

34. Ibid., p. 40.

35. Laqueur, *A History of Zionism*, p. 382.

36. Quoted in Sykes, pp. 106–107.

37. Ibid., p. 96.

38. For an excellent account of Betar's history and early evolution, see Yonathan Shapiro, *The Road to Power: Herut Party in Israel* (Albany: State University of New York Press, 1991), pp. 26–62. Shapiro discusses Betar's activities both in Poland, where it was established in 1931, with Jabotinsky at its head, and in the *Yishuv*.

39. Laqueur, *A History of Zionism*, p. 383.

40. Isaac, *Party and Politics*, p. 36.

41. The Irgun's founders included individuals from various nonsocialist Zionist parties who were fed up with the control of the Hagana exercised by Mapai and the Histadrut. It was soon dominated by Betaris, however. For details, see Shapiro, pp. 53–57.

42. Horowitz and Lissak, pp. 90–91.

43. For details see R. Melka, "Nazi Germany and the Palestine Question," and David Yisraeli, "The Third Reich and Palestine," both in Kedourie and Haim, *Palestine and Israel*. Even under these arrangements, departing Jews were able to recover only 25–35 percent of the assets they left behind. Nazi motivations in permitting Jews to leave and in cooperating in the transfer of capital, at least through 1937, included a desire to rid Germany of its Jews, the goal of increasing German exports, and satisfaction at seeing Jewish immigration into Palestine strain relations between Great Britain and the Arabs.

44. Janet L. Abu-Lughod, "The Demographic Transformation of Palestine," in I. Abu-Lughod, *The Transformation*, p. 146.

45. Ibid., pp. 146–149.

46. Fred Gottheil, "Arab Immigration into Pre-State Israel: 1922–1931," in Kedourie and Haim, *Palestine and Israel*, p. 146.

47. An important exposition of this theory, or myth, is provided by Joan Peters, *From Time Immemorial: The Origins of the Arab-Jewish Conflict over Palestine* (New York: Harper and Row, 1984). A major thesis of Peters's work is that the Arabs of Palestine cannot claim to be an indigenous population displaced by Jewish immigrants, since many Arabs arrived at roughly the same time as the Jews. There have been both more favorable and less favorable reviews of Peters's book. Among the former are Walter Reich in the *Atlantic* (July 1984); Bernard Gwertzman in the *New York Times* (May 12, 1984); and Daniel Pipes in *Commentary* (July 1984). Among the latter are Alexander Cockburn and Edward Said in the *Nation* (October 13, 1984); Norman G. Finkelstein in *In These Times* (September 5–11, 1984); Bill Farrell in the *Journal of Palestine Studies* (Fall 1984); and Ian and David Gilmour in the *London*

Review of Books (February 7, 1985). Unrelated to debates about the magnitude of Arab immigration to Palestine is Britain's importation during the war of thousands of unskilled workers from neighboring Arab countries in order to meet growing manpower needs and hold down rapidly rising wage scales. See Rachelle Taqqu, "Peasants into Workmen: Internal Labor Migration and the Arab Village Community under the Mandate," in Migdal, p. 265.

48. Yehoshua Porath, a review of Peters, in the *New York Review of Books* (January 16, 1986), p. 37. Porath, a leading Israeli authority on Palestine during the period of the British mandate, also states: "What is surprising is that Joan Peters still writes as if the Zionist myths were wholly true and relevant, notwithstanding all the historical work that modifies or discredits them."

49. See Abner Cohen, *Arab Border Villages in Israel* (Manchester: Manchester University Press, 1965); and Gabriel Baer, "The Office and Functions of the Village Mukhtar," in Migdal, pp. 103–123.

50. Baer, p. 104. For a detailed discussion of politics and administration in Palestinian village society during the period of the British mandate, see Ylana N. Miller, *Government and Society in Rural Palestine, 1920–1948* (Austin: University of Texas Press, 1985), pp. 71–89.

51. Waines, p. 228.

52. *Report of the Committee on Village Administration and Responsibility* (Jerusalem: Government Printing Press, 1941).

53. Hurewitz, *The Struggle*, pp. 35–36. See also Waines, pp. 217–218, and Henry Rosenfeld, "The Class Situation of the Arab National Minority in Israel," *Comparative Studies in Society and History* 20 (July 1978): 375ff.

54. There are some discrepancies in the figures reported by various sources. See Abdul Latif Tibawi, *Arab Education in Mandatory Palestine: A Study in Three Decades of British Administration* (London: Luzac, 1956), pp. 270–271; Hurewitz, *The Struggle*, p. 36; Porath, *The Emergence*, pp. 20–21; and Lesch, *Arab Politics*, pp. 56–57.

55. Lesch, *Arab Politics*, p. 57.

56. Shulamit Carmi and Henry Rosenfeld, "The Origins of the Process of Proletarianization and Urbanization of Arab Peasants in Palestine," *Annals of the New York Academy of Sciences* 220 (1974): 477. See also Henry Rosenfeld, "From Peasantry to Wage Labor and Residual Peasantry: The Transformation of an Arab Village," in Robert A. Manners (ed.), *Process and Pattern in Culture* (Chicago: Aldine Publishing Company, 1964); and Taqqu, pp. 266ff.

57. Lesch, *Arab Politics*, pp. 63–64; Hurewitz, *The Struggle*, p. 33.

58. Taqqu, p. 269.

59. Lesch, *Arab Politics*, pp. 61–63. See also Adnan Mohammad Abu-Ghazaleh, "Arab Cultural Nationalism in Palestine during the British Mandate," *Journal of Palestine Studies* 1 (1972): 37–63; and Matiel Mogannam, *The Arab Woman and the Palestine Problem* (London: Herbert Joseph, 1937), pp. 56–58.

60. Kimmerling, *Zionism and the Economy*, p. 55.

61. Ibid., p. 53. Original sources include *Statistical Abstract of Palestine, 1939* (Jerusalem: Government Printer, 1940) and Z. Abramovitz and Y. Gelfat, *The Arab Economy in Palestine and in the Middle East* (Hakibbutz Hameuchad, 1940).

62. Hurewitz, *The Struggle*, p. 32.

63. Porath, *The Emergence*, p. 90. See also Lesch, *Arab Politics*, pp. 84ff.

64. Porath, *The Emergence*, pp. 74–79, 129. See also Lesch, *Arab Politics*. These accounts, which are the most thorough available, summarize considerable quantities of primary source material. Other useful accounts are to be found in Hurewitz, *The Struggle*, pp. 52ff.; Waines; and Ann Mosely Lesch, "The Palestine Arab Nationalist Movement under the Man-

date," in William Quandt, Fuad Jabber, and Ann Mosely Lesch, *The Politics of Palestinian Nationalism* (Berkeley: University of California Press, 1973).

65. Porath, *The Emergence*, p. 111.

66. Ibid., p. 282. See also Lesch, *Arab Politics*, p. 93.

67. For an excellent account of the formation and evolution of the Supreme Muslim Council, see Uri Kupferschmidt, *The Supreme Muslim Council: Islam under the British Mandate in Palestine* (Leiden: Brill, 1987).

68. Established practice was for an assembly of religious officials to convene and nominate three candidates for the position of mufti. The mufti would then be selected from among these three by the proper authorities, formerly the Ottoman *sheikh al-Islam* but now the mandatory government. In 1921, all three of the candidates selected were allied with the Nashashibi family, and al-Hajj Amin polled only fourth in the voting. In addition to family rivalries, opposition to al-Hajj Amin was based on the fact that he had not had religious training and was not a member of the *ulama*. Nevertheless, the Husaynis organized a vigorous and effective campaign to demonstrate grass-roots support for al-Hajj Amin, and after much deliberation he was appointed by the British.

69. Porath, *The Emergence*, pp. 222ff. See also Lesch, *Arab Politics*, pp. 96–99.

70. Porath, *The Emergence*, p. 239.

71. Ibid., p. 243.

72. For a useful biographical portrait of al-Hajj Amin al-Husayni, see Majid Khadduri, *Arab Contemporaries: The Role of Personalities in Politics* (Baltimore: Johns Hopkins University Press, 1973), pp. 67–87. Khadduri's account is entitled "The Traditional (Idealistic) School—The Extremist: al-Hajj Amin al-Husayni." For a fuller account, which is also somewhat more sympathetic, see Philip Mattar, *The Mufti of Jerusalem: Al-Hajj Amin al-Husayni and the Palestine National Movement* (New York: Columbia University Press, 1988).

73. James Jankowski, "Egyptian Responses to the Palestine Problem in the Interwar Period," *International Journal of Middle East Studies* 12 (1980): 3.

74. See H. A. R. Gibb, "The Islamic Congress at Jerusalem, December, 1931," in *Survey of International Affairs: 1934* (Oxford, 1935), pp. 99–109.

75. Waines, p. 231.

76. Muhammad Amin al-Husayni, *Haqa'iq an Qadiyyat Filastin* [Truths regarding the Palestine Problem] (Cairo, 1954), p. 10; quoted in Yehoshua Porath, *The Palestine Arab National Movement: From Riots to Rebellion* (London: Frank Cass, 1977), pp. 94–95.

77. Porath, *The Palestine Arab National Movement*, p. 98.

78. Lesch, *Arab Politics*, p. 106.

79. Ibid., p. 111.

80. Porath, *The Palestine Arab National Movement*, p. 76.

81. Barbara Kalkas, "The Revolt of 1936: A Chronicle of Events," in I. Abu-Lughod, *The Transformation*, p. 248.

82. See, for example, Norman Rose, *The Gentile Zionists: A Study in Anglo-Zionist Diplomacy, 1929–1939* (London: Frank Cass, 1973), pp. 157–158.

83. James Jankowski, "The Government of Egypt and the Palestine Question, 1936–1939," *Middle East Studies* 17 (1981): 447. Jankowski observes that the consequences of Egypt's Palestine policy may have been most significant for Egypt itself, especially as a stimulus to the development of closer ties between Egypt and other Arab countries.

84. Elie Kedourie, "The Arab-Israeli Conflict," in *Arab Political Memoirs and Other Studies* (London: Frank Cass, 1974); reprinted in Laqueur and Rubin, pp. 565–566.

85. Furlonge, pp. 67 and 87.

86. Ibid., p. 94.

87. See, for example, Horowitz and Lissak, pp. 18ff.; Flapan, *Zionism and the Palestinians*, pp. 194ff.; and Kimmerling, *Zionism and the Economy*, pp. 41ff.

88. M. Golan, *Shimon Peres*, p. 7.

89. Sykes, p. 108.

90. Hyamson, quoted in Sykes.

91. Sykes, p. 109. Disagreement continues about whether or not Arab attacks on Jews were planned in advance. In any event, on the second day of the rioting, Arab leaders issued a manifesto calling upon their countrymen "to strive sincerely to quell the riot, avoid bloodshed and save life. . . . to return to quiet and peace, to endeavor to assist in the restoration of order." Quoted in Waines, p. 228. The manifesto was issued by Musa Kazim al-Husayni, al-Hajj Amin al-Husayni, Raghib al-Nashashibi, Mustafa al-Khalidi, and Arif Dajani.

92. Quoted and discussed in John Bagot Glubb, *Peace in the Holy Land* (London: Hodder and Stoughton, 1971), p. 281.

93. Quoted and discussed in Gwyn Rowley, *Israel into Palestine* (London: Mansell, 1984), p. 35.

94. Quoted and discussed in Richard N. Verdery, "Arab 'Disturbances' and Commissions of Inquiry," in I. Abu-Lughod, *The Transformation*, p. 290.

95. The entire letter is reprinted in Laqueur and Rubin, pp. 50–56.

96. Weizmann, p. 335.

97. Sykes, pp. 114–115.

98. For example, there was a meeting between David Ben Gurion and Musa al-Alami in March 1934. Both the Arab and the Jewish versions of these meetings are reprinted in Neil Caplan, *Futile Diplomacy, Volume II: Arab-Zionist Negotiations and the End of the Mandate* (London: Frank Cass, 1986), pp. 189–192.

99. Porath, *The Palestine Arab National Movement*, p. 238.

100. General Robert Haining; quoted in Lesch, *Arab Politics*, p. 223. For an informative summary of the Arab Revolt from the perspective of rural society in Palestine, see Y. Miller, pp. 121–138.

101. John Marlowe, *The Seat of Pilate* (London: Cresset Press, 1959), pp. 137–138.

102. Porath, *The Palestine Arab National Movement*, pp. 260ff.

103. Ibid., pp. 266–269.

104. Dispatch of January 2, 1939; quoted in ibid., p. 269.

105. Jabotinsky, House of Lords, February 11, 1937; quoted in Laqueur and Rubin, p. 59.

106. Peel Commission Report, pp. 110–111. For a useful account of the commission and its work, see Caplan, *Futile Diplomacy, II*, pp. 58ff.

107. Quoted in Sykes, p. 174.

108. Ibid.

109. Simons, pp. 12–13.

110. Teveth, "The Evolution," p. 27.

111. Ibid., pp. 31–32.

112. Ibid., p. 40.

113. For example, Ben Gurion told the Histadrut Council in February 1937 that "no one in Zionism proposes removing the Arabs from Palestine," and a few months after that he wrote in a letter to a colleague, "It's hard for me to believe in forcible transfer and it's hard for me to believe in voluntary transfer." He replied to Ussishkin, in a response that may not have been based entirely on principle, "If you repeat it [the proposal to transfer Arabs from Palestine to Iraq] to an Englishman you will cause us only damage. To them we must explain that we neither desire nor need to deny the Arabs the possibility of existence, and this can be proved in num-

bers." Ibid., pp. 27, 29, and 31. A different view of Zionist attitudes toward transfer is presented by Simons, an analyst who writes from a militant Zionist perspective. Simons contends that "very few people have had the courage to support *publicly* the transfer of Arabs from Palestine. Most leaders of the Zionist movement *publicly* opposed such transfers. However, a study of their confidential correspondence, private diaries, and minutes of closed meetings, made available to the public under the 'thirty year rule,' reveals [that many prominent Zionist leaders] were really in favor of transferring the Arabs from Palestine" (p. 211).

114. Marlowe, p. 147.

115. A thorough account of the conference and of the broader diplomatic maneuvering that it produced is provided by Caplan, *Futile Diplomacy*, II, pp. 85–113.

116. The White Paper is reprinted in Laqueur and Rubin, pp. 64–75. For additional discussion, see Ronald W. Zweig, *Britain and Palestine during the Second World War* (London: Royal Historical Society, 1986), pp. 44–50. See also Caplan, *Futile Diplomacy*, II, pp. 116–118.

117. The statement of the Jewish Agency issued in response to the MacDonald White Paper is reprinted in Laqueur and Rubin, pp. 76–77.

118. Ibid., p. 77.

119. Sykes, p. 199.

120. Land sales to Jews were completely prohibited in the northern Negev, the western Galilee, and the hilly regions of eastern Palestine, between the coastal plain and the Jordan River. In the Jezreel Valley, the eastern Galilee, and parts of the coastal plain, land could be purchased only with the approval of the high commissioner.

121. For details see Marlowe, p. 169, and Laqueur, *A History of Zionism*, pp. 534–535.

122. Quoted in Sykes, p. 223.

123. For additional information, see Zweig, pp. 71ff.

124. An account of these and other episodes, written from the Zionist point of view, is provided in Arthur Koestler, *Promise and Fulfillment* (London: Macmillan, 1949). A British version of these events is given by Sykes, pp. 220ff. See also Nicholas Bethell, *The Palestine Triangle: The Struggle between the British, the Jews and the Arabs, 1935–1948* (London: Andre Deutsch, 1979), pp. 76–100.

125. See Hurewitz, *The Struggle*, p. 141.

126. Ibid., pp. 124–125.

127. Although wholeheartedly committed to the struggle against Nazism, the Zionist movement was unable to provide much assistance to the Jews of Europe who were facing annihilation. Further, some critics, including many in present-day Israel, have charged that this is partly the result of misplaced priorities and, to a lesser extent, ambivalent attitudes. For a judicious and thoroughly researched analysis of this subject, see Dina Porat, *The Blue and Yellow Stars of David: The Zionist Leadership in Palestine and the Holocaust, 1939–1945* (Cambridge: Harvard University Press, 1990). Writing in the introduction to this important study, Porat states, "Ever since the end of the Second World War, the Israeli public has been traumatized by feelings of guilt concerning the Holocaust. The prevailing opinion has been that the Yishuv . . . failed to do what could have been done to rescue Jews in Nazi-occupied countries."

128. For a careful account of the negotiations for a Jewish army, see Michael J. Cohen, *Palestine: Retreat from the Mandate, The Making of British Policy, 1936–1945* (London: Paul Elek, 1978), pp. 98–124.

129. For a discussion of the origins and philosophy of the Stern Group, see Gorny, pp. 263–264 and 319–320. A useful summary is also provided by Michael J. Cohen, *Palestine and the Great Powers, 1945–1948* (Princeton: Princeton University Press, 1982), pp. 69–72.

130. For details, see Zweig, pp. 175–176.

131. The entire declaration is reprinted in Laqueur and Rubin, pp. 77–79.

132. Quoted in Hurewitz, *The Struggle*, p. 195.

133. Quoted in Sykes, p. 261. For additional discussion of the 1944 Labour Party Conference, see Simons, pp. 207–209. Following its electoral victory in 1945, the Labour Party did nothing to implement its 1944 resolutions on Palestine, and Britain resumed its attempts to limit Jewish immigration to the country.

134. The only major Arab leader to support Britain in spite of these considerations was King Abdullah of Transjordan, who remained loyal to Britain throughout the war years. For an important study of Abdullah's cooperation with the British, and of his secret dealings with the Zionist movement throughout the entire period of the mandate, see Avi Shlaim, *Collusion across the Jordan: King Abdullah, the Zionist Movement, and the Partition of Palestine* (Oxford: Oxford University Press, 1988).

135. Sykes, p. 124. For additional information about the mufti and his policies, see Khadduri, *Arab Contemporaries*, whose overall conclusion is that al-Hajj Amin used "negative and extreme methods . . . to the point of diminishing returns" (p. 84). For a more extended discussion, which also presents the mufti in a somewhat more sympathetic light, see Mattar, *The Mufti*. Mattar cites original and previously unpublished source material and endeavors to show that al-Hajj Amin was not a fanatic or extremist driven by hatred, as he is often portrayed.

136. An account of this meeting is published in Laqueur and Rubin, pp. 79–84.

137. From evidence submitted to the 1946 Anglo-American Committee of Inquiry by the Arab Office in Jerusalem; reprinted in Laqueur and Rubin, p. 95.

138. Michael J. Cohen, "The Zionist Perspective," in William Roger Louis and Robert W. Stookey (eds.), *The End of the Palestine Mandate* (Austin: University of Texas Press, 1986), p. 79.

139. A. L. Sachar, p. 425.

140. For an informed account of this illegal Jewish immigration to Palestine following the war, written by an activist in the Zionist underground who was one of its organizers, see Ze'ev Venia Hadari, *Second Exodus: The Full Story of Jewish Illegal Immigration to Palestine, 1945–1948* (London: Vallentine Mitchell, 1991).

141. In his response to Truman, the British prime minister, Clement Attlee, reminded the American president that both Roosevelt and Churchill had promised to consult the Arabs before taking any action affecting the future of Palestine, and he added that to break these promises could set the whole Middle East aflame. Truman followed with a conciliatory letter, expressing an understanding of Britain's position and promising to take no further action. For useful summaries of the diplomatic maneuvering associated with the demand for 100,000 immigration certificates, see M. J. Cohen, *Palestine and the Great Powers*, pp. 55–59; and Alan R. Taylor, *Prelude to Israel: An Analysis of Zionist Diplomacy, 1897–1947* (Beirut: Institute for Palestine Studies, 1970), pp. 89ff. Taylor observes that Truman's efforts to resettle more Jewish refugees in the United States and other countries were opposed by some Zionists on the grounds that they would weaken the case for a Jewish state. For an account by the man whom Truman assigned to coordinate his refugee assistance program, see Morris L. Ernest, *So Far So Good* (New York: Harper, 1948), pp. 176–177.

142. Bethell, p. 241.

143. David A. Charters, *The British Army and Jewish Insurgency in Palestine, 1945–47* (New York: St. Martin's Press, 1989), p. 54. According to Charters, Hagana militants, disillusioned with the negotiating process, urged the Jewish Agency in summer 1945 to allow active opposition to the British, after which there was enhanced cooperation with underground groups in "a campaign to extract concessions from the British" (p. 53). This "United Resistance Movement" collapsed in August 1946, however, and thereafter the Hagana appears to

have confined its activities solely to illegal immigration, and to have removed itself from the armed struggle against the British (p. 59), whereas the Irgun and the Stern Group intensified their terrorist operations (pp. 60–65). For an additional account suggesting that some terrorist operations may have been conducted with the knowledge, or participation, of mainstream Zionist institutions, see Kirk, pp. 209–218. Kirk observes, for example, that the Palmach participated in several attacks against British installations. He also reports on cooperation with the Irgun and the Stern Group, asserting that intercepted Jewish Agency communications reveal "collusion on a high level between the Agency Executive and the terrorist organizations whose activities they always officially deplored and declared themselves powerless to prevent." It may also be noted that Zionist leaders steadfastly refused to assist the British in identifying terrorists, not only insisting that terrorism must be combated by modifying the policies to which it was an understandable response, but adding as well that the Jews of the *Yishuv* could not be expected to assist the British by informing on one another. In June 1946, the British government reacted to the new terrorist activities by arresting the members of the Jewish Agency Executive who were in Palestine at the time. The detainees were released several weeks later.

144. Concerning the question of mainstream Zionist complicity in the bombing of the King David Hotel, Menachem Begin, leader of the Irgun, is reported to have claimed, "We carried out this very difficult operation at the request of the *Hagana*." See Bethell, p. 257. For a useful and balanced summary of the attack on the King David Hotel, see M. J. Cohen, *Palestine and the Great Powers*, pp. 90–93. Another informative account, which concludes that "Zionist terrorism offers a basic explanation of why the British were forced to retreat," is provided by William Roger Louis, "British Imperialism and the End of the British Mandate," in Louis and Stookey, pp. 10ff.

145. The report is reprinted in Laqueur and Rubin, pp. 84–94.

146. For further information about the Anglo-American Committee and its proceedings, see Amikam Nachmani, *Great Power Discord in Palestine: The Anglo-American Committee of Inquiry into the Problems of European Jewry and Palestine, 1945–1946* (London: Frank Cass, 1987), pp. 61–86 and 121–137. See also Ritchie Ovendale, *Britain, the United States, and the End of the Palestine Mandate, 1942–1948* (London: The Boydell Press, 1989), pp. 106–140.

147. See Flapan, *Zionism and the Palestinians*, p. 291.

148. For details, see Nachmani, pp. 205–210.

149. Sykes, pp. 301–302.

150. George Kirk; quoted in Sykes, p. 323.

151. For details, see Peter Grose, "The President versus the Diplomats," in Louis and Stookey.

152. Hurewitz, *The Struggle*, p. 305.

153. Writing later of the persistence of Zionist leaders, Truman states in his memoirs, "I do not think I ever had as much pressure and propaganda aimed at the White House as I had in this instance." See *Memoirs by Harry S Truman, Vol. II: Years of Trial and Hope* (Garden City: Doubleday, 1956), p. 158.

154. Grose reports that a cabinet meeting on November 11 discussed the countries whose delegations might be pressured to support partition; "The President," p. 45. Yet significant U.S. pressure on these countries came only in the forty-eight hours prior to the United Nations vote, adding to the drama that attended the meeting of the General Assembly. Indicative is U.S. action toward Liberia, an account of which is provided by M. J. Cohen, *Palestine and the Great Powers*, p. 297. "Liberia was a developing country, very much dependent on its rubber exports, a major part of which were bought by the Firestone Rubber Company in the United States. . . . [Former Secretary of State] Stettinius mobilized Harvey Firestone who, fearing a

Jewish boycott of his products, informed President Tubman of Liberia that if his country did not change its vote, the Firestone company would have to reconsider its plans to extend its rubber holdings in Liberia. The Liberian vote duly changed to support partition." Useful general accounts of the diplomatic maneuvers behind the adoption of the partition resolution are provided by Hurewitz, *The Struggle*, pp. 302–309; M. J. Cohen, *Palestine and the Great Powers*, pp. 292–300; and Taylor, pp. 102–107.

155. Although both sides accused them of partiality, the British appear to have placed high priority on not being drawn into the conflict and on arranging for the removal from Palestine of their considerable store of military equipment and arms. As expressed by Sir Alan Cunningham, high commissioner at the time, Britain's policy was "to remain neutral between two hotly contesting sides." See M. J. Cohen, *Palestine and the Great Powers*, p. 339.

156. For a discussion of *Tochnit Dalet*, see Simha Flapan, *The Birth of Israel: Myths and Realities* (New York: Pantheon Books, 1987), p. 42. Flapan notes that Plan D explicitly "provided for the seizure of areas in Galilee and on the way from Tel Aviv to Jerusalem that had been assigned to the Arab state or included in the international zone."

157. Flapan, *Zionism*, pp. 317–320. American and some contemporary Arab sources privately concluded that Israeli confidence was justified. See also Furlonge, pp. 152–153. Although Israeli forces did not have an adequate supply of weapons at the beginning of the war, the Hagana did have 30,000 men with wartime experience. An additional 4,000–5,000 armed men served under the command of the Irgun. The Arab armies were poorly trained, and many were also badly equipped. The most professional fighting force in the Arab world was the Arab Legion of Transjordan, which had only 4,500 men available for combat. See John Bagot Glubb, *A Soldier with the Arabs* (London: Hodder and Stoughton, 1957).

158. Flapan, *Zionism*, p. 303.

Part III. Routinization of the Conflict, 1948–1967

1. Chaim Herzog, *The Arab-Israeli Wars* (New York: Vintage Books, 1984), p. 106.

2. President Truman announced *de facto* recognition of Israel several hours after the Jewish state declared its independence. Three days later Moscow extended *de jure* recognition to the new state, temporarily making the Soviet emissary to Tel Aviv dean of the diplomatic corps in Israel. The U.S. thereafter raised its mission to an embassy, regaining diplomatic seniority. For details see A. L. Sachar, p. 450; and Herbert Feis, *The Birth of Israel: The Tousled Diplomatic Bed* (New York: Norton, 1969), pp. 60–63.

3. David Ben Gurion, "The Imperatives of the Jewish Revolution," in Hertzberg, *The Zionist Idea*, pp. 606–619. Ben Gurion was committed to a socialist as well as a Jewish Israel, and he believed in an ingathering of Jews residing in the Diaspora. Thus, he elsewhere defines the consummation of the Jewish revolution as "the concentration of the majority of our people in a homeland transformed into a Jewish socialist state." See also David Ben Gurion, *Ben Gurion Looks Back in Talks with Moshe Pearlman* (New York: Schocken Books, 1965), pp. 235ff.

4. Feis, p. 61.

5. Amnon Rubinstein, *The Zionist Dream Revisited* (New York: Schocken Books, 1984), p. 34.

6. The remarks are by Pinhas Lavon, at the time general secretary of the Histadrut. Lavon was a pacifist early in his career but subsequently became defense minister and took a much more hard-line attitude toward the Arabs. Lavon's statement is quoted in Tom Segev, *1949: The First Israelis* (New York: The Free Press, 1986), pp. 46–47.

7. Abraham Joshua Heschel, *Israel: An Echo of Eternity* (New York: Farrar, Straus and Giroux, 1967), p. 219.

5. The Palestinian Disaster and Basic Issues after 1948

8. This and other passages from Bernadotte's report to the General Assembly on September 16 are quoted in Khouri, pp. 81ff. For a fuller account, see Amitzur Ilan, *Bernadotte in Palestine, 1948* (New York: St. Martin's, 1989). See also Saadia Touval, *The Peace Brokers* (Princeton: Princeton University Press, 1982), pp. 38ff.

9. C. H. Dodd and M. E. Sales, *Israel and the Arab World* (New York: Barnes and Noble, 1970), p. 92.

10. Khouri, p. 294. See also Don Peretz, *Israel and the Palestine Arabs* (Washington: The Middle East Institute, 1958), p. 65.

11. The Tripartite Declaration is reprinted in Ralph H. Magnus (ed.), *Documents on the Middle East* (Washington: American Enterprise Institute, 1969), pp. 163–164. This is not to say that the United States and other countries supported Israel fully on territorial questions. In May 1949, for example, President Truman had criticized Israel for failing to compromise at the Lausanne Conference, and later that year he had again called upon Israel to make territorial concessions.

12. Glubb, *A Soldier with the Arabs*, p. 307.

13. Cited in Benjamin Shwadran, *Jordan: A State of Tension* (New York: Council for Middle Eastern Affairs Press, 1959), p. 297. For additional details see also Peter Gubser, *Jordan: Crossroads of Middle Eastern Events* (Boulder, Colorado: Westview Press, 1983), pp. 84–87. For a fuller account of King Abdullah's life and role in the construction of modern Jordan, see Mary C. Wilson, *King Abdullah, Britain and the Making of Jordan* (New York: Cambridge University Press, 1987).

14. Shaul Mishal, *West Bank/East Bank: The Palestinians in Jordan, 1949–1967* (New Haven: Yale University Press, 1978), pp. 1–2.

15. Abdullah had been meeting secretly with Zionist leaders for almost fifteen years and had cordial relations with several of them. For an important account of his negotiations with Jewish leaders, based partly on recently declassified official documents and focusing on the period following termination of the British mandate, see Shlaim. For another valuable study, dealing with secret talks during 1949 and 1950, see Itamar Rabinovich, *The Road Not Taken: Early Arab-Israeli Negotiations* (New York: Oxford University Press, 1991), pp. 111–167.

16. See Arthur R. Day, *East Bank/West Bank: Jordan and the Prospects for Peace* (New York: Council on Foreign Relations, 1986), pp. 19–20. Britain had initially been hesitant to support Abdullah's designs on Palestine, principally because of a reluctance to take a position against the majority of the Arab League. By mid-1948, however, British officials had concluded that Abdullah's annexation of Arab Palestine would be in their own country's strategic interest. For a fuller discussion, see Ilan Pappé, *Britain and the Arab-Israeli Conflict: 1948–51* (New York: St. Martin's Press, 1988), pp. 10–16.

17. From Ben Gurion's diaries, entry of January 16, 1949; quoted in Segev, *1949*, p. 15. See also Shlaim, p. 519. Israel's position was that it would support Jordanian control of Gaza only if this could be achieved with Egyptian consent.

18. Shlaim, pp. 537–538.

19. Quoted in Barry Rubin, *The Arab States and the Palestine Conflict* (Syracuse: Syracuse University Press, 1981), p. 214. Rubin provides a valuable account of Abdullah's diplomatic maneuvering between 1948 and 1951.

20. Sharabi, *Palestine and Israel*, p. 194.

21. Quoted in Khouri, p. 125.

22. Reported in *Keesing's Contemporary Archives* (London: Keesing's Publications, 1948–1973), p. 10101. The UN Economic Survey Mission to Palestine offered somewhat lower estimates, putting the number of refugees at 726,000 in the fall of 1949. Further, noting that some refugees were self-supporting, the Economic Survey recommended early in 1950 that the UN provide rations for only 625,000. For a useful and objective discussion see Peretz, *Israel and the Palestine Arabs*.

23. Terrence Prittie, *Israel: Miracle in the Desert* (New York: Praeger, 1968), p. 120. Prittie agrees that the United Nations Relief and Works Agency (UNRWA) may indeed have been feeding 750,000 Palestinians at the beginning of 1949 but adds, "UNRWA authorities found it next to impossible to distinguish between genuine refugees and the hordes of vagrants and unemployed who joined the bread lines." This difficulty was in fact acknowledged by some UN and Red Cross officials. For example, a November 1949 report of the International Committee of the Red Cross summarized a number of factors which it said made precise estimates "almost impossible." For details see Edward H. Buehrig, *The UN and the Palestinian Refugees: A Study in Non-Territorial Administration* (Bloomington: Indiana University Press, 1971), p. 31. For a detailed account of Israeli arguments supporting lower estimates of the number of refugees, see Walter Pinner, *How Many Arab Refugees* (London: Macgibbon and Key, 1959). Pinner contends that there were 539,000 Palestinian refugees by the end of 1948.

24. Benny Morris, *The Birth of the Palestinian Refugee Problem, 1947–1949* (Cambridge: Cambridge University Press, 1987), p. 1.

25. *Progress Report of the UN Mediator*, 3rd Session, 16 September 1948. See also Buehrig, p. 21.

26. Khouri, p. 135. Khouri summarizes this 1953 UNRWA report and other pertinent UN documents in his useful and balanced discussion. For a fuller discussion, see Milton Viorst, *Reaching for the Olive Branch: UNRWA and Peace in the Middle East* (Washington: The Middle East Institute, 1989), pp. 32–46.

27. See Ann Mosely Lesch and Mark Tessler, *Israel, Egypt and the Palestinians: From Camp David to Intifada* (Bloomington: Indiana University Press, 1989), pp. 96–97.

28. Nafez Nazzal, *The Palestinian Exodus from Galilee in 1948* (Beirut: Institute for Palestine Studies, 1978), p. 77. The interview was carried out in al-Ghaziyih, Lebanon.

29. Ibid., p. 83. The interview was carried out in Ain al- Hilweh Camp, Sidon, Lebanon.

30. Ibid., p. 45. The interview was carried out in Ain al- Hilweh Camp, Sidon, Lebanon.

31. Ibid., p. 69. The interview was carried out in Shatilla Camp, Beirut, Lebanon.

32. Ann Mosely Lesch, "Closed Borders, Divided Lives: Palestinian Writings," Universities Field Staff International Reports, Asia, no. 28, 1985, p. 1. See also Lesch and Tessler, p. 125.

33. Khouri, pp. 100–101.

34. From a 1963 speech to a contingent of Egyptian soldiers; quoted in Laqueur and Rubin, p. 140.

35. *Palestine Royal Commission Report*, July 1937 (London: H.M.S.O., 1937), p. 131.

36. The full text is reprinted in Laqueur and Rubin, pp. 94–104.

37. Hadawi, p. 48.

38. Edward Said, *The Question of Palestine* (New York: Vintage, 1980), p. 99.

39. Ibid., p. 13. The quoted passage is from Theodor Herzl, *Complete Diaries* (New York: Herzl Press, 1960), vol. I, p. 88.

40. Ibid., pp. 99–100. The quoted passage is from Joseph Weitz, *My Diary and Letters to the Children* (Tel Aviv: Massada, 1965), vol. II, pp. 181–182.

41. Fayez A. Sayegh, "Zionist Colonialism in Palestine"; partially reprinted in Laqueur and Rubin, pp. 167–168.

42. Frank Gervasi, *The Case for Israel* (New York: Viking, 1967), p. 11.

43. Some argue that the case for Israel is further strengthened by the fact that a small Jewish community remained in Palestine from Roman times until the emergence of modern Zionism. As expressed by James Parkes, a British historian and Christian theologian, Israel's "real title deeds [to Palestine] were written by the . . . heroic endurance of those who had maintained a Jewish presence in the land all through the centuries, and in spite of every discouragement. This page of history found no place in the constant flow of Zionist propaganda . . . [and thus permitted opponents of Zionism] to paint an entirely false picture of the wickedness of Jewry trying to establish a two-thousand year old claim to the country." See Parkes, *Whose Land*, p. 266. This point is also discussed in Samuel Katz, *Battleground: Fact and Fantasy in Palestine* (New York: Bantam Books, 1973), pp. 86ff. Katz summarizes the Jewish presence in Palestine during this period and writes, "Widely unknown, its significance certainly long ungrasped, is the no less awesome fact that throughout the eighteen centuries between the fall of the Second Jewish Commonwealth and the beginning of the Third, in our time, the tenacity of Jewish attachment to the land of Israel found continuous expression in the country itself."

44. Hadawi, p. 42. This position is also taken by a few Jews and was put forward for a time by a small number of Jewish organizations, such as the American Council for Judaism and American Jewish Alternatives to Zionism. For a Jewish expression of this point of view, see Elmer Berger, *Who Knows Better Must Say So!* (New York: American Council for Judaism, 1955).

45. Heschel, pp. 22 and 54.

46. Katz, pp. 84 and 86.

47. W. T. Mallison, Jr., "The Zionist-Israel Juridical Claims to Constitute the 'Jewish People' Nationality Entity and to Confer Membership in It: Appraisal in Public International Law," *George Washington Law Review* 32 (1964): 983–1075. This article is reprinted in John Norton Moore (ed.), *The Arab-Israeli Conflict, Volume I: Readings* (Princeton: Princeton University Press, 1974). Many of the works on international law cited in the present discussion are to be found in this useful four-volume collection of readings and documents.

48. The report is published by the Institute for Palestine Studies, 1968, and is reprinted in Moore, *The Arab-Israeli Conflict, I.*

49. Ben Halpern, "The Anti-Zionist Phobia: Legal Style," *Midstream* 2 (1965): 74–85; reprinted in Moore, *The Arab-Israeli Conflict, I.*

50. Arab jurists, reprinted in ibid., p. 316.

51. Ibid., pp. 321ff. A Palestinian lawyer who has written extensively on this point is Henry Cattan. See, for example, Henry Cattan, *Palestine, the Arabs and Israel* (London: Longman, 1969). In an appendix to this volume, entitled "Sovereignty over Palestine" and reprinted in Moore, *The Arab-Israeli Conflict, I*, Cattan states, "A study of Chapter XII of the Charter of the United Nations leaves no room for doubt that unless and until the Mandatory Power negotiates a trustee agreement in accordance with Article 79 and presents it to the General Assembly for approval, neither the General Assembly nor any other organ of the United Nations is competent to entertain, still less to recommend or enforce, any solution with regard to a mandated territory" (p. 213). Among the other authorities cited by both Cattan and the Arab jurists' seminar is Ian Brownlie, who writes, "It is doubtful if the United Nations 'has a capacity to convey title,' *inter alia* because the Organization cannot assume the role of territorial sovereign." See Ian Brownlie, *Principles of Public International Law* (Oxford: Clarendon Press, 1966), pp. 161–162.

52. Issa Nakhleh, "The Liberation of Palestine Is Supported by International Law and Justice," pamphlet published by the Permanent Mission of the Arab Higher Committee for

Palestine in New York in 1969, reprinted in Moore, *The Arab-Israeli Conflict, I,* p. 574. See also M. Cherif Bassiouni and Eugene M. Fisher, "The Arab-Israeli Conflict—Real and Apparent Issues: An Insight into Its Future from the Lessons of the Past," *St. John's Law Review* 44 (1970): 399–465, reprinted in Moore, *The Arab-Israeli Conflict, I.* Also relevant is Henry Cattan, "The Implementation of United Nations Resolutions on Palestine," in Ibrahim Abu-Lughod (ed.), *Palestinian Rights: Affirmation and Denial* (Wilmette, Illinois: Medina Press, 1982). Cattan argues that the international community itself recognizes the continuing validity of the Partition Resolution, since it is on this basis that it rejected the military occupation of Jerusalem by Israel and Jordan in 1948 (pp. 36–37).

53. Nathan Feinberg, *The Arab-Israeli Conflict in International Law* (Jerusalem, 1970), partially reprinted in Moore, *The Arab-Israeli Conflict, I,* p. 244.

54. For example, Feinberg cites S. Bastid, "La jurisprudence de la Cour Internationale de Justice," *R.A.D.I.,* tome 78 (Paris, 1952), p. 665.

55. Feinberg, *The Arab-Israeli Conflict,* pp. 246–247. It is interesting to note that some Israeli legal scholars have sought to differentiate between the valid exercise of sovereignty by Israel over parts of Palestine proposed for an Arab state, and the invalid actions of Jordan in this regard. The basis for this argument is that Israel acted in self-defense in the 1947–48 War, whereas Jordan acquired the West Bank through aggression against Israel. See, for example, Yehuda Zvi Blum, *Secure Boundaries and Middle East Peace* (Jerusalem: Hebrew University of Jerusalem Faculty of Law, 1971), pp. 88–91.

56. Julius Stone, *Israel and Palestine: Assault on the Law of Nations* (Baltimore: The Johns Hopkins University Press, 1981), pp. 62–65. Stone's work provides a useful summary of Israel's position in a number of disputes concerned with international law.

57. For an Arab account of the massacre, see Sabri Jiryis, *The Arabs in Israel* (Beirut: Institute of Palestine Studies, 1969), p. 91. For a useful summary by an Israeli scholar, see Morris, *The Birth,* pp. 113–115. See also Flapan, *The Birth of Israel,* pp. 94–96. For a fuller report, by the Red Cross representative who discovered the massacred bodies on April 10, see the account of Jacques de Reynier in Walid Khalidi (ed.), *From Haven to Conquest* (Beirut: Institute for Palestine Studies, 1971). See also Jacques de Reynier, *À Jerusalem un drapeau flottait sur la ligne de feu* (Neuchâtel: La Baconniere, 1950).

58. Quoted in Noam Chomsky, *The Fateful Triangle: The United States, Israel and the Palestinians* (Boston: South End Press, 1983), p. 96.

59. Menachem Begin, *The Revolt: Story of the Irgun* (New York: Henry Schuman, 1951), p. 162. For another contemporary perspective, see Jon Kimche, *The Seven Fallen Pillars* (New York: Praeger, 1953), p. 228. Kimche, a British journalist with pro-Zionist inclinations, reports that Irgun leaders justified their action in Zionist circles by arguing that "it led to the panic flight of the remaining Arabs in the Jewish state and so lessened the Jewish casualties." Kimche himself calls the massacre at Deir Yassin "the darkest stain on the Jewish record."

60. For a full account of this version of events, see Begin. Some of these assertions are also set forth in a 1969 report prepared by the Israeli Ministry of Foreign Affairs, a summary of which is to be found in *Myths and Facts 1976: A Concise Record of the Arab-Israeli Conflict* (Washington: Near East Report, 1976), pp. 58–59.

61. Sykes, p. 351.

62. Morris, *The Birth,* pp. 113–114. Morris's conclusion is not shared by Flapan, a prominent Israeli journalist and peace activist who wrote that the slaughter at Deir Yassin was carried out "in a cold and premeditated fashion"; *The Birth of Israel,* p. 94.

63. Glubb, *A Soldier with the Arabs,* p. 99.

64. See Nazzal, p. 29. See also Furlonge, p. 155. As in the case of Deir Yassin, the incident was condemned by the Jewish Agency.

65. Glubb, *A Soldier with the Arabs,* p. 99.

66. Partial support for this charge is provided by Morris, who reports that the attack on Deir Yassin was "undertaken with the reluctant, qualified consent of the *Hagana* commander in Jerusalem," and that Irgun and Stern Group commanders "from the first had intended to expel the village's inhabitants." *The Birth*, pp. 113–114. See also Flapan, *The Birth of Israel*, p. 94.

67. Sykes, p. 352.

68. Hal Draper, "The Origins of the Middle East Crisis," in Laqueur and Rubin, p. 295.

69. Sykes, p. 352.

70. Nazzal, p. 36. The village of Ain al-Zeitoun, which was located adjacent to Safad and had a population of 820, was attacked in May 1948 by forces of the Palmach, the elite "strike force" of the official Hagana. According to Nazzal's account, "Palmach soldiers rolled barrels filled with explosives down the hill to the village and threw hand grenades, killing and injuring many of the villagers." The two other villages where atrocities are reported by Nazzal's informants are al-Bassa and Majd al-Kurum, which were attacked, respectively, in May and October 1948.

71. Ibid., p. 33.

72. Ibid., pp. 73–74.

73. Furlonge, p. 155.

74. Edgar O'Ballance, *The Arab-Israeli War, 1948* (New York: Praeger, 1957), p. 64. O'Ballance elsewhere writes, "Many Israeli sympathizers were appalled at the ruthless way in which the Arab inhabitants were ousted from their homes and driven before advancing armies. . . . The Israelis made no excuse for it, as it was part of their plan for the reconquest of their Promised Land, in which there was no room for large, hostile, alien groups" (p. 209). As acknowledged by one Jewish observer quoted by Arab sources, "We, Jews, forced the Arabs to leave [their] cities and villages. . . . Some of them were driven out by force of arms; others were made to leave by deceit, lying and false promises." See Nathan Chofshi in the *Jewish Newsletter* (New York), February 9, 1959.

75. Rony E. Gabbay, *A Political Study of the Arab-Jewish Conflict* (New York: Gregory Lounz, 1959).

76. Furlonge, p. 155.

77. Flapan, *Birth of Israel*, p. 42.

78. Ibid.

79. Morris, *The Birth*, p. 62. For an additional Israeli perspective on Plan D, see Herzog, *The Arab-Israeli Wars*, pp. 32–33. Herzog writes, "The operational aspects of Plan D called for the securing of all areas allocated to the Jewish state under the United Nations Partition Resolution—plus areas of Jewish settlement outside those planned borders, in order to be in a suitable position to meet the invading Arab armies by deploying defenders across the axes of advance."

80. Benny Morris, "The Origins of the Palestinian Refugee Problem," in Lawrence J. Silberstein (ed.), *New Perspectives on Israeli History: The Early Years of the States* (Albany: State University of New York Press, 1991), p. 46.

81. Morris, *The Birth*, p. 62.

82. Morris, "The Origins," p. 46.

83. Uri Avnery, *Israel without Zionists: A Plea for Peace in the Middle East* (New York: Macmillan, 1968), p. 196.

84. Arthur Koestler, *Promise and Fulfillment: Palestine, 1917–1949* (New York: Macmillan, 1949), p. 207. These warnings did not threaten abuse by Jewish forces but rather mistreatment that would occur upon the arrival of "new contingents of savage Iraqis." See also Erskine B. Childers, "The Wordless Wish: From Citizens to Refugees," in I. Abu-Lughod, *The*

Transformation, 1971. Childers discusses the Koestler account and numerous others in order to document his charge that the Zionists deliberately sought to expel the Arabs from Palestine. A shorter account is also available in Erskine B. Childers, "The Other Exodus," *The Spectator*, May 12, 1961; reprinted in Laqueur and Rubin.

85. Jon Kimche and David Kimche, *Both Sides of the Hill* (London: Secker and Warburg, 1960), p. 228.

86. Aryeh Yitzhaki, *Yediot Aharonot*, April 14, 1972; quoted and discussed in Flapan, *The Birth of Israel*, p. 94.

87. From *Hasepher Hapalmach* [The Book of the Palmach] (Tel Aviv: Hakibbutz Hameuchad, 1953); translated in Khalidi, *Middle East Forum* 37 (November 1961): 82, and quoted in Nazzal, p. 106.

88. Morris, *The Birth*, p. 288.

89. Ibid., p. 207. See also Benny Morris, "Operation Dani and the Palestinian Exodus from Lydda and Ramleh in 1948," *Middle East Journal* 40 (Winter 1986): 82–109. Morris points out that the expulsion of Arabs from Lydda and Ramleh was motivated, in part, by a desire to clog the roads with civilians and thereby block the advance of the Arab legion. He also reports that the cabinet and others were not informed of Ben Gurion's expulsion decision, which caused considerable controversy in Zionist political circles when it later became known.

90. Benny Morris, *1948 and After: Israel and the Palestinians* (Oxford: Oxford University Press, 1990), p. 75. The document is entitled "The Emigration of the Arabs of Palestine in the Period 12/1/1947–6/1/1948." See also Benny Morris, "The Causes and Character of the Arab Exodus from Palestine: The Israel Defense Forces Intelligence Service Analysis of June 1948," *Middle Eastern Studies* 22 (January 1986): 5–19. For a recent Israeli account raising questions about the validity of this document and its conclusions, as presented by Morris, see Shabtai Teveth, "The Palestine Arab Refugee Problem and Its Origins," *Middle Eastern Studies* 26 (April 1990): 216–219.

91. Morris, *1948 and After*, p. 141. See also Benny Morris, "Yosef Weitz and the Transfer Committees, 1948–1949," *Middle Eastern Studies* 22 (October 1986): 522–561. Morris's account is again challenged by Teveth, who argues that Weitz had little influence in senior Zionist circles, and that his views accordingly deserve only limited attention. He writes, "Weitz was given to self-aggrandizement, desperately filling thousands of pages, in manuscript and in print, in diaries and letters, with his ideas and opinions, only to meet frustration at every turn." See Shabtai Teveth, "Charging Israel with Original Sin," *Commentary* 88 (September 1989): 31–32. For additional discussion, see Teveth, "The Palestine Arab Refugee Problem," pp. 231–236.

92. Morris, *The Birth*, pp. 149–150.

93. Segev, *1949*, p. 26.

94. Ibid.

95. Portions of Eban's speech are reprinted in Laqueur and Rubin.

96. Quoted in Sykes, p. 355.

97. Morris, *The Birth*, p. 293.

98. Ibid., p. 288.

99. Ibid., p. 128.

100. Ibid., p. 292. Even as Ben Gurion approved expulsions for Lydda and Ramleh during this period, he agreed, and perhaps even instructed, that the Arab population of Nazareth should be left in place.

101. Ibid., p. 286. For a forceful rebuttal to Morris's conclusion, which contends that the Israeli scholar's own documentation demonstrates the existence of a systematic Zionist plan to expel the Palestinians, see Norman Finkelstein, "Myths, Old and New," *Journal of Palestine*

Studies 81 (Autumn 1991): 66–89. This issue of the *Journal of Palestine Studies* also contains another critique of Morris's study and a strong response by Morris. A further rejoinder by Finkelstein appears in volume 82 of the journal.

102. Eban, 1958 speech, quoted in Laqueur and Rubin, p. 152. This statement is also quoted in Gabbay, p. 88.

103. Herzog, *The Arab-Israeli Wars*, p. 43.

104. Avnery, *Israel without Zionists*, pp. 193–194.

105. Sykes, p. 352. Sykes adds that, unlike the Arabs, Zionists were disinclined to dwell on atrocities committed against them because they did not wish to lower Jewish morale. Thus, "the transmissions from *Kol Yisrael*, run by people with experience of the morale-building techniques evolved in the war, concentrated on tales of strength and success and largely avoided subjects of grief."

106. Morris, *The Birth*, pp. 288, 364.

107. Sykes, p. 352. See also Morris, *The Birth*, p. 288.

108. Furlonge, p. 156.

109. Nazzal, p. 44.

110. Benny Morris, "Response to Finkelstein and Masalha," *Journal of Palestine Studies* 81 (Autumn 1991): 101.

111. This document is among the appendixes in Gervasi.

112. See Herzog, *The Arab-Israeli Wars*, p. 35. Herzog notes that the commander of the British forces also tried, unsuccessfully, to persuade the Arabs to remain in Haifa.

113. Quoted in Gervasi, p. 109; and also in *Myths and Facts*, p. 55.

114. Quoted in *Myths and Facts*. Childers charges that apologists for Israel have distorted the content of this article, which in an unquoted portion describes how Jewish forces gave the Arabs of Haifa an hour to leave the city. See Childers, "The Other Exodus," pp. 145–147; and Childers, "The Wordless Wish," pp. 188–190.

115. Avnery, *Israel without Zionists*, p. 194. See also Morris, *The Birth*, pp. 36–41. Morris discusses efforts by local Jewish leaders during the early months of the war to maintain peaceful relations with Arab communities in the northern coastal plain and the adjacent foothills of the West Bank.

116. Nazzal, p. 83.

117. See Teveth, "Charging Israel," pp. 29–30; and Teveth, "The Palestine Arab Refugee Problem," pp. 225–227. Teveth claims that the Arab states advised evacuation as early as April. He states that they did nothing to precipitate the flight from Palestine during the preceding months, although he adds that they also "did nothing to bar the refugees from entry."

118. Quoted in Teveth, "Charging Israel," p. 29. Teveth's analysis is put forward in response to the work of Morris, and he accordingly uses some of Morris's documentation to support his case.

119. Kenneth Bilby, *New Star in the New East* (New York: Doubleday, 1950), pp. 30–31.

120. REMP *Bulletin*, The Hague, January-March 1957, p. 10; quoted in Gervasi, p. 109. This report is one of several routinely cited in pro-Israeli works which discuss the refugee problem.

121. Herzog, *The Arab-Israeli Wars*, p. 38.

122. Nazzal, p. 47.

123. Edward Atiyah, *The Arabs* (London: Penguin Books, 1955), p. 183.

124. From a 1952 memorandum submitted to the League of Arab States by the Higher Arab Committee; quoted in Joseph B. Schechtman, *The Refugees in the World* (New York: Barnes, 1963), p. 197.

125. Childers, "The Other Exodus," p. 146. See also Said, pp. 100ff.

126. Morris, *The Birth*, p. 290. Morris's account has been challenged by the president of the Organization of Jews from Arab Countries, who states in a letter to the *New York Times* that while in Baghdad in 1948 he heard repeated radio broadcasts urging the Arabs of Palestine to leave their homes. See Richard Bernstein, "Birth of the Land of Israel: A History Revisited," *New York Times*, July 28, 1988.

127. Flapan, *The Birth of Israel*, p. 85.

128. Flapan suggests that some accounts quoted by Israeli sources may have been fabricated. Ibid., p. 86.

129. Sykes, p. 354.

130. Childers, "The Other Exodus," p. 146.

131. Flapan, *The Birth of Israel*, pp. 84–87. Flapan's account draws heavily upon Aharon Cohen, *Israel and the Arab World* (Hebrew) (Tel Aviv, 1964).

132. Morris, *The Birth*, p. 290.

133. July 30, 1948; note of Moshe Shertok, known as Moshe Sharett after Israeli independence. Portions of the note are reproduced in Buehrig, pp. 12–13.

134. Quoted in Marie Syrkin, "I. F. Stone Reconsiders Zionism," *Midstream* (October 1967); reprinted in Laqueur and Rubin.

135. See Eban, 1958 speech, quoted in Laqueur and Rubin, p. 156. The study was published by the Carnegie Endowment for International Peace in November 1957, under the title "Century of the Homeless Man."

136. May 1958 Report of a Special Study Commission to the Near East and Africa, sent by the Foreign Affairs Committee of the U.S. House of Representatives.

137. Katz, pp. 33–34. See also Heskel M. Haddad, "The Jewish Refugees from the Arab Countries," *Middle East Information Series* 16 (November 1971): 29–32. Jews who left the Arab countries have set up a number of organizations, such as the Organization of Jews from Arab Countries and the Association of Jewish Victims of Egyptian Persecution. These organizations have asserted the Jews' right to compensation for the property they left behind.

138. V. D. Segre, *Israel: A Society in Transition* (London: Oxford University Press, 1971), pp. 124–125.

139. See, for example, André Chouraqui, *Between East and West: The Jews of North Africa* (Philadelphia: Jewish Publication Society of North America, 1968). See also Mark Tessler and Linda Hawkins, "The Political Culture of Jews in Tunisia and Morocco," *International Journal of Middle East Studies* 11 (January 1980): 59–86.

140. For a detailed account of the mass exodus of Iraq's Jewish community, with special attention to Israeli involvement, see Abbas Shiblak, *The Lure of Zion: The Case of the Iraqi Jews* (London: Al Saqi Books, 1986). For an account by the Israeli most directly involved, see Shlomo Hillel, "Operation Ezra and Nehemiah," in Azriel Eisenberg and Leah Ain-Globe (eds.), *Home at Last* (New York: Bloch Publishing Company, 1977).

141. Rabinovich, *The Road Not Taken*, p. 27. For a fuller account of U.S.-Israeli discussions relating to the refugee problem, see Morris, *The Birth*, pp. 256ff.

142. Quoted in Khouri, p. 130.

143. Ibid., p. 163. The quoted document is from June 30, 1964. See also Allen, pp. 418–419.

144. See Morris, *The Birth*, p. 255. Morris quotes Walter Eytan, director general of the Foreign Ministry, who states, "It would be doing the refugees a disservice to let them persist in the belief that if they returned, they would find their homes or shops or fields intact. In certain cases, it would be difficult for them even to identify the sites upon which their villages once stood."

145. This was the main feature of the plan proposed by Joseph E. Johnson. Johnson, head of the Carnegie Endowment for International Peace, was made a special representative by the UN Conciliation Commission in 1961 and spent the next eighteen months searching for a way to make progress on the Palestine refugee problem. He estimated at the time that the number of refugees who would opt for repatriation, if given a choice, would probably not exceed 10 percent. For a useful summary, see Buehrig, p. 18–20.

146. Quoted in Khouri, p. 127.

147. Bilby, p. 231. Other accounts state that by 1949 public opinion was firmly opposed to any repatriation of the refugees and thus served to constrain those in the government who were willing to consider a political compromise. See Segev, *1949*, p. 33.

148. See Weitz, vol. III, pp. 293 and 302; quoted in Said, p. 102.

149. Britain's position on the refugee question was generally similar to that of the United States and the United Nations in 1948. For a useful account, based on recently released British, Israeli, and American archival materials, see Pappé, pp. 124–161.

150. In return for the strategic advantage that would accrue to Israel with acquisition of the Gaza Strip, the Jewish state would be expected to make satisfactory arrangements for the refugees residing in Gaza. In the American and British versions of this plan, it was assumed that these Palestinians would be permitted to return to their communities of origin. For details, see Morris, *The Birth*, pp. 266–275.

151. Rabinovich, *The Road Not Taken*, p. 57.

152. Quoted in Segev, *1949*, pp. 33–34.

153. Ibid., pp. 29–30.

154. For additional discussion of Israeli reactions to the possible repatriation of 100,000 Palestinians, see Morris, *The Birth*, pp. 280–282.

155. A Conciliation Commission report of September 1950 recorded the impression that Arab governments "are inclining more and more to the view that the problem cannot be fully solved by the return of the refugees to their homes." Quoted in Khouri, p. 130.

156. Ibid., p. 139.

157. Ibid., p. 145.

158. The United Nations lists the following Christian Holy Places in the Jerusalem area: Basilica of the Holy Sepulchre, Bethany, Cenacle, Church of St. Anne, Church of St. James the Great, Church of St. Mark, Deir es-Sultan, Tomb of the Virgin, House of Caiphas and Prison of Christ, Sanctuary of the Ascension, Pool of Bethesda, Birthplace of John the Baptist, Basilica of the Nativity, Milk Grotto, Shepherds Field, the Nine Stations of the Cross. For a useful summary, dealing also with the religious significance of Jerusalem for Jews and Muslims, see Richard Pfaff, *Jerusalem: Keystone of an Arab-Israeli Settlement* (Washington: American Enterprise Institute, 1969), pp. 6ff. A concise history of Jewish, Christian, and Muslim involvement in Jerusalem is to be found in Norman Kotker, *The Earthly Jerusalem* (New York: Charles Scribner's, 1969). A vivid description of present-day Jewish, Christian, and Muslim life in the city is provided by Grace Halsell, *Journey to Jerusalem* (New York: Macmillan, 1981). For additional information about Christian attitudes toward Jerusalem, see Joseph P. Brennan, "Jerusalem—A Christian Perspective," and Gabriel Grossmann, "The Christian Churches in Present-Day Israel," both in Oesterreicher and Sinai.

159. The direction of Muslim prayer is known as the *qibla*. The *qibla* was changed from Jerusalem to Mecca in 624, and this change may have been related to an emerging conflict between Muhammad and the Jewish communities of the Arabian Peninsula. See Ruthven, p. 75. See also Montgomery Watt, *Muhammad at Medina* (Oxford: Clarendon Press, 1956), pp. 198–202.

160. Muhammad is said to have tied al-Buraq to rings hammered into the Western Wall.

The wall is therefore called al-Buraq by Muslims and is considered sacred. While in heaven, Muhammad is supposed to have met with numerous Jewish and Christian prophets, including Jesus, John the Baptist, Abraham, Moses, and David. While there he also asked God to reduce the number of times that Muslims were to pray each day. Muhammad had originally taken on the obligation of fifty daily prayers, but God eventually consented that the number should be reduced to five. Many early Muslims reportedly viewed this episode as a dream rather than an actual occurrence. Nevertheless, Muhammad was able to describe some of the attributes of Jerusalem and, in any event, the story of his adventure eventually came to be regarded as a true miracle by believing Muslims. For a useful summary see Hava Lazarus-Yafeh, "The Sanctity of Jerusalem in Islam," in Oesterreicher and Sinai.

161. According to the *Encyclopedia Britannica*, which quotes Turkish census figures, Jerusalem in 1844 had 7,120 Jews, 5,000 Muslims, and 3,390 Christians. In 1876 the figures were 12,000, 7,560, and 5,470 respectively.

162. For a useful historical summary of Jerusalem's Islamic character and its situation under various Muslim rulers, see Abdul Latif Tibawi, "Jerusalem: Its Place in Islam and Arab History," in Ibrahim Abu-Lughod (ed.), *The Arab-Israeli Confrontation of June 1967: An Arab Perspective* (Evanston: Northwestern University Press, 1970).

163. The siege began in December 1947, but Jewish truck convoys managed to reach Jerusalem with some regularity until February 1948. During March and April a few convoys also reached the city, although the effects of the siege became more serious for the Jews of Jerusalem during this period. From April 22 until June 11, the beginning of the first truce, no overland supplies reached Jerusalem. Contact with other Jewish areas of Palestine was maintained only by a small plane, which regularly brought powdered milk, drugs, and ammunition from Tel Aviv. The water supply of West Jerusalem was also cut early in May, forcing the Jews to distribute rations of water that had been stored in cisterns. For a vivid account of the siege, written from a Zionist perspective, see Marie Syrkin, "The Siege of Jerusalem," in Oesterreicher and Sinai. For a fuller account of the Battle of Jerusalem, see Herzog, *The Arab-Israeli Wars*, pp. 38–45 and 59–68.

164. Speech of December 5, 1949; quoted in Gabriel Padon, "The Divided City: 1948–1967," in Oesterreicher and Sinai, p. 92.

165. Quoted in Khouri, p. 107.

166. Padon, p. 97.

167. Progress Report of the United Nations Conciliation Commission for Palestine, December 11, 1949–October 23, 1950; partially reprinted in Moore, *The Arab-Israeli Conflict*, III, see p. 515.

168. The Third Progress Report of the United Nations Conciliation Commission for Palestine, June 21, 1949; partially reprinted in ibid.; see p. 492.

169. Cattan, "The Implementation," pp. 36–37.

170. "Strife in the Holy Land" (New York: Arab Information Center, n.d.), pp. 12–13.

171. *Myths and Facts*, p. 98.

172. Yehuda Zvi Blum, *The Juridical Status of Jerusalem* (Jerusalem: Hebrew University of Jerusalem Papers on Peace Problems, 1974), p. 20. Blum also quotes pertinent UN documents from 1948 which acknowledge that establishment of an international regime for Jerusalem was being "obstructed by the Arab resistance" (p. 9). For another detailed and heavily documented presentation of the Israeli case, see Elihu Lauterpacht, *Jerusalem and the Holy Places* (London: Anglo-Israel Association, 1968); partially reprinted in Moore, *The Arab-Israeli Conflict*, I.

173. Shwadran, p. 298.

174. *Keesing's Contemporary Archives*, vol. 8 (1950–1952), p. 10812.

175. Malcolm Kerr, "The Changing Political Status of Jerusalem," in I. Abu-Lughod, *The Transformation*, p. 359.

176. From *Filastin*, May 19, 1953; quoted in Padon, p. 98.

177. Blum, *The Juridical Status*, p. 15.

178. Israeli officials acknowledged in 1967 that they had been smuggling military equipment to Mount Scopus. Some vehicles and guns had been smuggled in piece by piece and then reassembled in the Israeli enclave. See Khouri, pp. 221–222. See also Randolph S. Churchill and Winston S. Churchill, *The Six Day War* (Boston: Houghton Mifflin, 1967), p. 124.

179. Although most religious sites were in East Jerusalem, and hence under Jordanian control, there were also some complaints about Israel's record. In particular, Arabs claimed that the development and expansion of West Jerusalem had resulted in the desecration of a number of Arab cemeteries.

180. John M. Oesterreicher, "An Open Letter to His Excellency, the Ambassador of the Hashemite Kingdom of Jordan," January 1972; reprinted in Oesterreicher and Sinai, p. 252.

181. Ze'ev Vilnay, "Jerusalem in the Modern Era, 1860–1967," in Oesterreicher and Sinai, p. 27.

182. These charges are contained in an interministerial commission report prepared in October 1967, after Israel had taken control of East Jerusalem; discussed in Padon, p. 101.

183. Oesterreicher, "An Open Letter," in Oesterreicher and Sinai, p. 251.

184. Lauterpacht, p. 960. See also Kerr, "The Changing Political Status."

185. Michael C. Hudson, "The Arab State's Policies toward Israel," in I. Abu-Lughod, *The Transformation*, p. 313. Hudson notes that boycott decisions were often influenced by pragmatic considerations. For example, Arab states did not deny themselves the services of major international banks and airlines that also did business with Israel.

186. These development programs and alliances were of psychological as well as political significance to Israel at the time. They reduced the country's sense of isolation. They also gave many Israelis a sense of identification with the liberation struggles taking place in Africa and elsewhere. Some argued that economic and political development in the Jewish state could serve as a model for other emerging countries. See, for example, Michael Curtis and Susan Aurelia Gitelson (eds.), *Israel and the Third World* (New Brunswick, New Jersey: Transaction Books, 1976). Particularly relevant to the present discussion are chapters by E. Kanovsky ("Can Israel Serve as a Model for Developing Countries?") and Ehud Avriel ("Israel's Beginnings in Africa"). See also Leopold Laufer, *Israel and the Developing Countries: New Approaches to Cooperation* (New York: The Twentieth Century Fund, 1967); and Moshe Decter, *To Serve, to Teach, to Leave: The Story of Israeli Development Assistance Programs in Black Africa* (New York: American Jewish Congress, 1977).

187. For additional discussion of Israel's efforts to "leap over the Arab wall," see Gideon Rafael, *Destination Peace: Three Decades of Israeli Foreign Policy* (London: Weidenfeld and Nicolson, 1981), pp. 78ff. Rafael states that "when Israel's policy-makers realized that attempts at breaking the wall of Arab hostility were doomed to failure, they turned their sights elsewhere. Beyond the wall were important countries in the Middle East [Iran and Turkey] and Africa which were accessible to Israel." For a fuller account of Israeli foreign policy during the early years of statehood, see Uri Bialer, *Between East and West: Israel's Foreign Policy Orientation 1948–1956* (Cambridge: Cambridge University Press, 1990). Bialer discusses Israel's nonalignment during the first part of this period, based partially on its desire to maintain cordial relations with both the United States and the Soviet Union.

188. Hudson, "The Arab State's Policies," p. 314. See also Robert W. Macdonald, *The League of Arab States: A Study in the Dynamics of Regional Organization* (Princeton: Princeton University Press, 1965), pp. 119–120.

189. Nadav Safran, *From War to War: The Arab-Israeli Confrontation, 1948–1967* (New York: Pegasus, 1969), p. 43. See also Gervasi, pp. 134.

190. Quoted in Ernest Stock, *Israel on the Road to Sinai, 1949–1956* (Ithaca: Cornell University Press, 1967), p. 100.

191. Ibid., pp. 100–101.

192. Additional arguments pertaining to the 1888 Suez Canal Convention are set forth in Majid Khadduri, "Closure of the Suez Canal to Israeli Shipping," *Law and Contemporary Problems* 33 (1968): 147–157; reprinted in Moore, *The Arab-Israeli Conflict, I*.

193. See, for example, Shabtai Rosenne, *Israel's Armistice Agreements with the Arab States: A Juridical Interpretation* (Tel Aviv: International Law Association, Israeli Branch, 1951), p. 83. See also Nathan Feinberg, *The Legality of a 'State of War' after the Cessation of Hostilities under the Charter of the United Nations and the Covenant of the League of Nations* (Jerusalem: Magnes Press, 1961), pp. 41–42; and Simha Dinitz, "The Legal Aspects of the Egyptian Blockade of the Suez Canal," *Georgetown Law Journal* 45 (Winter 1956–57): 186.

194. The legal basis for this argument is set forth in Leo Gross, "Passage through the Suez Canal of Israel-Bound Cargo and Israeli Ships," *American Journal of International Law* 51 (1957): 530–568; reprinted in Moore, *The Arab-Israeli Conflict, I*. Gross states that measures concerning "the defense of Egypt and the maintenance of public order" authorized under Article 10 of the 1888 convention are restricted by the requirement of Article 11 that such measures "shall not interfere with the free use of the Canal."

195. Khouri, p. 207.

196. These and other arguments supportive of the Egyptian case are set forth in Burhan W. Hammad, "The Right of Passage in the Gulf of Aqaba," *Revue Égyptienne de Droit International* 15 (1959): 118–151; reprinted in Moore, *The Arab-Israeli Conflict, I*. See also M. Cherif Bassiouni, "Some Legal Aspects of the Arab-Israeli Conflict," in I. Abu-Lughod, *The Arab-Israeli Confrontation*, pp. 114–118.

197. Charles B. Selak, Jr., "A Consideration of the Legal Status of the Gulf of Aqaba," *American Journal of International Law* 52 (1958): 660–698; reprinted in Moore, *The Arab-Israeli Conflict, I*, p. 733.

198. Leo Gross, "The Geneva Conference on the Law of the Sea and the Right of Innocent Passage through the Gulf of Aqaba," *American Journal of International Law* 53 (1959): 564–594, reprinted in Moore, *The Arab-Israeli Conflict, I*.

199. Khouri, p. 209.

6. Israel and the Arab States through June 1967

1. For a detailed account of the Free Officers coup and Nasser's rise to power, see Joel Gordon, *Nasser's Blessed Movement: Egypt's Free Officers and the July Revolution* (New York: Oxford University Press, 1992).

2. Quoted in Raymond Baker, *Egypt's Uncertain Revolution under Nasser and Sadat* (Cambridge: Harvard University Press, 1978), p. 36. See also Walid Khalidi, trans., "Nasser's Memoirs of the First Palestine War," *Journal of Palestine Studies* 2 (1973): 19–26.

3. Quoted in Robert St. John, *The Boss: The Story of Gamal Abdel Nasser* (New York: McGraw-Hill, 1960), p. 36.

4. Mahmoud Riad, *The Struggle for Peace in the Middle East* (London: Quartet Books, 1981), p. 7. See also Miles Copeland, *The Game of Nations: The Amorality of Power Politics* (New York: Simon and Schuster, 1969), p. 68. Copeland cites U.S. intelligence sources that quote Nasser as stating that although he and his officers had been "humiliated" by the Israelis,

their resentments were "against our own superior officers, other Arabs, the British and the Israelis—in that order." For additional discussion, see Jean Lacouture and Simonne Lacouture, *Egypt in Transition* (London: Methuen, 1958), p. 233. Nasser was not the only member of the Free Officers group to take this position. General Muhammad Naguib, the most senior member of the group, privately told United States officials at the time of the coup that he was not interested in Palestine. For details see Copeland. See also Stock, p. 118. Stock notes that Naguib's attitude toward Israel changed a few months later, and, more generally, he asserts that "it is difficult to judge whether there was ever a sincere desire on Egypt's part to come to terms." Opposition to Nasser's moderation, in the military and in the country at large, is also discussed in Baker, pp. 36–37. Finally, some observers report that when the Wafd Party came to power early in 1950, it was also interested in making peace with Israel. See, for example, Gabbay, pp. 316–322. Gabbay states that the Wafd government did not feel bound by the policies of the previous regime but that the Israelis, at the time conducting secret negotiations with Jordan, were largely indifferent to the possibility of a dialogue with Cairo.

5. For an instructive summary of Israeli judgments about Egyptian intentions after the Free Officers coup but before Nasser's consolidation of power, see Rabinovich, *The Road Not Taken*, pp. 199–200. Rabinovich reports that senior Israeli officials took note of Egypt's growing interest in peace. Abba Eban, for example, delivered a memorandum to the U.S. secretary of state that read, in part, "There is evidence to show that Egyptian public opinion is increasingly aware of the need to reach a settlement with Israel. Israel's government has reached this conclusion on the basis of talks and contacts as well as a study of the Egyptian press." Similarly, Ben Gurion told American journalists that "wide circles in Egypt want peace with Israel, but they are afraid of their political rivals." On the other hand, Rabinovich also notes that these analyses "ran counter to the evaluation of at least some of the Israeli Foreign Ministry's experts."

6. Yair Evron, *The Middle East: Nations, Superpowers and Wars* (New York: Praeger, 1973), p. 34.

7. Richard Crossman, *Palestine Mission: A Personal Record* (New York: Harper and Bros., 1947); quoted in Baker, p. 37.

8. Evron, p. 33.

9. Press reports appearing in *Ma'ariv* and *Yediot Aharonot* on August 4, 1961, are summarized in Khouri, pp. 300–301, and in Stock, p. 122. A *Ma'ariv* report of May 25, 1961, is also mentioned by Evron.

10. See Michael Brecher, "Ben Gurion and Sharett: Contrasting Israeli Images of 'the Arabs,' " *New Middle East* 18 (March 1970). See also Stock, pp. 124–126. For a more comprehensive discussion, largely sympathetic to Sharett, see Gabriel Sheffer, "Resolution vs. Management of the Middle East Conflict: A Reexamination of the Confrontation between Moshe Sharett and David Ben-Gurion," Jerusalem Papers on Peace Problems, no. 32 (Jerusalem: Magnes Press, 1980). For an instructive account of the broader ideological differences relating to foreign policy among senior Israeli politicians, see Bialer, especially Part I.

11. An instructive account is provided by Ben Gurion's biographer, who presents an unflattering picture of Lavon and asserts that "the atmosphere at the top was being poisoned by the character of Pinhas Lavon." See Michael Bar-Zohar, *Ben Gurion: A Biography* (New York: Weidenfeld and Nicolson, 1978), p. 208.

12. For an informative account of the conflict between Lavon and Dayan, and of the larger issues of civilian-military relations raised by the Lavon Affair, see Yoram Peri, *Between Battles and Ballots: Israeli Military in Politics* (Cambridge: Cambridge University Press, 1983), pp. 233–236.

13. It is generally agreed that the architect of the sabotage plan was Benjamin Jibli, chief

of military intelligence. Jibli testified that Lavon had given the original order for the operation, and some, including Ben Gurion, never abandoned their conviction that this was in fact the case. There is a considerable body of Hebrew-language literature on the Lavon Affair, about which there continues to be disagreement. Helpful sources in English, written from differing perspectives, include Peri, pp. 232–240; Stock, pp. 117–126; Bar-Zohar, pp. 208–216; Ben Gurion, *Ben Gurion Looks Back*, pp. 206–215; M. Golan, *Shimon Peres*, pp. 32–34 and 110–115; and S. N. Eisenstadt, *Israeli Society* (New York: Basic Books, 1967), pp. 329–332.

14. Quoted in Bar-Zohar, p. 216.

15. Ibid., p. 222.

16. For a summary of the Anglo-Egyptian negotiations, see J. Gordon, pp. 168–172. Gordon also provides a useful summary of Egyptian-U.S. relations during the period of these negotiations.

17. Relevant Knesset proceedings and other Israeli documents are quoted in Stock, p. 118.

18. Evron, p. 41.

19. Ibid., pp. 28–30. See also Khouri, p. 200.

20. For additional discussion, see Lt. Gen. E. L. M. Burns, *Between Arab and Israeli* (London: Harrap and Co., 1962), pp. 33ff.; and Kenneth Love, *Suez: The Twice-Fought War* (New York: McGraw-Hill, 1969), pp. 86–87. Nasser himself claimed that whatever Egyptian assistance Palestinian infiltrators received was provided by his political enemies, most notably the Muslim Brothers. See Baker, p. 37. For an additional discussion, see Safran, *From War to War*, p. 45. Safran states, "Egyptian authorities tended at first merely to wink at infiltration."

21. Quoted in Stock, p. 123.

22. Ibid., p. 114. Stock reports that during the first two months of 1955 there were twenty-seven forays from Gaza, resulting in the deaths of seven Israelis and the wounding of twenty-four others. See also Earl Berger, *The Covenant and the Sword: Arab-Israeli Relations, 1948–1956* (London: Kegan Paul, 1965), p. 204. Supporters of Israel also emphasize the cumulative impact of Palestinian guerrilla raids. Stock, for example, states that by the end of 1953 "a mood of anger and frustration over the almost nightly violence had taken hold in Israel, fanned by detailed press reports on each incident" (p. 68). The basis for Israeli anger was also recorded by Moshe Dayan in a January 1955 *Foreign Affairs* article. According to Dayan, from 1949 to the middle of 1954 there had been an average of 1,000 cases of infiltration per month along Israel's various frontiers. Dayan's figure greatly exceeds the estimates provided by most pro-Israeli sources and, if accurate, undoubtedly includes numerous nonviolent border crossings by individual Palestinian peasants seeking to return to their villages inside Israel or to recover property left behind.

23. See, for example, Lacouture and Lacouture, p. 275. See also Anthony Nutting, *Nasser* (London: Constable, 1972), pp. 93–96; and Robert Stephens, *Nasser: A Political Biography* (London: Penguin Press, 1971), pp. 155–156.

24. Quoted in Chomsky, p. 467. Chomsky also cites an article by Israeli journalist Nahum Barnea, published in *Davar* on January 26, 1979, to the effect that Lavon gave orders which were "much more severe" than those leading to the sabotage operations in Egypt. Ibid., p. 20. This point, based in part on a discussion of Sharett's diary, is also made by Evron, p. 35. See also Hudson, "The Arab States' Policies," pp. 322–326.

25. Burns, p. 76.

26. Robert R. Bowie, *Suez 1956: International Crises and the Role of Law* (New York: Oxford University Press, 1974), p. 10.

27. In March 1954, Israel carried out a large-scale raid on the Jordanian town of Nahalin, resulting in the deaths of fourteen members of the Jordanian National Guard. The strike was

largely in retaliation for a murderous attack on an Israeli bus at Scorpion's Pass, on the road between Beersheba and Eilat. Nine Israeli civilians were killed. Israeli sources contend that the raid on Nahalin was not excessive, since the number of casualties on each side was roughly equivalent. They also note that the attack was of a military nature, being directed at a post of the National Guard. Arab sources insist that the Israeli raid was unjustified, since the Jordanian government had worked to reduce infiltration and had cooperated fully in an investigation of the Scorpion's Pass massacre, and also since the perpetrators of the act were never identified.

28. Burns, p. 47.

29. Interview with Nasser conducted by Erskine Childers; quoted in Peter Calvocoressi, *Suez: Ten Years After* (New York: Pantheon Books, 1967), p. 37.

30. Article in *Ha'aretz* on April, 17, 1964; quoted in Evron, p. 45. See also Terence Robertson, *Crisis: The Inside Story of the Suez Conspiracy* (New York: Athenaeum, 1965); and Calvocoressi, pp. 61–62.

31. An informative account of Glubb's ouster is provided by Uriel Dann, *King Hussein and the Challenge of Arab Radicalism: Jordan, 1955–1967* (Oxford: Oxford University Press, 1989), pp. 31–34. Dann writes, "Nasser did not persuade Hussein to dismiss Glubb. . . . But the dismissal delighted him and seemed to him as yet another proof of his ascending star."

32. Press release of July 19, 1956; quoted in Bowie, p. 14.

33. Some observers suggest that Nasser had for some time intended to nationalize the Suez Canal, and that the withdrawal of American support for the Aswan Dam was simply a pretext which the Egyptian president used to justify his action. Other observers disagree. Nasser himself maintained that Egypt had no prior plans to nationalize the canal, and that the decision to do so was not made until July 23, 1956. The Suez Canal Company's concession was due to expire in 1968, and in 1954 Egypt began planning for the takeover. Thus, a number of Egyptian personnel were already familiar with the administration of the company and the operation of the canal. For details see Robertson, p. 6.

34. Interview with Nasser conducted by Erskine Childers; quoted in Calvocoressi, p. 42.

35. Reprinted in Anthony Eden, *The Suez Crisis of 1956* (Boston: Beacon Press, 1968), pp. 55–56.

36. The United States was strongly opposed to military action against Egypt. Eisenhower responded to Eden's telegram by telling the British prime minister on July 31, "I have given you my own personal convictions, as well as that of my associates, as to the unwisdom of even contemplating the use of military force at this moment." The American president added that the use of force by others, unless it was absolutely clear that every peaceful means of resolving the conflict had been exhausted, could well lead to serious opposition from the people and government of the United States. See Calvocoressi, pp. 6–7. See also Anthony Nutting, *No End of a Lesson: The Inside Story of the Suez Crisis* (New York: Potter, 1967), pp. 110–113. Nutting reports that Eisenhower's attitude required Britain, France, and Israel to take "the most elaborate precautions to preserve absolute secrecy, even to the point of misleading our friends and 'enemies' alike."

37. For a broad overview of the Sinai-Suez War, with contributions by a number of Israeli scholars and politicians, see Selwyn Ilan Troen and Moshe Shemesh (eds.), *The Suez-Sinai Crisis, 1956: Retrospective and Reappraisal* (London: Frank Cass, 1990).

38. Quoted in Bowie, p. 89.

39. Ibid., p. 104.

40. Stock, p. 211.

41. Statement of February 2, 1957; quoted in Bowie, p. 91.

42. The document is reprinted in Dodd and Sales, pp. 124–126.

43. Ibid., pp. 127–128.

44. During the first part of 1957, Britain, France, and the United States sought Egyptian agreement for a political compromise that would restore a measure of international control to the Suez Canal. Then, when Cairo reopened the canal under an Egyptian authority, the three powers attempted to organize a shipowners' boycott. All of these efforts were unsuccessful. For details see Nutting, *No End*, pp. 167ff.

45. Bar-Zohar, p. 258.

46. Moshe Dayan, *Diary of the Sinai Campaign* (London: Weidenfeld and Nicolson, 1966), p. 204.

47. Interview with Nasser conducted by Erskine Childers; quoted in Calvocoressi, p. 58.

48. Riad, p. 10. See also Stock, p. 213. Ben Gurion subsequently acknowledged, in a moment of candor a decade later, that he had erred in his remarks following the Jewish state's successful military campaign: "I made a few mistakes in that speech, saying the Armistice Agreement was dead and buried, that Egypt would not be allowed to return to Sinai. I went too far . . . [but] the victory was too quick. I was too drunk with victory." See Bar-Zohar, p. 253.

49. Riad. Riad reports that Ben Gurion later stated that "Israel's aim in the Sinai operation was the liberation of that part of the homeland which was occupied by the invader. . . . In the 1948 War we did not attain all that we desired." In another account, Ben Gurion puts the matter somewhat differently: "I told [the Government] that we must destroy the bases of the *fedayeen* in Sinai. And this was our aim in invading Sinai, although we did not regard Sinai as part of Egypt. Not a single Egyptian lives in Sinai—only a number of Bedouin here and there. But—I told the Government—'You will not be able to stay there because Russia and America will not let us. . . . So you should not have any illusions that we are going to conquer the Sinai desert.' " See Calvocoressi, p. 71.

50. The story of the United Arab Republic is told in fascinating detail in Malcolm H. Kerr, *The Arab Cold War: Gamal 'Abd al-Nasir and His Rivals, 1958–1970* (London: Oxford University Press, 1971). Kerr's important study may be profitably read in conjunction with Dann, which examines the impact on Jordan of inter-Arab diplomacy and Nasser's growing influence in the years after the Sinai-Suez War.

51. Ibid., p. 32.

52. See Evron, p. 54. For a fuller discussion, see Bar-Zohar, pp. 304–305.

53. For additional details, see Safran, *From War to War*, p. 231.

54. Quoted in Khouri, p. 227.

55. Ibid., p. 224. UNTSO officials condemned the Syrians for installing and using heavy military equipment in this sector. At the same time, they also accused Israel of provocative behavior, arguing that the Jewish state frequently sent patrol boats close to the Syrian shore when there was no valid security reason for doing so. The UN Security Council strongly condemned Israel's retaliatory strike.

56. Some analysts point out that there is an important inconsistency in this Arab argument, since development of the Negev and other areas inside the Jewish state would make Israel less likely, rather than more likely, to covet the territory of its neighbors. Nevertheless, many Arabs saw Israel as an expansion-oriented power and so opposed any program that would add to its power or population. For additional discussion, see Evron, p. 53.

57. There is disagreement about whether the Arab scheme had value, apart from its goal of denying water to Israel. Some pro-Israeli sources claim that most of the water diverted under the Arab League plan would be wasted. See, for example, Prittie, pp. 61–62. Others state that the projected Banyas-Yarmouk canal would have permitted a substantial increase in irrigation

and agricultural development in the Jordan River Valley, opening up new lands for cultivation on both sides of the river. It also would have produced hydroelectric power for both Jordan and Syria. See, for example, Khouri, p. 228.

58. J. C. Hurewitz, *Middle East Politics: The Military Dimension* (New York: Praeger, 1969), p. 147.

59. Kerr, *The Arab Cold War*, p. 104. In addition to Kerr's important study, a valuable scholarly account of this period is provided by Itamar Rabinovich, *Syria under the Ba'th, 1963–1966: The Army-Party Symbiosis* (Jerusalem: Israel Universities Press, 1972). Another useful source is John Devlin, *The Ba'th Party: A History from Its Origins to 1966* (Stanford: Hoover Institution Press, 1976). Important studies dealing with the period prior to 1958 include Patrick Seale, *The Struggle for Syria: A Study in Post-war Arab Politics, 1945–1958* (London: Oxford University Press, 1965); and Gordon Torrey, *Syrian Politics and the Military (1945–1958)* (Columbus: Ohio State University Press, 1964).

60. Hurewitz, *Middle East Politics*, pp. 153–155. A convenient introduction to the two religious minorities is to be found in Michael C. Hudson, *Arab Politics: The Search for Legitimacy* (New Haven: Yale University Press, 1977), pp. 63–65.

61. Hurewitz, *Middle East Politics*, p. 153.

62. Gordon Torrey, "Aspects of the Political Elite in Syria," in George Lenczowski (ed.), *Political Elites in the Middle East* (Washington: American Enterprise Institute, 1975), p. 156.

63. See, for example, Evron, p. 65. For a fuller discussion, see Michael Van Dusen, "Political Integration and Regionalism in Syria," *Middle East Journal* 26 (Spring 1972): 123–136. See also John F. Devlin, *Syria: Modern State in an Ancient Land* (Boulder, Colorado: Westview Press, 1983), pp. 68–70.

64. Hudson, *Arab Politics*, p. 260. Hudson notes that Bathists also used the Syrian army's defeat in 1948, as well as their claims of a continuing Israeli threat, to justify calls for a complete restructuring of the Syrian political system.

65. Evron, p. 66.

66. Torrey, "Aspects," p.156. Evron also stresses the antipathy of the Syrian people toward the new regime in Damascus. As an indication of popular perceptions of the Bathists, he reports that a rumor circulated in Damascus at this time to the effect that the government had sold the Golan Heights to Israel for a large amount of money (p. 232).

67. Evron, p. 69.

68. For a thorough discussion of the Israeli economy during this period, see Eisenstadt, *Israeli Society*, pp. 71–142. Eisenstadt notes that government policies aimed at the absorption of new immigrants aggravated the situation. Immigrants were often employed in public works projects, such as road construction and the planting of forests, and were thus removed from the regular labor market (p. 128).

69. Quoted in Prittie, p. 46.

70. Eisenstadt, *Israeli Society*, p. 142.

71. Kimche, *Palestine or Israel*, p. 243.

72. Leonard Fein, *Politics in Israel* (Boston: Little, Brown, 1967), p. 162.

73. See, for example, Asher Arian, *Politics in Israel: The Second Generation* (Chatham, New Jersey: Chatham House Publishers, 1985), pp. 50–51.

74. A vivid comparison of these two generations is provided in Amos Elon, *The Israelis: Founders and Sons* (New York: Holt, Rinehart and Winston, 1971). Elon, a well-known Israeli writer, introduces his general account with a comparison of Eshkol and Dayan. He writes that Eshkol was "a man of the old, passing order of wider Jewish loyalties.... a sociable, rather garrulous, and marvelously witty, experienced party functionary ... [who had] spent most of his life as a trade union man." Dayan, by contrast, represented "a new locally bred, locally

oriented generation of hardened, morally disillusioned younger men, self-reliant, asking no man for sympathy and with little of their own to give. . . . tough and competent" (pp. 19–22).

75. See Arian, *Politics*, pp 8off. Noting that Revisionists had long been labeled "irresponsible opportunists, unworthy of support and likely to pose a danger to the Zionist cause," Arian outlines the historical events which produced bad blood between Herut and Labor Zionism. He also reports that in early Knesset debates, Ben Gurion refused to call Begin by name and referred to him as "the man sitting next to Mr. Bader." Another account of the personal animosity between Ben Gurion and Begin is provided in Fein, p. 90.

76. An indication of Eshkol's initial moderation is the prime minister's restraint in the face of Syrian attacks on Israeli farmers in August 1963. Instead of ordering a retaliatory strike, the Eshkol government submitted the matter to the UN Security Council. See Khouri, p. 223. Khouri argues that the change in Eshkol's attitude reflected both domestic political considerations and a growth in Arab military power and in the number of border incidents (p. 307).

77. Safran, *From War to War*, pp. 304–305. Safran reports that partly in response to criticism from Ben Gurion and others, Eshkol "tended to lean over backward and respond favorably to requests made by the professional heads of the defense establishment concerning budgetary allocations, permission to undertake retaliatory actions, and so on."

78. For a detailed account, see Helena Cobban, *The Palestine Liberation Organization: People, Power and Politics* (London: Cambridge University Press, 1984), pp. 23ff. For an excellent summary of the prior organizational activities of the young Palestinians who subsequently established Fatah, see Laurie A. Brand, *Palestinians in the Arab World: Institution Building and the Search for State* (New York: Columbia University Press, 1988), pp. 65–70. Most were active in the Palestinian Student Union in Egypt, which Brand calls "the training ground" for the leaders of Fatah and other Palestinian groups. Although Fatah's orientation was nationalist, other groups organized by Palestinians during this period had a pan-Arabist orientation. Some also had Marxist tendencies. Other useful introductions to Fatah and the PLO include Cheryl Rubenberg, *The Palestine Liberation Organization: Its Institutional Structure* (Belmont, Massachusetts: Institute of Arab Studies, 1983); Paul A. Jureidini and William Hazan, *The Palestinian Movement in Politics* (Lexington, Massachusetts: D. C. Heath, 1979); Richard J. Ward, Don Peretz, and Evan M. Wilson, *The Palestine State: A Rational Approach* (Port Washington, New York: Kennikat Press, 1977); and Quandt, Jabber, and Lesch.

79. Cobban, pp. 28–29.

80. The Executive Committee was reduced to eleven members when the constitution was revised in 1968. A later amendment increased the size of the committee to fourteen.

81. The fund was to seek financial assistance both from Palestinians and from Arab states. The PLO was also to receive a regular subvention from the Arab League, although officials complained that they received only a small percentage of the promised funding. See Quandt, Jabber, and Lesch, p. 68.

82. Ibid., p. 162.

83. Ibid.

84. For a fuller account, see Cobban, pp. 31–32. The decision to initiate commando raids against Israel was taken late in 1964 by a slender one-vote majority.

85. According to Israeli sources, Fatah raids launched directly across the Syrian-Israeli border did not begin until January 1966, and in the months that followed over three-fourths of the commando attacks still originated in Jordan. These sources also claim that a number of raids were launched from Lebanon. For details, see Khouri, pp. 230–231. Khouri also provides a useful summary of the most important Arab and Israeli military operations undertaken during this period.

86. Stock, p. 221. See also Evron, p. 67.

87. Quoted in Khouri, p. 232.

88. See Evron, p. 70–71. The static defense concept was championed by the left-wing Mapam Party. Evron notes that while this approach to security was not very popular in 1966 and 1967, it would be adopted and used with great success in 1968.

89. Anthony Carthew, "After the Raid on Es-Samu," *New York Times Magazine*, December 18, 1966, pp. 30, 81; quoted in Khouri, p. 237.

90. Interview with Jon Kimche; quoted in Kimche, *Palestine or Israel*, p. 250.

91. Ibid., pp. 245–246. Kimche does not identify the author of these remarks but states that this individual was later to hold one of the half-dozen most important posts in the country. The author states that he rechecked his views with "the most independent and unimpeachable sources . . . [and] deliberately avoided the declared opponents of Eshkol and Mapai."

92. *New York Times*, April 8, 1967; quoted in Khouri, p. 243.

93. Hisham Sharabi, "Prelude to War: The Crisis of May–June 1967," in I. Abu-Lughod, *The Arab-Israeli Confrontation*, p. 49.

94. Ibid. For a detailed discussion of the public statements made by various Israeli leaders during this period, see Walter Laqueur, *The Road to War: The Origins and Aftermath of the Arab-Israeli Conflict, 1967–8* (Baltimore: Penguin Books, 1968), pp. 87–90. See also Richard B. Parker, *The Politics of Miscalculation in the Middle East* (Bloomington: Indiana University Press, 1993), pp. 16–17.

95. For a detailed account of the delivery of the Soviet warning that Israeli troops were massing on the Syrian frontier, see Parker, especially chapter 1. Parker reports that the Soviet warning was delivered at least twice, in Cairo and in Moscow.

96. The entire speech, which Nasser delivered to the Advanced Air Headquarters, is reprinted in Laqueur and Rubin, pp. 169–174.

97. Riad, p. 17.

98. Muhammad Hasanayn Haykal, "An Armed Clash with Israel Is Inevitable—Why?" *Al-Ahram*, May 26, 1967; reprinted in Laqueur and Rubin, p. 181.

99. Ibrahim Abu-Lughod, "Israel's Arab Policy," in I. Abu-Lughod, *The Arab-Israeli Confrontation*, p. 90.

100. Sharabi, "Prelude to War," pp. 49–51. The Arabs were encouraged in this view by the Soviet Union. The Soviet premier told the UN after the war that in May his government had received intelligence reports to the effect that following the planned attack on Syria, Israel intended to "carry the fighting over into the territory of the United Arab Republic" (Egypt).

101. Riad, p. 17.

102. Eban's speech is reprinted in Laqueur and Rubin.

103. Parker, p. 8.

104. Ibid. Parker cites a number of Egyptian and Jordanian sources. See also Peter Mansfield, *Nasser's Egypt* (Baltimore: Penguin Books, 1969), p. 80.

105. Churchill and Churchill, p. 28.

106. Winston Burdett, *Encounter with the Middle East: An Intimate Report of What Lies behind the Arab-Israeli Conflict* (New York: Athenaeum, 1969), pp. 162–209.

107. For example, see Safran, *From War to War*, pp. 276–277. For additional discussion, see Parker, pp. 11–13. Parker reports that "for years conventional Washington wisdom has been that since the Soviets could not possibly have believed the report, they must have fabricated it for one or more of a variety of reasons." He also notes that some Arab writers have advanced the theory that the Soviets were "hoping to draw Nasser into a trap in order to be rid of him, because they saw him as an obstacle to the spread of Communism in the area."

108. Charles W. Yost, "The Arab-Israeli War: How It Began," *Foreign Affairs* 46 (1968): 304–320; also reprinted in Irene L. Gendzier (ed.), *A Middle East Reader* (New York: Pegasus, 1969), p. 371.

109. Parker, p. 13.

110. Ibid., pp. 18–19. The possibility of a deliberate Israeli deception is also proposed by Nutting, *Nasser*, pp. 397–398. Parker states that, as with other explanations, there is no direct evidence to support the theory that Israel engaged in a campaign of disinformation.

111. The statements by U Thant are cited by Yost.

112. See Parker, p. 15. Parker cites both Syrian and Egyptian sources, noting that some reports say Rabin's statement was made on the 11th, rather than the 12th.

113. *Middle East Record*, vol. 3, p. 187; quoted in Parker, p. 15. The most important press account attributing these remarks to Rabin is a United Press International dispatch of May 12, which reports that a "highly placed Israeli source" discussed the possibility of overthrowing the regime in Damascus if it did not cease its sponsorship of guerrilla activity.

114. Herzog, *The Arab-Israeli Wars*, p. 148. See also Churchill and Churchill, p. 29, who report that on May 10 Rabin "antagonized the Syrians by suggesting that his forces might attack Damascus and topple the regime of Nureddin Atassi." An additional perspective is provided by Eric Rouleau, a leading French journalist covering the Arab world. Rouleau also discusses the impact on Nasser of Rabin's remarks. See E. Rouleau, J. F. Held, and J. S. Lacouture, *Israel et les Arabes: Le troisième combat* (Paris, 1967), pp. 74ff.

115. Yitzhak Rabin, *The Rabin Memoirs* (Boston: Little, Brown, 1979), p. 66.

116. A private memorandum on the establishment of the UNEF, prepared in 1957 by former UN secretary-general Dag Hammarskjold, suggests a possible legal basis for delaying removal of the force from Egypt. Hammarskjold states that he had secured Nasser's agreement that the UNEF should not be removed until its task had been completed. Thus, upon receipt of an Egyptian request for its withdrawal, the General Assembly should be consulted and asked to determine whether the task of the UNEF had in fact been completed. Hammarskjold adds that if the Assembly were to judge the UNEF's task to be unfinished but the Egyptians should nonetheless insist upon its withdrawal, the request would have to be honored, but it would then be clear that Cairo was violating an agreement between itself and the UN. U Thant insisted in his own report on the removal of the UNEF that Hammarskjold's memorandum was a private, interpretative account prepared after the fact, and thus without practical relevance.

117. U Thant's defense of his decision is contained in his report to the UN, a copy of which appears in an appendix to Laqueur, *The Road to War*. Substantial portions of this report are also reprinted in Dodd and Sales, pp. 157–172. Useful summaries of the debate over the secretary-general's decision are to be found in Yost, and in Khouri, p. 246. See also Parker.

118. The UNEF contained 978 Indians, 795 Canadians, 579 Yugoslavs, 530 Swedes, 430 Brazilians, and 61 Norwegians.

119. A thorough discussion of the various explanations that have been advanced to account for the Egyptian decision is provided by Parker, chapter 4.

120. Mansfield, *Nasser's Egypt*, p. 80.

121. Yost, p. 80.

122. Parker, pp. 49–50.

123. Quoted in Yost, p. 374; and also in Churchill and Churchill, p. 30.

124. Riad, pp. 17–18. See also Parker. Parker notes that there was a rivalry and competition, as well as a friendship, between Nasser and Amer, which may have contributed to a tendency on Amer's part to act on general instructions with only limited consultation about the details of their implementation. In addition, Parker asserts that "whatever Nasser may have wanted, Amer wanted the total withdrawal of the UNEF from the beginning" (p. 71).

125. Yost, p. 376.

126. Riad, p. 18. Even those UNEF troops to be withdrawn from their positions along the Sinai frontier were not ordered out of Egyptian territory. Rikhye was rather asked to concentrate these forces inside the Gaza Strip.

127. Quoted in Parker, p. 74.

128. Ibid.

129. Haykal, "An Armed Clash," p. 182. See also Riad, and Mansfield, *Nasser's Egypt*, p. 81.

130. Eban, speech reprinted in Laqueur and Rubin, pp. 214–216.

131. See Stock, p. 228.

132. Nasser's speech is reprinted in Laqueur and Rubin. The other quotations by Nasser are cited in Eban's speech to the United Nations.

133. Shuqayri denied making this statement, although later Palestinian sources remember the PLO's first chairman as "the man who gave the Palestinians a bad name by threatening to throw the Jews into the sea." See Cobban, p. 31. Shuqayri is also reported to have stated that if the Arabs took Israel, the surviving Jews would be helped to return to their countries of origin, "but my estimation is that none will survive." See Churchill and Churchill, p. 52.

134. Katz, p. 184.

135. A thorough account of Israeli politics during this period of waiting is provided by Laqueur, *The Road to War*, pp. 126–180. A briefer summary is provided by Safran, *From War to War*, pp. 303–316.

136. This is reported in the fuller, Hebrew-language version of Rabin's memoirs.

137. Safran, *From War to War*, p. 312.

138. An excellent summary of civilian-military relations during this period is provided by Peri, pp. 244ff. It is also reported, according to Safran, that when Eshkol went on the radio to announce the cabinet's May 27 decision, "soldiers at the front smashed their transistors in a mixture of disgust and despair." Safran, *From War to War*, p. 315.

139. Peri, p. 250.

Part IV. The Palestinian Dimension Reemerges

1. For details, see Lesch and Tessler, pp. 225–228.

2. See Herzog, *The Arab-Israeli Wars*, pp. 182–183. See also Hussein, King of Jordan, *My 'War' with Israel* (New York: Morrow, 1969).

3. By December 1967, according to UN sources, 230,000 Palestinians had moved from the West Bank to the East Bank. Of these, 110,000 were already classified as refugees, having come to the West Bank from other parts of Palestine after 1948. Predictably, Israeli and Arab officials once again traded accusations about responsibility for the exodus of these Palestinians. On August 6, Israel and Jordan agreed that West Bank residents who had fled to Jordan would be permitted to return to their homes during the last two weeks in August. But while 130,000 Palestinians applied for repatriation, only 20,000 applications were processed and approved, and only 14,000 refugees actually returned to the West Bank during the period covered by the agreement. Several thousand also received authorization to return at a later date.

7. Postwar Diplomacy and the Rise of the Palestine Resistance Movement

4. For excerpts of Johnson's speech, see Magnus, pp. 204–205.

5. Ibid., p. 202. Statements by both Johnson and Kosygin are reprinted.

6. William B. Quandt, *Decade of Decisions: American Policy toward the Arab-Israeli Conflict* (Berkeley: University of California Press, 1977), p. 63.

7. For a detailed discussion, see Arthur S. Lall, *The UN and the Middle East Crisis,*

1967 (New York: Columbia University Press, 1968), pp. 116ff. See also Quandt, *Decade*, p. 65; and Khouri, p. 308.

8. The United States abstained from voting on the Jerusalem resolution. The U.S. Mission issued a statement declaring that Washington agreed with the resolution to the extent that it expressed the sense of the General Assembly that no action should be taken which would prejudice the future status of the city. The mission also stated that it would have voted for the resolution had certain modifications sought by the U.S. been incorporated.

9. Riad, p. 47. Riad reports that the Soviet Union urged the Arabs to vote for the Latin American draft, on the grounds that it called for termination of the state of belligerency but not for formal recognition of Israel or direct talks with the Jewish state. He also adds that Egypt favored the resolution but felt itself to be bound by the principle of Arab unity.

10. Gideon Rafael, "UN Resolution 242: A Common Denominator," *New Middle East* (June 1973), reprinted in Laqueur and Rubin, p. 349. Rafael was Israel's permanent representative to the United Nations in 1967. See also Rafael, *Destination Peace, pp.* 167–185.

11. Lall reports that many delegates from Non-Aligned countries, though fully in sympathy with the demand for Israeli withdrawal from occupied Arab territory, privately expressed dismay at the uncompromising position of the Arabs. See Lall, pp. 212–213.

12. August 31, 1967; parts of this editorial in the official Syrian newspaper are reprinted in Dodd and Sales, pp. 175–176.

13. See Khouri, p. 311. Khouri cites *New York Times* accounts to the effect that King Hussein expressed a willingness to terminate the state of belligerency, acknowledge Israel's armistice borders and its possession of Eilat, compromise on the issue of refugee repatriation, provide Israel with a corridor to the Western Wall, and demilitarize the West Bank.

14. From Nasser's address to the Arab Summit Conference in Khartoum on August 31. For additional excerpts, see Riad, p. 54.

15. The full text of the Khartoum resolutions is reprinted in Dodd and Sales, pp. 174–175.

16. Yehoshafat Harkabi, "Ending the Arab-Israeli Conflict," in Michael Curtis (ed.), *People and Politics in the Middle East* (New Brunswick, New Jersey: Transaction Books, 1971), p. 272. Harkabi placed particular emphasis on the resolution's affirmation of Palestinian rights, arguing that espousal of these rights is tantamount to an endorsement of politicide since the PLO and other Palestinian guerrilla groups "repeatedly declare that they reject a political solution and that their aim is the liquidation of the 'Zionist entity' " (p. 270). A slightly softer assessment is offered by Yitzhak Rabin, who also sees the Khartoum resolution as an expression of Arab militancy but does not interpret it as ruling out the existence of a Jewish state in Palestine. According to Rabin, the objective guiding the Arabs at Khartoum was "the creation of a Palestinian state not merely alongside Israel—in the West Bank and the Gaza Strip—but on all the territory allocated to an Arab state in the 1947 Partition Resolution!" See Rabin, p. 137.

17. Abba Eban, *An Autobiography* (New York: Random House, 1977), p. 445. Eban adds that "even if the Khartoum proposals had been accepted in a spirit of rhetorical intoxication, the Arab governments which had voted for them would find it very difficult to revoke them."

18. Herzog, *The Arab-Israeli Wars*, pp. 191 and 197.

19. See, for example, Quandt, *Decade*, p. 65.

20. See Khouri, pp. 312–313. Syria and Algeria were represented by their foreign ministers, rather than by their heads of state, and the Syrian representative boycotted the sessions and returned to Damascus before the conclusion of the summit.

21. Riad, pp. 54–57.

22. See, for example, Kamel S. Abu-Jaber, "United States Policy toward the June Conflict," in I. Abu-Lughod, *The Arab-Israeli Confrontation*, p. 164. See also Sharabi, *Palestine and Israel*, pp. 137–138. Another useful discussion is provided by Khouri, who asserts that "the summit conference, according to the view of most neutral observers, displayed a considerable amount of realism and moderation and had probably gone as far as it could go, considering . . . the violent opposition to any show of moderation by the more militant Syrian, Algerian and Palestinian leaders" (p. 313–314). An additional perspective on Egyptian behavior is provided by Baker, pp. 117–118. Baker writes, "That Nasser's policy toward Israel had in fact been a moderate one in the context of inter-Arab politics is clear from the historical record, as are the reasons for that moderation. Yet since the myth of Egyptian militancy was fostered by both the Egyptians and the Israelis—each for their own reasons—it has persisted."

23. See Khouri, p. 315.

24. A useful summary is provided by Isaac, *Party and Politics*, p. 148. Herut did not call for outright annexation of Sinai and the Golan, which were not part of the historic Land of Israel, but the party did urge that there be extensive Jewish settlement in each of the two territories.

25. Ibid., pp. 79–80. This interpretation of religious law was challenged by other orthodox Jews, including some within the NRP. It was the opinion of some that a higher religious duty is the saving of lives, and so withdrawal would be permitted were it to bring peace to the Jews and the State of Israel.

26. Ibid., p. 126. See also Laqueur, *The Road to War*, pp. 301–302; and David Kimche and Dan Bawley, *The Sandstorm: The Arab-Israeli War of June, 1967, Prelude and Aftermath* (London: Stein and Day, 1968), pp. 214–215.

27. An example is the speech which Gideon Rafael made at the United Nations in October. Rafael said, "Israel again declares that it is ready right here and now, tonight, under this very roof, to meet representatives of the U.A.R. and any other Arab state and to discuss with them all measures designed to ensure security for all and to lay the basis for a peaceful future." See Lall, p. 231.

28. See Keesing's Research Report, *The Arab-Israeli Conflict: The 1967 Campaign* (New York: Charles Scribner's, 1968), pp. 47–49.

29. Lall, p. 227.

30. Riad, p. 62.

31. All three drafts are reprinted in Lall, Appendixes 17–19.

32. Quoted in ibid., pp. 231 and 234.

33. The draft resolution is reprinted in full in ibid., Appendix 20.

34. Ibid., p. 247. See also Eban, *An Autobiography*, pp. 450–451.

35. Quoted in Eban, *An Autobiography*.

36. The U.S. draft resolution is reprinted in full in Lall, Appendix 21.

37. Riad, p. 62.

38. Lall, p. 250.

39. Riad reports that he nonetheless received private assurances from Lord Caradon that it was proper to understand the resolution as calling for a complete Israeli withdrawal. "The text means all and not some of the territories," he quotes the British diplomat as saying. "Proof of this is that the resolution in the preamble emphasizes the inadmissibility of the acquisition of territory by war. This is *my* language, Mr. Minister [addressing Riad], and I assure you the text conveys the meaning you want." Riad, p. 68.

40. See Touval, p. 145.

41. Lall, p. 264.

42. Ibid., p. 263.

43. Touval, p. 153.

44. Riad, p. 74.

45. Nasser's speech is reprinted in Laqueur and Rubin, pp. 189–194.

46. From a speech which Nasser delivered at Cairo University on April 25, 1968; quoted in Robert Stephens, *Nasser: A Political Biography* (London: Penguin Press, 1971), p. 510. See also Baker, pp. 116ff.

47. See Cobban, p. 45. Cobban's report is based on a 1983 interview with Khaled al-Hassan.

48. Cobban, p. 37. Cobban interviewed Arafat in 1979. Some observers, including analysts sympathetic to the Palestinian cause, question the veracity of Arafat's story.

49. Ehud Ya'ari, *Strike Terror: The Story of Fatah* (New York: Sabra Books, 1970), p. 150. See also Shaul Mishal, *The PLO under Arafat: Between Gun and Olive Branch* (New Haven: Yale University Press, 1986), pp. 8–9.

50. Whereas Palestinian sources place the size of the invading Israeli force at 10,000 to 15,000, a range which is accepted by several foreign observers, Israelis report that Karameh was attacked by no more than 1,000 to 1,500 IDF troops supported by 150 armored vehicles. There are similar discrepancies about the number of casualties sustained by each side. The most important Palestinian account of what happened at Karameh is provided by Abu Iyad (the *nom de guerre* of Salah Khalaf), who claims to have participated in the battle. See Abu Iyad with Eric Rouleau, *My Home, My Land: A Narrative of the Palestinian Struggle* (New York: Times Books, 1981), pp. 57–58. See also Abdallah Frangi, *The PLO and Palestine* (London: Zed Books, 1983), pp. 110–112; John Cooley, *Green March, Black September* (London: Frank Cass, 1973), pp. 100–101; and Cobban, pp. 41–42. A number of Israeli sources are summarized in Jillian Becker, *The PLO: The Rise and Fall of the Palestine Liberation Organization* (New York: St. Martin's Press, 1984), pp. 62–67. See also Daniel Dishon (ed.), *The Middle East Record, 1968* (Tel Aviv: Israel Universities Press, 1971), pp. 367–368.

51. Frangi, p. 111.

52. For a thorough description of Palestinian institution-building in Jordan during this period, see Brand, pp. 186–220. Brand also discusses Palestinian organizational activity in Egypt and Kuwait in the period following the June War. The presence of the Palestine resistance movement was also beginning to make itself felt in the refugee camps of Lebanon at this time, although that country did not become an important center of Palestinian organizational activity until the 1970s. For a summary of the Palestine resistance movement in Lebanon in 1968 and 1969, see Rosemary Sayigh, *Palestinians: From Peasants to Revolutionaries* (London: Zed Books, 1979), p. 156.

53. Brand, p. 198. Although the General Union of Palestinian Women was not licensed by the Jordanian government, chapters sprang up throughout the country, "from the refugee camps to the cities of Amman, Salt, Irbid, Aqaba and Karak." Brand also reports that "during the 1967–1971 period, the union participated widely in international conferences and symposia and thereby played an important informational role."

54. Ibid., p. 193.

55. Both the charter and the constitution approved at the Fourth PNC are appended in Becker, pp. 230–240. For additional discussion, see Quandt, Jabber, and Lesch, pp. 70 and 91–92; and Cobban, pp. 43–44, which also appends extracts of the charter. The terms "Palestine National Council" and "Palestine National Congress" are sometimes used interchangeably by authors writing about this period.

56. Adapted from Quandt, Jabber, and Lesch, p. 66. See also Rubenberg, *The Palestine Liberation Organization, p. 11*; and Cheryl Rubenberg, "The Structural and Political Context of the PLO's Changing Objectives in the Post-1967 Period," in Yehuda Lukacs and Abdalla

M. Battah (eds.), *The Arab-Israeli Conflict: Two Decades of Change* (Boulder, Colorado: Westview Press, 1988), pp. 94–95. There were several additional small splinter groups.

57. Somewhat different versions of this chart appear in Rubenberg, *The Palestine Liberation Organization*, pp. ii–iii; and in Becker, p. 241.

58. Abdallah Laroui, *The Crisis of the Arab Intellectual* (Berkeley: University of California Press, 1976), p. viii.

59. Abdallah Laroui, "The Arab Revolution between Awareness and Reality," *Mawaqif* 10 (July–August 1970): 138.

60. Ibid.

61. Kerr, *The Arab Cold War*, p. 135.

62. Fouad Ajami, *The Arab Predicament: Arab Political Thought and Practice since 1967* (New York: Cambridge University Press, 1981), p. 30.

63. Ibid., p. 32.

64. Sadeq al-Azm, *Al-Naqd al-Dhati Ba'd al-Hazima* [Self- Criticism after the Defeat] (Beirut, 1968), p. 133; quoted in Ajami, p. 34.

65. Adonis, "The Problems of Literature and the Intelligentsia," *Al-Adab* 6 (June 1968): 4–5; quoted in Ajami, p. 29.

66. Jiryis, *The Arabs in Israel*, p.175. Jiryis's study was first published in Hebrew, in Haifa, in 1966. It was then translated into Arabic, and subsequently into English and French as well, and was published both by the Arab League Office in Jerusalem, Jordan, and by the Palestine Research Center in Beirut.

67. Clovis Maksoud, "New Palestine: Grievance Redressed, Justice for Arab and Jew," *Mid East* (June 1970): 7–10.

68. Naseer H. Aruri, "Palestinian Nationalism since 1967: An Overview," in Lukacs and Battah, p. 75.

69. Ibid.

70. Alain Gresh, *The PLO: The Struggle Within, Toward an Independent Palestinian State* (London: Zed Books, 1985), p. 45.

71. "The Seven Points," passed by the Central Committee of Fatah, January 1969; reprinted in Laqueur and Rubin, pp. 372–373.

72. "An Interview with 'Abu Ammar' [Yasir Arafat]," *Free Palestine*, August 1969; reprinted in Laqueur and Rubin, pp. 373–379. See also Gresh, p. 44.

73. Ismail Shammout, *Palestine: Illustrated Political History* (Beirut: Palestine Liberation Organization, 1972), p. 43.

74. "Interview with Arafat," in Laqueur and Rubin, pp. 373–379.

75. Gresh, p. 44.

76. "The Seven Points," in Laqueur and Rubin, pp. 372–373.

77. Maksoud.

78. "Interview with Arafat," in Laqueur and Rubin, pp. 373–379.

79. *The Militant*, October 9, 1970; reprinted from "The Palestine Revolution and the Jews" (mimeo) (New York: Palestine Liberation Organization, 1969).

80. For additional discussion, see Mark Tessler, "Secularism in the Middle East? Reflections of Recent Palestinian Proposals," *Ethnicity* 2 (1975): 178–203.

81. Yehoshafat Harkabi, "The Palestinian National Covenant," in Michael Curtis et al. (eds.), *The Palestinians: People, History, Politics* (New Brunswick, New Jersey: Transaction Books, 1975); and Yehoshafat Harkabi, "Fedayeen Action and Arab Strategy," *Adelphi Papers* no. 53 (December 1968).

82. "Interview with Arafat."

83. "The Platform of the Popular Front for the Liberation of Palestine," reprinted in Laqueur and Rubin, pp. 379–383.

84. Harkabi, "The Palestinian National Covenant," pp. 151–152.

85. A few elements within the PLO also pointed out this "contradiction" and took what Harkabi and some others would consider a more logically consistent position. For example, the tiny Arab Liberation Front insisted that no state of Palestine should be brought into existence because it would constitute yet another division within the Arab world and hence an impediment to the realization of Arab unity. In this connection, too, a leader of Saiqa denied the existence of a separate Palestinian people and stated, "We speak about a Palestinian identity only for political reasons, because it is in the Arabs' national interest." See Becker, p. 73.

86. Quandt, Jabber, and Lesch, pp. 100–102.

87. Hisham Sharabi, *Arab Intellectuals and the West: The Formative Years* (Baltimore: Johns Hopkins University Press, 1970), p. 119.

88. Maksoud.

89. Quoted in *Arab News and Views*, February 1969, pp. 4–5. See also Gilbert Denoyan, *El Fatah Parle* (Paris: Editions Albin Michel, 1970), p. 212. Denoyan quotes a Fatah spokesman as saying, "All those who wish to remain in Palestine as Jewish Palestinian citizens equal to Christian and Muslim Palestinians can stay with us. The others, if they want to leave, will have the right to leave." For additional discussion, see Quandt, Jabber, and Lesch, pp. 102–103.

90. Quoted in Gresh, p. 44.

91. *Time* magazine, December 21, 1970.

92. Relevant statements are quoted in Quandt, Jabber, and Lesch, pp. 103–104. Ironically, perhaps, it is the more radical Palestinian factions, most notably PDFLP, that were most likely to speak, albeit vaguely, about the national rights of the Jews in Palestine.

93. Ibid., p. 106.

94. Ibid., p. 107.

95. Accounts of Egyptian strategic thinking and of Nasser's motivation for launching the War of Attrition are to be found in Riad, pp. 102ff., and Muhammad Hassanein Haykal, *The Sphinx and the Commissar* (London: Collins, 1977), pp. 188ff. The most thorough account, in Arabic, is the memoirs of Mahmoud Fawzi, the defense minister during this period. See Mahmoud Fawzi, *The Three-Year War* (Cairo: al-Mustaqbal al-Arabi, 1984). An additional perspective is provided in Karen Dawisha, *Soviet Foreign Policy towards Egypt* (New York: St. Martin's Press, 1979), pp. 49ff.

96. Herzog, *The Arab-Israeli Wars*, p. 214. A valuable account, written by a respected Israeli scholar, is Yaacov Bar Siman Tov, *The War of Attrition* (New York: Columbia University Press, 1980). Another important study, written by a U.S. State Department official who served in Israel during this period, is David A. Korn, *Stalemate: The War of Attrition and Great Power Diplomacy in the Middle East, 1967–1970* (Boulder, Colorado: Westview Press, 1992).

97. Israeli officials argued that the Soviet decision to intervene was actually made as early as the fall of 1969, and thus should not be seen as a response to Jerusalem's deep-penetration retaliatory strikes. For additional discussion, see Bar Siman Tov, pp. 145–146, and Korn, p. 194.

98. Herzog, *The Arab-Israeli Wars*, p. 216.

99. Having been designated to fill Eshkol's term, Meir continued as prime minister following the Labor Party's victory in the election of October 1969. Labor's platform in this election displayed greater flexibility toward the occupied territories than did that of its major rival, Gahal, but it nevertheless promised that "until peace comes, our forces will remain on all the cease fire lines," and that "Israel will never return to the armistice lines used before the Six Day War." See Arian, *Politics in Israel*, p. 248.

100. Rabin, p. 153.

101. Eban, *An Autobiography*, p. 463.

102. For details, see Quandt, *Decade*, pp. 89ff.

103. Riad, pp. 110–111.

104. Quoted in Korn, p. 161, and Quandt, *Decade*, p. 91.

105. Rabin, p. 162.

106. The ceasefire provisions of this proposal, sometimes described as the Second Rogers Initiative, were approved by the entire Israeli cabinet. The provisions dealing with negotiations, peace, and withdrawal were opposed by the six ministers belonging to Gahal, however, and the cabinet's endorsement of these provisions led to Gahal's resignation from the government. Even after Israel had approved the Rogers Plan, there was a sharp disagreement between Washington and Jerusalem about the precise wording of the instructions to be given to Gunnar Jarring as a basis for the new round of peace talks he was to conduct. For a detailed account of the diplomatic and political maneuvering associated with these events, see Korn, pp. 235–272. Valuable accounts are also to be found in Touval, pp. 165ff., and Quandt, *Decade*, pp. 99ff. Additional information on Israeli deliberations is to be found in Michael Brecher, *Decisions in Israel's Foreign Policy* (New Haven: Yale University Press, 1975), pp. 494ff.

107. Some sources put the number as high as 140,000, and one author reports a Lebanese claim that 170,000 Palestinians entered the country during and after the 1947–48 War. See David Gilmour, *Lebanon: The Fractured Country* (New York: St. Martin's, 1983), p. 86; and Harald Vocke, *The Lebanese War: Its Origins and Political Dimensions* (London: C. Hurst and Co., 1978), p. 35.

108. R. Sayigh, p. 151.

109. Some authors suggest that one reason for Beirut's caution was a fear that Israel was seeking an opportunity to modify its border with Lebanon in order to gain control of the waters of the Litani River. Gilmour, for example, summarizes Israeli sources stating that both Ben Gurion and Dayan had at one time envisioned the seizure of southern Lebanon for this purpose. See Gilmour, pp. 93 and 146.

110. *Middle East Record*, 1969/1970, p. 215.

111. Gilmour, p. 99.

112. Ibid., pp. 94–95.

113. R. Sayigh, pp. 158ff.

114. Cobban reports that for two decades the D. B. had "exercised a rigid control over every tiny detail of day-to-day life in the camps." See Cobban, p. 47. Sayigh describes some of the abuses associated with this situation. For example, she reports that following the liberation of one of the camps, a man was seen destroying a bed to which he had once been tied with a stone on his chest in the camp police station. See R. Sayigh, p. 161.

115. R. Sayigh, p. 161.

116. Gilmour, p. 95.

117. For example, about fifty guerrillas were killed or wounded in a battle a few weeks after the signing of the Cairo Agreement, and following the encounter the PLO issued a communiqué in Amman that blamed Saiqa and the PFLP for initiating the encounter with Lebanese forces. See R. Sayigh, p. 163.

118. Although the PLO tended to ignore the provision of the Cairo Agreement requiring it to obtain Lebanese approval for operations against Israel, respect for the agreement was made much more difficult by the fact that some guerrilla groups resisted PLO discipline and operated as independent commando units. Critics of the PLO pointed out that the Palestinians also disregarded other provisions of the Cairo Agreement. For example, despite clauses forbidding the Palestinians from amassing heavy weapons, they now acquired tanks and artillery.

119. The various accounts are summarized in Becker, p. 99.

120. Gilmour, p. 99.

121. Herzog, *The Arab-Israeli Wars*, p. 203. Herzog also gives the following statistics for the period from September 1968 through March 1969: of 534 incidents, 189 emanated from Jordan, 123 involved incursions from the Gaza Strip, 29 originated in the West Bank, and 47 occurred along the Suez Canal (p. 206).

122. Frangi, p. 115.

123. Quandt, *Decade*, p. 101.

124. Day, p. 59.

125. Hurewitz, *Middle East Politics*, p. 311.

126. Mishal, *West Bank/East Bank*, p. 93. Mishal notes that one important result of these Jordanian controls was the inability of the Palestinians to form an all–West Bank political leadership.

127. R. Sayigh, p. 111.

128. Quoted in ibid.

129. Frangi, p. 115.

130. Becker, p. 75.

131. "Interview with Arafat," in Laqueur and Rubin, pp. 373–379.

132. Frangi, p. 116.

133. Cobban, pp. 48–49.

134. Ibid., p. 49.

135. See Quandt, Jabber, and Lesch, p. 125. Quandt reports that the Jordanians later claimed to have documents indicating that Fatah, along with the more radical organizations, had decided to attempt a coup d'etat in September of 1970.

136. Palestinians were also angered by Hussein's conciliatory statements to the Western press at this time, telling an interviewer from the *New York Times*, for example, that he would accept limited changes in the pre-1967 border between Israel and Jordan and was willing to consider an international administration for East Jerusalem. For details, see Rafik Halabi, *The West Bank Story* (New York: Harcourt Brace Jovanovich, 1981), p. 93.

137. Quandt, Jabber, and Lesch, p. 124. See also Cobban.

138. Henry Kissinger, *The White House Years* (Boston: Little, Brown, 1979), pp. 595–596.

139. Frangi, p. 116.

140. Becker, p. 76. See also Mishal, *The PLO under Arafat*, p. 15; and Rowley, *Israel into Palestine*, p. 53. Mishal states that the Palestinians suffered 3,500 casualties in September 1970. Rowley reports that 2,600 commandos were killed.

141. Frangi, p. 118.

142. Mishal, *The PLO under Arafat*, p. 15.

143. Frangi. See also Gresh, p. 111.

144. Abu Iyad, p. 98.

145. Ann Mosely Lesch, *Political Perceptions of the Palestinians in the West Bank and the Gaza Strip* (Washington: The Middle East Institute, 1980), p. 39.

8. Israel, the Palestinians, and the Occupied Territories in the 1970s

1. A good discussion of Israeli actions in East Jerusalem in 1967, and of the response of the city's Palestinian population, is to be found in Halabi, pp. 29ff. See also Rowley, pp. 70ff.; and David Kroyanker, *Developing Jerusalem: 1967–1975* (Jerusalem: The Jerusalem Foundation, 1975).

2. For a useful introduction, see Rowley, p. 58.

3. Howard M. Sachar, *A History of Israel, Volume II: From the Aftermath of the Yom Kippur War* (New York: Oxford University Press, 1987), p. 12. For good accounts of the Allon Plan, see Mishal, *The PLO under Arafat,* pp. 129–132; and Mark A. Heller, *A Palestinian State: The Implications for Israel* (Cambridge, Massachusetts: Harvard University Press, 1983), pp. 35–36. See also Rowley, p. 126. For additional information about Allon's own ideological orientation, see Real Jean Isaac, *Israel Divided: Ideological Politics in the Jewish State* (Baltimore: Johns Hopkins University Press, 1976), pp. 115–116.

4. Mishal, *The PLO,* p. 130.

5. Isaac, *Party and Politics,* p. 148. For an additional summary account of Gahal's performance in the 1969 elections, see William Frankel, *Israel Observed: An Anatomy of the State* (New York: Thames and Hudson, 1980), pp. 49–50. Useful information about this and subsequent Knesset elections is also provided by Asher Arian, *Politics in Israel,* pp. 133ff.; and for a fuller account of the 1969 elections, see the contributions in Asher Arian (ed.), *The Elections in Israel—1969* (Jerusalem: Jerusalem Academic Press, 1972). See also Don Peretz, "Israel's 1969 Election Issues: The Visible and the Invisible," *Middle East Journal* 24 (1970): 31–71.

6. For a useful discussion of the different definitions of territorial compromise that existed within the Labor Alignment, see Isaac, *Israel Divided,* pp. 110ff. For a general account of the Labor Party at this time, see Myron J. Aronoff, *Power and Ritual in the Israeli Labor Party: A Study in Political Anthropology* (Amsterdam: Van Gorcum, 1977). See also Peter Medding, *Mapai in Israel: Political Organization and Government in a New Society* (Cambridge: Cambridge University Press, 1972).

7. Halabi, p. 38.

8. Eban, *An Autobiography,* p. 453.

9. *The Israel Administration in Judea, Samaria and Gaza* (Tel Aviv: The Ministry of Defense, 1968), p. 5.

10. *Jerusalem Post Weekly,* December 7, 1970; quoted in Isaac, *Israel Divided,* pp. 116–117.

11. For an excellent discussion of Israel's policies toward its Arab citizens, see Ian Lustick, *Arabs in the Jewish State* (Austin: University of Texas Press, 1980). See also Sammy Smooha, *Israel: Pluralism and Conflict* (Berkeley: University of California Press, 1978). For differing perspectives on the political circumstances of Arabs in Israel in the 1960s, see Jacob Landau, *The Arabs in Israel* (London: Oxford University Press, 1969), and Jiryis. For a general overview and summary, see Lesch and Tessler, pp. 89–124.

12. Yehoshua Arieli, "Annexation and Democracy," *New Outlook,* July 1969; reprinted in Laqueur and Rubin, p. 451.

13. Halabi, p. 81.

14. For additional details, see Lesch and Tessler, pp. 229–230.

15. Israeli spokesmen sometimes assert that this "thinning out" was motivated by a desire to reduce overcrowding and improve the living conditions of refugees in Gaza, although they usually acknowledge that Palestinians opposed their "development" efforts.

16. Halabi, p. 82. Joining critics of Sharon's actions, Halabi expresses serious doubts about the wisdom of Israel's policies. He asserts that occupation was having a "malignant, brutalizing effect" on Israeli society and complains that many Israelis were now prepared to justify collective punishment and assaults on innocent civilians in the name of security. At the same time, he also notes that the residents of Gaza suffered at the hands of Palestinian commandos, whom he calls "terrorists" and describes as sworn enemies of the State of Israel. According to his analysis, "The inhabitants of Gaza felt themselves being crushed between the hammer of repression and the anvil of terror" (p. 79).

17. Ibid., pp. 54ff.

18. For a useful discussion of the West Bank's traditional elite, see Emile Sahliyeh, *In Search of Leadership: West Bank Politics since 1967* (Washington: The Brookings Institution, 1987), pp. 21–41. See also Halabi. Halabi gives a good account of the *modus vivendi* worked out between Moshe Dayan, the Israeli defense minister, and Hamdi Kenan and Sheikh Muhammad Ali Jabari, traditional leaders in Nablus and Hebron respectively.

19. Some details of Hussein's plan are provided by Heller, pp. 52–53, and by Sahliyeh, *In Search*, pp. 35–36. To enhance the attractiveness of his proposed United Arab Kingdom, Hussein established a ministry for the West Bank and increased financial assistance to a number of the region's municipalities and public institutions. He also attempted to be more conciliatory to the Palestinians in other ways, appointing a prime minister of Palestinian descent and adding several new cabinet members of Palestinian origin.

20. Sahliyeh, *In Search*, pp. 36–40. The response of the PLO to the elections, including its arguments in favor of a boycott and against the Hussein plan, is discussed in Gresh, pp. 114–118.

21. There is an extensive literature on the war of October 1973. Particularly helpful, from differing perspectives, are Chaim Herzog, *The War of Atonement: October 1973* (Boston: Little, Brown, 1975); Ze'ev Schiff, *October Earthquake: Yom Kippur, 1973* (Tel Aviv: University Publishing Projects, 1974); Michael Handel, *Perception, Deception, and Surprise: The Case of the Yom Kippur War* (Jerusalem: The Hebrew University Press, 1975); Muhammad Haykal, *The Road to Ramadan* (New York: The New York Times Book Company, 1975); Saad al-Shazly, *The Crossing of the Suez* (San Francisco: American Mideast Research, 1980); Naseer Aruri (ed.), *Middle East Crucible: Studies on the Arab-Israeli War of October, 1973* (Wilmette, Illinois: Medina Press, 1975); and Galia Golan, *The Soviet Union and the Arab-Israeli War of October, 1973* (Jerusalem: The Hebrew University Press, 1974).

22. Herzog, *The War of Atonement*, p. 97.

23. For details, see Quandt, *Decade*, pp. 183ff.

24. Responding to urgent appeals from the Egyptians, the Soviet Union threatened to intervene to save the Egyptian Third Army, and this in turn produced a tense standoff between the United States and the USSR. Washington issued a worldwide military alert, bringing the superpowers close to a military confrontation on October 25–26.

25. More than 6,000 Israelis were killed or wounded during the eighteen days of fighting, a figure far higher than that associated with any of the country's previous wars.

26. Useful accounts of the Israeli elections of December 1973 are brought together in Asher Arian (ed.), *The Elections in Israel—1973* (Jerusalem: Jerusalem Academic Press, 1975). See also Don Peretz, "The War Election and Israel's Eighth Knesset," *Middle East Journal* 28 (1974): 111–125; and Asher Arian, "Were the 1973 Elections in Israel Critical?" *Comparative Politics* 8 (1975): 152–165.

27. The entire Agranat Commission report is reprinted in Laqueur and Rubin, pp. 487–498. The quoted passage appears on p. 489.

28. H. Sachar, *A History, II*, pp. 3–4. See also Herzog, *The War of Atonement*, p. 280. Herzog states, "It would seem inconceivable to a Western reader that any Minister of Defense— however able, however brilliant and however effective—could avoid ministerial responsibility for what occurred."

29. Donna Robinson Divine, "Why This War," *International Journal of Middle East Studies* 7 (1976): 523–543.

30. Sadat had also sought a diplomatic breakthrough in 1971, taking action that some considered as dramatic as his expulsion of Soviet advisors the following year. Early in 1971, he gave an interview to *Newsweek* editor Arnaud de Borchgrave, in which he stated that Egypt was ready to recognize and make peace with Israel. De Borchgrave flew to Jerusalem with this

information and told Prime Minister Golda Meir that Sadat would soon repeat his offer of peace to UN envoy Gunnar Jarring. Meir dismissed Sadat's overture, however, leading some Israeli analysts, as well as de Borchgrave, to conclude that "Mrs. Meir here missed the greatest opportunity to prevent the [1973] war." See Herzog, *The War of Atonement*, p. 18.

31. This policy was announced publicly in a speech in Damascus on March 8, 1972, by President Hafez al-Assad, who stated that the price of Syrian acceptance of UN 242 was not only complete Israeli withdrawal from Arab lands captured in 1967 but also recognition of the rights of the Palestinians. For details, see Khouri, pp. 367–368. Khouri also asserts, on the basis of personal interviews, that Syrian officials had for some time privately expressed a willingness to accept UN 242 under the conditions set forth in Assad's speech.

32. The Egyptian president's threats were dismissed not only in Egypt but in Israel as well, where analysts took note of Sadat's declared intention to go to war but concluded that he was incapable of translating them into action. See Herzog, *The War of Atonement*, pp. 26 and 279.

33. See Riad, pp. 228ff.

34. Quoted in Shazly, p. 175.

35. Herzog, *The War of Atonement*, p. 22.

36. For an overview of the nature and consequences of the Arabs' new oil wealth, see the contributions in Naiem A. Sherbiny and Mark Tessler (eds.), *Arab Oil: Impact on the Arab Countries and Global Implications* (New York: Praeger Publishers, 1976).

37. Farouk A. Sankari, "The Character and Impact of Arab Oil Embargoes," in ibid., pp. 270ff.

38. A thorough account of Kissinger's efforts is provided by Quandt, *Decade*, pp. 207ff. Other useful accounts include Edward R. F. Sheehan, *The Arabs, Israelis, and Kissinger: A Secret History of American Diplomacy in the Middle East* (New York: Reader's Digest Press, 1976), and Matti Golan, *Secret Conversations with Henry Kissinger: Step-by-Step Diplomacy in the Middle East* (New York: Quadrangle Books, 1976).

39. For details, see Gresh, pp. 167–171; Franji, pp. 140–142; and Cobban, p. 62.

40. Gresh, p. 168.

41. Ibid.

42. Ibid., p. 161. The interview was granted to an American Jewish journalist, Paul Jacobs, and was published on March 22, 1974. Hawatmeh explained his decision by saying, "I do not see why we should accept that Arab reactionaries should start a dialogue with the most extremist Israeli circles and forbid progressive [Palestinian] forces to do the same with progressive Israeli forces." Jacobs described the interview as a historic event, "because, for the first time, a Palestinian leader of this importance no longer demands the destruction of the State of Israel as a pre-condition for dialogue and even an agreement between Israelis and Palestinians; because, for the first time, a Palestinian PLO leader made a distinction not only between the Israeli government and the Israeli people but also right-wing and left-wing Zionists; and because Hawatmeh agreed that his statement be published first in an Israeli paper." See Jacobs's statement to *Le Nouvel Observateur*, March 24, 1974, quoted in Gresh. For additional information about Jacobs's efforts to foster a dialogue between "progressive" Palestinians and Israelis, see Paul Jacobs, *Between the Rock and the Hard Place* (New York: Random House, 1970).

43. Franji, pp. 139–140.

44. The Rabat summit conference resolution of October 29, 1974, is reprinted in Laqueur and Rubin, p. 518. For additional information about the Rabat summit, and about the PLO's accomplishments in the international arena in general during this period, see Gresh, pp. 179ff., and Franji, pp. 142ff. See also Mishal, *The PLO*, pp. 18ff.

45. See Mishal, *The PLO*, p. 19. Mishal bases his account of the secret clauses of the Rabat resolution on a newspaper account published in Cairo in *Akhbar al-Yawm*.

46. Arafat's UN address is reprinted in Laqueur and Rubin, pp. 504–518. For a fuller account of Arafat's visit to the United Nations, see Franji, pp. 143–145.

47. These are UN General Assembly resolutions 3236 (XXIX) and 3237 (XXIX) respectively, both of which are printed in *United Nations Monthly Chronicle* 11 (December 1974): 36–37.

48. "For the Rights of Palestinians: Work of the Committee on the Exercise of the Inalienable Rights of the Palestinian People," United Nations document, n.d., p. 8.

49. Eban, *An Autobiography*, p. 585.

50. For example, the left-oriented Israeli magazine *New Outlook* published an editorial in its issue of July–August 1975 declaring that "growing sections within the PLO . . . openly advocate a peaceful solution to the conflict based on partition according to the 1967 borders. Pursuit of this path would be in Israel's best interest—these elements would be encouraged by an Israeli recognition of the Palestinians and a willingness to negotiate with them."

51. The United States voted against the resolution, and the American ambassador to the United Nations, Daniel Patrick Moynihan, declared, "The United States . . . does not acknowledge, it will never abide by, and it will never acquiesce in this infamous act."

52. *Toward Peace in the Middle East: Report of a Study Group* (Washington: The Brookings Institution, 1975). For a summary, see Quandt, *Decade*, pp. 290–292. The report also recommends that "Palestinian refugees should be helped to resettle in a newly formed Palestinian entity if they so choose," adding that this and all other recommendations are contingent upon the Palestinians' accepting Israel's right to exist.

53. Quandt, *Decade*, p. 290.

54. "United States Policy in the Middle East, November 1974–February 1976," *Selected Documents* (Washington: United States Department of State, 1976), pp. 59ff. For additional accounts, see Quandt, *Decade*, p. 278, and Khouri, 381.

55. The ascendancy of a new, pro-PLO urban elite is discussed by Sahliyeh, *In Search*, pp. 42ff. See also Halabi, pp. 110ff.

56. A thorough account of the PNF is provided by Sahliyeh, *In Search*, pp. 51–63. See also Mishal, *The PLO*, p. 106.

57. Sahliyeh, *In Search*, pp. 91–95.

58. Quoted in Gresh, p. 182. Most Communist parties adhered closely to the political line of the Soviet Union, which advocated the creation of an independent Palestinian state alongside Israel.

59. For details about the 1976 West Bank elections, see Sahliyeh, *In Search*, pp. 63ff. See also Mishal, *The PLO*, pp. 107ff., and Halabi, p. 117ff.

60. Halabi, p. 118.

61. See Sahliyeh, *In Search*. See also Moshe Ma'oz, *Palestinian Leadership in the West Bank* (London: Frank Cass, 1984).

62. The number of Palestinians in Lebanon at this and other points in time is subject to dispute, particularly since there has been no census in the country since the entrance of roughly 120,000 Palestinian refugees in 1947–48. For additional information, see chapter 7, note 107. See also Cobban, p. 280, note 22.

63. Useful background is provided by Michael C. Hudson, "Developments and Setbacks in the Palestine Resistance Movement, 1967–1971," *Journal of Palestine Studies* 1 (Spring 1972): 64–84.

64. Iliya Harik, "Lebanon: Anatomy of Conflict," American Universities Field Staff Reports, no. 49, 1981, p. 13. Harik argues that Lebanese factions might have been able to resolve

their differences, or at least restrict them to the political arena, had it not been for disruptions caused by a strong PLO presence in the country. For a less scholarly exposition of the argument that the Palestinian presence undermined the stability of Lebanon, written by a supporter of the country's Maronite Christian community, see Vocke.

65. See, for example, Michael C. Hudson, *Lebanon: The Precarious Republic* (New York: Random House, 1968); and Walid Khalidi, *Conflict and Violence in Lebanon: Confrontation in the Middle East* (Cambridge: Harvard Center for International Affairs, 1979).

66. Cobban, p. 65.

67. From an interview with Helena Cobban. For further discussion, see Cobban, pp. 65ff. Cobban reports that late in 1975 Fatah, the dominant faction within the PLO, "was still trying to avoid full-scale involvement in the Lebanese fighting" (p. 67), and that "Fatah leaders tried everything possible to avoid being forced to fight the Syrians" (p. 77).

68. Ibid., p. 68. See also Rashid Khalidi, *Under Siege: PLO Decisionmaking during the 1982 War* (New York: Columbia University Press, 1986), p. 25.

69. For details of the agreement reached between Israel and the Maronite Christian community in Lebanon in March 1976, see Ze'ev Schiff and Ehud Ya'ari, *Israel's Lebanon War* (New York: Simon and Schuster, 1984), pp. 11ff. See also Itamar Rabinovich, *The War for Lebanon, 1970–1983* (Ithaca: Cornell University Press, 1984); and Jonathan Randall, *Going All the Way: Christian Warlords, Israeli Adventurers, and the War in Lebanon* (New York: Vintage Books, 1984). For a detailed account of the Syrian role in the Lebanese civil war, see Adeed Dawisha, *Syria and the Lebanese Crisis* (London: Macmillan, 1980).

70. The Arab Deterrent Force originally included small contingents from other Arab countries, including units from Arab peacekeeping forces previously sent to Lebanon. The Arab states understood that the ADF would be dominated by Syria, however, and most non-Syrian units quietly withdrew within a year or two.

71. Estimates of the total number of Lebanese killed range between 60,000 and 80,000, with the number of wounded being perhaps three times higher.

72. R. Khalidi, *Under Siege*, pp. 29, 30–31.

73. Selim Nassib with Caroline Tisdall, *Beirut: Frontline Story* (London: Pluto Press, 1983), p. 22. See also R. Khalidi, *Under Siege*, p. 32.

74. R. Khalidi, *Under Siege*, pp. 32–33.

75. Quoted in Nassib.

76. Gresh, p. 206.

77. Widespread use of the term "earthquake" is discussed by Isaac, *Party and Politics*, pp. 11ff. See also Don Peretz, "The Earthquake: Israel's Ninth Knesset Election," *Middle East Journal* 31 (1977): 251–266. For a fuller discussion of the 1977 election, see the contributions in Howard R. Penniman (ed.), *Israel at the Polls: The Knesset Elections of 1977* (Washington: American Enterprise Institute, 1979).

78. See, for example, Yehuda Ben-Meir, *National Security Decision-Making: The Israeli Case* (Boulder, Colorado: Westview Press, 1986), p. 111.

79. Benjamin Akzin, "The Likud," in Penniman, pp. 104–106. See also Isaac, *Party and Politics*, pp. 156–158.

80. Yigal Allon, "The Case for Defensible Borders," *Foreign Affairs* 55 (1976): 38–53. Although the main features vary only in minor ways, Allon in fact introduced several different versions of his peace plan. For additional information, see Heller, pp. 35–36, and Mishal, *The PLO*, pp. 129–132.

81. See, for example, Moshe Dayan, "After All, What about the Mountain Ridge?" *Yediot Aharonot*, February 13, 1981; quoted and discussed in Heller, p. 35. See also Isaac, *Israel Divided*, pp. 116ff. Isaac discusses apparent contradictions in Dayan's views; while he

repeatedly associated himself with Labor's position of "territories for peace" and argued that keeping the territories would lead to greater Arab hostility, he also urged that the West Bank be economically linked to Israel and later recommended that Israeli law be extended to the territories. In 1969, Dayan had called Israel's acceptance of UN 242 "a fatal mistake" (p. 128).

82. These positions on issues of territorial compromise were articulated by some of the more hard-line leaders of the Labor Alignment as early as 1970 and 1971. For example, Prime Minister Golda Meir told U.S. officials on March 13, 1971, that Israel must retain Sharm al-Sheikh, and an access road to it, that Gaza must not return to Egyptian rule, and that Israeli forces must remain on the Golan Heights. For details, see Quandt, *Decade*, pp. 138–139.

83. See *Jerusalem Post*, May 31, 1974; quoted and discussed in Isaac, *Party and Politics*, pp. 124–125.

84. For a good summary of the scandals and leadership problems that plagued Labor at this time, and of their impact on the 1977 election, see Myron J. Aronoff, "The Decline of the Israeli Labor Party: Causes and Significance," in Penniman. See also Isaac, *Party and Politics*, pp. 121ff. Isaac argues that Labor's declining fortunes were also very much the result of the diminishing appeal of its socialist ideology. According to this analysis, the ideology itself appeared outdated, since socialist experiments in the Soviet Union and elsewhere had failed; and the party was also hurt by growing sympathy for the Palestinian cause among socialist regimes in Europe, with the result that the Israeli Labor movement was increasingly isolated within the Socialist International.

85. For an account of the DMC, see Efraim Torgovnik, "A Movement for Change in a Stable System," in Penniman. See also Arian, *Politics in Israel*, pp. 89ff.

86. See Asher Arian, "The Electorate: Israel 1977," in Penniman, especially pp. 77ff. See also Arian, *Politics in Israel*, pp. 139ff.

87. Empirical research on the attitudes toward Arabs held by Israelis of Afro-Asian origin was done by Yochanan Peres in the late 1960s. See Yochanan Peres and Zipporah Levy, "Jews and Arabs: Ethnic Group Stereotypes in Israel," *Race* 10 (April 1969): 479–492; and Yochanan Peres, "Ethnic Relations in Israel," *American Journal of Sociology* 76 (May 1971): 1021–1047. For a more recent treatment, see Moshe Shokeid, *Distant Relations: Ethnicity and Politics among Arabs and North African Jews in Israel* (New York: Praeger, 1982). A comprehensive scholarly examination of the circumstances of Israeli Jews of Afro-Asian origin, including a review of research on their attitudes and stereotypes about Arabs, is provided by Smooha, especially pp. 151ff. A vivid portrait presented from a journalistic and literary perspective, based on interviews conducted among Jews from Morocco living in the development town of Bet Shemesh, is offered by Amos Oz, *In the Land of Israel* (New York: Vintage, 1984), especially pp. 27ff.

88. For an instructive exchange of differing scholarly opinions on the subject of Jewish life in Arab North Africa, see Lawrence Rosen, "Muslim-Jewish Relations in a Moroccan City," *International Journal of Middle East Studies* 3 (October 1972): 435–449; and Norman A. Stillman, "The Moroccan Jewish Experience: A Revisionist View," *Jerusalem Quarterly* 9 (Fall 1979): 111–123. See also Mark Tessler, "The Identity of Religious Minorities in Non-Secular States: Jews in Tunisia and Morocco and Arabs in Israel," *Comparative Studies in Society and History* 20 (July 1978): 359–373; and Mark Tessler and Linda Hawkins, "The Political Culture of Jews in Tunisia and Morocco," *International Journal of Middle East Studies* 11 (January 1980): 59–86. For more comprehensive accounts of Jews in Arab and Muslim countries, see Norman A. Stillman, *The Jews of Arab Lands: A History and Source Book* (Philadelphia: Jewish Publication Society of America, 1979); and Bernard Lewis, *The Jews of Islam* (Princeton: Princeton University Press, 1984).

89. Peres, for example, suggests that the stereotypes of Arabs reflected in his surveys may

result from scapegoating and self-hatred, which in turn are the result of difficulties associated with absorption and modernization. See Y. Peres, "Ethnic Relations." See also Moshe Lissak, *Social Mobility in Israeli Society* (Jerusalem: Israel Universities Press, 1969). Although he does not place emphasis on stereotypes of Arabs, Lissak, too, takes the view that the attitudes and behavior patterns of immigrants to Israel from Arab and Muslim countries have been determined principally by social and economic disadvantages resulting from the difficulties of absorption, rather than by cultural or historical factors. For a thorough account of the material, educational, and political disadvantages that continued to characterize Jews of Afro-Asian origin on the eve of the 1977 election, see Smooha.

90. This point is discussed in Peter Grose, *A Changing Israel* (New York: Vintage, 1985), pp. 86ff. Grose illustrates his analysis with the remarks of a young Afro-Asian bank teller: "[In the past] my mother cleaned this bank after hours while Ashkenazi girls were bank tellers. Now this bank is being cleaned after hours by [Arab] laborers who come by bus from a village east of Jerusalem. I am a teller."

91. From remarks made by Ben Gurion in the mid-1960s; quoted in Nissim Rejwan, "The Two Israels: A Study in Europocentrism," *Judaism* 16 (Winter 1967): 97–108. For a fuller discussion, see also Smooha, pp. 86ff. Among the additional quotations offered by Smooha is Golda Meir's rhetorical inquiry in an address to the Zionist Federation of Great Britain in 1964, "Shall we be able to elevate these immigrants to a suitable level of civilization?"; and the following passage written by Abba Eban in 1969: "One of the great apprehensions which afflict us when we contemplate our cultural scene is the danger lest the predominance of immigrants of Oriental origin force Israel to equalize its cultural level with that of the neighboring Arab world . . . and [thereby] drag us into an unnatural Orientalism."

92. For accounts of Likud's emergence during and after the 1977 elections, see Efraim Torgovnik, "Likud 1977–1981: The Consolidation of Power," in Robert O. Freedman (ed.), *Israel in the Begin Era* (New York: Praeger, 1982); David Pollock, "Likud in Power: Divided We Stand," in ibid.; and Mark Tessler, "The Political Right in Israel: Its Origins, Growth and Prospects," *Journal of Palestine Studies* 15 (Winter 1986): 12–55.

93. From a speech to the Knesset on December 28, 1977; reprinted in Laqueur and Rubin, p. 607.

94. There is a growing literature on Gush Emunim. Excellent overviews are provided by David Newman (ed.), *The Impact of Gush Emunim: Politics and Settlement in the West Bank* (London: Croom Helm, 1985); and Ian Lustick, *For the Land and the Lord: Jewish Fundamentalism in Israel* (New York: Council on Foreign Relations, 1988). See also Uriel Tal, "Foundations of a Political Messianic Trend in Israel," *Jerusalem Quarterly* 35 (1985): 44–55; Ehud Sprinzak, "Fundamentalism, Terrorism and Democracy: The Case of the Gush Emunim Underground," Occasional Papers of the Smithsonian Institution's Wilson Center, no. 4, 1986; and Ian Lustick, "Israel's Dangerous Fundamentalists," *Foreign Policy* 68 (Fall 1987): 118–139.

95. For discussions of Israel's religious parties in general and the NRP in particular, see Mark Tessler, "Religion and Politics in the Jewish State of Israel," in Emile Sahliyeh (ed.), *Religious Resurgence and Politics in the Contemporary World* (Albany: State University of New York Press, 1990); Stewart Reiser, *The Politics of Leverage: The National Religious Party of Israel and Its Influence on Foreign Policy* (Cambridge, Massachusetts: Harvard University Center for Middle East Studies, 1984); Daniel J. Elazar, "Religious Parties and Politics in the Begin Era," in Freedman, *Israel*; Daniel J. Elazar and Janet Aviad, "Religion and Politics in Israel: The Interplay of Judaism and Zionism," in Michael Curtis (ed.), *Religion and Politics in the Middle East* (Boulder, Colorado: Westview Press, 1981); and Isaac, *Party and Politics*, pp. 59–90.

96. In an interview in *Ha'aretz* on December 17, 1974, Rabin had stated openly that Israel's goal was to divide Egypt from Syria and the rest of the Arabs. Both Israel's strategy and Syrian opposition to the second Sinai agreement are discussed by Quandt, *Decade*, pp. 261ff. See also M. Golan, *Secret Conversations*, pp. 229ff.

97. See Baker, pp. 154–156 and 165–168. See also John Waterbury, *The Egypt of Nasser and Sadat: The Political Economy of Two Regimes* (Princeton: Princeton University Press, 1983), pp. 229–230.

98. Baker, p. 168.

99. An authoritative account of U.S. efforts to foster an agreement between Israel and Egypt following the election of Jimmy Carter is provided by William B. Quandt, *Camp David: Peacemaking and Politics* (Washington: The Brookings Institution, 1986). See also Jimmy Carter, *Keeping Faith: Memoirs of a President* (New York: Bantam Books, 1982); Cyrus Vance, *Hard Choices: Critical Years in America's Foreign Policy* (New York: Simon and Schuster, 1983); and Steven L. Spiegel, *The Other Arab-Israeli Conflict: Making America's Middle East Policy, from Truman to Reagan* (Chicago: University of Chicago Press, 1985).

100. Quandt, *Camp David*, p. 139.

101. See Mark Tessler, "Moroccan-Israeli Relations and the Reasons for Moroccan Receptivity to Contact with Israel," *Jerusalem Journal of International Relations* 10 (Spring 1988): 76–108. For a fuller account, see Moshe Dayan, *Breakthrough: A Personal Account of the Egypt-Israel Peace Negotiations* (New York: Knopf, 1981).

102. Excerpts from Sadat's speech are reprinted in Laqueur and Rubin, pp. 592–601.

103. See Quandt, *Camp David*, and Carter, *Keeping Faith*. See also Ismail Fahmy, *Negotiating for Peace in the Middle East* (Baltimore: Johns Hopkins University Press, 1983); Ezer Weizman, *The Battle for Peace* (New York: Bantam Books, 1981); and Dayan, *Breakthrough*.

104. Sadat declared that he was also encouraged to continue the negotiations by the efforts of a newly formed peace movement in Israel. Known as Peace Now, the movement had held a huge rally in Tel Aviv on the eve of Camp David, urging the Israeli government to seize this historic opportunity for peace. Sadat stated that he thought about this demonstration on those occasions when he despaired of obtaining any concessions from Israel.

105. *The Camp David Summit* (Washington: U.S. Department of State, 1978).

106. Quandt, *Camp David*, pp. 247ff. Begin told Carter that he would spell out his position in a letter, but when it was eventually delivered this letter stated that the moratorium on new Israeli settlements in the West Bank and Gaza would last only for the three months envisioned for negotiating a peace treaty with Egypt.

107. For example, see Franji, p. 170. See also Walid W. Kazziha, *Palestine in the Arab Dilemma* (New York: Barnes and Noble, 1979), pp. 106–107.

108. Hussein's questions and the United States' answers are given in Quandt, *Camp David*, pp. 388–396.

109. The Palestinian inhabitants of the occupied territories also refused to participate in the autonomy talks, even though, in the case of Palestinians from the West Bank, it is not clear how they might have done so without being part of a Jordanian delegation. In any event, in the summer of 1979, the U.S. consul in East Jerusalem approached a number of West Bank mayors but received a firm refusal when he urged them to join in the peace process. Although it had produced no results, Israel subsequently protested this action, claiming that it went beyond the limits of acceptable consular activity.

110. "West Bank Palestinians: Reactions to Camp David," quoted in Laqueur and Rubin, p. 625.

111. Franji, p. 168.

112. Quoted in Laqueur and Rubin, p. 626.

113. Mishal, *The PLO*, pp. 130–131. The four settlements in areas from which Labor expressed a willingness to withdraw were all founded and settled illegally by religious fundamentalists. These communities are Qiryat Arba, adjacent to Hebron; Qedumim, near Nablus; Ofra, near Ramallah; and Ma'aleh Adumim, on the road between Jerusalem and Jericho. Work on the latter three, which one analyst describes as "renegade antposts" until they were formally sanctioned by the Begin government in July 1977, was begun in 1975, with a leading role played by Gush Emunim. See Geoffrey Aronson, *Israel, Palestinians and the Intifada: Creating Facts on the West Bank* (London: Kegan Paul International, 1990), p. 66.

114. Figures are given in Meron Benvenisti, *The West Bank Data Project, 1987 Report: Demographic, Economic, Legal, Social and Political Developments in the West Bank* (Jerusalem: The Jerusalem Post, 1987), p. 55. See also Halabi, p. 210.

115. Comprehensive information about the Begin government's settlement drive is provided by the West Bank Data Project, directed by Meron Benvenisti, former deputy mayor of Jerusalem. Benvenisti's study includes detailed information about the legal and administrative procedures employed to acquire Arab land for Israeli settlement. See Meron Benvenisti, *The West Bank Data Project: A Survey of Israel's Policies* (Washington: The American Enterprise Institute, 1984); and Benvenisti, *The West Bank Data Project, 1987 Report*. Other useful studies include William W. Harris, *Taking Root: Israeli Settlement in the West Bank, the Golan, and Gaza-Sinai, 1967–1980* (New York: John Wiley, 1980); David Ott, *Palestine in Perspective: Politics, Human Rights and the West Bank* (London: Quartet, 1980); Ian Lustick, "Israel and the West Bank after Elon Moreh: The Mechanisms of De Facto Annexation," *Middle East Journal* 35 (Autumn 1981): 557–577; Halabi, especially pp. 208–238; Rowley, especially pp. 57–94; and Don Peretz, *The West Bank: History, Politics, Society, and Economy* (Boulder, Colorado: Westview Press, 1986), especially pp. 59–78.

116. Peretz, *The West Bank*, p. 66.

117. See Franji, p. 178. Franji claims that there was not a single case of a Palestinian being allowed to sink a new well for agricultural purposes, and that only seven new wells for drinking water had been permitted. See also Peretz, *The West Bank*, pp. 65ff.

118. Peretz, *The West Bank*, p. 62. For a fuller discussion, see also Lustick, "Israel and the West Bank."

119. Matityahu Drobles, *The Master Plan for the Development of Settlement in Judea and Samaria* (Jerusalem: Jewish National Fund, 1978); and Matityahu Drobles, *Strategy, Policy and Plans for Settlement in Judea and Samaria* (Jerusalem: World Zionist Organization, 1980). For a summary and discussion, see Rowley, pp. 62–69; G. Aronson, pp. 95–97; and Elisha Efrat, *Geography and Politics in Israel since 1967* (London: Frank Cass, 1988), pp. 75ff.

120. This was roughly $100,000 U.S. per family at 1978 exchange rates. Projected budgetary allocations included 30 percent for permanent housing, 45 percent for means of production, and the remainder for infrastructure, temporary housing, water, and miscellaneous. For a detailed study of the actual cost of West Bank settlements, see Aaron Dehter, *How Expensive Are West Bank Settlements?* (Jerusalem: The Jerusalem Post, 1987).

121. See Benvenisti, *The West Bank Data Project: A Survey*, p. 6.

122. *Judea-Samaria and the Gaza District since 1967* (Jerusalem: Israel Information Center, 1986).

123. See, for example, Arye Bregman, *Economic Growth in the Administered Areas, 1968–1973* (Jerusalem: Bank of Israel Research Department, 1974); Abba Lerner and Haim Ben Shahar, *The Economics of Efficiency and Growth: Lessons from Israel and the West Bank* (Cambridge: Ballinger, 1975); Arye Bregman, "The Economic Development of the Administered Areas," in Daniel J. Elazar (ed.), *Self-rule/Shared Rule* (Ramat Gan: Turtledove Publish-

ing, 1979); and Shmuel Sandler with Hillel Frisch, "The Political Economy of the Administered Territories," in Daniel J. Elazar (ed.), *Judea, Samaria, and Gaza: Views of the Present and the Future* (Washington: American Enterprise Institute, 1982).

124. Sandler with Frisch, p. 136.

125. Bakir Abu Kishk and Izzat Ghurani, "Housing," in Emile A. Nakhleh (ed.), *A Palestinian Agenda for the West Bank and Gaza* (Washington: American Enterprise Institute, 1980), pp. 77ff.

126. Fathiyya Said Nasru, *West Bank Education in Government Schools, 1967–1977* (Birzeit: Birzeit University Publications, 1977), p. 22. See also Khalil Mahshi and Ramzi Rihan, "Education: Elementary and Secondary," in E. Nakhleh, *A Palestinian Agenda*, pp. 40ff.; and Emile A. Nakhleh, *The West Bank and Gaza: Toward the Making of a Palestinian State* (Washington: American Enterprise Institute, 1979), pp. 54–58.

127. One Palestinian scholar seeks to offer a more balanced view of the situation prior to 1967, noting that "while the prevailing view of stagnation and regional discrimination under those regimes is basically correct, it nevertheless disguises a substantial amount of differentiation and mobility that was taking place during the same period." See Salim Tamari, "The Palestinians in the West Bank and Gaza: The Sociology of Dependency," in Khalil Nakhleh and Elia Zureik (eds.), *The Sociology of the Palestinians* (New York: St. Martin's Press, 1980), p. 95.

128. Nasru, p. 58. Nasru also noted that the dropout rate had increased since 1967 and that it was higher in districts close to the Israeli border.

129. For studies by an American economist and a British economist, both of whom report improvements in the standard of living of West Bank and Gaza residents, see Vivian Bull, *The West Bank: Is It Viable?* (Lexington: D. C. Heath, 1975); and Brian Van Arkadie, *Benefits and Burdens: A Report on West Bank and Gaza Strip Economies since 1967* (New York: Carnegie Endowment for International Peace, 1977).

130. Both Israeli and Palestinian analysts draw on data provided by the *Administered Territories Statistics Quarterly*, published by the Central Bureau of Statistics in Israel. For discussions, see Heller, pp. 85–86; and Ghassan Harb, "Labor and Manpower," in E. Nakhleh, *A Palestinian Agenda*, pp. 94–95. See also Sarah Graham-Brown, "The Economic Consequences of Occupation," in Naseer H. Aruri (ed.), *Occupation: Israel over Palestine* (Belmont, Massachusetts: Association of Arab-American University Graduates, 1983), pp. 206ff.

131. Heller notes that a significant portion of this theoretically available capital is not invested because, among other things, of political uncertainty and a reluctance to use the Israeli banking system. See Heller, p. 91. See also Van Arkadie, pp. 106–110.

132. Tamari, "The Palestinians," p. 91.

133. Jamil Hilal, "Class Transformation in the West Bank and Gaza," *MERIP Reports* 53 (December 1976): 10.

134. Franji, p. 178.

135. Ibrahim Oweiss, "Economics of Israeli Settlements in the Occupied Arab Territories," in *Israeli Settlements in the Occupied Arab Territories* (Tunis: League of Arab States, 1987), p. 256. See also Jamil Hilal, *The West Bank: The Socio-Economic Structure, 1948–1974* (Beirut: Palestine Liberation Organization Research Center, 1975), p. 252. Hilal gives slightly different figures but reports the same general trend. He also notes a decline in the relative contribution to GNP of the agricultural sector.

136. Tamari, "The Palestinians," p. 96.

137. With multiplier effects taken into consideration, the contribution to GNP would be even higher. As a result of the multiplier effect, wages in Israel alone accounted for nearly half

of the growth in the territories' GNP between 1967 and 1974. See Van Arkadie, pp. 163–164. Van Arkadie also notes that this income financed the importation of goods produced in Israel, and that the trend was for the territories to become a "dormitory economy" (p. 74).

138. See Graham-Brown, p. 200. See also Lesch and Tessler, p. 250.

139. For a fuller discussion, see Lesch and Tessler, pp. 154ff.

Part V. The High Price of Stalemate

9. Violent Confrontations in the Early 1980s

1. Walid Khalidi, "Regiopolitics: Toward a U.S. Policy on the Palestine Problem," *Foreign Affairs* 59 (Summer 1981).

2. "Weekly Media Abstract," published by the Media Analysis Center, Prime Minister's Office Building, Jerusalem, December 29, 1980.

3. Ibid. The citations for the quoted passages are *al-Watan* (Kuwait), November 8, 1980, and the *Los Angeles Times*, October 26, 1980. The "Weekly Media Abstract" of April 21, 1981, stated that the PLO "is aware of the powerful wishful thinking element of Europe where an assessment of the PLO's substance is concerned," and "feeds this element by planting disinformation which is avidly gobbled up in Europe."

4. See Tessler, "Moroccan-Israeli Relations."

5. Israeli arguments that the Fahd Plan does not constitute a deviation from traditional Saudi (and Arab) opposition to the existence of a Jewish state in the Middle East are summarized in "Weekly Media Abstract," November 9, 1981. Although little interest in the Saudi plan was shown by either the Likud government or the Labor opposition, there were some dissenting voices in Israel. For example, Amos Elon, the Israeli writer, stated in an article in *Ha'aretz*, "There is something shocking, frightening, if not downright despair-producing in the vulgar, and certainly not tactically useful Israeli response to the eight-point plan of Saudi Crown Prince Fahd. . . . Are we so accustomed to war that we are simply afraid of peace? Are we so taken aback, so angered and unsure of ourselves that we do not even bother to examine whether the Saudi plan . . . is a first step, an opening to a process of negotiation?" See *Ha'aretz*, November 13, 1981. Similarly, Israeli journalist Yoel Marcus called Jerusalem's out-of-hand dismissal of the Fahd Plan "a grave mistake" and complained that if the PLO were suddenly to offer to negotiate with Israel, "the government would undoubtedly declare a day of national mourning." See *Yediot Aharonot*, November 6, 1981. For additional discussion, see Chomsky, pp. 75–76.

6. Although it was circulated and signed, the Israeli military censor would not permit the petition to be published.

7. For a fuller discussion of the political left in Israel at this time, see Lesch and Tessler, pp. 164–173.

8. For a discussion, see Isaac, *Party and Politics*, p. 80. Oz VeShalom also argued that *pikuach nefesh* was the "controlling" principle, meaning that saving lives took precedence over all other religious commandments, and that return of the occupied territories was not only permitted but thus required, if this would indeed lead to the saving of Jewish and other lives.

9. Quoted in Lesch and Tessler, p. 153. See also Charles S. Liebman and Eliezer Don-Yehiya, *Religion and Politics in Israel* (Bloomington: Indiana University Press, 1984), p. 94. Raising questions about the majoritarian character of Rabbi Shlomo's views, Liebman and Don-Yehiya state that many Israeli rabbis within the religious Zionist camp do not accept a

messianic theology, but "they have generally been silent on this point since the Six-Day War." Further complicating the situation, the argument that Jewish law prohibits surrender of the West Bank and Gaza is rejected by the ultraorthodox Agudat Yisrael party. Though at this time a member of the Begin government's parliamentary coalition, Aguda continued to reject the messianism of Gush Emunim and the NRP and to insist that its attitude toward the occupied territories was not determined by spiritual or theological considerations.

10. Quoted in Lesch and Tessler, p. 151.

11. Arian, *Politics in Israel*, p. 43.

12. H. M. Sachar, *A History, II*, p. 126.

13. Ibid., p. 128. See also Naomi Chazan, "Domestic Developments in Israel," in William B. Quandt (ed.), *The Middle East: Ten Years after Camp David* (Washington: The Brookings Institution, 1988). Chazan points out that Begin approved the attack on the Iraqi reactor shortly after a meeting with Anwar Sadat of Egypt, "thus suggesting, for domestic consumption, that the peace with Egypt had not weakened Israel's military strength or undermined its resolve" (p. 169).

14. Peri, p. 261. For a fuller account of the 1981 election, see Dan Caspi, Abraham Diskin, and Emanuel Gutmann (eds.), *The Roots of Begin's Success: The 1981 Israeli Elections* (London: Croom Helm, 1984); and see especially Shlomo Aronson and Nathan Yanai, "Critical Aspects of the Elections and Their Implications," in ibid.

15. These and other provisions of the coalition agreement are reprinted in Laqueur and Rubin, pp. 622–623. As noted, much of the coalition agreement also dealt with religious issues, with the new government committing itself to work for the extension of orthodox Jewish law in a number of areas.

16. Arian, *Politics in Israel*, p. 201. For additional information about Sharon's emergence as the dominant figure in the cabinet, see H. M. Sachar, *A History, II*, p. 169.

17. H. M. Sachar, *A History, II*, p. 154.

18. Ibid., p. 155.

19. Benvenisti, *West Bank Data Project, 1987*, p. 55.

20. Quoted in H. M. Sachar, *A History, II*, p. 156.

21. For details, see Jonathan Kuttab and Raja Shehadeh, *Civilian Administration in the Occupied West Bank* (Ramallah: Law in the Service of Man, 1982).

22. Menachem Milson, "How to Make Peace with the Palestinians," *Commentary* (May 1981). See also Menachem Milson, "The Palestinians in the Peace Process," *Forum* 42/43 (1981).

23. Paid ad in *Ha'aretz*, November 27, 1981.

24. *Jerusalem Post*, November 26, 1981.

25. For details, see Benny Morris, "IDF Source Tells How— and Why—Books Are Banned," *Jerusalem Post*, April 6, 1982.

26. From an interview with a foreign correspondent; quoted in Ann Mosely Lesch, "Israeli Occupation Policies: Reflections on the West Bank and Gaza Strip," paper presented at the 1982 annual meeting of the Middle East Studies Association.

27. For example, Ariel Sharon stated in March 1982, "The PLO is now in a critical situation on the West Bank because of the opposition it encounters from the village leagues. This is the most positive development in the areas since 1967." Quoted in the *Jerusalem Post*, March 22, 1982.

28. *Davar*, November 27, 1982. See also Lesch, "Israeli Occupation Policies," p. 25. Another indication of the artificial nature of the league based in Beit Sahour is provided by the Israeli writer Amos Elon, who visited its office in March 1982 and found it empty except for several guards paid by the Israelis. See *Ha'aretz*, March 19, 1982.

29. Zvi Barel, in *Ha'aretz*, May 5, 1982.

30. For example, in mid-April 1982, residents of Bethlehem and nearby Beit Sahour claimed that five members of the local village league, armed with Uzi submachine guns, beat up a guard and the dean of students of Bethlehem University and then, continuing their rampage, attacked a religious club and a coffee house in Beit Sahour. Local witnesses also reported that the group used a Landrover of the type issued to the leagues for their local patrols. For details, see the *Jerusalem Post*, April 19, 1982.

31. Lesch and Tessler, p. 265.

32. Some analysts suggest that King Hussein turned against the Israeli-sponsored leagues because he feared they might undermine his own influence in the West Bank, as well as that of the PLO. See David Richardson, "Leagues out of Their Depth," *Jerusalem Post Magazine*, March 19, 1982. Following Jordan's condemnation of the leagues, Mustafa Doudin, leader of the Dura village league and a former Jordanian cabinet minister, issued a public statement in which he declared, "King Hussein is my king, I swore the oath of loyalty to him."

33. *Ha'aretz*, March 12, 1984.

34. H. M. Sachar, *A History, II*, p. 160. Sachar, who offers a useful summary of Israel's village league policy, places heavy responsibility for the failure of this policy on opposition from Jordan. He states, "Without Hashemite approval, overt or tacit, no moderate alternative to the PLO appeared to be viable in the territories."

35. For a detailed discussion, see Waterbury, especially pp. 144–157. Waterbury notes that foreign capital tended to cluster in three areas that had little to do with direct production: investment companies, banks, and tourism.

36. *Al-Ahram al-Iqtisadi*, July 21, 1980; quoted in Waterbury, p. 146.

37. For details, see Waterbury, p. 363. Waterbury reports that there was some speculation in Egypt at this time that Sadat's crackdown may have resulted in part from Begin's urging that the Egyptian president disarm the most vocal critics of Camp David. Waterbury also suggests that Sadat's actions against Egyptian Copts may have been designed, at least partially, to give the appearance of evenhandedness and to counter charges that he was acting against Islam.

38. Members of Takfir wal-Higra, translated as Repentance and Holy Flight, had kidnapped a former Egyptian cabinet minister in July 1977 and then killed this individual when the government refused their demand that detained Muslim activists be released. Most of the group's top leaders and several hundred of its followers were subsequently arrested and remained in prison at the time of Sadat's assassination. For details about Takfir wal-Higra, see Saad Eddin Ibrahim, "Islamic Militancy as a Social Movement: The Case of Two Groups in Egypt," in Ali E. Hillal Dessouki (ed.), *Islamic Resurgence in the Arab World* (New York: Praeger Publishers, 1982). For a fuller account of the views held by those who killed the Egyptian president, see Johannes J. G. Jansen, *The Neglected Duty: The Creed of Sadat's Assassins and Islamic Resurgence in the Middle East* (New York: Macmillan, 1986). Jansen observes that the movement did not attach priority to the liberation of Jerusalem and the Holy Land. Its spokesmen rather declared that it is "more important to fight an enemy who is near than an enemy who is far away," and therefore "we must concentrate on the real problem of Islam, the establishment of God's law, beginning in our own country" (p. 18). Jansen also discusses other Islamic attitudes toward Israel and points out that Muslim scholars at Cairo's al-Azhar Islamic University declared in May 1979 that the conclusion of a peace treaty with Israel is not contrary to Islamic law (p. 44).

39. Mark N. Cooper, *The Transformation of Egypt* (Baltimore: The Johns Hopkins University Press, 1982), p. 257. See also J. J. G. Jansen, p. 1. Jansen quotes an Egyptian religious official who states, "Their real aim was not only to assassinate [Sadat] . . . wasn't the real aim of the whole operation that they wanted to seize power in Egypt?"

40. Excerpts from the inaugural address are reprinted in Laqueur and Rubin, pp. 632–633. Mubarak also stated in his address that Egypt would "spare no effort . . . [to] put the Palestinian people along the beginning of the correct course for achieving their legitimate rights."

41. H. M. Sachar, *A History, II*, p. 150. Almost half of the Members of Knesset from Labor abstained, and many who did vote against the Golan annexation bill were drawn from the Alignment's Mapam wing. Begin was able to secure from the Knesset Foreign Affairs and Defense Committee a waiver of the mandatory waiting period between the first and second readings, thus enabling the bill to pass the Knesset in a single day.

42. For additional discussion, see Lesch and Tessler, p. 161.

43. Ibid., p. 160.

44. H. M. Sachar, *A History, II*.

45. Ibid.

46. *Ha'aretz*, March 15, 1982.

47. It was later discovered that nearly 500 grenades had been smuggled into Yamit by Stop the Withdrawal militants.

48. Quoted in Lesch and Tessler, pp. 24–25.

49. *Al-Fajr Jerusalem*, April 23–29, 1982. *Al-Fajr Jerusalem*, which describes itself as a "Palestinian Weekly," is an English-language newspaper published in East Jerusalem. It is a subsidiary of *al-Fajr*, an Arabic-language daily published in East Jerusalem.

50. Ibid., April 30–May 6, 1982.

51. See the *Jerusalem Post*, April 15, 1982; April 18, 1982; April 19, 1982; April 30, 1982; May 5, 1982.

52. "Road to Nowhere," editorial in the *Jerusalem Post*, May 12, 1982.

53. *The Karp Report: An Israeli Government Inquiry into Settler Violence against Palestinians on the West Bank*. An English-language version of the report, made public in February 1984, has been published by the Institute for Palestine Studies of Washington, D.C.

54. See also H. M. Sachar, *A History, II*, p. 163.

55. *Jerusalem Post*, February 9, 1984. In 1982, when the report was shelved and the government declined to act on its findings, Karp resigned from her post as head of the commission of inquiry.

56. *The Karp Report*, p. 42.

57. Ibid., p. 43.

58. Yosef Goell, "Minister beyond the Limits," *Jerusalem Post*, April 19, 1982. Goell stated that his information came from informants who had recently returned from reserve duty in the West Bank. He added that despite the relaxation of proper standards, the overwhelming majority of officers and men serving in the territories "have certainly not sought to take advantage of any loosening of control from the top."

59. Quoted in the *Jerusalem Post*, March 28, 1982.

60. *Time* magazine, May 17, 1982. The poll was conducted between April 4 and 15. Interestingly, although it reported overwhelming support for the PLO, only half of the respondents thought that the independent Palestinian state they sought should be headed by Yasir Arafat.

61. For details, see *Al-Hamishmar*, April 30, 1982.

62. *Ha'aretz*, March 22, 1982.

63. Sylvie Keshet in *Yediot Aharonot*, May 4, 1982.

64. Quoted in M. Thomas Davis, *40 Km into Lebanon: Israel's 1982 Invasion* (Washington, D.C.: National Defense University Press, 1987), p. 68.

65. Most of the casualties were civilians, including both residents of the high-rise build-

830 | Notes for Pages 569–576

ings containing PLO offices and men and women in the adjacent streets. The deaths of so many innocent civilians provoked widespread international condemnation and led the United States to delay delivery of a scheduled shipment of F-16 fighter planes. See Schiff and Ya'ari, *Israel's Lebanon War*, p. 100.

66. H. M. Sachar, *A History, II*, p. 166.

67. Schiff and Ya'ari, *Isreal's Lebanon War*, p. 97.

68. Davis, p. 76. Lebanese police sources give higher figures, reporting 210 killed and 250 wounded. See Franklin Lamb (ed.), *Reason Not the Need: Eyewitness Chronicles of Israel's War in Lebanon* (Nottingham, England: Spokesman for the Bertrand Russell Peace Foundation, 1984), p. 2.

69. Portions of the speech are reprinted in Laqueur and Rubin, pp. 652–656.

70. Quoted in Schiff and Ya'ari, *Israel's Lebanon War*, p. 66.

71. See ibid., p. 76. Schiff and Ya'ari, leading Israeli journalists who shared Israel's 1982 Journalist of the Year Award for their coverage of the war in Lebanon, provide a detailed account of the Begin government's efforts to obtain American approval for an invasion of Lebanon. See also Ze'ev Schiff, "The Green Light," *Foreign Policy* 50 (Spring 1983): 73–85. Haig's view is presented in his book *Caveat: Realism, Reagan and Foreign Policy* (New York: Macmillan, 1984).

72. Davis, p. 84. For additional discussion, see Michael C. Hudson, "The United States' Involvement in Lebanon," in Halim Barakat (ed.), *Toward a Viable Lebanon* (London: Croom Helm, 1988), pp. 213–215.

73. An excellent account of the Israeli government's pursuit of a *casus belli*, and of PLO attempts to avoid giving Israel an excuse to invade Lebanon, is provided by Schiff and Ya'ari, *Israel's Lebanon War*, pp. 55, 91–107.

74. Ibid., p. 95.

75. Ibid., p. 92. See also pp. 101–102.

76. Ibid., p. 98. See also H. M. Sachar, *A History, II*, p. 175.

77. Schiff and Ya'ari, *Israel's Lebanon War*, p. 105. Two ministers from the Liberal Party wing abstained. All others supported the decision to launch Operation Peace for Galilee.

78. Richard Gabriel, *Operation Peace for Galilee: The Israeli-PLO War in Lebanon* (New York: Hill and Wang, 1984), p. 67. See also Schiff and Ya'ari, *Israel's Lebanon War*, pp. 114–115.

79. Quoted in Efraim Inbar, "The 'No Choice War' Debate in Israel," *Journal of Strategic Studies* 12 (March 1989): 24.

80. See R. Khalidi, *Under Siege*, pp. 51ff. See also Schiff and Ya'ari, *Israel's Lebanon War*, pp. 137ff.

81. Amnon Kapeliouk, *Al-Hamishmar*, July 16, 1982; quoted in Lamb, p. 116. Schiff and Ya'ari also give a powerful account of the destruction at Ain al-Hilweh, adding, "Israeli soldiers watching the devastation seemed to become inured to the din and the smoke and the smell of death. Sensibilities became dulled; the destruction engendered a chilling tedium." Some of the destruction, here and elsewhere, was the result of the use of cluster bombs, which the Israelis dropped in violation of the agreement under which these munitions had been purchased from the United States. See Davis, p. 84.

82. The report, from June 23, 1982, is cited in Michael Jansen, *The Battle of Beirut: Why Israel Invaded Lebanon* (London: Zed Press, 1982), p. 19. Illustrating the great variation of available reports, another source gives Red Cross figures estimating that 90 percent of all three camps were destroyed. See Lamb, p. 13.

83. Christopher Walker, *The Times*, July 9, 1982; quoted in M. Jansen, p. 24. Jansen summarizes many Israeli, Palestinian, Lebanese, and international sources and attempts to sort out contradictory reports concerning casualty figures.

84. M. Jansen, pp. 21, 24.

85. See R. Khalidi, *Under Siege*, pp. 58–60. See also Yezid Sayigh, "Palestinian Military Performance in the 1982 War," *Journal of Palestine Studies* 12 (Summer 1983): 3–24. A favorable Israeli assessment of the PLO's performance in direct clashes with the IDF is offered by Itamar Rabinovich, *The War for Lebanon, 1970–1983* (Ithaca: Cornell University Press, 1984), p. 151.

86. See R. Gabriel, pp. 116–117.

87. Ibid., pp. 85–87. Relying on Israeli sources, Gabriel reports that the IDF took special care in the areas of Tyre and Sidon, where "it reduced the speed with which the Israelis were able to overcome enemy opposition." Gabriel also provides an extended discussion of IDF behavior throughout the course of the war, concluding, "It is clear from examining the ethical conduct of the Israeli forces on the battlefield toward civilians and the PLO that the IDF has been more restrained than any modern army that comes to mind." See ibid., p. 176. These claims, which were regularly advanced by Israeli spokesmen during the summer of 1982, are rejected by Palestinian sources, as well as some others. Some acknowledge that Israeli soldiers were indeed instructed not to harm civilians but add that these instructions had little meaning in the face of orders to advance, firing, into refugee camps and other heavily populated areas. For further discussion, see M. Jansen, pp. 21–22.

88. Abraham Rabinovich, *Jerusalem Post*, June 18, 1982; quoted in M. Jansen, p. 15.

89. Shemtov made this statement to the Knesset on June 29, 1982; quoted in Inbar, p. 26.

90. Schiff and Ya'ari report not only that Sharon did this deliberately but also that most members of the cabinet may not have understood the implications of their decision so far as conflict with the Syrians was concerned. *Israel's Lebanon War*, p. 156.

91. Quoted in Shai Feldman and Heda Rechnitz-Kijner, "Deception, Consensus and War: Israel in Lebanon," Occasional Papers of the Jaffee Center for Strategic Studies of Tel Aviv University, no. 27, October 1984, p. 16.

92. Ibid.

93. Sharon told a press conference on June 20, "Israel hopes Lebanon will become the second Arab state to sign a peace treaty with Israel." He repeated this to the Knesset Foreign Affairs and Defense Committee several days later, and on June 29 Begin told the Knesset that Israel was seeking to achieve "the expulsion of the terrorists and the establishment of a Lebanese government which, we hope, will sign a peace treaty with Israel." The implications of such a situation, he elaborated in a July speech, would be "a continuum of peace between Israel, Egypt and Lebanon, and even joint tourist packages." See Feldman and Rechnitz-Kijner, p. 18.

94. Some Shiite Muslims expressed these views to Israeli journalists, and more generally, as noted earlier, neither the PLO's Muslim nor its Druze allies made any serious attempt to assist the Palestinians in their confrontation with the IDF. The deterioration of PLO relations with Lebanese Sunnis, Shia, and Druze is discussed in R. Khalidi, *Under Siege*, pp. 18–19 and 115.

95. Schiff and Ya'ari, *Israel's Lebanon War*, pp. 41–42.

96. Quoted in Feldman and Rechnitz-Kijner, p. 19.

97. Ze'ev Schiff, *Ha'aretz*, April 7, 1982; quoted in Feldman and Rechnitz-Kijner, p. 21. The authors give equal credit to Alex Fishman, military correspondent of *Al-Hamishmar*, who presented the essence of Sharon's plan and debated it in detail at least four months before the invasion of Lebanon.

98. Schiff and Ya'ari, *Israel's Lebanon War*, pp. 60–61, present a good account of the evidence for and against this proposition. They conclude it is most likely that "Begin had been assured, or had convinced himself, that the upcoming operation was not really a war at all but a sharply defined and contained ground operation."

99. Feldman and Rechnitz-Kijner, p. 18.

100. For further discussion, see H. M. Sachar, A History, II, p. 191.

101. Feldman and Rechnitz-Kijner, p. 19.

102. Ibid.

103. Quoted in the New York Times, August 29, 1982, p. E19. See also Lesch and Tessler, p. 197.

104. R. Khalidi, Under Siege, p. 46.

105. Amos Perlmutter, "Begin's Rhetoric and Sharon's Tactics," Foreign Affairs 61 (Fall 1982): 68.

106. Yoel Marcus, "The War Is Inevitable," Ha'aretz, March 26, 1982; quoted in Chomsky, p. 199.

107. A particularly passionate denunciation of the war and its architects, written while the war was still in progress, is offered by the Israeli journalist Jacobo Timerman. See Jacobo Timerman, The Longest War (New York: Knopf, 1982). According to Timerman, "During previous wars the questions were postponed. The wars were short. The questions did not challenge the permanent values of the state. . . . But Sharon's War is long, confused, and now for the first time questions are unsheathed during the fighting. For the first time they pose the possibility that the moral and institutional foundations of the state have been affected" (p. 22). For additional discussion and a more analytical treatment, see Myron J. Aronoff, Israeli Visions and Divisions: Cultural Change and Political Conflict (New Brunswick, New Jersey: Transaction Publishers, 1989), pp. 32ff. Aronoff emphasizes the impact of the war on preexisting divisions in Israeli society, stating that "the unprecedented lack of consensual support for this war dramatically expressed the polarized ideological perceptions of reality of many Israelis."

108. Quoted in Lesch and Tessler, p. 38. See also Schiff and Ya'ari, Israel's Lebanon War, pp. 204–205. The authors report that Deputy Chief of Staff Moshe Levi "was aghast at the sullen mood among the men." Having just lost ten men in battles along the Beirut-Damascus highway, a company commander asked Levy, "What does the Beirut-Damascus highway have to do with peace in the Galilee anyway?" He also demanded to know, "Why do we find ourselves on the attack and hear IDF spokesmen announce that it was the Syrians who opened fire?" Additional discussion is provided in Timerman, pp. 68–69.

109. Quoted in Ehud Ya'ari, "Israel's Dilemma in Lebanon," Middle East Insight 3 (April–May 1984): 18–23. A particularly moving lament of the senseless loss of life brought on by the unnecessary war is expressed in a letter to the Jerusalem Post by Ya'acov Guterman, quoted in Timerman, pp. 100–101. Guterman, whose only son died in the battle for Beaufort Castle, wrote, "I remained with a prayer in my heart that reasonable and concerned people in Israel and abroad would prevent them from this madness, but my desire and the desire of the sons was not fulfilled. . . . With unabashed effrontery, Menachem Begin, Ariel Sharon, Rafael Eitan and the ministers who voted for the war in Lebanon sloganized 'Peace for Galilee' when there had been no shots in Galilee for over a year. . . . "

110. Schiff and Ya'ari, Israel's Lebanon War, p. 301.

111. Ibid., p. 218. The authors report that Israel's political establishment for a time seemed to treat this aspect of the war as a "spectator sport," before it realized that "such actions were offensive to the sensibilities of others."

112. Ibid., p. 211.

113. R. Khalidi, Under Siege, p. 65.

114. Schiff and Ya'ari, Israel's Lebanon War, p. 207.

115. R. Khalidi, Under Siege, pp. 116–120, 127–129.

116. Ibid., p. 163. Khalidi reports that even the PLO minority opposed to withdrawal accepted the inevitable when, in the face of increasingly intense Israeli attacks, they issued a

last appeal to the president of Syria and this appeal went unanswered. The Palestinians, who had told Assad they would hold out in Beirut if he instructed them to do so, were informed by Syrian officials that Assad would not respond. Khalidi states that at this point, on August 10, the decision to withdraw from Beirut became unanimous. Ibid., p. 165.

117. R. Gabriel, pp. 156–159. See also Davis, p. 100. Even higher casualty figures are given by Schiff and Ya'ari, who similarly describe Sharon's orders as "contrary to any scrutable logic." The Israeli journalists also note, however, that Sharon was probably motivated by the fact that an agreement on the Habib plan was in sight, since, over the defense minister's objections, the Israeli cabinet had the day before approved the plan in principle, subject only to "suggestions for a number of amendments." *Israel's Lebanon War*, p. 225.

118. Quoted in H. M. Sachar, *A History, II*, p. 190.

119. For details, see Schiff and Ya'ari, *Israel's Lebanon War*, pp. 11–30.

120. The Lebanese army was in a state of advanced disorganization by September 1982. Some Maronite leaders advocated that it be reconstituted as a thoroughly Christian force. Bashir Gemayel, choosing a slightly less radical course, was planning to merge the Phalange militia and the regular Lebanese army into a single force that would be loyal to him alone. See ibid., pp. 245–246.

121. Although Haddad at first denied that his forces were present at Sabra and Shatilla, he later told an Israeli interviewer that it was possible that some of his men did join the Phalange. Evidence placing some of his men in the camps is summarized by Lamb, pp. 104, 111. For a different conclusion, see *The Beirut Massacre: The Complete Kahan Commission Report*, with an introduction by Abba Eban (New York: Karz-Cohl, 1983), pp. 51–52.

122. Lamb, p. 104.

123. See *The Beirut Massacre*, p. 22.

124. See Lamb, pp. 537–631, for firsthand accounts, many by foreign doctors and nurses who were working in Beirut. Interviews with a number of these same individuals, as well as several others, can also be found in *Witness of War Crimes in Lebanon: Testimony Given to the Nordic Commission, Oslo, October 1982* (London: Ithaca Press, 1983), pp. 114–134. Additional testimony, based on interviews with Palestinians and foreign medical personnel who were inside the camps during the massacre, is provided in Nassib with Tisdall, pp. 138ff.

125. *The Beirut Massacre*, p. 45. See also M. Jansen, p. 106. Jansen suggests that perhaps 1,000 people were slaughtered in Sabra and Shatilla and that almost 1,000 more, mostly women and children, were put on trucks, driven away, and very possibly murdered.

126. *The Beirut Massacre*.

127. Lamb, p. 111.

128. Schiff and Ya'ari, *Israel's Lebanon War*, p. 264.

129. Testimony quoted in Lamb, p. 541.

130. Testimony quoted in ibid., pp. 548–549.

131. *The Beirut Massacre*, p. 54.

132. Ibid., p. 58.

133. Ibid., p. 63.

134. Ibid., p. 60.

135. Ibid., p. 63.

136. *Israel in Lebanon: The Report of the International Commission to Enquire into Reported Violations of International Law by Israel during Its Invasion of Lebanon* (London: Ithaca Press, 1983), p. 169. The discussion pertains to Geneva Convention IV, particularly articles 29, 32, and 147.

137. Ibid., p. 181. As an illustration of such dehumanization, the commission's report contains a quotation by the Israeli writer A. B. Yehoshua: "When one speaks about extermi-

nation and purification, when Palestinians are called two-legged animals [by Begin], there is no wonder that an [Israeli] soldier permits that such horrors will be committed near him." Yehoshua's assessment is reprinted from *Ha'olam Hazeh*, September 22, 1982.

138. Lamb, p. 100.

139. Schiff and Ya'ari, *Israel's Lebanon War*, p. 257, report that while the number of armed Palestinians in the camps after September 1 is not known with precision, observers on the scene put the number at a few dozen Palestinian fighters and up to 200 armed men working out of defensive bunkers. See also R. Khalidi, *Under Siege*, p. 179, who states that most of these individuals were part-time members of the self-defense militias of the camps, and that the Israelis would never have introduced only a small contingent of Phalange forces had they not known very well that the Palestinians' numbers and power were extremely limited.

140. *The Beirut Massacre*, p. 54.

141. Schiff and Ya'ari, *Israel's Lebanon War*, p. 258.

142. Ibid., p. 259.

143. See Schiff and Ya'ari for a discussion of Sharon's meetings with Phalange leaders on September 15, the day before the massacre began. Ibid., pp. 255–256. While the Israeli defense minister stressed the need to destroy whatever was left of the PLO's political and military infrastructure in West Beirut, including the camps, the authors report that there is no evidence he encouraged the Phalange to use violence against Palestinian civilians.

144. Ibid., p. 258.

145. Ibid., p. 250.

146. Ibid., p. 263. Levy's remarks, made in a cabinet meeting, drew no response from other ministers present. Levy himself expressed concern at least partly because of the criticism which would be directed against Israel, stating, "No one is going to believe that we went in there to maintain order, and we'll bear the blame. . . . "

147. Ibid., pp. 271–272. A useful summary of these events is also provided by Lamb, pp. 105–112.

148. Schiff and Ya'ari, *Israel's Lebanon War*, pp. 274–275.

149. For a fuller discussion of Israeli condemnations of the Begin government's actions in Lebanon following the massacre at Sabra and Shatilla and publication of the Kahan Commission report, see Aronoff, *Israeli Visions*, pp. 34ff. Aronoff notes that leftist Knesset members often called the government fascist and that leaders of the Labor Alignment sometimes used terms such as "neo-fascist" or "Peronist" when describing the Begin government.

150. Schiff and Ya'ari, *Israel's Lebanon War*, p. 285.

151. Yitzhak Rabin, "In the Aftermath of the War in Lebanon: Israel's Objectives," in Joseph Alpher (ed.), *Israel's Lebanon Policy: Where To?* (Tel Aviv: Jaffee Center for Strategic Studies, 1984), p. 40.

152. These and other public opinion poll data are summarized in Feldman and Rechnitz-Kijner, pp. 61–63.

153. William P. Bundy, "A Portentous Year," *Foreign Affairs* 62, no. 3 (Fall 1982): 509.

10. Futile Diplomacy in the Mid-1980s

1. The text of Ronald Reagan's September 1, 1982, address to the American people appears in the *New York Times*, September 2, 1982. It is reprinted in Laqueur and Rubin, pp. 656–663; and it may also be found, along with accompanying talking points sent by Reagan to the Israeli prime minister and to Arab governments, in Quandt, *The Middle East*, pp. 461–470.

2. For additional discussion, see William Quandt, "U.S. Policy toward the Arab-Israeli Conflict," in Quandt, *The Middle East*, p. 365. Quandt, a highly respected analyst of U.S. policy toward the Middle East, writes that although Reagan's peace initiative was addressed to the larger Arab-Israeli conflict, and to the Palestinian problem in particular, it was "predicated on the belief that the problems of Lebanon were on their way to a solution."

3. "Middle East Peace Initiative," Secretary Shultz's Statement before the Senate Foreign Relations Committee on September 10, 1982. For additional information, see Dan Tschirgi, *The American Search for Mideast Peace* (New York: Praeger, 1989), p. 178.

4. Most of these points were also made in Shultz's congressional testimony on September 10. For additional discussion, see Lesch and Tessler, pp. 199–200. See also Alan J. Kreczko, "Support Reagan's Initiative," *Foreign Policy* (Winter 1982/1983): 393.

5. From a September 2 communiqué by the Israeli government, which was reprinted in the *New York Times*, September 3, 1982.

6. Ibid.

7. For a fuller discussion and for citations from the Israeli press reporting on these developments, see Chomsky, pp. 349–355. See also Lesch and Tessler, pp. 194ff.; Tschirgi, p. 180; and Khouri, pp. 438–439.

8. Ben Meir's comments, broadcast by Israeli radio on September 2, are quoted in Emile Sahliyeh, *The PLO after the War in Lebanon* (Boulder, Colorado: Westview Press, 1986), p. 77. Going even farther, Chaim Druckman, at the time a Member of Knesset from the National Religious Party, a partner in Begin's coalition, stated that Israel should annex the West Bank in order "to prove by action that it rejects the Reagan plan." Ibid.

9. For example, see William Safire's comment in the *New York Times*, September 13, 1982.

10. Quoted in Lesch and Tessler, p. 201. Similarly, Victor Shemtov, leader of the dovish Mapam wing of the Alignment, stated that the Reagan Plan had "positive elements" and thus should be examined seriously. Quoted in Sahliyeh, *The PLO after the War*, p. 77. Such sentiments were also widely expressed in the Israeli press. For example, the independent daily *Ha'aretz* editorialized on September 6 that the government was making a big mistake by refusing to consider the U.S. initiative.

11. For example, see Chomsky, pp. 112 and 345. Chomsky cites statements by Yitzhak Rabin and by Uzi Shimoni, head of the public information branch of the Labor Alignment.

12. Samuel Lewis, "The United States and Israel: Constancy and Change," in Quandt, *The Middle East*, p. 246.

13. Ibid., p. 247. For additional discussion, see Joseph Sisco, "Middle East: Progress or Lost Opportunity," *Foreign Affairs* 61 (1983): 631–633. The specificity of the Reagan Plan with respect to final status issues was aimed at Jordan in particular. King Hussein had been deeply disappointed that Henry Kissinger's shuttle diplomacy in the mid-1970s had produced a partial Israeli withdrawal from Sinai and the Golan Heights but had not addressed Israel's control of the West Bank. According to Sisco, former U.S. under secretary of state for Near East and South Asian affairs, "Hussein has always wanted to know 'what light is at the end of the tunnel,' and the Reagan proposals provide him for the first time with the U.S. preferences" (p. 632).

14. Quoted in Lesch and Tessler, p. 210.

15. Quoted in Sahliyeh, *The PLO after the War*, p. 93; and Tschirgi, p. 181.

16. Kemal Kirisci, *The PLO and World Politics: A Study of the Mobilization of Support for the Palestinian Cause* (London: Frances Pinter, 1986), p. 119.

17. The Final Statement of the 1982 Fez summit is reprinted in Laqueur and Rubin, pp. 663–665. It may also be found in Quandt, *The Middle East*, pp. 471–472.

18. For a discussion of Syria's growing isolation in the Arab world and its response to the hostile attitude of the Reagan administration, see Moshe Ma'oz, *Asad: The Sphinx of Damascus* (New York: Weidenfeld and Nicolson, 1988), pp. 168–169. For a critical analysis of the U.S. failure to consider Syrian interests during this period, see George W. Ball, *Error and Betrayal in Lebanon: An Analysis of Israel's Invasion of Lebanon and Its Implications for U.S.-Israeli Relations* (Washington: Foundation for Middle East Peace, 1984), pp. 66–67. Ball contrasts the diplomacy of Secretary of State George Shultz and the Reagan administration with that of Henry Kissinger in 1974–75, Kissinger having been "sharply aware of the need to gauge what President Asad needed." For additional background about Syria's role in Lebanon, see A. Dawisha.

19. Most of the Palestinian rejectionist factions were either Syrian or Libyan clients and, according to Sahliyeh, they "maintained special relationships with their respective Arab custodians and adhered strictly to the policies dictated by those countries." As a result, familiar differences between the PLO's rejectionist minority and its moderate mainstream took on additional significance following the war in Lebanon, since this division could more easily be exploited by Syria, Libya, or any other Arab state seeking to manipulate the Palestinian question for its own purposes. For additional discussion, see Sahliyeh, *The PLO after the War*, p. 89.

20. See ibid., pp. 101ff., for an excellent summary of the views of the Palestinian rejectionist camp, including the political and ideological differences among its constituent groups. For further discussion and background, see Aaron David Miller, *The PLO: The Politics of Survival* (New York: Praeger, 1983); John W. Amos, *Palestinian Resistance: Organization of a National Movement* (New York: Pergamon, 1980), pp. 58–59 and 81–84; and Muhammad Y. Muslih, "Moderates and Rejectionists within the Palestine Liberation Organization," *Middle East Journal* 20 (Spring 1976): 127–140.

21. Sahliyeh, *The PLO after the War*, pp. 91–92.

22. Ibid., p. 101.

23. Khalil Shikaki, "The Intifada and the Transformation of Palestinian Politics," Universities Field Staff International Reports, no. 18, 1989–1990, p. 3.

24. Ibid. Furthermore, a split within Fatah in the summer of 1983 removed a hard-line minority that in the past had challenged Arafat's policies from inside his own faction. According to Shikaki, "This served to strengthen [further] the hands of the more moderate elements within the PLO." For a fuller discussion, see also Yezid Sayigh, "Struggle Within, Struggle Without: The Transformation of PLO Politics since 1982," *International Affairs* 65 (Spring 1989): 247–271.

25. Sahliyeh, *The PLO after the War*, p. 93.

26. Ibid., pp. 94–95.

27. Quoted in Lesch and Tessler, p. 201. Another Jordanian attempt to convince Americans that the Arabs were truly interested in peace was an article by Crown Prince Hassan in *Foreign Affairs*. Hassan stated, "I am not holding the Arabs blameless for the depth and duration of Arab-Israeli conflict. For too long Arab states thought the monumental injustice perpetrated against the Palestinian people in 1948 was the only reality. . . . Today, we understand that the Palestinian problem must be dealt with *in the context* of the existence of Israel." See Hassan Ibn Talal, "Jordan's Quest for Peace," *Foreign Affairs* 60 (Spring 1982): 802–813.

28. Arafat's remarks were made in an interview with the Italian daily *Republica*; quoted in Sahliyeh, *The PLO after the War*, p. 96.

29. Quoted in the *New York Times*, October 23 and October 24, 1982.

30. For further discussion, see Tessler, "Moroccan-Israeli Relations." See also Tschirgi, p. 182.

31. See Quandt, *The Middle East*, p. 367. See also Sisco, pp. 634–635.

32. See Sahliyeh, *The PLO after the War*, p. 121.

33. A detailed account of rejectionist efforts to prevent the PNC meeting from taking place is presented by Cobban, pp. 131–133.

34. Quoted in Sisco, pp. 633–634.

35. Quoted in Cobban, p. 133.

36. Quoted in ibid., pp. 134–135. The political program adopted by the PNC, dated February 22, 1982, is reprinted in Laqueur and Rubin, pp. 679–683.

37. Sahliyeh, *The PLO after the War*, p. 111.

38. Ibid., pp. 109 and 110. The latter resolution produced a sharp protest from the Egyptian government, which described the PLO statement as interference in Egyptian affairs. For additional discussion of the vagueness and compromise that characterized these and other PNC resolutions, see Ibrahim Abu-Lughod, "Flexible Militancy: Report on the Sixteenth Palestine National Council," *Journal of Palestine Studies* 12 (Summer 1983): 25–40; Cheryl Rubenberg, "The PLO Response to the Reagan Initiative: The PNC at Algiers," *American-Arab Affairs* 4 (February 1983): 53–69; and Patrick Seale, "PLO Strategies: Algiers and After," *World Today* 39 (April 1983): 137–143.

39. Cobban, p. 135. See also Sahliyeh, *The PLO after the War*, p. 109. Sahliyeh describes the PNC statement as a "qualified rejection" of the American plan, noting that it was "designed to permit Arafat some freedom to try to improve the Reagan initiative and to keep the door open for a dialogue with the United States." For additional discussion, see Tschirgi, p. 186, and Frangi, pp. 249–253.

40. See Trudy Rubin, "Why Hussein Hurries for Mideast Talks," *Christian Science Monitor*, January 25, 1983. For additional discussion, see Lesch and Tessler, pp. 212–213.

41. Results of the poll, published in *Bayader al-Siyassi*, February 12, 1983, are summarized in Sahliyeh, *The PLO after the War*, p. 128.

42. Hussein's statement is reprinted in the *New York Times*, April 11, 1983. It is also reprinted in Laqueur and Rubin, pp. 686–691.

43. Quoted in Quandt, *The Middle East*, p. 367. For a fuller account, see Karen Elliott House, "Hussein's Decision," *Wall Street Journal*, April 14, 1983, and April 15, 1983.

44. Sahliyeh, *The PLO after the War*, p. 129.

45. For further discussion, see ibid., p. 132. According to Sahliyeh, "The failure of U.S. diplomatic efforts to bring about an Israeli troop withdrawal from Lebanon made it exceedingly difficult for Jordan to believe that the United States would be able to convince the Likud government to withdraw from the West Bank and Gaza Strip without an open U.S.-Israeli confrontation— an option the Reagan Administration was unwilling to undertake."

46. See Lesch and Tessler, p. 203; and Quandt, *The Middle East*, pp. 366–368. See also William B. Quandt, "Reagan's Lebanon Policy: Trial and Error," *Middle East Journal* 38 (Spring 1984): 241–242.

47. Tschirgi, p. 180. The importance of Hussein's lack of confidence that the United States would press for acceptance of the principles it had articulated has also been emphasized by Harold Saunders, former U.S. deputy assistant secretary of state for Near East and South Asian affairs. Moreover, according to Saunders, Hussein's doubts about the U.S. did not begin with the 1982 Reagan Plan. In remarks at a conference sponsored by the Council on Foreign Relations and held at Tel Aviv University in September 1984, Saunders suggested that an important reason why Hussein rejected participation in the Camp David autonomy talks was his belief that the United States would be unable to deliver a fair settlement in that context. See *Prospects for Peace in the Middle East: The View from Israel* (New York: Council on Foreign Relations, 1985), p. 31.

48. Shimon Shamir, "Israeli Views of Egypt and the Peace Process: The Duality of Vision," in Quandt, *The Middle East*, p. 210. See also Ian Lustick, "Israeli Politics and American Foreign Policy," *Foreign Affairs* 61 (Winter 1982/83).

49. Tschirgi, p. 188.

50. Ibid., p. 187.

51. Quoted in Sahliyeh, *The PLO after the War*, p. 130. Both al-Wazir and Arafat were interviewed by Radio Monte Carlo, al-Wazir on April 1, 1983, and Arafat on February 3, 1983.

52. S. W. Lewis, "The United States and Israel," p. 247.

53. In mid-March, the U.S. Defense Department made public a letter sent to Secretary of Defense Caspar Weinberger by the commandant of the Marine Corps, in which many of the American complaints were spelled out. The Israelis, for their part, accused U.S. and other international forces in Lebanon of providing sanctuary for Lebanese guerrilla groups carrying out raids against the IDF. These strains in American-Israeli relations led Washington to suspend delivery of some F-16 aircraft for which Israel had contracted the preceding year. For additional discussion, see Tschirgi, pp. 194–195.

54. Excerpts from the Israeli-Lebanese agreement are reprinted in Laqueur and Rubin, pp. 691–694. For a summary and assessment of the May 17 agreement, especially as it relates to security considerations, see Frederic C. Hof, *Galilee Divided: The Israel-Lebanon Frontier, 1916–1984* (Boulder, Colorado: Westview Press, 1988), pp. 105–111.

55. Quoted in Schiff and Ya'ari, *Israel's Lebanon War*, p. 296.

56. Ibid., p. 297.

57. Ibid.

58. From an interview in *Newsweek*, May 30, 1983, p. 76; quoted in Tschirgi, p. 196.

59. Khouri, p. 444.

60. Expressing Washington's mistaken belief that Syrian interests could be ignored and that Assad could be bullied into accepting the Israeli-Lebanese agreement, Habib told a British journalist about this time, "We know Syria won't willingly accept the terms of this accord. It must now accept them unwillingly." Reported by Patrick Seale in the *Observer*, October 30, 1983; quoted in Gilmour, p. 187.

61. See Gilmour, p. 188.

62. See Randall, p. 296.

63. Weinberger's remarks were made in a speech to the American Jewish Committee in New York and in answers to questions following the speech. Reported in the *New York Times*, May 14, 1983, and quoted in Robert O. Freedman, "Focus Lebanon: The Middle East, January–October 1983," in Robert O. Freedman (ed.), *The Middle East since Camp David* (Boulder, Colorado: Westview Press, 1984), pp. 239–240.

64. Freedman, *The Middle East*, p. 235. In addition to urging caution on the Syrians, this theme was also stressed by a Soviet delegation that visited Israel in May 1983, to attend ceremonies marking the thirty-eighth anniversary of the defeat of Nazi Germany. Members of the delegation reaffirmed Moscow's support of Israel's right to live in peace and security and stated that the USSR favored a peace treaty between Israel and Lebanon, although only after all IDF troops had been withdrawn. Ibid., p. 239. For a fuller discussion, see Robert O. Freedman, "The Soviet Union and the Crisis in Lebanon: A Case Study of Soviet Policy from the Israeli Invasion to the Abrogation of the 17 May Agreement," in Halim Barakat (ed.), *Toward a Viable Lebanon* (London: Croom Helm, 1988), pp. 232–276.

65. Quoted in Gilmour, p. 195. For additional discussion, see Ball, p. 78. Ball summarizes the flawed logic of the Reagan administration as follows: "The fact that the Druze obtained arms from Syrians made them, *ipso facto*, surrogates of the Syrians. Since the Syrians in turn

obtained arms from Moscow, they thus became instruments of the Kremlin. It therefore followed, Q. E. D., that a successful repulse of the Maronite invaders would be a triumph for a Soviet Union that was 'seeking to take over the Middle East'—and ultimately, of course, the world." See also Hudson, "The United States' Involvement," p. 229, who characterizes U.S. policy as blinded by ideological distortions. According to Jonathan C. Randall, senior foreign correspondent for the *Washington Post*, "Were the Reagan Administration not so ideologically anti-Soviet—and the 1984 elections so near—a rational solution might be found in an international conference, with European and Soviet participation, on the overall Mideast problem, not just Lebanon" (p. 303).

66. According to Schiff and Ya'ari, "When the IDF left the area it was with full realization that Jumblatt's men would roll up the Phalange almost effortlessly, taking a great stride toward realizing the dream of a Druze canton (without Israeli help) and leaving the U.S. Marine position in Khalde airport an easy target." *Israel's Lebanon War*, p. 298.

67. Gilmour, p. 193.

68. Schiff and Ya'ari, *Israel's Lebanon War*, p. 298.

69. See Tschirgi, p. 197.

70. Reagan's remarks were reported in the *Washington Post*, October 25 and October 28, 1983; quoted in C. D. Smith, p. 272. Reagan also stated, "If Lebanon ends up under the tyranny of forces hostile to the West, not only will our strategic position in the Eastern Mediterranean be threatened, but also the stability of the entire Middle East." Quoted in Ball, p. 76. On November 19, George Shultz insisted that Lebanon was under assault from Arab radicals and that "the primary obstacle to the internal reconstruction [of Lebanon] is the presence of outside, non-Lebanese forces." Reported in U.S. Department of State, Current Policy no. 528.

71. Ball, p. 80.

72. Quoted in Hof, p. 110.

73. Schiff and Ya'ari, *Israel's Lebanon War*, p. 299.

74. Although the withdrawal of the IDF was not completed until June, the decision to pull Israeli troops out of Lebanon was taken by the cabinet in January, with the vote being 16 to 6. The cabinet specified that there would be three phases to the withdrawal, the first to be carried out within five weeks of its decision. It also specified that efforts to arrive at political arrangements would continue during the withdrawal.

75. Sartawi had advanced the argument that the Arabs should endeavor to strengthen the Israeli peace camp. He had asserted, for example, that Israel would not have been able to annex the Golan Heights had there been at least ten representatives of the peace movement in the Knesset. His views in this regard were expressed in an article in *Le Monde*, January 22, 1982, which is reprinted in "Dr. Sartawi Speaks His Mind," *New Outlook* (March 1982): 15–16. See also Simha Flapan, "Dr. Sartawi—And the Dilemma of Israeli-Palestinian Dialogue," *New Outlook* (March 1982): 17–22.

76. For a fuller discussion, see Sahliyeh, *The PLO after the War*, pp. 142–152. See also Mishal, *The PLO*, p. 173; and Gresh, pp. 236–240.

77. Sahliyeh, *The PLO after the War*, p. 147. Abu Musa even surpassed the PLO charter of 1968 in his uncompromising attitude, declaring that all Jews who had settled in Israel since its establishment would be required "to return to their countries of origin." Quoted in Gresh, p. 237.

78. Sahliyeh, *The PLO after the War*, pp. 149–150.

79. Arafat made this statement to Radio Monte Carlo on November 18, 1983; quoted in ibid., p. 169.

80. See Schiff and Ya'ari, *Israel's Lebanon War*, p. 297.

81. In February 1982, government troops under the command of Assad's brother, Rifat, had brutally suppressed a rebellion led by the Muslim Brotherhood in the Syrian city of Hamma. Estimates of the number of rebels killed range from 5,000 to 25,000. This massacre and other Syrian actions against Islamic groups led anti-Syrian Sunni forces in Lebanon to support Arafat against Damascus. Giving additional logic to this alliance are reports that several years earlier Arafat may have provided arms to the Brotherhood in Hamma. See Becker, p. 224.

82. For a firsthand account, see Joseph B. Treaster, "Arafat's Soldiers Lose Stronghold," *New York Times*, November 7, 1983.

83. Quoted in Sahliyeh, *The PLO after the War*, p. 170.

84. Ibid., p. 169.

85. Mordechai Nissan, "The Begin Legacy," *Jerusalem Post*, September 11, 1983; quoted in S. N. Eisenstadt, *The Transformation of Israeli Society* (Boulder, Colorado: Westview Press, 1985), p. 529.

86. Shulamit Hareven, quoted in Eisenstadt, *The Transformation*, p. 530.

87. H. M. Sachar, *A History, II*, pp. 211–212. For additional discussion, see Emmanuel Gutmann, "Begin's Israel: The End of an Era," *International Journal* 38 (1983): 690–699; and Avram Schweitzer, *Israel: The Changing National Agenda* (London: Croom Helm, 1986), pp. 138ff.

88. Quoted in Aronoff, *Israeli Visions*, p. 36. Aronoff provides a thorough discussion of these tensions and divisions. Among the sources upon which he draws is Israeli satirical cartoonist Jacob Kirschen, who in February 1983 had one of his characters say: "I dreamt we went mad, with half of us thinking the other half fascist and the other half thinking that the first half are cowards and traitors. I dreamt about political murder and violent Knesset 'debating' about violent street 'debating' " (p. 35).

89. The cost of the war in Lebanon has been estimated at more than $5 billion. For additional discussion, see Haim Barkai, "Reflections on the Economic Cost of the Lebanon War," *Jerusalem Quarterly* 37 (1986): 95–106.

90. See Gerald M. Steinberg, "Large Scale National Projects as Political Symbols: The Case of Israel," *Comparative Politics* 19 (April 1987): 331–346.

91. For additional information, see H. M. Sachar, *A History, II*, pp. 212–215. See also Eisenstadt, *The Transformation*, p. 516.

92. Evidence that the accused terrorists were indeed operating within the mainstream of the settler movement was subsequently provided by the statements of some defendants implicating Gush Emunim leader Moshe Levinger, Tehiya MK Eliezer Waldman, and others. See Mark Tessler, "The Political Right in Israel: Its Origins, Growth and Prospects," *Journal of Palestine Studies* 58 (Winter 1986): 49–52. See also Eisenstadt, *The Transformation*, pp. 550–551.

93. Shubert Spero, "Messianism in Context," *Jerusalem Post*, June 17, 1984.

94. *Jerusalem Post*, July 11, 1985.

95. Statement by Yossi Dayan, a leader of the Kach Party headed by Meir Kahane; quoted in Tessler, "The Political Right," p. 51.

96. *Jerusalem Post*, July 23, 1985. Although the three-judge panel that handed down the sentences emphasized the gravity of the crimes that had been committed, they also made a number of statements declaring that they were influenced by "humanitarian and extraordinary personal" considerations. One judge stated of the defendants, for example, "They are mostly men of Torah and labor, who left behind them an easy way of life and went, with their families . . . [to contribute] to the causes of state, security, settlement and welfare."

97. *Jerusalem Post*, July 23, 1985. All sentences included the time defendants had been in custody since their arrest, and most were eligible to have their sentences reduced by one-third for good behavior. One right-wing MK, Geula Cohen of Tehiya, declared that "such lenient sentences prove that our cause for clemency is just."

98. Quoted in H. M. Sachar, *A History*, II, p. 215.

99. For a discussion of the changes over time in the proportion of Knesset seats held by the two leading parties, see Arian, *Politics in Israel*, pp. 165ff.

100. For additional discussion, see Raphael Israeli, "The Israeli Elections of 1984: Issues and Factions," *Middle East Review* (Special Report) 1 (1984/1985). According to Israeli, Afro-Asian Jews belonging to Aguda came to the realization that "they had been used as vote-getters, rather than accepted as genuine participants in the party's leadership" (p. 4). In addition to these defections from Aguda, Shas also received votes from religious Jews of Afro-Asian origin who had previously supported Likud or who had voted for Tami in 1981. Tami's leader, Aharon Abuhatzeira, had broken with the NRP in 1981, and his party won three Knesset seats in the balloting of that year. He was subsequently convicted of financial misconduct, however, costing his party many votes in 1984. In that year, Tami won only a single seat in the Knesset.

101. Itzhak Galnoor, "The 1984 Elections in Israel: Political Results and Open Questions," *Middle East Review* (Summer 1986): 51–53.

102. For additional discussion, see Tessler, "The Political Right," pp. 29–30. See also H. M. Sachar, *A History*, II, pp. 222.

103. Quoted in H. M. Sachar, *A History*, II, p. 222. Sachar, a knowledgeable and objective observer, describes this notion as a "crypto-Fascist" idea.

104. C. Paul Bradley, *Parliamentary Elections in Israel: Three Case Studies* (Grantham, New Hampshire: Thompson and Rutter, 1985), p. 154. See also Gregory Mahler, *Israel: Government and Politics in a Maturing State* (New York: Harcourt Brace Jovanovich, 1990), p. 114.

105. Morasha also received support from Poalei Agudat Yisrael, a tiny ultraorthodox workers' party which had maintained an independent organizational structure but usually participated in elections jointly with Aguda. The party submitted a separate list of candidates in the 1981 elections but did not receive enough votes to obtain a seat in the Knesset. Although Poalei Aguda remained a minuscule faction, its endorsement of Morasha in 1984 suggested that religious parties committed to territorial maximalism, in the tradition of Gush Emunim, had some support not only among orthodox Jews but among the ultraorthodox as well. For further discussion, see Tessler, "The Political Right," pp. 35–36.

106. These quotations were recorded by officials of the New Israel Fund, a Jewish organization devoted to combating racism and political extremism in Israel. They were publicized in an NIF newsletter dated October 14, 1985. For additional discussion, see Tessler, "The Political Right," pp. 30–31. See also H. M. Sachar, *A History*, II, pp. 223–224; Gabriel Sheffer, "Kahane, Kahanism and Racism," *Israel Yearbook*, 1985, pp. 68–72; Ehud Sprinzak, "Kach and Meir Kahane: The Emergence of Jewish Quasi-Fascism," *Patterns of Prejudice* 19 (1985); and Robert I. Friedman, "The Sayings of Rabbi Kahane," *New York Review of Books*, February 13, 1986. For a thorough analysis of Kach and the growth of parties to the right of Likud more generally, see Ehud Sprinzak, *The Ascendance of Israel's Radical Right* (New York: Oxford University Press, 1991). Sprinzak offers detailed profiles of many of the radical right's most important personalities.

107. Some of these findings were reported in "The Popularity of Various Political Lists among Youth," Dahaf poll, Van Leer Institute, Jerusalem, May 1985. For additional discussion, see Galnoor, p. 52.

108. These themes are given forceful expression in the concluding chapters of a major synthetic work by one of Israel's most prominent sociologists. See Eisenstadt, *The Transformation*.

109. Interview published in *Al-Ahram*, December 23, 1983; quoted in Sahliyeh, *The PLO after the War*, p. 178.

110. Sahliyeh, *The PLO after the War*, p. 179. See also Gresh, p. 240.

111. Sahliyeh, *The PLO after the War*, p. 182.

112. The results are given in *al-Fajr*, December 9, 1983. See also Gresh, p. 239.

113. Interview broadcast on Radio Monte Carlo, December 30, 1983; quoted in Sahliyeh, *The PLO after the War*, p. 184.

114. Mishal, *The PLO*, pp. 173–174.

115. Hani al-Hasan, interview in *Filastin al-Thawra*, April 21, 1984; quoted in ibid., p. 174.

116. Interview on Jordan television, January 2, 1984; quoted in Sahliyeh, *The PLO after the War*, p. 185.

117. Six of the vacant seats were reserved for Muslims and two for Christians. Although political parties remained banned and organized campaigning was not permitted, more than 100 individuals competed for the eight vacant seats. Three of the seats in the former category were won by Islamic activists. For additional discussion, see Robert B. Satloff, *Troubles on the East Bank: Challenges to the Domestic Stability of Jordan* (New York: Praeger, 1986), p. 50. New parliamentary elections were held in November 1989, with 647 candidates contesting the seats representing Jordanian citizens and Palestinian refugees residing in the East Bank. Thirty-four of these seats were won by the Muslim Brotherhood, and twelve were won by Communists and others identified with the political left.

118. *Jordan Times*, October 2, 1984; quoted in Day, p. 42. There were many additional calls at this time for an opening up of Jordanian political life. For example, many deputies in the reconvened parliament argued for the legalization of political parties and for more general political and constitutional freedoms. For an informative discussion of the nature and limits of Hussein's commitment to democracy at this time, see also Satloff, *Troubles*, pp. 72–74. Satloff notes that new government appointments were marked by a virtual absence of men tied to the Jordanian security apparatus, and that this was an important departure from past practice, but adds that there nevertheless was little evidence that the reconvening of parliament and other moves toward democracy heralded a new era in the kingdom's political life. Some additional progress was made in spring 1986, when the parliament passed legislation expanding the assembly from 60 to 142 seats, half of which would be chosen from the East Bank and 11 more of which would be set aside for the previously disenfranchised residents of Palestinian refugee camps in the East Bank. For additional discussion, see Emile Sahliyeh and Mark Tessler, "Experimentation with Democracy: The Cases of Jordan and Tunisia," paper presented at the 1990 meeting of the American Political Science Association.

119. Reflecting the same preoccupation with the Soviet Union that was leading the U.S. to become involved in the Lebanese civil war at this time, the strategic cooperation agreement between the U.S. and Israel provided for a "joint political-military group to enhance United States–Israeli cooperation" and specified that this group should give "priority attention to the threat to our mutual interests posed by increased Soviet involvement in the Middle East." The agreement itself promised an increase in U.S. military aid to Israel, negotiations for an accord on reciprocal duty-free trade, Israeli access to secret American electronic technology, and U.S. assistance to help Israel develop the Lavi fighter aircraft. For additional discussion, see Khouri, pp. 449–451. According to Khouri, even the most pro-Western Arabs were embittered by this agreement. See also Sahliyeh, *The PLO after the War*, pp. 187–188.

120. Sahliyeh, *The PLO after the War*, p. 198. For additional discussion of the PNC meeting from the Jordanian point of view, see Day, pp. 135–136. Day notes that the conference was also a success for Hussein, being an opportunity "to assert the maximum Jordanian influence over the PLO."

121. West Bank Palestinians elected to the PLO Executive Committee included Fahd Qawasmeh and Muhammad Milhem, the former mayors of Hebron and Halhoul respectively, and Bishop Elias Khouri of Ramallah. In addition, Sheikh Abdul Hamid al-Sayeh, former head of the Islamic Council in Jerusalem, was selected as speaker of the PNC. Three seats on the Executive Committee were left open, to be filled later by the Popular Front, the Democratic Front, and Saiqa.

122. "Resolution 242," *al-Fajr Jerusalem*, November 30, 1984.

123. The February 11, 1985, agreement is reprinted in Quandt, *The Middle East*, pp. 471–472.

124. From Hussein's address to the American Enterprise Institute in Washington, D.C., on June 2, 1985; quoted in the *Jordan Times*, June 2, 1985.

125. Following a two-day meeting in Tunis, the PLO Executive Committee issued a statement that described the Hussein-Arafat accord as "a logical outcome of Palestine National Council resolutions, Arab summit resolutions and UN resolutions concerning the Palestinian problem."

126. "The Palestinian-Jordanian Accord," *al-Fajr Jerusalem*, February 15, 1985.

127. Samuel W. Lewis, "Israel: The Peres Era and Its Legacy," *Foreign Affairs* 65 (1987): 599.

128. The inner cabinet, established in May 1985, consisted of ten ministers, five from Labor and five from Likud. Peres finally persuaded this body to accept arbitration in a pressurized all-night session on January 12–13, 1986. According to Labor, Likud's opposition was not based only, or perhaps even primarily, on a commitment to retention of Taba. As stated in an editorial in the *Jerusalem Post*, Likud did not want Labor to get credit for improving relations with Egypt and preferred to maintain the cold peace rather than see an increase in Peres's prestige and an improvement in the chances for talks dealing with the West Bank and Gaza. *Jerusalem Post*, International Edition, September 24, 1985. In addition, there was strong sentiment within the Israeli settler movement, and among some in Likud, that Taba should not be returned under any conditions. During the negotiations in Beersheba, for example, some Israelis demonstrated with signs declaring "Taba! The last grain of sand from the vast Sinai! Not to be returned!" For a fuller discussion of the Taba issue, see Lesch and Tessler, pp. 43–60. For a useful Israeli perspective, see also Ruth Lapidoth, "The Taba Controversy," *Jerusalem Quarterly* 37 (1986): 37–38.

129. Shimon Peres, "Palestinians in Perspective," *Jerusalem Post*, October 7, 1983.

130. For an analysis of the February 11 agreement reflecting these judgments, see Barry Rubin, "The PLO's Intractable Foreign Policy," Policy Papers of the Washington Institute for Near East Policy, 1985, pp. 25–32. Rubin writes that the PLO's stance "totally negated Jordan's effort to create a new approach . . . [and] was a formula for continued deadlock and revolutionary posturing" (p. 27). See also Sahliyeh, *The PLO after the War*, pp. 220–221.

131. Michael Eilan and David Landau, "Shultz to Tell Hussein It's Time to Name Names," *Jerusalem Post*, May 12, 1985. The article refers to a visit to Israel, Egypt, and Jordan being undertaken by the U.S. secretary of state.

132. "Hanna Siniora and Fayez Abu Rahmeh: The Palestinian-Jordanian Joint Delegation," *Journal of Palestine Studies* 53 (Autumn 1985): 4, 7.

133. Ibid., p. 17.

134. For a summary of the Egyptian reaction to this incident, see Saad Eddin Ibrahim,

"Domestic Developments in Egypt," in Quandt, *The Middle East*, p. 35. Ibrahim notes that Egypt's most prominent lawyers volunteered to defend Khater and that there were popular protests when his death sentence was first announced, and also a few days later when the government claimed that he had committed suicide in his prison cell.

135. Ibid. For a similar Egyptian view, see Abdel Monem Said Aly, "Egypt: A Decade after Camp David," in Quandt, *The Middle East*, p. 89. American reactions to Egypt's handling of the *Achille Lauro* affair are summarized in Bob Woodward, *Veil: The Secret Wars of the CIA, 1981–1987* (New York: Simon and Schuster, 1987), pp. 414–416. See also Hermann F. Eilts, "The United States and Egypt," in Quandt, *The Middle East*, p. 128. Contributing to the restoration of cordial relations between the two countries was U.S. assistance in helping Cairo to recover a hijacked Egypt Air plane in Malta several months later.

136. A survey of reactions in the occupied territories is provided by Said al-Ghazali, "Unanimous Rejection of Peres' Plan," *al-Fajr Jerusalem*, October 25, 1985.

137. Sahliyeh, *The PLO after the War*, pp. 246.

138. Emile Sahliyeh, "Jordan and the Palestinians," in Quandt, *The Middle East*, p. 311.

139. Quoted in the *New York Times*, October 31, 1985.

140. In his statement, broadcast on November 7, 1985, Arafat reaffirmed earlier PLO decisions to refrain from terrorism, declared that all PLO institutions and factions were to abide by these decisions, and promised that the PLO would take measures to deter any deviations. He also stated that condemnations of terrorism cannot be one-sided, and so Israel, too, must be compelled to stop "all acts of terrorism inside and outside the occupied territories." Finally, he declared that Palestinians have "the right to resist the Israeli occupation of their land in any way possible in order to achieve a withdrawal." The full text of Arafat's statement is reprinted in *Journal of Palestine Studies* 58 (Winter 1986): 214–216.

141. Hussein's address is reprinted in *Journal of Palestine Studies* 60 (Summer 1986): 206–232.

142. Interview in *al-Fajr Jerusalem*, February 21, 1986.

143. The survey, sponsored by *al-Fajr*, *Newsday*, and the Australian Broadcasting Corporation, was carried out by Professor Mohammed Shadid of an-Najah National University in Nablus. For details, see Mohammed Shadid and Rick Seltzer, "Political Attitudes of Palestinians in the West Bank and Gaza Strip," *Middle East Journal* 42 (Winter 1987): 16–32. Angered by the survey's findings and strongly encouraged by the government in Amman, Israel responded by withdrawing the work permit of Professor Shadid.

144. S. W. Lewis, "Israel," p. 601.

145. Hirsh Goodman, "Limited Mission Accomplished," *Jerusalem Post*, July 25, 1986. For a fuller discussion, see Tessler, "Moroccan-Israeli Relations." The final communiqué issued by Hassan and Peres is reprinted in the *New York Times*, July 25, 1986.

146. For an account of Israeli-Egyptian cooperation in a variety of areas, including tourism, trade, and scientific and cultural programs, see Lesch and Tessler, pp. 61–85. For a presentation of survey data indicating that most Egyptians favored peace with Israel in the mid-and late 1980s, see Mark Tessler and Jamal Sanad, "Will the Arab Public Accept Peace with Israel," in Efraim Karsh and Gregory Mahler (eds.), *Israel at the Crossroads* (London: I. B. Tauris, 1993). This chapter reports that peace with Israel was favored by 70 percent of the 300 respondents in a representative sample of Egyptians interviewed in 1988, whereas only 14 percent opposed peace and the remainder were unsure.

147. The text of this agreement, known as the "London Document," was published in the Israeli newspaper *Ma'ariv* on January 1, 1988. It specified that the agreement was between the government of Jordan and the foreign minister of Israel, pending approval of the government of Israel. Parts of the agreement were to be made public upon this approval, whereas

others were to be treated "with great confidentiality." Key provisions of the London Document dealt with an international conference, which would be convened by the UN secretary-general and include the five permanent members of the Security Council. Consistent with Israel's past insistence upon direct peace talks, negotiations at this conference were to be conducted "in bilateral committees in a direct manner."

148. S. W. Lewis, *Israel*, p. 602.

149. *Jerusalem Post*, International Edition, May 23, 1987; quoted in Don Peretz, *Intifada: The Palestinian Uprising* (Boulder, Colorado: Westview Press, 1990), p. 30.

150. *Kol Ha'ir* (Jerusalem), October 24, 1986; quoted in G. Aronson, pp. 310–311.

151. S. W. Lewis, *Israel*, p. 601.

152. These comments were made by Yossi Sarid, an MK from the Citizens' Rights Movement, in *Davar*, August 4, 1986; quoted in G. Aronson, p. 319. The policies that defined the "iron fist" were approved by the cabinet on August 4, 1985. For a fuller discussion, see ibid., pp. 315–319. Aronson's account draws heavily on reports from the Israeli press.

153. Quoted in *Newsweek*, February 17, 1986.

154. *Jerusalem Post*, International Edition, May 23, 1987; quoted in Peretz, *Intifada*, p. 30.

155. For additional discussion, see Tessler and Lesch, pp. 260–262.

156. Shadid and Seltzer.

157. Said al-Ghazali, "Fundamentalist Groups See Islam as Changing the World," *al-Fajr Jerusalem*, July 19, 1987. See also Elaine Ruth Fletcher, "Islamization of the Conflict," *Jerusalem Post Magazine*, January 29, 1988.

11. The Intifada and Beyond

1. See Kenneth W. Stein, "The *Intifadah* and the 1936–1939 Uprising: A Comparison of the Palestinian Arab Communities," Occasional Paper Series of the Carter Center of Emory University, vol. 1, no. 1 (1990). See also M. Khalid al-Azhari, "Thawra 1936 wa Intifada 1987" [The 1936 Revolt and the 1987 Intifada], *Shu'un Filastinya* (October 1989): 3–26. For accounts of the intifada from differing perspectives, see David McDowall, *Palestine and Israel: The Uprising and Beyond* (Berkeley: University of California Press, 1989); Yossi Melman and Dan Raviv, *Beyond the Uprising: Israelis, Jordanians, and Palestinians* (Westport, Connecticut: Greenwood Press, 1989); Zachary Lockman and Joel Beinin (eds.), *Intifada: The Palestinian Uprising against Israeli Occupation* (Boston: South End Press, 1989); Jamal Nassar and Roger Heacock (eds.), *Intifada: Palestine at the Crossroads* (New York: Praeger, 1990); Ze'ev Schiff and Ehud Ya'ari, *Intifada: The Palestinian Uprising—Israel's Third Front* (New York: Simon and Schuster, 1990); Don Peretz, *Intifada: The Palestinian Uprising* (Boulder: Westview Press, 1990); Rex Brynen (ed.), *Echoes of the Intifada: Regional Repercussions of the Palestinian-Israeli Conflict* (Boulder: Westview Press, 1991); and F. Robert Hunter, *The Palestinian Uprising* (Berkeley: University of California Press, 1991).

2. Emile A. Nakhleh, "The West Bank and Gaza: Twenty Years Later," *Middle East Journal* 42 (Spring 1988): 210.

3. See, for example, "A Pogrom Situation in the West Bank," *Jerusalem Post*, July 23, 1987.

4. Figures are from a BBC report entitled "Around the Arab World," broadcast on July 18, 1987; quoted in Kamal Nasser, "Israeli Water Policies Deprive Palestinians," *al-Fajr Jerusalem*, August 16, 1987. Quoting Israeli sources, Nasser's account also reports that Israel has drilled seventeen wells in the Jordan Valley since 1967 while refusing to authorize Palestinians

to dig any new wells for agricultural purposes. As a result, according to an Israeli Civil Administration report discussed in Jerusalem's *al-Quds* newspaper on July 30, 1987, 81.4 percent of the West Bank's water is consumed by Israelis.

5. The proposed new well, for which funds were being raised in the United States under the banner of "Water for Jerusalem," was to be drilled to a depth of 900–1000 meters, whereas Arab wells rarely exceed a depth of 100 meters. Thus, according to Palestinians, the new project threatened to deplete the wells currently serving Bethlehem and other Arab communities in the southern portion of the West Bank. For an account of these Palestinian concerns, see Khalil Touma, "Bethlehem Plan Further Threatens Scarce Water Resources," *al-Fajr Jerusalem*, July 26, 1987. Among those in Israel opposed to the plan was the head of the Civil Administration in the West Bank, Ephraim Sneh. Sneh resigned his position in September 1987, largely, according to the Israeli press, because of differences with his superiors about the proposed water-drilling project. For additional discussion, see Peretz, *Intifada*, pp. 29 and 32.

6. Quoted in Peretz, *Intifada*, p. 37.

7. Ann Mosely Lesch, "The Palestinian Uprising—Causes and Consequences," United Field Staff International Reports, Asia, no. 1, 1988–89, p. 4.

8. Quoted in *al-Fajr Jerusalem*, December 20, 1987.

9. Lesch, "The Palestinian Uprising," p. 4.

10. Nakhleh, "The West Bank and Gaza," p. 222.

11. Ibid., p. 215. Nakhleh also cites other Palestinian sources and concludes that "an evident gap is developing between indigenous Palestinians on the one hand and expatriate leadership on the other" (p. 23). Criticism of expatriate leadership was also expressed by *al-Fajr* in an editorial following the Eighteenth PNC meeting. The paper declared, "We will not be satisfied by the PLO leaders simply kissing and making up. . . . The Palestinian leadership must conduct an honest and tough critique of the events of the past, of our position at present, and where we want to go from here." *Al-Fajr Jerusalem*, April 19, 1987. For additional discussion, see McDowall, pp. 119–120.

12. *Al-Fajr Jerusalem*, November 15, 1987, p. 5.

13. Nakhleh, "The West Bank and Gaza," p. 210.

14. Hirsh Goodman, "When Extremism Eclipses Reason," *Jerusalem Post* (International Edition), October 24, 1987; quoted in Peretz, *Intifada*, p. 35.

15. Nakhleh, "The West Bank and Gaza," p. 214.

16. Lesch, "The Palestinian Uprising," p. 4.

17. See Salim Tamari, "The Palestinian Movement in Transition: Historical Reversals and the Uprising," in Brynen, pp. 16ff.

18. Quoted in Peretz, *Intifada*, p. 39.

19. Daoud Kuttab, in *al-Fajr Jerusalem*, May 31, 1987; quoted in McDowall, p. 105.

20. Mark Tessler, "The Palestinian Uprising and the Israeli Response: Human Rights, Political and Security Dimensions," *Wisconsin International Law Journal* 8 (Spring 1990): 309.

21. See Lesch, "The Palestinian Uprising," p. 5. Lesch estimates that the army could maintain control of only about 100 villages at any one time.

22. Daoud Kuttab, "A Profile of the Stonethrowers," *Journal of Palestine Studies* 67 (Spring 1988): 18–20.

23. Lesch, "The Palestinian Uprising," p. 5.

24. *Jerusalem Post*, February 8, 1988.

25. Lesch, "The Palestinian Uprising," p. 6.

26. A useful discussion is provided by Tamari, a Palestinian scholar who reminds readers that many myths have arisen about the local committees and that to some extent their activities "remain more expressions of revolutionary *élan* than substantive programs of social change."

While Tamari makes clear that this does not diminish the magnitude of the organizational accomplishments of the local committees, he suggests that there remains a gap between their radical rhetoric and their declared objective of revolutionary change. See Tamari, "The Palestinian Movement," p. 25.

27. See Daoud Kuttab, "Beyond the Intifada: The Struggle to Build a Nation," *The Nation*, October 17, 1988. See also Don Peretz, *Intifada*, pp. 88–89.

28. See Tamari, "The Palestinian Movement." See also Kuttab, "A Profile," p. 21. Kuttab reports that the grass-roots organizations which developed during the 1980s "took the form of labor unions, student councils, women's committees, and young people's social action committees. The latter, especially the pro-Fatah Shabibah youth social action committees, gradually developed in virtually every village, camp, and neighborhood."

29. For further discussion, see Tamari, "The Palestinian Movement." Tamari draws, in part, upon Lisa Taraki, "Mass Organizations in the West Bank," unpublished manuscript. For a fuller account of grass-roots organizations in the West Bank and Gaza, focusing in particular on the labor movement and the women's movement, see Joost Hiltermann, *Behind the Intifada: Labor and Women's Movements in the Occupied Territories* (Princeton: Princeton University Press, 1991).

30. Quoted in McDowall, p. 118. For additional discussion, see Ziad Abu-Amr, "The Intifada and Its Leadership," *The Return: An International Palestinian Monthly Magazine* 1 (August 1989): 13–16.

31. Peretz, *Intifada*, pp. 89–90.

32. The text of the fourteen-point memorandum is reprinted in *Journal of Palestine Studies* 67 (Spring 1988): 63–65.

33. Kuttab, "A Profile," p. 20.

34. Peretz, *Intifada*, p. 90. Peretz reports that these "strike forces" usually contained ten to fifteen members. According to Peretz and other sources, the youth patrols also performed functions related to the maintenance of public order and safety, such as mediating disputes, preventing crime, and cracking down on known drug dealers. See also the *New York Times*, May 20, 1989.

35. Nafez Assaily, "Intifada: Palestinian Nonviolent Protest—An Affirmation of Human Dignity and Freedom," report published by the Palestinian Center for the Study of Non-Violence, May 31, 1988.

36. The Israelis distributed a number of fraudulent leaflets early in 1988 in an attempt to confuse Palestinians and disrupt the intifada. This effort appears to have had little success, however. Palestinians reported that the bogus directives could be identified by their style and content. See Lesch, "The Palestinian Uprising," p. 7. See also Peretz, *Intifada*, p. 91.

37. For discussions of the position of Islamic groups in the West Bank and Gaza prior to the intifada, see Lesch and Tessler, pp. 260–262; Emile Sahliyeh, "The West Bank and Gaza Strip," in Shireen Hunter (ed.), *The Politics of Islamic Revivalism* (Bloomington: Indiana University Press, 1988); and Mohammad Shadid, "The Muslim Brotherhood Movement in the West Bank and Gaza," *Third World Quarterly* 10, no. 2 (1988). For additional background, see Nels Johnson, *Islam and the Politics of Meaning in Palestinian Nationalism* (London: Keegan Paul, 1982).

38. For example, David Shipler, a *New York Times* correspondent based in Jerusalem, was told by an Israeli officer in Gaza that the IDF was providing funds to Islamic activists in order to build them up as an alternative to the PLO. See David Shipler, *Arab and Jew: Wounded Spirits in a Promised Land* (New York: Times Books, 1986), pp. 176–177. See also Peretz, *Intifada*, p. 104.

39. Elie Rekhess, "The Rise of the Palestinian Islamic Jihad," *Jerusalem Post*, October 21, 1987.

40. Ibid.

41. Ibid.

42. Quoted in Gail Pressberg, "The Uprising: Causes and Consequences," *Journal of Palestine Studies* 67 (Spring 1988): 44.

43. Peretz, *Intifada*, pp. 93 and 102.

44. For further discussions, see Robert Satloff, "Islam and the Palestinian Uprising," *Orbis* (Summer 1989): 389–401; Elie Rekhess, "The Islamic Intifada," *Jerusalem Post*, July 12, 1989; and Jean-Francois Legrain, "A Defining Moment: Palestinian Islamic Fundamentalism," in James Piscatori (ed.), *Islamic Fundamentalisms and the Gulf Crisis* (Cambridge: American Academy of Arts and Sciences, 1991).

45. A good summary of the Hamas charter is provided by Peretz, *Intifada*, pp. 104–106. The text of the charter is reprinted, with commentary, in Raphael Israeli, "The Charter of Allah: The Platform of the Islamic Resistance Movement (Hamas)," in Yonah Alexander and Abraham H. Foxman (eds.), *The 1988–1989 Annual on Terrorism* (Amsterdam: Kluwer Academic Publishers, 1990). Despite the militancy of Hamas and other Palestinian groups operating under the banner of Islam, there are differences of opinion among Muslims about whether an accommodation with the Jewish state is prohibited by Islamic law. As noted earlier in connection with the assassination of Anwar Sadat, some Islamic radicals in Egypt do not attach priority to the liberation of Jerusalem and the Holy Land, and scholars at Cairo's al-Azhar Islamic University have declared that the conclusion of a peace treaty with Israel is not contrary to Islamic law. See J. J. G. Jansen, pp. 18 and 44.

46. See Mordechai Bar-On, "Israeli Reactions to the Palestinian Uprising," *Journal of Palestine Studies* 68 (Summer 1988): 49–50. Bar-On, an Israeli Member of Knesset from the leftist Citizens' Rights Movement, notes that Rabin's statements to this effect demonstrated that he failed to understand the utterly novel nature of the Palestinian uprising.

47. The names and ages of those killed are given in Ann Mosely Lesch, "Uprising for Palestine," *Journal of South Asian and Middle Eastern Studies* 11 (Summer 1988): 11–13. The causes of death are also given. A summary of relevant information through the summer of 1988 is also provided in Ronald R. Stockton, "Intifada Deaths," *Journal of Palestine Studies* 70 (Winter 1989): 101–108.

48. Rabin's new policy was actually introduced on January 4, 1988, but was not made public until several weeks later. According to the *Jerusalem Post* of January 26, 1988, Rabin stated that the use of force was necessary "to instill fear of the IDF [among the Palestinians]."

49. According to one report, thirty-four Palestinians died in tear-gas–related incidents between the beginning of the intifada and March 1988. See Lesch, "Uprising for Palestine."

50. *Al-Fajr Jerusalem*, August 28, 1988, p. 1. Reviewed by Israeli censors, the paper is a generally reliable source of information about the occupied territories. Although broadly in agreement, specific figures differ from one source to another. For example, Stockton gives somewhat lower figures than *al-Fajr*, reporting that "at least 287 Palestinians had been killed by October 31, 1988." According to Israeli figures reported in *Yediot Aharonot* on April 25, 1988, more than two hundred Palestinians were killed between December 1987 and April 1988. The Human Rights Report of the United States Department of State, claiming to have consulted both Israeli and Palestinian sources, puts the figure at 366 for all of 1988. See *Country Reports on Human Rights Practices for 1988: Report Submitted to the Committee on Foreign Relations of the U.S. Senate and the Committee on Foreign Affairs of the U.S. House of Representatives* (Washington, D.C.: U.S. Department of State, February 1989), p. 1377.

51. *Al-Fajr Jerusalem*, June 12, 1989, p. 1. Israeli sources give lower figures, indicating that 450–475 Palestinians had been killed by June 1989.

52. The Israeli government refused official comment on the operation in Tunis. The only cabinet member to denounce the assassination of Abu-Jihad publicly at this time was Ezer Weiz-

man. For a summary of the different reactions of Israeli leaders, see Peretz, *Intifada*, pp. 61–62. Peretz also cites press accounts which report that the assassination was planned at a time when Israeli leaders felt "increasing desperation" over their inability to halt the intifada.

53. For additional information about Palestinian reactions, see the statements of the PLO and of the UNLU, both of which are reprinted in *Journal of Palestine Studies* 68 (Summer 1988): 182- 184. The latter declaration promised that the assassination of Abu-Jihad would "strengthen our determination to march ahead with our mighty popular revolution."

54. *New York Times*, June 24, 1989.

55. See Judith Gabriel, "Israel's Policy of Deportation," *The Return* 1, no. 3 (October 1988): 6–10, 30. Gabriel gives the names of thirty-four Palestinians said to have been deported as of August 1988 and lists twenty-six more for whom deportation orders had been issued. The U.S. State Department Human Rights Report observed that "these deportations contravene the Fourth Geneva Convention in the view of the United States." See *Country Reports*, p. 1379.

56. *Country Reports*.

57. Ibid., pp. 1376–1387.

58. Palestinian sources put the figures for the same period as high as 550 houses and 5,000 persons. See Judith Gabriel, "Israel's Use of House Demolitions: Collective Punishment on the Rise," *The Return* 1, no. 11 (July 1989): 16–19.

59. The report states that convicted soldiers "received light punishments, ranging from suspended sentences to imprisonment for two and one-half months" (p. 1379).

60. Quoted in the *Jerusalem Post*, October 5, 1988.

61. Quoted in the *Jerusalem Post*, September, 8, 1988.

62. See, for example, Asher Wallfish, "Shomron: Intifada Can't Be Eradicated," *Jerusalem Post*, January 11, 1989. Similarly, Colonel Nehemia Dayan, chief education officer of the IDF, was quoted in a Voice of Jerusalem newscast on April 10, 1988, to the effect that "the defense forces cannot handle the root of the matter [in the occupied territories], since the Israeli-Palestinian conflict requires a political, not a military, solution." A comparison between the intifada and the anticolonial nationalist struggles in Algeria and other countries is also offered by Emmanuel Sivan, a senior Israeli scholar. See Sivan, "Israel's Decolonization Crisis," *New Outlook* (December 1989): 16–19.

63. Quoted in the *Jerusalem Post*, February 29, 1988.

64. Quoted in the *Jerusalem Post*, January 12, 1989.

65. Aaron Hart, "The Unrest That Makes Peace More Remote," *Jerusalem Post*, January 28, 1988. Aaron Hart is a pen name.

66. Quoted in Joel Brinkley, "Israeli Defense Chief Sees Failure in Quelling Uprising," *New York Times*, December 5, 1989.

67. All figures are quoted in ibid., which notes that forty- five Israelis had also lost their lives as a result of violence associated with the intifada. As in the past, Palestinian sources put the number of deaths higher. According to *al-Fajr Jerusalem* of November 13, 1989, 716 Palestinians had been killed by Israelis since the beginning of the uprising.

68. Quoted in Brinkley.

69. Quoted in the *Jerusalem Post*, August 21, 1988. In the same statement, Cohen also complained about the Association for Civil Rights in Israel, which opposes the deportation of Palestinians. She called ACRI "a racist political organization working mainly for Arabs' rights under the guise of working for civil rights in general."

70. Quoted in the *Jerusalem Post*, August 21, 1988.

71. Quoted in the *Jerusalem Post*, September 11, 1988.

72. Quoted in the *Jerusalem Post*, September 5, 1988.

73. Shubert Spero, "Losing the 'Intifada' Game," *Jerusalem Post*, January 24, 1989.

74. Quoted in the *Jerusalem Post*, January 27, 1988. Rabin expressed concern over the

abuses reported in the press at this time but insisted that these were exceptions and isolated incidents. He acknowledged, however, in response to continuing complaints, that some soldiers implemented the government's policies with considerable enthusiasm, perhaps accounting for some of the unintended excesses. He also acknowledged that some soldiers were distressed by the actions they had witnessed or in which they had taken part.

75. For details, see the *Jerusalem Post*, February 11, 1988.

76. Quoted in the *Jerusalem Post*, February 15, 1988.

77. Quoted in the *Jerusalem Post*, February 11, 1988.

78. *Jerusalem Post*, October 17, 1988.

79. For additional information, see Asher Wallfish, "The Perils of Talking to the Troops," *Jerusalem Post*, January 23, 1988.

80. Ami Dar, "Shooting and Defecating," *Jerusalem Post*, February 21, 1989. Earlier expressions of such views, by other reservists serving the territories, include Ronit Mitlon, "The Wild West: A Reservist's Monologue," *Ha'aretz Weekly Supplement*, March 11, 1988; and Dan Sagir, "This Isn't the Way to Suppress the Uprising," *Ha'aretz*, August 26, 1988.

81. Quoted in the *Jerusalem Post*, September 30, 1988.

82. An account of this program is provided by Tom Segev, "The Comparison," *Ha'aretz*, May 5, 1989.

83. Ibid.

84. In an April 1989 poll, for example, almost 55 percent of the respondents expressed this view, in contrast to 38 percent who disapproved of using harsher methods and, in most cases, expressed the opinion that it was not possible to suppress the intifada by military means. Findings are reported in *Yediot Aharonot*, April 28, 1989.

85. Giora Goldberg, Gad Barzilai, and Efraim Inbar, "The Impact of Intercommunal Conflict: The Intifada and Israeli Public Opinion," Policy Studies of the Leonard Davis Institute, The Hebrew University of Jerusalem, no. 43, February 1991, pp. 17 and 41.

86. Ze'ev Schiff, *Security for Peace: Israel's Minimal Security Requirements in Negotiations with the Palestinians* (Washington: The Washington Institute for Near East Policy, 1989), pp. 14–15. See also Ze'ev Schiff, "The Year of the Club," *Ha'aretz* weekly magazine, April 1988.

87. Uri Avnery, "The Intifada: Substance and Illusion," *New Outlook* (December 1989): 13.

88. For additional discussion, see Victor Cygielman, "The Impact of Two Years of the Intifada," *New Outlook* (December 1989). According to Cygielman, "For young Israelis born around 1967, it was as normal and easy to travel from Tel Aviv to Nablus (West Bank) as it was to travel from Tel Aviv to Nazareth (Galilee). In their eyes, both were Arab cities under Israeli rule, and they did not stop to ponder over distinctions" (p. 5).

89. *Jerusalem Post*, September 11, 1988.

90. Neri Livneh, "Border of Fear," *Hadashot*, September 29, 1989.

91. Cygielman.

92. Rehavam Ze'evi, the founder of Moledet and author of its platform, spelled out his views about transfer in *Ha'aretz*, August 17, 1988. The case for transfer was also set forth in publications of the Israeli settler movement. For example, a March 1988 article in the settler press sought to establish an ethical foundation for the removal of Palestinians, writing that the expulsion of Arabs from the West Bank and Gaza would be "a righteous and just act . . . [because a nation] has the moral right to defeat its enemies and banish them." See Yitzhak Shilat, "The Fear of Employing Force Stems from Moral Weakness," *Nekuda*, March 1988. For a useful introduction to the notion of transfer and its occasional emergence in Zionist political discourse, see Shabtai Teveth, "The Evolution."

93. For several years prior to the intifada, a few declarations and statements by personalities of the extreme right had sought, largely without success, to give legitimacy to the notion of transfer and to initiate a national debate on the subject. See, for example, Israel Eldad, "Transfer as a 'Zionist' Solution," *Ha'aretz*, July 9, 1987; and Avishai Erlich, "Is Transfer an Option?" *Israeli Democracy* 1 (Winter 1987): 36–38.

94. *Jerusalem Post*, August 12, 1988. The format of the poll may have had the effect of somewhat inflating support for the notion of transfer. Respondents were asked what Israel should do to preserve its democratic character should it retain the occupied territories. Other possible responses, in addition to the removal of Palestinians, included giving political rights to Palestinians, and hence endangering Israel's Jewish character, and the view that it is acceptable to compromise Israeli democracy.

95. Heller, pp. 147–148. For a more recent analysis, undertaken in collaboration with a leading Palestinian scholar, see also Mark A. Heller and Sari Nusseibeh, *No Trumpets, No Drums: A Two-State Settlement of the Israeli-Palestinian Conflict* (New York: Hill and Wang, 1991). Similar arguments are advanced by Ze'ev Schiff, a leading Israeli analyst of military affairs, in an important study completed in 1989. Schiff discusses in substantial detail the security arrangements that should accompany Israel's withdrawal from the West Bank and Gaza and the establishment in these territories of a Palestinian political entity. See Schiff, *Security for Peace*. For additional discussion of the military significance of the West Bank, see Aryeh Shalev, *The West Bank: Line of Defense* (New York: Praeger, 1985).

96. Quoted in Ron Ben-Yishai, "What Do the Generals Think about Territorial Compromise," *Yediot Aharonot*, June 10, 1988, Supplement, pp. 6–7. See also "Generals Dismiss the Security Value of the West Bank," *Ha'aretz*, May 31, 1988. For additional discussion, including an account of the April 12, 1988, press conference at which formation of the Council for Peace and Security was announced, see Bar-On, p. 58.

97. Quoted in Dore Gold, "The Generals and the Areas," *Jerusalem Post*, June 10, 1988.

98. Quoted in Ben-Yishai. Also quoted in "Israeli Officers Argue the West Bank Is a Liability," *Newsweek*, May 30, 1988.

99. Abba Eban, "Israel: Hardly the Monaco of the Middle East," *New York Times Magazine*, January 2, 1989.

100. Ben-Yishai.

101. Shlomo Slutsky, "They Don't Believe the IDF Spokesman," *Hadashot*, March 18, 1989.

102. A summary of findings is provided by Ronit Matalon, "Without a Norm," *Ha'aretz*, February 19, 1988, Supplement. See also Bar-On, pp. 51–52; and Ayala Pines, "Israeli Burnout and the Intifada," *New Outlook* (December 1989): 35–36. For a poignant account by an Israeli anthropologist, based on his own experience while serving with his IDF reserve unit in the Hebron area in mid-1988, see Eyal Ben-Ari, "Masks and Soldiering: The Israeli Army and the Palestinian Uprising," *Cultural Anthropology* 4 (1989): 372–389. A particularly forceful statement of the relationship between these problems and Israel's military preparedness was put forward by Martin Van Crefeld, a military historian at the Hebrew University of Jerusalem. Crefeld asserted, with hyperbole, that the IDF had become "a disintegrating structure that has totally lost its deterrent capability." Charging that Israeli soldiers in the territories felt abandoned, he argued that they were increasingly operating not as a unified structure seeking to carry out an assigned mission but as isolated "bands that try to protect themselves and to cover up their acts so that the high command and the media don't discover [what they've done]." Quoted in Roli Rozen, "The Era of Conventional Wars Has Come to an End, and the Future Battlefield Is the Intifada," *Ha'aretz*, Weekend Supplement, May 12, 1989.

103. Quoted in the *Jerusalem Post*, October 25, 1988.

104. Ben-Yishai. The meeting took place in March 1988.

105. Cited in Ben-Yishai. There is also evidence of similar conclusions being reached among much of the general public. For example, 78 percent of those interviewed in a Dahaf Institute public opinion poll conducted in the spring of 1988 agreed that Israel would be able to defend itself were it to withdraw from the occupied territories.

106. Schiff, *Security for Peace*, p. 15.

107. For details, see Peretz, *Intifada*, p. 169.

108. Ibid., p. 171.

109. In yet another survey, conducted by the Gallup Organization in October 1989 on behalf of the Institute for Palestine Studies, 39 percent of all respondents and 45 percent of those who described themselves as "informed" about the Middle East favored the creation of an independent Palestinian state in the West Bank and Gaza, as opposed to 21 percent and 24 percent, respectively, who opposed such a state. See "A Gallup/IPS Survey regarding the Conflict between Israel and the Palestinians," *Journal of Palestine Studies* 74 (Winter 1990): 75–86. For a discussion of U.S. public opinion based on earlier surveys, see Fouad Moughrabi, "American Public Opinion and the Palestine Question," *Journal of Palestine Studies* 58 (Winter 1986): 56–75.

110. At the Arab summit, the PLO had initially requested creation of a fund providing $300–400 million, primarily to help Palestinians in the occupied territories who were unable to work because of the intifada. For additional information, including Palestinian complaints about the difficulty of actually obtaining some of the payments promised by Arab countries, see Paul Noble, "The PLO in Regional Politics," in Brynen, pp. 142 and 161.

111. Hussein's speech at the summit appealed for aid to Jordan, as well as Syria, the other "front-line" state, arguing that support for the PLO did not absolve the Arab world from a responsibility to acknowledge the special burdens assumed by Jordan. For additional discussion, see Lamis Andoni, "Jordan," in Brynen, p. 170. Andoni, a well-known Amman-based journalist, reports that "Jordanian officials, who did not hide their bitterness at the Arab 'apathy' to Jordan's concerns, later described the Algiers summit resolutions as having 'finalized the separation which started in the 1974 Rabat Arab summit between Jordan and the West Bank into a permanent divorce.' "

112. Ibid., p. 173.

113. Mahdi F. Abdul-Hadi, "The Jordanian Disengagement: Causes and Effects," Paper of the Palestinian Academic Society for the Study of International Affairs, Jerusalem, September 1988, p. 6.

114. Maher Abukhater, "Hussein's Measures Are Pressure Tactics," *al-Fajr Jerusalem*, August 7, 1988. For additional discussion, see Youssef Ibrahim, "Jordan's West Bank Moves Upsetting Daily Life," *New York Times*, October 18, 1988.

115. Quoted in Ben-Yishai.

116. Peretz provides an informative account of the claims by some Israeli and American Jewish leaders that the intifada had been planned by PLO officials residing outside the West Bank and Gaza. He reports, for example, that officials of the Israeli embassy in Washington gave American Jewish leaders a closed-door briefing in which they claimed to have evidence of PLO involvement based on intercepted communications. Peretz adds, however, that within a few weeks Yitzhak Rabin "acknowledged that the uprising had been spontaneously generated—led and organized from within the territories, not from abroad." For additional discussion, see Peretz, *Intifada*, p. 174.

117. *Jerusalem Post* (International Edition), August 27, 1988; quoted in Peretz, *Intifada*, p. 136.

118. Shikaki, pp. 4–5.

119. For additional information, see David Remnick, "Gorbachev Prods Arafat on Recognizing Israel," *Washington Post*, April 11, 1988.

120. Shikaki, p. 5.

121. See Bassam Abu Sharif, "Prospects of a Palestinian-Israeli Settlement," reprinted in *Journal of Palestine Studies* 69 (Autumn 1988): 272–275; also reprinted in Peretz, *Intifada*, pp. 208–210.

122. Reprinted in Peretz, *Intifada*, pp. 204–207.

123. On September 13, for example, Arafat issued such a call in an address in Strasbourg, France, to socialist deputies of the European Parliament, adding that the conference should also be based on recognition of the Palestinians' right to self-determination. The address is reprinted in *Journal of Palestine Studies* 70 (Winter 1989): 206–213.

124. According to an Egyptian official, the meeting sought to show Israelis that there was "an Arab partner ready for negotiation." On October 24, the day after the Aqaba meeting, the PLO issued a statement calling on the Arab citizens of Israel to take part in the elections and urging all Israelis to vote for parties that "represent the real peace choice." See *New York Times*, October 25, 1988.

125. The "Palestinian Declaration of Independence," issued by Yasir Arafat in the name of the PNC on November 15, 1988, is reprinted in *Journal of Palestine Studies* 70 (Winter 1989): 213–216; also reprinted in Peretz, *Intifada*, pp. 211–214.

126. The Political Communiqué of the PNC, dated November 15, 1988, is reprinted in *Journal of Palestine Studies* 70 (Winter 1989): 216–223; also reprinted in Peretz, *Intifada*, pp. 215–219. For additional discussion, see Rashid Khalidi, "The 19th PNC Resolutions and American Policy," *Journal of Palestine Studies* 74 (Winter 1990): 29–42.

127. *New York Times*, March 22, 1989.

128. In March, for example, the U.S. State Department issued statements questioning the PLO's commitment to carry out its renunciation of terrorism. See the *New York Times*, March 3, 1989. At the same time, the Israeli defense minister reported a few weeks later that Fatah, Arafat's own faction within the PLO, had not engaged in attacks in Israel in five months. See the *Washington Post*, March 29, 1989. The most serious terrorist episode during this period took place in July, when a Palestinian grabbed the steering wheel of an Israeli bus traveling from Jerusalem to Tel Aviv and caused the bus to plunge into a ravine, killing fourteen passengers. Islamic Jihad, which is not affiliated with the PLO, claimed responsibility for the incident, and the following week Arafat issued a statement expressing regret over the loss of life.

129. Arafat's interview was carried live on French television (TF1). For a transcript, see *Journal of Palestine Studies* 74 (Winter 1990): 144–146.

130. The survey asked a representative sample of 653 Jewish Israelis the following question: "On the basis of Arafat's recent claims [to recognize Israel], and on the condition that he keeps his promise to stop terrorism, are you in favor of or against negotiations with the PLO?" For a discussion of this and other relevant public opinion polls bearing on Israeli attitudes toward negotiations with the PLO, see Tessler, "The Palestinian Uprising," pp. 361ff. See also Bar-On, especially pp. 52–53.

131. *New York Times*, April 2, 1989.

132. The poll was conducted by the Dahaf Institute late in April and was reported in *Yediot Aharonot*, April 28, 1989.

133. For example, a *New York Times* poll asked the same questions in April 1987 and found that talks with the PLO were favored by only 42 percent of the Israelis interviewed.

134. Goldberg, Barzilai, and Inbar, p. 11. The authors note, interestingly, that this shift was not perceived by most respondents, who often claimed that their attitudes had moved to

the right even though their answers to specific policy questions revealed that their views had in fact moved in the opposite direction. For additional discussion of these data, see Gad Barzilai, Giora Goldberg, and Efraim Inbar, "Israeli Leadership and Public Attitudes toward Federal Solutions for the Arab-Israeli Conflict before and after Desert Storm," *Publius* 21 (Summer 1991): 191–209.

135. Barzilai, Goldberg, and Inbar, p. 49. Based on these findings, the authors report that there is "an emerging group of Likud doves," which is "very large when we take into consideration the expected hawkish tendency" (p. 52). In comparison with other Likud supporters, these doves are older, better educated, and less religious and have higher incomes.

136. Interview in *Davar*, September 29, 1989. The most prominent Likud politician to call for a dialogue with the PLO was Shlomo Lahat, the mayor of Tel Aviv and a political maverick who does not share his party's foreign-policy orientation. Lahat told an interviewer during the 1988 election campaign, even before the Nineteenth PNC: "I believe a Palestinian state is inevitable. I believe, unfortunately, that the PLO represents the Palestinian people. I know that the price of peace and real security is withdrawal [from the occupied territories]." Lahat also stated that despite his advocacy of territorial compromise and negotiations with the PLO, "I advocate voting Likud, because only the Likud will be able to advance such a peace process." See the *Jerusalem Post*, September 14, 1988.

137. *The West Bank and Gaza: Israel's Options for Peace* (Tel Aviv: Tel Aviv University, 1989). The report is based on a six-month investigation by Tel Aviv University's Jaffee Center for Strategic Studies. A summary account is given in the *New York Times*, March 9, 1989.

138. Among those calling publicly for repeal of the 1986 law were Ora Namir, one of the Labor MKs who attended the meeting in Paris; Haim Ramon, chairman of the Alignment's Knesset faction; and Abba Eban, who also stated that "Israel should accept the PLO for talks." For additional discussion, see Dvorah Getzler and Asher Wallfish, "Tied Vote Scuttles Bill on Contacts with PLO," *Jerusalem Post*, January 12, 1989; Michel Zlotowski, "MKs, PLO Nearly 'Together,'" *Jerusalem Post*, January 15, 1989; and Paul Montgomery, "Israelis and Palestinians: Frank Talks," *New York Times*, February 3, 1989.

139. Schiff, *Security for Peace*, pp. 1–3.

140. Philip Mattar, "The Critical Moment for Peace," *Foreign Policy* 76 (Fall 1989): 141–159.

141. According to the daily reports of the Foreign Broadcast Information Service, there was a meeting in Italy in late April between Yasir Abd Rabbo of the PLO Executive Committee and Israel Gat of the Labor Party's Foreign Relations Department, and a subsequent meeting in Paris between Ibrahim al-Sus of the PLO and Avraham Tamir, former director general of the Israeli Foreign Ministry. In July, public confirmation of these and other meetings was offered by Yossi Beilin, deputy finance minister and aide to Labor Alignment leader Shimon Peres. Beilin acknowledged that "for two and a half months, clear, official and unequivocal negotiations have been under way between [the PLO and] the Israeli government headed by Yitzhak Shamir, via the Americans." Further, addressing his remarks to hard-liners of the Israeli right, Beilin added that "whoever doesn't admit or recognize this, whoever tries to ignore it, is like a small boy who closes his eyes and thinks the world doesn't see him." See the *New York Times*, July 13, 1989.

142. Quoted in *al-Fajr Jerusalem*, July 10, 1989.

143. The text of Mubarak's ten points is presented in *Journal of Palestine Studies* 73 (Autumn 1989): 145–146.

144. Early in January, Ezer Weizman, Israeli science minister and leader of the Yahad faction of the Labor Alignment, was called from Tunis on behalf of the PLO by Ahmed Tibi, an Arab citizen of Israel. Tibi solicited advice about how the PLO might respond to the Baker

proposals, and Weizman consulted with Shimon Peres before responding. Weizman was subsequently dismissed from Israel's inner cabinet because of this contact with the PLO. See the *New York Times*, January 3, 1990.

145. New disturbances began on May 20 when an Israeli, said to be emotionally disturbed, shot and killed seven Palestinian laborers from Gaza who were waiting in Rishon Le-Zion to be picked up and taken to work. In the unrest that followed, confrontations with the IDF resulted in the deaths of at least seven more Palestinians and left dozens of others seriously wounded. See the *New York Times*, May 21, 1990.

146. See the *New York Times*, March 21, 1990.

147. The chronologies of the *Middle East Journal* and the *Journal of Palestine Studies* provide a convenient source of information about events during this period. They also identify journalistic and other sources where fuller accounts are available.

148. For a comparison of the different attitudes toward the Gulf crisis adopted by various Arab countries and an assessment of the determinants of differing Arab positions, see David Garnham, "Explaining Middle Eastern Alignments during the Gulf War," *Jerusalem Journal of International Relations* 13 (Fall 1991): 63–83. For additional discussion of the anger that led many ordinary Arab citizens to look favorably on Saddam Hussein, see Mark Tessler, "Anger and Governance in the Arab World: Lessons from the Maghrib and Implications for the West," *Jerusalem Journal of International Relations* 13 (Fall 1991): 7–33.

149. As early as August 14, the *New York Times* reported that some PLO officials were deeply disturbed about the injury to relations with the Gulf states that would be caused by Arafat's support for Iraq. Some also worried that the credibility of Palestinian denunciations of Israel's occupation of the West Bank and Gaza would be undermined by the appearance of PLO support for Iraq's occupation of Kuwait. In late August, for example, Juwayyid al-Ghusayn, a member of the PLO Executive Committee and chairman of the Palestine National Fund, stated that Iraq's occupation of Kuwait was illegal; and PLO spokesman Bassam Abu Sharif stated that the Palestinian organization "cannot possibly support the usurpation of one Arab country by another." See the *New York Times*, September 4, 1990.

150. *New York Times*, October 16, 1990. For a fuller discussion of the costs to the PLO of Palestinian support for Saddam Hussein and Iraq, see Lamis Andoni, "The PLO at the Crossroads," *Journal of Palestine Studies* 81 (Autumn 1991): 54–65.

151. Yaron London, "Farewell Husayni, Nusaybah and All Other 'Authentic' Leaders," *Yediot Aharonot*, August 14, 1990. See also Yehoshua Porath, "Why Do They Support Him?" *Ha'aretz*, August 19, 1990. According to Porath, a prominent scholar, "Those who think that the Palestinian desire for a state is strong enough to cause them to be satisfied with 20 percent of Palestinian territory and give up the rest . . . are unable to explain the comprehensive Palestinian support for Saddam Hussein and their willingness to see their houses and villages victims of chemical weapons attack so long as Israel is destroyed."

152. The United Nations proposed to send a delegation to Jerusalem to investigate the incident, but the Israeli government refused to allow the visit. Yitzhak Shamir also rejected a personal appeal from George Bush asking that the visit be permitted to take place.

153. Barzilai, Goldberg, and Inbar, pp. 204–205.

154. Ze'ev Schiff, "Israel after the War," *Foreign Affairs* 70 (Spring 1991): 27, 29.

155. Ibid.

156. Another 11 percent of the respondents interviewed in 1991 favored formulas involving shared rule by Israel, Jordan, and the Palestinians, and an additional 12 percent had either no opinion or no clear preference. For details, see Barzilai, Goldberg, and Inbar, p. 204.

157. Gideon Levy, "If You Ask Me, This Place Is Pure Peacefulness," *Ha'aretz*, September 6, 1991.

158. For details about the fate of Kuwait's Palestinian community during and after the Gulf crisis, see Ann Mosely Lesch, "Palestinians in Kuwait," *Journal of Palestine Studies* 80 (Summer 1991): 42–54. See also "Nowhere to Go: The Tragedy of the Remaining Palestinian Families in Kuwait," Report of Middle East Watch, October 23, 1991.

159. For additional discussion, see Salim Tamari "Eyeless in Judea: Israel's Strategy of Collaborators and Forgeries," *Middle East Report* 164–165 (May-August 1990): 39–44; and Joost Hiltermann, "The Enemy inside the Intifada," *The Nation*, September 10, 1990, pp. 229–234. For an interesting account by an Israeli analyst, see Hillel Frisch, "Between Diffusion and Territorial Consolidation in Rebellion: Striking at the Hard Core of the Intifada," *Terrorism and Political Violence* 3 (Winter 1991): 55–56.

160. Salim Tamari, "The Next Phase: Problems of Transition," in *Palestinian Assessments of the Gulf War and Its Aftermath* (Jerusalem: Palestinian Academic Society for the Study of International Affairs, April 1991), p. 15.

Bibliography

Abdul-Hadi, Mahdi F. "The Jordanian Disengagement: Causes and Effects." Paper of the Palestinian Academic Society for the Study of International Affairs, Jerusalem, September 1988.

Abramov, Zalman. *Perpetual Dilemma: Jewish Religion in the Jewish State.* Rutherford, New Jersey: Fairleigh Dickinson University Press, 1976.

Abramovitz, Z., and Y. Gelfat. *The Arab Economy in Palestine and in the Middle East.* Hakibbutz Hameuchad, 1940.

Abu-Amr, Ziad. "The Intifada and Its Leadership." *The Return: An International Palestinian Monthly Magazine* 1 (August 1989): 13–16.

Abu-Ghazaleh, Adnan Mohammad. "Arab Cultural Nationalism in Palestine during the British Mandate." *Journal of Palestine Studies* 1 (1972): 37–63.

Abu Iyad, with Eric Rouleau. *My Home, My Land: A Narrative of the Palestinian Struggle.* New York: Times Books, 1981.

Abu-Jaber, Kamel S. "United States Policy toward the June Conflict." In Ibrahim Abu-Lughod, ed., *The Arab-Israeli Confrontation of June 1967: An Arab Perspective.* Evanston: Northwestern University Press, 1970.

Abu Kishk, Bakir, and Izzat Ghurani. "Housing." In Emile A. Nakhleh, ed., *A Palestinian Agenda for the West Bank and Gaza.* Washington: American Enterprise Institute, 1980.

Abu-Lughod, Ibrahim. "Flexible Militancy: Report on the Sixteenth Palestine National Council." *Journal of Palestine Studies* 12 (Summer 1983): 25–40.

———, ed. *The Arab-Israeli Confrontation of June 1967: An Arab Perspective.* Evanston: Northwestern University Press, 1970.

———. *Palestinian Rights: Affirmation and Denial.* Wilmette, Illinois: Medina Press, 1982.

———. *The Transformation of Palestine: Essays on the Origin and Development of the Arab-Israeli Conflict.* Evanston: Northwestern University Press, 1971.

Abu-Lughod, Janet L. "The Demographic Transformation of Palestine." In Ibrahim Abu-Lughod, ed., *The Transformation of Palestine: Essays on the Origin and Development of the Arab-Israeli Conflict.* Evanston: Northwestern University Press, 1971.

Abu Sharif, Bassam. "Prospects of a Palestinian-Israeli Settlement." Reprinted in *Journal of Palestine Studies* 69 (Autumn 1988): 272–275.

Abukhater, Maher. "Hussein's Measures Are Pressure Tactics." *Al-Fajr Jerusalem,* August 7, 1988.

Ahmed, J. M. *The Intellectual Origins of Egyptian Nationalism.* London: Oxford University Press, 1960.

Ajami, Fouad. *The Arab Predicament: Arab Political Thought and Practice since 1967.* New York: Cambridge University Press, 1981.

Akzin, Benjamin. "The Likud." In Howard Penniman, ed., *Israel at the Polls: The Knesset Elections of 1977.* Washington: American Enterprise Institute, 1979.

Alexander, Yonah, and Abraham H. Foxman, eds. *The 1988–1989 Annual on Terrorism.* Amsterdam: Kluwer Academic Publishers, 1990.

Allen, Richard. *Imperialism and Nationalism in the Fertile Crescent.* London: Oxford University Press, 1974.

Allon, Yigal. "The Case for Defensible Borders." *Foreign Affairs* 55 (1976): 38–53.

Alpher, Joseph, ed. *Israel's Lebanon Policy: Where To?* Tel Aviv: Jaffee Center for Strategic Studies, 1984.

Aly, Abdel Monem Said, "Egypt: A Decade after Camp David." In William B. Quandt, ed., *The Middle East: Ten Years after Camp David.* Washington: The Brookings Institution, 1988.

Amin, Osman. *Mohammed Abduh.* Washington: American Council of Learned Societies, 1953.

Amos, John W. *Palestinian Resistance: Organization of a National Movement.* New York: Pergamon, 1980.

Andoni, Lamis. "Jordan." In Rex Brynen, ed., *Echoes of the Intifada: Regional Repercussions of the Palestinian-Israeli Conflict.* Boulder, Colorado: Westview Press, 1991.

———. "The PLO at the Crossroads." *Journal of Palestine Studies* 81 (Autumn 1991): 54–65.

Antonius, George. *The Arab Awakening.* New York: Capricorn Books, 1965.

Arian, Asher. *Politics in Israel: The Second Generation.* Chatham, New Jersey: Chatham House, 1985.

———. "Were the 1973 Elections in Israel Critical?" *Comparative Politics* 8 (1975): 152–165.

———, ed. *The Elections in Israel—1969.* Jerusalem: Jerusalem Academic Press, 1972.

———. *The Elections in Israel—1973.* Jerusalem: Jerusalem Academic Press, 1975.

Arieli, Yehoshua. "Annexation and Democracy." *New Outlook* (July 1969).

Armajani, Yahya. *Middle East, Past and Present.* Englewood Cliffs: Prentice-Hall, 1970.

Aronoff, Myron J. *Israeli Visions and Divisions: Cultural Change and Political Conflict.* New Brunswick, New Jersey: Transaction Publishers, 1989.

———. *Power and Ritual in the Israeli Labor Party: A Study in Political Anthropology.* Amsterdam: Van Gorcum, 1977.

Aronson, Geoffrey. *Israel, Palestinians and the Intifada: Creating Facts on the West Bank.* London: Kegan Paul International, 1990.

Aronson, Shlomo, and Nathan Yanai. "Critical Aspects of the Elections and Their Implications." In Dan Caspi, Abraham Diskin, and Emanuel Gutmann, eds., *The Roots of Begin's Success: The 1981 Israeli Elections.* London: Croom Helm, 1984.

Aruri, Naseer H. "Palestinian Nationalism since 1967: An Overview." In Yehuda Lukacs and Abdalla M. Battah, eds., *The Arab-Israeli Conflict: Two Decades of Change.* Boulder, Colorado: Westview Press, 1988.

———, ed. *Middle East Crucible: Studies on the Arab-Israeli War of October, 1973.* Wilmette, Illinois: Medina Press, 1975.

————. *Occupation: Israel over Palestine.* Belmont, Massachusetts: Association of Arab-American University Graduates, 1983.

Assaily, Nafez. "Intifada: Palestinian Nonviolent Protest—An Affirmation of Human Dignity and Freedom." Jerusalem: Report Published by the Palestinian Center for the Study of Non-Violence, 1988.

Atias, M. *The Book of Documents of the National Council of Knesset Israel, 1918–1948.* Jerusalem: R. H. Cohen, 1953.

Atiyah, Edward. *The Arabs.* London: Penguin Books, 1955.

Avineri, Shlomo. *The Making of Modern Zionism: The Intellectual Origins of the Jewish State.* New York: Basic Books, 1981.

Avnery, Uri. "The Intifada: Substance and Illusion." *New Outlook* (December 1989).

————. *Israel without Zionists: A Plea for Peace in the Middle East.* New York: Macmillan, 1968.

al-Azhari, M. Khalid. "Thawra 1936 Wa Intifada 1987" [The 1936 Revolt and the 1987 Intifada] (Arabic). *Shu'un Filastinya* (October 1989): 3–26.

al-Azm, Sadeq. *Al-Naqd al-Dhati Ba'd al-Hazima* [Self-Criticism after the Defeat] (Arabic). Beirut, 1968.

al-Azmeh, Aziz. "Islamic Legal Theory and the Appropriation of Reality." In Aziz al-Azmeh, ed., *Islamic Law: Social and Historical Contexts.* London: Routledge, 1988.

Azzam, Salem, ed. *Islam and Contemporary Society.* London: Longman and the Islamic Council of Europe, 1982.

Baer, Gabriel. "The Office and Functions of the Village Mukhtar." In Joel Migdal, ed., *Palestinian Society and Politics.* Princeton: Princeton University Press, 1980.

Baker, Raymond. *Egypt's Uncertain Revolution under Nasser and Sadat.* Cambridge: Harvard University Press, 1978.

Ball, George W. *Error and Betrayal in Lebanon: An Analysis of Israel's Invasion of Lebanon and Its Implications for U.S.-Israeli Relations.* Washington: Foundation for Middle East Peace, 1984.

Bamberger, Bernard J. *The Story of Judaism.* New York: Union of American Hebrew Congregations, 1957.

Bar-On, Mordechai. "Israeli Reactions to the Palestinian Uprising." *Journal of Palestine Studies* 68 (Summer 1988): 46-65.

Bar Siman Tov, Yaacov. *The War of Attrition.* New York: Columbia University Press, 1980.

Bar-Zohar, Michael. *Ben Gurion: A Biography.* New York: Weidenfeld and Nicolson, 1978.

Barakat, Halim, ed. *Toward a Viable Lebanon.* London: Croom Helm, 1988.

Barkai, Haim. "Reflections on the Economic Cost of the Lebanon War." *Jerusalem Quarterly* 37 (1986): 95–106.

Barnai, Jacob. *The Jews in Palestine in the Eighteenth Century.* Tuscaloosa: University of Alabama Press, 1992.

Barnes, John, and David Nicholson, eds. *The Leo Amery Diaries, Vol. 1: 1896–1929.* London: Hutchinson, 1980.

Barzilai, Gad; Giora Goldberg; and Efraim Inbar. "Israeli Leadership and Public Attitudes toward Federal Solutions for the Arab-Israeli Conflict before and after Desert Storm." *Publius* 21 (Summer 1991): 191–209.

Bassiouni, M. Cherif. "Some Legal Aspects of the Arab-Israeli Conflict." In Ibrahim Abu-

Lughod, ed., *The Arab-Israeli Confrontation of June 1967: An Arab Perspective*. Evanston: Northwestern University Press, 1970.

Bassiouni, M. Cherif, and Eugene M. Fisher. "The Arab-Israeli Conflict—Real and Apparent Issues: An Insight into Its Future from the Lessons of the Past." *St. John's Law Review* 44 (1970): 399–465.

al-Bazzaz, Abd al-Rahman. "Islam and Arab Nationalism." In Sylvia G. Haim, ed., *Arab Nationalism: An Anthology*. Berkeley: University of California Press, 1962.

Becker, Jillian. *The PLO: The Rise and Fall of the Palestine Liberation Organization*. New York: St. Martin's Press, 1984.

Beeri, Eliezer. *The Beginnings of the Israeli-Arab Conflict, 1882–1911* (Hebrew). Tel Aviv: Sifriat Poalim, 1985.

Begin, Menachem. *The Revolt: Story of the Irgun*. New York: Henry Schuman, 1951.

The Beirut Massacre: The Complete Kahan Commission Report. New York: Karz-Cohl, 1983.

Ben-Ari, Eyal. "Masks and Soldiering: The Israeli Army and the Palestinian Uprising." *Cultural Anthropology* 4 (1989): 372-389.

Ben-Arieh, Yehoshua. "The Growth of Jerusalem in the Nineteenth Century." *Annals of the Association of American Geographers* 65 (1975): 252–269.

———. "The Population of the Large Towns in Palestine during the First Eighty Years of the Nineteenth Century According to Western Sources." In Moshe Ma'oz, ed., *Studies on Palestine during the Ottoman Period*. Jerusalem: Magnes Press, 1975.

Ben Gurion, David. *Ben Gurion Looks Back in Talks with Moshe Pearlman*. New York: Schocken Books, 1965.

Ben-Meir, Yehuda. *National Security Decision-Making: The Israeli Case*. Boulder, Colorado: Westview Press, 1986.

Ben-Yishai, Ron. "What Do the Generals Think about Territorial Compromise" (Hebrew). *Yediot Aharonot*, June 10, 1988, Supplement, pp. 6–7.

Benvenisti, Meron. *The West Bank Data Project: A Survey of Israel's Policies*. Washington: The American Enterprise Institute, 1984.

———. *The West Bank Data Project, 1987 Report: Demographic, Economic, Legal, Social and Political Developments in the West Bank*. Jerusalem: The Jerusalem Post, 1987.

Berger, Earl. *The Covenant and the Sword: Arab-Israeli Relations, 1948–1956*. London: Kegan Paul, 1965.

Berger, Elmer. *Who Knows Better Must Say So!* New York: American Council for Judaism, 1955.

Bernstein, Richard. "Birth of the Land of Israel: A History Revisited." *New York Times*, July 28, 1988.

Berque, Jacques. *Les arabes d'hier à demain*. Paris: Éditions du Seuil, 1960.

Bertrand, Louis. *Devant l'Islam*. Paris: Plon, 1926.

Bethell, Nicholas. *The Palestine Triangle: The Struggle between the British, the Jews and the Arabs, 1935–1948*. London: Andre Deutsch, 1979.

Bialer, Uri. *Between East and West: Israel's Foreign Policy Orientation 1948–1956*. Cambridge: Cambridge University Press, 1990.

Bilby, Kenneth. *New Star in the New East*. New York: Doubleday, 1950.

Bill, James, and Carl Leiden. *Politics of the Middle East*. Boston: Little, Brown, 1979.

Blum, Yehuda Zvi. *The Juridical Status of Jerusalem*. Jerusalem: Hebrew University of Jerusalem Papers on Peace Problems, 1974.

———. *Secure Boundaries and Middle East Peace*. Jerusalem: Hebrew University of Jerusalem Faculty of Law, 1971.

Blumberg, Arnold. *Zion before Zionism, 1838–1881*. Syracuse: Syracuse University Press, 1985.

———, ed. *A View from Jerusalem, 1849–1858: The Consular Diary of James and Elizabeth Anne Finn*. Cranbury, New Jersey: Associated University Press, 1980.

Bourguiba, Habib. *Introduction to the History of the National Movement*. Tunis: Ministry of Cultural Affairs and Information, 1962.

Bowie, Robert R. *Suez 1956: International Crises and the Role of Law*. New York: Oxford University Press, 1974.

Bradley, C. Paul. *Parliamentary Elections in Israel: Three Case Studies*. Grantham, New Hampshire: Thompson and Rutter, 1985.

Brand, Laurie A. *Palestinians in the Arab World: Institution Building and the Search for State*. New York: Columbia University Press, 1988.

Brecher, Michael. "Ben Gurion and Sharett: Contrasting Israeli Images of 'the Arabs.' " *New Middle East* 18 (March 1970).

———. *Decision in Israel's Foreign Policy*. New Haven: Yale University Press, 1975.

Bregman, Arye. "The Economic Development of the Administered Areas." In Daniel J. Elazar, ed., *Self-rule/Shared Rule*. Ramat Gan: Turtledove Publishing, 1979.

———. *Economic Growth in the Administered Areas, 1968–1973*. Jerusalem: Bank of Israel Research Department, 1974.

Brennan, Joseph P. "Jerusalem—A Christian Perspective." In John M. Oesterreicher and Anne Sinai, eds., *Jerusalem*. New York: The John Day Company, 1974.

Brinkley, Joel. "Israeli Defense Chief Sees Failure in Quelling Uprising." *New York Times*, December 5, 1989.

Brinton, Jasper Yates. *The Mixed Courts of Egypt*. New Haven: Yale University Press, 1968.

Brockelman, Carl. *History of the Islamic Peoples*. New York: Capricorn Books, 1960.

Brown, Leon Carl. *The Tunisia of Ahmed Bey*. Princeton: Princeton University Press, 1974.

Brownlie, Ian. *Principles of Public International Law*. Oxford: Clarendon Press, 1966.

Brynen, Rex, ed. *Echoes of the Intifada: Regional Repercussions of the Palestinian-Israeli Conflict*. Boulder, Colorado: Westview Press, 1991.

Buehrig, Edward H. *The UN and the Palestinian Refugees: A Study in Non-Territorial Administration*. Bloomington: Indiana University Press, 1971.

Bull, Vivian. *The West Bank: Is It Viable?* Lexington: D. C. Heath, 1975.

Bulliet, Richard. *Conversion to Islam in the Medieval Period: An Essay in Quantitative History*. Cambridge: Harvard University Press, 1979.

Bundy, William P. "A Portentous Year." *Foreign Affairs* 62 (Fall 1984): 485–520.

Burdett, Winston. *Encounter with the Middle East: An Intimate Report of What Lies behind the Arab-Israeli Conflict*. New York: Athenaeum, 1969.

Burns, Lt. Gen. E. L. M. *Between Arab and Israeli*. London: Harrap and Co., 1962.

Calvocoressi, Peter. *Suez: Ten Years After*. New York: Pantheon Books, 1967.

Caplan, Neil. *Futile Diplomacy, Volume I: Early Arab-Zionist Negotiation Attempts, 1913–1931*. London: Frank Cass, 1983.

————. *Futile Diplomacy, Volume II: Arab-Zionist Negotiations and the End of the Mandate*. London: Frank Cass, 1986.

————. "The Yishuv, Sir Herbert Samuel, and the Arab Question in Palestine, 1921–1925." In Elie Kedourie and Sylvia G. Haim, eds., *Zionism and Arabism in Palestine and Israel*. London: Frank Cass, 1982.

Caplan, Samuel, and Harold U. Ribalow, eds. *The Great Jewish Books and Their Influence on History*. New York: Horizon Press, 1952.

Carmi, Shulamit, and Henry Rosenfeld. "The Origins of the Process of Proletarianization and Urbanization of Arab Peasants in Palestine." *Annals of the New York Academy of Sciences* 220 (1974).

Carter, Jimmy. *The Blood of Abraham: Insights into the Middle East*. New York: Houghton-Mifflin, 1985.

————. *Keeping Faith: Memoirs of a President*. New York: Bantam Books, 1982.

Carthew, Anthony. "After the Raid on Es-Samu." *New York Times Magazine*, December 18, 1966.

Caspi, Dan; Abraham Diskin; and Emanuel Gutmann, eds., *The Roots of Begin's Success: The 1981 Israeli Elections*. London: Croom Helm, 1984.

Cattan, Henry. "The Implementation of United Nations Resolutions on Palestine." In Ibrahim Abu-Lughod, ed., *Palestinian Rights: Affirmation and Denial*. Wilmette, Illinois: Medina Press, 1982.

————. *Palestine, the Arabs and Israel*. London: Longman, 1969.

Charters, David A. *The British Army and Jewish Insurgency in Palestine, 1945–47*. New York: St. Martin's Press, 1989.

Chazan, Naomi. "Domestic Developments in Israel." In William B. Quandt, ed., *The Middle East: Ten Years after Camp David*. Washington: The Brookings Institution, 1988.

Childers, Erskine B. "The Other Exodus." *The Spectator*, May 12, 1961.

————. "The Wordless Wish: From Citizens to Refugees." In Ibrahim Abu-Lughod, ed., *The Transformation of Palestine: Essays on the Origin and Development of the Arab-Israeli Conflict*. Evanston: Northwestern University Press, 1971.

Chomsky, Noam. *The Fateful Triangle: The United States, Israel and the Palestinians*. Boston: South End Press, 1983.

Chouraqui, André. *L'Alliance israelite universelle et la renaissance contemporaine juive*. Paris: Presses Universitaires de France, 1965.

————. *Between East and West: The Jews of North Africa*. Philadelphia: Jewish Publication Society of North America, 1968.

Churchill, Randolph S., and Winston S. Churchill. *The Six Day War*. Boston: Houghton Mifflin, 1967.

Cobban, Helena. *The Palestine Liberation Organization: People, Power and Politics*. London: Cambridge University Press, 1984.

Cohen, Abner. *Arab Border Villages in Israel*. Manchester: Manchester University Press, 1965.

Cohen, Aharon. *Israel and the Arab World* (Hebrew). Tel Aviv, 1964.

Cohen, Michael J. *Palestine: Retreat from the Mandate, The Making of British Policy, 1936–1945*. London: Paul Elek, 1978.

————. *Palestine and the Great Powers, 1945–1948*. Princeton: Princeton University Press, 1982.

————. "The Zionist Perspective." In William Roger Louis and Robert W. Stookey, eds., *The End of the Palestine Mandate*. Austin: University of Texas Press, 1986.

Cohn, Norman. "Medieval Millenarianism: Its Bearing on the Comparative Study of Millenarian Movements." In Sylvia Thrupp, ed., *Millenarian Dreams in Action.* New York: Schocken Books, 1970.

———. *The Pursuit of the Millennium.* London: Mercury Books, 1950.

Congrès de l'Afrique du Nord. Paris: Comité d'organisation du congrès, 1908–1909.

Cooley, John. *Green March, Black September.* London: Frank Cass, 1973.

Cooper, Mark N. *The Transformation of Egypt.* Baltimore: The Johns Hopkins University Press, 1982.

Copeland, Miles. *The Game of Nations: The Amorality of Power Politics.* New York: Simon and Schuster, 1969.

Coulson, Noel J. *Conflicts and Tensions in Islamic Jurisprudence.* Chicago: University of Chicago Press, 1969.

———. *A History of Islamic Law.* Edinburgh: Edinburgh University Press, 1964.

Country Reports on Human Rights Practices for 1988: Report Submitted to the Committee on Foreign Relations of the U.S. Senate and the Committee on Foreign Affairs of the U.S. House of Representatives. Washington, D.C.: U.S. Department of State, February 1989.

Crossman, Richard. *Palestine Mission: A Personal Record.* New York: Harper and Brothers, 1947.

Cudsi, Alexander S., and Ali E. Hillal Dessouki, eds. *Islam and Power.* Baltimore: Johns Hopkins University Press, 1981.

Curtis, Michael, ed. *People and Politics in the Middle East.* New Brunswick, New Jersey: Transaction Books, 1971.

———. *Religion and Politics in the Middle East.* Boulder, Colorado: Westview Press, 1981.

Curtis, Michael, et al., eds. *The Palestinians: People, History, Politics.* New Brunswick, New Jersey: Transaction Books, 1975.

Curtis, Michael, and Susan Aurelia Gitelson, eds. *Israel and the Third World.* New Brunswick, New Jersey: Transaction Books, 1976.

Cygielman, Victor. "The Impact of Two Years of the Intifada." *New Outlook* (December 1989).

Daniel-Rops, Henri. *Israel and the Ancient World.* Garden City: Doubleday Image Books, 1964.

Dann, Uriel. *King Hussein and the Challenge of Arab Radicalism: Jordan, 1955–1967.* Oxford: Oxford University Press, 1989.

Dar, Ami. "Shooting and Defecating." *Jerusalem Post,* February 21, 1989.

Davis, M. Thomas. *40 Km into Lebanon: Israel's 1982 Invasion.* Washington, D.C.: National Defense University Press, 1987.

Dawisha, Adeed. *Syria and the Lebanese Crisis.* London: Macmillan, 1980.

Dawisha, Karen. *Soviet Foreign Policy towards Egypt.* New York: St. Martin's Press, 1979.

Dawn, C. Ernest. "The Rise of Arabism in Syria." *Middle East Journal* 16 (1962): 145–168.

Day, Arthur R. *East Bank/West Bank: Jordan and the Prospects for Peace.* New York: Council on Foreign Relations, 1986.

Dayan, Moshe. "After All, What about the Mountain Ridge?" (Hebrew). *Yediot Aharonot,* February 13, 1981.

———. *Breakthrough: A Personal Account of the Egypt-Israel Peace Negotiations.* New York: Knopf, 1981.

————. *Diary of the Sinai Campaign.* London: Weidenfeld and Nicolson, 1966.

Decter, Moshe. *To Serve, to Teach, to Leave: The Story of Israeli Development Assistance Programs in Black Africa.* New York: American Jewish Congress, 1977.

Dehter, Aaron. *How Expensive Are West Bank Settlements?* Jerusalem: The Jerusalem Post, 1987.

DeLima, N. "On Labor in Palestine." In *The Jewish National Fund: From the Beginnings of Its Activities in Palestine until the Purchases of the Valley* (Hebrew). Jerusalem: Initiating Committee, 1939.

Denoyan, Gilbert. *El Fatah Parle.* Paris: Éditions Albin Michel, 1970.

Dessouki, Ali E. Hillal, ed. *Islamic Resurgence in the Arab World.* New York: Praeger Publishers, 1982.

Devlin, John F. *The Ba'th Party: A History from Its Origins to 1966.* Stanford: Hoover Institution Press, 1976.

————. *Syria: Modern State in an Ancient Land.* Boulder, Colorado: Westview Press, 1983.

Dinitz, Simha. "The Legal Aspects of the Egyptian Blockade of the Suez Canal." *Georgetown Law Journal* 45 (Winter 1956–57).

Dishon, Daniel, ed. *The Middle East Record, 1968.* Tel Aviv: Israel Universities Press, 1971.

Divine, Donna Robinson. "Why This War." *International Journal of Middle East Studies* 7 (1976): 523–543.

Dodd, C. H., and M. E. Sales. *Israel and the Arab World.* New York: Barnes and Noble, 1970.

Drobles, Matityahu. *The Master Plan for the Development of Settlement in Judea and Samaria.* Jerusalem: Jewish National Fund, 1978.

————. *Strategy, Policy and Plans for Settlement in Judea and Samaria.* Jerusalem: World Zionist Organization, 1980.

Eban, Abba. *An Autobiography.* New York: Random House, 1977.

————. "Israel: Hardly the Monaco of the Middle East." *New York Times Magazine,* January 2, 1989.

Eden, Anthony. *The Suez Crisis of 1956.* Boston: Beacon Press, 1968.

Efrat, Elisha. *Geography and Politics in Israel since 1967.* London: Frank Cass, 1988.

Eilan, Michael, and David Landau. "Shultz to Tell Hussein It's Time to Name Names." *Jerusalem Post,* May 12, 1985.

Eilts, Hermann F. "The United States and Egypt." In William B. Quandt, *The Middle East: Ten Years after Camp David.* Washington: The Brookings Institution, 1988.

Eisenberg, Azriel, and Leah Ain-Globe, eds. *Home at Last.* New York: Bloch Publishing Company, 1977.

Eisenstadt, S. N. *Israeli Society.* New York: Basic Books, 1967.

————. *The Transformation of Israeli Society.* Boulder, Colorado: Westview Press, 1985.

Elazar, Daniel J. "Religious Parties and Politics in the Begin Era." In Robert O. Freedman, ed., *Israel in the Begin Era.* New York: Praeger, 1982.

————, ed. *Judea, Samaria, and Gaza: Views of the Present and the Future.* Washington: American Enterprise Institute, 1982.

————. *Self-rule/Shared Rule.* Ramat Gan: Turtledove Publishing, 1979.

Elazar, Daniel J., and Janet Aviad. "Religion and Politics in Israel: The Interplay of Judaism and Zionism." In Michael Curtis, ed., *Religion and Politics in the Middle East.* Boulder, Colorado: Westview Press, 1981.

Eldad, Israel. "Transfer as a 'Zionist' Solution" (Hebrew). *Ha'aretz*, July 9, 1987.

Elon, Amos. *The Israelis: Founders and Sons*. New York: Holt, Rinehart and Winston, 1971.

Erlich, Avishai. "Is Transfer an Option?" *Israeli Democracy* 1 (Winter 1987): 36–38.

Ernest, Morris L. *So Far So Good*. New York: Harper, 1948.

Esposito, John. "Law in Islam." In Yvonne Yazbeck Haddad, Byron Haines, and Ellison Findly, eds., *The Islamic Impact*. Syracuse: Syracuse University Press, 1984.

Esposito, John L. *Islam: The Straight Path*. New York: Oxford University Press, 1988.

———, ed. *Islam and Development*. Syracuse: Syracuse University Press, 1980.

Ettinger, M., ed. *Book of the Economy of the Yishuv, 1947* (Hebrew). Tel Aviv: HaVaad HaLeumi, 1947.

Evron, Yair. *The Middle East: Nations, Superpowers and Wars*. New York: Praeger, 1973.

Fahmy, Ismail. *Negotiating for Peace in the Middle East*. Baltimore: Johns Hopkins University Press, 1983.

Fanon, Frantz. *A Dying Colonialism*. New York: Grove Press, 1965.

al Faruqi, Isma'il. "Islam as Culture and Civilization." In Salem Azzam, ed., *Islam and Contemporary Society*. London: Longman and the Islamic Council of Europe, 1982.

Fawzi, Mahmoud. *The Three-Year War* (Arabic). Cairo: al-Mustaqbal al-Arabi, 1984.

Federbush, Simon. "The Talmud." In Samuel Caplan and Harold U. Ribalow, eds., *The Great Jewish Books and Their Influence on History*. New York: Horizon Press, 1952.

Fein, Leonard. *Politics in Israel*. Boston: Little, Brown, 1967.

Feinberg, Nathan. *The Arab-Israeli Conflict in International Law*. Jerusalem, 1970.

———. *The Legality of a 'State of War' after the Cessation of Hostilities under the Charter of the United Nations and the Covenant of the League of Nations*. Jerusalem: Magnes Press, 1961.

Feis, Herbert. *The Birth of Israel: The Tousled Diplomatic Bed*. New York: Norton, 1969.

Feldman, Shai, and Heda Rechnitz-Kijner. "Deception, Consensus and War: Israel in Lebanon." Occasional Papers of the Jaffee Center for Strategic Studies of Tel Aviv University, no. 27, October 1984.

Finkelstein, Norman. "Myths, Old and New." *Journal of Palestine Studies* 81 (Autumn 1991): 66–89.

Flapan, Simha. *The Birth of Israel: Myths and Realities*. New York: Pantheon Books, 1987.

———. "Dr. Sartawi—and the Dilemma of Israeli-Palestinian Dialogue." *New Outlook* (March 1982).

———. *Zionism and the Palestinians*. London: Croom Helm, 1979.

Fletcher, Elaine Ruth. "Islamization of the Conflict." *Jerusalem Post Magazine*, January 29, 1988.

"For the Rights of Palestinians: Work of the Committee on the Exercise of the Inalienable Rights of the Palestinian People." United Nations document, n.d.

Frangi, Abdallah. *The PLO and Palestine*. London: Zed Books, 1983.

Frankel, William. *Israel Observed: An Anatomy of the State*. New York: Thames and Hudson, 1980.

Freedman, Robert O., ed. *Israel in the Begin Era*. New York: Praeger, 1982.

———. *The Middle East since Camp David*. Boulder, Colorado: Westview Press, 1984.

———. "The Soviet Union and the Crisis in Lebanon: A Case Study of Soviet Policy from the Israeli Invasion to the Abrogation of the 17 May Agreement." In Halim Barakat, ed., *Toward a Viable Lebanon*. London: Croom Helm, 1988.

Friedman, Isaiah. *Germany, Turkey and Zionism: 1897–1918.* London: Oxford University Press, 1977.

Friedman, Robert I. "The Sayings of Rabbi Kahane." *New York Review of Books,* February 13, 1986.

Frisch, Hillel. "Between Diffusion and Territorial Consolidation in Rebellion: Striking at the Hard Core of the Intifada." *Terrorism and Political Violence* 3 (Winter 1991).

Fromkin, David. *A Peace to End All Peace: Creating the Modern Middle East, 1914–1922.* New York: Henry Holt, 1989.

Furlonge, Geoffrey. *Palestine Is My Country: The Story of Musa Alami.* London: John Murray, 1969.

Gabbay, Rony E. *A Political Study of the Arab-Jewish Conflict.* New York: Gregory Lounz, 1959.

Gabriel, Judith. "Israel's Policy of Deportation." *The Return: An International Palestinian Monthly Magazine* 1, no. 11 (October 1988): 6–10.

———. "Israel's Use of House Demolitions: Collective Punishment on the Rise." *The Return: An International Palestinian Monthly Magazine* 1, no. 3 (July 1989): 16–19.

Gabriel, Richard. *Operation Peace for Galilee: The Israeli-PLO War in Lebanon.* New York: Hill and Wang, 1984.

"A Gallup/IPS Survey regarding the Conflict between Israel and the Palestinians." *Journal of Palestine Studies* 74 (Winter 1990): 75–86.

Galnoor, Itzhak. "The 1984 Elections in Israel: Political Results and Open Questions." *Middle East Review* (Summer 1986).

Garnham, David. "Explaining Middle Eastern Alignments during the Gulf War." *Jerusalem Journal of International Relations* 13 (Fall 1991): 63–83.

Gendzier, Irene L., ed. *A Middle East Reader.* New York: Pegasus, 1969.

Gervasi, Frank. *The Case for Israel.* New York: Viking, 1967.

Getz, A., ed. *Statistical Handbook of Jewish Palestine, 1947.* Jerusalem: Jewish Agency, 1947.

Getzler, Dvorah, and Asher Wallfish. "Tied Vote Scuttles Bill on Contacts with PLO." *Jerusalem Post,* January 12, 1989.

al-Ghazali, Said. "Fundamentalist Groups See Islam as Changing the World." *Al-Fajr Jerusalem,* July 19, 1987.

———. "Unanimous Rejection of Peres' Plan." *Al-Fajr Jerusalem,* October 25, 1985.

Gibb, H. A. R. *Arabic Literature.* Oxford: Oxford University Press, 1926.

———. "The Islamic Congress at Jerusalem, December, 1931." In *Survey of International Affairs: 1934.* Oxford, 1935.

———. *Mohammedanism.* New York: Oxford University Press, 1962.

———. *Studies on the Civilization of Islam.* Boston: Beacon Press, 1962.

Gil, Moshe. *A History of Palestine, 634–1099.* Cambridge: Cambridge University Press, 1992.

Gilmour, David. *Lebanon: The Fractured Country.* New York: St. Martin's Press, 1983.

Glubb, John Bagot. *Peace in the Holy Land: An Historical Analysis of the Palestinian Problem.* London: Hodder and Stoughton, 1971.

———. *A Soldier with the Arabs.* London: Hodder and Stoughton, 1957.

Golan, Galia. *The Soviet Union and the Arab-Israeli War of October, 1973.* Jerusalem: The Hebrew University Press, 1974.

Golan, Matti. *Secret Conversations with Henry Kissinger: Step-by-Step Diplomacy in the Middle East.* New York: Quadrangle Books, 1976.

———. *Shimon Peres: A Biography.* London: Weidenfeld and Nicolson, 1982.

Gold, Dore. "The Generals and the Areas." *Jerusalem Post*, June 10, 1988.

Goldberg, Giora; Gad Barzilai; and Efraim Inbar. "The Impact of Intercommunal Conflict: The Intifada and Israeli Public Opinion." Policy Studies of the Leonard Davis Institute, The Hebrew University of Jerusalem, no. 43, February 1991.

Goldman, Solomon. "The Hebrew Bible." In Samuel Caplan and Harold U. Ribalow, eds., *The Great Jewish Books and Their Influence on History.* New York: Horizon Press, 1952.

Goodman, Hirsh. "Limited Mission Accomplished." *Jerusalem Post*, July 25, 1986.

———. "When Extremism Eclipses Reason." *Jerusalem Post* (International Edition), October 24, 1987.

Gordon, David. *North Africa's French Legacy.* Cambridge: Harvard Middle Eastern Monograph Series, 1962.

Gordon, Joel. *Nasser's Blessed Movement: Egypt's Free Officers and the July Revolution.* New York: Oxford University Press, 1992.

Gorny, Yosef. *Zionism and the Arabs, 1882–1948: A Study of Ideology.* New York: Oxford University Press, 1987.

Gottheil, Fred. "Arab Immigration into Pre-State Israel: 1922-1931." In Elie Kedourie and Sylvia G. Haim, eds., *Palestine and Israel in the 19th and 20th Centuries.* London: Frank Cass, 1982.

Graham-Brown, Sarah. "The Economic Consequences of Occupation." In Naseer H. Aruri, ed., *Occupation: Israel over Palestine.* Belmont, Massachusetts: Association of Arab-American University Graduates, 1983.

Granott, A. *Agrarian Reform and the Record of Israel.* London: Eyre and Spottiswoode, 1956.

———. *The Land System in Palestine: History and Structure.* London: Eyre and Spottiswoode, 1952.

Grayzel, Solomon. *A History of the Jews.* New York: New American Library, 1968.

Gresh, Alain. *The PLO: The Struggle Within, Toward an Independent Palestinian State.* London: Zed Books, 1985.

Grose, Peter. *A Changing Israel.* New York: Vintage, 1985.

———. "The President versus the Diplomats." In William Roger Louis and Robert W. Stookey, eds., *The End of the Palestine Mandate.* Austin: University of Texas Press, 1986.

Gross, Leo. "Passage through the Suez Canal of Israel-Bound Cargo and Israeli Ships." *American Journal of International Law* 51 (1957): 530–568.

———. "The Geneva Conference on the Law of the Sea and the Right of Innocent Passage through the Gulf of Aqaba." *American Journal of International Law* 53 (1959): 564–594.

Grossmann, Gabriel. "The Christian Churches in Present-Day Israel." In John M. Oesterreicher and Anne Sinai, eds., *Jerusalem.* New York: The John Day Company, 1974.

Gubser, Peter. *Jordan: Crossroads of Middle Eastern Events.* Boulder, Colorado: Westview Press, 1983.

Gutmann, Emmanuel. "Begin's Israel: The End of an Era." *International Journal* 38 (1983): 690–699.

Ha'am, Ahad. *Nationalism and the Jewish Ethic.* Edited with an introduction by Hans Kohn. New York, 1962.

Hadari, Ze'ev Venia. *Second Exodus: The Full Story of Jewish Illegal Immigration to Palestine, 1945–1948.* London: Vallentine, Mitchell, 1991.

Hadawi, Sami. *Bitter Harvest: Palestine 1914–1967.* New York: The New World Press, 1967.

Haddad, Heskel M. "The Jewish Refugees from the Arab Countries." *Middle East Information Series* 16 (November 1971): 29–32.

Haddad, Yvonne Yazbeck; Byron Haines; and Ellison Findly, eds. *The Islamic Impact.* Syracuse: Syracuse University Press, 1984.

Haig, Alexander. *Caveat: Realism, Reagan and Foreign Policy.* New York: Macmillan, 1984.

Haim, Sylvia G., ed. *Arab Nationalism: An Anthology.* Berkeley: University of California Press, 1962.

Halabi, Rafik. *The West Bank Story.* New York: Harcourt Brace Jovanovich, 1981.

Halper, Jeffrey. *Between Redemption and Revival: The Jewish Yishuv of Jerusalem in the Nineteenth Century.* Boulder, Colorado: Westview Press, 1991.

Halpern, Ben. "The Anti-Zionist Phobia: Legal Style." *Midstream* 2 (1965): 74–85.

Halsell, Grace. *Journey to Jerusalem.* New York: Macmillan, 1981.

Hammad, Burhan W. "The Right of Passage in the Gulf of Aqaba." *Revue Égyptienne de Droit International* 15 (1959): 118–151.

Handel, Michael. *Perception, Deception, and Surprise: The Case of the Yom Kippur War.* Jerusalem: The Hebrew University Press, 1975.

Hanna, Paul L. *British Policy in Palestine.* Washington: American Council on Public Affairs, 1942.

Harb, Ghassan. "Labor and Manpower." In Emile A. Nakhleh, ed., *A Palestinian Agenda for the West Bank and Gaza.* Washington: American Enterprise Institute, 1980.

Harel, Menashe. "The Jewish Presence in Palestine throughout the Ages." In John M. Oesterreicher and Anne Sinai, eds., *Jerusalem.* New York: John Day, 1974.

Harik, Iliya. "Lebanon: Anatomy of Conflict." American Universities Field Staff Reports, Asia, no. 49, 1981.

Harkabi, Yehoshafat. "Fedayeen Action and Arab Strategy." Adelphi Papers. no. 53, December 1968.

———. "The Palestinian National Covenant." In Michael Curtis et al., eds., *The Palestinians: People, History, Politics.* New Brunswick, New Jersey: Transaction Books, 1975.

Harris, William W. *Taking Root: Israeli Settlement in the West Bank, the Golan, and Gaza-Sinai, 1967–1980.* New York: John Wiley, 1980.

Hart, Aaron. "The Unrest That Makes Peace More Remote." *Jerusalem Post*, January 28, 1988.

Hassan Ibn Talal, "Jordan's Quest for Peace." *Foreign Affairs* 60 (Spring 1982): 802–813.

Hattis, Susan Lee. *The Bi-National Idea in Palestine during Mandatory Times.* Haifa: Shikmona, 1970.

Haykal, Muhammad. *The Road to Ramadan.* New York: The New York Times Book Company, 1975.

Haykal, Muhammad Hassanein. "An Armed Clash with Israel Is Inevitable—Why?" (Arabic) *Al-Ahram*, May 26, 1967.

———. *The Sphinx and the Commissar*. London: Collins, 1977.

Heller, Mark A. *A Palestinian State: The Implications for Israel*. Cambridge, Massachusetts: Harvard University Press, 1983.

Heller, Mark A., and Sari Nusseibeh. *No Trumpets, No Drums: A Two-State Settlement of the Israeli-Palestinian Conflict*. New York: Hill and Wang, 1991.

Hertzberg, Arthur. *The French Enlightenment and the Jews*. Philadelphia: Jewish Publication Society, 1968.

———. "Ideological Evolution." In *Israel Pocket Library: Zionism*. Jerusalem: Keter Publishing House, 1973.

———. *The Zionist Idea*. New York: Atheneum, 1970.

Herzl, Theodor. *Complete Diaries*. New York: Herzl Press, 1960.

———. *Palais Bourbon: Bilder aus dem franzosischen Parlamentsleben*. Leipzig, 1895.

Herzog, Chaim. *The Arab-Israeli Wars*. New York: Vintage Books, 1984.

———. *The War of Atonement: October 1973*. Boston: Little, Brown, 1975.

Heschel, Abraham Joshua. *Israel: An Echo of Eternity*. New York: Farrar, Straus and Giroux, 1967.

Hilal, Jamil. "Class Transformation in the West Bank and Gaza." *MERIP Reports* 53 (December 1976): 10.

———. *The West Bank: The Socio-Economic Structure, 1948–1974*. Beirut: Palestine Liberation Organization Research Center, 1975.

Hillel, Shlomo. "Operation Ezra and Nehemiah." In Azriel Eisenberg and Leah Ain-Globe, eds., *Home at Last*. New York: Bloch Publishing Company, 1977.

Hiltermann, Joost. *Behind the Intifada: Labor and Women's Movements in the Occupied Territories*. Princeton: Princeton University Press, 1991.

———. "The Enemy inside the Intifada." *The Nation*, September 10, 1990.

Hirschberg, Haim Z'ew. "The Ottoman Period (1517–1917)." In *Israel Pocket Library: History until 1880*. Jerusalem: Keter Publishing House, 1973.

Hitti, Philip K. *Islam and the West*. Princeton: Van Nostrand, 1962.

Hof, Frederic C. *Galilee Divided: The Israel-Lebanon Frontier, 1916–1984*. Boulder, Colorado: Westview Press, 1988.

Holt, P. M. *Egypt and the Fertile Crescent, 1516–1922: A Political History*. Ithaca: Cornell University Press, 1966.

Horowitz, Dan, and Moshe Lissak. *Origins of the Israeli Polity: Palestine under the Mandate*. Chicago: University of Chicago Press, 1978.

Hourani, Albert. *Arabic Thought in the Liberal Age: 1798–1939*. London: Oxford University Press, 1962.

House, Karen Elliott. "Hussein's Decision." *Wall Street Journal*, April 14, 1983 and April 15, 1983.

Hudson, Michael C. *Arab Politics: The Search for Legitimacy*. New Haven: Yale University Press, 1977.

———. "The Arab States' Policies toward Israel." In Ibrahim Abu-Lughod, ed., *The Transformation of Palestine: Essays on the Origin and Development of the Arab-Israeli Conflict*. Evanston: Northwestern University Press, 1971.

———. "Developments and Setbacks in the Palestine Resistance Movement, 1967–1971." *Journal of Palestine Studies* 1 (Spring 1972): 64–84.

———. "Islam and Political Development." In John Esposito (ed.), *Islam and Development*. Syracuse: Syracuse University Press, 1980.

———. *Lebanon: The Precarious Republic*. New York: Random House, 1968.

———. "The United States' Involvement in Lebanon." In Halim Barakat, ed., *Toward a Viable Lebanon*. London: Croom Helm, 1988.

Hunter, F. Robert. *Egypt under the Khedives, 1805–1879: From Household Government to Modern Bureaucracy*. Pittsburgh: University of Pittsburgh Press, 1984.

———. *The Palestinian Uprising*. Berkeley: University of California Press, 1991.

Hunter, Shireen, ed. *The Politics of Islamic Revivalism*. Bloomington: Indiana University Press, 1988.

Hurewitz, J. C. *Middle East Politics: The Military Dimension*. New York: Praeger, 1969.

———. *The Struggle for Palestine*. New York: Schocken Books, 1976.

al-Husayni, Muhammad Amin. *Haqa'iq ar Qadiyyat Filastin* [Truths regarding the Palestine Problem] (Arabic). Cairo, 1954.

Hussein, King of Jordan. *My 'War' with Israel*. New York: Morrow, 1969.

Hyamson, Albert M. *Palestine under the Mandate*. London: Methuen, 1950.

Ibrahim, Saad Eddin. "Domestic Developments in Egypt." In William B. Quandt, *The Middle East: Ten Years after Camp David*. Washington: The Brookings Institution, 1988.

———. "Islamic Militancy as a Social Movement: The Case of Two Groups in Egypt." In Ali E. Hillal Dessouki, ed., *Islamic Resurgence in the Arab World*. New York: Praeger Publishers, 1982.

Ibrahim, Youssef. "Jordan's West Bank Moves Upsetting Daily Life." *New York Times*, October 18, 1988.

Ilan, Amitzur. *Bernadotte in Palestine, 1948*. New York: St. Martin's, 1989.

Inbar, Efraim. "The 'No Choice War' Debate in Israel." *Journal of Strategic Studies* 12 (March 1989).

Ingrams, Doreen. *Palestine Papers 1917–1922: Seeds of Conflict*. London: John Murray, 1972.

Isaac, Real Jean. *Israel Divided: Ideological Politics in the Jewish State*. Baltimore: Johns Hopkins University Press, 1976.

———. *Party and Politics in Israel: Three Visions of a Jewish State*. New York: Longman, 1981.

Israel in Lebanon: The Report of the International Commission to Enquire into Reported Violations of International Law by Israel during Its Invasion of Lebanon. London: Ithaca Press, 1983.

Israel Pocket Library: History until 1880. Jerusalem: Keter Publishing House, 1973.

Israel Pocket Library: History from 1880. Jerusalem: Keter Publishing House, 1973.

Israel Pocket Library: Zionism. Jerusalem: Keter Publishing House, 1973.

Israeli, Raphael. "The Charter of Allah: The Platform of the Islamic Resistance Movement (Hamas)." In Yonah Alexander and Abraham H. Foxman, eds., *The 1988–1989 Annual on Terrorism*. Amsterdam: Kluwer Academic Publishers, 1990.

———. "The Israeli Elections of 1984: Issues and Factions." *Middle East Review* (Special Report) 1 (1984/1985).

The Israeli Administration in Judea, Samaria and Gaza. Tel Aviv: Ministry of Defense, 1968.

Israeli Settlements in the Occupied Arab Territories. Tunis: League of Arab States, 1987.

Jacobs, Paul. *Between the Rock and the Hard Place*. New York: Random House, 1970.

Jankowski, James. "Egyptian Responses to the Palestine Problem in the Interwar Period." *International Journal of Middle East Studies* 12 (1980): 1–38.

———. "The Government of Egypt and the Palestine Question, 1936–1939." *Middle East Studies* 17 (1981).

Jansen, Johannes J. G. *The Neglected Duty: The Creed of Sadat's Assassins and Islamic Resurgence in the Middle East*. New York: Macmillan, 1986.

Jansen, Michael. *The Battle of Beirut: Why Israel Invaded Lebanon*. London: Zed Press, 1982.

Jiryis, Sabri. *The Arabs in Israel*. Beirut: The Institute for Palestine Studies, 1969.

Johnson, Nels. *Islam and the Politics of Meaning in Palestinian Nationalism*. London: Kegan Paul, 1982.

Judea-Samaria and the Gaza District since 1967. Jerusalem: Israel Information Center, 1986.

Jureidini, Paul A., and William Hazan. *The Palestinian Movement in Politics*. Lexington, Massachusetts: D. C. Heath, 1979.

Kalkas, Barbara. "The Revolt of 1936: A Chronicle of Events." In Ibrahim Abu-Lughod, ed., *The Transformation of Palestine: Essays on the Origin and Development of the Arab-Israeli Conflict*. Evanston: Northwestern University Press, 1971.

The Karp Report: An Israeli Government Inquiry into Settler Violence against Palestinians on the West Bank (Hebrew). Published in English in 1984 by the Institute for Palestine Studies, Washington, D.C.

Katz, Samuel. *Battleground: Fact and Fantasy in Palestine*. New York: Bantam Books, 1973.

Kazziha, Walid W. *Palestine in the Arab Dilemma*. New York: Barnes and Noble, 1979.

Keddie, Nikki. *An Islamic Response to Imperialism: Political and Religious Writings of Sayyid Jamal ad-Din al-Afghani*. Berkeley: University of California Press, 1983.

Kedourie, Elie. "The Arab-Israeli Conflict." In *Arab Political Memoirs and Other Studies*. London: Frank Cass, 1974.

Kedourie, Elie, and Sylvia G. Haim, eds. *Palestine and Israel in the 19th and 20th Centuries*. London: Frank Cass, 1982.

———. *Zionism and Arabism in Palestine and Israel*. London: Frank Cass, 1982.

Keesing's Research Report. *The Arab-Israeli Conflict: The 1967 Campaign*. New York: Charles Scribner's, 1968.

Kerr, Malcolm H. *The Arab Cold War: Gamal 'Abd al-Nasir and His Rivals, 1958–1970*. London: Oxford University Press, 1971.

———. "The Changing Political Status of Jerusalem." In Ibrahim Abu-Lughod, ed., *The Transformation of Palestine: Essays on the Origin and Development of the Arab-Israeli Conflict*. Evanston: Northwestern University Press, 1971.

Khadduri, Majid. *Arab Contemporaries: The Role of Personalities in Politics*. Baltimore: Johns Hopkins University Press, 1973.

———. "Closure of the Suez Canal to Israeli Shipping." *Law and Contemporary Problems* 33 (1968): 147–157.

Khairallah, Chedley. *Le Mouvement Jeune Tunisien.* Tunis: Bonici, n.d.

Khalidi, Rashid. *British Policy towards Syria and Palestine: 1906–1914.* London: Ithaca Press, 1980.

———. "The 19th PNC Resolutions and American Policy." *Journal of Palestine Studies* 74 (Winter 1990): 29–42.

———. *Under Siege: PLO Decisionmaking during the 1982 War.* New York: Columbia University Press, 1986.

Khalidi, Walid. *Conflict and Violence in Lebanon: Confrontation in the Middle East.* Cambridge: Harvard Center for International Affairs, 1979.

———. "Regiopolitics: Toward a U.S. Policy on the Palestine Problem." *Foreign Affairs* 59 (Summer 1981): 1050–1063.

———, ed. *From Haven to Conquest: Readings in Zionism and the Palestine Problem until 1948.* Beirut: Institute for Palestine Studies, 1971.

———, trans. "Nasser's Memoirs of the First Palestine War." *Journal of Palestine Studies* 2 (1973): 3–32.

Khouri, Fred J. *The Arab-Israeli Dilemma.* Syracuse: Syracuse University Press, 1985.

Kimche, David, and Dan Bawley. *The Sandstorm: The Arab-Israeli War of June, 1967, Prelude and Aftermath.* London: Stein and Day, 1968.

Kimche, Jon. *Palestine or Israel.* London: Secker and Warburg, 1973.

———. *The Seven Fallen Pillars.* New York: Praeger, 1953.

Kimche, Jon, and David Kimche. *Both Sides of the Hill* London: Secker and Warburg, 1960.

Kimmerling, Baruch. *Zionism and the Economy.* Cambridge: Schenkman, 1983.

———. *Zionism and Territory: The Socio-Territorial Dimensions of Zionist Politics.* Berkeley: University of California, Institute of International Studies, 1983.

Kirisci, Kemal. *The PLO and World Politics: A Study of the Mobilization of Support for the Palestinian Cause.* London: Frances Pinter, 1986.

Kirk, George. *A Short History of the Middle East: From the Rise of Islam to Modern Times.* New York: Praeger, 1964.

Kissinger, Henry. *The White House Years.* Boston: Little, Brown, 1979.

Koestler, Arthur. *Promise and Fulfillment: Palestine, 1917–1949.* London: Macmillan, 1949.

Korn, David A. *Stalemate: The War of Attrition and Great Power Diplomacy in the Middle East, 1967–1970.* Boulder, Colorado: Westview Press, 1992.

Kotker, Norman. *The Earthly Jerusalem.* New York: Charles Scribner's, 1969.

Kreczko, Alan J. "Support Reagan's Initiative." *Foreign Policy* (Winter 1982/1983): 140–153.

Kressel, Getzel. "Zionist Congresses." In *Israel Pocket Library: Zionism.* Jerusalem: Keter Publishing House, 1973.

Kritzeck, James, ed. *Anthology of Islamic Literature.* New York: Meridian, 1964.

Kroyanker, David. *Developing Jerusalem: 1967–1975.* Jerusalem: The Jerusalem Foundation, 1975.

Kupferschmidt, Uri. *The Supreme Muslim Council: Islam under the British Mandate in Palestine.* Leiden: Brill, 1987.

Kuttab, Daoud. "Beyond the Intifada: The Struggle to Build a Nation." *The Nation,* October 17, 1988.

———. "A Profile of the Stonethrowers." *Journal of Palestine Studies* 67 (Spring 1988): 14–23.

Kuttab, Jonathan, and Raja Shehadeh. *Civilian Administration in the Occupied West Bank*. Ramallah: Law in the Service of Man, 1982.

Lacouture, Jean, and Simonne Lacouture. *Egypt in Transition*. London: Methuen, 1958.

Lall, Arthur S. *The UN and the Middle East Crisis, 1967*. New York: Columbia University Press, 1968.

Lamb, Franklin, ed. *Reason Not the Need: Eyewitness Chronicles of Israel's War in Lebanon*. Nottingham, England: Spokesman for the Bertrand Russell Peace Foundation, 1984.

Landau, Jacob. *The Arabs in Israel*. London: Oxford University Press, 1969.

Landes, David. *Bankers and Pashas: International Finance and Economic Imperialism in Egypt*. Cambridge: Harvard University Press, 1958.

Lapidoth, Ruth. "The Taba Controversy." *Jerusalem Quarterly* 37 (1986).

Laqueur, Walter. *A History of Zionism*. New York: Schocken Books, 1976.

———. *The Road to War: The Origins and Aftermath of the Arab-Israeli Conflict, 1967–8*. Baltimore: Penguin Books, 1968.

Laqueur, Walter, and Barry Rubin, eds. *The Israel-Arab Reader: A Documentary History of the Middle East Conflict*. New York: Penguin Books, 1984.

Laroui, Abdallah. "The Arab Revolution between Awareness and Reality" (Arabic). *Mawaqif* 10 (July-August 1970).

———. *The Crisis of the Arab Intellectual*. Berkeley: University of California Press, 1976.

Laskier, Michael. *The Alliance Israelite Universelle and the Jewish Communities of Morocco: 1862–1962*. Albany: State University of New York Press, 1983.

Laufer, Leopold. *Israel and the Developing Countries: New Approaches to Cooperation*. New York: The Twentieth Century Fund, 1967.

Lauterpacht, Elihu. *Jerusalem and the Holy Places*. London: Anglo-Israel Association, 1968.

Lazarus-Yafeh, Hava. "The Sanctity of Jerusalem in Islam." In John M. Oesterreicher and Anne Sinai, eds., *Jerusalem*. New York: John Day, 1974.

Legrain, Jean-Francois. "A Defining Moment: Palestinian Islamic Fundamentalism." In James Piscatori, ed., *Islamic Fundamentalisms and the Gulf Crisis*. Cambridge: American Academy of Arts and Sciences, 1991.

Lenczowski, George, ed. *Political Elites in the Middle East*. Washington: American Enterprise Institute, 1975.

Lerner, Abba, and Haim Ben Shahar. *The Economics of Efficiency and Growth: Lessons from Israel and the West Bank*. Cambridge: Ballinger, 1975.

Lesch, Ann Mosely. *Arab Politics in Palestine, 1917–1939: The Frustration of a Nationalist Movement*. Ithaca: Cornell University Press, 1979.

———. "Closed Borders, Divided Lives: Palestinian Writings." Universities Field Staff International Reports, Asia, no. 28 (1985).

———. "Israeli Occupation Policies: Reflections on the West Bank and Gaza Strip." Paper presented at the 1982 annual meeting of the Middle East Studies Association.

———. "The Palestinian Uprising—Causes and Consequences." Universities Field Staff International Reports, Asia, no. 1 (1988–89).

———. "Palestinians in Kuwait." *Journal of Palestine Studies* 80 (Summer 1991): 42–54.

————. *Political Perceptions of the Palestinians in the West Bank and the Gaza Strip.* Washington: The Middle East Institute, 1980.

————. "Uprising for Palestine." *Journal of South Asian and MiddleEastern Studies* 11 (Summer 1988): 3–20.

Lesch, Ann Mosely, and Mark Tessler. *Israel, Egypt and the Palestinians: From Camp David to Intifada.* Bloomington: Indiana University Press, 1989.

Levy, Gideon. "If You Ask Me, This Place Is Pure Peacefulness" (Hebrew). *Ha'aretz*, September 6, 1991.

Lewis, Bernard. *The Arabs in History.* New York: Harper, 1966.

————. *The Jews of Islam.* Princeton: Princeton University Press, 1984.

Lewis, Samuel W. "Israel: The Peres Era and Its Legacy." *Foreign Affairs* 65 (1987): 582–610.

————. "The United States and Israel: Constancy and Change." In William B. Quandt, ed., *The Middle East: Ten Years after Camp David.* Washington: The Brookings Institution, 1988.

Lewison, Ludwig, ed. *Theodore Herzl: A Portrait for His Age.* Cleveland and New York: World Publishing Company, 1955.

Lewy, Guenter. *Religion and Revolution.* New York: Oxford University Press, 1974.

Lichtenstadter, Ilse. *Introduction to Classical Arabic Literature.* New York: Schocken Books, 1976.

Liebman, Charles S., and Eliezer Don-Yehiya. *Religion and Politics in Israel.* Bloomington: Indiana University Press, 1984.

Lissak, Moshe. *Social Mobility in Israeli Society.* Jerusalem: Israel Universities Press, 1969.

Livneh, Neri. "Border of Fear" (Hebrew). *Hadashot*, September 29, 1989.

Lockman, Zachary, and Joel Beinin, eds. *Intifada: The Palestinian Uprising against Israeli Occupation.* Boston: South End Press, 1989.

London, Yaron. "Farewell Husayni, Nusaybah and All Other 'Authentic' Leaders" (Hebrew). *Yediot Aharonot*, August 14, 1990.

Louis, William Roger, and Robert W. Stookey, eds. *The End of the Palestine Mandate.* Austin: University of Texas Press, 1986.

Love, Kenneth. *Suez: The Twice-Fought War.* New York: McGraw-Hill, 1969.

Lukacs, Yehuda, and Abdalla M. Battah, eds. *The Arab-Israeli Conflict: Two Decades of Change.* Boulder, Colorado: Westview Press, 1988.

Lustick, Ian. *Arabs in the Jewish State.* Austin: University of Texas Press, 1980.

————. *For the Land and the Lord: Jewish Fundamentalism in Israel.* New York: Council on Foreign Relations, 1988.

————. "Israel and the West Bank after Elon Moreh: The Mechanisms of De Facto Annexation." *Middle East Journal* 35 (Autumn 1981): 557–577.

————. "Israeli Politics and American Foreign Policy." *Foreign Affairs* 61 (Winter 1982/83): 379–399.

————. "Israel's Dangerous Fundamentalists." *Foreign Policy* 68 (Fall 1987): 118–139.

Macdonald, Robert W. *The League of Arab States: A Study in the Dynamics of Regional Organization.* Princeton: Princeton University Press, 1965.

McDowall, David. *Palestine and Israel: The Uprising and Beyond.* Berkeley: University of California Press, 1989.

Magnus, Ralph, H., ed. *Documents on the Middle East.* Washington: American Enterprise Institute, 1969.

Mahler, Gregory. *Israel: Government and Politics in a Maturing State.* New York: Harcourt Brace Jovanovich, 1990.

Mahler, Raphael. *A History of Modern Jewry: 1780–1815.* New York: Schocken Books, 1971.

Mahshi, Khalil, and Ramzi Rihan. "Education: Elementary and Secondary." In Emile A. Nakhleh, ed., *A Palestinian Agenda for the West Bank and Gaza.* Washington: American Enterprise Institute, 1980.

Maksoud, Clovis. "New Palestine: Grievance Redressed, Justice for Arab and Jew." *Mid East* (June 1970): 7–10.

Mallison, W. T., Jr. "The Zionist-Israel Juridical Claims to Constitute the 'Jewish People' Nationality Entity and to Confer Membership in It: Appraisal in Public International Law." *George Washington Law Review* 32 (1964): 983–1075.

Mandel, Neville J. *The Arabs and Zionism before World War I.* Berkeley: University of California Press, 1976.

Manners, Robert A., ed. *Process and Pattern in Culture.* Chicago: Aldine Publishing Company, 1964.

Mansfield, Peter. *The Arabs.* Middlesex: Penguin Books, 1978.

———. *Nasser's Egypt.* Baltimore: Penguin Books, 1969.

Ma'oz, Moshe. *Asad: The Sphinx of Damascus.* New York: Weidenfeld and Nicolson, 1988.

———. *Palestinian Leadership in the West Bank.* London: Frank Cass, 1984.

———, ed. *Studies on Palestine during the Ottoman Period.* Jerusalem: Magnes Press, 1975.

Marcus, Yoel. "The War Is Inevitable" (Hebrew). *Ha'aretz,* March 26, 1982.

Marlowe, John. *The Seat of Pilate.* London: Cresset Press, 1959.

Marmorstein, Emile. "European Jews in Muslim Palestine." In Elie Kedourie and Sylvia G. Haim (eds.), *Palestine and Israel in the 19th and 20th Centuries.* London: Frank Cass, 1982.

Matalon, Ronit. "The Wild West: A Reservist's Monologue" (Hebrew). *Ha'aretz, Weekly Supplement,* March 11, 1988.

———. "Without a Norm" (Hebrew). *Ha'aretz,* February 19, 1988, Supplement.

Mattar, Philip. "The Critical Moment for Peace." *Foreign Policy* 76 (Fall 1989): 141–159.

———. *The Mufti of Jerusalem: Al-Hajj Amin al-Husayni and the Palestine National Movement.* New York: Columbia University Press, 1988.

Medding, Peter. *Mapai in Israel: Political Organization and Government in a New Society.* Cambridge: Cambridge University Press, 1972.

Melka, R. "Nazi Germany and the Palestine Question." In Elie Kedourie and Sylvia G. Haim, eds., *Zionism and Arabism in Palestine and Israel.* London: Frank Cass, 1982.

Melman, Yossi, and Dan Raviv. *Beyond the Uprising: Israelis, Jordanians, and Palestinians.* Westport, Connecticut: Greenwood Press, 1989.

Memmi, Albert. *Portrait du colonisé, précédé du portrait du colonisateur.* Paris: Gallimard, 1957.

Micaud, Charles A., with Leon Carl Brown and Clement Henry Moore. *Tunisia: The Politics of Modernization.* New York: Praeger, 1964.

Migdal, Joel, ed. *Palestinian Society and Politics.* Princeton: Princeton University Press, 1980.

Miller, Aaron David. *The PLO: The Politics of Survival.* New York: Praeger, 1983.

Miller, Ylana N. *Government and Society in Rural Palestine, 1920–1948.* Austin: University of Texas Press, 1985.

Milson, Menachem. "How to Make Peace with the Palestinians." *Commentary* (May 1981): 25–35.

———. "The Palestinians in the Peace Process." *Forum* 42/43 (1981).

Mishal, Shaul. *West Bank/East Bank: The Palestinians in Jordan, 1949–1967.* New Haven: Yale University Press, 1978.

———. *The PLO under Arafat: Between Gun and Olive Branch.* New Haven: Yale University Press, 1986.

Mogannam, Matiel. *The Arab Woman and the Palestine Problem.* London: Herbert Joseph, 1937.

Montgomery, Paul. "Israelis and Palestinians: Frank Talks." *New York Times,* February 3, 1989.

Moore, John Norton, ed. *The Arab-Israeli Conflict, Volume I: Readings.* Princeton: Princeton University Press, 1974.

———. *The Arab-Israeli Conflict, Volume II: Readings.* Princeton: Princeton University Press, 1974.

———. *The Arab-Israeli Conflict, Volume III: Documents.* Princeton: Princeton University Press, 1974.

———. *The Arab-Israeli Conflict, Volume IV: The Difficult Search for Peace (1975–1988), Part One.* Princeton: Princeton University Press, 1991.

———. *The Arab-Israeli Conflict, Volume IV: The Difficult Search For Peace (1975–1988), Part Two.* Princeton: Princeton University Press, 1991.

Morris, Benny. *The Birth of the Palestinian Refugee Problem, 1947–1949.* Cambridge: Cambridge University Press, 1987.

———. "The Causes and Character of the Arab Exodus from Palestine: The Israel Defense Forces Intelligence Service Analysis of June 1948." *Middle Eastern Studies* 22 (January 1986): 5–19.

———. "IDF Source Tells How—and Why—Books Are Banned." *Jerusalem Post,* April 6, 1982.

———. *1948 and After: Israel and the Palestinians.* Oxford: Oxford University Press, 1990.

———. "Operation Dani and the Palestinian Exodus from Lydda and Ramleh in 1948." *Middle East Journal* 40 (Winter 1986): 82–109.

———. "The Origins of the Palestinian Refugee Problem." In Lawrence J. Silberstein, ed., *New Perspectives on Israeli History: The Early Years of the State.* Albany: State University of New York Press, 1991.

———. "Response to Finkelstein and Masalha." *Journal of Palestine Studies* 81 (Autumn 1991): 98–114.

———. "Yosef Weitz and the Transfer Committees, 1948–1949." *Middle Eastern Studies* 22 (October 1986): 522–561.

Moughrabi, Fouad. "American Public Opinion and the Palestine Question." *Journal of Palestine Studies* 58 (Winter 1986): 56–75.

Mus, Paul. *Le destin de l'union française: de l'Indochine à l'Afrique.* Paris, 1954.

Muslih, Muhammad Y. "Moderates and Rejectionists within the Palestine Liberation Organization." *Middle East Journal* 20 (Spring 1976): 127–140.

———. *The Origins of Palestinian Nationalism.* New York: Columbia University Press, 1988.

Myths and Facts 1976: A Concise Record of the Arab-Israeli Conflict. Washington: Near East Report, 1976.

Mzali, Mohammed-Salah, and Jean Pignon, eds. *Kheredine, homme d'état: mémoires.* Tunis: Maison Tunisienne de l'Édition, 1971.

Nachmani, Amikam. *Great Power Discord in Palestine: The Anglo-American Committee of Inquiry into the Problems of European Jewry and Palestine, 1945–1946.* London: Frank Cass, 1987.

Naff, Thomas. "Toward a Muslim Theory of History." In Alexander S. Cudsi and Ali E. Hillal Dessouki, eds., *Islam and Power.* Baltimore: Johns Hopkins University Press, 1981.

Nakhleh, Emile A. *The West Bank and Gaza: Toward the Making of a Palestinian State.* Washington: American Enterprise Institute, 1979.

———. "The West Bank and Gaza: Twenty Years Later." *Middle East Journal* 42 (Spring 1988): 209–226.

———, ed. *A Palestinian Agenda for the West Bank and Gaza.* Washington: American Enterprise Institute, 1980.

Nakhleh, Khalil, and Elia Zureik, eds. *The Sociology of the Palestinians.* New York: St. Martin's Press, 1980.

Nasr, Seyyed Hossein. "Islamic Education and Science: A Summary Appraisal." In Yvonne Yazbeck Haddad, Byron Haines, and Ellison Findly (eds.), *The Islamic Impact.* Syracuse: Syracuse University Press, 1984.

———. *Science and Civilization in Islam.* Cambridge: Harvard University Press, 1968.

Nasru, Fathiyya Said. *West Bank Education in Government Schools, 1967–1977.* Birzeit: Birzeit University Publications, 1977.

Nassar, Jamal, and Roger Heacock, eds. *Intifada: Palestine at the Crossroads.* New York: Praeger, 1990.

Nasser, Kamal. "Israeli Water Policies Deprive Palestinians." *Al-Fajr Jerusalem,* August 16, 1987.

Nassib, Selim, with Caroline Tisdall. *Beirut: Frontline Story.* London: Pluto Press, 1983.

Nazzal, Nafez. *The Palestinian Exodus from Galilee in 1948.* Beirut: Institute for Palestine Studies, 1978.

Newman, David, ed. *The Impact of Gush Emunim: Politics and Settlement in the West Bank.* London: Croom Helm, 1985.

Nicholson, R. A. *A Literary History of the Arabs.* Cambridge: Cambridge University Press, 1969.

Nissan, Mordechai. "The Begin Legacy." *Jerusalem Post,* September 11, 1983.

Noble, Paul. "The PLO in Regional Politics." In Rex Brynen, ed., *Echoes of the Intifada: Regional Repercussions of the Palestinian-Israeli Conflict.* Boulder, Colorado: Westview Press, 1991.

"Nowhere to Go: The Tragedy of the Remaining Palestinian Families in Kuwait." New York: Report of Middle East Watch, October 1991.

Nutting, Anthony. *The Arabs.* New York: Mentor, 1964.

———. *Nasser.* London: Constable, 1972.

———. *No End of a Lesson: The Inside Story of the Suez Crisis.* New York: Potter, 1967.

O'Ballance, Edgar. *The Arab-Israeli War, 1948.* New York: Praeger, 1957.

Oesterreicher, John M., and Anne Sinai, eds. *Jerusalem.* New York: John Day, 1974.

Ott, David. *Palestine in Perspective: Politics, Human Rights and the West Bank.* London: Quartet, 1980.

Ovendale, Ritchie. *Britain, the United States, and the End of the Palestine Mandate, 1942–1948.* London: The Boydell Press, 1989.

Oweiss, Ibrahim. "Economics of Israeli Settlements in the Occupied Arab Territories." In *Israeli Settlements in the Occupied Arab Territories.* Tunis: League of Arab States, 1987.

Oz, Amos. *In the Land of Israel.* New York: Vintage, 1984.

Padon, Gabriel. "The Divided City: 1948–1967." In John M. Oesterreicher and Anne Sinai, eds., *Jerusalem.* New York: John Day, 1974.

Pappé, Ilan. *Britain and the Arab-Israeli Conflict: 1948–51.* New York: St. Martin's Press, 1988.

Parker, Richard B. *The Politics of Miscalculation in the Middle East.* Bloomington: Indiana University Press, 1993.

Parkes, James. *A History of the Jewish People.* Baltimore: Penguin Books, 1964.

———. *Whose Land: A History of the Peoples of Palestine.* Middlesex: Penguin Books, 1970.

Penniman, Howard R., ed. *Israel at the Polls: The Knesset Elections of 1977.* Washington: American Enterprise Institute, 1979.

Peres, Shimon. "Palestinians in Perspective." *Jerusalem Post,* October 7, 1983.

Peres, Yochanan. "Ethnic Relations in Israel." *American Journal of Sociology* 76 (May 1971): 1021–1047.

Peres, Yochanan, and Zipporah Levy. "Jews and Arabs: Ethnic Group Stereotypes in Israel." *Race* 10 (April 1969): 479–492.

Peretz, Don. "The Earthquake: Israel's Ninth Knesset Election." *Middle East Journal* 31 (1977): 251–266.

———. *The Government and Politics of Israel.* Boulder, Colorado: Westview Press, 1979.

———. *Intifada: The Palestinian Uprising.* Boulder, Colorado: Westview Press, 1990.

———. *Israel and the Palestine Arabs.* Washington: The Middle East Institute, 1958.

———. "Israel's 1969 Election Issues: The Visible and the Invisible." *Middle East Journal* 24 (1970): 31–71.

———. "The War Election and Israel's Eighth Knesset." *Middle East Journal* 28 (1974): 111–125.

———. *The West Bank: History, Politics, Society and Economy.* Boulder, Colorado: Westview Press, 1986.

Peri, Yoram. *Between Battles and Ballots: Israeli Military in Politics.* Cambridge: Cambridge University Press, 1983.

Perlmutter, Amos. "Begin's Rhetoric and Sharon's Tactics." *Foreign Affairs* 61 (Fall 1982): 67–83.

Peters, Joan. *From Time Immemorial: The Origins of the Arab-Jewish Conflict over Palestine.* New York: Harper and Row, 1984.

Pfaff, Richard. *Jerusalem: Keystone of an Arab-Israeli Settlement.* Washington: American Enterprise Institute, 1969.

Pickthall, Marmaduke. *The Meaning of the Glorious Koran.* London: Knopf, 1930.

Pines, Ayala. "Israeli Burnout and the Intifada." *New Outlook* (December 1989).

Pinner, Walter. *How Many Arab Refugees*. London: Macgibbon and Key, 1959.

Piscatori, James, ed. *Islamic Fundamentalisms and the Gulf Crisis*. Cambridge: American Academy of Arts and Sciences, 1991.

Polk, William. *The Opening of South Lebanon*. Cambridge: Harvard University Press, 1963.

———. *The United States and the Arab World*. Cambridge: Harvard University Press, 1969.

Pollock, David. "Likud in Power: Divided We Stand." In Robert O. Freedman, ed., *Israel in the Begin Era*. New York: Praeger, 1982.

Porat, Dina. *The Blue and Yellow Stars of David: The Zionist Leadership in Palestine and the Holocaust, 1939–1945*. Cambridge: Harvard University Press, 1990.

Porath, Yehoshua. *The Emergence of the Palestinian-Arab National Movement: 1918–1929*. London: Frank Cass, 1974.

———. "The Land Problem as a Factor in Relations between Arabs, Jews, and the Mandatory Government." In Gabriel Ben-Dor, ed., *The Palestinians and the Middle East Conflict*. Ramat Gan: Turtledove, 1978.

———. *The Palestine Arab National Movement: From Riots to Rebellion*. London: Frank Cass, 1977.

———. "Why Do They Support Him?" (Hebrew). *Ha'aretz*, August 19, 1990.

Pressberg, Gail. "The Uprising: Causes and Consequences." *Journal of Palestine Studies* 67 (Spring 1988): 38–50.

Prittie, Terrence. *Israel: Miracle in the Desert*. New York: Praeger, 1968.

Prospects for Peace in the Middle East: The View from Israel. New York: Council on Foreign Relations, 1985.

Quandt, William; Fuad Jabber; and Ann Mosely Lesch. *The Politics of Palestinian Nationalism*. Berkeley: University of California Press, 1973.

Quandt, William B. *Camp David: Peacemaking and Politics*. Washington: The Brookings Institution, 1986.

———. *Decade of Decisions: American Policy toward the Arab-Israeli Conflict*. Berkeley: University of California Press, 1977.

———. "Reagan's Lebanon Policy: Trial and Error." *Middle East Journal* 38 (Spring 1984): 237–254.

———, ed. *The Middle East: Ten Years after Camp David*. Washington: The Brookings Institution, 1988.

Rabin, Yitzhak. *The Rabin Memoirs*. Boston: Little, Brown, 1979.

Rabinovich, Itamar. *The Road Not Taken: Early Arab-Israeli Negotiations*. New York: Oxford University Press, 1991.

———. *Syria under the Ba'th, 1963–1966: The Army-Party Symbiosis*. Jerusalem: Israel Universities Press, 1972.

———. *The War for Lebanon, 1970–1983*. Ithaca: Cornell University Press, 1984.

Rafael, Gideon. *Destination Peace: Three Decades of Israeli Foreign Policy*. London: Weidenfeld and Nicolson, 1981.

———. "UN Resolution 242: A Common Denominator." *New Middle East* (June 1973).

Raisin, Jacob S. *The Haskalah Movement in Russia*. New York: The Jewish Publication Society of America, 1913.

Randall, Jonathan C. *Going All the Way: Christian Warlords, Israeli Adventurers, and the War in Lebanon*. New York: Vintage Books, 1984.

Rein, Natalie. *Daughters of Rachel: Women in Israel.* New York: Penguin Books, 1980.

Reiser, Stewart. *The Politics of Leverage: The National Religious Party of Israel and Its Influence on Foreign Policy.* Cambridge: Harvard University Center for Middle East Studies, 1984.

Rejwan, Nissim. "The Two Israels: A Study in Europocentrism." *Judaism* 16 (Winter 1967): 97–108.

Rekhess, Elie. "The Islamic Intifada." *Jerusalem Post*, July 12, 1989.

———. "The Rise of the Palestinian Islamic Jihad." *Jerusalem Post*, October 21, 1987.

Remnick, David. "Gorbachev Prods Arafat on Recognizing Israel." *Washington Post*, April 11, 1988.

Report of the Committee on Village Administration and Responsibility. Jerusalem: Government Printing Press, 1941.

Reviv, Hanoch. "Until the Monarchy." In *Israel Pocket Library: History until 1880.* Jerusalem: Keter Publishing House, 1973.

Reynier, Jacques de. *À Jerusalem un drapeau flottait sur la ligne de feu.* Neuchatel: La Baconniere, 1950.

Riad, Mahmoud. *The Struggle for Peace in the Middle East.* London: Quartet Books, 1981.

Richardson, David. "Leagues out of Their Depth." *Jerusalem Post Magazine*, March 19, 1982.

Robertson, Terence. *Crisis: The Inside Story of the Suez Conspiracy.* New York: Athenaeum, 1965.

Rodinson, Maxime. *Mohammed.* New York: Vintage Books, 1974.

Rodrigue, Aron. *French Jews, Turkish Jews: The Alliance Israelite Universelle and the Politics of Jewish Schooling in Turkey, 1860–1925.* Bloomington: Indiana University Press, 1990.

———. *De l'instruction à l'émancipation: les enseignants de l'alliance israelite universelle, 1860–1939.* Paris: Calmann-Levi, 1989.

Ro'i, Yaacov. "The Zionist Attitude to the Arabs 1908–1914." In Elie Kedourie and Sylvia G. Haim, eds., *Palestine and Israel in the 19th and 20th Centuries.* London: Frank Cass, 1982.

Rose, Norman. *The Gentile Zionists: A Study in Anglo-Zionist Diplomacy, 1929–1939.* London: Frank Cass, 1973.

Rosen, Lawrence. "Muslim-Jewish Relations in a Moroccan City." *International Journal of Middle East Studies* 3 (October 1972): 435–449.

Rosenfeld, Henry. "The Class Situation of the Arab National Minority in Israel." *Comparative Studies in Society and History* 20 (July 1978): 374–407.

———. "From Peasantry to Wage Labor and Residual Peasantry: The Transformation of an Arab Village." In Robert A. Manners, ed., *Process and Pattern in Culture.* Chicago: Aldine Publishing Company, 1964.

Rosenne, Shabtai. *Israel's Armistice Agreements with the Arab States: A Juridical Interpretation.* Tel Aviv: International Law Association, Israeli Branch, 1951.

Rouleau, E.; J. F. Held; and J. S. Lacouture. *Israel et les Arabes: Le troisième combat.* Paris, 1967.

Rowley, Gwyn. *Israel into Palestine.* London: Mansell, 1984.

Rozen, Roli. "The Era of Conventional Wars Has Come to an End, and the Future

Battlefield Is the Intifada" (Hebrew). *Ha'aretz*, Weekend Supplement, May 12, 1989.

Rubenberg, Cheryl. *The Palestine Liberation Organization: Its Institutional Structure.* Belmont, Massachusetts: Institute of Arab Studies, 1983.

———. "The PLO Response to the Reagan Initiative: The PNC at Algiers." *American-Arab Affairs* 4 (February 1983): 53–69.

———. "The Structural and Political Context of the PLO's Changing Objectives in the Post-1967 Period." In Yehuda Lukacs and Abdalla M. Battah, eds., *The Arab-Israeli Conflict: Two Decades of Change.* Boulder, Colorado: Westview Press, 1988.

Rubin, Barry. *The Arab States and the Palestine Conflict.* Syracuse: Syracuse University Press, 1981.

———. "The PLO's Intractable Foreign Policy." Policy Papers of the Washington Institute for Near East Policy, 1985.

Rubin, Trudy. "Why Hussein Hurries for Mideast Talks." *Christian Science Monitor*, January 25, 1983.

Rubinstein, Amnon. *The Zionist Dream Revisited.* New York: Schocken Books, 1984.

Ruedy, John. "Dynamics of Land Alienation." In Ibrahim Abu-Lughod, ed., *The Transformation of Palestine: Essays on the Origin and Development of the Arab-Israeli Conflict.* Evanston: Northwestern University Press, 1971.

Ruthven, Malise. *Islam in the World.* New York: Oxford University Press, 1984.

Sachar, Abram Leon. *A History of the Jews.* New York: Knopf, 1964.

Sachar, Howard M. *The Course of Modern Jewish History.* New York: Dell Publishing Company, 1977.

———. *A History of Israel: From the Rise of Zionism to Our Time.* New York: Knopf, 1979.

———. *A History of Israel, Volume II: From the Aftermath of the Yom Kippur War.* New York: Oxford University Press, 1987.

Safran, Nadav. *Egypt in Search of Political Community: An Analysis of the Intellectual and Political Evolution of Egypt, 1804–1952.* Cambridge: Harvard University Press, 1961.

———. *From War to War: The Arab-Israeli Confrontation, 1948–1967.* New York: Pegasus, 1969.

Sagir, Dan. "This Isn't the Way to Suppress the Uprising" (Hebrew). *Ha'aretz*, August 26, 1988.

Sahliyeh, Emile. *In Search of Leadership: West Bank Politics since 1967.* Washington: The Brookings Institution, 1987.

———. "Jordan and the Palestinians." In William B. Quandt, ed., *The Middle East: Ten Years after Camp David.* Washington: The Brookings Institution, 1988.

———. *The PLO after the War in Lebanon.* Boulder, Colorado: Westview Press, 1986.

———. "The West Bank and Gaza Strip." In Shireen Hunter, ed., *The Politics of Islamic Revivalism.* Bloomington: Indiana University Press, 1988.

———, ed. *Religious Resurgence and Politics in the Contemporary World.* Albany: State University of New York Press, 1990.

Sahliyeh, Emile, and Mark Tessler. "Experimentation with Democracy: The Cases of Jordan and Tunisia." Paper presented at the 1990 meeting of the American Political Science Association.

Said, Edward. *The Question of Palestine*. New York: Vintage, 1980.

Sandler, Shmuel, with Hillel Frisch. "The Political Economy of the Administered Territories." In Daniel J. Elazar, ed., *Judea, Samaria, and Gaza: Views of the Present and the Future*. Washington: American Enterprise Institute, 1982.

Sankari, Farouk A. "The Character and Impact of Arab Oil Embargoes." In Naiem A. Sherbiny and Mark Tessler, eds., *Arab Oil: Impact on the Arab Countries and Global Implications*. New York: Praeger Publishers, 1976.

Satloff, Robert. "Islam and the Palestinian Uprising." *Orbis* (Summer 1989): 389–401.

———. *Troubles on the East Bank: Challenges to the Domestic Stability of Jordan*. New York: Praeger, 1986.

Sayigh, Rosemary. *Palestinians: From Peasants to Revolutionaries*. London: Zed Books, 1979.

Sayigh, Yezid. "Palestinian Military Performance in the 1982 War." *Journal of Palestine Studies* 12 (Summer 1983): 3–24.

———. "Struggle Within, Struggle Without: The Transformation of PLO Politics since 1982." *International Affairs* 65 (Spring 1989): 247–271.

al-Sayyid, Afaf Lutfi. *Egypt under Cromer: A Study in Anglo-Egyptian Relations*. London: John Murray, 1968.

Schacht, Joseph. *An Introduction to Islamic Law*. Oxford: Clarendon Press, 1964.

Schechtman, Joseph B. *The Refugees in the World*. New York: Barnes, 1963.

Schiff, Ze'ev. "The Green Light." *Foreign Policy* 50 (Spring 1983): 73–85.

———. "Israel after the War." *Foreign Affairs* 70 (Spring 1991): 19–33.

———. *October Earthquake: Yom Kippur, 1973*. Tel Aviv: University Publishing Projects, 1974.

———. *Security for Peace: Israel's Minimal Security Requirements in Negotiations with the Palestinians*. Washington: The Washington Institute for Near East Policy, 1989.

———. "The Year of the Club" (Hebrew). *Ha'aretz* weekly magazine, April 1988.

Schiff, Ze'ev, and Ehud Ya'ari. *Intifada: The Palestinian Uprising—Israel's Third Front*. New York: Simon and Schuster, 1990.

———. *Israel's Lebanon War*. New York: Simon and Schuster, 1984.

Scholch, Alexander. "The Demographic Development of Palestine, 1850–1882." *International Journal of Middle Eastern Studies* 17 (November 1985): 485–505.

Schuon, Frithjof. *Understanding Islam*. New York: Roy, 1963.

Schweitzer, Avram. *Israel: The Changing National Agenda*. London: Croom Helm, 1986.

Seale, Patrick, "PLO Strategies: Algiers and After." *World Today* 39 (April 1983): 137–143.

———. *The Struggle for Syria: A Study in Post-War Arab Politics, 1945–1958*. London: Oxford University Press, 1965.

Segev, Tom. "The Comparison" (Hebrew). *Ha'aretz*, May 5, 1989.

———. *1949: The First Israelis*. New York: The Free Press, 1986.

Segre, V. D. *Israel: A Society in Transition*. London: Oxford University Press, 1971.

Selak, Charles B., Jr. "A Consideration of the Legal Status of the Gulf of Aqaba." *American Journal of International Law* 52 (1958): 660–698.

Shadid, Mohammad. "The Muslim Brotherhood Movement in the West Bank and Gaza." *Third World Quarterly* 10, no. 2 (1988).

Shadid, Mohammed, and Rick Seltzer. "Political Attitudes of Palestinians in the West Bank and Gaza Strip." *Middle East Journal* 42 (Winter 1988): 16–32.

Shafir, Gershon. *Land, Labor and the Origins of the Israeli-Palestinian Conflict, 1882–1914*. Cambridge: Cambridge University Press, 1989.

Shalev, Aryeh. *The West Bank: Line of Defense*. New York: Praeger, 1985.

Shamir, Shimon. "Israeli Views of Egypt and the Peace Process: The Duality of Vision." In William B. Quandt, ed., *The Middle East: Ten Years after Camp David*. Washington: The Brookings Institution, 1988.

Shammout, Ismail. *Palestine: Illustrated Political History*. Beirut: Palestine Liberation Organization, 1972.

Shapiro, Yonathan. *The Road to Power: Herut Party in Israel*. Albany: State University of New York Press, 1991.

Sharabi, Hisham B. *Arab Intellectuals and the West: The Formative Years*. Baltimore: Johns Hopkins University Press, 1970.

———. *Nationalism and Revolution in the Arab World*. Princeton: Van Nostrand, 1966.

———. *Palestine and Israel: The Lethal Dilemma*. New York: Pegasus, 1969.

———. "Prelude to War: The Crisis of May–June 1967." In Ibrahim Abu-Lughod, ed., *The Arab-Israeli Confrontation of June 1967: An Arab Perspective*. Evanston: Northwestern University Press, 1970.

Shaw, Stanford. "The Ottoman Census System and Population, 1831–1914." *International Journal of Middle Eastern Studies* 9 (August 1978): 325–338.

al-Shazly, Saad. *The Crossing of the Suez*. San Francisco: American Mideast Research, 1980.

Sheehan, Edward R. F. *The Arabs, Israelis, and Kissinger: A Secret History of American Diplomacy in the Middle East*. New York: Reader's Digest Press, 1976.

Sheffer, Gabriel. "Kahane, Kahanism and Racism." *Israel Yearbook*, 1985.

———. "Resolution vs. Management of the Middle East Conflict: A Reexamination of the Confrontation between Moshe Sharett and David Ben-Gurion." Jerusalem: Magnes Press, Jerusalem Papers on Peace Problems, 1980.

Sherbiny, Naiem A., and Mark Tessler, eds. *Arab Oil: Impact on the Arab Countries and Global Implications*. New York: Praeger Publishers, 1976.

Shiblak, Abbas. *The Lure of Zion: The Case of the Iraqi Jews*. London: Al Saqi Books, 1986.

Shikaki, Khalil. "The Intifada and the Transformation of Palestinian Politics." Universities Field Staff International Reports, Asia, no. 18, 1989–1990.

Shilat, Yitzhak. "The Fear of Employing Force Stems from Moral Weakness" (Hebrew). *Nekuda*, March 1988.

Shipler, David. *Arab and Jew: Wounded Spirits in a Promised Land*. New York: Times Books, 1986.

Shlaim, Avi. *Collusion across the Jordan: King Abdullah, the Zionist Movement, and the Partition of Palestine*. Oxford: Oxford University Press, 1988.

Shokeid, Moshe. *Distant Relations: Ethnicity and Politics among Arabs and North African Jews in Israel*. New York: Praeger, 1982.

Shwadran, Benjamin. *Jordan: A State of Tension*. New York: Council for Middle Eastern Affairs Press, 1959.

Silberstein, Lawrence J., ed. *New Perspectives on Israeli History: The Early Years of the State*. Albany: State University of New York Press, 1991.

Silver, Abba Hillel. *A History of Messianic Speculation in Israel*. New York: Macmillan, 1927.

Simons, Chaim. *International Proposals to Transfer Arabs from Palestine, 1895–1947: A Historical Survey.* Hoboken, New Jersey: Ktav Press, 1988.

Siniora, Hanna, and Fayez Abu Rahmeh. "The Palestinian-Jordanian Joint Delegation." *Journal of Palestine Studies* 53 (Autumn 1985): 3–18.

Sisco, Joseph. "Middle East: Progress or Lost Opportunity." *Foreign Affairs* 61 (1983): 611–640.

Sivan, Emmanuel. "Israel's Decolonization Crisis." *New Outlook* (December 1989): 16–19.

Slutsky, Shlomo. "They Don't Believe the IDF Spokesman" (Hebrew). *Hadashot*, March 18, 1989.

Slutsky, Yehuda. *Preface to the History of the Israeli Labor Movement* (Hebrew). Tel Aviv: Am Oved, 1973.

———. "Under British Rule (1917–1948)." In *Israel Pocket Library: History from 1880.* Jerusalem: Keter Publishing House, 1973.

———. "Under Ottoman Rule (1880–1917)." In *Israel Pocket Library: History from 1880.* Jerusalem: Keter Publishing House, 1973.

Smith, Charles D. *Palestine and the Arab-Israeli Conflict.* New York: St. Martin's, 1992.

Smith, Wilfred Cantwell. *Islam in Modern History.* Princeton: Princeton University Press, 1957.

Smooha, Sammy. *Israel: Pluralism and Conflict.* Berkeley: University of California Press, 1978.

Soustelle, Jacques. *The Long March of Israel.* New York: American Heritage Press, 1969.

Spero, Shubert. "Losing the 'Intifada' Game." *Jerusalem Post*, January 24, 1989.

———. "Messianism in Context." *Jerusalem Post*, June 17, 1984.

———. "Fundamentalism, Terrorism and Democracy: The Case of the Gush Emunim Underground." Occasional Papers of the Smithsonian Institution's Wilson Center, no. 4, 1986.

———. "Kach and Meir Kahane: The Emergence of Jewish Quasi-Fascism." *Patterns of Prejudice* 19 (1985).

Spiegel, Steven L. *The Other Arab-Israeli Conflict: Making America's Middle East Policy, from Truman to Reagan.* Chicago: University of Chicago Press, 1985.

Sprinzak, Ehud. *The Ascendance of Israel's Radical Right.* New York: Oxford University Press, 1991.

St. John, Robert. *The Boss: The Story of Gamal Abdel Nasser.* New York: McGraw-Hill, 1960.

Statistical Abstract of Palestine, 1939. Jerusalem: Government Printing Press, 1940.

Stein, Kenneth W. "The *Intifadah* and the 1936–1939 Uprising: A Comparison of the Palestinian Arab Communities." Occasional Paper Series of the Carter Center of Emory University, vol. 1, no. 1, 1990.

———. *The Land Question in Palestine, 1917–1939.* Chapel Hill: University of North Carolina Press, 1984.

———. "Legal Protection and Circumvention of Rights for Cultivators in Mandatory Palestine." In Joel Migdal, ed., *Palestinian Society and Politics.* Princeton: Princeton University Press, 1980.

Stein, Leonard. *The Balfour Declaration.* London: Vallentine, Mitchell, 1961.

Steinberg, Gerald M. "Large Scale National Projects as Political Symbols: The Case of Israel." *Comparative Politics* 19 (April 1987): 331–346.

Stephens, Robert. *Nasser: A Political Biography*. London: Penguin Press, 1971.

Stillman, Norman A. *The Jews of Arab Lands: A History and Source Book*. Philadelphia: Jewish Publication Society of America, 1979.

———. "The Moroccan Jewish Experience: A Revisionist View." *Jerusalem Quarterly* 9 (Fall 1979): 111–123.

Stock, Ernest. *Israel on the Road to Sinai, 1949–1956*. Ithaca: Cornell University Press, 1967.

Stockton, Ronald R. "Intifada Deaths." *Journal of Palestine Studies* 70 (Winter 1989): 101–108.

Stone, Julius. *Israel and Palestine: Assault on the Law of Nations*. Baltimore: The Johns Hopkins University Press, 1981.

A Survey of Palestine. Jerusalem: Government of Palestine, 1946.

Sussman, Zvi. *Wage Differentials and Equality within the Histadruth: The Impact of Egalitarian Ideology and Arab Labour on Jewish Wages in Palestine*. Ramat Gan: Massada, 1947.

Sykes, Christopher. *Crossroads to Israel, 1917–1948*. Bloomington: Indiana University Press, 1965.

Syrkin, Marie. "The Siege of Jerusalem." In John M. Oesterreicher and Anne Sinai, eds., *Jerusalem*. New York: John Day, 1974.

Tal, Uriel. "Foundations of a Political Messianic Trend in Israel." *Jerusalem Quarterly* 35 (1985): 44–55.

Tamari, Salim. "Eyeless in Judea: Israel's Strategy of Collaborators and Forgeries." *Middle East Report* 164–165 (May-August 1990): 39–44.

———. "The Next Phase: Problems of Transition." In *Palestinian Assessments of the Gulf War and Its Aftermath*. Jerusalem: Palestinian Academic Society for the Study of International Affairs, April 1991.

———. "The Palestinian Movement in Transition: Historical Reversals and the Uprising." In Rex Brynen, ed., *Echoes of the Intifada: Regional Repercussions of the Palestinian-Israeli Conflict*. Boulder: Westview Press, 1991.

———. "The Palestinians in the West Bank and Gaza: The Sociology of Dependency." In Khalil Nakhleh and Elia Zureik, eds., *The Sociology of the Palestinians*. New York: St. Martin's Press, 1980.

Taqqu, Rachelle. "Peasants into Workmen: Internal Labor Migration and the Arab Village Community under the Mandate." In Joel Migdal, ed., *Palestinian Society and Politics*. Princeton: Princeton University Press, 1980.

Taylor, Alan R. *Prelude to Israel: An Analysis of Zionist Diplomacy, 1897–1947*. Beirut: Institute for Palestine Studies, 1970.

Tessler, Mark. "Anger and Governance in the Arab World: Lessons from the Maghrib and Implications for the West." *Jerusalem Journal of International Relations* 13 (Fall 1991): 7–33.

———. "The Identity of Religious Minorities in Non-Secular States: Jews in Tunisia and Morocco and Arabs in Israel." *Comparative Studies in Society and History* 20 (July 1978): 359–373.

———. "Moroccan-Israeli Relations and the Reasons for Moroccan Receptivity to Contact with Israel." *Jerusalem Journal of International Relations* 10 (Spring 1988): 76–108.

———. "The Palestinian Uprising and the Israeli Response: Human Rights, Political and

Security Dimensions." *Wisconsin International Law Journal* 8 (Spring 1990): 301–386.

———. "The Political Right in Israel: Its Origins, Growth and Prospects." *Journal of Palestine Studies* 58 (Winter 1986): 12–55.

———. "Religion and Politics in the Jewish State of Israel." In Emile Sahliyeh, ed., *Religious Resurgence and Politics in the Contemporary World*. Albany: State University of New York Press, 1990.

———. "Secularism in the Middle East? Reflections of Recent Palestinian Proposals." *Ethnicity* 2 (1975): 178–203.

Tessler, Mark, and Linda Hawkins. "The Political Culture of Jews in Tunisia and Morocco." *International Journal of Middle East Studies* 11 (January 1980): 59–86.

Tessler, Mark, and Jamal Sanad. "Will the Arab Public Accept Peace with Israel." In Efraim Karsh and Gregory Mahler, eds., *Israel at the Crossroads*. London: I. B. Tauris, 1993.

Teveth, Shabtai. "Charging Israel with Original Sin." *Commentary* 88 (September 1989): 24–33.

———. "The Evolution of 'Transfer' in Zionist Thinking." Occasional Papers of the Moshe Dayan Center of Tel Aviv University, no. 107, May 1989.

———. *Moshe Dayan: The Soldier, the Man, the Legend*. London: Quartet Books, 1974.

———. "The Palestine Arab Refugee Problem and Its Origins." *Middle Eastern Studies* 26 (April 1990): 214–249.

Tibawi, Abdul Latif. *Arab Education in Mandatory Palestine: A Study in Three Decades of British Administration*. London: Luzac, 1956.

———. "Jerusalem: Its Place in Islam and Arab History." In Ibrahim Abu-Lughod, ed., *The Arab-Israeli Confrontation of June 1967: An Arab Perspective*. Evanston: Northwestern University Press, 1970.

Timerman, Jacobo. *The Longest War*. New York: Knopf, 1982.

Torgovnik, Efraim. "Likud 1977–1981: The Consolidation of Power." In Robert O. Freedman, ed., *Israel in the Begin Era*. New York: Praeger, 1982.

———. "A Movement for Change in a Stable System." In Howard Penniman, ed., *Israel at the Polls: The Knesset Elections of 1977*. Washington: American Enterprise Institute, 1979.

Torrey, Gordon. "Aspects of the Political Elite in Syria." In George Lenczowski, ed., *Political Elites in the Middle East*. Washington: American Enterprise Institute, 1975.

———. *Syrian Politics and the Military (1945–1958)*. Columbus: Ohio State University Press, 1964.

Touma, Khalil. "Bethlehem Plan Further Threatens Scarce Water Resources." *Al-Fajr Jerusalem*, July 26, 1987.

Touval, Saadia. *The Peace Brokers*. Princeton: Princeton University Press, 1982.

Toward Peace in the Middle East: Report of a Study Group. Washington: The Brookings Institution, 1975.

Treaster, Joseph B. "Arafat's Soldiers Lose Stronghold." *New York Times*, November 7, 1983.

Troen, Selwyn Ilan, and Moshe Shemesh, eds. *The Suez-Sinai Crisis, 1956: Retrospective and Reappraisal*. London: Frank Cass, 1990.

Truman, Harry S. *Memoirs, Vol. II: Years of Trial and Hope*. Garden City: Doubleday, 1956.

Tschirgi, Dan. *The American Search for Mideast Peace*. New York: Praeger, 1989.

"United States Policy in the Middle East, November 1974–February 1976." In *Selected Documents*. Washington: United States Department of State, 1976.

Van Arkadie, Brian. *Benefits and Burdens: A Report on West Bank and Gaza Strip Economies since 1967*. New York: Carnegie Endowment for International Peace, 1977.

Van Dusen, Michael. "Political Integration and Regionalism in Syria." *Middle East Journal* 26 (Spring 1972): 123–136.

Vance, Cyrus. *Hard Choices: Critical Years in America's Foreign Policy*. New York: Simon and Schuster, 1983.

Verdery, Richard N. "Arab 'Disturbances' and Commissions of Inquiry." In Ibrahim Abu-Lughod, ed., *The Transformation of Palestine: Essays on the Origin and Development of the Arab-Israeli Conflict*. Evanston: Northwestern University Press, 1971.

Vereté, Mayir. "The Balfour Declaration and Its Makers." In Elie Kedourie and Sylvia G. Haim, eds., *Palestine and Israel in the 19th and 20th Centuries*. London: Frank Cass, 1982.

Vilnay, Ze'ev. "Jerusalem in the Modern Era: 1860–1967." Translated from the Hebrew by Claire Remba. In John M. Oesterreicher and Anne Sinai, eds., *Jerusalem*. New York: John Day, 1974.

Viorst, Milton. *Reaching for the Olive Branch: UNRWA and Peace in the Middle East*. Washington: The Middle East Institute, 1989.

Vital, David. *The Origins of Zionism*. Oxford: Oxford University Press, 1975.

———. *Zionism: The Formative Years*. Oxford: Oxford University Press, 1982.

Vocke, Harald. *The Lebanese War: Its Origins and Political Dimensions*. London: C. Hurst and Company, 1978.

Von Grunebaum, Gustav E. *Modern Islam*. Berkeley: University of California Press, 1962.

Waines, David. "The Failure of the Nationalist Resistance." In Ibrahim Abu-Lughod, ed., *The Transformation of Palestine: Essays on the Origin and Development of the Arab-Israeli Conflict*. Evanston: Northwestern University Press, 1971.

Wallfish, Asher. "The Perils of Talking to the Troops." *Jerusalem Post*, January 23, 1988.

———. "Shomron: Intifada Can't Be Eradicated." *Jerusalem Post*, January 11, 1989.

Ward, Richard J.; Don Peretz; and Evan M. Wilson. *The Palestine State: A Rational Approach*. Port Washington, New York: Kennikat Press, 1977.

Waterbury, John. *The Egypt of Nasser and Sadat: The Political Economy of Two Regimes*. Princeton: Princeton University Press, 1983.

Watt, Montgomery, *Muhammad: Prophet and Statesman*. London: Oxford University Press, 1961.

———. *Muhammad at Medina*. Oxford: Clarendon Press, 1956.

Weitz, Joseph. *My Diary and Letters to the Children* (Hebrew). Tel Aviv: Massada, 1965.

Weizman, Ezer. *The Battle for Peace*. New York: Bantam Books, 1981.

Weizmann, Chaim. *Trial and Error*. New York: Schocken Books, 1966.

Werblowsky, R. J. Zwi. "Jewish Messianism." In *Encyclopedia of Religion*, vol. 9. New York: Macmillan, 1987.

The West Bank and Gaza: Israel's Options for Peace. Tel Aviv: Report of the Jaffee Center for Strategic Studies of Tel Aviv University, 1989.

Wilson, Mary C. *King Abdullah, Britain and the Making of Jordan*. New York: Cambridge University Press, 1987.

Witness of War Crimes in Lebanon: Testimony Given to the Nordic Commission, Oslo, October 1982. London: Ithaca Press, 1983.

Woodward, Bob. *Veil: The Secret Wars of the CIA, 1981–1987.* New York: Simon and Schuster, 1987.

Ya'ari, Ehud. "Israel's Dilemma in Lebanon." *Middle East Insight* 3 (April–May 1984): 18–23.

———. *Strike Terror: The Story of Fatah.* New York: Sabra Books, 1970.

Yisraeli, David. "The Third Reich and Palestine." In Elie Kedourie and Sylvia G. Haim, eds., *Zionism and Arabism in Palestine and Israel.* London: Frank Cass, 1982.

Yost, Charles W. "The Arab-Israeli War: How It Began." *Foreign Affairs* 46 (1968): 304–320.

Zborowski, Mark, and Elizabeth Herzog. *Life Is with People: The Culture of the Shtetl.* New York: Schocken Books, 1952.

Ziadeh, Nicola. *Origins of Nationalism in Tunisia.* Beirut: American University of Beirut Press, 1962.

Zlotowski, Michel. "MKs, PLO Nearly 'Together.' " *Jerusalem Post,* January 15, 1989.

Zweig, Ronald W. *Britain and Palestine during the Second World War.* London: Royal Historical Society, 1986.

Zwergbaum, Aharon. "Zionist Organization." In *Israel Pocket Library: Zionism.* Jerusalem: Keter Publishing House, 1973.

Index

MARK TESSLER, Professor of Political Science and Director of the Center for International Studies at the University of Wisconsin–Milwaukee, has spent more than six years in the Middle East, doing research in Tunisia, Israel, the West Bank, Egypt, and Morocco. He is coauthor of *Political Elites in Arab North Africa* and (with Ann Mosely Lesch) of *Israel, Egypt, and the Palestinians: From Camp David to Intifada*.